Tulsian's
ADVANCED MANAGEMENT ACCOUNTING

FOR CA (FINAL)

with Quick Revision Book

CA (Dr.) P.C. TULSIAN

M.Com., Ph.D., FCA, PGDFM

Additional Director (Former)
Board of Studies
The Institute of Chartered Accountants of India, New Delhi
Head
Department of Commerce
Ramjas College
University of Delhi
DELHI

Recipient of an Award for 'Exemplary Services contributed to the cause of Profession' by The Institute of Chartered Accountants of India, New Delhi

CA BHARAT TULSIAN

Chartered Accountant

Assistant Manager, KPMG
Alumnus of Sri Ram College of Commerce (SRCC), University of Delhi, DELHI
Recipient of An Award for the ***'Best Article on Foreign Exchange'*** *in All India by The Institute of Chartered Accountants of India, New Delhi*

S. CHAND & COMPANY PVT. LTD.
(AN ISO 9001 : 2008 COMPANY)
RAM NAGAR, NEW DELHI - 110 055

S. CHAND & COMPANY PVT. LTD.

(An ISO 9001:2008 Company)

Head Office: 7361, RAM NAGAR, NEW DELHI - 110 055

Phone: 23672080-81-82, 9899107446, 9911310888 Fax: 91-11-23677446

www.schandpublishing.com; e-mail: helpdesk@schandpublishing.com

Branches

Ahmedabad : Ph: 27541965, 27542369, ahmedabad@schandpublishing.com
Bengaluru : Ph: 22268048, 22354008, bangalore@schandpublishing.com
Bhopal : Ph: 4274723, 4209587, bhopal@schandpublishing.com
Chandigarh : Ph: 2625356, 2625546, chandigarh@schandpublishing.com
Chennai : Ph: 28410027, 28410058, chennai@schandpublishing.com
Coimbatore : Ph: 2323620, 4217136, coimbatore@schandpublishing.com (Marketing Office)
Cuttack : Ph: 2332580, 2332581, cuttack@schandpublishing.com
Dehradun : Ph: 2711101, 2710861, dehradun@schandpublishing.com
Guwahati : Ph: 2738811, 2735640, guwahati@schandpublishing.com
Hyderabad : Ph: 27550194, 27550195, hyderabad@schandpublishing.com
Jaipur : Ph: 2219175, 2219176, jaipur@schandpublishing.com
Jalandhar : Ph: 2401630, 5000630, jalandhar@schandpublishing.com
Kochi : Ph: 2378740, 2378207-08, cochin@schandpublishing.com
Kolkata : Ph: 22367459, 22373914, kolkata@schandpublishing.com
Lucknow : Ph: 4026791, 4065646, lucknow@schandpublishing.com
Mumbai : Ph: 22690881, 22610885, mumbai@schandpublishing.com
Nagpur : Ph: 6451311, 2720523, 2777666, nagpur@schandpublishing.com
Patna : Ph: 2300489, 2302100, patna@schandpublishing.com
Pune : Ph: 64017298, pune@schandpublishing.com
Raipur : Ph: 2443142, raipur@schandpublishing.com (Marketing Office)
Ranchi : Ph: 2361178, ranchi@schandpublishing.com
Siliguri : Ph: 2520750, siliguri@schandpublishing.com (Marketing Office)
Visakhapatnam : Ph: 2782609, visakhapatnam@schandpublishing.com (Marketing Office)

First Edition 2012
Revised Edition 2013; Reprint 2014; Revised Edition 2015
Reprint 2016

ISBN : 978-93-848-5763-9 **Code :** 1007C 549

This book is for sale in India & other SAARC countries only.

PRINTED IN INDIA

By Vikas Publishing House Pvt. Ltd., Plot 20/4, Site-IV, Industrial Area Sahibabad, Ghaziabad-201010 and Published by S.Chand & Company Pvt. Ltd., 7361, Ram Nagar, New Delhi -110 055.

Preface to the Fourth Edition

We are thankful to the Readers and Teachers for their response and encouragement given to the Third Edition. This edition is thoroughly revised and substantially expanded; all chapters have been updated and expanded.

Salient Features

The book adopts a fresh and novel approach to the study of **Advanced Management Accounting**. for the students of CA Final Course (Group-II). It has been written in a teach yourself style strictly following a student-friendly approach, and is essentially meant to serve as a tutor at home. Among the important features of this book include:

	(A) PEDAGOGICAL FEATURES
Simple Language	The Text is presented in the simplest language "meant to serve beginners".
Heading for each Paragraph	Each paragraph has been arranged under a suitable heading for easy retention of concepts.
Tabular form	Wherever possible the text matter relating to a particular topic/sub-topic has been presented in a Tabular Form.
Eye-catching Screens	All important equations, formulae, figures and practical steps have been presented in screen format to catch the eye.
Uniform Format of Chapter	Each chapter has been uniformly organised under suitable headings, viz., Text Supported by Suitable Illustrations, Solved Problems.
	(B) DISTINCTIVE FEATURES
Exhibits	Over 110 exhibits to acquaint students with various accounting treatment and formats.
Illustrations	Over 400 Illustrations have been provided for a better understanding of the text.
Solved Problems	Over 500 solved problems along with necessary working notes and alternative solution have been provided throughout the text.

TULSIAN'S QUICK REVISION FOR ADVANCED MANAGEMENT ACCOUNTING	
Section A	Fully Solved Scanner Chapter-Wise [Advanced Management Accounting]
Section B	Fully Solved Scanner Chapter-Wise [Operations Research]
Section C	Revision One Day Before Examination Important Theory Questions with Answers [Advanced Management Accounting]
Section D	Revision One Day Before Examination Important Theory Questions with Answers [Operations Research]

Acknowledgements

We wish to express our sincere thanks to several individuals who have been a source of inspiration and support personally and professionally including Dr. R. P. Tulsian, Dr. M. M. Goyal, Dr. S. C. Garg, Dr. Tanushree Jain, Ms. Madhu Aggarwal, Dr. Rajeev Goyal, Dr. S.N. Gupta, Dr. S.S. Lamba, Dr. Sarita Jain, Dr. Usha Jain, Dr. V. K. Aggarwal, Dr. V. P. Bansal, Dr. Vibha Jain, Dr. Savita Gopal, Dr. S.C. Gupta, Dr. S.P. Gupta, Dr. Naresh Gupta, Dr. Amit Singhal, Dr. J.B. Gupta, Dr. Madhu Gupta, Dr. Sushma Aggarwal, Dr. Renu Gupta, Dr. Manju Gupta, Dr. C.P. Gupta Dr. S. Z. H. Zaidi. CA M.K. Aggarwal, CA S.K. Aggarwal, CA N D Gupta, CA Naveen Gupta, CA Anil Jindal, CA Madhu Sudan Goyal, CA Vinod Aggarwal, CA Sunil Gupta, CA Arun Jain, CA Virender Aggarwal, CA. S.K. Gupta, CA Ishwar Khemka, CA Prem Bansal, CA Ashish Gupta, CA M.K. Sharda, CA Rajeev Rastogi. CA Atul Gupta, CA Kuldeep Bhardwaj, CA Neeraj Chabra, CA Kishore Paul, CA Pradeep Narang, CA S.K. Gupta, CA R. Devarajan, CA Tapas Dutta, CA Arnav Chakrabarty, CA Seema Gupta, CA Shilpa Aggarwal, CA Vishal Pandey, Ms. Nidhi Singh, Dr. N.N. Sen Gupta, Prof. J.P. Sharma, CA Pallavi, CA Antima Jain, CA Piyush Tulsian , CA Swati Tulsian, CA Piyush and CA **Prarthana Mittal.**

Special word of thanks is also due to our favourite students **Piyush, Pranav, Arushi and Aman Mittal** who provided incisive comment and useful feedback.

We must conclude that this book would never has been written without the support, encouragement and prodding of our family members. Many thanks to them.

Any criticisms or suggestions for further improvement of the book will be gratefully acknowledged and appreciated.

CA (Dr.) PC Tulsian
pctulsian@gmail.com

CA Bharat Tulsian
bharattulsian88@gmail.com

CONTENTS

SECTION-A : ADVANCED MANAGEMENT ACCOUNTING

SECTION-B : OPERATIONS RESEARCH

TULSIAN'S QUICK REVISION
FOR ADVANCED MANAGEMENT ACCOUNTING
FOR CA FINAL

SECTION A

FULLY SOLVED SCANNER CHAPTERWISE
(CA PROFESSIONAL EXAMINATION PROBLEMS WITH AUTHENTIC SOLUTIONS)

SECTION A : SCANNER FOR MANAGEMENT ACCOUNTING

SECTION B

SCANNER FOR OPERATIONS RESEARCH

SECTION C

IMPORTANT THEORY QUESTIONS WITH ANSWERS

SECTION D

IMPORTANT THEORY QUESTIONS WITH ANSWERS

SECTION E

QUESTION PAPERS

Section–A

ADVANCED MANAGEMENT ACCOUNTING

1 Management Accounting – An Overview

LEARNING OBJECTIVES

After studying this chapter, you should be able to understand:

- Meaning of Management Accounting
- Features of Management Accounting
- Basic Objective of Management Accounting
- Functions of Management Accounting
- Scope of Management Accounting
- Distinction between Financial Accounting and Management Accounting
- Distinction between Cost Accounting and Management Accounting
- Tools and Techniques of Management Accounting
- Services performed by Management Accountants

1.0 MEANING OF MANAGEMENT ACCOUNTING

Management Accounting is concerned with providing the required **accounting and non-accounting** information to the management at various levels to assist them in **managerial** planning, control and decision-making so as to achieve organizational goals & objectives in efficient manner.

Management Accounting *or* **Managerial Accounting** is concerned with the provisions and use of accounting information to managers within organizations, to provide them with the basis to make informed business decisions that will allow them to be better equipped in their management and control functions.

According to The Chartered Institute of Management Accountants (CIMA), *Management Accounting is "the process of identification, measurement, accumulation, analysis, preparation, interpretation and communication of information used by management to plan, evaluate and control within an entity and to assure appropriate use of and accountability for its resources. Management accounting also comprises the preparation of financial reports for non-management groups such as shareholders, creditors, regulatory agencies and tax authorities"*

According to The Institute of Management Accountants(IMA), *"Management Accounting is a profession that involves partnering in management decision making, devising planning and performance management systems,and providing expertise in financial reporting and control to assist management in the formulation and implementation of an organization's strategy."*

According to The American Institute of Certified Public Accountants(AICPA) , *Management Accounting as practice extends to the following three areas:*

- ***Strategic Management****—Advancing the role of the management accountant as a strategic partner in the organization.*

- ***Performance Management****—Developing the practice of business decision-making and managing the performance of the organization.*
- ***Risk Management****—Contributing to frameworks and practices for identifying, measuring, managing and reporting risks to the achievement of the objectives of the organization.*

According to The Institute of Certified Management Accountants(ICMA), "A management accountant applies his or her professional knowledge and skill in the preparation and presentation of financial and other decision oriented information in such a way as to assist management in the formulation of policies and in the planning and control of the operation of the undertaking."

2.0 FEATURES OF MANAGEMENT ACCOUNTING

1. Management Accounting is forward-looking, instead of historical;
2. It is model based with a degree of abstraction to support decision making generally, instead of case based;
3. It is designed and intended for use by managers within the organization, instead of being intended for use by shareholders, creditors, and public regulators;
4. It is usually confidential and used by management, instead of publicly reported;
5. It is computed by reference to the needs of managers, instead of by reference to general financial accounting standards.
6. Management accounting knowledge and experience can be obtained from varied fields and functions within an organization, such as information management, treasury, efficiency auditing, marketing, valuation, pricing, logistics, etc.
7. Management Accountants are seen as the "value-creators" amongst the accountants. They are much more interested in taking decisions that will affect the future of the organization.

3.0 BASIC OBJECTIVE OF MANAGEMENT ACCOUNTING

The basic objective of management accounting is to provide the necessary information to the management in such a manner as to facilitate:

(a) the formulation of policies
(b) planning the activities (i.e. what is to be done how and when)
(c) controlling the operations (i.e. what can be done to ensure adherence to planned activities)
(d) decision making (i.e. selection of optimal alternative among a set of alternatives after evaluation)

4.0 FUNCTIONS OF MANAGEMENT ACCOUNTING

Management accounting performs the following functions:

1. Identification	Management accounting identifies the business transactions.
2. Measurement	It measures the identified business transactions in terms of common measurement unit (i.e. the rulling currency of a country)
3. Accumulation	It accumulates the measured business transactions in a manner useful to the users.
4. Analysis	It establishes the relationship between the various items *or* a group of items.
5. Preparation & Interpretation	It is concerned with explaining the meaning and significance of the relationship so established by the analysis.
6. Communication	It is concerned with the reporting of summarised, analysed and interpreted information to the users to make reasoned decisions.

5.0 SCOPE OF MANAGEMENT ACCOUNTING

The scope of management accounting is wider than financial accounting and cost accounting and includes the following:

1. Financial Accounting	Management accounting uses financial information provided by financial accounting to forecast and plan for future.
2. Cost Accounting	Management accounting uses cost information provided by cost accounting for profit planning and decision-making.
3. Budgeting	Management accounting uses budgeting to prepare various budgets and to exercise budgetary central.
4. Financial Management	Management accounting uses financial planning, organisation and control which fall under financial management.
5. Tax Management	Management accountant is concerned with tax accounting, tax planning, payment of advance tax, TDS, prompt filing of tax returns which fall under tax management.
6. Quantitative Techniques	Management accountant makes use of various quantitative techniques such as linear programming for product mix decision, assignment problems, transportation problems, simulation, Queing theory.
7. Statistical tools	Management accounting uses various statistical tools like graphs, tables, charts etc. to prepare various reports.
8. Internal control & Internal Audit	Management accountant makes use of internal control and internal check systems for smooth functioning of financial system.
9. Tools of Financial Analysis	Management accountant makes use of various tools of financial analysis like ratio analysis, cash flow statement to analyse and interpret the financial data.
10. Electronic Data Processing	Management accounting uses the computers to record, process and analyse the various financial and cost data.

6.0 DISTINCTION BETWEEN FINANCIAL ACCOUNTING AND MANAGEMENT ACCOUNTING

Financial accounting differs from management accounting in the following respects:

Basis of Distinction	***Financial Accounting***	***Management Accounting***
1. Objective	Its objective is to provide information above financial performance and financial position of the business to the external users like share-holders Govt. Agencies etc.	Its objective is to provide information to the internal user (i.e. management) for managerial decision-making.
2. Emphasis – Reporting/control	Its emphasis is on reporting and not on control.	Its emphasis is on planning, controlling and decision making.
3. Legal Requirements	It is compulsory.	It is optional.

Basis of Distinction	*Financial Accounting*	*Management Accounting*
4. Information-Historical/ Projected	It presents only historical information.	It presents both historical and projected information for future decision-making.
5. Monetary/Non-Monetory Information	It presents only monetary information.	It presents both monetory and non-monotary information.
6. Accounting Principles	It is governed by GAPP (i.e. Generally Accepted Accounting Principles).	It is not governed by GAPP.
7. Frequency of Report	It presents generally Annual reports.	It presents daily, weekly, monthly, quarterly, half yearly reports as per the need of management.
8. Coverage of Report	Financial Accounting Reports relate to the entire organisation.	Management Accounting Reports relate to various segments of the organisation (i.e. Deptt, Division Product, Function Responsibility Centres).
9. Accuracy Vs. Timeliness in Reports	Its emphasis is on the accuracy.	Its emphasis is on prompt and timely reporting even if less accurate.
10. General Vs. Special Purpose Reports	It generaters general purpose reports like Income Statement, Balance Sheet Cash Flow Statement.	It generates special purpose reports *e.g.* Performance Report of Sales Manager, Production Manager etc.
11. Publication and Audit	Financial Statements are published for general public and sent to sharholders and are required to be audited by chartered accountants.	Management Accounting statements are *neither* published *nor* required to be audited by chartered accountants.
12. Use of Other Disciplines	It does not make use of other disciplines.	It makes use of other disciplines like Statistics, Operation Research.

7.0 DISTINCTION BETWEEN COST ACCOUNTING AND MANAGEMENT ACCOUNTING

Cost accounting differs from management accounting in the following respects:

Basis of Distinction	*Cost Accounting*	*Management Accounting*
1. Objective	Its objective is to ascertain cost, to analysis cost and to control	Its objective is to provide information to the internal user (i.e. management) for managerial decision-making.

Basis of Distinction	Cost Accounting	Management Accounting
2. Emphasis-Control/Decision Making	Its emphasis is on control-control of material cost, labour cost and overheads.	Its emphasis is on planning, controlling and decision-making.
3. Scope	Its scope is limited to providing cost information for managerial uses.	Its scope is broader than that of cost accounting since it makes uses of financial information, cost information, and other information.
4. Use of Technique	It does not use financial accounting techniques.	It makes use of financial accounting techniques such as Ratio Analysis, Cash Flow Statement etc.
5. Legal Requirement	It is compulsory in case of manufacturing industries as per The Companies Act, 1956.	It is optional.

8.0 TOOLS AND TECHNIQUES OF MANAGEMENT ACCOUNTING

Some of the important tools and techniques of management accounting are as follows:

1. Ratio Analysis	**Ratio Analysis** is the process of identifying strengths and weaknesses of the enterprise by logically establishing the significant relationship between the items of Income Statement or Balance Sheet or both to provide a meaningful understanding of the financial performance and financial position of an enterprise and interpreting the results thereof in order to derive meaningful conclusions. It may be Cross Sectional *or* Time Series Analysis.
2. Comparative Financial Statement (for Horizontal Analysis	**Comparative Financial Statements** may refer to— (a) Financial Statements of an enterprise for two or more successive accounting periods, *or* (b) Financial Statements of different enterprises for the same accounting periods, *or* (c) Financial Statements of an enterprise and an industry to which the enterprise belongs, for the same accounting period, *or*
3. Common size Financial State-ments (for Vertical Analysis)	**Common Size Financial Statements** are those in which figures reported are converted into percentages to some common base such as Net Sales for Income Statement and Total Assets for Balance Sheet.
4. Funds Flow Statement	The **Funds Flow Statement** consists of two terms **'Fund'** and **'Flow'**. Fund may be interpreted as cash or working capital or all financial resources. Flow means change. Therefore, when the term 'Fund' is interpreted as 'working capital', the Funds Flow Statement means statement of changes in working capital. This statement contains the sources of funds, uses of funds and the changes in net working capital indicating the difference between the total sources and total uses. This statement is also known as Statement of Sources and Applications of Funds, or Statement of Sources and Uses of Working Capital.

5. Cash Flow Statement	The **Cash Flow Statement** means the statement of changes in cash and Cash equivalents. It shows— 1. Net Cash flows from Operating Activities; 2. Net Cash flows from Investing Activities; 3. Net Cash flows from Financing Activities; 4. Net Change in Cash and Cash Equivalents.
6. Trend Percentage	**Trend Percentage** analysis is a time series analysis to determine the trend of the financial data over a series of years. The working of the trend percentage analysis involves the following three steps: **Steps 1** *Selection of a base year* **Steps 2** *Assignment of an index number of 100 to each item of the base year.* **Steps 3** *Calculation of percentage relationship that each item of eac year bears to the same item in the base year.*
7. Standard Costing	**Standard Costing** is a system which involves— (a) Fixation of standards for each element of cost. (b) Comparison of actual costs with standard costs to ascertain the variances. (c) Analysis of variances to ascertain the reasons for the variances. (d) Presenting information to the appropriate level of management to decide upon the corrective action to be taken.
8. Budgetory Control	**Budgetory Control** is a system which involves— (a) Establishment of budgeted performance for each activity of the business for the budget period. (b) Comparison of actual performace with the budgeted performance to ascertain variances (c) Analysis of variances to ascertain the reasons for the variance. (d) Taking corrective action.
9. Marginal Costing	**Marginal Costing** is the practice of charging all variable costs to operations, processes or products and writing off all fixed costs against profits in the period in which they arise.
10. Break even Analysis (or Cost-Volume- Profit Analysis	**Break Even Analysis** is a technique used for studying the relationship between Cost, Volume and Profit at different levels of operations. It is also called Cost-Volume-Profit Analysis (*or* CVP Analysis).
11. Differential Costing	**Differential Costing** is a technique of decision-making in which differential costs of various alternatives are compared with the differential revenues for the purposes of choosing between competing alternatives. So long as the incremental revenues exceed incremental costs, the decision should be in favour of the proposal.
12. Just in Time [JIT]	**JIT** system involves– (a) Installing a system of receiveing **requisite quantity** of products/ spare parts/materials of **required quality** from its suppliers on the **exact date and at the exact time** and **at the exact place** and thereby reducing inventory carrying costs (b) Reducing the machine setup time so as to make even small production runs economical and thereby reducing (i) the amount of WIP inventory & inventory carrying costs(ii) the amount of defective products & scrap costs (iii) Product Obsolescence.

13. Target Costing	**Target Costing** is a cost management technique which aims to design & produce a product with specified functionality and quality at expected cost not exceeding the target cost to ensure the target margin and target level of customer satisfaction at target selling price".
14. Total Quality Management[TQM]	**TQM** is a **continuous process** of quality improvement where **commitment** come from top management to bring TQM **culture** in the entire organization by making 'quality' a part of everyone's job with the **cooperation** and involvement of all Employees & **control** procedures with a view to **focus on customer** by delivering products or services of consistent high quality in a timely fashion and thereby reducing the costs associated with scraps, spoilage & defectives.
15. Throughput Accounting (TA)	**Throughput Accounting (TA)** is a method of performance measurement which relates production and other costs to throughput (i.e. usage of key resources by various products.) It recognizes the interdependencies of modern production processes. For any given product, customer or supplier, it is a tool to measure the contribution per unit of constrained resource.
16. Life Cycle Costing	**Life Cycle Costing** estimates, tracks and accumulates the costs over a product's entire life cycle from its inception to abandonment or from the initial R & D stage till the final customer servicing and support of the product with a view to determine whether the profits earned during the manufacturing phase will cover the costs incurred during pre and post manufacturing stages.
17. Balanced Scorecard	**Balanced Scorecard** is an approach which provides information relating to financial and non-financial measures from four different perspectives(i.e. **Customer Perspective, Internal Business Perspective, Innovation & Learning Perspective, Financial Perspective**) to management to assist in strategy formulation and implementation .
18. Value Chain Analysis	**Value Chain Analysis** is a continuous process of identifying Value Chain (i.e. a linked set of value creating activities from the basic raw materials and components sources to the ultimate end use of the product or service delivered to the customer) which will yield the maximum competitive advantage and applying the organization's resources to each linked process so as to achieve cost effectiveness.
19. Manufacturing Resources Planning (MRP)	**MRP** is a production scheduling system which specifies: 1. When what quantity of finished products should be produced on the basis of **The Master Production Schedule.** 2. What quantity of sub-assemblies, components and materials is required for each finished product as per **The Bill of Material File.** **3. Inventory** of sub-assemblies, components and materials in hand as per **The Inventory File.** **4.** The sequence of operations required to manufacture components, sub-assemblies and finished products as per **The Routing File.** **5.** The production time of sub-assemblies and components produced internally and lead times for externally acquired items as per**The Master Parts File.**

20. Enterprise Resource Planning (ERP)	**Enterprise Resource Planning (ERP)** software is a single integrated software that runs off a single database which attempts to integrate all departments and functions (like Manufacturing, Selling and Distribution, Payables, Receivables, Inventory etc.) across the enterprise into a single computer system so that various departments can more easily & quickly share information and communicate with each other.
21. Business Process Re-engineering	**Business Process Re-engineering** involves redesigning the business processes by substantially improving the current methods of performing business processes and introducing new methods of performing business processes by focusing on (a) simplification, (b) cost reduction, (c) improved quality and (d) enhanced customer satisfaction
22. Value Engineering	**Value Engineering** involves (i) Identifying improved product designs that reduces the product's costs without sacrificing functionality/ quality(ii) Eliminating unnecessary Non-Value added activities that increase the product's cost and for which customers are not prepared to pay extra.
23. Computer–Aided Manufacturing (CAM)	**Computer–Aided Manufacturing (CAM)** involves carrying out the manufacturing process by a range of machinery which are linked together with a single integrated computer software with the help of Computer Numerical Control (CNC) and robotics with a view to achieve the goal of high speed & accuracy.CNC machines are programmable machine tools.
24. Synchronous Manufacturing	The concept of '**Synchronous Manufacturing**' was started in 1984. It has been defined as an all-encompassing manufacturing management philosophy that includes a consistent set of principles, procedures, and techniques where every action is evaluated in terms of the common global goal of the organisation to focus on those areas of operations where there exist potential global improvements
25. Benchmarking	**Benchmarking** is the process of identifying and learning from the best practices anywhere in the world so as to find out how the product, service or activity can be improved and ensure that the improvements are implemented.
26. Down sizing	**Down Sizing** means that if any present activity or service does not provide target profit or provide loss, we have the following two options– **Option 1:** Either to reduce the present level of activity. **Option 2:** Sub-contract the existing activity to outside agency.
27. Tear-down Analysis [Reverse Engineering]	**Reverse Engineering** involves examining competitor's products in order to identify opportunities for product improvement and cost reduction with a view to incorporate relative advantage of competitor's product to the product design.
28. Divestment Strategy	**Divestment** involves a strategy of selling off or shedding business operations to divert the resources, so released, for other purposes. Selling off a business segment or product division is one of the frequent forms of divestment strategy. It may also include selling off

	or giving up the control over a subsidiary where by the wholly owned subsidiaries may be floated as independently quoted companies.
29. Resource Consumption Accounting (RCA)	**Resource Consumption Accounting (RCA)** is formally defined as a dynamic, fully integrated, principle-based, and comprehensive management accounting approach that provides managers with decision support information for enterprise optimization. RCA emerged as a management accounting approach around 2000 and was subsequently developed at CAM-I the Consortium for Advanced Manufacturing–International, in a Cost Management Section *RCA interest group*
30. Managerial Risk Accounting	**Managerial Risk Accounting** is concerned with the generation, dissemination and use of risk related accounting information to managers within organisation to enable them to judge and shape the risk situation of the organisation according to the objectives of the organisation.

9.0 SERVICES PERFORMED BY MANAGEMENT ACCOUNTANTS

Following are the primary tasks/ services performed by management accountants:

1. Cost Analysis
2. Cost Allocation
3. Cost Benefit Analysis
4. Cost-Volume-Profit Analysis
5. Life Cycle Cost analysis
6. Client Profitability Analysis
7. IT Cost Transparency
8. Price Modeling
9. Product Profitability
10. Strategic Planning
11. Strategic Management Advise
12. Business Metrics Development
13. Annual Budgeting
14. Capital Budgeting
15. Buy *vs.* Lease Analysis
16. Geographic *vs.* Industry or Client Segment Reporting
17. Sales Management Scorecards
18. Sales and Financial Forecasting
19. Internal Financial Presentation and Communication

THEORETICAL QUESTIONS

1. What is meant by Management Accounting? State its main features and basic objective.
2. State the scope of Management Accounting.
3. Distinguish between Financial Accounting and Management Accounting
4. Distinguish between Cost Accounting and Management Accounting.
5. Enumerate any five techniques of Management Accounting.

2 Marginal Costing

LEARNING OBJECTIVES

After studying this chapter, you should be able to understand:

- What is Marginal Costing?
- What is Direct Costing?
- What is Differential Costing?
- What is Absorption Costing?
- What is 'Marginal Cost'?
- What are Fixed Costs?
- What are Variable Costs?
- What are Semi-Variable Cost/Semi-Fixed Costs?
- Methods of Segregating the Semi-Variable Cost
- What is Marginal Cost Equation?
- What is Contribution?
- What is 'Profit Volume Ratio' (*OR* P/V Ratio)
- What is Break Even Analysis?
- What is Break Even Point?
- What is Margin of Safety?
- What is Break-Even Chart?
- Relationship Between Angle of Incidence, Break-even Level and Margin of Safety
- Merged Plant/Company
- Overall P/V Ratio and B.E.P. for the Company Selling Various Products in Various Sales Mix Ratios
- What is Key Factor / Budget Factor / Limiting Factor?
- Advantages of Marginal Costing
- Limitations of Marginal Costing
- Circumstances Under Which it may be Justifiable to Sell at a Price Below Marginal Cost for a Limited Period
- Circumstances under which it may be Justifiable to Sell at a Price Below Total Cost But above Marginal Cost
- Cost Indifference Point

1.0 WHAT IS MARGINAL COSTING?

Meaning	(a) Marginal costing is the practice of charging all marginal costs to operations processes *or* products and writing off all fixed costs against the profits in the period in which they arise. (b) **CIMA, London,** defines the Marginal Costing as "*the ascertainment of marginal costs and of the effect on profit of changes in volume or type of output by differentiating between fixed costs and variable costs*". (c) Marginal costing is a technique used for managerial decision making and not a system of costing like job costing *or* process costing.

Basic Features	(a) All costs are **classified on variability** basis as fixed costs and variable costs. (b) Only **variable costs** are treated **as product costs** and hence are charged to operations, processes *or* products. (c) All **fixed costs** are treated **as period costs** and hence are written off against profits in the period in which they arise.

HOW TO PREPARE INCOME STATEMENT UNDER MARGINAL COSTING

INCOME STATEMENT UNDER MARGINAL COSTING

	Particulars	₹	₹
A	Sales		×××
B	*Less:* Variable Cost of Sales:		
	(a) Direct Material Cost	×××	
	(b) Direct Labour Cost	×××	
	(c) Direct Expenses	×××	
	(d) Variable Production Overheads	×××	
	Variable Cost of Goods produced	×××	
	Add: Opening Stock	×××	
	Less: Closing Stock	(×××)	
	Variable Cost of Goods sold	×××	
	Add: Variable Administration Overheads	×××	
	Add: Variable Selling and Distribution Overheads	×××	
	Variable Cost of Sales		×××
C	Contribution [A – B]		×××
D	*Less:* Fixed Overheads:		
	Fixed Production Overheads	×××	
	Fixed Administration Overheads	×××	
	Fixed Selling and Distribution Overheads	×××	×××
E	Profit under Marginal Costing (C – D)		×××

2.0 WHAT IS DIRECT COSTING?

Meaning	(a) Direct costing is the practice of charging all direct costs to operations, processes *or* products and writing off all indirect costs against the profits in the period in which they arise. (b) **CIMA, London,** defines the 'Direct Costing' as "*the practice of charging all direct costs to operations, processes or products, leaving all indirect costs to be written off against profits in the period in which they arise*".
Basic Features	(a) All costs are **classified as direct costs and indirect costs.** (b) Only **direct costs** are treated as **product costs** and hence are charged to operations, processes *or* products. (c) All **indirect costs** are treated as **period costs** and hence are written off against the profits in the period in which they arise.
How different from Marginal Costing	Direct Costing differs from Marginal Costing in the sense that some fixed costs could be considered to be direct costs in appropriate circumstances.

3.0 WHAT IS DIFFERENTIAL COSTING?

Meaning of Differential Costing	Differential Costing is a technique of decision-making in which differential costs of various alternatives are compared with the differential revenues for the purposes of choosing between competing alternatives. So long as the incremental revenues exceed incremental costs, the decision should be in favour of the proposal.
Meaning of Differential Cost	Differential Cost is the net increase *or* decrease in total cost which results from any variation in level of operations. It includes both fixed and variable costs. It is termed as **incremental cost** when the cost increases and as **decremental cost** when the cost decreases.
How Different Marginal Cost	Differential Cost differs from the Marginal Cost in the sense that Marginal Cost includes the material, labour, direct expenses and variable overheads *whereas* Differential Cost includes both fixed and variable costs.
Applications	Some of the areas in which differential cost technique is used are – whether to process further *or* not, whether to accept an additional order at lower than existing price.

4.0 WHAT IS ABSORPTION COSTING?

Meaning	(a) Absorption Costing is the practice of charging all variable manufacturing costs (*i.e.* Direct Material Cost, Direct Labour Cost, Direct Expenses and Variable Production Overheads) and fixed production overheads to operations, processes *or* products and writing off all administration, selling and distribution overheads against the profits in the period in which they arise. **Note:** *The fixed production overheads are absorbed at a rate predetermined on the basis of normal capacity utilization and not on the basis of actual production.* (b) **CIMA, London**, defines the '*Absorption Costing' as 'the practice of charging all costs, both variable and fixed, to operations, processes or products.*
Basic Features	(a) All costs are **classified on functional basis** as Production costs, Administration costs, Selling costs, Distribution costs. (b) All **variable manufacturing costs and fixed production overheads** are treated **as product costs** and hence are charged to operations, processes *or* products. (c) All **administration, selling and distribution overheads** are treated **as period costs** and hence, are written off against the profits in the period in which they arise.

DISTINCTION BETWEEN ABSORPTION COSTING AND MARGINAL COSTING

Absorption Costing differs from Marginal Costing in the following respects:

Basis of Distinction	Absorption Costing	Marginal Costing
1. **Product Costs**	**All variable manufacturing costs and fixed production overheads**	**Only variable manufacturing costs** are treated as product costs

	are treated as product costs and hence, are charged to product, processes *or* operations.	and hence, are charged to products, processes *or* operations.
2. **Period Costs**	**Only administration, selling and distribution overheads** are treated as **period costs** and hence, are written off against the profits in the period in which they arise.	**All fixed costs i.e. Production/Administration/Selling/Distribution Overheads** are treated as **period costs** and hence are written off against profits in the period in which they arise.
3. **Value of Stock**	Value of closing stock ***includes*** **fixed production overheads.**	Value of closing stock ***comprises*** **only variable costs.**
4. **Under/over Recovery**	Under/over recovery of fixed overheads **generally arises.**	The question of under/over recovery of fixed overheads **does not arise.**
5. **Basis of Managerial Decisions**	Managerial Decisions are based on **total profit** *i.e.* excess of total sales revenue over total costs.	Managerial Decisions are based on **contribution** *i.e.* excess of sales revenue over over variable costs.

HOW TO PREPARE INCOME STATEMENT UNDER ABSORPTION COSTING

INCOME STATEMENT UNDER ABSORPTION COSTING

	Particulars	₹	₹
A	Sales		×××
B	*Less:* Manufacturing Cost of Goods sold:		
	(a) Direct Material Cost	×××	
	(b) Direct Labour Cost	×××	
	(c) Direct Expenses	×××	
	(d) Variable Production Overheads	×××	
	(e) Fixed Production Overheads	×××	
	Total Cost of Goods Produced	×××	
	Add: Opening Stock @	×××	
	Less: Closing Stock @	(×××)	
	Standard Cost of Goods Sold	×××	
	Add: Under-absorbed Fixed Production Overheads	×××	
	Less: Over-absorbed Fixed Production Overheads	(×××)	
	Adjusted Manufacturing Cost of Goods sold		×××
C	Gross Profit (A – B)		×××
D	*Less:* Administration, Selling & Distribution Overheads:		
	Variable Administration Overheads	×××	
	Fixed Administration Overheads	×××	
	Variable Selling and Distribution Overheads	×××	
	Fixed Selling and Distribution Overheads	×××	×××
E	Profit under Absorption Costing (C – D)		×××

RECONCILIATION OF PROFIT UNDER MARGINAL COSTING WITH THE PROFIT UNDER ABSORPTION COSTING

STATEMENT SHOWING THE RECONCILIATION OF PROFIT

	Particulars	₹
A	Profit under Marginal Costing	xxxx
B	*Add:* Fixed Production Overheads included in Closing Stock @ ₹	xxxx
C	*Less:* Fixed Production Overheads included in Opening Stock @ ₹	xxxx
D	Profit under Absorption Costing [A + B – C]	xxxx

Illustration 1. Tulsian Ltd. provides you the following information:

Normal Capacity	2,00,000 units
Opening Stock	40,000 units
Units Produced	1,70,000 units
Units sold	2,00,000 units
Selling Price per unit	₹ 25
Direct Material Cost per unit	₹ 4
Direct Labour Cost per unit	₹ 4
Variable Production Overheads per unit	₹ 2
Fixed Production Overheads	₹ 8,00,000
Variable Administration Overheads per unit sold	₹ 0.50
Fixed Administration Overheads	₹ 1,00,000
Variable Selling & Distribution Overheads per unit sold	₹ 1.50
Fixed Selling & Distribution Overheads	₹ 2,00,000

Required:

(a) Prepare Income Statement using (i) Absorption Costing and (ii) Marginal Costing

(b) Prepare a Statement reconciling the difference in profit if any.

Solution: **INCOME STATEMENT UNDER ABSORPTION COSTING**

	Particulars		₹
A	Total Sales [2,00,000 × ₹ 25]		50,00,000
B	*Less:* Manufacturing Cost of Goods Sold:		
	Direct Material Cost	(1,70,000 × ₹ 4)	6,80,000
	Direct Labour Cost	(1,70,000 × ₹ 4)	6,80,000
	Variable Production Overheads	(1,70,000 × ₹ 2)	3,40,000
	Fixed Production Overheads	(1,70,000 × ₹ 4)	6,80,000
	Total Cost of Goods Produced	(1,70,000 × ₹ 14)	23,80,000
	Add: Opening Stock	(40,000 × ₹ 14)	5,60,000
	Less: Closing Stock	(10,000 × ₹ 14)	(1,40,000)
	Standard Cost of Goods sold		28,00,000
	Add: Under-absorbed fixed Production Overheads	(30,000 × ₹ 4)	1,20,000
	Adjusted Cost of Goods sold		29,20,000
C	Gross Profit [A – B]		20,80,000
D	*Less:* Administration and Selling and Distribution Overheads:		
	Variable Administration Overheads	(2,00,000 × ₹ 0.50)	1,00,000
	Fixed Administration Overheads		1,00,000
	Variable Selling and Distribution Overheads	(2,00,000 × ₹ 1.50)	3,00,000
	Fixed Selling and Distribution Overheads		2,00,000
			7,00,000
E	Profit under Absorption Costing [C – D]		13,80,000

Working Notes:

(i) Fixed Mfg. overheads per unit $= \frac{\text{Fixed Mfg Overheads}}{\text{Normal Capacity}}$

$= \frac{₹\ 8,00,000}{₹\ 2,00,000} = ₹\ 4$

(ii) Mfg. Cost per unit for valuation of stock = ₹ 4 + ₹ 4 + ₹ 2 + ₹ 4 = ₹ 14

INCOME STATEMENT UNDER MARGINAL COSTING

	Particulars	₹
A	Total Sales [2,00,000 × ₹ 25]	50,00,000
B	*Less:* Total Variable Cost of Sales:	
	Direct Material Cost (1,70,000 × ₹ 4)	6,80,000
	Direct Labour Cost (1,70,000 × ₹ 4)	6,80,000
	Variable Production Overheads (1,70,000 × ₹ 2)	3,40,000
	Variable Manufacturing Cost of Goods produced (1,70,000 × ₹ 10)	17,00,000
	Add: Opening Stock (40,000 × ₹ 10)	4,00,000
	Less: Closing Stock (10,000 × ₹ 10)	(1,00,000)
	Variable Cost of Goods Sold 20,00,000	
	Add: Variable Administration Overheads	1,00,000
	Add: Variable Selling and Distribution Overheads	3,00,000
		24,00,000
C	Contribution [A – B]	26,00,000
D	*Less:* Fixed Overheads:	
	(a) Fixed Production Overheads	8,00,000
	(b) Fixed Administration Overheads	1,00,000
	(c) Fixed Selling and Distribution Overheads	2,00,000
		11,00,000
E	Profit under Marginal Costing [C – D]	15,00,000

Note: Variable Manufacturing Cost per unit for valuation of stock = ₹ 4 + ₹ 4 + ₹ 2 = ₹ 10

STATEMENT SHOWING THE RECONCILIATION OF PROFIT

	Particulars	₹
A	Profit under Marginal Costing	15,00,000
B	*Add:* Fixed Production Overheads included in Closing Stock @ ₹ 4	40,000
C	*Less:* Fixed Production Overheads included in Opening Stock @ ₹ 4	(1,60,000)
D	Profit under Absorption Costing [A + B – C]	13,80,000

5.0 WHAT IS 'MARGINAL COST'?

Meaning	**CIMA, London,** defines the 'Marginal Cost' as "*the amount at any given volume of output by which aggregate costs are changed if the volume of output is increased or decreased by one unit. In practice this is measured by the total variable cost attributable to one unit*". **Note:** In this context, a unit may be single article, a batch of articles, an order, a stage of production capacity, a process *or* a department. It relates to the change in output in the particular circumstances under consideration.

Computation

In practice, Marginal Cost is measured by the total variable cost attributable to one unit. It is computed as follows:

COMPUTATION OF MARGINAL COST/VARIABLE COST

Particulars	₹
Direct Materials Cost	×××
Direct Labour Cost	×××
Direct Expenses	×××
Variable Production Overheads	×××
Variable Administration Overheads	×××
Variable Selling & Distribution Overheads	×××
Total Variable Cost	×××

6.0 WHAT ARE FIXED COSTS?

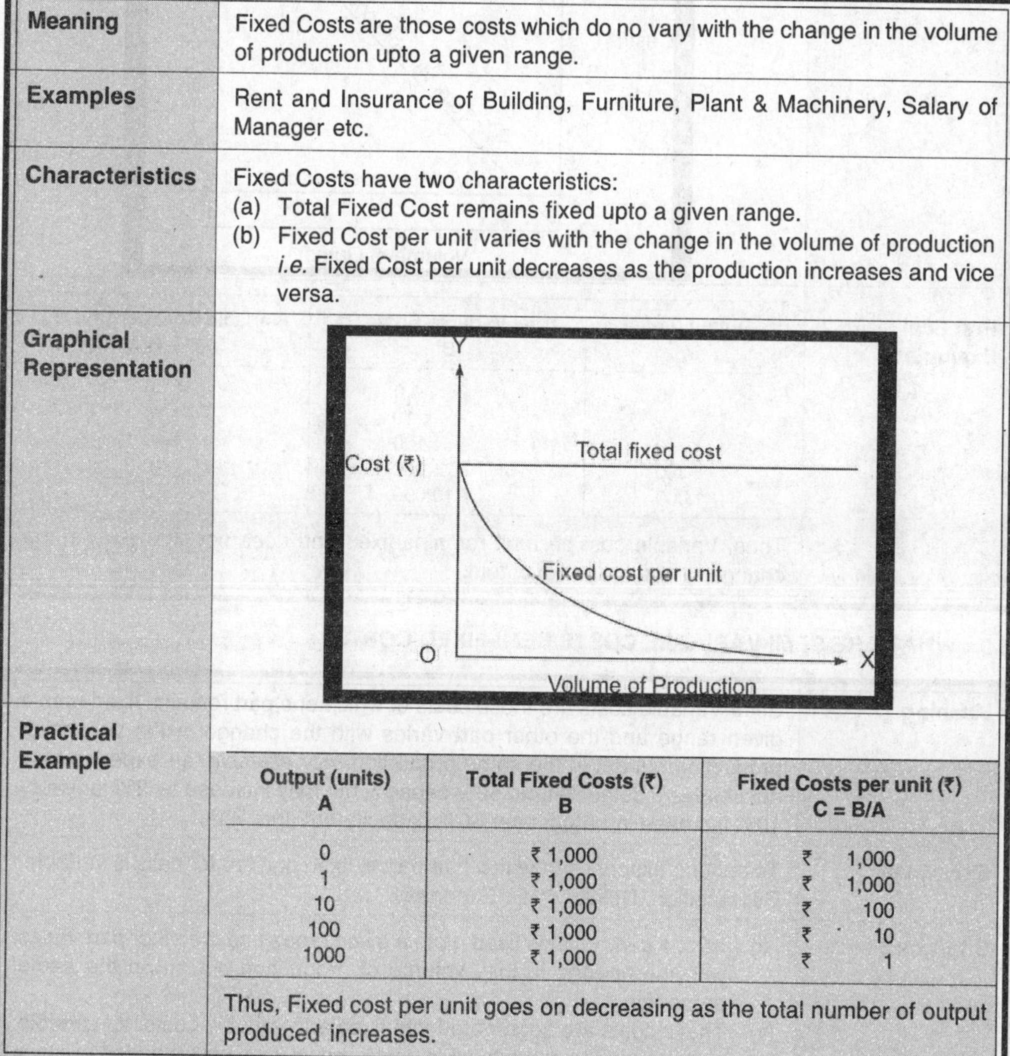

Meaning

Fixed Costs are those costs which do no vary with the change in the volume of production upto a given range.

Examples

Rent and Insurance of Building, Furniture, Plant & Machinery, Salary of Manager etc.

Characteristics

Fixed Costs have two characteristics:

(a) Total Fixed Cost remains fixed upto a given range.

(b) Fixed Cost per unit varies with the change in the volume of production *i.e.* Fixed Cost per unit decreases as the production increases and vice versa.

Graphical Representation

Practical Example

Output (units) A	Total Fixed Costs (₹) B	Fixed Costs per unit (₹) C = B/A
0	₹ 1,000	₹ 1,000
1	₹ 1,000	₹ 1,000
10	₹ 1,000	₹ 100
100	₹ 1,000	₹ 10
1000	₹ 1,000	₹ 1

Thus, Fixed cost per unit goes on decreasing as the total number of output produced increases.

7.0 WHAT ARE VARIABLE COSTS?

Meaning

Variable costs are those costs which vary in direct proportion to the volume of production.

Examples

Direct Material Costs, Direct Labour Cost, Direct Expenses, and Variable Overheads.

Characteristics

Variable Costs have two characteristics:

(a) Total Variable Costs vary in direct proportion to the volume of production *i.e.* total variable costs decrease as the production decreases and vice versa.

(b) Variable Cost per unit remains fixed.

Graphical Representation

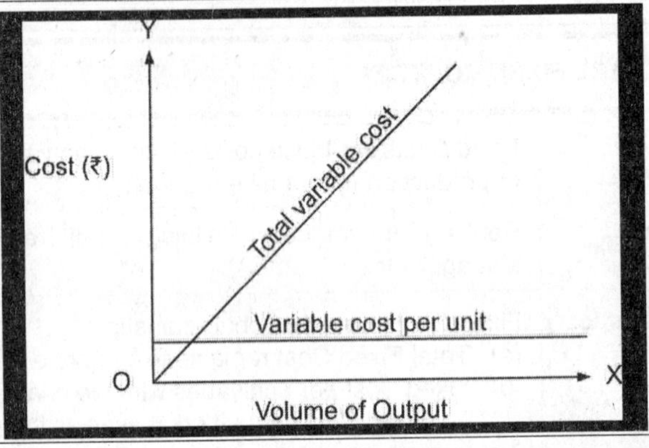

Y
Cost (₹)
Total variable cost
Variable cost per unit
O
X
Volume of Output

Practical Example

Output (units) A	Total Variable Costs (₹) B	Variable Cost per Unit (₹) C = B/A
0	₹ 0	₹ 0
1	₹ 10	₹ 10
10	₹ 100	₹ 10
100	₹ 1,000	₹ 10
1,000	₹ 10,000	₹ 10

Thus, Variable cost per unit remains fixed and does not change with the changes in the volume of output.

8.0 WHAT ARE SEMI-VARIABLE COSTS/SEMI-FIXED COSTS?

Meaning

Semi-Variable costs are those costs of which one part remains fixed upto a given range and the other part varies with the change in the volume of production but not in the same proportion. *For example*, an expense may not change if output is upto 50% capacity but may increase by 2% for every 10% increase in output over 50% capacity but upto 70%.

Examples

Telephone expenses of which hire part is fixed and fee for calls is variable, Depreciation, Delivery Van Expenses

Characteristics

(i) Its one part remains fixed upto a given range and the other part varies with the change in the volume of production but not in the same proportion.

(ii) These costs are segregated into fixed and variable costs. Its variable part is added to other variable costs and its fixed part is added to other fixed costs.

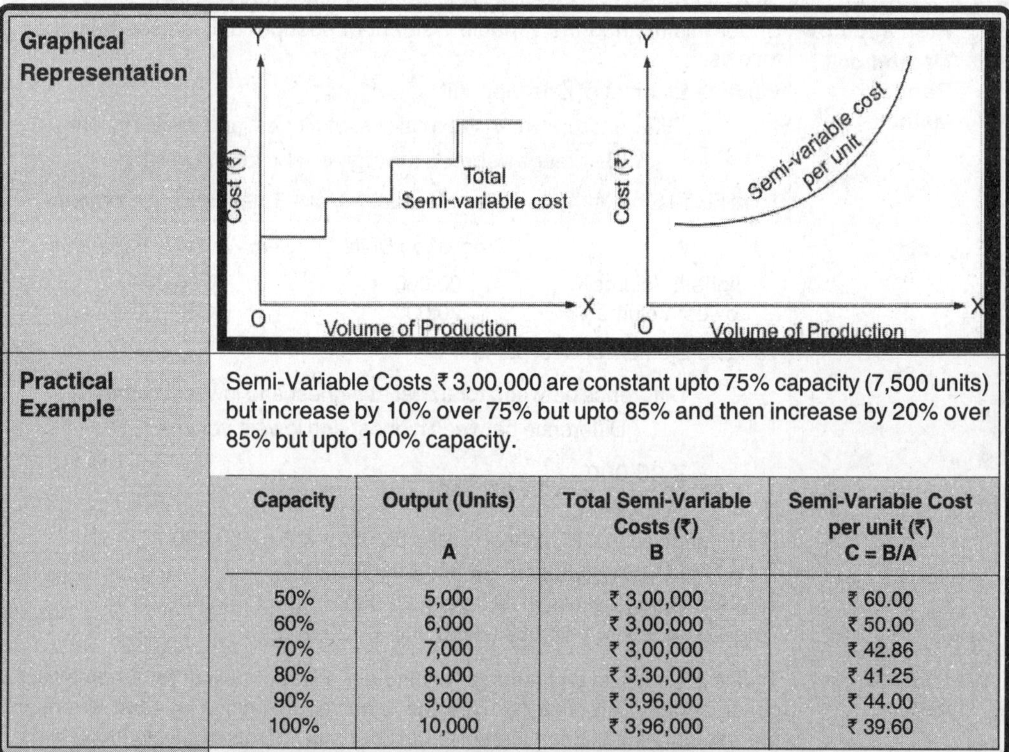

Graphical Representation

Practical Example

Semi-Variable Costs ₹ 3,00,000 are constant upto 75% capacity (7,500 units) but increase by 10% over 75% but upto 85% and then increase by 20% over 85% but upto 100% capacity.

Capacity	Output (Units) A	Total Semi-Variable Costs (₹) B	Semi-Variable Cost per unit (₹) C = B/A
50%	5,000	₹ 3,00,000	₹ 60.00
60%	6,000	₹ 3,00,000	₹ 50.00
70%	7,000	₹ 3,00,000	₹ 42.86
80%	8,000	₹ 3,30,000	₹ 41.25
90%	9,000	₹ 3,96,000	₹ 44.00
100%	10,000	₹ 3,96,000	₹ 39.60

9.0 METHODS OF SEGREGATING THE SEMI-VARIABLE COST

Semi-variable cost can segregated into fixed cost and variable cost by any of the following five methods:

1. Comparison by Level of Activity Method

Under this method the variable element of cost per unit is ascertained as follows:

$$\text{Variable Element of Cost per unit} = \frac{\text{Change in Total Semi - Variable Cost}}{\text{Change in the Level of activity/output}}$$

Total Fixed Element = Total Semi-variable cost – Total Variable Element

Example:

Month	*Production units*	*Semi-variable expenses* ₹
Jan.	100	200
Feb.	150	250
Difference	50	50

$$\text{Variable Cost} = \frac{\text{Change in Total Semi – Variable Cost}}{\text{Change in Output}} = \frac{₹\,50}{50 \text{ units}}$$

= ₹ 1 per unit.

Total Variable Cost in Jan. (100 × ₹ 1) = ₹ 100

Fixed Element = Total semi-variable cost – Total variable element

= ₹ 200 – ₹ 100 = ₹ 100

Total Variable Cost in Feb. (150 × ₹ 1) = ₹ 150

Fixed Element = ₹ 250 – ₹ 150 = ₹ 100

2. High and Low Method *or* Range Method

Under this method the variable element of cost per unit is ascertained as follows:

Variable Element of Cost per unit

$$= \frac{\text{Difference between the total cost at highest and lowest volume}}{\text{Difference between the highest and lowest volume}}$$

Total Fixed Element = Total Semi-Variable Cost – Total Variable Element

Example

	Production Units	*Semi-Variable Expenses*
Highest Volume	30,000	₹ 80,000
Lowest Volume	20,000	₹ 60,000

Variable Element of Cost per unit

$$= \frac{\text{Difference between total cost at highest and lowest volume}}{\text{Difference between highest and lowest volume}}$$

$$= \frac{₹\ 20,000}{10,000} = ₹\ 2 \text{ per unit}$$

Total Variable Cost at highest level = 30,000 × ₹ 2 = ₹ 60,000
Total Fixed Cost = ₹ 80,000 – ₹ 60,000 = ₹ 20,000
Total Variable Cost at lowest level = 20,000 × ₹ 2 = ₹ 40,000
Total Fixed Cost = ₹ 60,000 – ₹ 40,000 = ₹ 20,000

3. Least Square Method

This is a statistical technique of finding out a line of best fit for a number of observations. This method uses the linear equation $y = a + bX$; where b represents the variable element of cost per unit, 'a' represents the total fixed cost, 'Y' represents the total cost, 'X' represents the volume of output. The total cost is thus split into fixed and variable elements by solving this equation. To calculate value of 'b', the following steps are suggested:

PRACTICAL STEPS IN COMPUTING THE VALUE OF '*B*'

Step 1 → *Denote level of output by X and Semi-Variable Cost by Y*

Step 2 → *Calculate* $\Sigma X, \Sigma Y, \Sigma X^2$ *and* ΣXY

Step 3 → *Calculate Variable Cost per unit as follows:*

$$= \frac{N\Sigma XY - \Sigma X.\Sigma Y}{N\Sigma X^2 - (\Sigma X)^2}$$

Step 4 → *Variable Cost at given level of output*
= Output at that level × Variable Cost per unit

Step 5 → *Fixed Cost = Total Cost at given level – Total Variable Cost*

Illustration 2. Calculate the Fixed Expenses with the help of least squares method. The semi-variable expenses for six months are as under:

Month	*Machine Hours*	*Semi-Variable Expenses (₹)*
Jan.	200	1,400
Feb.	150	1,300
March	100	1,200
April	300	1,600
May	250	1,500
June	400	1,800

Solution: **CALCULATION OF ΣX, ΣY, ΣX² AND ΣXY**

Month	*Machine Hours*	*Semi-Variable Expenses*		
	X	*Y*	X^2	*XY*
Jan.	200	1,400	40,000	2,80,000
Feb.	150	1,300	22,500	1,95,000
March	100	1,200	10,000	1,20,000
April	300	1,600	90,000	4,80,000
May	250	1,500	62,500	3,75,000
June	400	1,800	1,60,000	7,20,000
	$\Sigma X = 1{,}400$	$\Sigma Y = 8{,}800$	$\Sigma X^2 = 3{,}85{,}000$	$\Sigma XY = 21{,}70{,}000$

N = (No. of Months) = 6

$$\text{Variable Cost per Unit} = \frac{N\Sigma XY - \Sigma X.\Sigma Y}{N\Sigma X^2 - (\Sigma X)^2}$$

$$= \frac{(6 \times 21{,}70{,}000) - (1{,}400 \times 8{,}800)}{(6 \times 3{,}85{,}000) - (1400)^2}$$

$$= \frac{130{,}20{,}000 - 123{,}20{,}000}{3{,}50{,}000}$$

$$= \frac{7{,}00{,}000}{3{,}50{,}000} = ₹\ 2$$

A.	Total cost for Jan.	₹ 1,400
B.	Variable cost for Jan (200 × ₹ 2)	400
C.	Fixed cost (A – B)	1,000

4. Analytical Method	Under this method an attempt is made to judge empirically the proportion of variable cost and fixed cost. The degree of variability is determined for each item of semi-variable cost. Once this has been done, the method is easy to apply.
Example:	Suppose in the last month the total semi-variable expenses amount to ₹ 10,000. If the degree of variability is assumed to be 60%, then variable element = 60% of ₹ 10,000 = ₹ 6,000. Fixed element = ₹ 10,000 – ₹ 6,000 = ₹ 4,000 Now in future months, the fixed element will remain constant, but the variable element will vary according to the change in production volume. Thus, if in the next month production increases by 50%, the total semi-variable expenses will be: Fixed element of ₹ 4,000 *plus* variable element of ₹ 9,000 (*i.e.* ₹ 6,000 + 50% of ₹ 6,000).
5. Graphical Method	Variable and Fixed Elements of cost are ascertained with the help of a graph as follows: **PRACTICAL STEPS INVOLVED IN GRAPHICAL METHOD** **Step 1 →** *Plot output on X-axis and semi-variable costs an Y-axis.* **Step 2 →** *Plot several points indicating total semi-variable cost corresponding to different levels of output.* **Step 3 →** *Draw a straight line through the points plotted. This is the total semi-variable cost line. The point at which this total semi-variable cost line cuts Y-axis indicates the total fixed cost.*

Step 4 → *Draw a line parallel to X-axis from the fixed cost point. This is the fixed cost line which indicates the same fixed cost at different levels of output.*

Step 5 → *Ascertain the variable cost by deducting the fixed cost from total semi-variable cost.*

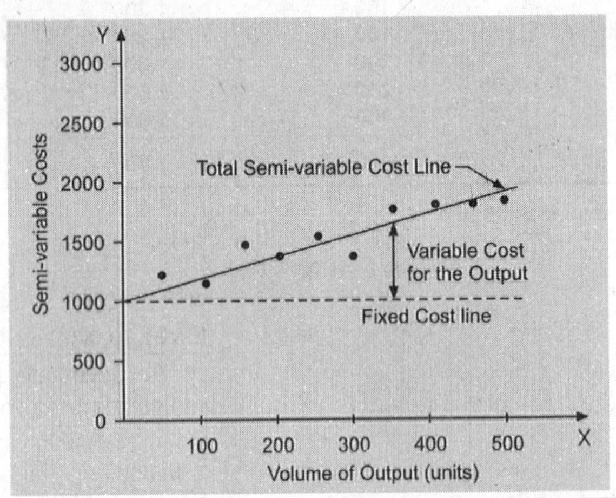

Illustration 3. PCT Ltd. provides you the following information:

Activity Level	10,000 Hours	20,000 Hours	30,000 Hours
Overheads (₹)	3,00,000	4,20,000	5,40,000

Required:

(a) Calculate Variable Overheads Rate per hour
(b) Calculate Fixed Overheads
(c) Calculate Total Overheads at a level of 25,000 hours.
(d) Calculate the Activity Level at which the Standard Overhead Rate of ₹ 15 per hour has been fixed.

Solution:

(a) Variable Overheads Rate per hour $= \dfrac{\text{Difference in Overheads}}{\text{Difference in Activity Level}}$

$$= \frac{5{,}40{,}000 - 3{,}00{,}000}{30{,}000 \text{ Hours} - 10{,}000 \text{ Hours}} = ₹\ 12 \text{ per hour}$$

(b) Fixed Overheads = Total Overheads – Total Variable Overheads
= ₹. 3,00,000 – (10,000 hours × ₹ 12) = ₹. 1,80,000

(c) Total Overheads at 25,000 Hours = ₹. 1,80,000 + (25,000 hours × ₹ 12) = ₹. 4,80,000

(d) Activity Level at which Overhead Rate has been fixed $= \dfrac{\text{Fixed Overheads}}{\text{Fixed Overhead Rate per Hour}}$

$$= \frac{1{,}80{,}000}{15 - 12} = 60{,}000 \text{ Hours}$$

10.0 WHAT IS MARGINAL COST EQUATION?

Meaning	Marginal Cost equation explains that the total sales *minus* total variable cost is the contribution towards fixed costs and profit. Marginal Cost equation can be developed as follows:

	Total Sales = Total Cost + Profit *or,* Total Sales = Total Variable Cost + Total Fixed Cost + Profit *or,* Output × Selling Price per unit = (Output × Variable Cost per unit) + Total Fixed Cost + Profit *or,* $SO = VO + F + P$ *where,* S = Selling Price Per Unit O = Output V = Variable Cost Per Unit F = Total Fixed Costs P = Profit *or,* $SO - VO = F + P$ *or,* $O(S - V) = F + P$ (Marginal Cost Equation)
Usefulness	On the basis of marginal cost equation, any unknown figure (*say* Output, Selling Price Per unit, Variable Cost per unit, Fixed Cost *or* Profit) may be ascertained with the help of other known figures. Profit at given level of output: $P = O(S - V) - F$ Output required to earn a given level of profit: $O = \frac{F + P}{S - V}$

Illustration 4. Selling Price per unit is ₹ 10, Variable Cost per unit is ₹ 6. Fixed Costs ₹ 2,000. Calculate the Profit *or* loss if the firm produces and sells (a) 400 units (b) 500 units (c) 600 units.

Solution: S = ₹ 10, V = ₹ 6, F = ₹ 2,000

(a) P = 400 (₹ 10 – ₹ 6) – ₹ 2,000 = – ₹ 400

(b) P = 500 (₹ 10 – ₹ 6) – ₹ 2,000 = 0

(c) P = 600 (₹ 10 – ₹ 6) – ₹ 2,000 = ₹ 400

Illustration 5. Selling Price per unit ₹ 10, Variable cost per unit ₹ 6, Fixed Cost ₹ 2,000. Calculate the number of units to be produced and sold to earn (a) zero profit (b) ₹ 400 (c) ₹ 500

Solution: S = ₹ 10, V = ₹ 6, F = ₹ 2,000

(a) $O = \frac{F + P}{S - V} = \frac{2{,}000 + 0}{10 - 6}$ = 500 units

(b) $O = \frac{F + P}{S - V} = \frac{2{,}000 + 400}{10 - 6}$ = 600 units

(c) $O = \frac{F + P}{S - V} = \frac{2{,}000 + 500}{10 - 6}$ = 625 units

11.0 WHAT IS CONTRIBUTION?

Meaning	(a) Contribution is the difference between the Total Sales Value and Total Variable Cost. (b) Contribution is basically that portion of sales which remains after recovering variable costs and is available towards fixed costs and profits.
Is the Contribution Equal to Profit?	The contribution may *or* may not be equal to profit depending upon the amount of fixed costs. If the fixed costs are zero, the contribution is equal to profit. If the contribution is more than fixed costs, there will be profit, if it is equal to fixed costs, there will be no profit, and if it is less than fixed costs, there will be loss.

Computation	It can be computed as follows: 1. Contribution = Total Sales Value – Total Variable Costs. *or,* $C = SO - VO$ 2. Contribution = Fixed Cost + Profit *or,* $C = F + P$ 3. Contribution = Fixed Cost – Loss *or,* $C = F - L$

Illustration 6. Calculate Contribution in each of the following cases:

Case (a) Selling Price Per Unit ₹ 10, Variable Cost Per Unit ₹ 6.
Case (b) Total Sales ₹ 6,000, Total Variable Cost ₹ 3,600
Case (c) Fixed Costs ₹ 2,000, Profit ₹ 400
Case (d) Fixed Costs ₹ 2,000, Profit 0
Case (e) Fixed Costs ₹ 2,000, Loss ₹ 400

Solution:

(a) Contribution per unit = Selling Price per unit – Variable Cost per unit
= ₹ 10 – ₹ 6 = ₹ 4

(b) Contribution = Total Sales – Total Variable Cost = ₹ 6,000 – ₹ 3,600 = ₹ 2,400

(c) Contribution = Fixed Costs + Profit = ₹ 2,000 + ₹ 400 = ₹ 2,400

(d) Contribution = Fixed Costs + Profit = ₹ 2,000 + 0 = ₹ 2,000

(e) Contribution = Fixed Costs – Loss = ₹ 2,000 – ₹ 400 = ₹ 1,600

12.0 WHAT IS 'PROFIT VOLUME RATIO' (*OR* P/V RATIO)?

Meaning	P/V Ratio is the ratio of Contribution to Sales and is usually expressed as a percentage.
Computation	It can be computed as follows: 1. $\text{P/V Ratio (in \%)} = \frac{\text{Contribution}}{\text{Sales}} \times 100$ 2. $\text{P/V Ratio (in \%)} = \frac{\text{Sales} - \text{Variable Cost}}{\text{Sales}} \times 100$ 3. $\text{P/V Ratio (in \%)} = \frac{\text{Fixed Costs} + \text{Profit}}{\text{Sales}} \times 100$ 4. $\text{P/V Ratio (in \%)} = 100 - \left(\frac{\text{Variable Cost}}{\text{Sales}} \times 100\right)$ 5. $\text{P/V Ratio (in \%)} = \frac{\text{Change in Profit}}{\text{Change in Sales}} \times 100$
What Indicates?	P/V Ratio indicates the effect on profit for a given change in the sales.
Uses	(a) P/V Ratio facilitates the determination of – (i) Variable cost for any given sales volume (ii) Contribution for any given sales volume (iii) Sales volume for any given variable cost (iv) Sales volume required to earn desired profit (v) Break-Even Point (vi) Fixed costs for any given Break-Even Point

	(b) P/V Ratio measures the profitability of each product, operation, process, factory, sales area etc. (c) P/V Ratio facilitates managerial decision-making regarding the choice of product, choice of process etc.
How to Improve?	(a) by reducing variable cost, *or* (b) by increasing the selling price, *or* (c) by reducing variable cost and increasing the selling price, *or* (d) by improving Sales Mix (*i.e.* by increasing the sales of products having higher P/V Ratio and reducing the sales of products having lower P/V Ratio)

Illustration 7. Calculate P/V Ratio in each of the following cases:

Case (a) Contribution ₹ 3, Sales ₹ 15

Case (b) Sales ₹ 10 and Variable Cost ₹ 4

Case (c) Variable Cost ₹ 4, and Contribution ₹ 4

Case (d) Variable Cost to Sales Ratio 40%

Case (e) Fixed Cost ₹ 2,000, Profit ₹ 400, Sales ₹ 6,000

Case (f)

	Year I	*Year II*
Sales	₹ 4,50,000	₹ 5,10,000
Profit	₹ 60,000	₹ 75,000

Case (g)

	Year I	*Year II*
Sales	₹ 1,50,000	₹ 70,000
Total Cost	₹. 1,20,000	₹. 80,000

Solution:

Case (a) $\text{P/V Ratio} = \dfrac{\text{Contribution}}{\text{Sales}} \times 100 = \dfrac{3}{15} \times 100 = 20\%$

Case (b) $\text{P/V Ratio} = \dfrac{\text{Sales} - \text{Variable Cost}}{\text{Sales}} \times = \dfrac{10-4}{10} \times 100 = 60\%$

Case (c) $\text{P/V Ratio} = \dfrac{\text{Contribution}}{\text{Variable Cost} + \text{Contribution}} \times 100 = \dfrac{4}{4+4} \times 100 = 50\%$

Case (d) P/V Ratio = 100 – Variable Cost to Sales Ratio = 100 – 40% = 60%

Case (e) $\text{P/V Ratio} = \dfrac{\text{Fixed Cost} + \text{Profit}}{\text{Sales}} \times 100 = \dfrac{2{,}000 + 400}{6{,}000} \times 100 = 40\%$

Case (f) $\text{P/V Ratio} = \dfrac{\text{Change in Profit}}{\text{Change in Sales}} \times 100 = \dfrac{75{,}000 - 60{,}000}{5{,}10{,}000 - 4{,}50{,}000} \times 100 = 25\%$

Case (g) $\text{P/V Ratio} = \dfrac{\text{Change in Profit}}{\text{Change in Sales}} \times 100 = \dfrac{-10{,}000 - 30{,}000}{70{,}000 - 1{,}50{,}000} \times 100 = 50\%$

Illustration 8. Selling Price per unit ₹ 10, Variable Cost per unit ₹ 4
Calculate P/V ratio in each of following cases:

(a) If selling price is reduced by 20%
(b) If selling price is increased by 20%
(c) If variable cost is decreased by 25%
(d) If variable cost is increased by 25%
(e) If selling price and variable cost are reduced by 20% and 25% respectively.
(f) If selling price and variable cost are increased by 20% and 25% respectively.

Solution:

$$\text{New P/V Ratio} = \frac{\text{New Selling Price} - \text{Variable cost}}{\text{New Selling Prioe}} \times 100$$

(a) $\text{New P/V Ratio} = \dfrac{(10 - 20\%\text{ of }10) - 4}{(10 - 20\%\text{ of }10)} \times 100 = 50\%$

(b) $\text{New P/V Ratio} = \dfrac{(10 + 20\%\text{ of }10) - 4}{(10 + 20\%\text{ of }10)} \times 100 = 66\frac{2}{3}\%$

$\text{New P/V Ratio} = \dfrac{\text{Selling Price} - \text{New Variable Cost}}{\text{Selling Price}} \times 100$

(c) $\text{New P/V Ratio} = \dfrac{10 - (4 - 25\%\text{ of }4)}{10} \times 100 = 70\%$

(d) $\text{New P/V Ratio} = \dfrac{10 - (4 + 25\%\text{ of }4)}{10} \times 100 = 50\%$

$\text{New P/V Ratio} = \dfrac{\text{New Selling Price} - \text{New Variable Cost}}{\text{New Selling Price}} \times 100$

(e) $\text{New P/V Ratio} = \dfrac{(10 - 20\%\text{ of }10) - (4 - 25\%\text{ of }4)}{(10 - 20\%\text{ of }10)} \times 100 = 62.5\%$

(f) $\text{New P/V Ratio} = \dfrac{(10 + 20\%\text{ of }10) - (4 + 25\%\text{ of }4)}{10 + 20\%\text{ of }10} \times 100 = 58.33\%$

13.0 WHAT IS BREAK EVEN ANALYSIS?

Meaning	Break Even Analysis is a technique used for studying the relationship between Cost, Volume and Profit at different levels of operations. It is also called Cost-Volume-Profit Analysis (*or* CVP Analysis).
Usefulness	It is used to determine– (a) the amount of profit/loss at various volume of operations (b) the volume of operations required to earn a target profit (c) the effect of change in variable cost on profit (d) the effect of change in fixed cost on profit (e) the effect of change in selling price on profit (f) the effect of change in sales volume on profit

14.0 WHAT IS BREAK EVEN POINT?

Meaning	(a) Break Even Point refers to that volume of operation at which total sales revenue is just equal to total cost (*i.e.* Fixed Cost and Variable Cost). (b) It is the point at which there is *neither* profit *nor* loss. (c) It is the point at which contribution (*i.e.* Sales – Variable Costs) is just equal to fixed costs.
How to Calculate	B.E.P. can be expressed in terms of number of units, value *or* percentage of sales. 1. $\text{B.E.P (in units)} = \dfrac{\text{Fixed Costs}}{\text{Contribution Per Unit}}$ 2. $\text{B.E.P (in value)} = \dfrac{\text{Fixed Cost}}{\text{Contribution per unit}} \times \text{Selling Price Per Unit}$ *or* $= \dfrac{\text{Fixed Cost}}{\text{P/V Ratio}}$ 3. $\text{B.E.P (in \%)} = \dfrac{\text{Fixed Cost}}{\text{Total Contribution}} \times 100$ *or,* $= \dfrac{\text{B.E.P. (in value)}}{\text{Total Sales (in value)}} \times 100$

<table>
<tr><td></td><td>

or, $= \dfrac{\text{B.E.P. (in units)}}{\text{Total Sales (in units)}} \times 100$

4. Cash B.E.P. (units) $= \dfrac{\text{Cash Fixed Costs}}{\text{Contribution per unit}}$

or, $= \dfrac{\text{Total Fixed Cost} - \text{Non Cash Fixed Costs}}{\text{Contribution per unit}}$

5. Cash B.E.P (₹) $= \dfrac{\text{Cash Fixed Costs}}{\text{P/V Ratio}}$

Note: Non-Cash Fixed Costs are those fixed costs which do not involve any Cash Outflow. *For Example*, Depreciation, Write off of Deferred Revenue Expenditure, Intangible Assets, etc., Notional Rent for Owner's Building.

</td></tr>
<tr><td>Profitability Before and After Reaching B.E.P.</td><td>Before reaching B.E.P., the firm incurs losses and after reaching B.E.P. the firm earns profits.</td></tr>
</table>

Illustration 9. Selling Price per unit ₹ 10, Variable Cost per unit ₹ 6, Fixed Costs ₹ 2,000, Actual Sales ₹ 20,000. Fixed costs include Depreciation ₹ 300, Deferred Revenue Expenditure w/o ₹ 100.

Calculate Break-Even Point (in units), Break Even Point (in value), Break-Even Point (in %) and Cash Break Even

Solution:

$$\text{B.E.P. (in units)} = \frac{\text{Fixed Costs}}{\text{Contribution per unit}} = \frac{2{,}000}{10-6} = 500 \text{ units}$$

$$\text{B.E.P. (in value)} = \frac{\text{Fixed Costs}}{\text{Contribution per unit}} \times \text{Selling Price per unit}$$

$$= \frac{2{,}000}{10-6} \times ₹\ 10 = ₹\ 5{,}000$$

or
$$= \frac{\text{Fixed Costs}}{\text{P/V Ratio}} = \frac{2{,}000}{40\%} = ₹\ 5{,}000$$

Note: $\text{P/V Ratio} = \dfrac{\text{Contribution}}{\text{Sales}} \times 100 = \dfrac{10-6}{10} \times 100 = 40\%$

$$\text{B.E.P. (in \%)} = \frac{\text{B.E.P. (in units)}}{\text{Actual Sales (in units)}} \times 100 = \frac{500}{2{,}000} \times 100 = 25\%$$

or
$$= \frac{\text{Actual B.E.P (in Rs)}}{\text{Actual Sales (in Rs)}} \times 100 = \frac{5{,}000}{20{,}000} \times 100 = 25\%$$

or
$$= \frac{\text{Fixed Costs}}{\text{Total Contribution}} \times 100 = \frac{2{,}000}{8{,}000} \times 100 = 25\%$$

Note: Total Contribution = Total Sales – Total Variable Cost = ₹ 20,000 – ₹ 12,000 = ₹ 8,000

$$\text{Cash B.E.P (units)} = \frac{\text{Cash Fixed Costs}}{\text{Contribution per unit}} = \frac{2{,}000 - (300+100)}{10-6} = 400 \text{ units}$$

$$\text{Cash B.E.P (₹)} = \frac{\text{Cash Fixed Costs}}{\text{P/V Ratio}} = \frac{2{,}000 - (300+100)}{40\%} = ₹\ 4{,}000$$

Illustration 10. Selling Price per unit ₹ 10, Variable Cost per unit ₹ 4, Fixed Costs ₹ 35,000. Calculate New B.E.P. in each of the following cases:

(a) If selling price is reduced by 20%
(b) If variable cost is decreased by 25%
(c) If fixed cost is increased by 20%
(d) If selling price and variable cost are decreased by 20% and 25% respectively and fixed cost is increased by 20%

Solution:

(a) $$\text{New P/V Ratio} = \frac{\text{New Selling Price} - \text{Variable Cost}}{\text{New Selling Rice}} \times 100$$

$$= \frac{(10 - 20\% \text{ of } 10) - 4}{(10 - 20\% \text{ of } 10)} \times 100 = 50\%$$

$$\text{New B.E.P.} = \frac{\text{Fixed Cost}}{\text{New P/V Ratio}} = \frac{35{,}000}{50\%} = ₹\ 70{,}000$$

(b) $$\text{New P/V Ratio} = \frac{\text{Selling Price} - \text{New Variable Cost}}{\text{Selling Price}} \times 100$$

$$= \frac{10 - (4 - 25\% \text{ of } 4)}{10} \times 100 = 70\%$$

$$\text{New B.E.P.} = \frac{\text{Fixed Costs}}{\text{New P/V Ratio}} = \frac{35{,}000}{70\%} = ₹\ 50{,}000$$

(c) $$\text{P/V Ratio} = \frac{10 - 4}{10} \times 100 = 60\%$$

$$\text{New B.E.P.} = \frac{\text{New Fixed Costs}}{\text{P/V Ratio}} = \frac{35{,}000 + 20\% \text{ of } 35{,}000}{60\%} = ₹\ 70{,}000$$

(d) $$\text{New P/V Ratio} = \frac{\text{New Selling Price} - \text{New Variable Cost}}{\text{New Selling Price}} \times 100$$

$$= \frac{(10 - 20\% \text{ of } 10) - (4 - 25\% \text{ of } 4)}{10 - 20\% \text{ of } 10} \times 100 = 62.5\%$$

$$\text{New B.E.P.} = \frac{\text{New Fixed Costs}}{\text{New P/V Ratio}} = \frac{35{,}000 + 20\% \text{ of } 35{,}000}{62.5\%} = ₹\ 67{,}200$$

Illustration 11. The cost of production of a product per unit is as follows:

	₹
Direct Materials	5
Direct Wages	4
Production Overheads (40% Fixed)	5
Administration Overheads (Fixed)	1
	15

The figures given above are based on an output of 1,00,000 units : Selling Price per unit is ₹ 20. What is the Break-even-Point?

Solution:

Step 1 → Fixed Overheads = Fixed Production Overheads + Fixed Adm. Overheads
= (1,00,000 × ₹ 2) + (1,00,000 × ₹ 1) = ₹ 3,00,000

Step 2 → Contribution per unit = Selling Price – Variable Cost
= ₹ 20 – (₹ 5 + ₹ 4 + ₹ 3) = ₹ 8

Step 3 → $$\text{B.E.P (Units)} = \frac{\text{Fixed Overheads}}{\text{Contribution per unit}} = \frac{3{,}00{,}000}{8} = 37{,}500 \text{ units}$$

B.E.P. (₹) = 37500 units × ₹ 20 = ₹ 7,50,000

Illustration 12. Calculate Break Even Sales from the following information:

	Year I	Year II
Total Sales	₹. 20,000	₹. 30,000
Total Cost	₹. 17,600	₹. 21,600

Solution:

(a) Profit/Volume Ratio = $\frac{\text{Difference in Profit}}{\text{Difference in Total Sales}} \times 100 = \frac{8,400 - 2,400}{30,000 - 20,000} \times 100 = 60\%$

(b) Fixed Costs = Contribution – Profit = 60% of ₹ 20,000 – ₹ 2,400 = ₹ 9,600

(c) Break-Even Point = $\frac{\text{Fixed Costs}}{\text{P/V Ratio}} = \frac{9,600}{60\%}$ = ₹ 16,000

Illustration 13. Profit Volume Ratio 40%. Break Even Sales ₹. 2,50,000. Calculate Fixed Costs.

Solution:

Fixed Cost = Break Even Sales × P/V Ratio = ₹ 2,50,000 × 40% = ₹ 1,00,000

15.0 WHAT IS MARGIN OF SAFETY?

Meaning	(a) Margin of Safety is the difference between the Actual Sales and the Break Even Sales (b) At any level of margin of safety, fixed costs are zero since fixed costs are already recovered upto Break-even point. (c) At any level of margin of safety, the contribution (*i.e.* Sales – Variable Costs) is equal to profits since fixed costs are zero.
How to Calculate	Margin of Safety can be expressed in terms of number of units, value *or* percentage of sales.
	1. Margin of Safety (in units) = Actual Sales (in units) – Break Even Sales (in units) *or,* $= \frac{\text{Profit}}{\text{Contribution per unit}}$ 2. Margin of Safety (in value) = Actual Sales (in value) – Break Even Sales (in value) *or,* $= \frac{\text{Profit}}{\text{Contribution per unit}} \times \text{Selling Price per unit}$ *or,* $= \frac{\text{Profit}}{\text{P/V Ratio}}$ *or,* = Margin of Safety (in units) × Selling Price per unit 3. Margin of Safety (in % of Sales) $= \frac{\text{Margin of Safety (in units)}}{\text{Actual Sales (in units)}} \times 100$ *or,* $= \frac{\text{Margin of Safety (in Rs)}}{\text{Actual Sales (in Rs)}} \times 100$ *or,* $= \frac{\text{Profit}}{\text{Total Contribution}} \times 100$ *or,* = 100 – Break Even Sales (in %)

How to Improve	Margin of Safety can be improved — (a) by increasing the selling price provided the demand is inelastic so as to absorb the increased prices (b) by increasing the sales volume provided the capacity is available (c) by reducing variable cost (d) by reducing fixed cost (e) by improving the sales mix

Tutorial Notes:

1. *Fixed Costs are used as numerator in the formulae for B.E.P.*
2. *Profit is used as numerator in the formulae for Margin of Safety.*
3. *Same denominators (i.e., Contribution per unit, P/V Ratio, Total Contribution) are used in the formulae for B.E.P. and Margin of Safety.*

Illustration 14. Selling Price per unit ₹ 10, Variable Cost per unit ₹ 6. Fixed Cost ₹ 2,000, Actual Sales ₹ 20,000. Calculate Margin of Safety (in units), Margin of Safety (in value) and Margin of Safety (in %).

Solution:

MARGINAL COST SHEET

A	Actual Sales (in units)	2,000
B	Selling Price Per unit	₹ 10
C	Total Sales (A x B)	₹ 20,000
D	*Less:* Total Variable Cost (2000 x ₹ 6)	₹ 12,000
E	Total Contribution (C – D)	₹ 8,000
F	*Less:* Fixed Costs	₹ 2,000
G	Profit	₹ 6,000

$$\text{Margin of Safety (in units)} = \frac{\text{Profit}}{\text{Contribution per unit}} = \frac{6,000}{10-6} = 1500 \text{ units}$$

$$\text{Margin of Safety (in value)} = \frac{\text{Profit}}{\text{Contribution per unit}} \times \text{Selling Price per unit}$$

$$= \frac{6,000}{10-6} \times ₹\ 10 = ₹\ 15,000$$

$$\text{Margin of Safety (in \%)} = \frac{\text{Margin of Safety (in units)}}{\text{Actual Sales (in units)}} \times 100 = \frac{1500}{2000} \times 100 = 75\%$$

$$or, \quad = \frac{\text{Margin of Safety (in value)}}{\text{Actual Sales (in value)}} \times \frac{15,000}{20,000} \times 100 = 75\%$$

$$or, \quad = \frac{\text{Profit}}{\text{Total Contribution}} \times 100 = \frac{6,000}{8,000} \times 100 = 75\%$$

Illustration 15. Calculate Margin of Safety in each of the following alternative cases :

(a) Profit ₹. 2,400, Contribution per unit ₹. 6
(b) Break- Even Sales 1600 units, Actual Sales 2000 units
(c) Profit ₹. 2,400, P/V Ratio 60%
(d) Break-Even Sales 30%, Actual Sales ₹ 20,000
(e) Profit ₹. 4,800, Total Contribution ₹. 19,200
(f) Break- Even Sales 70%.
(g)

	Year I	*Year II*
Total Sales	₹. 20,000	₹. 30,000
Total Profit	₹. 2,400	₹. 8,400

Solution:

(a) $\text{Margin of Safety} = \frac{\text{Profit}}{\text{Contribution per unit}} = \frac{2,400}{6} = 400 \text{ units}$

(b) Margin of Safety = Actual Sales (in units) – B.E.P. (in units)
= 2000 units – 1600 units = 400 units

(c) $\text{Margin of Safety} = \frac{\text{Profit}}{\text{P/V Ratio}} = \frac{2,400}{60\%} = ₹.\ 4,000$

(d) Margin of Safety = Actual Sales – B.E.P.
= ₹. 20,000 – 30% of ₹. 20,000 = ₹. 14,000

(e) Margin of Safety = $\frac{\text{Profit}}{\text{Total Contribution}} \times 100 = \frac{4,800}{19,200} \times 100 = 25\%$

(f) Margin of Safety = 100 % – B.E.P. (in %) = 100 % – 70% = 30%

(g) (i) Profit/Volume Ratio = $\frac{\text{Difference in Profit}}{\text{Difference in Total Sales}} \times 100 = \frac{8,400 - 2,400}{30,000 - 20,000} \times 100 = 60\%$

(ii) Fixed Costs = Contribution – Profit
Taking the figures relating to 20X1
A Contribution = 60% of ₹ 20,000 = ₹ 12,000
B Profit = ₹ 20,000 – ₹ 17,600 = ₹ 2,400
C Fixed Costs [A – B] = ₹ 9,600

(iii) Break-Even Point = $\frac{\text{Fixed Costs}}{\text{P/V Ratio}} = \frac{9,600}{60\%}$ = ₹ 16,000

(iv) Margin of Safety = Actual Sales – Break-Even Sales
For 20X1= ₹ 20,000 – ₹ 16,000 = ₹ 4,000
For 20X2 = ₹ 30,000 – ₹ 16,000 = ₹ 14,000

16.0 WHAT IS BREAK-EVEN CHART?

Meaning	Break Even Chart is a graphical representation of the Break Even Analysis (*or* Cost, Volume – Profit Relationship).
What Does it show?	It shows— (a) Variable Cost at various levels of activity (b) Fixed Cost at various levels of activity (c) Total Cost at various levels of activity (d) Profit/Loss at various levels of activity (e) Break-even Point (f) Margin of Safety (g) Angle of Incidence (h) Loss Area (i) Profit Area
What is Angle of Incidence?	It is the angle between total sales line and total cost line drawn in the case of break-even chart. It indicates the rate at which profits are being earned. The larger the angle, the higher the rate of profit *or* vice-versa.
How to Prepare?	**PRACTICAL STEPS IN THE PREPARATION OF BREAK EVEN CHART** **Step 1 →** *Take Production & Sales (in units) on X-axis* **Step 2 →** *Take Cost & Sales (in ₹) on Y-axis.* **Step 3 →** *Draw Fixed Cost line as horizontal line* **Step 4 →** *Draw Total Cost line starting from the point of fixed cost* **Step 5 →** *Draw Sales Line starting from the point of origin.* **Step 6 →** *Locate the point where Total Sales line cuts the Total Cost line. This point is known as Break Even Point.* **Step 7 →** *Draw the perpendicular from B.E.P. on X-axis. The point at which this perpendicular touches X-axis gives us B.E.P (in units)* **Step 8 →** *Draw the perpendicular from B.E.P. on Y-axis. The point at which this perpendicular touches Y-axis gives us B.E.P. (in ₹)*

Uses	(a) Break-Even Chart facilitates the determination of: (i) Break-Even Point (ii) Margin of Safety (iii) Angle of incidence (iv) Sales required to earn a desired amount of profit (v) Fixed Cost, Variable Cost, Total Cost, Sales, Profit at various level of operations. (b) Break even Chart can be used to show the effect of any of the following changes on profit: (i) Change in the Sales Volume (ii) Change in the Selling Price (iii) Change in the Variable Costs (iv) Change in the Fixed Costs (c) Break Even Chart facilitates Inter-firm comparision
Assumptions	Break-even Analysis is based on the following assumptions: (a) All costs can be separated into fixed and variable components. (b) Fixed costs will remain constant. (c) Variable cost will change in direct proportion to the volume of output. In other words, variable cost per unit will remain constant. (d) Selling price of the product will remain constant. (e) There is only one product *or* in the case of multiple products, the sales mix will remain constant. (*i.e.*, sales of various products will always be in some predetermined proportions). (f) Entire production will be sold. (g) Productivity and Operating efficiency will remain constant. (h) Product specifications and methods of manufacturing and selling will remain constant. (i) General price level will remain constant.
Limitations	Break even analysis is fundamentally a static analysis as it assumes almost everything constant (*e.g.*, constant total fixed costs, variable cost per unit, selling price, productivity, sales mix in case of multi products etc.). The limitations which make the assumptions to be unrealistic are given below: (a) All costs can not be separated into fixed and variable components with accuracy. (b) Fixed costs may change because of change in management policy *or* after a range of activity. (c) Variable cost per unit may change because of operation of law of increasing returns *or* decreasing returns. (d) Selling price may change because of increase *or* decrease in output, market demand & supply, competition etc. (e) In case of multiple products, the sales mix need not necessarily be constant. (f) In case of multiple products, separate break even points are to be calculated. This poses a problem of apportionment of fixed costs to each product. (g) Entire production need not necessarily be sold in practice. (h) A Breakeven chart assumes that business condition will not change. This is hardly so. (i) A break-even chart does not consider the amount of capital employed in the business, a very important factor for determining profitability of a concern.

Cash Break-even Chart	Cash Break-even Chart is a graphical representation of the Cost, Volume-Profit Relationship under which, only cash fixed costs are considered. Non-cash items like depreciation etc. are excluded from the fixed cost for computation of cash break-even point. It depicts the level of output or sales at which the sales revenue will be equal to total cash cost. It is computed as under: $$\text{Cash BEP (Units)} = \frac{\text{Cash Fixed Cost}}{\text{Contribution Per Unit}}, \text{Cash BEP (₹)} = \frac{\text{Cash Fixed Cost}}{\text{P/V Ratio.}}$$

Illustration 16. Selling Price per unit ₹ 12, Variable Cost per unit ₹ 6. Fixed Cost ₹ 2,400.

Calculate Break Even Point (in units) and (in value) with the help of Break Even Chart.

Solution:

In order to determine BEP, it will be necessary to compute total cost and sales at varying levels as follows:

Output	*Variable Cost* (₹)	*Fixed Cost* (₹)	*Total Cost* (₹)	*Sales* (₹)
100	600	2,400	3,000	1,200
200	1,200	2,400	3,600	2,400
300	1,800	2,400	4,200	3,600
400	2,400	2,400	• 4,800	4,800
500	3,000	2,400	5,400	6,000
600	3,600	2,400	6,000	7,200
700	4,200	2,400	6,600	8,400
800	4,800	2,400	7,200	9,600

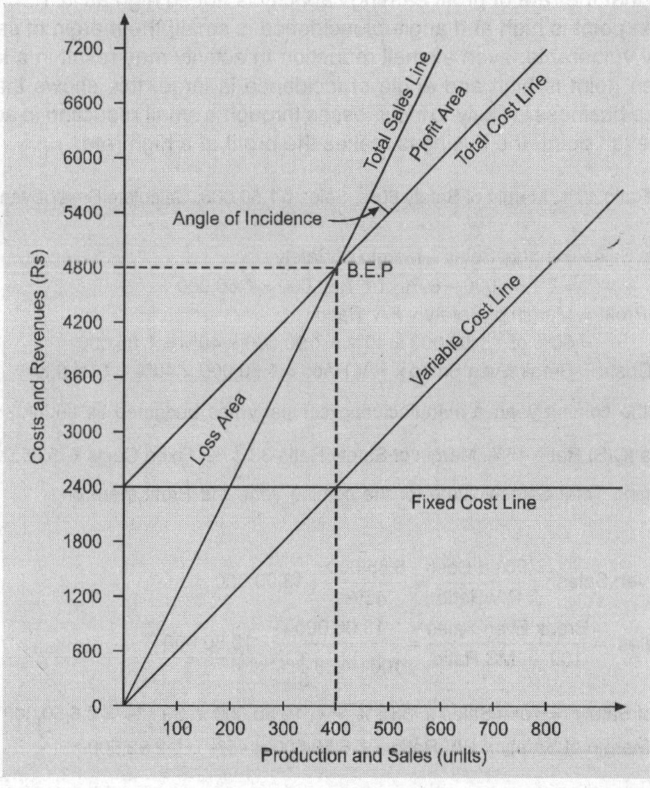

B.E.P. (in units) = 400 units

B.E.P (in ₹) = ₹ 4,800

Verification:

$$\text{B.E.P. (in units)} = \frac{\text{Fixed Costs}}{\text{Contribution Per Unit}} = \frac{2,400}{12-6} = 400 \text{ units}$$

$$\text{B.E.P. (in ₹)} = \frac{\text{Fixed Costs}}{\text{P/V Ratio}} = \frac{2,400}{[(12-6)/12)]} = ₹\ 4,800$$

17.0 RELATIONSHIP BETWEEN ANGLE OF INCIDENCE, BREAK-EVEN LEVEL AND MARGIN OF SAFETY

The relationship between Angle of Incidence, Break-even Level and Margin of Safety can be shown as follows:

	Situation		Effect on	
Case	**Break Even Point**	**Angle of Incidence**	**Margin of Safety**	**Rate of Profit**
1	Low	Large	Large	High
2	Low	Small	Large	Low
3	High	Small	Low	Low
4	High	Large	Low	High

1. If the break-even point is low and angle of incidence is large, the margin of safety is large and the business enjoys financial stability. A low break-even point indicates that the business could be run profitably even if there is a fall in sales, unless the sales are very low.
2. If the break-even point is low and angle of incidence is small, the conclusions are the same as in 1 above except that the rate of profit earning capacity is not so high as in 1.
3. If the break-even point is high and angle of incidence is small, the margin of safety is low. The business is very vulnerable, even a small reduction in activity may result in a loss.
4. If the break-even point is high and angle of incidence is large, this shows that the margin of safety is low. The business is likely to incur losses through a small reduction in activity. However, after the break-even point, the business makes the profit at a high rate.

Illustration 17. P/V Ratio 40%, Margin of Safety 60%, Sales ₹ 1,50,000. Calculate Break Even Sales, Fixed Cost and Net Profit.

Solution: Break Even Sales = Actual Sales – Margin of Safety

= ₹ 1,50,000 – 60% of ₹ 1,50,000 = ₹ 60,000

Profit = Margin of Safety × P/V Ratio

= 60% of ₹ 1,50,000 × 40% = ₹ 90,000 × 40% = ₹ 36,000

Fixed Costs = Break Even Sales × P/V Ratio = ₹ 60,000 × 40% = ₹ 24,000

Illustration 18. For the coming year, a manufacturing company has budgeted as under:

Contribution / Sales (C/S) Ratio 45%, Margin of Safety Ratio $33\frac{1}{3}$ %, Fixed Costs ₹. 5,85,000

Required: Determine Total Sales-volume for the coming year and Profit there on.

Solution:

Step 1→ Break Even Sales $= \frac{\text{Fixed Cost}}{\text{P/V Ratio}} = \frac{5,85,000}{45\%} = 13,00,000$

Step 2→ Total Sales $= \frac{\text{Break Even Sales}}{100 - \text{MS Ratio}} = \frac{13,00,000}{100 - 33\frac{1}{3}\%} = 19,50,000$

Step 3→ Margin of Safety = Total Sales × $33\frac{1}{3}\%$ = ₹. 19,50,000 × $33\frac{1}{3}\%$ = ₹ 6,50,000

Step 4→ Profit = Margin of Safety × P/V Ratio = ₹ 6,50,000 × 45% = ₹ 2,92,500.

Illustration 19. P/V Ratio 40%, Margin of Safety 20%, Break even point ₹ 200 crores. Calculate Total Sales, Fixed Cost and Profit.

Solution:

(a) Total Sales = $\frac{\text{Break Even Sales}}{100 - \text{MS Ratio}} = \frac{200 \text{ crores}}{100\% - 20\%}$ = ₹ 250 crores

(b) Fixed Costs = Break Even Sales × P/V Ratio = ₹. 200 crores × 40% = ₹ 80 crores

(c) Net Profit = Margin of Safety × P/V Ratio = (20% of ₹ 250 crores) × 40% = ₹. 20 crores

Illustration 20. Break Even Sales ₹. 16,000, Total Cost ₹. 17,600, Break Even Sales 1600 units. Margin of Safety 400 units, Calculate Fixed Cost.

Solution:

Step 1→ Break Even Sales (%) = $\frac{\text{Break Even Sales (units)}}{\text{Actual Sales (units)}} \times 100 = \frac{1,600}{1,600 + 400} \times 100$ = 80%

Step 2→ Total Sales = $\frac{\text{Break Even Sales (₹)}}{\text{Break Even Sales (\%)}} = \frac{6,000}{80\%}$ = ₹. 20,000

Step 3→ Profit = Total Sales – Total Cost = ₹ 20,000 – ₹ 17,600 = ₹. 2,400

Step 4→ Margin of Safety (₹) = Total Sales × (100 – BEP%) = ₹. 20,000 × 20% = ₹. 4,000.

Step 5→ P/V Ratio = $\frac{\text{Profit}}{\text{Margin of Safety (₹)}} \times 100 = \frac{2,400}{4,000} \times 100$ = 60%

Step 6→ Fixed Costs = BEP (₹) × P/V Ratio = ₹. 16,000 × 60% = ₹. 9,600

Illustration 21. Margin of Safety ₹. 64,000, Total Cost ₹. 41,600, Margin of Safety 6,400 units, Break even Sales 1,600 units, calculate Fixed Costs.

Solution:

Step 1→ Margin of Safety (%) = $\frac{\text{Margin of Safety (units)}}{\text{Actual Sales (Units)}} \times 100 = \frac{6,400}{6,400 + 1,600} \times 100$ = 80%

Step 2→ Total Sales = $\frac{\text{Margin of Safety (₹)}}{\text{Margin of Safety (\%)}} = \frac{64,000}{80\%}$ = ₹. 80,000

Step 3→ Profit = Total Sales – Total Cost = ₹. 80,000 – ₹. 41,600 = ₹. 38,400

Step 4→ P/V Ratio = $\frac{\text{Profit}}{\text{Margin of Safety (₹)}} = \frac{38,400}{64,000} \times 100$ = 60%

Step 5→ Break Even Sales = Total Sales × (100 – MS%) = ₹ 80,000 × 20% = ₹ 16,000

Step 6→ Fixed Costs = BEP × P/V Ratio = ₹ 16,000 × 60% = ₹ 9,600.

Illustration 22. The following information is given by Tushar Ltd.

Sales ₹ 80,000, Cost (2/3rd variable) ₹ 72,000

(a) Calculate the P/V Ratio, Break-Even Point, Margin of Safety and Profit at the existing level

(b) Calculate the effect of

(i) 10% decrease in selling price
(ii) 10% increase in selling price
(iii) 10% decrease in variable cost
(iv) 10% increase in variable cost
(v) 10% decrease in fixed cost
(vi) 10% increase in fixed cost
(vii) 10% *decrease* in selling price accompained by 10% *decrease* in variable costs
(viii) 10% *increase* in selling price accompained by 10% *increase* in variable costs
(ix) 10% decrease in sales volume
(x) 10% increase in sales volume
(xi) 20% Increase in sales volume, 10% decrease in selling price, 10% decrease in variable cost and 10% increase in fixed cost

Solution:

P/V Ratio = $\frac{\text{Contribution}}{\text{Sales}} \times 100$

B.E.P. (₹) = $\frac{\text{Fixed Costs}}{\text{P/V Ratio}}$

Margin of Safety (M.S.) (in ₹) = $\frac{\text{Profit}}{\text{P/V Ratio}}$

Particulars	*Present*	*(i)*	*(ii)*	*(iii)*	*(iv)*	*(v)*
Sales	80,000	72,000	88,000	80,000	80,000	80,000
Less: Variable Cost	(48,000)	(48,000)	(48,000)	(43,200)	(52,800)	(48,000)
Contribution	32,000	24,000	40,000	36,800	27,200	32,000
Less: Fixed Cost	(24,000)	(24,000)	(24,000)	(24,000)	(24,000)	(21,600)
Profit	8,000	0	16,000	12,800	3,200	10,400

Particulars	*(vi)*	*(vii)*	*(viii)*	*(ix)*	*(x)*	*(xI)*
Sales	80,000	72,000	88,000	72,000	88,000	86,400
Less: Variable Cost	(48,000)	(43,200)	(52,800)	(43,200)	(52,800)	51,840
Contribution	32,000	28,800	35,200	28,800	35,200	34,560
Less: Fixed Cost	(26,400)	(24,000)	(24,000)	(24,000)	(24,000)	26,400
Profit	5,600	4,800	11,200	4,800	11,200	8,160

(a) **At existing level**

$$\text{P/V Ratio} = \frac{32,000}{80,000} \times 100 = 40\%$$

B.E.P. (₹) = ₹ 24,000/40% = ₹ 60,000

M.S. (₹) = ₹ 8,000/40% = ₹ 20,000

(b) (i) **10% decrease in Selling Price**

$$\text{P/V Ratio} = \frac{24,000}{72,000} \times 100 = 33\frac{1}{3}\%$$

B.E.P (₹) = ₹ 24,000/ $33\frac{1}{3}\%$ = ₹ 72,000

M.S. (₹) = ₹ 0/ $33\frac{1}{3}\%$ = 0

(ii) **10% increase in Selling Price**

$$\text{P/V Ratio} = \frac{40,000}{88,000} \times 100 = 45.45\%$$

B.E.P (₹) = ₹ 24,000/45.45% = ₹ 52,800

M.S. (₹) = ₹ 16,000/45.45% = ₹ 35,200

(iii) **10% decrease in Variable Cost**

$$\text{P/V Ratio} = \frac{36,800}{80,000} \times 100 = 46\%$$

B.E.P. (₹) = ₹ 24,000/46% = ₹ 52,174

M.S. (₹) = ₹ 12,800/46% = ₹ 27,826

(iv) **10% increase in Variable Cost**

$$\text{P/V Ratio} = \frac{27,200}{80,000} \times 100 = 34\%$$

B.E.P (₹) = ₹ 24,000/34% = ₹ 70,588

M.S. (₹) = ₹ 3,200/34% = ₹ 9,412

(v) **10% decrease in Fixed Cost**

$$\text{P/V Ratio} = \frac{32,000}{80,000} \times 100 = 40\%$$

B.E.P. (₹) = ₹ 21,600/40% = ₹ 54,000

M.S (₹) = ₹ 10,400/40% = ₹ 26,000

(vi) **10% increase in Fixed Cost**

$$\text{P/V Ratio} = \frac{32,000}{80,000} \times 100 = 40\%$$

B.E.P. (₹) = ₹ 26,400/40% = ₹ 66,000

M.S. (₹) = ₹ 5,600/40% = ₹ 14,000

(vii) **10% decrease in Selling Price accompanied by 10% decrease in Variable Cost**

$$\text{P/V Ratio} = \frac{28{,}800}{72{,}000} \times 100 = 40\%$$

B.E.P. (₹) = ₹ 24,000/40% = ₹ 60,000

M.S. (₹) = ₹ 4,800/40% = ₹ 12,000

(viii) **10% increase in Selling Price accompanied by 10% increase in Variable Costs**

$$\text{P/V Ratio} = \frac{35{,}200}{88{,}000} \times 100 = 40\%$$

B.E.P. (₹) = ₹ 24,000/40% = ₹ 60,000

M.S. (₹) = ₹ 11,200/40% = ₹ 28,000

(ix) **10% decrease in Sales Volume**

It means 10% decrease in sales units and hence both Present sales value and variable costs will decrease by 10%

Solution same as in case (vii)

(x) **10% increase in Sales Volume**

It means 10% increase in sales units and hence both present sales value and variable cost will increase by 10%.

Solution same as in case (viii)

(xi) **P/V Ratio** = $\frac{34{,}560}{86{,}400} \times 100 = 40\%$

BEP (₹) = ₹ 26,400 / 40% = ₹ 66,000

M.S. (₹) = ₹ 8,160 / 40% = ₹ 20,400

Illustration 23. You are given the following information for the coming year of PCT Ltd.

Sales (units)		2000
Selling Price per unit	₹.	10
Marginal cost per unit	₹.	4
Fixed cost	₹.	9,600
Income tax rate		50%

You are required :

(a) To evaluate the effect of 10% decrease in selling price accompanied by a similar decrease in the variable cost but 20% increase in physical sales volume.

(b) To evaluate the effect of 10% increase in selling price accompanied by a similar increase in the variable costs but 20% decrease in physical sales volume.

(c) To compute the sales (in units) as well as sales (in ₹.) to earn ₹. 12,000 after income taxes.

(d) To compute the sales (in units & ₹.) to earn ₹. 11,520 after income taxes if there is 10% increase in fixed cost.

(e) To compute the sales (in units & ₹.) to earn 20% on sales after income tax.

Solution:

	Particulars	*Present*	*(a)*	*(b)*	*(c)*	*(d)*	*(e)*
A.	Sales (in units)	2,000	2,400	1,600	5,600	5,600	x
B.	Sales Price unit	₹. 10	₹. 9	₹. 11	₹. 10	₹. 10	₹. 10
C.	Total Sales (A x B)	20,000	21,600	17,600	56,000	56,000	10 x
D.	*Less :* Marginal Cost	8,000	8,640	7,040	22,400	22,400	4 x
E.	Contribution (C – D)	12,000	12,960	10,560	33,600	33,600	6 x
F.	*Less :* Fixed Cost	9,600	9,600	9,600	9,600	10,560	9,600
G.	Profit before tax (E – F)	2,400	3,360	960	24,000	23,040	6 x – 9,600
H.	*Less :* Tax	1,200	1,680	480	12,000	11,520	3 x – 4,800
I.	Profit after Tax (G – H)	1,200	1,680	480	12,000	11,520	3 x – 4,800

Working Notes :

(i) *For case (c) & (d)*

$$\text{P/V Ratio} = \frac{\text{Contribution}}{\text{Sales}} \times 100$$

$$\text{Sales} = \frac{\text{Contribution}}{\text{P/V Ratio}} = \frac{33{,}600}{60\%} = 56{,}000$$

$$\text{Sales (in units)} = \frac{\text{Sales (in ₹)}}{\text{Sales Price/Unit}} = \frac{56{,}000}{10} = 5{,}600 \text{ units}$$

(ii) *For case (e)*

3 x - 4,800 = 20% of 10 x

x = 4800

Desired sales (in units) = 4,800

Desired sales (in ₹.) = 4,800 x 10 = ₹. 48,000

Illustration 24. The following information is given by Bharat Ltd.

Selling Price per unit ₹ 10, Variable Cost per unit ₹ 6, Fixed Costs ₹ 24,000

You are required to calculate:

(a) Profit-Volume Ratio (b) Break-even Sales (in units) and (in rupees) (c) Profit when sales are 10% above the Break-even Sales (d) Sales to earn profit of ₹ 4,000 (e) Sales to earn profit @ 10% on sales (f) Sales to earn profit of ₹. 2 per unit (g) New B.E.P. if selling price is reduced by 10% (h) New Selling Price if existing quantity of B.E.P. is to be brought down by 20% (i) New selling price if existing value of BEP is to brought down by 40% (j) Margin of Safety Sales if profit is ₹. 60,000.

Solution:

(a) $$\text{Profit-Volume Ratio} = \frac{\text{Contribution}}{\text{Sales}} \times 100 = \frac{10-6}{10} \times 100 = 40\%$$

(b) $$\text{B.E.P. (in units)} = \frac{\text{Fixed Costs}}{\text{Contribution Per Unit}} = \frac{24{,}000}{4} = 6{,}000 \text{ Units}$$

$$\text{B.E.P. (in ₹)} = \frac{\text{Fixed Costs}}{\text{P/V Ratio}} = \frac{24{,}000}{40\%} = ₹\ 60{,}000$$

(c) **Profit when Sales are 6,600 units** (*i.e.* 6,000 + 10% of 6,000)

A	No. of Sales units	6,600
B	Selling Price per unit	₹ 10
C	Total Sales	₹ 66,000
D	*Less:* Variable Cost (6,600 × ₹ 6)	₹ 39,600
E	Contribution	₹ 26,400
F	*Less:* Fixed Costs	₹ 24,000
G	Profit	₹ 2,400

Alternatively Profit on 600 units = (600 × ₹ 10) × 40% = ₹ 2,400

(d) **Sales to earn a profit of ₹ 4,000**

$$\text{Desired Sales (in Units)} = \frac{\text{Fixed Cost + Desired Profit}}{\text{Contribution Per Unit}} = \frac{24{,}000 + 4{,}000}{4} = 7{,}000 \text{ units}$$

$$\text{Desired Sales (in ₹)} = \frac{\text{Fixed Cost + Desired Profit}}{\text{P/V Ratio}} = ₹\ 70{,}000$$

(e) **Sales to earn profit @ 10% on sales**

Let Desired Sales be X and hence Desired Profit is 10% of X

$$\text{Desired Sales (in ₹)} = \frac{\text{Fixed Cost + Desired Profit}}{\text{P/V Ratio}}$$

$$X = \frac{24{,}000 + 10\% \text{ of } X}{40\%}$$

$$.4X = ₹\ 24{,}000 + .X$$

$$.4X - .X = ₹\ 24{,}000$$

$$X = ₹\ 24{,}000/.3 = ₹\ 80{,}000$$

$$\text{Desired Sales (in Units)} = ₹\ 80{,}000/₹\ 10 = 8{,}000 \text{ units}$$

(f) **Sales to earn a profit of ₹. 2 per unit**

Let Desired Sales be x and hence Desired Profit is ₹. 2x.

$$\text{Desired Sales (in units) } x = \frac{\text{Fixed Cost + Desired Profit}}{\text{Contribution Per Unit}} = \frac{24{,}000 + 2x}{4}$$

X = ₹. 24,000/2 = 12,000 units.

Desired Sales (in ₹.) = 12,000 × ₹. 10 = ₹. 1,20,000

(g) New Contribution = (₹ 10 – ₹ 1) – ₹ 6 = ₹ 3

$$\text{B.E.P. (in units)} = \frac{\text{Fixed Costs}}{\text{Contribution Per Unit}} = \frac{24{,}000}{3} = 8{,}000 \text{ units}$$

$$\text{B.E.P. (in ₹)} = \frac{\text{Fixed Costs}}{\text{Contribution Per Unit}} \times \text{Selling Price per unit}$$

$$= \frac{24{,}000}{3} \times ₹\,9 = ₹\,72{,}000$$

(h) $$\text{B.E.P. (in units)} = \frac{\text{Fixed Costs}}{\text{Contribution Per Unit}} = \frac{\text{Fixed Costs}}{\text{New Selling Price – Variable Cost}}$$

Let New Selling Price be *X*, New B.E.P. = 80% of 6000 = 4800 units

$$4{,}800 = \frac{24{,}000}{X - 6}$$

$$4{,}800\,(X - ₹\,6) = ₹\,24{,}000$$

$$X - ₹\,6 = ₹\,24{,}000/4{,}800 = ₹\,5$$

$$X = ₹\,5 + ₹\,6 = ₹\,11$$

(i) $$\text{BEP (₹.)} = \frac{\text{Fixed Cost}}{\text{P/V Ratio}}, \text{ Let P/V Ratio be X}$$

$$60\% \text{ of ₹. } 60{,}000 = \frac{24{,}000}{X}$$

$$X = ₹\,24000 / ₹\,36000 = \frac{2}{3} \text{ or } 66\frac{2}{3}\%$$

$$\text{P/V Ratio} = \frac{\text{S.P. per unit – Variable Cost per unit}}{\text{S. P. per unit}} = \frac{X - 6}{X} = \frac{2}{3}$$

X = ₹. 18

(j) $$\text{Margin of Safety} = \frac{\text{Profit}}{\text{P/V Ratio}} = \frac{60{,}000}{40\%} = 1{,}50{,}000$$

Illustration 25. Tushar Ltd. provides you the following information.

Fixed Expenses ₹ 4,000, Break Even Point ₹ 10,000

You are required to Calculate:

(a) P/V Ratio
(b) Profit when Sales are ₹ 20,000
(c) Sales to earn profit of ₹ 6,000
(d) New Break Even Point if selling price is reduced by 20%
(e) New Break-Even Point if variable cost is increased by 25%

Solution:

(a) $$\text{P/V Ratio} = \frac{\text{Fixed Cost}}{\text{Break Even Sales}} \times 100 = \frac{4{,}000}{10{,}000} \times 100 = 40\%$$

(b) Profit = Contribution – Fixed Cost = (40% of ₹ 20,000) – ₹ 4,000 = ₹ 4,000

(c) $$\text{Desired Sales} = \frac{\text{Fixed Cost + Desired Profit}}{\text{P/V Ratio}} = \frac{4{,}000 + 6{,}000}{40\%} = ₹\,25{,}000$$

(d) $$\text{New P/V Ratio} = \frac{\text{New Selling Price – Variable Cost}}{\text{New Selling Price}} \times 100 \text{ (Let Old SP = ₹ 100)}$$

$$= \frac{80 - 60}{80} \times 100 = 25\%$$

New B.E.P. = ₹ 4,000/25% = ₹ 16,000

(e) New P/V Ratio $= \frac{\text{Selling Price} - \text{New Variable Cost}}{\text{Selling Price}} \times 100$ (Let Old SP = ₹ 100)

$= \frac{₹\,100 - (₹\,60 + 25\% \text{ of } ₹\,60)}{₹\,100} \times 100 = \frac{25}{100} \times 100 = 25\%$

New B.E.P. = ₹ 4,000/25% = ₹ 16,000

Illustration 26. The following information in given by Seema Ltd:

Profit ₹ 12,000, Fixed Cost ₹ 24,000, Margin of Safety ₹ 30,000

You are required to Calculate:

(a) Profit Volume Ratio (b) Break Even Sales and Actual Sales (c) Profit when sales are 10% above the Break Even Sales (d) Sales to earn profit of ₹ 4,000 (e) Sales to earn profit @ 10% on sales (f) New B.E.P. if selling price is to be reduced by 10% (g) New B.E.P. if variable cost is to be increased by 25% (h) Sales to earn the same amount of profit if the selling price is reduced by 10% (i) Profit if selling price, variable cost and fixed cost increase by 20% 25% and 25% respectively with corresponding decrease in sales volume by 10%.

Solution:

(a) Profit Volume Ratio $= \frac{\text{Profit}}{\text{Margin of Safety}} \times 100 = \frac{12{,}000}{30{,}000} \times 100 = 40\%$

(b) B.E.P. $= \frac{\text{Fixed Cost}}{\text{P/V Ratio}} = \frac{24{,}000}{40\%} = ₹\,60{,}000$

Actual Sales = B.E.P. + Margin of Safety = ₹ 60,000 + ₹ 30,000 = ₹ 90,000

(c) Profit = Contribution – Fixed Cost

= [40% of (₹ 60,000 + 10% of ₹ 60,000)] – ₹ 24,000 = ₹ 2,400

(d) Desired Sales $= \frac{\text{Fixed Cost} + \text{Desired Profit}}{\text{P/V Ratio}} = \frac{24{,}000 + 4{,}000}{40\%} = ₹\,70{,}000$

(e) Sales to earn profit @ 10% on sales

Let Desired Sales be X and hence Desired Profit is 10% of X

$$\text{Desired Sales (in ₹)} = \frac{\text{Fixed Cost} + \text{Desired Profit}}{\text{P/V Ratio}}$$

$$X = \frac{24{,}000 + 10\% \text{ of } X}{40\%}$$

$$.4X = ₹\,24{,}000 + .X$$

$$.4X - .X = ₹\,24{,}000$$

$$X = ₹\,24{,}000/.3 = ₹\,80{,}000$$

(f) New P/V Ratio $= \frac{\text{New Selling Price} - \text{Variable Cost}}{\text{New Selling Price}} \times 100$

$= \frac{(100 - 10) - 60}{(100 - 10)} \times 100 = 33\frac{1}{3}\%$

New B.E.P. $= ₹\,24{,}000/33\frac{1}{3}\% = ₹\,72{,}000$

(g) New P/V Ratio $= \frac{\text{Selling Price} - \text{New Variable Cost}}{\text{Selling Price}} \times 100$

$= \frac{100 - (60 + 25\% \text{ of } 60)}{100} \times 100 = 25\%$

New B.E.P. = ₹ 24,000/25% = ₹ 96,000

(h) New P/V Ratio $= \frac{\text{New Selling Price} - \text{Variable Cost}}{\text{New Selling Price}} \times 100$

$= \frac{(100 - 10) - 60}{(100 - 10)} \times 100 = 33\frac{1}{3}\%$

Desired Sales $= \frac{\text{Fixed Costs} + \text{Desired Profit}}{\text{New P/V Ratio}}$

$= \frac{24{,}000 + 12{,}000}{33\frac{1}{3}\%} = ₹\,1{,}08{,}000$

(i) Existing Sales = ₹ 90,000
New Sales = ₹ 90,000 × 90% × 120% = ₹ 97,200
New Variable Cost = ₹ 90,000 × 90% × 75% = ₹ 60,750
New Contribution = ₹ 97,200 – ₹ 60,750 = ₹ 36,450
New Fixed Cost = ₹ 24000 × 125% = ₹ 30,000
New Profit = ₹ 36,450 – ₹ 30,000 = ₹ 6,450

Illustration 27. PCT (1) Ltd. provides you the following information:

	Year 1	*Year 2*
Total Sales	₹ 20,000	₹ 30,000
Total Cost	₹ 17,600	₹ 21,600

Required: Calculate the following:

(a) the Profit/volume ratio; (b) Fixed costs; (c) Break-Even Point; (d) Margin of Safety; (e) the Amount of profit/loss when sales are ₹ 50,000; (f) the Amount of sales required to earn a profit of ₹ 59,040; (g) the Amount of sales required to earn profit @ 10% on sales; (h) the Amount of profit for the year 3 after taking into consideration the 10% decrease in selling price but 20% increase in physical sales volume and fixed costs, (i) the percentage increase in Selling Price that would be needed over the sales value of year 2 to earn a Margin of Safety of 60%.

Solution:

(a) $\text{Profit/Volume Ratio} = \dfrac{\text{Difference in Profit}}{\text{Difference in Total Sales}} \times 100 = \dfrac{8{,}400 - 2{,}400}{30{,}000 - 20{,}000} \times 100 = 60\%$

(b) Fixed Costs = Contribution – Profit

Taking the figures relating to year 1

A Contribution = 60% of ₹ 20,000 = ₹ 12,000
B Profit = ₹ 20,000 – ₹ 17,600 = ₹ 2,400
C Fixed Costs [A – B] = ₹ 9,600

(c) $\text{Break-Even Point} = \dfrac{\text{Fixed Costs}}{\text{P/V Ratio}} = \dfrac{9{,}600}{60\%} = ₹\ 16{,}000$

(d) Margin of Safety = Actual Sales – Break-Even Sales
For year 1= ₹ 20,000 – ₹ 16,000 = ₹ 4,000
For year 2 = ₹ 30,000 – ₹ 16,000 = ₹ 14,000

(e) Profit/Loss at Sales of ₹ 50,000
Profit = Contribution – Fixed Costs = 60% of ₹ 50,000 – ₹ 9,600 = ₹ 20,400

(f) Sales required to earn a profit of ₹ 59,040

$\text{Desired Sales} = \dfrac{\text{Fixed Costs + Desired Proft}}{\text{P/V Ratio}} = \dfrac{9{,}600 + 59{,}040}{60\%} = ₹\ 1{,}14{,}400$

(g) **Sales required to earn Profit @ 10% on Sales**

Suppose, Desired Sales = *x*. Hence desired profit = 10% of *x* = 0.1*x*

$\text{Desired Sales} = \dfrac{\text{Fixed Costs + Desired Proft}}{\text{P/V Ratio}}$

$x = \dfrac{9{,}600 + .1x}{60\%}$

$.6x = ₹\ 9{,}600 + .1x$

$x = ₹\ 9{,}600/.5 = ₹\ 19{,}200$

(h)		
A.	Sales [90% of (30,000 + 20% of 30,000)]	32,400
B.	*Less* : Variable cost [40% of (30,000 + 20% of 30,000)]	14,400
C.	Contribution [A – B]	18,000
D.	*Less* : Fixed costs [9,600 + 20% of ₹ 9,600]	11,520
E.	Profit [C – D]	6,480

(i) 60% Margin of Safety means BEP = 40%. Let New sales be X

$\text{New BEP (\%)} = \dfrac{\text{New Fixed Costs}}{\text{New Contribution}} = \dfrac{9{,}600}{X - 12{,}000} = 40\%$

$$0.4X - ₹\,4{,}800 = ₹\,9{,}600$$

$$X = \frac{14{,}400}{0.40} = ₹\,36{,}000$$

$$\text{\% Increase in Selling Price} = \frac{\text{New Sales} - \text{Existing Sales}}{\text{Existing Sales}} \times 100 = \frac{(36{,}000 - 30{,}000)}{30{,}000} \times 100 = 20\%$$

Illustration 28. PCT (2) Ltd. provides you the following information for the year 2013.

	First Half	*Second Half*
	₹	₹
Sales	20,000	30,000
Profit Earned	7,200	13,200

You are required to calculate the following, assuming that the fixed costs remain constant during each of the half year:

(a) The P/V ratio, fixed cost, break-even point and margin of safety for first half, second half and for the whole year.
(b) The amount of profit/loss when sales for the year are ₹ 60,000.
(c) The amount of sales required to earn a profit of ₹ 59,040.
(d) The amount of sales required to earn a profit of 10% on sales.
(e) The amount of profit for the year 2014 assuming anticipated 10% increase in selling price but 20% decrease in physical sales volume and fixed costs.

Solution:

(a) (i) $\text{P/V Ratio} = \frac{\text{Difference in Profit}}{\text{Difference in Sales}} \times 100 = \frac{6{,}000}{10{,}000} \times 100 = 60\%$

(ii) Fixed Costs = Contribution – Profit

Taking the figures relating to the first half of the year

A. Contribution = [60% of ₹ 20,000] = ₹ 12,000
B. Profit = ₹ 7,200
C. Fixed Costs for first half [A – B] = ₹ 4,800

Fixed costs for the whole year = ₹ 4,800 × 2 = ₹ 9,600

(iii) $\text{Break Even Point} = \frac{\text{Fixed Costs}}{\text{P/V Ratio}}$

For First half = ₹ 4,800/60% = ₹ 8,000
For Second half = ₹ 4,800/60% = ₹ 8,000
For the whole year = ₹ 9,600/60% = ₹ 16,000

(iv) Margin of Safety = Actual Sales – B.E.P. Sales

For First half = ₹ 20,000 – ₹ 8,000 = ₹ 12,000
For Second half = ₹ 30,000 – ₹ 8,000 = ₹ 22,000
For the whole year = ₹ 50,000 – ₹ 16,000 = ₹ 34,000

(b)		
A.	Contribution [60% of ₹ 60,000]	₹ 36,000
B.	*Less* : Fixed Costs	₹ 9,600
C.	Profit [A – B]	₹ 26,400

(c) $\text{Desired Sales} = \frac{\text{Fixed Costs} + \text{Desired Profit}}{\text{P/V Ratio}} = \frac{9{,}600 + 59{,}040}{60\%} = ₹\,1{,}14{,}400$

(d) Let Desired Sales be *X*, Desired Profit = 10% of *x* = .1*x*

$$\text{Desired Sales} = \frac{\text{Fixed Costs} + \text{Desired Profit}}{\text{P/V Ratio}}$$

$$x = \frac{9{,}600 + .1x}{60\%}$$

$$.6x = ₹\,9{,}600 + .1x$$

$$x = ₹\,9{,}600/.5 = ₹\,19{,}200$$

		Proposed
(e) A.	Sales [110% of (₹ 50,000 – 20% ₹ 50,000)]	₹ 44,000
B.	*Less* : Variable cost [40% (₹ 50,000 – 20% of 50,000)]	16,000
C.	Contribution [A – B]	28,000
D.	*Less* : Fixed Costs (₹ 9,600 – 20% of ₹ 9,600]	7,680
E.	Profit [C – D]	20,320

Illustration 29. X Ltd. furnishes you the following information relating to the half year ended 30th Sept. 2013:

	₹.
Fixed Expenses	45,000
Sales Value	1,50,000
Profit	30,000

During the second half of the year the company has projected a loss of ₹. 10,000.

Calculate :

(i) The margin of safety for six months ending on 30th Sept. 2013 :

(ii) Expected sales volume for the second half of the year assuming that the P/V ratio and fixed expenses remain constant in the second half year also.

(iii) The break even point and margin of safety for the whole year 2013-2014.

Solution:

(i) *Calculation of Margin of Safety*

		₹.
A.	Fixed Expenses	45,000
B.	Profit	30,000
C.	Contribution [A + B]	75,000
D.	Sales	1,50,000
E.	P/V Ratio = $\frac{75,000}{1,50,000} \times 100 = 50\%$	50%

F. Break-even point = $\frac{\text{Fixed}}{\text{P/V Ratio}} = \frac{45,000}{50\%}$ = ₹. 90,000

G. Margin of Safety = ₹. 1,50,000 – ₹. 90,000 = ₹. 60,000

(ii) *Expected Sales Volume for Second Half*

		₹.
A.	Fixed Expenses	45,000
B.	Loss	(–) 10,000
C.	Contribution [A – B]	35,000
D.	P/V Ratio :	50%
E.	Sales : $\left[\frac{\text{Contribution}}{\text{P/V Ratio}} = \frac{35,000}{50\%}\right]$	₹. 70,000

(iii) *Break Even Point and Margin of Safety for the year 20X1-20X2*

		₹.
A.	Fixed expenses for the full year [₹. 45,000 5 2]	90,000
B.	Profit (₹. 30,000 – ₹. 10,000)	20,000
C.	Contribution [A + B]	1,10,000
D.	Sales (₹. 1,50,000 + ₹. 70,000)	2,20,000
E.	P/V Ratio :	50%

F. Break-even point : $\frac{\text{Fxied Cost}}{\text{P/V Ratio}} = \frac{90,000}{50\%}$ = ₹. 1,80,000

G. Margin of Safety = ₹. 2,20,000 – ₹. 1,80,000 = ₹. 40,000

Illustration 30. A company had incurred fixed expenses of ₹. 4,50,000, with sales of ₹. 15,00,000 and earned a profit of ₹. 3,00,000 during the first half year. In the second half, it suffered a loss of ₹. 1,50,000.

Calculate :

(i) The profit-volume ratio, break-even point and margin of safety for the first half year.

(ii) Expected sales-volume for the second half year assuming that selling price and fixed expenses remained unchanged during the second half year.

(iii) The break-even point and margin of safety for the whole year.

Solution:

(i) Profit volume ratio, break-even point and margin of safety (for the first half year)

$$\text{Profit-volume Ratio} = \frac{\text{Contribution}}{\text{Sales}} \times 100 = \frac{(\text{Fixed Expenses} + \text{Profit})}{\text{Sales}} \times 100$$

$$= \frac{(4,50,000 + 3,00,000)}{15,00,000} \times 100 = 50\%$$

$$\text{Break-even Point} = \frac{\text{Fixed Expenses}}{\text{P/V Ratio}} = \frac{4,50,000}{50\%} = ₹.\ 9,00,000$$

Margin of Safety = Actual sales – Break-even sales = ₹. 15,00,000 – ₹. 9,00,000
= ₹. 6,00,000

(ii) *Expected Sales -Volume (for the second half year assuming that selling price and fixed expenses remained unchanged during the second half year).*

$$\text{Expected sales volume} = \frac{\text{Fixed Expenses} - \text{Loss}}{\text{P/V Ratio}} = \frac{4,50,000}{50\%} = ₹.\ 6,00,000$$

(iii) *Break-even point and margin of safety (for the whole year)*

$$\text{Break even point} = \frac{\text{Fixed expenses for the whole year}}{\text{P/V Ratio}}$$

$$= \frac{9,00,000}{50\%} = ₹.\ 18,00,000$$

$$\text{Margin of safety} = \frac{\text{Profit for the year}}{\text{P/V Ratio}} = \frac{3,00,000 - 1,50,000}{50\%} = ₹.\ 3,00,000$$

Alternative Method :

Margin of safety = Sales above the break-even point
= Actual sales – Break-even sales
= [₹. 15,00,000 + ₹. 6,00,000] – ₹. 18,00,000 = ₹. 3,00,000

Illustration 31. A single product company sells its products at ₹. 60 per unit. In 2013, the company operated at a margin of safety of 40%. The fixed costs amounted to ₹. 3,60,000 and the variable cost ratio to sales was 80%.

In 2014, it is estimated that the variable cost will go up by 10% and the fixed costs will increase by 5%.

Find the selling price required to be fixed in 2014 to earn the same P/V ratio as in 2013.

Assuming the same selling price of ₹. 60 per unit in 2014 find the number of units required to be produced and sold to earn the same profit as in 2013.

Solution:

Selling price to be fixed in 2014

Variable cost per unit in 2014 = ₹. 52.80 (i.e. ₹. 48 + ₹. 4.80)
Fixed cost in 2014 = ₹. 3,78,000 (i.e. ₹. 3,60,000 + ₹. 18,000)
P/V ratio in 2013 = 20%

Since P/V ratio is 20%, therefore variable cost is 80%.

$$\text{Hence, the required selling price} = \frac{52.80}{80\%} = ₹.\ 66$$

Number of units to be produced and sold in 2014 to earn the same profit as in 2013.

Profit in 2013 *[Refer to Working Note (iii)]*	₹. 2,40,000
Fixed cost in 2014	₹. 3,78,000
Desired contribution in 2014 (₹. 2,40,000 + ₹. 3,78,000)	₹. 6,18,000

Contribution per unit in 2014 = Selling price per unit – Variable cost per unit
= ₹. 60 – ₹. 52.80 = ₹. 7.20

Number of units to be produced and sold in 2014 $= \frac{\text{Fixed cost + Desired Profit}}{\text{Contribution per unit}}$

$= \frac{6,18,000}{7.20} = 85,833.33$ units

Working Notes:

(i) P/V ratio $= \frac{\text{(Selling Price – Variable Cost)}}{\text{Selling price}} \times 100$

$= \frac{(60 - 48)}{60} \times 100 = \frac{12}{60} \times 100 = 20\%$

(ii) Number of units sold (in 2013)

Break-even point $= \frac{\text{Fixed-even point}}{60\%} = \frac{3,60,000}{12} = 30,000$ units

Since, margin of safety is 40%, therefore break-even point is 60% of units sold.

or, No. of units sold $= \frac{\text{Break-even point}}{60\%} = \frac{30,000 \text{ units}}{60\%} = 50,000$ units

(iii) Profit earned in 2013

Profit = [Total contribution on the sale of 50,000 units – Fixed costs]
= [(50,000 units × ₹. 12) – ₹. 3,60,000]
= [₹. 6,00,000 – ₹. 3,60,000] = ₹. 2,40,000

Illustration 32. A company sells its product at ₹. 15 per unit. In a period, if it produces and sells 8,000 units, it incurs a loss of ₹. 5 per unit. If the volume is raised to 20,000 units, it earns a profit of ₹. 4 per unit. Calculate breakeven point both in terms of rupees as well as in units.

Solution:

Average cost at 8,000 units volume :
= Selling price per unit + Loss component per unit
= ₹. 15 + ₹. 5 = ₹. 20

Average cost at 20,000 unit volume
= Selling price per unit – Profit component per unit
= ₹. 15 – ₹. 4 = ₹. 11

Total cost at 8,000 units volume = 8,000 × ₹. 20 = ₹. 1,60,000
Total cost at 20,000 units volume = 20,000 × ₹. 11 = ₹. 2,20,000

Variable Cost per unit $= \frac{\text{Change in the total cost}}{\text{Change in the volume of production}}$

$= \frac{2,20,000 - 1,60,000}{20,000 \text{ units} - 8,000 \text{ units}}$

$= \frac{60,000}{12,000 \text{ units}} =$ ₹. 5

Fixed Cost = Total Cost – Variable Cost = ₹. 1,60,000 – ₹. 40,000 = ₹. 1,20,000

P/V Ratio $= \frac{\text{Fixed Costs}}{\text{P/V Ratio}} \times 100 = \frac{1,20,000}{66\frac{2}{3}\%} \times 100 = 66\frac{2}{3}\%$

Break-even point (Rupees) $= \frac{\text{Fixed Costs}}{\text{P/V Ratio}} = \frac{1,20,000}{66\frac{2}{3}\%} =$ ₹. 1,80,000

Break-even point (in units) $= \frac{\text{Fixed Costs}}{\text{S.P. – V.C.}} = \frac{\text{Fixed Costs}}{\text{Contribution per unit}}$

$= \frac{1,20,000}{15 - 5} = \frac{1,20,000}{10} = 12,000$ units.

Illustration 33. A company has three factories situated in North, East and South with its Head Office in Mumbai. The Management has received the following summary report on the operations of each factory for a period :

(₹. in 000)

	Sales		*Profit*	
	Actual	*Over/(Under) Budget*	*Actual*	*Over/(Under) Budget*
North	1,100	(400)	135	(180)
East	1,450	150	210	90
South	1,200	(200)	330	(110)

Calculate for each factory and for the company as a whole for the period :
(i) The Fixed Costs (ii) Break-Even Sales

Solution: **(i) STATEMENT SHOWING CALCULATION OF FIXED COSTS**

(₹. '000)

Region	*Actual Sales* A	*P/V Ratio* B	*Contribution* C = A × B	*Actual Profit* D	*Fixed Cost* E = C − D
North	1,100	45	495	135	360
East	1,450	60	870	210	660
South	1,200	55	660	330	330
	3,750	54	2,025	675	1,350

(ii) STATEMENT SHOWING CALCULATION OF BREAK-EVEN SALES

(₹. '000)

Region	*Fixed Cost* A	*P/V Ratio* B	*Break-even sales* C = A/B
North	360	45	800
East	660	60	1,100
South	330	55	600
			2,500

Break-Even Sales (company as whole) : $\frac{\text{F.C.}}{\text{P/V Ratio}} = \frac{1,350}{54\%}$ = 2,500 *(in ₹. '000)*

Working Note: **STATEMENT SHOWING CALCULATION OF PROFIT VOLUME RATIO**

Region	*Sales*			*Profit*			*P/V Ratio*
	Actual	*Over/ (Under) Budget*	*Budgeted Sales*	*Actual*	*Over/ (Under) Budget*	*Budgeted Profit*	$\frac{\text{(Diff. between profit)}}{\text{(Diff. between sales)}} \times 100$
North	1,100	(400)	1,500	135	(180)	315	(180/400 × 100) = 45%
East	1,450	150	1,300	210	90	120	(90/150 × 100) = 60%
South	1,200	(200)	1,400	330	(110)	440	(110/200 × 100) = 55%

Illustration 34. A company budgets a production of 10,000 units. The variable cost is estimated at ₹ 2 per unit. The fixed costs are estimated ₹ 60,000. The selling price is fixed to earn a profit of 25% on cost.

You are required to:

(i) Compute break-even point in terms of units and sales; and
(ii) Compute how many units must be produced and sold to earn a profit of ₹ 60,000.

Solution:

Step 1 → Selling Price per unit = Variable Cost + Fixed Cost + Profit
= ₹ 2 + (₹ 60,000/10,000) + 25% of ₹ 8 = ₹ 10

Step 2 → Contribution per unit = Sales – Variable Cost = ₹ 10 – ₹ 2 = ₹ 8

Step 3 → BEP (Units) = $\frac{\text{Fixed Costs}}{\text{Contribution per unit}} = \frac{60,000}{8}$ = 7,500 units

BEP (₹) = 7,500 units × ₹ 10 = ₹ 75,000

Step 4 → Desired Sales Units = $\frac{\text{Fixed Costs} + \text{Desired Profits}}{\text{Contribution per unit}} = \frac{60,000 + 60,000}{8}$ = 15,000 units

Illustration 35. Quality Products Ltd., manufactures and markets a single product. The following data are available:

Materials per unit	₹. 16	Dealer's Margin per unit	10% on Selling Price
Conversion Costs (variable) per unit	12	Selling Price per unit	40

Fixed Cost : ₹. 5 lakhs
Present Sales : 90,000 units
Capacity utilisation : 60 per cent

There is acute competition. Extra efforts are necessary to sell. Suggestions have been made for increasing sales :

Proposal I By reducing selling price by 5 per cent.
Proposal II By increasing dealer's margin by 25 per cent over the existing rate.

Which of these two suggestions you would recommend, if the company decides to maintain the present profit ? Give reasons.

Solution: **STATEMENT SHOWING THE EVALUATION OF PROPOSALS**

	Particulars	*Present*		*Proposal I*	*Proposal II*
A	Selling Price		₹. 40	₹. 38	₹. 40
B	*Less :* Variable Costs :				
	Material	16		16.00	16.00
	Conversion cost	12		12.00	12.00
	Dealer's margin	4		3.80	5.00
			32	31.80	33.00
C	Contribution per unit (A – B)		8	6.20	7.00
D	Present/Required Contribution		7,20,000	7,20,000	7,20,000
E	Sales (units) required to maintain present contribution (D/C)		90,000	1,16,129	1,02,857

Recommendation: The proposal II is recommended since the contribution per unit (i.e. ₹. 7) is higher than that under proposal I and the sales (in units) (i.e. 102857) required to earn the same level of existing profit are lower than that under proposal I.

Illustration 36. The following data relate to a manufacturing company:
Plant capacity : 4,00,000 units per annum. Present utilisation: 40%

Actuals for the year 20X1 were:

Selling Price	₹ 50 per unit	Variable Manufacturing Costs	₹ 15 per unit
Material Cost	20 per unit	Fixed Costs	27 lakhs

In order to improve capacity utilisation the following two alternative proposals are considered:

I Reduce selling price by 10%
II Spend additionally ₹ 3 lakhs on sales promotion.

Required: How many units should be sold to earn a profit of ₹ 5 lakhs per year under each of these proposals?

Solution:

	Particulars	*Proposal I*	*Proposal II*
A	Selling Price	₹ 45	₹ 50
B	*Less:* Variable Costs: (₹ 20 + ₹ 15)	₹ 35	₹ 35
C	Contribution per unit (A – B)	₹ 10	₹ 15
D	Fixed Costs	27,00,000	30,00,000

E	No. of units to be sold to earn a profit of ₹ 5 lakhs:		
	$= \frac{\text{Fixed Costs + Desired Profit}}{\text{Contribution per unit}}$	$\frac{27,00,000+5,00,000}{10}$	$\frac{30,00,000+5,00,000}{15}$
		3,20,000 units	2,33,333 units

Illustration 37. The following data relates to a manufacturing company :

Plant capacity : 4,00,000 units per annum, Present utilization : 40%

Actuals for the year 20XI were : Selling price ₹. 50 per unit; Materials Cost ₹. 20 per unit; Variable Manufacturing Costs ₹ 15 per unit; Fixed Costs ₹ 27 lakhs.

In order to improve capacity utilization the following proposal is considered :

Reduce Selling Price by 10% and Spend additionally ₹. 3 lakhs on Sales Promotion.

How many units should be produced and sold in order to increase profit by ₹. 8 lakhs per year?

Solution:

Let the desired sales (in units) be x

A	Desired sales (in units)		x
B	Revised Selling Price (₹. 50 *less* 10%)		₹ 45 per unit
C	Total Sales (A × B)		45 x
D	*Less :* Variable Cost		
	Material Cost @ ₹. 20	20 x	
	Variable Manufacturing Cost @ ₹. 15	15 x	35 x
E	Revised Contribution (C – D)		10 x
F	*Less :* Total Fixed Costs		
	Present fixed costs	₹. 27,00,000	
	Additional Promotion Expenses	₹. 3,00,000	30,00,000
G	Profit (E – F)		10 x – 30,00,000

10 x – 30,00,000 = ₹. 5,00,000 (desired profit given)

10 x = ₹. 30,00,000 + ₹. 5,00,000

x = ₹. 35,00,000/10 = 3,50,000 units

Working Notes:

(i) Existing Loss = Sales – Variable Costs – Fixed Costs

= (4,00,000 × 40% × ₹ 50) – (4,00,000 × 40% ₹ 35) – ₹ 27,00,000

= ₹. 3,00,000

(ii) Desired Profit = ₹. 8,00,000 – ₹ 3,00,000 = ₹. 5,00,000

Illustration 38. Titan Engineering is operating at 70 per cent capacity and presents the following information :

Break-even point	₹. 200 crores
P/V Ratio	40 per cent
Margin of safety	20 per cent

Titan's management has decided to increase production to 95 per cent capacity level with the following modifications :

(i) The selling price will be reduced by 8 per cent.

(ii) The variable cost will be reduced by 5 per cent on sales.

(iii) The fixed cost will increase by ₹. 25%, including depreciation on additions, but excluding interest on additional capital.

(iv) Additional capital of ₹. 50 crores will be needed for capital expenditure and working capital.

Required: (a) Indicate the sales figure that will be needed to earn 50% increase in the present profit and also meet 20 per cent interest on the additional capital. (b) What will be the revised. (i) Break-even point; (ii) P/V Ratio; (iii) Margin of safety.

Solution:

Assuming that the present selling price is ₹. 100 crores

			₹. *(Crores)*
(a)	A	Revised selling price will be (8% *less*)	92.00
	B	Revised variable costs (55% of ₹. 92)	50.60

C Contribution (₹. 92.00 – ₹. 50.60) 41.40

D New P/V Ratio = $\frac{41.40}{92.00} \times 100 = 45\%$

E Revised fixed costs

Present fixed cost	80
Increase in fixed costs	20
Interest at 20 per cent on additional capital (₹. 50 crores x 20%)	10
Total revised fixed costs	110

F Revised required sales $= \frac{\text{Revised Fixed Cost + Expected Profit}}{\text{P/V Ratio}}$

$= \frac{\text{110 crores + 30 crores}}{45\%} = \text{311.11 crores}$

(b) (i) Revised Break-even Point = $\frac{\text{Fixed Costs}}{\text{P/V Ratio}} = \frac{\text{110 crores}}{45\%} = \text{244.44 crores}$

(ii) P/V Ratio = 45%

(iii) Revised Margin of Safety = Revised Sales – Revised break-even Sales
= ₹. 311.11 crores – ₹. 244.44 crores = ₹. 66.67 crores

Working Notes :

(i) Total Sales = Break-even sales + Margin of safety
= ₹. 200 crores + 25% of ₹. 200 crores = ₹. 250 crores

(ii) P/V Ratio = 40%

(iii) Variable Cost = 60% of Sales = 60% of ₹. 250 crores = ₹. 150 crores

(iv) Fixed Cost = Break-even Sales x P/V Ratio = ₹. 200 crores x 40% = ₹. 80 crores

(v) Total Cost = ₹. 150 crores + ₹. 80 crores = ₹. 230 crores

(vi) Profit = Total Sales – Total costs = ₹. 250 crores – ₹. 230 crores = ₹. 20 crores.

Alternatively, Profit = Margin of Safety x P/V Ratio = 50 x 40% = ₹. 20 crores

Illustration 39. Tulsian (1) Ltd. provides you the following information:

Year I		*Year II*	
Sales	₹. 15,00,000	Sales	₹. 5,00,000
Total Profit	₹. 3,60,000	Total Cost	₹. 5,40,000

During the next year III, the Selling Price and Variable Cost are expected to be reduced by 20% and 33-1/3% respectively and Fixed Costs are expected to increase by 25%.

Required:

(a) Estimate the Profit if Sales Units are expected to increase by 100%.
(b) Estimate the Sales in order to increase Profit by ₹. 2,40,000 per year.
(c) Estimate the Sales so as to earn a return of 25% on Sales.
(d) Estimate the Sales so as to earn a return of 30% on Capital Employed. Working Capital is 25% of Sales and 20% of Capital Employed.
(e) Estimate the BEP for the next year III.

Solution:

(a)

		₹.	
A.	Sales	8,00,000	(₹. 5,00,000 x 200% x 80%)
B.	*Less:* Variable Cost	4,00,000	(₹. 3,00,000 x 200% x 66-2/3%)
C.	Contribution (A – B)	4,00,000	
D.	*Less:* Fixed Cost	3,00,000	(2,40,000 x 125%)
E.	Profit (C – D)	1,00,000	

(b) Desired Sales = $\frac{\text{New Fixed Costs + Expected Profit}}{\text{New P/V Ratio}}$

Desired Sales = $\frac{\text{3,00,000 + 2,00,000 (i.e. 2,40,000 − 40,000)}}{50\%}$ = ₹. 10,00,000

(c) Desired Sales = $\dfrac{\text{New Fixed Costs + Expected Profit}}{\text{New P/V Ratio}}$

Let Sales be x, $x = \dfrac{3,00,000 + 0.25x}{50\%}$ = ₹. 12,00,000

(d) Desired Sales = $\dfrac{\text{New Fixed Costs + Expected Profit}}{\text{New P/V Ratio}}$

Let Sales be x, Working Capital = 0.25x, Capital Employed = 0.25x / 20% = 1.25x

Desired Return on Capital Employed = 30% of 1.25x = 0.375 X

$X = \dfrac{3,00,000 + 0.375X}{50\%}$ = ₹. 24,00,000

(e) New BEP = $\dfrac{\text{New Fixed Cost}}{\text{New P/V Ratio}} = \dfrac{(2,40,000 \times 125\%)}{50\%}$ = ₹. 6,00,000

Working Notes:

(i) Profit Volume Ratio = $\dfrac{\text{Change in Profit}}{\text{Change in Sales}} \times 100 = \dfrac{-40,000 - 3,60,000}{5,00,000 - 15,00,000} \times 100 = 40\%$

(ii) Fixed Costs = Contribution – Profit = 40% of ₹. 15,00,000 – ₹. 3,60,000 = ₹. 2,40,000

(iii) New P/V Ratio = $\dfrac{\text{New Selling Price – New Variable Cost}}{\text{New Selling Price}} \times 100$

$= \dfrac{[(10 - 20\% \text{ of } 10) - (6 - 33\frac{1}{3}\% \text{ of } 6)]}{(10 - 20\% \text{ of } 10)} \times 100 = 50\%$

(iv) New Fixed Costs = ₹. 2,40,000 + 25% of ₹. 2,40,000 = ₹. 3,00,000

Illustration 40. Tulsian (2) Ltd provides you the following information for the year 2010:

Margin of Safety ₹. 64,000, Total Cost ₹. 41,600, Margin of Safety 6,400 Units, Break-Even Sales 1,600 Units. During the next year, the Selling Price is expected to be reduced by 10% and Variable Costs and Fixed Costs are to be increased by 12.5% and 20% respectively.

Required:

(a) Estimate the Profit if Sales Units are expected to increase by 20%.
(b) Estimate the Sales in order to increase Profit by 20%.
(c) Estimate the Sales so as to earn 20% on Sales.
(d) Estimate the Sales so as to earn a Profit of ₹. 2 Per Unit.
(e) Estimate the BEP for the next year.

Solution:

(a)

		₹.	
A.	Sales	86,400	(₹. 80,000 x 120% x 90%)
B.	*Less:* Variable Cost	43,200	(₹. 32,000 x 120% x 112.5%)
C.	Contribution (A – B)	43,200	
D.	*Less:* Fixed Cost	11,520	(₹. 9,600 x 120%)
E.	Profit (C – D)	31,680	

(b) Desired Sales = $\dfrac{\text{New Fixed Costs + Expected Profit}}{\text{New P/V Ratio}}$

$= \dfrac{(9,600 \times 120\%) + (38,400 \times 120\%)}{50\%}$ = ₹. 1,15,200

(c) Desired Sales = $\dfrac{\text{New Fixed Costs + Expected Profit}}{\text{New P/V Ratio}}$

Let Sales be x, $x = \dfrac{(9,600 \times 120\%) + 0.20x}{50\%} \Rightarrow X = \dfrac{11,520}{0.30}$ = ₹. 38,400

(d) Desired Sales (Units) = $\dfrac{\text{New Fixed Costs + Expected Profit}}{\text{Contribution Per Unit}}$

Let Sales Units be x, $x = \dfrac{(9,600 \times 120\%) + 2x}{(9 - 4.5)}$ = 4,608 Units

Desired Sales (₹.) = 4,608 Units × ₹. 9 = ₹. 41,472

(e) New BEP = $\frac{\text{New Fixed Cost}}{\text{New P/V Ratio}} = \frac{(9{,}600 \times 120\%)}{50\%}$ = ₹. 23,040

Working Notes:

(i) Margin of Safety (%) = $\frac{\text{Margin of Safety (Units)}}{\text{Actual Sales (Units)}} \times 100 = \frac{6{,}400}{6{,}400 + 1{,}600} \times 100 = 80\%$

(ii) Total Sales = $\frac{\text{Margin of Safety (₹)}}{\text{Margin of Safety (\%)}} = \frac{64{,}000}{80\%}$ = ₹. 80,000

(iii) Profit = Total Sales – Total Cost = ₹. 80,000 – ₹. 41,600 = ₹. 38,400

(iv) P/V Ratio = $\frac{\text{Profit}}{\text{Margin of Safety}} \times 100 = \frac{38{,}400}{64{,}000} \times 100 = 60\%$

(v) Break-Even Sales = Total Sales × (100 – Margin of Safety %) = ₹. 80,000 × 20% = ₹. 16,000

(vi) Fixed Costs = BEP × P/V Ratio = ₹. 16,000 × 60% = ₹. 9,600

(vii) New P/V Ratio = $\frac{\text{New Selling Price} - \text{New Variable Cost}}{\text{New Selling Price}} \times 100$

$= \frac{[(10 - 10\% \text{ of } 10) - (4 + 12.5\% \text{ of } 4)]}{(10 - 10\% \text{ of } 10)} \times 100 = \frac{9 - 4.50}{9} = 50\%$

Illustration 41. Tulsian (3) Ltd provides you the following information for the current year :

Margin of Safety ₹. 64,000, Total Cost ₹. 41,600, Margin of Safety 6,400 Units, Break-Even Sales 1,600 Units. During the next year, Variable Costs and Fixed Costs are expected to be increased by 25% and 20% respectively.

Required:

(a) Estimate the percentage change in Sales Volume in Units that will be needed to earn 20% increase in the present profit.

(b) Estimate the percentage change in Sales Volume in Units that will be needed to earn 20% increase in the present profit if the Selling Price is also expected to be reduced by 10%

(c) Estimate the percentage change in Selling Price that will be needed to earn 20% increase in the present profit.

(d) Estimate the percentage change in Selling Price that will be needed to earn 20% increase in the present profit if the Sales Volume in Units is also expected to be increased by 20%

(e) Estimate the percentage change in Selling Price that will be needed to earn a Margin of Safety of 80%.

(f) Estimate the percentage change in Selling Price that will be needed to earn a Margin of Safety of 80% if the Sales Volume in Units is also expected to be increased by 20%

Solution:

	(a)	*(b)*	*(c)*	*(d)*
A. No. of Sales Units	X	X	8,000	9,600
B. Selling Price Per Unit	₹. 10	₹. 9	X	X
C. Sales [A x B]	₹. 10X	₹. 9X	₹. 8,000X	₹. 9,600X
D. *Less:* Total Variable Cost	₹. 5X	₹. 5X	₹. 40,000	₹. 48,000
E. Contribution [C – D]	₹. 5X	₹. 4X	₹. 8,000X – ₹. 40,000	₹. 9,600X – ₹. 48,000
F. *Less:* Total Fixed Costs	₹. 11,520	₹. 11,520	₹. 11,520	₹. 11,520
G. Profit [E – F]	₹. 5X – ₹. 11,520	₹. 4X – ₹. 11,520	₹. 8,000X – ₹. 51,520	₹. 9,600X – ₹. 59,520

(a) ₹. 5X – ₹. 11,520 = ₹. 46,080

X = 11,520 Units

Percentage change required in Sales Units = $\frac{\text{(New Sales Units – Old Sales Units)}}{\text{Old Sales Units}} \times 100$

$= \frac{(11{,}520 - 8{,}000)}{8{,}000} \times 100$ = 44% Increase

(b) ₹. 4X – ₹. 11,520 = ₹. 46,080
X = 14,400 Units

$$\text{Percentage change required in Sales Units} = \frac{(\text{New Sales Units} - \text{Old Sales Units})}{\text{Old Sales Units}} \times 100$$

$$= \frac{(14{,}400 - 8{,}000)}{8{,}000} \times 100 = 80\% \text{ Increase}$$

(c) ₹. 8,000X – ₹. 51,520 = ₹. 46,080
X = ₹. 12.2

$$\text{Percentage change required in selling price} = \frac{(\text{New Selling Price} - \text{Old Selling Price})}{\text{Old Selling Price}} \times 100$$

$$= \frac{(12.2 - 10)}{10} \times 100 = 22\% \text{ Increase}$$

(d) ₹. 9,600X – ₹. 59,520 = ₹. 46,080
X = ₹. 11

$$\text{Percentage change required in selling price} = \frac{(\text{New Selling Price} - \text{Old Selling Price})}{\text{Old Selling Price}} \times 100$$

$$= \frac{(11 - 10)}{10} \times 100 = 10\% \text{ Increase}$$

(e) 80% Margin of Safety means BEP = 20%, BEP Units = 20% of 8,000 = 1,600 Units, Let new S.P be X

$$\text{New BEP} = \frac{\text{New Fixed Cost}}{\text{New Contribution per Unit}} = \frac{(9{,}600 \times 120\%)}{X - 5} = 1{,}600 \text{ Units}$$

1,600X – 8,000 = 11,520
X = ₹. 19,520 / 1,600 = 12.2

$$\text{Percentage change required in selling price} = \frac{(\text{New Selling Price} - \text{Old Selling Price})}{\text{Old Selling Price}} \times 100$$

$$= \frac{(12.2 - 10)}{10} \times 100 = 22\% \text{ Increase}$$

(f) 80% Margin of Safety means BEP = 20%, BEP Units = 20% of 9,600 = 1,920 Units, Let new S.P be X

$$\text{New BEP} = \frac{\text{New Fixed Cost}}{\text{New Contribution per Unit}} = \frac{(9{,}600 \times 120\%)}{X - 5} = 1{,}920 \text{ Units}$$

1,920X – 9,600 = 11,520
X = ₹. 21,120 / 1,920 = 11

$$\text{Percentage change required in selling price} = \frac{(\text{New Selling Price} - \text{Old Selling Price})}{\text{Old Selling Price}} \times 100$$

$$= \frac{(11 - 10)}{10} \times 100 = 10\% \text{ Increase}$$

Working Notes:

(i) $\text{Margin of Safety (\%)} = \frac{\text{Margin of Safety (Units)}}{\text{Actual Sales (Units)}} \times 100 = \frac{6{,}400}{6{,}400 + 1{,}600} \times 100 = 80\%$

(ii) $\text{Total Sales} = \frac{\text{Margin of Safety (₹)}}{\text{Margin of Safety (\%)}} = \frac{64{,}000}{80\%} = ₹.\ 80{,}000$

(iii) Existing Profit = Total Sales – Total Cost = ₹. 80,000 – ₹. 41,600 = ₹. 38,400

(iv) $\text{P/V Ratio} = \frac{\text{Profit}}{\text{Margin of Safety}} \times 100 = \frac{38{,}400}{64{,}000} \times 100 = 60\%$

Margin of Safety ₹. 64,000

(v) Break-Even Sales = Total Sales × (100 – Margin of Safety %) = ₹. 80,000 x 20% = ₹. 16,000

(vi) Fixed Costs = BEP × P/V Ratio = ₹. 16,000 × 60% = ₹. 9,600

(vii) New Fixed Cost = ₹. 9,600 × 120% = ₹. 11,520

(viii) Existing Selling Price = ₹. 80,000/8,000 Units = ₹. 10

(ix) Existing Variable Cost = ₹. 10 × 40% = ₹. 4

(x) New Variable Cost = ₹. 4 × 125% = ₹. 5

(xi) New Profit = ₹. 38,400 × 120% = ₹. 46,080

Illustration 42. Tulsian (4) Ltd. currently operating at 75% capacity is producing 1,500 Units and provides you the following information:

Units	2,000	1,500
Sales reduced by Prime Cost	₹. 36,000	₹. 27,000
Overheads I	₹. 3 per unit	₹. 4 per unit
Overheads II	₹. 2 per unit	₹. 2 per unit
Overheads III	₹. 7 per unit	₹. 9 per unit

Required: Calculate Break Even Point.

Solution:

		2,000 Units	1,500 Units
A.	Selling Price – Prime Cost	18 (₹. 36,000 / 2,000)	18 (₹. 27,000/1,500)
B.	*Less:* Variable Overheads II	2	2
	Variable Overheads III	1	1
		3	3
C.	Contribution [A – B]	15	15
D.	Fixed Overheads I	6,000 (2,000 × ₹. 3)	6,000 (2,000 × ₹. 3)
	Fixed Overheads III	12,000	12,000
		18,000	18,000
E.	Break Even Point = $\frac{\text{Fixed Cost}}{\text{Contribution/Unit}}$	= $\frac{18,000}{15}$ = 1,200 Unis	= $\frac{18,000}{15}$ = 1,200 Units

Working Note:

(i) Variable Overheads III per Unit $= \frac{\text{Change in the Amount of Overheads}}{\text{Change in Activity Level}}$

$= \frac{(2,000 \times 7) - (1,500 \times 9)}{2,000 - 1,500}$ = ₹ 1 per Unit

(ii) Fixed Overheads III = ₹. 14,000 – (2,000 x ₹ 1) = ₹. 12,000

Illustration 43. A company has a P/V Ratio of 40 per cent (a) By what percentage must sales be increased to offset 10 per cent reduction in selling price to maintain the same amount of contribution (b) By what percentage must selling price be increased to offset 25% increase in variable cost so as to maintain the same amount of contribution (c) By what percentage must selling price be increased to offset 25% increase in variable cost so as to maintain the same P/V Ratio (d) By what percentage must variable cost be decreased to offset 25% reduction in selling price so as to maintain the same amount of contribution (e) By what percentage must variable cost be decreased to offset 25% reduction in selling price so as to maintain the same P/V Ratio?

Solution:

(a) Let the present selling price per unit be ₹ 100

	Present	Revised
Selling Price per unit	₹ 100	₹ 90
Variable Cost per unit	₹ 60	₹ 60
Contribution per unit	Rs 40	₹ 30

% of increase in Sales required to offset

$$= \frac{\text{Present Contribution} - \text{Revised Contribution}}{\text{Revised Contribution}} \times 100$$

$$= \frac{40 - 30}{30} \times 100 = 33\frac{1}{3}\%$$

(b) Let the present selling price per unit be ₹ 100

A. Present Selling Price per unit	₹ 100
B. *Less* : Present Variable cost per unit @ 60%	₹ 60
C. Present Contribution per unit [A – B]	₹ 40
Revised variable cost [₹ 60 + 25% of ₹ 60]	75
Add : Present contribution per unit	40
Revised selling price	115

Increase in selling price required to offset = ₹ 115 – ₹ 100 = ₹ 15

% of increase in selling price required to offset

$$= \frac{\text{Revised Selling Price} - \text{Present Selling Price}}{\text{Present Selling Price}} \times 100$$

$$= \frac{115 - 100}{100} \times 100 = 15\%$$

(c) Let the Revised Selling Price be X

$$\text{Desired P/V Ratio} = \frac{\text{Revised Selling Price} - \text{Revised Variable Cost}}{\text{Revised Selling Price}} \times 100$$

$$40\% = \frac{X - (60 + 25\% \text{ of } 60)}{X} \times 100$$

$$0.4X - X = ₹\ 75$$

$$X = ₹\ 75/.6 = ₹\ 125$$

% of increase in selling price required to offset

$$= \frac{\text{Revised Selling Price} - \text{Present Selling Price}}{\text{Present Selling Price}} \times 100$$

$$= \frac{125 - 100}{100} \times 100 = 25\%$$

(d) Let the present price per unit be ₹ 100

	Present	Revised	
A. Selling Price per unit	₹ 100	₹ 75	(i.e. ₹ 100 – ₹ 25)
B. Contribution	₹ 40	₹ 40	
C. Variable Cost (A – B)	₹ 60	₹ 35	

% of decrease in variable cost required to offset

$$= \frac{\text{Present Variable Cost} - \text{Revised Variable Cost}}{\text{Present Variable Cost}} \times 100$$

$$= \frac{60 - 35}{60} \times 100 = \frac{25}{60} \times 100 = 41.67\%$$

(e) Let Revised Variable cost be X

$$\text{Desired P/V Ratio} = \frac{\text{Revised Selling Price} - \text{Revised Variable Cost}}{\text{Revised Selling Price}} \times 100$$

$$40\% = \frac{75 - X}{75} \times 100$$

$$40\% \text{ of } ₹\ 75 = ₹\ 75 - X$$

$$X = ₹\ 75 - ₹\ 30 = ₹\ 45$$

% of decrease in Variable Cost required to offset

$$= \frac{\text{Present Variable Cost} - \text{Revised Variable Cost}}{\text{Present Variable Cost}} \times 100$$

$$= \frac{60 - 45}{60} \times 100 = 25\%$$

18.0 MERGED PLANT/COMPANY

Sales, Variable Cost, Contribution and Fixed Cost	Whenever management decides to merge two or more plants/companies operating at same/different capacity level, first the sales, variable cost, contribution and fixed cost of each individual plant/company should be calculated at 100% capacity and then these figures should be totalled so as to calculate Sales, Variable Cost, Contribution and Fixed Cost (including additional fixed expenses involved in the merger) of the merged plant.
P/V Ratio	$= \frac{\text{Total Contribution of all Plants/Companies at 100\% Capacity}}{\text{Total Sales of all Plants/Companies at 100\% Capacity}} \times 100$
B.E.P. (in value)	$= \frac{\text{Fixed Cost of all Plants /Companies + Additional Fixed Cost of Merger (if any)}}{\text{P/V Ratio of Merged Plant/Company}}$
Capacity Utilization at B.E.P.	$= \frac{\text{BEP of a Merged Plant/Company}}{\text{Total Sales of a Merged Plant/Company at 100\% Capacity}} \times 100$
Profit at a given capacity utilization	A. Sales at a given capacity utilization — xxxx B. *Less :* Variable Costs at a given capacity utilization — xxxx C. Contribution at a given capacity utilization [A – B] — xxxx D. *Less :* Fixed costs of a Merged Plant/Company — xxxx E. Profit at a given capacity utilization [C – D] — xxxx
Sales required to earn a given profit	$= \frac{\text{Fixed Cost of a Merged Plant/Company + Desired Profit}}{\text{P/V Ratio of a Merged Plant/Company}}$
Capacity Utilization at required sales	$= \frac{\text{Required Sales}}{\text{Total Sales of a Merged Plant/Company at 100\% Capacity}} \times 100$

Illustration 44. A, B and C are three similar plants under the same management who want them to be merged for better operation. The details are as under:

	Plant A at 100% ₹ *(in lakhs)*	*Plant B at 70%* ₹ *(in lakhs)*	*Plant C at 50%* ₹ *(in lakhs)*
Turnover	300	280	150
Variable Cost	200	210	75
Fixed Cost	70	50	62

Required:

(a) Compute the Capacity of the merged plant for break even;

(b) Compute the Profit of the merged plant at 75% capacity .

(c) Compute the Capacity utilisation of the merged plant to earn a profit of ₹. 28 lakhs,

(d) Compute the percentage increase in selling price necessary to sustain an increase in Fixed Overheads by 6% when the merged plant is working at a capacity to earn a profit of ₹. 28 Lakhs.

Solution: **TURNOVER AND COST STATEMENT OF THREE PLANTS AT 100%**

(Figures in lakhs)

Particulars	*Individual Plants at 100% capacity*			*Merged Plant at*
	A	*B*	*C*	*100% Capacity*
A. Sales	300	400	300	1,000
B. *Less:* Variable Cost	200	300	150	650
C. Contribution [A – B]	100	100	150	350
D. Fixed Cost	70	50	62	182

Basic Calculations:

$$\text{P/V Ratio of Merged Plant} = \frac{\text{Contribution of Merged Plant}}{\text{Turnover of Merged Plant}} \times 100 = \frac{350 \text{ lakhs}}{1{,}000 \text{ lakhs}} \times 100 = 35\%$$

$$\text{Break Even Point (after merger)} = \frac{\text{Fixed Cost}}{\text{P/V Ratio}} = \frac{182 \text{ lakhs}}{35\%} = ₹.\ 520 \text{ lakhs}$$

(i) Capacity of the merged plant at Break Even Point

$$\frac{\text{Turnover at Break Even Point}}{\text{Turnover of Merged Plant at 100\% Capacity}} \times 100 = \frac{520 \text{ lakhs}}{1{,}000 \text{ lakhs}} \times 100 = 52\%$$

(ii) Profit at 75 % Capacity of the merged plant

= Contribution – Fixed Cost = (750 × 35%) – 182 = ₹. 80.5 Lakhs

(iii) Capacity of the Merged Plant to earn a required profit of ₹. 28 lakhs

$$\text{Desired Turnover} = \frac{\text{Fixed Cost + Desired Profit}}{\text{P/V Ratio}} = \frac{182 \text{ Lakhs} + 28 \text{ Lakhs}}{35\%} = ₹.\ 600 \text{ Lakhs}$$

$$\frac{\text{Turnover at Break Even Point}}{\text{Turnover of Marged Plant at 100\% Capacity}} \times 100 = \frac{600 \text{ lakhs}}{1{,}000 \text{ lakhs}} \times 100 = 60\%$$

(iv) $$\text{\% of Increase in Selling Price} = \frac{6\% \text{ of } 182 \text{ Lakhs}}{600 \text{ Lakhs}} \times 100 = 1.82\%$$

19.0 OVERALL P/V RATIO AND B.E.P. FOR THE COMPANY SELLING VARIOUS PRODUCTS IN VARIOUS SALES MIX RATIOS

1. WHERE EITHER INDIVIDUAL SALES OF EACH PRODUCT OR INDIVIDUAL SALES MIX RATIO OF EACH PRODUCT AND TOTAL SALES OF ALL THE PRODUCTS ARE GIVEN

(a) $$\text{Overall P/V Ratio} = \frac{\text{Total Contribution of all the Products}}{\text{Total Sales of all the Products}} \times 100$$

(b) $$\text{Overall B.E.P.} = \frac{\text{Total Fixed Cost of all the Products}}{\text{Overall P/V Ratio}}$$

2. WHERE SALES MIX RATIO IS GIVEN WITH REFERENCE TO VALUE

(a) Overall P/V Ratio = Weighted P/V Ratio of Product 1 + Weighted P/V Ratio of Product 2 .... + Weighted P/V Ratio of Product N

Note: Weighted P/V Ratio of a Product = Sales Value Mix Ratio × Individual P/V Ratio of a product.

(b) $$\text{Overall B.E.P. (in Value)} = \frac{\text{Total Fixed Cost of all the products}}{\text{Overall P/V Ratio}}$$

(c) Individual B.E.P. (in Value) for a Product = Individual Sales Value Mix Ratio × Overall B.E.P. (in value)

(d) Individual B.E.P. (in Qty.) for a Product = $\frac{\text{Individual BEP (in Value)}}{\text{Selling Price of a Product}}$

(e) Overall B.E.P. (in Qty.) = Individual BEP (in Qty.) of Product 1 + Individual B.E.P. (in Qty) of Product 2 + ...

3. WHERE SALES MIX RATIO IS GIVEN WITH REFERENCE TO QUANITY

(a) Weighted Contribution of a product
= Individual Sales Quantity Mix Ratio × Individual Contribution per unit

(b) Total Weighted Contribution of all the products
= Weighted contribution of a Product 1 + Weighted contribution of Product 2 and so on.

(c) Overall B.E.P. (in units) = $\frac{\text{Total Fixed Cost of all Products}}{\text{Total Weigthted contribution per unit}}$

(d) Individual B.E.P. (in units) for a product
= Individual Sales Qty. Mix Ratio × Overall B.E.P. (in units)

(e) Individual B.E.P. (value) for a product
= Individual B.E.P. (in units) × Selling Price per unit of a product

(f) Overall B.E.P (in value) = Individual BEP (Value) of Product 1 + Individual BEP (Value) of Product 2 + ...

(g) Overall P/V Ratio = $\frac{\text{Total Fixed Cost of all the Products}}{\text{Overall BEP (in Value)}}$

Illustration 45. The budgeted income statement by product lines on Multi Products Ltd. for 20X1 is as follows:

	Product A	*Product B*	*Product C*
Sales	₹. 2,00,000	₹. 5,00,000	₹. 3,00,000
Variable Expenses :			
Cost of goods sold	90,000	2,70,000	1,50,000
Selling	30,000	90,000	45,000
Fixed Expenses :			
Selling	36,000	90,000	54,000
Administrative	16,000	40,000	24,000
Income before Tax	28,000	10,000	27,000
Income Tax @ 40%	11,200	4,000	10,800
Net Income	16,800	6,000	16,200

All products are manufactured in the same facilities under common administrative control. Fixed expenses are allocated among the products in proportion of their budgeted sales volume.

Required:

(a) Compute the budgeted breakeven point of the company as a whole from the data provided.

(b) What would be the effect on Budgeted Income if half of the budgeted sales volume of product B were shifted to product A and C in equal rupee amounts, so that the total budgeted sales in rupees remain the same.

(c) What would be the effect of the shift in the product-mix suggested in (b) above on the budgeted break-even point of the whole company ?

Solution: **(a) CALCULATION OF BUDGETED *BEP* FOR THE COMPANY AS A WHOLE**

$$\text{Overall P/V Ratio} = \frac{\text{Total Contribution}}{\text{Total Sales}} \times 100 = \frac{80{,}000 + 1{,}40{,}000 + 1{,}05{,}000}{10{,}00{,}000} \times 100 = \frac{3{,}25{,}000}{10{,}00{,}000} \times 100 = 32.5\%$$

$$\text{Overall BEP} = \frac{\text{Total Fixed Costs}}{\text{Overall P/V Ratio}} = \frac{52{,}000 + 1{,}30{,}000 + 78{,}000}{32.5\%} = \frac{2{,}60{,}000}{32.5\%} = ₹\ 8{,}00{,}000$$

(b) STATEMENT SHOWING THE EFFECT ON BUDGETED INCOME IF HALF THE SALES OF PRODUCT B IS SHIFTED EQUALLY TO PRODUCTS A AND C

	Particulars	*Product A* ₹	*Product B* ₹	*Product C* ₹	*Total* ₹
A	Sales	3,25,000	2,50,000	4,25,000	10,00,000
B	Total cost				
	Cost of goods sold	1,46,250	1,35,000	2,12,500	4,93,750
	Selling	48,750	45,000	63,750	1,57,500
	Fixed Expenses : (apportioned according to sales) @ 18%	58,500	45,000	76,500	1,80,000
	Administrative @ 8%	26,000	20,000	34,000	80,000
		2,79,500	2,45,000	3,86,750	9,11,250
C	Income before Tax [A – B]	45,500	5,000	38,250	88,750
D	Income Tax @ 40%	18,200	2,000	15,300	35,500
E	Net Income [C – D]	27,300	3,000	22,950	53,250

The original budgeted income is ₹ 39,000. Hence, the income would increase by ₹.14,250 as a result of the proposed change.

(c) EFFECT OF SHIFT IN THE PRODUCT MIX ON BUDGETED B.E.P.

$$\text{Overall P/V Ratio} = \frac{\text{Total Contribution}}{\text{Total Sales}} \times 100$$

$$= \frac{1,30,000 + 70,000 + 1,48,750}{10,00,000} \times 100 = \frac{3,48,750}{10,00,000} \times 100 = 34.875\%$$

$$\text{Overall Break-even point} = \frac{\text{Total Fixed Costs}}{\text{Overall P/V Ratio}} = \frac{2,60,000}{34.875\%} = \text{Rs } 7,45,520$$

Thus, the break-even point will stand reduced to sales of ₹ 7,45,520 from ₹ 8,00,000 as result of shift in the total production mix.

Illustration 46. Tulsian Ltd. manufactures three products X, Y and Z. The unit selling price of these products are ₹ 50, ₹ 30 and ₹ 20 respectively. The corresponding Variable Cost to Sales Ratio is 20%, 30% and 50%. The total fixed costs are ₹ 59,83,000.

Required: Calculate Overall Break Even Point (in Qty.) and (in Value), Overall P/V Ratio, Productwise Break Even Point (in Qty) and (in value) if (a) the proportion (Quantitywise) in which these products are manufactured and sold are 20%, 30% and 50% respectively (b) the proportion (valuewise) in which these products are manufactured and sold are 20%, 30% and 50% respectively.

Solution:

(a) If Sales Quantity Mix Ratio is 20%, 30% and 50% respectively.

STATEMENT SHOWING THE CALCULATION OF WEIGHTED CONTRIBUTION

Particulars	*X*	*Y*	*Z*	*Total*
A. Selling Price per cent	50	30	20	
B. *Less* : Variable Cost per cent	10	9	10	
C. Contribution	40	21	10	
D. Sales Mix (in Qty.) Ratio	0.20	0.30	0.50	
E. Weighted Contribution (C × D)	8	6.3	5	19.3

$$\text{Overall Break Even Qty.} = \frac{\text{Total Fixed Costs}}{\text{Overall Contribution per Unit}} = \frac{59,83,000}{19.3} = 3,10,000 \text{ units}$$

PRODUCT-WISE BEP (IN QTY.) & (IN VALUE)

	BEP (in Qty)	SP Per unit	BEP (in value)
X 3,10,000 × 0.20	= 62,000 units	₹ 50	31,00,000
Y 3,10,000 × 0.30	= 93,000 units	₹ 30	27,90,000
Z 3,10,000 × 0.50	= 1,55,000 units	₹ 20	31,00,000
	3,10,000 units		89,90,000

$$\text{Overall P/V Ratio} = \frac{\text{Total Fixed Cost}}{\text{Overall BEP (in value)}} \times 100 = \frac{59{,}83{,}000}{89{,}90{,}000} \times 100 = 66.5517\%$$

$$\textit{Alternatively,} = \frac{\text{Weighted Contribution per unit}}{\text{Weighted Selling per unit}} \times 100 = \frac{19.3}{(50 \times 0.20) + (30 \times 0.30) + (20 \times 0.50)} \times 100$$

$$= \frac{19.3}{29.0} \times 100 = 66.5517\%$$

$$\text{Overall BEP (in Value)} = \frac{\text{Total Fixed Cost}}{\text{Overall P/V Ratio}} = \frac{59{,}83{,}000}{66.5517\%} = ₹\ 89{,}90{,}000$$

(b) If Sales Value Mix Ratio is 20%, 30% and 50% respectively.

STATEMENT SHOWING THE CALCULATION OF WEIGHTED P/V RATIO

	X	Y	Z	Total
A. Sales Value Mix Ratio	0.20	0.30	0.50	
B. P/V Ratio	0.80	0.70	0.50	
C. Weighted P/V Ratio	0.16	0.21	0.25	0.62

Overall P/V Ratio = 62%

$$\text{Overall BEP (in value)} = \frac{\text{Total Fixed Cost}}{\text{Overall P/V Ratio}} = \frac{59{,}83{,}000}{62\%} = 96{,}50{,}000$$

PRODUCT-WISE BEP (IN QTY.) & (IN VALUE)

BEP (in Value)		Selling Price per unit	BEP (in Qty.)
X ₹ 96,50,000 × 0.20	= ₹ 19,30,000	₹ 50	38,600 units
Y ₹ 96,50,000 × 0.30	= ₹ 28,95,000	₹ 30	96,500 units
Z ₹ 96,50,000 × 0.50	= ₹ 48,25,000	₹ 20	2,41,250 units
	₹ 96,50,000		3,76,350 units

$$\text{Overall Contribution per unit} = \frac{\text{Total Fixed Cost}}{\text{Overall BEP (in Qty.)}} = \frac{59{,}83{,}000}{3{,}76{,}350} = 15.8974$$

$$\text{Overall BEP (in Qty.)} = \frac{\text{Total Fixed Cost}}{\text{Overall Contribution per unit}} = \frac{₹\ 59{,}83{,}000}{₹\ 15.8974} = 3{,}76{,}350$$

Illustration 47. Find the overall break-even point and overall P/V Ratio for the following three products of Tulsian Ltd.:

	Product X	Product Y	Product Z
Sales Value Mix Ratio	20%	30%	50%
Variable Cost to Sales Ratio	50%	30%	20%
Total Fixed Costs ₹ 35,500			

Solution:

STATEMENT SHOWING THE CALCULATION OF P/V RATIO

Product	*X*	*Y*	*Z*	*Total*
A. Sales Mix Ratio	20%	30%	50%	100%
B. P/V Ratio (100 – Variable Cost Ratio)	50%	70%	80%	
C. Weighted P/V Ratio (A × B)	0.10	0.21	0.40	0.71

Overall P/V Ratio = 71%

$$\text{Overall Break-even point} = \frac{\text{Total Fixed Costs}}{\text{Overall P/V Ratio}} = \frac{35{,}500}{0.71} = 50{,}000$$

Illustration 48. A Company sells two products, J and K. The sales mix is 4 units of J and 3 units of K. The contribution margin per unit are ₹ 40 for J and ₹ 20 for K. Fixed Costs are ₹ 3,08,000 per month. Compute the break-even point.

Solution:

Let 4x = No. of units of J. Then 3x = No. of units of K

$$\text{BEP in x units} = \frac{\text{Fixed Cost}}{\text{Contribution}} = \frac{3{,}08{,}000}{[(4 \times 40) + (3 \times 20)]} = 1{,}400 \text{ units}$$

Break even point of Product J = 4 × 1,400 = 5,600 units
Break even point of Product K = 3 × 1,400 = 4,200 units

20.0 WHAT IS KEY FACTOR / BUDGET FACTOR / LIMITING FACTOR?

Meaning	Key Factor is a factor which limits the activities of an undertaking. The extent of its influence must first be assessed while preparing functional budgets and taking decisions about the profitability of a product.
Examples	Some of the examples of key factor are: (a) Shortage of raw material (b) Shortage of labour (c) Plant Capacity available (d) Sales Capacity available (e) Cash available
Product Mix Decisions	Contribution per unit of key factor $\left(\text{i.e. } \frac{\text{Contribution per unit}}{\text{Key Factor per unit}}\right)$ must be considered to decide upon the priority of products to be produced and sold. The product having largest contribution per unit of key factor is ranked first and the product having second largest contribution per unit of key factor is ranked second and so on. To decide upon the priority of products, the following guidelines may be used:

Case	**Basis for deciding upon the priority of products**
(a) **If Maximum Sales (in units) is a limiting factor**	(a) Contribution per unit
(b) **If Maximum Sales (in value) is a limiting factor**	(b) Profit-volume ratio (or P/V Ratio)
(c) **If Raw-material is a limiting factor**	(c) Contribution per unit of raw-material required to produce one unit of a product
(d) **If Labour Hour is a limiting factor**	(d) Contribution per unit of labour hour required to produce one unit of a product
(e) **If Machine Hour is a limiting factor**	(e) Contribution per unit of machine hour required to produce one unit of a product

	(f) **If there is heavy demand for the product**	(f) Profit/Volume Ratio (or P/V Ratio)
	(g) **If there is low demand for the product**	(g) Low Break even point

Illustration 49. *X* Ltd. which produces two products using the same raw-material and production facilities, provides you the following information:

	Product A ₹	*Product B* ₹
Selling Price per unit	100	80
Material @ ₹ 2 per kg	20	10
Labour @ ₹ 3 per hour	15	30
Variable Overheads @ ₹ 4 per machine hour	40	16
Total Fixed Overheads: ₹ 6,00,000		

Required: Comment on the profitability of each product when:

(a) Sales Quantity is limited;
(b) Sales Value is limited;
(c) Raw-material is in short supply;
(d) Labour hours are limited;
(e) Production Capacity (in terms of Machine Hours) is limited;
(f) there are heavy demand conditions;
(g) there are low demand conditions.

Solution: **STATEMENT SHOWING THE CONTRIBUTION PER UNIT OF KEY FACTOR**

	Particulars	*Product A* ₹	*Product B* ₹
A.	Selling Price per unit	100	80
B.	*Less:* Variable Cost		
	Material	20	10
	Labour	15	30
	Variable overheads	40	16
		75	56
C.	Contribution per unit (A – B)	25	24
D.	P/V Ratio $\left(\frac{\text{Contribution}}{\text{Sales}} \times 100\right)$	25%	30%
E.	Contribution per kg of Material $\left(\frac{\text{Contribution per unit}}{\text{Raw-material required per unit}}\right)$	$\frac{25}{10}$ = ₹ 2.5	$\frac{24}{5}$ = ₹ 4.8
F.	Contribution per labour hour $\left(\frac{\text{Contribution per unit}}{\text{Labour hours required per unit}}\right)$	$\frac{25}{5}$ = ₹ 5	$\frac{24}{10}$ = ₹ 2.4
G.	Contribution per Machine hour $\left(\frac{\text{Contribution per unit}}{\text{Machine hrs required per unit}}\right)$	$\frac{25}{10}$ = ₹ 2.5	$\frac{24}{4}$ = ₹ 6
H.	Break Even Point $\left(\frac{\text{Fixed Overheads}}{\text{Contribution per unit}}\right)$	$\frac{6,00,000}{25}$ = 24,000 units	$\frac{6,00,000}{24}$ = 25,000 units

(a) When sales quantity is limited, Product *A* is more profitable because its contribution per unit is higher than that of Product *B*.

(b) When sales value is limited, Product *B* is more profitable because its P/V Ratio is higher than that of Product *A*

(c) When Raw-Material is in short supply, Product *B* is more profitable because its contribution per kg. of raw-material is higher than that of Product *A*.

(d) When Labour hours are limited, Product A is more profitable because its contribution per labour hour is higher than that of Product *B*.

(e) When production capacity in terms of machine hours is limited, Product *B* is more profitable because its contribution per machine hour is higher than that of Product *A*

(f) When there are heavy demand conditions, Product *B* is more profitable because its P/V Ratio is higher than that of Product *A*.

(g) When there low demand conditions, Product *A* is more profitable because its Break Even Point is lower than that of Product *B*.

21.0 ADVANTAGES OF MARGINAL COSTING

1. Constant Product Cost	Marginal costing permits to have constant product cost since marginal cost per unit is constant from one period to another period within a short span of time. If fixed cost is included, the product cost will change from one period to another depending upon the volume of output.
2. No Under/ Over Overheads	Marginal costing avoids the under/over recovery of overheads since fixed overheads are treated as period costs and hence are written off to Profit & Loss Account.
3. Break Even Analysis	Marginal costing facilitates to carry out break even analysis Break-even analysis is used to determine – (a) the amount of profit/loss at various volume of operations (b) the volume of operations required to earn a target profit (c) the effect of change in variable cost, fixed cost, selling price, sales volume on profit.
4. Control of Costs	Segregation of costs into fixed and variable helps the management to exercise control over costs. The management can compare the actual costs with the budgeted costs and take corrective action through variance analysis.
5. Decision-Making	Marginal Costing facilitates the management to take various decision such as – (a) *Product Decisions:* Choice of Products, Discontinuation of a Product. (b) *Make or Buy Decision:* Whether to produce a particular component in the factory *or* to buy from outside source (c) Whether to Export *or* Not (d) Whether to Process further *or* not (e) Whether to Retain *or* Replace an existing Machine (f) Whether to Lease *or* Buy a Fixed Asset (g) Whether to Shut Down *or* Continue

22.0 LIMITATIONS OF MARGINAL COSTING

1. Segregation into Fixed and Variable – a difficult task	It is difficult to classify all the costs into fixed and variable with accuracy since some costs have no relation to volume of output *or* even with the time. *For example*, management's decision regarding bonus to workers may not be directly related to time *or* output.
2. Ignores Fixed Overheads	Always pricing the products ignoring fixed overheads may not be appropriate especially in the long run.

3. **Not Appropriate for Job/Contract Costing**	It can not be easily applied in Job/Contract costing. Fixed overheads cannot be ignored while valuing WIP.
4. **Assumption regarding behaviour of costs**	Some of assumptions regarding the behaviour of costs are not necessarily true in real life. *e.g.* Variable costs may change due to shortage of material, labour, bulk purchases.
5. **Apportionment of Fixed Costs**	In case of multiple products, separate break even points are to be calculated. This poses a problem of apportionment of fixed costs to each product.
6. **Ignores Time Factor & Investment**	It ignores Time Factor & Investment.

23.0 CIRCUMSTANCES UNDER WHICH IT MAY BE JUSTIFIABLE TO SELL AT A PRICE BELOW MARGINAL COST FOR A LIMITED PERIOD

1. Where goods are of perishable nature
2. Where stocks have been accumulated in large quantities and the market prices have fallen
3. To introduce a new product
4. To maintain sales of the profitable products in case the sales of these products is linked to the sale of product to be sold below marginal cost
5. To capture foreign markets
6. To obviate shut down costs
7. To retain future market
8. To eliminate competitors from the market

24.0 CIRCUMSTANCES UNDER WHICH IT MAY BE JUSTIFIABLE TO SELL AT A PRICE BELOW TOTAL COST BUT ABOVE MARGINAL COST

1. To avoid the risk of loss of market in favour of competitors
2. To avoid the deterioration and depreciation of Plant & Machinery
3. To avoid the situation of incurring the advertising and selling expenses
4. To avoid the additional cost of recruitment and training of skilled and trained staff again on the re-opening.

25.0 COST INDIFFERENCE POINT

Meaning	It refers to that level of activity at which the total cost (i.e., fixed cost + Variable cost) of the two alternative is the same. Management is indifferent as to the choice out of two alternatives at this point.
How to Calculate	Cost Indifference Point may be calculated as under: **Method 1:** Treat the Cost-Indifference Point be X and equate the Total Cost of one alternative with that of another alternative as follows: $V_1 * X + F_1 = V_2 * X + F_2$ *Where,* V_1 = Variable Cost per unit under Alternative 1 F_1 = Fixed Cost under Alternative 1 V_2 = Variable Cost per unit under Alternative 2 F_2 = Fixed Cost under Alternative 2 **Method 2:** $\text{Cost Indifference Point} = \dfrac{\text{Fixed Cost under Alternative 1} - \text{Fixed Cost under Alternative 2}}{\text{Variable Cost per unit under Alternative 2} - \text{Varable Cost per unit under Alternative 1}}$

Interpretation	Case	Which Alternative to be used?
	1. *At Activity Level below the Indifference Point*	1. Alternative with Lower Fixed Costs
	2. *At Activity Level above the Indifference Point*	2. Alternative with Lower Variable Cost
	3. *At Activity Level equal to the Indifference Point*	3. Any Alternative

Illustration 50. Tulsian Ltd. has the choice of buying Machine *X* or Machine *Y* or Machine *Z*. Following are the Cost details:

	Machine X	*Machine Y*	*Machine Z*
Fixed Cost	₹ 3,00,000	₹ 5,80,000	₹ 10,00,000
Variable Cost	₹ 140	₹ 70	₹ 40

Required:

(a) Compute the Cost Indifference Points for each of the pair of machines.
(b) What do the Cost Indifference Points suggest as a course of action in this regard?
(c) If the management expects to produce 8,700 units, which machine would be most economical?

Solution

(a) $$\text{Cost Indifference Point} = \frac{\text{Difference in Fixed Cost}}{\text{Difference in Variable Cost Per Unit}}$$

$$\text{CIP between Machine X and Machine Y} = \frac{5,80,000 - 3,00,000}{140 - 70} = 4,000 \text{ Units}$$

$$\text{CIP between Machine Y and Machine Z} = \frac{10,00,000 - 5,80,000}{70 - 40} = 14,000 \text{ Units}$$

$$\text{CIP between Machine X and Machine Z} = \frac{10,00,000 - 3,00,000}{140 - 40} = 7,000 \text{ Units}$$

(b) **Interpretation of Cost Indifference Point**

Activity Level	*Which Machine is Economical*
1 If Activity Level = Indifference Point	Any of the Machines
2 If Activity Level < Indifference Point	Machine with Lower Fixed Cost
3 If Activity Level > Indifference Point	Machine with Lower Variable Cost Per Unit

Inference from above computations:

From 0 to 4,000 Units,	Use Machine X
From 4,001 to 14,000 Units,	Use Machine Y
Above 14,000 Units	Use Machine Z

(c) For 8,700 Units, Machine Y would be most economical.

Illustration 51. The following are cost data for three alternative ways of processing the clerical work for cases brought under the LC Court System:

	A *Manual* *(₹)*	*B* *Semi Automatic* *(₹)*	*C* *Fully Automatic* *(₹)*
Monthly Fixed Costs			
Occupancy	15,000	15,000	15,000
Maintenance contract	0	5,000	10,000
Equipment lease	0	25,000	1,00,000
	15,000	45,000	1,25,000

Unit variable costs (per report):			
Supplies	40	80	20
Labour	(5 hrs × 40) or 200	(1 hr × 60) or 60	(0.25hr × 80) or 20
	240	140	40

***Required*:**

(i) Calculate cost indifference points. Interpret your results.

(ii) If the present case load is 600 cases and it is expected to go up to 850 cases in near future, which method is most appropriate on cost considerations?

Solution:

(i) COST INDIFFERENCE POINTS BETWEEN WAYS OF PROCESSING THE CLERICAL WORK

Particulars	*A and B (₹)*	*A and C (₹)*	*B and C (₹)*
I. Differential Fixed Costs:	30,000 (₹ 45,000 – ₹ 15,000)	1,10,000 (₹ 1,25,000 – ₹ 15,000)	80,000 (₹ 1,25,000 – ₹ 45,000)
II. Differential Variable Costs per case:	100 (₹ 240 – ₹ 140)	200 (₹ 240 – ₹ 40)	100 (₹ 140 – ₹ 40)
III. Cost Indifference Point: [I/II] (Differential Fixed Costs/Differential Variable Costs)	300 Cases	550 Cases	800 Cases

Interpretation of results

Case	*Which Alternative to be used*
1. At activity level below the Indifference Point	1. Alternative with Lower Fixed Costs
2. At Activity Level above the Indifference Point	2. Alternative with Lower Variable Cost
3. At Activity Level equal to the Indifference Point	3. Any Alternative

Thus, if expected number of cases is below 300, Alternative A should be used. If expected number of cases are between 301 and 800 use Alternative B. If expected number of cases is above 800, use alternative C.

(ii) Present case load is 600. Therefore, alternative B is suitable. As the number of cases is expected to go upto 850 cases, alternatives C is most appopriate.

Illustration 52. Find the cost break-even points between each pair of plants where cost functions are:

Plant A : ₹ 3,00,000 + ₹ 6x

Plant B : ₹ 4,50,000 + ₹ 5x

Plant C : ₹ 7,50,000 + ₹ 4x

(Where x denotes No. of units produced)

Also suggest the range of output for which the plants will be profitable.

Solution:

Plant A & B:

Assumption constant selling price per unit between each pair Plant A and Plant B

₹ 3,00,000 + ₹ 6 x = 4,50,000 + ₹ 5 x

₹ 6 x – ₹ 5 x = ₹ 1,50,000

x = 1,50,000

Plant A is better for output between 0 and 1,50,000 units

Plant B is better beyond 1,50,000 units

Plant B & C :

₹ 4,50,000 + ₹ 5 x = ₹ 7,50,000 + ₹ 4 x
x = 3,00,000

Plant B is better for output between 1,50,000 and 3,00,000
Plant C is better beyond 3,00,000 units

Plant A & C :

₹ 3,00,000 + ₹ 6x = ₹ 7,50,000 + ₹ 4 x
x = 2,25,000

Plant A is better for output between 0 and 2,25,000
Plant C is better beyond 2,25,000

Range of Output	*Economical Plant*
0 to 1,50,000 units	*Plant A*
1,50,001 units to 3,00,000 units	*Plant B*
Above 3,00,000 units	*Plant C*

Illustration 53. Two firms A & Co. and B & Co. sell the same type of product in the same market. Their budgeted Profit & Loss Account for the year ending 31st March, 20X1 are as follows :

	A & Co.		*B & Co.*	
	₹	₹	₹	₹
Sales		5,00,000		6,00,000
Variable costs	4,00,000		4,00,000	
Fixed costs	30,000	4,30,000	70,000	4,70,000
Net Profit		70,000		1,30,000

Required:

(a) Calculate sales volume at which both the firms will earn equal profit.
(b) State which firm is likely to earn greater profits in condition of :
(i) heavy demand for the product
(ii) low demand for the product

Give reasons.

Solution: **(a) SALES VOLUME AT WHICH WITH THE FIRMS WILL EARN EQUAL PROFIT**

	A & Co.	*B & Co.*
A. Sales (₹)	5,00,000	6,00,000
B. *Less :* Variable costs (₹)	4,00,000	4,00,000
C. Contribution (₹) [A – B]	1,00,000	2,00,000
D. P/V Ratio $\left[\frac{\text{Contribution}}{\text{Sales}} \times 100\right]$	20%	33-1/3%

E. Sales Volume $= \frac{\text{Difference in F.C.}}{\text{Difference in P/V Ratio}}$

(For both the firms to earn equal profit) $= \frac{40,000}{13.33\%}$

= 3,00,000

(b) The P/V ratio of B & Co. at 33-1/3% is higher than that of A & Co. at 20% and therefore B & Co. will earn higher profit if the sales volume exceeds ₹ 3,00,000 level.

In fact for each additional unit of product's sale above ₹ 3,00,000 the profit of B & Co. will rise by ₹ 33-1/3% which exceeds by ₹ 13-1/3, the profit of A & Co. under similar conditions. However below that level, profit for A & Co. will be greater. We can, therefore, generally conclude that B & Co. likely to earn higher profits under conditions of heavy demand for the product above ₹ 3,00,000. On the other hand, A & Co. is likely to earn higher profits under conditions of low demand for the product (below ₹ 3,00,000).

Illustration 54. A Practising Chartered Accountant now spends ₹ 0.90 per km. On taxi fares for his clients work. He is considering two other alternatives, the purchase of a new small car *or* an old bigger car.

Items	*New Small Car* ₹	*Old Bigger Car* ₹
Purchase Price	35,000	20,000
Sales Price, after 5 years	19,000	12,000
Repairs and Servicing, per annum	1,000	1,200
Taxes and Insurance, per annum	1,700	700
Petrol consumption, per litre	10 kms.	7 kms.
Petrol Price, per litre	3.50	3.50

He estimates that he travels 10,000 km annually, which of the three alternative will be cheapest? If his practice expands and has to do 19,000 km. Per annum, what should be his decision ? At how many km. per annum will the cost of the two cars break-even? Ignore interest and income-tax.

Solution

COMPARATIVE COSTS OF ALTERNATIVE MODES OF CONVEYANCE

Particulars	*New Small Car* ₹	*Old Bigger Car* ₹	*Taxi* ₹
A. Fixed Costs per annum :			
Depreciation	3,200	1,600	
Repairs & Servicing	1,000	1,200	
Taxes & insurance	1,700	700	
	5,900	3,500	
B. Variable Costs per annum :			
(a) Petrol : 10,000 km.	3,500	5,000	
(b) Petrol : 19,000 km.	6,650	9,500	
C. Total Cost : [A + B]			
(a) 10,000 km	9,400	8,500	9,000
(b) 19,000 km	12,550	13,000	17,100

Recommendation: An old bigger car is the cheapest for his present practice. However, if his practice, expands, a new small car will be the cheapest.

$$\text{Cost Break-even Point} = \frac{\text{Difference in Fixed Costs}}{\text{Difference in Variable Cost of two car}}$$

$$= \frac{5{,}900 - 3{,}500}{0.50 - 0.35} = \frac{2{,}400}{0.15} = 16{,}000 \text{ km}$$

Illustration 55. Y Company has just been incorporated and plans to produce a product that will sell for ₹ 10 per unit. Preliminary market surveys show that demand will be around 10,000 units per year.

The Company has the choice of buying one of two machines, each of which has a capacity of 10,000 units per year. Machine 'A' would have fixed costs of ₹ 30,000 per year and would yield a profit of ₹ 30,000 per year on the sale of 10,000 units. Machine 'B' would have fixed costs of ₹ 18,000 per year and yield a profit of ₹ 22,000 per year on the sale of 10,000 units. Variable costs behave linearly for both machines.

Required :

(a) Break-even sales for each machine. (b) Sales level where both machines are equally profitable, (c) Range of sales where one machine is more profitable than the other.

Solution:

In the present problem sales, fixed overhead and profit are given. From this information variable cost can be arrived at :

(a) STATEMENT SHOWING BREAK EVEN SALES FOR EACH MACHINE

Particulars	*Machine A*	*Machine B*
A. Total Fixed cost (₹)	30,000	18,000
B. Total Profit (₹)	30,000	22,000

C. Total Contribution (₹) [A + B]	60,000	40,000
D. Total Sales (₹) (10,000 ₹ 10)	1,00,000	1,00,000
E. Total Variable Cost (₹)	40,000	60,000
F. P/V Ratio	60%	40%
G. Variable Cost per unit (₹) [Total Variable Cost/10,000]	4.00	6.00
H. Contribution per unit (₹) [Selling Price – Variable Cost]	6.00	4.00
I. Break-even Sales units = Fixed Cost ÷ Contribution per unit	5,000 units	4,500 units
J. Break-even Sales (in ₹) = [BES (Units) ₹ 10]	₹ 50,000	₹ 45,000

(b) Sales Level where Both the Machines are Equally Profitable.

It is now a question of indifference point, i.e., the point at which total cost of the two given machines will be equal. At this point profitability of the two machines will be equal. Suppose sales at which cost indifference point occurs is equal to x. Therefore, at this level total cost will be the same,

$$₹\ 30{,}000 + 4x = ₹\ 18{,}000 + 6x \text{ or } x = 6{,}000 \text{ units}$$

Proof

	Data of 6,000 units	
	Machine A	*Machine B*
Sales	₹ 60,000	₹ 60,000
Less : Variable Cost	24,000	36,000
Contribution	36,000	24,000
Less : Fixed cost	30,000	18,000
Profit	6,000	6,000

(c) It is clear from (b) that at the level of 6,000 units, both the machines are equally profitable. Contribution per unit of A is more than B, but fixed cost of A is also more than B. Advantage of higher contribution per unit of A will be realised after recovery of fixed cost of A, i.e. ₹ 30,000 . Therefore, upto 6,000 units B is more profitable. After 6,000 units Machine A is more profitable. To support the above, profitability of the two machines at two different levels (5,000 units and 7,000 units) is given below :

Particulars	*5,000 units*		*7,000 units*	
	A	B	A	B
Contribution	30,000	20,000	42,000	28,000
Less : Fixed cost	30,000	18,000	30,000	18,000
Profit	—	2,000	12,000	10,000

Therefore, up to 6,000 units, B is more profitable than A due to lower fixed cost. However, beyond 6,000 units A is more profitable than B due to better P/V Ratio.

Illustration 56. A Company proposes to install a machine for the manufacture of a component which at present is being purchased at ₹ 24 each. There are two alternatives, namely (a) installation of an automatic machine and (b) installation of a semi-automatic machine. The details of the two machines are as under :

	Automatic Machine	*Semi-Automatic Machine*
Initial cost of machine (₹)	9,00,000	6,00,000
Life	10 Years	10 Years
Fixed overheads other than depreciation On machines (per annum) (₹)	1,62,000	84,000
Variable expenses for the component (₹)	12	15

The Company charges depreciation on straight line method. Scrap value of the machine at the end of life is nil. The demand for the components at present is 20,000 units per annum. This demand is expected to increase to 40,000 units.

Required :

(a) For each of the two volumes of output namely 20,000 and 40,000 units, state with supporting calculations whether the components should be purchased or manufactured by installation of machine. If your decision is an favour of installation of machine, which model will you advice?

(b) At what Volume of output should the company change over from purchase of components to manufacture by installation of (I) semi-automatic machine and (ii) automatic machine.

(c) At what volume of manufacture of the components will the Company switch over from installation of one type of machine to the other ?

Solution **(a) STATEMENT SHOWING THE COST PER UNIT UNDER VARIOUS ALTERNATIVES**

Particulars	20,000 units		40,000 units	
	Automatic Machine	*Semi-Automatic Machine*	*Automatic Machine*	*Semi-Automatic Machine*
Variable cost (₹)	12.00	15.00	12.00	15.00
Fixed overheads other than depreciation	8.10	4.20	4.05	2.10
Depreciation (₹)	4.50	3.00	2.25	1.50
Total cost of manufacture (₹)	24.60	22.20	18.30	18.60
Cost of Buying per unit (₹)	24.00	24.00	24.00	24.00

It is profitable to install semi-automatic machine at the production level of 20,000 units. However at the volume of 40,000 units, automatic machine should be installed.

(b) STATEMENT SHOWING THE CHANGE OVER FROM PURCHASE TO MANUFACTURE

Particulars	*Automatic-Machine*	*Semi-Automatic Machine*
A. Purchase price of component	₹ 24.00	₹ 24.00
B. Variable costs of manufacture	₹ 12.00	₹ 15.00
C. Saving [A – B]	₹ 12.00	₹ 9.00
D. Total fixed costs (including depreciation)	₹ 2,52,000	₹ 1,44,000
E. Number of units at which change over is effected [D/C]	21,000	16,000

(c) STATEMENT SHOWING SWITCHOVER FROM ONE TYPE OF MACHINE TO THE OTHER

	Automatic Machine	*Semi-Automatic*	*Difference Machine*
A Variable cost	₹ 12	₹ 15	₹ 3
B. Total fixed cost (including Depreciation)	₹ 2,52,000	₹ 1,44,000	₹ 1,08,000
C. Number of units at which switch over is effected [Difference in Fixed Costs/Difference in Variable Costs per unit			36,000 units

Working Note : *Calculation of fixed overheads per unit and Depreciation per unit*

Particulars	20,000 units		40,000 units	
	Automatic Machine	*Semi-Automatic Machine*	*Automatic Machine*	*Semi-Automatic Machine*
A. Fixed Overheads (₹)	1,62,000	84,000	1,62,000	84,000
B. Depreciation (₹)	90,000	60,000	90,000	60,000
C. No. of units	20,000	20,000	40,000	40,000
D. Fixed OH per unit (₹) [A/C]	8.10	4.20	4.05	2.10
E. Depreciation per Unit [B/C]	4.50	3.00	2.25	1.50

Illustration 57. Standard Pump Ltd., manufacturing petrol and diesel operated pumps. The company wants to have a customer survey before marketing the pumps. You are asked to work out the economics of choice between the two types of pumps. The Company provides you the following data :

	Petrol-operated pump 'X'	*Diesel-operated pump 'Y'*
Selling price (₹)	8,000	17,750
Cost of fuel per litre (₹)	8	3
Operating hours per litre	20	40

Using above data, answer following questions :

(i) How many hours the pumps should run so that the customer willing to buy is indifferent in choice between X and Y ? Assume that fuel cost has linear function with respect to time.

(ii) Assuming the price of X remains unchanged, and the customer wants to run the pump for 10,000 hours, how much he will be willing to pay for Y ?

(iii) If Standard Pump Ltd., offers to convert a petrol-operated pump to diesel-operated one after 10,000 hours of operation of the former, how much customer will be willing to pay for the modification of the pump?

(iv) If there is a saving of ₹ 3,250 in operating cost of Y over its life, how many hours the customer should expect to run the pumps so as to be in different in choice ?

(v) If there is a restriction on the fuel supply to the extent of 700 litres for both petrol and diesel, what will be customer's preference either for petrol - operated or diesel operated one? Ignore interest on capital.

(vi) How many hours the pumps should run so that the operating cost per hour would be 50 paise per hour in case of each pump set?

Solution

(i) Calculation of Indifference Point

Let the operating hours be x

Total cost of Pump X = ₹ 8,000 + $\frac{8}{20}x$ ....*Equation I*

Total cost of Pump Y = ₹ 17,750 + $\frac{3}{40}x$. ....Equation II

Equation both the equation to find out value of x

$$8{,}000 + 0.40x = 17{,}750 + 0.075x$$
$$0.325x = 9{,}750$$
$$x = 9750/.325 = 30{,}000 \text{ hours}$$

(ii) Calculation of Maximum Price for pump Y

Let the maximum price for pump Y = x

Thus, 8,000 + (0.40 10,000) = x + 0.075 10,000

x = 12,000 – 750 = ₹ 11,250

(iii) Calculation of Conversion cost after 10,000 hours

A. Hours still to be operated to reach indifference point = 30,000 – 10,000 = 20,000

B. Revenue Saving per hour = $\frac{8}{20} - \frac{3}{40} = 0.325$

C. Max. Saving after conversion [A B] [20,000 .325] = 6,500

The customer will be willing to pay upto ₹ 6,500 for modification.

(iv) Calculation of Required operating hours

Let the required operation hours be x

₹ 8,000 + 0.40x – (17,750 + 0.075x) = ₹ 3,250

0.325 x = ₹ 17,750 + ₹ 3,250 – ₹ 8,000

x = ₹ 13,000/0.325 = 40,000

(v) Choice in case of limited fuel

		Pump X	*Pump Y*
A.	Selling price	8,000	17,750
B.	Cost of fuel	700 8 = 5,600	700 3 = 2,100
C.	Total Cost [A + B]	13,600	19,850
D.	Operating hours	700 20 = 14,000	700 40 = 28,000
E.	Operating cost per hour [C/D]	0.97	0.71

Decision — Customer's preference will be for Pump Y since its operating cost is less than that of Pump X.

(vi) $\frac{17750 + 0.075}{x} = 0.50 \Rightarrow x = 41{,}765;$ $\frac{8000 + 40x}{x} = 0.50 \Rightarrow x = 80{,}000$

Illustration 58. Tulsian Ltd. owns two factories, one at Delhi and the other at Noida. Both factories produce and sell same product with the same Selling Price of ₹ 200 Per Unit. The following are the other cost details:

	Delhi Plant	**Noida Plant**
Capacity Operated	75%	83-1/3%
Actual Sales	₹ 30 Lacs	₹ 50 Lacs
Total Fixed Cost	₹ 15 Lacs	₹ 8.1 Lacs
Depreciation	₹ 3 Lacs	₹ 2.1 Lacs
Profit / (Loss)	(₹ 3 Lacs)	₹ 1.90 Lacs

Required:

(a) Calculate Break-Even-Point for each Plant.
(b) Calculate Cash Break-Even-Point for each Plant.
(c) Calculate Cost Indifference Point
(d) In case Total Output is to be increased by 7,000 Units, how much output should be increased from which Plant and why?
(e) In case Total Output is to be curtailed by 7,000 Units, from which Plant should it be curtailed and why?
(f) Determine Combined BEP for the company as a whole adopting each of the following three approaches:
   (i) Constant Sales-Mix in the ratio of capacities of Plants.
   (ii) Variable Sales-Mix producing from more profitable Plant first.
   (iii) Using Actual Sales Ratio as the basis.

Solution

	Delhi Plant	**Noida Plant**
(a) BEP (Units) = $\frac{\text{Fixed Costs}}{\text{Contribution Per Unit}}$	$\frac{15,00,000}{(200-120)}$ = 18,750 Units	$\frac{8,10,000}{(200-160)}$ = 20,250 Units
BEP (₹) = $\frac{\text{Fixed Costs}}{\text{P/V Ratio}}$	$\frac{15,00,000}{40\%}$ = ₹ 37,50,000	$\frac{8,10,000}{20\%}$ = ₹ 40,50,000
(b) Cash BEP (Units) = $\frac{\text{Cash Fixed Costs}}{\text{Contribution Per Unit}}$	$\frac{12,00,000}{(200-120)}$ = 15,000 Units	$\frac{6,00,000}{(200-160)}$ = 15,000 Units
Cash BEP (₹) = $\frac{\text{Cash Fixed Costs}}{\text{P/V Ratio}}$	$\frac{12,00,000}{40\%}$ = ₹ 30,00,000	$\frac{6,00,000}{20\%}$ = ₹ 30,00,000

(c) Cost Indifference Point = $\frac{\text{Difference in Fixed Cost}}{\text{Difference in Variable Cost Per Unit}} = \frac{15,00,000 - 8,10,000}{160 - 120}$ = 17,250 Units

At Cost Indifference Point of 17,250 units the management has choice either to produce at Delhi Plant or Noida Plant. Upto 17,250 units Noida Plant is more economical than Delhi Plant due to lower Fixed Cost and beyond 17,250 units Delhi Plant is more economical than Noida Plant due to lower Variable Cost.

(d) If Total Output is to be increased by 7,000 Units, first 5,000 units should be produced from Delhi Plant so as to use its capacity fully because per unit contribution of ₹ 80 from Delhi Plant is higher than per unit contribution of ₹ 40 from Noida Plant. Remaining 2,000 units should be produced from Noida Plant.

(e) In case output is to be curtailed by 7,000 units, entire curtailment should be from Noida Plant because it has lower per unit contribution of ₹ 40 per unit as compared with ₹ 80 from Delhi Plant.

(f) (i) Constant Sales-Mix in the Ratio of Capacities of Plants:

$$\text{Combined P/V Ratio} = \frac{\text{Total Contribution from the two Plants at Full Capacity}}{\text{Total Sales of the two Plants at Full Capacity}}$$

$$= \frac{[(200 - 120) \times 20,000] + [(200 - 160) \times 30,000]}{[(200 \times 20,000) + (200 \times 30,000)]}$$

$$= \frac{(16,00,000 + 12,00,000)}{(40,00,000 + 60,00,000)} \times 100 = 28\%$$

$$\text{Combined BEP (₹)} = \frac{\text{Combined Fixed Cost}}{\text{Combined P/V Ratio}} = \frac{15,00,000 + 8,10,000}{28\%} = ₹\ 82,50,000$$

(f) (ii) Using Variable Sales-Mix producing from more profitable Plant first:

Combined Fixed Cost is to be recovered first from more Profitable Plant (i.e. Delhi) and then from Noida Plant Contribution from Full Capacity of Delhi Plant = 20,000 Units x ₹ 80 = ₹ 16,00,000.

Contribution required from Noida Plant = Combined Fixed Cost – ₹ 16,00,000
= ₹ 23,10,000 – ₹ 16,00,000 = ₹ 7,10,000

Units required from Noida Plant to meet the balance Fixed Cost = ₹ 7,10,000 / ₹ 40 = 17,750 Units

Combined BEP = Sales of Units at Full Capacity of Profitable Plant (i.e. Delhi Plant)
+ Sales of Units required from Noida Plant to meet the balance Fixed Cost
= (20,000 Units × ₹ 200) + (17,750 Units × ₹ 200) = ₹ 75.50 Lacs

(f) (iii) Using Actual Sales Ratio as the basis:

$$\text{Combined P/V Ratio} = \frac{\text{Total Contribution from the two Plants at Actual Capacity}}{\text{Total Sales of the two Plants at Actual Capacity}}$$

$$= \frac{[(200 - 120) \times 15{,}000] + [(200 - 160) \times 25{,}000]}{[(200 \times 15{,}000) + (200 \times 25{,}000)]}$$

$$= \frac{(12{,}00{,}000 + 10{,}00{,}000)}{(30{,}00{,}000 + 50{,}00{,}000)} \times 100 = 27.50\%$$

$$\text{Combined BEP (₹)} = \frac{\text{Combined Fixed Cost}}{\text{Combined P/V Ratio}} = \frac{15{,}00{,}000 + 8{,}10{,}000}{27.50\%} = ₹\ 84 \text{ Lacs}$$

Working Notes:

	Delhi Plant	**Noida Plant**
Actual Sales Units	= ₹ 30 Lacs/₹ 200 = 15,000	= ₹ 50 Lacs/₹ 200 = 25,000
Full Capacity	= 15,000/75% = 20,000	= 25,000/83-1/3% = 30,000
Variable Cost	= ₹ 30 Lacs – ₹ 15 Lacs	= ₹ 50 Lacs – ₹ 8.10 Lacs
(Sales – Fixed Cost – Profit)	– (₹ 3 Lacs) = ₹ 18 Lacs	– ₹ 1.90 Lacs = ₹ 40 Lacs
Variable Cost Per Unit	= Total Variable Cost/Sales units	= Total Variable Cost/Sales units
	= ₹ 18 Lacs/15,000	= ₹ 40 Lacs/25,000
	= ₹ 120 Per Unit	= ₹ 160 Per Unit

Break Even Point in Case of Semi-Variable Costs

Illustration 59. Calculate Break-Even-Point for a train journey between Delhi and Jaipur where cost of an Engine is ₹ 80,000 and of Bogie is ₹ 16,000. Capacity of a bogie is 70 passengers and each ticket is priced at ₹ 600. Variable Cost per ticket is ₹ 100.

Solution:

Step 1: Let BEP (in terms of Bogies) be X

$$X = \frac{\text{Fixed Cost + Cost of Bogies}}{\text{Contribution Per Bogie}} = \frac{(80{,}000 + 16{,}000X)}{(500 \times 70)}$$

$$35000X = 80000 + 16000X$$

$$X = 80000 / 19000 = 4.21 \text{ rounded off to next integer } 5$$

Step 2: BEP (in term of passengers) $\frac{\text{Fixed Cost + Cost of 5 Bogies}}{\text{Contribution Per Passenger}} = \frac{[80{,}000 + (16{,}000 \times 5)]}{500}$

$$= 320 \text{ Passengers}$$

Verification:

$$\text{Profit} = \text{Contribution} - \text{Cost of Engine} - \text{Cost of 5 Bogies}$$

$$= [(320 \times ₹\ 500) - ₹\ 80{,}000 - (₹\ 16{,}000 \times 5)] = 0$$

Illustration 60. Calculate Break-Even Level of Students from the following information:

Picnic Charges per student ₹ 820
Cost of Snacks per student ₹ 140
Entrance Fee per student ₹ 550
Cost of Costumes per student ₹ 60
Rent per bus ₹ 1300
Special Permit Fee ₹ 100 per bus
Prizes to Students for Games ₹ 520
Allowance to each Teacher ₹ 100

Maximum Capacity of a bus 50 (excluding 2 seats reserved for the teachers accompanying the students).

Solution:

Step 1: Let BEP (in terms of Buses) be X

$$X = \frac{\text{Fixed Cost + Semi-Fixed Cost of Buses}}{\text{Contribution Per Bus}} = \frac{(520 + 3{,}100X)}{(70 \times 50)}$$

$$3{,}500X = 520 + 3{,}100X$$

$$X = 520/400 = 1.3 \text{ rounded off to next integer } 2$$

Step 2: BEP (in term of passengers) $\frac{\text{Fixed Cost + Cost of 2 Buses}}{\text{Contribution Per Student}} = \frac{(520 + 6{,}200)}{70} = 96 \text{ Students}$

Verification:

Profit = Revenue – Variable Costs – Cost of Prizes – Semi-Fixed Cost of 2 Buses
= [(₹ 820 × 96) – (₹ 750 × 96) – ₹ 520 – (₹ 3,100 × 2)] = 0

Working Note:

Semi-Fixed Cost per bus = Rent + Permit Fee + Allowance + Cost of Snacks for Teachers + Entrance Fee for Teachers + Cost of Costumes for Teachers
= ₹ 1,300 + ₹ 100 + (₹.100 × 2) + (₹ 140 × 2) + (₹ 550 × 2) + (₹ 60 × 2)
= ₹ 3,100

Illustration 61. Bharat Ltd. provides you the following information :

		1000 units	*1500 units*	*2000 units*	*2500 units*	*3000 units*
Sales	₹	50,000	75,000	1,00,000	1,25,000	1,50,000
Direct Material Cost	₹	30,000	45,000	60,000	75,000	90,000
Units		0–1000	1001–2000	2001–2500	2501–3000	3001 & above
Semi-Variable Overheads	₹	2,000	4,000	4,000	6,000	6,000
Fixed Overheads	₹	20,000	20,000	20,000	20,000	20,000

Required: Calculate the Break-Even Point

Solution:

$$\text{Break-Even Point} = \frac{\text{Fixed Cost + Initial Semi-Variable Cost}}{\text{Contribution per unit}} = \frac{20,000 + 2,000}{50 - 30} = 1,100$$

At the break-even point of 1,100, there will be under recovery of semi-variable overheads to the extent of ₹ 2,000 [i.e. ₹ 4,000 – ₹ 2,000)]

To recover ₹ 2,000, 100 units $\left[\text{i.e. } \frac{2,000}{20}\right]$ should be added to the above B.E.P.

Hence, B.E.P. is = 1,100 + 100 = 1,200

Verification:

A.	Sales for 1200 units [1200 × ₹ 50]		₹ 60,000
B.	*Less* : Direct Material Cost [1200 × ₹ 30]	36,000	
	Semi-variable Overheads	4,000	
			40,000
C.	Contribution [A – B]		20,000
D.	*Less* : Fixed cost		20,000
E.	Profit		Nil

Note: Semi variable overheads vary @ ₹ 200 for every 100 units

Illustration 62. Calculate the break-even number of candidates from the following information :

	₹
Fee collected per candidate	100
Variable cost per candidate	60
One Supervisor for every 100 candidates at the rate of	400
Fixed Cost	40,000

Solution:

A.	Fees collected		100
B.	*Less* : Variable Costs:		
	Variable Cost	60	
	Supervision Cost	4	64
C.	Contribution [A – B]		36
D.	Fixed Cost		40,000
E.	B.E.P. [Fixed Costs/Contribution per unit] [₹ 40,000/₹ 36] = 1111.11 Units		

If B.E.P. is taken as 1111.11 candidates, there would be under recovery of supervisors cost to the extent of ₹ 355.56 as follows:

Supervision Cost recovered	(1111.11 × ₹ 4)	4,444.44
Actual Supervision Cost	(1200 × ₹ 4)	4,800.00
Under reocvery		355.56

To recover ₹ 355.56, 8.89 candidates $\left[\text{i.e. } \frac{355.56}{40}\right]$ should be added to the above B.E.P.

Hence, B.E.P. is = 1111.11 + 8.89 = 1120 candidates

Verification:

A.	Fees collected for 1120 candidates [1120 × ₹ 100]		1,12,000
B.	*Less*: Variable cost [1120 × ₹ 60]	67,200	
	Supervision Cost [12 × 400]	4,800	72,000
C	Contribution [A – B]		40,000
D	*Less* : Fixed cost		40,000
E	Profit [C – D]		Nil

Break-Even Analysis with Use of Probability

Illustration 63. X Ltd. which makes only one product sells 10,000 units of its product making a loss of ₹ 10,000. The variable cost per unit of the product is ₹ 8 and the fixed cost is ₹ 30,000. The company has estimated the following demand level of its product as under :

Sales (units)	10,000	12,000	14,000	16,000	18,000
Probability	0.10	0.15	0.20	0.30	0.25

Required:

(a) What is the probability that the company will at least break-even in the period?
(b) What is the probability that the company will continue to make losses?
(c) What is the probability that the company will make a profit of at least ₹ 6,000?

Solution:

Total Contribution = Fixed Cost – Losses = ₹ 30,000 – ₹ 10,000 = ₹ 20,000
Contribution per unit = ₹ 20,000/10,000 = ₹ 2

$$\text{B.E.P.} = \frac{\text{Fixed Cost}}{\text{Contribution per unit}} = \frac{30,000}{2} = 15,000 \text{ units}$$

(a) *Probability that sales will equal or exceed 15,000 units*

16,000 units	0.30
18,000 units	0.25
	0.55 or 55%

(b) *Probability that sales will be less than 15,000 units*

10000 units	0.10
12000 units	0.15
14000 units	0.20
	0.45 *or* 45%

(c) Sales (units) to earn ₹ 6,000 $= \frac{\text{Fixed Cost + Desired Profit}}{\text{Contribution per unit}}$

$$= \frac{30,000 + 6,000}{2} = 18,000 \text{ units}$$

Probability that sales will equal *or* exceed 18,000 units is 25%.

Illustration 64. X Ltd. which makes only one product sells 20,000 units of its product making a contribution of ₹ 1,00,000. The variable cost per unit is ₹ 10.

The company has estimated the fixed costs as follows:

Fixed Cost p.a. (₹)	50,000	60,000	70,000	80,000	90,000
Probability	0.1	0.3	0.3	0.1	0.2

Required:
(a) What is the probability that the comapny will break-even in the period ?
(b) What is the probability that the company will continue to make losses ?
(c) What is the probability that the comany will make a profit of at least ₹ 25,000 ?

Solution:

Total Contribution = ₹ 1,00,000

(a) Minimum Fixed Costs to Break-even = ₹ 1,00,000,
Probability that Fixed Costs will be ₹ 1,00,000 is nil

(b) Minimum Fixed Costs to continue to make losses = Above ₹ 1,00,000
Probability that Fixed Cost will exceed ₹ 1,00,000 is nil

(c) Minimum Fixed Costs to make a profit of ₹ 25,000 = ₹ 75,000
Probability that Fixed Cost will be ₹ 75,000 or less

50,000	60,000	70,000	
0.1	0.3	0.3	= 0.7 *or* 70%

SOLVED PROBLEMS I

Problem 1.

	Year 1	Year 2	
Sales	₹ 3,00,000	Decrease in selling price & Decrease in fixed cost	
M/S Ratio	25%	M/S Ratio	40%
P/V Ratio	$33\frac{1}{3}\%$	P/V Ratio	30%

Required: (a) Decreased sales amount in year 2 (b) New profit in year 2 (c) Decreased fixed cost in year 2 and (d) New BEP in year 2

Solution:

Margin of Safety = 25% of ₹ 3,00,000 = ₹ 75,000

Profit = Margin of Safety × P/V Ratio = ₹ 75,000 × $33^1/_3$ % = ₹ 25,000

Position in year 1

A. Sales	₹ 3,00,000
B. *Less* : Variable cost @ 66.2/3%	₹ 2,00,000
C. Contribution [A – B]	₹ 1,00,000
D. *Less* : Profit $33\frac{1}{2}$ % of ₹ 75,000	₹ 25,000
E. Fixed cost [C – D]	₹ 75,000

Position in Year 2

(a) *Decreased sales amount :* Let the decreased sales amount be X

A. Sales	X
B. *Less* : Variable cost	2,00,000
C. Contribution	X – 2,00,000

or, X – 2,00,000 = 30% of X

or, X = 2,00,000/.7 = 2,85,714

(b) *New profit in year 2*

New Margin of Safety = 40% of ₹ 2,85,714 = ₹ 1,14,286

Profit = 1,14,286 × 30% = ₹ 34,286

(c) *Decreased fixed cost in year 2*

	₹
A. Sales	2,85,714
B. *Less* : Variable cost @ 70%	2,00,000
C. Contribution @ 30%	85,714
D. *Less* : Profit	34,286
E. Fixed cost (C – D)	51,428

(d) *New B.E.P. in year 2* = $\frac{\text{Fixed Costs}}{\text{P/V ratio}} = \frac{51,428}{30\%}$ = ₹ 1,71,427

Problem 2. The following is a summary of the trading results of a company selling electrical appliances for the year ended 31st December 2013 during which 80,000 units were sold :

		₹ *(Lakhs)*
Sales		96
Costs :		
Material	36	
Labour :		
Direct	15	
Indirect	6	
Other costs	18	75
Profit		21

Taking into consideration the following matters, prepare a summary of the expected results for the following year:

(a) The selling price is to be reduced by ₹ 7.50.
(b) Sales volume is expected to be increased by 40%.
(c) Suppliers have agreed to give a discount of 5% on all purchases of materials.
(d) Direct workmen are to be paid an incentive bonus of 2½ % in order to stimulate production. Indirect labour is not expected to increase during the following year.
(e) Other costs vary directly with production except to the extent of ₹ 3 lakhs which is considered 'fixed' and an additional expense of ₹ 1 lakh will arise due to rent in respect of an extension to the factory.
(f) You are to assume that there are no stock or work-in-progress as at 31st December.

Solution: **SUMMARY OF EXPECTED RESULTS FOR THE YEAR 2014**

		₹
A	Sales Revenue [(80,000 × 140%) × (₹ 120 – ₹ 7.50)]	1,26,00,000
B	*Less :* Total Costs :	
	Material Cost [(80000 × 140%) × (₹ 45 – ₹ 2.25)]	47,88,000
	Direct Labour Cost [(80000 × 140%) × (₹ 18.75 × 102.50%)]	21,52,500
	Indirect Labour Cost	6,00,000
	Other Variable Costs [(80000 × 140%) × ₹ 18.75)]	21,00,000
	Other Fixed Costs [₹ 3,00,000 + ₹ 1,00,000]	4,00,000
		1,00,40,500
C	Profit (A – B)	25,59,500

Problem 3. X Ltd. had prepared the following budget for the year 2014 based on full capacity utilisation.

		₹ *(lakhs)*
Sales of whole production		40.00
Direct Materials	8.00	
Direct Wages	12.00	
Direct Consumables	4.00	24.00
Gross Profit		16.00
Commission	2.00	
Delivery	1.20	
Maintenance	0.80	
Depreciation	1.60	
Salaries and Indirect Wages	5.20	
Other Costs	2.40	13.20
Net Profit		2.80

Commission and delivery costs are fixed as to 50%. The remaining 50% varies directly with sales. Maintenance cost are also fixed and variable in the same proportion with reference to production as in the case of commission. All other indirect costs are fixed.

Owing to current uncertainties in the economic situation, It is now envisaged that during 2014 only 60% of production will be achieved and all of it will be sold.

You are required to :

(a) Prepare a revised budget for 2014 and Statement of Present Profit on Marginal Costing Basis; and
(b) Determine the break-even level of production.

Solution: **(a) REVISED BUDGET FOR 2014 AT 60% CAPACITY**

	Particulars		*(₹ in lakhs)*
A	Sales		24.00
B	*Less :* Costs :		
	Direct Materials	4.80	
	Direct Wages	7.20	
	Direct Consumables	2.40	14.40
C	Gross Profit (A – B)		9.60
D	*Less :* Expenses		
	Commission [1.00 + 60% of 1.00]	1.60	
	Delivery [.60 + 60% of .60]	0.96	
	Maintenance [.40 + 60% of .40]	0.64	
	Depreciation	1.60	
	Salaries and Indirect Wages	5.20	
	Other Costs	2.40	12.40
E	Net Loss (C – D)		2.80

STATEMENT OF PRESENT PROFIT (ON MARGINAL COSTING BASIS)

	Particulars		*(₹ in lakhs)*
A	Sales		40.00
B	*Less :* Variable Costs :		
	Direct Materials	8.00	
	Direct Wages	12.00	
	Direct Consumables	4.00	
	Commission	1.00	
	Delivery	0.60	
	Maintenance	0.40	26.00
C	Contribution (A – B)		14.00
D	*Less :* Fixed Costs :		
	Commission	1.00	
	Delivery	0.60	
	Maintenance	0.40	
	Depreciation	1.60	
	Salaries and Indirect Wages	5.20	
	Other Costs	2.40	11.20
E	Profit (C – D)		2.80

(b) *Break-even Level of Production*

P/V Ratio : $\frac{\text{Contribution}}{\text{Sales}} \times 100 = \frac{14}{40} \times 100 = 35\%$

BEP sales $= \frac{\text{Fixed Expenses}}{\text{P/V Ratio}} = \frac{11.20 \text{ lakhs}}{35\%}$ = ₹ 32,00,000 *or* 80% of full capacity of 40,00,000

Problem 4. A factory is currently working at 50% capacity and produces 10,000 units of product P, the unit cost of which is ₹ 180 comprised as follows :

	₹
Direct Material	100
Direct Labour	30
Factory Overhead	30 (40% Fixed)
Administrative Overhead	20 (50% Fixed)

The selling price per unit is ₹ 200

If the capacity is increased to 60%, the raw material cost will increase by 2% and selling price falls by 2%. At 80% capacity, raw material cost increases by 5% and selling price falls by 5%.

Required: Work out the total costs and profit for the three capacity levels and prepare a brief note for the management on the profitability of these levels of performance with your recommendation.

Solution: STATEMENT SHOWING TOTAL COSTS AND PROFIT AT VARIOUS CAPACITY LEVELS

	Particulars	Capacity		
		50% 10,000 Units	*60% 12,000 Units*	*80% 16,000 Units*
A.	Sales (₹)	20,00,000	23,52,000	30,40,000
B.	Total Variable Costs :			
	Direct Material (₹)	10,00,000	12,24,000	16,80,000
	Direct Labour (₹)	3,00,000	3,60,000	4,80,000
	Factory Overhead (₹)	1,80,000	2,16,000	2,88,000
	Administration Overhead (₹)	1,00,000	1,20,000	1,60,000
		15,80,000	19,20,000	26,08,000
	Factory Overhead (10,000 × 12)	1,20,000	1,20,000	1,20,000
	Administration Overhead (10,000 × 10)	1,00,000	1,00,000	1,00,000
C.	Total Fixed Cost (₹)	2,20,000	2,20,000	2,20,000
D.	Total Cost (₹) (B + C)	18,00,000	21,40,000	28,28,000
E.	Profit (₹) (A – D)	2,00,000	2,12,000	2,12,000
F.	Profit Margin (%) $\left(\frac{\text{Profit}}{\text{Sales}} \times 100\right)$ 100	10%	9.01%	6.97%

Brief Note (for Management on the profitability) :

From the above total cost and profit statement the following two facts are apparent :

(a) The profit margin at 50% capacity is 10%, at 60% capacity it is 9.01% and at 80% capacity it is 6.97%. It means that profit margin shows a downward trend as capacity increases from 50% onwards.

(b) At 50% capacity the concern's total profit is ₹ 2,00,000, whereas at 60% and 80% capacities it is ₹ 2,12,000. Therefore it is clear that as we move from 50% to 60% capacity, the profit increases by ₹ 12,000, whereas there is no change in the profitability when the capacity is increased from 60% to 80% level.

On the basis of above two facts, it is advisable for management to increase its production upto 60% level of operation inspite of a slight decrease in profit margin.

Problem 5. From the following figures, find the break-even volume :

Selling price per tonne ₹ 69.50, Fixed Expenses ₹ 18.02 lakhs, Variable Cost per tonne ₹ 35.50

If this volume represents 40% capacity, what is the additional profit for an added production of 40% capacity, the selling price of which is 10% lower for 20% capacity production and 15% lower, than the existing price, for the other 20% capacity.

Solution:

$$\text{Break-even Volume} = \frac{\text{Fixed Cost}}{\text{Contribution per tonne}} = \frac{18.02 \text{ lakhs}}{34} = 53{,}000 \text{ tonnes}$$

Additional Profit for additional 40% capacity :

Present Break-even level of 53,000 tonnes represent 40% capacity. Additional production for another 40% capacity, i.e., 53,000 tonnes.

		First 20% Capacity	Second 20% Capacity
A	Selling Price per tonne	69.50	69.500
B	*Less :* Deduction	6.95	10.425
C	Revised Selling Price (A – B)	62.55	59.075
D	*Less :* Variable Cost	35.50	35.500
E	Profit per tonne (C – D)	27.05	23.575
F	Total Profit (26,500 × E)	7,16,825	6,24,737.50

Additional Profit over additional 40% capacity = ₹ 7,16,825 + ₹ 6,24,737.50

= ₹ 13,41,562.50

Problem 6. Repographics Ltd. manufactures a document reproducing machine which has a variable cost structure as follows :

Material ₹ 40, Labour ₹ 10, Overhead ₹ 4 and a Selling Price of ₹ 90.

Sales during the current year are expected to be ₹ 13,50,000 and Fixed Overheads ₹ 1,40,000.

Under a wage agreement, an increase of 10% is payable to all direct workers from the beginning of the forthcoming year, whilst Material costs are expected to increase by $7^1/_2$%, Variable Overhead Costs by 5% and Fixed Overhead Costs 3%.

You are required to calculate : (a) The new selling price if the Current Profit/Volume Ratio is to be maintained ; and (b) The quantity to be sold during the forthcoming year to yield the same amount of profit as the current year assuming the selling price to remain as ₹ 90.

Solution: Let the Selling Price for next year be x.

(a) STATEMENT SHOWING THE CALCULATION OF NEW SELLING PRICE

	Particulars	Present ₹	Proposed ₹
A	Selling Price per unit	90.00	x
B	*Less :* Variable costs per unit :		
	Material	40.00	43.00
	Labour	10.00	11.00
	Overhead	4.00	4.20
		54.00	58.20
C	Contribution per unit (A – B)	36.00	x – 58.20

D P/V Ratio $\frac{\text{Contribution}}{\text{Sales}} \times 100 = \frac{x - 58.20}{x} \times 100 = 40\%$

$x - 58.20 = .4\,x$

$.6x = 58.20$

$x = 58.20/.6 =$ ₹ 97

Let the No. of Units to be sold be x.

(b) STATEMENT SHOWING THE QUANTITY TO BE SOLD TO YIELD THE SAME PROFIT

	Particulars	Present ₹	Proposed ₹
A	No. of units	15,000	x
B	Selling Price per unit	90	90
C	Total Sales (A × B)	13,50,000	90 x
D	*Less :* Variable costs	8,10,000	58.20 x
E	Contribution (C - D)	5,40,000	31.80 x
F	*Less :* Fixed costs	1,40,000	1,44,200
G	Profit (E - F)	4,00,000	31.80 x – 1,44,200

31.80 x – 1,44,200 = ₹ 4,00,000

x = 5,44,200/31.80 = 17,113 units

Problem 7. A Japanese soft drink company is planning to establish a subsidiary company in India to produce mineral water. Based on the estimated annual sales of 40,000 bottles of the mineral water, cost studies produced the following estimates for the Indian subsidiary :

	Total Annual costs	*Percent of Total Annual Cost which is variable*
Material	2,10,000	100%
Labour	1,50,000	80%
Factory Overheads	92,000	60%
Administration Expenses	40,000	35%

The Indian production will be sold by manufacturer's representatives who will receive a commission of 8% of the selling price. No portion of the Japanese office expenses is to be allocated to the Indian subsidiary.

You are required to : (i) Compute the selling price per bottle to enable the management to realise an estimated 10% profit on sale proceeds in India. (ii) Calculate the break-even point in Rupee sales as also in number of bottles for the Indian subsidiary on the assumption that the selling price is ₹ 14 per bottle.

Solution: **(i) COMPUTATION OF SELLING PRICE PER BOTTLE**

Let the selling price per bottle be x

A.	Selling price per bottle		x
B.	No. of Bottles		40,000
C.	Total Sales (A x B)		40,000 x
D.	*Less :* Total Costs		
	Material	2,10,000	
	Labour	1,50,000	
	Factory Overheads	92,000	
	Adm. Expenses	40,000	
	Commission @ 8% of Sales	3200 x	4,92,000 + 3,200 x
E.	Profit (C – D)		40,000 x – (4,92,000 + 3200 x)

40,000 x – (4,92,000 + 3,200 x) = 10% of 40,000 x (given)

32,800 x = 4,92,000 *or,* x = 4,92,000/32,800 = ₹ 15 per bottle

(ii) Computation of Break Even Point

		Total	*Per unit*
A	No. of Bottles	40,000	1
B	Selling Price per unit (₹)	14	14
C	Total Sales Revenue (₹) (A x B)	5,60,000	14
D	*Less :* Variable costs (₹)		
	Materials	2,10,000	5.25
	Labour (80% of ₹ 1,50,000)	1,20,000	3.00
	Factory Overhead (60% of ₹ 92,000)	55,200	1.38
	Administration expenses (35% of ₹ 40,000)	14,000	0.35
	Commission (₹ 40 x 14,000 x 8%)	44,800	1.12
		4,44,000	11.10
E	Contribution (₹) [C – D]	1,16,000	2.90
F	Fixed Costs (₹)	92,800	

(₹ 1,50,000 x 20%) + (₹ 92,000 x 40%) + (₹ 40,000 x 65%) = ₹ 92,800

$$\text{P/V Ratio} = \frac{\text{Sales} - \text{Variable Cost}}{\text{Sales}} \times 100 = \frac{5{,}60{,}000 - 4{,}44{,}000}{5{,}60{,}000} \times 100 = 20.714\%$$

$$\text{Break-Even Point (in Rupees sales)} = \frac{\text{Fixed Cost}}{\text{P/V Ratio}} = \frac{92{,}800}{20.7142\%} = ₹\ 4{,}48{,}000$$

$$\text{Break-Even-Point (in number of bottles)} = \frac{\text{Fixed Costs}}{\text{Contribution per bottle}} = \frac{92{,}800}{2.90} = 32{,}000 \text{ bottles}$$

Problem 8. Modern Sports Ltd. has for the past several years produced boxing gloves which are sold at ₹ 28 per pair. Higher costs in recent years have made management to consider about the adequacy of this selling price.

The labour rate was increased from ₹ 1.75 per hour to ₹ 2.25 per hour and the cost of leather has gone up from ₹ 1.10 to ₹ 2.15 per square foot during the last five years. Fixed expenses have increased 25% from the level of ₹ 18,000 five years ago. Over the same period, variable overhead has increased 30%, or ₹ 3 per pair of gloves. Each glove requires 1.5 sq. ft. of leather and one hour direct labour.

Required : Calculate the selling price that the company has to charge under the new cost structure to break-even at the same number of units as five years ago.

Solution:

Selling Price of a pair of Boxing Gloves = ₹ 28

One glove requires : 1.5 sq. ft. of leather; 1 hour of direct labour.

Therefore, a pair requires : 2 sq. ft. of leather; 2 hours of direct labour.

Now two marginal cost statements are being made, one at old and other at new prices to find out the new selling price.

Old Marginal Cost Statement (Per pair of Gloves)	₹	*New Marginal Cost Statement (Per pair of Gloves)*	₹
Leather (1.10 × 3)	3.30	Leather (2.15 × 3)	6.45
Labour (1.75 × 2)	3.50	Labour (2.25 × 2)	4.50
Variable Overheads (3/30%)	10.00	Variable Overheads (₹ 10 + ₹ 3)	13.00
Marginal Cost	16.80	Marginal Cost	23.95
Contribution	11.20	Contribution *[Refer to W.N. (ii)]*	14.00
Selling Price	28.00	Selling Price	37.95

New Selling price should, therefore, be ₹ 37.95 per pair of gloves.

Working Notes :

(i) Variable overheads : 30% Increase = ₹ 3

Old variable overheads are therefore = 3/30% = ₹ 10.

(ii) Old Break-even point $= \frac{\text{Fixed Cost}}{\text{Contribution per unit}} = \frac{18,000}{11.20} = 1,607$ units approx.

New contribution per unit to maintain Break-even at old level :

$$\text{BEP} = \frac{\text{Fixed Cost}}{\text{Contribution per unit}}$$

$$1,607 = \frac{18,000 + 4,500}{x} \quad or,\ 1,607\,x = 22,500 \quad or,\ x = 14$$

Problem 9. Sturdy Horse Ltd., a cycle manufacturing company has drawn up a programme for the manufacture of a new product for the purpose of fuller utilisation of its capacity. The scheme envisages the manufacture of baby tricycle fitted with a bell. The company estimates the sales of tricycles at 10,000 during the first year and expects that from the second year onwards the sales estimates will stabilise at 20,000 tricycles. Since the Company has no provision for the manufacture of the small bells specially required for the tricycles, the requirement of the bells is initially proposed to be met by way of purchase from the market at ₹ 8 each. However if the Company desires to manufacture the bell in its factory by installation of new equipment, it has two alternative proposals as under.

	Super X Machine	*Janata Machine*
Initial Cost of machine	₹ 3,00,000	₹ 2,00,000
Life	10 years	10 years
Fixed overheads other than depreciation on Machines (per annum)	₹ 54,000	₹ 28,000
Variable expenses per bell	₹ 4.00	₹ 5.00

Depreciation on machine should be charged on straight line basis.

Required:

(i) For each of the two levels of output namely 10,000 and 20,000 bells state with suitable workings whether the Company should purchase the bells from market or install new equipment for manufacture of bells. If your decision is in favour of the installation of new equipment, which of the two new machines should be installed?

(ii) What would be your decision in case the forecast of requirement from the second year onwards is estimated at 40,000 bells instead of 20,000 bells.

(iii) At what volume of bells will the installation of the two machines break-even?

Solution:

(i) COST-BENEFIT ANALYSIS OF TWO MACHINES AT OUTPUT LEVEL OF 10,000 AND 20,000 UNITS

Output / Details	10,000 units		20,000 units	
	Super-X ₹	Janata ₹	Super-X ₹	Janata ₹
A. Cost of Buying @ ₹ 8 form Market	80,000	80,000	1,60,000	1,60,000
B. Cost of Manufacturing				
Variable cost	40,000	50,000	80,000	1,00,000
Depreciation on Machine	30,000	20,000	30,000	20,000
Fixed Overhead	54,000	28,000	54,000	28,000
Total Cost	1,24,000	98,000	1,64,000	1,48,000
C. Decision	Buy from Market		Instal Janata Machine	

(ii) BUY/MANUFACTURE DECISION AT LEVEL OF 40,000 UNITS

	Particulars	Super-X ₹	Janata ₹
A.	Cost of Buying @ ₹ 8	3,20,000	3,20,000
B.	Manufacturing Costs :		
	Variable Cost	1,60,000	2,00,000
	Depreciation on Machinery	30,000	20,000
	Fixed Overhead	54,000	28,000
	Total Cost of Manufacture	2,44,000	2,48,000
C.	Cost Saving on Manufacture	76,000	72,000

D. **Decision.** As Super-X, Machine results in higher cost saving, it should be installed at an estimated volume of 40,000 units.

(iii) BREAK-EVEN VOLUME OF TWO MACHINES

It is that volume of production at which a manufacture is indifferent as to which machine he should install as total cost on both machine is the same. This point is known as cost indifference point.

Let Break-even volume = x units.

Cost on Super X Machine for 'x' units = $54{,}000 + 30{,}000 + 4x = 84{,}000 + 4x$ ....Eq. I

Cost on Janata Machine for 'x' units = $20{,}000 + 28{,}000 + 5x = 48{,}000 + 5x$ ....Eq. II

At cost indifference point, total cost under two alternative will be equal. Therefore,

$$84{,}000 + 4x = 48{,}000 + 5x \text{ or } x = 36{,}000 \text{ units.}$$

Therefore, so at 36,000 units, the installation of the two machines will break-even.

SOLVED PROBLEMS II

Problem 10. A firm has invested ₹ 5,00,000 in its plant and sets a 30% annual return on investment. Fixed costs at present are ₹ 4,00,000 p.a. and variable cost is ₹ 15 per Unit. In the previous year, the firm produced and sold 50,000 units @ ₹ 25 each and earned a profit of ₹ 1,00,000. How can management achieve their target profit goal by varying different variables like fixed costs, variable costs, quantity sold or price per unit ?

Solution:

Desired profit = 30% of ₹ 5,00,000 = ₹ 1,50,000

Let the variable to be changed be x in each case :

Particulars	*If Fixed Cost to be Changed (a)*	*If Variable Cost to be changed (b)*	*If Quantity Sold to be changed (c)*	*It Selling Price per unit to be changed (d)*
A Sales (units)	50,000	50,000	x	50,000
B Selling Price per unit	25	25	25	x
C Total Sales (A × B)	12,50,000	12,50,000	25 x	50000 x
D *Less* : Variable costs	7,50,000	x	15 x	7,50,000
E Contribution (C – D)	5,00,000	12,50,000 – x	10x	50,000 x –7,50,000
F *Less* : Fixed costs	x	4,00,000	4,00,000	4,00,000
G Profit (E – F)	5,00,000 – x	8,50,000 – x	10 x – 4,00,000	50,000 - 11,50,000

Case (a) 5,00,000 – x = ₹ 1,50,000

x = ₹ 3,50,000

The desired profits can be achieved by reducing the fixed costs by ₹ 50,000 (i.e. ₹ 4,00,000 - ₹ 3,50,000)

Case (b) 8,50,000 – x = ₹ 1,50,000

x = ₹ 7,00,000

Variable cost per unit = ₹ 7,00,000/50,000 = ₹ 14 per unit

The desired profits can be achieved by reducing the variable cost by ₹ 1 (i.e. ₹ 15 - ₹ 14)

Case (c) 10 x – 4,00,000 = 1,50,000

x = (1,50,000 + 4,00,000)/10 = 55,000 units

The desired profit can be achieved by increasing the sales volume (in units) by 5000 units (i.e. 55,000 – 50,000)

Case (d) 50,000 x – 11,50,000 = ₹ 1,50,000 = (₹ 1,50,000 + ₹ 11,50,000)/50,000 = ₹ 26

The desired profit can be achieved by increasing the selling price per unit by ₹ 1 (i.e. ₹ 26 – ₹ 25)

Problem 11. A company has an opening stock of 6,000 units of output. The production planned for the current period is 24,000 units and expected sales for the current period amount to 28,000 units. The selling price per unit of output is ₹ 10. Variable cost per unit is expected to be ₹ 6 per unit while it was only ₹ 5 per unit during the previous period. The total fixed costs for the current peirod is ₹ 86,000. What is the break-even volume for the current period if (a) FIFO system is followed (b) LIFO system is followed.

Solution:

Step 1 : Statement showing units produced and sold

			FIFO	*LIFO*
Units in Opening Stock	6,000	Units sold : from op. Stock	6,000	4,000
Current production	24,000	Units out of Current Production	22,000	24,000
		Closing stock	2,000	2,000
Total	30,000	Total	30,000	30,000

Step 2 : Break-even point is the level of sales at which contribution is just enough to meet fixed overheads.

	FIFO	*LIFO*
A. Fixed overhead	₹ 86,000	86,000
B. *Less* : Contribution from opening stock FIFO [6,000 units × (₹ 10 – ₹ 5), LIFO [4000 units × ₹ 10 – ₹ 5]	30,000	20,000
C. Fixed overhead to be recovered by current production to breakeven	56,000	66,000
D. Contribution per unit from current production [₹ 10 – ₹ 6]	₹ 4	₹ 4
E. B.E.P. from current production FIFO [₹ 56,000/4], LIFO [₹ 66,000/4]	14,000	16,500
F. B.E.P. (in units) FIFO [6,000 + 14,000], LIFO [4000 + 16500]	20,000	20,500

Problem 12. Bal Bharti Public School has a total of 150 students consisting of 5 sections with 30 students per section. The school plans for a picnic around the city during the week-end to places such as the zoo, the amusement park, the planetarium etc. A private transport operator has come forward to lease out the buses for taking the students. Each bus will have a maximum capacity of 50 (excluding 2 seats reserved for the teachers accompanying the students). The school will employ two teachers for each bus, paying them an allowance of ₹ 50 per teacher. It will also lease out the required number of buses. The following are the other cost estimates:

	Cost per student ₹
Breakfast	5
Lunch	10
Tea	3
Entrance fee at zoo	2

Rent ₹ 650 per bus
Special permit fee ₹ 50 per bus.
Block Entrance fee at the planetarium ₹ 250.
Prizes to students for games ₹ 250.
No costs are incurred in respect of the accompanying teachers (except the allowance of ₹ 50 per teacher).

Required :

(a) Prepare a flexible budget estimating the total cost for the levels of 30, 60, 90, 120 and 150 students. Each item of cost is to be indicated separately.
(b) Compare the average cost per student at these levels.
(c) What will be your conclusions regarding the break-even level of students if the school proposes to collect ₹ 45 per student ?

Solution:

BAL BHARTI PUBLIC SCHOOL
(a) FLEXIBLE BUDGET TO ESTIMATE THE TOTAL COST

	Level of Students *Particulars*	*30* ₹	*60* ₹	*90* ₹	*120* ₹	*150* ₹
A	*Variable Costs :*					
	Breakfast	150	300	450	600	750
	Lunch	300	600	900	1,200	1,500
	Tea	90	180	270	360	450
	Entrance fee	60	120	180	240	300
		600	1,200	1,800	2,400	3,000
B.	*Semi-Fixed Costs :*					
	Rent of bus	650	1,300	1,300	1,950	1,950
	Permit fee	50	100	100	150	150
	Allowance to teachers	100	200	200	300	300
		800	1,600	1,600	2,400	2,400
C.	*Fixed Costs :*					
	Block entrance fee at planetarium	250	250	250	250	250
	Prizes to students for games	250	250	250	250	250
		500	500	500	500	500
D.	Total Cost [A + B + C]	1,900	3,300	3,900	5,300	5,900
(b)	**Average Cost per Student** [Total Cost/ No. of students]	₹ 63.33	₹ 55	₹ 43.33	₹ 44.17	₹ 39.33

(c) **Break even level :**

∴ Contribution per student= ₹ 45 – ₹ 20 = ₹ 25

Since the semi-fixed cost changes for every 50 students, fixed costs + semi-fixed costs for three levels of students to be covered are :

	Level	*Upto 50*	*51 to 100*	*101 to 150*
		₹	₹	₹
A.	Fixed Costs (including semi-fixed costs)	1,300	2,100	2,900
B.	Contribution per student	25	25	25
C.	B.E.P. [Fixed cost/Contribution per unit]	52	84	116

The number of students required to recover fixed costs at levels upto 50, 51 to 100 and 101 to 150 are 52, 84 and 116 respectively. The figure of 52 students lies outside the first level i.e. upto 50, but the remaining figures 84 and 116 are within their prescribed levels. Therefore, 84 and 116 students represent two breakeven points.

Problem 13. Frazer Ltd. Manufactures and sells a product, the selling price and raw material cost of which have remained unchanged during the past two years. The following are the relevant data:

	Year 1	*Year 2*
Quantity sold (kgs.)	*100*	*150*
	₹	₹
Sales value	20,000	?
Raw materials	10,000	?
Direct wages	3,000	?
Factory overheads	5,000	5,700
Profit	2,000	2,550

During year 2, direct wage rates increased by 50%, but there was a saving of ₹ 300 in fixed factory overheads. ***Required:*** What quantity (in kgs.) the company should have produced and sold in year 2 in order to maintain the same amount of net profit per kg. as it earned during year 1 ?

Solution: STATEMENT SHOWING THE QUANTITY TO BE PRODUCED AND SOLD DURING YEAR 2

	Particulars	₹	₹
A	Selling price per kg. (₹ 20,000/100 kg)		200
B	Variable Costs per kg.		
	Raw Materials	100	
	Direct wages $\left[\frac{₹\ 3,000}{100\ kg} \times 150\%\right]$	45	
	Variable factory overhead [(₹ 6,000 – ₹ 5,000)/(150 – 100)]	20	165
C	Contribution per kg (A – B)		35
D	*Less :* Profit required per kg (₹ 2,000/100 kg.)		20
E	Balance contribution per kg for meeting fixed costs (C – D)		15
F	Total fixed costs		2,700
G	Quantity of kgs. Produced and sold (₹ 2,700/15)		180 kgs.

Working Notes :

(i) Calculation of Variable Factory Overhead per kg.

		₹
A	Total Factory overheads in year 2	5,700
B	*Add :* Savings in fixed factory overheads	300
C	Total Factory overheads in year 2 before saving [A + B]	6,000
D	*Less :* Total factory overheads in year 1	5,000
E	Increase in factory overhead [C – D]	1,000

$$\therefore \text{ Variable Factory Overhead per kg.} = \frac{\text{Increase in factory overhead}}{\text{Increase in quantity}} = \frac{6000-5000}{150-100} = \text{Rs. } 20$$

(ii) Calculation of Fixed Factory Overhead :

		Year 1	*Year 2*
		₹	₹
A	Total factory overheads	5,000	5,700
B	*Less :* Variable factory overheads	2,000	3,000
C	Fixed Factory Overheads (A – B)	3,000	2,700

Problem 14. A company manufactures and sells a product, the price of which is controlled by the Government. Raw material required for this product is also made available at a fixed controlled price. The following figures have been called for the previous two accounting years of the company :

	Year I	*Year II*
Quantity sold (tonnes)	1,26,000	1,44,000
Price per tonne	₹ 185	₹ 185
	(₹ In thousands)	
Sales Value	23,310	26,640
Raw Materials	11,340	12,960
Direct Labour	1,512	1,872
Factory, Administration and Selling Expenses	9,702	11,232
Profit	756	576

During *Year II* direct labour rates increased by 8-1/3%. Increases in factory, administration and selling expenses during the year were ₹ 8,10,000 on account of factors other than the increased quantities produced and sold. The managing director desires to know, what quantity if they had produced and sold would have given the company the same net profit per tonne in *Year II* as it earned during *Year I.* Advise him.

Solution:STATEMENT SHOWING THE QUANTITY TO BE PRODUCED AND SOLD DURING YEAR II

	Particulars	₹	₹
A	Selling Price		185.00
B	Variable Costs : Material *[Refer to W.N. (i)]*	90.00	
	Labour *[Refer to W.N. (ii)]*	13.00	
	Variable Overhead *[Refer to W.N. (iii)]*	40.00	143.00
C	Contribution (A – B)		42.00
D	Profit required (i.e. 7,56,000/1,26,000)		6.00
E	Balance contribution per tonne for meeting Fixed Costs (C – D)		36.00
F	Fixed Costs (Note 4)		54,72,000
G	Quantity required (54,72,000/36)		1,52,000 tonnes

Working Notes :

(i) Materials cost per tone in Year II : 1,29,60,000/1,44,000 = ₹ 90

(ii) Labour cost per tonne in Year II : 18,72,000/1,44,000 = ₹ 13

(iii) Variable portion of factory, administration and selling expenditure etc.

A Total in Year II	₹ 1,12,32,000
B Increase otherwise than on account of increased turnover	8,10,000
C Amount spent in Year I	97,02,000
D Increase (A – B – C)	7,20,000
E Increase in quantity sold	18,000 tonnes
F Increase (or variable expenses) per tonne (7,20,000/18,000)	₹ 40

(iv) Fixed portion of factory, administration and selling expenses :

A Total in Year II	₹ 1,12,32,000
B Variable expenses @ ₹ 40 per tonne	57,60,000
C Fixed portion (A – B)	54,72,000

Problem 15. Tulsian Ltd. provides you the following information:

Sales	20,000 units
Direct Material	₹ 20,000
Direct Wages	₹ 20,000
Direct Expenses	₹ 8,000
Factory Overheads (15% Variable)	₹ 40,000
Office & Adm. Expenses (80% fixed)	₹ 40,000
Selling & Distribution Expenses (75% fixed)	₹ 40,000
Commission to Dealer	4%
Tax Rate	40%

Required : Calculate the selling price per unit in each of the following alternative cases :

Case (a) If it is decided to earn an overall profit after tax of ₹ 14,400

Case (b) If it is decided to earn an overall profit after tax @ 7.2% on sales.

Case (c) If it is decided to earn 20% return after tax on capital employed. (Note : Net fixed Assets ₹ 32,000 and working capital 20% of sales)

Case (d) If it is decided to earn profit after tax @ 10% on total cost.

Solution: Let the selling price be X

STATEMENT SHOWING THE COMPUTATION OF PROFIT AFTER TAX

A	No. of units	20,000
B	Selling Price per unit (₹)	x
C	Total Sales (A × B)	20,000 x
D	*Less :* Variable cost of sales :	
	Direct Material	20,000
	Direct Wages	20,000
	Direct Expenses	8,000
	Variable Factory Overheads	6,000
	Variable Office & Adm. Expenses	8,000
	Variable Selling & Dist. Expenses	10,000
	Commission to dealer @ 4% on sales	800 x
		72,000 + 800 x
E	Contribution (C – D)	19200 x – 72,000
F	*Less :* Fixed Costs :	
	Fixed Factory Overheads	34,000
	Fixed Office Adm. Expenses	32,000
	Fixed Selling & Distribution Expenses	30,000
		96,000
G	Profit before tax (E – F)	19200 x – 1,68,000
H	*Less :* Tax @ 40%	7680 x – 67,200
I	Profit after tax (G – H)	11,520 x – 1,00,800

(a) *Selling Price per unit under Case (a)*

11520 x – 1,00,800 = 14,400 (given)

11,520 x = 14,400 + 1,00,800

x = 115200/11520 = ₹ 10 per unit

(b) *Selling Price per unit under Case (b)*

11520 x – 1,00,800 = 7.2% of 20000 x

11520 x – 1440 x = 1,00,800

x = 1,00,800/10080 = ₹ 10 per unit

(c) *Selling Price per unit under Case (c)*

Capital Employed = Net Fixed Assets + Working capital

= ₹ 32,000 + 20% of 20000 x

= ₹ 32,000 + 4000 x

Desired Return on capital Employed = 20% of (32,000 + 4,000 x)

= 6400 + 800 x

Thus, 11520 x – 100800 = 6,400 + 800 x

11520 x – 800 x = 6,400 + 1,00,800

10720 x = 107200

x = 1,07,200/10720 = ₹ 10 per unit

(d) *Selling Price per unit under Case (d)*

Total cost = Variable Cost + Fixed Cost

= ₹ 72,000 + 800 x + ₹ 96,000

= ₹ 1,68,000 + 800 x

$$11520\,x - 1{,}00{,}800 = 10\% \text{ of } (1{,}68{,}000 + 800\,x)$$
$$11520\,x - 1{,}00{,}800 = 16{,}800 + 80\,x$$
$$11440\,x = 16{,}800 + 1{,}00{,}800$$
$$x = ₹\ 117600/11440 = ₹\ 10.28 \text{ per unit}$$

Problem 16. The existing cost structure of an article, the selling price of which is ₹ 600, is as follows :
Direct Material : 50% of the total cost
Direct Labour : 33 1/3% of Prime cost
Overhead : Balance of the total cost

Due to anticipated increase in existing material price by 25% and in the existing labour rate by 10%, the existing profit would come down by 30% if the selling price remains unchanged. A tender for the supply of above article is to be placed.

Required : Prepare (a) present statement of profit per article and (b) suggest the tender price so that (i) the same percentage of profit on cost as at present had to be earned and (ii) the same amount of profit as at present had to be earned.

Solution: Let x be the total present cost

STATEMENT SHOWING THE PRESENT AND ANTICIPATED COST STRUCTURE

	Present	*Anticipated*	
Direct Material Cost	.50 x	.5 x + 25% of .5 x =	.625 x
Direct Labour Cost	.25 x	.25 x + 10% of .25 x =	.275 x
Overhead	.25 x		.250 x
Total cost	x		1.150 x

Present Profit = ₹ 600 – x. Anticipated profit at same selling price = ₹ 600 – 1.150 x

$$₹\ 600 - 1.150\,x = 70\% \text{ of } (₹\ 600 - x)$$
$$₹\ 600 - 1.150\,x = ₹\ 420 - .7x$$
$$.7\,x - 1.150\,x = ₹\ 420 - ₹\ 600 = ₹\ 180$$
$$x = ₹\ 180/.45 = ₹\ 400$$

(a) PRESENT STATEMENT OF PROFIT PER ARTICLE

A	Selling Price per unit		₹ 600
B	*Less :* Total cost per unit		
	(a) Direct Material cost (50% of ₹ 400)	₹ 200	
	(b) Direct Labour cost (25% of ₹ 400)	100	
	(c) Overheads	100	400
C	Profit per article (A - B)		200

(b) STATEMENT OF REVISED SELLING PRICE

	Particulars	*If same % of Profit is to be earned*	*If same amount of profit is to be earned*
A	Direct Material Cost (125% of ₹ 200)	250	250
B	Direct Labour Cost (110% of ₹ 100)	110	110
C	Overheads	100	100
D	Total Anticipated Cost (A + B + C)	460	460
E	*Add :* Profit (50% of ₹ 460)	230	200
F	Revised Selling Price (D + E)	690	660

SOLVED PROBLEMS III

Problem 17. A single product manufacturing company has an installed capacity of 3,00,000 units per annum. The normal capacity utilization of the company is 90%. The company has prepared the following budget for a year:

Variable Factory Costs	₹ 33 per unit
Variable Selling and Administration Costs	₹ 9 per unit
Fixed Factory Costs	₹ 21,60,000
Fixed Selling and Administration Costs	₹ 7,56,000
Selling Price per unit	₹ 60

The actual production, sales, price and cost data relating to the year under review are as given below:

Production	2,40,000 units
Sales	2,25,000 units
Finished Goods Stock in the beginning of the year:	15,000 units
Actual Factory Variable Costs exceeded the budget by	₹ 1,20,000

Required:

(i) Calculate the Budgeted Profit and Break Even Point in units.

(ii) What increase in selling price was necessary during the year under review to maintain the budgeted point?

(iii) Prepare statements showing the actual profit during the year under review by using (1) Absorption Costing Method and (2) Marginal Costing Method.

Solution:

(i) **STATEMENT SHOWING BUDGETED PROFIT AND B.E.P**

A. Normal Capacity Utilization (3,00,000 × 90%)		2,70,000
B. Contribution per unit [₹ 60 – (₹ 33 + ₹ 9)]		₹ 18
B. Total Contribution [2,70,000 × ₹ 18)]		₹ 48,60,000
D. *Less:* Fixed Costs:		
Factory Costs	₹ 21,60,000	
Selling and Administration Costs	₹ 7,56,000	₹ 29,16,000
E. Profit [C – D]		₹ 19,44,000

$$\text{Break-even point (in units)} = \frac{\text{Fixed Costs}}{\text{Contribution per unit}} = \frac{29,16,000}{18} = 1,62,000$$

(ii) **1. ACTUAL VARIABLE COST PER UNIT**

	₹	₹
Budgeted Factory Costs	33.00	
Increase in Factory Costs per unit (1,20,000/2,40,000)	0.50	33.50
Selling and Administration Costs		9.00
		42.50

(ii) **2. SELLING PRICE REQUIRED TO MAINTAIN THE BUDGETED PROFIT**

A. Total Contribution required (₹)	₹ 48,60,000
B. Actual Production (units)	₹ 2,40,000
C. Contribution desired per unit (A ÷ B) (₹)	₹ 20.25
D. Variable Cost per unit (₹)	₹ 42.50
E. Selling Price required to maintain budgeted profit (C + D) (₹)	₹ 62.75
F. Increase in Selling Price necessary ₹ (62.75 – 60)	₹ 2.75

(iii) 1. PROFITABILITY BASED ON ABSORPTION COSTING METHOD

Particulars		₹
A. Sales (2,25,000 units @ ₹ 60)		1,35,00,000
B. *Less:* Manufacturing Cost of Goods Sold:		
Variable Factory Cost: (2,40,000 units × ₹ 33)	79,20,000	
Increase in Cost	1,20,000	
Fixed Factory costs (2,40,000 units × ₹ 8)	19,20,000	
Total Production costs	99,60,000	
Less: Closing Stock (30,000 units × 99,60,000)/2,40,000	12,45,000	
	87,15,000	
Add: Opening Stock 15,000 units × ₹ 41*	6,15,000	
Standard Cost of goods sold		93,30,000
Less: Under absorption of factory fixed overheads (2,40,000 – 2,70,000 units) × ₹ 8		2,40,000
Adjusted Manufacturing Cost of Goods Sold		95,70,000
C. Gross Profit [A – B]		39,30,000
D. *Less:* Selling and Administration Costs:		
Variable Costs: [2,25,000 units × ₹ 9]	20,25,000	
Fixed Costs	7,56,000	27,81,000
E. Profit under Absorption costing		11,49,000

Note: Cost of Opening Stock (per unit) = Variable Factory Cost per unit + Fixed Overhead Recovery Rate = ₹ 33 per unit + ₹ 8 per unit = ₹ 41 per unit.

2. PROFITABILITY BASED ON MARGINAL COSTING METHOD

Particulars	₹	₹
A. Sales (2,25,000 units @ ₹ 60)		1,35,00,000
B. *Less:* Variable Cost of Sales:		
Variable Cost (2,40,000 units × ₹ 33)	79,20,000	
Increase in Cost	1,20,000	
Total	80,40,000	
Less: Closing Stock [(30,000 × 80,40,000)/2,40,000]	10,05,000	
	70,35,000	
Add: Opening Stock (15,000 units × ₹ 33)	4,95,000	
Production Variable Costs of Goods Sold	75,30,000	
Variable Selling and Admin (2,25,000 × ₹ 9)	20,25,000	95,55,000
C. Contribution [A – B]		39,45,000
D. *Less:* Fixed Overheads: Factory	21,60,000	
Selling & Administration	7,56,000	29,16,000
E. Profit [C – D]		10,29,000

Working Notes:

(i) Fixed overhead Recovery Rate = ₹ 21,60,000/2,70,000 = ₹ 8

(ii) Closing Stock = ₹ 15,000 + ₹ 2,40,000 – ₹ 2,25,000 = ₹ 30,000

Problem 18. A Ltd. makes and sells a single product. The company's trading results for the year are:

Figs. – ₹ '000 (Year 2010)

Sales		3,000
Direct materials	900	
Direct labour	600	
Overheads	900	2,400
Profits		600

For the year 2011, the following are expected:

(i) Reduction in the selling price by 10%.
(ii) Increasing in the quantity sold by 50%.
(iii) Inflation of direct material cost by 8%.
(iv) Price inflation in variable overhead by 6%.
(v) Reduction of fixed overhead expenses by 25%.

It is also known that

(a) In 2009, overhead expenditure totalled to ₹ 8,00,000.
(b) Total overhead cost inflation for 2010 has been 5% more than 2009.,
(c) Production and sales volumes have been 25% higher in 2010 than in 2009.

Your are required to:

(i) Prepare a statement showing the estimated trading results for 2011.
(ii) Calculate the Break-even point for 2010 and 2011.
(iii) Comment on the BEP and profits of the 2010 and 2011.

Solution:

(i) **STATEMENT SHOWING TRADING RESULTS**

Particulars		*2010*	*2011*	
A. Sales:		3,000	4,050	(3,000 × 150% × 90%)
B. *Less:* Variable Costs:	Direct Material	900	1,458	(900 × 150% × 108%)
	Direct Labour	600	900	(600 × 150%)
	Variable Overhead	300	477	(300 × 150% × 106%)
Total Variable Cost		1,800	2,835	
C. Contribution [A – B]		1,200	1,215	
D. *Less:* Fixed Overheads		600	450	(600 × .75)
E. Profit [C – D]		600	765	

(ii)

		2010	2011
P/V Ratio	$\frac{\text{Contribution}}{\text{Sales}} \times 100$	$\frac{1200}{3000} \times 100 = 40\%$	$\frac{1215}{4,050} \times 100 = 30\%$
BEP	$\frac{\text{Fixed Cost}}{\text{P/V Ratio}}$	$\frac{600}{40\%} = 1,500$	$\frac{450}{30\%} = 1,500$

(iii)

Particulars	*2010*	*2011*	*% Change*
BEP	1,500	1,500	No Change
Fixed Overheads	600	450	$\frac{450-600}{600} \times 100 = (25\%)$
P/V Ratio	40%	30%	$\frac{30-40}{40} \times 100 = (25\%)$
Profit	600	765	$\frac{765-600}{600} \times 100 = 27.5\%$

Both Fixed Cost and P/V ratio have declined by 25% equally. So BEP sales remains the same.

The Contribution is only ₹ 1,215 in 2011 though quantity is increased by 50%. This is due to increase in production cost and decrease in Selling price. This is more than made up by decrease in fixed cost so that overall profit has increased by 27.5%.

Working Note: Calculation of Variable Overheads and Fixed overheads

Total Overheads for same Production in 2010 = 800 × 105% = 840

Variable Overheads for 2010 = $\frac{900-840}{125-100} \times 125 = 300$

Fixed Overheads for 2010 = 900 – 300 = 600

Problem 19. The trading results of ZED Ltd. for I and II are as follows:

	Year I ₹	Year II ₹
Material	1,60,000	2,05,200
Wages	96,000	1,32,000
Variable Overheads	40,000	46,000
Fixed Overheads	50,000	54,800
Total Costs	3,46,000	4,38,000
Profit	54,000	90,000
Sales	4,00,000	5,28,000

Selling Price was enhanced by 10% in Year II. Material Prices and Wage Rates to have increased by 8% and 10% respectively.

Required: Prepare a Statement showing how much each factor has contributed to the variation in profit.

Solution:

Particulars	*Year I* ₹ *(a)*	*Year II* ₹ *(b)*	*Difference figure* ₹ *(c) = (b) – (a)*	*Due to Price Change* ₹ *(d)*	*Due to volume Change* ₹ *(c)*	*Due to other Factors* ₹ *(f) = (c) – (d) – (e)*
A. Sales	4,00,000	5,28,000	1,28,000	48,000	80,000	—
B. *Less:* Total Costs:						
Material	1,60,000	2,05,200	45,200	15,200	32,000	(–2,000)
Wages	96,000	1,32,000	36,000	12,000	19,200	4,800
Variable Overheads	40,000	46,000	6,000	—	8,000	(–2,000)
Fixed Overheads	50,000	54,800	4,800	—	—	4,800
Total Costs	3,46,000	4,38,000	92,000	27,200	59,200	5,600
C. Profit [A – B]	54,000	90,000	36,000	20,800	20,800	(–5,600)

Working Notes:

(i) Rise in Sales Figures of Year II due to 10% increase in selling price

$$= ₹\ 5{,}28{,}000 \times \frac{10}{110} = ₹\ 48{,}000$$

(ii) Rise in the figure of sales volume = (₹ 5,28,000 – ₹ 4,00,000) – ₹ 48,000 = ₹ 80,000

(iii) Percentage rise in the figure of sales volume = $\frac{₹\ 80{,}000}{₹\ 4{,}00{,}000} \times 100 = 20\%$

(iv) Increase in material prices = $\frac{₹\ 2{,}05{,}200}{108} \times 8 = ₹\ 15{,}200$

(v) Increase in wages = $\frac{₹\ 1{,}32{,}000}{110} \times 10 = ₹\ 12{,}000$

(vi) Increase in material, wages and overheads by 20% due to rise in sales volume are ₹ 32,000; ₹ 19,2000 and ₹ 8,000 respectively.

Problem 20. A company produces and sells four types of dolls for children. It also produces and sells a set of dress kit for the dolls. The company has worked out the following estimates for the next year:

Doll	Estimated Demand Units	Standard Material Cost (₹)	Standard Labour Cost (₹)	Estimated Selling Price Per Unit (₹)
A	50,000	20	15	60
B	40,000	25	15	80
C	35,000	32	18	100
D	30,000	50	20	120
Dress Kit	2,00,000	15	5	50

To encourage the sale of dress kits, a discount of 20% in its price offered if it were to be purchased along with the doll. It is expected that all the customers, buying dolls will also buy the dress kit.

The company's factory has effective capacity of 2,00,000 labour hours per annum on a single-shift basis and it produces all the products on that basis. The labour hour rate is ₹ 15 Overtime labour has to paid at double the normal rate.

Variable cost works out to 40% of direct labour cost. Fixed costs are ₹ 30 lakhs per annum.

There will be no inventory at the end of the year.

Your are to draw a conservative estimate of the year's profitability.

Solution:

STATEMENT OF CONSERVATIVE ESTIMATE OF THE YEAR'S PROFITABILITY

Particulars	Doll A	Doll B	Doll C	Doll D	Dress Kit
A. Estimated Demand (units)	50,000	40,000	35,000	30,000	2,00,000
B. Selling Price per unit:	60	80	100	120	50
C. *Less:* Variable Costs per unit					
Material Cost per unit	20	25	32.00	50	15
Labour Costs	15	15	18.00	20	5
Variable Costs @ 40%	6	6	7.20	8	2
Total Variable Costs	41	46	57.20	78	22
D. Contribution per unit	19	34	42.80	42	28
E. Total Contribution (A × D)	9,50,000	13,60,000	4,98,000	12,60,000	56,00,000
F. *Less:* Discount on dress kits [1,55,000 × ₹ 50 × 20%]					(15,50,000)
G. Net Contribution	9,50,000	13,60,000	14,98,000	12,60,000	40,50,000
H. Total Net Contribution (₹)	91,18,000				
I. *Less:* Overtime Premium (₹) (38,666,66 hrs × ₹ 15)	(5,80,000)				
J. *Less:* Fixed Cost (₹)	(30,00,000)				
K. Profit (₹)	55,38,000				

Working Note: Total labour hours required to meet estimated demand of four types of dolls and their dress kit.

Doll	Estimated Demand (units)	*Std Labour time per doll [Labour Cost/₹ 15]	Total Labour hours
A	B	C	D = B × C
A	50,000	1 hr	50,000.00
B	40,000	1 hr	40,000.00
C	35,000	1.2 hrs	42,000.000
D	30,000	1.33333 hrs	40,000.00
Dress Kit	2,00,000	0.33333 hrs	66,666.66

Total labour hours to meet estimated demand	2,38,666.66
Less: Normal Hours Available	2,00,000.00
Overtime Hours needed	38,666.66

Problem 21. Tulsian Fashion is high fashion women's garments manufacture. It is planning to introduce a new fashion garment in the market in the forthcoming Diwali season. Four maters of cloth material are required layout the dress pattern. After cutting, some material remains that can be sold as a cut-piece. The left-over material can also be used to manufacture a matching cap and handbag.

Tulsian Fashion expects to sell 2,500 dresses, if matching caps and handbags are not provided and 500 more if matching caps and handbag are made available. The market research indicates that the cap and/or handbag cannot be sold independently, but only as accessories with the dress.

The following combination of sales is expected:

Completer Sets of Dress, Cap and Handbag	68%
Dress and Cap only	12%
Dress and Handbag only	09%
Dress only	11%
	100%

The material used in the dress costs ₹ 60 per meter. The cost of cutting the dress, if the cap and handbag are not manufactured, is estimated at ₹ 20 a dress and the resulting remnants can be sold for ₹ 5 for each dress cut out.

If the cap and handbag are to be manufactured, it requires a more delicate and skillful cutting and hence cutting cost will increase by ₹ 8 per dress.

The selling prices and the other cost to complete the three items, one they are cut, are as follows:

	Selling Price per unit	*Other Costs per Unit*
Dress	400.00	48.00
Cap	29.00	6.50
Handbag	18.00	3.00

Other costs per unit excludes the cost of material and cutting.

You are required to prepare as statement showing:

(a) Should the company go in for caps and handbags along with dresses? Substantiate your answer.

(b) What are the non-quantitative factors that could influence the company's decision to manufacture caps and handbags that match the dress?

Solution:

(a) **STATEMENT SHOWING PROFITABILITY**

Particulars	*If Matching Caps and Handbags are not provided with Dresses*	*If Matching Caps and Handbag are provided with Dresses*
A. Expected Sales (pieces)	2,500	3,000
	₹	₹
B. Sales Revenue	10,00,000 (2,500 dresses × ₹ 400)	13,11,180 (Refer to working note 2)
C. *Less:* Costs:		
Materials (Refer to working note 3)	5,87,500	7,18,350
Cutting	50,000 (2,500 dresses × ₹ 20)	81,360 Refer to working note 4)
Other	1,20,000 (2,500 dresses × ₹ 48)	1,66,530 (Refer to working note 5)
Total Costs	7,57,500	9,66,240
D. Operating Profit [B – C]	2,42,500	3,44,940

Since, the company can earn an additional profit of ₹ 1,02,440 (₹ 3,44,940 – ₹ 2,42, 500) if matching caps and handbags are provided along with dresses. Therefore, the company should go for manufacturing matching caps and handbags and provided them along with dresses.

Working Notes:

(i) Expected Sales in forthcoming season, if caps and handbags are provided with dresses:

Complete sets of dress, cap and handbag	(68% of 3,000)	2,040 dresses
Dress and cap only	(12% of 3,000)	360 dresses
Dress and handbag only	(9% of 3,000)	270 dresses
Dress only	(11% of 3,000)	330 dresses
		3,000 dresses

(ii) Sales Revenue of Expected Sales, if caps and handbags are provided with dresses:

	₹
Complete set of dress, cap and handbag (2,040 dresses × ₹ 447)	9,11,880
Dress and cap only (360 dresses × ₹ 429)	1,54,440
Dress and handbag only (270 dresses × ₹ 418)	1,12,860
Dress only (330 dresses × ₹ 400)	1,32,000
	13,11,180

(iii) Material For 2,500 dresses = 2,500 dresses × 4 meters × (₹ 60 per meter – ₹ 5) = ₹ 5,87,500

(iv) For 3,000 dresses [(2,670 dresses × 4 meter × ₹ 60 per meter) + 330 dresses × (4 meters × ₹ 60 per meter – ₹ 5)] ₹ 7,18,350

(v) Cutting Costs for 3,000 dresses (2,670 dresses × ₹ 28 + 330 dresses × ₹ 20) ₹ 81,360

(vi) Other costs for 3,000 Dresses

	₹
Complete set of dress, cap and handbag (2,040 Dresses × ₹ 57.50)	1,17,300
Dress and Cap only (360 dresses × ₹ 54.50)	19,620
Dress and handbag only (270 dresses × ₹ 51)	13,770
Dress only (330 dresses × ₹ 48)	15,840
	1,66,530

(b) Non-quantitative factors that could influence the company's decision to manufacture caps and handbags that match the dress are:

1. Reliability for various estimates of costs, sales and prices.
2.. Proper consideration of quality in terms of design, colour and durability.
3. Timing of production and distribution of four combination i.e. complete set of dress, dress and cap dress and handbags and dress only has been planned suitably in advance.
4. Effect on the production, sales of other product lines of Tulsian Fashions has to be examined.

Problem 22. The financial controller of ACE Ltd. has prepared the following estimated of working results for the year ending 31st March, 2010.

		Year ending 31.3.2010
Direct Material	₹/unit	16.00
Direct Wages	₹/unit	40.00
Variable Overheads	₹/unit	12.00
Selling Price	₹/unit	125.00
Fixed Expenses	₹	6,75,000 per annum
Sales	₹	25,00,000 per annum

During the year 2010-2011, it is expected that the material prices and variable overheads will go up by 10% and 5% respectively. As a result of re-engineering of business processes, the overall direct labour efficiency will increase by 12%, but the wage rate will go up by 5%. The fixed overheads are also expected to increase by ₹ 1,25,000.

The Vice-President-Manufacturing states that the same level of output as obtained in 2009-2010 should be maintained in 2010-2011 also and effort should be make to maintain the same level of profit by suitably increasing the selling price.

The Vice President-Marketing states that the market will not absorb any increases in the selling price. On the other hand, he proposes that publicity involving advertisement expenses as given below will increase the quantity of sales as under:

Advertisement Expenses (₹)	80,000	1,94,000	3,20,000	4,60,000
Additional Units of Sales	2,000	4,000	6,000	8,000

Required:

(a) Present an Income Statement for the year 2010-2011.

(b) Find the revised price and the percentage of increase in the price for 2010-2011, if the views of the Vice-President Manufacturing are accepted.

(c) Evaluate the four alternative proposals put forth by the Vice-President-Marketing. Determine the best output level to the budgeted and prepare an overall income Statement for 2010-2011 at the level of output.

Solution:

(a) INCOME STATEMENT FOR THE YEAR 2010-2011

Particulars	₹
A. Sales Revenue [20,000 units × ₹ 125]	25,00,000
B. *Less:* Variable Cost [20,000 units × ₹ 67.70]	13,54,000
C. Total Contribution [A – B]	11,46,000
D. *Less:* Fixed Expenses	8,00,000
E. Profit	3,46,000

(b) STATEMENT FOR DETERMINING REVISED PRICE AND THE PERCENTAGE OF INCREASE IN THE PRICE FOR 2010-2011 BASED ON THE VIEWS OF VICE PRESIDENT MANUFACTURING.

Particulars	₹
A. Variable Cost (20,000 units × ₹ 67.70)	13,54,000
B. Fixed Expenses	8,00,000
C. Profit	4,65,000
D. Desired Sales Revenue [A + B + C]	26,19,000
E. Revised Selling Price (per unit) (₹ 26,19,000/20,000 units)	130.95
F. Percentage increase in Selling Price = $\frac{₹\ 130.95 - ₹\ 125}{₹\ 125} \times 100 = 4.76\%$	

(c) EVALUATION OF FOUR ALTERNATIVE PROPOSALS OF VICE-PRESIDENT – MARKETING

Particulars	₹	₹	₹	₹
A. Additional Units of sales	2,000	4,000	6,000	8,000
B. Contribution per unit (₹)	57.30	57.30	57.30	57.30
C. Total Contribution (₹) [A + B]	1,14,600	2,29,200	3,43,800	4,58,400
D. *Less:* Advertisement Expenses (₹)	(80,000)	(1,94,000)	(3,20,000)	(4,60,000)
F. Additional Profit/(Loss)	34,600	35,200	23,800	(1,600)

Evaluation of four alternatives: Since the additional profit is maximum at the additional sales of 4,000 units, therefore the second alternative is adjudged as the best out of the four alternatives proposed by the Vice President of Marketing. Hence the concern should produce and sell 24,000 units during the year 2010-2011.

OVERALL INCOME STATEMENT FOR 2010-2011

A. Output and sales		24,000 units
B. Selling Price per unit		₹ 125
C. Sales Revenue [A × B]		30,00,000
D. *Less:* Variable Cost [24,000 units × ₹ 67.70]		(16,24,800)
E. Contribution [C – D]		13,75,200
F. *Less:* Advertisement Expenses	₹ 1,94,000	
Fixed expenses	₹ 8,00,000	(9,94,000)
G. Profit [E – F]		3,81,200

Working Note:

(i) Number of units produced and sold for the year 2009-2010 = $\frac{\text{Total Sales Revenue}}{\text{Selling price per unit}}$

$= \frac{₹\ 25,00,000}{₹\ 125 \text{ p.u.}} = 20,000 \text{ units}$

(ii) **Statement of Variable Cost per unit**

Year	*2009–2010*	*2010-2011*	
	₹	₹	
Direct Material	16	17.60	(₹ 16 + 10% × ₹ 16)
Direct Wages	40	37.50	(₹ 40 × 100/112 × 105/100)
Variable Overheads	12	12.60	(₹ 12 + 5% × ₹ 12)
Variable Cost per unit	68	67.70	

(iii) Contribution per unit during 2010-2011 = Selling price – Variable costs = ₹ 125 – ₹ 67.70 = ₹ 57.30

(iv) Profit in 2009-2010

Contribution per unit = S.P. – V.C. = ₹ 125 – ₹ 68 = ₹ 57

Total Contribution = (20,000 units × ₹ 57) = ₹ 11,40,000

Less: Fixed expenses = ₹ 6,75,000

Profit = ₹ 4,65,000

Problem 23. Ret Ltd., a retail store buys computers form Comp Ltd. and sells them in retail. Comp Ltd. Pay Ret Ltd. a commission of 10% on the selling price at which Ret Sells to the outside market. This commission is paid at the end of the month in which Ret Ltd. submits a bill for the commission. Ret Ltd. sells the computers to its customers at its store at ₹ 30,000 per piece. Comp Ltd. has a policy of not taking back computer once dispatched from its factory. Comp Ltd. sells a minimum of 100 computers to its customers.

Comp Ltd. charges prices to Ret Ltd. as follows:

₹ 29,000 per unit, for order quantity 100 units to 140 units.

₹ 26,000 per unit, for the entire order, if the quantity is 141 to 200 units. Ret Ltd. cannot order less than 100 or more than 200 units from Comp Ltd.

Due to the economic recession, Ret Ltd. will be forced to offer as a free gift, a digital camera costing it ₹ 4,500 per piece, which is compatible with the computer. These cameras are sold by another Co., Photo Ltd. only in boxes, where each box contains 50 units. Ret Ltd. can order the cameras only in boxes and these cameras cannot be sold without the computer.

In its own store, Ret Ltd. can sell 110 units of the computer. At another far of location, Ret Ltd. can sell upto 80 units of the computer (along with its free camera), provided it is willing to spend ₹ 5,000 per unit on shipping costs. In this market also, the selling price that each unit will fetch is ₹ 30,000 per unit.

You are required to:

(i) State what is Ret's best strategy along with supporting calculations.

(ii) compute the break-even point in units, considering only the above costs.

Solution:

PROFITABILITY AT DIFFERENT SALES LEVELS

A. Sales Units	110	140	150	190
B. Gross Margin per unit	4,000	4,000	7,000	7,000
C. Total Gross Margin (Excluding Shipping Cost)	4,40,000	5,60,000	10,50,000	13,30,000
D. *Less:* Shipping Cost (₹) For Sales beyond 110 units		1,50,000 (30 × 5,000)	2,00,000 (40 × 5,000)	4,00,000 (80 × 5,000)
E. Contribution (₹ [C – D]	4,40,000	4,10,000	8,50,000	9,30,000
F. *Less:* Fixed Cost (Cost of cameral)	6,75,000	6,75,000	6,75,000	9,00,000
G. Profit [E – F]	–2,35,000	–2,65,000	1,75,000	30,000

Best Strategy is sales level at 150 units since the profit is maximum at this level.
The variations of profits is due to incremental fixed cost.

From the profits at different levels, it is seen that the BEP lies between 151 and 190 and fixed cost will be ₹ 9,00,000 when Four Boxes of Cameras are purchased.

$$\text{Let BEP} = \text{X units} = \frac{\text{Fixed Costs + Shipping Cost}}{\text{Contribution Margin/unit}}$$

$$= \frac{₹\ 9,00,000 + (X - 110) \times ₹\ 5,000}{₹\ 7,000}$$

$$X = ₹\ 3,50,000/2000 = 175 \text{ units}$$

Note: There will be no BEP if three boxes of Cameras are purchased.

Working Note:

(i) Margin of Dealer (upto 140 units) = 10% of ₹ 30, 000 + (₹ 30,000 – ₹, 29,000) = ₹ 4,000
Margin of (upto 200 units) = 10% of ₹ 30,000 + (₹ 30,000 – ₹ 26,000) = ₹ 7,000

Problem 24. The Budget Controller of PCT (Exam.) Ltd. a Manufacturing Organisation producing three products has compiled the following data for the preparation of the annual budget for the year 2011.

Raw Materials	*Price / Kg.*	*Raw Material Per Unit*		
	₹	*Product A*	*Product B*	*Product C*
RM 1	5	1	6	12
RM 2	2	6	—	14
RM 3	3	6	10	2
Direct Labour:	*Rate/Hour* ₹			
Dept. 1	2	9	4	4
Dept. 2	3	3	4	2
Dept. 3	4	2	5	4
Factory Overheads Variable ₹ / Unit	4	8	6	
Sales Value (₹ Lacs)		346.50	275.40	263.25
Opening Stock of Finished Goods (Units)		1200	800	1000

Fixed Factory Overheads Rate Per Direct Labour Hour:

Dept. 1 ₹ 5, Dept. 2 ₹ 3, Dept. 3 ₹ 6,

The following policies have been laid down for the budget year 2011 -

(i) Fixed Factory Overheads will be absorbed on Direct Labour Hour basis.
(ii) Administration Overheads are absorbed at the rate of 20% of Factory Cost.
(iii) Selling and Distribution Overheads (one-third variable) are recovered at the rate of 25% of the cost of production including Administration Overheads.
(iv) The mark-up on Cost of Sales for Profit is: Product 'A' 10%, Product 'B' 20%, Product 'C' 30%.
(v) Inventories of Finished Goods will be reduced by 25% on 31.12.2011
(vi) The Finished Goods Inventories are valued on marginal cost basis. The marginal costs of the opening stocks on 1.1.2010 were: Product 'A' ₹ 80, Product 'B' ₹ 120 and Product 'C' ₹ 140.

Required: (a) The number of units of each product estimated to be sold in the Budget year.
(b) The number of units of each product proposed to be produced in the Budget year.
(c) The Contribution to Sales Ratio envisaged for each of the products.
(d) Valuation of Opening and Closing Stock of Finished Goods on marginal cost basis.

Solution

(a) BUDGETED SALES UNITS

	Particulars	*A*	*B*	*C*
A	Direct Material Cost:			
	RM 1	5	30	60
	RM 2	12	—	28
	RM 3	18	30	6
		35	60	94
B	Direct Labour Cost:			
	Dept. 1	18	8	8
	Dept. 2	9	12	6
	Dept. 3	8	20	16
		35	40	30
C	Factory Overheads:			
	Variable Factory Overheads	4	8	6
	Fixed Factory Overheads:			
	Dept. 1	45	20	20
	Dept. 2	9	12	6
	Dept. 3	12	30	24
		70	70	56
D	Factory Cost (A + B + C)	140	170	180
E	Administration Overheads @ 20%	28.00	34.00	36.00
F	Cost of Production (D + E)	168.00	204.00	216.00
G	Selling and Distribution Overheads @ 25%	42.00	51.00	54.00
H	Cost of Sales (F + G)	210.00	255.00	270.00
I	Profit	21.00	51.00	81.00
J	Selling Price (H + I)	231.00	306.00	351.00
K	Sales Value	346,50,000	275,40,000	263,25,000
L	Budgeted Sales Units (K / J)	1,50,000	90,000	75,000

(b) NUMBER OF BUDGETED PRODUCTION UNITS

	A	B	C
Budgeted Sales Units	1,50,000	90,000	75,000
Add: Closing Stock (Units)	900	600	750
Less: Opening Stock (Units)	1,200	800	1,000
	1,49,700	89,800	74,750

(c) CONTRIBUTION TO SALES RATIO = (SELLING PRICE – VARIABLE COST)/SELLING PRICE)

		A	B	C
A	Selling Price	231	306	351
B	*Less:* Variable Costs:			
	Direct Material Cost:	35	60	94
	Direct Labour Cost:	35	40	30
	Variable Factory Overheads	4	8	6
	Variable Selling and Distribution Expenses	14	17	18
		88	125	148
C	Contribution (A – B)	143	181	203
D	Contribution to Sales Ratio = (Selling Price Variable Cost)/Selling Price	61.90%	59.15%	57.83%

(d) VALUATION OF OPENING AND CLOSING STOCKS

A. Closing Stock (Units)	900	600	750
B. Marginal Cost Per Unit (Direct Material + Direct Labour + Variable Factory OH)	74.00	108.00	130.00
C. Closing Stock (₹) [A x B]	66,600	64,800	97,500
D. Opening Stock (Units)	1,200	800	1,000
E. Marginal Cost Per Unit (Direct Material + Direct Labour + Variable Factory OH)	80	120	140
F. Value of Opening Stock [D x E]	96,000	96,000	1,40,000

Problem 25. Tulsian Ltd. Provides you the following information:

Production Capacity	*33-1/3%*	*50%*
Sales (units)	9000	15000
Production (units)	10000	15000
Direct Material	110000	165000
Direct Labour	180000	230000
Production Overheads (including depreciation)	110000	125000
Depreciation on Production Machinery	20000	20000
Administrative Expenses	20950	20950
Selling & Distribution Expenses	38000	50000

Variable labour cost becomes 50% higher for activity in excess of 19,000 units due to the necessity for overtime working. The variable element of selling and distribution expenses is a function of sales. All other costs with a variable element are a function of production volume.

During 2009-10, All goods produced were sold @ ₹ 40 for ₹ 7,20,000

During 2010-11, Direct Material Price is expected to increase by ₹.1 with 5% inefficiency (wasting allowance), Direct Wage Rate is expected to increase by 12-1/2% with 25% increase in productivity of variable labour input, Fixed Production Overheads and Fixed Selling and Distribution Overheads are expected to increase by 20%.

Required:

(a) Prepare Income Statement for the year 2009-10 and 2010-11 assuming the same level of output and sales as in 2009-10.

(b) What percentage change in selling price is required during 2010-11 to earn the same profit as earned during 2009-10?

(c) How many units are required to be produced and sold during 2010-11 to earn the same profit as earned during 2009-10?

(d) Evaluate the following proposals and suggest the best proposal and also calculate Break-Even Point under that Proposal.

(i) Marketing Manager proposes that publicity involving advertisement expenses will increase the sales as under:

Advertisement Expenses (₹)	10,000	20,000	30,000	50,000	85,000
Additional Units of Sales	1,000	2,000	3,000	8,000	12,000

(ii) Production Manager proposes to increase the sales by 50% by reducing selling price by 5% on all units sold.

Solution:

(a) INCOME STATEMENT

Particulars	*2009-10*	*2010-11*
A. No. of Sales Units	18,000	18,000
B. Selling Price Per Unit	40	40
C. Sales [A x B]	7,20,000	7,20,000
D. *Less:* Total Variable Cost @ ₹ 26 / ₹ 26.60	4,68,000	4,78,800
E. Contribution [C – D]	2,52,000	2,41,200
F. *Less:* Total Fixed Costs	2,00,950	2,26 ,950
G Profit [E – F]	51,050	14,250

(b) PERCENTAGE CHANGE REQUIRED IN SELLING PRICE

Let the new Selling Price be X

A.	No. of Sales Units	18,000
B.	Selling Price Per Unit	X
C.	Sales [A x B]	18,000X
D.	*Less:* Total Variable Cost @ ₹ 26.60	4,78,800
E.	Contribution [C – D]	18,000X – 4,78,800
F.	*Less:* Total Fixed Costs	2,26,950
G.	Profit [E – F]	18,000X – 7,05,750

$$18{,}000X - 7{,}05{,}750 = 51{,}050$$

$$X = 7{,}56{,}800 / 18{,}000 = ₹\ 42.044$$

$$\text{Percentage change required in selling price} = \frac{(\text{New Selling Price} - \text{Old Selling Price})}{\text{Old Selling Price}} \times 100$$

$$= \frac{(42.044 - 40)}{40} \times 100 = 5.11\%$$

(c) UNITS REQUIRED TO BE PRODUCED AND SOLD

Let the new Sales Units be X

$$X = \frac{\text{Fixed Cost + Desired Profit + Overtime}}{\text{Contribution per unit (excluding overtime)}} = \frac{₹\ 2{,}26{,}950 + 51{,}050 + (X - 19{,}000) \times 4.5}{₹\ 40 - ₹\ 26.60}$$

$$= 1{,}92{,}500/8.9 = 21{,}629.21 \text{ Units}$$

(d) (i) EVALUATION OF FIVE ALTERNATIVE PROPOSALS OF MARKETING MANAGER

A	Additional Units of Sales	1,000	2,000	3,000	8,000	12,000
B	Contribution Per unit [₹ 40 – ₹ 26.60]	13.40	13.40	13.40	13.40	13.40
C	Total Contribution [A x B]	13,400	26,800	40,200	1,07,200	1,60,800
D	*Less:* Overtime @ 4.50 (For Output in excess of 19000 units)	0	4,500	9,000	31,500	49,500
E	*Less:* Advertisement Expenses	10,000	20,000	30,000	50,000	85,000
F	Additional Profit [C – D – E]	3,400	2,300	1,200	25,700	26,300

Evaluation: Out of these proposals the fifth proposal of 12,000 additional Units seems to be the best since the additional profit is maximum at that level.

(d) (ii) EVALUATION OF PROPOSAL OF PRODUCTION MANAGER AND FIFTH PROPOSAL OF MARKETING MANAGER

Particulars	*Proposal (Production Manager)*	*5th Proposal (Marketing Manager)*
A. No. of Sales Units	27,000	30,000
B. Selling Price Per Unit	38	40
C. Sales [A x B]	10,26,000	12,00,000
D. *Less:* Total Variable Costs:		
Variable Cost (excluding overtime) @ ₹ 26.60	7,18,200	7,98,000
Overtime [(27,000 – 19,000) x ₹ 4.50]	36,000	
Overtime [(30,000 – 19,000) x ₹ 4.50]		49,500
	7,54,200	8,47,500
E. Contribution [C – D]	2,71,800	3,52,500
F. *Less:* Total Fixed Costs:		
Advertisement Expenses	—	85,000
Other Fixed Costs	2,26,950	2,26,950
	2,26,950	3,11,950
G. Profit [E – F]	44,850	40,550

Recommendation: Proposal 1 is suggested since the profit under this Proposal is more than that under Proposal 2 by ₹ 4300. Break-Even Point (units) under Proposal 1

$$\text{BEP} = \frac{\text{Fixed Cost} + \text{Overtime}}{\text{Contribution per unit (excluding overtime)}} = \frac{₹\ 2{,}26{,}950 + (X - 19{,}000) \times 4.5}{₹\ 38 - ₹\ 26.60}$$

= 1,41,450 / 6.9 = 20500 Units

BEP (₹) = 20,500 units × ₹ 38 = ₹ 7,79,000

Working Notes

(i) Segregation of Fixed and Variable Cost

Variable Cost Per Unit = Change in Cost/Change in Units

Direct Material Cost Per unit = (₹ 1,65,000 – ₹ 1,10,000)/(15,000 – 10,000) = ₹ 11

Direct Labour Cost Per unit = (₹ 2,30,000 – ₹ 1,80,000)/(15,000 – 10,000) = ₹ 10

Fixed Labour Cost = ₹ 1,80,000 – (₹ 10 × 10,000) = ₹ 80,000

Production Overheads (excluding dep.) Per unit = (₹ 1,05,000 – ₹ 90,000)/(15000 – 10000) = ₹ 3

Fixed Production Overheads (excluding dep.) = ₹ 90,000 – (3 × 10,000) = ₹ 60,000

Selling & Distribution Expenses Per unit = (₹ 50,000 – ₹ 38,000)/(15000 – 9000) = ₹ 2

Fixed Selling & Distribution Expenses = ₹ 38,000 – (2 × 9,000) = ₹ 20,000

(ii) Calculation of Variable Cost Per Unit

	2009-10	2010-11	
Direct Material	11	12.6	[(11 + 1) x 105%]
Direct Labour	10	9	(10 × 112.5% × 100/125)
Variable Production Overheads	3	3	
Variable Selling & Distribution Expenses	2	2	
Total Variable Cost/Unit upto 19000 units	26	26.6	
Overtime	—	4.5	(10 × 112.5% × 100/125 × 50%)
Total Variable Cost/Unit beyond 19000 units	26	31.1	

(iii) Calculation of Total Fixed Cost

	2009-10	2010-11	
Production Labour	80,000	90,000	(80,000 × 112.5%)
Production Overheads (excluding depreciation)	60,000	72,000	(60,000 × 120%)
Depreciation on Production Machinery	20,000	20,000	
Administrative Expenses	20,950	20,950	
Selling & Distribution Expenses	20,000	24,000	(20,000 × 120%)
Total Fixed Cost	2,00,950	2,26,950	

Problem 26. ABC Ltd. can produce 4,00,000 units of a product per annum at 100% capacity. The variable production costs are ₹ 40 per unit and the variable selling expenses are ₹ 12 per sold unit. The budgeted fixed production expenses were ₹ 24,00,000 per annum and the fixed selling expenses were ₹ 16,00,000. During the year ended 31st March, 2008, the company worked at 80% of its capacity. The operating data for the year are as follows:

Production	3,20,000 units
Sales @ ₹ 80 per unit	3,10,000 units
Opening stock of finished goods	40,000 units

Fixed production expenses are absorbed on the basis of capacity and fixed selling expenses are recovered on the basis of period.

You are required to prepare Statements of Cost and Profit for the year ending 31st March, 2008:

(i) On the basis of marginal costing

(ii) On the basis of absorption costing.

Solution: **STATEMENT OF COST AND PROFIT UNDER MARGINAL COSTING**
FOR THE YEAR ENDING 31ST MARCH, 2008

Output = 3,20,000 units

Particulars	*₹ in lacs*	*₹ in lacs*
A. *Sales:* [3,10,000 units @ ₹ 80]		248.00
A. *Less*: Variable Cost of Sales:		
Variable Cost of Production (3,20,000 × ₹ 40)	128.00	
Add: Opening Stock 40,000 units @ ₹ 40	16.00	
Less: Closing Stock [(3,20,000 + 40,000 – 3,10,000) @ ₹ 40 = 50,000 units @ ₹ 40]	20.00	
Variable Cost of production of 3,10,000 units	124.00	
Add: Variable Selling Expenses @ ₹ 12 per unit	37.20	161.20
C. Contribution [A – B]		86.80
D. *Less*: Fixed Production Cost	24.00	
Fixed Selling Expenses	16.00	40.00
E. Actual Profit under Marginal Costing		46.80

(ii) **STATEMENT OF COST AND PROFIT UNDER ABSORPTION COSTING**
FOR THE YEAR ENDING 31ST MARCH, 2008

Output = 3,20,000 units

Particulars	*₹*	*₹ (in lacs)*
A. Sales: [3,10,000 units @ ₹ 80]		248.00
B. *Less:* Cost of Goods Sold		
Variable Cost of Production (3,20,000 @ ₹ 40)	128.00	
Add: Fixed Cost of Production absorbed 3,20,000 units @ ₹ 6	19.20	
Production Cost of 3,20,000 units	147.20	
Add: Opening Stock: [40,000 × 1,47,20,000/3,20,000]	18.40	
Less: Closing Stock: [50,000 × 1,47,20,000/3,20,000]	23.00	142.60
C. Gross Profit [A – B]		105.40
D. *Less:* Selling Expenses:		
Variable: [₹ 12 × 3,10,000 units]	37.20	
Fixed	16.00	53.20
E. Unadjusted profit		52.20
F. *Less*: Fixed Production Overheads under absorbed:		4.80
G. Actual Profit under Absorption Costing		47.40

Working Notes:

(i) Absorption Rate for Fixed Cost of Production $= \frac{₹\ 24,00,000}{4,00,000} = ₹\ 6$ per unit

(ii) Fixed Production Overhead under absorbed = ₹ (24,00,000 – 19,20,000) = ₹ 4,80,000.

Problem 27. PQ Ltd. reports the following cost structure at two capacity levels:

	(100% capacity) 2,000 units	1,500 units
Production Overheads I	₹ 3 per unit	₹ 4 per unit
Production Overheads II	₹ 2 per unit	₹ 2 per unit

If the selling price, reduced by direct material and labour is ₹ 8 per unit, what would be its break-even point?

Solution:

COMPUTATION OF BREAK-EVEN POINT IN UNITS:

	2,000 units	1,500 units
Production Overhead I: (Fixed)	₹ 6,000	₹ 6,000
	(2,000 units × ₹ 3 per unit)	(1,500 units × ₹ 4 per unit)
A. Selling Price – Material and labour	₹ 8	₹ 8
B. Production Overhead II (Variable Overhead)	2	2
C. Contribution per unit (A) – (B)	6	6

D. Break - even point = $\frac{\text{Fixed Cost}}{\text{Contribution per unit}} = \frac{6,000}{6}$ = 1,000 units

Problem 28. CAS Ltd. is manufacturing and selling two products Splash and Flash at selling price of ₹ 3 and ₹ 4 respectively. The following sales strategy has been outlined for the year:

(i) Sales planned for year will be ₹ 7.20 lakhs in the case of Splash and ₹ 3.50 lakhs in the case of Flash.
(ii) To meet competition, the selling price of Splash will be reduced by 20% and that of Flash by 12 ½ %.
(iii) Break– even is planned at 60% of the total sales of each product.
(iv) Profit for the year to be achieved is planned as ₹ 69,120 in the case of Splash and ₹ 17,500 in the case of Flash. This would be possible by launching a cost reduction programme and reducing the present annual fixed expenses of ₹ 1,35,000 allocated as ₹ 1,08,000 to Splash and ₹ 27,000 to Flash.

Required:

(a) Calculate the total number of units of Splash and Flash to be sold during the year and Number of units to be sold of Splash and Flash to break-even.
(b) Calculate the reduction in fixed expenses product-wise that is envisaged by the Cost Reduction Programme

Solution

CALCULATION OF NO. OF UNITS TO BE SOLD AND BEP (UNITS)

	Particulars	*Splash*	*Flash*
A	Sales	₹ 7,20,000	₹ 3,50,000
B	Selling Price / Unit (Revised)	₹ 2.4 (80% of ₹ 3)	₹ 3.5 (87.5% of ₹ 4)
C	Sales Units (A / B)	3,00,000	1,00,000
D	BEP %	60%	60%
E	BEP Units (C × D)	1,80,000	60,000

CALCULATION OF REDUCTION IN FIXED EXPENSES PRODUCT-WISE

	Particulars	*Splash*	*Flash*
A	Margin of Safety (Units) [Sales Units × (100 – BEP%) × Selling Price]	2,88,000 (3,00,000 × 40% × 2.4)	1,40,000 (1,00,000 × 40% × 3.5)
B	Profit (given)	69,120	17,500
C	Previous Fixed Cost (given)	1,08,000	27,000
D	New P/V Ratio [(Profit / MS) × 100]	24%	12.5%
E	Break– Even Sales [Sales Units x BEP% x Selling Price]	₹ 4,32,000 (3,00,000 × 60% x 2.4)	₹ 2,10,000 (1,00,000 × 60% × 3.5)
F	Revised Fixed Cost (BES × P/V Ratio)	1,03,680	26,250
G	Reduction in Fixed Cost (C – E)	4,320	750

Problem 29. Explain and illustrate Cash Break-even Chart.

Solution

(i) Cash break-even chart is a graphical representation of the Cost, Volume-Profit Relationship under which, only cash fixed costs are considered. Non-cash items like depreciation etc. are excluded from the fixed cost for computation of cash break-even point. It depicts the level of output or sales at which the sales revenue will equal to total cash outflow. It is computed as under:

$$\text{Cash BEP (Units)} = \frac{\text{Cash Fixed Cost}}{\text{Contribution Per Unit}}, \quad \text{Cash BEP (Rs.)} = \frac{\text{Cash Fixed Cost}}{\text{P / V Ratio.}}$$

Example: Fixed Cost (including Depreciation of ₹ 10,000) ₹ 30,000

Selling Price per unit ₹ 10, Variable Cost per unit ₹ 6

$$\text{Cash BEP (Units)} = \frac{₹\ 30,000 - ₹10,000}{₹10 - ₹6} = 5000 \text{ units}$$

$$\text{Cash BEP (₹)} = \frac{₹\ 30,000 - ₹10,000}{40\%} = ₹\ 50,000$$

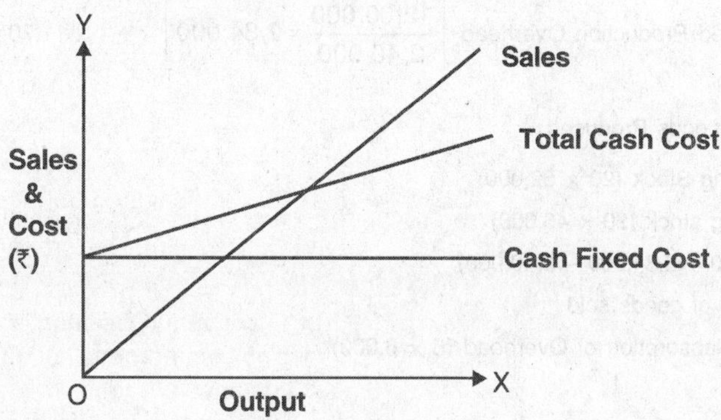

Problem 30. X Ltd. provides you the following information:

Normal Capacity	2,40,000 units
Opening Stock	52,000 units
Units produced	2,34,000 units
Units sold	2,40,000 units
Direct material cost per unit	₹ 6
Direct labour cost per unit	₹ 6
Variable manufacturing overhead per unit	₹ 3
Fixed manufacturing overheads	₹ 12,00,000
Variable Administration overhead per unit	₹ 0.80
Fixed Administration overhead	₹ 1,20,000
Variable selling and distribution overhead per unit sold	₹ 2.00
Fixed selling and distribution overheads	₹ 2,40,000
Selling price per unit	₹ 35

Required:

(a) Prepare Income Statement using

(i) Absorption Costing

(ii) Marginal Costing.

(b) Prepare a statement reconciling the difference in profit, if any.

(c) Calculate break-even-point and margin of safety.

(d) How many units are to be sold to earn a profit of 25% on cost ?

Solution

(i) STATEMENT UNDER ABSORPTION COSTING

Particulars	₹	₹
A. Total Sales (24,000 × 35)		**84,00,000**
B. *Less:* Manufacturing Cost of Goods sold		
Direct Material Cost (2,34,000 × 6)		14,04,000
Direct Labour Cost = (2,34,000 × 6)		14,04,000
Variable Manufacturing Overhead (2,34,000 x 3)		7,02,000
Fixed Production Overhead $\left[\frac{12,00,000}{2,40,000} \times 2,34,000\right]$	11,70,000	
Total Cost of goods Produced		**46,80,000**
Add: Opening Stock (20 × 52,000)		10,40,000
Less: Closing stock (20 × 46,000) (52,000 + 2,34,000 – 2,40,000)		9,20,000
Adjusted Cost of goods sold		48,00,000
Add: Under-absorption of Overhead (5 × 6,000)		30,000
		48,30,000
C Gross Profit [A – B]		35,70,000
D Less: Variable Administration Overhead (0.80 × 2,40,000)	1,92,000	
Fixed Administration Overhead	1,20,000	
Variable Selling & Distribution Overhead (2 x 2,40,000)	4,80,000	
Fixed Selling & Distribution Overhead	2,40,000	10,32,000
E Profit under Absorption Costing		**25,38,000**

(ii) STATEMENT UNDER MARGINAL COSTING

Particulars	₹	₹
A Total Sales (2,40,000 × 35)		**84,00,000**
B Less: Total Variable Cost		
Direct Material	14,04,000	
Direct Labour	14,04,000	
Variable Manufacturing Overhead	7,02,000	35,10,000
Add: Opening Stock (52,000 units × ₹.15)		7,80,000

Less: Closing Stock (46,000 units × ₹ 15)	6,90,000
Variable Cost of Goods Sold	**36,00,000**
Add: Variable Administration Overheads	1,92,000
Add: Variable Selling and Distribution Overheads	4,80,000
Total Variable Cost	**42,72,000**
C Contribution [*A* – *B*]	41,28,000
D *Less:* Fixed Cost	
Manufacturing (5 × 2,40,000)	12,00,000
Administration	1,20,000
Selling & Distribution	2,40,000
E Profit under Marginal Costing [*C* – *D*]	15,60,000
	25,68,000

(b) RECONCILIATION STATEMENT

Particulars	₹
A. Profit under Marginal Costing	25,68,000
B. *Add:* Fixed Manufacturing Overhead in Closing Stock (46,000 units × ₹ 5)	2,30,000
C. *Less:* Fixed Manufacturing Overhead in Opening Stock 52,000 units × ₹.5	2,60,000
D. Profit under Absorption Costing [A + B – C]	**25,38,000**

(c) Calculation of Break-Even-Point and Margin of Safety

$$\text{P/V Ratio} = \frac{\text{Contribution}}{\text{Sales}} \times 100 = \frac{41{,}28{,}000}{84{,}00{,}000} \times 100 = 49.142\%$$

Contribution Per Unit ₹.35 – ₹.17.80 = ₹.17.20

$$\text{BEP (in ₹)} = \frac{\text{Fixed Cost}}{\text{P/V Ratio}} = \frac{15{,}60{,}000}{49.142\%} = \text{Rs. } 31{,}74{,}474 \text{ (Approximately)}$$

$$\text{BEP (in ₹)} = \frac{\text{Fixed Cost}}{\text{Contribution Per Unit}} = \frac{₹\,15{,}60{,}000}{₹\ 17.20} = 90698 \text{ units (Approximately)}$$

Margin of Safety = Total Sales – Break-Even Sales

= 84,00,000 – 31,74,474 = ₹.52,25,526

Margin of Safety % = 62.21%

(d) Sales Units to earn 25% Profit on Cost i.e., 20% on Sales

$$\text{Sales} = \frac{\text{Fixed Cost} + \text{Desired Profit}}{\text{P/V Ratio}}$$

Let Sales Value be x

$$x = \frac{15{,}60{,}000 + 20\% \text{ of } x}{49.142\%} \text{ or}$$

$$\frac{x}{1} = \frac{15,60,000 + .2x}{.49142} \text{ or } .49142x - .2x = 15,60,000$$

$$x = \frac{15,60,000}{.29142} = \text{Rs. } 53,53,466$$

$$\text{Sales Units} = \frac{53,53,466}{₹\ 35} = 1,52,956 \text{ Units Approx.}$$

Problem 31. Jay Kay Limited is a single product manufacturing company. The following information relates to the months of May and June, 2011:

	May ₹	*June* ₹
(i) Budgeted Costs and Selling prices:		
Variable manufacturing cost per unit	2.00	2.20
Total fixed manufacturing cost		
(based on budgeted output of 25,000 units per month)	40,000	44,000
Total fixed marketing cost	14,000	15,400
Selling price per unit	5.00	5.50
(ii) Actual production and sales:	*Units*	*Units*
Production	24,000	24,000
Sales	21,000	26,500

(iii) There was no stock of finished goods at the beginning of May, 2011. There was no wastage or loss of finished goods during May or June, 2011.

(iv) Actual costs incurred corresponded to those budgeted for each month.

You are required to calculate the relative effects on the monthly operating profits of applying: (*a*) Absorption costing and (*b*) Marginal costing.

Solution

(*a*) **QUANTITY TALLY**

Particulars		*May 2011*	*June 2011*
Opening Stock	units	—	3,000
Production	units	24,000	24,000
Total	units	24,000	27,000
Sales	units	21,000	26,500
Closing Stock	units	3,000	500
Fixed manufacturing overheads	₹	40,000	44,000
Budgeted output	units	25,000	25,000
Fixed overheads absorption rate per unit	₹	1.60	1.76

(i) PROFITABILITY BASED ON ABSORPTION COSTING

Particulars	*May 2011* ₹	*June 2011* ₹
A. Sales:		
May: 21,000 units @ ₹ 5.00	1,05,000	
June: 26,500 units @ ₹ 5.50		1,45,750
B. Production Costs:		
Variable: May 24,000 units @ ₹ 2.00	48,000	
June 24,000 units @ ₹ 2.20		52,800
Fixed: May 24,000 units @ ₹ 1.60	38,400	
June 24,000 units @ ₹ 1.76		42,240
Total Production Costs	86,400	95,040

C. *Add:* Opening Stock		
May Nil		
June 3,000 units @ Res. 3.60* 10,800		
Total	86,400	1,05,840
D. *Less:* Closing stock		
May 3,000 units @ ₹ 3.60*	10,800	
June 500 units @ ₹ 3.96*		1,980
E. Production Cost of Goods sold [B + C – D]	75,600	1,03,860
F. Marketing fixed costs	14,000	15,400
G. Total Cost of Goods Sold	89,600	1,19,260
H. Profit (Sales – COGS) [A – G]	15,400	26,490
Budgeted Output	25,000 units	
Actual Output	24,000 units	
Shortfall 1, 000 units		
Under recovery of fixed overheads		
May 1,000 units @₹	1.60	1,600
June 1,000 units @ ₹ 1.76	1,760	
Net Profit	13,800	24,730
*Total cost = VC + FC		
May 2.00 + 1.60 = 3.60		
June 2.20 + 1.76 = 3.96		

(ii) PROFITABILITY BASED ON MARGINAL COSTING

Particulars			*May 2011* ₹	*June 2011* ₹
A. Sales			1,05,000	1,45,750
Production cost - Variable			48,000	52,800
Add: Opening Stock				
May Nil				
June 3,000 units @ ₹ 2.00				6.000
Total			48,000	58,800
Less: Closing Stock				
May 3,000 units § ₹ 2.00			6,000	
June 500 units @ ₹ 2.20				1,100
B. Variable Cost of Goods Sold			42,000	57,700
C. Contribution [A – B]			63,000	88,050
D. *Less:* Fixed costs:				
Production	40,000	44,000		
Marketing	14,000	15,400	54,000	59,400
E. Net Profit [C – D]			9,000	28,650

Problem 32. A Pharmaceutical company produces formulations having a shelf life of one year. The company has an opening stock of 30,000 boxes on 1st January, 2011 and expected to produce 1, 30,000 boxes as was in the just ended year of 2010, Expected sale would be 1, 50,000 boxes. Costing department has worked out escalation in cost by 25% on variable cost and 10% on fixed cost. Fixed cost for the year 2010 is ₹ 40 per unit. New price announced for 2011 is ₹ 100 per box. Variable cost on opening stock is Rs40 per box. You are required to compute breakeven volume for the year 2011.

Solution

Shelf life is one year hence opening stock of 30,000 boxes is to be sold first. Contribution on these boxes is 30,000(100 – 40) = ₹ 18,00,000

In the question production of 2010 is same as in 2011. Hence fixed cost for the year 2010 is ₹ 52,00,000 (1,30,000 × 40). Therefore fixed cost for the year 2011 is ₹ 57,20,000 (52, 00,000 + 10% of 52, 00,000).

Variable Cost for the year 2011 (₹ 40 + 25% of ₹ 40) = ₹ 50 per Unit

Hence Contribution per unit during 2011 is ₹ 50 (100 – 50)

Break even volume is the volume to meet the fixed cost i.e. fixed cost equals to contribution. Therefore, remaining fixed cost of ₹ 39,20,000 (₹ 57,20,000 – ₹ 18,00,000) to be recovered from production during 2011.

Production in 2011 to reach BEP = ₹ 39,20,000/50 = 78,400 units

Therefore BEP for the year 2011 is 1,08,400 boxes (30000 + 78400)

3 Relevant Costing

Learning Objectives

After studying this chapter, you should be able to understand:

- Relevant Cost
- Sunk Costs
- Opportunity Cost
- Out of Pocket Costs
- Differential Cost
- Discretionary Costs
- Type of Relevant Information
- Relevant Cost for Materials
- Relevant Cost per Labour and Overheads
- Relevant Cost for Machine

1.0 RELEVANT COST

Meaning	Relevant costs are those expected future costs which differ under different alternatives.
Examples	In case of whether to retain or replace an old machine, the realizable value and dismantling cost of old machine are relevant costs but the present written down book value of old machine is irrelevant cost.
Importance	Relevant cost analysis helps in drawing the attention of managers to those elements of costs which are relevant for the decision.
Two Common Pit Falls in Relevant Cost Analysis	Two comment pit falls in Relevant Cost Analysis are as follows: (a) First Pit fall is to assume that all variable costs are relevant. All variable costs are not relevant. Variable costs which remain unchanged under different alternatives are irrelevant but variable costs which differ under different alternatives are relevant. (b) Second Pit fall is to assume that all fixed costs are irrelevant. All fixed costs are not irrelevant. Fixed costs which remain unchanged under different alternatives are irrelevant but fixed costs which differ under different alternatives are relevant.
Practical Example	X Ltd. proposes to re-arrange plant facilities and estimates its future costs under two alternatives choices, are as under:

Particulars	Do not re-arrange ₹	₹-arrange ₹
Direct Materials Cost/unit	20.00	20.00
Direct Labour Cost/unit	10.00	9.00
Production Overheads	1,00,000	1,00,000
Additional Overheads	—	10,000

Identify the Relevant and Irrelevant Costs

Solution:

Cost	Relevant	Reason
1. Direct Material Cost	Irrelevant	It remains unchanged
2. Direct Labour Cost	Relevant	It differs under both the alternatives.
3. Production Overheads	Irrelevant	These remain unchanged.
4. Additional Overheads	Relevant	These differ under both the alternatives.

2.0 SUNK COSTS

Meaning	Sunk Costs are the historical costs which have already been incurred by decision made in past and can not be changed by any decision made in the future. Sunk costs are irrelevant in decision making because these are past costs.
Example	Written down value of machine already purchased is sunk cost,
Are all Irrelevant Costs Sunk Costs?	**No.** *for example*, when a comparison of two alternative production methods using the same material cost is made, material cost, is irrelevant cost because it does not differ under both the alternatives but it is not a sunk cost because material cost is the future cost to be incurred.

3.0 OPPORTUNITY COST

Meaning	Opportunity cost is the cost of next best alternative of resources. It is the measure of benefits foregone by rejecting the second best alternative of resources in favour of the best. It is the value of opportunity lost by diversion of an input factor from one use to another. It is also defined as the maximum contribution that is forgone by using the scarce resources for a particular purpose.
Examples	1. The opportunity cost of using a machine to produce a particular product is the foregone earnings that would have been possible if the machine was used to produce other products. 2. The opportunity cost of funds invested in a business is the interest that could have been earned by investing the funds in bank deposit. 3. The opportunity cost of one's time is the salary which he would have earned by his profession.
Uses	Opportunity cost concept is helpful to the management in making profitability calculations when one or more of the inputs required by two or more of the alternatives courses of action is already available.

	1. **Decision Making:** Opportunity costs apply to the use of scarce resources, where resources are not scarce, there is no sacrifice from the use of these resources. Where a course of action requires the use of scarce resources, it is necessary to incorporate the lost profit which will be foregone from using scarce resources. If resources have no alternatives use only the additional cash flow resulting from the course of action should be included in decision making as relevant cost. 2. **Cost Control:** The conventional variance analysis will report an adverse usage variance and adverse sales volume variance. However, the failure to achieve the budgeted optimum level of output may be due to inefficient usage of scarce resources. The foregone contribution should therefore be charged to the manager responsible for controlling the usage of scarce resources and not to the sales manager because the failure to achieve the budgeted sales is due to the failure to use scarce resources efficiently. Thus if resources are scarce, the usage variance should reflect the acquisition cost *plus* budgeted contribution per unit of the scarce resources. If the lost sales are made good in subsequent periods, the real opportunity cost will consist of lost interest arising from delay in receiving the net cash-flows and not the foregone contribution.

Illustration 1

Estimated direct material requirements of a business concern viz., CAS Ltd. for the year 2011-12 are 2,00,000 units. Unit cost for orders below 2,40,000 units is ₹ 10. When size of order equals 2,40,000 units or more the concern received a discount of 5% on the above quoted per unit price. Keeping in view the following two alternaves:

(i) Buy 2,40,000 units at the start of the year;

(ii) Buy 20,000 units per month.

Calculate the opportunity cost, if the concern has the facility of investing surplus funds in government bonds at the rate of 10% interest.

Solution

Average investment in inventory under the given two alternatives are:

(i) (2,40,000 units × ₹ 9.50)/2 = ₹ 11,40,000

(ii) (20,000 units × ₹ 10)/2 = ₹ 1,00,000

Difference between the average investment in inventory ₹ 10,40,000

The concern can invest ₹ 10,40,000 at 10 percent and can earn ₹ 1,04,000 as interest annually. The sum of ₹ 1,04,000 is an opportunity foregone if alternative (i) is chosen.

Hence ₹ 1,04,000 is the opportunity cost of the 2,40,000 units purchase order.

$$\text{Opportunity Cost per unit} = \frac{1{,}04{,}000}{2{,}40{,}000} = 0.433$$

Net Benefit per unit = 0.50 – 0.433 = 0.067 per unit

Note: *₹ 1,04,000 would not ordinarily be recorded in the accounting system as it is a foregone cost.*

4.0 OUT OF POCKET COSTS

Meaning	Out of pocket cost is that portion of costs which involves payments to outsiders i.e., it gives rise to cash expenditure as opposed to such costs as depreciation, which do not involve any cash expenditure.

Uses	Out of pocket costs are relevant for decision making (i.e., Make or Buy Decisions, Pricing Decisions), Controlling/Reducing costs.
Examples	Commission to salesman on sales, transport expenses, Carriage Inward on purchase of component.

5.0 DIFFERENTIAL COST

Meaning	Differential cost is the change (increase or decrease) in the total cost (variable as well as fixed) due to change in the level of activity, technology or production process or method of production.
How differs from Marginal Cost?	Differential cost includes both fixed and variable cost but marginal cost represents only variable cost.
Differential Cost or Incremental Cost Technique	It is a technique used in the preparation of ad-hoc information in which only income differences between alternative courses of action are taken into consideration. This technique is applicable to situations where fixed costs alter. This technique is of particular use in short term problems which are non-repetitive, one time, ad hoc problems. The essential pre-requisite for making managerial decisions by using incremental cost technique, is to compare the incremental costs with incremental revenues. So long as the incremental revenue is greater than incremental costs, the decision should be in favour of the proposal.
Applications of Differential Cost/ Incremental Cost techniques in making managerial decisions	The important areas in which incremental cost analysis could be used for managerial decision making are as under: 1. Whether to process a product further or not 2. Whether to an accept an additional order from a special customer at lower than existing price or not 3. Whether to retain or replace decisions 4. Whether to reduce or maintain price decision 5. Whether to discontinue a product, suspend or close down a segment of the business or not 6. Whether to introduce a new product or not 7. How to optimize investment plan out of multiple alternatives 8. Whether to open new sales territory and branch or not 9. Submitting tenders 10. Whether to make or buy decisions 11. Whether to lease or buy decisions

Illustration 2

Tulsian Ltd. is planning either to produce or buy the component 'PQR'. If it decides to produce component 'PQR' then it has to install system facilities for that in its factory. The following information is provided for the production of components at various levels:

Particulars	*Production Level (in units)*			
	1,00,000	1,50,000	2,00,000	2,50,000
Variable Costs	2,50,000	3,73,500	5,06,000	6,27,500
Fixed Production Overheads	1,00,000	1,35,000	1,75,000	1,75,000

This component can be purchased from the market at following prices

Order Quantity	1,00,000	1,50,000	2,00,000	2,50,000
Price	3.40	3.35	3.30	3.25

Required: Comment whether the company should produce the component or buy it form the market when the estimated requirements of the component are (a) 1,00,000 units, (b) 1,50,000 units, (c) 2,00,000 units, (d) 2,50,000 units.

Solution

STATEMENT SHOWING THE RELEVANT COST OF MAKE OR BUY

Particulars	*Case (a)*	*Case (b)*	*Case (c)*	*Case (d)*
A. Relevant (incremental) cost when the component is produced	3,50,000	5,08,500	6,81,000	8,02,500
B. Relevant (incremental) costs when the component is purchased	3,40,000	5,02,500	6,60,000	8,12,500
C. Differential Cost (A – B).	10,000	6,000	21,000	(10,000)
D. Recommendation:	Purchase	Purchase	Purchase	Make

Illustration 3

ACE Ltd. has an inventory of 5,000 units of product left over from last years' production. This model is no longer in demand. It is possible to sell these at reduced prices through the normal distribution channels. The other alternative is to ask someone to take them on "as is where is" basis. The latter alternative will cost the company ₹ 5,000.

The company produced 2,40,000 units of the product, last year, when the unit costs were as under.

Variable Manufacturing Cost	***6.00***
Fixed Manufacturing Cost	***1.00***
Variable Selling & Distribution Cost	***3.00***
Fixed Selling & Distribution Cost	***1.50***
Total Cost	***11.50***
Selling Price per Unit	***14.00***

Required: Should the company scrap the items or sell them at a reduced price? If you suggest the latter, what minimum price would your recommend?

Solution

A. Cost if sold through normal distribution channels @ ₹ 3	₹ 15,000
B. Cost if the stock is disposed off by asking someone to take then on "as is where is basis",	(₹ 5,000)
C. Differential Cost [A – B]	₹ 10,000
D. Differential Cost per unit [₹ 10,000/5,000]	₹ 2

Recommendation: Hence, if the company can get anything more than ₹ 2 per unit, then it is worthwhile to sell the stock of 5,000 units and earn an additional contribution.

Note: Historical cost of ₹ 11.50 per unit of 5,000 units of a product is irrelevant (as it is a sunk cost) for determining the recommended price per unit.

6.0 DISCRETIONARY COSTS

Meaning	Discretionary costs are the costs— (a) Which are incurred at the discretion of management (b) Which can be avoided by the managerial decision (c) Which arise from periodic (usually yearly) decisions regarding the maximum outlay to be incurred. (d) Which are not tied to a clear cause and effect relationship between inputs and outputs. The note worthy feature of discretionary costs is that managers are seldom confident that the "correct" amounts are being spent.
Examples	Advertising, Research and Development, Public Relations, Executive Training, Teaching, Health Care and Management Consulting Services.
How to Control	To control discretionary costs control points/ parameters may be established. But these points need to be devised individually. *For example*, Research and Development costs may be controlled by establishing dates for submitting major reports to management. For advertising and sales promotion, such costs may be controlled by pre-setting targets. In the case of employees benefits, such costs may be controlled by calling a meeting of employees union and making them aware that the company would meet only the fixed costs and the variable costs should be met by them.

Illustration 4

ZED Ltd. operates two shops. Product A is manufactured in Shop-1 and customer's job against specific orders are being carried out in Shop 2. Its annual statement of income is:

Particulars	*Shop–1 (Product-A)* ₹	*Shop–2 (Job Works)* ₹	*Total* ₹
Sales/Income	1,25,000	2,50,000	3,75,000
Material	40,000	50,000	90,000
Wages	45,000	1,00,000	1,45,000
Depreciation	18,000	31,500	49,500
Power	2,000	3,500	5,500
Rent	5,000	30,000	35,000
Heat and Light	500	3,000	3,500
Other Expenses	4,500	2,000	6,500
Total	1,15,000	2,20,000	3,35,000
Net Income	10,000	30,000	40,000

The depreciation charges are for machines used in the shops. The rent and heat and light are apportioned between the shops on the basis of floor area occupied. All other costs are current expenses idenfied with the output in a particular shop.

A valued customer has given a job to manufacture 5,000 units of X for Shop-2. As the company is already working at its full capacity, it will have to reduce the output of product-A by 50% to accept the said job. The customer is willing to pay ₹ 25 per unit of X. The material and labour will cost ₹ 10 and ₹ 18 respectively per unit. Power will be consumed on the job just equal to the power saved on account of reduction of output of A. In addition the company will have to incur additional overheads of ₹ 10,000.

You are required to compute the following in respect of this job.

(a) Differential Cost; (b) Full Cost; (c) Opportunity Cost; and (d) Sunk Cost.

Advise whether the company should accept the job.

Solution

(a) DIFFERENTIAL COST OF THE JOB

Particulars	*Relevant Cost of Producing 'X'* ₹	*Relevant Cost of Producing 'A'* ₹
Material Cost	50,000	20,000
Labour Cost	90,000	22,500
Additional Overheads	10,000	—
Other expenses	—	2,250
Total	1,50,000	44,750

Differential Cost of the job = ₹ 1,05,250

Note: Depreciation, rent, heat and light and power are not going to affect the costs.

(b) **Full Cost of the Jobs:**

	₹
Relevant Cost of Producing 'X' [as above at (a)]	1,50,000
Depreciation	9,000
Power	1,000
Rent	2,500
Heat and Light	250
Total	1,62,750

(c) **Opportunity Cost of taking the order:**

	₹
Sale of Product A	62,500
Less: Relevant Cost of Producing 'A' [as above at (a)]	44,750
Opportunity Cost	17,750

(d) **Sunk Cost of the jobs:**

	₹
Depreciation	9,000
Power*	1,000
Rent	2,500
Heat and Light	250
Total	12,750

* If a student treats power as a relevant cost, in that case it would not appear here.

Advise: The company should not accept the job as there will be a cash disadvantage of ₹ 42,750 as computed below:

	₹	₹
A Differential Revenue [5,000 units @ ₹ 25]	1,25,000	
Less: Sale of Product A	62,500	62,500
B Differential Cost		1,05,250
C Cash Disadvantage [A – B]		42,750

7.0 TYPE OF RELEVANT INFORMATION

There are two types of relevant information:

(i) Quantitative Information
(ii) Qualitative Information

(i) Quantitative Information: Quantitative information or factors are outcomes that are measured in numerical terms. Numerical terms may be financial or non-financial. Non-financial numerical information includes raw material required per unit of output. Example of financial information is cost of direct material/direct labour.

(ii) Quantitative Information: Quantitative information or factors are outcomes that are difficult to measure accurately in numerical terms. *For example*, Job Satisfaction.

8.0 RELEVANT COST FOR MATERIALS

Item	*Relevant Cost of Materials*
1. Material having *no Regular use* and lying is Stock (i.e., Obsolete Material)	Relevant cost = Expected Net Realizable value = Disposal Value – Disposal Expenses **Tutorial Notes** *(i) Book value of such material is sunk cost and hence irrelevant for decision-making.* *(ii) Current Replacement Price is irrelevant since such material is already lying in stock and is having no regular use. [Refer to Illustration 5]*
2. Material in *Regular use* and is lying in Stock	(a) ***If Current Activities are to be kept intact*** – Relevant Cost = Current Purchase Price (or Replacement Cost) (b) ***If Current Activities are to be discontinued*** – Relevant Cost = Contribution lost due to disontinuance of current activity. ***Note:*** *Here, Contribution = Sales – Variable Cost (other than Material Costs)* **Tutorial Notes** *(i) Book value of such material is sunk cost and hence irrelevant for decision-making.* *(ii) Current Replacement Price is irrelevant since such material is already lying in stock and is having no regular use. [Refer to Illustration 6]*
3. Material having no Regular use and is lying in Stock and a substitute Material can be used for it	(a) ***If Purchase Price of Substitute Material*** (*say X*) is more than Net Realizable value of material already in stock (*say Y*) – Relevant Cost = Net Realizable Value (Y) (b) ***In other case,*** Relevant Cost = Purchase Price of Substitute Material (X) **Tutorial Note** *In the case, the material which is already in stock should be sold out and the substitute material should be purchased. [Refer to Illustration 7]*
4. Material Already in the Stock having Alternative use and some other Material can also be used for that Alternative use	There may be situation when some other material can also be used as a substitute for the alternative use instead of material already in the stock, in such circumstances the relevant cost would be **higher** of the following two: (a) Net Realisable Value of Material already the stock, *or* (b) Purchase Price of material which can be used as substitute for alternative use. *[Refer to Illustration 8]*

Illustration 5

X Ltd. received an offer from Y Ltd. for delivery of product AB. One unit of product AB require one unit of raw material A which was purchased by X Ltd. for ₹ 100 per unit. Currently it is lying with X Ltd. with no alternative use. It can be resold in the market @ ₹ 70 per unit but for this purpose X Ltd. has to incur ₹ 5 per unit on raw material A to make it in re-salable condition. However product A can be procured at market @ ₹ 120 per unit. Identify the sunk cost, replacement cost and net realisable value per unit in the above case and the cost which is relevant for decision making.

Solution

1. **Sunk Cost/Historical Cost:** The cost at which product A was purchased i.e. ₹ 100.
2. **Net Realisable Value:** The amount that can be realised by the sale of product A after deducting costs which are necessary to make it resalable.
   ₹ 70 – ₹ 5 = ₹ 65 per unit
3. **Replacement cost:** Current Purchase Price of product X from the market = in this case it is ₹ 120 per unit.
   In this solution, the net releasible value is the relevant cost for decision making.

Illustration 6

X Ltd. receives an order from Y Ltd. for delivery of product AB. One unit of product AB requires one unit of raw material A as input. Material A is in stock of X Ltd. It was purchased @ ₹ 100 per unit. It can be resold at ₹ 70 per unit after incurring cost of ₹ 5 per unit to make it resalable. Raw material A is also used in the production of product AC. One unit of Product AC requires one unit of raw material A. However one unit of Product AC gives contribution margin of ₹ 90 per unit (ignoring cost of raw material A) Raw material A can be currently purchased from the open market at a cost of ₹ 120 per unit.

You are required to calculate relevant cost in following alternative cases:

Case (a) Order should not affect the production of product AC and raw material currently in stock can be used either for product AB or product AC.

Case (b) Order can be completed only after affecting current production of product AC and raw material in stock can be used either for product AB or product AC.

Solution

Relevant Cost in Case (a)

As order should not affect the production of product AC therefore raw material currently in stock shall be used for the production of product AB. However requirement of raw materials for the production of product AB will be met through purchases from the market. Hence relevant cost in this case would be replacement cost of raw material A and in this case it is ₹ 120 per unit.

Relevant Cost in Case (b)

As order affect the production of product AC therefore raw material in stock will be used for the production of product AB. In this case contribution loss per unit of raw material A will became relevant cost. In this case relevant cost would be ₹ 90 per unit.

Illustration 7

X Ltd. receives an offer from Y Ltd. for delivery of product AB. In the production of product AB, Raw material A is used. One unit of product AB requires one unit of material A. However X Ltd. has already in stock, raw material A which was purchased for ₹ 100. The current cost of raw material A is ₹ 120. The material lying in stock with X Ltd. could be resold in the market at ₹ 70 but after incurring cost of ₹ 5 on it. Material X has no other alternative use. You are required to determine relevant cost of material A in each of the following alternative cases:

Case (a) ***If raw material B can be used instead of raw material A as a substitute and current cost of raw material B is ₹ 80 and it is not in stock with X Ltd.***

Case (b) ***If raw material B can be used instead of raw material A as a substitute and current cost of raw material B is ₹ 60 and it is not in stock with X Ltd.***

Solution

Case (a)

Purchase Price of substitute raw material = ₹ 80

Net Realisible Value of raw material A already in stock = ₹ 70 – ₹ 5 = ₹ 65

₹ 80 – ₹ 65 = ₹ 15

As it is greater than zero, therefore it is advisable to use raw material A which is already in the stock and in this case the relevant cost would be net realisible value of raw material A i.e. ₹ 65.

Case (b)

₹ 60 – ₹ 65 = – ₹ 5

Now as this is less than zero, it is advisable to purchase substitute raw material B from the market and sale raw material A. In this case relevant cost would be ₹ 60.

Illustration 8

X Ltd. get contract from Y Let. for supply of Product AB. Material P is used in the production of Product AB. Material P is already in stock with X Ltd. However material P is also used in the production of Product CD with is regularly produced by X Ltd. Production of Product AB is to be undertaken in such a manner so that regular production of Production CD is affected. Material P was purchased for ₹ 100 per unit. Another material Q is also available which can be used as substitute for material P in the production of Product CD. The purchase price of material Q is ₹ 90 per unit and it is not is stock with X Ltd. You are required to compute relevant cost in each of the following cases:

Case (a) ***When the material P can be resold in the market for ₹ 85 per unit after incurring cost of ₹ 5 per unit necessary to make it in re-saleable condition.***

Case (b) ***When the material P can be resold in the market for ₹ 98 per unit after incurring cost of ₹ 5 per unit necessary to make it in re-saleable condition.***

Solution

Case (a)

Relevant cost would be higher of the following:

Net Realisable Value of Material P, i.e., ₹ 85 per unit – ₹ 5 per unit = ₹ 80 per unit

OR

Purchase Price of Material Q = ₹ 90 per unit

Hence Relevant cost in ₹ 90 per unit.

Case (b)

Relevant cost would be higher of the following:

Net Realisable Value of Material P i.e., ₹ 98 per unit – ₹ per unit = ₹ 93 per unit

OR

Purchase Price of Material Q = ₹ 90 per unit

Hence Relevant Cost is ₹ 93 per unit

9.0 RELEVANT COST FOR LABOUR AND OVERHEADS

1. Labour ***(a) Casual Labour (i.e., Not on Regular Pay Roll)***	(a) ***If Casual Labour is in short supply*** Relevant Cost = Variable Labour cost + Contribution Lost (b) ***If Casual Labour is available is abundance*** Relevant Cost = Variable Labour Cost **Tutorial Note** *Unless other wise indicated in question, labour is presumed to be casual and not permanent. [Refer to Illustration 9]*
(b) Permanent Labour (i.e., on Regular Payroll)	(a) ***If Permanent Labour is idle (i.e., not used any where)*** Relevant Cost = Nil (b) ***If Permanent Labour is not idle*** Relevant Cost = Contribution lost due to removing labour from regular activity. **Tutorial Note** *The use of phrases like 'The labour can not be retrenched, Labour is entitled to Idle Time Wages etc., indicate that the labour is permanent. [Refer to Illustration 10]*
2. Overheads ***(a) Fixed overheads***	Relevant Cost = Differential Fixed Overheads to be incurred in future.
(b) Variable Overheads	Relevant Cost = Differential Variable Overheads to be incurred in future

Illustration 9

X Ltd. receives an offer from Y Ltd. for the delivery of product AB. Each unit of product AB requires one hour of labour type A. X Ltd. kept Type A labour on casual basis. Type A labour is paid at @ ₹ 20 per hour. However type A labour is also engaged in the production of product CD whose 1 unit also requires an hour of Type A labour. Thc selling price of product CD is ₹ 50 per unit and variable cost of producing CD (including labour cost) is ₹ 25 per unit.

You are required to calculate relevant cost of labour in each of the following alternative cases:

Case (a) Type A labour supply is in abundant.

Case (b) Type A labour supply is in short and for producing product AB production of product CD is to be given.

Solution

Case (a)

Relevant cost in this case would be ₹ 20

Case (b)

Relevant cost in this case would be

Variable cost per labour hour			₹ 20
Contribution lost (Selling Price)		₹ 50	
Less: Variable cost (Excluding labour)	₹ 25		
Less: Labour cost	₹ 20	₹ 45	
Contribution			₹ 5
Relevant Cost in this case			₹ 25

Illustration 10

X Ltd. receives an offer from Y Ltd. for supply of product AB. Each unit of product AB requires an hour of Type B labour. Type B labour is permanently employed by X Ltd. This Type B labour is currently engaged in the production of product CD which also requires an hour of Type B labour and whose selling price is ₹ 50 per unit and variable cost is ₹ 20 per unit (excluding labour cost). The Type B labour is paid a rate of ₹ 10 per hour (irrespective of the fact that they are engaged or not). You are required to calculate relevant cost in each of the following cases:

***Case (a)** When the Type B labour is idle and fulfilling the order will not affect regular activity.*

***Case (b)** When the Type B labour is not idle and production of one unit of product AB can be achieved only after forgoing the production of product CD.*

Solution

Case (a) When the permanent labour is idle and order can be fulfilled without affecting the regular activity then the relevant cost in this case would be zero.

Case (b) When the permanent labour is not idle then the relevant cost would be contribution forgone by forgoing the regular activities.

Contribution forgone

Selling price per unit	₹ 50
Less: Variable cost of production	(₹ 20)
Contribution forgone	₹ 30

Relevant cost in this cost would be ₹ 30.

In this case labour cost is not considered since it is fixed in nature.

10.0 RELEVANT COST FOR MACHINE

1. Machine having no Alternative use and is already lying with the firm	**Relevant Cost** = Resale Value of Machine before the offer – Resale Value after the completion of the offer
2. Purchase of New Machine for the offer and Transfer of Machine to existing business after the completion of offer	**Relevant Cost** = Current Purchase Price at the time of offer – Replacement cost of machine after the completion of the offer.
3. Purchase of New Machine for the offer and no alternative use after the completion of offer	**Relevant Cost** = Current Purchase Price at the time of offer – Resale Value after the completion of offer *[Refer to Illustration 11]*

Illustration 11

X Ltd. receives an offer from Y Ltd. for supply of product AB. The completion of this offer would require the use of machine A. Now this machine is already with X Ltd. However it has no other alternative use. The current realisable value of machine A is ₹ 70,000. However after using it for the order it expected realisable value would fall to ₹ 40,000. Calculate the relevant cost of machine to be charged to the order.

Solution

The relevant cost in this case would be difference in resale values.

In this case it would be ₹ 70,000 – ₹ 40,000 = ₹ 30,000.

Hence ₹ 30,000 would be relevant cost for machine A that would be charged to the order.

Note: *In some cases machine become unusable after offer. In such case relevant cost would be determined as follows.*

Relevant cost: Current replacement cost today – Estimated Resale Value at the end of the offer.

Illustration 12

Estimated direct material requirement of a business concern viz., X Ltd. for the year 2011-12 are 1,00,000 units. Unit cost for orders below 1,20,000 units is ₹ 10. When size of order equals 1,20,000 units or more the concern received a discount of 2% on the above quoted per unit price. Keeping in view the following two alternatives:

1. ***Buy 1,20,000 units at the start of the year.***
2. ***Buy 10,000 units per month.***

Required: Calculate the opportunity cost. If the concern has the facility of investing surplus funds in government bonds at the rate of 12% interest.

Solution

Let Working capital be (introduced)	₹ 12,00,000
Alternative 1: Purchase 1,20,000 units at begining of year	
Cost to be incurred (1,20,000 × ₹ 9.8)	11,76,000
Surplus	24,000
Interest (24,000 × 12%)	2,880
Amount left at the end of year with interest	26,880

Alternative 2: Calculation of Interest if purchased in every month

Working capital = 12,00,000

Raw Material	*10,000 × 12 = 1,20,000 units*	
1st January	11,00,000 × 12% × 1/12	11,000
1st February	10,00,000 × 12% × 1/12	10,000
1st March	9,00,000 × 12% × 1/12	9,000
1st April	8,00,000 × 12% × 1/12	8,000
1st May	7,00,000 × 12% × 1/12	7,000
1st June	6,00,000 × 12% × 1/12	6,000
1st July	5,00,000 × 12 % × 1/12	5,000
1st August	4,00,000 × 12% × 1/12	4,000
1st September	3,00,000 × 12% × 1/12	3,000
1st October	2,00,000 × 12% × 1/12	2,000
1st November	1,00,000 × 12% × 1/12	1,000
		66,000

Opportunity cost for Alternative 1 equal to benefit of Alternative 2 i.e. ₹ 66,000.

Opportunity cost of Alternative 2 equal to benefit of Alternative 1 i.e. ₹ 26,880.

COMPREHENSIVE ILLUSTRATION

Illustration 13

X Ltd. receives an order from Y Ltd. for supply of 1,00,000 units of product AB. The following information is available regarding the cost of producing product AB.

Raw material: Product AB would require 3 types of raw material; P, Q and R respectively. Raw material P has no alternative use and is lying is stock with X Ltd. 1 unit of Raw material P is require to produce 1 unit of product AB.

The information regarding Raw material P is as follows

Original Cost	:	***₹ 2 per unit***
Current Resale Value	:	***₹ 1.50 per unit***
Current Replacement Cost	:	***₹ 2.50 per unit***

Raw material Q is regularly used by X Ltd. 1 unit of Raw Material Q is required to produce one unit of Product AB. Company also produces product CD by using semi-skilled labour and acceptance of this offer shall result in production of product CD to the extent of 25000 units. One unit of Q is required to produce one unit of CD. Raw material Q currently in stock is 50,000 units. The following information is available in regard to raw material Q.

Original cost	:	***₹ 2 per unit***
Realisable value	:	***₹ 1.50 per unit***
Replacement cost	:	***₹ 2.50 per unit***
Contribution lost per unit in respect of product CD	:	***₹ 5.00 per unit***

Raw material R is already in stock and have no alternative use. However instead of product R a substitute material R_1 could be used. One unit of R is required to produce one unit of product AB. Similarly instead of R, R_1 could be used and one unit of R_1 is required to produce one unit of product AB.

The information regarding product R and R_1 is as follows.

	R	***R_1***
Original Cost	***3***	***–***
Current Replacement Cost	***3.50***	***2.50***
Net Realisable Value	***3.00***	***–***

Labour: Production of AB require three types of labour.

1. ***Semi-skilled labour***
2. ***Skilled labour***
3. ***Highly skilled labour.***

Semi-skilled labour is casual in nature and abundant in supply and can be acquired at @ ₹ 5 per hour. 2 hours of semi-skilled labour is required to produce one unit of product AB. Skilled labour is casual in nature and in short supply. Regular production of X Ltd. is affected if skilled labour is used to produce product AB. 1 hour of Skilled labour is required to produce 1 unit of product AB.

Wage rate for skilled labour is ₹ 10 per hour and contribution lost is ₹ 2 per hour.

Highly skilled labour is permanently employed by X Ltd. 0.25 hour is required to produce one unit of product AB. 14000 hours of highly skilled labour is lying idle with X Ltd. However if they are engaged in production of AB Ltd, then contribution forgone from regular activity will be ₹ 27 per hours.

Machine: Two machine would be required to produce product AB.

Both Machine A and Machine B will have no alternative use after the completion of this order.

Machine A is currently in stock. It was purchased for ₹ 80,000 and have currently estimated realisable value of ₹ 50,000. Its estimated realisable value after its use for order is ₹ 20,000. Machine B have to be procured from the market. It current replacement cost is ₹ 80,000. It would have no alternative use after completion of the order and will have estimated realisable value of ₹ 20,000 after completion of the contract.

Required: Determine the relevant cost of the contract.

Solution

A. Machine Cost:

Raw Material P [1,00,000 × ₹ 1.50 per unit]	1,50,000
Raw Material Q: [75,000 × 2.50]	1,87,500
[25,000 × 5.00]	1,25,000
Raw Material R_1 [1,00,000 × 2.50]	2,50,000
Raw Material Cost	7,12,500

B. Labour Cost:

Semi-skilled Labour [1,00,000 × 2 × ₹ 5]	10,00,000
Skilled-Labour [1,00,000 × (₹ 10 + ₹ 2)]	12,00,000
Highly Skilled Labour: [14,000 × 0]	0
[11000 × 27]	2,97,000
Labour Cost	24,97,000

C. Machine Cost:

Machine A [₹ 50,000 – ₹ 20,000]	30,000
Machine B [₹ 80,000 – ₹ 20,000]	60,000
Machine Cost	90,000

D. Total Relevant Cost (A + B + C) 32,99,500

Illustration 14

A Ltd. has recently conducted a market research at a cost of ₹ 1,00,000 and found the market for product PQ with an annual demand of 50,000 unit at a price of ₹ 45 per unit. However the demand will last only for a year.

The following information is provided in this respect.

RAW MATERIAL – Each unit of Product PQ would require 3 types of Raw material A, B & C respectively. Raw material A is regularly used by the A Ltd. and stocks are replaced as they are used. However the current stock of Raw material B is the result of overbuying for an earlier contract. The material B is not used regularly by A Ltd. and any excess stock of material B would be disposed off. The company does not carry any stock of Material C and the units of Raw material C would be specially purchased.

Raw Material	*Quantity required per unit of PQ.*	*Current Stock Level*	*Cost per unit of Raw Material*		
			Original Cost ₹	*Current Replacement Cost* ₹	*Current Resale Value* ₹
A	1.00	40000	3.00	4.00	2.50
B	1.50	30000	2.00	2.50	1.80
C	0.50	0	–	10.00	–

LABOUR – Production of each unit of Product PQ would require 1 hour of skilled labour and 3 hours of unskilled labour. Current wage rate are ₹ 8 per hour for skilled labour and ₹ 5 per hour for unskilled labour. The skilled labour would be required to transferred from another job on which they are earning a contribution of ₹ 3 per hour. However unskilled labour are available in abundant. In addition to this, one foreman would be required to devote all his working time for one year in supervision of the production of Product PQ. He is currently paid an annual salary of

₹ 1,80,000. The foreman is due to retire immediately on an annual pension of ₹ 1,00,000 payable by the company.

OVERHEAD – A predetermined rate of recovery for overhead is in operation and the fixed overheads are recovered fully from the regular production at ₹ 8 per hour. Variable overhead costs for Product PQ are estimated at ₹ 5 per unit produced.

Required: You are required to compute a cost for product PQ with all details of materials, labour overhead, etc. on the basis of relevant cost and suggest whether production of product PQ should be undertaken or not.

Solution

Details of Relevant Costs

(A) Market Research Cost

It is sunk cost and have no relevance for decision making.

(B) RAW MATERIAL COSTS

(a) Raw Material A

As raw material A is regularly and stocks are replaced as they are used. Hence the relevant cost in this case would be current replacement cost = 50,000 × ₹ 4 = ₹ 2,00,000

(b) Raw material B

Material B is not regularly used by the company. However some of the stock is already lying in the stock with the company. In respect of material lying in the stock, the relevant cost is net realisable value. In the case of new purchases the current replacement cost is relevant cost.

Therefore:

30,000 × ₹ 1.80 = ₹ 54,000

45,000 × ₹ 2.50 = ₹ 1,12,500

(c) Raw Material C

This material is not used by the company and it is also neither lying in the stock so relevant cost is current replacement cost of raw material C

Hence 25000 × ₹.10 = ₹ 2,50,000

Total Raw material cost = ₹ 2,00,000 + ₹ 54,000 + ₹ 1,12,500 + ₹ 2,50,000 = ₹ 6,16,500

(C) LABOUR COST

(a) Skilled Labour

Wage rate for skilled labour is ₹ 8 per hour. If product PQ were not manufactured and the skilled labour were not transferred, they would have given a clean contribution of ₹ 3 per hour. So total relevant cost in respect of skilled labour is ₹ 11 per hour (i.e. ₹ 8 + ₹ 3)

Total Skilled Labour Cost = 50,000 × ₹ 11 = ₹ 5,50,000

(b) Unskilled labour

There is no contribution loss in respect of unskilled labour since it is available in the abundance. The relevant cost in respect of unskilled labour is only the amount payable to them per hour. Hence total Unskilled Labour Cost = 1,50,000 × ₹ 5 = ₹ 7,50,000

(c) Foreman Cost

Relevant cost in respect of Foreman = ₹ 1,80,000 – ₹ 1,00,000 = ₹ 80,000

Total Labour Cost = ₹ 5,50,000 + ₹ 7,50,000 + ₹ 80,000 = ₹ 13,80,000

(D) OVERHEAD COST

Fixed overhead have been fully recovered from existing production. So its rate of recovery is not relevant.

Variable Overhead = 50,000 × ₹ 5 = ₹ 2,50,000
Total Overhead Cost = ₹ 2,50,000

(E) Total Relevant Cost = (A) + (B) + (C) + (D)

₹ 0 + ₹ 6,16,500 + ₹ 13,80,000 + ₹ 2,50,000 = ₹ 22,46,500

(F) Estimated Revenues = 50,000 × ₹ 45 = 22,50,000

Conclusion: As estimated revenues are more than total relevant costs so production should be undertaken.

Illustration 15

Mahila Griha Udyog Industries is considering to supply its products—a special range of namkeens—to a departmental store. The contract will last for 50 weeks, and the details are given below:

		₹
Material:	***X (in stock-at original cost)***	***1,50,000***
	Y (on order–on contract)	***1,80,000***
	Z (to be ordered)	***3,00,000***
Labour:	***Skilled***	***5,40,000***
	Non-skilled	***3,00,000***
	Supervisory	***1,00,000***
General Overheads		***10,80,000***
Total cost		***26,50,000***
Price offered by department store		***18,00,000***
Net Loss		***8,50,000***

Should the contract be accepted if the following additional information is considered?

(i) Material X is an obsolete material. It can only be used on another product, the material for which is available at ₹ 1,35,000 (Material X requires some adaptation to be used and costs ₹ 27,000).

(ii) Material Y is ordered for some other product which is no longer required. It now has a residual value of ₹ 2,10,000)

(iii) Skilled labour can work on other contracts which are presently operated by semi-skilled labour at a cost of ₹ 5,70,000.

(iv) Non-skilled labour are specifically employed for this contract.

(v) Supervisor staff will remain whether or not the contract is accepted. Only two of them can replace other positions where the salary is ₹ 35,000.

(vi) Overheads are charged at 200% of skilled labour. Only ₹ 1,25,000 would be avoidable, if the contract is not accepted.

Solution

STATEMENT OF RELEVANT COST OF MAHILA GRIHA UDYOG INDUSTRIES IF THE CONTRACT IS ACCEPTED/REJECTED

Particulars	*Relevant Costs (if Contract is accepted)* ₹	*Relevant Costs (if Contract is rejected)* ₹
A. Cash Inflows:		
Contract Price	18,00,000	—
Sale of Material Y	—	2,10,000
Total Cash Inflows:	18,00,000	2,10,000
B. Cash Outflows:		
Material X substitute	1,35,000	—
Adaptation required for the use of obsolete material X	—	27,000
Material Z	3,00,000	
Replacement of semi-skilled labour by skilled labour	5,70,000	—
Non-skilled labour cost	3,00,000	—
Supervisory staff cost	35,000	—
Avoidable overheads	1,25,000	—
Total Cash outflow:	14,65,000	27,000
C. Net Cash Inflow: [A – B]	3,35,000	1,83,000

Conclusion: The contract should be accepted as it yields a net incremental cash inflow of ₹ 1,52,000 (i.e. ₹ 3,35,000 – ₹ 1,83,000).

Working Notes:

(i) Material Y will have to be paid for whether or not the contract is accepted, therefore its cost is irrelevant. The relevant cost figure here is that which has an opportunity cost of ₹ 2,10,000. This means that the company can resell material Y at this price.

(ii) Regarding material X, if the contract is accepted, alterative material will have to be purchased for the other product at a cost of ₹ 1,35,000. If the contract is rejected material X will be adapted for a product not included in the list of special range of namkeens at a cost of ₹ 27,000.

(iii) The relevant skilled labour cost of ₹ 5,70,000 is the extra cost to the company because of this contract. It is the replacement cost of semi skilled labour by skilled labour.

(iv) Non-skilled labour cost is the incremental cost of the contract.

(v) If the company accepts the contract is will have to pay ₹ 35,000 for two position that the supervisory staff can replace.

(vi) Only ₹ 1,25,000 of avoidable overheads are relevant to this contract.

Illustration 16

Ranka has been offered a contract by Excel Ltd. to build for it five special Guest Houses for use by top management. Each Guest House will be an independent one. The contract will be for a period of one year and the offer price is ₹ '1' crore. In addition Excel Ltd. will also provide 2 grounds of land free of cost for the purpose of construction. The Chief Accountant of Ranka Builders has prepared an estimate on the basis of which he has advised that the contract should not be accepted at the price offered. His estimate was as follows:

	₹ In Lacs
Land (3 Grounds at ₹ 20 lacs each)	***60***
Drawings and design	***7***
Registration	***10***
Cement and Sand	***6***
Bricks and Tiles	***4***
Steel	***10***
Other (including interior decoration)	***10***
Labour-Skilled	***12***
—Unskilled	***8***
—Supervisor's Salary	***5***
Overheads General	***12***
Depreciation	***6***
Total Cost	***150***

The Accountant also provides the following information:

Land: The total requirement of land is 3 grounds costing ₹ 20 lacs per ground Excel Ltd. will provide 2 grounds free of cost.

Drawing and Design: These have already been prepared and 50% of the cost has already been incurred.

Materials:

(i) Cement and sand are already in stock and are in regular use. If used for this contract, they have to be replaced at a cost of ₹ 8 lacs.

(ii) Bricks and tiles represent purchases made several months before for a different contract. They could be sold readily for a net ₹ 5 lacs after meeting all further expensed

(iii) Others: Materials worth ₹ 2 lacs relating to interior decoration are in stock for which no alternative use is expected in the near future. However they can be sold for ₹ 1 lac.

Labour:

(i) Skilled workers will be transferred to this project from another 'project. The project manager claimed that if the men where returned to him, he could have earned the company an additional ₹ 2 lacs in terms of profits.

(ii) The supervisor undertakes various tasks in the sites and his pay and continuity of employment will not be affected by the new contract if the contract is taken, he will devote half of his time.

Overheads:

(i) The equipment that would be used on the contract was bought one year before for ₹ 30 lacs and is expected to last for five years. It can also be used on other contracts and the current replacement price will be ₹ 32 lacs and in a year's time it will be ₹ 25 lacs.

(ii) The general overheads includes both specific and absorbed overheads. If the contract is not undertaken, ₹ 4 lacs of the same can be avoided.

Ranka Builders has also on hand another project, which would not be executed if the contract from Excel Ltd. were to be accepted. The estimated profit on that project is ₹ 10 lacs.

In the light of information given above, you are required to indicate with reasons whether the contract from Excel Ltd. should be accepted or not.

Solution

STATEMENT OF RELEVANT COSTS ON THE ACCEPTANCE OF CONTRACT FROM EXCEL LTD.

[₹ *in Lacs*]

S. No.	*Particulars*	*Basis for the cost to be relevant* ₹	*Relevant cost if contract is accepted* ₹	*Irrelevant cost if the contract is accepted* ₹
1.	Land cost		20	
2.	Drawings and design		—	7 (Sunk cost)
3.	Registration	Incremental	10	—
	Materials:			
	Cement and Sand	Replacement	8	
	Bricks and Tiles	Opportunity	5	
	Steel	Incremental	10	
	Others		9	
5.	Labour			
	Skilled	Opportunity	12 + 2	
	Unskilled	Incremental	8	
	Supervisor's salary			5 (Sunk cost)
6.	Overheads:			
	General	Relevant (avoidable)	4	
	Depreciation		—	6 (Sunk cost)
	Replacement cost of machine		7	
7.	Estimated Profit foregone on other project	Opportunity foregone	10	
	Total		105	

Decision: Since the offer price of contract is ₹ 100 lacs and its total relevant cost is ₹ 105 lacs; these figures clearly shows that the offer should not be accepted.

Working notes:

(i) Cost of 1 ground of Land

	₹ (Lacs)
Total cost of 3 grounds of land	60
Cost of grounds of land will be borne by Excel Ltd.	40
Cost of 1 grounds of land will be borne by M/s Ranka Builders	20

(ii) Others material cost is ₹ 10 lacs, it includes material worth ₹ 2 lacs, relating to interior decoration, which is a sunk cost, this material can be sold for ₹ 1 lac, (which is a relevant opportunity cost) and ₹ 8 lacs. Material is an incremental cost. Hence total relevant cost of others material is ₹ 9 lacs. (₹ 8 lacs, incremental + ₹ 1 lac. opportunity cost).

(iii) Since the equipment can also be used on this contract. Its current replacement price is ₹ 32 lacs, and after one year its cost will be ₹ 25 lacs. Therefore the relevant opportunity cost of machine is: ₹ 7 lacs. (₹ 32 lacs – ₹ 25 lacs).

Illustration 17

A company had nearly completed a job relating to construction of a job relating to construction of a specialised equipment, when it discovered that the customer had gone out of business. At this stage, the position if the job was as under:

	₹
Original cost estimate	***1,75,200***
Cost incurrent so far	***1,48,500***

Costs to be incurred	***29,700***
Progress payment received from original customer	***1,00,000***

After searches, a new customer for the equipment has been found. He is interested to take the equipment, if certain modifications are carried out. The new customer wanted the equipment in its original condition, but without its control device and with certain other modifications. The costs of these additions and modifications are estimated as under:

		₹
Direct materials (at cost)		***1,050***
Direct Wages.	***Dept. A***	***15 man days***
	Dept. B	***25 man days***
Variable overheads		***25% of direct wages in each department***
Delivery costs		***₹ 1,350***

Fixed overheads will be absorbed at 50% of direct wages in each department.

The following additional information is available:

1. ***The direct materials required for the modification are in stock and if not used for modification of this order, they will be used in another job in place of materials that will now cost ₹ 2,250.***
2. ***Department A is working normally and hence any engagement of labour will have to be paid at the direct wage rate of ₹ 120 per man day.***
3. ***Department B is extremely busy. Its direct wages rate is ₹ 100 per man day and it is currently yielding a contribution of ₹ 3.20 per rupee of direct wages.***
4. ***Supervisory overtime payable for the modification is ₹ 1,050.***
5. ***The cost of the control device that the new customer does not require is ₹ 13,500. If it is taken out, it can be used in another job in place of a different mechanism. The latter mechanism has otherwise to be bought for ₹ 10,500. The dismantling and removal of the control mechanism will take one man day in department A.***
6. ***If the convention is not carried out, some of the materials in the original equipment can be used in another contract in place of materials that would have cost ₹ 12,000. It would have taken 2 man days of work in department A to make them suitable for this purpose. The remaining materials will realise ₹ 11,400 as scrap. The drawings, which are included as part of the job can he sold for ₹ 1,500***

Required: Calculate the minimum price, which the company can afford to quote for the new customer:

Solution

STATEMENT OF MINIMUM PRICE WHICH THE COMPANY CAN AFFORD TO QUOTE FOR THE NEW CUSTOMER (BASED ON RELEVANT COST)

Particulars	₹
Cost to be incurred to bring the equipment in its original condition.	29,700
Opportunity Cost of the direct material	2,250
Direct Wages:	
Dept A: [15 man days × ₹ 120]	1,800
Dept. A: [25 man days × ₹ 100]	2,500
Opportunity Cost of Contribution lost by Department B (₹ 2,500 × ₹ 3.2)	8,000
Variable Overheads [25% (₹ 1,800 + ₹ 2,500)]	1,075
Delivery Costs	1,350
Supervisory overtime payable for modification	1,050
Cost Control device to be used in another job (W.N)	(10,350)
Net Loss on Material Cost savings, in the original equipment (WN)	11,700
Opportunity Cost of remaining materials which can be sold as scrap	11,400
Opportunity Cost of sale of drawings	1,500
Total Minimum Price which may be quoted	61,975

Working Notes:

(i) *Cost of Control Device to be used in another job*:

		₹
A	Cost of control device	10,500
B	*Less*: Dismantling and removal (1 man day × ₹ 120)	(120)
C	*Less*: Variable cost (25% × ₹ 120)	(30)
D	Balance Cost of Control Device [A – B – C]	10,350

(ii) *Net Loss on Material Cost Saving of Equipment*

A	Loss on Material Cost Saving of Equipment	12,000
B	*Less*: Conversion Cost (2 man days × ₹ 120)	(240)
C	*Less*: Variable Overheads (25% × ₹ 240)	(60)
D	Net Loss on Material Cost Saving of Equipment [A – B – C]	11,700

SOLVED PROBLEMS

Problem 1

X Ltd. manufactures desks. Material is currently used to make chairs which provide contribution of ₹ 10 per chair. 2 kg of material is required for each chair.

Required: What is the minimum price per desk

(i) if material is in plenty

(ii) if material is scarce.

The following information is provided for 1 Desk.

	Cost per unit (₹)
Material (3 kg @ ₹ 4)	12
Labour	10
VO	8
Allocated FO	4
	34

Solution

(i) If material is in plenty

Minimum Price = ₹ 12 + ₹ 10 + ₹ 8 = ₹ 30

(ii) If Material is scarce

Minimum Price = ₹ 12 + ₹ 10 + ₹ 8 + [(₹ 10/2) × 3kg)] = ₹ 45

Problem 2

The book cost of ₹ 4 per kg is a historic (Sunk) cost and therefore irrelevant to the valuation. However there are two opportunities for this material.

1. Realise the material A and obtain future revenue of ₹ 2 per kg
2. Use the material A as a substitute for material X and thus save a cost of ₹ 6 per kg.

Where is the relevant value of material A?

Solution

A possible saving in cost is the same as a benefit receivable. The opportunity cost of using material A in the contract is the greater of the two opportunities foregone, i.e. ₹ 6 per kg.

Thus, Relevant Value of Material A = 500 kg × ₹ 6 = ₹ 3,000

Problem 3

X Ltd. has been approached by a customer who would like a special job to be done for him and is willing to pay ₹ 22,000 for it. The job would require the following materials:

Material	*Total Units Required*	*Units Already in stock*	*Book Value of Units in Stock ₹/Unit*	*Realisable Value ₹/unit*	*Replacement Cost ₹/Unit*
A	1,000	0	–	–	6
B	1,000	600	2	2.5	5
C	1,000	700	3	2.5	4
D	200	200	4	6	9

(i) Material B is used regularly by X Ltd. and if the stocks are required for this job, they would need to be replaced to meet other production demand.

(ii) Material C and D are in stocks as the result of previous excess purchase and they have a restricted use. No other use could be found for material C but material D could be used in another job as substitute for 300 units of material E which currently cost ₹ 5 per unit (of which the company has no units in stock at the moment).

Required: What are the relevant costs of material, in deciding whether or not to accept the contract? Assume all other expenses on this contract to be specially incurred besides the relevant cost of material is ₹ 550.

Solution

STATEMENT OF COST AND BENEFITS

Particulars	₹
Revenue (Given)	22,000
Less: Relevant costs	
Material (as per working note)	(15,450)
Other cost	(550)
Net benefit	6,000

It is better to accept the job because revenue ₹ 22,000 is sufficient to cover the relevant costs and to provide net incremental benefit in addition to regular activities (to the company) for the next period.

Working Notes

(i) Relevant cost for materials

	₹
(a) Material 'A'	
Out of Stock: Replacement cost (1000 Qty. @ ₹ 6)	6,000
(b) Material 'B'	
(i) Out of stock: Replacement cost (400 Qty. @ ₹ 5)	2,000
(ii) Regular use: Replacement cost (600 Qty. @ ₹ 5)	3,000
	5,000
(c) Material 'C'	
(i) Out of stock: Replacement cost (300 Qty. @ ₹ 4)	1,200
(ii) Obsolete: Opportunity cost (700 Qty. @ ₹ 2.5)	1,750
	2,950

(d) Material 'D' (Sub. use)

Opp. cost higher of other alternative, i.e.	
(i) Sale: 6 × 200 =	1,200
or	*or*
(ii) Substitute use (E) (300 × 5)	1,500
	1,500
Total relevant cost for material (A, B, C & D)	**15,450**

Problem 4

A division of Rhine Autos has received an enquiry from one of its major customers for a special order for a component that will require 1,000 skilled labour hours and that will incur other variable costs of ₹ 8,000. Skilled labour is currently in short supply and if the company accepts the order then it will be necessary to reduce production of components P. Details of the cost per unit and the selling price of component P are as follows:

	₹	₹
Selling Price		88
Less: Direct labour (4 Hours at ₹ 10 per hour)	40	
Other variable costs	12	52
Contribution to profits		36

Required: The minimum selling price the company should accept for the special order.

Solution

STATEMENT OF RELEVANT COST

Particulars	₹
Direct Labour Cost (1000 hrs × 10 per hour)	10,000
Other Variable Cost	8,000
Benefit to be lost	9,000
Minimum price	27,000

W.N. 1:

Benefit to be lost

Contribution to profit (p) = 36

Contribution lost due to acceptance of offer per labour hour = $\frac{36}{4}$ = ₹ 9 per hour

Total contribution lost = 1000 hr × ₹ 9 per hour = 9,000.

Problem 5

ABC Ltd. is tendering for a six-month contract, which would require the use of a specialist machine. The machine was purchased four years ago for ₹ 90,000 and now has a net book value of ₹ 35,000. ABC Ltd. was about to sell the machine for ₹ 40,000 but if they used it on this contact they can sell it after the six months for ₹ 25,000. The variable cost of operating the machine for six months would be ₹ 60,000. Ignoring interest costs identify the relevant cost of using the machine on the contract.

Solution

Relevant cost for contract

	₹
Cost to be incurred	60,000
Add: Benefit to be lost (40,000 – 25,000)	15,000
Obsolete	
Total relevant cost	**75,000**

Problem 6

A Company is considering the costs for a special order. The order would require 1,250 kg of material D. This material is readily available and regularly used by the company. There are 265 kg of material D in stock which costs ₹ 795 last week. The current market price is ₹ 3.24 per kg.

Material D is normally used to make product X. Each unit of X requires 3 kg of material D and if material D costed at ₹ 3 per kg, each unit of X yields a contribution of ₹ 15.

The cost of material D is to be included in the costing of the special order which is nearest to

A. ₹ 3990 B. ₹ 4050 C. ₹ 10,000 D. ₹ 10,300

Solution

The material is readily available and the use of the materials will necessitate their replacement. The relevant cost is therefore the replacement cost of ₹ 4050 (1,250 kg at ₹ 3.24).

Answer = B.

Problem 7

Engineers Ltd. is just ready to deliver a machine specially designed for Durables & Co. When it is learnt that the latter has gone bankrupt, an enquiry comes from another firm Steady Enterprises, which can accept the machine meant for Durables & Co. if certain alterations are done to suit Steady Enterprises' needs and the price is attractive.

The following factors prevail:

(a) Costs incurred on the machine for Durables & Co.	Amount (₹)
Direct materials	5,60,000
Direct labour	4,00,000
Variable overhead	1,40,000
Fixed overhead	3,00,000
Fixed selling and distribution overhead	1,00,000
Total	**15,00,000**

Notes: If the negotiation with Steady Enterprises fails, part of the material used may be dealt with as under:

(i) Brass materials – could be sold as scrap for ₹ 1,00,000

(ii) Steel material – could be sold as scrap for ₹ 26,000, but to sell it as scrap some 100 hours labour will be hired at ₹ 10 per hour to bring it to saleable condition.

(iii) Balance materials will have to be removed at a cost of ₹ 5,000, but will have a "nil" sale value.

Price quoted to Durables & Co. was ₹ 18,00,000.

To cater to Steady Enterprises needs, the alteration cost will be:

Particulars	*Department A*	*Department M*
Direct material	₹ 10,000	₹ 5,000
Direct labour	10 men for 2 months @ ₹ 3,000 per man per month	6 women for 2 months 2,000 per women per month
Variable overhead	20% of direct labour cost	25% of direct labour cost
Fixed overhead	60% of direct labour cost	50% of direct labour cost

Notes:

(i) Materials required are already in stock and valued at cost. If the work for Steady Enterprises is not undertaken, the company has the following choice:
- Material for Department M, will be used for another job.
- Material for Department A, lying as it is for some years, will remain put on quick sale for ₹ 3,000.

The present market prices for the materials for M and A are ₹ 12,000 and ₹ 6,000 respectively.

(ii) Department M is currently working at full capacity earning a contribution of ₹ 3 towards fixed overhead and profit per ₹ 1 of labour.

(iii) Department A is presently working at 40% of its capacity, but as per agreement with the Union, its present work force of 24 women cannot be reduced. A worker in this department gets ₹ 2,000 a month as wages. In order to utilize its labour, Department A undertakes some off-loading work for ₹ 32,500 per month from a sister concern when the workload in Department A falls below 50% capacity. Variable cost associated with the off-loading work is ₹ 4,000 per month. The conversion work for Steady Enterprises will mean 25% additional workload for Department A for two months.

The pattern and specification of the original machine could be sold to a customer for ₹ 60,000. For supervision of the job for Steady Enterprises, a temporary Supervisor would be needed for 2 months at an agreed salary of ₹ 10,000. He will be a person deputed by Steady Enterprises. The company charges all indirect and supervisory salaries to fixed overhead.

Durables & Co. has already made an earnest money deposit of ₹ 1,80,000 for the machine. As per terms of the contract this deposit stands forfeited and Engineers Ltd. is now free to treat the sum as miscellaneous income. Taxation may be ignored.

Required: Engineers Ltd. seeks your advice for the minimum price, based on relevant costs only, for the quotation it will make to Steady Enterprises.

Solution

STATEMENT OF RELEVANT COST

Particulars	(₹)
Cost to be incurred [as per working note (iii)]	3,40,000
Benefit to be lost [as per working note (ii)]	1,85,000
Less: Benefit to be achieved (Saving in removal cost)	(5,000)
Minimum Price	5,20,000

Working Notes

(i) Cost incurred of ₹ 15,00,000 to be termed as sunk cost due to past cost, hence ignored.

(ii) **Benefit to be lost:**

	₹
Sale of brass material	1,00,000
Sale of steel material (26,000 – 100 × 10)	25,000
Sale of pattern and specification	60,000
Total	**1,85,000**

(iii) **Cost to be incurred:**

Material	
Department M (regular use)	12,000
Department A (obsolete):	
Resale value	3,000
Labour: (Lab. cost + Contribution lost)	
M: (60,000 + 1,80,000)	2,40,000
A: benefit lost	57,000

Variable overhead:	
M (600 × 10 × 2)	12,000
A (500 × 6 × 2)	6,000
Supervisor's salary	10,000
Total	**3,40,000**

Benefit Lost:

Total capacity	24 Women
Utilize 40%	9.6 Women
Spare 60%	14.4 Workers

If work of Steady Enterprises cannot be achieved then present utilisation would be 40% and spare will be 60%

If we are interested to accept the offer of Steady Enterprises

Present labour utilised = 40%

Steady (6/24 × 100) = 25%

Total Work Load = 65%

Now Spare (100% – 65%) = 35%

Benefit lost due to Steady Enterprises P.M.

Revenue	32,500
Variable cost	4,000
	28,500

The Benefit lost (28,500 × 2 month) = 57,000

Problem 8

You are the management accountant of a publishing and printing company who is supposed to quote for the production programme for the local village fair. The work would be carried out in addition to the normal work of the company. Because of the existing commitments some weekend working would be required to complete the printing of the programme. A trainee accountant has produced the following cost estimate based upon the resources required as specified by the production manager:

Particulars		₹
Direct material	Paper (book value)	5,000
	Inks (purchase price)	2,400
Direct labour	Skilled 250 hours @ ₹ 4.00	1,000
	Unskilled 100 hours @ R. 3.50	350
Variable overheads	350 hours @ ₹ 4.00	1,400
Printing press depreciation	200 hours @ ₹ 2.50	500
Fixed production costs	350 hours @ ₹ 6.00	2,100
Estimating department cost		400
		13,150

You are aware that considerable publicity could be obtained for the company if you are able to win this order and the price quoted must be very competitive.

The following notes are relevant to the cost estimate above:

1. The paper to be used is currently in stock at a value of ₹ 5,000. It is of an unusual colour, which has not been used for some time. The replacement price of the paper is ₹ 8,000. Whilst

the scrap value of that in stock is ₹ 2,500. The production manager does not foresee any alternative use for the paper if it is not used for the village fair programmes.

2. The inks required are not held in stock. They would have to be purchased in bulk at a cost of ₹ 3,000. 80% of the ink purchases would be used in printing the programmes. No other use is foreseen for the remainder.
3. Skilled direct labour is in short supply, and to accommodate the printing of the programmes 50% of the time required would be worked at weekends for which a premium of 25% above the normal hourly rate is paid. The normal hourly rate is ₹ 4.00 per hour.
4. Unskilled labour is presently under-utilized and at present 200 hours per week is recorded as idle time. If the printing work is carried out at a weekend, 25 unskilled hours would have to occur at this time, but the employees concerned would be given two hours time off (for which they would be paid) in lieu of each hour worked.
5. Variable overhead represents the cost of operating the printing pressed and binding machines.
6. When not being used by the company the printing press is hired to outside companies for ₹ 6.00 per hour. This earns a contribution of ₹ 3.00 per hour. There is unlimited demand for this facility.
7. Fixed production costs are those incurred by and absorbed into production, using an hourly rate based on budgeted activity.
8. The cost of the estimating department represent time spent in discussions with the village fair committee concerning the printing of its programme.

Required: Prepare a revised cost estimate using the opportunity cost approach, showing clearly the minimum price that the company should accept for the order. Give reasons for each resource valuation in your cost estimate. Explain the relevance of opportunity costs in decision-making.

Solution

STATEMENT OF MINIMUM PRICE

Particulars	₹
Costs to be incurred:	
Paper	2,500
Ink	3,000
Direct labour	
Skilled [As per working note (i)]	1,125
Unskilled [As per working note (ii)]	—
Variable overheads (350 × 4)	1,400
Printing Press (3 × 200 hr.)	600
Minimum Price (Total)	8,625

Working Notes:

(i) Skilled labour hours

Total	250 hours	
50%	50%	
Week days	Weekend	
Total	[(125 hr × ₹ 4) + 125 × ₹ (4 + 1)] = ₹ 1,125	

(ii) Unskilled:

Under-utilized = 200 labour hours during week days

Available:		
Utilized:	75 hours	Weekend
Balance	125	Weekdays
Required	25	Weekend

= 50 hours weekdays out of balance 125 weekdays hours. We give time off of 50 hours during week in lieu of 25 working at weekend.
Still available Weekhours = 125 – 50 = 75 hours.

(iii) The cost of estimating department always to be termed as sunk cost.

Problem 9

A company has been making an order for a customer, but the customer has gone into liquidation, and there is no prospect that any money will be obtained from the winding up of the company.

Costs incurred to-date in manufacturing the machine are ₹ 50,000 and progress payments of ₹ 15,000 have been received from the customer prior to the liquidation.

The Sales department has found another company willing to buy the machine for ₹ 34,000 once it has been completed. To complete the work, the following costs would be incurred:

(a) Materials these have been bought at a cost of ₹ 6,000. They have no other use, and if the machine is not finished, they would be sold for scrap for ₹ 2,000.

(b) Further labour costs would be ₹ 8,000. Labour is in short supply, and if the machine is not finished, the work force would be switched to another job, which would earn ₹ 30,000 in revenue, and incur direct costs of ₹ 12,000 not including direct labour, of ₹ 8,000 and absorbed (fixed) overhead of ₹ 8,000.

(c) Consultancy fees ₹ 4,000. If the work is not completed, the consultant's contract would be cancelled at a cost of ₹ 1,500.

(d) General overheads of ₹ 8,000 would be added to the cost of the additional work.

Required: Prepare a statement showing the economics of the proposition. Should the new customer's offer be accepted?

Note: Labour cost of ₹ 8,000 would be paid if the machine is completed.

Labour cost of ₹ 8,000 would be paid if we do the under mentioned job by utilising such labour and we have to incur material cost of ₹ 12,000 so that the contribution from utilizing such labour in the another job would be sale of ₹ 30,000 – direct material cost ₹ 12,000 – direct labour cost ₹ 8,000 = ₹ 10,000. Absorb fixed overheads are always irrelevant.

Solution

STATEMENT OF COST BENEFIT

Particulars	*W.N. No.*	₹
Revenue		34,000
Less: Relevant Cost		
Material	(ii)	2,000
Labour	(iii)	18,000
Consultancy fee	(iv)	2,500
General overhead/Additional		–
Benefits		11,500

It is better to accept the offer for the completion of machine because incremental revenue is sufficient to cover the relevant cost.

Working Notes:

(i) Past cost of ₹ 50,000 is Sunk Cost.

(ii) **Material:**
Book Value = 6,000 (obsolete)
Scrap Sale value = 2,000
Relevant cost = 2,000.

(iii) **Labour:**

		₹
	Revenue	30,000
	(–) Direct cost.	(12,000)
Labour	(–) Labour cost	(8,000)
(Casual + Busy)	Contribution	10,000
	Offer labour cost	8,000
	+ Cont. lost	10,000
		18,000

(iv) Cost to be incurred due to acceptance of offer	4,000
Less: benefit to be achieved due to acceptance of offer	1,500
Relevant cost	2,500

(v) General overhead always to be termed as sunk cost because change in apportionment does not change in *total cash* outflow.

Problem 10

JB Ltd. is a small specialist manufacturer of electronic components and much of its output is used by the makers of aircraft for both civil and military purposes. One of the few aircraft manufacturers has offered a contract to JB Ltd. for the supply, over the next twelve months, of 400 identical components. The data relating to the production of each component is as follows:

Material requirements:

3 kilograms Material M1	– See note 1 below
2 kilograms Material P2	– See note 2 below
1 part no. 678	– See note 3 below

Notes:

1. Material M1 is in continuous use by the company, 1,000 kg are currently held in stock at a book value of ₹ 4.70 per kg but it is known that future purchases will cost ₹ 5.50 per kg.
2. 1,200 kg of Material P 2 are held in stock. The original cost of this material was ₹ 4.30 per kg but as the material has not been required for the last two years and it has been written down to ₹ 1.50 per kg scrap value. The only foreseeable alternative use is as a substitute for Material P 4 (in current use) but this would involve further processing cost of ₹ 1.60 per kg. The current cost of material P 4 is ₹ 3.60 per kg.
3. It is estimated that part no. 678 could be brought for ₹ 50 each.

Labour requirements: Each component would require five hours of skilled labour and five hours of semi-skilled labour. An employee possessing the necessary skills is available and is currently paid ₹ 5 per hour. A replacement would however to be obtained at a rate of ₹ 4 per hour for the work which would otherwise be done by the skilled employee. The current rate for semi-skilled work is ₹ 3 per hour and an additional employee could be appointed for this work.

Overhead: JB Ltd. absorbs overhead by a machine hour rate, currently ₹ 20 per hour of which ₹ 7 is for variable overhead and ₹ 13 for fixed overhead. If this contract is undertaken, it is estimated that fixed costs will increase for the duration of the contract by ₹ 3,200. Spare machine capacity is available and each component would require four machine hours.

A price of ₹ 145 per component has been suggested by the large company which makes aircraft.

Required: State wheather or not the contract should be accepted and support your conclusion with appropriate figures for presentation to management.

Solution

STATEMENT OF COST AND BENEFIT

Particulars	*Working Note No.*	₹
Revenue (145 × 400)		58,000
Less: Relevant Costs:		
Material	(i)	(28,200)
Labour	(ii)	(14,000)
Overhead	(iii)	(14,400)
Net benefit		1,400

Advice: It is better to accept the offer because incremental revenue is sufficient to cover the cost.

Working Notes:

	₹
(i) Relevant cost for material	
M1 (3 × 400 × 5.5) (Regular use: Current price)	6,600
[P2 (2 kg × 400 = 800 kg) [800 × 2 (Sub. Use)]	1,600
Part no. 678 (₹ 50 × 400)	20,000
Total	**28,200**

	₹
(ii) Relevant cost for labour	
Skilled [5 hrs × (5 – 1) × 400]	8,000
Semi skilled [5 hrs × 400 × 3]	6,000
Total	**14,000**

Skilled labour cost	**₹ per hr**
Cost to be incurred	500
Less: Benefit to be achieved due to acceptance of offer	(100)
Relevant cost	400

(iii) Overhead cost	₹
Variable overhead	
(₹ 7 × 4 × 400)	11,200
Fixed cost	3,200
	14,400

Problem 11

Novel Accessories have been manufacturing a joy figurate to be fitted on car bonnets. One of the figurate resembles a tiny model of Ashokan pillar with the Lion capital. As the car fitted with these have been mistaken by the public as belonging to Government dignitaries, on a complaint, the police authorities have banned the use of this on car bonnets. The company is now left with an inventory of 8,000 units of this figurette and manufacturing costs per unit are as follows:

	₹
Material	1.20
Labour	0.80
Fixed overheads	0.50
Total	**2.50**

Prior to being banned the selling price was ₹ 3 per unit. The alternative courses of action:

(i) Sell the units as scrap metal for ₹ 6,500.

(ii) Rework them by putting a base under them which would allow them to be sold as Drawing Room curios at a price of ₹ 3.20 each. Such work would require ₹ 2 per unit of additional labour and a fixed overhead charge of ₹ 1 each would be entailed in terms of the company's absorption costing system. No further materials would be required.

(iii) Melt them down and use the metal as a substitute in a strong selling line where the metal currently used costs 50 per cent more than the material used in the figurate. This process would incur a materials loss of three eights of the original metal.

Required: You are required to examine each of these alternatives and arrive at the decisions, which would result in the greatest benefit to the company.

Solution

STATEMENT OF COMPARATIVE BENEFIT

A_0 *Sale as Scrap*		A_1 *Rework*		A_2	
	₹		₹		₹
Revenue	6,500	Revenue	25,600	Saving in	9,000
Less: Cost	Nil	– Cost		Cost of material	
		Material	–	(1.2 × 150%) × 8000 × 5/8)	
		Labour (8,000 × 2)	16,000		
		Fixed overhead	(Sunk cost)		
Net benefit	6,500		9,600		9,000

It is better to select the A[1] alternative.

Problem 12

The Z Company owns and operates a chain of 25 stores. Budgeted data for the Garden Stores is as follows:

	₹
Annual sales	4,25,000
Annual cost of goods sold and other operating expenses	3,82,000
Annual building ownership costs (not included above)	20,000

The company can lease the building to a large flower shop for ₹ 4,000 per month.

Decide whether to continue operations of this store or to lease using.

1. The total project (or comparative statement approach)
2. The incremental (or relevant cost) approach
3. The opportunity cost approach.

Solution

(i) Comparative Approach

STATEMENT OF COMPARATIVE COST

A1 : Store	₹	*A2 : Lease*	₹
Revenue	4,25,000	Revenue	48,000
Less: Cost	(3,82,000)	*Less:* Cost	—
Building Cost	—		
Net benefit	**43,000**	**Net benefit**	**48,000**

It is better to select A2 option is lease.

(ii) Differential Approach

STATEMENT OF COST AND BENEFIT

Particulars	*A1*
Difference in revenue (4,25,000 – 48,000)	3,77,000
Difference in cost	3,82,000
Net benefit on A1 over A2	(5,000)

A1 has less benefit than A2 by 5,000.

(iii) Opportunity Lost Approach

STATEMENT OF COST AND BENEFIT

Revenue	48,000
– Cost to be incurred	–
– Opportunity Cost	(43,000)
	5,000

Working Notes:

(i) Net benefit in A2 over A1 — 5,000

(ii) For Opportunity Cost Approach

Benefit of A1 = Opportunity Cost of A2

Revenue	4,25,000
– Cost	(3,82,000)
Benefit of A1	43,000

Becomes opportunity cost for A2.

(iii) Building ownership cost to be termed as *sunk cost* due to future obligation already decided.

Problem 13

A Company accepts a one-year contract which will require four skilled employees. The four skilled employees could be recruited on a one-year contract at a cost of ₹ 40,000 per employee. The employees would be supervised by an existing manager who earns ₹ 60,000 per annum. It is expected that supervision of the contract would take 10% of the manager's time.

Instead of recruiting new employees, the company could retrain some existing employees who currently earn ₹ 30,000 per year. The training would cost ₹ 15,000 in total. If these employees were used they would need to be replaced at a total cost of ₹ 1,00,000.

The relevant labour cost of the contract is:

A ₹ 1,00,000
B ₹ 1,15,000
C ₹ 1,35,000
D ₹ 1,41,000
E ₹ 1,66,000

Solution

Incremental cost of new employees = ₹ 40,000 × 4 = ₹ 1,60,000

Supervision is not an incremental cost.

Incremental costs of retaining

Training	₹ 15,000
Replacement cost	₹ 1,00,000
	₹ 1,15,000

Retaining is the cheaper alternative and therefore the relevant cost of the contract is ₹ 1,15,000.

Problem 14

You have received a request from EXE Plc. to provide a quotation for the manufacture of a specialised piece of equipment. This would be a one-off order, in excess of normal budgeted production. The following cost estimate has already been prepared:

Particulars			₹
Direct materials			
Steel	10 sq metre at ₹ 5.00 per sq metre	1	50
Brass fittings		2	20
Direct labour			
Skilled	25 hours at ₹ 8.00 Per hour	3	200
Semi-skilled	10 hours at ₹ 5.00 per hour	4	50
Overhead	35 hours at ₹ 10.00 per hour	5	350
Estimate time		6	100
			770
Administrative overhead			
At 20% of production cost		7	154
			924
Profit at 25% of total cost Selling price		8	231
Selling price			**1,155**

Notes:

1. The steel is regularly used, and has a current stock value of ₹ 5.00 per sq metre. There are currently 100 sq meters in stock. The steel is readily available at a price of ₹ 5.50 per sq metre.
2. The brass fittings would have to be bought specifically for this job: a supplier has quoted price of ₹ 20 for the fittings required.
3. The skilled labour is currently employed by your company and paid at a rate of ₹ 8.00 per hour. If this job were undertaken it would be necessary either to work 25 hours overtime which would be paid at time plus one half or to reduce production of another product which earns a contribution of ₹ 13.00 per hour.
4. The semi-skilled labour currently has sufficient paid idle time to be able to complete this work.
5. The overhead absorption rate includes power costs which are directly related to machine usage. If this job was undertaken, it is estimated that the machine time required would be 10 hours. The machines incur power costs of ₹ 0.75 per hour. There are no other overhead costs which can be specifically identified with this job.
6. The cost of the estimating time is that attributed to the four hours taken by the engineers to analyze the drawings and determine the cost estimate given above.
7. It is company policy to add 20% on to the production cost as an allowance against administration costs associated with the jobs accepted.
8. This is the standard profit added by your company as part of its pricing policy.

Required: On the basis of relevant cost, prepare the lowest cost estimate that could be used as the basis for a quotation. Explain briefly your reasons for using each of the values in your estimate.

Solution

CALCULATION OF MINIMUM SELLING PRICE

Particulars	₹
Direct materials: Steel	55.00
Brass Fittings	20.00
Direct Labour: Skilled	300.00
Semi-skilled	—
Overhead	7.50
Estimating time	—
Administration	—
Relevant cost of the order	**382.50**

Notes:

(i) Using the materials for the order will result in them having to be replaced. Therefore, future cash outflows will increase by ₹ 55.

(ii) Future cash outflows of ₹ 20 will be incurred.

(iii) The required labour hours can be obtained by reducing production of another product involving a lost contribution before deducting the labour cost of ₹ 21 (₹ 13 + ₹ 8) per hour (Note: that the labour cost will be incurred for all alternatives and therefore is not an incremental cash flow). Alternatively, the company can pay additional wages involving overtime of ₹ 300 (25 hours × ₹ 12). Therefore the latter course of action is the most economical and the incremental cash flows from undertaking the order will be ₹ 300.

(iv) No incremental cost is involved since the alternative is paid idle time.

(v) The only incremental cost is power consisting of 10 hours at ₹ 0.75 per hour.

(vi) Estimating time is a sunk cost.

(vii) Administration does not involve any incremental cash flows.

Problem 15

The production manager of your organization has approached you for some costing advice on project X, a one-off order form overseas that he intends to tender for. The costs associated with the project are as follows:

	₹
Material A	4000
Material B	8000
Direct labour	6000
Supervision	2000
Overheads	12000
	32000

You ascertain the following:

(i) Material A is in stock and the above was the cost. There is now no other use for material A, other than the above project, within the factory and it would cost ₹ 1,750 to dispose of. Material B would have to be ordered at the cost shown above.

(ii) Direct labour costs of ₹ 6000 relate to workers that will be transferred to this project from another project. Extra labour will need to be recruited to the order project at a cost of ₹ 7000.

(iii) Supervision cost has been charged to the project on the basis of 33-1/3% of labour costs and will be carried out by existing staff within their normal duties.

(iv) Overheads have been charged to the project at the rate of 200% on direct labour.

(v) The company is currently operating at a point above break-even.

(vi) The project will need the utilization of machinery that will have no other use to the company after the project has finished. The machinery will have to be purchased at a cost of ₹ 10000 and then disposed of for ₹ 5,260 at the end of the project.

The production manger tells you that the overseas customer is prepared to pay up to a maximum of ₹ 30,000 for the project and a competitor is prepared to accept the order at that price. He also informs you the minimum that he can charge is ₹ 40,000 as the above costs show ₹ 32,000, and this does not take into consideration the cost of the machine and profit to be taken on the project.

Required:

(a) *Cost the project for the production manager, clearly stating how you have arrived at your figures and giving reasons for the exclusion of other figures.*

(b) *Write a report to the production manager stating whether the organization should go ahead with the tender for the project, the reasons why and the price, bearing in mind that the competitor is prepared to undertake the project for ₹ 30000.*

Note: *The project should only be undertaken if it shows a profit.*

(c) *State four non-monetary factors that should be taken into account before tendering for this project.*

(d) *What would be your advice if you were told that the organization was operating below break-even point? Give reasons for your advice.*

Solution

(a)

Particulars	*Relevant Costs of the project*
Material A	(1,750)
Material B	8,000
Direct labour	7,000
Net cost of machinery	4,750
Relevant cost	18,000
Contract price	30,000
Contribution	12,000

Notes:

(i) *There is saving in material cost of ₹ 1,750 if material A is not used.*

(ii) *The actual cost of material B represents the incremental cost.*

(iii) *The hiring of the labour on the other contract represents the additional cash flows of undertaking this contract.*

(iv) *The net cost of purchasing the machinery represents the additional cash flows associated with the contract.*

(v) (a) *Supervision and overheads will still continue even if the contract is not accepted and are therefore irrelevant.*

(b) The report should indicate that the cost given in the question do not represent incremental cash flows arising from undertaking the contract. As the company is operating at an activity level in excess of break-even point any sales revenue in excess of ₹ 18,000 incremental costs will provide an additional contribution which will result in an increase in profits. Assuming that the company has spare capacity, and that a competitor is prepared to accept the order at ₹ 30000, then a tender price slightly below ₹ 30,000 would be appropriate.

(c) Before accepting the contract the following non-monetary factors should be considered.

(i) *Is there sufficient spare capacity to undertake the project?*

(ii) *Is the overseas customer credit worthy?*

(iii) *Has the workforce the necessary skills to undertake the project?*

(iv) *Is the contract likely to result in repeat business with the customer?*

(d) If the company were operating below the break-event point, acceptance of the order would provide a further contribution towards fixed costs and reduce the existing loss. In the short term it is better to accept the order and reduce the total loss but if, in the long run, there are not enough orders to generate sufficient contributions to cover total fixed cost, and then the company will not survive.

Problem 16

Intervero Ltd., a small engineering company, operated a job order costing system. It has been invited lo tender for a comparatively large job, which is outside the range of its normal activities, and since there is surplus capacity, the management is keen to quote as low a price as possible. It is decided that the opportunity should be treated in isolation without any possibility of its leading to further work of a similar nature (although such a possibility does exist). A low price will not have repercussions on Intervero's regular work. The estimating department has spent 100 hours on work in connection with the quotation and they have incurred traveling expense of ₹ 550 in connection with a visit to the prospective customers' factory. The following cost estimates has been prepared on the basis of their study.

	Inquiry 205 H 81 Cost Estimate (₹)
Direct material and components:	
2,000 units of A at ₹ 25 per unit	50,000
200 units of B at ₹ 10 per unit	2,000
Other material and components to be bought	12,500
	64,500
Direct labour:	
700 hrs. of skilled labour at ₹ 3.50 per hour	2,450
1,500 hrs of unskilled labour at ₹ 2 per hour	3,000
Overhead:	
Department P-200 hrs. at ₹ 25 per hour	5,000
Department Q-400 hrs. at ₹ 20 per hour	8,000
Estimating department:	
100 hours at ₹ 5 per hour	500
Travelling expenses	550
Planning department:	
300 hrs. at ₹ 5 per hour	1,500
	85,500

The following information has been brought together:

1. **Material A:** This is a regular stock item. The stock holding is more than sufficient for this job. The material currently held has an average cost of ₹ 25 per unit but the current replacement cost is ₹ 20 per unit.
2. **Material B:** A stock of 4,000 units of B is currently held in the stores. This material is slow moving and the stock is the residue of a batch bought seven years ago at a cost of ₹ 10 per unit. B currently costs ₹ 24 per unit but the resale value is only ₹ 18 per unit. A foreman has pointed out that B could be used as a substitute for another type of regularly used raw material which costs ₹ 20 per unit.
3. **Direct Labour:** The work force is paid on a time basis. The company has adopted no redundancy policies which mean that skilled workers are frequently moved to jobs which do not make proper use of their skills. The wages included in the cost estimate are for the mix of

labour which the job ideally requires. It seems likely, if the job is obtained then most of the 2,200 hours of direct labour will be performed by skilled staff receiving ₹ 3.50 per hour.

4. **Overhead: Department P:** It is a department of Intervero Ltd., that is working at full capacity. The department is treated as a profit centre and it uses a transfer price of ₹ 25 per hour for charging out its processing time to other departments. This charge is calculated as follows:

Particulars	₹
Estimated variable cost per machine hour	10
Fixed departmental overhead	8
Departmental profit	7
Total	**25**

Department P's facilities are frequently hired out to other firms and a charge of ₹ 30 per hour is made. There is a steady demand from outside customers for the use of these facilities.

5. **Overhead: Department Q** uses a transfer price of ₹ 20 for charging out machine processing time to other Department. This charge is calculated as follows:

Particulars	₹
Estimated variable cost per machine hour	8
Fixed departmental overhead	9
Departmental profit	3
Total	**20**

6. **Estimating department:** This department charges out its time to specific jobs using a rate of ₹ 5 per hour. The average wage rate within the department is ₹ 2.50 per hour but the higher rate is justified as being necessary to cover departmental overheads and the work done on unsuccessful quotations.
7. **Planning department:** This department also uses a charging out rate which is intended to cover all departmental costs.
8. The offer received for the above contract is ₹ 70,000.

Required: You are required to restate the cost estimate by using an opportunity cost approach. Make any assumptions that you deem to be necessary and briefly justify each of the figures that you give.

Solution

STATEMENT OF COST OF INTEVERO LTD.

Particulars	₹
Direct material:	
A: 2,000 units @ ₹ 20 (Refer to Working Note 1)	40,000
B: 200 units @ ₹ 20 (refer to Working Note 2)	4,000
Direct labour (skilled)	12,500
Direct labour (unskilled) (refer to Working Note 3)	Sunk

Overheads:	
Dept. P: 200 hrs @ ₹ 30 (refer to Working Note 4)	6,000
Dept. Q: 400 hrs. @ ₹ 8	3,200
Estimating department	Sunk
Planning department	Sunk
Total cost	**65,700**

Working Notes:

(i) *Material A is a regularly used item. Therefore, the present stock is not meant for this contract. Hence, the replacement cost is considered.*

(ii) *Material B will be sold if not used for this contract. Therefore, the resale value (₹ 20 or ₹ 18 whichever is more should be considered).*

(iii) *The entire job will be performed by skilled workers (unskilled jobs also). This implies skilled workers are idle at present and since the company follows no redundancy policy and their wages will be paid on time basis whether the contract is accepted or not. Hence they are treated as a sunk cost.*

(iv) ***Department** P is a profit centre and is working at full capacity at present and has a steady demand from outside for its facilities at ₹ 30 per hour. Therefore, we should consider this ₹ 30 per hr. as relevant (out of pocket cost ₹ 10 + opportunity cost of ₹ 20).*

(v) ***Department Q:** only the out of pocket costs being the variable overheads of ₹ 8 per hr, should be considered.*

(vi) *All other costs mentioned are sunk costs.*

Conclusion: We should accept this offer.

Problem 17

AB Limited has just completed production of an item of special equipment for a customer – ST Limited, only to be notified that the customer has gone into liquidation. After much effort the sales manager has managed lo locate one potential buyer, VW Limited, that has indicated that it might be prepared to buy machine if certain conversion work could be carried out.

The selling price of the machine to the original buyer has been fixed at ₹ 25,300 and had included as estimated normal profit markup of 10% on total costs. The costs incurred in the manufacture of the machine were:

Particulars	(₹)
Direct Material	9,500
Direct Wages	6,000
Overheads: Variable	1,500
Fixed Production	5,000
Fixed, Selling and Administration	1,000
Total	**23,000**

If the machine is converted production, management estimates that the following extra work would be needed.

Direct Material at Cost ₹ 1,600

The materials for the conversion are at stock. If not needed for the conversion, they could be used in the production of another machine in place of materials that would currently cost ₹ 1,900.

Direct Wages

Department L: 3 men for 4 weeks at ₹ 75 per man/week

Department M: 1 man for 4 weeks at ₹ 60 per man/week

The conversion would be carried out in two departments. Department L is currently extremely busy and it is estimated that its contribution to overhead and profits is ₹ 2.50 per ₹ 1 of labour.

Department M is very short of work. For organisational reason its labour force cannot be reduced below its present level of four employees, all of whom are paid at the standard wage of ₹ 60 per week. The load of work on these employees is however only 40% of their standard capacity.

Variable Overhead

20% of direct wages

Fixed Production Overhead:

Department L: 83-1/3% of direct wages.

Department M: 25% of direct wages.

The following additional information is available:

1. In the original machine there are three types of basic materials:
   (a) Type P would be sold to a scrap merchant for ₹ 1,500.
   (b) Type Q would be sold to the scrap merchant for ₹ 1,000 but it would cost ₹ 90 to put it into a suitable condition for sale.
   (c) Type R would need to be scrapped at a cost to AB limited of ₹ 300.
2. The design and specification of the original machine could be sold overseas for a sum of ₹ 750 if the machine is scrapped.
3. An additional temporary supervisor would have to be engaged for the conversion work at a cost of ₹ 450. It is the company's normal practice to charge supervision to fixed overhead.
4. Customer ST Limited paid a non-returnable deposit to the company of 12% of the selling price.

Required: You are required to calculate the minimum price the AB Limited should accept from VW Limited for the converted machine.

Solution

STATEMENT OF RELEVANT COST

Particulars	*W.N. No.*	*Amount (₹)*
Cost to be incurred	(ii)	5,728
Add: Benefit to be lost	(iii)	3,160
Less: Benefit to be achieved	(iv)	(300)
Minimum price		8,588

Working Notes:

(i) Cost incurred ₹ 23,000 is past cost

(ii) **Cost to be incurred** — ₹

(a) Material (Sub use) — 1,900

(b) Labour*

Labour cost + Contribution lost

L (900 + 2250) — 3,150

M (1 × 4 × 60): permanent & idle — –

(c)	Variable overhead 20% of wages	
	L (20% of 75 = 15) × 3 × 4 = 180	
	M (20% of 60 = 12) × 1 × 4 = 48	228
	Additional supervisor salary	450
	Cost to be incurred	5,728
	*Labour cost (3 × 4 × 75) = ₹ 900	
	Contribution lost = (2.5 × 900) = 2,250	
(iii)	**Benefit to be lost:**	
	Sale of Material "p"	1,500
	Sale of Material Q(1,000 – 90)	910
	Sale of Design	750
		3,160
(iv)	**Benefit to be achieved**	
	Removal Cost of 'R'	300
	Total	**300**

Problem 18

Tiptop Textile manufactures a wide range of fashion fabrics. The company is considering whether to add a further product the 'Superb' to the range. A market research survey recently undertaken at a cost of ₹ 50,000 suggests that demand for the 'Superb' will last for only one year, during which 50,000 units could be sold at ₹ 18 per unit.

Production and sale of 'Superb' would take place evenly throughout the year. The following information is available regarding the cost of manufacturing 'Superb'.

Raw Material: Each 'Superb' would require three types of raw material Posh, Flash and Splash. Quantities required, current stock levels and cost of each raw material are shown below. Posh is used regularly by the company and stocks are replaced as they are used. The current stock of Flash is the result of overbuying-for an earlier contract. The material is not used regularly by Tiptop Textiles and any stock that was not used to manufacture 'Superb' would be sold. The company does not carry a stock of Splash and the units required would be specially purchased.

Raw Material	*Quantity Reqd. Per Unit of*	*Current Stock Level (meters)*	*Cost Per Meter of Raw Material*		
			Original Cost (₹)	*Current Replacement Cost (₹)*	*Current Resale Value (₹)*
Posh	1.00	1,00,000	2.10	2.50	1.80
Flash	2.00	60,000	3.30	2.80	1.10
Splash	0.5	0	–	5.50	5.00

Labour: Production of each 'Superb' would require a quarter of an hour of skilled labour and two hours of unskilled labour. Current wage rates are ₹ 3 per hour for skilled labour and ₹ 2 per hour for unskilled labour. In addition, one foreman would be required to devote all his working time for one year in supervision of the production of Superb. He is currently paid an annual salary of ₹ 15,000. Tiptop Textiles is currently finding it very difficult to get skilled labour. The skilled workers needed to manufacture 'Superb' were transferred from another job on which they were learning a contribution surplus of ₹ 1.50 per labour hour, comprising sales revenue of ₹ 10.00 less skilled labour

Wages of ₹ 3.00 and other variable costs of ₹ 5.50. It would not be possible to employ additional skilled labour during the coming year.

If 'Superb' are not manufactured, the company expects to have an available 2,00,000 surplus unskilled labour hours during the coming year. Because the company intends to expand in future, it has decided not to terminate the services of any unskilled worker in the foreseeable future. The foreman is due to retire immediately on an annual pension payable by the company of ₹ 6,000. He has been prevailed upon to stay on for a further year and to defer his pension for one year in return for his annual salary.

Machinery: Two machines would be required to manufacture 'Superb' MT 4 and MT 7. Details of each machine are as under:

	Start of the year Amount (₹)	*End of the year Amount (₹)*
MT 4: Replacement cost	80,000	65,000
Real value	60,000	47,000
MT 7: Replacement cost	13,000	9,000
Resale value	11,000	8,000

Straight-line depreciation has been charged on each machine for each year of its life. Tiptop Textiles owns a number of MT 4 machines, which are used regularly on various products. Each MT 4 is replaced as soon as it reaches the end of its usual life.

MT 7 machines are no longer used and the one which would be used for 'Superb' is the only one the company now has. If it was not used to produce 'Superb', it would be sold immediately.

Overheads: A predetermined rate of recovery for overhead is in operation and the fixed overheads are recovered fully from the regular production at ₹ 3.50 per labour hour. Variable overhead costs for Superb are estimated at ₹ 1.20 per unit produced. For the decision-making, incremental costs based upon relevant cost and opportunity costs are usually computed.

Require: You are required to compute such a cost sheet for 'Superb' with all details of material, labour, overhead, etc., substantiating the figures with necessary explanations.

Solution

STATEMENT OF COST AND BENEFIT

Particulars	*Working Note*	₹
Revenue: (18 × 50,000)		9,00,000
Less: Relevant Cost		
Material	(ii)	4,40,500
Labour	(iii)	56,250
Foreman Salary: (15,000 – 6,000)	(iv)	9,000
Variable Overhead: 1.2 × 50,000	(vi)	60,000
Machinery	(v)	18,000
	Net Benefit	**3,16,250**

It is better to accept the production of Superb.

Working Notes:

(i) Market survey of ₹ 50,000 is sunk cost

(ii) Relevant Cost for Material

Particulars			₹
Posh	1 mtr × 50,000 × 2.5		1,25,000
(Regular use)	Current purchase cost		
Flash	Out of stock: CPP		
Requirement		40,000 × 2.8	1,12,000
= 50,000 × 2 = 1,00,000		60,000 × 1.1	66,000
	Obsolete : Resale Value		
Splash	Stock		
Reg: 50,000 × 0.5 = 25,000	Out of stock: CPP	(25,000 × 5.5)	
	Replacement cost		1,37,500
	Total relevant cost		**4,40,500**

(iii) **Skilled labour** (1/4 hour × 50,000) × (3 + 1.5)* — 56,250

Unskilled Labour (permanent & idle) — Nil

***Contribution lost for skilled labour**

Revenue	10
– Labour	(3)
– Other V.C.	(5.5)
Contribution/hour	1.5

(iv) **Pension**

If Superb is not to be produced.

Salary	15,000
– benefit to be achieved by nonpayment of pension	(6,000)
Relevant cost	9,000

(v) **Machinery Cost**

MT4 (Regular use)	
Current Purchase cost	80,000
– transfer to regular stock	(65,000)
Difference of replacement cost	15,000
MT7	
Benefit to be lost	11,000
– benefit achieved	(8,000)
Difference Resale value	3,000

(vi) **Variable Overhead always to be incurred during the actual working hours**

Labour cost = Rate × Actual pay hour.

Variable overhead = Rate × Actual working hour

Variable overhead = % on labour it means % to be applied on rate.

Problem 19

Aylett and Co. Ltd. has been offered a contract, if accepted would significantly increase next year's activity levels. The contract requires the production of 20,000 kg of product X and specifies a contract price of ₹ 100 per kg The resources used in the production of each kg of X include the following:

Resources per kg. of Product X	
Labour grade	1 2 hours
Grade	2 6 hours
Materials	A 2 units
	B 1 Liter

Grade 1 labour is highly skilled and although it is currently under-utilised in the firm it is Aylett's policy to continue to pay grade 1 labour in full. Acceptance of the contract would reduce the idle-time of grade 1 labour. Idle time payments are treated as non-production overheads.

Grade 2 is unskilled labour with a high turnover and may be considered a variable cost. The Costs to Aylett of each type of labour are:

Grade 1 ₹ 4 per hour

Grade 2 ₹ 2 per hour

The materials required to fulfill the contract would be drawn from those materials already in stock. Material A are widely used within the firm and any usage for this contract will necessitate replacement. Material B were purchased to fulfill an expected order that was not received, if material B is not used for the contract, it will be sold. For accounting purposes FIFO is used. The various values and costs for A and B are:

VALUE AND COSTS FOR MATERIALS A AND B

	A *Per unit* ₹	*B* *Per Liter* ₹
Book Value	8	30
Replacement cost	10	32
Net realisable value	9	25

A single recover rate for fixed factory overheads is used throughout the firm even through some fixed production overheads could be attributed to single products or departments. The overhead is recovered per productive labour hour and initial estimates of next year's activity, which excludes the current contract, show fixed production overheads of ₹ 6,00,000 and productive labour hours of 3,00,000. Acceptance of the contract would increase fixed production overheads by ₹ 2,28,000. Variable production overheads are accurately estimated at ₹ 3 per productive hour.

Acceptance of the contract would be expected to encroach on the sale and production of another product Y, that is also made by Aylett Ltd. It is estimated that sales of Y, would then decrease by 5,000 units in the next year only. However this forecast reduction in sales of Y would enable attributable fixed factory overheads of ₹ 58,000 to be avoided. Information on Y is as follows:

Particulars	*Per unit*
Sales price	₹ 70
Labour – grade 2	4 hours
Materials – relevant costs	₹ 12

All activity undertaken by Aylett is job costed using full, absorption, costing in order to derive a profit figure for each contract. If the contract for X is accepted it will be treated as a separate job for routine costing purposes. The decision to accept or reject the contract will be taken in sufficient time to enable its estimated, effects to be incorporated in the next year's budgets and also in the calculations carried out to derive the overhead recovery rate to be used in the forthcoming year.

Required: Advise Aylett on the desirability of the contract.

Solution

STATEMENT OF COST AND BENEFIT

Particulars	*Working Note No.*	₹
Revenue [20,000 × 100]		20,00,000
Less: Relevant Cost		
Material	(i)	(9,00,000)
Labour	(ii)	(2,40,000)
Avoidable Fixed Cost		(2,28,000)
Variable Overhead 3 × (40,000 + 1,20,000 hr)		(4,80,000)
Opportunity Cost (benefit lost) on sale of Y	(iii)	(1,32,000)
Net benefit		20,000

Conclusion: It is better to accept the offer of 2,00,000 unit of "X" due to incremental net benefit of ₹ 20,000.

Working Notes:

(i) Relevant Cost for Material

	₹
A: [2 unit × 20,000 × 10]	4,00,000
(Regular use: Replacement cost)	
B: Obsolete Resale Value [1 ltr. × 20,000 × 25]	5,00,000
Total	9,00,000

(ii) Relevant Cost for Labour

Grade - I	
(permanent: not busy) [2 hr. × 20,000 × 4]	Nil
Grade - II	
(Casual + not busy) [6 hr × 20,000 × 2]	2,40,000
Total	2,40,000

(iii) Benefit from Sale of 5000 Unit of Y

	₹
Revenue [5,000 × ₹ 70]	3,50,000
Less: Material [12 × 5,000]	(60,000)
Labour [4 hours × 5,000 × 2]	(40,000)
Variable overhead [4 hour × 5,000 × 3]	(60,000)
Fixed overhead (Avoidance) inrelation with 'Y'	(58,000)
Profit	**1,32,000**

Problem 20

W Ltd. is to produce a new product in a short-term venture which will utilize some obsolete materials and expected spare capacity. The new product will be advertised in Quarter 1 with production and sales taking place in Quarter II. No further production or sales are anticipated.

Sales volumes are uncertain but will be to some extent a function of sales price. The possible sales volumes and the advert. Costs associated with each potential sales price are as follows:

Sales Price ₹ 20 Per Units		*Sales Price ₹ 25 Per Unit*		*Sales Price ₹ 40 Per Unit*	
Sales volume (Units 000's)	*Prob.*	*Sales volume (Units 000's)*	*Prob.*	*Sales volume (Units 000's)*	*Prob.*
4	0.1	2	0.1		
6	0.4	5	0.2	3	0.5
8	0.5	6	0.2	10	0.2
–	–	8	0.5	15	0.3
–	–		0.5		0.3
Adv. Cost ₹ 20,000		₹ 50,000		₹ 1,00,000	

The resources used in the production of each unit of the product are:

Production Labour:

Grade – I 2 hours
Grade – II 1 hours

Materials:

X - 1 unit
Y - 2 units

The normal cost per hour of labour is

Grade – I – ₹ 2, Grade – II – ₹ 3

However, before considering the effects of the current venture there is expected to be 4,000 hours of idle time for each grade of labour in Quarter II. Idle time is paid at the normal rates.

Material X is in stock at a book value of ₹ 8 per unit but is widely used within the firm and any usage for the purpose of this venture will require replacing. Replacement cost is ₹ 9 per unit.

Material Y is obsolete stock. There are 16,000 units in stock.

At a book value of ₹ 3.50 per unit and any stock not used will have to be disposed of at a cost to W Ltd of ₹ 3 per unit. Further quantities of Y can be purchased for ₹ 4 per unit.

Overhead recovery rates are:

Variable overhead ₹ 2 per direct labour hour worked. Fixed overhead ₹ 3 per direct labour hour worked. Total fixed overheads will not alter as a result of the current venture.

Feedback from advertising will enable the exact demand to be determined at the end of Quarter I and production in Quarter II will be set to equal that demand. However, it is necessary to decide now on the sales price in order that it can be incorporated into the advertising campaign.

Required: Calculate the expected money value of the venture at each sale price and on the basis of this, advice W Ltd. of its best course of action.

Solution

Selling price = ₹ 25 Expected sale = 6,800 [4,000 × 0.1 + 6,000 × 0.4 + 8,000 × 0.5]
Selling price = ₹ 20 Expected sale = 6,400 [2,000 × 0.1 + 5,000 × 0.2 + 6,000 × 0.2 + 8,000 × 0.5]
Selling price = ₹ 40 Expected sale = 8,000 [3,000 × 0.5 + 10,000 × 0.2 + 15,000 × 0.3]

STATEMENT OF COMPARATIVE COST & BENEFIT

	S.P. = 20	S.P. = 25	S.P. = 40
Quantity	Qty = 6800	Qty. = 6,400	Qty. = 8,000
Revenue	1,36,000	1,60,000	3,20,000
Less: Cost			
Labour	(27,600)	(24,800)	(36,000)
Material	(20,400)	(19,200)	(24,000)
Variable overhead	(40,800)	(38,400)	(48,000)
	(2 × (2 hr + 1 hr) × 6800	(2 × 3hr × 6,400)	(2 × 3 × 8,000)
Advertising cost	(20,000)	(50,000)	(1,00,000
Benefit	27,200	27,600	1,12,000

It is better to select the selling price 40 with a quantity 8,000 units because of higher benefit.

Working Notes:

(i) Calculation of Labour Cost

	Qty. 6,800	Qty. 6,400	Qty. 8,000
Grade I	2 hr × 6,800	2 hr × 6,400	2 hr × 8,000
	= 13,600 hr	= 12,800 hr	16,000 hr
Less: Idle hours	4,000 hr	4,000 hr	4,000 hr
Extra hours needed	9,600	8,800	12,000
Cost per hour	₹ 2	₹ 2	₹ 2
(a) Extra cost	₹ 19,200	₹ 17,600	₹ 24,000
Grade II	1 hr × 6,800 = 6,800 hr	6,400 × 1hr = 6,400 hr	8,000 × 1hr = 8,000 hr
Less: Idle hour	(4,000)	(4,000)	(4,000)
	= 2,800	= 2,400	= 4,000
(b) Extra Cost (2,800 × ₹ 3)	= ₹ 8,400	(2,400 × 3) = ₹ 7,200	(4,000 × 3) = 12,000
Total Labour Cost (a + b)	27,600	24,800	36,000

(ii) Relevant Cost for Material

		Qty. 6,800		6,400		8,000
X: Regular use						
(i)	6,800 × 1 × 9 =	61,200	6,400 × 1 × 9 =	57,600	8,000 × 1 × 9 =	72,000
(ii)	Y 6,800 × 2 × 3 =	(40,800)	6,400 × 2 × 3 =	(38,400)	8,000 × 2 × 3 =	(48,000)
Total Material Cost (i + ii)		20,400		19,200		24,000

Note: In case of Y: benefit to be advised

Problem 21

A construction company has accepted contract AX and work thereon is about to begin. However, the company has received an offer for another contract BX. The company cannot, due to certain constraints, take up both the contracts simultaneously. In case the company is desirous of taking up contract BX, it can get the first contract AX rescinded upon payment of a penalty for ₹ 70,000.

ESTIMATES RELATING TO CONTRACT A AND B

Particulars	*Contract AX* ₹	*Contract BX* ₹
* Material X - in stock at original cost	54,000	–
Material Y - in stock at original cost	–	62,000
** Material X - firm orders placed at original cost	76,000	–
Material X - not yet ordered (at current cost)	1,50,000	–
Material Z- not yet ordered (at current cost)		1,78,000
Labour - to be engaged and paid for	2,15,000	2,75,000
Site Management costs	85,000	85,000
Travel and other expenses (To be incur)	17,000	14,000
Depreciation of plant	24,000	32,000
Interest on capital at 12%	12,800	16,000
Head office exp. allocated to contracts	31,690	33,100
Total	6,65,490	6,95,100
Contract price	7,20,000	8,80,000
Estimated Profit	54,510	1,84,900

The following additional information is available:

- Material X is not in regular use. It can be used as a substitute for other materials, which are currently quoted at 10% less than the original cost of X.
- Material Y is in regular use and its price has doubled since it was purchased. Its net realizable value if sold will be its new price less 15% it can, however, be kept in store for use in other contracts to be taken up in the next year.
- If contracts AX is undertaken, a part of the plant having spare capacity can be hired out for a rental of ₹ 15,000. It is the policy of the company to charge notional interest on the estimated working capital at 12% per annum.
- Either of two contracts can be completed by 31 st March 2003, which is the close of the company's financial year. Site management cost is fixed.
- ** If the order of material of ₹ 76,000 which has been placed for contract AX, now the order may be cancelled upon on payment of ₹ 7,600 as penalty.

Required: Using the relevancy of cost concept, prepare a comparative statement to show the net benefit resulting from each contract; advice the management of the company as to which of two contracts should be undertaken.

Solution

STATEMENT OF COST AND BENEFIT

Particulars	*AX* ₹	*BX* ₹
Revenue	7,20,000	8,80,000
Less: Cost		
Material (X)	(48,600)	(1,24,000)
Material (X)	(76,000)	(1,78,000)
Material (X) cost to be incurred	(1,50,000)	
Labour	(2,15,000)	(2,75,000)
Site management cost sunk (Central place)	—	—

Travel & other expenses	(17,000)	(14,000)
Depreciation	—	—
Interest on capital (Not to be taken as opportunity cost in short term	—	—
Head office expenses	—	—
Benefit	2,13,400	2,89,000
+ Benefit achieved due to offer	15,000	
Total benefit	**2,28,400**	**2,89,000**

STATEMENT OF FINAL COST AND BENEFIT (IN FAVOUR OF BX OVER AX)

		₹
Incremental Revenue	(2,89,000 – 2,28,400)	60,600
Less: Penalty in cancellation of AX	70,000	
Penalty on cancellation of "X" order	7,600	(77,600)
Net Benefit		**(17,000)**

Decision: It is not better to accept the contract "BX" after cancellation contract "AX" because the incremental revenue 60,600 is not sufficient to cover the penalty cost of ₹ 77,600.

Working Notes:

(i) *Site Management cost is fixed, hence to be termed as opportunity cost (future obligation and sunk cost).*

(ii) *Interest on capital is although called opportunity cost but to be considered in long term. Investment decision.*

(iii) *Head office expense allocation also to be termed as sunk because change in opportunity does not amount to change in cash outflows.*

Problem 22

A company manufactures a wide range of fashion fabric. The company is considering whether to add a further product "BEST" to the range. A market researcher survey recently undertaken at a cost of ₹ 1,00,000 suggest that demand for "BEST" will last for only year during which 50,000 unit could be sold at ₹ 1,000 per unit.

The following information is available regarding the cost of manufacture "BEST".

Raw material: Each product requires four types of raw material M1, M2, M3, M4 .

M1: For every unit of best, one kg of M1 is required. At present material M1 is not available in stock. Current resale value of M1, is ₹ 2 per kg and Current replacement cost of M1 is ₹ 2 kg.

M2: Each unit of best requires two units of M2. The current stock of M2 are 1,50,000 units lying in godown, which has no other use. The current resale value is ₹ 2 per unit or it can be used in place of another material R2, current replacement cost of R 2 is ₹ 3 per unit.

Current replacement cost of M2 is ₹ 4 Per unit.

M3: Material M3 is also in stock but it is unlikely that any additional supply can be obtained for some considerable time because of an industrial dispute. At present time material M3 can be used normally in producing a product Z which has selling price = 450 per unit and total variable cost (excluding cost of material M3) is 100 per unit and one unit of Z requires five units of M3. Each unit of best requires one unit of M3. Current stock available = 2,00,000 units of M3.

Current resale value of M3 = 20 per unit

Current replacement value of M3 – not applicable

Original cost of M3 = ₹ 10 per unit

M4: Current stock = 20,000 units

Each unit of Best requires one unit of M4, if Best is not to be produced then material of M4 need to be disposed at a cost to the Co. of ₹ 2 per unit.

Current replacement cost = 5 per unit.

Labour: Each product requires 2 hour of skilled (grade I), 3 hours unskilled and 4 hours of Semi-skilled labour, Skilled labour (Grade I) rate ₹ 1 per hour and skilled labour (Grade I) is employed on a casual basis.

Unskilled labour is under-utilised & company's policy is to continue to pay unskilled labour (not to be retrenched) current wage rate = 2 per hour.

Semi-skilled labour is presently engaged in meeting the demand for product "L" which required 4 hour of semi-skilled labour. The contribution from sale of 1 unit of "L" = 24 current wage rate of semi-skilled = 2 per hour semi-skilled labours are in short supply.

Supervisory labour cost = ₹ 2,00,000

Supervisory staff will remain whether or not the contract is accepted. Only two of them can replace the other position where salary is ₹ 90,000 if contract not to be accepted.

Foreman Labour Cost: 2,40,000.

Foreman can work on other contracts, which are presently operated by semi-skilled labour at cost of ₹ 2,70,000.

Each product of Best would require 5 hours of highly skilled labour (Grade II). An employee possessing necessary skills is currently paid ₹ 5 per hour. A replacement would however to be obtained at rate of 4 per hour for the work, which would otherwise, were be done by Highly skilled employee (Grade II).

Machinery: One machines would be required to manufacture "Best" i.e., MT 7.

DETAILS OF EACH MACHINE ARE AS UNDER:

	Start of the year ₹	*End of the year* ₹
MT 7: Replacement cost	13,000	9,000
Resale value	11,000	8,000

MT 7 machines are no longer used and the one which would be used for 'Best' is the only one the company now has. If it was not used to produce 'Best', it would be sold immediately.

Overheads: A predetermined rate of recovery for overhead is in operation and the fixed overheads are recovered fully from the regular production at ₹ 3.50 per labour hour. Variable overhead costs for Best are estimated at ₹ 1.20 per unit produced. For the decision-making, incremental costs based upon relevant cost and opportunity costs are usually computed.

Acceptance of the contract would be expected to encroach on the sale and production of another product, Y that is also made by Co. It is estimated that sales of Y, would then decrease by 5,000 units in the next year only. However, this forecast reduction in sales of Y would enable attributable fixed factory overheads of ₹ 58,000 to be avoided. Information on Y is as follows:

	Per Unit
Sales price	₹ 70
Labour-(GradeX)	4 hours (normal rate is 1.00 per hour)
Variable overhead	₹ 1.2 per hour
Materials – relevant costs	₹ 12

All activities undertaken by Co. is job costed using full, absorption, costing in order to derive a profit figure for each contract. If the contract for Best is accepted it will be treated as a separate job for routine costing purposes. The decision to accept or reject the contract will be taken in sufficient time to enable its estimated, effects to be incorporated in the next year's budgets and also in the calculations carried out to derive the overhead recovery rate to be used in the forthcoming year.

Required: Advise Co. on the desirability of the contract.

You are required to compute a cost sheet for 'Best' with all details of material, labour, overhead, etc., substantiating the figures with necessary explanations.

Solution

STATEMENT OF COST FOR 50,000 UNITS OF "BEST"

Particulars	*Working Note No.*	₹
Revenue		5,00,00,000
Less: Relevant cost		
Material	(ii)	(40,10,000)
Labour:		
Grade I and others	(iii)	(20,60,000)
Grade II	(iv)	(10,00,000)
Machinery	(v)	(3,000)
Overheads	(vi)	(60,000)
Opportunity cost	(vii)	(1,88,000)
Net Benefit		**4,26,79,000**

It is better to accept the offer as it results in net benefit of ₹ 4,26,79,000.

Working Notes:

(i) Market survey cost of ₹ 1,00,000 is *termed* as sunk cost and thus has no relevance for future decision.

(ii) Material:

	₹	₹
M1: Requirement 1 × 50,000 = 50,000 kg		
Cost to be incurred due to acceptance of offer (2 × 50,000)	1,00,000	1,00,000
M2: Requirement 2 × 50,000 = 1,00,000 units		
Cost to be incurred due to acceptance of offer =	Nil	Nil
Add: Benefit lost due to acceptance of offer =	3,00,000	3,00,000
Scrap = 2,00,000 *or* used in place of R 2		
Saving = 3 × 10,00,000		
M3: Requirement 1 × 50,000 = 50,000 units		
Cost to be incurred due to acceptance of offer	Nil	
Add: Benefit lost (10,000 units of Z)		
Selling Price	45,00,000	
Variable Cost	10,00,000	35,00,000
Original cost of material to be considered as sunk cost.		
M4: Requirement (1 × 50,000) = 50,000 units		
Cost to be incurred due to acceptance of offer (30,000 × 5)	1,50,000	
Less: Benefit to be achieved due to acceptance of offer i.e. (2 × 20,000)	(40,000)	1,10,000
Relevant cost of Material for 50,000 units = (1,00,000 + 3,00,000 + 35,00,000 + 1,10,000)		**40,10,000**

Labour: Grade I and Others

(iii) Labour

Grade – 1

Skilled – (Requirement 2 × 50,000 = 1,00,000 hrs.)

Skilled labour is of casual nature

A. Relevant cost to be incurred due to acceptance of offer (1 × 1,00,000) = ₹ 1,00,000

Unskilled – (Requirement 3 × 50,000 = 1,50,000 hrs.)

Unskilled labour is of permanent nature, i.e. they cannot be retrenched hence their cost is to be termed as sunk cost for the purpose of calculating cost of Best = Nil

Semi-Skilled – (Requirement 4 × 50,000 = 2,00,000 hrs.)

Labour hrs is of casual nature	
Cost to be incurred due to acceptance of offer (2 × 2,00,000) =	4,00,000
Add: Benefit lost due to acceptance of offer (24/4 × 2,00,000) =	12,00,000
B. Relevant cost due to acceptance of offer	16,00,000

Note 1: Semi-skilled labour is presently engaged in the production of product L which requires 4 units of semi-skilled labour for one unit of product L. So the contribution loss due to acceptance of offer will be equal to contribution which will be otherwise earned (if the offer would not be accepted and the semi skilled labour will be engaged in meeting the demand of L)

Supervisory Labour Cost:

C. Benefit lost due to acceptance of offer	90,000

(As due to the acceptance of offer it will not be possible to save ₹ 90,000 and new recruitments will have to be done at a cost of ₹ 90,000 therefore it will be charged from offer.)

Note 2: As it is given in the question that the supervisor/staff will remain whether or not the contract is accepted, so it will be termed as sunk cost due to future obligation has already been decided so it is not relevant for decision.

Only the cost of two Supervisors is relevant for decision-making because if the contract is not accepted, two supervisors can replace other position as they would not be required then.

Foreman Labour Cost:

D. Increase in outflow of cost due to acceptance of offer	30,000
(i.e. ₹ 2,70,000 in place of ₹ 2,40,000 therefore ₹ 30,000 will	2,40,000
become relevant cost hence, charged from the offer)	2,70,000
Relevant cost of labour for 50,000 units of Best (A + B + C + D)	20,60,000

(iv) **Grade II**

Highly skilled labour: Requirement (5 × 50,000) =	2,50,000 hrs.
Labour is of casual nature	
Cost to be incurred due to acceptance of offer (4 x 2,50,000) =	₹ 10,00,000
Relevant cost	₹ 10,00,000

(v) **Machinery**

MT 7: Machinery is of no use	
Hence difference in resale value becomes benefit lost (11,000 – 8,000)	3,000
Relevant cost of machinery for 50,000 units of Best	3,000

(iv) Cost to be incurred due to acceptance of offer, i.e. Variable overhead (1.2 × 50,000)	60,000
(vii) **Opportunity Cost:**	
Benefit lost due to acceptance of offer	₹
Selling price of "Y" (5,000 × 70)	3,50,000
Less: Labour (4 hr × 1 × 5,000)	(20,000)
Material (12 × 5,000)	(60,000)
Variable overheads (1.2 × 5,000 × 4hr × 1)	(24,000)
Fixed cost	(58,000)
Opportunity cost for 50,000 units of Best	1,88,000

Problem 23

A company in the civil engineering industry with headquarters located 22 miles from Delhi undertakes contracts anywhere in India.

The company has had its tender for a job in north-east India accepted at ₹ 2,88,000 and work is due to begin in March. However, the company has also been asked to undertake a contract is ₹ 3,52,000. Both of the contracts cannot be taken simultaneously because of constraints on staff site management personnel and on plant available. An escape clause enables the company to withdraw from the contract in the north-east, provided notice is given before the end of November and an agreed penalty of ₹ 28,000 is paid.

The following estimates have been submitted by the company's quantity surveyor:

Cost estimates	*North-east (₹)*	*South west (₹)*
Materials:		
In stock at original cost, Material X	21,600	
In stock at original cost Material		24,800
Firm orders placed at original cost, Material X	30,400	
Not yet ordered - current cost, Material X	60,000	
Not yet ordered – current cost, Material Z		71,200
Labour - hired locally	86,000	1,10,000
Site management	34,000	34,000
Staff accommodation and travel for site management	6,800	5,600
Plan on site – depreciation	9,600	12,800
Interest on capital, 8%	5,120	6,400
Total local contract costs	2,53,520	2,64,800
Headquarters cost allocated at rate of 5% on total contract costs	12,676	13,240
	2,66,196	2,78,040
Contract price	2,88,000	3,52,000
Estimated profit	21,804	73,960

Notes:

(i) X,Y and Z are three building material. Material X is not in common use and would not realize much money if re-sold; however, it can be used on other contracts but only as a substitute for another material currently quoted at a 10% less than the original cost of X. The price of Y, a material in common use, has doubled since it was purchased; its net realizable value if re-sold would be its new price less 15% to cover disposal cost. Alternatively it could be kept for use on other contracts in the following financial year.

(ii) With the construction industry not yet recovered from the recent recession, the company is confident that manual labour, both skilled and unskilled, could be hired locally on a subcontracting basis to meet the needs of each of the contracts.

(iii) The plant which would be needed for the south west contract has been owned for some years and ₹ 12,800 is the year's depreciation on a straight-line basis. If the north-east contract is undertaken, less plant will be required but the surplus plant will be hired out for the period of the contract at a rental of ₹ 6,000.

(iv) It is the company's policy to charge all contracts with notional interest at 8% on estimated working capital involved in contracts. Progress payments would be receivable from the contractee.

(v) Salaries and general costs of operating the small headquarters amount to about ₹ 1,08,000 each year. There are usually ten contracts being supervised at the same time.

(vi) Each of the two contracts is expected to last from March to February which, coincidently, is the company's financial year.

(vii) Site management is treated as a fixed cost.

You are required, as the management accountant to the company,

(a) to present comparative statements to show the net benefit to the company of undertaking the more advantageous of the two contracts;

(b) to explain the reasoning behind the inclusion in (or omission from) your computed financial statements, of each item given in the cost estimate and the notes relating thereto.

Solution

Particulars	*North-east* (₹)	*South coast* (₹)
Material X from stock (i)	19,440	
Material Y from stock (ii)		49,600
Firm orders of Material X (iii)	27,360	
Material X not yet ordered (iv)	60,000	
Material Z not yet ordered (v)		71,200
Labour (vi)	86,000	1,10,000
Site management (vii)	—	—
Staff accommodation and travel for site management (viii)	6,800	5,600
Plant rental received (ix)	(6,000)	—
Penalty clause (x)	—	28,000
	1,93,600	2,64,400
Contract Price	2,88,000	3,52,000
Net Benefit	94,400	87,600

(b)

(i) *If material X is not used on the North East contract the most beneficial use is to use it as a substitute material thus avoiding future purchases of ₹ 19,440 (0.9 × 21600). Therefore by using the stock quantity of material X the company will have to spend ₹ 19,440 on the other materials.*

(ii) *Material Y is in common use and the company should not dispose of it. Using the materials on the South west contract will mean that they will have to be replaced at a cost of ₹ 49,600 (₹ 24,800 × 2). Therefore the future cash flow impact of taking on the contract is ₹ 49,600.*

(iii) *It is assumed that with firm orders for materials it is not possible to cancel the purchase. Therefore the cost will occur whatever future alternative is selected. The materials will be used as substitute material if they are not used on the contract and therefore, based on the same reasoning as note (i) above, the relevant cost is the purchase price of the substitute material (0.9 × ₹ 30,400).*

Problem 24

A limited has been offered a contract that, if accepted, would significantly increase next year's activity level. The contract requires the production of 20,000 kgs. of product X and specifies a contract price of ₹ 1,000 per kg. The resources required in the production of each kg. of X include the following:

	Resources per kg of X
Labour:	
Grade 1	2 hours
Grade 2	6 hours
Materials:	
A	2 units
B	1 litre

Grade I labour is highly skilled and although currently under-utilized in the firm, it is A's policy to continue to pay Grade I labour in full. Acceptance of the contract would reduce the idle time of Grade I labour. Idle time payments are treated as non-production overheads. Grade 2 is unskilled with a high turnover, and may be considered a variable cost.

The cost to A for each type of labour are:

Grade I ₹ 40 per hour; Grade 2 ₹ 20 per hour.

The materials required to fulfil the contract would be drawn from the materials already in stock. Material A is widely used within the firm and any usage for the contract will necessitate replacement. Material B was purchased to fulfil an expected order that was not received. If, material B is not used for the contract, it will be sold.

For accounting purposes FIFO is used. The various values and costs for A and B are as follows:

	A *Per unit (₹)*	*B* *Per unit (₹)*
Book value	8	300
Replacement cost	100	320
Net realizable value	90	250

A single recovery rate for fixed factory overheads is used throughout the firm, even though some of these costs could be attributed to a particular product or department. The overhead is recovered by applying a pre-determined rsio per productive labour hour. Initial estimates of next year's activity, which exclude the current contract, show fixed production overhead of ₹ 60,00,000 and production labour hours of 3,00,000. Acceptance of the contract would increase fixed production overheads by ₹ 22,80,000.

Variable production overheads are accurately estimated at ₹ 30 per productive labour hour.

Acceptance of the contract would encroach on the resources used to produce and sale another product Y, which is also made by A Limited. It is estimated that the sale of Y would then decrease by 5,000 units in the next year only. However, this reduction in sale of Y would enable attributable fixed factory overhead of ₹ 5,80,000 to be avoided. Information on Y is as follows:

	Per unit
Selling price	₹ 700
Labour Grade 2	4 hours
Materials relevant variable costs	₹ 120

Required: Advise A Limited on the desirability of the acceptance of the contract purely on economic consideration. Show your calculations. ***(May 2002)***

Solution

RELEVANT COSTS AND BENEFIT ANALYSIS FROM THE ACCEPTANCE OF THE CONTRACT

Particulars	*(₹.'000)*
A. Sales revenue: (20,000 kgs × ₹ 1,000)	20,000
B. Relevant Costs:	
Labour:	
Grade 1	NIL
Grade 2 (20,000 kgs. × 6 hours × 20)	2,400
Material A (20,000 kgs. × 2 units × ₹ 100)	4,000
Material B (20,000 kgs. × 1 litre × ₹ 250)	5,000
Variable production overhead (20,000 kgs. x 8 hours x ₹ 30)	4,800
Total variable cost	16,200
Incremental fixed costs	2,280
	18,480
Add: Loss of contribution on product Y	1,320
Total relevant cost:	19,800
C. Excess of relevant revenue over Relevant Cost [A – B]	200

Advice to A Limited: to accept the contract, as it will enhance the pre-tax operating income by ₹ 2,00,000.

Working Notes:

(i) Relevant cost of labour Grade : Nil, labour cost for Grade I labour as it will not be affected by the decision. Grade 2 : ₹ 20 per hour

(ii) Relevant cost of material

Material A : ₹ 100 per unit, the replacement cost because the material is widely used.

Material B : ₹ 250 per unit, the net realisable value, being the opportunity cost.

(iii) STATEMENT OF LOSS OF CONTRIBUTION FROM THE REDUCTION IN SALE OF PRODUCT Y.

Particulars	₹	₹
A. Sales revenue per unit:		700
B. Variable cost per unit		
Grade 2 labour: (4 hours x ₹ 20)	80	
Materials relevant variable costs	120	
Variable production overheads: (4 hours x ₹ 30)	120	320
C. Contribution per unit: {(A) – (B)		380
D. Loss of contribution from the reduction in sale of 5,000 units (5,000 untis × ₹ 380)		19,00,000
E. *Less:* Avoidable fixed factory overhead cost		(5,80,000)
Net Loss		13,20,000

4 Marginal Costing — Decision Making

Learning Objectives

After studying this chapter, you should be able to understand:

- Decision-Making Process
- Cost Concepts Associated with Decision-Making
- Product Mix Decisions
- Make or Buy Decision
- Manufacturing or Sub-Contracting Decision
- Acceptance of an Offer and Submission of a Tender
- Whether to Accept Export Order or not
- Shut Down or Continue Decision
- Expand or Contract Decision
- Whether to Drop or Add a Product Line
- How to Decide Whether to Process Further or Not
- Optimising Investment Plan
- Pricing Decision
- Pricing under Different Market Structures
- New Product Pricing Strategies
- Price Discrimination Strategies
- Geographic Pricing Strategies
- Pareto Analysis
- Different Selling Prices
- Replacement Decision

1.0 DECISION-MAKING PROCESS

Decision-making is the process of choosing the best among the available alternatives. A decision-making process involves the following practical steps:

Step 1: *Define the problem in clear terms*
Step 2: *Identify the possible alternatives*
Step 3: *Determine the evaluation criterion on the basis of which possible alternatives are to be evaluated*
Step 4: *Evaluate the possible alternatives on the basis of evaluation eriterion considering financial factors such as commercial cost-benefit analysis and non-financial factors such as social cost-benefit analysis*
Step 5: *Rank the evaluated alternatives in order of priorities*
Step 6: *Select the most profitable alternative (s) as per requirements of the business.*

2.0 COST CONCEPTS ASSOCIATED WITH DECISION-MAKING

Certain cost are associated with decision-making, let us first understand them. Cost can be classified according to their nature and information needs of the management in the following manner:

1. By Element	Under this classification costs are classified into (a) Direct Costs and (b) Indirect Costs according to elements viz., Materials, Labour and Expenses.
2. By Function	Under this classification costs are classified as: Production Cost; Administration Cost: Selling Costs; Distribution Cost; Research Cost; Development Cost etc.
3. By Behaviour	Under this classification costs are classified as Fixed; Variable and Semi Variable Costs. Fixed costs can be further classified as Committed and Discretionary Costs.
4. By Normality	Under this classification costs are classified as Normal Costs and Abnormal Costs.
5. By Controllability	Under this Classification costs are classified as Controllable Costs and Uncontrollable costs.

Management of a business house requires cost information for decision making under different circumstances. *For example* they require such information for fixing selling price, controlling and reducing costs. To perform all these functions a classification of cost according to their nature and information needs is an essential pre-requisite of the management.

The break up of the aggregate costs into relevant types, is an essential pre-requisite of decision making as well as of controlling costs. Classification of costs on different bases is thus necessary for various purposes. For the purpose of decision-making and control, costs are distinguished on the basis of their relevance to different type of decisions and control functions. The importance of distinguishing costs are direct or indirect lies in the fact that direct costs of a product or an activity can be accurately allocated while indirect costs have to be apportioned on the basis of certain assumptions. This is so because direct costs are controllable at the operational level whereas indirect costs are not amenable to such control.

2.1 Relevant Cost

Meaning	Relevant costs are those expected future costs which differ under different alternatives.
Examples	In case of whether to retain or replace an old machine, the realizable value and dismantling cost of old machine are relevant costs but the present written down book value of old machine is irrelevant cost.
Importance	Relevant cost analysis helps in drawing the attention of managers to those elements of costs which are relevant for the decision.
Two Common Pit Falls in Relevant Cost Analysis	Two comment pit falls in Relevant Cost Analysis are as follows: (a) First Pit fall is to assume that all variable costs are relevant. All variable costs are not relevant. Variable costs which remain unchanged under different alternatives are irrelevant but variable costs which differ under different alternatives are relevant. (b) Second Pit fall is to assume that all fixed costs are irrelevant. All fixed costs are not irrelevant. Fixed costs which remain unchanged under different alternatives are irrelevant but fixed costs which differ under different alternatives are relevant.

Practical Example	X Ltd. proposes to re-arrange plant facilities and estimates its future costs under two alternatives choices, are as under:		
	Particulars	***Do not re-arrange* ₹**	***₹-arrange* ₹**
	Direct Materials Cost/unit	20.00	20.00
	Direct Labour Cost/unit	10.00	9.00
	Production Overheads	1,00,000	1,00,000
	Additional Overheads	—	10,000
	Identify the Relevant and Irrelevant Costs **Solution:**		
	Cost	***Relevant***	***Reason***
	1. Direct Material Cost	Irrelevant	It remains unchanged
	2. Direct Labour Cost	Relevant	It differs under both the alternatives.
	3. Production Overheads	Irrelevant	These remain unchanged.
	4. Additional Overheads	Relevant	These differ under both the alternatives.

2.2 Sunk Costs

Meaning	Sunk Costs are the historical costs which have already been incurred by decision made in past and can not be changed by any decision made in the future. Sunk costs are irrelevant in decision making because these are past costs.
Example	Written down value of machine already purchased is sunk cost,
Are all Irrelevant Costs Sunk Costs?	**No.** *for example*, when a comparison of two alternative production methods using the same material cost is made, material cost, is irrelevant cost because it does not differ under both the alternatives but it is not a sunk cost because material cost is the future cost to be incurred.

2.3 Opportunity Cost

Meaning	Opportunity cost is the cost of next best alternative of resources. It is the measure of benefits foregone by rejecting the second best alternative of resources in favour of the best. It is the value of opportunity lost by diversion of an input factor from one use to another. It is also defined as the maximum contribution that is forgone by using the scarce resources for a particular purpose.
Examples	1. The opportunity cost of using a machine to produce a particular product is the foregone earnings that would have been possible if the machine was used to produce other products. 2. The opportunity cost of funds invested in a business is the interest that could have been earned by investing the funds in bank deposit. 3. The opportunity cost of one's time is the salary which he would have earned by his profession.
Uses	Opportunity cost concept is helpful to the management in making profitability calculations when one or more of the inputs required by two or more of the alternatives courses of action is already available.

	1. **Decision Making:** Opportunity costs apply to the use of scarce resources, where resources are not scarce, there is no sacrifice from the use of these resources. Where a course of action requires the use of scarce resources, it is necessary to incorporate the lost profit which will be foregone from using scarce resources. If resources have no alternatives use only the additional cash flow resulting from the course of action should be included in decision making as relevant cost. 2. **Cost Control:** The conventional variance analysis will report an adverse usage variance and adverse sales volume variance. However, the failure to achieve the budgeted optimum level of output may be due to inefficient usage of scarce resources. The foregone contribution should therefore be charged to the manager responsible for controlling the usage of scarce resources and not to the sales manager because the failure to achieve the budgeted sales is due to the failure to use scarce resources efficiently. Thus if resources are scarce, the usage variance should reflect the acquisition cost *plus* budgeted contribution per unit of the scarce resources. If the lost sales are made good in subsequent periods, the real opportunity cost will consist of lost interest arising from delay in receiving the net cash-flows and not the foregone contribution.

Illustration 1. Estimated direct material requirements of CAS Ltd. for the year are 2,00,000 units. Unit cost for orders below 2,40,000 units is ₹ 10. When size of order equals 2,40,000 units or more the concern received a discount of 5% on the above quoted per unit price. Keeping in view the following two alternaves:

(i) Buy 2,40,000 units at the start of the year;
(ii) Buy 20,000 units per month.

Calculate the opportunity cost, if the concern has the facility of investing surplus funds in government bonds at the rate of 10% interest.

Solution: Average investment in inventory under the given two alternatives are:

(i) (2,40,000 units × ₹ 9.50)/2	= ₹	11,40,000
(ii) (20,000 units × ₹ 10)/2	= ₹	1,00,000
Difference between the average investment in inventory	₹	10,40,000

The concern can invest ₹ 10,40,000 at 10 percent and can earn ₹ 1,04,000 as interest annually. The sum of ₹ 1,04,000 is an opportunity foregone if alternative (i) is chosen.

Hence ₹ 1,04,000 is the opportunity cost of the 2,40,000 units purchase order.

$$\text{Opportunity Cost per unit} = \frac{1,04,000}{2,40,000} = 0.433$$

Net Benefit per unit = 0.50 – 0.433 = 0.067 per unit

Note: ₹ 1,04,000 would not ordinarily be recorded in the accounting system as it is a foregone cost.

2.4 Out of Pocket Costs

Meaning	Out of pocket cost is that portion of costs which involves payments to outsiders i.e., it gives rise to cash expenditure as opposed to such costs as depreciation, which do not involve any cash expenditure.
Uses	Out of pocket costs are relevant for decision making (e.g. price fixation during recession, make or buy decisions), controlling or reducing costs.
Examples	Commission to salesman on sales, transport expenses, Carriage Inward on purchase of component.

2.5 Differential Cost

Meaning	Differential cost is the change (increase or decrease) in the total cost (variable as well as fixed) due to change in the level of activity, technology or production process or method of production.
How differs from Marginal Cost?	Differential cost includes both fixed and variable cost but marginal cost represents only variable cost.
Differential Cost or Incremental Cost Technique	It is a technique used in the preparation of ad-hoc information in which only income differences between alternative courses of action are taken into consideration. This technique is applicable to situations where fixed costs alter. This technique is of particular use in short term problems which are non-repetitive, one time, ad hoc problems. The essential pre-requisite for making managerial decisions by using incremental cost technique, is to compare the incremental costs with incremental revenues. So long as the incremental revenue is greater than incremental costs, the decision should be in favour of the proposal.
Applications of Differential Cost/ Incremental Cost techniques in making managerial decisions	The important areas in which incremental cost analysis could be used for managerial decision making are as under: 1. Whether to process a product further or not 2. Whether to an accept an additional order from a special customer at lower than existing price or not 3. Whether to retain or replace decisions 4. Whether to reduce or maintain price decision 5. Whether to discontinue a product, suspend or close down a segment of the business or not 6. Whether to introduce a new product or not 7. How to optimize investment plan out of multiple alternatives 8. Whether to open new sales territory and branch or not 9. Submitting tenders 10. Whether to make or buy decisions 11. Whether to lease or buy decisions

Illustration 2. Tulsian Ltd. is planning either to produce or buy the component 'PQR'. If it decides to produce component 'PQR' then it has to install system facilities for that in its factory. The following information is provided for the production of components at various levels:

Particulars	*Production Level (in units)*			
	1,00,000	1,50,000	2,00,000	2,50,000
Variable Costs	2,50,000	3,73,500	5,06,000	6,27,500
Fixed Production Overheads	1,00,000	1,35,000	1,75,000	1,75,000

This component can be purchased from the market at following prices

Order Quantity	1,00,000	1,50,000	2,00,000	2,50,000
Price	3.40	3.35	3.30	3.25

Required: Comment whether the company should produce the component or buy it form the market when the estimated requirements of the component are (a) 1,00,000 units, (b) 1,50,000 units, (c) 2,00,000 units, (d) 2,50,000 units.

Solution: **STATEMENT SHOWING THE RELEVANT COST OF MAKE OR BUY**

Particulars	Case (a)	Case (b)	Case (c)	Case (d)
A. Relevant (incremental) cost when the component is produced	3,50,000	5,08,500	6,81,000	8,02,500
B. Relevant (incremental) costs when the component is purchased	3,40,000	5,02,500	6,60,000	8,12,500
C. Differential Cost (A – B).	10,000	6,000	21,000	(10,000)
D. Recommendation:	Purchase	Purchase	Purchase	Make

Illustration 3. ACE Ltd. has an inventory of 5,000 units of product left over from last years' production. This model is no longer in demand. It is possible to sell these at reduced prices through the normal distribution channels. The other alternative is to ask someone to take them on "as is where is" basis. The latter alternative will cost the company ₹ 5,000.

The company produced 2,40,000 units of the product, last year, when the unit costs were as under.

Variable Manufacturing Cost	6.00
Fixed Manufacturing Cost	1.00
Variable Selling & Distribution Cost	3.00
Fixed Selling & Distribution Cost	1.50
Total Cost	11.50
Selling Price per Unit	14.00

Required: Should the company scrap the items or sell them at a reduced price? If you suggest the latter, what minimum price would your recommend?

Solution:

A. Cost if sold through normal distribution channels @ ₹ 3	₹ 15,000
B. Cost if the stock is disposed off by asking someone to take then on "as is where is basis",	₹ 5,000
C. Differential Cost [A – B]	₹ 10,000
D. Differential Cost per unit [₹ 10,000/5,000]	₹ 2

Recommendation: Hence, if the company can get anything more than ₹ 2 per unit, then it is worthwhile to sell the stock of 5,000 units and earn an additional contribution.

Note: Historical cost of ₹ 11.50 per unit of 5,000 units of a product is irrelevant (as it is a sunk cost) for determining the recommended price per unit.

2.6 Discretionary Costs

Meaning	Discretionary costs are the costs— (a) Which are incurred at the discretion of management (b) Which can be avoided by the managerial decision (c) Which arise from periodic (usually yearly) decisions regarding the maximum outlay to be incurred. (d) Which are not tied to a clear cause and effect relationship between inputs and outputs. The note worthy feature of discretionary costs is that managers are seldom confident that the "correct" amounts are being spent.
Examples	Advertising, Research and Development, Public Relations, Executive Training, Teaching, Health Care and Management Consulting Services.
How to Control	To control discretionary costs control points/ parameters may be established. But these points need to be devised individually. *For example,* research and development costs may be controlled by establishing dates for submitting major reports to management. For advertising and sales promotion, such costs may be controlled by pre-setting targets. In the case of employees benefits, such costs may be controlled by calling a meeting of employees union and making them aware that the company would meet only the fixed costs and the variable costs should be met by them.

Illustration 4. ZED Ltd. operates two shops. Product A is manufactured in Shop-1 and customer's job against specific orders are being carried out in Shop 2. Its annual statement of income is:

Particulars	*Shop–1 (Product-A)* ₹	*Shop–2 (Job Works)* ₹	*Total* ₹
Sales/Income	1,25,000	2,50,000	3,75,000
Material	40,000	50,000	90,000
Wages	45,000	1,00,000	1,45,000
Depreciation	18,000	31,500	49,500
Power	2,000	3,500	5,500
Rent	5,000	30,000	35,000
Heat and Light	500	3,000	3,500
Other Expenses	4,500	2,000	6,500
Total	1,15,000	2,20,000	3,35,000
Net Income	10,000	30,000	40,000

The depreciation charges are for machines used in the shops. The rent and heat and light are apportioned between the shops on the basis of floor area occupied. All other costs are current expenses idenfied with the output in a particular shop.

A valued customer has given a job to manufacture 5,000 units of X for Shop-2. As the company is already working at its full capacity, it will have to reduce the output of product-A by 50% to accept the said job. The customer is willing to pay ₹ 25 per unit of X. The material and labour will cost ₹ 10 and ₹ 18 respectively per unit. Power will be consumed on the job just equal to the power saved on account of reduction of output of A. In addition the company will have to incur additional overheads of ₹ 10,000.

You are required to compute the following in respect of this job.

(a) Differential Cost; (b) Full Cost; (c) Opportunity Cost; and (d) Sunk Cost.

Advise whether the company should accept the job.

Solution: **(a) DIFFERENTIAL COST OF THE JOB**

Particulars	*Relevant Cost of Producing 'X'* ₹	*Relevant Cost of Producing 'A'* ₹
Material Cost	50,000	20,000
Labour Cost	90,000	22,500
Additional Overheads	10,000	—
Other expenses	—	2,250
Total	1,50,000	44,750

Differential Cost of the job = ₹ 1,05,250

Note: Depreciation, rent, heat and light and power are not going to affect the costs.

(b) **Full Cost of the Jobs:**

	₹
Relevant Cost of Producing 'X' [as above at (a)]	1,50,000
Depreciation	9,000
Power	1,000
Rent	2,500
Heat and Light	250
Total	1,62,750

(c) **Opportunity Cost of taking the order:**

	₹
Sale of Product A	62,500
Less: Relevant Cost of Producing 'A' [as above at (a)]	44,750
Opportunity Cost	17,750

(d) **Sunk Cost of the jobs:**

	₹
Depreciation	9,000
Power*	1,000
Rent	2,500
Heat and Light	250
Total	12,750

* If a student treats power as a relevant cost, in that case it would not appear here.

Advise: The company should not accept the job as there will be a cash disadvantage of ₹ 42,750 as computed below:

		₹	₹
A	Differential Revenue [5,000 units @ ₹ 25]	1,25,000	
	Less: Sale of Product A	62,500	62,500
B	Differential Cost		1,05,250
C	Cash Disadvantage [A – B]		42,750

Illustration 5. Mahila Griha Udyog Industries is considering to supply its products—a special range of namkeens—to a departmental store. The contract will last for 50 weeks, and the details are given below:

		₹
Material:	X (in stock-at original cost)	1,50,000
	Y (on order–on contract)	1,80,000
	Z (to be ordered)	3,00,000
Labour:	Skilled	5,40,000
	Non-skilled	3,00,000
	Supervisory	1,00,000
General Overheads		10,80,000
Total cost 26,50,000		
Price offered by department store		18,00,000
Net Loss		8,50,000

Should the contract be accepted if the following additional information is considered?

(i) Material X is an obsolete material. It can only be used on another product, the material for which is available at ₹ 1,35,000 (Material X requires some adaptation to be used and costs ₹ 27,000).

(ii) Material Y is ordered for some other product which is no longer required. It now has a residual value of ₹ 2,10,000)

(iii) Skilled labour can work on other contracts which are presently operated by semi-skilled labour at a cost of ₹ 5,70,000.

(iv) Non-skilled labour are specifically employed for this contract.

(v) Supervisor staff will remain whether or not the contract is accepted. Only two of them can replace other positions where the salary is ₹ 35,000.

Overheads are charged at 200% of skilled labour. Only ₹ 1,25,000 would be avoidable, if the contract is not accepted.

Solution: **STATEMENT OF RELEVANT COST OF MAHILA GRIHA UDYOG INDUSTRIES IF THE CONTRACT IS ACCEPTED/REJECTED**

Particulars	*Relevant Costs (if contract is accepted)* ₹	*Relevant Costs (if contranct is rejected)* ₹
A. Cash Inflows:		
Contract Price	18,00,000	—
Sale of Material Y	—	2,10,000
Total Cash Inflows:	18,00,000	2,10,000
B. Cash Outflows:		
Material X substitute	1,35,000	—
Adaptation required for the use of obsolete material X	—	27,000

Particulars	*Relevant costs (if contract is accepted)* ₹	*Relevant costs (if contranct is rejected)* ₹
Material Z	3,00,000	
Replacement of semi-skilled labour by skilled labour	5,70,000	—
Non-skilled labour cost	3,00,000	—
Supervisory staff cost	35,000	—
Avoidable overheads	1,25,000	—
Total Cash outflow:	14,65,000	27,000
C. Net Cash Inflow: [A – B]	3,35,000	1,83,000

Conclusion: The contract should be accepted as it yields a net incremental cash inflow of ₹ 1,52,000 (i.e. ₹ 3,35,000 – ₹ 1,83,000).

Working Notes:

(i) Material Y will have to be paid for whether or not the contract is accepted, therefore its cost is irrelevant. The relevant cost figure here is that which has an opportunity cost of ₹ 2,10,000. This means that the company can resell material Y at this price.

(ii) Regarding material X, if the contract is accepted, alterative material will have to be purchased for the other product at a cost of ₹ 1,35,000. If the contract is rejected material X will be adapted for a product not included in the list of special range of namkeens at a cost of ₹ 27,000.

(iii) The relevant skilled labour cost of ₹ 5,70,000 is the extra cost to the company because of this contract. It is the replacement cost of semi skilled labour by skilled labour.

(iv) Non-skilled labour cost is the incremental cost of the contract.

(v) If the company accepts the contract is will have to pay ₹ 35,000 for two position that the supervisory staff can replace.

(vi) Only ₹ 1,25,000 of avoidable overheads are relevant to this contract.

Illustration 6. Ranka has been offered a contract by Excel Ltd. to build for it five special Guest Houses for use by top management. Each Guest House will be an independent one. The contract will be for a period of one year and the offer price is ₹ One crore. In addition excel Ltd. will also provide 2 grounds of land free of cost for the purpose of construction. The Chief Accountant of Ranka Builders has prepared an estimate on the basis of which he has advised that the contract should not be accepted at the price offered. His estimate was as follows:

	₹ In Lacs
Land (3 Grounds at ₹ 20 lacs each)	60
Drawings and design	7
Registration	10
Cement and Sand	6
Bricks and Tiles	4
Steel	10
Other (including interior decoration)	10
labour-Skilled	12
—Unskilled	8
—Supervisor's Salary	5
Overheads General	12
Depreciation	6
Total Cost	150

The Accountant also provides the following information:

Land: The total requirement of land is 3 grounds costing ₹ 20 lacs per ground Excel Ltd. will provide 2 grounds free of cost.

Drawing and Design: These have already been prepared and 50% of the cost has already been incurred.

Materials:

(i) Cement and sand are already in stock and are in regular use. If used for this contract, they have to be replaced at a cost of ₹ 8 lacs.

(ii) Bricks and tiles represent purchases made several months before for a different contract. They could be sold readily for a net ₹ 5 lacs after meeting all further expensed

(iii) **Others:** Materials worth ₹ 2 lacs relating to interior decoration are in stock for which no alternative use is expected in the near future. However they can be sold for ₹ 1 lac.

Labour:

(i) Skilled workers will be transferred to this project from another 'project. The project manager claimed that if the men where returned to him, he could have earned the company an additional Ps. 2 lacs in terms of profits.

(ii) The supervisor undertakes various tasks in the sites and his pay and continuity of employment will not be affected by the new contract if the contract is taken, he will devote half of his time.

Overheads:

(i) The equipment that would be used on the contract was bought one year before for ₹ 30 lacs and is expected to last for five years. It can also be used on other contracts and the current replacement price will be ₹ 32 lacs and in a year's time it will be ₹ 25 lacs.

(ii) The general overheads includes both specific and absorbed overheads. if the contract is not undertaken, ₹ 4 lacs of the same can be avoided.

Ranka Builders has also on hand another project, which would not be executed if the contract from Excel Ltd. were to be accepted. The estimated profit on that project is ₹ 10 lacs.

In the light of information given above, you are required to indicate with reasons whether the contract from Excel Ltd. should be accepted or not.

Solution:

STATEMENT OF RELEVANT COSTS ON THE ACCEPTANCE OF CONTRACT FROM EXCEL LTD.

[₹ in Lacs]

S. No.	*Particulars*	*Basis for the cost to be relevant* ₹	*Relevant cost if contract is accepted* ₹	*Irrelevant cost if the contract is accepted* ₹
1.	Land cost		20	
2.	Drawings and design		—	7 (Sunk cost)
3.	Registration	Incremental	10	—
	Materials:			
	Cement and Sand	Replacement	8	
	Bricks and Tiles	Opportunity	5	
	Steel	Incremental	10	
	Others		9	
5.	Labour			
	Skilled	Opportunity	12 + 2	
	Unskilled	Incremental	8	
	Supervisor's salary			5 (Sunk cost)
6.	Overheads:			
	General	Relevant (avoidable)	4	
	Depreciation		—	6 (Sunk cost)
	Replacement cost of machine		7	
7.	Estimated Profit foregone on other project	Opportunity foregone	10	
	Total		105	

Decision: Since the offer price of contract is ₹ 100 lacs and its total relevant cost is ₹ 105 lacs; these figures clearly shows that the offer should not be accepted.

Working notes:

(i) Cost of 1 ground of Land

	₹ (Lacs)
Total cost of 3 grounds of land	60
Cost of grounds of land will be borne by Excel Ltd.	40
Cost of 1 grounds of land will be borne by M/s Ranka Builders	20

(ii) Others material cost is ₹ 10 lacs, it includes material worth ₹ 2 lacs, relating to interior decoration, which is a sunk cost, this material can be sold for ₹ 1 lac, (which is a relevant opportunity cost) and ₹ 8 lacs. Material is an incremental cost. Hence total relevant cost of others material is ₹ 9 lacs. (₹ 8 lacs, incremental + ₹ 1 lac. opportunity cost).

(iii) Since the equipment can also be used on this contract. Its current replacement price is ₹ 32 lacs, and after one year its cost will be ₹ 25 lacs. Therefore the relevant opportunity cost of machine is: ₹ 7 lacs. (₹ 32 lacs – ₹ 25 lacs).

Illustration 7. A company had nearly completed a job relating to construction of a job relating to construction of a specialised equipment, when it discovered that the customer had gone out of business. At this stage, the position if the job was as under:

	₹
Original cost estimate	1,75,200
Cost incurrent so far	1,48,500
Costs to be incurred	29,700
Progress payment received from original customer	1,00,000

After searches, a new customer for the equipment has been found. He is interested to take the equipment, if certain modifications are carried out. The new customer wanted the equipment in its original condition, but without its control device and with certain other modifications. The costs of these additions and modifications are estimated as under:

		₹
Direct materials (at cost)		1,050
Direct Wages.	Dept. A	15 man days
	Dept. B	25 man days
Variable overheads		25% of direct wages in each department
Delivery costs		₹ 1,350

Fixed overheads will be absorbed at 50% of direct wages in each department.

The following additional information is available:

1. The direct materials required for the modification are in stock and if not used for modification of this order, they will be used in another job in place of materials that will now cost ₹ 2,250.
2. Department A is working normally and hence any engagement of labour will have to be paid at the direct wage rate of ₹ 120 per man day.
3. Department B is extremely busy. Its direct wages rate is ₹ 100 per man day and it is currently yielding a contribution of ₹ 3.20 per rupee of direct wages.
4. Supervisory overtime payable for the modification is ₹ 1,050.
5. The cost of the control device that the new customer does not require is ₹ 13,500. If it is taken out, it can be used in another job in place of a different mechanism. The latter mechanism has otherwise to be bought for ₹ 10,500. The dismantling and removal of the control mechanism will take one man day in department A.
6. If the convention is not carried out, some of the materials in the original equipment can be used in another contract in place of materials that would have cost ₹ 12,000. It would have taken 2 man days of work in department A to make them suitable for this purpose. The remaining materials will realise ₹ 11,400 as scrap. The drawings, which are included as part of the job can he sold for ₹ 1,500

Required: Calculate the minimum price, which the company can afford to quote for the new customer:

Solution:

STATEMENT OF MINIMUM PRICE WHICH THE COMPANY CAN AFFORD TO QUOTE FOR THE NEW CUSTOMER (BASED ON RELEVANT COST)

Particulars	₹
Cost to be incurred to bring the equipment in its original condition.	29,700
Opportunity Cost of the direct material	2,250
Direct Wages:	
Dept A: [15 man days × ₹ 120]	1,800
Dept. A: [25 man days × ₹ 100]	2,500
Opportunity Cost of Contribution lost by Department B (₹ 2,500 × ₹ 3.2)	8,000
Variable Overheads [25% (₹ 1,800 + ₹ 2,500)]	1,075
Delivery Costs	1,350
Supervisory overtime payable for modification	1,050
Cost Control device to be used in another job (W.N)	(10,350)
Net Loss on Material Cost savings, in the original equipment (WN)	11,700
Opportunity Cost of remaining materials which can be sold as scrap	11,400
Opportunity Cost of sale of drawings	1,500
Total Minimum Price which may be quoted	61,975

Working Notes:

(i) *Cost of Control Device to be used in another job:*

		₹
A	Cost of control device	10,500
B	*Less*: Dismantling and removal (1 man day × ₹ 120)	(120)
C	*Less*: Variable cost (25% × ₹ 120)	(30)
D	Balance Cost of Control Device [A – B – C]	10,350

(ii) *Net Loss on Material Cost Saving of Equipment*

A	Loss on Material Cost Saving of Equipment	12,000
B	*Less*: Conversion Cost (2 man days × ₹ 120)	(240)
C	*Less*: Variable Overheads (25% × ₹ 240)	(60)
D	Net Loss on Material Cost Saving of Equipment [A – B – C]	11,700

3.0 PRODUCT MIX DECISIONS

Product mix decisions involve deciding upon the priority of products to be produced and sold so as to maximize the profit. For the purposes of understanding, Product Mix Decisions may be studied under the following six headings:

1. Product Mix Decision when there is only one key factor
2. Product Mix Decision when there is only one key factor and product specific fixed costs are also given
3. Product Mix Decision where there are more than one key factors
4. Product Mix Decision when there are more than one level of activity
5. Product Mix Decision when a product passes through various departments and departmental hours are limited
6. Product Mix Decision when Sales Demand of two or more products at different Selling prices are given

3.1 Product Mix Decision when there is only one key factor

Let us first understand what is key factor?

Meaning of Key Factor	Key Factor is a factor which limits the activities of an undertaking. The extent of its influence must first be assessed while preparing functional budgets and taking decisions about the profitability of a product.
Examples of Key Factor	Some of the examples of key factor are: (a) Shortage of Raw Material (b) Shortage of Labour Hours (c) Machine Capacity available (d) Sales Capacity available (e) Cash available
Basis of Decision	The product mix decision should be taken on the basis of contribution per unit of key factor $\left(\text{i.e. } \frac{\text{Contribution per unit}}{\text{Key factor per unit}}\right)$.
Procedure	The following procedure may be followed to decide the most profitable product mix. **Step 1:** *Calculate the Contribution per unit of key factor* $= \frac{\text{Contribution per unit}}{\text{Key Factor per unit}}$ **Step 2:** *Assign the Ranking (say I, II, III) to various products on the basis of contribution per unit of key factor [e.g. Rank I to largest contribution, Rank II to second largest contribution and so on]*

<table>
<tr><td></td><td colspan="2">Step 3: First allocate the key factor resources (say Material, Labour Hours, Machine Hours) to meet the committed sales of products (if any)
Step 4: Then allocate the balance of key factor resources to products ranked on the basis of contribution per unit of key factor [e.g. First allocate to Rank I Product upto maximum sales demand, then allocate to Rank II Product and so on]
Step 5: Find out the quantity of each product to which key resources have been allocated and total contribution for such product mix. This is called the most profitable product mix.
Step 6: Calculate the profit for the suggested product mix.</td></tr>
<tr><td rowspan="9">Basis for Deciding upon Priority of Products</td><td colspan="2">To decide upon the priority of products, the following guidelines may be used:</td></tr>
<tr><td>Case</td><td>Basis for deciding upon the Priority of Products</td></tr>
<tr><td>(a) If maximum sales (in units) is a limiting factor</td><td>(a) Contribution per unit</td></tr>
<tr><td>(b) If maximum sales (in value) is a limiting factor</td><td>(b) Profit-volume ratio (or P/V Ratio)</td></tr>
<tr><td>(c) If raw-material is a limiting factor</td><td>(c) Contribution per unit of raw-material required to produce one unit of a product</td></tr>
<tr><td>(d) If labour hour is a limiting factor</td><td>(d) Contribution per unit of labour hour required to produce one unit of a product</td></tr>
<tr><td>(e) If machine hour is a limiting factor</td><td>(e) Contribution per unit of machine hour required to produce one unit of a product</td></tr>
<tr><td>(f) If there is heavy demand for the product</td><td>(f) Profit/Volume Ratio (or P/V Ratio)</td></tr>
<tr><td>(g) If there is low demand for the product</td><td>(g) Low Break even point</td></tr>
</table>

Illustration 8. *X* Ltd. which produces two products using the same raw-material and production facilities, provides you the following information:

	Product A ₹	*Product B* ₹
Selling Price per unit	100	80
Material @ ₹ 2 per kg	20	10
Labour @ ₹ 3 per hour	15	30
Variable Overheads @ ₹ 4 per machine hour	40	16
Total Fixed Overheads: ₹ 6,00,000		

Required: Comment on the profitability of each product when:

(a) Sales Quantity is limited;
(b) Sales Value is limited;
(c) Raw-material is in short supply;
(d) Labour hours are limited;
(e) Production Capacity (in terms of Machine Hours) is limited;
(f) there are heavy demand conditions;
(g) there are low demand conditions.

Solution: **STATEMENT SHOWING THE CONTRIBUTION PER UNIT OF KEY FACTOR**

Particulars	Product A ₹	Product B ₹
A. Selling Price per unit	100	80
B. *Less:* Variable Costs:		
Material	20	10
Labour	15	30
Variable overheads	40	16
	75	56
C. Contribution per unit (A – B)	25	24
D. P/V Ratio $\left(\frac{\text{Contribution}}{\text{Sales}}\times 100\right)$	25%	30%
E. Contribution per kg of Material $\left(\frac{\text{Contribution per unit}}{\text{Raw-material required per unit}}\right)$	$\frac{25}{10}$ = ₹ 2.5	$\frac{24}{5}$ = ₹ 4.8
F. Contribution per Labour Hour $\left(\frac{\text{Contribution per unit}}{\text{Labour hours required per unit}}\right)$	$\frac{25}{5}$ = ₹ 5	$\frac{24}{10}$ = ₹ 2.4
G. Contribution per Machine Hour $\left(\frac{\text{Contribution per unit}}{\text{Machine hrs required per unit}}\right)$	$\frac{25}{10}$ = ₹ 2.5	$\frac{24}{4}$ = ₹ 6
H. Break Even Point $\left(\frac{\text{Fixed Overheads}}{\text{Contribution per unit}}\right)$	$\frac{6,00,000}{25}$ = 24,000 units	$\frac{6,00,000}{24}$ = 25,000 units

(a) When sales quantity is limited, Product *A* is more profitable because its contribution per unit is higher than that of Product *B*.

(b) When sales value is limited, Product *B* is more profitable because its P/V Ratio is higher than that of Product *A*

(c) When Raw-Material is in short supply, Product *B* is more profitable because its contribution per kg. of raw-material is higher than that of Product *A*.

(d) When Labour hours are limited, Product A is more profitable because its contribution per labour hour is higher than that of Product *B*.

(e) When production capacity in terms of machine hours is limited, Product *B* is more profitable because its contribution per machine hour is higher than that of Product *A*

(f) When there are heavy demand conditions, Product *B* is more profitable because its P/V Ratio is higher than that of Product *A*.

(g) When there low demand conditions, Product *A* is more profitable because its Break Even Point is lower than that of Product *B*.

Illustration 9. COJIH Ltd. is manufacturing three household products *A*, *B* and *C*, and selling them in a competitive market. Details of current demand, selling price and cost structure are given below:

	A	B	C
Expected Demand *(Units)*	10,000	12,000	20,000
Selling Price per unit *(₹)*	20	16	10
Variable Cost per unit *(₹)*			
Direct Materials *(₹ 10/kg.)*	6	4	2
Direct Labour *(₹ 15/Hr.)*	3	3	1.50
Variable overheads	2	1	1
Fixed Overhead per unit *(₹)*	5	4	2

The Company is frequently affected by acute scarcity of raw material and high labour turnover. During the next period it is expected to have one of the following situations:

(a) Raw materials available will be only 12,100 kg.

(b) Direct labour hours available will be only 5,000 hrs.

(c) It may be possible to increase sales of any one product by *25%* without any additional Fixed costs but by spending ₹ 20,000 on advertisement. There will be no shortage of materials or labour.

Required: Suggest the best production plan in each case and the resultant profit that the company would earn according to your suggestion.

Solution: STATEMENT SHOWING THE CONTRIBUTION AND RANKING OF THE PRODUCT

Particulars	*Products*		
	A	*B*	*C*
A Selling Price per unit (₹)	20	16	10
B *Less:* Variable Cost per unit (₹)			
Direct Material	6	4	2.00
Direct Labour	3	3	1.50
Variable Overheads	2	1	1.00
Total Variable Cost per unit	11	8	4.50
C Contribution per unit (₹) [A – B]	9	8	5.50
D P/V Ratio *or* Contribution/Sales Ratio	45%	50%	55%
Ranking			
With no limiting factor (on the basis of profitability)	III	II	I
With raw material as limiting factor			
Raw material required per unit [Raw Material Cost / Price per kg.]	0.6 kg	0.4 kg.	0.2 kg.
Contribution per kg. of raw material	₹.15	₹ 20	₹ 27.50
Ranking when Raw Material is a limiting factor	III	II	I
With labour as limiting factor:			
Labour hours required per unit [Labour Cost / Wages per hour]	1/5 hr.	1/5 hr	1/10 hr.
Contribution per labour hour	₹ 45	₹ 40	₹ 55
Ranking when labour hour is a limiting factor	II	III	I

(a) STATEMENT SHOWING THE PROFITABILITY WHEN RAW MATERIAL AVAILABLE IS 12,100 KG.

Product	*No. of Units*	*Raw material required*	*Contribution per unit* ₹	*Total Contribution* ₹
C	20,000	4,000 kg.	5.50	1,10,000
B	12,000	4,800 kg.	8.00	96,000
A	5,500	3,300 kg.	9.00	49,500
			Total Contribution	2,55,500
			Less : Total Fixed Costs	1,38,000
			Net Profit	1,17,500

Total Fixed Costs

A.	10,000	₹ 5	= ₹	50,000
B.	12,000	₹ 4	= ₹	48,000
C.	20,000	₹ 2	= ₹	40,000
			₹	1,38,000

(b) STATEMENT SHOWING THE PROFITABILITY WHEN LABOUR HOURS AVAILABLE IS 5,000 HOURS

Product	No. of Units	Labour Hours required	Contribution per unit ₹	Total Contribution ₹
C	20,000	2,000	5.50	1,10,000
A	10,000	2,000	9.00	90,000
B	5,000	1,000	8.00	40,000
			Total Contribution	2,40,000
			Less: Fixed cost	1,38,000
			Net Protit	1,02,000

(c) No shortage of material and labour. Most profitable product C is to be selected for 25% more production and Sale, i.e. 25% of 20,000 *or* 5,000 units

Extra 5,000 units will fetch an additional contribution of ₹ (5,000 ₹ 5.50) *or* ₹ 27,500, which is more than additional expenditure on advertisement of ₹ 20,000.

STATEMENT SHOWING THE PROFITABILITY WHEN THERE IS NO SHORTAGE

Product		No. of Units	Contribution per unit ₹	Total Contribution ₹
A		10,000	9.00	90,000
B		12,000	8.00	96,000
C		25,000	5.50	1,37,500
			Total Contribution	3,23,500
	Less : Fixed Costs		1,38,000	
	Advertisement Expenses		20,000	1,58,000
			Net Profit	1,65,500

Illustration 10. (a) A firm produces 5 different products from a single raw material. Raw material is available in abundance at ₹ 6 per kg. The labour rate is ₹ 8 per hour for all products. The plant capacity is 21,000 labour hours for the budget period. Production facilities can produce all the products. The factory overhead rate is ₹ 8 per hour, comprising ₹ 5.60 per hour as fixed overhead and ₹ 2.40 per hour as variable overhead. The Selling Commission is 10 percent of the product price. Given the follwing information, you are to suggest a suitable sales mix which will maximise the Company's profits. Determine the profits that will be earned at the Selected Sales mix.

Product	*Market Demands (units)*	*Selling Price per unit (₹)*	*Labour Hours required per unit*	*Raw Material required per unit (in gms.)*
A	4,000	32.00	1.00	700
B	3,600	30.00	0.80	500
C	4,500	48.00	1.50	1,500
D	6,000	36.00	1.10	1,300
E	5,000	44.00	1.40	1,500

(b) Assume, in above situation, 3,500 hours of overtime working is possible. It will result in additional fixed overheads of ₹ 20,000, a doubling of labour rates and a 50 percent increase in variable overheads. Do you recommend the overtime working ?

Solution: **(a) STATEMENT SHOWING THE CONTRIBUTION AND RANKING OF THE PRODUCT**

Particulars	*Products*				
	A	*B*	*C*	*D*	*E*
A. Selling Price per unit (₹)	32	30	48	36	44
B. *Less :* Variable Costs per unit :					

Direct Material	4.20	3.00	9.00	7.80	9.00
Direct Labour	8.00	6.40	12.00	8.80	11.20
Variable Overhead	2.40	1.92	3.60	2.64	3.36
Selling Commission	3.20	3.00	4.80	3.60	4.40
Total Variable Cost	17.80	14.32	29.40	22.84	27.96
C. Contribution per unit (₹) [A – B]	14.20	15.68	18.60	13.16	16.04
D. Labour Hrs. required for each unit	1.00	0.80	1.50	1.10	1.40
E. Contribution per hour (₹) [C/D]	14.20	19.60	12.40	11.96	11.46
F. Ranking	II	I	III	IV	V

STATEMENT SHOWING THE SUGGESTED SUITABLE SALES MIX AND PROFITABILITY AT THE SUGGESTED SALES MIX

Product (in order of ranking)	*Suitable Sales Mix (Limited to Market Demands) Units*	*Labour hours required*	*Contribtuion per unit ₹*	*Total Contribution ₹*
B	3,600	2,880	15.68	56,448
A	4,000	4,000	14.20	56,800
C	4,500	6,750	18.60	83,700
D	6,000	6,600	13.16	78,960
E	550	770*	16.04	8,822
	Total Contribution			2,84,730
	Less : Factory Fixed Overheads [21,000 × ₹ 5.60]			1,17,600
	Total Profits			1,67,130

* Balance labour hours (i.e. 21,000 – 20,230 = 770 hours] will be used in the production of Product E.

(b) STATEMENT SHOWING THE EVALUATION OF OVERTIME WORKING TO PRODUCE 2,500 UNITS OF PRODUCT 'E'

Particulars		₹
A. Sales (2,500 units at ₹ 44)		1,10,000
B. *Less* : Variable Cost:		
Variable Costs per unit	27.96	
Increase in labour rate (₹ 8.00 1.4)	11.20	
Increase in overhead (₹ 1.20 1.4)	1.68	
	40.84	
Total Variable Costs [2,500 units ₹ 40.84]		1,02,100
C. Additional Contribution		7,900
D. *Less* : Increase in Fixed Cost		20,000
E. Loss		(12,100)

Recommendations: The proposal for overtime is to be rejected as it will result in reduction in profits by ₹ 12,100.

Illustration 11. PCT Ltd. provides you the following data for three products:

	A	*B*	*C*	Total
Selling Price per unit (₹)	10	10	10	
Raw Material Cost per unit [@₹ 0.50 per kg]	2.00	1.25	0.80	
Direct Labour [@₹ 2 per hour]	1.00	3.00	4.00	
Variable Overheads per hour	2.00	0.50	0.60	
Possible Maximum Sales (units)	2,000	200	4,000	
Fixed Costs (₹)				9,600
Minimum Committed Sales	20 units	40 units	—	

Required: If maximum availability of raw material is 7,000 kg, suggest that product mix which will yield maximum profit and also ascertain profit at suggested product mix.

Solution: **STATEMENT SHOWING THE CONTRIBUTION AND RANKING**

Particulars	*Product A Per Unit*	*Product B Per Unit*	*Product C Per Unit*
A. Sales (₹)	10.00	10.00	10.00
B. *Less:* Variable Costs (₹)			
Raw-Material Costs	2.00	1.25	0.80
Direct Labour Costs	1.00	3.00	4.00
Variable Overheads	1.00	0.75	1.20
	4.00	5.00	6.00
C. Contribution (₹)	6.00	5.00	4.00
D. Raw-material required per unit	4.00	2.50	1.60
E. Contribution per unit of Raw-Material (₹) [C/D]	1.50	2.00	2.50
F. Ranking	III	II	I

Suggested Product Mix: In case Raw-Material is in Short Supply, Contribution per Unit of Key factor (i.e. Raw Material here) is the deciding factor and accordingly first *C*, then *B* and lastly *A*.

STATEMENT SHOWING THE ALLOCATION OF RAW MATERIAL FOR MOST PROFITABLE PRODUCT MIX

A.	Total Raw Material Available		7,000 kg.
B.	*Less :* Raw Material required for – 20 units of product 'A' [20 4]	80 kg.	
	– 40 units of product 'B' [40 2.50]	100 kg.	180 kg.
C.	Balance Raw Material [A – B]		6,820 kg
D.	*Less :* Raw Material required for 4000 units of C (i.e. Maximum Sales) [4,000 1.6 = 6,400 kg.]		6,400 kg
E.	Balance Raw Material [6,820 kg. – 6,400 kg]		420 kg
F.	*Less :* Raw Material required for 160 units of B [160 2.5 kg]		400 kg
G.	Balance Raw Material [420 kg – 400 kg]		20 kg
H.	Maximum possible production of product 'A' with the balance [20/4]		5 units

Thus, Product Mix should be A 25 units, B 200 units, C 4,000 units

STATEMENT SHOWING THE PROFITABILITY OF SUGGESTED PRODUCT MIX

Particulars	*Product A*	*Product B*	*Product C*	*Total*
A. Units	25	200	4,000	
B. Selling Price per unit	10	10	10	
C. Total Sales (₹) [A B]	250	2,000	40,000	42,250
D. *Less :* Variable Cost (₹)	100	1,000	24,000	25,100
E. Contribution (₹) [C – D]	150	1,000	16,000	17,150
F. *Less :* Fixed costs (₹)				9,600
G. Profit (₹) [E – F]				7,550

Illustration 12. M/s PL Agro Ltd., engaged in agricultural activities has 500 hectares of virgin land, which can be used for growing jointly or individually tea, coffee, and cardamom. The yield per hectare of the different crops and their selling prices per kg. are as under :

	Yield (kgs.)	*Selling Price (₹ per kg.)*
Tea	2,500	25
Coffee	625	50
Cardamonm	125	300

The relevant cost data are given below :

(a) *Variable Cost per kg. :*

	Tea (₹)	*Coffee* (₹)	*Cardamom* (₹)
Labour charges	10.00	12.50	150.00
Packing material	2.50	2.50	12.50
Other costs	5.00	1.25	25.00

(b) *Fixed Cost per annum :* Cultivation and growing cost ₹ 16,00,000, Administrative cost ₹ 4,50,000, Land revenue ₹ 2,75,000, Repairs and maintenance ₹ 5,00,000, Other costs ₹ 6,75,000.

The policy of the Company is to produce and sell all the three kinds of products and the maximum and minimum area to be cultivated per product is as follows:

	Maximum Area (Hectares)	*Minimum Area (Hectares)*
Tea	320	240
Coffee	100	60
Cardamom	60	20

Required: Calculate the priority of production, the most profitable product mix and the maximum profit which can be achieved.

Solution: STATEMENT SHOWING THE CONTRIBUTION AND RANKING OF THE PRODUCT

Particulars	*Tea* ₹	*Coffee* ₹	*Cardamom* ₹
A. Selling Price per kg.	25.00	50.00	300.00
B. *Less:* Variable Costs :			
Labour Charges	10.00	12.50	150.00
Packing Material	2.50	2.50	12.50
Other Costs	5.00	1.25	25.00
Total Variable Cost	17.50	16.25	187.50
C. Contribution per kg. [A – B]	7.50	33.75	112.50
D. Output per hectare	2500	625	125
E. Contribution per hectare [C D]	18,750	21,093.75	14,062.50
F. Ranking on the basis of contribution per hectare	II	I	III

Therefore, to maximise profit, subjects to other constraints, if any, the order of priority of production would be, coffee, tea, cardamom.

STATEMENT SHOWING THE CALCULATION OF MAXIMUM PROFIT AT SUGGESTED PRODUCT MIX

Particulars	*A Maximum Area (Hectare)*	*B Yield per hectare*	*C = A B Production Kg.*	*D Contribution Per kg.*	*E = C D Total* ₹
Tea	320	2500	8,00,000	7.50	60,00,000
Coffee	100	625	62,500	33.75	21,09,375
Cardamom	60	125	7,500	112.50	8,43,750
A. Total Contribution					89,53,125
B. *Less :* Fixed cost					35,00,000
C. Profit [A – B]					54,53,125

Illustration 13. A farmer owns an orchard which has an area of 350 acres on which he grows apples, apricots, cherries and plums.Of the total areas, 250 acres of land are unsuitable for growing apples & plums and are suitable only for apricots and cherries. On the remainting 100 acres of land, any of the four fruits can be grown.

The marketing policy requires that in each season all the four types of fruits must be produced and quantity of any one type should not be less than 12,000 boxes.

It is also essential that the area devoted to anyone should be in terms of complete acres and not in fraction of an acre. There are no physical or marketing limitations and there is an adequate supply of all types of labour.

The details regarding the selling price, production and costs are given below :

	Apples	*Apricots*	*Cherries*	Plums
Selling price per box (in ₹)	10	10	20	30
Seasons yield per acre (in boxes)	500	150	100	200
Weight per box (kgs.)	30	30	40	20
Material per acre. (₹)	180	70	60	100
Labour growing per acre. (₹)	200	150	100	130
Harvesting and packing per box (₹)	1	1	2	3
Transport per box (₹)	2	2	1	3

Fixed Overheads each season:

Cultivation and growing ₹ 58,000, Harvesting ₹ 68,000, Transport ₹ 5,000, Administration ₹ 42,000, Land Revenue ₹ 9,000.

Required: Advise the farmer on the area to be allotted to each item in order to earn the maximum total profit and what is that total profit ?

Solution: I. STATEMENT SHOWING THE CONTRIBUTION AND RANKING OF THE PRODUCT

Particulars	*Apples*	*Apricots*	*Cherries*	*Plums*
A. No. of Boxes per Acre	500	150	100	200
B. Selling Price per Box. (₹)	10	10	20	30
C. Sellign Price per Acre (₹) [A B]	5,000	1,500	2,000	6,000
D. *Less:* Marginal Cost (₹)				
(a) Material Cost per acre	180	70	60	100
(b) Labour Cost per acre				
(i) Growing	200	150	100	130
(ii) Harvesting & Packing	500	150	200	600
(iii) Transport	1,000	300	100	600
Total Marginal Cost per acre	1,880	670	460	1,430
E. Contribution per acre (₹) [C – D]	3,120	830	1,540	4,570
F. Priority as per Contribution per arce	II	IV	III	I

II. STATEMENT SHOWING THE ALLOCATION OF AREA SUITABLE FOR APRICOTS AND CHERRIE ONLY

A. Total such area	250
B. *Less :* Area for Min. Qty of Apricots (i.e. the product having lesser contribution) [12000/150]	80
C. Balance to be used for product having greater Contribution i.e. Cherries [A – B]	170

III. STATEMENT SHOWING THE ALLOCATION OF AREA SUITABLE FOR EVERY FRUIT

A. Total Such Area	100
B. *Less :* Minimum Qty of Apples (i.e. the product having lesser Contribution) [12000/500]	24
C. Balance to be used for product having greater contribution i.e. plums [A – B]	76

IV. STATEMENT SHOWING THE MAXIMUM TOTAL PROFITS AT SUGGESTED PRODUCT MIX

Particulars	*Apples*	*Apricots*	*Cherries*	*Plums*	Total
A. Area in Acres	24	80	170	76	
B. Contribution/Acre (₹)	3,120	830	1,540	4,570	
C. Total Contribution (A B)	74,880	66,400	2,61,800	3,47,320	7,50,400
D. *Less :* Fixed costs					1,82,000
E. Profit [C – D]					5,68,400

Illustration 14. XY Ltd. makes and sell two products: X and Y. The budgeted selling price of X is ₹ 1,800 and that of Y is ₹ 2,160. Variable costs associated with producing and selling the X are ₹ 900 and with Y ₹ 1,800. Annual fixed production and selling costs of XY Ltd. are ₹ 88,000.

The company has two production/sales option. The X and Y can be sold *either* in the ratio of two X to three Y *or* in the ratio of one X to two Y. Find the optimal product mix.

Solution: **CONTRIBUTION PER UNIT**

Particulars	*Product X* ₹	*Product Y* ₹
A. Budgeted Selling Price per unit	1,800	2,160
B. *Less*: Variable Cost per unit	900	1,800
C. Contribution per unit	900	360

TOTAL CONTRIBUTION

Option I (2 units X and 3 units Y)		*Option II (1 unit X and 2 units Y)*
A. Total Contribution = (2 × ₹ 900) + (3 × ₹ 360)	2,880	1620 = (1 unit × ₹ 900) + (2 units × ₹ 360)

Decision: Optimum Mix is 2 units of X and 3 units of Y since total contribution under this option is more than that under option II.

3.2 Product Mix Decision when there is Only one Key Factor and Product Specific Fixed Cost are also given

When product specific fixed costs are given, product mix decision should be taken using Total Profit (i.e. Total Contribution – Total Fixed Cost) Analysis. The product mix which gives maximum profits should be selected. Ranking per unit of key factor may be used to develop various product combinations.

Illustration 15. Tulsian Ltd provides you the following information.

	X	*Y*	*Z*
Selling Price per unit	₹ 550	₹ 630	₹ 690
Direct Material Cost per unit	₹ 180	₹ 160	₹ 300
Direct Labour Cost per unit	₹ 160	₹ 220	₹ 140
Variable Overheads per unit	₹ 110	₹ 140	₹ 145
Specific Fixed Overheads	—	2000	4,780
General Fixed Overheads ₹ 20,000			

Required: Find out the most profitable product mix

(a) If maximum labour hours available are 1617 hours @₹ 20 per hour

(b) If Demand is limited to 100 units of X, 115 units of Y and 135 units of Z with production facility being limited to 215 units for X, Y and Z put together.

Solution: **STATEMENT SHOWING CONTRIBUTION PER UNIT AND RANKING**

Particulars	*X*	*Y*	*Z*	*Total*
A. Selling Price per unit	550	630	690	
B. *Less:* Variable Cost per unit				
Direct Material Cost	180	160	300	
Direct Labour Cost	160	220	140	
Variable Overheads	110	140	145	
	450	520	585	
C. Contribution per unit [A + B]	100	110	105	
D. Direct Labour Hour per unit	8	11	7	

Particulars	X	Y	Z	Total
E. Contribution per Labour Hour	12.5	10	15	
F. Ranking on the basis of contribution per unit	3	1	2	
G. Ranking on the basis of Contribution per Labour Hour	2	3	1	
H. General Fixed Overheads	—	—	—	20,000
I. Specific Fixed Overheads	—	2,000	4,780	6,780
Total fixed overheads				26,780
J. BEP (Units) (for only 1 product at a time)	$\frac{20,000}{100} = 200$	$\frac{22,000}{110} = 200$	$\frac{24,780}{105} = 236$	
K. Maximum Permissible Output	$\frac{1617}{8} = 202$	$\frac{1617}{11} = 147$	$\frac{1617}{7} = 231$	

Part (a) **If maximum Labour Hours available are 1617 hours Ranking on the basis of contribution per Labour Hours is to be considered.**

Rank 1 Product Z should not be produced since 231 < BEP

Rank 2 Product X should be produced since 202 > BEP

Profit on 202 units of product X = Contribution – fixed cost

= (202 × 100) – ₹ 20,000 = ₹ 200

Part (*b*) **If Demand is limited,** Ranking on the basis of contribution per unit is to be considered

Particulars	X	Y	Z	Total	Fixed Cost	Profit (Loss)
Contribution per unit	100	110	105	—	—	—
Option I (Units)	—	115	100	215	—	—
Contribution (₹)	—	12,650	10,500	23,150	26,780	(3,630)
Option II (Units)	100	115	—	215	—	—
Contribution (₹)	10,000	12,650	—	22,650	22,000	650
Option III (Units)	80	—	135	215	—	—
Contribution (₹)	8,000	—	14,175	22,175	24,780	(2,605)

Recommendation: The most profitable product mix is: 100 Units of product X and 115 units of Product Y.

3.3 Product Mix Decision when there are more than one Key Factors

When there are more than one key factor, the product mix decision should be taken using linear programming techniques. A trial and error technique suggested below may or may not yield the same results as linear programming techniques. Suppose there are two key factors (*say Material and Labour hours*), the following practical steps may be followed to decide the product mix.

Step 1: *Calculate Contribution per unit of material*

Step 2: *Assign the Ranking (say I, II, III) to various products on the basis of Contribution per unit of material. (e.g. Rank I to largest contribution, Rank II to second largest contribution and so on)*

Step 3: *Calculate Contribution per labour hour*

Step 4: *Assign the Ranking (say I, II, III) to various products on the basis of contribution per labour hour*

Step 5: *First allocate the Material to products ranked on the basis of contribution per unit of material (e.g. First allocate to Rank I Product upto Maximum Sales Demand, then allocate to Rank II Product only upto Maximum Sales Demand and so on) as if labour hour is not a key factor.*

Step 6: *Allocate the Labour Hours to products ranked on the basis of contribution per labour hour (e.g. First allocate to Rank I Product upto Maximum Sales Demand, then allocate*

to Rank II Product upto Maximum Sales Demand and so on) as if material is not a key factor.

Step 7: *Find out the product to which both the key factor resources are allocated fully to meet the maximum sales demand under Step 5 and Step 6.*

Step 8: *Find out the balance quantity of both the key factor resources available for the remaining products.*

Step 9: *Make one equality for one key factor resource and another equality for another key factor resource*

Step 10: *Solve both the equations to get units of both the remaining products*

Step 11: *Calculate the Contribution and Net Profit for the calculated product mix.*

Illustration 16. Tulsian Ltd. can produce three different products from the same raw material using the same production facilities. The relevant details are as follows:

Particulars	*X*	*Y*	*Z*
Maximum Market Demand (units)	6000	4000	3000
Selling Price per unit (₹)	125	100	200
Raw-Material as % of Sales Value	80%	60%	75%
Labour Cost per unit	12	20	6

Overhead Rate is ₹ 5 per hour of which 60% is fixed. Maximum Raw Material available 1,00,000 kg @ ₹ 10 per kg. Maximum Production hours available 18,400@₹ 8 per hour.

Required:

(a) Find out the Product Mix to yield maximum profit and determine the Profit at the selected product Mix

(b) Assume, in above situation 1500 hours of overtime working is possible and additional 7000 kg of raw material is available at 5% extra rate. It will result in additional fixed overheads of ₹ 1,000, 50% increase in labour rates and 20% increase in variable overheads. Do you recommend the overtime working?

Solution:

Step 1: Statement showing the Contribution per unit of key factor and Ranking of the product

	Particulars	*X*	*Y*	*Z*
A.	Selling Price per unit (₹)	125	100	200
B.	*Less*: Variable Cost per unit (₹):			
	Material	100	60	150
	Labour	12	20	16
	Variable Overheads @ ₹ 2 per hour	3 (1.5 × ₹ 2)	5 (2.5 × ₹ 2)	4 (2 × ₹ 2)
		115	85	170
C	Contribution per unit [A – B]	10	15	30
D	Raw-material required per unit (kg) [Raw-Material Cost/₹ 10]	10	6	15
E	Contribution per kg of Raw-material [C/D]	1	2.5	2
F	Ranking on the basis of contribution per kg of Raw-material	III	I	II
G	Labour Hours required per unit (₹)	1.5	2.5	2
H	Contribution per labour hour [C/G]	6.66	6	15
I	Ranking in the basis of Contribution per Labour Hour	II	III	I

Step 2: Statement showing Allocation of Material on the basis of Contribution per unit of Raw-Material as if Labour Hour is not a key factor.

Particulars	*Product units*	*Raw-material units*
A. Total Available		1,00,000
B. *Less*: For product Y (Rank I)	4000	(24,000)
C. Balance Available [A – B]		76,000
D. *Less*: For Z (Rank II)	3,000	(45,000)
E. Balance Available [C – D]		31,000
F. *Less*: For *X* (Rank III)	3,100	(31,000)
G. Balance available		—

Step 3: Statement showing Allocation of Labour Hours on the basis of Contribution per Labour Hour as if Raw-Material is not key factor

Particulars	*Product units*	*Labour Hours*
A. Total Available		18,400
B. *Less*: For Z (Rank I)	3,000	(6,000)
C. Balance available [A – B]		12,400
D. *Less*: For X (Rank II)	6,000	(9,000)
E. Balance available		3,400
F. *Less*: For Y (Rank III)	1,360	(3,400)
G. Balance available		—

Step 4: Identify the product to which both Material and Labour Hours have been allocated fully to meet maximum sales demand i.e. Project Z (3000 units)

Step 5: Balance Qty of Material and Labour

	Material	*Labour*
Total Available	1,00,000	18,400
Less: For 3000 units of Z	(45,000) (3000 × 15 kg)	(6,000) (3000 × 2 hours)
Balance for X and Y	55,000	12,400

Step 6: *Calculation of units of product X and Y to be produced*

Since the slope of objective function comprising Product X and Y $\left(\text{i.e. } \frac{10}{15}\right)$ is between the slope of the material constraint $\left(\text{i.e. } \frac{10}{6}\right)$ and labour hours constraint $\left(\text{i.e. } \frac{1.5}{2.5}\right)$, the solution can be obtained by solving the two constraints as equality.

Let X be the units of product X and Y be the units of product Y

$10X + 6Y = 55{,}000$ ... *Equation I for Material*

$1.5X + 2.5Y = 12{,}400$ ... *Equation II for Labour Hours*

Multiplying eq II by 2.4

$3.6X + 6Y = 29{,}760$ ...*Equation III*

Subtracting eq. III for eq I

$6.4X = 25{,}240$

$X = 25{,}240/6.4 = 3943.75$ units

Putting Value of X is eq. I, we get

$Y = (55{,}000 - 39{,}437.50)/6 = 2{,}593.75$

STATEMENT OF PROFIT AT MOST PROFITABLE MIX

Particulars A	*Product Units* B	*Raw-material* C	*Labour Hours* D	*Contribution per Unit* E	*Total Contribution* F = B × E
A. Total Available		1,00,000	18,400		
B. *Less*: for X	3943	(39,430)	(5914.5)	10	39,430
for Y	2594	(15,564)	(6,485)	15	38,910
for Z	3000	(45,000)	(6,000)	30	90,000
		6	(0.5)		1,68,340
Less: Fixed Overheads (18400 Hours × ₹ 3 per hours)					(55,200)
Net Profit					1,13,140

Part (b) **STATEMENT SHOWING THE REVISED CONTRIBUTION PER UNIT**

	Particulars	*Product X* ₹	*Product Y* ₹	*Product Z* ₹
A	Selling Price per unit	125	100	200
B	*Less*: Variable Cost per unit:			
	Material	105.00	63	157.50
	Labour	18.00	30	24.00
	Variable overheads	3.60	6	4.80
		126.60	99	186.30
C	Contribution per unit [A – B]	(1.60)	1	13.70

Product X can not been recommended since it has negative contribution of ₹ 1.60.

Product Z can not be produced further since it has already been produced upto maximum sales demand.

Y can not be recommended because there will be additional net loss of ₹ 400 as shown below:

Maximum Additional output possible: 1500 Hours/2.5 = 600 units

7000 kg/6 = 1166.7 units whichever is lower

Additional contribution on 600 units = 600 × ₹ 1 = ₹ 600

Less: Additional fixed overheads = ₹ 1000

Additional net Loss = (₹ 400)

Recommendation: In view of above, overtime working is not recommendable at all.

Illustration 17. X Ltd. supplies spare parts to an air craft company Y Ltd. The production capacity of X Ltd. facilitates production of any one spare part for a particular period of time. The following are the cost and other information for the production of the two different spare parts A and B:

Per unit	*Part A*	*Part B*
Alloy usage	1.6 kgs.	1.6 kgs.
Machine Time : Machine A	0.6 hrs.	0.25 hrs.
Machine Time : Machine B	0.5 hrs.	0.55 hrs.
Target Price (₹)	145	115

Total hours available: Machine A 4,000 hours, Machine B 4,500 hours

Alloy available is 13,000 kgs. @ ₹ 12.50 per kg.

Variable overheads per machine hour: Machine A : ₹ 80, Machine B : ₹ 100

(a) You are required to identify the spare part which will optimise contribution at the offered price.

(b) If Y Ltd. reduces target price by 10% and offers ₹ 60 per hour of unutilised machine hour, what will be the total contribution from the spare part identified above?

(c) Calculate the total contribution of most profitable mix it both the parts can be produced and supplied.

Solution:

Part (a)

Step 1: Statement showing the Contribution per unit of key factor and Ranking of Spare Part

	Particulars	*Part A*	*Part B*
A	Target Price per unit (₹)	145	115
B	*Less*: Variable Cost per unit (₹):		
	Alloy Usage (1.6 × ₹ 12.50)	20	20
	Variable Overheads		
	Machine A	48	20
	Machine B	50	55
		118	95
C	Contribution per unit [A – B]	27	20
D	Machine A time per unit	0.6 hour	0.25 hour
E	Contribution per Machine A hour	45	80
F	Ranking on the basis of contribution per Machine A hour	II	I
G	Machine B time per unit	0.5 hrs.	0.55 hrs.
H	Contribution per Machine B hour	54	36.36
I	Ranking on the basis of Contribution per machine B hour	I	II
J	Maximum Output as per Machine A	6666.67	16000
K	Maximum Output as per Machine B	9000	8181.81
L	Max Permissible Output on both machines	6666	8181

Step 2: Allocation of Machine Hours to 6666 units of part A
Maximum Contribution = 6666 × ₹ 27 = ₹ 1,79,982

Step 3: Allocation of Machine Hours to 8181 units of Part B
Maximum Contribution = 8181 × ₹ 20 = ₹ 1,63,620

Part (b) If Y Ltd reduces target Price by 10% of Part A

	Machine A	*Machine B*
Total Hours Available	4,000	4,500
Less: Used for 6666 Parts of A	(3999.6)	(3333)
	0.4	1167
Additional Contribution for unutilized Machine Hour		
Machine A (0.4 × ₹ 60)		24
Machine B (1167 × 60)		70020
		70044
Contribution after Reduction in Target Price [6666 × (₹ 27 – ₹ 14.50)]		83,325
Total Contribution from spare Part A identfied		1,53,369

Recommendation: X Ltd. should not accept the 2nd offer since there will be net Loss of ₹ 26,613 (i.e. ₹ 1,79,982 – ₹ 1,53,369)

Part (c) Most profitable spare part mix it both the parts can be produced and supplied.

Since the slope of objective function comprising Part A and Part B $\left(\text{i.e. } \frac{27}{20}\right)$ is between the slope of the Machine A constraint $\left(\text{i.e. } \frac{0.6}{0.25}\right)$ and Machine B constraint, $\left(\text{i.e. } \frac{0.5}{0.55}\right)$, the solution can be obtained by solving the two constraints as equality.

$$0.6A + 0.25B = 4000 \text{ Hours} \quad \text{...Eq I (Machine A Hours)}$$
$$0.5A + 0.55B = 4500 \text{ Hours} \quad \text{...Eq II (Machine B Hours constraint)}$$

Multiplying Eq II by 1.2

$$0.6A + 0.66B = 5400 \text{ hours} \quad \text{...Eq III}$$

Subtracting eq. I from eq. III

0.41B = 1400 hours
B = 1400/0.41 = 3414.63

Putting Value of B in eq. I

A = (4000 – 853.66)/0.6 = 5243.90 units

	Particulars	*Machine A*	*Machine B*	*Contribution per unit*	*Total Contribution*
A	Total Available Hours	4000	4500		
B	Used for 5243 Units of Part A	(3145.8)	(2621.5)	27	1,41,561
	Used for 3414 Units of part B	(85.35)	(1877.70)	20	68,280
	Total				2,09,841

3.4 Product Mix Decision when there are more than One Level of Activity

When there are more than one level of activity, the following practical steps may be followed to decide the most profitable level of activity:

Step 1: *Assign the Ranking (say I, II, III) to various products on the basis of Contribution per unit of key factor (e.g. Rank I to largest contribution, Rank II to second largest contribution and so on)*

Step 2: *Calculate the Product Mix at each level of activity (say machine hours)*

Step 3: *Calculate the Total Contribution and Net Profit (i.e. Total Contribution – Fixed Cost) of each product mix at each level of activity*

Step 4: *Select the level of activity having Maximum Net Profit.*

Illustration 18. The relevant data of X Ltd. for its three products A, B and C are as under:

Particulars	*A*	*B*	*C*
Direct Material (₹/Unit)	260	300	250
Direct Labour (₹/Unit)	130	270	260
Variable Overheads (₹/Unit)	110	230	180
Selling Price (₹/Unit)	860	1,040	930
Machine Hours required (Per Unit)	12	6	3
Maximum Demand (Units)	250	300	1800

The estimated fixed overheads at four different levels of 3,600; 6,000; 8,400; and 10,800 machine hours are ₹ 1,00,000; ₹ 1,50,000; ₹ 2,20,000 and ₹ 3,00,000 respectively.

You are required to find out (i) the most profitable product-mix at each level and (ii) the level of activity where the profit would be maximum.

Solution:

Step 1: **RANKING OF THREE PRODUCTS A, B AND C**

	Particulars	*A*	*B*	*C*
A.	Selling Price per unit (₹)	860	1,040	930
B.	*Less*: Variable Cost per unit (₹)	500	800	690
C.	Contribution per unit [A – B]	360	240	240
D.	Machine hrs. required per unit	12	6	3
E.	Contribution per machine hour (₹) [C/D]	30	40	80
F.	Ranking	III	II	I
G.	Maximum Demand (units)	250	300	1,800
H.	Max. Hours required (G × D)	3,000	1,800	5,400

Scheme of Distribution of Hours: First produce C upto 5400 Hours, then produce Product B upto 1,800 Hours and then produce Product A upto 3,000 Hours.

(i) **STATEMENT OF THE MOST PROFITABLE PRODUCT MIX AT EACH LEVEL OF MACHINE HOURS**

Product (mix)	Max Demand	Machine Hours			
		3,600	6,000	8,400	10,800
C	1800	1,200 units (3,600 hrs/ 3 hrs p.u.)	1,800 units (5,400 hrs/ 3 hrs p.u.)	1,800 units	1,800 units
B	300	—	100 units (600 hrs/ 6 hrs p.u.)	300 units (1800 hrs/ 6 hrs p.u.)	300 units
A	250	—	—	100 units (1,200 hrs/ 12 hrs p.u.)	250 units (3,000 hrs/ 12 hrs p.u.)

(ii) **STATEMENT OF LEVEL OF ACTIVITY WHERE THE PROFIT WOULD BE MAXIMUM**

Level of Activity (Machine hours)	C units (1)	Contribution @ ₹ 240 (2)	B units (3)	Contribution @ ₹ 240 (4)	A units (5)	Contribution @ ₹ 360 (6)	Total Contribution (₹) (7) = (2) + (4) + (6)	Fixed Cost (₹) (8)	Net Profit (₹) (7) – (8)
3,600	1,200	2,88,000	—	—	—	—	2,88,000	1,00,000	1,88,000
6,000	1,800	4,32,000	100	24,000	—	—	4,56,000	1,50,000	3,06,000
8,400	1,800	4,32,000	300	72,000	100	36,000	5,40,000	2,20,000	3,20,000
10,800	1,800	4,32,000	300	72,000	250	90,000	5,94,000	3,00,000	2,94,000

Recommendation: At 8,400 machine hour level of capacity the company would earn maximum profit i.e. ₹ 3,20,000

3.5 Product Mix Decision when a Product passes through various Departments and Departmental Hours are limited

When a product passes through various departments and departmental hours are limited, the following practical steps may be followed to decide the most profitable product mix:

Step 1: *Calculate Total Labour Hours available in each department*

Step 2: *Calculate Department-wise and total hours required per unit of each product*

Step 3: *Calculate the maximum output of each product possible in each individual department*

Step 4: *Calculate the maximum output of each product possible considering the hours available in all the departments*

*[**Note:** Minimum of Maximum output (as per step 3) can be produced by utilizing the available hours in all the departments.]*

Step 5: *Calculate Contribution per hour for each product.*

Step 6: *Rank the product on the basis of contribution per hour.*

Step 7: *Calculate the profit for the product mix*

Illustration 19. ZED Ltd. manufactures two products P and Q and sells them at ₹ 215 and ₹ 320 per unit respectively. The variable costs per unit are as under:

	Product-P	Product-Q
Raw Materials:		
Material-X	22.00	28.00
Material-Y	8.00	32.00

Direct Wages (₹ 6 per labour hour):		
Department-A	36.00	54.00
Department-B	18.00	36.00
Department-C	54.00	—
Department-D	—	72.00
Variable Overheads	23.00	14.30

The company procures raw materials against import licence. The company operates at single shift a day of 8 hours for 300 days in a year. The number of workmen engaged are 30, 16, 18 and 24 in departments A, B, C and D respectively. Neither the workers are subject to transfer from one department to another nor any new recruitment is possible at present. Fixed costs are ₹ 12,000 per month.

You are required to find out the following:

(a) The product-mix to yield maximum profit

(b) The most profitable product if only one product is to be manufactured. Whether the answer will differ if licence to import raw materials is released only for ₹ 1,80,000.

Solution:

Step 1: Total Labour Hours Available = No. of Workmen × Days × Hour per day

In Department A = 30 × 300 × 8 = 72,000
In Department B = 16 × 300 × 8 = 38,400
In Department C = 18 × 300 × 8 = 43,200
In Department D = 24 × 300 × 8 = 57,600

Step 2: Computation of hours required per unit of each product (Wages/Wage Rate per hour)

Departments	*Product-P*	*Product-Q*
A	36/6 = 6	54/6 = 9
B	18/6 = 3	36/6 = 6
C	54/6 = 9	—
D	—	72/6 = 12
Total hours per unit:	18	27

Step 3: Statement showing Maximum Output permissible

Department	*Hours available*	*Product P*		*Product Q*	
		Hrs. required/ Unit	*Maximum output in Units*	*Hrs. required/ Unit*	*Maximum output in Units*
	(a)	*(b)*	*(c) = (a)/(b)*	*(d)*	*(e) = (a)/(d)*
A	72,000	6	12,000	9	8,000
B	38,400	3	12,800	6	6,400
C	43,200	9	4,800*	—	—
D	57,600	—		12	4,800*

*This shows that either 4,800 units of product P or Q can be obtained by utilising the available hours in the four departments.

Step 4: Productwise Contribution per hour

	Particulars	*Product-P* ₹	*Product-Q* ₹
A	Selling Price per unit	215	320
B	*Less:* Material Cost/unit: P: (₹ 22 + ₹ 8), Q: (₹ 28 + ₹ 32)	30	60
	Wages/unit: P: (₹ 36 + 18 + ₹ 54), Q: (₹ 54 + ₹ 36 + ₹ 72)	108	162
	Variable Overheads/unit	23	14.30
	Total Variable Cost/unit	161	236.30

	Particulars	Product-P ₹	Product-Q ₹
C	Contribution per unit [A – B]	54	83.70
D	Labour Hours required per unit	18	27
E	Contribution per labour hour [C/D]	3	3.10

Step 5: Though the contribution per labour of Product Q is better but there is a constraint viz., the numbers of workers in each department can neither be interchanged nor newly recruited, hence due to this following alternatives would arise which may help in deciding about the product mix to yield maximum profit.

Alternative I: Producing 4,800 units of Product Q and utilising the remaining available hours of labour for making units of Product P.

Alternative II: Producing 4,800 units of Product P and utilising the remaining available hours of labour for making units of Product Q.

Step 6: **Statement of Product Mix under Alternative I**

Department	*Available Hours*	*Hrs. required/ for 4,800 units of Q*	*Remaining hours*	*Hrs. per Unit of Product P*	*Units of Product*
	(a)	*(b)*	*(c) = (a) – (b)*	*(d)*	*(e) = (c)/(d)*
A	72,000	43,200	28,800	6	4,800
B	38,400	28,800	9,600	3	3,200
C	43,200	—	43,200	9	4,800
D	57,600	57,600	Nil	—	—

The above table shows that out of the available hours under alternative I; 4,800 units of Product Q and 3,200 units of Product P can be made.

Step 7: **Statement of Product Mix under Alternative II**

Department	*Available Hours*	*Hrs. required/ for 4,800 units of P*	*Remaining hours*	*Hrs. per Unit of Product Q*	*Units of Product*
	(a)	*(b)*	*(c) = (a) – (b)*	*(d)*	*(e) = (c)/(d)*
A	72,000	28,800	43,200	9	4,800
B	38,400	14,400	24,000	6	4,000
C	43,200	43,200	—	—	—
D	57,600	—	57,600	12	4,800

The above table shows that out of the available hours under alternative II; 4,800 units of Product P and 4,000 units of Product Q can be made.

Step 8: **Statement showing Profit under Alternatives I and II**

Products	*Alternative I*			*Alternative II*		
	Units	*Contribution p.u. (₹)*	*Amount ₹*	*Units*	*Contribution p.u. (₹)*	*Amount ₹*
P	3,200	54.00	1,72,800	4,800	54.00	2,59,200
Q	4,800	83.70	4,01,760	4,000	83.70	3,34,800
Total Contribution:			5,74,560			5,94,000
Less: Fixed cost p.a.			(1,44,000)			(1,44,000)
Profit			4,30,560			4,50,000

Decision: *Alternative II is the most profitable product mix.*

Answer to Part (b)

STATEMENT OF MOST PROFITABLE PRODUCT IF ONLY ONE PRODUCT IS TO BE MANUFACTURED

Products	*P*	*Q*
Contribution per unit (₹): A	54.00	83.70
Maximum possible output (in units): (B)	4,800	4,800
Total Contribution: (A) × (B)	2,59,200	4,01,760

Product Q is to be preferred

STATEMENT OF MOST PROFITABLE PRODUCT IF ONLY ONE PRODUCT IS TO BE MANUFACTURED AND LICENCE TO IMPORT THE RAW MATERIAL IS ONLY FOR MATERIALS WORTH ₹ 1,80,000

Products	*P*	*Q*
Raw material required p.u. (₹)	30	60
Permissible output in units of imported material of ₹ 1,80,000	6,000	3,000
Maximum output possible in the available hours	4,800	4,800
Output possible keeping in view the availability of imported material and labour hours (Units)	4,800	3,000
Contribution per unit (₹)	54	83.70
Total Contribution (₹)	2,59,200 (4,800 units × ₹ 54)	2,51,100 (3,000 units × ₹ 83.70)

Product P is to be preferred (i.e. answer differs) because of import licence restriction, which is only available for purchasing material worth only ₹ 1,80,000

3.6 Product Mix decision when Sales Demand of Two or More Products at different Selling Prices are given

When a firm can produce two or more products from the same production facilities and the demand of each product is affected by the change in their prices, the management may have to choose price mix which will give the maximum profit, particularly when the production capacity is limited. In such a situation, the firm should compute all the possible combinations and select a price-mix which yield the maximum profitability.

When sales demands of two or more products at different selling prices are given, the following practical steps may be followed to decide the most profitable price and quantity of each product:

[Practical Steps when there is no Key Factor]

Step 1: *Calculate Total Contribution of each product at each selling price*
Step 2: *Select the Selling price of each product at which total contribution is maximum*

Method I [Practical Steps when there is key Factor (Say Labour Hours)]

Step 1: *Calculate Total Contribution and Total Hours of each product at each Selling Price.*
Step 2: *Calculate Total Contribution and Total Labour Hours of both the products at all possible Price Combinations*
Step 3: *Select the Combination at which the Total Contribution is maximum and Total Labour Hours required for both the products are within the given limit..*

Method II [Practical Steps when there is Key Factor (say Labour Hours)]

Step 1: *Calculate Total Contribution and Incremental Contribution of each product at each selling price*
Step 2: *Calculate Total Labour hours and Incremental Labour hours of each product at each selling price*
Step 3: *Calculate Incremental Contribution per Incremental Labour Hours*

Step 4: *Assign Rank I to largest incremental contribution per incremental labour hour of any product, Rank II to second largest incremental contribution per incremental labour hour (of any product and so on).*

Step 5: *Allocate labour hours to Rank I product upto maximum sales demand, then allocate to Rank II product upto maximum sales demand and so on till the labour hours are exhausted*

Step 6: *Calculate total contribution of each product to which labour hours have been allocated as per Step 5*

Step 7: *Calculate the Profit for the suggested Product Mix.*

Illustration 20. Tulsian Ltd. manufactures and markets two products A and B, the demand in the market of which fluctuates with the prices quoted. As a result of the deliberations of its recent sales conference the following data were agreed upon as a working basis:

	Product A			*Product B*		
Selling Price per unit (₹)	32	30	28	22	20	19
Expected demand per Month (Nos.)	900	1,000	1,500	1,600	2,000	3,000

8 labour hours are required to produce product A and 4 labour hours to produce product B and the maximum capacity of the factory is restricted to 20,000 labour hours per month. The variable cost per unit for Product A and Product B are ₹ 20 and ₹ 14 respectively

Fixed Overheads are ₹ 32,400 per quarter.

You are required to compute the possible combinations and arrive at a proper price mix for maximum profitability.

Solution

CALCULATION OF TOTAL CONTRIBUTION AND TOTAL LABOUR HOURS OF EACH PRODUCT AT DIFFERENT PRICES

Product	*Product A*			*Product B*		
A. Expected Demand	900	1,000	1,500	1,600	2,000	3,000
B. Selling Price per unit (₹)	32	30	28	22	20	19
C. Variable Cost per unit (₹)	20	20	20	14	14	14
D. Contribution per unit (₹) [B – C]	12	10	8	8	6	5
E. Labour Hours per unit	8	8	8	4	4	4
F. Total Contribution (₹) [A × D]	10,800	10,000	12,000	12,800	12,000	15,000
G. Total Labour Hours required [A × E]	7,200	8,000	12,000	6,400	8,000	12,000

TOTAL CONTRIBUTION AND TOTAL LABOUR HOURS OF BOTH THE PRODUCTS AT ALL POSSIBLE PRICE COMBINATIONS

Products A Selling Price (₹)	*Products B Selling Price (₹)*	*Total Contribution (₹)*	*Labour Hrs. Required*
32	22	23,600*	13,600**
32	20	22,800	15,200
32	**19**	**25,800**	**19,200**
30	22	22,800	14,400
30	20	22,000	16,000
30	19	25,000	20,000
28	22	24,800	18,400
28	20	24,000	20,000
28	19	27,000	24,000

* (₹ 10,800 + ₹ 12,800), ** (7,200 + 6,400)

Recommendation: The above computations show that the maximum contribution of ₹ 25,800 is possible at 19,200 labour hours. Therefore, profitable *price mix* is A ₹ 32 and B ₹ 19.

Illustration 21. Universe Ltd. manufactures two products X and Y. It is facing severe competition in the market. The monthly sales potential in units at different selling prices as anticipated by the Sales Manager are as under:

Product-X		*Product-Y*	
Selling Price per unit ₹	*Sales Potential (in units)*	*Selling Price per unit* ₹	*Sales Potential (in units)*
110	5,000	78	30,000
108	7,500	77	32,000
107	8,000	75	35,000
103	8,400	72	40,000
96	9,000	69	45,000

The total costs as disclosed by the budgets of the company are as follows:

	Product X		*Product Y*	
Output and Sales per month (units)	5,000	9,000	30,000	45,000
Total Costs per month (₹ In lacs)	5	6.6	18	25.5
Labour hours needed per month	20,000	36,000	60,000	90,000

You are required to find out the selling price and units to be sold to earn maximum profit where (a) labour hours are available without any restriction and (b) only 95,000 hours are available

Solution:

TOTAL CONTRIBUTION AND TOTAL LABOUR HOURS OF EACH PRODUCT AT DIFFERENT PRICES

	Particulars	Product X					Product Y				
A	Expected Demand	5,000	7,500	**8,000**	8,400	9,000	30,000	32,000	35,000	**40,000**	45,000
B	Selling Price Per Unit (₹)	110	108	107	103	96	78	77	75	72	69
C	Variable Cost Per Unit (₹)	40	40	40	40	40	50	50	50	50	50
D	Contribution/ Unit (₹) [B – C]	70	68	67	63	56	28	27	25	22	19
E	Labour Hours Per Unit	4	4	4	4	4	2	2	2	2	2
F	Total Contribution [A x D]	3,50,000	5,10,000	5,36,000	5,29,200	5,04,000	8,40,000	8,64,000	8,75,000	8,80,000	8,55,000
G	Total Labour Hrs Req. [A x E]	20,000	30,000	32,000	33,600	36,000	60,000	64,000	70,000	80,000	90,000

TOTAL CONTRIBUTION AND TOTAL LABOUR HOURS OF BOTH THE PRODUCTS AT DIFFERENT PRICE COMBINATIONS

Price Combinations	*Price of Product X*	*Price of Product Y*	*Units X*	*Units Y*	*Total Contribution of Both Products*	*Total Labour hours for Both Products*
1	110	78	5,000	30,000	11,90,000*	80,000**
2	110	77	5,000	32,000	12,14,000	84,000
3	110	75	5,000	35,000	12,25,000	90,000
4	110	72	5,000	40,000	12,30,000	1,00,000
5	110	69	5,000	45,000	12,05,000	1,10,000
6	108	78	7,500	30,000	13,50,000	90,000
7	108	77	7,500	32,000	13,74,000	94,000
8	108	75	7,500	35,000	13,85,000	1,00,000
9	108	72	7,500	40,000	13,90,000	1,10,000
10	108	69	7,500	45,000	13,65,000	1,20,000
11	**107**	78	**8,000**	**30,000**	13,76,000	**92,000**
12	**107**	77	**8,000**	**32,000**	14,00,000	**96,000**

Price Combinations	Price of Product X	Price of Product Y	Units X	Units Y	Total Contribution of Both Products	Total Labour hours for Both Products
13	107	75	8,000	35,000	14,11,000	1,02,000
14	**107**	**72**	**8,000**	**40,000**	**14,16,000**	1,12,000
15	107	69	8,000	45,000	13,91,000	1,22,000
16	103	78	8,400	30,000	13,69,200	93,600
17	103	77	8,400	32,000	13,93,200	97,600
18	103	75	8,400	35,000	14,04,200	1,03,600
19	103	72	8,400	40,000	14,09,200	1,13,600
20	103	69	8,400	45,000	13,84,200	1,23,600
21	96	78	9,000	30,000	13,44,000	96,000
22	96	77	9,000	32,000	13,68,000	1,00,000
23	96	75	9,000	35,000	13,79,000	1,06,000
24	96	72	9,000	40,000	13,84,000	1,16,000
25	96	69	9,000	45,000	13,59,000	1,26,000

*(3,50,000 + 8,40,000), **(20,000 + 60,000)

STATEMENT SHOWING PROFIT

Particulars	*No Labour Hour Constraint*	*Labour Hour Constraint of 95,000 Hours*
Contribution from Product X	5,36,000 (i.e. 8000 x 67)	5,36,000 (i.e. 8000 x 67)
Contribution from Product Y	8,80,000 (i.e. 40,000 x 22)	8,50,500 (i.e. 31,500 x 27)
Total Contribution	14,16,000	13,86,500
Less: Fixed Cost	6,00,000	6,00,000
Profit	8,16,000	7,86,500

Working Notes:

(i) COMPUTATION OF VARIABLE COST P.U. AND FIXED COST (P.M.) OF TWO PRODUCTS "X" AND "Y"

Products	*X* ₹	*Y* ₹
Variable Cost per unit	40	50
$\left(\frac{\text{Change in total costs of a product}}{\text{Change in the output of the product}}\right)$	$\left(\frac{1,60,000}{4,000 \text{ units}}\right)$	$\left(\frac{7,50,000}{15,000 \text{ units}}\right)$
Fixed Cost (Total Cost – Variable Cost)	3,00,000 (₹ 5,00,000 – ₹ 2,00,000)	3,00,000 (₹ 18,00,000 – ₹ 15,00,000)

(ii) Allocation of 95,000 Labour Hours

Total Labour hours available	95,000
Less: Utilized for 8000 units of Product X (32000/4)	32,000
Balance Utilized for 31,500 units of Product Y (63000/2)	63,000

Illustration 22. Zilmil Ltd. makes two products 'Brightly; and 'Lightly'. Both the products use the same labour force, the size of which is restricted to 78,000 hours per month. The estimated production and sales, cost etc. per month are as follows:

	Brightly		*Lightly*	
Production and Sales (in Nos.)	12,000	16,000	40,000	48,000
Cost per month (₹)	34,00,000	38,00,000	62,00,000	66,80,000
Labour Hours needed p.m.	24,000	32,000	40,000	48,000

The company is considering pricing option in a highly competitive market. It has estimated sales demand at various selling prices:

Brightly:

Selling Price per unit (₹)	276	272	268	264	260	254
Sales demand per month	12,000	14,000	16,000	18,000	20,000	22,000

Lightly:

Selling Price per unit (₹)	163	162	161	160	156	152
Sales demand per month	40,000	42,000	44,000	46,000	48,000	50,000

You are required to compute profit maximizing price and quantity for each product.

Solution:

Step 1: Ranking on the basis of Incremental Contribution per Labour Hour

Brightly

Unit Price (₹)	*Contribution per unit (₹)*	*Volume (Units)*	*Total Contribution (₹ in '000)*	*Incremental Contribution (₹ '000)*	*Labour hours*	*Incremental labour hours*	*Incremental Contribution per labour hour ₹*	*Rank*
A	*B*	*C*	*D*	*E*	*F*	*G*	*H = E/G*	*I*
276	176	12,000	2,112	2,112	24,000	24,000	88	2
272	172	14,000	2,408	296	28,000	4,000	74	6
268	168	16,000	2,688	280	32,000	4,000	70	7
264	164	18,000	2,952	264	36,000	4,000	66	8
260	160	20,000	3,200	248	40,000	4,000	62	9
254	154	22,000	3,388	188	44,000	4,000	47	10

Lightly

Unit Price (₹)	*Contribution per unit (₹)*	*Volume (Units)*	*Total Contribution (₹ in '000)*	*Incremental Contribution (₹ '000)*	*Labour hours*	*Increment labour hours*	*Incremental contribution per labour hour*	*Rank*
A	*B*	*C*	*D*	*E*	*F*	*G*	*H = E/G*	*I*
163	103	40,000	4120	4,120	40,000	40,000	103	1
162	102	42,000	4284	164	42,000	2,000	82	3
161	101	44,000	4444	160	44,000	2,000	80	4
160	100	46,000	4600	156	46,000	2,000	78	5
156	96	48,000	4608	8	48,000	2,000	4	11
152	92	50,000	4600	(8)	50,000	2,000	(4)	Loss

Step 2: As the labour time is scarce source (time available 78,000 hours), the decision has to be taken on the basis of ranks based upon Incremental Contribution per Labour Hour.

Product	*Price*	*Incremental Volume*	*Incremental labour hours*	*Balance hours*	*Incremental contribution (in 000 ₹)*
Lightly	163	40,000	40,000	38,000	4120
Brightly	276	12,000	24,000	14,000	2112
Lightly	162	2,000	2,000	12,000	164
Lightly	161	2,000	2,000	10,000	160
Lightly	160	2,000	2,000	8,000	156
Brightly	272	2,000	4,000	4,000	296
Brightly	268	2,000	4,000		280
Total					7,288

Hence product mix is Brightly – 16,000 units and Lightly 46,000 units

	₹
Optimal Contribution per month	72,88,000
Fixed Costs per month	(60,00,000)
Profit	12,88,000

Working Notes:

	Brightly	*Lightly*
(i) Variable Cost per unit	$\frac{(38,00,000 - 34,00,000)}{(16,000 - 12,000)}$ = Rs 100	$\frac{(66,80,000 - 62,00,000)}{(48,000 - 40,000)}$ = Rs 60
(ii) Fixed Cost (₹)	22,00,000	38,00,000

4.0 MAKE OR BUY DECISION

4.1 Basis of Make or Buy Decision

A decision as to whether to make the component or buy the component from an outside supplier should be based on Marginal Cost Analysis.

4.2 Considerable Factors

The following factors should be considered in Make or Buy decisions.

Cost Factors	Non-Cost Factors
1. **Marginal Cost of making** the component	1. **Capacity of Supplier**—Ensure whether the supplier has capacity to supply the requirements.
2. **Contribution lost** due to non-manufacture of a product which is currently produced using the facilities which now to be used for making the component	2. **Reliability of Supplier**—Ensure whether the supplier can be relied upon for the quality of goods to be supplied.
3. **Cost of buying** the component from an outside supplier	3. **Timely Delivery**—Ensure whether the supplier will make timely delivery of the components.
4. **Benefits** resulting **from** the utilization of the **capacity released** due to discontinuance of the manufacturing of the component (e.g. rental income from hiring out the capacity released, contribution from production of new product by using capacity released	4. **More than one Supplier**—Ensure that more than one supplier is available to reduce the risk of outside buying.
5. **Reduction in Fixed** costs on buying the component.	5. **Possible use of released production capacity and facilities due** to discontinuance of the manufacturing of the component

4.3 Relative Economics of Make *or* Buy

The relative economics of the "Make *vs.* Buy" decision is management control:
Generally for taking a Make *vs.* Buy decision comparison is made between the supplier's price and the marginal cost of making *plus* the opportunity cost. Make vs. buy decision is a strategic decision, and,

therefore, both short-term as well as long-term thinking about various costs and other aspects needs to be done.

A company generally buy a component instead of making it under following situations:

1. If it costs less to buy rather than to manufacture it internally;
2. If the return on the necessary investment to be made to manufacture is not attractive enough;
3. If the company does not have the requisite skilled manpower to make;
4. If the concern feels that manufacturing internally will mean additional labour problem;
5. If adequate managerial manpower is not available to take charge of the extra work of manufacturing;
6. If the component shows much seasonal demand resulting in a considerable risk of maintaining inventories;
7. If transport and other infrastructure facilities are adequately available;
8. If there is risk of technological obsolescence for the component such that it does not encourage capital investment in the component.
9. If the process of making is confidential or patented.

4.4 Practical Steps In Make or Buy Decision

Step 1: *Calculate the Relevant Cost of manufacturing the component*
*[**Note:** Fixed overheads are not relevant cost but contribution lost due to non-manufacture of a product which is currently produced using the facilities which now to be used for making the component is relevant cost. Thus, lost contribution becomes relevant cost when the firm is working at its full capacity.]*

Step 2: *Calculate the Relevant Cost of buying the component as follows:*
A. Cost of Buying the Component from an outside supplier
B. Less: Benefits resulting from the utilization of the capacity released due to discontinuance of manufacturing of the component (e.g. Rental Income from hiring out the capacity released, contribution from production of new product by using capacity released)
C. Less: Reduction in Fixed Costs (if any) due to discontinuance of manufacturing of the component.

Step 3: *Compare the Relevant Cost of manufacturing with the Relevant Cost of Buying.*

Step 4: *Make the component if Relevant Cost of Manufacture is less than the Relevant Cost of Buying*

or

Buy the component if Relevant Cost of Manufacture is more than the Relevant Cost of Buying.

4.5 Format of Statement Showing the Relevant Cost to Make and Buy

STATEMENT SHOWING THE RELEVANT COST TO MAKE AND BUY

Particulars	*Make*	*Buy and Released Capacity remains idle*	*Buy and Released Capacity is rented out*	*Buy and Released Capacity is used for another Product*
Variable Cost of Mfg	xxx	—	—	—
Cost of Buying	—	xxx	xxx	xxx
Reduction in Fixed Cost	—	(xxx)	(xxx)	(xxx)
Rental Income	—	—	(xxx)	—
Contribution from Another Product	—	—	—	(xxx)
Relevant cost	xxx	xxx	xxx	xxx

Illustration 23. A machine manufactures 10,000 units of a part at a total cost of ₹ 21 of which ₹ 18 is variable. This part is readily available in the market at ₹ 19 per unit.

If the part is purchased from the market then the machine can either be utilised to manufacture a component in same quantity contributing ₹ 2 per component or it can be hired out at ₹ 21,000.

Recommend which of the alternative is profitable.

Solution: **STATEMENT SHOWING THE RELEVANT COST TO MAKE AND BUY**

Particulars	*Make*	*Buy and Released Capacity used for other product*	*Buy and Released Capacity rented out*
Variable Cost of Mfg [10000 × ₹ 18]	1,80,000	—	—
Cost of Buying [10000 × ₹ 19]	—	1,90,000	1,90,000
Contribution from another component [10000 × ₹ 2]	—	(20,000)	—
Rental Income	—	—	(21,000)
Relevant Cost	1,80,000	1,70,000	1,69,000

Recommendation: The part should be bought from outside and released capacity should be hired out since it will result in net saving of ₹ 11,000 (i.e. ₹ 1,80,000 – ₹ 1,69,000).

Illustration 24. Tulsian Ltd. manufactures 10,000 units of component 'X' per month. The total cost of a manufactured component is ₹ 100 as follows:

	₹
Material	10
Labour @ ₹ 10 per hour	40
Overheads (40% variable)	50
	100

An outside supplier has offered the same component at ₹ 80 *plus* 10% GST *plus* Delivery Cost of ₹ 2. If the component is bought, fixed overheads to the extent of 60% could be avoided if the capacity remains idle.

Required:

(a) Should the component be made or bought assuming that the released capacity remains idle

(b) Determine the level of production of component X at which Tulsian Ltd. would be indifferent between buying and producing the component. If the future volume level were predicted to decrease, would that influence the decision taken in Part (a)?

(c) Evaluate the following two alternatives available to the manufactures:

(i) Rent out the released capacity at ₹ 1 per hour

(ii) Manufacture a new product 'Y' which can be sold at ₹ 73 per unit. The unit cost of product 'Y' is ₹ 60 as follows:

	₹
Material	30
Labour @₹ 10 per hour	20
Variable overheads	10
	60

Solution: **STATEMENT SHOWING THE RELEVANT COST TO MAKE AND BUY**

Particulars	*Make*	*Buy and Released Capacity remains idle*	*Buy and Released Capacity is rented out*	*Buy and released Capacity is used for product another*
Variable Cost of Mfg. [₹ 10 + ₹ 40 + ₹ 20] [10000 × ₹ 70]	7,00,000	—	—	—
Cost of Buying [₹ 80 + ₹ 8 + 2] [10000 × ₹ 90]	—	9,00,000	9,00,000	9,00,000
Reduction in Fixed Overheads [10000 × ₹ 30 × 60%]	—	(1,80,000)	—	—

Rental Income [10000 × 4 × ₹ 1]	—	—	(40,000)	—
Contribution from Product 'Y' [20,000 × (₹ 73 – ₹ 60)]	—	—	—	(2,60,000)
	7,00,000	7,20,000	8,60,000	6,40,000

(a) The component should be manufactured since the cost of manufacturing is less than that of buying from outside.

(b) Indifference Point can be obtained by equating following two equations:

(Variable Mfg Cost per unit × Volume) + Avoidable Fixed costs ...Eq I

Cost of Buying per unit × Volume ...Eq. II

Let volume in units be X

₹ 70 X + ₹ 1,80,000 = ₹ 90 X

X = ₹ 1,80,000/20 = 9,000 units

If the volume falls below 9,000 units, then Tulsian Ltd. would prefer to buy, since the total cost of buying will be lower than the total cost of manufacturing.

(c) The component should be bought from outside and the released capacity used to produce Product 'Y' since this decision will result in saving of ₹ 60,000 (i.e. ₹ 7,00,000 – ₹ 6,40,000)

Working Notes:

(i) Released Capacity (in hours) = 10000 × ₹ 40/₹ 10 = 40,000 hours

(ii) Max No. of units of product 'Y' = 40,000/2 = 20000 units

(iii) Fixed Overhead is not relevant cost.

Illustration 25. Auto Parts Ltd. has an annual production of 90,000 units for a motor component. The component's. cost structure is as below:

	₹
Materials	270 per unit
Labour (25% fixed)	180 per unit
Expenses :	
Variable	90 per unit
Fixed	135 per unit
Total	675 per unit

(a) The Purchase Manager has an offer from a supplier who is willing to supply the component at ₹ 540. Should the component be purchased and production stopped ?

(b) Assume the resources now used for this component's manufacture are to be used to produce another new product for which the selling price is ₹ 485.

In the latter case, the material price will be ₹ 200 per unit. 90,000 units of this product can be produced, at the same cost basis as above for labour and expenses. Discuss whether it would be advisable to divert the resources to manufacture that new product, on the footing that the component presently being produced would, instead of being produced, be purchased from the market.

Solution:

(a) STATEMENT OF THE VARIABLE MFG. COST AND PURCHASE COST OF COMPONENT

Particulars	*Per unit* ₹	*Total for 90,000 Units* ₹
Materials	270	2,43,00,000
Labour	135	1,21,50,000
Expenses	90	81,00,000
Total variable cost (when component is produced)	495	4,45,50,000
Cost of purchase (When component is purchased)	540	4,86,00,000
Difference, excess of purchase price over variable cost	45	40,50,000

Advice: If the component is purchased from the outside supplier, the Company will have to pay ₹ 45 per unit more and on 90,000 units that Company will have to spend ₹ 40,50,000 more. Therefore, the Company should not stop the production of the component.

(b) STATEMENT OF CONTRIBUTION PER UNIT IF THE RESOURCES ARE USED FOR NEW PRODUCT

Particulars	₹	₹
A. Selling Price of the new product per unit		485
B. *Less :* Materials Cost	200	
Labour (Variable)	135	
Expenses (Variable)	90	425
C. Contribution per unit [A – B]		60
D. Loss per unit if present component is purchased [₹ 540 – ₹ 495]		45
E. Saving per unit [₹ 60 – ₹ 45]		15
F. Total Saving [90,000 ₹ 15]		13,50,000

Advice: If the Company diverts its resources for the production of another new product, it will benefit by ₹ 15 (i.e. ₹ 60 – 45 per unit). On 90,000 units, the Company will 'save' ₹ 13,50,000. Therefore, it is advisable to divert the resources to manufacture the new product and the component presently being produced should be purchased from the market.

Illustration 26. Part No. X - 293 used in the assembly of a product manufactured by your company has during the past three years been a bought-out item. The current price of this part is ₹ 120. Transportation and other delivery costs account for ₹ 15 per piece. GST at 10 per cent is added to the invoice price.

Your company had been manufacturing this part earlier but decided subsequently to discontinue its own manufacture. There is sufficient unutilised capacity which can be used, if it is decided to manufacture this part again in its own plant. Annual requirements of this part are 6,000 units.

Prepare a study to enable the management to come to decision on a proposal to manufacture the part within its own plant. The following estimates are available :

	Part No. X - 293 *Estimated cost per unit*
Raw Materials	₹ 96
Direct Wages	8
Overheads at 800 per cent of Direct Wages	64
Total Cost	168
Mark-up for return on investment @12%	12
	180

In addition, special tools, jigs and fixtures required to manufacture this part are needed to be acquired at a cost of ₹ 1,50,000. These are to be amortised over 5 years.

The overhead rate is the budgeted recovery rate for products manufactured by the Company. The variable portion of this amounts to 100 per cent of direct wages.

Required: Make your recommendations.

Solution: **COST INCURRED TO BUY THE REQUIREMENTS OF PART X - 293**

Particulars	*Per unit*	*Total*
Purchase Price (₹)	120.00	7,20,000
Transportation and Delivery Charges	15.00	90,000
GST	12.00	72,000
	147.00	8,82,000

COST INCURRED TO MANUFACTURE 6,000 UNITS OF PART X - 293

Particulars	*Per unit*	*Total*
Raw Materials (₹)	96.00	5,76,000
Direct Wages	8.00	48,000
Variable Overheads	8.00	48,000
Special Tools, jigs, etc. (1/5 of the total investment)	5.00	30,000
Interest, say @ 12% on the investment in special tools	3.00	18,000
	120.00	7,20,000

The manufacture of the part by the Company itself will result in a savings of ₹ 1,62,000. The Company, before taking the decision, should consider the following points :

(i) Whether a saving of ₹ 1,62,000 is worth the trouble the Company will have to take in purchasing and installing a new plant and increase in fixed overheads on account of interest etc.

(ii) Whether the spare capacity can be utilised for some other purpose.

(iii) Need for maintenance of quality and regularity of supplies.

The Company should, therefore, consider whether the spare capacity with the company can be put to some other use. If not, manufacture of the part X - 293 may be undertaken.

Illustration 27. A Company is considering the possibility of purchasing from a supplier a component it now makes. The supplier will provide the components in the necessary quantities at a unit price of ₹ 9. Transportation and storage cost would be negligible.

The Company produces the components from a single raw material in economic lots of 2,000 units at a cost of ₹ 2 per unit. Average annual demand is 20,000 units. The annual holding cost is ₹ 0.25 per unit and the minimum stock level is set at 400 units. Direct labour costs for the component are ₹ 6 per unit, fixed manufacturing overhead is charged at a rate of ₹ 3 per unit based on a normal activity of 20,000 units. The Company also hires the machine on which the components are produced at a rate of ₹ 200 per month.

Required : Should the Company make the components?

Solution:

The cost of placing an order, when component is purchased, is not given. This can be found out by EOQ formula.

$$\text{EOQ} = \sqrt{\frac{2 \times \text{Annual consumption} \times \text{Cost of placing an order}}{\text{Cost of carrying one unit of inventory of one year}}}$$

Substituting the given information :

$$2{,}000 = \sqrt{\frac{2 \times 20{,}000 \times x}{0.25}} \quad \textit{or,} \quad x = ₹\ 25$$

Cost of Placing an order = ₹ 25

Average stock level = Minimum stock level + 1/2 EOQ = 400 + 1/2 (2,000) = 1,400 units

COMPARISON OF ANNUAL COSTS

Make	₹	*Buy*	₹
(i) Storage cost [1400 0.25]	350	Purchase Cost :	
(ii) Ordering cost [(20,000 ÷ 2,000) 25]	250	[20,000 ₹ 9]	1,80,000
(iii) Material cost [20,000 ₹ 2]	40,000		
(iv) Labour cost [20,000 ₹ 6]	1,20,000		
(v) Rental charges [₹ 200 12]	2,400		
	1,63,000		1,80,000

Recommendation: The Company should make the component till it has some alternative use for existing capacity. Since the cost to manufacture the component is less than the cost to buy from outside. Labour cost has been presumed to be variable cost. Fixed cost being sunk cost is not relevant for decision making.

Illustration 28. Part No. 4466 is manufactured by PCT (Exam.) Ltd. and is used extensively in the Company's finished products. The annual requirement for this component is 12,000 units. The lowest price quotation so far required from an outside supplier is ₹ 21.50 per unit. This is being considered as the Company wants to discontinue manufacture of this component and buy it from outside. You are asked to help the Company for taking a decision. In this connection, the following figures are supplied to you :

The expenses when Part No. 4466 was in production for 12,000 units were as under :

Materials	₹ 3,50,000
Direct labour	4,00,000
Indirect labour	1,60,000
Lighting	20,000
Power	30,000
Depreciation	2,00,000
Insurance	15,000
Miscellaneous	27,000

Fringe benefits to labour work out normally 15% of total labour costs. Discontinuing the production of this component would not any way permits the disposal of any of the factory's assets.

The following proportion of expenses can be avoided, if manufacture of Part No. 4466 is stopped:

	Percentage
Materials	30
Direct Labour	35
Indirect labour	25
Power	20

When the part is purchased from an outside supplier, shipping charge would average 75 paise per unit and indirect labour cost would be increased by ₹ 20,000 annually for receiving, inspecting and handling the purchased parts.

Required: Prepare a schedule showing the relating costs of buying and making Part No. 4466 and give your recommendation.

Solution:

(i) STATEMENT OF SAVING IN EXPENSES, IF MANUFACTURE OF PART NO. 4466 IS STOPPED

Particulars	₹
Material (30% of ₹ 3,50,000)	1,05,000
Direct labour (35% of ₹ 4,00,000)	1,40,000
Indirect labour (25% of ₹ 1,60,000)	40,000
Power (20% of ₹ 30,000)	6,000
Fringe benefits 15% of (₹ 1,40,000 + ₹ 40,000)	27,000
Total	3,18,000

(ii) STATEMENT SHOWING THE COST OF BUYING PART NO. 4466

Particulars	₹
Lowest price (12,000 ₹ 21.50)	2,58,000
Shipping charges (12,000 ₹ 0.75)	9,000
Additional indirect labour cost	20,000
Fringe benefit (15% of 20,000)	3,000
Total	2,90,000
Incremental profit on decision to buy (₹ 3,18,000 – ₹ 2,90,000)	28,000

Recommendation : The company should buy the component from outside since the decision to buy will result in saving of ₹ 28,000 (i.e. ₹ 3,18,000 – ₹ 2,90,000).

Illustration 29. The Company at present manufactures component 'X' one unit of which is required for each unit of Product 'A'. The budgeted output of Product 'A' are 1,20,000 units. The cost details for 10,000 units of component 'X' are as under :

Direct materials	₹ 24,000
Direct labour @ ₹ 5 per hour	30,000
Variable overheads	18,000
Fixed overheads	18,000
Total	90,000

The component 'X' however is available for purchase at the market at ₹ 8.00 each. In the event of the Company deciding to purchase the component 'X' from market, the Company has two alternatives for the use of the capacity so released as under.

(a) Rent out the released capacity at ₹ 1 per hour.

(b) Manufacture component 'Y' which can be sold at ₹ 8.00 per unit. The cost data of this component for 10,000 units are :

Direct materials	₹ 30,000
Direct labour @ ₹ 5 per hour	15,000
Factory variable overheads	9,000
Other variable overheads	21,000
Total	75,000

Required:

(i) Make an appraisal of proposal to manufacture component 'X' and state whether the component 'X' should be manufactured in the factory or purchased from the market. Assume that no alternative use of spare capacity is available.

(ii) Evaluate the alternative use of the spare capacity and state whether to manufacture or buy the component 'X' and if your decision is to buy the component 'X', which of the two alternatives for the use of spare capacity will you prefer ?

Solution: **(i) STATEMENT SHOWING THE RELEVANT COST OF MAKE OR BUY**

Particulars	*Cost of decision to Manufacture (₹)*	*Cost of decision to Buy (₹)*
Direct material	2,88,000	
Direct labour	3,60,000	
Variable overhead	2,16,000	
Cost of Buying @ ₹ 8	—	9,60,000
Net Relevant Cost	8,64,000	9,60,000

Since the capacity is existing, it is profitable to make the product. Fixed cost of product 'X' is irrelevant to decision, because this facility has to be provided for Product A.

(ii) STATEMENT SHOWING THE RELEVANT COST OF MAKE OR BUY

Particulars	*Make*	*Buy if released Capacity is rented out*	*Buy if released capacity is used for product 'Y'*
Variable Cost of Mfg. @ ₹ 7.20	8,64,0000	—	—
Cost of Buying @ ₹ 8	—	9,60,000	9,60,000
Rental Income [72,000 ₹ 1]	—	(72,000)	—
Total contribution for product 'Y'	—	—	(1,20,000)
	8,64,000	8,88,000	8,40,000

Recommendation: The company should buy component 'X' from outside and released capacity should be used to produce product 'Y' since this decision will result in net saving of ₹ 24,000 (i.e. ₹ 8,64,000 – ₹ 8,40,000).

Working Notes :

(i) Released capacity (in hours) = $\frac{30,000}{\text{Rs. } 5} \times \frac{1,20,000}{10,000}$ = 72,000 Hours

(ii) Hours to be required to produce 10000 units of 'Y' = ₹ 15,000/₹ 5 = 3,000 Hours

(III) Max. Number of units of 'Y' = $\frac{72,000}{3,000}$ × 10,000 = 2,40,000 Units

(iv) Contribution per unit of 'Y' [₹ 8 – (₹ 3 + ₹ 1.5 + ₹ 0.9 + ₹ 2.1)] = ₹ 0.50

(v) Total contribution for 2,40,000 units of 'Y' = 2,40,000 ₹ 0.50 = ₹ 1,20,000

Illustration 30. A Company proposes to install a machine for the manufacture of a component which at present is being purchased at ₹ 24 each. There are two alternatives, namely (a) installation of an automatic machine and (b) installation of a semi-automatic machine. The details of the two machines are as under :

	Automatic Machine	*Semi-Automatic Machine*
Initial cost of machine (₹)	9,00,000	6,00,000
Life	10 Years	10 Years
Fixed overheads other than depreciation On machines (per annum) (₹)	1,62,000	84,000
Variable expenses for the component (₹)	12	15

The Company charges depreciation on straight line method. Scrap value of the machine at the end of life is nil. The demand for the components at present is 20,000 units per annum. This demand is expected to increase to 40,000 units.

Required:

(a) For each of the two volumes of output namely 20,000 and 40,000 units, state with supporting calculations whether the components should be purchased or manufactured by installation of machine. If your decision is an favour of installation of machine, which model will yoU advice?

(b) At what Volume of output should the company change over from purchase of components to manufacture by installation of (I) semi-automatic machine and (ii) automatic machine.

(c) At what volume of manufacture of the components will the Company switch over from installation of one type of machine to the other ?

Solution: **(a) STATEMENT SHOWING THE COST PER UNIT UNDER VARIOUS ALTERNATIVES**

	20,000 units		*40,000 units*	
Particulars	*Automatic Machine*	*Semi-Automatic Machine*	*Automatic Machine*	*Semi-Automatic Machine*
Variable Cost (₹)	12.00	15.00	12.00	15.00
Fixed Overheads other than depreciation	8.10	4.20	4.05	2.10
Depreciation (₹)	4.50	3.00	2.25	1.50
Total cost of manufacture (₹)	24.60	22.20	18.30	18.60
Cost of Buying per unit (₹)	24.00	24.00	24.00	24.00

It is profitable to install semi-automatic machine at the production level of 20,000 units. However at the volume of 40,000 units, automatic machine should be installed.

(b) STATEMENT SHOWING THE CHANGE OVER FROM PURCHASE TO MANUFACTURE

Particulars	*Automatic-Machine*	*Semi-Automatic Machine*
A. Purchase Price of component	₹ 24.00	₹ 24.00
B. Variable Costs of manufacture	₹ 12.00	₹ 15.00
C. Saving [A – B]	₹ 12.00	₹ 9.00
D. Total Fixed Costs (including depreciation)	₹ 2,52,000	₹ 1,44,000
E. Number of units at which change over is effected [D/C]	21,000	16,000

(c) STATEMENT SHOWING SWITCHOVER FROM ONE TYPE OF MACHINE TO THE OTHER

	Automatic Machine	*Semi-Automatic*	*Difference Machine*
A Variable Cost	₹ 12	₹ 15	₹ 3
B. Total Fixed Cost (including Depreciation)	₹ 2,52,000	₹ 1,44,000	₹ 1,08,000
C. Number of units at which switch over is effected [Difference in Fixed Costs/Difference in Variable Costs]			36,000 units

Working Note : *Calculation of Fixed Overheads per unit and Depreciation per unit*

	20,000 units		*40,000 units*	
Particulars	*Automatic Machine*	*Semi-Automatic Machine*	*Automatic Machine*	*Semi-Automatic Machine*
A. Fixed Overheads (₹)	1,62,000	84,000	1,62,000	84,000
B. Depreciation (₹)	90,000	60,000	90,000	60,000
C. No. of units	20,000	20,000	40,000	40,000
D. Fixed OH per unit (₹) [A/C]	8.10	4.20	4.05	2.10
E. Depreciation per Unit [B/C]	4.50	3.00	2.25	1.50

Illustration 31. Product 'A' takes five hours to produce on a particular machine and it has a selling price of ₹ 50 and a marginal cost of ₹ 35.

On the same machine, another product 'B' can be made at two hours at a marginal cost of ₹ 5 per unit. Supplier's price of product 'B' is ₹ 10 per unit.

Assuming that machine hour is the key factor, advise whether product 'B' could be bought out or manufactured.

Solution: **STATEMENT SHOWING THE RELEVANT COST TO MAKE AND BUY**

Particulars	*Make* ₹	*Buy* ₹
Marginal Cost of Mfg	5	—
Contribution lost [2 hours × ₹ 3 per hour]	6	—
Cost of Buying	—	10
	11	10

Advise: Product 'B' should be bought from outside since the cost of buying is less than that of making.

Working Note: Contribution per hour of product 'A' = (₹ 50 – ₹ 35)/5 = ₹ 3 per unit

4.6 Make or Buy Decision when there is a Key Factor

When more than one component are manufactured and there is a key factor (*say Machine Hours*), excess of Purchase Price over Variable Cost of Manufacturing per unit of key factor should be used to assign the ranking for manufacturing. The component of which variable cost of manufacturing is more than the cost of buying, should be bought from outside whether there is a key factor a not.

Illustration 32. Delhi Equipment Ltd. manufacture four components, the cost particulars of which are given below:

	Components			
	A (₹)	*B* (₹)	*C* (₹)	*D* (₹)
Direct Material	80	100	100	120
Direct Labour	20	25	25	30
Variable Overhead	10	12	15	10
Fixed Overhead	15	23	20	20
	125	160	160	180
Output per Machine Hour (units)	4	2	3	3

The key factor is shortage of machine capacity.

Required: Advise management as to whether they should continue to produce all *or* some of these components (which are used in its main product) *or* they should buy them from a supplier who has quoted the following prices:

A = ₹ 115; B = ₹ 175; C = ₹ 135; D = ₹ 185.

Solution: **STATEMENT SHOWING CONTRIBUTION, RANKING AND DECISION**

	Particulars	*Components*			
		A	*B*	*C*	*D*
A.	Purchase Price per unit (₹)	115	175	135	185
B.	Variable Cost of Manufacturing per unit (₹)				
	Direct Material	80	100	100	120
	Direct Labour	20	25	25	30
	Variable Overhead	10	12	15	10
	Marginal Cost per unit	110	137	140	160
C.	Contribution per unit (₹) [A – B]	5	38	(5)	25
D.	Machine hour per unit	0.25	0.50	0.33	0.33
E.	Contribution per unit of Machine Hour (₹)	20	76	(15)	75
F.	Ranking for Manufacturing	III	I		II
G.	Decision	Mfg.	Mfg.	Buy	Mfg.

The above analysis shows :

(i) Component C should be purchased from outside whether there is a key factor or not since its marginal cost is more than its purchase price. Purchasing from outside will push up the profitability by ₹ 15 per machine hour.

(ii) In case shortage of machine capacity is the key factor (as given in the question), the management must decide about the ranking of the three components. The above analysis for manufacturing should be in the order of B, D and A.

Illustration 33. Agrocaps Ltd., engaged in manufacturing agricultural machinery, is preparing its annual budget for the coming year. The company has a metal pressing capacity of 20,000 hours, which will be insufficient for manufacture of all requirements of components A, B, C, and D.

The Company has the following choices :

(i) Buy the components entirely from outside suppliers.
(ii) Buy from outside suppliers and/or use a partial second shift.

The data for the current year are given below:

	Standard production cost per unit			
	A	*B*	*C*	*D*
Variable Costs (₹) :				
Direct Materials	37	27	25	44
Direct wages	10	8	22	40
Direct expenses	10	20	10	60
Fixed overhead (₹)	5	4	11	20
Total production costs (₹)	62	59	68	164
Requirements (in units)	2,000	3,500	1,500	2,800

Direct expenses relate to the use of the metal presses which costs ₹ 10 per hour, to operate. Fixed overheads are absorbed as a percentage of direct wages.

Supply of all or any part of the total requirements can be obtained at following prices, each delivered to the factory: A at ₹ 60, B at ₹ 59, C at ₹ 52 and D at ₹ 168.

Second shift operations would increase direct wages by 25 per cent over the normal shift and fixed overhead by ₹ 500 for each 1,000 (or part thereof) second shift hours worked.

You are required to present, with calculations:

(a) Which component, and what quantities should be manufactured in the 20,000 hours of press time available?
(b) Whether it would be profitable to make any of the balance of components required on a second shift basis instead of buying them from outside suppliers.

Solution:

(a) COMPONENTS AND THEIR QUANTITIES TO BE MANUFACTURED IN THE 20,000 HOURS OF PRESS TIME AVAILABLE (SINGLE SHIFT OPERATION)

A. Available capacity for metal pressing	20,000
B. *Less :* Utilized to produce 2,800 units of D [2,800 6]	16,800
C. Balance hours available [A – B]	3,200
D. *Less :* Utilized to produce 2000 units of A [2,000 1]	2,000
E. Balance hours available [C – D]	1,200
F. Utilized to produce 600 units of B, for the balance hours available [600 2]	1,200
G. Balance hours available [E – F]	Nil

So, in 20,000 hours of press time available, all the requirements of components D and A and only 600 units of B can be manufactured. The balance requirement of component B i.e. 2,900 (3,500 – 600) units will have to be bought out or manufactured in the second shift.

(b) Since the purchase price of component C (i.e. ₹ 52) is lower than the marginal cost of manufacturing (i.e. ₹ 57) in even single shift, it will not be profitable to make it, hence it would be purchased from outside.

Now it is to be seen whether 2,900 units of B should be produced in the second shift or bought from outside. The comparative position is given below:

COST OF PRODUCING 2,900 UNITS OF COMPONENT B IN SECOND SHIFT

	Particulars	₹
A.	Variable cost per unit on single shift basis	55.00
B.	*Add :* Increase in direct wages per unit	2.00
C.	Variable Cost per unit [A + B]	57.00
D.	Total Variable Costs for 2,900 units [2,900 x ₹ 57]	1,65,300
E.	Additional Fixed cost for 5800 hours [i.e. 2,900 x 2] @ ₹ 500 for every 1000 hours or part thereof	3,000
F.	Total Cost for producing 2,900 units of B in Second shift [D + E]	1,68,300
G.	Bought out price for 2,900 units of B [2,900 x ₹ 59]	1,71,100
H.	Disadvantage in buying [F – G]	(2,800)

Recommendation: Since the cost of manufacturing balance quantity of component B i.e. 2,900 in second shift is less by ₹ 2,800, it is profitable to make it on a second shift basis instead of buying from outside suppliers.

Working Notes:

(i) *Calculation of Press Hours required:*

	A	*B*	*C*	*D*
Direct Expenses per unit	₹ 10	₹ 20	₹ 10	₹ 60
No. of press hours per unit [Direct expenses/10]	1	2	1	6

(ii) *Comparison of Marginal Cost of production per unit with Bought out price per unit*

	A	*B*	*C*	*D*
Marginal (variable) costs (₹) :				
Direct Material	37	27	25	44
Direct Wages	10	8	22	40
Direct expenses	10	20	10	60
Marginal Cost per unit (₹)	57	55	57	144
Bought out price (₹)	60	59	52	168
Excess of bought out price over Marginal cost	3	4	(5)	24
Press Hours per unit	1	2	1	6
Excess of bought out price per Unit of limiting factor (i.e. press hour) (₹)	3	2	(5)	4

The bought-out price for component C is ,lower by ₹ 5 then the marginal cost of production and so it should be purchased from outside.

In case the remaining components A, B and D are bought, their ranking in terms of loss per unit of limiting factors (press hour) would be D (highest loss per unit), A and B. the capacity available should, therefore, be deployed for making D first and then A and thereafter B.

4.7 When Make or Buy Decision becomes a Capital Budgeting Decision

If capital equipments are required to be purchased for manufacturing the component, Make or Buy decision remains no longer short run operating decision and it becomes a Capital Budgeting Decision. In such a case Capital Budgeting technique should be used to evaluate Make or Buy Decision.

Illustration 34. A firm needs a component in an assembly operation. If it wants to do the manufacturing itself, it would need to buy a machine for ₹ 4 lakhs which would last for 4 years with no salvage value. Manufacturing costs in each of the 4 years would be ₹ 6 lakhs, ₹ 7 lakhs, ₹ 8 lakhs and 10 lakhs respectively. If the firm had to buy the component from a supplier the component would cost ₹ 9 lakhs, ₹ 10 lakhs, ₹ 11 lakhs and ₹ 14 lakhs respectively in each of the 4 years. However, the machine would occupy floor space which could have been used for another machine. This latter machine could be hired at no cost to manufacture an item, the sale of which would produce net cash flows in each of the 4 years of ₹ 2 lakhs; it is impossible to find room for both the machines and there are no other external effects. The cost of capital is 10% and PV factor for each of the 4 years is 0.909, 0.826, 0.751 and 0.683 respectively. Should the firm make the component or buy from outside?

Solution: **EVALUATION OF MAKE OR BUY PROPOSAL**

Year	*Present Value Factor at 10%*	*When the Component is manufactured*		*When the Component is bought*	
		Cash outflow (Capital cost, Manufacturing cost + Opportunity cost)	*Present value of Cash Outflows*	*Cash Outflow (cost of buying)*	*Present Value*
0	1.000	4	4.000	—	—
1	0.909	6 + 2	7.272	9	8.181
2	0.826	7 + 2	7.434	10	8.260
3	0.751	8 + 2	7.510	11	8.261
4	0.683	10 + 2	8.196	14	9.562
			34.412		34.264

Advise: The firm should buy the component from outside since it will result in saving of ₹ 0.148 lakh (i.e.₹ 34.412 lakhs – ₹ 34.264 lakhs)

Note: The loss of ₹ 2 lakhs cash inflow for each of the 4 years due to inability of the firm to operate another machine when it manufactures the component is to be treated as an opportunity cost.

5.0 MANUFACTURING OR SUB-CONTRACTING DECISION

5.1 Basis of Decision

When the firm has limited capacity to manufacture, whether to manufacture or sub-contract decision should be taken on the basis of **Excess of Sub-Contract Price over the Variable Manufacturing Cost per hour.**

5.2 Products to be Sub-contracted

Products of which sub contract price is less than the variable manufacturing costs or products for which processing hours can not be allocated fully, should always be sub-contracted.

5.3 Practical Steps in Manufacturing or Sub-Contracting Decision

The following practical steps may be followed to find out what is to be manufactured and what is to be sub-contracted so as to maximize the profit.

Step 1: *Calculate Contribution per unit treating Sub-contract Price as Selling Price, as under: Contribution per unit = Sub-contract Price – Variable Cost of manufacturing*

Step 2: *Calculate processing hours required per unit*

Step 3: *Calculate Contribution per processing hour*

Step 4: *Decide upon the ranking of the products to be manufactured on the basis of Contribution per processing hour.*

Step 5: *Allocate the available processing hours in the order of ranking of the products to be manufactured*

Step 6: *Sub-contracting strategy should be adopted for other products. In other words, the products in respect of which contribution per processing hour is negative and the products for which processing hours can not be allocated fully, should be sub-contracted.*

Illustration 35. Jindal Furnishers Ltd., manufacturer one type of sofa set exclusively, the set contains the following seven components :

One sofa, two centre tables and four chairs.

These components can be either manufactured by the Company or sub-contracted and the following are the relevant data :

	Sofa	Table	Chair
Direct Material Cost per component	₹ 1,000	500	550
Direct Labour Hours per component	100	50	10
Sub-contract Price per component	₹ 2,500	1,000	750

Sales of sofa sets are currently 8,000 per period, each set selling for ₹ 7,500. A capacity constraint of 5,00,000 direct labour hours obliges the Company to sub-contract some components.

The variable overheads vary with direct labour hours worked and are incurred at rate of ₹ 2 per hour. Fixed costs are ₹ 17,50,000 per period and labour costs ₹ 5.50 per hour.

Required: What should be the strategy as to own manufacturing and sub-contracting ?

Solution: **STATEMENT SHOWING THE CONTRIBUTION PER HOUR FOR DIFFERENT COMPONENTS BY MANUFACTURING AND NOT SUB-CONTRACTING AND RANKING**

Particulars	*Sofa*	*Table*	*Chair*
A. Sub-Contract Price	₹ 2,500	₹ 1,000	₹ 750
B. *Less :* Variable Cost of own manufacturing:			
Direct Material Cost	1,000	500	550
Direct Labour Cost	550	275	55
Variable Overhead	200	100	20
	1,750	875	625
C. Contribution [A – B]	750	125	125
D. Hour required per component	100	50	10
E. Contribution per hour	7.5	2.5	12.5
F. Ranking for Manufacturing	II	III	I

STATEMENT SHOWING THE ALLOCATION OF HOURS

A. Total hours available	5,00,000
B. *Less :* hours required to produce 32,000 chairs for 8000 sets [32,000 10]	3,20,000
C. Balance to produce Sofa	1,80,000
D. Hours required per Sofa	100
E. No. of Sofas to be manufactured	1,800
F. Balance of Sofas to be sub-contracted (8000 – 1800)	6,200
G. No. of Tables to be sub-contracted (8000 2)	16000

Thus, the following strategy should be adopted

	Sofa	*Table*	*chair*
Own manufacturing	1,800	—	32,000
Sub-contracting	6,200	16,000	—

Illustration 36. Motor Components Ltd. have secured an order for 3,000 components per week from a car manufacturer but there is a shortage of available skilled labour capacity which is restraining the Company from producing the entire quantity within the Company.

Production, cost and sales information of Motor Components Ltd. are as under :

Sales price of complete component	₹ 1,500
Skilled Labour capacity per week	7,500 hours
Production Labour rate per hour	₹ 120
Variable Production overhead	₹ 50% of labour cost
Fixed Overhead	₹ 5,00,000 per week
Testing cost for complete component	₹ 20

Each component is finally assembled from three section, make up of one or more parts as under:

	Section I	*Section II*	*Section III*
Part per section	5	4	1
Material cost per part	₹ 60	₹ 40	₹ 20
Production labour minutes per part	18 mins.	15 mins.	30 mins.
The sub-contract price for component of ₹ 1,400 made up as	₹ 700	₹ 500	₹ 200

The two production strategies available are :

(a) to produce as many completed components as possible within the existing weekly skilled labour capacity and sub-contract the remaining complete components, and

(b) produce as many of the three sections of the components as possible and subcontract the remaining section.

Required: Advise which of the above two production strategies would be more profitable for the Company.

Solution:

EVALUATION OF STRATEGY (A)

Time taken : Section I = 5 part 18 minutes	1.50 hrs.
Section II = 4 part 15 minutes	1.00 hrs.
Section III = 1 part 30 minutes	0.50 hrs.
Total time taken by the component	3.00 hrs.

No. of components to be produced in 7,500 hrs. = 7,500 ÷ 3 = 2,500 Nos.

Complete components to be produced in 7,500 hrs. = (7,500 hrs. ÷ 3)	2,500 units
Complete components to be sub-contracted (3,000 – 2,500)	500 units
	3,000 units

STATEMENT SHOWING THE PROFITABILITY UNDER STRATEGY (A)

Particulars	₹
A. Total Cost of producing 2500 units	
Material Cost {(300 + 160 + 20) 2500}	12,00,000
Labour Cost {(180 + 120 + 60) 2500}	9,00,000
Variable Cost {(90 + 60 + 30) 2500}	4,50,000
Testing (2500 x ₹ 20)	50,000
Total Variable Cost	26,00,000
Fixed Cost :	5,00,000
	31,00,000
B. Total Cost of sub-contracting 500 units	
Cost of sub contracting 500 units = 500 (700 + 500 + 200)	7,00,000
Testing of sub contracting units (500 20)	10,000
	7,10,000
C. Total Cost of manufacturing 2,500 units and Sub contracting 500 units [A + B]	38,10,000
D. Total Sales [3,000 ₹ 1,500]	45,00,000
E. Profit [D – C]	6,90,000

EVALUATION OF STRATEGY (B)
STATEMENT SHOWING CONTRIBUTION PER HOUR IN DIFFERENT SECTIONS BY MANUFACTURING AND NOT SUB-CONTRACTING AND RANKING

Particulars	*Sections*		
	I	*II*	*III*
A. Sub - contract Price	700	500	200
B. *Less:* Variable Cost of own manufacture			
Material Cost	₹ 300	₹ 160	₹ 20
Labour Cost @ ₹ 120 per hour	180	120	60
Variable Production Overhead 50% of labour cost	90	60	30
	570	340	110
C. Contribution before testing	130	160	90
D. Labour hours per section	1.5	1	1/2
E. Contribution per hour	86.67	160	180
F. Ranking for manufacturing	III	II	I

STATEMENT SHOWING THE ALLOCATION OF 7,500 HOURS

A.	Total hours available	7,500
B.	*Less :* hours utilized to produce 3000 contracts of section III (3,000 1/2)	(1,500)
C.	Balance hours available [A – B]	6,000
D.	Less : Hours utilized to produce to 3000 components of Section II (3,000 1)	(3,000)
E.	Balance hours available to produce 2000 components of Section [2,000 1.5]	3,000

Thus, the following strategy should be adopted :

	Section I	*Section II*	*Section III*
Own manufacturing	2,000	3,000	3,000
Sub-Contracting	1,000	—	—

STATEMENT SHOWING THE PROFITABILITY UNDER STRATEGY (B)

₹ (in lakhs)

	Particulars		₹
A.	Total Variable Cost of own manufacturing:		
	Section I [2,000 ₹ 570]	11.40	
	Section II [3000 ₹ 340]	10.20	
	Section III [3000 ₹ 110]	3.30	24.90
B.	Total Variable Cost of Sub-contracting 1000 components of Section I [1000 700]		7.00
C.	Testing Fee [3000 ₹ 20]		0.60
D.	Fixed Cost		5.00
E.	Total Cost		37.50
F.	Total Sales [3000 ₹ 1,500]		45.00
G.	Profit under strategy (b)		7.50

Decision : Strategy (b) should be adopted since it will increase profit by ₹ 60,000 per week (i.e. ₹ 7,50,000 – ₹ 6,90,000)

Illustration 37. HAXY Ltd. manufactures four products P, Q, R and S. The direct cost of production are estimated at :

	P	*Q*	*R*	*S*
Materials	₹ 36	₹ 38	₹ 42	₹ 24
Labour :				
Assembly (at ₹ 4 per hour)	8	12	16	16
Machinists (at ₹ 6 per hour)	12	24	18	36

Total Fixed Costs are dependent on output levels, as follows :

Production (Units)	*Total Fixed Costs*
Upto 50,000	₹ 4,00,000
50,001 to 75,000	5,00,000
75,001 to 1,00,000	6,00,000

The Sales Director estimates that demand for their products in the next year will be as follows:

	P	*Q*	*R*	*S*
Units	18,000	30,000	27,000	15,000
Selling price per unit (₹)	68	90	91	94

The Production Manager states that the capacity of existing machines is 2,10,000 hours per annum, though this will be increased to 3,00,000 hours in two years time when new plant which is currently on order will be delivered. Meanwhile, a local firm has offered to manufacture any of the products on a Sub-contract basis at the following prices :

P ₹ 63; Q ₹ 80; R ₹ 72 S ₹ 82

Required :

(a) Advise the management to what extent the services of the sub-contractor should be utilised in order to meet the expected demand of P, Q, R, S

(b) Prepare a Statement showing the profit you would expect if your advise is followed.

(c) What will be your advise if existing fixed costs are fully avoidable on sub-contracting?

Solution:

Part (a) STATEMENT SHOWING THE CONTRIBUTION PER UNIT AND RANKING OF PRODUCT IF PRODUCT ARE MANUFACTURED

	Particulars	*P*	*Q*	*R*	*S*
A.	Sub-contract Price (₹)	63	80	72	82
B.	*Less* : Variable Cost of in house manufacturing:				
	Material	36	38	42	24
	Labour				
	Assembly (at ₹ 4 per hour)	8	12	16	16
	Machinists (at ₹ 6 per hour)	12	24	18	36
	Total Variable Cost	56	74	76	76
C.	Contribution [A – B]	7	6	(4)	6
D.	Hours per unit (Machinist)	2 hrs	4 hrs	3 hrs	6 hrs
E.	Contribution per hour [C/D]	3.50	1.5		1
F.	Ranking, if only, contribution per hour is considered	I	II		III

STATEMENT SHOWING THE ALLOCATION OF 2,10,000 HOURS

A.	Total hours available	2,10,000
B.	*Less* : Hours utilized to produce 18,000 units of P [18000 2]	(36,000)
C.	Balance hours [A – B]	1,74,000
D.	*Less* : Hours utilized to produce 30,000 units of Q [30,000 4]	(1,20,000)
E.	Balance hours utilized to produce 9,000 units of S [9000 6]	54,000

Thus, the following strategy could be adopted :

	P	Q	R	S
Own manufacturing	18,000	30,000	—	9,000
Sub-contracting	—	—	27,000	6,000

(b) STATEMENT SHOWING THE PROFIT BY MANUFACTURING 50,000 UNITS AND 57,000 UNITS

Products	*Units*	*Total Contribution*	*Units*	*Total Contribution*
P	18,000	2,16,000	18,000	2,16,000
Q	30,000	4,80,000	30,000	4,80,000
S	2,000	36,000	9,000	1,62,000
	50,000	7,32,000	57,000	8,58,000
Less : Fixed Cost		4,00,000		5,00,000
		3,32,000		3,58,000
Add : Profit by Sub-contracting :				
R		5,13,000 (27,000 × ₹ 19)		5,13,000 (27,000 × ₹ 19)
S		1,56,000 (13,000 × ₹ 12)		72,000 (6,000 × ₹ 12)
		6,69,000		5,85,000
Net Profit		10,01,000		9,43,000

(c) STATEMENT SHOWING THE PROFIT BY SUB-CONTRACTING ALL UNITS

Product	*Selling Price*	*Sub-Contract Price*	*Contribution*	*Units*	*Total Contribution*
P	60	63	5	18,000	90,000
Q	90	80	10	30,000	3,00,000
R	91	72	19	27,000	5,13,000

S	94	82	12	15,000	1,80,000
				Total Contribution	10,83,000
				Less: Fixed Costs (since there is no production)	—
				Total Profit	10,83,000

Advise: As this profit is more than ₹ 10,01,000 all the units should be sub-contracted and there should be no in house manufacturing.

Illustration 38. T T D Ltd. manufacture a single product on normal working capacity of 8,000 units per annum. The sales manager has projected a sale of 10,000 units for the next year at a price of ₹ 250 per unit.
The operating budget for the next year is as under :

	₹ *lacs*	₹ *lacs*
Sales 8,000 units @ ₹ 250 each		20. 00
Cost of production :		
Raw Materials	12.00	
Direct Wages	3.00	
Works Overheads (50% fixed)	1.40	
Administration Overhead (all fixed)	0.60	
Selling and distribution overheads (80% fixed)	1.00	18.00
	Profit	2.00

In order to increase the production to meet the sales demand two proposals have been put forward as under:

(i) Sub-contracting the production of 2,000 units at ₹ 225 per unit

(ii) Installing an additional machine which will entail the following expenses :

(a) Cost of the machine ₹ 2,00,000 : Life 20 years

(b) Recruitment of ten workers including direct workers to operate the machine at a wage rate ₹ 500 each p.m. Add 25% towards fringe benefits. (None of the existing workers will be used for this purpose)

(c) Interest on capital required for the purchase of the machine - 15% p.a.

The following additional fixed expenses will be incurred in respect of both the alternatives.

Administration expenses	₹ 10,000 p.a.
Selling and distribution expenses	₹ 20,000 p.a.

Required :

(i) A statement showing the respective profitability of the two methods of increasing the production.

(ii) Comments upon the choice of the two methods of increasing the production.

Solution: **STATEMENT OF COMPARATIVE PROFITABILITY**

	Particulars	*Sub-contracting* ₹	*Installing an Additional Machine* ₹
A	Sales [2,000 units 250]	5,00,000	5,00,000
B	Cost of Sub-contracting [2,000 225]	4,50,000	—
C	Raw Materials [12,00,000/8000] = 150 per unit		3,00,000
D	Direct Wages 10 workers: [60,000 + 25% of 60,000]		75,000
E	Depreciation [2,00,000/20]		10,000
F	Variable Works Overhead – [70000/8,000] = ₹ 8.75 per unit		17,500
G	Interest on capital @ 15% on 2,00,000		30,000
H	Additional Admn. Overhead	10,000	10,000
I	Additional Selling and Distribution Overhead	20,000	20,000
J	Variable Selling and Distribution overhead –	5,000	5,000
K	Total Cost [B + C + D + E + F + G + H + I + J]	4,85,000	4,67,500
L	Profit	15,000	32,500
M	Percentage of Profit on Sales [Profit 100/Sales]	3%	6.5%

(ii) Comments

Methods of installing an additional machine is more profitable. But the profitability on 2,000 additional units is 6.5% which is less than 10% profitability on 8,000 budgeted units for the next year.

Fixed cost by installing an additional machine

	₹
Direct Wages	75,000
Depreciation	10,000
Interest on capital	30,000
Total	1,15,000

If the additional sales of 2,000 units is temporary, installing an additional machine is not profitable as it involves the fixed expenses of ₹ 1,15,000 per annum and if this cannot be dispensed with, then Sub-contracting is profitable. If there is long term prospect, installing an additional machine is more profitable.

6.0 ACCEPTANCE OF AN OFFER AND SUBMISSION OF A TENDER

6.1 Basis of Decision

When a firm having surplus capacity receives an offer from a special or export market, a decision as to whether to accept or not to accept the offer should be taken on the basis of the **Incremental Revenue and Cost Analysis.**

6.2 Practical Steps In a Decision as to whether or not to accept the Offer

Step 1: *Ascertain whether Surplus Capacity is available.*

Step 2: *Ascertain whether Fixed Costs have already been recovered or not*
*(**Note:** Profit at current operating capacity indicates that fixed costs have already been recovered)*

Step 3: *Calculate Incremental Cost for additional output*

Incremental Cost = Total Cost for Existing and Additional Output less Total Cost for Existing Output

Step 4: *Calculate Average Incremental Cost per unit*

$$\text{Average Incremental Cost} = \frac{\text{Incremental Cost}}{\text{Additional Output}}$$

Step 5: *Compare Average Incremental Cost with Offer Price per unit.*

Step 6: *Accept the offer if Offer Price is more than the Average Incremental Cost*
Reject the offer if Offer Price is less than the Average Incremental Cost.

***Notes:**(i) Export Benefits (if any) should be treated as part of export offer price.*
(ii) Any Additional Cost to be incurred on accepting the after should be treated as part of Incremental Cost.

Illustration 39. Somesh of Agra presently operates its plant at 80% of the normal capacity to manufacture a product only to meet the demand of Government of Tamil Nadu under a rate contract.

He supplies the product for ₹ 4,00,000 and earns a profit margin of 20% on sale realisations.

Direct cost per unit is constant.

The indirect costs as per his budget projections are:

Indirect costs	20,000 units (80% capacity) ₹	22,500 units (90% capacity) ₹	25,000 units (100% capacity) ₹
Variable	80,000	90,000	1,00,000
Semi-variable	40,000	42,500	45,000
Fixed	80,000	80,000	80,000

He has received an order for the product equal to 20% of its present operations. Additional packing charges on this order will be ₹ 1,000. Arrive at the price to be quoted for the export order to give him a profit margin of 10% on the export price.

Solution:

Step 1: Computation of Differential Cost of Production of 4000 Additional Units

Particulars	*20000 units* ₹	*24000 units* ₹	*Differential cost of 4000 units* ₹
Direct Cost @₹ 6	1,20,000	1,44,000	24,000
Indirect costs:			
Variable @ ₹ 4	80,000	96,000	16,000
Semi-variable	40,000	44,000	4,000
Fixed	80,000	81,000	1,000
Total	3,20,000	3,65,000	45,000

Step 2: Computation of Selling price per unit to be quoted

Differential Cost of 4000 units	₹ 45,000
Add: Profit being 1/9th of cost	₹ 5000
Sales Value of 4000 units	₹ 50,000

Selling price per unit = ₹ 50,000/4000 = ₹ 12.50 per unit

Working Notes:

(i) Prime Cost at 80% capacity = Cost of Sales – Indirect Cost
= (₹ 4,00,000 – 20%) – (80,000 + 40,000 + 80,000) = ₹ 1,20,000

(ii) Semi-variable Cost at 96% capacity = ₹ 40,000 + $\frac{45,000 - 40,000}{20\%} \times 16\%$ = ₹ 44,000

Illustration 40. A small scale manufacturer produces an article at the operated capacity of 10,000 units while the normal capacity of his plant is 14,000 units. Working at a profit margin of 20% on sales realization, he has formulated his budget as under:

	10,000 units	*14,000 units*
Sales Realization	₹ 2,00,000	₹ 2,80,000
Variable overheads	50,000	70,000
Semi-variable overheads	20,000	22,000
Fixed overheads	40,000	40,000

He gets an order for a quantity equivalent to 20% of the operated capacity and even on this additional production, profit margin is desired at the same percentage on Sales Realization as for production to operated capacity.

Assuming prime cost is constant per unit of production, what should be the minimum price to realise this objective ?

Solution: **(i) STATEMENT SHOWING THE COMPUTATION OF PRIME COST**

Particulars		₹
A. Sales at operated capacity		2,00,000
B. *Less :* Profit Margin (20% of sales)		40,000
C. Cost of Sales [A – B]		1,60,000
D. *Less :* Overheads :		
Variable Overhead	₹ 50,000	
Semi-Variable Overhead	20,000	
Fixed Overheads	40,000	1,10,000
E. Prime Cost [C – D]		50,000

(ii) STATEMENT SHOWING DIFFERENTIAL COST FOR 2,000 UNITS

	Cost of 10,000 units	*Cost of 12,000 units*	*Diff. Cost for 2,000 units*
Prime Cost	₹ 50,000	₹ 60,000	₹ 10,000
Variable Cost	50,000	60,000	10,000
Semi-variable overhead	20,000	21,000	1,000
Fixed Overheads	40,000	40,000	—
	1,60,000	1,81,000	21,000

A review of semi-variable overhead for 10,000 units and 14,000 units reveals that increase of 4,000 units leads to an increase of 2,000. Therefore, increase of 2,000 units will lead to increase of ₹ 1,000 in semi-variable overhead.

Differential cost for additional 2000 units (i.e. ₹ 21,000 ÷ 2,000)	₹ 10.500
Profit : 20% of sales or 25% of cost	2.625
Hence, minimum selling price to realise the given objective	= 13.125

Illustration 41. Indian plastics manufactures and sells 60,000 buckets (at 60% capacity) on a selling price of ₹ 16 per piece. Its cost of sales per piece is:

	₹
Direct Materials	5.00
Direct Wages	1.65
Works Overheads	5.00 (50% fixed)
Selling Overheads	0.40 (25% varying)

During the current year, it intends to produce the same number but anticipates that the fixed charges will go up by 10 per cent , while rates of Direct Labour and Direct Material will increase by 3.1/33 per cent and 6 per cent respectively. There is no scope for increasing the selling price due to keen competition. Under this situation, it obtains from Indian Railways an offer for a further 20 per cent of its capacity.

Required: What minimum price per piece should be quoted to the Railway to ensure that it earns an overall profit of ₹ 2,27,200.

Solution: STATEMENT SHOWING THE CALCULATION OF PRICE FOR THE SPECIAL ORDER OF 20,000 UNITS

	Particulars	₹
A.	Desired Profit	2,27,200
B.	Profit on 60,000 units expected during the Current year (60,000 3.32)	1,99,200
C.	Additional Profit to be ensured (A – B)	28,000
D.	Contribution required per unit (₹ 28,000/20,000)	1.40
E.	Variable cost per unit	9.60
F.	Minimum price per unit (D + E)	11.00

Working Note :

STATEMENT SHOWING THE COMPARATIVE PROFITABILITY FOR TWO YEARS FOR 60,000 UNITS

	Particulars	*Previous year* ₹	*Current Year (prior to acceptance of special order)* ₹
A.	Selling Price per Unit	16.00	16.00
B.	*Less:* Variable Costs per unit:	—	—
	(a) Direct Materials	5.00	5.30
	(b) Direct Labour	1.65	1.70
	(c) Variable expenses		
	(d) Works Overheads	2.50	2.50
	(e) Sales Overheads	0.10	0.10
		9.25	9.60
C.	Contribution per unit (A – B)	6.75	6.40
D.	Fixed Costs per unit		
	(a) Works Overheads	2.50	2.75
	(b) Selling Overheads	.30	.33
		2.80	3.08
E.	Profit per unit (C – D)	3.95	3.32

7.0 WHETHER TO ACCEPT EXPORT ORDER OR NOT

If surplus capacity is available accept the export order if export price (along with export incentives) is more than the incremental cost of producing export order quantity otherwise not. Present fixed costs are not relevant for export order decision. It should be ensured that dumping in export market at a price lower than local price should not have any adverse effect on local sales.

Change in profit due to acceptance of export order may be calculated as follows:

Profit on Export Order = (Net Export Price per unit – Marginal Cost per unit) × Export Order Quantity

Illustration 42. A manufacturer of certain product has been selling exclusively in the Indian market upto now. He has just received his first export enquiry and wants to quote as competitively as the circumstances will allow. His latest Indian Cost Sheet is:

	₹
Raw materials/unit	34
Direct labour/unit	13
Services ($33^1/_3$% fixed)/unit	6
Fixed Works overhead/unit	7
Fixed Office Overhead/unit	2
	62
Profit earned in India	6
Indian Selling Price	68

Management is thinking of quoting a selling price somewhere between ₹ 62 and ₹ 68 per unit for this export order. One of the Directors suggests quoting an even lower price based on the principles of Marginal Costing. As the Firm's Accountant, you are requested to compute the lowest, the management could quote on these principles assuming additional Expenses like special packing insurance etc. will amount to ₹ 4 per unit.

Solution: **STATEMENT SHOWING THE LOWEST PRICE FOR THE EXPORT ENQUIRY**

Raw Materials/unit	₹ 34
Direct Labour/unit	₹ 13
Services/unit	₹ 4
Additional Expenses//unit	₹ 4
Marginal Cost/unit	₹ 55

The cost sheet would depend on the assumptions made. The above is one illustrative cost sheet based on the principles of Marginal Costing, using the figures given in the latest "total" cost sheet. The assumptions are given below :

Notes :

(i) It is assumed that sufficient manufacturing capacity exists not to disrupt the supplies now being made to the Indian market, while fulfilling this export order. If any such disruption takes place, the negative costs of this disruption will be another direct opportunity cost of fulfilling this export order.

(ii) Certain direct costs of this export order like import duties in the foreign country, special commissions etc. would have to be separately calculated and added on to the above Marginal Cost of ₹ 51 before the selling price is finally fixed. We would have to carefully determine whether the quoted price should be on FOB or CIF basis.

(iii) The benefit available from exports, such as cash subsidy that may be available, should be added to the available price.

(iv) On the above basis, any price above ₹ 55 will be that lowest possible price which can be quoted by the Company.

Illustration 43. X Ltd. operating at 80% levels of capacity, provides you the following information :

Units produced & sold	2000
	₹
Direct Materials	2,000
Direct Labour	2,000
Direct Expenses	1,600
Overheads (80% fixed)	12,000
Total Cost	17,600
Total Cost per unit	8.80
Profit per unit	1.20
Selling price per unit	10.00

This company receives an offer from Canada for the purchase of above product to be produced on idle capacity at present at a price of ₹ 4 per unit.

If this export order is executed, the Company will have to incure the following expenses :

(i) Special packing charge of fifty paise per unit;
(ii) Insurance ₹ 500.
(iii) Freight ₹ 750.

At the same time, the company shall get the import quota for an item of which cost price in Indian Rupees is ₹ 100 in Canada and the market price in India is ₹ 300. The import quota is granted @ 50% of the export price to be received in foreign exchange.

Required: Should the Company accept or reject the export order ?

Solution:

I. *Benefits associated with acceptance of Export Order*		
A. Revenues Realised [(500 ₹ 4)]		₹ 2,000
B. Entitlement to an import Quota [₹ 2,000 50%] = ₹ 1,000		
C. Premium on Import Quota [₹ 1,000 (₹ 300 – ₹ 100)%]		₹ 2,000
D. Total Revenues (A + C)		₹ 4,000
II. *Costs associated with acceptance of Export Order*		
A. Variable Cost of Mfg.		₹
Direct Material [₹ 2,000 500/2000]	500	
Direct Labour [₹ 2,000 500/2000]	500	
Direct Expenses [₹ 1,600 500/2000]	400	
Overheads [₹ 2,400 500/2000]	600	2,000
B. Extra Out of Pocket Costs		
Packing (500 ₹ 0.50)	250	
Insurance	500	
Freight	750	1,500
C. Total out of Pocket costs		3,500
III. Net Benefits associated (I – II)		500

Recommendation: Yes, the Company should accept the export order since the Company will gain ₹ 500 by doing so.

Illustration 44. A company manufacturing electric motors at a price of ₹ 6,900 each, made up as under :

	₹
Direct Material	3,200
Direct Labour	400
Variable Overheads	1,000
Fixed Overheads	200
Depreciation	200
Variable Selling Overheads	100
Royalty	200
Profit	1,000
	6,300
Central Excise Duty	600
	6,900

(i) A foreign buyer has offered to buy 200 such motors at ₹ 5,000 each. As a Cost Accountant of the Company would you advise acceptance of the offer ?

(ii) What should the Company quote for a motor to be purchased by a company under the same management, if it should be at cost

Solution: **STATEMENT SHOWING THE RELEVANT COST PER UNIT FOR EXPORT**

Particulars	₹
A. Direct Material	3,200
B. Direct Labour	400
C. Variable Overhead	1,000
D. Royalty (Considering it is paid on production basis)	200
	4,800

Recommendation:

(i) Offer from foreign buyer should be accepted since this decision will yield an incremental profit of ₹ 40,000 [i.e., (₹ 5,000 – 4,800) 200] This will further increase by export incentive *minus* the cost of extra packing required for export. It should be noted that no excise duty is leviable on exports.

(ii) Following price should be quoted for a motor to be purchased by a company under the same management.

Price (excluding excise duty)		₹ 6,300
Less : Profit	₹ 1,000	
Variable selling overhead	₹ 100	1,100
Price to be quoted		5,200

Note. : Excise duty should be added wherever payable.

Illustration 45. Z Ltd. having an installed capacity of 10,000 units of a product is currently operating at 70% utilisation. The cost & Price structures are as follows :

Capacity Utilisation	*Unit (Costs)* (₹)	*Unit Price* (₹)
60%	160	200
70%	150	194
80%	148	190
90%	144	
100%	142	

The Company has received an order for 2,000 units from Canada at a price of ₹ 130 per unit.
Required: Advise the Company as to whether the export order should be accepted or not.

Solution **STATEMENT SHOWING THE DIFFERENTIAL COST PER UNIT**

Capacity Utilisation (%)	*Production (in units)*	*Unit cost* (₹)	*Total Costs* (₹)	*Differential Cost* (₹)	*Differential Cost/Unit* (₹)
60	6,000	160	9,60,000	—	—
70	7,000	150	10,50,000	90,000	90
80	8,000	148	11,84,000	1,34,000	134
90	9,000	144	12,96,000	1,12,000	112
100	10,000	142	14,20,000	1,24,000	124

STATEMENT SHOWING THE ADDITIONAL PROFIT FROM EXPORT

	Particulars		₹
A.	Sales of 2000 units [2,000 ₹ 130]		2,60,000
B.	*Less:* Cost of producing 2000 units		
	First 1,000	1,34,000	
	Next 1,000	1,12,000	2,46,000
C	Net Profit		14,000

Recommendation: The company should accept the export order since it will increase the existing profit by ₹ 14,000.

Illustration 46. X Ltd. having an installed capacity of 1,00,000 units of a product is currently operating at 70% utilization. At current level of input prices, the FOB unit costs (after taking credit for applicable export incentives) work-out as follows:

Capacity utilization %	*FOB unit costs* ₹
70	97
80	92
90	87
100	82

The Company has received three foreign offers from different sources as under :
Source A : 5,000 units at ₹ 55 per unit FOB
Source B : 10,000 units at ₹ 52 per unit FOB
Source C : 10,000 units at ₹ 51 per unit FOB
Required : Advise the Company so to whether any or all the export orders should be accepted or not.

Solution:

STATEMENT SHOWING DIFFERENTIAL COSTS AT DIFFERENT CAPACITY UTILISATION LEVELS

Capacity Utilisation Per cent	*Production at different levels of capacity utilisation units*	*FOB unit Costs* ₹	*Total Costs* ₹	*Differential Costs* ₹	*Differential Cost per unit* ₹
70	70,000	97	67,90,000	—	—
80	80,000	92	73,60,000	5,70,000	57
90	90,000	87	78,30,000	4,70,000	47
100	1,00,000	82	82,00,000	3,70,000	37

Evaluation of Various possibilities'

I. If export order from source 'A' only is accepted		
A. Incremental Revenue @ ₹ 55	₹ 2.75 lacs	
B. Incremental costs @ ₹ 57	₹ 2.85 lacs	
C. Net Gain (loss) (A – B)	(₹ 0.10 lacs)	
II. If export order from source 'B' only is accepted		
A. Incremental Revenue @ ₹ 52	₹ 5.20 lacs	
B. Incremental Costs @ ₹ 57	₹ 5.70 lacs	
C. Net Gain (loss) (A – B)	(₹ 0.50 lacs)	
III. If export order from source 'C' only is accepted		
A. Incremental Revenue @ ₹ 51	₹ 5.10 lacs	
B. Incremental Cost @ ₹ 57	₹ 5.70 lacs	
C. Net Gain (loss) (A – B)	(₹ 0.60 lacs)	
IV. If all export orders are accepted		
A. Incremental Revenue		
On 5000 units @ ₹ 55	2.75	
On 10000 units @ ₹ 52	5.20	
On 10000 units @ ₹ 51	5.10	13.05
B. *Less :* Incremental Cost		
On 10000 units @ ₹ 57	5.70	
On next 10000 units @ ₹ 47	4.70	
On next 5000 units @ ₹ 37	1.85	12.25
C. Net Gain [A – B]		0.80

It is obvious from the above statement that the Company will gain only when all the three export orders are accepted. If the Company accepts export orders only for one or two of the three sources, it will lose. Therefore, the Company should accept all the three exports orders.

Illustration 47. A Company is at present working at 90% of its capacity and producing 13,500 units per annum. It operates a Flexible Budgetary Control System. The following figures are obtained from its budget:

Particulars	*Capacity utilisation*	
	90%	*100%*
Sales	(₹) 15,00,000	(₹) 16,00,000
Fixed Expenses	3,00,500	3,00,600
Semi-fixed Expenses	97,500	1,00,500
Semi-Variable Expenses	1,45,000	1,49,500
Units Manufactured	13,500	15,000

Labour and material costs per unit are constant under the present conditions. Profit margin is 10%.

Required:

(a) Determine the differential cost of producing 1,500 units by increasing capacity utilisation to 100 per cent.

(b) What would you recommend as an export price for these 1,500 units after considering that overseas prices are much lower than inland prices.

Solution:

Basic Calculations :

STATEMENT SHOWING THE COMPUTATION OF COST OF MATERIAL AND LABOUR

Particulars		₹
A. Sales at 90% Capacity		15,00,000
B. *Less :* Profit Margin (10%)		1,50,000
C. Total Cost [A – B]		13,50,000
D. *Less:* Expenses:		
Fixed	3,00,500	
Semi-fixed	97,500	
Variable	1,45,000	
		5,43,000
E. Cost of Materials & Labour at 90% capacity		8,07,000
F. Cost of Materials & Labour at 100% capacity [₹ 8,07,000 100/90]		8,96,667

(a) STATEMENT SHOWING THE DIFFERENTIAL COST

Particulars	*90%* *13,500 units* ₹	*100%* *15,000 units* ₹	*Differencial Cost of 1,500 units* ₹
Materials and Labour	8,07,000	8,96,667	89,667
Variable Expenses	1,45,000	1,49,500	4,500
Semi-fixed Expenses	97,500	1,00,500	3,000
Fixed Expenses	3,00,500	3,00,600	100
	13,50,000	14,47,267	97,267

(b) Minimum Price for Export = 97,267/1,500 = ₹ 64.84 per unit

At the minimum price of ₹ 64.84 per unit, there will be no additional profit to the Company. A price below this may be considered, if there is a possibility of getting some benefits because of exports e.g., export incentive or subsidy from the Government.

It has been presumed in the above case that utilisation of full capacity would not require any additional capital investment and also sufficient care has been taken to see that the goods exported are not dumped in the home market.

Illustration 48. A Ltd., operating at 75% level of activity produces and sells two products X and Y. The cost sheets of these two products are as under :

	Product X	*Product Y*
Units produced and sold	3,000	2,000
	Per Unit	*Per Unit*
	₹	₹
Direct Materials	10	20
Direct Labour	20	20
Factory Overheads (40% fixed)	25	15
Administration and selling overheads (60% fixed)	40	25
Total cost per unit	95	80
Selling price per unit	115	95

Factory overheads are absorbed on the basis of machine hour which is the limiting factor. The machine hour rate is ₹ 10 per hour.

The Company receives an offer from Japan for the purchase of product X at a price of ₹ 87.50 per unit. Alternatively, the Company has another offer form Bangkok for the purchase of product Y at a price of ₹ 77.50 per unit. In both the cases, a special packing charge of ₹ 2.50 per unit has to be borne by the Company. The Company can accept either of the two export orders by utilising the balance of 25% of its capacity.

Required : Advise the Company with detailed workings as to which proposal should be accepted and prepare a statement showing the overall profitability of the Company after incorporating the export propoosal suggested by you.

Solution: **STATEMENT SHOWING THE EVALUATION OF TWO EXPORT PROPOSALS**

Particulars	*Offer from Japan for Product X*	*Offer from Bangkok for Product Y*
A. Export Price per unit (₹)	87.50	77.50
B. *Less:* Variable costs per unit (₹) :		
Direct materials	10.00	20.00
Direct labour	20.00	20.00
Variable factory overheads	15.00	9.00
Variable administration and selling overheads	16.00	10.00
Special packing charges	2.50	2.50
	63.50	61.50
C. Contribution per unit (₹) [A – B]	24.00	16.00
D. Machine hours required per unit	2.5	1.5
E. Contribution (₹) per machine hour [C/D]	9.6	10.67

Recommendation: Since machine hour is the limiting factor and the product Y yields a better contribution per machine hour, the surplus machine hours (3,500 hours) (Refer to working note 2) should be utilised to produce 2,333 units of product Y (3,500/1.5 hours = 2333.33 units). Hence the export proposal from Bangkok should be accepted.

STATEMENT SHOWING THE OVERALL PROFITABILITY

Particulars	*Product X Home*	*Product Y Home*	*Product Y Export*	*Total*
A. Sales Volume (in units)	3,000	2,000	2,333	
B. Contribution per unit (₹)	54	36	16	
C. Contribution (₹) [A B]	1,62,000	72,000	37,328	2,71,328
D. *Less :* Fixed Cost (₹)				1,44,000
E. Profit (₹) [C – D]				1,27,328

Working Notes:

(i) *Calculation of Machine Hours Available to Produce Additional Units*

Products	*X*	*Y*
A. Factory overheads per unit	25	15
B. Machine hour Rate (₹)	10	10
C. Machine hours per unit [A/B]	2.5	1.5
D. Units produced	3,000	2,000
E. Total machine hours utilised at 75% level of activity		10,500 hours
F. Total machine hours at 100% level of activity [10500 100/75]		14,000 hours
G. Machine hours available for being utilised to produce product X or Y for export (14,000 hours – 10,500 hours)		3,500 hours

(ii) *Calculation of Fixed Cost*

		₹
A	Fixed Factory Overheads X : ₹ 10 3,000 = ₹ 30,000 Y : ₹ 6 2,000 = ₹ 12,000	42,000
B	Fixed Administration and Selling Overheads X : ₹ 24 3,000 = ₹ 72,000 Y : ₹ 15 2,000 = ₹ 30,000	1,02,000
C	Total Fixed Cost [A + B]	1,44,000

Illustration 49. A company currently operating at 80% capacity has the following particulars :

	₹
Sales	32,00,000
Direct Materials	10,00,000
Direct Labour	4,00,000
Variable Overheads	2,00,000
Fixed Overheads	13,00,000

An export order has been received that would utilise half the capacity of the Factory. The order cannot be split, i.e. it has either to be taken in full and executed at 10% below the normal domestic prices, or rejected totally. The alternatives available to the Management are :

I Reject the order and continue with the domestic sales only; (as at present), or

II Accept the offer, split capacity between overseas and domestic sales and turn away excess domestic demand, or

III Increase capacity, so as to accept the export order and maintain the present domestic sales by :
   (a) buying an equipment that will increase capacity by 10%. This will result in an increase of ₹ 1,00,000 in fixed costs, and
   (b) work overtime to meet balance of required capacity. In that case labour will be paid at one and a half times the normal wage rate.

Required : Prepare a Comparative Statement of Profitability and suggest the best alternative.

Solution: **STATEMENT OF COMPARATIVE PROFITABILITY UNDER VARIOUS ALTERNATIVES**

Particulars	*Alternatives*		
	I ₹	*II* ₹	*III* ₹
A. Total Sales :			
Domestic Sales [*Working Note (i)*]	32,00,000	20,00,000	32,00,000
Sales Export [*Working Note (ii)*]	—	18,00,000	18,00,000
	32,00,000	38,00,000	50,00,000
B. *Less:* Total Variable Cost:			
Direct Materials *[Working Note (iii)]*	10,00,000	12,50,000	16,25,000
Direct Labour *[Working Note (iii)]*	4,00,000	5,00,000	7,00,000
Variable Overhead *[Working Note (iii)]*	2,00,000	2,50,000	3,25,000
	16,00,000	20,00,000	26,50,000
C. Contribution [A – B]	16,00,000	18,00,000	23,50,000
D. *Less :* Fixed Overheads	13,00,000	13,00,000	14,00,000
E. Profit [A – B]	3,00,000	5,00,000	9,50,000

Suggestion : Alternative III is the best as it would give the highest profits.

Working Notes :

(i) Sales revenue at 100% capacity = ₹ 32,00,000   100/80 = ₹ 40,00,000

(ii) Sales revenue from export order at 50% capacity = ₹ 20,00,000 – 10% of ₹ 20,00,000 = ₹ 18,00,000

(iii) Material Cost, Labour cost & Variable Overheads

	100%	130%
Direct Material Cost	10,00,000 x 100/80 = 12,50,000	10,00,000 130/80 = 16,25,000
Direct Labour cost	4,00,000 x 100/80 = 5,00,000	4,00,000 110/80 = 5,50,000
		+ 4,00,000 x 20/80 150% = 1,50,000
		7,00,000
Variable Overhead	2,00,000 x 100/80 = 2,50,000	2,00,000 x 130/80 = 3,25,000

Illustration 50. A manufacturing company currently operating at 80% capacity has received an export order from Middle East, which will utilise 40% of the capacity of the factory. The order has to be either taken in full and executed at 10% below the current domestic prices or rejected totally.
The current sales and cost data are given below :

Sales ₹ 16.00 lakhs	Variable Overheads ₹ 0.60 lakhs
Direct Material ₹ 5.80 lakhs	Fixed Overheads ₹ 5.20 lakhs
Direct Labour ₹ 2.40 lakhs	

The following alternative are available to the management :

A. Continue with domestic sales and reject the export order
B. Accept the export order and allow the domestic market to starve to the extent of excess demand
C. Increase capacity so as to accept the export order and maintain the domestic demand by :

(i) Purchasing additional plant and increasing 10% capacity and thereby increasing fixed overheads by ₹ 65,000 and
(ii) Working overtime at one and half time the normal rate to meet balance of the required capacity.

Required: Evaluate each of the above alternatives and suggest the best one.

Solution:

(a) STATEMENT OF PROFITABILITY WHEN DOMESTIC SALES ARE CONTINUED & THE EXPORT ORDER IS REJECTED

Particulars	*(₹ in lakhs)*
A. Sales	16.00
B. *Less :* Variable cost [5.80 + 2.40 + .60]	8.80
C. Contribution [A – B]	7.20
D. *Less :* Fixed cost	5.20
E. Profit [C – D]	2.00

(b) STATEMENT OF PROFITABILITY WHEN EXPORT ORDER IS ACCEPTED WITHOUT INCREASE IN CAPACITY

It is given that export order will utilize the 40% of the capacity. It is therefore necessary to work out 100% capacity (₹ 16 lakhs ÷ 80% = ₹ 20 lakhs)

Particulars	*(₹ in lakhs)*
A. Domestic sales (60% of ₹ 20 lakhs)	12.00
B. Export sales (40% of ₹ 20 lakhs 90%)	7.20
C. Total Sales [A + B]	19.20
D. *Less :* Variable Cost [8.80 100/80]	11.00
E. Contribution [C – D]	8.20
F. *Less :* Fixed costs	5.20
G. Profit [E – F]	3.00

(c) STATEMENT OF PROFITABILITY WHEN CAPACITY IS REVISED

Particulars		*(₹ in lakhs)*
A. Domestic Sales		16.00
B. Export Sales		7.20
C. Total Sales [A + B]		23.20
D. *Less :* Variable costs :		
Direct Materials [5.80 120/80]		8.70
Direct Labour [2.40 120/80]	3.60	
Add : Extra for overtime working :		
10% additional increase in capacity with overtime working		
[3.60 10/120 1/2]	0.15	3.75
Variable Overhead [0.60 120/80]		0.90
Total Variable cost		13.35

E. Contribution [C – D]	9.85
F. *Less* : Fixed cost (5.20 + 0.65)	5.85
G. Profit [E – F]	4.00

Recommendation : The company should increase the capacity so as to accept export order and maintain the domestic demand since this decision will maximise the profits

Illustration 51. X Ltd. produces 10,000 units per annum by employing 50% of the factory capacity. The selling price of the unit is ₹ 5 and the total costs were :

	₹
Materials	10,000
Wages	20,000
Fixed overheads	11,000
Variable overheads	4,000
	45,000

Variable overhead maintain a constant ratio to the number of units produced. The company accepts an export order for an additional 10,000 units at a selling price of ₹ 3.88 each.

The increased volume of purchases reduces the material prices by 2-1/2%. Wage rates remain constant, but due to the employment of new workers there is a drop in labour efficiency of 5% on all production.

Required: Prepare a statement showing the variation of net profits resulting from the acceptance of the order.

Solution STATEMENT SHOWING THE PROFITABILITY BEFORE AND AFTER THE ACCEPTANCE OF ORDER

Particulars	*50% Capacity 10,000 units* ₹	*100% Capacity 20,000 units* ₹
A. Sales Revenue	50,000	88,800
B. *Less* : Variable Costs :		
(a) Material Cost	10,000	19,500
(b) Wages	20,000	42,105
(c) Variable Overheads	4,000	8,000
	34,000	69,605
C. Contribution (A – B)	16,000	19,195
D. *Less* : Fixed Cost	11,000	11,000
E. Net Profit (C – D)	5,000	8,195

The total profit will increase by ₹ 3,195 by accepting an additional offer of 10,000 units.

Working Note : *Calculation of Wages*

For 19,000 (i.e. 20,000 *minus* 5% of ₹ 20,000) units wages payable = ₹ 40,000

For 20,000 units, wages payable $\left(\frac{40,000 \times 20,000}{19,000}\right)$ = ₹ 42,105

Illustration 52. X Ltd. produces product 'A' for which the Company has an assured market. The output for the next year has been budgeted at 1,20,000 units at 92% capacity utilisation. The cost sheet based output is as under:

Selling Price	₹ 100
Direct Materials	21
One Component 'X' [Material ₹ 2.40, Labour ₹ 3.00, Variable overheads ₹ 1.80]	9
Direct Wages @ ₹ 5 per hour	20
Factory Overheads (50% fixed)	24
Selling & Distribution Overheads (75% variable)	12
Administration Overheads	4
Total Costs	90

The factory overheads are applied on the basis of direct labour hours.

The Board was of the view that steps should be taken to utilise the idle capacity to improve the profitability of the Company. The following proposal was accordingly put up before the Board for consideration :

An order has been received from abroad of 500 units of Product B per month at ₹ 120 per unit. The cost data are : direct materials ₹ 40 per unit, direct labour 8 hours per unit, selling and distribution overheads applicable to this product order is ₹ 10 per unit and the variable factory overheads are chargeable on the basis of direct labour hours.

Required :

(i) Prepare a statement showing the profitability of the Company as originally evisaged in the budget.
(ii) Evaluate the export order and state whether it is acceptable or not.
(iii) How many units of Product 'B' can be exported if the demand exists for the same ?

Solution: (i) STATEMENT SHOWING THE PROFITABILITY OF THE COMPANY AS ORIGINALLY ENVISAGED.

Particulars		₹
A. Sales [1,20,000 ₹ 100]		1,20,00,000
B. *Less :* Variable Costs :		
Direct Material [1,20,000 ₹ 21]	₹ 25,20,000	
Direct Wages [1,20,000 ₹ 20]	24,00,000	
Component X's variable cost @ ₹ 7.20 per unit	8,64,000	
Factory overhead @ ₹ 12 per unit	14,40,000	
S & D. Overhead @ ₹ 9 per unit	10,80,000	83,04,000
C. Contribution [A – B]		36,96,000
D. Fixed Overheads :		
Factory	₹ 14,40,000	
Selling and Distribution	3,60,000	
Component 'X'	2,16,000	
Administration	4,80,000	24,96,000
E. Profit as per original budget [C – D]		12,00,000

(ii) STATEMENT SHOWING THE EVALUATION OF EXPORT ORDER

Particulars		₹
A. Selling Price		120.00
B. *Less :* Variable Costs :		
Direct Material	₹ 40.00	
Direct Labour [8 ₹ 5]	40.00	
Selling and Distribution Overhead	10.00	
Factory Overhead [60% of Direct labour cost]	24.00	114.00
C Contribution [A – B]		6.00

Recommendation: The export order should be accepted since this decision will increase the profit by ₹ 3,000 (i.e. 500 ₹ 6)

(iii) STATEMENT SHOWING THE MAX. UNITS OF PRODUCT 'B' WHICH CAN BE EXPORTED

A. Total hours to be used by Product A (1,20,000 4 hrs.)	4,80,000
B. Total hours used by X [1,20,000 0.6 hrs i.e. (3 ÷ 5)]	72,000
C. Hours available at 92% capacity [A + B]	5,52,000
D. Hours at 100% [5,52,000 100/92)]	6,00,000
E. Hours remaining to be utilized [D – C]	48,000
F. Hours required per unit of Product 'B'	8
G. Maximum No. of units of Product 'B' [E/F]	6,000

Illustration 53. A company which works at a capacity utilisation of 60% expects its turnover for the year 20X1 at ₹ 86.40 lacs. If the Company works at 100% capacity, the sales - cost relationship will be as under :

Factory Cost : Two-thirds of Sales Value
Prime Cost : 75% of Factory Cost
Selling & Administration Expenses (75% Variable) : 20% of Sales Value.
The factory Overheads will vary according to the Operating Capacity in the following manner :

Operating Capacity	60%	80%	100%	120%
Factory Overhead (₹ lacs)	19.80	21.60	24.00	30.00

The company receives an offer from abroad for a value of ₹ 19.80 lacs. The prime cost of this order is estimated at ₹ 12 lacs and the selling and administration expenses applicable to this order is ₹ 90,000. This order will occupy 40% of the capacity of the plant.

The Marketing Director estimates that by the time the new order materialises, the Company's own sales will increase to 80% of the capacity.

Required : Prepare statement to show :

(i) Profitability at the present capacity utilisation of 60%.

(ii) Profitability based on the Marketing Director's estimates of increase in the Company's own sales to 80% capacity.

(iii) Evaluation of the export order with advice as to whether the Company should accept the export or not.

Solution **STATEMENT SHOWING THE PROFITABILITY AT 100%, 60%, & 80% CAPACITY**

Particulars	*At 100%*	*At 60%*	*At 80%*
A. Sales at 100% capacity	₹ 144.00	86.40	115.20
B. Prime Cost (75% of 2/3rd of Sales at 100%))	72.00	43.20	57.60
C. Factory Overheads (given)	24.00	19.80	21.60
D. Factory Cost [B + C]	96.00	63.00	79.20
E. Selling and Administration Expenses (20% of sales)			
— Variable [75% of 20% of sales]	21.60	12.96	17.28
— Fixed	7.20	7.20	7.20
F. Total Cost of Sales [D + E]	124.80	83.16	103.68
G. Profit [A – F]	19.20	3.24	11.52

STATEMENT SHOWING THE EVALUATION OF EXPORT ORDER

	₹
A. Sales	19.80
B. Prime Cost	12.00
C. Factory Overheads (Factory Overheads at 120%, *Less* Factory Overheads at 80%)	8.40
D. Factory Cost {B + C]	20.40
E. Selling and Administration Expenses	0.90
F. Cost of Sales {D + E}	21.30
G. Loss [A – F]	1.50

Recommendation: Export order should not be accepted since this decision involves a loss of ₹ 1,50,000. However, if fixed portion of factory overheads is excluded, it will be profitable to accept the order.

8.0 SHUT DOWN OR CONTINUE DECISION

8.1 Basis of Decision

A decision as to whether to shut down or continue should be based on the **marginal cost analysis.**

8.2 Considerable Factors

The following major factors should be considered in shut down or continue decision:

Cost Factors	Non-Cost Factors
1. Present Contribution 2. Present Fixed Costs 3. Fixed Costs if plant is shut down 4. Additional Costs of plant shut down e.g. (extra maintenance Costs, Compensation on long-term contracts, Redundancy Payments) 5. Costs to be incurred on re-opening (e.g. Overhauling the plant, recruitment and training of staff, cost of technological obsolenscence)	1. Loss of expereinced employees on shut down 2. Loss of Customers on shut down 3. Loss of Suppliers on shut down 4. Loss of Reputation on shut down

8.3 Practical Steps In Shut Down or Continue Decision

Step 1: *Calculate Operating Losses if Plant is continued*
= Present Sales – Present Variable Costs – Present Fixed Costs

Step 2: *Calculate Operating Losses if Plant is shut down*
= Fixed Costs if Plant is shut down + Additional Costs of Plant shut down

Step 3: *Continue the Plant if operating losses of continued Plant are* ***less than*** *those of shut down plant.*

OR

Shut Down the Plant if operating losses of continued Plant are ***more than*** *those of shut down Plant.*

In otherwords, if present contribution is sufficient to cover the avoidable fixed cost, continue the operations, otherwise shut down.

8.4 Shut Down Point

Shut Down Point refers to that level of activity at which operating losses are just equal to fixed costs if the plant is shut down. At this point the management would be indifferent as to shut down or continue decision. Shut Down Point may be calculated as follows:

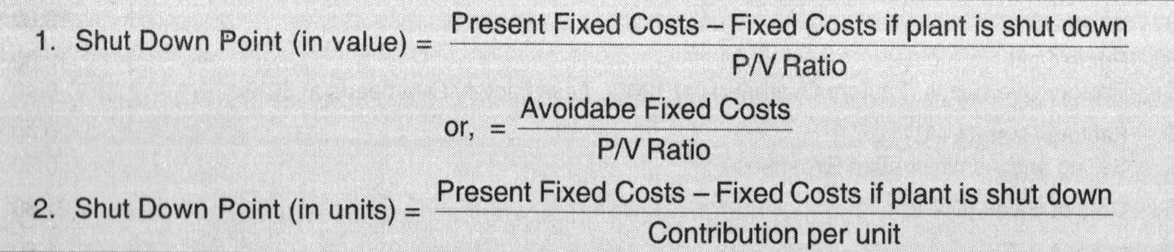

1. Shut Down Point (in value) = $\frac{\text{Present Fixed Costs – Fixed Costs if plant is shut down}}{\text{P/V Ratio}}$

or, = $\frac{\text{Avoidabe Fixed Costs}}{\text{P/V Ratio}}$

2. Shut Down Point (in units) = $\frac{\text{Present Fixed Costs – Fixed Costs if plant is shut down}}{\text{Contribution per unit}}$

Shut Down or Continue Decision on the basis of Shut Down Point

Actual Level of Activity	Whether to Shut Down or Continue
If Actual Sales = Shut Down Point	*Either* Shut Down *or* Continue
If Actual Sales > Shut Down Point	Continue
If Actual Sales < Shut Down Point	Shut Down

Illustration 54. Universe Ltd. manufactures 20,000 units of 'X' in a year at its normal production capacity. The unit cost as to variable costs and fixed costs at this level are ₹ 13 and ₹ 4 respectively. Selling Price per unit is ₹ 20.

Due to trade depression, it is expected that only 2,000 units of 'X' can be sold during the next year. The management plans to shut-down the plant. The fixed costs for the next year then is expected to be reduced to ₹ 33,000. If the plant is shut down, plant maintenance would cost ₹ 8,000 and on reopening of the factory, cost of overhauling the plant and cost of training and engagement of new personnel would amount to ₹ 3,000 and ₹ 1,000 respectively. Should the plant to be shut-down? What is the shut-down point?

Solution: **STATEMENT OF SHOWING OPERATING LOSSES**

Particulars	*If Plant is operated* ₹	*If Plant is shut down* ₹
A. Sales [2000 × ₹ 20]	40,000	—
B. *Less*: Variable Cost [2000 × ₹ 13]	(26,000)	—
C. Contribution [A – B]	14,000	—
D. *Less*: Fixed Costs	(80,000)	33,000
Additional shut down cost (8,000 + 3,000 + 1,000)	—	12,000
E. Operating losses	66,000	45,000

Recommendation: The plant should be shut down since operating losses of shut down plant are less than those of continued plant.

$$\text{Shut-down Point} = \frac{\text{Total Fixed Cost} - \text{Shut Down Costs}}{\text{Contribution per unit}} = \frac{80,000 - 45,000}{20 - 13} = 5,000 \text{ units}$$

Plant should be shut down since the Actual Sales (i.e. 2,000 units) are less than Shut-down Point (i.e. 5,000 units)

Illustration 55. (a) X Ltd. provides you the following information :

1.	Production and Sales at present	25,000 units
2.	Sales at present	₹ 6,25,000 p.a.
3.	P/V ratio	20%
4.	Fixed Costs at present	₹ 4,80,000 p.a.
5.	Fixed Cost when the plant is shut down	₹ 3,60,000 p.a.

Required : Advise the Company whether the plant should be shut down & calculate the Shut Down Point.

(b) If in the above part (a) the existing sales (in units) are reduced by 5%, shall your decision be changed ?

Solution

Part (a)

Particulars	*If Plant Is Continued* ₹	*If Plant is Shut Down* ₹
A. Sales	6,25,000	Nil
B. *Less* : Variable cost @ 80%	5,00,000	Nil
C. Contribution @ 20% (A – B)	1,25,000	Nil
D. Fixed Costs	4,80,000	3,60,000
E. Operating Losses (C – D)	3,55,000	3,60,000

Recommendation: Since the operating losses, if shut down are larger than those, if not shut down, the plant should not be shut down.

$$\text{Shut Down Point} = \frac{\text{Fixed Costs at Present} - \text{Fixed Cost if Shut Down}}{\text{P/V Ratio}}$$

$$= \frac{4,80,000 - 3,60,000}{20\%} = \frac{1,20,000}{20\%} = ₹\ 6,00,000$$

$$\text{Shut Down Point (in units)} = \frac{6,00,000}{25} = 24,000 \text{ Units}$$

Plant should not be shut down since the Actual Sales (i.e. 25,000 units) are more than the shut down point (i.e. 24,000 units)

Verification:

		₹
A.	Sales [24,000 ₹ 25]	6,00,000
B.	Variable costs @ 80%	4,80,000
C.	Contribution [A – B]	1,20,000
D.	Fixed costs	4,80,000
E.	Operating Losses [C – D]	3,60,000

Part (b)

Particulars		*If Plant is Continued* ₹	*If Plant is Shut Down* ₹
A.	Sales [23,750 ₹ 25]	5,93,750	—
B.	Variable costs	4,75,000	—
C.	Contribution [A – B]	1,18,750	—
D.	*Less :* Fixed Costs	4,80,000	3,60,000
E.	Operation Losses [C – D]	(3,61,250)	3,60,000

Recommendation: Since the operating losses, if shut down, are lesser than those if plant is continued, the plant should be shut down.

Note : Shut Down Point (i.e. ₹ 6,00,000) will remain same as calculated in Part (a).

Illustration 56. A paint manufacturing company manufactures 2,00,000 per annum medium-seized tins of "Spray Lac Paints" when working at normal capacity. It incurs the following cost of manufacturing per unit.

Direct Material	₹ 7.80
Direct Labour	2.10
Variable Overhead	2.50
Fixed Overhead	4.00
Product Cost (per unit)	16.40

Each unit (tin) of the product is sold for ₹ 21 with variable selling and administrative expenses of 60 paise per tin.

During the next quarter only 10,000 units can be produced and sold.

Management plans to shut down the plant estimating that the fixed manufacturing cost can be reduced to ₹ 74,000 for the quarter.

When the plant is operating, the fixed overheads are incurred at a uniform rate throughout the year. Additional costs of plant shut-down for the quarter are estimated at ₹ 14,000.

Required :

(a) express your opinion, along with the calculation, as to whether the plant should be shut down during the quarter, and

(b) calculate the shut down point for quarter in units of products (i.e. in terms of number of tins)

Solution:

(₹ in lakhs)

Particulars		*If Continued*	*If Shut Down*
A.	Sales (10000 ₹ 21)	2.10	—
B.	*Less :* Variable Costs		
	Direct Material Costs	0.78	
	Direct labour Costs	0.21	
	Variable Overheads	0.25	
	Selling & Adm. Expenses	0.06	
		1.30	—
C.	Contribution (A – B)	0.80	—
D.	*Less :* Fixed costs	2.00	0.74 + 0.14 = .88
E.	Loss	(1.20)	(0.88)

(a) *Opinion* — The decision to shut-down is more advantageous to the company than the decision to continue since the costs of decision to shut down are less than the costs of decision to continue.

(b) $$\text{Shut Down Point (units)} = \frac{\text{Fixed Costs } (\textit{if continued}) - \text{Fixed Cost } (\textit{if shut down})}{\text{Contribution per unit}}$$

$$= \frac{2{,}00{,}000 - 88{,}000}{8} = 14{,}000$$

Note : Contribution per unit = ₹ 80,000/10,000 = ₹ 8 per unit.

Illustration 57. SBP Ltd. had the following annual flexible budget for the year ending 31st March :

	80% Capacity (₹ lakhs)	*60% Capacity (₹ lakhs)*
Direct Material Cost	2.00	1.50
Direct Labour Cost	2.00	1.50
Direct Expenses	1.60	1.20
Manufacturing Expenses	4.00	3.85
Office & Admn. Expenses	4.00	3.80
Selling & Distribution Expenses	4.00	3.75
Sales	20.00	15.00

Owing to adverse trading conditions, the Company has been operating at 50% capacity, realising budgeted selling prices.

Owing to acute competition, it has become inevitable to reduce price by 15% even to maintain the sales at the existing level. The directors are considering whether or not their factory should be closed down until the trade recession has passed. A market research consultant had advised that in about a year's time, there is every indication that sales volume will increase to 75% of normal capacity and the revenues to be produced @ 10% less than the budgeted revenues.

If the Directors decide to close down the factory for year, it is estimated that :

(a) the present fixed costs would be reduced to ₹ 2 lakhs p.a.

(b) closing down costs (redundancy payments etc.) would amount to ₹ 0.50 lakhs.

(c) necessary maintenance of plant would cost ₹ 20,000 p.a.

(d) on reopening of the factory, the cost of overhauling the plant, training and engagement of new personnel, would amount to ₹ 30,000 and ₹ 10,000 respectively.

Required: As a Chartered Accountant, Suggest the Board of Directors whether or not they should shut down the factory:

Solution:

The Directors,
SBP Ltd.
New Delhi
Dear Sirs,

As desired, we have analysed the cost implications of the decision of temporary closure of the factory in view of the trade recession. We find that if the factory is run at 50% capacity and with reduced selling prices, the loss likely to be incurred in one full year (the estimated period of recession), would be around ₹ 3.975 lakhs as detailed below :

₹ (in lakhs)

	Particulars	*If Continue*
A	Sales [(20 50/80) – 15% of 12.5]	10.625
B	*Less :* Variable Costs:	
	Direct Materials	1.250
	Direct labour	1.250
	Direct Expenses	1.000
	Manufacturing Expenses	0.375
	Office & Administrative Expenses	0.500
	Selling & Distribution Expenses	0.625
		5.000

	Particulars	*If continue*
C	Contribution [A – B]	5.625
D	*Less :* Fixed Costs	
	Manufacturing Expenses	3.40
	Office & Adm. Expenses	3.20
	Selling & Distribution Expenses	3.00
		9.60
E	Loss (D – C)	3.975

If the factory is closed, the following costs will be incurred :

Particulars	*(₹ in lakhs)*
Fixed Costs	2.00
Closing down Costs	0.50
Maintenance Costs	0.20
Cost of Overhauling the plant, training and engagement of staff	0.40
	3.10

It is obvious from the above, that despite the fact that running at 50% capacity would imply a loss of ₹ 3.975 lakhs, it is better to close down the factory since in that case the loss would be lower.

In our view, even if running the factory entailed a somewhat bigger loss as compared to the loss incurred by closing it down temporarily, it may be better to keep the factory in operation. This is because a closure, even if temporary, results in the loss of regular and old customers, suppliers and skilled personnel. This coupled with a loss of goodwill in the market, may give rise to substantial losses at the time of restarting the factory.

We trust that the above analysis would be helpful to you in reaching an appropriate decision in the matter. We shall be glad to provide any further assistance that may be required in this regard.

Your faithfully,
X & Co.
Chartered Accountants

Working Note : *Calculation of Expenses (₹ in lakhs)*

	Mfg. Expenses	*Adm. Expenses*	*Selling Expenses*
A. Amount At 60%	3.85	3.80	3.75
B. Amount At 80%	4.00	4.00	4.00
C. Amount At 20%	0.15	0.20	0.25
D. Amount At 50%	0.375	0.50	0.625
	[0.15 50/20]	[0.20 50/20]	[0.25 50/20]

Illustration 58. A Ltd. is experiencing recessionary difficulties and as a result its directors are considering whether or not the factory should be closed down till the recession has passed.

A flexible budget is compiled giving the following details:

Particulars	*Fixed Costs*		*Total Costs at Production Capacity*			
	Close down ₹	*Normal* ₹	*40%* ₹	*60%* ₹	*80%* ₹	*100%* ₹
Factory Overheads	6,000	8,000	10,000	11,000	12,000	13,000
Administration Overheads	3,500	5,500	6,500	7,000	7,500	8,000
Selling & Dist. Overheads	3,000	5,000	7,000	8,000	9,000	10,000
Miscellaneous	500	500	1,500	2,000	2,500	3,000
Direct Labour	—	—	10,000	15,000	20,000	25,000
Direct Material	—	—	12,000	18,000	24,000	32,000
Total	13,000	19,000	47,000	61,000	75,000	91,000

The following additional information has been supplied to you :

(i) Present sales at 50% capacity are estimated at ₹ 30,000 per annum.

(ii) Estimated costs of closing down are ₹ 4,500. In addition, maintenance of plant and machinery is expected to amount to ₹ 800 per annum.
(iii) Costs of reopening after being closed down are estimated to be ₹ 2,000 for overhauling of machines and getting ready and ₹ 1,400 for training of personnel.
(iv) Market research investigations reveal that sales should take an upward swing to around 70% capacity at prices which would produce revenue of ₹ 1,00,000 in approximately twelve months' time.

Required: Advise the Directors whether to close down for twelve months or continue operations indefinitely.

Solution:

STATEMENT OF PROFIT (LOSS)

	Particulars		*(Percentage capacity levels)* 0 ₹	50 ₹	70 ₹
A	Sales		Nil	30,000	1,00,000
B	Costs :				
	Variable Costs		Nil	35,000	49,000
	Fixed Costs		13,000	19,000	19,000
	Special shut-down costs :				
	Closing down	4,500			
	Plant Maintenance	800			
	Cost of reopening & overhauling	2,000			
	Training	1,400	8,700		
	Total Costs		21,700	54,000	68,000
C	Profit (loss) [A – B]		(21,700)	(24,000)	32,000

Recommendation: Loss will be a sum of ₹ 1300 more (i.e. ₹ 24,000 – ₹ 21,700) if the plant is not closed down. The difference being insignificant, it may be advisable to continue the operation on account of non-financial considerations.

Working Notes :

(i) Variable Costs for 1% capacity level $= \dfrac{\text{Change in costs}}{\text{Change in capacity levels}} = \dfrac{61{,}000 - 47{,}000}{60\% - 40\%}$ = ₹ 700

(ii)		
	A. Total Costs at 40% capacity (given)	47,000
	B. *Less :* Fixed Costs (given)	19,000
	C. Variable Costs at 40%	28,000
	D. *Add :* Additional Variable Cost for 10% (₹ 700 10)	7,000
	E. Total Variable Costs at 50%	35,000
	F. *Add :* Additional Variable Cost for 20% (₹ 700 20)	14,000
	G. Total Variable Costs at 70% [E + F]	49,000

Illustration 59. Easy-going Ltd. is a big company with many departments producing and selling a number of products and making profits regularly year by year. Recently the Personnel Department of the Company undertook a manpower planning exercise and found to its dismay that the whole company was overstaffed by about 50% and the average age of staff and workers was on the wrong side of 45. This discovery has rudely shaken the management. If feels that mass scale retrenchment and recruitment of young professionals to cope with the changing technologies will be the ultimate solution.

But apprehending the repercussions of such a drastic step both inside and outside, the Company is thinking of introducing a voluntary retirement scheme. For this purpose, as an experimental measure, the Company wants to start with the Doledrums Department which markets a product, almost at the verge of its life cycle. For this Department, summarised annual figures are as follows:

	50%	70% (₹ 000)	90%
Direct Labour	560	784	1,008
Direct Material	400	560	720
Production Overhead	320	384	448
Administration, Marketing & Distribution	240	272	304

Three strategies have been advocated.

Strategy A:

Close down the Department for 3 years. The new product line would not come in for 3 years and then would be capital - intensive, rather than labour intensive.

(i) Redundancy payments would be ₹ 1,10,000 but this would need to be augmented by ₹ 50,000 to make the deal acceptable to work force:

(ii) The existing overhead costs would be reduced by ₹ 1,44,000 per annum :

(iii) Extra costs of retaining, overhauling the idle equipment etc. on reopening would be ₹ 80,000; and

(iv) Extra annual costs during the closed years for maintenance would be ₹ 16,000.

Strategy B:

Allow the Department on run down naturally without interference.

(i) Production: Year 1 : 70%, Year 2 : 60%, Year 3 : 50%

(ii) Redundancy payments arising at the end of year 3 - ₹ 40,000 :

(iii) Sales Revenue: Year 1 : ₹ 18,30,000, Year 2 : ₹ 15,35,000, Year 3 : ₹ 12,15,000,

(vi) Extra Retaining Cost ₹ 20,000

Strategy C:

Flood the market in the terminal years at reduced prices, causing financial embarrassment to competitors.

(i) Production 90% overall years ;

(ii) Redundancy and retaining payment at the end of year 3 - ₹ 75,000 :

(iii) Sales Revenue: Year 1 ₹ 23,72,000, Year 2 ₹ 23,42,000, Year 3 ₹ 23,22,000

(iv) Compensation on long-term contracts ₹ 25,000

(v) Extra advertisement per annum ₹ 40,000

Required : Calculate the losses that will be incurred under each strategy.

Solution:

Strategy A :

Redundancy Costs	₹ 1,60,000
Overhead in 3 years [(₹ 3,20,000 – 1,44,000) 3]	5,28,000
Extra costs retaining overhauling etc.	80,000
Extra annual costs for closed 3 years [16,000 3]	48,000
Loss over 3 years	8,16,000

Strategy B :

Loss in year 1 [₹ 20,00,000 – 18,30,000]	₹ 1,70,000
Loss in year 2 [₹ 17,60,000 – 15,35,000]	2,25,000
Loss in year 3 [₹ 15,20,000 – 12,15,000]	3,05,000
Redundancy payments in 3 years	40,000
Extra retaining cost	20,000
Loss over a period of 3 years	7,60,000

Strategy C :

Loss in year 1 [₹ 24,80,000 – ₹ 23,72,000]	₹ 1,08,000
Loss in year 2 [₹ 24,80,000 – ₹ 23,42,000]	1,38,000
Loss in year 3 [₹ 24,80,000 – ₹ 23,22,000]	1,58,000
Compensation on long-term contracts	25,000
Extra advertisements p.a. [i.e. ₹ 40,000 3]	1,20,000
Redundancy and retaining payment	75,000
Loss over 3 years	6,24,000

Working Notes:

(i) Variable Overhead at 20% capacity = Overheads at 90% – Overhead at 70%
= (₹ 4,48,000 + 3,04,000) – (₹ 3,84,000 + ₹ 2,72,000)
= ₹ 7,52,000 – ₹ 6,56,000 = ₹ 96,000

(ii) Variable Overheads at 90% = ₹ 96,000 × 90/20 = ₹ 4,32,000

(iii) Fixed Overheads at 90% = ₹ 7,52,000 – ₹ 4,32,000 = ₹ 3,20,000

(iv) Variable Cost at 60% = (₹ 10,08,000 + ₹ 7,20,000 + ₹ 4,32,000)   60/90 = ₹ 14,40,000

Illustration 60. X Y Z Ltd. has to date spent ₹ 75,000 on a research project and it expects that when completed in a further year the results of that research can be sold for ₹ 1,00,000. In trying to decide whether to proceed, the business identifies the additional expenses necessary to complete the research :

Materials ₹ 30,000. This materials (already in store and paid for is very toxic and will have to be disposed off in sealed containers at a cost of R. 2,500.

Labour ₹ 20,000. The research project uses highly skilled labour taken from the production department of the Company. If they were working on normal production, the Company could earn ₹ 25,000 additional contribution to profit in the next year after paying the skilled labour.

Research staff. ₹ 30,000. The research unit will be closed down after the project has been completed and voluntary retirement pay has already been agreed at ₹ 12,500.

General overheads. ₹ 20,000. The research unit is apportioned a share of the total fixed costs of the business.

The Management Accountant of the Company has presented the following analysis and recommended against continuation, since the analysis that the Company would lose ₹ 25,000 more by continuing the project than by abandoning now.

The Managing Director seeks your opinion as the group Management Accountant about the analysis presented by the Management Accountant.

Particulars	*Abandon now*	*Complete the project*
Sales	—	₹ 1,00,000
Costs to date	₹ 75,000	₹ 75,000
Additional costs :		
Materials		30,000
Labour		20,000
Research staff		30,000
Overheads		20,000
Loss in contribution		25,000
Net Loss	75,000	1,00,000

Solution

The analysis presented by the Management Accountant does not speak about his expertise in presenting decision-making data. He has not considered the sunk cost, relevant and irrelevant cost and opportunity cost concepts. The conclusions drawn by the Management Accountant are incorrect due to the following reasons :

(i) The Company has already spent ₹ 75,000 on a research project. The Company cannot retrieve the amount already spent, if the Company discontinues the project. It is sunk cost, and irrelevant for decision making.

(ii) The materials worth ₹ 30,000 purchased in the past is still lying in store and it has no substitute use. Thus ₹ 30,000 is again a sunk cost and the same cannot be considered for decision analysis. The amount of ₹ 2,500 spent on disposing it off will have to be taken into consideration.

(iii) If the research project is abandoned, labour cost of ₹ 20,000 is not relevant as the same will be used by production department. If the research projects continued, it is necessary to consider the contribution foregone (opportunity cost of ₹ 25,000).

(iv) Salaries of research staff will be saved if the research project is abandoned. This is relevant to this decision. The voluntary retirement pay has already been agreed and it forms part of sunk cost and, therefore, it is irrelevant to this decision analysis.

(v) Apportionment of general overheads to research project is irrelevant as it is a fixed overhead. This cost will continue to be incurred by the production department irrespective of whether the research project is continued or not. The correct analysis is given below :

STATEMENT SHOWING RELEVANT COST OF CONTINUING OR DISCONTINUING THE RESEARCH PROJECT

Particulars	*Abandon the project*	*Complete the project*
A. Sale Proceeds from Research (₹)	—	1,00,000
B. Relevant Costs (₹) :		
Disposal Cost of Material	2,500	—
Labour	—	25,000
Research Staff Cost	—	30,000
Total Cost	2,500	55,000
C. Profit/(Loss) (₹) [A – B]	(2,500)	45,000

If the project is abandoned, the company's loss will be ₹ 2,500. However, if the research project is completed, the company will earn a profit of ₹ 45,000. Therefore, company should continue the project.

Illustration 61. In the year I the turnover of a company, which operated at a marging of safety of 25% amounted to ₹ 9,00,000 and its profit volume ratio was 33 – 1/3%. During the year II, the company estimated that although the same volume of sales as in the year I would be maintained, the sales value would go down due to decrease in selling price. There will be no change in variable costs. The company proposes to reduce its fixed costs through an intensive cost reduction programme. These changes will alter the profit volume ratio and margin of safely to 30% and 40% respectively in the year II

Even if the company closed down its operations in the year II, it would incur a minimum fixed cost of ₹ 50,000.

Required:

(i) Present a comparative statement indicating the sales, variable costs, fixed costs and profit for both the years.

(ii) At what minimum sales will the company be better off by locking up in business in the year II.

Solution: **COMPARATIVE STATEMENT**

Particulars	*Year I* ₹	*Year II* ₹
A. Sales	9,00,000	8,57,143
B. *Less:* Variable costs	(6,00,000)	(6,00,000)
C. *Less:* Fixed costs	(2,25,000)	(1,54,286)
D. Profit [A – B – C]	75,000	1,02,857

(ii) Minimum sales at which the company will be better off by locking up business in the year II

$$\text{Shut-down point} = \frac{\text{Avoidable Fixed Costs}}{\text{P/V Ratio}} = \frac{1{,}54{,}286 - 50{,}000}{30\%} = 3{,}47{,}620$$

Working Notes:

(i) *For the year I*

		₹
A	Sales (given)	9,00,000
B	*Less*: Variable Cost (66 – 2/3% of ₹ 9,00,000)	6,00,000
C	Contribution [A – B]	3,00,000
D	*Less*: Fixed Cost [BEP × P/V Ratio] [(75% of ₹ 9,00,000) × 33 – 1/3%]	2,25,000
E	Profit [C – D]	75,000

(ii) *For the year II*

A	Sales (assume X)	X
B	*Less*: Variable Cost	6,00,000
C	Contribution	X – 6,00,000

X – 6,00,000 = 30% of X

X = 6,00,000/0.70 = ₹ 8,57,143

Fixed Cost = BEP × P/V Ratio = (60% of ₹ 8,57,143) × 30% = ₹ 1,54,286

9.0 EXPAND OR CONTRACT DECISION

9.1 Basis of Decision

A decision as to expansion or contraction of capacity should be based on pre and post Total Profit Analysis.

9.2 Considerable Factors

While taking a decision as to whether the capacity should be expended or contracted, the following factors should be considered.

Decision as to Expansion of Capacity	*Decision as to Contraction of Capacity*
1. Additional Fixed Expenses to be incurred. 2. Possible decrease in selling price due to increase in production.	1. Loss of Contribution 2. Saving in Fixed Costs

3. Whether the demand is sufficient to absorb the increased production.	3. Additional cost of Contraction (e.g. extra maintenance cost, Compensation as long-term contracts, Redundancy payments etc.) 4. Loss of Experienced Employees 5. Loss of Customers 6. Loss of Suppliers 7. Loss of Reputation

9.3 Practical Steps in Expand or Contract Decision

Step 1: *Calculate Total Profit before Expansion/Contraction of Capacity*
Step 2: *Calculate Total Profit after Expansion/Contraction of Capacity*
Step 3: *Expand/Contract the Capacity if Steps 2 > Step 1*
Do not Expand/Contract the Capacity if Step 2 < Step 1

Illustration 62. A factory is currently working at 50% capacity and produces 10,000 units of product P, the unit cost of which is ₹ 180 comprised as follows :

	₹
Direct Material	100
Direct Labour	30
Factory Overhead	30 (40% Fixed)
Administrative Overhead	20 (50% Fixed)

The selling price per unit is ₹ 200

If the capacity is increased to 60%, the raw material cost will increase by 2% and selling price falls by 2%. At 80% capacity, raw material cost increases by 5% and selling price falls by 5%.

Required : Work out the total costs and profit for the three capacity levels and prepare a brief note for the management on the profitability of these levels of performance with your recommendation.

Solution: STATEMENT SHOWING TOTAL COSTS AND PROFIT AT VARIOUS CAPACITY LEVELS

Particulars	*Capacity*		
	50% 10,000 Units	*60% 12,000 Units*	*80% 16,000 Units*
A. Sales (₹)	20,00,000	23,52,000	30,40,000
B. Total Variable Costs :			
Direct Material (₹)	10,00,000	12,24,000	16,80,000
Direct Labour (₹)	3,00,000	3,60,000	4,80,000
Factory Overhead (₹)	1,80,000	2,16,000	2,88,000
Administration Overhead (₹)	1,00,000	1,20,000	1,60,000
	15,80,000	19,20,000	26,08,000
Factory Overhead (10,000 12)	1,20,000	1,20,000	1,20,000
Administration Overhead (10,000 10)	1,00,000	1,00,000	1,00,000
C. Total Fixed Cost (₹)	2,20,000	2,20,000	2,20,000
D. Total Cost (₹) (B + C)	18,00,000	21,40,000	28,28,000
E. Profit (₹) (A – D)	2,00,000	2,12,000	2,12,000
F. Profit Margin (%) $\left(\frac{\text{Profit}}{\text{Sales}} \times 100\right)$	10%	9.01%	6.97%

Brief Note (for Management on the profitability):

From the above total cost and profit statement the following two facts are apparent :

(a) The profit margin at 50% capacity is 10%, at 60% capacity it is 9.01% and at 80% capacity it is 6.97%. It means that profit margin shows a downward trend as capacity increases from 50% onwards.

(b) At 50% capacity the concern's total profit is ₹ 2,00,000, whereas at 60% and 80% capacities it is ₹ 2,12,000. Therefore it is clear that as we move from 50% to 60% capacity, the profit increases by ₹ 12,000, whereas there is no change in the profitability when the capacity is increased from 60% to 80% level.

On the basis of above two facts, it is advisable for management to increase its production upto 60% level of operation inspite of a slight decrease in profit margin.

Illustration 63. Titan Engineering is operating at 70 per cent capacity and presents the following information:

Break-even point	₹ 200 crores
P/V Ratio	40 per cent
Margin of safety	20 per cent

Titan's management has decided to increase production to 95 per cent capacity level with the following modifications:

(i) The selling price will be reduced by 8 per cent.
(ii) The variable cost will be reduced by 5 per cent on sales.
(iii) The fixed cost will increase by ₹ 20 crores, including depreciation on additions, but excluding interest on additional capital.
(iv) Additional capital of ₹ 50 crores will be needed for capital expenditure and working capital.

Required: (a) Indicate the sales figure, with the working, that will be needed to earn ₹ 10 crores over and above the present profit and also meet 20 per cent interest on the additional capital. (b) What will be the revised. (i) Break-even point; (ii) P/V Ratio; (iii) Margin of safety.

Solution:

Assuming that the present selling price is ₹ 100 crores

			₹ (Crores)
(a)	A	Revised Selling Price will be (8% *less*)	92.00
	B	Revised Variable Costs (55% of ₹ 92)	50.60
	C	Contribution (₹ 92.00 – ₹ 50.60)	41.40
	D	New P/V Ratio = $\frac{41.40}{92.00} \times 100 = 45\%$	
	E	Revised Fixed Costs	
		Present Fixed Cost	80
		Increase in Fixed Costs	20
		Interest at 20 per cent on additional capital (₹ 50 crores x 20%)	10
		Total Revised Fixed Costs	110

F Revised Required Sales $= \frac{\text{Revised fixed cost + Expected profit}}{\text{P/V Ratio}}$

$= \frac{\text{110 crores + 30 crores}}{45\%} = ₹\ 311.11$ crores

(b) (i) Revised Break-even Point $= \frac{\text{Fixed Costs}}{\text{P/V Ratio}} = \frac{\text{110 crores}}{45\%} = ₹\ 244.44$ crores

(ii) P/V Ratio = 45%

(iii) Revised margin of safety = Revised sales – Revised break-even sales
= ₹ 311.11 crores – ₹ 244.44 crores
= ₹ 66.67 crores

Working Notes :

(i) Total sales = Break-even sales + Margin of Safety
= ₹ 200 crores + 25% of ₹ 200 crores = ₹ 250 crores

(ii) P/V Ratio = 40%

(iii) Variable Cost = 60% of Sales = 60% of ₹ 250 crores = ₹ 150 crores

(iv) Fixed Cost = Break-even Sales   P/V Ratio = ₹ 200 crores   40%
= ₹ 80 crores

(v) Total Cost = ₹ 150 crores + ₹ 80 crores = ₹ 230 crores

(vi) Profit = Total Sales – Total costs = ₹ 250 crores – ₹ 230 crores
= ₹ 20 crores.

Alternatively, Profit = Margin of Safety   P/V Ratio = 50   40% = ₹ 20 crores

Illustration 64. Unique Products manufactures and sells in a year 20,000 units of a particular product to definite customers at a price of ₹ 100 per unit. The concern has a capacity to produce 25,000 units of the product per annum. To produce beyond 25,000 units per annum, the concern will have to install a new equipment at a cost of ₹ 15 lakhs. The equipment will have a life span of 10 years and will have no residual value. There is an offer from a client to purchase 10,000 units of the product regularly at a price of ₹ 90 per unit. The order, if accepted, will have to be over and above the existing level of production of 20,000 units.

The cost structure is as under:

	₹ Per unit
Direct Material	30
Direct Labour	20
Variable Overhead	10
Profit	20

During the coming year, it has been estimated that the cost of direct material, as compared to the current year will increase by 10%. Because of certain wage agreement direct labour cost will increase by 25%. Fixed overheads will increase by 10%. If the new order for 10,000 units is accepted, fixed overheads will increase further by ₹ 60,000 due to increased administrative charges.

You are required to analyse whether the concern should accept the order or instead of that try to secure order for the balance unused capacity, as available now, through some sales promotion expenses which will be ₹ 50,000 per annum. Ignore financial charges for the new investment.

Solution: **COMPARATIVE PROFIT STATEMENT (BASED ON REVISED COST STRUCTURE)**

	Proposal 1	*Proposal 2*	*Proposal 3*
	Sell 20,000 units only	*Secure orders for 5,000 additional units (unused capacity) and sell 25,000 units*	*Accept the new order for 10,000 additional units and sell 30,000 units*
Particulars	₹	₹	₹
A. Total Sales	20,00,000 (20,000 units × ₹ 100	25,00,000 (25,000 units × ₹ 100	29,00,000 (20,000 units × ₹ 100) + (10,000 units × ₹ 90)
B. *Less*: Total Costs:			
Direct Material	6,60,000 (20,000 units × ₹ 33)	8,25,000 (25,000 units × ₹ 33)	9,90,000 (30,000 units × ₹ 33)
Director Labour	5,00,000 (20,000 units × ₹ 25)	6,25,000 (25,000 units × ₹ 25)	7,50,000 (30,000 units × ₹ 25)
Variable Overheads	2,00,000 (20,000 units × ₹ 10)	2,50,000 (25,000 units × ₹ 10)	3,00,000 (30,000 units × ₹ 10)
Fixed Overheads	4,40,000 (₹ 4,00,000 + ₹ 40,000)	4,40,000	4,40,000
Add: Administrative Charges	—	—	60,000
Add: Sales Promotion Expenses	—	50,000	—
Depreciation (New equipment)			1,50,000
Total Costs	18,00,000	21,90,000	26,90,000
C Profit [A – B]	2,00,000	3,10,000	2,10,000

Analysis: The above analysis clearly shows that profit is maximum under proposal 2. Therefore, it is advisable for the concern to produce and sell 25,000 units@₹ 100 per unit and utilise its full production capacity.

Illustration 65. JBC Ltd, a manufacturing company having a capacity of 60,000 units has prepared a following cost sheet:

Direct Material Per Unit	₹	12.5
Direct Wages Per Unit	₹	5

Semi-Variable Cost	₹ 30,000 Fixed + 0.50 Per Unit
Factory Overheads Per Unit	₹ 10 (50% Fixed)
Selling and Administration Overheads Per Unit	₹ 8 (25% Variable)
Selling Price Per Unit	₹ 40

During the year 2011, the sales volume achieved by the company was 50,000 units. The company has launched an expansion program as under:

(a) The capacity will be increased to 1,00,000 units.
(b) The cost of investment on expansion is ₹ 5 Lakhs which is proposed to be financed through financial institution at 12% per annum.
(c) The depreciation rate on new investment is 10% based on straight line.
(d) The additional fixed overheads will amount to ₹ 2 Lakhs upto 80,000 units and will increase ₹ 80,000 more beyond 80,000 units.

After the expansion, the company has two alternatives for operating the expanded plant as under:

(i) Sales can be increased upto 80,000 units by spending ₹ 50,000 on special advertisement campaign to explore a new market.
(ii) Sales can be increased upto 1,00,000 units subject to the following:
 (a) Reduction of selling price by ₹ 4 per unit on all the units sold.
 (b) The direct material cost would go down by 4%due to discount on bulk buying.
 (c) By increasing the variable selling and administration expenses by 4%.

Required:

(i) Construct a Flexible Budget at the Level 50,000 Units, 80,000 Units and 1,00,000 Units of Production and select the best Profitable level of operation.
(ii) Calculate Break-Even-Point both before and after expansion.

Solution:

FLEXIBLE BUDGET

	Particulars	*50,000 Units* ₹	*80,000 Units* ₹	*1,00,000 Units* ₹
A	No. of Units	50,000	80,000	1,00,000
B	Selling Price Per Unit	40	40	36
C	Sales [A x B]	20,00,000	32,00,000	36,00,000
D	*Less:* Variable Costs:			
	Direct Material @ ₹ 12.50/ 12.50/ 12.00	6,25,000	10,00,000	12,00,000
	Direct Wages @ ₹ 5	2,50,000	4,00,000	5,00,000
	Semi-Variable Cost (Variable) @ ₹ 0.50	25,000	40,000	50,000
	Variable Factory Overheads @ ₹ 5	2,50,000	4,00,000	5,00,000
	Variable Selling &Adm. OH @ ₹ 2/ 2/ 2.08	1,00,000	1,60,000	2,08,000
	Total Variable Cost	12,50,000	20,00,000	24,58,000
E	Contribution [C – D]	7,50,000	12,00,000	11,42,000
F	*Less:* Total Fixed Costs:			
	Fixed Factory Overheads (₹ 5 x 60,000)	3,00,000	3,00,000	3,00,000
	Fixed Selling & Adm. OH (₹ 6 x 60,000)	3,60,000	3,60,000	3,60,000
	Semi-Variable Cost (Fixed)	30,000	30,000	30,000
	Additional Fixed OH (due to expansion)	0	2,00,000	2,80,000
	Interest	0	60,000	60,000
	Depreciation	0	50,000	50,000
	Special Advertisement Expenses	0	50,000	0
	Total Fixed Costs	6,90,000	10,50,000	10,80,000
G	Profit [E – F]	60,000	1,50,000	62,000

Advice: Activity Level of 80,000 Units is most Profitable Level since the profit is maximum at that level.

(ii) **CALCULATION OF BREAK-EVEN-POINT**

$$\text{BEP (Units)} = \frac{\text{Fixed Costs}}{\text{Contribution Per Unit}} = \frac{6,90,000}{15} \quad \frac{10,50,000}{15} \quad \frac{10,80,000}{11.42}$$

= 46,000 Units   70,000 Units   94,571 Units

$$BEP (₹) = \frac{(Fixed\ Costs\ x\ Sales)}{Total\ Contribution}$$

At 50,000 Units Level : (₹ 6,90,000 x ₹ 20,00,000)/₹ 7,50,000 = ₹ 18,40,000
At 80,000 Units Level : (₹ 10,50,000 x ₹ 32,00,000)/₹ 12,00,000 = ₹ 28,00,000
At 1,00,000 Units Level : (₹ 10,80,000 x ₹ 36,00,000)/₹ 11,42,000 = ₹ 34,04,553

10.0 WHETHER TO DROP OR ADD A PRODUCT LINE

When a firm manufacturing a number of products finds that one or more of its products is or are un-remunerative from the profitability point of view, the firm may consider the following two alternatives:

Alternative I: To drop the un-remunerative product and to leave the capacity unutilised.

Alternative II: To drop the un-remunerative product and to utilise the capacity for the manufacture of a more remunerative product (which may be Existing Product or New Product).

Decision Criteria for Alternative I

If the contribution of product proposed to be dropped is less than the avoidable fixed costs due to discontinuance of this product, then DROP the Product, otherwise not

Decision Criteria for Alternative II

If the contribution of the product proposed to be dropped is less than the contribution of the product proposed to be produced by utilizing the released capacity, then DROP the Product, otherwise not.

Illustration 66. The Novelties Ltd, is not keen on making special efforts to push the sales of product B, on of the three main products it deals in, since product B is not considered to be as profitable as the other two. The selling prices and cost of the three products are :

Product	*Selling Price*	*Direct Material*	*Direct Labour*		
			Dept. X	*Dept. Y*	*Dept. Z*
	₹	₹	₹	₹	₹
A	340	50	40	10	10
B	290	30	10	40	10
C	320	40	10	10	40

Overhead rates for each department per rupee of direct labour are as follows:

	Dept. X	*Dept. Y*	*Dept. Z*
	₹	₹	₹
Variable Overheads	1.20	0.40	1.00
Fixed Overheads	1.20	2.00	1.40
Total	2.40	2.40	2.40

Required : What will be your advice about the profitability of product B ? Give reasons.

Solution: STATEMENT OF THE COST AND CONTRIBUTION OF VARIOUS PRODUCTS OF NOVELTIES LTD.

Particulars	*A* ₹	*B* ₹	*C* ₹
A. Selling price	340	290	320
B. *Less :* Variable Costs:			
Direct Material	50	30	40
Direct Labour	60	60	60
Variable Overhead	62	38	56
Total Variable Cost	172	128	156

Particulars	A ₹	B ₹	C ₹
C. Contribution [A – B]	168	162	164
D. *Less :* Fixed Overheads	82	106	88
E. Profit [C – D]	86	56	76
F. P/V Ratio	49.4%	55.86%	51.25%

The attitude of 'the Novelties Ltd', towards product 'B' appears to be based on wrong considerations. Product B gives, as the above statement shows, a contribution only slightly less that than that of others in terms of rupees. In terms of percentage Product B has the maximum profit volume ratio.

It appears that due to the inequitable apportionment of fixed overhead cost, the profit of product B is low in comparision to products A and C. This probably has resulted in the attitude of indifference the company has towards product B. But that is not the right approach, as long as a product gives good contribution, it should be encouraged.

Working Notes : *Calculation of Variable and Fixed Overheads*

	Dept. X ₹		Dept. Y ₹		Dept. Z ₹		Total ₹
(i) Variable Overheads							
A	40	1.20	10	0.40	10	1.00	62
B	10	1.20	40	0.40	10	1.00	38
C	10	1.20	10	0.40	40	1.00	56
(ii) Fixed Overheads :							
A	40	1.20	10	2.00	10	1.40	82
B	10	1.20	40	2.00	10	1.40	106
C	10	1.20	10	2.00	40	1.40	88

Illustration 67. The costs per unit of the three products *A, B* and *C* of a company are given below :

	Product A ₹	Product B ₹	Product C ₹
Direct Materials	20	16	18
Direct Labour	12	14	12
Variable Expenses	8	10	6
Fixed Expenses	6	6	4
	46	46	40
Profit	18	14	12
Selling Price	64	60	52
No. of Units produced	10,000	5,000	8,000

Production arrangements are such that if one product is given up, the production of the others can be raised by 50%. The directors propose that C should be given up because the profit from that product is the lowest.

Required: Present suitable analysis of the data indicating whether the proposal should be accepted.

Solution:

Fixed Expenses = (10,000 × ₹ 6) + (5,000 × ₹ 6) + (8,000 × ₹ 4) = ₹ 1,22,000

STATEMENT SHOWING THE PRODUCTWISE CONTRIBUTION

Particulars	A ₹	B ₹	C ₹
Selling Price per unit	64	60	52
Marginal Cost per unit	(40)	(40)	(36)
Contribution per unit	24	20	16
Total Contribution	2,40,000	1,00,000	1,28,000

(a) STATEMENT SHOWING THE PROFITABILITY IF A IS GIVEN UP

Particulars	*A*	*B*	*C*	*Total*
A. Present Units	—	5,000	8,000	
B. Additional Units	—	2,500	4,000	
C. Total Units [A + B]	—	7,500	12,000	
D. Contribution per unit		20	16	
E. Contribution (₹) [C D]	—	1,50,000	1,92,000	3,42,000
F. *Less :* Fixed cost (₹)				1,22,000
G. Total Profit (₹) [E – F]				2,20,000

(b) STATEMENT SHOWING THE PROFITABILITY IF B IS GIVEN UP

Particulars	*A* ₹	*B* ₹	*C* ₹	*Total* ₹
A. Present units	10,000	—	8,000	
B. Additional Units	5,000	—	4,000	
C. Total units [A + B]	15,000	—	12,000	
D. Contribution per unit	24	—	16	
E. Total Contribution (₹)	3,60,000	—	1,92,000	5,52,000
F. *Less :* Fixed cost				1,22,000
G. Total Profit [E – F]				4,30,000

(c) STATEMENT SHOWING THE PROFITABILITY IF C IS GIVEN UP

Particulars	*A* ₹	*B* ₹	*C* ₹	*Total* ₹
A. Present units	10,000	5,000	—	
B. Additional Units	5,000	2,500	—	
C. Total Units [A + B]	15,000	7,500	—	
D. Contribution per unit	24	20	—	
E. Total Contribution (₹)	3,60,000	1,50,000	—	5,10,000
F. *Less :* Fixed cost				1,22,000
G. Total Profit [E – F]				3,88,000

Recommendation: If product B is given up, the profit is the maximum since the total contribution of B is lowest. The proposal to give up product C is therefore, not advisable.

Illustration 68. Alpha Ltd. has prepared the following budget estimates for the year :

Sales (in units)	*Product A* 6,000 ₹/Unit	*Product B* 16,000 ₹/Unit
Selling Price	40	64
Direct Materials	12	22
Direct Wages @ ₹ 1 per hour	8	12
Variable overheads	4	6
Fixed Overheads	8	12
Total cost	32	52
Profit	8	12

After finalisation of the above budget estimated, it is observed that one-third of the production capacity is still idle. In order to improve the performance, the following proposals are under consideration :

(i) Product A will be discontinued and the capacity so released will be used for product B. The selling price of Product B will, however, have to be reduced by ₹ 2 per unit in order to increase the volume of sales.

(ii) Product B will be discontinued and the capacity so released will be diverted to the production of product C. The particulars relating to per unit of product C are as under :

Selling Price	₹ 52	Direct Labour	₹ 10
Direct Material	₹ 15	Variable Overheads	₹ 5

(iii) The idle capacity will be utilised for meeting an export demand for product D. The particulars relating to per unit of product D are as under :

Selling Price	₹ 72	Direct Labour	₹ 20
Direct Materials	₹ 40	Variable Overheads	₹ 10

(iv) The idle capacity will be hired out by fixing a price in such a way that the same rate of profit per direct labour hour as obtained in the budget estimates is achieved.

Required: Prepare a statement showing the profitability of the products A and B as envisaged in the budget estimates. Also evaluate each of the above four proposals separately and prepare statements showing the profitability under each proposal.

Solution:

Basic Calculations :

	Products A	Products B	Total
Direct Labour hours per unit	8	12	
Number of units	6,000	16,000	
Direct Labour hours utilised	48,000	1,92,000	2,40,000
Idle Capacity [$2,40,000 \times \frac{3}{2} \times \frac{1}{3}$]		1,20,000	
Fixed Cost	48,000	1,92,000	2,40,000

(a) BUDGETED STATEMENT OF PROFITABILITY

Particulars	*Product A*	*Product B*	*Total*
A. Output (units)	6,000	16,000	
B. Selling Price per unit (₹)	40	64	
C. Variable Cost per unit (₹) :			
Direct Material	12	22	
Direct Wages	8	12	
Variable Overheads	4	6	
	24	40	
D. Contribution per unit (₹) [B – C]	16	24	
E. Total Contribution (₹) [A D]	96,000	3,84,000	4,80,000
F. *Less :* Fixed Cost			2,40,000
G. Profit (₹)			2,40,000

(b) Evaluation of Proposal (i)

Spare Capacity because of discontinuing Product A = 48,000 hours
Spare capacity released will produce product B = 48,000/12 = 4,000 units
Hence, Production will be entirely of Product B = 16,000 + 4,000 = 20,000 units

STATEMENT SHOWING THE PROFITABILITY UNDER PROPOSAL (i)

A. Output (in units)		20,000
B. Selling Price per unit (₹)		62
C. Variable Cost per unit (₹) :		
Direct Materials	22	
Direct Wages	12	
Variable Overheads	6	
		40
D. Contribution per unit (₹) [B – C]		22
E. Total Contribution (₹) [A D]		4,40,000
F. *Less :* Fixed Cost (₹)		2,40,000
G. Profit (₹) [E – F]		2,00,000

Evaluation of Proposal (ii)

Spare capacity because of discontinuing Product B = 16,000 × 12 = 1,92,000 hrs.

Spare capacity will be used for production of Product C = $\frac{1,92,000}{10}$ = 19,200 units

STATEMENT SHOWING THE PROFITABILITY UNDER PROPOSAL (ii)

Particulars	*Product A*	*Product C*	*Total*
A. Output (Units)	6,000	19,200	
B. Selling Price per unit (₹)	40	52	
C. Variable cost per unit :			
Direct Material	12	15	
Direct Labour	8	10	
Variable Overheads	4	5	
	24	30	
D. Contribution per unit [B – C]	16	22	
E. Total Contribution (₹) [A × D]	96,000	4,22,400	5,18,400
F. *Less :* Fixed Costs			2,40,000
G. Profit [E – F]			2,78,400

Evaluation of Proposal (iii)

STATEMENT SHOWING THE PROFITABILITY UNDER PROPOSAL (iii)

Particulars	*Product A*	*Product B*	*Product D*	*Total*
A. Output (units)	6,000	16,000	6,000	
B. Selling Price per unit (₹)	40	64	72	
C. Variable Cost per unit :				
Direct Materials	12	22	40	
Direct Labour	8	12	20	
Variable Overheads	4	6	10	
	24	40	70	
D. Contribution per unit [B – C]	16	24	2	
E. Total Contribution [A × D]	96,000	3,84,000	12,000	4,92,000
F. *Less :* Fixed Costs				2,40,000
G. Profit [E – F]				2,52,000

Evaluation of Proposal (iv)

STATEMENT SHOWING THE PROFITABILITY UNDER PROPOSAL (iv)

	₹
A. Budgeted Profit	2,40,000
B. Budgeted Direct Labour Hours	2,40,000
C. Profit per Direct Labour hour [A/B]	1
D. Idle Capacity (Direct Labour Hours)	1,20,000
E. Additional profit by hiring out the idle capacity [1,20,000 × ₹ 1]	1,20,000
F. Profit as per the estimate	2,40,000
G. Total profits after hiring out the idle capacity [E + F}	3,60,000

Recommendation: Since, Proposal (iv) is giving the highest budgeted profit, and therefore, Proposal (iv) is recommended.

Illustration 69. E Ltd. is engaged in the manufacturing of three products in its factory. The following budget estimates are prepared for the next year :

	Product		
	A	*B*	*C*
Sales (Units)	10,000	25,000	20,000
Selling Price Per Unit (₹)	40	75	85
Direct Material Per Unit (₹)	10	14	18
Direct Wages Per Unit @ ₹ 2 Per Hour	8	12	10
Variable Overhead Per Unit (₹)	8	9	10
Fixed Overhead Per Unit (₹)	16	18	20
Profit / (Loss)	(2)	22	27

After the finalisation of the above manufacturing schedule, it is observed that presently only 80% capacity being utilised by these three products. The production activities are made at the same platform and it may be inter changebale among products according to requirement. In order to improve the profitability of the company the following three proposals are put for consideration:

(a) Discontinue Product A and capacity released may be used for either Product B or C or equally shared. The Fixed Cost of Product A is avoidable. Expected changes in Material Cost and Selling Price subject to the utilisation of Product A's capacity are as under:

Product B: Material Cost increased by 10% and Selling Price reduced by 2%.
Product C: Material Cost increased by 5% and Selling Price reduced by 5%.

(b) Discontinue Product A and Divert the capacity so released and the idle capacity to produce a new Product D for meeting export demand whose per unit cost data are as follows:

	₹
Selling Price	60
Direct Material	28
Direct Wages @ ₹ 3 Per Hour	12
Variable Overhead	6
Fixed Cost (Total)	1,05,500

(c) Product A, B and C are continuosly run and hire out the idle capacity fixing a price in such a way that the same rate of profit per direct labour hour is obtained in the original budget estimates.

Required:

(i) Prepare a Statement of Profitability of Products A, B and C in existing situation.
(ii) Evaluate the above Proposals independently and calculate the overall Profitability of the Company under each Proposal.
(iii) Which Proposal should be accepted, if the company wants to maximise its Profit?

Solution

(i) **STATEMENT OF PROFITABILITY**

	Particulars	*Product A*	*Product B*	*Product C*	*Total*
A	Selling Price Per Unit	40	75	85	
B	*Less:* Variable Cost:				
	Direct Material Cost	10	14	18	
	Direct Wages @ ₹ 2 Per Hour	8	12	10	
	Variable Overhead	8	9	10	
	Total Variable Cost	26	35	38	
C	Contribution Per Unit [A – B]	14	40	47	
D	Sales Units	10,000	25,000	20.000	
E	Total Contribution [C x D]	1,40,000	10,00,000	9,40,000	20,80,000
F	*Less:* Fixed Cost	1,60,000	4,50,000	4,00,000	10,10,000
G	Profit/(Loss) [E – F]	–20,000	5,50,000	5,40,000	10,70,000
H	Labour Hours Per Unit	4	6	5	
I	Total Labour Hours [D x H]	40,000	1,50,000	1,00,000	2,90,000
J	Profit Per Direct Labour Hour [G / I]				3.6897

Proposal (a)

(ii)

STATEMENT OF PROFITABILITY

		Proposal I If Used for Product B			*Proposal II If Used for Product C*			*Proposal III If Used for Both Equally*		
		Product B	*Product C*	*Total*	*Product B*	*Product C*	*Total*	*Product B*	*Product C*	*Total*
A	Sales Units	31,667	20,000		25,000	28,000		28,333	24,000	
B	Selling Price	73.50	85.00		75.00	80.75		73.50	80.75	
C	Variable Cost	36.40	38.00		35.00	47.90		36.40	47.90	
D	Contribution/Unit	37.10	47.00		40.00	32.85		37.10	32.85	
E	Total Contribution	11,74,846	9,40,000	21,14,846	10,00,000	9,19,800	19,19,800	10,51,154	7,88,400	18,39,554
F	*Less:* Fixed OH			8,50,000			8,50,000			8,50,000
G	Profit [E – F]			12,64,846			10,69,800			9,89,554

Hence Capacity released should be used only for production of Product B since overall Profitability (i.e.12,64,845.70) is maximum.

Proposal (b)

A	Total Labour Hours at 80% Level	2,90,000
B	Total Labour Hours at 100% Level (2,90,000 x 100/80)	3,62,500
C	Idle Labour Hours (B – A)	72,500
D	Capacity Released from Product A(10,000 x 4)	40,000
E	Total available Labour Hours [C + D]	1,12,500
F	Units of Product D [E/4]	2,8125
G	Contribution Per Unit (60 – 28 – 12 – 6)	14
J	Total Contribution [F x G]	3,93,750
K	*Less:* Fixed Cost	1,05,500
L	Profit/(Loss) [J – K]	2,88,250

OVERALL PROFITABILITY

	Particulars	*Product B*	*Product C*	*Product D*	*Total*
A	Contribution	10,00,000	9,40,000	3,93,750	2,33,3750
B	*Less:* Fixed Cost	4,50,000	4,00,000	1,05,500	9,55,500
C	Profit [B – C]	5,50,000	5,40,000	2,88,250	13,78,250

Proposal (c)

A	Profit as Per Original Estimate	10,70,000.00
B	Profit from Hiring Idle Capacity [72,500 x 3.6897]	2,67,503.25
C	Total [A + B]	13,37,503.25

(iii) Proposal (b) should be accepted if Company wants to maximise its Profit.

11.0 HOW TO DECIDE WHETHER TO PROCESS FURTHER OR NOT

To decide whether to process further *or* not incremental revenue after further processing should be compared with further processing costs.

Case	Decision
I. If Incremental Revenue exceeds Further Processing Costs	Product should be processed further and should be sold after further processing because the overall income will increase by the difference between the incremental revenue and further processing costs.
II. If Incremental Revenue is less than the Further Processing Costs	Product should not be processed further and should be sold at split off point because the overall income will decrease by the difference between the further processing costs and incremental revenue if the products are processed further.

Tutorial Note: *Apportionment of Joint Costs is not relevant in decision-making regarding further processing of joint or by-products*

Illustration 70. Tulsian Ltd. operates a chemical process which produces four products – *P*, *Q*, *R*, and *S* from a basic raw material provides you the following data:

1. Basic raw Material 1,25,000 units @ ₹ 2
2. Initial Processing Wages ₹ 1,50,000
3, Initial Processing Overheads ₹ 1,00,000
4. Output, Selling Prices and Additional Processing Costs:

Product	*Output (Units)*	*Selling Price per unit at split off point (₹)*	*Selling Price per unit after further processing (₹)*	*Additional Processing Costs after split off (₹)*
P	10,000	40	70	2,50,000
Q	20,000	30	65	3,00,000
R	30,000	20	40	7,50,000
S	40,000	10	20	2,00,000

5. Joint Costs are to be apportioned on the basis of Net Realizable value.

Required:

(*a*) State with supporting calculations as to whether any *or* all the products should be further processed *or* not so that the company can maximize its profits.

(*b*) Prepare a statement showing the product - wise and total profitability based on your recommendation in part (*a*).

Solution:

(*a*) **STATEMENT SHOWING THE CALCULATION FOR FUTHER PROCESSING DECISION**

Products	*P* ₹	*Q* ₹	*R* ₹	*S* ₹
A. Selling Price per unit after further processing	70	65	40	20
B. Selling Price per unit at split off point	40	30	20	10
C. Incremental Selling price (A – B)	30	35	20	10
D. Total incremental Revenue (C × units)	3,00,000	7,00,000	6,00,000	4,00,000
E. *Less:* Further Processing Costs	2,50,000	3,00,000	7,50,000	2,00,000
F. Incremental Profit (Loss) (*D*) – E)	50,000	4,00,000	(1,50,000)	2,00,000

Recommendation: Product '*R*' should not be further processed since its further processing results in a loss of ₹ 1,50,000 and hence it should be sold at split off point. Product '*P*', '*Q*', and '*S*' should be sold after further processing.

(*b*) **STATEMENT SHOWING THE PROFITABILITY**

(if products 'P', 'Q' and 'S' are sold after further processing and product 'R' is sold at split off point)

Product	*Output (units)* A	*Sales Value* B	*Joint Costs apportioned* C	*Further Processing Costs* D	*Total Costs* ₹ E = C + D	*Profit (Loss)* ₹ F = B – E
P	10,000	7,00,000	90,000	2,50,000	3,40,000	3,60,000
Q	20,000	13,00,000	2,00,000	3,00,000	5,00,000	8,00,000
R	30,000	6,00,000	90,000	—	90,000	5,10,000
S	40,000	8,00,000	1,20,000	2,00,000	3,20,000	4,80,000
		34,00,000	5,00,000	7,50,000	12,50,000	21,50,000

Comment: The overall profit will increase by ₹ 1,50,000 if recommendations are accepted.

Working Note:

STATEMENT SHOWING THE APPORTIONMENT OF JOINT COSTS (NET REALIZABLE VALUE)

Products	*Output (units)*	*Selling Price per unit*	*Sales Value after further processing*	*Further Processing Costs*	*Net Realizable Value at split of point*	*Joint cost apportioned [in the ratio of 45 : 100 : 45 : 60]* ₹
		₹	₹	₹	₹	
	A	*B*	*C = A × B*	*D*	*E = C – D*	*F =* $\frac{Rs\ 5,00,000}{Rs\ 25,00,000} \times E$
P	10,000	70	7,00,000	2,50,000	4,50,000	90,000
Q	20,000	65	13,00,000	3,00,000	10,00,000	2,00,000
R	30,000	40	12,00,000	7,50,000	4,50,000	90,000
S	40,000	20	8,00,000	2,00,000	6,00,000	1,20,000
					25,00,000	5,00,000

12.0 OPTIMISING INVESTMENT PLAN

When multiple alternatives of investment opportunities having similar risks are available, one can use incremental cost and revenue approach to find out the optimum investment plan as follows: In this case we increase the total investment by increment till such time the incremental rate of return falls below the cut off rate given. The cut off rate is the minimum rate of return expected from the investment.

Step 1: *Arrange the Projects in ascending order*
Step 2: *Calculate the Incremental Investment*
Step 3: *Calculate the Incremental Net Profit*
Step 4: *Calculate the Rate of Return on Incremental Investment as follows:*

$$Rate = \frac{Incremental\ Net\ Profit}{Incremental\ Investment} \times 100$$

Step 5: *Compare the Rate of Return on Incremental Investment with Cut-off Rate*
*[**Note:** Cut off Rate is the minimum rate of return expected from the investment]*
Step 6: *Select the Projects (upto Maximum Amount available for Investment) on which the Rate of Return exceeds the cut off rate.*

Illustration 71. A company has ₹ 2,00,000 to invest and it can earn 14% by investing the sum in company deposits. It also has got an opportunity to invest this sum in five projects as under:

	Projects				
	A ₹	*B* ₹	*C* ₹	*D* ₹	*E* ₹
Total Investment	20,000	60,000	1,00,000	1,60,000	2,00,000
Annual Net Profit	1,000	8,400	15,600	24,240	28,640
Rate of Return	5%	14%	15.6%	15.15%	14.3%

Find the Optimum Investment Plan.

Solution: **RATE OF RETURN ON INCREMENTAL INVESTMENT**

Particulars	*Projects*				
	A ₹	*B* ₹	*C* ₹	*D* ₹	*E* ₹
Incremental Investment	20,000	40,000	40,000	60,000	40,000
Incremental Net Profit	1,000	7,400	7,200	8,640	4,400
Rate of Return on Incremental Investment	5%	18.5%	18%	14.4%	11.0%

Looking at the figures above, we find that project B, C and D are the most profitable projects because if the rate of return is more than the cut off rate of 14%. The following table will prove the facts. It may be observed here that the total income is the highest figure if the funds are invested in project its B, C and D and the balance available in other company deposits at 14%.

Total Funds available	2,00,000
Funds Invested in Project B, C, D	1,40,000
Balance Invested in Deposits	60,000
Income from Projects (₹ 7,400 + ₹ 7,200 + ₹ 8,640)	23,240
Income from Deposits (₹ 60,000 × 14%)	8,400
Total Income	31,640

13.0 PRICING DECISION

13.1 Meaning of Pricing Decision

Pricing decision mainly involves the determination of the price to be charged by the organisation for its products and services. Pricing policy mainly covers the following decisions:

1. What should be the Pricing Strategy?
2. What should be the Wholesalers' Discounts?
3. What should be the Retailers' Discounts?
4. What should be the Quantity Discount Terms?
5. What should be the Cash Discount Terms?
6. What should be the Credit Period Terms?

13.2 Factors affecting Pricing Decision

The major factors affecting the pricing decision are as follows:

1. Pricing Objective	The Pricing objectives should always be in conformity with the overall objectives of the firm. The pricing objective may be: (a) To earn desired profit on cost (b) To earn desired Return on Investment (c) To maximize Market share (d) To prevent competitor's entry by following penetration pricing policy (e) To build up goodwill of the organisation as a supplier of quality goods and services at reasonable prices
2. Cost	Cost sets the lower limit of the price while value to consumers sets the upper limit. Normally the product price should not be less than its cost unless it is necessary under special circumstances, (like to capture a specific market, to make the entry of competitor difficult)
3. Degree of Market Competition	Degree of competition affects the degree of pricing freedom enjoyed by the organisation in the market. In monopoly market, firm enjoys complete pricing freedom and becomes the price maker. In competitive market, firm does not enjoy complete pricing freedom and must set the price in line with the competitors.
4. Degree of Price Elasticity of Demand	Price elasticity of demand refers to the degree of responsiveness of change in demand due to change in the price of the product. In case of inelastic demand, the firm can fix higher price without much loss of demand. In case of elastic demand, the firm can get larger revenue by lowering price.

	Note: Availability of substitutes of the product also affects the elasticity.
5. Govt. Price Controls	Govt. may decide to fix the price substantially lower than the cost. Govt. may direct the firms to manufacture a particular product to the levels of licensed capacity.

13.3 Features of a Good Pricing Policy/General Guidelines to be used in adopting a Pricing Policy

A Good Pricing Policy should—

(a) provide an incentive to producer for adopting improved technology and maximising production;
(b) encourage optimum utilisation of resources;
(c) work towards better balance between demand and supply;
(d) promote exports; and
(e) avoid adverse effects on the rest of the economy.

13.4 Pricing Techniques

The various pricing techniques are shown below:

1. Cost-plus Price Technique
2. Marginal Cost Pricing Technique
3. Return on Investment Technique
4. Competitive Pricing Technique
5. Incremental Pricing Technique

13.5 Cost-plus Price Technique

Meaning	Under Cost-plus Price Technique, a fixed percentage of profit is added to the historical cost.
Suitability	This technique is suitable: (a) where an enterprise is entering a new technological area. (b) where the customer has no choice but to accept the cost-plus price.
Advantages	1. It assures the recovery of total cost (i.e. variable cost and fixed cost) 2. It assures a fixed percentage of profit. 3. It is easy to understand and thus it is normally used in Govt. purchases.
Disadvantages	1. It does not encourage the manufacturers to reduce the cost of product. 2. It encourages inefficiencies of manufacturers. 3. It does not differentiate between the use of high technology and low technology. 4. It ignores demand. 5. It fails to reflect competition adequately. 6. It introduces an artificial and arbitrary element in allocation of common costs of multi products firms 7. It does not facilitate advance budgeting in the absence of price.

13.6 Marginal Cost Pricing Technique

Meaning	Under Marginal Cost Pricing Technique, price is fixed as equal to marginal cost. It is a short-term pricing policy.

Suitability	Marginal Cost Pricing Technique is suitable: (a) where enterprise is operating in conditions of excess installed capacity (b) where there is a cut-throat competition (c) where new product is to be introduced in the market (d) where there is no demand of the product at full cost. This situation may arise from wrong investment decision.

13.7 Return on Investment Pricing

Meaning	Under Return on Investment Pricing Technique a certain percentage of capital employed is added to the historical total cost. This percentage varies from industry to industry depending upon its nature. Capital Employed = Fixed Assets + Working Capital
Advantages	1. It assures the recovery of total cost (i.e. variable cost and fixed cost) 2. It assures a fair return on investment. 3. It is easy to understand. 4. It makes provision of ploughing back of profits. 5. It is useful for performance measurement.
Issues Involved	1. The basis on which capital employed is computed. 2. Which items should be covered in the return on capital? 3. What rate of return can be regarded as fair?

Illustration 72. Tulsian Ltd. provides you the following information:

Sales	20,000 units
Direct Material	₹ 20,000
Direct Wages	₹ 20,000
Direct Expenses	₹ 8,000
Factory Overheads (15% Variable)	₹ 40,000
Office & Adm. Expenses (80% fixed)	₹ 40,000
Selling & Distribution Expenses (75% fixed)	₹ 40,000
Commission to Dealer	4%
Tax Rate	40%

Required: Calculate the Selling Price per unit in each of the following alternative cases :

Case (a) If it is decided to earn an overall profit after tax of ₹ 14,400

Case (b) If it is decided to earn an overall profit after tax @ 7.2% on sales.

Case (c) If it is decided to earn 20% return after tax on capital employed. (**Note:** Net Fixed Assets ₹ 32,000 and Working Capital 20% of sales)

Case (d) If it is decided to earn profit after tax @ 10% on total cost.

Solution: Let the selling price be X

STATEMENT SHOWING THE COMPUTATION OF PROFIT AFTER TAX

A	No. of units	20,000
B	Selling Price per unit (₹)	x
C	Total Sales (A × B)	20,000 x
D	*Less :* Variable Cost of sales :	
	Direct Material	20,000
	Direct Wages	20,000
	Direct Expenses	8,000
	Variable Factory Overheads	6,000
	Variable Office & Adm. Expenses	8,000
	Variable Selling & Dist. Expenses	10,000
	Commission to dealer @ 4% on sales	800 x
		72,000 + 800 x

E	Contribution (C – D)	19200 x – 72,000
F	*Less :* Fixed Costs :	
	Fixed Factory Overheads	34,000
	Fixed Office Adm. Expenses	32,000
	Fixed Selling & Distribution Expenses	30,000
		96,000
G	Profit before tax (E – F)	19200 x – 1,68,000
H	*Less :* Tax @ 40%	7680 x – 67,200
I	Profit after tax (G – H)	11,520 x – 1,00,800

(a) *Selling Price per unit under Case (a)*

11520 x – 1,00,800 = 14,400 (given)

11,520 x = 14,400 + 1,00,800

x = 115200/11520 = ₹ 10 per unit

(b) *Selling Price per unit under Case (b)*

11520 x – 1,00,800 = 7.2% of 20000 x

11520 x – 1440 x = 1,00,800

x = 1,00,800/10080 = ₹ 10 per unit

(c) *Selling Price per unit under Case (c)*

Capital Employed = Net Fixed Assets + Working capital

= ₹ 32,000 + 20% of 20000 x

= ₹ 32,000 + 4000 x

Desired Return on Capital Employed = 20% of (32,000 + 4,000 x) = 6400 + 800 x

Thus, 11520 x – 100800 = 6,400 + 800 x

11520 x – 800 x = 6,400 + 1,00,800

10720 x = 107200

x = 1,07,200/10720 = ₹ 10 per unit

(d) *Selling Price per unit under Case (d)*

Total cost = Variable Cost + Fixed Cost

= ₹ 72,000 + 800 x + ₹ 96,000

= ₹ 1,68,000 + 800 x

11520 x – 1,00,800 = 10% of (1,68,000 + 800 x)

11520 x – 1,00,800 = 16,800 + 80 x

11440 x = 16,800 + 1,00,800

x = ₹ 117600/11440 = ₹ 10.28 per unit

Illustration 73. Find out the selling price of an article whose costs for production and sale of 1,00,000 units are:

Material ₹ 50,000, Labour ₹ 40,000, Production Overheads are absorbed @ 100% of Prime cost, Administration Overheads are absorbed @ ₹ 0.70 per unit produced, Selling and Distribution Overheads are recovered @10% on sales.

The fixed portion of capital employed is ₹ 30,000 and the varying portion is 40% of sales. A profit of 8% net on capital employed after payment of tax at 40% of the earnings is desired.

Solution:

A.	Selling Price (Assume)	X	
B.	Sales Units	1,00,000	
C.	Total Sales	1,00,000X	
D.	*Less:* Costs		
	Prime Cost ₹ 50,000 + ₹, 40,000	90,000	
	Production Overheads (100% of 90,000)	90,000	
	Administration Overheads (1,00,000 × 0.70)	70,000	
	Selling and Dist Overheads (10% of 1,00,000X)	10,000X	
		10,000X + 2,50,000	
E.	Profit before Tax	90,000X – 2,50,000	
F.	*Less:* Tax @ 40%	36,000X – 1,00,000	
G.	Profit After Tax	54,000X – 1,50,000	...(Eq. I)

Capital Employed = ₹ 30,000 + 40% of 1,00,000X = 30,000 + 40,000X

Return on Capital Employed = 8% (30,000 + 40,000X) = 2,400 + 3,200X ...(Eq. II)

Equation Eq I and II we get X = ₹ 3

Hence, Selling Price = ₹ 3

Illustration 74. Prepare Cost Sheet based on the following data and consider the price that you would quote for an export order of 25,000 pieces.

Raw Material -	5,000 Kgs. @ ₹ 13.90 per Kg.
Direct Labour -	7,500 Hrs. Normal @ ₹ 4.00 per hour
	25% overtime at double the normal rate.

Factory overheads - 80% of direct wages.
Selling and Distribution cost - 40% of direct wages
Office & Adm. Cost - 20% of direct wages
Additional Fixed Capital Investment to be made - ₹ 25,000
Normal Net Return on Capital employed expected - 50%
Increase in working capital : 10% of the Sales Value

Solution:

COST SHEET

Particulars	₹
A. Raw Materials (5,000 ₹ 13.90)	69,500
B. Direct Labour [(7,500 ₹ 4.00) + (7,500 25% ₹ 8)]	45,000
C. Prime Cost (A + B)	1,14,500
D. Factory Overheads (45,000 80/100)	36,000
E. Factory Cost (C + D)	1,50,500
F. Office & Adm. Cost (45,000 20/100)	9,000
G. Cost of Production (E + F)	1,59,500
H. Selling & Distribution Cost (45,000 40/100)	18,000
I. Cost of Sales (G + H)	1,77,500
J. Normal Expected Return on Capital Employed (25,000 50/100)	12,500
	1,90,000
K. Return on Increase in Working Capital (10% of Sales 50% i.e. 5% of sales *or* 1/19th of Cost)	10,000
L. Desired Sales for 25,000 [J + K]	2,00,000
M. Selling Price per piece (2,00,000/25,000)	₹ 8

Illustration 75. For quoting consultancy fee, it has been decided to provide for bonus at 20% of the fee payable to the officers and have a profit mark up at 25% on the total cost inclusive of such bonus. For a particular assignment, the cost has been estimated at ₹ 75,000. Compute the fee that should be charged, to provide for the aforesaid two elements.

Solution:

Let the consultancy fee be x
Thus,

A. Cost (excluding bonus)	₹ 75,000
B. *Add :* Bonus	0.2x
C. Total Cost [A + B]	₹ 75,000 + 0.2x
D. *Add :* Profit @ 25%	25% of (₹ 75,000 + 0.2x)
E. Consultancy Fee [C + D]	₹ 93,750 + 0.25x
	₹ 93,750 + 0.25x = x
	x = ₹ 93,750/0.75 = ₹ 1,25,000

Therefore, the various elements of consultancy fee will be as under :

A. Cost	₹ 75,000
B. *Add :* Bonus [20% of ₹ 1,25,000]	₹ 25,000
C. Total Cost [A + B]	₹ 1,00,000
D. *Add :* Profit [25% of ₹ 1,00,000]	₹ 25,000
E. Consultancy fee [C + D]	₹ 1,25,000

Illustration 76. An organisation manufactures a product, particulars of which are detailed below:

Annual Production (Units)	20,000
Cost per annum (₹):	
Material	50,000
Other variable cost	60,000
Fixed cost	40,000
Apportioned Investment (₹)	1,50,000

Determine the unit selling price under two strategies mentioned below. Assume that the organisation's Tax rate is 40%—

(a) 20% return on investment.

(b) 6% profit on list sales, when trade discount is 40%.

Solution:

(a) SELLING PRICE TO YIELD 20% RETURN ON INVESTMENT

	Particulars	₹
A	Selling price	X
B	Sales units	20,000
C	Total Sales [A × B]	20,000 X
D	*Less*: Cost [50,000 + 60,000 + 40,000]	1,50,000
E	Profit before tax [C – D]	20,000 X – 1,50,000
F	*Less*: Tax @ 40%	(8000X – 60,000)
G	Profit after tax	12000X – 90,000
	Profit after tax = 20% Return on Investment 12000X – 90000 = 20% of ₹ 1,50,000 = ₹ 30,000 X = (₹ 30,000 + 90,000)/12000 = ₹ 10	

(b) SELLING PRICE TO YIELD 6% PROFIT ON LIST SALES

	Particulars	₹
A	Selling Price	X
B	Sales units	20,000
C	Total Sales at list price	20,000X
D	*Less*: Trade Discount @40%	8000X
E	Total Sales after trade discount	12000X
F	*Less*: Cost [50,000 + 60,000 + 40,000]	1,50,000
G	Profit before tax (E – F)	12,000X – 1,50,000
H	*Less*: Tax @40%	4800X – 60,000
I	Profit after tax	7200X – 90,000

Profit after tax = 6% of list sales
7200X – 90,000 = 6% of 20,000X
6000X = 90,000
X = 90,000/6000 = ₹ 15
Net Selling Price = ₹ 15 – 40% of ₹ 15 = ₹ 9

Illustration 77. The existing cost structure of an article, the selling price of which is ₹ 600, is as follows :

Direct Material : 50% of the total cost
Direct Labour : 33 $^1/_3$% of Prime cost
Overhead : Balance of the total cost

Due to anticipated increase in existing material price by 25% and in the existing labour rate by 10%, the existing profit would come down by 30% if the selling price remains unchanged. A tender for the supply of above article is to be placed.

Required : Prepare (a) present statement of profit per article and (b) suggest the tender price so that (i) the same percentage of profit on cost as at present had to be earned and (ii) the same amount of profit as at present had to be earned.

Solution: Let x be the total present cost

STATEMENT SHOWING THE PRESENT AND ANTICIPATED COST STRUCTURE

	Present	Anticipated	
Direct Material Cost	0.50 x	0.5 x + 25% of 0.5 x =	0.625 x
Direct Labour Cost	0.25 x	0.25 x + 10% of 0.25 x =	0.275 x
Overhead	0.25 x		0.250 x
Total cost	x		1.150 x

Present Profit = ₹ 600 – x. Anticipated profit at same selling price = ₹ 600 – 1.150 x

₹ 600 – 1.150 x = 70% of (₹ 600 – x)

₹ 600 – 1.150 x = ₹ 420 – 0.7x

0.7 x – 1.150 x = ₹ 420 – ₹ 600 = ₹ 180

x = ₹ 180/0.45 = ₹ 400

(a) PRESENT STATEMENT OF PROFIT PER ARTICLE

A	Selling Price per unit		₹ 600
B	*Less :* Total Cost per unit		
	(a) Direct Material cost (50% of ₹ 400)	₹ 200	
	(b) Direct Labour cost (25% of ₹ 400)	100	
	(c) Overheads	100	400
C	Profit per article (A – B)		200

(b) STATEMENT OF REVISED SELLING PRICE

	Particulars	*If same % of Profit is to be eamed*	*If same amount of profit is to be eamed*
A	Direct Material Cost (125% of ₹ 200)	250	250
B	Direct Labour Cost (110% of ₹ 100)	110	110
C	Overheads	100	100
D	Total Anticipated Cost (A + B + C)	460	460
E	*Add :* Profit (50% of ₹ 460)	230	200
F	Revised Selling Price (D + E)	690	660

Illustration 78. New product company is contemplating to launch a new product in the market. The estimated cost details are as follows :

(i) Material cost per unit : ₹ 40

(ii) Labour cost per unit : ₹ 36

(iii) Production overheads are to be calculated from following data :

Production Departments	*Hourly overhead Rate (₹)*	*Normal monthly Hours for over-head rates*	*Fixed overhead included in overhead (₹)*	*Time to be taken by new product (hours)*
A	3.60	30,000	36,000	5
B	4.80	20,000	12,000	2.5
C	6.00	40,000	60,000	4

(iv) Annual Administration and Selling Expenses — ₹ 2,50,000. (applicable to the new product.)

(v) Estimated Sales Quantity : 50,000 per annum.

Required : (a) Based on the above information prepare a cost-sheet and find out the unit selling price with a profit margin of 40% on total cost.

(b) A foreign buyer offers to buy additional 10,000 units of the new product at ₹ 125 per unit. Advise management whether this offer is acceptable.

Solution

Basic Calculations :

COMPUTATION OF DEPARTMENT-WISE OVERHEAD RATES

Particulars	*A* ₹	*B* ₹	*C* ₹
A. Total Monthly Overheads (Full Overhead Rate x Normal Hours)	1,08,000	96,000	2,40,000
B. Fixed Overheads	36,000	12,000	60,000
C. Variable Overheads [A – B]	72,000	84,000	1,80,000
D. Variable Overhead Rate [Variable Overhead/Normal Hours]	2.40	4.20	4.50
E. Fixed Overhead Rate [Fixed Overhead/Normal Hours]	1.20	0.60	1.50

(a) STATEMENT SHOWING THE COMPUTATION OF SELLING PRICE PER UNIT

	Particulars		₹
A	Direct Material		40.00
B	Direct Labour		36.00
C	Variable Overheads :		
	Departments : A [₹ 2.40 5 Hrs.]	12.00	
	B [₹ 4.20 2.5 Hrs]	10.50	
	C [₹ 4.50 4 Hrs]	18.00	40.50
D	Variable Cost of Production [A + B + C]		116.50
E	Fixed Overheads :		
	Department A [₹ 1.20 5 Hrs]	6.00	
	B [₹ 0.60 2.5 Hrs.]	1.50	
	C [₹ 1.50 4 Hrs.]	6.00	13.50
F	Total Cost of Production [D + E]		130.00
G	Administrative and Selling Overhead (₹ 2,50,000/50,000 pcs)		5.00
H	Total Cost of Sales [F + G]		135.00
I	*Add :* 40% Mark-up on Cost		54.00
J	Suggested Selling Price [H + I]		189.00

(b) Advice:

The price offered by the foreign buyer is ₹ 125 per unit. It is more than the variable cost per unit of ₹ 116.50. Thus, there is an extra contribution of ₹ 8.50 per unit. Presuming that the total fixed overheads will be recovered on domestic sales, the overall profit of the Company would go up by ₹ 85,000 (i.e. 10,000 ₹ 8.50). Hence, the offer should be accepted.

Illustration 79. X Ltd. is engaged solely in coating other manufacturers metal fabrications with a preservative. The fabrications are not the property of X Ltd., and their value does not appear in their accounts.

They have prepared the following budget for the twelve months ending 31st December, 2014 :

Elements	*Quantity*	*Value*
Preservative	50,000 units	2,00,000
Direct labour	1,50,000 hours	1,50,000
Variable overhead @ ₹ 1 per hour		1,50,000
Variable cost		5,00,000
Fixed overhead		2,50,000
Total Cost :		7,50,000
Profit		1,50,000
Sales		9,00,000

Variable overhead may be taken to vary in direct proportion to direct labour hours.

Early in April , 2014 the company was asked to quote for coating for a new customer, the contract to be completed by the 31st July, 2014. It has been estimated that each fabrication unit will require 1 unit of preservative and 7 direct labour hours to complete and you are asked to calculate a selling price.

It was, however, felt that consideration has to be taken that difficulty has always been experienced in obtaining regular supplies of preservative and that labour is in short supply in summer months because of the incidence of holidays and high absenteeism:

Required:

(a) Calculate on each of the following assumptions a price for the new contract below which it would not pay to sell :

   (i) Assuming normal absorption costing principles with fixed overhead cost based on variable cost and a profit loading based on total cost.

   (ii) Assuming direct material is the only factor limiting production.

   (iii) Assuming direct labour is the only factor limiting production.

(b) State which price you would recommend to obtain profit at the same level as the budget considering the delivery period.

(c) Assuming there is no limiting factor and the contract is not a part of the budgeted turnover what is the minimum price above which there will be an increase in total contribution. Give reasons.

Solution

(a) (i) CALCULATION OF CONTRACT PRICE WHEN FIXED COST IS ABSORBED ON THE BASIS OF VARIABLE COST AND PROFIT IS BASED ON TOTAL COST

Particulars	₹
A. Material (1 ₹ 4)	4.00
B. Direct Labour (7 ₹ 1)	7.00
C. Variable Overhead (7 ₹ 1)	7.00
D. Total Variable Cost (A + B + C)	18.00
E. Fixed Overhead @ 50% of Variable Cost	9.00
F. Total Cost (D + E)	27.00
G. Profit @ 20% of Total Cost	5.40
H. Selling Price for new product (F + G)	32.40

(a) (ii) CALCULATION OF CONTRACT PRICE WHEN FIXED COST AND PROFIT ARE CALCULATED ON THE BASIS OF MATERIAL AND MATERIAL IS THE LIMITING FACTOR

Particulars	₹
A. Material (1 ₹ 4)	4.00
B. Direct Labour (7 ₹ 1)	7.00
C. Variable Overhead (7 ₹ 1)	7.00
D. Total Variable Cost (A + B + C)	18.00
E. Fixed Overhead @ 125% of Material Cost	5.00
F. Total Cost (D + E)	23.00
G. Profit @ 75% of Material cost	3.00
H. Selling Price for new product (F + G)	26.00

(a) (iii) CALCULATION OF CONTRACT PRICE WHEN FIXED COST AND PROFIT ARE CALCULATED ON THE BASIS OF LABOUR AND LABOUR IS THE LIMITING FACTOR

Particulars	₹
A. Material (1 ₹ 4)	4.00
B. Direct Labour (7 ₹ 1)	7.00
C. Variable Overhead (7 ₹ 1)	7.00
D. Total Variable Cost (A + B + C)	18.00
E. Fixed Overhead @ 166-2/3% of Labour Cost	11.67
F. Total Cost (D + E)	29.67
G Profit @ 100% of Labour cost	7.00
H. Selling Price for new product (F + G)	36.67

(b)

A.	Possible No. of units which can be coated without disturbance during May to July 1,50,000 x 1/7 x 3/12 = 5,357 Units	
B.	No. of units which could not be coated because of holidays & absenteeism (say)	357 units (assumed)
C.	Effective No. of Units	5000 units
D.	Variable Cost @ ₹ 18 (5,000 x ₹ 18)	₹ 90,000
E.	Fixed cost for 3 months (2,50,000 x 3/12)	₹ 62,500
F.	Total Cost (D + E)	₹ 1,52,500
G.	Profit for 3 months (1,50,000 x 3/12)	₹ 37,500
H.	Total Sales Revenue for 500 units	₹ 1,90,000
I.	Selling Price per Unit (1,90,000/5000)	₹ 38

(c) When there is no limiting factor and the contract is not a part of the budgeted turnover, any price above the variable cost of ₹ 18 per unit will increase the total contribution since the fixed overheads are recovered in the budgeted production.

Illustration 80. The Park Institute of Correspondence Studies teaches wholly through the correspondence Method. This is done by the production of self-study packs which enable students to prepare for professional qualifications.

Each course of study was sold at the price of ₹ 15 last year and a total of 10,000 units were produced and sold. The production costs of the various courses offered by the Institute are the same.

The variable cost of producing a study course last year was :

	₹
Direct Materials	5.00
Direct Labour	6.00
Other Direct Costs (mainly postage)	0.60
Variable Overheads	0.40

The Fixed Overhead for the Institute during the year was ₹ 20,000.

During the coming year the costs of the organisation are expected to increase by the following:

	%
Direct Materials	20.00
Direct Labour	16.67
Other Direct Costs	66.67
Variable Overheads	25.00
Fixed Overheads	5.00

Market research has shown that when the Institute increases the price of its courses to its students, as long as the increase is kept below 17.5% this is unlikely to have an effect on the number of units sold. However, for every 1% price are raised above at 17.5% increase, the number of units sold can be expected to fall by 2%.

Required

For the coming year.

(a) The selling price of the study courses if the number of study courses sold and the annual profits are to remain as before.

(b) The number of units that the organisation would have to sell if it did not change the price charged for these, but maintained the profit level attained in the previous year.

Solution:

(a) *Computation of Selling Price*

			₹
A.	Contribution per unit [₹ 15 – 12]		3
B.	Total Contribution [10,000 ₹ 3]		30,000
C.	*Less* : Fixed Cost		20,000
D.	Profit [B – C]		10,000
E.	New Variable Costs :	Material (5 1.2)	6.00
		Labour (6 1.1667)	7.00
		Other Direct Costs (0.60 1.667)	1.00
		Variable Overheads (0.40 1.25)	0.50
			14.50

F. New Contribution required = (Profit + Fixed Costs)/10,000
= [₹ 10,000 + (₹ 20,000 1.05]/10,000 = ₹ 3.10 per unit

G. New Selling Price = New Variable Cost + New Contribution = ₹ 14.50 + ₹ 3.10 = ₹ 17.60

There is an increase of ₹ 2.60 on the previous price of ₹ 15 i.e., a 17.33% increase, which is below 17.5%, the threshold above which price elasticity of demand becomes relevant.

(b) *Number of units to be sold* = $\frac{\text{New Fixed Costs + Desired profit}}{\text{New Contribution per unit}} = \frac{21,000 + 10,000}{\text{Rs. } 15 - \text{Rs } 14.50}$ = 62,000 units

Illustration 81. A local government authority owns and operates a leisure centre with numerous sporting facilities, residential accommodation, a cafeteria and a sports shop. The summer season lasts for 20 weeks including a peak period of 6 weeks corresponding to the school holidays. The following budgets have been prepared for the next summer season :

Accommodation

60 single rooms let on daily basis.
35 double rooms let on daily basis at 160% of the single room rate.
Fixed costs ₹ 29,900.
Variable costs ₹ 4 per single room per day and ₹ 6.40 per double room per day.

Sports Centre

Residential guests each pay ₹ 2 per day and casual visitors ₹ 3 per day for the use of facilities.
Fixed costs ₹ 15,500.

Sports Shop

Estimated contribution ₹ 1 per person per day.
Fixed costs ₹ 8,250.

Cafeteria

Estimated contribution ₹ 1.50 per person per day.
Fixed costs ₹ 12,750.
During the summer season the centre is open 7 days a week and the following activity levels are anticipated.
Double rooms fully booked for the whole season.
Single rooms fully booked for the peak period but at only 80% of capacity during the rest of the season.
30 casual visitors per day on average

You are required :

(a) Calculate the charges for single and double rooms assuming that the authority wishes to make a ₹ 10,000 profit on accommodation;
(b) Calculate the anticipated total profit for the leisure centre as whole for the season;

Solution: **(a) STATEMENT SHOWING THE CALCULATION OF CHARGE FOR ROOMS**

Particulars	₹
A. Single Room Days for 6 weeks [60 6 7]	2,520
B. Single Room Days for 14 weeks [60 14 7 80%]	4,704
C. Total Single Room Days [A + B)	7,224
D. Total Double Room Days [35 20 7]	4,900
E. Variable Cost for Single Room Days [7224 4]	28,896
F. Variable Cost for Double Room Days [4900 6.40]	31,360
G. Total Variable Cost [E + F]	60,256
H. Fixed Cost	29,900
I. Total Cost [G + H]	90,156
J. Desired Profit	10,000
K. Desired Sales Revenue [I + J]	1,00,156

Let the charge for Single Room Day be X
: Charge for Double Room Day will be 1.6 X
Thus, 7224X + (4,900 x 1.6 X) = 1,00,156
15064 X = 1,00,156
X = 1,00,156/15,064 = ₹ 6.65
Charge for Double Room = ₹ 6.65 x 1.6 = ₹ 10.64

(b) Statement showing Calculation for Total Anticipated Profit

Residential Guests for Single Room	7,224
Residential Guests for Double Room (4900 x 2)	9,800
Total Residential Guests	17,024
Casual Visitors [30 20 7]	4,200

STATEMENT SHOWING THE TOTAL ANTICIPATED PROFIT

Particulars	*Sports Centre*	*Sports Shop*	*Cafeteria*	*Total*
A. Residential Guests	17,024	17,024	17,024	
B. Casual visitors	4,200	4,200	4,200	
C. Contribution per R. Guest (₹)	₹ 2	₹ 1	₹ 1.50	
D. Contribution per casual visitor (₹)	₹ 3	₹ 1	₹ 1.50	
E. Total Contribution from R. Guests (₹) [A C]	34,048	17,024	25,536	76,608
F. Total Contribution from casual visitors [B D]	12,600	4,200	6,300	23,100
G. Total Contribution (₹) [E + F]	46,648	21,224	31,836	99,708
H. *Less* : Fixed costs (₹)	15,500	8,250	12,750	36,500
I. Profit (₹) [G – H]	31,148	12,974	19,086	63,208

Illustration 82. The share of production and the cost-based fair price computed separately for a common product for each of the four companies in an industry are as follows :

	Company			
	A	*B*	*C*	*D*
Share of Production (%)	40	25	20	15
Direct Materials *(₹ per unit)*	15	18	17	19
Direct Labour *(₹ per unit)*	10	12	14	16
Depreciation *(₹ per unit)*	30	20	16	10
Other Overheads *(₹ per unit)*	30	30	28	24
	85	80	75	69
20% Return on Capital Employed (₹ per unit)	63	43	35	23
Fair price (₹ per unit)	148	123	110	92

Capital employed per unit is worked out as follows:

	Company			
	A	*B*	*C*	*D*
Net Fixed Assets (₹ per unit)	300	200	160	100
Working Capital (₹ per unit)	14	15	15	15
Total (₹ per unit)	314	215	175	115

Required: What should be the uniform price that should be fixed for the common product?

Solution:

Let the total output be 100 units. In such a case the total sales value of the output of 100 units can be computed as follows:

Product	*Total Output (units)*	*Fair price per unit @ 20% return on capital employed (₹)*	*Sales value ₹*
1	*2*	*3*	*4 = 2 3*
A	40	148	5,920
B	25	123	3,075
C	20	110	2,200
D	15	92	1,380
	100		12,575

$$\text{Uniform Selling Price per unit} = \frac{\text{Total Sales Value}}{\text{Total Output}} = \frac{12,575}{100} = ₹\ 125.75 \text{ per unit}$$

Illustration 83. CAS Ltd. is about to introduce a new product with the following estimates:

Price per unit (in rupees)	30.00	31.50	33.00	34.50	36.00	37.50	39.00
Demand (in thousand units)	400	380	360	340	315	280	240

Costs:

Direct Material	₹ 12 per unit	Selling Expenses	10% on Sales
Direct Labour	₹ 3 per unit	Fixed Production Overheads	₹ 14,40,000
Variable Overhead	₹ 3 per unit	Administration Expenses	₹ 10,80,000

Judging from the estimates, determine the tentative price of the new product to earn maximum profit.

Solution:

CAS LTD.
STATEMENT FOR DETERMINING TENTATIVE PRICE OF THE NEW PRODUCT, FROM ESTIMATES, TO EARN MAXIMUM PROFIT

Price per unit (₹)	*Demand (in lakhs of unit)*	*Sales Revenue (in ₹ lakhs)*	*Variable Costs (in ₹ lakhs) (₹ 18 p.u. + 10% of selling price)*	*Contribution (in ₹ lakhs)*
A	B	C	D	E = C – D
30.00	4.00	120.00	84.00	36.00
31.50	3.80	119.70	80.37	39.33
33.00	3.60	118.80	76.68	42.12
34.50	3.40	117.30	72.93	44.37
36.00	3.15	113.40	68.04	45.36
37.50	2.80	105.00	60.90	44.10
39.00	2.40	93.60	52.56	41.04

The tentative price of the new product should be ₹ 36 per unit. At this price the profit of CAS Ltd. is maximum, (i.e. ₹ 20,16,000) as follows:

Maximum Profit = Maximum Contribution – (Fixed Production Overhead + Administration Expenses)
= ₹ 45,36,000 – (₹ 14,40,000 + ₹ 10,80,000) = ₹ 20,16,000

Illustration 84. ABC Ltd. has developed a new product which is about to be launched into the market. The variable cost of selling the product is ₹ 17 per unit. The marketing department has estimated that at a selling price of ₹ 25, annual demand would be 10,000 units. However, if the selling price is set above ₹ 25, sales demand would fall by 500 units for each ₹ 0.50 increase above ₹ 25. Similarly, if the price is below ₹ 25, demand would increase by 500 units for each ₹ 0.50 stepped reduction in price below ₹ 25.

Required: (a) Determine the price which would maximise ABC Ltd.'s profit in the next year.

(b) The break-even point of a manufacturing company is ₹ 1,60,000. Fixed cost is ₹ 48,000. Variable cost is ₹ 12 per unit. Determine the contribution-margin ratio.

Solution

(a) STATEMENT SHOWING THE TOTAL CONTRIBUTION AT VARIOUS SELLING PRICES

Selling Price Per unit ₹ A	*Variable Cost per unit* ₹ B	*Contribution per unit* ₹ C = A – B	*Sales Volume (units)* ₹ D	*Total Contribution* ₹ E = D C
25.00	17	8.00	10,000	80,000
24.50	17	7.50	10,500	78,750
24.00	17	7.00	11,000	77,000
25.50	17	8.50	9,500	80,750

26.00	17	9.00	9,000	81,000
26.50	17	9.50	8,500	80,750
27.00	17	10.00	8,000	80,000
27.50	17	10.50	7,500	78,750

From the above statement it is quite apparent that the total contribution would be maximum at a selling price of ₹ 26 per unit and sales demand of 9,000 units.

(b) Contribution margin ratio = $\frac{\text{Fixed Cost}}{\text{BEP Sales}} \times 100 = \frac{48,000}{1,60,000} \times 100 = 30\%$

Note : This problem could also be solved using differentiation.

Illustration 85. Electromatic Excellers Ltd. specialises in the manufacture of novel transistors. They have recently developed a technology to design a new radio transistor capable of being used as an emergency lamp also. They are quite confident of selling all of the 8,000 units that they would be making in a year. The capital equipment that would be required will cost ₹ 25 lakhs. It will have an economic life of 4 years and no significant terminal salvage value.

During each of the first four years promotional expenses are planned as under:

Year	*1*	*2*	*3*	*4*
Advertisement (₹)	1,00,000	75,000	60,000	30,000
Other expenses (₹)	50,000	75,000	90,000	1,20,000

Variable costs of producing and selling the unit would be ₹ 250 per unit.

Additional fixed operating costs incurred because of this new product are budgeted at ₹ 75,000 per year.

The company's profit goals call for a discounted rate of return of 15% after taxes on investments on new products. The income tax rate on an average works out to 40%. You can assume that the straight line method of depreciation will be used for tax and reporting. Work out an initial selling price per unit of the product that may be fixed for obtaining the desired rate of return on investment.

Solution:

Step 1: Computation of Present Value of Cash Inflows after tax (assuming Selling Price be X)

A	Selling Price	X
B	No. of Sales Units	8000
C	Total sales [A × B]	8000 X
D	*Less*: Variable cost (8000 × ₹ 250)	(20,00,000)
	Advertisement and other exp.	(1,50,000)
	Additional fixed cost	(75,000)
	Depreciation (₹ 25,00,000/4)	(6,25,000)
E	Earning before tax [C – D]	8000 X – 28,50,000
F	*Less*: Tax @ 40%	(3200X – 11,40,000)
G	Earning after tax [E – F]	4800X – 17,10,000
H	*Add*: Depreciation (being Non-cost item)	6,25,000
I	Cash flow after tax [G + H]	4800X – 10,85,000
J	PV of CFAT = (4800X – 10,85,000) × 3.0079 = 14437.92X × 3263571.50	

Step 2: Computation of Selling Price

PV of CFAT = PV of cash out flow

14437.92 X – 3263571.50 = ₹ 25,00,000

X = (₹ 25,00,000 + 3263571.50)/14437.92

= ₹ 399.20 per unit

13.8 Competitive Pricing Technique

When a company sets its price mainly on the consideration of what its competitors are charging, its pricing policy under such a situation is called competitive pricing or competition-oriented pricing. Under such a pricing the concern may charge same prices or prices lower or higher than its competitors by a certain percentage. Competitive price so determined does not maintain a rigid relation between its price, cost or demand. Its own costs or demand may change, but the concern maintains its price because its competitors maintain their prices. Conversely, the concern will change its price when its competitors change their price, even if its own costs or demand have not altered. Different type of competitive in vogue are as follows:

(i) **Going Rate Pricing:** It is a competitive pricing method under which a firm tries to keep its price at the average level charged by the industry. The use of such a practice of pricing is specially useful where it is difficult to measure costs. Adoption of going rate pricing will not only yield fair return but would be least disruptive for industry's harmony.

(a) **In a Competitive Market:** The concern selling a homogeneous product in a highly competitive market has actually very little choice about the setting of its price. The concern which is going to charge more than the going rate would attract virtually no customers. The concern should not charge less because it can dispose of its entire output at the going rate. The major challenge before such a concern is good cost control. Since promotion and personnel selling are not in the picture, the major marketing costs arise in physical distribution.

(b) **In Pure Oligopoly,** where a few large concerns dominate the industry, the concern also tends to charge the same price as is being charged by its competitors. Since there are only a few concerns, each firm is quite aware of others' prices, and so are the buyers.

This does not mean that the going price in an oligopoly market will be perpetuated indefinitely. It cannot, since industry costs and demand change over time. Usually, the industry takes collective action to raise the price, or in rare cases, to lower the price. This is done when one firm assumes the role of price leader. The others follow any change in price by the leader.

(ii) **Sealed Bid Pricing:** Competitive pricing also dominates in those situations where firms compete for jobs on the basis of bids, such as original equipment manufacture and defence contract work. The bid is the firms offer price, based on expectations of how competitors will price rather than on a rigid relation based on the concern's own costs or demand. The objective of the firm in the bidding situation is to get the contract, and this means that it hopes to set its price lower than that set by any of the other bidding firms. Even when it is anxious to get a contract in order to keep the plant busy, it can not quote price below marginal cost without worsening its position. On the other hand, if it raises its price above marginal cost, it increases its potential profit but reduces its chance of getting the contract.

The main obstacle in the use of formal bidding theory is guessing the probability of getting the contract at various bidding levels. This estimate requires information about what the competitors are likely to bid, and to know all about this is really a difficult task. Therefore, the concern has to rely on conjecture, trade gossip or past bidding history.

13.9 Incremental Pricing Technique

Incremental pricing is used because it involves comparison of the impact of decisions on revenues and cost. If a pricing decision results in a greater increase in revenue than in costs, it is favourable.

The following points will be useful to show how this technique gives consideration to all repercussions of a decision.

1. This technique considers changes in costs rather than in average cost. **Overhead allocations are irrelevant**.
2. This technique necessitates consideration being given to possible complementary relations in demand. Sale of one product may lead to the sale of a complementary product. This **overall effect on profitability has to be evaluated**.
3. **The opportunity costs should be covered by the incremental revenue.** A price which results in an incremental revenue which in turn merely covers the incremental costs is not sufficient. If the opportunity foregone is greater than incremental revenue, the decision is not sound.
4. The decision should take into account the short run and long run effects. A high price may increase its immediate profits but may lead to loss of revenue in the long run owing to competitors snatching the business.
5. In fixing prices consideration should be given to price volume relationship. The responsiveness of the market to the price should be such that the volume is increased so that fuller utilisation of plant is achieved.
6. Consideration should also be given to the evaluation of **uncertainty**. The decision taken should be able to maximise the **expected value**.

14.0 PRICING UNDER DIFFERENT MARKET STRUCTURES

Monopoly	1. There is a single seller who sells unique products having no close substitutes. 2. A firm has considerable control over price and thus, is **price maker**. 3. Price is greater than marginal cost at equilibrium point. 4. Average Revenue (AR) is greater than Marginal Revenue (MR) 5. A firm earns Super Normal Profits
Monopolistic Competition	1. There are large number of sellers who sell similar products 2. A firm has some control over the price and thus, is price maker to some extent. 3. Price is greater than marginal cost at equilibrium point. 4. Average Revenue (AR) is greater than Marginal Revenue (MR) 5. A firm earns only normal profits in the long run.
Perfect Competition	1. There are infinitely large number of sellers. 2. A firm has no control over the price since price is determined at industry level. 3. Price is equal to MC at equilibrium point. 4. Average Revenue (AR) is equal to Marginal Revenue (MR). 5. A firm earns only normal profits in the long run.
Oligopoly	1. There are a few large sellers occuping a major share of the market. 2. Each firm studies the potential reaction of competitors and consumers before increasing or decreasing the selling price. 3. Normally Rival firm react to price decrease and not to price increase.

Illustration 86. In a purely competitive market, 10,000 pocket computers can be manufactured and sold and a certain profit is generated. It is estimated that 2000 pocket computers need be manufactured and sold in monopoly market to earn the same profit. Profit under both the conditions is targeted at ₹ 20,00,000. The variable cost per computer is ₹ 1,000 and the total fixed cost is ₹ 3,70,000.

Required : Find out the unit selling price both under monopoly and competitive condition.

Solution: LET THE UNIT SELLING PRICE UNDER MONOPOLY BE *x* AND UNDER COMPETITIVE CONDITION BE *y*.

Particulars	*Monopoly*	*Competitive*
A. Selling Price per unit	*x*	y
B. No. of units	2000	10,000
C. Total Sales [A B]	2000 *x*	10,000 y
D. *Less :* Variable Cost @ ₹ 1000	20,00,000	100,00,000
E. Contribution [C – D]	2000 *x* – 20,00,000	10,000 y – 100,00,000
F. *Less :* Fixed Costs	3,70,000	3,70,000
G. Profit [E – F]	2000 *x* – 23,70,000	10000 y – 103,70,000

Monopoly Price

2000 *x* – 23,70,000 = ₹ 20,00,000

2000 *x* = 43,70,000

x = ₹ 43,70,000/2000 = ₹ 2,185 per unit

Competitive Price

10000 y – 103,70,000 = ₹ 20,00,000

10000 y = 1,23,70,000

y = 123,70,000/10,000 = ₹ 1,237 per unit

15.0 NEW PRODUCT PRICING STRATEGIES

When a new product is launched in the market, the manufacturer enjoys flexibility in the matter of price setting. The price decision at this stage has long-run implications because an inappropriate price can adversely affect the demand and profitability of the product. At this stage, the firm has to particularly keep in view the long-run returns and profits rather than the immediate profits. Pricing a new product may become further difficult if the firm is inexperienced, and the data regarding the effect of price on demand is not available to the firm.

There are two strategies to the pricing of a new product. They are: I) Skimming Pricing Policy and II) Penetration Pricing Policy. The two approaches are just opposite to each other. Let us study these approaches in detail.

1. Skimming Pricing Policy

Meaning	Skimming Pricing means using a high introductory price to skim the 'cream' of the demand.
For example	Innovators like Sony and Nokia use this strategy to market their top end high tech. Under Skimming Pricing a manufacturer skims the market (or *takes butter out of the milk)* by launching a new product at a high price and later reducing the price gradually in order to tag new market segments. Skimming price is appropriate for a product that is a real innovation (a product that represents a significant departure from established ways of doing things). The price is set at a level which is higher in the range of expected prices. The firm can continue with this policy for an indefinite period, *or* reduce the price subsequently for other segments of the market.
Suitable Conditions	Skimming pricing is suitable for an innovative product under the following conditions: 1. When the demand for product is inelastic i.e. the buyers are not sensitive to price. 2. When there exists an elite class of buyers who value high price and buy irrespective of price. 3. When marketer does not expect competition soon after launching the product. 4. When marketer can not increase the production capacity as the demand increases.
Advantages	Skimming pricing has two advantages: 1. It enables the firm to recoup their research and development expenditure within a short period of time. 2. It may discourage large firms from entering the field particularly when the market is not large enough to attract the big competitors. While percentage margins may be attractive, the total rupee profits could be too small to attract large firms.
Effect	If the firm adopts the skimming pricing strategy, its sales volume in units will be low but the sales volume in value will be high, and profits will also be high. High Price → Low Sales Volume (in Units) → High Sales Volume in (Value) → High Profit

2. Penetration Pricing Policy

Meaning	Penetration pricing means using lower initial price to capture as large a market as possible. Under penetration pricing policy, a low initial price is set to reach the mass' market immediately.
Suitable Conditions	Penetration pricing is said to be more suitable when the following conditions exists: 1. When the demand for product is highly elastic i.e. buyers are sensitive to price. 2. When there is no segment or their is only a small segment of customers who buy irrespective of price. 3. When marketer expects strong competition soon after launching the product. 4. When marketer can increase the production capacity as the demand increases.
Advantages	Penetration pricing has two advantages: 1. It may discourage other firms from entering the field. The required investment in production and marketing may be too great relative to the anticipated low profit margin. 2. Due to low prices, the innovator may get a strong hold on the market making it difficult for competitors to cut into it.
Effect	If the firm adopts the penetration pricing strategies, its volume (in units) as well as (in value) will be high and profits will also be high. Low Price → Low Sales Volume (in Value) → High Sales Volume (in units) → High Profit

Distinction between Skimming Pricing and Penetration Pricing

Skimming Pricing differs from Penetration pricing in the following respects:

Basis of Distinction	Skimming Princing	Penetration Pricing
1. Price Elasticity of Demand	It is suitable when the demand for product is **inelastic** i.e. the buyers are not sensitive to price.	It is suitable when the demand for product is **highly elastic** i.e. buyers are sensitive to price.
2. Existence of elite class of Buyers	It is suitable when there exists an **elite class** of buyers who value high price and buy irrespective of price.	It is suitable when there is no *segment or* there is only a **small segment** of customers who buy irrespective of price.
3. Competition	It is suitable when marketer does expects **no competition** soon after launching the product.	It is suitable when marketer expects **strong competition** soon after launching the product.
4. Production Capacity	It is suitable when marketer **can not increase** the production capacity as the demand increases.	It is suitable when marketer **can increase** the production capacity as the demand increases.

16.0 PRICE DISCRIMINATION STRATEGIES

Price discrimination means charging different prices and it many be on the basis of customer, product, place or time.

Basis	1. **On the basis of Customer:** In this case, the same product is charged at different prices to different customers. It is, however, potentially disruptive of customer relations. 2. **On the basis of Product Version:** In this case, a slightly different product is charged at a different price regardless of its cost-price relationship. If, for example, a table with wooden top can be sold at ₹ 1400, a table with sunmica top costing ₹ 200 extra is sold at ₹ 1500. The higher premium in the latter case does not necessarily reflect the higher production cost. 3. **On the basis of Place:** An example of this method is the seats in cinema theatre where the front seats are charged at lower rates than the back seats. 4. **On the basis of Time:** An example of this method is the practice of giving off-season concession in sale of fans or refrigerators just after the summer season and in sale of woollen garments just after the winter season 5. On the basis of elasticity of demand.
Conditions	Price discrimination is possible if the following conditions are satisfied: 1. the market must be capable of being segmented for price discrimination; 2. the customers should not be able to resell the product of the segment paying higher price; and 3. the chance of competitors' underselling in the segment of higher prices should not be possible.

17.0 GEOGRAPHIC PRICING STRATEGIES

In pricing, a seller must consider the costs of shipping goods to the buyer. Pricing policies may be established whereby the buyer pays all the freight expense, the seller bears the entire cost, or the seller and buyer share this expense. The strategy chosen can influence the geographic limits of a firm's market, locations of its production facilities, sources of its raw materials, and its competitive strength in various geographic markets.

1. **Uniform Delivered Pricing**	Under uniform delivered pricing, the same delivered price is quoted to all buyers regardless of their locations. Uniform delivered pricing is typically used where freight costs are a small part of the seller's total cost. This strategy is also used by many retailers who believe "free" delivery is an additional service that strengthens their market position.
2. **Zone-Delivered Pricing**	Zone-delivered pricing divides a seller's market into a limited number of broad geographic zones and then sets a uniform delivered price for each zone.
3. **Point-of-Production Pricing**	In a widely used geographic pricing strategy, the seller quotes the selling price at the point of production and the buyer selects the mode of transportation and pays all freight costs. This method of pricing is referred as FOB factory pricing.
4. **Freight-Absorption Pricing**	Under freight-absorption pricing, a manufacturer will quote to the customer a delivered price equal to its factory price *plus* the freight costs that would be charged by a competitive seller located near that customer.

18.0 PARETO ANALYSIS

Meaning	Vilfredo Pareto, an Italian economist observed that about 70–80% of value was represented by 30–20% of volume. This phenomenon, can be observed in many different business situations. The management can use it in a number of different circumstances to direct management attention to the key control mechanism or planning aspects.
Usefulness of Pareto Analysis	Pareto analysis is useful: 1. To prioritize problems, goals, and objectives 2. To identify root causes 3. To select and define key quality improvement programs 4. To select key customer relations and service programs 5. To select key employee relations improvement programs 6. To select and define key performance improvement programs 7. To maximise research and product development time 8. To verify operating procedures and manufacturing processes 9. To product or services sales and distribution 10. To allocate physical, financial and human resources
Application of Pareto Analysis	The Pareto Analysis is generally applicable to the following business situations: **1. Pricing of a product:** In the case of a firm dealing with multi products, it would not be possible for it to analyse price-volume relationships for all of them. In practice, in case of such firm approximately 20% of products may account for about 80% of total sales revenue. Pareto Anaysis is used for analysing the firm estimated sales revenues from various products and it might indicate that approximately 80% of its total sales revenue is earned from about 20% of its products. Such analysis helps the top management to delegate the pricing decision for approximately 80% of its products to the lower levels of management, thus freeing themselves to concentrate on the pricing decisions for products approximately 20% which are essential for the company's survival. Thus, a firm can adopt more sophisticated pricing methods for small proportion of products that jointly accounts for approximately 80% of total sales revenue. For the remaining 80% of the products which account for 20% of total sales revenue the firm may use cost based pricing method. **2. Customer Profitability:** In practice it is often found that approximately 20% of customers generate 80% of the profit. There will always be some customers who are less profitable than others, just as some products are less profitable than others. Such an analysis is useful tool for evaluation of the portfolio of customer profile. **3. Stock Control:** In practice approximately 20% of the total quantity of stock may account for about 80% of its value. The outcome of such analysis is that by concentrating on small proportion of stock items that jointly accounts for 80% of the total value, a firm may well be able to control most of monetary investment in stocks. **4. Application in Activity Based Costing:** In Activity Based Costing it is often said that 20% of an organisation cost drivers are responsible for 80% of the total cost. By analysing, monitoring and controlling those cost drivers that cause most cost, a better control and understanding of overheads will be obtained.

5. **Quality Control:** Pareto analysis seeks to discover from an analyşis of defect report or customer complaints which "vital few" causes are responsible for most of the reported problems. Often, 80% of reported problems can usually be traced to 20% of the various underlying causes. By concentrating once efforts on rectifying the vital 20%, one can have the greatest immediate impact on product quality.

The Pareto Analysis indicates how frequently each type of failure (defect) occurs. The purpose of the analysis is to direct management attention to the area where the best returns can be achieved by solving most of quality problems, perhaps just with a single action.

Example: A Toy company performs a Pareto analysis, given a set of 'defect types' and frequencies of their occurrence. The sample data consists of information about 200 defective items. The items have been classified by their 'defect types' as follows:

Defect Types	*No. of Types*
Cracks (due to mishandling of raw material)	40
Improper shapes	30
Incomplete	20
Surface scratches	100
Other (due to bad quality raw material)	10

Frequency table indicating the frequency of occurrence of defects in decreasing order of their occurrence will be as follows:

Defect type	*No. of items*	*%*	*Cummulative%*
Surface scratches	100	50	50
Cracks	40	20	70
Improper shape	30	15	85
Incomplete	20	10	95
Other	10	5	100

The purpose of Pareto analysis in this example, is to direct attention to the area where best returns can be achieved by solving most of the quality problems, perhaps just with a single action. In this case, use of good quality raw material say plastic may solve 50% of problems and if raw material is handled properly at least 70% the problems may be overcome.

19.0 DIFFERENT SELLING PRICES

Use of differential selling price which is above, the marginal cost but below the total cost is resorted to in order to absorb surplus capacity. This can be done in the following two ways:

(i) Use the surplus capacity to produce the same product which may be sold at a price above marginal cost in a different market. *For example* Dumping of goods in the export market. The articles sold in the home market will recover all fixed expenses. Since price reduction in the home market is injurious to the normal sales, it is not resorted to. Any reduction in the selling prices in the export market will not affect the price prevailing in the home market.

Example *(₹ in lacs)*

Sales	*Home Market*	*Export Market*	*Total*
Sales	100	15	115
Less: Marginal cost	40	10	50

Contribution	60	5	65
Less: Fixed cost	50	—	50
Profit	10	5	15

(ii) Use the surplus capacity to produce different product which may be sold at a price above its marginal cost in the same or different market. The overall profitability will thus increase.
Note: The manufacture of different product, however, should be confined to surplus capacity and it should not have the possibility of becoming a major product at the low price at which it is sold. If it becomes so there will be a reduction in profit as illustrated below:

Example: (*Assuming Surplus Capacity is 10%*)

	Condition 1		*Condition 2*	
	Product A	*Product B*	*Product A*	*Product B*
Capacity	90%	10%	60%	40%
Sales	18,000	4,000	12,000	16,000
Marginal cost	12,000	3600	8,000	14,400
Gross margin	6,000	400	4,000	1600
Fixed expenses	4,000	—	4,000	—
Profit	2,000	400	—	1600
Total Profit	2,400		1600	

Illustration 87. Prompt Printers Ltd. uses a scheme of pricing based on cost-plus. All the overheads are charged, based on direct labour and based on the total cost arrived at the selling price is fixed.

The following figures are from the annual budget for prepared by the Company:

Sales	₹ 10,00,000
Direct material	1,80,000
Direct labour	3,20,000
Factory Superintendent's salary	30,000
Commission paid on sales	50,000
Foremen's salaries	60,000
Insurance	10,000
Advertisement	20,000
Depreciation on assets	30,000
Administration expenses	90,000
Variable factory costs :	
Repairs and maintenance	60,000
Tools Consumed	40,000
Miscellaneous supplies	10,000

The company has submitted a tender quoting ₹ 10,000 on a large order with a cost of ₹ 1,800 direct material and ₹ 3,200 direct labour. The customer strikes the business at ₹ 8,900 on a take it or leave it' basis. If the Company accepts the order, the sale for the next year would be ₹ 10,08,900. The Company is reluctant to accept the order as it would be against its policy of accepting an order below cost.

As a Cost Accountant of the Company, you are required to give your recommendation with supporting figures to explain that the price offered would not be below cost and a sizable profit also could be made.

Solution:

It is given in the question that all the overheads (both fixed and variable) are charged on direct labour. Therefore, it is necessary to determine the overhead recovery rate from the data given in the annual budget for. Further, profit for the budget year can be determined as under :

STATEMENT SHOWING THE COMPUTATION OF PROFIT AS % OF COST AND OVERHEAD RECOVERY RATE

Particulars		₹
A. Direct Material		₹ 1,80,000
B. Direct Labour		3,20,000
C. Variable Factory Costs :		
Repairs and maintenance	₹ 60,000	
Tools consumed	40,000	
Miscellaneous supplies	10,000	
Commission (5% of sales)	50,000	1,60,000
D. Fixed Overheads :		
Factory supdt. Salary	30,000	
Foremen's salaries	60,000	
Insurance	10,000	
Advertisement	20,000	
Depreciation on assets	30,000	
Administration expenses	90,000	2,40,000
E. Total Cost of Sales [A + B + C + D]		9,00,000
F. Sales		10,00,000
G. Profit [F – E]		1,00,000

Overhead Recovery Rate = (Total Overheads ÷ Direct labour) 100
= (₹ 4,00,000 ÷ ₹ 3,20,000) 100 = 125%

Profit as % of Cost = Profit/Cost of sales = 1,00,000/9,00,000 = 1/9

If budgeted pattern of overhead recovery and profit margin is adopted, the quotation will work out as under:

A. Direct Material	₹ 1,800
B. Direct Labour	3,200
C. Overhead (125% of ₹ 3,200)	4,000
D. Total Cost of Sales [A + B + C]	9,000
E. Profit (1/9 of ₹ 9,000)	1,000
F. Price to be quoted	10,000

From the above, following two points should be noted :

(a) The Company does not differentiate between fixed overhead and variable overhead :

(b) If the above tender is accepted, the sales will go up from ₹ 10,00,000 to ₹ 10,08,900. It means this is an additional activity. Therefore, fixed overhead should be disregarded in working out the price for quotation purpose.

The revised profit will be as follows :

Price Offered (Incremental Revenue)		₹ 8,900
Direct Material	₹ 1,800	
Direct Labour	3,200	
Variable Overhead (excl. sales commission)	1,100	
Commission (5% of 8,900)	445	
Incremental Cost		6,545
Surplus (Incremental revenue *less* incremental cost)		2,355

Recommendation: The above computation shows that the price offered by the customer (₹ 8,900 i.e. incremental revenue) is much more than the incremental cost (₹ 6,545). Therefore, the Company should accept the order. Normally, cost *plus* basis (both fixed cost and variable cost) of pricing is most suitable basis of price quotation at normal activity level. But in the present case acceptance of order will lead to additional sales. Thus, in such case, only marginal cost is considered.

Working Notes :

(i) Variable overheads exclusive commission at sales of ₹ 10,00,000
= ₹ 1,60,000 – ₹ 50,000 = ₹ 1,10,000

(ii) Variable overhead at sales of ₹ 10,000 = $\frac{1,10,000}{10,00,000} \times 10,000$ = ₹ 1,100.

Comments on the Pricing Policy of the Company

When overheads are capable of being distinguished as variable and fixed. It is wrong to club them together and charge overheads indiscriminately as a percentage of direct labour. Cost plus, as a basis of pricing, is allright for normal activity; but for incremental activity, the relevant cost is only the marginal cost and the profit on marginal activity, is normally greater than that of the original activity. Taking the whole cost and basing the price on cost plus will be misleading. It will result in loosing valuable profit opportunity for earning an additional profit.

20.0 REPLACEMENT DECISION (i.e. DECISION WHETHER TO RETAIN OR REPLACE THE EXISTING MACHINE)

20.1 Replacement Decision In case the Remaining Useful Life of the Existing Machine and the Useful Life of the New Machine are same.

In such a case Incremental Approach should be adopted as follows :

Step 1: *Calculate Incremental Contribution as follows :*

Particulars	*Existing Machine*	*New Machine*	*Incremental (New – Old)*
A. Units Produced	xxx	xxx	
B. Selling Price per unit	xxx	xxx	
C. *Less* : Direct Material Cost per unit	(xxx)	(xxx)	
D *Less* : Direct Labour Cost per unit	(xxx)	(xxx)	
E. *Less* : Variable Overheads per unit	(xxx)	(xxx)	
F. Contribution per unit [B – C – D – E]	xxx	xxx	
G. Total Contribution [A x F]	xxx	xxx	**xxx**

Step 2: *Calculate Incremental Depreciation (assuming Straight Line Method of Depreciation)*

Particulars	*Existing Machine*	*New Machine*	*Incremental (New – Old)*
A. Cost of Machine	xxx	xxx	
B. Freight, Carriage & Installation Exp.	xxx	xxx	
C. Workers' Training Expenses	xxx	xxx	
D. *Less*: Subsidy from Govt.	(xxx)	(xxx)	
E. *Less*: Estimated Salvage Value	(xxx)	(xxx)	
F. Depreciable Amount [A +B + C– D – E]	xxx	xxx	
G. Useful Life (Years)	xxx	xxx	
H. Depreciation [F/G]	xxx	xxx	**xxx**

Note: In case of any other method of depreciation (*say Written Down Value*), depreciation should be calculated accordingly.

Step 3 : *Calculate Incremental Salvage Value and Tax Advantage*

Particulars	*Existing Machine*	*New Machine*	*Incremental (New – Old)*
A. Book Value at the end Useful Life	xxx	xxx	
B. *Less*: Cash Salvage Value at the end of Useful Life	(xxx)	(xxx)	xxx
C. Short Term Capital Loss (Gain) [A – B]	xxx	xxx	
D. Tax on Loss (Profit) [C x Tax Rate]	xxx	xxx	xxx

Step 4 : *Calculate Incremental Cash Outflow*

	Particulars	*Amount*
A.	Purchase Price of New Machine	xxx
B.	Freight, Carriage & Installation Expenses	xxx
C.	Workers' Training Expenses	xxx
D.	*Less*: Subsidy from Govt.	(xxx)
E.	Incremental Working Capital	xxx
F.	*Less*: Net Sale Proceeds of Existing Machine (Current Realizable Value – Disposal Charges)	(xxx)
G.	*Less* : Tax Saving on Loss on Sale of Existing Machine (Book Value – Net Current Realizable Value)	(xxx)
or		
	Add : Tax on Profit on Sale of Existing Machine (Net Current Realizable Value – Book Value)	xxx
H.	**Incremental Cash Outflow**	**xxx**

20.2 Worth Noting Points to be kept in mind while taking Replacement Decision

At the time of taking the decision whether to retain or replace the existing machine, the following points should be kept in mind:

Item	*How to Treat*
1. Consultant' s Fees as to study the problem of Retain or Replace.	Treat as sunk cost since it is bound to occur whether the existing machine is retained or replaced.
2. Allocation of Fixed Overheads from other Departments	Treat as irrelevant cost since it does not affect the decision to retain or replace
3. Undepreciated Book Value of Existing Machine.	Treat as irrelevant cost since it does not affect the decision to retain or replace.
4. Loss on Sale of Existing Machine.	Treat as irrelevant cost since it does not affect the decision to retain or replace.
5. Tax Saving on Loss on Sale of Existing Machine.	Treat as Cash Inflow
6. Market Value of Existing Machine.	Treat as Cash Inflow if its Current Market Value is more than the Exchange Value offered by supplier of New Machine.
7. Exchange Value offered by Suppliers of New Machine	Treat as Cash Inflow if Exchange Value is more than the Current Market value of the existing machine
8. Cost of Disposal and Dismantling the Existing Machine.	Treat as Cash Outflow
9. Release of Working Capital on Sale of Existing Machine.	Treat as Cash Inflow
10. Cost of New Machine.	Treat as Cash Outflow
11. Expenses on Freight, Carriage & Installation of New Machine.	Treat as Cash Outflow
12. Expenses on Training of Workers for New Machine.	Treat as Cash Outflow

13. Working Capital required if New Machine is Installed.	Treat as Cash Outflow
14. Retrenchment Compensation	Treat as Cash Outflow
15. Tax saving on Retrenchment Compensation (if it is given that Retrenchment compensation is deductible for tax)	Treat as Cash Inflow

Illustration 88. Tulsian Ltd. is considering the replacement of its existing machine by the new one. A consultant who has charged a fee of ₹ 25,000 supplies the following information in this regard:

	Existing Machine	*New Machine*
1. Annual Machine Hours	8,000	5,000
2. Machine Hours required per unit	1 Hour	0.5 Hour
3. Material required per unit	5 kg	4 kg
4. Material Cost per kg.	₹ 2	₹ 3
5. Labour Hours required per unit	4 Hours	3 Hours
6. Labour Cost per unit	₹ 40	₹ 30
7. Variable Overheads per unit	₹ 10	₹ 10
8. Fixed Cash Expenses per unit	₹ 10	₹ 8
9. Fixed Overheads per unit (Allocations from other Departments)	₹ 3	₹ 2.4
10. Selling Price per unit	₹ 100	₹ 120
11. Book Value of Existing Machine (Purchased 3 years ago)	₹ 2,52,000	
12. Cost of New Machine		₹ 4,30,000
13. Useful Life	8 years	5 years
14. Freight, Carriage & Installation Exp.		₹ 10,000
15. Workers' Training Expenses incurred to put the asset to use		₹ 20,000
16. Subsidy from Govt.		₹ 50,000
17. Estimated Salvage Value at the end of useful Life.	₹ 2,000	₹ 10,000
18. Cash Salvage Value at the end of useful Life.	₹ 1,500	₹ 15,000
19. Current Realizable Value	₹ 10,600	
20. Cost of Dismantling & Removal	₹ 600	
21. Working Capital required	₹ 40,000	₹ 1,00,000

Other Information:

Method of Depreciation: Straight Line Method
Rate on Income Tax: 30 %
Company's Cost of Capital: 10 %
Exchange Value of Old Machine offered by Suppliers of New Machine : ₹ 9,000
Annuity Factor @ 10% for 5 and 8 years are ₹ 3.791 and ₹ 5.335 respectively.
PV Factor @ 10 % for 5th and 8th year are ₹ 0.621 and ₹ 0.467 respectively.

	Year 1	*Year 2*	*Year 3*	*Year 4*	*Year 5*
Present Value Factors @ 60%	0.625	0.391	0.244	0.153	0.095
Present Value Factors @ 65%	0.606	0.367	0.223	0.135	0.082

Required: Should the Company replace the existing machine ?

Solution:

(a) STATEMENT SHOWING THE CALCULATION OF INCREMENTAL CASH INFLOW AFTER TAXES (CFAT)

Particulars	₹
A. Incremental Contribution	3,60,000
B. *Less*: Incremental Depreciation	(30,000)
C. *Less*: Incremental Cash Fixed Cost (₹ 80,000 – ₹ 80,000)	-
D. Incremental Earning before Tax	3,30,000
E. *Less*: Tax @ 30%	(99,000)
F. Incremental Earning after Tax	2,31,000
G. *Add*: Incremental Depreciation	30,000
H. Incremental Cash Flow after Taxes (CFAT) (for years other than last year)	**2,61,000**
I. *Add*: Release of Incremental Working Capital	60,000
J. *Add*: Incremental Cash Salvage Value at the end of Useful Life	13,500
K. *Less*: Incremental Tax	(1,650)
L. Total Incremental CFAT for the last year	**3,32,850**

STATEMENT SHOWING THE INCREMENTAL NET PRESENT VALUE

Particulars	*Year*	*PV factor at 10%*	*Amount*	*PV*
Purchase Price of New Machine	0	1	(4,30,000)	(4,30,000)
Freight, Carriage & Installation Exp.	0	1	(10,000)	(10,000)
Workers' Training Expenses	0	1	(20,000)	(20,000)
Subsidy from Govt.	0	1	50,000	50,000
Incremental Working Capital	0	1	(60,000)	(60,000)
Net Sale Proceeds of Existing Machine (₹ 10,600 – ₹ 600)	0	1	10,000	10,000
Tax saving on Loss on Sale of existing machine 30% of ₹.2,42,000 (₹ 2,52,000 – ₹ 10,000)	0	1	72,600	72,600
Incremental CFAT for 1 - 4 years	1 to 4	3.170	2,61,000	8,27,370
Incremental CFAT for 5th year	5	0.621	3,32,850	2,06,700
Incremental NPV				**6,46,670**

Recommendation: The New Machine should be purchased since the NPV is positive.

Working Note:

(i) Calculation of Incremental Contribution

Particulars	*Existing Machine*	*New Machine*	*Incremental (New – Old)*
A. Units Produced [Annual Machine Hrs./(MH per unit]	8,000	10,000	
B. Selling Price per unit	100	120	
C. *Less* : Material Cost per unit (Qty ∞ Rate)	(10)	(12)	
D. *Less* : Labour Cost per unit (Hour ∞ Rate)	(40)	(30)	
E. *Less* : Variable Overheads per unit	(10)	(10)	
F. Contribution per unit [B – C – D – E]	40	68	
G. Total Contribution (A x D)	3,20,000	6,80,000	**3,60,000**

(ii) Calculation of Incremental Depreciation

Particulars	*Existing Machine*	*New Machine*	*Incremental (New – Old)*
A. Book Value/Cost of Machine	2,52,000	4,30,000	
B. *Add* : Freight, Carriage & Installation Exp.		10,000	
C. *Add* : Workers' Training Expenses		20,000	
D. *Less* : Subsidy from Govt.		(50,000)	
E. *Less* : Estimated Salvage Value	(2,000)	(10,000)	
F. Depreciable Amount [A + B + C – D – E]	2,50,000	4,00,000	
G. Useful Life	5 yrs	5 yrs	
H. Depreciation [F/G]	50,000	80,000	**30,000**

(iii) Calculation of Incremental Salvage Value and Tax Advantage

Particulars	*Existing Machine*	*New Machine*	*Incremental (New – Old)*
A. Book Value at the end of useful life	2,000	10,000	
B. *Less*: Cash Salvage Value at the end of useful life	(1,500)	(15,000)	**(13,500)**
C. Short Term Capital Loss (Gain)	500	(5,000)	
D. Tax on Loss (Profit) @ 30 %	150	(1,500)	**(1,650)**

(*iv*) Consultant's fees has been treated as sunk cost.

(*v*) Since the fixed overheads are allocation from other departments, differential fixed overheads other than depreciation are irrelevant.

(*vi*) Exchange Value of old machine offered by Suppliers of New Machine is irrelevant since the current realizable value (*i.e.*, ₹ 10,600) is more than the exchange value (*i.e.*, ₹ 9,000).

20.3 Replacement Decision In case the Remaining Useful Life of the Existing Machine and the Useful Life of the New Machine are different.

In such a case Annualised Present Value Approach should be adopted.

The practical steps involved in the regard are given below :

Step 1: *Calculate the Present Value of Cash Flows After Tax (CFAT) at the given discount rate.*

Step 2: *Calculate Annualized Equivalent Present Value as follows :*

Annualized Equivalent Present Value = Total Present Value/Present Value Factor of Annuity of ₹ 1 at given Rate of Interest at the end of the life of the project.

Or

Annualized Equivalent Present Value = Total Present Value × Capital Recovery Factor at given Rate of Interest at the end of the life of the project.

Note : *Capital Recovery Factor is equal to the reciprocal of Present Value Factor of Annuity of ₹ 1 at given Rate of Interest at the end of the life of the project.*

Note : *Annualized Equivalent Present Value is the Equated Annual Instalment of present value over the useful life of the project.*

Step 3: *Select the Project as follows :*

When Net Present value of Cash Inflows is considered	Select the project having the highest Annualized Equivalent Present Value
When Present value of Cash Outflows is considered	Select the project having the lowest Annualized Equivalent Present Value

Illustration 89. S Engineering Company is considering to replace or repair a particular machine, which has just broken down. Last year this machine costed ₹ 20,000 to run and maintain. These costs has been increasing in real

terms in recent years with the age of the machine. A further useful life of 5 years is expected, if immediate repairs of ₹ 19,000 are carried out. If machine is not repaired it can be sold immediately to realise about ₹ 5000. (Ignore loss/ gain on such disposal)

Alternatively, the company can buy a new machine for ₹ 49,000 with an expected life of 10 years with no salvage value after providing depreciation on straight line basis. In case, running and maintenance costs reduce to ₹ 14,000 each year and are not expected to increase much in real terms for few years at least.

S Engineering Company regards a normal return of 10 % p.a. after tax as a minimum requirement on any new investment. Take corporate tax rate of 30 % and assume that depreciation on straight line basis will be accepted for tax purpose also. Given cumulative present value of ₹.1 p.a. at 10 % for 5 years ₹ 3.791 and for 10 years ₹ 6.145.

Required : Considering capital budgeting techniques, which alternative will you choose?

Solution:

STATEMENT SHOWING THE CALCULATION OF ANNUAL CASH COST AFTER TAX SAVING

Particulars	*Repair Proposal*	*Replace Proposal*
Running and Maintenance Cost	20,000	14,000
Depreciation	—	4,900
Total Cost	20,000	18,900
Less: Tax Saving @ 30%	(6,000)	(5,670)
Cost after Tax Saving	14,000	13,230
Less: Depreciation being non-cash cost	—	(4,900)
Annual Cash Cost after Tax Saving	14,000	8,330

STATEMENT SHOWING ANNUALIZED PRESENT VALUE OF CASH OUTFLOW

Particulars	*Year*	*PV factor*	*Repair Proposal*		*Replace Proposal*	
			Amount	*PV*	*Amount*	*PV*
Cost of Immediate Repairs			19,000			
Less: Tax Saving @ 30 %			5,700			
	0	1	13,300	13,300		
Cost of New Machine	0	1			49,000	49,000
Less: Net Sale Proceeds of Old Machine	0	1			(5,000)	(5,000)
Annual Cash Cost after Tax Saving	1 to 5/1 to 10	3.791/ 6.145	14,000	53,074	8,330	51,188
PV of Cash Outflow				66,374		95,188
Annuity Factor for 5/10 years		3.791/ 6.145		3.791		6.145
Annualized PV of Cash Outflow (PV / Annuity Factor)				**17,508**		**15,490**

Recommendation : Replacement Proposal should be preferred over Repair Proposal since Replacement Proposal has lower annualized PV of cash outflow.

SOLVED PROBLEMS

Problem 1. R Ltd. will produce 3,00,000 kgs. of S and 6,00,000 kgs. of Y from an input of 9,00,000 kgs. of raw material Z.

The selling price of S is ₹ 8 per kg and that of Y is ₹ 6 per kg.

Processing costs amount to ₹ 54 lacs per month as under:

Raw material Z 9,00,000 kgs. at ₹ 3 per kg	₹ 27,00,000
Variable processing costs	₹ 18,00,000
Fixed processing costs	₹ 9,00,000
Total	₹ 54,00,000

There is an offer to purchase 60,000 kgs of Y additionally at a price of ₹ 4 per kg. The existing market for Y will not be affected by accepting the offer. But the price of S is likely to be decreased uniformly on all sales.

Find the minimum reduced average price for S to sustain the increased sales.

Solution: Since S and Y are produced simultaneously from an input of raw material Z, therefore when additional 60,000 kgs of Y will be produced then 30,000 kgs. of S will also be produced simultaneously. The input of material Z required for these additional 60,000 kgs of Y and 30,000 kgs. of S will be 90,000 kgs. of material Z. Hence the cost of processing 90,000 kgs. of material will be as follows:

	Particulars	₹
A	Cost of Raw material Z (90,000 kgs × ₹ 3)	2,70,000
B	Variable processing cost (90,000 kgs × ₹ 2)	1,80,000
C	Total Cost of Processing [A + B]	4,50,000
D	*Less*: Sales revenue from 60,000 kgs. of Y (60,000 kgs × ₹ 4)	2,40,000
E	Balance cost to be recovered [C + D]	2,10,000
F	Current sales revenue from the sale of 3,00,000 kgs. of S (3,00,000 kgs × ₹ 8)	24,00,000
G	Total sales revenue to be earned from the sale of S (3,00,000 kgs. + 30,000 kgs.)	26,10,000
H	Minimum price per kg of S to recover (₹ 26,10,000/3,30,000 kgs.)	7.91

Problem 2. A 'Company can produce and sell at its maximum capacity 20,000 units of a product. The sale price is ₹ 100. The present sales is 15,000 units. To produce over 20,000 units and upto another 10,000 units some balancing equipments are to be installed at a cost of ₹ 10 lakhs and the same will have a life span of 10 years.

The current cost structure is as under:

Direct material	30% of sale value
Direct labour	20% of sale value
Variable overheads	₹ 20 per unit
Profit	₹ 15 per unit

The present cost is estimated to go up due to price escalation as under :

10% in Direct material from present level of 30%

25% in Direct labour from present level of 20%

₹ 50,000 in Fixed overheads per year.

There is a concrete proposal from a party to take 10,000 units additionally over the present level of output on a long-term basis at a unit price of ₹ 90. Apart from the investment of ₹ 10 lakhs, as shown above, the fixed overheads will increase by ₹ 50,000 due to additional Administrative expenses.

The Company is in a dilemma as to whether to accept the order for 10,000 units or to use the present unused capacity of 5,000 units for which there will be additional selling expenditure of ₹ 50,000.

Ignore financing charges and give your recommendation.

Solution: **STATEMENT OF PROFITABILITY FOR VARIOUS ALTERNATIVES**

	Alternatives	*I* *Rejecting the proposal for the purchase of 10,000 units and continuing with present level of sales only*	*II* *Rejecting the proposal for the purchase of 10,000 units from a party and attaining the maximum capacity by incurring additional selling expenditure*	*III* *Accepting the proposal of the party to take 10,000 units @ ₹ 90 per unit by installing a balancing equipment and continuing with present level of sales*	*IV* *Accepting the proposal of party to take 10,000 units @ ₹ 90 per unit by installing a balancing equipment and attaining able capacity by incurring additional selling expenditure*
	Sales (units)	*15,000* ₹	*20,000* ₹	*25,000* ₹	*30,000* ₹
A	Sales value:	15,00,000 (15,000 × ₹ 100)	20,00,000 (20,000 × ₹ 100)	24,00,000 (15,000 × ₹ 100 + 10,000 × ₹ 90)	29,00,000 (20,000 × ₹ 100 + (10,000 × ₹ 90)
B	*Variable costs:*				
	Direct materials (33% of sales value)	4,95,000	6,60,000	8,25,000	9,90,000
	Direct labour (25% of sale value)	3,75,000	5,00,000	6,25,000	7,50,000
	Variable overheads (@ ₹ 20 per unit)	3,00,000	4,00,000	5,00,000	6,00,000
	Total variable costs:	11,70,000	15,60,000	19,50,000	23,40,000
C	Fixed costs:				
	Fixed overheads	2,75,000	2,75,000	2,75,000	2,75,000
	Additional selling Exp.	—	50,000	—	50,000

Depreciation for balancing equipment	—	—	1,00,000	1,00,000
Additional adminstrative Exp.	—	—	50,000	50,000
Total fixed costs:	2,75,000	3,25,000	4,25,000	4,75,000
D Total Costs [B + C]	14,45,000	18,85,000	23,75,000	28,15,000
E Profit: [A – D]	55,000	1,15,000	25,000	85,000

Note: For computing the material and labour cost under alternatives III & IV the notional sale price of ₹ 100 is taken for additional 10,000 units.

***Recommendations*:** Alternative II is the best as it gives maximum profit.

Working Note:

	₹
Fixed Overheads:	
A Present Sales: (15,000 units × ₹ 100)	15,00,000
B Variable Cost (30% of sales)	4,50,000
Direct labour (20% of sales)	3,00,000
Variable overheads (₹ 20 per unit)	3,00,000
Total Variable Costs:	10,50,000
C Contribution: [A – B]	4,50,000
D Profit: (15,000 units × ₹ 15)	2,25,000
E Fixed Overheads: [C – D]	2,25,000
F *Add*: Additional Fixed Overheads due to price escalation	50,000
G Total Fixed Overheads [E + F]	2,75,000

Problem 3. A company produces four products A, B, C and D which are marketed in cartons. Of the total of 20 machines installed, 8 are suitable for manufacturing all the products and the remaining 12 machines are not suitable for the manufacture of products A and D.

Each machine is in production for 300 days per year and each is used on a given product in terms of full days and not in fractions of days. The Company however, has no problem in obtaining adequate supplies of labour and raw materials.

The marketing policy is that all four products should be sold and the minimum annual production should be 3,000 cartons for each product. Fixed costs budgeted amount to ₹ 50 lacs. Production cost price data are as under:

	A	*B*	*C*	*D*
Production/machine (Cartons per day)	14	4	3	6
	₹	₹	₹	₹
Selling Price/Carton	810	790	845	1290
Costs : Process 1				
Direct Material /day/machine	140	52	45	84
Direct Labour/day/machine	224	148	90	132
Costs : Process II				
Direct Material/Carton	30	30	30	30
Direct Labour/Carton	240	216	300	360
Variable overheads/Carton	390	390	300	720

Required: Calculate the optimum product mix and the maximum profit at optimum product mix.

Solution STATEMENT SHOWING CONTRIBUTION PER MACHINE DAY AND RANKING OF THE PRODUCT

Particulars	*A*	B	C	*D*
A. Cartons per day per machine	14	4	3	6
B. Minimum Sales	3,000	3,000	3,000	3,000
C. No. of Days for Minimum Sales (B/A)	215	750	1,000	500
D. Sales per Carton	₹ 810	₹ 790	₹ 845	₹ 1,290
E. Variable Costs per Carton (₹):				
Process 1 : Direct Material	10	13	15	14
Direct Wages	16	37	30	22

Process 2 : Direct Materials	30	30	30	30
Direct Labour	240	216	300	360
Variable Overheads	390	390	300	720
	686	686	675	1,146
F. Contribution per Carton (₹)	124	104	170	144
G. Contribution per Machine day [F A]	1,736	416	510	864
H. Ranking	I	IV	III	II

STATEMENT SHOWING THE ALLOCATION OF MACHINE DAYS

Particulars	*All Machine*	*Other Machine*
A. No. of Machines	8	12
B. No. of Days per machine	300	300
C. Total No. of Machine Days	2,400	3,600
D. For Minimum Sales of 'D'	500	—
E. Balance for 'A'	1,900	
F. For Minimum Sales of B		750
G. Balance for 'C'		2,850

STATEMENT SHOWING THE PROFITABILITY AT OPTIMUM PRODUCT MIX

Particulars	*A*	*B*	*C*	*D*	*Total*
A. Machine Days	1,900	750	2,850	500	6,000
B. Production/day (Cartons)	14	4	3	6	
C. Total Cartoon	26,600	3,000	8,550	3,000	
D. Contribution/cartoon	124	104	170	144	
E. Total Contribution [C D]	32,98,400	3,12,000	14,53,500	4,32,000	54,95,900
F. *Less* : Fixed Costs					50,00,000
G. Profit [E – F]					4,95,900

Problem 4. Something More Ltd. Is considering adding to its product line. After a lot of deliberations between the Sales and Production Personnel, it is decided that products, P, Q and R would be the most desirable additions to the Company's product range on account of the technical competency, marketing potential and production flexibility as regards these products. In fact P, Q and R can all be made on the same kind of plant as that is already in use and therefore as regards production, all products can be readily interchanged. However, it is considered necessary to build further plant facilities to cater for additional production.

In this connection the following data are relevant :

Particulars	*Product P*	*Product Q*	*Product R*
Direct Materials per unit	₹ 100	₹ 120	₹ 90
Direct Labour per unit	50	70	90
Variable Overheads per unit	50	130	100
Selling Price per unit	350	420	370
Demand in units per cost period (on the basis of the above selling price)	200	125	750
Machine Hours required per unit of production	15	5	3

It is felt that initially extra plant, facilities can be built to operate at the following five different levels of activity, viz, 1,800,2,300, 2,800, 3,300 and 3,800 machine hours per cost period. The fixed overhead costs for a cost period relevant to these five different levels of activity are estimated at ₹ 15,000, ₹ 20,000, ₹ 26,000, ₹ 33,000 and ₹ 39,000 respectively.

Required: Advise, with supporting figures, the product or products to be manufactured and in what quantities at each of the five contemplated levels of activity in order to maximise the profits at each level and also indicate the level of activity that would seem most desirable to be pursued for such maximization of profits.

Solution:

STATEMENT SHOWING CONTRIBUTION PER UNIT AND CONTRIBUTION PER HOUR AND RANKING OF THE PRODUCT

Particulars	P	Q	R
A. Selling Price per unit (₹)	350	420	370
B. Variable Costs per unit (₹) :			
Direct Material	100	120	90
Direct Labour	50	70	90
Variable overheads	50	130	100
Total	200	320	280
C. Contribution per unit (₹) [A – B]	150	100	90
D. Hrs. required for one unit	15	5	3
E. Contribution per hour (₹) [C/D]	10	20	30
F. Ranking	III	II	I

STATEMENT SHOWING PRODUCTION OF P, Q, R BASED ON CONTRIBUTION PER UNIT

Level of activity (in hours)	*Product P (Maximum units = 200 Maximum hrs. to be utilized 200 15 = 3000 hours)*			*Product Q (Maximum units = 125 Maximum hrs. to be utilized = 125 5 = 625 hours)*			*Product R (Maximum units = 750 Maximum hrs. to be utilised = 750 3 = 2250 hours)*					
	Hrs. used	*Units produ-Ced*	*Contri-bution made ₹*	*Hrs. used*	*Units produ-ced*	*Contri-bution made ₹*	*Hrs. used*	*Units prod-uced*	*Contri-bution made ₹*	*Total Contri-bution ₹*	*Fixed Cost ₹*	*Profit ₹*
1,800							1,800	600	54,000	54,000	15,000	39,000
2,300				50	10	1000	2,250	750	67,500	68,500	20,000	48,500
2,800				550	110	11,000	2,250	750	67,500	78,500	26,000	52,500
3,300	420 5*	28	4,200	625	125	12,500	2,250	750	67,500	84,200	33,000	51,200
3,800	915 10*	61	9,150	625	125	12,500	2,250	750	67,500	89,150	39,000	50,150

* (These hours are used to produce incomplete units for which profit will be realised only in the next period (year or quarter). These hours are to be disregarded for profit for this period.

Level of Activity at which profit is maximum: Maximum profit of ₹ 52,500 will be made when 750 units of R and 110 units of Q are produced at activity level of 2,800 Hours.

Problem 5. COJIG Ltd. producing products 'PIE' and 'SIGMA' using a single production process, has the following cost data :

	PIE	*SIGMA*
Selling Price per unit *(₹)*	20	30
Variable Cost per unit *(₹)*	11	16
Machine Hours required per unit production *(hrs.)*	1	2
Market Demand (units)	1 lakh	2.5 lakhs

Total Machine Hours available — 4 lakhs

Fixed cost per annum — ₹ 26 lakhs

Considering the limiting factors of machine hours and market limitations, you are required to:

(a) indicate the best combination of products to give optimum contribution;

(b) show the additional machinery requirement to be augmented on rental basis at an annual rent of ₹ 1.5 lakhs per machine to provide additional capacity of 30,000 hours per machine ;

(c) suggest the change in number of machines to be rented if the annual rental charges reduce to ₹ 1,25,000 per machine.

Solution

(a) STATEMENT SHOWING THE CONTRIBUTION, RANKING, OPTIMUM PRODUCT MIX AND PROFITABILITY AT OPTIMUM PRODUCT MIX

	Particulars	*Products*		
		PIE	*SIGMA*	*Total*
A	Selling Price per unit (₹)	20	30	
B	Variable Cost per unit (₹)	11	16	
C	Contribution per unit (₹) [A – B]	9	14	
D	Machine hours required per Unit	1	2	
E	Contribution per machine hour. (₹) [C/D]	9	7	
F	Ranking	I	II	
G	Production towards market Demand (units)	1,00,000	1,50,000	2,50,000
H	Total Hours required [G D]	1,00,000	3,00,000	4,00,000
I	Total Contribution (₹) [G C]	9,00,000	21,00,000	30,00,000

(b) STATEMENT OF REQUIREMENTS OF ADDITIONAL MACHINES ON RENTAL BASIS

	Particulars	
A	Annual rent per machine having capacity of 30,000 hours (₹)	1,50,000
B	No. of units of SIGMA to be produced to meet up market demand (additional)	1,00,000
C	Requirement of machine hours for production [1,00,000 2 Hours]	2,00,000
D	Number of machines required [(2,00,000 ÷ 30,000) = 6.67 i.e. (6 + 1)]	7
E	Total net contribution of 6 rented machines with utilisation of full capacity (₹) [(30,000 6 Machines ₹ 7) – (₹ 1,50,000 6 Machines)]	3,60,000
F	Total net contribution of 7 rented Machines leaving idle capacity of 10,000 hours (₹) [(30,000 6 Machines ₹ 7) + (20,000 1 Machine ₹ 7) – (₹ 1,50,000 7 Machines)]	3,50,000
G	Incremental net margin (₹) (E – F)	₹ 10,000

In the light of (E), (F) and (G) of above statement only 6 additional machines are to be augmented on rental basis.

(c) Change in Number of Machines to be rented

		₹
(i)	Net Contribution of 6 rented machines [(30,000 6 Machines ₹ 7) – (₹ 1,25,000 6 Machines)]	5,10,000
(ii)	Net Contribution 7 rented machines [(30,000 6 Machines ₹ 7) + (₹ 20,000 1 Machine ₹ 7) – (₹ 1,25,000 7 Machines)]	5,25,000
(iii)	Incremental Net Margin [(ii) – (i)]	15,000

Suggestion: 7 additional machines should be augmented on rental basis as this decision will increase the net margin by ₹ 15,000.

Problem 6. An engineering company is engaged in producing four products through operations at welding and pressing departments. Products WI and W2 are produced by welders in the welding department whereas products P1 and P2 are produced by press-operators in the pressing department. Due to specific skill requirements, the welders and press-operators can only work in their own department. The following relevant data are available in respect of the products :

Products	*W1*	*W2*	*P1*	*P2*
Hours required per unit	4	4	5	2
Selling Price per unit (₹)	48	50	77	69
Direct Material Cost per unit (₹)	18	22	32	44
Direct Labour Hourly rate (₹)	4	4	4	4
Variable Overhead Rate per unit (₹)	2	2	3	3

The Company incurs ₹ 50,000 per annum towards fixed costs. The maximum available hours are 20,000 and 16,000 for welding and pressing departments respectively. The demands keep on fluctuating but the minimum demands which are to be met as per management's decision are 2,000 units of WI, 2,500 units of W2, 1,800 units of PI and 2,200 units of P2.

The production manager suggests that the welders and press-operators can be trained to perform both welding and pressing jobs so that excess demand of any of the products can be met. This decision is going to increase the burden of fixed costs by ₹ 5,000 per annum.

Required : Prepare the profitability statement for optimum product-mix and recommend with reasons and appropriate workings whether it is advisable to train the welders and press-operators as suggested by the production manager.

Solution: **STATEMENT SHOWING OPTIMUM PRODUCT MIX BEFORE TRAINING**

Particulars	*Welding 20,000 hours*		*Pressing 16,000 hours*	
	WI	*W2*	*PI*	*P2*
A. Selling Price per unit (₹)	48	50	77	69
B. *Less :* Variable Cost per unit:				
Material (₹)	18	22	32	44
Labour (₹)	16	16	20	8
Variable Overhead (₹)	2	2	3	3
Total Variable Cost (₹)	36	40	55	55
C. Contribution per unit (₹) [A – B]	12	10	22	14
D. Labour hours per unit	4	4	5	2
E. Contribution per hour (₹) [C/D]	3	2.5	4.4	7
F. Ranking	I	II	II	I
G. Minimum Production (units)	2,000	2,500	1,800	2,200
H. Labour hours needed for min. produc.	8,000	10,000	9,000	4,400
I. Labour hours used for min. produc.	8,000 +10,000 = 18,000		9,000 + 4,400 = 13,400	
J. Balance hours available	20,000 – 18,000 = 2,000		16,000 – 13,400 = 2,600	
K. Product to be produced	WI		P2	
L. Units to be produced	2,000 ÷ 4 = 500		2,600 ÷ 2 = 1,300	
	WI	W2	P1	P2
Hence, Product-Mix	= 2,000 + 500 = 2,500	2,500	1,800	= 2,200 + 1,300 = 3,500

STATEMENT SHOWING THE PROFITABILITY BEFORE TRAINING

Product	*Product-mix units*	*Hours*		*Contribution*	
		Per unit	*Total*	*Per hour* ₹	*Total* ₹
WI	2,500	4	10,000	3.00	30,000
W2	2,500	4	10,000	2.50	25,000
PI	1,800	5	9,000	4.40	39,600
P2	3,500	2	7,000	7.00	49,000
				Total	1,43,600
				Less : Fixed Costs	50,000
				Net Profit	₹ 93,600

STATEMENT SHOWING OPTIMUM PRODUCT MIX AFTER TRAINING

After training the capacity will be taken as a whole at 36,000 labour hours because of interchangeability of available labour force. The ranking will be done on the basis of contribution per hour among all the four products, since a workman is trained to work in any of the departments.

Product	W1	W2	PI	P2
Maximum hours	36,000 hours as a whole			
Hours needed for minimum production	8,000	10,000	9,000	4,400
		(Total hours = 31,400 hours)		
Balance hours	(36,000 – 31,400 hours = 4,600 hours)			
Product priority (Ranking)	III	IV	II	I
Product in balance hours	P2 (I rank) : 4,600 ÷ 2 = 2,300 units			
Product mix (units)	2,000	2,500	1,800	2,200 + 2,300 = 4,500

STATEMENT SHOWING THE PROFITABILITY AFTER TRAINING

Product	*Product-mix*	*Hours*		*Contribution*	
	units	*Per unit*	*Total*	*Per hour* ₹	*Total* ₹
W1	2,000	4	8,000	3.00	24,000
W2	2,500	4	10,000	2.50	25,000
P1	1,800	5	9,000	4.40	39,600
P2	4,500	2	9,000	7.00	63,000
				Total	1,51,600
				Less : Fixed Costs	55,000
				Net Profit	96,600

Recommendation: Since the net profit after training will increase by ₹ 3,000 (₹ 96,600 – ₹ 93,600), it is advisable to train the welders and press operators as suggested by the production manager.

Problem 7. On a turnover of ₹ 20 crores in year I, a large manufacturing company earned a profit of 10% before interest and depreciation which were fixed. The product mix was as under :

Products	*Mix % to Total Sales*	*P/V Ratio (%)*	*Raw Material as % of Sales Value*
P	10	30	40%
Q	30	20	35%
R	20	40	50%
S	40	10	60%

Interest and depreciation amounted to ₹ 150 lacs and ₹ 77 lacs respectively.

Due to fluctuations in prices in the International Market, the company anticipates that the cost of raw materials which are imported will increase by 10% during year II. The company has been able to secure a licence for the import of raw materials of a value of ₹ 1,023 lacs at year II prices. In order to counteract the increase in costs of raw materials, the company is contemplating to revise its product mix. The market survey report recently prepared indicates that the sales potential of each of the products P, Q and R can be increased up to 30% of the total sales value of year I. There is no inventory of finished goods or work in process in both the years.

Required:

(i) Set an Optimal Product Mix for year II and find the profitability.

(ii) What percentage increase in Overall Price is required in year II to raise the sales value to maintain the margin of safety at 10%.

Solution:

Part (i)

(a) STATEMENT SHOWING ORIGINAL AND REVISED MATERIAL COST

Product	*Mix % to Total Sales*	*Sales (₹ lacs)*	*Raw material as % on Sales Value*	*Existing Cost of Raw Material*	*Increased Cost of Raw Material after 10% increase*
P	10	200	40	80	88
Q	30	600	35	210	231

R	20	400	50	200	220
S	40	800	60	480	528
		2,000		970	1,067

(b) STATEMENT SHOWING OTHER VARIABLE COST

(₹/lacs)

Product	*Sales*	*Existing P/V Ratio %*	*Variable Cost*	*Material Cost*	*Other Variable Cost*
A	*B*	*C*	*D*	*E*	*F = D – E*
P	200	30	140	80	60
Q	600	20	480	210	270
R	400	40	240	200	40
S	800	10	720	480	240
	2000		1,580	970	610

(c) STATEMENT SHOWING CONTRIBUTION TO MATERIAL RATIO AND RANKING OF PRODUCTS ON THIS BASIS

(₹ in lacs)

Products	*Sales*	*Other Variable Cost*	*Revised Material cost*	*Total Variable Cost*	*Contribution*	*P/V Ratio*	*Contribution to Material Ratio*	*Ranking based on contribution to sales*
A	*B*	*C*	*D*	*E*	*F = B – E*			
P	200	60	88	148	52	26%	59.09%	II
Q	600	270	231	501	99	16.5%	42.86%	III
R	400	40	220	260	140	35%	63.64%	I
S	800	240	528	768	32	4%	6.06%	IV
	2,000	610	1,067	1,677	323			

(d) STATEMENT SHOWING MAXIMUM SALES POTENTIAL OF INDIVIDUAL PRODUCTS

(₹ in lacs)

P	30% of ₹ 2,000 = 600
Q	30% of ₹ 2,000 = 600
R	30% of ₹ 2,000 = 600
S	40% of ₹ 2,000 = 800

(e) STATEMENT SHOWING ALLOCATION OF RAW MATERIAL BASED ON CONTRIBUTION TO SALES RATIO

Product	*Rank as per Statement (c)*	*Sales ₹ in lacs*	*Material Required*	*Working for determining value of material required*	*Balance raw Material (₹ in lacs)*
Balance Raw Material					1,023
R	I	600	330	(i.e. 220/400 600)	693
P	II	600	264	(i.e. 88/200 600)	429
Q	III	600	231	(i.e. 231/600 600)	198
S	IV	300	198		Nil
			1,023		

(f) STATEMENT SHOWING THE TOTAL CONTRIBUTION IN YEAR I

Product	*Sales (₹ in lacs)*	*P/V ratio %*	*Contribution (₹ in lacs)*
P	200	30	60
Q	600	20	120

Product	Sales (₹ in lacs)	P/V ratio %	Contribution (₹ in lacs)
R	400	40	160
S	800	10	80
	2,000		420

(g) STATEMENT SHOWING THE COMPUTATION OF FIXED OVERHEAD

A	Present Contribution		₹.420 (lakhs)
B	*Less* : Profit @ 10% of sales (10% of 2000)		200
C.	Fixed overheads other than Interest & Depreciation		220
D.	*Add* : Interest	150	
	Depreciation	77	227
E.	Total fixed overheads [C + D]		447

(h) STATEMENT SHOWING THE OPTIMUM MIX AND PROFITABILITY AT OPTIMUM MIX

Product	*Optimum sales ₹ in lacs*	*Revised P/V Ratio %*	*Contribution (₹ in lacs)*
P	600	26	156
Q	600	16.5	99
R	600	35	210
S	300	4	12
		Total	477
		Less : Fixed cost	447
		Profit	30

Contribution = Sales x P/V ratio = 600 lacs x 26% = 156 lacs.

(ii) ***Required percentage increase in overall price in 20X2***

Break Even Sales = Fixed Cost / P/V Ratio = 447 / (477 ÷ 2,100) = ₹ 1,967.92 lacs.

Actual Sales = 1,967.92/.90 = ₹ 2,186.58 lacs

Optimum Sales = ₹ 2100 lacs

Required Increase in Sales value = ₹ 2,186.58 lacs – ₹ 2,100 lacs = ₹ 86.58 lacs

Required percentage of increase in sales price = $\frac{86.58}{2,100}$ × 100 = 4.123%

Problem 8. Bloom Ltd. makes 3 products, A, B and C. The following information is available:

	(Figures in Rupees per unit)		
	A	*B*	*C*
Selling Price (peak-season)	550	630	690
Selling Price (off-season)	550	604	690
Material Cost	230	260	290
Labour (peak-season)	110	120	150
Labour (off-season)	100	99	149
Variable Production Overhead	100	120	130
Variable Selling Overhead (only for peak-season)	10	20	15
Labour hours required for one unit of production	8	11	7 (hours)

Material Cost and Variable Production Overheads are the same for the peak-season and off-season. Variable selling overheads are not incurred in the off-season. Fixed costs amount to ₹ 26,780 for each season, of which ₹ 2,000 is towards salary for special technician, incurred only for product B, and ₹ 4,780 is the amount that will be incurred on after-sales warranty and free maintenance of only product C, to match competition.

Labour force can be interchangeably used for all the products. During peak-season, there is labour shortage and the maximum labour hours available are 1,617 hours. During off-season, labour is freely available, but demand is limited to 100 units of A, 115 units of B and 135 units of C, with production facility being limited to 215 units for A, B and C put together.

You are required to:

(i) Advise the company about the best product mix during peak-season for maximum profit.

(ii) What will be the maximum profit for the off-season?

Solution:

(PEAK SEASON)
STATEMENT OF CONTRIBUTION AND BEP (IN UNITS)

Particulars	*Product A*	*Product B*	*Product C*	*Total*
A. Selling Price per unit	550	630	690	
B. Variable Costs per unit:				
Direct Material	230	260	290	
Direct Labour	110	120	150	
Variable Production Overhead	100	120	130	
Variable Selling Overhead	10	20	15	
Total Variable Cost	450	520	585	
C. Contribution / unit (A – B)	100	110	105	
D. Direct Labour hours required per unit	8	11	7	
E. Contribution per Labour Hour (C / D)	12.5	10	15	
F. Ranking	II	III	I	
General Fixed Overhead				20,000
Specific Fixed overhead	—	2,000	4,780	6,780
G. Total Fixed Overhead				26,780
H. BEP (units) (for only 1 Product at a time) (G/C)	$\frac{20,000}{100} = 200$	$\frac{22,000}{110} = 200$	$\frac{24,780}{105} = 236$	

Maximum units that can be produced of product C with limited labour hours 1,617 = 1617/7 = 231

Since 231 < Break Even units, Bloom Ltd. cannot produce C.

Next Rank = A

Maximum units of A that can be produced with limited labour hours = 1,617/8 = 202 units.

Since 202 > Break Even units of A (200) Bloom Ltd. can produce A.

Profit will be ₹ 200 [i.e., (₹ 202 × 100) – ₹ 20,000]

STATEMENT OF CONTRIBUTION AND DEMAND (OFF SEASON)

Figures ₹ per unit

Particulars	*Product A*	*Product B*	*Product C*
A. Selling Price	550	604	690
Direct Material	230	260	290
Direct Labour	100	99	149
Production-Variable Overhead	100	120	130
B. Total Variable Cost	430	479	569
C. Contribution per unit (A – B)	120	125	121
Ranking	3	1	2
Maximum demand	100	115	135

STATEMENT OF PROFITABILITY UNDER DIFFERENT OPTIONS
(LIMIT OF PRODUCTION = 215 UNITS)

Particulars	*A*	*B*	*C*	*Total*	*Fixed Cost*	*Profit (loss)*
Contribution per unit	120	125	121			
Option 1: Units	—	115	100	215		
Contribution (₹)	—	14,375	12,100	26,475	26,780	(305)

Particular	A	B	C	Total	Fixed Cost	Profit (loss)
Option 2: Units	100	115	—	215		
Contribution (₹)	12,000	14,375	—	26,375	22,000	4,375
Option 3: Units	80	—	135	215		
Contribution (₹)	9,600	—	16,335	25,935	24,780	1,155

Best strategy is to produce 100 units of Product A and 115 units units of product during off season since Maximum Profit = ₹ 4,375.

(i) Best strategy for peak-season is to produce 202 units of A.

(ii) Maximum profit for off-season ₹ 4,375.

Problem 9. All Play and Notwork Ltd. are specialists in the manufacture of sports goods. They manufacture croquet mallets but purchase the wooden balls, iron arches and stakes required to complete a croquet set.

Mallets consist of a head and handle. Handles use 1.5 board feet per handle at ₹ 40 per board foot. Spoilage loss is negligible for the manufacture of handles.

Heads frequently split and create considerable scrap. A head requires 0.20 board feet of high quality lumber costing ₹ 70 per board foot. Spoilage normally works out to 20% of the completed heads. 4% of the spoiled heads can be salvaged and sold as scrap at ₹ 10 per spoiled head.

In the department machining and assembling the mallets, 12 men work 8 hours per day for 25 days in a month. Each worker can machine and assemble 15 mallets per uninterrupted 50 minutes time frame. In each 8 hours working day, 15 minutes are allowed for coffee-break, 8 minutes on an average for training and 9 minutes for supervisory instructions. Besides 10% of each day is booked as idle time to cover checking in and checking out changing operations, getting materials and other miscellaneous matters. Workers are paid at a comprehensive rate of ₹ 6 per hour.

The department is geared to produce 40,000 mallets per month and the monthly expenses of the department are as under:

Processing costs amount to ₹ 54 lacs per month as under:

	₹
Finishing and painting of the mallets	50,800
Lubricating oil for cutting machines	300
Depreciation for cutting machine	700
Repairs and maintenance	100
Power to run the machines	200
Plant Manager's salary	2,700
Other overheads allocated to the department	1,20,000

As the mallets are machined and assembled in lots of 500, prepare a total cost sheet for one lot and advise the management on the selling price to be fixed per mallet in order to ensure a minimum 20% margin on the selling price.

Solution:

ALL PLAY AND NOWORK LTD.
COST SHEET OF ONE LOT OF 500 CROQUET MALLETS

Particulars	₹	₹	₹
A Direct Material			
Handles (1.5 feet × 500 units × ₹ 40)		30,000	
Heads (1.20 × 500 × 0.20 × ₹ 70)	8,400		
Less: Scrap recovery (4% × 100 × ₹ 10)	40	8,360	38,360
B Direct Labour: $\left(\frac{8 \text{ hrs.} \times 6}{120} \times 500\right)$			200
C **Prime Cost**			38,560
D Factory and Other Overheads: Variable			
Finishing and painting $\left(\frac{50{,}800}{40{,}000} \times 500\right)$			635

Particulars	₹	₹	₹
Fixed $\left(\frac{1,24,000}{36,000} \times 500\right)$			1,722
E Total Cost			40,917
Price quotation:			
Cost per mallet (₹ 40,917/500 units)			81.834
Add: Profit 25% on cost			20.458
Selling price			102.29

Working notes:

(i) Since 20% of completed heads are spoiled, output of 1 unit requires input of 1 + 0.20 = 1.20 units; so, total heads processed: 1.20 x 500 = 600, of which spoiled heads are 100.

(ii) Total time in a day: 8 x 60 — 480 minutes

Less: Idle time	48 minutes	
Coffee break	15 minutes	
Instructions	9 minutes	
Training	8 minutes	80 minutes
Productive time per day:		400 minutes

Therefore, mallets to be produced per man per day: $\left(\frac{400}{50} \times 15\right) = 120$ units

(iii) Finishing and painting overheads are assumed to be variable for the production of 40,000 mallets.

(iv) All the other expenses are fixed and are to be absorbed by 36,000 mallets of monthly production. Since mallets are produced at the rate of 120 mallets per man day, so total monthly production will be: = 120 units x 12 men x 25 days = 36,000 mallets.

Problem 10. A company has prepared the following budget for the forthcoming year:

	₹ *laks*
Sales	20.00
Direct Materials	3.60
Direct Labour	6.40
Factory Overheads:	
Variable	2.20
Fixed	2.60
Administration Overheads	1.80
Sales Commission	1.00
Fixed Selling Overheads	0.40
Total costs	18.00
Profit	2.00

The policy of the company in fixing selling prices is to charge all overheads other than the prime costs on the basis of percentage of direct wages and to add a mark up of one-ninth of total costs for profit.

While the company is confident of achieving the budget drawn up as above, a new customer approached the company directly for execution of a special order. The direct materials and direct labour costs of the special order are estimated respectively at ₹ 36,000 and ₹ 64,000. This special order is in excess of the budgeted sales as envisaged above. The company submitted a quotation of ₹ 2,00,000 for the special order based on its policy. The new customer is willing to pay a price of ₹ 1,50,000 for the special order. The company is hesitant to accept the order below total cost as, according to the company management, it will lead to a loss.

You are required to state your arguments and advise the management on the acceptance of the special order.

Solution:

ANALYSIS OF COST AND PROFIT

Particulars	*₹ (lakhs)*
Direct Material	3.60
Direct Labour	6.40
Prime Cost	10.00
Overheads:	
Variable Factory Overheads	2.20
Fixed Factory Overheads	2.60
Administration Overheads	1.80
Selling Commission	1.00
Fixed Selling Overheads	0.40
	8.00
Total Cost	18.00
Profit	2.00
Rate of Profit on Costs (2/18) = 1/9	

Overhead absorption rate based on direct wages = (8.00 / 6.40) = 125% of Direct Wages

Break up of New Order:	₹
Direct Materials	36,000
Direct Labour	64,000
Overheads 125% of direct wages	80,000
Total Costs	1,80,000
Profit@ 1/9 on cost	20,000
Selling Price	2,00,000

The following points emerge:

(i) Factory overheads only are to be recovered on the basis of direct wages.

(ii) The special order is a direct order. Hence commission is not payable.

(iii) The budgeted sales are achieved Hence all fixed overheads are recovered. Hence, no fixed overheads will be chargeable to the special order.

Based on the above, the factory variable overheads recovery rate may be calculated as under:

Total Variable Factory Overheads ₹ 2.20 lakhs
Direct Wages ₹ 6.40 lakhs
Factory Overhead rate = (2.20 / 6.40) × 100 = 34.375%

Applying this rate the cost of the special order will be as under:

Particular	₹
Direct Materials	36,000
Direct labour	64,000
Overheads 34.375% of direct wages	22,000
Total Costs	1,22,000
Price offered	1,50,000
Margin	28,000 (more than 1/9)

Hence, the order is acceptable at the price of ₹ 1,50,000.

Problem 11. X is a multiple product manufacturer. One product line consists of motors and the company produces three different models. X is currently considering a proposal from a supplier who wants to sell the company blades for the motors line.

The company currently produces all the blades it requires. In order to meet customer's needs, X currently produces three different blades for each motor model (nine different blades).

The supplier would charge ₹.25 per blade, regardless of blade type. For the next year X has projected the costs of its own blade production as follows (based on projected volume of 10,000 units):

Direct Materials	₹.75,000
Direct Labour	₹.65,000

Variable Overheads	₹.55,000
Fixed Overheads:	
Factory Supervision	₹ 35,000
Other Fixed Cost	₹.65,000
Total Production Costs	₹.2,95.000

Assume (1) the equipment utilized to produce the blades has no alternative use and no market value, (2) the space occupied by blade production will remain idle if the company purchases rather than makes the blades, and (3) factory supervision costs reflect the salary of a production supervisor who would be dismissed from the firm if blade production ceased.

(i) Determine the net profit or loss of purchasing (rather than manufacturing), the blades required for motor production in the next year.

(ii) Determine the level of motor production where X would be indifferent between buying and producing the blades. If the future volume level were predicted to decrease, would that influence the decision?

(iii) For this part only, assume that the space presently occupied by blade production could be leased to another firm for ₹.45,000 per year. How would this affect the make or buy decision?

Solution:

This is a make or buy decision.

COST OF MAKING THE BLADES

A. Direct Materials (₹.75,000 / 10,000 units)	₹ 7.50
B. Direct Labour (₹ 65,000 / 10,000 units)	₹ 6.50
C. Variable Overhead, (₹ 55,000 / 10,000)	₹ 5.50
D. Supervision (₹ 35,000 / 10,000)	₹.3.50
E. Total Cost [A + B + C + D]	₹.23.00

Compare the cost to make the blades for 10,000 motors. ₹ 23.00, with the cost to buy, ₹ 25.00. There is a net loss of ₹ 2.00 if 'X' chooses to buy the blades.

(b) 'X will be indifferent between buying and making the blades when the total costs for making and buying will be equal at the volume level where the variable costs per unit times the volume plus the fixed avoidable costs are equal to the supplier's offered cost of ₹.25.00 per unit times the volume.

(Direct materials + Direct labour + Variable overhead) × Volume + Supervision = Cost to buy x Volume. Let volume in units = x

$$(7.50 + 6.50 + 5.50) \times x + 35{,}000 = 25.00\ x$$
$$19.50\ x + 35{,}000 = 25.00\ x$$
$$35{,}000 = 25.00 \times x - 19.50 \times x$$
$$35{,}000 = 5.50 \times x$$
$$x = 6{,}364 \text{ units of blades}$$

As volume of production decreases, the average per unit cost of in house production increases. If the volume falls below 6,364 motors, then 'X' would prefer to buy the blades from the supplier.

(c) If the space presently occupied by blade production could be leased to another firm for ₹.45,000 per year, 'X' would face an opportunity cost associated with in house blade production for the 10,000 units of ₹.4.50 per unit.

Now cost to take = 23.00 + 4.50 = 27.50

Now 'X' should buy because the cost to make, 27.50, is higher than the cost to buy, 25.00.

Problem 12. XYZ Limited is currently manufacturing 5,000 units of the product 'XY 100' annually, making full use of its machine capacity. The selling price and total costs per unit associated with 'XY 100' are as follows:

	₹	₹
Selling Price per unit		900
Costs per unit:		
Direct Materials	200	
Variable Machine Operating Costs (₹ 100 per machine hour)	150	
Manufacturing Overhead Costs	180	
Marketing and Administrative Costs	200	730
Operating income per unit of 'XY 100'		170

XYZ Limited can sell additional 3,000 units of 'XY 100', if it can outsource those additional units.

ABC Limited, a supplier of quality products, has agreed to supply upto 6,000 units of 'XY 100' per year at a price of ₹ 650 per unit delivered at XYZ's factory.

XYZ Limited can use its facility to produce an alternative product 'XY 200'. It can sell up to 12,000 units of 'XY 200' annually. Estimated selling price and total costs per unit to manufacture and sell 12,000 units of 'XY 200' are as follows:

	₹	₹
Selling price per unit		600
Costs per unit:		
Direct Materials	200	
Variable Machine Operating Costs (₹ 100 per machine hour)	50	
Manufacturing Overhead costs	60	
Marketing and Administrative Costs	110	420
Operating Income per unit of 'XY 200'		180

Other information pertaining to the operation of XYZ Limited is as follows:

(a) XYZ Limited use machine hours as the basis for assigning fixed manufacturing overhead. The fixed manufacturing overhead for the current year is ₹ 3,00,000. These costs will not be affected by the product-mix decision.

(b) Variable marketing and administrative costs per unit for various products are as follows:

Manufactured	'XY 100'	₹ 80
Purchased	'XY 100'	₹ 40
Manufactured	'XY 200'	₹ 60

Fixed marketing and administrative costs for the current year is ₹ 6,00,000. These costs will not be affected by the product-mix decision.

Required: Calculate the quantity of each product that XYZ Limited should manufacture and/or purchase to maximize operating income.

Step 1: Calculation of Variable Mfs Overheads

		XY 100	XY 200
A	Total Manufacturing Overheads	₹ 180	₹ 60
B	Fixed manufacturing overhead per unit [₹ 3,00,000/5000] [₹ 3,00,000/12000]	₹ 60	₹ 25
C	Variable Manufacturing Overheads per unit [A – B]	₹ 120	₹ 35

Step 2: Ranking between manufactured "XY 100" and manufactured "XY 200"

		Manufactured 'XY 100' ₹	*Manufactured 'XY 200'* ₹
A	Selling Price per unit	900	600
B	*Less*: Total Variable Cost		
	Direct Material	200	200
	Variable Machine Operating Costs	150	50
	Variable Manufacturing Overheads	120	35
	Variable Cost of Production	470	285
	Variable Marketing and Administrative cost	80	60
	Total Variable Cost per unit:	550	345
C	Contribution per unit: [A – B]	350	255
D	Machine hours required per unit	1.50	0.50
	Contribution per hour [C/D]	233	510
F	Ranking	II	I

Step 3: Ranking between manufactured "XY 100" and purchased "XY 100"

		Manufactured 'XY 100' ₹	*Purchased 'XY 100'* ₹
A	Selling price per unit	900	600
B	*Less*: Total Variable Cost per unit		
	Variable Cost of production	470	—

	Purchase Price	—	650
	Variable Marketing and administrative cost	80	40
	Total Variable Cost per unit: (A)	550	690
C	Contribution per unit: [A – B]	350	(90)
D	Ranking	I	II

Step 4: Allocation of available 7,500 machine hours

"XY 200" : 12,000 units × 0.50 hours or 6,000 hours

"XY 100" : (7,500 – 6,000) hours = 1,500 hours

Step 5: Quantity of each product that XYZ Limited should manufacture and/or purchase to maximise operating income

Manufactured "XY 200"	12,000 units
Manufactured "XY 100". [1,500 hours/1.5 hours]	1,000 units
Purchased "XY 100"	6,000 units
Maximum number of units which ABC can supply.	

Problem 13. Paints ltd. manufactures 2,00,000 tins of paint at normal capacity. It incurs the following manufacturing costs per unit:

Particulars	₹
Direct Material	7.80
Direct Labour	2.10
Variable Overhead	2.50
Fixed Overhead	4.00
Production Cost /unit	16.40

Each unit is sold for ₹ 21, with an additional variable selling overhead incurred at ₹ 0.60 per unit.

During the next quarter, only 10,000 units can be produced and sold. Management plans to shut down the plant estimating that the fixed manufacturing cost can be reduced to ₹ 74,000 for the quarter.

When the plant is operating, the fixed overheads are incurred at a uniform rate throughout the year. Additional costs of plant shut down for the quarter are estimated at ₹ 14,000.

You are required:

(i) To advise whether it is more economical to shut down the plant during the quarter rather than operate the plant.

(ii) Calculate the shut down point for the quarter in terms of numbering units.

Solution:

Contribution per tin = S.P – V.C = 21 – (7.8 + 2.1 + 2.5 + 0.6) = ₹ 8 per tin.

Particulars	*If plant is continued*	*If Plant is shut Down*
A. Contribution (10,000 × ₹ 8)	80,000	—
B. Fixed Costs	2,00,000 [2,00,000 × ₹ 4× 1/4]	(74,000)
C. Shut Down Costs	—	(14,000)
D. Loss	(1,20,000)	(88,000)

Advise: The company is advised to shut down and save ₹ 32,000

$$\text{Shut-down point (number of units)} = \frac{\text{Avoidable Fixed Cost}}{\text{Contribution per unit}} = \frac{2,00,000 - 88,000}{8}$$

$$= \frac{1,12,000}{8} = 14,000 \text{ units.}$$

Problem 14. TQM Limited makes engines for motor cars for its parent company and for two other motor car manufacturers.

On 31st December, the company has sufficient work order for January and one further order for 21,000 engines. Due to recession in the economy, no further order are expected until May when it is hoped economic prospect for the motor car industry will have improved. Recently factory has been working at only 75% of full capacity and the order for 21,000 engines represents about one month production at this level of activity.

The board of directors are currently considering following two options:

(i) Complete the order in February and close the factory in March and April.

OR

(ii) Operate at 25 per cent of full capacity for each of three months of February, March and April.

The costs per month at different levels of activities are as follows:

Particulars	*At 75% (₹)*	*At 25% (₹)*	*Idle (₹)*
Direct Material	5,25,000	1,75,000	—
Direct Labour	5,23,600	1,73,250	
Factory Overheads:			
Indirect Material	8,400	4,900	4,900
Indirect Labour	1,01,500	59,500	
Indirect Expenses:			
Repairs and Maintenance	28,000	28,000	
Others Expenses	52,500	34,300	26,600
Office Overheads:			
Staff Salaries	1,48,400	98,000	67,550
Other Overheads	28,000	19,950	11,200

Other information is as follows:

- Material cost and labour cost will not be incurred where there is no production.
- On the reopening of the factory, one time cost of training and engagement of new personnel would be ₹.65,800 and overhauling cost of plant would be ₹ 14,000.
- Parent company can purchase engines from open market at reasonable price.

Required:

(i) To express your opinion, along with calculations, as to whether the plant should be shut down during the month of March and April or operate 25% of full capacity for three months.

(ii) To list and comment on cost and non-costs factors which might to relevant to the discussion.

Solution: (i)

EVALUATION OF BOTH THE OPTIONS

Particulars	*Option At 75% in Feb and close in March and April (₹)*	*I Option II At 25% each from Feb – April (₹)*
A. Direct Material	5,25,000	5,25,000
B. Direct Labour	5,23,600	5,19,750
C. Factory Overheads:		
Indirect Material	8,400	14,700
Two months idle	9,800	
Indirect Labour	1,01,500	1,78,500
Training cost	65,800	
Indirect Exp.:		
Repairs & Maintenance	28,000	84,000
Over hauling cost	14,000	
Others Expenses	52,500	1,02,900
Idle [26,600 × 2]	53,200	
D. Office Overheads		
Staff Salaries	1,48,400	2,94,000
Idle (67,550 × 2)	1,35,100	
Other Overheads	28,000	59,850
Idle	22,400	
E. Total Overhead Cost	6,67,100	7,33,950
F. Total Cost	17,15,700	17,78,700

Advise: The more economic course of action is to operate at 75% capacity for a month only, and close the plant for March and April. This option will save (₹.17,78,700 – ₹.17,15,700) = ₹.63,000.

(ii) Cost Factors and Non Cost Factors

In regard to the decision on close down of operations or continuing with operations, the factors to be considered are:

(a) Cost factors:

1. The proposal which involves the lower total costs will be selected.
2. If the company has contracted the purchases from high quality and high price suppliers, a change in the procurement policy to 'shop around' may be considered to obtain economics in purchases.
3. The services of unskilled labour, if any, who do not require re-training may be dispensed with. They may be recruited and put on work without incurring training cost on re-opening of the factory. This will save training and idle time cost.
4. The possibility of wage freeze may reluctantly be considered as an extreme measure.

(b) Non-cost factors:

1. If the skilled workers are discharged, it may be difficult to get them back on rolls when the factory is re-opened. Skilled workers may be scarce and training and orientation costs may be heavy on re-opening of the factory. Thus it is advisable to continue operations in the interests of these types of workers.
2. Even though the closure is temporary in nature, the competitors may usurp the market and the company may lose a sizable market share on re-opening. To avoid this situation, continuance of production is better.
3. It is advisable to continue operations to avoid heavy depreciation of plant and machinery and obsolescence risk.
4. Regular customers may switch over to competitor's products and may not return after re-opening of the factory. This may result in reduction in sales.

Problem 15. Fairbilt Furniture Ltd. manufactures three products: Tables, Chairs and Cabinets. The company is in the process of finalizing the plans for the coming year; hence the executives thought it would be prudent to have a look at the product-wise performance during the current year. The following information is furnished:

	Tables	*Chairs*	*Cabinets*
Unit Selling Price	80	60	36
Direct Material	28	24	16
Direct Labour	20	12	12
Factory Overheads:			
Variable	8	6	4
Fixed	8	6	1.28
Cost of Production	64	48	33.28
Selling, Distribution and General Administration Expenses:			
Variable	4	2	2
Fixed	4	6	1.52
Unit cost (i)	72	56	36.80
Unit profit (loss) (ii)	8	4	(0.80)
Sales volume (units)	10,000	15,000	15,000
Profit (loss)	80,000	60,000	(12,000)

For the coming period, the selling prices and the cost of three products are expected to remain unchanged. There will be an increase in the sales of tables by 1,000 units and the increase in sales of cabinets is expected to be 8,000 units. The sales of chairs will remain to be unchanged. Sufficient additional capacity exists to enable the increased demands to be met without incurring additional fixed costs. Some among the executives contend that it will be unwise to go for additional production and sale of cabinets, since it is already making losses at ₹.0.80 per unit. The suggestion is that cabinets should be eliminated altogether.

Do you agree? Substantiate with necessary analysis and determine the product wise and overall profits for the coming year.

Solution:

Note: Reconciliation of the figures given for 'cabinets' reveals the fact that the selling price is 36(36.80 – 0.80)

FAIRBILT FURNITURE LTD.

STATEMENT SHOWING PRODUCT-WISE CONTRIBUTION AND TOTAL PROFIT

Particular	*Tables Per unit*	*Total*	*Chairs Per unit*	*Total*	*Cabinets Per unit*	*Total*	*Total*
Sales Volume (units)		10,000		15,000		15,000	
Selling Price (₹)	80	8,00,000	60	9,00,000	36	5,40,000	22,40,000
Direct Material	28	2,80,000	24	3,60,000	16	2,40,000	8,80,000
Direct Labour	20	2,00,000	12	1,80,000	12	1,80,000	5,60,000
Variable Factory OH	8	80,000	6	90,000	4	60,000	2,30,000
Variable Selling OH	4	40,000	2	30,000	2	30,000	1,00,000
Total Variable Cost	60	6,00,000	44	6,60,000	34	5,10,000	17,70,000
Contribution	20	200,000	16	240,000	2	30,000	470,000
Fixed Factory OH		80,000		90,000		19,200	1,89,200
Fixed Selling OH		40,000		90,000		22,800	1,52,800
Total Fixed Overheads							3,42,000
Total Profit							128,000

The above analysis shows the cabinets make a contribution of ₹.2 per unit. The loss sustained in the previous year is because of the falling sales volume below breakeven level.

FAIRBILT FURNITURE LTD.

Budgeted Performance for the Coming Year

Particulars	*Tables*	*Chairs*	*Cabinets*
Unit Contribution (₹)	20	16	2
Sales Volume (Units)	11,000	15,000	23,000
Total Contribution (₹)	2,20,000	2,40,000	46,000
Less: Fixed Cost (₹)	1,20,000	1,80,000	42,000
Profit (₹)	1,00,000	60,000	4,000

The company makes a total profit of ₹.1,64,000 if all the products are continued. However, if the production of cabinets is discontinued, there will be an adverse effect on the overall profit of the company. This is because cabinets also contribute toward meeting the fixed costs of the company.

Problem 16. Panchwati Cement Ltd. produces '43 grade' cement for which the company has an assured market. The output for 2004 has been budgeted at 1,80,000 units at 90% capacity utilisation. The cost sheet based on output (per unit) is as follows:

	₹
Selling price	130
Direct material	30
Component 'EH'	9.40
Direct Wages @ ₹ 7 per hour	28
Factory overhead (50% fixed)	24
Selling and distribution overheads (75% variable)	16
Administrative overhead (fixed)	5

The factory overheads are applied on the basis of direct labour hours.

To utilise the idle capacity and to improve the profitability of the company, the following proposals were put up before the Board of Directors for consideration:

(i) An order has been received from abroad for 500 units of product '53 grade' cement per month at ₹ 175 per unit. The cost data are:
Direct material ₹ 56 per unit, Direct Labour 10 hours per unit, selling and distribution overhead application to this product order is ₹ 14 per unit and Variable Factory Overhead are chargeable on the basis of direct labour hours.

(ii) The company at present manufactures component 'EH', one unit of which is required for each unit of product '43 grade'. The cost details for 15,000 units of component 'EH' are as follows:

	₹
Direct materials	30,000
Direct labour	52,500
Variable overheads	25,500
Fixed overheads	33,000
Total	1,41,000

The component 'EH' however is available for purchase at the market at ₹ 7.90 per unit.

(iii) In the event of company deciding to purchase the component 'EH' from market, the company has two alternatives for the use of the capacity so released, which are as under:
(a) Rent out the released capacity at ₹ 1 per hour.
(b) Manufacture component 'GYP' which can be sold at ₹ 8 per unit. The cost data of this component for 15,000 units are:

	₹
Direct materials	42,000
Direct labour	31,500
Factory variable overheads	13,500
Other variable overheads	25,500
Total	1,12,500

Required:

(i) Prepare a statement showing profitability of the company envisaged in the budget.
(ii) Evaluate the export order and state whether it is acceptable or not.
(iii) Make an appraisal of proposal to manufacture component 'EH' and state whether the component 'EH' should be manufactured in the factory or purchased from the market. Assume that no alternative use of spare capacity is available.
(iv) Evaluate the alternative use of the spare capacity and state whether to manufacture or buy the component 'EH' and if your decision is to buy the component 'EH', which of the two alternatives for the use of spare capacity will you prefer?

Solution:

(i) STATEMENT SHOWING PROFITABILITY AS PER ORIGINAL BUDGET

	Particulars	*[₹ in lacs]*
A.	Sales (1,80,000 units × ₹ 130)	234.00
B.	*Less*: Variable Costs:	
	Direct Material (1,80,000 units × ₹ 30)	54.00
	Component 'EH' (Variable cost = ₹ 7.20 per unit)	12.96
	Direct wages (1,80,000 units × ₹ 28)	50.40
	Variable Factory overheads (1,80,000 units × ₹ 24 × 50%)	21.60
	Variable Selling and distribution (1,80,000 units × ₹ 24 × 50%)	21.60
	Total Variable Cost	160.56
C.	Contribution [A – B]	73.44
D	*Less*: Fixed Costs:	
	Fixed Factory Overheads	21.60
	Fixed Selling and Distribution Overheads	7.20
	Component 'EH'@2.20	3.96
	Administrative Overheads	9.00
		41.76
E	Profit [C – D]	31.68

(ii) STETEMENT OF EVALUTION OF EXPORT ORDER

	Particulars	₹
A	Export Order price per unit	175
B	*Less*: Variable Costs:	
	Direct Material	56
	Direct Labour (10 hours × ₹ 7 per hour)	70
	Variable Factory Overhead (₹ 3 × 10 labour hours)	30
	Selling and Distribution Overheads	14
	Total Variable Cost	170
C	Contribution [A – B]	5

Since the product earns contribution of ₹ 5 per unit, it should be accepted.

Total units 500 (per month) = 6000 units per (annum)

Therefore additional contribution (6000 units × ₹ 5) = ₹ 30,000

Total hours on product '43 grade' (1,80,000 units × 4) = 7,20,000 Hrs

Total hours on component 'EH' (1,80,00 units × 0.5*) = 90,000 Hrs

$$\frac{\text{Direct Labour Cost}}{\text{Number of units produced} \times \text{Labour rate per hour}} = \frac{52{,}500}{15{,}000 \text{ units} \times 7 \text{ per hour}} = 0.5 \text{ Hrs}$$

Total hours utilised at 90% capacity = 7,20,000 hours + 90,000 hours = 8,10,000 hours

$$100\% \text{ Capacity Hours} = \frac{8{,}10{,}000 \text{ hours} \times 100}{90} = 9{,}00{,}00 \text{ Hrs}$$

Balance hours available = 90,000 hours p.a

Hours required for export order 60,000 hours.

Decision: Both contribution per unit of export order and availability of capacity confirm its acceptance.

(iii) Component 'EH' make or buy

	Make (₹)	Buy (₹)
Variable cost of mfg. [30,000 + 52500 + 25,500] × 12	12,96,000	—
Cost of Buying		14,22,000
	12,96,000	14,22,000

Decision: If the capacity remains idle it is profitable to make since cost of In-hours manufacturing component is less than that of buying.

(iv) ALTERNATIVE USE OF THE SPARE CAPACITY

	Particulars	Make	Buy if spare capacity is rented out	Buy if share capacity is used for another component
		₹	₹	₹
A	Variable Cost of mfg	12,96,000	—	—
B	Cost of Buying	—	14,22,000	14,22,000
C	Rental Income [90,000 hours × ₹ 1]	—	(90,000)	—
D	Contribution from another component [(90,000 hrs/0.3 × ₹ 0.50]	—	—	(1,50,000)
E	Relevant cost	12,96,000	13,32,000	12,72,000

Recommendation: Component 'EH' should be purchased and spare capacity should be used to manufacture component GYP since it will result in net saving of ₹ 24,000 (i.e. ₹ 12,96,000 – ₹ 12,72,000).

Problem 17. The Officer's Recreation Club of a large public sector undertaking has a cinema theatre for the exclusive use of themselves and their families. It is a bit difficult to get good motion pictures for show and so picture are booked as and when available.

The theatre has been showing the pictures "Blood Bath" for the past two weeks. This picture, which is strictly for adults only has been a great hit and the Manager of the theatre is convinced that the attendance will continue to be above normal for another two weeks, if the show of "Blood Bath is extended. However, another popular movie, eagerly looked forward to by both adults and children alike, "Appu on the Airbus" is booked for next two weeks. Even if "Blood Bath" is extended, the theatre has to pay the regular rental on "Appu on the Airbus" as well.

Normal attendance at the theatre is 2,000 patrons per week, approximately one-fourth of whom are children under the age of 12. Attendance for "Blood Bath" has been 50% greater than the normal total. The manager believes that this would taper off during the second two weeks, 25% below that of the first two weeks, during the third week and 33-1/3% below that of first two weeks, during the fourth week. Attendances for "Apu on the Airbus" would be expected to be normal throughout its run, regardless of the duration.

All runs at the theatre are shown at a regular price of ₹ 2 for adults and ₹ 1.20 for children under 12. The rental charge for "Blood Bath" is ₹ 900 for one week or ₹ 1,500 for two weeks. The rental charge for 'Appu on Air Bus' is ₹ 750 for one week or ₹ 1,200 for two weeks. All other operating costs are fixed ₹ 4,200 per week, except for the cost of potato wafers and cakes, which average 60% of their selling price, sales of potato wafers and cakes, regularly average ₹ 1.20 per patron, regardless of age.

The manager can arrange to show "Blood Bath" for one week and "Appu on the Airbus" for the following week; or he can extend the show of "Blood Bath" for two weeks or else he can show "Appu on the Airbus for two weeks as originally booked.

Required: Show by computation, the most profitable course of action he has to pursue.

Solution

STATEMENT SHOWING THE COMPARATIVE PROFITABILITY OF THREE PROPOSALS

Particulars	*Show "Blood Bath" for second two weeks* ₹	*Show "Appu on the Airbus" for two weeks* ₹	*Show "Blood Bath" for another one week and "Appu On the Airbus" for the following week.* ₹
A. Earnings :			
(a) Sales of tickets			
– Adults @ ₹ 2.00	8,500	6,000	7,500
– Children @ ₹ 1.20	—	1,200	600
(b) Sales of eatable @ ₹ 1.20 per patron	5,100	4,800	5,100
Total earnings (a + b)	13,600	12,000	13,200
B. Incremental costs :			
(a) Rental charges of "Blood Bath"	1,500	—	900
(b) Cost of eatables (60% of selling price) i..e. @ ₹ 0.72 per patron	3,060	2,880	3,060
Total incremental cost (A + B)	4,560	2,880	3,960
C. Incremental Profit [A – B]	9,040	9,120	9,240

Recommendations : It is seen from the above statement that the incremental profit is maximum when both the pictures are shown for one week. The manager of the theatre should show "Blood Bath" for one week and "Appu on the Airbus" for next one week.

Working Notes:

(i) *Calculation of Attendance for Blood Bath*

		Third Week	Fourth Week	Total
Normal attendance Adults	2,000			
50% greater	1,000			
Total	3,000			
Less : Attendance 25% for 3rd week	750	2,250		
Fourth week (3,000 *less* 33 - 1/3% for 4th week)			2000	4,250

(ii) *Calculation of Attendance for Appu on Airbus*

Adult : 75% of Normal attendances [75% of 2000]	1500
Children : 25% of Normal attendance [25% of 2000]	500

Rent for "Appu on the Air bus" is ₹ 750 for one week or ₹ 1,200 for two weeks. This item of expenditure is committed cost as the theatre has to pay rent on this picture even though it is not screened. This cost has not been taken into consideration in arriving at a decision.

(iii) Calculation of Total Attendance

Adults :			
Third week	2,250	1,500	2,250
Fourth week	2,000	1,500	1,500
Total : Adults	4,250	3,000	3,750
Children :			
Third week	—	500	—
Fourth week	—	500	500
Total : Children	—	1,000	500
Grand total (Adult + Children)	4,250	4,000	4,250

Similarly another item of committed cost is operation cost of ₹ 4,200. This is also not relevant in the present decision.

Problem 18. A company manufacturing a highly successful line of cosmetics intends to diversify the product line to achieve fuller utilisation of its plant capacity. As a result of considerable research made, the company has been able to develop a new product called "EMO". EMO is packed in tubes of 50 gram capacity and is sold to the whole sellers in cartons of 24 tubes at ₹ 240 per carton. Since the company uses its spare capacity for the manufacture of EMO, no additional fixed expenses will be incurred. However the cost accountant has allocated a share of ₹ 4,50,000 per month as fixed expenses to be absorbed by EMO as a fair share of the company's present fixed costs to the new product for costing purposes. The company estimates the production and sale of EMO at 3,00,000 tubes per month and on this basis the following cost estimates have been developed:

	₹ per carton
Direct Materials	108
Direct Wages	72
Overheads	54
Total Costs	234

After a detailed market survey the company is confident that the production and sales of EMO can be increased to 3,50,000 tubes per month and ultimately to 4,50,000 tubes per month.

The company at present has a capacity for the manufacture of 3,00,000 empty tubes and the cost of the empty tubes if purchased from outside will result in a saving of 20% in material and 10% in direct wages and variable overhead costs of EMO. The price at which the outside firm is willing to supply the empty tubes is ₹ 1.35 per empty tube. If the company desires to manufacture empty tubes in excess of 3,00,000 tubes, a new machine involving an additional fixed overheads of ₹ 30,000 per month will have to be installed.

Required:

(i) State by showing your workings whether the company should make or buy the empty tubes at each of the three volumes of production of EMO namely, 3,00,000; 3,50,000 and 4,50,000 tubes,

(ii) At what volume of sales will it be economical for the company to install the additional equipment for the manufacture of empty tubes?

(iii) Evaluate the profitability on the sale of EMO at each of the aforesaid three levels of output based on your decision and showing the cost of empty tubes as a separate element of cost.

Solution: **COST OF MANUFACTURING / BUYING OF 300,000 EMPTY TUBES OF EMO**

Particulars	*Empty Tube Cost* ₹	*If Empty Tubes are made* ₹	*If Empty Tubes are purchased* ₹
Direct Materials	0.90	2,70,000	—
Direct Wages	0.30	90,000	—
Variable Overheads	0.075	22,500	—
Purchase Price	1.35	—	4,05,000
Total		3,82,500	4,05,000

Since manufacturing capacity is available for the manufacture of 3,00,000 empty tubes at a cost of ₹ 3,82,500 whereas the total cost of purchase of tubes is higher, i.e., ₹ 4,05,000, the company should manufacture the empty tubes for a production volume of 3,00,000 EMO tubes.

Beyond 3,00,000 empty tubes, the company has to install a new machine involving a total additional fixed overheads of ₹ 30,000. The cost of making and buying the additional tubes 50,000 and 1,50,000 units of empty tubes will be as under :

Additional empty tubes		*50,000 tubes*		*1,50,000 tubes*	
	Per tube ₹	*Make* ₹	*Buy* ₹	*Make* ₹	*Buy* ₹
Direct materials	0.90	45,000		1,35,000	—
Direct wages	0.30	15,000		45,000	—
Variable overheads	0.075	3,750		11,250	—
Additional overheads		30,000		30,000	—
Purchase price	1.35	—	67,500	—	2,02,500
Total		93,750	67,500	2,21,250	2,02,500

The above statement shows that the cost of buying additional empty tubes at both the levels is lower than the cost of their manufacture. Therefore, if the company increases production to 3,50,000 tubes of EMO, 3,00,000 tubes should be made in the factory and additional 50,000 tubes should be purchased at ₹ 67,500.
If the company increases production to 4,50,000 tubes of EMO, 3,00,000 empty tubes should be made in the factory and additional 1,50,000 tubes should be purchased at a cost of ₹ 2,02,500.

(ii) Additional fixed overheads to be incurred on a new machine: ₹ 30,000. Savings per unit if empty tubes are made in the factory instead of buying: ₹ 1.35 - ₹ 1.275 = ₹ .075

Minimum additional quantity of empty tubes to be made to recover the additional fixed costs:

$$\frac{30,000}{0.075} = 4,00,000 \text{ empty tubes}$$

Thus the company should sell 3,00,000 + 4,00,000 = 7,00,000 tubes of EMO per month to warrant justification for the installation of the new machine for the manufacture of empty tubes.

(iii) EVALUATION OF THE PROFITABILITY ON SALE OF EMO AT THE THREE LEVELS

Particulars	*Per tube* ₹	*3,00,000 tubes* ₹	*3,50,000 tubes* ₹	*4,50,000 tubes* ₹
Sales (₹ 240/24 tubes)	10	30,00,000	35,00,000	45,00,000
Direct Materials	3.60	10,80,000	12,60,000	16,20,000
Direct Wages	2.70	8,10,000	9,45,000	12,15,000
Variable Overheads	0.675	2,02,500	2,36,250	3,03,750
Empty Tubes made	1.275	3,82,500	3,82,500	3,82,500
Empty Tubes purchased	1.35	—	67,500	2,02,500
Total Costs		24,75,000	28,91,250	37,23,750
Profit		5,25,000	6,08,750	7,76,250

Working notes:

(i) Variable Overheads per tube ₹
Overheads per tube ₹ 54/24 tubes = 2.25
Fixed overheads allocated for 3,00,000 tubes: ₹ 4,50,000
Fixed overheads per tube = (₹ 4,50,000/3,00,000) = ₹ 1.50
Variable Overheads per tube = ₹ 2.25 – ₹ 1.50 = ₹ 0.75.

(ii) Direct wages per tube = ₹ 72/24 tubes = ₹ 3

(iii) Direct materials per tube = ₹ 108/24 tubes = ₹ 4.50

(iv) Cost of making one empty tube:

Particulars	Cost per tube of EMO ₹	Costs in respect of empty tube ₹	Cost of empty tube ₹	Cost per tube of EMO without empty tube ₹
Direct Materials	4.50	20	0.90	3.60
Direct Wages	3.00	10	0.30	2.70
Variable Overheads	0.75	10	0.075	0.675
	8.25		1.275	6.975

Problem 19. CARCARE CORPORATION has just today paid for and installed a special machine for polishing cars at one of its prestigious outlets. It is the first day of the company's fiscal year.

The machine costs ₹ 20,000. Its annual operating costs total ₹ 15,000 exclusive of 'depreciation. The machine will have a four-year useful life and a zero terminal disposal value.

After the machine has been used for one day, a machine salesman walks in. He offers a different machine that promises to do the same job at a yearly operating cost of ₹.9,000, exclusive of depreciation. The new machine will cost ₹ 24,000 in cash, duly installed. The "old" machine is unique and can be sold outright for only ₹ 10,000 *minus* ₹ 2,000 removal cost. The new machine, like the old one, will have a four-year useful life and zero terminal disposal value.

For simplicity, ignore income taxes interest and present value considerations.

Sales, all in cash, will be ₹ 1,50,000 annually and other cash costs will be ₹ 1,10,000 annually, regardless of this decision.

Required:

(a) Prepare a statement of cash receipts and disbursements for each of the four years under both alternatives. What is the cumulative difference in cash flows for the four years taken together?

(b) Prepare Income Statements for each of the four years under both alternatives. Assume straight line depreciation. What is the cumulative difference in operating income for the four years taken together?

(c) What are the irrelevant items in your presentations in requirements (a) and (b)? Why are they irrelevant?

(d) Suppose the cost of the "old" machine was ₹ 10,00,000 rather than ₹ 20,000. Nevertheless, the old machine can be sold outright for only ₹ 10,000 minus ₹.2,000 removal cost. Would the net differences in requirements (a) and (b) change? Explain.

(e) "To avoid a loss, we should keep the old machine." What is the role of book value in decisions about replacement of machines?

Solution:

(a) STATEMENT OF CASH RECEIPTS, DISBURSEMENTS AND CUMULATIVE DIFFERENCE IN CASH FLOWS FOR FOUR YEARS TAKEN TOGETHER UNDER BOTH ALTERNATIVES

(₹ In thousands)

Particulars	*Keep Old Machine*			*Buy New Machine*			
	Year 1	*2nd, 3rd and 4th each year*	*All 4 years*	*Year 1*	*2nd, 3rd and 4th each year*	*All 4 years*	*Cumulative difference in cash flows for four years taken together*
A. Total Receipts:							
Sales, Revenue	150	150	600	150	150	600	
Sale old equipment	—	—	—	8	—	8	
Total Receipts:	150	150	600	158	150	608	
B. Total Disbursements							
Annual Operating Cost	15	15	60	9	9	36	
Other cash costs	110	110	440	110	110	440	
Purchase cost of "old" machine	20	—	20	20	—	20	
Purchase of "new" machine	—	—	—	24	—	24	
Total Disbursements	145	125	520	163	119	520	
C. Net Cash in-flows: (A) – (B)	5	25	80	(5)	31	88	08

INCOME FOR EACH OF THE FOUR YEARS AND CUMULATIVE DIFFERENCE IN OPERATING INCOME

(₹ In thousands)

Particular	*Keep Old Machine*		*Buy New Machine*			*Cumupative difference in operating income*
	1st, 2nd, 3rd and 4th each year	*All 4 years*	*year 1*	*2nd, 3rd and 4th each year*	*All 4 years*	
A. Sale Revenue	150	600	150	150	600	
B. *Less* costs:						
Annual Operating Cost	15	60	9	9	36	
Other Cash Costs	110	440	110	110	440	
Depreciation	5	20	6	6	24	
Loss on the disposal of old machine	—	—	12	—	12	
	130	520	137	125	512	
C. Operating Income: (A) – (B)	20	80	13	25	88	08

(c) The purchase cost of old machine ₹ 20,000; the sale revenue ₹ 1,50,000 and other cash costs of ₹ 1,10,000 as irrelevant items for the presentation in requirements (a) and (b) above. These items are irrelevant because their amounts are common to both the alternatives.

(d) The net difference in requirements under (a) and (b) will not change if the cost of 'old' machine becomes ₹ 10,00,000 instead of ₹ 20,000. This is so because the cost of old machine is common for both the alternatives.

(d) In the decision about the replacement of machine the book value of the machine is irrelevant because it is a past (historical) cost. All past costs are down the drains. Nothing can change what has already happened. As apparent from (a) and (b) above; we can completely ignore the cost of old machine i.e. ₹ 20,000 and still have a correct analysis.

Working note:

(i) Depreciation as per SLM = (Cost – Terminal value) / Useful life
On Old Machine = (₹ 20,000 – 0)/4 = ₹ 5,000
On New Machine = (₹ 24,000 – 0)/4 = ₹ 6,000

(ii) Loss on the disposal of old machine = ₹ 20,000 – (₹ 10,000 – ₹ 2,000) = ₹ 12,000

Problem 20. A businessman-employs 20 swing machinists, but he is aware that ten are the better workers than others. He is considering to conduct a training programme for his ten less efficient mechanists to increase their efficiency to be equal to that achieved by "better" workers. Relevant data are as follows;

- There is one sewing machine for each machinist.
- All the machinists are engaged on similar work and are paid Rs2.20 each good garment produced on piece work system.
- To rectify each rejected garment costs ₹ 4, this work is done by subcontractor.
- Garment machining department operates 2,000 hours a year.
- Average output per machinist (on the basis of all 20 machinists) is 12 good garments with one rejected per worker per hour. However 10 less efficient machinists' averages only 10 good garments with 1.5 rejected per worker per hour.
- Depreciation of each sewing machine is Rs10,000 per year and the variable cost of power, cleaning and preventive maintenance is ₹ 5 per hour per machine.
- Fixed production overhead other than depreciation is ₹ 20 per machine hour.
- Selling price per garment is Rs18.
- Direct material cost per garment is ₹ 12.
- Training will not reduce productive hours.
- There is no problem in selling increased output.

You are required

(a) To prepare a statement of comparative costs for the "better" worker and the "less efficient" workers excluding material costs.

(b) To find out the benefit derived over a one year period, if Rs1,00,000 is spent on a training course for the "less efficient" workers to match the efficiency with the "better" workers.

Solution:

(a) Average output of all 20 machinist is 12 good units and 1 rejected piece while average output of 10 "less efficient' workers is 10 good units and 1.5 rejected pieces. Hence average output of 10 "better worker" is 14 good units and 0.5 rejected piece.

STATEMENT SHOWING ANNUAL COMPARATIVE COST FOR THE "BETTER MACHINIST" AND THE "LESS EFFICIENT' MACHINIST EXCLUDING DIRECT MATERIAL COST.

Particulars	*Better*	*Less Worker Efficient worker*
Good Units		
(14 × 2,000 × 10 efficient workers)	2,80,000	
(10 × 2,000 × 10 less efficient worker)		2,00,000
Rejects after correction		
(2,000 hrs × 0.5 × 10)	10,000	
(2,000 hrs × 1.5 × 10)		30,000
Labour cost		
(2,80,000 × 2.20)	6,16,000	
(2,00,000 × 2.20)		4,40,000
Rectification Cost		
(10,000 × 4)	40,000	
(30,000 × 4)		120000
Variable Production Cost (2000 × 5 × 10)	1,00,000	1,00,000
Total Variable Cost (Excluding Direct Material Cost)	7,56,000	6,60,000

(b) **STATEMENT OF BENEFIT FROM TRAINING**

A. Sales		
(2,90,000 × 18)	52,20,000	
(2,30,000 × 18)		41,40,000
B. *Less:* Variable costs:		
Direct Material		
(2,90,000 × 12)	34,80,000	
(2,30,000 × 12)		27,60,000
Variable Cost as per (a)	7,56,000	6,60,000
	42,36,000	34,20,000
C. Contribution [A – B]	9,84,000	7,20,000

D. Benefit from training = Increase in contribution After training – Cost of training
= (₹ 9,84,000 – ₹ 7,20,000) – ₹ 1,00,000 = ₹ 1,64,000

Problem 21. A company operates its plant on single shift basis. It can produce upto 8,000 units of output per month without overtime. The fixed costs on single shift basis of operation amount to ₹ 30,000 per month. The average variable cost per unit is ₹ 10.

The output can be increased upto 15,000 units per month by working overtime. This entails no increase in fixed costs, but the variable costs per unit during overtime will be ₹ 12 in excess 8,000 units upto the capacity of 75, 000 units.

If a second shift is worked, the maximum capacity of the second shift is 8,000 units per month. The variable cost on second shift operation is ₹ 10.50 per unit and the incremental fixed : cost involved in the second shift is ₹ 6,000 per month.

Required:

(i) If the company's demand for the product is 10,000 units, should the company work overtime or second shift?

(ii) At what level of output will the company consider working second shift instead of working overtime? State the range of output for overtime working and second shift operation.

(iii) During a particular month, the company predicted its demand to be 14,000 units and worked second shift. At the end of the month it was discovered that the company's demand was only 11,000 units and the company accordingly produced only 11,000 units. Calculate the cost of prediction error.

Solution:

(I) COMPARATIVE STATEMENT OF COST
(when demand for the product is 10,000 units)

Particulars	*Working overtime for producing 2,000 units*	*Working second shift for producing 2,000 units*
Variable Cost	24,000	21,000
Fixed Cost	NIL	6,000
Total Cost	24,000	27,000

* 8000 units in fact are produced in the single shift.

Decision: Resorting to overtime for producing additional 2,000 units and 8,000 units in the single shift will be beneficial to the extent of ₹ 3,000 (i.e., ₹ 27,000 – ₹ 24,000)

[ii) Range of output for overtime working and second shift operation:

Let X be the number of units at which their total cost under overtime working and second shift operation equalises, i.e. X units × ₹ 12 + ₹ 30,000 = X units × ₹ 10.50 + ₹ 36,000

On solving the above relation we get X = 4,000 units.

Range	*Method to be adopted*
Above 8,000 units but less than 12,000 units	Overtime working
At 12,000 units	Any one method may be adopted
12,001 to 16,000 units	Second shift working

(iii) Computation of Prediction Error:

COST STATEMENT OF PRODUCING 11,000 UNITS

Particulars	*Options*	
	Working overtime for producing 3000 additional units ₹	*Working second shift for producing 3,000 additional units* ₹
Cost of Producing 8,000 units in first shift {8,000 units × ₹ 10 + ₹ 30,000}	1,10,000	1,10,000
Additional cost of producing 3,000 units	36,000 (3,000 units × ₹ 12)	37,500 (3,000 units × ₹ 10.50 + ₹ 6,000)
Total Cost	1,46,000	1,47,500

Prediction error: A comparison of total cost of producing 11,000 units under overtime working and second shift working clearly shows a difference of ₹ 1,500 (₹ 1,47,500 – ₹ 1,46,000). The difference of ₹ 1,500 is due to prediction error.

Problem 22. A Ltd produces and markets a range of consumer durable appliances. It ensures after sales service through X Ltd. The big appliances are serviced at customer's residence while small appliances are serviced at workshop of X Ltd

The material supplied to X Ltd. is charged at cost at 10%. X Ltd. charges customers at 25% over the above price. For labour, the company receives 10% of the rate fixed for work done under the after-sales service agreement and 15% of the rate fixed in case of jobs not covered under the agreement from X Ltd. 60% by value of the total work undertaken by X Ltd was for big appliances and rest accounted for small appliances during the previous year.

The company decides to carry out all or some of the work itself and has chosen one area in the first instance. During the previous year the company earned a profit of ₹ 2,16,000 as detailed below from X Ltd. for the area chosen:

	Material ₹	*Labour ₹*
Under after-sales service agreement	60,000	1,00,000
For jobs not covered under the agreement	20,000	36,000

The company forecasts same volume of work in that area for the ensuing period. The following three options are under consideration of the management:

(1) To set up a local service centre to provide service for small appliances only. The existing system is to continue for big appliances.
(2) To set up a local service centre to provide service for big appliances only. The existing system is to continue for small appliances.
(3) To set up a local service centre to provide service to all appliances. The existing system then stands withdrawn.

The relevant costs for carrying out jobs under the above options are as under:

	(₹ '000')		
	Option-1	*Option-2*	*Option-3*
Heat, rent light etc.	125	50	150
Management costs	108	83	150
Service staff costs	230	440	750
Transport costs	25	220	230

You are required to find out the most profitable option.

Solution:

STATEMENT SHOWING VALUE OF TOTAL WORK UNDERTAKEN BY X LTD. AT CUSTOMER'S PRICE

Particualrs	*(₹ '000)*
Material Cost (for appliances covered under agreement)	825
Material Cost (for appliances not covered under agreement)	275
Labour Cost (for appliances covered under agreement)	1,000
Labour Cost (for appliances not covered under agreement)	240
Total Receipts	2,340

Break up of receipts:		
Big appliances	60%	1,404
Small appliances	40%	936

PROFITABILITY STATEMENT

(₹ '000')

Particulars	*Option 1*	*Option 2*	*Option 3*
A. Revenue:			
Big appliancoo	129.6 (60% x ₹ 216)	1,404	1,404
Small appliances	936	86.4 (40% x ₹ 216)	936
	1,065.6	1,490.4	2,340
B. Costs:			
Material	320 (40% x (825+275)	480 60% x (825 + 275)	800 (825 + 275)
	137.5%	137.5%	137.5%
Heat, Rent, Light etc.	125	50	150
Management Costs	108	83	150
Service Staff Costs	230	440	750
Transport Costs	25	220	230
Total Costs:	808	1,273	2,080
C. Profit [A – B]	257.6	217.4	260

Recommendation: Option 3 is most profitable one,

Working Notes:

(i) Material and labour cost (for appliances under after sales agreement): ₹

(i) Cost of Material per unit charged to customer's by X Ltd. [100 × 110% × 125%] 137.50

Cost of material charged to customer's by X Ltd.

$\left(\frac{60{,}000}{10}\right) \times 137.50$ 8,25,000

(ii) Cost of labour charged to customer by X Ltd.

$\left(\frac{1{,}00{,}000}{10}\right) \times 100$ 10,00,000

(ii) Material and Labour cost (for appliances not covered under sales agreement): ₹

Cost of material charged to customer by X Ltd.

$\left(\frac{20{,}000}{10}\right) \times 137.50$ 2,75,000

Cost of labour charged to customer by X Ltd.

$\left(\frac{36{,}000}{15}\right) \times 100$ 2,40,000

Problem 23. K. Ltd. manufactures and sells a range effort goods. Management is considering a proposal for an advertising campaign, which would cost the company ₹ 3,00,000. The marketing department has put forward the following two alternative sales budgets for the following year.

	Product ('000 units)			
	A	*B*	*C*	*D*
Budget 1-Without Advertising	216	336	312	180
Budget – 2 With Advertising	240	372	342	198

Selling prices and variable production costs are budgeted as follow:

	Product (₹ Per unit)			
	A	B	C	D
Selling prices	11.94	14.34	27.54	23.94
Variable Production Costs:				
Direct material	5.04	6.60	15.24	12.48
Direct Labour	2.04	2.04	3.36	3.18
Variable overheads	0.72	0.72	1.20	1.08

Other Data:

(1) The variable overheads are absorbed on a machine hour basis at a rate of ₹ 1.20 per machine hour,

(2) Fixed overheads total ₹ 30,84,000 per annum.

(3) Production capacity during the budget period 8,15,000 machine hours.

(4) Products A and C could be bought in at ₹ 10.68 per unit and ₹ 24 per unit respectively.

Required:

(i) Determine whether investment in the advertising campaign would be worthwhile and how production facilities would be best utilised.

(ii) Explain the assumptions and reasoning behind your advise. ***(May 1996)***

Solution

STATEMENT OF PRODUCT RANKING AND MACHINE HOURS REQUIRED UNDER BUDGET-1 AND BUDGET-2

Particulars	*Products*				*Total*
	A	*B*	*C*	*D*	
Selling Price (₹)	11.94	14.34	27.54	23.94	
Less: Variable cost (₹)	7.80	9.36	19.80	16.74	
Contribution (₹)	4.14	4.98	7.74	7.20	
Time in machine (Hrs.)	0.6	0.6	1	0.9	
	$\left(\frac{0.72}{1.20}\right)$	$\left(\frac{0.72}{1.20}\right)$	$\left(\frac{1.20}{1.20}\right)$	$\left(\frac{1.08}{1.20}\right)$	
Contribution per machine hour (₹)	6.9	3.3	7.79	8	
Ranking	IV	I	III	II	
Budget-I (Mc. Mrs.) (without Advt.)	1,29,600	2,01,600	3,12,000	1,62,000	8,05,200
Budget –2 (Mc.Hrs.) (with Advt.)	1,44,000	2,23,200	3,42,000	1,78,200	8,87,400

Available budget hours viz. 8,15,000 hours are sufficient for Budget-1. However there is a shortfall of 72,400 hours (8,87,400 – 8,15,000) to meet Budget-2, targets. These additional machine hours requirement may be met by way of purchasing either additional units of product A or C, so that the extra cost of buying machine hours is minimum.

Products	*A*	*C*
Additional buying in cost p.u. (₹)	2.88 (₹ 10.68 – ₹ 7.80)	4.20 (₹ 24 – ₹ 19.80)
Additional buying cost p.u. per machine hour(₹)	4.80 (₹ 2.88/0.6 hrs.)	4.20 (₹.4.20/1hr.)

Since additional buying cost per machine hour is minimum in the case of production C, therefore it is advisable to purchase 72,400 units of product C and thus meet fully the gap in the machine hours requirement i.e. 72,400. The extra cost of buying 72,400 machine hours wouid come to ₹ 3,04,080 (72,400 hours × ₹ 4.20)

(i) EVALUATION OF INVESTMENT IN ADVERTISEMENT CAMPAIGN

	Products				*Total*
	A	*B*	*C*	*D*	
A. Additional sales volume ('000 units):	24	36	30	18	
B. Unit Contribution (₹):	4.14	4.98	7.74	7,20	
C. Additional Contribution (₹, '000): (B × A)	99.36	179.28	232.20	129.60	640.44
Less: Extra machine buying cost (₹.'000)	—	—	—	—	304.08
Less: Cost of advertisement (₹.'000)					300.00
Additional Profit					36.36

The generation of additional profit clearly shows that the investment in advertisement campaign is worthwhile.

STATEMENT OF PRODUCTION FACILITIES UTILISATION

Product	*Machine hours utilised*
A	1,44,000
B	2,23,200
C	2,69,600
D	1,78,000
Total	8,15,000

(ii) Assumptions:

1. Fixed costs (other than advertising) will remain unchanged.
2. Variable cost has linear relationship with the volume of production.
3. Prices and efficiency will remain unchanged at all levels of output.
4. Sales estimates are sound.

Reasoning: The reasoning behind the above advice is based on the fact that the additional revenue exceeds the additional relevant costs and the costs are minimised by buying in product C.

Problem 24. SWEET DREAMS LTD. manufactures and markets three products A, Band C in the State of Haryana and Rajasthan. At the end of first half of year I the following absorption based profit statement has been drawn by the accountant

(₹ In '000)

		Haryana	*Rajasthan*	*Total*
Sales		3,000	900	3,900
Manufacturing Cost of Sales		2,331	699	3,030
Gross Profit		669	201	870
Administration Expenses	(A)	120	36	156
Selling Expenses	(B)	184	169	353
Total Expenses		304	205	509
Net Profit		365	(4)	361

(A) The expenses are constant and common to both the States. They stand allocated on th$ basis of sales.
(B) The expenses are semi-fixed but specifically relate to the respective State,

The management is worried to note that the decision taken to market the products in Rajasthan to utilise idle capacity has proved wrong and wish to cover only Haryana State. The incharge marketing division is not satisfied with the above way of profit presentation. He is of the firm opinion that sales effected in the State of Rajasthan is contributing profits. For the next half year he expects no increase in demand in Haryana while for Rajasthan he anticipates to sell B or C more by 50% of existing sales. This will utilise the idle capacity in full.

The product-wise relevant details for the first half of year I are:

	A	*B*	*C*
Sales (in ₹ '000):			
Haryana	1,200	900	900
Rajasthan	300	300	300
Variable Costs (as a % on sales):			
Manufacturing	40	35	30
Selling	3	2	2
Specific fixed manufacturing expenses (in ₹ '000)	570	470	610

You are required to:

(a) Prepare a State-wise profit statement for the first half of year I using contribution approach. Also offer your views on the contention of the management and opinion expressed by incharge marketing division.
(b) Prepare a productwise profit statement for the' same period using contribution approach.
(c) Submit your well thought out' recommendation as to which product should be produced to utilise idle capacity. ***(Nov 1996)***

Solution

(a) STATE WISE PROFIT STATEMENT FOR THE FIRST HALF OF YEAR I USING CONTRIBUTION APPROACH

(₹ '000)

	Particulars	*Haryana*	*Rajasthan*	*Total*
A.	Sales:	3,000	900	3,900
B.	Variable Costs:			
	Manufacturing	1,065	315	1,380

	Selling:	72	21	93
	Total:	1,137	336	1,473
C.	Contribution: [A – B]	1,863	564	2,427
D.	Specified fixed cost: (Manufacturing)	1,266	384	1,650
	Selling	112	148	260
	Total:	1,378	532	1,910
E.	Net Contribution: [C – D]	485	32	517
F.	*Less*: Common fixed costs (Administration)			156
			361	
G.	P/V Ratio (in%) (C/S × 100)	62.1	62.87	62.23

Views: The contention of the management is not valid i.e. the state of Rajasthan shows ₹.32,000 as contribution to meet the common fixed costs. In case only Haryana state is covered the net profit of the concern would go down from ₹.3,61,000 to ₹.3,29,000.

In view of the above position, the statement made by the incharge of the marketing division appears to be correct.

(b) PRODUCTWISE PROFIT STATEMENT FOR THE FIRST HALF OF YEAR I USING CONTRIBUTION APPROACH

(Fig in ₹ '000)

	Production	*A*	*B*	*C*	*Total*
A.	Total Sales of Haryana and Rajasthan	1,500	1,200	1,200	3,900
B.	*Less:* Variable Cost:				
	Manufacturing:				
	((1500 × 40%)				
	(1200 × 35%)				
	(1200 × 30%)	600	420	360	1,380
	Selling:				
	(1500 × 3%)				
	(1200 × 2%)				
	(1200 × 2%)	45	24	24	93
	Total:	645	444	384	1,473
C.	Contribution: [A – B]	855	756	816	2,427
D.	Specified Fixed Cost:				
	Manufacturing	570	470	610	1,650
	Selling	100	80	80	260
	Total:	670	550	690	1,910
E.	Net Contribution: D – E]	185	206	126	517
F.	*Less*: Common Fixed Adm. Exp.				156
G.	Net Profit				361
H.	P/V ratio (Contribution/Sales) × 100	57%	63%	68%	62.23%

(c) Recommendation for utilising idle capacity:

A review of the above P/V ratio's shows that the increase of output of product C in Rajasthan is the best. The increase of production after utilising the idle capacity in Rajasthan to the extent of ₹.1,50,000 (i.e. 50% of ₹.3,00,000) would increase the contribution of the company in the state of Rajasthan by ₹.I.02,000 (68% × ₹.I.50,000).

Working Notes:

(i) VARIABLE MANUFACTURING AND SELLING COSTS (IN ₹ '000):

Product	Sales		Mfg. Costs			Selling Costs		
	Haryana	Rajasthan	% of Sales	Haryana	Rajasthan	%of Sales	Haryana	Rajasthan
A	1,200	300	40	480	120	3	36	9
B	900	300	35	315	105	2	18	6
C	900	300	30	270	90	2	18	6
Total:				1.065	315		72	21

(ii) SPECIFIED FIXED EXPENSES (IN ₹ '000):

Particulars	Manufacturing			Selling		
	Haryana	Rajasthan	Total	Haryana	Rajasthan	Total
A. Total Manufacturing Cost of sales	2,331	699	3,030	184	169	353
B. *Less*: Variable Mfg & Selling Costs	1,065	315	1,380	72	21	93
C. Specified Fixed Cost [A – B]	1,266	384	1,650	112	148	260

(iii) PRODUCTWISE SPECIFIED FIXED SELLING EXPENSES (IN ₹ '000):

	Total	A	B	C
Fixed selling expenses of Haryana and Rajasthan apportioned in proportion of their sales, viz., (15 : 12 : 12)	260	100	80	80

Problem 25. A Company manufactures two products 'X' and T. Company's fixed cost per annum is ₹ 5 lacs. These products are sold for ₹ 288 per unit of 'X' and ₹ 432 per unit of Y. Standard cost data are:

	Product 'X' ₹	Product 'Y' ₹
Direct Raw Material	40	80
Direct wages ₹ 8 per hour in Departments:		
1	48	72
2	24	48
3	72	–
4	–	96
Variable overhead	32	28

The Company operates 8 hours shift for 300 days in a year. Number of workers engaged by each department is given below:

Department	1	2	3	4
No. of Workers	45	24	27	36

Required:

(a) How many units of each product should be manufactured and what is the resultant maximum profit, if numbers of employees cannot be increased or transferred?

(b) If only one product is to be manufactured by the Company, which of the products would give the maximum profit and what is the amount of such profit?

Solution

CONTRIBUTION ANALYSIS

Particulars		*Product X* ₹	*Product Y* ₹
A. Selling Price		288	432
B. Variable Costs:			
Direct materials		40	80
Direct Labour:	Dep't. 1	48	72
	Dep't. 2	24	48
	Dep't. 3	72	–
	Dep't. 4	–	96
Variable Overheads		32	28
Total Variable Costs		216	324
C. Contribution per unit [A – B]		72	108

The direct labour hours required to manufacture the two products in each of the four departments at the wage rate of ₹ 8 per hour are as under:

Department	*Product X*		*Product Y*	
	Wage cost	*Hours/unit*	*Wage cost*	*Hours/unit*
1	48	6	72	9
2	**24**	**3**	**48**	**6**
3	72	9	–	–
4	–	–	96	12

Department 3 is used only for product X and department 4 is used only for product Y. Hence, these two departments will determine the maximum production of these two products as under:

Department 3: Maximum available hours = Workers x Hours/day x days/year
= 27 x 8 x 300 = 64,800 hours

Maximum possible production of product X: $\frac{64,000}{9 \text{ hrs per unit}}$ = 7,200 units

Department 4: Maximum available hours = Workers x Hours/day x days/year
= 36 x 8 x 300 = 86,400 hours

Maximum possible production of product Y: $\frac{86,400}{12 \text{ hrs per unit}}$ = 7,200 units

The company can produce 7,200 units each of products X and Y provided departments 1 and 2 have capacity to process this quantity of output.

We can check the capacity of departments land 2 as under:

Department 1: Maximum available hours = Workers x Hours/day x days/year
= 45 x 8 x 300 = 1,08,000 hours

Hours required to produce 7,200 units each of X and Y:

Product X = 7,200 x 6 hours = 43,200 hours
Product Y = 7,200 x 9 hours = 64,800 hours
Total = 1,08,000 hours

Department 1 has capacity to produce 7,200 units each of products X and Y.

Department 2: Maximum available hours = Workers x Hours/day x days/year
= 24 x 8 x 300 = 57,600 hours

Hours required to produce 7,200 units each of X and Y:

Product X = 7,200 x 3 hours = 21,600 hours
Product Y = 7,200 x 6 hours = 43,200 hours
Total = 64,800 hours

Department 2 has scarce capacity.

Since department 2 capacity is scarce, link the contribution to the key factor of department 2 hours as under:

		Product X	Product Y
Contribution per unit		72	108
Department 2 hours per unit	Hours	3	6
Contribution per hour of Department 2	₹	24	18
Rank		1	2

Optimal Product Mix:

Product	*Max. units*	*Lab. Hours/unit*	*Prod. units*	*Hours used*	*Balance hours*	*Cont./unit ₹*	*Total cont. ₹*
X	7,200	3	7,200	21,600	36,000	72	5,18,400
Y	7,200	6	6,000	36,000	–	108	6,48,000
Total Optimal Contribution							11,66,400
Fixed costs							5,00,000
Optimal Profit							6,66,400

Alternative Solution:

The maximum possible production of product X is 7,200 units and that of product Y is 7,200 units. The following two methods shall be used to determine the optimal profit:

(a) Produce 7,200 units of product X and use the balance capacity to produce product Y.

(b) Produce 7,200 units of product Y and use the balance capacity to produce product X.

Profitability based on (a):

Direct labour hours are scarce in Department 2.		
Maximum available hours in Department 2		57,600
Product X requires 7,200 x 3 =		21,600 hours
Balance hours on Y		36,000
Production of Y 36,000 ÷ 6 =		6,000 units
Contribution:	X 7,200 units @ ₹ 72	₹ 5,18,400
	Y 6,000 units @ ₹ 108	₹ 6,48,000
	Total	₹ 11,66,400
	Fixed costs	₹ 5,00,000
	Profit	₹ 6,66,400

Profitability based on (b):

Maximum available hours in Department 2		57,600
Product Y requires 7,200 x 6 =		43,200 hours
Balance hours on x		14,400
Production of x 14,400 ÷ 3 =		4,800 units
Contribution:	x 4,800 x 72	₹ 3,45,600
	Y 7,200 x 108	₹ 7,77,600
	Total	₹ 11,23,200
	Fixed costs	₹ 5,00,000
	Profit	₹ 6,23,200

Profitability of (a) is better.

Problem 26. A firm furnishes the following information:

Capacity in Unit	*Unit Cost* ₹	*Unit Price* ₹
2,000	40	100
3,000	35	95
4,000	34	94
5,000	32	–
6,000	31	–

At present the firm is operating at 4,000 units capacity and has received an order for 2,000 units from an export market at ₹ 28 per unit. Should the order be accepted? *(May 2000)*

Solution

STATEMENT OF INCREMENT COST AND INCREMENTAL REVENUE

Capacity in units (a)	*Unit cost ₹ (b)*	*Total cost ₹ (c) = (a) × (b)*	*Incremental cost ₹ (d)*	*Unit price ₹*	*Total Revenue (a) × (e)*	*Incremental Revenue ₹ ₹ (f)- (g)*
200	40	80,000	–	100	2,00,000	–
3000	35	1,05,000	25,000	95	2,85,000	85,000 (₹
4000	34	1,36,000	31,000	94	3,76,000	91,000
5000	32	1,60,000	24,000	–	–	
6000	31	1,86,000	26,000	–	–	

Decision: At 4,000 units capacity told sales revenue is ₹ 3,76,000 and the total cost is ₹ 1,36,000 leaving a profit of ₹ 2,40,000. The profit figure at this level clearly shows that the fixed expenses stand fully recovered. Hence, we have to take incremental cost for further levels of output. For an additional sales of 2,000 units incremental cost is ₹ 50,000 (₹ 1,86,000 – ₹, 1,36,000) and the cost per unit is ₹ 25 $\left(\frac{50,000}{2,000 \text{ units}}\right)$

Since the price quoted per unit is ₹ 28, which is more than ₹ 25, therefore, the order should be accepted.

Problem 27. A Company produces three products from an imported material. The Cost Structure per unit of the products are as under:

	Product		
	A ₹	*B* ₹	*C* ₹
Sales Value	200	300	250
Direct Material	50	80	60
Direct Wages ₹ 6 per hour	60	120	108
Variable Overheads	30	60	54

Out of Direct Material 80% is of the Imported material @ ₹ 10 per kg.

Prepare a statement showing comparative Profitability of the three products under the following scenarios.

(i) Imported Material is in restricted supply.

(ii) Production Capacity is limiting factor.

(iii) When maximum sales potential of products A and B are 1,000 units each and that of product 'C' is 500 units for specific requirement, availability of imported material is restricted to 10.000 kgs per month, how the profit could be maximised? ***(Nov 1997)***

Solution

(i) STATEMENT OF PROFITABILITY

Particulars	*Product A*	*Product B*	*Product C*
A. Sales Value p.u. (₹):	200	300	250
B. Direct Material (₹)	50	80	60
Direct Wages (₹)	60 (10 hrs.x 6)	120 ₹ (20 hrs. x ₹ 6)	108 (18 hrs.x ₹.6)
Variable Overheads (₹)	30	60	54
Total Variable Cost (₹):	140	260	222
C. Contribution p.u. (₹): [A – B]	60	40	28
D. P/V Ratio: $\left(\frac{C}{S} \times 100\right)$	30%	13.33%	11.2%
E. Contribution per kg. of Imported Material (₹)	15	6.25	5.83
F. Contribution per hour of Production (₹)	6 (₹.60/10 hrs.)	2 (₹.40/20 hrs.)	1.6 (₹.28/18 hrs.)

(i) When imported material is in restricted supply then product 'A' is most profitable as its contribution pre kilogram is maximum.

(ii) Even when production capacity is limited, product 'A' is the most profitable one.

(iii) STATEMENT FOR MAXIMISED PROFIT

Particulars	*Product A*	*Product B*	*Product C*
Maximum sales (units)	1,000	1,000	500
Requirement of imported material per unit (kg)	4	6.4	4.8
Total requirement of imported material for maximum sales (kg)	4,000	6,400	2,400
Contribution per kg (₹)	15	6.25	5.83
For maximising profit 10,000 kg of imported material is to be used for manufacturing those products where contribution per kg is maximum. But 500 units of C must be produced to meet specific requirement. Hence the material utilised will be (kg)	4,000	3,600	2,400
No. of units	1,000	562	500
Maximum profit (₹)	60,000	22,480	14,000

Working Note:

Value of imported and indigenous material and quantity of imported material consumed p.u.

Products	*A*	*B*	*C*
Value of imported material p.u. (₹)	40	64	48
Value of indigenous material p.u. (₹)	10	16	12
Quantity of imported material consumed p.u. (kg)	4	6.4	4.8

Problem 28. X Ltd. has two factories, one at Lucknow and another at Pune producing 7,200 tonnes and 10,800 tonnes of a product against the maximum production capacity of 9,000 and 11,880 tonnes respectively at Lucknow and Pune.

10% of the raw material introduced is lost in the production process. The maximum quantity of raw material, available locally are 6,000 and 13,000 tonnes at ₹ 720 and ₹ 729 per tonne at Lucknow and Pune respectively. For the additional needs a supplier of Bhopal is ready to supply raw material at our factory site at ₹ 792 per tonne.

Other variable costs of the production process are ₹ 22.32 lacs and ₹ 32.94 lacs and fixed costs are ₹ 18 lacs and ₹ 24.84 lacs respectively for Lucknow and Pune factory.

The output is sold at a selling price ofRs. 1,450 and ₹ 1,460 per tonne by Lucknow and Pune factory respectively.

You are required to compute the cost per tonne and net profit earned in respect of each factory.

Can you suggest any other alternative production plan for both the factories without any change in present total output of 18,000 tonnes whereby the company may earn optimum profit.

Solution

STATEMENT OF COST PER TONNE AND NET PROFIT EARNED IN RESPECT OF EACH FACTORY

Particulars	Lucknow	Pune
A. Present production	7,200 tonnes	10,800 tonnes
B. Total Costs:	₹	₹
Cost of raw material (₹ in lakhs)	59.04	87.48
Other variable costs (₹ in lakhs)	22.32	32.94
Fixed costs (₹ in lakhs)	18.00	24.84
Total cost (₹ in lakhs)	99.36	145.26
C. Cost per tonne (₹): [B/A]	1,380	1,345
D. Selling price (₹ Per tonne:	1,450	1,460
E. Net Profit per tonne (₹): [D – C]	70	115
F. Total Net Profit (₹ in lakhs) [A × E]	5.04	12.42

Total Profit of the company = (₹ 5.04 fakhs + ₹ 12.42 lakhs) ₹ 17.46 lakhs

ALTERNATIVE PRODUCTION PLAN TO EARN OPTIMUM

Particulars	Lucknow	Pane
Maximum production capacity (tonnes)	9,000	11,880
Present production (tonnes)	7,200	10,800
	₹	₹
Cost per tonne of output:	800	810
A. Cost per tonne of output manufactured from locally purchased raw material:		
B Cost per tonne of output manufactured from material Purchased from Bhopal:	880	880
C. Other variable cost (₹):	310 $\left(\frac{22.32 \text{ lakhs}}{7{,}200 \text{ tonnes}}\right)$	305 $\left(\frac{32.94 \text{ lakhs}}{10{,}800 \text{ tonnes}}\right)$
D. Selling price per tonne (₹):	1,450	1,460
E. Contribution per tonne of Output: [(D) – {(A) + (C)}	340	345
F. Contribution per tonne of Output: [(D) – {(B) + (C)}] (When material was purchased from Bhopal)	260	275

The priority to produce 18,000 tonnes of total output is as below as apparent from the above data:

	Priority
Pune factory (local purchase of raw material)	1st
Lucknow factory (local) purchase of raw material)	2nd
Pune factory (raw material purchased from Bhopal)	3rd
Lucknow factory (raw material purchased from Bhopal)	4th

SUGGESTED ALTERNATIVE PRODUCTION PLAN

Production priority.	Raw material Input (in tonnes)	Output (in tonnes)		
		Lucknow	Pune	Total
I 11,700 tonnes	13,000	–	11,700	11,700
II 5,400 tonnes	6,000	5,400	–	5,400
III (11,880 – 11,700) = 180 tonnes	200		180	180
IV 720 tonnes balancing figure (18,000 – 17,280 tonnes)	800	720	–	720
	20,000	6,120	11,800	18,000

Working Notes:

Particulars	Lucknow	Pane
(i) Present production output (tonnes)	7,200	10,800
Total raw material required for present production (tonnes) [present output/90%]	8,000	12,000
Raw material produced locally (tonnes)	6,000	12,000
Raw material product from Bhopal	2,000	–
Cost of raw material purchased locally and from Bhopal (₹ In lacs)	59.04 (₹ 720 x 6,000 + ₹ 792 x 2,000)	87.48 (12,000 x ₹ 729)
(ii) Cost per tonne of output manufactured from locally purchased raw material (in ₹)	800 $\left(720 \times \frac{100}{90}\right)$	810 $\left(729 \times \frac{100}{90}\right)$
(iii) Cost per tonne of ouiput manufactured from material purchased from Bhopal (in ₹)	880 $\left(729 \times \frac{100}{90}\right)$	880

Problem 29. A company has two plants - one at Sambalpur and the other at Bilaspur, where production of goods takes place,

The basic raw material requirement is 80% of the finished product, by weight. Such materials are available locally, but are limited to 6,000 M.T. at ₹ 1,800 per M.T. at Sambalpur and 16,000 M.T. at ₹ 2,000 per M.T. at Bilaspur. Any extra requirements, will have to be procured from Jamshedpur at ₹ 2,500 per M. T. Other details are as under:

	For unit at Sambalpur	*For unit at Bilaspur*
Annual output (M. T.)	12,000	15,000
Capacity utilisation (%)	80	60
Other variables (₹ lacs)	156	192
Fixed cost (₹ lacs)	108	120

You are required to determine:

(i) The cost break-up of each unit per M. T. of output;

(ii) The quantity of production at each unit from the availability of local supplies of basic raw material only, by keeping the same total production of the company, as a whole:

(iii) Cost savings, if any, as per the revised schedule of production.

Solution

(i) STATEMENT OF COST BREAK-UP

Particulars	Sambalpur Total Cost (₹ Lacs)	Bilaspur Cost per M. T. of output (₹)	Total cost (₹ Lacs)	Cost per M. T. of output (₹)
A. Material cost	198 [(6,000 M.T. × ₹ 1,800) + (3,600 M.T. × ₹ 2,500)]	1,650 (₹ 198 lacs/ 12,000 M.T.)	240 (12,000 M.T. × ₹ 12,000)	1,600 (₹ 240 lacs/15,000 M.T.)
B. Other variables	156	1,300 (156 lacs/ 12,000 M.T.)	192	1,280 (192 lacs/ 15,000 M.T.)
C. Fixed Cost	108	900 (108 lacs/ 12,000 M.T.)	120	800 (120 lacs/ 15,000 M.T,)
Total Cost [A + B + C]	462	3,850	552	3,680

Working Notes:

(i) POSSIBLE OUTPUT

Particulars	Sambalpur	Bilaspur
Annual output (M.T.)	12,000	15,000
Maximum possible output (M.T.)	15,000 (12,000/80%)	25,000 (15,000/60%)
Basic raw material requirement (M.T.)	9,600 (12,000 x 80%)	12,000 (15,000 x 80%)
Material available locally (M.T.)	6,000	16,000
Possible output from local material (M.T.)	7,500 (6,000/80%)	20,000 (16,000/80%)

(ii) QUANTITY OF PRODUCTION AT EACH UNIT FROM THE AVAILABILITY OF LOCAL SUPPLIES OF BASIC RAW MATERIAL

Particulars	Sambalpur	Bilaspur
Maximum output/possible (M.T.)	15,000	25,000
Material cost/M.T. of output from locals (₹)	1,440 (6,000 x ₹ 1,800) / 7,500 M.T.	1,600
Other variables/M.T. of output (₹)	1,300	1,280
Total variable cost/ M.T. of output Ranking	2,740	2,880
Possible output (M.T.) from local supplies of basic raw material (*Balancing figure*)	7,500	19,500

(iii) COST SAVING AS PER REVISED SCHEDULE OF PRODUCTION:

Particulars	Sambalpur (₹.lacs)	Bilaspur (₹.lacs)	Total (₹ lacs)
Total Variable Cost of output (Refer to part ii)	205.5 (7,500 M.T. x ₹ 2,740)	561.6 (19,500 M.T. x ₹.2,880)	767.1
Fixed Cost	108.0	120,0	228.0
A. Total Cost: (A)	313.5	681.6	995.1
B. Previous Total Cost: (as per (i) above)	462.0	552.0	1014.0
C. Cost savings: [B – A]	148.5	(129.6)	18.9

5 Budgeting and Budgetary Control

Learning Objectives

After studying this chapter, you should be able to understand:

- Meaning of the term 'Budget'
- Meaning of Budgeting
- Meaning of Budgetary Control
- Objectives of Budgetary Control System
- Practical Steps Involved in the Preparation of Budgets
- Advantages of Budgetary Control System
- Limitations of Budgetary Control System
- Types of Budgets
- Functional Budgets
- Sales Budget
- Production Budget
- Plant Utilisation Budget
- Direct Material Purchase Budget
- Direct Labour Cost Budget
- Factory Overheads Budget or Production/Manufacturing Overheads Budget
- Production Cost Budget
- Ending Inventory Budget
- Cost of Goods Sold Budget
- Administrative Cost Budget
- Selling and Distribution Cost Budget
- Research and Development Cost Budget
- Capital Expenditure Budget
- Cash Budget
- Master Budget
- Control Ratios
- Zero Base Budgeting
- Performance Budgeting

1.0 MEANING OF THE TERM 'BUDGET'

1.1 Meaning

According to C.I.M.A., London. ***"A budget is a financial and/or quantitative statement, prepared and approved prior to a defined period of time, of the policy to be pursued during that period for the purpose of attaining a given objective. It may include income, expenditure and the employment***

of capital." A budget is a plan covering all phases of operations for a definite period in the future. It is the form of quantitative expression of policies, plans, objectives and goals laid down in advance by top management for the concern as a whole and for each sub-division thereof (e.g. Sales, Production, Purchase).

1.2 Characteristics — The main characteristics of a budget are:

1. **Prepared in Advance** — It is prepared in advance and is derived from the long-term strategy of the organisation.
2. **Relates to Future** — It is related to future period for which objectives or goals have already been laid down
3. **Expressed in Quantitative/Financial Terms** — It is expressed in quantitative form, physical or monetary units, or both.

2.0 MEANING OF BUDGETING

Budgeting is the art of building budgets. Budgeting is a process of (i) making budgets and (ii) making use of budgets for further planning, co-ordinating and control purposes.

3.0 MEANING OF BUDGETARY CONTROL

Budgetary control is a technique of control with the use of budgets.

According to C.I.M.A., London ***"Budgetary control is the establishment of budgets relating to the responsibilities of executives to the requirements of a policy and the continuous comparison of actual with budgeted results either to secure by individual action the objective of that policy or to provide a basis for revision."***

The fundamental **principles of budgetary control** may be stated as under:

1. Establishing planned performance, for each of the activities of the business for the budget period.
2. Measurement of actual performance during the budget period.
3. Continuous Comparison of the actual performance with planned performance.
4. Ascertainment of the variances and analysis of reasons therefor, and
5. Taking corrective action such as revision of budget in the light of changed circumstances.

Budgetary control forms an integral part of any management control system. In a budgetary control system, each of the large number of budgets monitors actual performance relating to target (budgeted) level of performance for a sub-goal of the firm's activities. **For example,** comparison of budgeted and actual sales shows whether the performance in relation to the sale sub-goal is satisfactory or not. The attainment of the sub-goal in turn contributes to the achievement of overall goal of satisfactory level of profit. Thus, budgeting is viewed as a process constructing a set of sub-goals for a given goal of profit attainment.

4.0 OBJECTIVES OF BUDGETARY CONTROL SYSTEM

The objectives of Budgetary Control System are given below:

4.1 Main Objective

To achieve firm's objectives effectively and efficiently

4.2 Auxiliary to Main Objective

1. To determine targets of performance for each section or department of the business for the budget period.
2. To lay down the responsibilities of each of the executives and other personnel so that every one knows what is expected of him and how he will be judged.
3. To co-ordinate the various activities of the business.
4. To provide a basis for the comparison of actual performance with the predetermined targets.
5. To ascertain the variance (i.e., differences between actual performance and budgeted performance) and analyse the reasons therefor.
6. To take the necessary corrective action.
7. To provide a basis for revision of current & future policies.
8. To draw up long-range plans with a fair measure of accuracy.

9. To ensure the best use of all available resources to maximise profit or production subject to the budget (or limiting) factors.
10. To centralise control.
11. To decentralise responsibility to each manager.
12. To show the management where action is needed to remedy a situation.
13. To act as a guide for management decisions when unforeseeable conditions affect the budget.
14. To engender a spirit of careful forethought, assessment of what is possible and an attempt at it. It leads to dynamism without recklessness.
15. To plan and control income and expenditure of manufacturing or training operations so that the most practicable profits are obtained.
16. To plan and control capital expenditure in the most profitable direction.
17. To plan and control the financing of the business so that adequate working capital, including liquid resources are available for carrying out the policy of the business.
18. To plan and control expenditure on research and development.
19. To combine the ideas of all levels of management in the preparation of the firm's plans.

5.0 PRACTICAL STEPS INVOLVED IN THE PREPARATION OF BUDGETS

The following practical steps are involved in the preparation of budgets:

Step 1: APPOINTMENT OF BUDGET CONTROLLER

Although the Chief Executive is finally responsible for the budget programme, it is better if a large part of the supervisory responsibility is delegated to a special official designated as Budget Controller or Budget Director. Such a person should have knowledge of the technical details of the business and should report directly to the President or the Chief Executive of the organisation.

Step 2: FORMULATION OF BUDGET COMMITTEE

Composition	The Budget Controller is assisted in his work by the Budget Committee. The Committee consists of all the Heads of various departments, viz., Production, Sales, Finance, Personnel, Purchase, etc. with the Managing Director as its Chairman. It is generally the responsibility of the Budget Committee to submit, discuss and finally approve the budget figures. Each head of the department should have his own Sub-committee with executives working under him as its members. Each member will prepare his own budget which will be discussed at the committee meeting before a final shape is given for co-ordinated action.
Functions	The important functions of a budget committee are as follows: (a) To define general policies of the management; (b) To receive and review budget estimates; (c) To approve budget estimates; (d) To analyse variances and recommend corrective action where necessary; and (e) To co-ordinate budget programme.

Step 3: FIXATION OF BUDGET PERIOD

The period covered by a budget is known as budget period. There is no general rule governing the selection of the budget period. The length of the budget period depends upon the nature of the plan and circumstances of the business. **For example,** industries which are subject to fashion change use short budget period whereas industries involving long-term expenditure with relatively little change in product design use long budget periods. **For example,** (i) a shoe industry uses short-term budgets and (ii) a telephone manufacturing company uses long-term budgets. Normally, one year is a normal period for budget because it coincides with the accounting year. A common practice however, is to have a series of budget periods. Thus, sales budget may cover the next five years while production and cost budgets may cover only one year. The capital expenditure budget may cover even 5 to 10 years; the yearly budgets may also be broken down into monthly periods. Long-term budgets may be supplemented by short term budgets. Thus, **For example,** a long-term budget for three to five years may be supplemented by short-term budgets for one year or less.

For control purposes, the budget period may be divided into shorter periods. The period of time covered by a budget and the resulting comparative statement of actual and budgeted expenditure should be largely determined by the requirements and outlook of the persons whose activities are planned in the budget. **For example,** a foreman may need a weekly budget and report on certain costs because he exercises day-to-day control over such expenditure. The departmental manager with a broader outlook, may not be interested in short-term fluctuations. Normally, the control period covers a month.

Step 4: IDENTIFICATION OF BUDGET FACTOR (OR KEY FACTOR OR LIMITING FACTOR)

Meaning

The factor which sets a limit to the total activity is known as budget factor, key factor or limiting factor. **For example,** if production can not be increased inspite of heavy demand, due to non-availability of raw-material/power, raw-material/power is called here key factor. The key factors should be correctly identified and their extent of influence must first be carefully assessed.

It would be desirable to prepare first the budget relating to this particular factor, and then prepare the other budgets. An illustrative list of key factors in certain industries is given below:

Examples

Item	Budget Factor (or Key Factor)
(a) **Materials**	(i) Availability of supplies. (ii) Restrictions imposed by the Government like, quotas.
(b) **Labour**	(i) Shortage in certain key processes.
(c) **Plant and machinery**	(i) Insufficient capacity for lack of space. (ii) Bottlenecks in certain key processes.
(d) **Sales**	(i) Low market demand. (ii) Insufficient advertising due to lack of funds.
(e) **Finance**	(i) Long-term finance. (ii) Short-term funds.
(f) **Management**	(i) Lack of managerial time for additional work.

Examples of Key Factor in Specific Industries

Industry	Key Factor
Motor Car	Sales demand
Aluminium	Power
Petroleum Refinery	Supply of crude oil
Electro-optics	Skilled technicians
Hydro power generation	Monsoon

Aim	A key factor is not necessarily a permanent factor. It is often a temporary one. In the long run, it may be possible for the management to overcome the limitations imposed by a factor by raising funds necessary to finance capital expenditure, finding alternative sources of raw material or substitutes for raw materials; in the short run by working overtime, hiring equipment, etc. Thus, the aim of locating limitations is to seek harmony among the various factors of production from the beginning and to maintain it throughout the budget period.

STEP 5: IDENTIFICATION OF BUDGET CENTRES

It is a well known saying that "costs are the best controlled at the point of incurrence." Thus, for example, in the case of production cost the point of control will be at the supervisor or operator level. In this way, suitable areas of control have to be selected. These areas should not be too large because the span of control should be limited. Normally, the areas chosen should conform to the natural responsibilities of executives. Such areas are known as budget centres. A budget which refers to a budget centre is a department budget. A budget centre may again consist of a number of cost centres representing different groups of machines.

STEP 6: PREPARATION OF BUDGET MANUAL

Meaning	The budget manual is a schedule, document or booklet which shows, in written forms budgeting organisation and procedures. The manual should be well written and indexed, a copy thereof may be given to each departmental head for guidance.
Contents	Budget Manual should include the following matters: 1. Introduction: A brief explanation of the principle of budgetary control system, its objectives and benefits. 2. Procedure to be adopted in operating the system. For example, 'distribution instruction', will specify as to whom various budget schedules are to be sent. 3. Definition of duties and responsibilities of (a) operational executives, (b) budget committee and (c) budget controller. 4. Nature, type and specimen forms of various reports. It also specifies the persons responsible for the preparation of the reports and the programme of distribution of the reports to the various officers. 5. The account code and classification used by the company. 6. The budget calendar showing the dates for completion of each part of the budget and submission of reports. 7. The budget periods and control periods. 8. The follow-up procedures.
Advantages	The following are the advantages of Budget Manual: 1. An overall well co-ordinated plan, provided by budgetary control system, shows what role each manager is expected to play in maximising the profits. 2. Any problem arising from the operation of a budgetary control system can be settled through the manual. 3. New employees get acquainted with the procedure involved in the operation of the system by referring to manual. 4. Methods and procedures become standardised. 5. Since co-ordination is maintained, there is no overlapping of instructions. There is in other words synchronization of all efforts which leads to the attainment of the objectives with minimum of friction.

STEP 7: PREPARATION OF VARIOUS BUDGETS

6.0 ADVANTAGES OF BUDGETARY CONTROL SYSTEM

The advantages of budgetary control system are as follows:

1. Facilitates the carrying on of Business Activities in efficient manner	The use of budgetary control system enables the management of a business concern to conduct its business activities in the efficient manner.
2. Facilitates Control of Expenditure	It is a powerful instrument used by business houses for the control of their expenditure. It infact provides a yardstick for measuring and evaluating the performance of individuals and their departments.
3. Reveals Deviations	It reveals the deviations to management, from the budgeted figures after making a comparison with actual figures.
4. Facilitates Effective Utilisation of Resources	Effective utilisation of various resources like men, material, machinery and money is made possible, as the production is planned after taking them into account.
5. Facilitates Revision of Plans	It helps in the review of current trends and framing of future policies.
6. Facilitates Implementation of Standard Costing System	It creates suitable conditions for the implementation of standard costing system in a business organisation.
7. Inculcates Feeling of Cost Consciousness	It inculcates the feeling of cost consciousness among workers.

7.0 LIMITATIONS OF BUDGETARY CONTROL SYSTEM

The limitations of budgetary control system are as follows:

1. Estimates	Budgets may or may not be true, as they are based on estimates.
2. Rigidity	Budgets are considered as rigid document.
3. No Automatic Execution	Budgets cannot be executed automatically.
4. Lack of Staff co-operation	Staff co-operation is usually not available during budgetary control exercise.
5. Expensive	Its implementation is quite expensive.

8.0 TYPES OF BUDGETS

8.1 Budgets may be classified on various basis as follows:

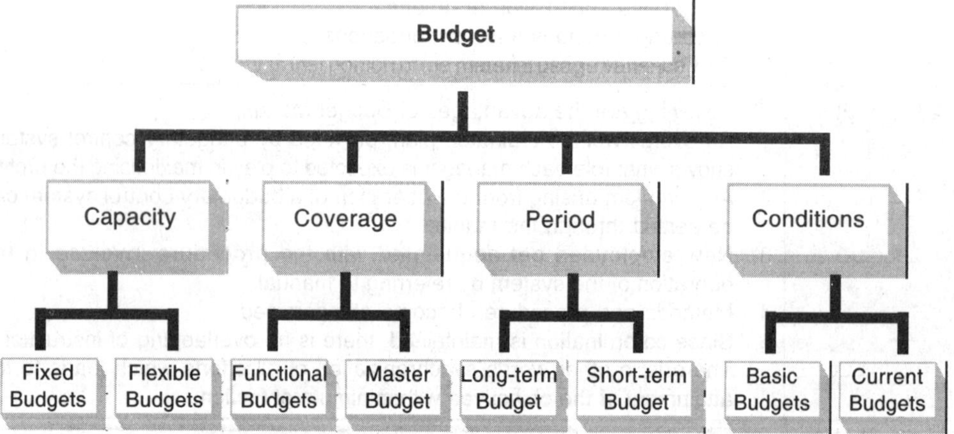

Let us discuss these various types of Budgets one by one.

FIXED BUDGET

Meaning	*According to C.I.M.A. London* ***"a fixed budget is a budget designed to remain unchanged irrespective of the level of activity actually attained".*** Fixed Budget is used as an effective tool of cost control. In case, the level of activity attained is different from the level of activity for budgeting purposes, the fixed budget becomes ineffective because it does not give due consideration to cost behaviour at different levels of activity. Such as budget is quite suitable for fixed expenses.
Features	The main features of a fixed budget are as follows: 1. It is prepared for one fixed level of activity. 2. It does not change with the change in the level of activity. 3. Expenses are not classified into fixed, variable and semi-variable.

FLEXIBLE BUDGET

Meaning	*According to C.I.M.A., London* ***"a flexible budget is a budget which, by recognising the difference between fixed, semi-variable and variable costs is designed to change in relation to the level of activity attained."*** In a flexible budgetary control system, a series of budgets are prepared one for each of a number of alternative production levels or volumes. Flexible budgets represent the amount of expenses that is reasonably necessary to achieve each level of output specified. In other words, the allowances given under flexible budgetary control system serve as a standard of what costs should be at each level of output. It is more realistic and practicable because it gives due consideration to cost behaviour at different levels of activity.
Features	The main features of flexible budget are as follows: 1. It is prepared for different levels of activity. 2. It changes with the change in the level of activity. 3. Expenses are classified into fixed, variable and semi-variable. Semi-variable expenses are further segregated into fixed and variable expenses.
Need	The need for preparation of flexible budgets arises in the following circumstances: 1. In case of industries where there are seasonal fluctuations in sales and/or production-for example, in soft drinks industry; 2. In case of a company which keeps on introducing new products or make changes in the design of its products frequently; 3. In case of industries engaged in make-to-order business like ship-building; 4. In case of an industry which is influenced by changes in fashion; 5. When there are general changes in sales. 6. In the case of new business venture due to its typical nature it may be difficult to forecast the demand of a product accurately. 7. Where the business is dependent upon the mercy of nature, e.g., a person dealing in wool trade may have enough market if temperature goes below the freezing point. 8. In the case of labour intensive industry where the production of the concern is dependent upon the availability of labour.

DISTINCTION BETWEEN FIXED BUDGET AND FLEXIBLE BUDGET

Fixed Budget differs from Flexible Budget in the following respects:

Basis of Distinction	Fixed Budget	Flexible Budget
1. Change with Activity	It does not change with actual volume of activity achieved. Thus, it is known as rigid or inflexible budget.	It can be recasted on the basis of activity level to be achieved. Thus, it is not rigid.
2. One Level or different levels of activity	It operates on one level of activity and under one set of conditions. It assumes that there will be no change in the prevailing conditions, which is unrealistic.	It consists of various budgets for different levels of activity.
3. Utility of Variance Analysis	Since all costs like-fixed, variable and semi-variable are related to only one level of activity, variance analysis does not give useful information.	Here analysis of variance provides useful information as each cost is analysed according to its behaviour.
4. Decision Making	If the budgeted and actual activity levels differ significantly, then the aspects like cost ascertainment and price fixation do not give a correct picture.	Flexible budgeting at different levels of activity, facilitates the ascertainment of cost, fixation of selling price and tendering of quotations.
5. Basis of Comparison	Comparison of actual performance with budgeted targets will be meaningless specially when there is a difference between the two activity levels.	It provides a meaningful basis of comparison of the actual performance with the budgeted targets.

OTHER BUDGETS

Functional Budgets	Budgets which relate to the individual functions in an organization are known as Functional Budgets. For example, purchase budget; sales budget; production budget; plant-utilisation budget and cash budget.
Master Budget	It is a consolidated summary of the various functional budgets. It serves as the basis upon which budgeted P & L A/c and forecasted Balance Sheet are built up.
Long-term Budgets	The budgets which are prepared for periods longer than a year are called long-term budgets. Such budgets are helpful in business forecasting and forward planning. Capital expenditure budget and Research and Development budget are examples of long-term budgets.
Short-term Budgets	Budgets which are prepared for period upto a year are known as short-term budgets. Cash budget is an example of short-term budget. Such type of budgets are prepared in cases where a specific action has to be immediately taken to bring any variation under control, as in cash budgets.

Basic Budget	A budget which remains unaltered over a long period of time is called basic budget.
Current Budget	A budget which is established for use over a short period of time and is related to the current conditions is called current budget.

FORMAT OF FLEXIBLE BUDGET

A simplest format of a Flexible Budget is given below:

Particulars	*Capacity Level*		
	60%	*80%*	*90%*
A. Sales (in units)	....	....	....
B. Selling Price per unit	....	....	....
C. Total Sales (A × B)	....	....	....
D. Variable Cost of Sales :			
(a) Direct Material @ ..... per unit	....	....	....
(b) Direct Labour @ ..... per unit	....	....	....
(c) Direct Expenses @ ..... per unit	....	....	....
(d) Production Overheads @ ..... per unit	....	....	....
(e) Adm. Overheads @ ..... per unit	....	....	....
(f) Selling & Distribution Overheads @ ..... per unit	....	....	....
	....	....	....
E. Contribution (C – D)	....	....	....
F. Fixed Costs:			
(a) Production Overheads	....	....	....
(b) Adm. Overheads	....	....	....
(c) Selling & Distribution Overheads	....	....	....
	....	....	....
G. Profit (E – F)	....	....	....

Illustration 1. PCT Ltd. provides you the following information at 80% capacity:

Production and Sales	2,000 units
Direct Material	₹ 1.00 per unit
Direct Labour	₹ 1.00 per unit
Direct Expenses	₹ 0.80 per unit
Production Overheads (15% variable)	₹ 2.00 per unit
Administrative overheads (80% fixed)	₹ 2.00 per unit
Selling & Distribution Overheads (25% variable)	₹ 2.00 per unit
Total Cost	₹ 8.80 per unit
Profit per unit	₹ 1.20 per unit
Selling Price	₹ 10.00 per unit

Required: Draw up a Flexible Budget at 60% and 90% capacity.

Solution: **FLEXIBLE BUDGET**

Particulars	*Capacity Level*		
	60%	*80%*	*90%*
A. Sales (in units)	1,500	2,000	2,250
B. Selling Price per unit	₹ 10	₹ 10	₹ 10
C. Total Sales (A × B)	15,000	20,000	22,500
D. Variable Cost of Sales :			
(a) Direct Material @ ₹ 1.00 per unit	1,500	2,000	2,250
(b) Direct Labour @ ₹ 1.00 per unit	1,500	2,000	2,250

Particulars	Capacity Level		
	60%	80%	90%
(c) Direct Expenses @ ₹ 0.80 per unit	1,200	1,600	1,800
(d) Production Overheads @ ₹ 0.30 per unit	450	600	675
(e) Adm. Overheads @ ₹ 0.40 per unit	600	800	900
(f) Selling & Distribution Overheads @ ₹ 0.50 per unit	750	1,000	1,125
	6,000	8,000	9,000
E. Contribution (C – D)	9,000	12,000	13,500
F. Fixed Costs :			
(a) Production Overheads [2000 units × (85% of ₹ 2.00)]	3,400	3,400	3,400
(b) Adm. Overheads [2000 units × (80% of ₹ 2.00)]	3,200	3,200	3,200
(c) Selling & Distribution Overheads [2000 units × (75% of ₹ 2.00)]	3,000	3,000	3,000
	9,600	9,600	9,600
G. Profit (E – F)	(600)	2,400	3,900

Illustration 2. Tulsian Ltd. manufactures two Products and provides you the following information:

	Product 'A'	Product 'B'
(a) Standard Data:		
Selling Price Per Unit	₹ 30	₹ 40
Direct Material :		
— X @ ₹ 3 per Unit	2 Units	4 Units
— Y @ ₹ 1 per Unit	1 Unit	2 Units
Direct Labour per unit :		
In P Dept.,	2 hours @ ₹ 1 per hour	1 hour @ ₹ 2 per hour
In Q Dept.	1 hour @ ₹ 3 per hour	1 hour @ ₹ 3 per hour
Overheads (65.2% fixed)	@ ₹ 2.50 per hour	@ 2.50 per hour
(b) Normal Capacity at 100%	10,000 units	8,000 units

Required: (a) Prepare Standard Cost Sheet for Product 'A' and Product 'B'; (b) Prepare Flexible Budget for Product 'A' at 50% and 75% level of capacity; (c) Prepare Flexible Budget for product 'B' at 75% and 100% level of capacity.

Solution:

(a) STANDARD COST SHEET

Particulars	Product 'A'	Product 'B'
A. Selling Price per unit	₹ 30.00	₹ 40.00
B. *Less:* Variable Cost:		
(i) Direct Material :		
— X	6.00	12.00
— Y	1.00	2.00
(ii) Direct Labour :		
— P Dept.	2.00	2.00
— Q Dept.	3.00	3.00
(iii) Variable Overheads	2.61	1.74
	14.61	20.74
C. Contribution (A – B)	15.39	19.26
D. *Less:* Fixed Overheads	4.89	3.26
E. Profit (C – D)	10.50	16.00

(b) & (c) FLEXIBLE BUDGET

Particulars	Product A 50%	Product 'A' 75%	Product 'B' 75%	Product B 100%
A. Sales (in units)	5,000	7,500	6,000	8,000
B. Selling Price per Unit	₹ 30	₹ 30	₹ 40	₹ 40
C. Total Sales (A × B)	1,50,000	2,25,000	2,40,000	3,20,000
D. Variable Cost of Sales :				
(i) Direct Material : X	30,000	45,000	72,000	96,000
Y	5,000	7,500	12,000	16,000
(ii) Direct Labour :				
P Dept.	10,000	15,000	12,000	16,000
O Dept.	15,000	22,500	18,000	24,000
(iii) Variable Overheads	13,050	19,575	10,440	13,920
	73,050	1,09,575	1,24,440	1,65,920
E. Contribution (C – D)	76,950	1,15,425	1,15,560	1,54,080
F. Fixed Overheads	48,900	48,900	26,080	26,080
G. Profit (E – F)	28,050	66,525	89,480	1,28,000

Illustration 3. PCT Ltd. provides you the following information :
Production and Sales at 60% capacity

	₹
Variable Expenses :	
Production	1,50,000
Administration	1,50,000
Selling & Distribution	1,20,000
Semi-Variable Expenses :	
Production	50,000
Administration	60,000
Selling & Distribution	70,000
Fixed Expenses :	
Production	3,40,000
Administration	3,20,000
Selling & Distribution	3,00,000
Total Sales	15,00,000

Note: *Semi-variable expenses are constant between 55% and 75% of capacity, increasing by 10% if the capacity exceeds 75% but does not exceed 90% of capacity and by 20% if the capacity exceeds 90% of capacity.*

Required: Prepare a Flexible Budget at 70%, 80%, and 100% capacity level.

Solution: **FLEXIBLE BUDGET**

Particulars	Capacity Level 70%	80%	100%
A. Total Sales	17.5	20.00	25.00
B. *Variable Expenses :*			
(i) Production	1.75	2.00	2.50
(ii) Administration	1.75	2.00	2.50
(iii) Selling & Distribution	1.40	1.60	2.00
	4.90	5.60	7.00
C. *Semi-Variable Expenses :*			
(i) Production	0.50	0.55	0.60
(ii) Administration	0.60	0.66	0.72
(iii) Selling & Distribution	0.70	0.77	0.84
	1.80	1.98	2.16

Particulars	Capacity Level		
	70%	80%	100%
D. *Fixed Expenses :*			
(i) Production	3.4	3.4	3.4
(ii) Administration	3.2	3.2	3.2
(iii) Selling & Distribution	3.0	3.0	3.0
	9.6	9.6	9.6
E. Total Expenses (B + C + D)	16.3	17.18	18.76
F. Profit (A – E)	1.2	2.82	6.24

Illustration 4. PCT Ltd. provides you the following information :

Production Capacity	*Costs & Sales (₹ lakhs)*	
	At 80%	*At 60%*
Direct Materials	2.00	1.50
Direct Labour	2.00	1.50
Direct Expenses	1.60	1.20
Production Overheads	4.00	3.85
Administrative Overheads	4.00	3.80
Selling & Distribution Overheads	4.00	3.75
Sales	20.00	15.00

Required : Draw up a Flexible Budget at 50% and 90% capacity.

Solution: **FLEXIBLE BUDGET (IN LAKHS OF RUPEES)**

Particulars	*Capacity Level*			
	50%	*60%*	*80%*	*90%*
A. Sales	12.5	15.00	20.00	22.50
B. Variable Cost of Sales :				
(a) Direct Material	1.25	1.50	2.00	2.25
(b) Direct Labour	1.25	1.50	2.00	2.25
(c) Direct Expenses	1.00	1.20	1.60	1.80
(d) Production Overheads	.375	0.45	0.60	.675
(e) Adm. Overheads	.500	0.60	0.80	.900
(f) Selling & Distribution Overheads	.625	0.75	1.00	1.125
	5.00	6.00	8.00	9.00
C. Contribution (A – B)	7.5	9.00	12.00	13.50
D. Fixed Costs :				
(a) Production Overheads	3.4	3.4	3.4	3.4
(b) Adm. Overheads	3.2	3.2	3.2	3.2
(c) Selling & Distribution Overheads	3.0	3.0	3.0	3.0
	9.6	9.6	9.6	9.6
E. Profit (C – D)	(2.1)	(.60)	2.4	3.9

Working Note: STATEMENT SHOWING THE CALCULATION OF FIXED AND VARIABLE EXPENSES

A *Particulars*	*B* *Variable Costs at 20%*	*C = B × 80/20* *Variable Costs at 80%*	*D* *Total cost at 80%*	*E = D – C* *Fixed Cost*
Direct Material	0.50	2.00	2.00	Nil
Direct Labour	0.50	2.00	2.00	Nil
Direct Expenses	0.40	1.60	1.60	Nil

Production Overheads	0.15	0.60	4.00	3.4
Adm. Overheads	0.20	0.80	4.00	3.2
Selling & Distribution OH	0.25	1.00	4.00	3.0
	2.00	8.00	17.60	9.6

Illustration 5. From the following information, prepare Budget for 2014 and 2015 taking 2013 as base year.

Actual Data :

Sales	2,000 units at 50% capacity
Selling Price per unit	₹ 10.00
Direct Material per unit	₹ 1.00
Direct Labour per unit	₹ 1.00
Direct Expenses per unit	₹ 0.80
Production Overheads per unit (85% fixed)	₹ 1.00
Adm. Overheads per unit (20% variable)	₹ 1.00
Selling & Distribution Overheads per unit (75% fixed)	₹ 1.00

2014 PROSPECTS :

Sales	20% increase in volume together with 10% decrease in selling price
Direct Material	5% price increase with 5% Inefficiency
Additional Plant (Subject to Depreciation @ 15%)	₹ 2,000
Direct Labour	10% increase in Wage Rates and 5% increase in Productivity

2015 ANTICIPATIONS TAKING 2013 AS BASE YEAR

Sales	20% decrease in sales volume together with 10% increase in sale price.
Direct Materials	5% price decrease
Direct Labour	10% decrease in wage rates, and 5% decrease in productivity

Solution:

BUDGET FOR THE YEAR 2014 AND 2015

	Particulars	*2014*	*2015*
A.	Sales (Units)	2,400	1,600
B.	Selling Price per unit	₹ 9	₹ 11
C.	Total Sales Revenue (A × B)	21,600	17,600
D.	Variable Cost of Sales:		
	(a) Direct Material [2400 × ₹ 1 × 105% × 105%] [1600 × Re1 × 95%]	2,646	1,520
	(b) Direct Labour *[Refer to Working Note]*	2,514	1,516
	(c) Direct Expenses @ ₹ 0.80 per unit	1,920	1,280
	(d) Production Overheads @ ₹ 0.15 per unit	360	240
	(e) Adm. Overheads @ ₹ 0.20 per unit	480	320
	(f) Selling & Distribution Overheads @ ₹ 0.25 per unit	600	400
		8,520	5,276
E.	Contribution (C – D)	13,080	12,324
F.	Fixed Costs:		
	(a) Production Overheads (Including 15% depreciation on plant)	2,000	2,000
	(b) Adm. Overheads	1,600	1,600
	(c) Selling & Distribution Overheads	1,500	1,500
		5,100	5,100
G.	Profit (E – F)	7,980	7,224

Working Note: *Calculation of Direct Labour Cost*

$$= \frac{\text{Revised Output}}{\text{Present Output}} \times \frac{\text{Present Direct}}{\text{Labour Cost}} \times \frac{(100 \pm \text{Change in Wage Rate})}{100} \times \frac{100}{100 \pm \text{Change in Productivity}}$$

$$\textit{for 2014} = \frac{2,400}{2,000} \times ₹\,2,000 \times \frac{(100+10)}{100} \times \frac{100}{(100+5)} = ₹\,2,514$$

$$\text{for 2015} = \frac{1,600}{2,000} \times ₹\,2,000 \times \frac{(100-10)}{100} \times \frac{100}{(100-5)} = ₹\,1,516$$

Illustration 6. Tulsian Ltd. provides you the following information:

Production Capacity	*33-1/3%*	*50%*
Sales (units)	9,000	15,000
Production (units)	10,000	15,000
Direct Material (₹)	1,10,000	1,65,000
Direct Labour (₹)	1,80,000	2,30,000
Production Overheads (including depreciation) (₹)	1,10,000	1,25,000
Depreciation on Production Machinery (₹)	20,000	20,000
Administrative Overheads (₹)	20,950	20,950
Selling & Distribution Overheads (₹)	38,000	50,000

Variable labour cost becomes 50% higher for activity in excess of 19,000 units due to the necessity for overtime working. The variable element of selling and distribution expenses is a function of sales. All other costs with a variable element are a function of production volume.

During 2012-13, All goods produced were sold @ ₹ 40 for ₹ 7,20,000

During 2013-14, Selling price is expected to decrease by 5% Direct Material price is expected to increase by ₹ 1 with 5% inefficiency (wasting allowance), Direct Wage rate is expected to increase by 12–1/2% with 25% increase in productivity of variable labour input, Fixed Production Overheads and Fixed Selling and Distribution Overheads are expected to increase by 20%.

Required: Prepare Budget for the year 2013-14 if Sales and Output are expected to increase by (a) 1000 units, and (b) 50%

Solution:

BUDGET FOR THE YEAR 2013 - 14

	Particulars	*(a)*	*(b)*
A	Sales Units	19,000	27,000
B	Selling Price Per Unit (₹)	38	38
C	Sales (A x B)	₹ 7,22,000	₹ 10,26,000
D	Variable Cost of Sales:		
	(a) Direct Material Cost @ ₹ 12.60	2,39,400	3,40,200
	(b) Direct Labour Cost @ ₹ 9	1,71,000	2,43,000
	(c) Overtime @ ₹ 4.50	0	36,000
	(d) Variable Production Overheads @ ₹ 3	57,000	81,000
	Variable Cost of Goods Produced	4,67,400	7,00,200
	Add: Variable Selling and Distribution Overheads @ ₹ 2	38,000	54,000
	Variable Cost of Sales	5,05,400	7,54,200
E	Contribution [C – D]	2,16,600	2,71,800
F	*Less:* Fixed Overheads:		
	(a) Fixed Labour Cost	90,000	90,000
	(b) Fixed Production Overheads	72,000	72,000

(c) Depreciation on Production machinery	20,000	20,000
(d) Fixed Administration Overheads	20,950	20,950
(e) Fixed Selling and Distribution Overheads	24,000	24,000
	2,26,950	2,26,950
G Profit / (Loss) [E – F]	(10,350)	44,850

Working Notes:

(i) *Segregation of Fixed and Variable Cost*

Variable Cost Per Unit = Change in Cost/Change in Units

Direct Material Cost Per unit = (₹ 1,65,000 – ₹ 1,10,000)/(15000 – 10000) = ₹ 11

Direct Labour Cost Per unit = (₹ 2,30,000 – ₹ 1,80,000) / (15000 – 10000) = ₹ 10

Fixed Labour Cost = ₹ 1,80,000 – (₹ 10 x 10,000) = ₹ 80,000

Variable Production Oh. (excluding dep.) Per unit = (₹ 1,05,000 – ₹ 90,000)/(15000 – 10000) = ₹ 3

Fixed Production Overheads (excluding dep.) = ₹ 90,000 – (3 x 10,000) = ₹ 60,000

Variable Selling & Distribution Overheads Per unit = (₹ 50,000 – ₹ 38,000)/(15000 – 9000) = ₹ 2

Fixed Selling & Distribution Overheads = ₹ 38,000 – (2 x 9,000) = ₹ 20,000

(ii) *Calculation of Variable Cost Per Unit*

	2012-13	2013-14	
Direct Material	11	12.6	[(11 + 1) x 105%]
Direct Labour	10	9	(10 x 112.5% x 100 / 125)
Variable Production Overheads	3	3	
Variable Selling & Distribution Expenses	2	2	
Total Variable Cost/Unit upto 19000 units	26	26.6	
Overtime	—	4.5	(10 x 112.5% x 100/125 x 50%)
Total Variable Cost/Unit beyond 19000 units	26	31.1	

(iii) *Calculation of Total Fixed Cost*

	2012-13	2013-14	
Production Labour	80,000	90,000	(80,000 x 112.5%)
Production Overheads (excluding depreciation)	60,000	72,000	(60,000 x 120%)
Depreciation on Production Machinery	20,000	20,000	
Administrative Overheads	20,950	20,950	
Selling & Distribution Overheads	20,000	24,000	(20,000 x 120%)
Total Fixed Cost	2,00,950	2,26,950	

9.0 FUNCTIONAL BUDGETS

A functional budget is one which relates to functions of a business as, **For example,** production budget relating to the manufacturing function. Functional budgets are prepared for each function and they are subsidiary to the master budget of the business. The various types of the functional budgets to be prepared will vary according to the size and nature of the business. The various commonly used functional budgets are:

1. Sales budget;
2. Production budget;
3. Plant utilisation budget;
4. Direct material usage budget;
5. Direct material purchase budget;
6. Direct labour (personnel) budget;
7. Factory overhead budget;
8. Production cost budget;
9. Ending-inventory budget;
10. Cost of goods sold budget;
11. Selling and distribution cost budget;
12. Administration expenses budget;
13. Research and development cost budget;
14. Capital expenditure budget;
15. Cash budget;
16. Master budget-Budgeted Income Statement and Budgeted Balance Sheet.

The important functional budgets (also known as Schedules to Master Budget) and the Master budget are discussed and illustrated on the next pages.

10.0 SALES BUDGET

<table>
<tr><td>Meaning</td><td colspan="2">Sales budget represents the physical quantities and values of total sales (which may be distributed product-wise, period-wise, area-wise, Salesman-wise, etc.) to be achieved during the budget period. Sales Budget provides answers to the questions like:
1. What is it to be sold? (say Product X, Product Y)
2. When is it to be sold? (say 1st Quarter, 2nd Quarter)
3. Where is it to be sold? (say Northern Region, Southern Region)
4. By whom is it to be sold? (say Salesman P, Salesman Q)</td></tr>
<tr><td>Purpose</td><td colspan="2">The purpose of sales budget is not an attempt to estimate or guess what the actual sales will be, but rather to develop a plan with clearly defined objectives towards which the operational effort is directed in order to attain or exceed the objective.</td></tr>
<tr><td>Basis</td><td colspan="2">Sales Budget is based on sales forecast. Sales forecast reflects the environmental and competitive situation of the available customer demand. Sales Budget shows how the management intends to react to this environmental and competitive situation. Sales forecast is passive but sales budget is active.</td></tr>
<tr><td rowspan="3">Factors</td><td colspan="2">The following factors should be considered while preparing Sales Budget:</td></tr>
<tr><td>Organisational Factors</td><td>Environmental Factors</td></tr>
<tr><td>Past sales figures and trends
Salesmen's estimates
Plant capacity
Orders in hand
Proposed expansion or discontinuation of products
Availability of material or supplies
Relative Products profitability
Financial aspect
Cost of distribution of goods
Quality of Sales Force</td><td>General Economic Conditions
General trade prospects
General Political Conditions & their impact on market
Seasonal & Cyclical fluctuations
Potential market
Degree of competition
Government controls, rules and regulations relating to the industry</td></tr>
<tr><td>Who is Respon-sible</td><td colspan="2">The Sales Director/Manager is directly responsible for the preparation and execution of sales budget.</td></tr>
<tr><td>Useful-ness</td><td colspan="2">Sales budget serves as a basis for the preparation of production budget and other budgets.</td></tr>
</table>

DISTINGUISH BETWEEN SALES FORECAST AND SALES BUDGET

Basis of Distinction	Sales Forecast	Sales Budget
1. Meaning	Sales forecast provides **probable sales** figures which can be.	Sales Budget provides **planned sales** figures which are planned to be achieved during the budget period.
2. Reflection	It reflects the environmental situtation.	It reflects how the management intends to react to this environment situation.
3. Basis	It is the basis for Sales Budget.	It is not the basis of sales forecast

10.2 Format of Sales Budget

A simplest format of a Sales Budget is given below:

SALES BUDGET (IN UNITS & ₹)
for the Budget period ending.....

Product / Period	Product 'A'			Product 'B'		
	Units	Rate ₹	Amount ₹	Units	Rate ₹	Amount ₹
Ist Quarter	.....	.....	.....	.....	.....	.....
2nd Quarter	.....	.....	.....	.....	.....	.....
3rd Quarter	.....	.....	.....	.....	.....	.....
4th Quarter	.....	.....	.....	.....	.....	.....
	.....	.....	.....	.....	.....	.....

Illustration 7. P.C.T. Ltd. provides you the following figures for the year I :

		Product A	Product B
Sales (in units) :	Ist Quarter	1,250	1,600
	IInd Quarter	2,950	800
	IIIrd Quarter	2,700	1,000
	IVth Quarter	3,100	600
Selling Price per unit		₹ 24	₹ 50
Targets for year II :			
Sales Quantity increase (decrease)		(20%)	25%
Selling Price increase (decrease)		25%	(20%)

Sales area *X*, *Y* and *Z* respectively produce 10%, 20%, 70% of Product '*A*' sales and 70%, 20% and 10% of Product '*B*' sales.

Required: Prepare Sales Budget for the year II.

Solution: **SALES BUDGET (IN TOTAL) FOR THE YEAR II**

Product / Period	Product 'A'			Product 'B'		
	Units	Rate ₹	Amount ₹	Units	Rate ₹	Amount ₹
Ist Quarter	1,000	30	30,000	2,000	40	80,000
2nd Quarter	2,360	30	70,800	1,000	40	40,000
3rd Quarter	2,160	30	64,800	1,250	40	50,000
4th Quarter	2,480	30	74,400	750	40	30,000
	8,000		2,40,000	5,000		2,00,000

SALES BUDGET (AREA-WISE)

Product & Area / Period	Product 'A'				Product 'B'			
	X ₹	Y ₹	Z ₹	Total ₹	X ₹	Y ₹	Z ₹	Total ₹
Ist Quarter	3,000	6,000	21,000	30,000	56,000	16,000	8,000	80,000
2nd Quarter	7,080	14,160	49,560	70,800	28,000	8,000	4,000	40,000
3rd Quarter	6,480	12,960	45,360	64,800	35,000	10,000	5,000	50,000
4th Quarter	7,440	14,880	52,080	74,400	21,000	6,000	3,000	30,000
Total	24,000	48,000	1,68,000	2,40,000	1,40,000	40,000	20,000	2,00,000

11.0 PRODUCTION BUDGET

Meaning	Production budget normally represents physical quantities of the total production (which may be distributed product-wise, period-wise, plant-wise) to be produced during the budget period along with the budgeted opening & closing inventory of products. Production budget provides answer to the questions like: 1. When is it to be produced ? (*say product X, product Y*) 2. What is it to be produced? (*say 1st Quarter, 2nd Quarter*) 3. Where it is to be produced? (*say Plant I, Plant II*) 4. At what levels inventory of products are to be maintained? (*say level of opening & closing inventory*)
Basis	Production Budget is generally based on Sales Budget.
Factors	The following factors should be considered while preparing production budget: 1. Sales requirements as per sales budget. 2. Inventory Policies (*such as stable minimum inventory policy or variable inventory policy*) 3. Production Policy (*such as stable production policy or variable production policy*) 4. Availability of Plant Capacity 5. Availability of Inputs such as Raw-materials, labour. 6. Manufacturing cycle (*i.e., the time gap between the purchase of raw-material and the production of finished goods*). 7. Make or Buy Policy 8. Sub-contracting Policy
Who is Responsible	The production director or manager is directly responsible for the preparation and execution of production budget.
Usefulness	Production budget serves as a basis for the preparation of cost budgets (*such as Material Cost Budget, Labour Cost Budget, Cost of Goods Sold Budget*), Cash Budget and other Budgets.

FORMAT OF PRODUCTION BUDGET

A simplest format of a Production Budget is given below:

PRODUCTION BUDGET (IN UNITS)

for the Budget period ending......

Product & Period / *Particulars*	*Product X*				*Product Y*			
	I Qtr.	*II Qtr.*	*III Qtr.*	*IV Qtr.*	*I Qtr.*	*II Qtr.*	*III Qtr.*	*IV Qtr.*
A. Budgeted Sales	.....	.....	.....	.....	.....	.....	.....	.....
B. *Add* : Budgeted Closing Stock of Finished Goods	.....	.....	.....	.....	.....	.....	.....	.....
C. *Less* : Budgeted Opening Stock of Finished Goods	.....	.....	.....	.....	.....	.....	.....	.....
D. Budgeted Production	.....	.....	.....	.....	.....	.....	.....	.....

Illustration 8 PCT Ltd. provides you the following information:

	Product A	Product B
Sales (in units) as per Sales Budget :		
1st Quarter 2014	1,000	2,000
2nd Quarter 2014	2,360	1,000
3rd Quarter 2014	2,160	1,250
4th Quarter 2014	2,480	750
Stock Position as on 1.1.2014 :		
Percentage of 1st Quarter 2014 sales	20%	100%
Stock Position ending 1st, 2nd and 3rd Quarter		
Percentage of Next Quarter's sales	50%	50%
Stock Position on 31.12.2014	2,200	1,000

Required: Prepare Production Budget for the year 2014.

Solution: **PRODUCTION BUDGET FOR THE YEAR 2014**

Particulars / Product & Period	Product 'A'				Product 'B'			
	1st Q.	2nd Q.	3rd Q.	4th Q.	Ist Q.	2nd Q	3rd Q.	4th Q.
A. Budgeted Sales	1,000	2,360	2,160	2,480	2,000	1,000	1,250	750
B. *Add :* Closing Stock	1,180	1,080	1,240	2,200	500	625	375	1,000
C. *Less :* Opening Stock	200	1,180	1,080	1,240	2,000	500	625	375
D. Units to be produced (A + B – C)	1,980	2,260	2,320	3,440	500	1,125	1,000	1,375

12.0 PLANT UTILISATION BUDGET

Meaning	Plant Utilisation Budget represents, in terms of working hours, weight or other convenient units of plant facilities required to carry out other programmes laid down in the production budget.
Purposes	The main purposes of this budget are: 1. To determine the load on each process, cost or groups of machines for the budget period. 2. To indicate the processes or cost centres which are overloaded so that corrective action may be taken such as: (i) Working overtime, (ii) Sub-contracting, (iii) Expansion of production facility, etc. 3. To detail the sales and production budget where it is not possible to increase the capacity of any of the overloaded process. 4. Where surplus capacity is available in any of the processes, to make effort to boost sales to utilise the surplus capacity.

Illustration 9. Three articles X, Y and Z are produced in a factory. They are through two cost centres A and B. From the data furnished, compile a statement for Budgeted Machine Utilisation in both the centres.

(a) *Sales Budget for the year*

Product	*Annual budgeted Sales (units)*	*Opening Stock of finished products (units)*	*Closing Stock of finished Products*
X	4,800	600	Equivalent to 2 Months' Sales
Y	2,400	300	Equivalent to 2 Months' Sales
Z	2,400	800	Equivalent to 2 Months' Sales

(b) *Machine Hours per unit of products :*

Product	*Machine Hour Per Unit Cost Centre*	
	A	*B*
X	30	70
Y	200	100
Z	30	20

(c) *Total No. of Machines:*

Cost Centres	*No.*
A	284
B	256
	540

(d) Total working hours during the year : Estimated 2,500 hours per machine.

Solution: **PRODUCTION BUDGET (IN UNITS)**

	Particulars	*Product X*	*Product Y*	*Product Z*
A.	Budgeted Sales	4,800	2,400	2,400
B.	*Add :* Closing Stock	800	400	400
C.	*Less :* Opening Stock	600	300	800
D.	Units to be produced (A + B – C)	5,000	2,500	2,000

MACHINE UTILISATION BUDGET

Product	*Cost Centre A*		*Cost Centre B*	
	Total Machine Hours	*No. of Machines Required*	*Total Machine Hours*	*No. of Machines Required*
X	1,50,000	60	3,50,000	140
Y	5,00,000	200	2,50,000	100
Z	60,000	24	40,000	16
	7,10,000	284	6,40,000	256

Working Notes:

(i) *Calculation of Machine hours*

Machine Hours = Total Production × Hours per unit
e.g. For product 'X' in cost centre 'A' = 5,000 × 30 = 1,50,000
In cost centre 'B' = 5,000 × 70 = 3,50,000

(ii) *Calculation of No. of Machines*

e.g. for Product 'X' in Cost Centre 'A' = $\frac{\text{Total Machine Hrs}}{\text{Hours per Machine}} = \frac{1,50,000}{2,500} = 60$

13.0 DIRECT MATERIAL PURCHASE BUDGET

Meaning	Direct material purchase budget represents the physical quantities and cost of total materials (*which may be distributed item-wise, period-wise, plant-wise*), to be purchased during the budget period. Direct material purchase budget provides answers to the questions like:

	1. What is to be purchased? (*say Material 'P', Material 'Q'*) 2. When is it to be purchased? (*say 1st Quarter, 2nd Quarter*) 3. Where is it to be purchased? (*say Plant I, Plant II*) 4. At what levels inventory of products are to be maintained? (*say level of opening & closing inventory*)
Basis	Direct Material Purchase Budget is generally based on Production Budget.
Factors	The following factors should be considered while preparing direct material purchase budget: 1. Production requirements as per production budget. 2. Inventory Policies regarding stocks of each item of raw-material required. 3. Quality standards for each item of material. 4. Standard requirement of each item of material required after considering normal loss in process. 5. Standard Prices for each item of materials required. 6. Economic Order Quality. 7. ₹-order Level. 8. Safety Stocks. 9. Inefficiency (i.e. Wasting Allowance) in the use of material
Who is Responsible	The purchase director or manager is directly responsible for the preparation and execution of Direct Material Purchase Budget.
Usefulness	1. To plan the purchases and place long-term contracts where necessary, taking into consideration the market position and trend in prices, 2. To plan the finances required for purchase, 3. Direct Material Purchase Budget facilitates the preparation of Cost of Goods produced Budget or Production Cost Budget, Cash Budget and other budgets.

FORMAT OF DIRECT MATERIAL PURCHASE BUDGET

A simplest format of Direct Material Purchase Budget is given below:

DIRECT MATERIAL PURCHASE BUDGET (QUANTITY AND VALUE)

Particulars	*Material X*	*Material Y*
A. Budgeted Usage (for Production):		
For Product 'A'	....	....
For Product 'B'	....	....
Total	....	....
Add: ......% Inefficiency (if any)	....	....
Total Usage	....	....
B. *Add:* Closing Stock of Material		....
C. *Less:* Opening Stock of Material		....
D. Budgeted Purchases (Units) [A + B – C]		....
E. Rate per Unit (₹)		....
F. Budgeted Purchases (₹) (D × E)		....

Illustration 10. A manufacturing company provides you the following information:

	Product A	*Product B*
Material X @ ₹ 3 per unit	2 units	4 units
Material Y @ ₹ 1 per unit	1 unit	2 units
Units to be produced as per Production Budget	10,000	4,000
Inventory of Raw Material:		
	Material X	*Material Y*
Opening Stock as on 1.1.2014	12,000 units	2,000 units
Estimated Closing Stock as on 31.12.2014	16,000 units	4,000 units

Required : Prepare Direct Material Usage and Purchase Budget for the year 2014.

Solution:DIRECT MATERIALS USAGE AND PURCHASE BUDGET FOR THE BUDGET YEAR 2014

Particulars		*Material X*		*Material Y*
A. Budgeted Usage (for production):				
For Product 'A'	(10,000 × 2)	20,000	(10,000 × 1)	10,000
For Product 'B'	(4,000 × 4)	16,000	(4,000 × 2)	8,000
B. Total		36,000		18,000
C. *Add :* Closing Stock		16,000		4,000
D. *Less :* Opening Stock		12,000		2,000
E. Budgeted Purchases (Units) [B + C – D]		40,000		20,000
F. Rate per Unit		₹ 3		₹ 1
G. Budgeted Purchases (₹) (E × F)		₹ 1,20,000		₹ 20,000

Illustration 11. Assuming that the Material Prices are expected to increase by 10% and 2% inefficiency (i.e. 2% wasting allowance) is expected in the use of materials, in Illustration 10, prepare Direct Material Usage and Purchase Budget.

Solution: DIRECT MATERIALS USAGE AND PURCHASE BUDGET FOR THE BUDGET YEAR 2014

Particulars		*Material X*		*Material Y*
A. Budgeted Usage (for production):				
For Product 'A'	(10,000 x 2)	20,000	(10000 x 1)	10,000
For Product 'B'	(4,000 x 4)	16,000	(4000 x 2)	8,000
Total		36,000		18,000
Add: 2% Inefficiency		720		360
Total Usage		36,720		18,360
B. *Add :* Closing Stock		16,000		4,000
C. *Less :* Opening Stock		12,000		2,000
D. Budgeted Purchases (Units) [A + B – C]		40,720		20,360
E. Rate per Unit (₹)		3.3		1.1
F. Budgeted Purchases (₹) (D × E)		1,34,376		22,396

14.0 DIRECT LABOUR COST BUDGET

Meaning	Direct Labour Cost Budget represents the hours and cost of total labour force (*which may be distributed item-wise, period-wise, plant-wise, department-wise*) required during the budget period. Direct labour cost provides answers to the questions like: 1. What type of labour is required? (*say skilled, semi-skilled, unskilled*) 2. When is it required? (*say 1st Quarter, 2nd Quarter*) 3. Where is it required? (*say Plant I, Plant II*)

Basis	Direct Labour Cost Budget is generally based on Production Budget.
Factors	The following factors should be considered while preparing Direct Labour Cost Budget: 1. Production Requirement (*as per production Budget*) 2. Quality standard for each type of labour 3. Standard requirements of each type of labour required. 4. Standards rates for each type of labour required 5. Increase/Decrease in Labour Efficiency (Productivity)
Who is Responsible	The personnel director or manager is directly responsible for the preparation and execution of Direct Labour Cost Budget. It reveals the labour cost to be incurred in the manufacture, to facilitate preparation of manufacturing cost budgets and cash budgets for financing the wage bill.
Usefulness	1. Direct Labour Cost Budget facilitates the preparation of Cost of Goods Produced Budget/Production Cost Budget, Cash Budget and other budgets. 2. It enables the personnel department to plan ahead in recruitment and training of workers so that labour turnover can be reduced to minimum.

FORMAT OF MAN POWER BUDGET AND DIRECT LABOUR COST BUDGET

A simplest format of Man Power Budget and Direct Labour Cost Budget are given below:

MAN POWER BUDGET SHOWING LABOUR HOURS AND NUMBER OF WORKERS

Particulars	*Dept. P*	*Dept. Q*
A. Hours Required		
For Product 'A'	....	....
For Product 'B'	....	....
Total Budgeted Hours Required	....	....
Adjustment for Increase in Efficiency	....	....
B. Hours during Budget Period	....	....
C. Budgeted No. of Workers (A/B)	....	....

DIRECT LABOUR COST BUDGET

Particulars	*Dept. P*			*Dept. Q*		
	Hours Required	*Rate ₹*	*Amt. ₹*	*Hours Required*	*Rate ₹*	*Amt. ₹*
For Product 'A'	....	....	....	....	....	....
For Product 'B'	....	....	....	....	....	....
			....			....

Illustration 12. A factory works 8 hours per day, 6 days in a week and budget period is one year and during each quarter, lost hours due to leave, holidays and other causes are estimated to be 124 hours.

	Product 'A'	*Product 'B'*
Direct Labour per unit		
In P Dept. @ ₹ 1	2 hours	1 hour
In Q Dept. @ ₹ 3	1 hour	2 hours
Units to be produced as per production budget	10,000	4,000

Required : Prepare (a) Man Power Budget, showing Direct Labour hours and number of workers; and (b) Man Power Budget showing labour cost.

Solution: MAN POWER BUDGET SHOWING LABOUR HOURS AND NUMBER OF WORKERS

Particulars		Dept. P		Dept. Q
A. Hours Required				
For Product 'A'	(10,000 × 2)	20,000	(10,000 × 1)	10,000
For Product 'B'	(4,000 × 1)	4,000	(4000 × 2)	8,000
Total Budgeted Hours Required		24,000		18,000
B. Hours during Budget Period		2,000		2,000
C. Budgeted No. of Workers (A/B)		12		9

MAN POWER BUDGET SHOWING LABOUR COST

Particulars	Dept. P			Dept. Q		
	Hours Required	Rate ₹	Amt. ₹	Hours Required	Rate ₹	Amt. ₹
For Product 'A'	20,000	1	20,000	10,000	3	30,000
For Product 'B'	4,000	1	4,000	8,000	3	24,000
			24,000			54,000

Note : *Budgeted Working Hours = (8 × 6 × 52) – (124 × 4) = 2000 Hours*

Illustration 13. Assuming that the Wage Rates are expected to increase by 30% and 25% increase in labour productivity is expected and lost hours due to leave etc. are estimated to be 24 hours during each quarter, in Illustration 12, prepare Man Power Budget showing Labour Hours and Number of Workers and Direct Labour Cost Budget.

Solution: MAN POWER BUDGET SHOWING LABOUR HOURS AND NUMBER OF WORKERS

Particulars		Dept. P		Dept. Q
A. Hours Required				
For Product 'A'	(10,000 × 2)	20,000	(10,000 × 1)	10,000
For Product 'B'	(4,000 × 1)	4,000	(4,000 × 2)	8,000
Total Budgeted Hours Required		24,000		18,000
Adjustment for Increase in Efficiency	(Hours × 100/125)	19,200		14,400
B. Hours during Budget Period		2,400		2,400
C. Budgeted No. of Workers (A/B)		8		6

Note: *Budgeted Working Hours = (8 × 6 × 52) – (24 × 4) = 2400 Hours*

DIRECT LABOUR COST BUDGET

Particulars	Dept. P			Dept. Q		
	Hours Required	Rate ₹	Amt. ₹	Hours Required	Rate ₹	Amt. ₹
For Product 'A'	16,000	1.3	20,800	8,000	3.9	31,200
For Product 'B'	3,200	1.3	4,160	6,400	3.9	24,960
			24,960			56,160

Illustration 14. Tulsian Ltd. manufactures two products A and B. Product A requires 4 hours and Product B requires 3 hours. Budgeted Wage Rate is ₹ 8 per hour. Overtime Premium is 50% and is payable, if a worker works for more than 40 hours a week. There are 150 workers. The Production Manager has estimated the production of Product A to be 5,200 Units and Product B 11,320 Units. The Target Productivity Ratio (or Efficiency Ratio) for the Productive Hours worked by the direct worker in actually manufacturing the product is 80%. In addition, the non-productive downtime is budgeted at 20% of the productive hours worked. There are twelve 5 days week in the Budget period.

Required: Prepare Wages Budget for Direct Workers.

Solution: **WAGES BUDGET FOR DIRECT WORKERS**

Particulars		*Rate*	*Total Wages*
Standard Hours for Product A (5200 Units x 4 Hours)	20,800		
Standard Hours for Product B (11320 Units x 3 Hours)	33,960		
Total Standard Hours	54,760		
Total Standard Hours at 80% efficiency (54760 / 0.80)	68,450		
Add: Non-productive time (20% of 68450)	13,690		
Total Hours Required	82,140		
Less: Total Labour Hours (150 Workers x 40 Hours Per week x 12 Weeks)	72,000	8	5,76,000
Overtime	10,140	12	1,21,680
			6,97,680

15.0 FACTORY OVERHEADS BUDGET OR PRODUCTION/MANUFACTURING OVERHEADS BUDGET

Meaning of Factory Overheads	Factory Overheads represent all the indirect costs incurred in connection with the manufacture of a product. **For example** — Cost of indirect materials used in production, cost of indirect labour used in production, Factory Rent, Salary of Works Manager, Depreciation of Plant & Machinery used in factory.
Meaning of Factory Overheads Budget	Factory Overheads Budget represents the amount of total factory overheads (*which may be distributed element-wise, variability-wise, period-wise, plant-wise*) to be incurred during the budget period. Factory overheads Budget provides answers to the questions like: 1. on what item of factory overheads, it is to be incurred? (*say Indirect Material, Indirect Labour, Indirect Expenses*) 2. When is it to be incurred? (*say 1st Quarter, 2nd Quarter*) 3. Where it is to be incurred? (*say Plant I, Plant II*) Factory or manufacturing Overheads include the cost of indirect material, indirect labour and indirect expenses. Manufacturing overheads may be classified into (i) Fixed Overheads i.e., which tend to remain constant irrespective of change in the volume of output (ii) Variable Overheads i.e., which tend to vary with the output, and (iii) Semi-variable Overheads, i.e., which are partly variable and partly fixed.
How to Estimate Factory Overheads	Fixed manufacturing overheads can be estimated on the basis of the past information and knowledge of any change which may occur during the ensuring budget period. Variable overheads are estimated after considering the scheduled production and operating conditions in the budget period.
How to Prepare?	The factory overhead budget is prepared by integrating the separate budgets of all the production departments.
Who is Responsible?	Production Director/Manager is directly responsible for the preparation and execution of overall factory overheads budget.
Usefulness	The Factory Overhead Budget is useful for calculating the pre-determined overhead recovery rates.

FORMAT OF FACTORY OVERHEADS BUDGET

A simplest format of Factory Overheads Budget is given below:

FACTORY OVERHEADS BUDGET

for the Budget period ending ......

Period	*First Quarter* ₹	*Second Quarter* ₹	*Third Quarter* ₹	*Fourth Quarter* ₹	*Year Total* ₹
Variable :					
1. Spoilage	....	....	....	....	....
2. Indirect material	....	....	....	....	....
3. Printing & Stationery	....	....	....	....	....
4. Postage & Telegram	....	....	....	....	....
Total	....	....	....	....	....
Semi-Variable :					
1. Repair & Maintenance :					
— Factory building	....	....	....	....	....
— Factory furniture	....	....	....	....	....
— Factory Plant & equipment	....	....	....	....	....
2. Light, Power & heat	....	....	....	....	....
3. Water	....	....	....	....	....
4. Telephone	....	....	....	....	....
Total	....	....	....	....	....
Fixed :					
1. Wages & salaries	....	....	....	....	....
2. Rent, rates, taxes & lease expenses	....	....	....	....	....
3. Depreciation on :					
— Factory building	....	....	....	....	....
— Factory furniture	....	....	....	....	....
— Factory Plant & equipment	....	....	....	....	....
4. Insurance					
— Factory building	....	....	....	....	....
— Factory furniture	....	....	....	....	....
— Factory Plant & equipment	....	....	....	....	....
Total	....	....	....	....	....
Grand Total	....	....	....	....	....

Illustration 15. Factory Overheads are applied on the basis of direct labour hours:

	Dept. P	*Dept. Q*
	₹	₹
Fixed Overheads	48,000	18,000
Variable Overheads per labour hour	0.50	1.50
Direct Labour hours required as per direct labour hours budget :		
For Product A	20,000	10,000
For Product B	4,000	8,000

Required: Prepare Factory Overhead Cost Budget.

Soltuion: **FACTORY OVERHEADS COST BUDGET**

Particulars	*Dept.P*			*Dept. Q*		
A. Total Fixed OH	₹ 48,000			₹ 18,000		
B. Budgeted Hours	24,000			18,000		
C. Fixed OH Rate per hour (A/B)	₹ 2.00			₹ 1.00		
D. Variable OH Rate per Hour	₹ 0.50			₹ 1.50		
E. Total OH Rate per hour (C + D)	₹ 2.50			₹ 2.50		
	Product A	*Product B*	*Total*	*Product A*	*Product B*	*Total*
F. Budgeted Hours	20,000	4,000	24,000	10,000	8,000	18,000
G. Budgeted Fixed OH (C × F) @ ₹ 2.00	40,000	8,000	48,000	10,000	8,000	18,000
H. Budgeted Variable OH (D × F) @ ₹ 0.50	10,000	2,000	12,000	15,000	12,000	27,000
I. Total Budgeted OH [G + H]	50,000	10,000	60,000	25,000	20,000	45,000

16.0 PRODUCTION COST BUDGET

Meaning of Production Cost	Production Cost generally represents the aggregate of direct material cost, direct labour cost, direct expenses and factory overheads. Sometimes, administration expenses are treated as part of production cost.
Meaning of Production Cost Budget	Production Cost Budget represents the amount of total production cost (*which may be distributed element-wise, period-wise, product-wise*) to be incurred during the budget period. Production Cost Budget provides answers to the questions like: 1. What amount is to be incurred on material cost? 2. What amount is to be incurred on labour cost? 3. What amount is to be incurred on production overheads? 4. When is it to be incurred? (*say 1st Quarter, 2nd Quarter*)
Basis	Production Cost Budget is based on: 1. Direct Material Cost Budget; 2. Direct Labour Cost Budget; 3. Production overheads Budget.
Usefulness	The Production Cost Budget facilitates the preparation of Ending Inventory Budget and Goods Sold Budget.

FORMAT OF PRODUCTION COST BUDGET

A simplest format of Production Cost Budget is given below:

PRODUCTION COST BUDGET
for the Budget period ending......

Period / *Product*	*Product W* ₹	*Product X* ₹	*Product Y* ₹	*Product Z* ₹	*Total* ₹
1st Quarter					
Direct Material	.....	.....	.....	.....	.....
Direct Labour Cost	.....	.....	.....	.....	.....
Direct Expenses	.....	.....	.....	.....	.....
Prime Cost	.....	.....	.....	.....	.....
Production Overheads	.....	.....	.....	.....	.....
Production Cost	.....	.....	.....	.....	.....
2nd Quarter					

17.0 ENDING INVENTORY BUDGET

Meaning	Ending Inventory Budget represents the physical quantities and cost of closing stocks of each item of raw-materials and finished goods to be at the end of the budget period. Ending Inventory Budget provides answers to the questions like: 1. What is the quantity, unit cost and total cost of each item of raw-material at the end of budget period? 2. What is the quantity, unit cost and total cost of each item of finished goods at the end of budget period?
Basis	Ending Inventory budget is based on: 1. Production Budget; 2. Direct Material Purchase Budget; 3. Production Cost Budget.
Usefulness	Ending Inventory Budget facilitates the preparation of Cost of Goods Sold Budget, Budgeted Income Statement and Budgeted Balance Sheet.

FORMAT OF ENDING INVENTORY BUDGET

A simplest format of Ending Inventory Budget is given below:

ENDING INVENTORY BUDGET
for the Budget period ending ......

Period	*First Quarter*			*Second Quarter*			*Third Quarter*			*Fourth Quarter*			*Year Total*	
Ending Inventory	*Units*	*Rate* ₹	*Amt.* ₹	*Units*	*Rate* ₹	*Amt.* ₹	*Units*	*Rate* ₹	*Amt.* ₹	*Units*	*Rate* ₹	*Amt.* ₹	*Units*	*Amt.* ₹
Materials:														
A	....	....	....	....	....	....	....	....	....	....	....	....	....	....
B	....	....	....	....	....	....	....	....	....	....	....	....	....	....
Total			....			....			....			....		....
Work-in-progress:														
X	....	....	....	....	....	....	....	....	....	....	....	....	....	....
Y	....	....	....	....	....	....	....	....	....	....	....	....	....	....
Total			....			....			....			....		....

Finished goods														
X	......	......	......	......	......	......	......	......	......	......	......	......	......	......
Y	......	......	......	......	......	......	......	......	......	......	......	......	......	......
Total			......			......			......			......		......

Note: *Ending Inventory Budget showing the Computation of Unit Costs of WIP & Finished Goods*

	WIP — X			*WIP — Y*			*Finished Goods — X*			*Finished Goods — Y*		
Element of Costs	*Equi-valent* Units	Unit Cost	Amt.	*Equi-valent* Units	Unit Cost	Amt.	*Equi-valent Units*	Unit Cost	Amt.	*Equi-valent Units*	Unit Cost	Amt.
Material *A*	....	....	....	....	....	....	....	....	....	....	....	....
Material *B*	....	....	....	....	....	....	....	....	....	....	....	....
Direct Labour	....	....	....	....	....	....	....	....	....	....	....	....
Factory Overhead	....	....	....	....	....	....	....	....	....	....	....	....
Total			....			....			....			....

18.0 COST OF GOODS SOLD BUDGET

Meaning of Cost of Goods Sold	Cost of Goods Sold (COGS) represents the Cost of Goods produced *plus* cost of opening stock of finished goods *minus* cost of closing stock of finished goods.
Meaning of Cost of Goods Sold Budget	The cost of goods sold budget represents the total cost of goods (*which may be distributed product-wise, period-wise, area-wise*) to be sold during the budget period. If adjustments for opening and closing stock of finished goods are made in the Production Cost Budget, the budget will be called Cost of Goods Sold Budget.
Basis for the preparation	Cost of Goods sold Budget is based on — 1. Production Cost Budget; 2. Ending Inventory Budget for Current Budget Period; 3. Ending Inventory Budget for Previous Budget Period.

FORMAT OF COST OF GOODS SOLD BUDGET

A simplest format of Cost of Goods Sold Budget is given below:

COST OF GOODS SOLD BUDGET
for the Budget period ending......

Period / *Particulars*	*Product X* (₹)	*Product Y* (₹)	*Total* (₹)
A. Direct Material Purchased	.... (As per Direct Material	Purchases Budget)	....
Add : Opening Stock of Mat.	....	....	....
Less : Closing Stock of Mat.	.... (As per Ending	Inventory Budget)........	
B. Direct Labour	.... (As per Direct	Labour Budget)	....
C. Direct Expenses	.... (As per Direct	Expenses Budget)........	
D. Prime Cost (A + B + C)	....	....	....
E. Production Overheads	.... (As per Production	Overheads Budget)	....

Period / Particulars	Product X (₹)		Product Y (₹)		Year Total (₹)
F. Total Production Cost incurred	....	....	....	....	....
Add : Opening Stock of WIP-X	....	....	....	....	....
Less : Closing Stock of WIP-X	....	(As per Ending Inventory Budget)........			
G. Cost of Goods Produced	....	....	....	....	....
Add : Opening Stock of FG-X	....	....	....	....	....
Less : Closing Stock of FG-X	....	(As per Ending Inventory Budget)........			
H. Cost of Goods Sold	....	....	....	....	....

Illustration 16. X Ltd. provides you following information:

	Product A	*Product B*
Direct Materials :		
X @ ₹ 3 per unit	2 units	4 units
Y @ ₹ 1 per unit	1 unit	2 units
Direct Labour per unit :		
In P Dept.	2 hours @ ₹ 1 per hour	1 hour @ ₹ 2 per hour
In Q Dept.	1 hour @ ₹ 3 per hour	1 hour @ ₹ 3 per hour
Production Overheads :		
Fixed	@ ₹ 1.63 per hour	@ ₹ 1.63 per hour
Variable	@ ₹ 0.87 per hour	@ ₹ 0.87 per hour
Units to be produced as per Production Budget	10,000	4,000
Estimated Closing Stock of Finished Goods	2,200	1,000
Opening Stock of Finished Goods	200	2,000
Valuation of Opening Stock	@ ₹ 25	@ ₹ 37.5

Required : Prepare Cost of Goods Sold Budget.

Solution: **COST OF GOODS SOLD BUDGET FOR THE BUDGET PERIOD**

Particulars	*Product 'A'* ₹	*Product 'B'* ₹	*Total* ₹
A. Direct Materials consumed :			
Material : X	60,000	48,000	1,08,000
Y	10,000	8,000	18,000
B. Direct Labour Incurred :			
Dept. 'P'	20,000	8,000	28,000
Dept. 'Q'	30,000	12,000	42,000
C. Production Overheads :			
Fixed	48,900	13,040	61,940
Variable	26,100	6,960	33,060
D. Cost of Goods Produced (A + B + C)	1,95,000	96,000	2,91,000
E. Adjustment for Opening & Closing Inventory of Finished Goods:			
(a) *Add :* Opening Stock	5,000	75,000	80,000
(b) *Less :* Closing Stock *	(42,900)	(24,000)	(66,900)
F. Cost of Goods Sold (D ± E)	1,57,100	1,47,000	3,04,100

* *Calculation of Closing Stock*

$$\text{For Product 'A'} = \frac{\text{Total Cost of Goods Produced}}{\text{Units Produced}} \times \text{Closing Stock} = \frac{1{,}95{,}000}{10{,}000} \times 2{,}200 = 42{,}900$$

$$\text{For Product 'B'} = \frac{96{,}000}{4{,}000} \times 1{,}000 = 24{,}000$$

19.0 ADMINISTRATIVE COST BUDGET

Meaning of Administrative Cost	Administrative Cost refer to those Costs which are incurred in connection with formulation of the policy, directing the organisation and controlling the operations of an undertaking which is not related directly to production, selling and distribution, research or development activity or function. **Examples** of such costs are salaries of the office staff. Rent/depreciation of Office Building, depreciation, repairs, maintenance, insurance of office furniture & machinery, printing and stationary, postage, telephone, etc.
Meaning of Administrative Cost Budget	Administrative Cost Budget represent the amount of total office & administrative expenses (*which may be distributed element-wise, variability-wise, period-wise, area-wise*) to be incurred during the budget period. Office & Administrative Cost budget provides answers to the questions like: 1. On what items of office & administrative expenses, it is to be incurred? (*say salaries, depreciation, stationary, postage*) 2. When is it to be incurred? (*say 1st Quarter, 2nd Quarter*) 3. Where is it to be incurred? (*say Office I, Office II*)
How to Estimate	Fixed Administrative Expenses can be estimated on the basis of the past information and knowledge of any changes which may occur during the ensuing Budget period.
How to Prepare	Administrative expenses Budget is prepared by integrating the separate budgets of all the administrative offices.
Who is responsible	Administration Director/Manager is directly responsible for the preparation and execution of overall Office & Administrative Cost Budget.
Usefulness	Administrative Cost Budget is useful for calculating the pre-determined Administrative Overhead Rates.

FORMAT OF ADMINISTRATIVE COST BUDGET

A simplest format of Administrative Cost is given below:

ADMINISTRATIVE COST BUDGET
for the Budget period ending......

Period / Nature of Office & Adm. Costs	*First Quarter (₹)*	*Second Quarter (₹)*	*Third Quarter (₹)*	*Fourth Quarter (₹)*	*Year Total (₹)*
Variable :					
1. Repair & Maintenance :					
— Office building	....	....	....	....	....
— Office furniture equipment	....	....	....	....	....
2. Light & power	....	....	....	....	....
3. Water	....	....	....	....	....
4. Telephones	....	....	....	....	....
Total Variable Costs	....	....	....	....	....
Fixed :					
1. Wages & Salaries	....	....	....	....	....
2. Rent, rates & taxes	....	....	....	....	....
3. Depreciation on :					
— Office building	....	....	....	....	....
— Office furniture & equipment	....	....	....	....	....

Period / Nature of Office & Adm. Costs	First Quarter (₹)	Second Quarter (₹)	Third Quarter (₹)	Fourth Quarter (₹)	Year Total (₹)
4. Insurance on :					
— Office building	....	....	....	....	....
— Office furniture & equipment	....	....	....	....	....
— Cash in transit	....	....	....	....	....
5. Travelling expenses	....	....	....	....	....
6. Audit fees	....	....	....	....	....
7. Professional service fees	....	....	....	....	....
8. Bank Charges	....	....	....	....	....
9. Director's fees	....	....	....	....	....
10. Donations	....	....	....	....	....
11. Legal costs	....	....	....	....	....
12. Printing & stationary	....	....	....	....	....
13. Postage & Telegram	....	....	....	....	....
Total Fixed Costs	....	....	....	....	....
Grand Total	....	....	....	....	....

Illustration 17. A department of Company X attains Sales of ₹ 6,00,000 at 80 per cent of its normal capacity and its expenses are given below :

	₹
Administrative Costs :	
Office Salaries	90,000
General Expenses	2 per cent of sales
Depreciation	7,500
Rates and Taxes	8,750
Selling Costs :	
Salaries	8 per cent of sales
Travelling Expenses	2 per cent of sales
Sales Office	1 per cent of sales
General Expenses	1 per cent of sales
Distribution Costs :	
Wages	15,000
Rent1 per cent of sales	
Other Expenses	4 per cent of sales

Required : Draw up Flexible Administration, Selling and Distribution Costs Budget, operating at 90 per cent, 100 per cent and 110 per cent of normal capacity.

Solution: **FLEXIBLE BUDGET OF DEPARTMENT ... OF COMPANY 'X'**

Particulars	*Basis*	*Level of activity*			
		80% ₹	*90%* ₹	*100%* ₹	*110%* ₹
Sales		6,00,000	6,75,000	7,50,000	8,25,000
Expenses :					
Administrative Costs :					
Office Salaries	Fixed	90,000	90,000	90,000	90,000
General Expenses	2% of Sales	12,000	13,500	15,000	16,500
Depreciation	Fixed	7,500	7,500	7,500	7,500
Rates & Taxes	Fixed	8,750	8,750	8,750	8,750
Total Administration Costs		1,18,250	1,19,750	1,21,250	1,22,750

Particulars	*Basis*	*Level of activity* 80% ₹	90% ₹	100% ₹	110% ₹
Selling Costs :					
Salaries	8% of Sales	48,000	54,000	60,000	66,000
Travelling Expenses	2% of Sales	12,000	13,500	15,000	16,500
Sales Office Expenses	1% of Sales	6,000	6,750	7,500	8,250
General Expenses	1% of Sales	6,000	6,750	7,500	8,250
Total Selling Costs		72,000	81,000	90,000	99,000
Distribution Costs :					
Wages	Fixed	15,000	15,000	15,000	15,000
Rent	1% of Sales	6,000	6,750	7,500	8,250
Other Expenses	4% of Sales	24,000	27,000	30,000	33,000
Total Distribution Costs		45,000	48,750	52,500	56,250
Total Administrative Selling and Dist. Costs		2,35,250	2,49,500	2,63,750	2,78,000

Note: *In the absence of information it has been assumed that office salaries, depreciation, rates and taxes and wages remain the same at 110% level of activity also. However, in practice some of these costs may change if present capacity is exceeded.*

20.0 SELLING AND DISTRIBUTION COST BUDGET

Meaning of Selling Costs	Selling costs are defined as the cost of seeking, to create and stimulate demand and of securing orders. Thee costs are, therefore, incurred to maintain and increase the level of sales. All expenses connected with advertising, sales promotion, sales office, salesmen, credit collection, market research, after sales service, etc are generally grouped together to form part of the responsibility of the sales manager. While making a budget, selling costs are divided into fixed and variable. Semi-variable costs should also be separated into variable and fixed elements. Using the past experience as a guide, consideration should be given to the future trend of sales, possible changes in competition, etc., in pre-determination of selling costs.
Meaning of Distribution Cost	Distribution cost has been defined as the cost of the sequence of operations which begins with making the packet product available for dispatch and ends with making the re-conditioned return empty package, if any, available for re-use. It also includes: (a) expenditure incurred in transporting articles to central or local storage. (b) expenditure incurred in moving articles to and from prospective customers as in case of goods on sale or return basis. (c) expenditure relating to pipes, mains and services which may be regarded as equivalent of packing and transportation in case of gas, electricity and water industry.
Meaning of Selling & Distribution Cost Budget	Selling & Distribution Cost Budget represents the amount of total selling & distribution cost (*which may be distributed element-wise, variability-wise, period-wise, area-wise*) to be incurred during the budget period. Selling & Distribution Cost Budget provides answers to the questions like: 1. on what items of selling cost/distribution cost it is to be incurred (*say advertising, transportation*)

	2. when is it to be incurred? (*say 1st Quarter, 2nd Quarter*) 3. where is it to be incurred? (*say Sales Office I, Sales Office II, Warehouse I, Warehouse II*)
How to estimate S & D Costs	Fixed selling & distribution costs can be estimated on the basis of the past information and knowledge of any changes which may occur during the ensuing budget period. Variable selling & distribution costs can be estimated after considering the scheduled sales and operating conditions in the budget period.
How to prepare	Selling & Distribution Cost is prepared by integrating the separate budgets of all the Sales Offices and Distribution Offices.
Who is Responsible	Sales Director/Manager is directly responsible for the preparation and execution of overall Selling & Distribution Cost Budget.
Usefulness	Selling & Distribution Cost Budget is useful for calculating the pre-determined Selling and Distribution Overheads Rates.

FORMAT OF SELLING & DISTRIBUTION COST BUDGET

A simplest format of Selling & Distribution Cost Budget is given below:

SELLING COSTS BUDGET

for the Budget period ending.....

Product & Area / *Nature of Selling Costs*	*Basis of Apportionment (₹)*	*Product X*		*Product Y*	
		North (₹)	*South (₹)*	*North (₹)*	*South (₹)*
Variable :					
1. Salesmen's commission	....	....	....	....	....
2. Salesmen's stationery	....	....	....	....	....
3. Salesmen's postage & Telegram	....	....	....	....	....
4. Bad debts	....	....	....	....	....
Total Variable Costs	....	....	....	....	....
Semi-variable :					
1. Repair & Maintenance :					
— Sales office	....	....	....	....	....
— Show rooms	....	....	....	....	....
— Furniture & equipment	....	....	....	....	....
2. Light & Power	....	....	....	....	....
3. Water	....	....	....	....	....
4. Telephones	....	....	....	....	....
Total Semi-variable Costs	....	....	....	....	....
Fixed :					
1. Wages & Salaries	....	....	....	....	....
2. Rent, rates, taxes & lease exp.	....	....	....	....	....
3. Depreciation on :					
— Saies Office	....	....	....	....	....
— Show rooms	....	....	....	....	....
— Furniture & Equipment	....	....	....	....	....

Nature of Selling Costs / Product & Area	Basis of Apportionment (₹)	Product X		Product Y	
		North (₹)	South (₹)	North (₹)	South (₹)
4. Insurance :					
— Sales Office	....	....	....	....	....
— Show-Rooms	....	....	....	....	....
— Furniture & equipment	....	....	....	....	....
5. Advertising	....	....	....	....	....
6. Travelling	....	....	....	....	....
Total Fixed Costs	....	....	....	....	....
Grand Total	....	....	....	....	....

DISTRIBUTION COSTS BUDGET

For the Budget period ending.....

Nature of Selling Costs / Product & Area	Basis of Apportionment (₹)	Product X		Product Y	
		North (₹)	South (₹)	North (₹)	South (₹)
Variable :					
1. Outside transport	....	....	....	....	....
2. Owned transport	....	....	....	....	....
3. Fuel & Oil	....	....	....	....	....
Total Variable Costs	....	....	....	....	....
Semi-Variable :					
1. Repair & maintenance :					
— Owned vehicles	....	....	....	....	....
— Storage & warehouse	....	....	....	....	....
2. Light & power	....	....	....	....	....
3. Water	....	....	....	....	....
4. Telephones	....	....	....	....	....
Total Semi-variable Costs	....	....	....	....	....
Fixed :					
1. Wages & Salaries	....	....	....	....	....
2. Rent, rates, taxes :					
— Store house	....	....	....	....	....
— Warehouse	....	....	....	....	....
3. Depreciation on :					
— Store Building	....	....	....	....	....
— Furniture & Equipment	....	....	....	....	....
4. Licences & Insurance :					
— Stores building	....	....	....	....	....
— Store Fur. & Equp.	....	....	....	....	....
— Vehicles	....	....	....	....	....
Total Fixed Costs	....	....	....	....	....
Grand Total	....	....	....	....	....

Illustration 18. P.C.T. Ltd. provides you the following information :

Sales Area	*Product X* ₹	*Product Y* ₹	*Total Sales* ₹
A	25,000	50,000	75,000
B	50,000	75,000	1,25,000
C	75,000	1,25,000	2,00,000

Direct Selling & Distribution Costs :

Area	*A*	*B*	*C*
Amount (₹)	15,050	15,500	9,450

Indirect Selling & Distribution Costs :

Advertising & General Administration	18,000
Carriage & Warehousing	9,900
Credit control Dept.'s Expenses	4,400

Budgeted Analysis of Sales is as follows :

	Product X		*Product Y*	
Area	*Sales Volume*	*No. of orders*	*Sales Volume*	*No. of orders*
A	4,000	600	4,000	800
B	8,000	1,000	6,000	1,000
C	12,000	400	10,000	600

As per cost manual, (a) the basis of apportionment of selling & distribution costs to product shall be the Sales values. (b) The basis of apportionment of indirect selling & distribution costs to sales area shall be as follows :

Advertising & General Administration	Sales values
Carriage & Warehousing	Sales volume
Credit Control Dept's Expenses	No. of orders

Required : Prepare a Selling & Distribution Cost Budget (a) by Sales areas and (b) by products.

Solution: (a) SELLING & DISTRIBUTION COSTS BUDGET (BY SALES AREAS)

Item of Costs	*Basis of Apportionment*	*Total*	*Sales Areas*		
			A ₹	*B* ₹	*C* ₹
A. Direct Costs	Actual	40,000	15,050	15,500	9,450
B. Indirect Costs					
— Adv. & G. Adm.	Sales Value 3 : 5 : 8	18,000	3,375	5,625	9,000
— Carriage & Warehousing	Sales Volume 4 : 7 : 11	9,900	1,800	3,150	4,950
— Credit Control Dept.'s Expenses	No. of Orders 7 : 10 : 5	4,400	1,400	2,000	1,000
		32,300	6,575	10,775	14,950
C. Total Costs (A + B)		72,300	21,625	26,275	24,400

(b) SELLING & DISTRIBUTION COSTS BUDGET (BY PRODUCTS)

Item of Costs	Basis of Apportion-ment	Product X				Product Y			
		A	B	C	Total	A	B	C	Total
A. Direct Costs	Sales Value	5,017	6,200	3,544	14,761	10,033	9,300	5,906	25,239
B. Indirect Costs	Sales Value	2,192	4,310	5,606	12,108	4,383	6,465	9,344	20,192
C. Total Costs (A + B)		7,209	10,510	9,150	26,869	14,416	15,765	15,250	45,431

21.0 RESEARCH AND DEVELOPMENT COST BUDGET

Meaning of Research Costs	Research costs are the costs of researching for new or improved production, new application of materials or improved methods, processes, system or services. Research may be *either* pure research *or* applied research. **Pure research** refers to the research directed towards improving understanding in a particular field without regard to its specific uses. **Applied research** refers to the research which is directed towards practical application of exciting knowledge with a view to gain same specified objectives. An organisation has to strike balance between pure research and applied research after achieving a trade off between the possible costs and possible benefits associated with each research.
Meaning of Development Costs	Development follow research and refers to the commercial application of knowledge gained by research. Development costs are the costs of the process, which begin with the implementation of the decision to produce a new or improved products or to employ a new or improved method and ends with commencement of formal production of that product or by that method.
Research and Development Aotivitics	In order to servive and grow in the existing competitive market, it has become essential to undertake research and development activities. Research and Development activities include: 1. Search for new product and new manufacturing process; 2. Improvement and redesign of existing products, processes and equipments; 3. Finding new uses of existing products; 4. Performance testing of product keeping in view the requirements of customers; 5. Solving technical problems arising in manufacture and application of existing products.
Meaning of Research & Development Cost Budget	Research & Development Cost Budget represents the amount of total research & development costs (*which may be distributed period-wise*) to be incurred during the budget period. Research & Development Cost Budget provides answers to the questions like: 1. On what item of Research & development cost, it is to be incurred? (*say salaries of staff, laboratory experts, survey expenses, Research material expenses*) 2. When it is to be incurred? (*say 1st Quarter, 2nd Quarter*) 3. Where it is to be incurred? (*say Research Center I, Research Center II*)

How to prepare	Research & Development Cost Budget is prepared by integrating the separate budgets of all the research centers.
Methods used for Allocation of R&D Costs	The methods used for allocation of R&D Cost are as follows: 1. A percentage based on total sales value method. This method is good if sales value is steady from year to year. 2. A percentage based on net profit. 3. A total sum is estimated on the basis of past experience and future R&D plans and policies. 4. A sum is fixed on the basis of resources available with the company. 5. All factors which affect the importance of R&D are considered. **For example,** factors like demand for existing products, competitors, economic conditions, etc., are considered and a amount of R&D budget is estimated.

22.0 CAPITAL EXPENDITURE BUDGET

Meaning	Capital expenditure budget represents the amount of expenditure or fixed assets (*which may distributed period-wise, area-wise, item-wise*) to be incurred during the budget period. This budget provides answers to the questions like: 1. What type of fixed assets are to be acquired? (*say land, building, plant & machinery, furniture*) 2. When these assets are to be acquired? (*say 1st Quarter, 2nd Quarter*) 3. Where these assets are to be acquired? (*say Plant I, Office I*)
Factors	This budget should be prepared after considering the following factors: 1. Capital Development Plans; 2. Modernisation Plans; 3. Renovation Plans; 4. Expansion Plans; 5. Replacement Plans; 6. Available of Long-term Funds; 7. Expected Future Earnings; 8. Overheads on production facilities of certain departments as indicated by the Plant Utilization Budget.
Usefulness	Capital expenditure Budget facilitates— 1. The preparation of Cash Budget, Budgeted Income Statement (e.g. Budgeted Depreciation on Budgeted Capital Expenditure), Budgeted Balance Sheet, Budgeted Cash Flow Statement 2. The calculation of Budgeted Rate of Return on Capital employed.

FORMAT OF CAPITAL EXPENDITURE BUDGET

A simplest format of Capital Expenditure Budget is given below:

CAPITAL EXPENDITURE BUDGET

for the Budget period ending....

Period / *Capital Expenditure*	*First Quarter* (₹)	*Second Quarter* (₹)	*Third Quarter* (₹)	*Fourth Quarter* (₹)	*Year Total* (₹)
Land & building	....	....	....	....	....
Plant & machinery	....	....	....	....	....
Furniture	....	....	....	....	....
Other fixed assets	....	....	....	....	....

Capital Expenditure \ Period	First Quarter (₹)	Second Quarter (₹)	Third Quarter (₹)	Fourth Quarter (₹)	Year Total (₹)
A Total Capital Expenditure	....	....	....	....	....
B Cost of fixed assets to be financed by other than cash	....	....	....	....	....
C Current Cash Expenditure (A – B)	....	....	....	....	....

23.0 CASH BUDGET

Meaning	Cash Budget represents the amount of estimated cash inflows, estimated cash outflows (*which may be distributed period-wise, item-wise*) and deficits/surplus over a given budget period. Cash budget provides answers to the questions like: 1. What are the likely cash inflows? 2. What are the likely cash outflows? 3. When will there be situations of surplus? 4. When will there be situations of deficits? 5. Where will there be situation of surplus/deficit? (*say Region I, Region II*)
Basis	Cash Budget is based on— 1. Sales Budget; 2. Direct Material Purchase Budget; 3. Direct Labour Cost Budget; 4. Production Overheads Budget; 5. Administrative Cost Budget; 6. Selling & Distribution Cost Budget; 7. Capital Expenditure Budget. 8. Research & Development Cost Budget.
Basic Purpose	Cash Budget serves as a device for planning and controlling the sources and uses of cash to ensure the availability of cash at a time when it is needed.
Importance	The importance of preparing a Cash Budget are summarised as follows: 1. It enables the management to determine the timings when there is likely to be a surplus/shortage of cash. 2. It enables the management to determine the quantum of surplus/shortage of cash. 3. It enables the management to determine the period for which the situation of shortage/surplus is likely to be continued. 4. It enables the management to prepare the borrowing schedule. 5. It enables the management to prepare the repayment schedule well in advance. 6. It enables the management to plan for dividend payment well in advance. 7. It enables the management to plan for financing the expansion/modernisation of the existing plant. 8. It enables the management to plan for financing a new project. 9. It enables the management to take advantage of cash discount. However, it should be well understood that the Cash Budget is only as much useful as the accuracy of the forecasts that are used in its preparation.
Methods of Preparation	Two popular methods of preparing Cash Budget are: 1. Receipts and Payments Method 2. Adjusted Net Income Method

RECEIPTS AND PAYMENTS METHOD

The practical steps involved in the preparation of Cash Budget as per Receipts and Payments Method are as follows;

PRACTICAL STEPS INVOLVED IN THE PREPARATION OF CASH BUDGET

Step 1: *Ascertain the Opening Balance*

Step 2: *Identify, Analyse and Estimate the Cash Inflows such as:*

(a) **Operating Cash inflows** (i.e. Cash inflows relating to operating activities such as cash sales, collection from debtors and trading commission).

(b) **Investing Cash inflows** (i.e. Cash inflows relating to investing activities such as sale of investments, sale of fixed assets, interest and dividend on investments).

(c) **Financing Cash inflows** (i.e. Cash inflows relating to financing activities such as proceeds from issue of shares, debentures).

Step 3: *Identify, Analyse and Estimate the Cash Outflows such as:*

(a) **Operating Cash outflows** (i.e. Cash outflows relating to operating activities such as cash purchases, payment to creditors, payment of operating expenses).

(b) **Investing Cash outflows** (i.e. Cash outflows relating to investing activities such as purchase of investments, purchase of fixed assets).

(c) **Financing Cash outflows** (i.e. Cash outflows relating to financing activities such as redemption of shares and debentures, payment of interest, tax and dividend).

Step 4: *Estimate the Net Cash Inflow and Outflow.*

In case of deficit, necessary arrangement should be made to finance the deficit. In case of surplus, necessary arrangement should be made to invest the surplus.

SPECIMEN OF CASH BUDGET AS PER RECEIPTS AND PAYMENTS METHOD

CASH BUDGET

for the Budget period ending.....

Particulars	*Period*			
	April (₹)	*May (₹)*	*June (₹)*	*July (₹)*
A. Total Cash Available:				
1. Opening Cash Balance	....	....	....	....
2. Cash Sales	....	....	....	....
3. Collections from Debtors	....	....	....	....
4. Proceeds from Issue of Shares/Debentures	....	....	....	....
5. Proceeds from Sale of Fixed Assets	....	....	....	....
6. Misc. Non-operating Incomes received	....	....	....	....
Total (1 + 2 + 3 + 4 + 5 + 6)	....	....	....	....
B. Total Cash Payments:				
7. Cash Purchases of Material	....	....	....	....
8. Payments to Suppliers of Materials	....	....	....	....
9. Payments of Direct Labour Wages	....	....	....	....
10. Payment of Production Overheads (Excluding Non-Cash Costs like Depreciation)	....	....	....	....
11. Payment of Administration Expenses (Excluding Non-Cash Costs like Depreciation)	....	....	....	....

Particulars	Period			
	April (₹)	May (₹)	June (₹)	July (₹)
12. Payment of Selling and Distribution Expenses (Excluding Non-Cash Costs like Depreciation)	....	....	....	....
13. Redemption of Redeemable Pref. Shares/Debentures/Buy Back of Shares	....	....	....	....
14. Purchase of Fixed Asset	....	....	....	....
15. Misc. Non-operating Expenses paid	....	....	....	....
16. Advance Payment of Income-tax	....	....	....	....
17. Payment of Dividend (Interim or Final)	....	....	....	....
Total Cash Payments (7 + ... + 17)	....	....	....	....
18. Surplus (Shortage) (A – B)	....	....	....	....
19. Effects of Short-term Financing and Investing				
Proceeds of Short-term Borrowings	....	....	....	....
Proceeds of Marketable Securities	....	....	....	....
Less : Repayment of loan principal	(.......)	(.......)	(.......)	(.......)
Less : Repayment of interest on loan	(.......)	(.......)	(.......)	(.......)
Less : Investment in Marketable Securities	(.......)	(.......)	(.......)	(.......)
20. Closing Cash Balance (18 ± 19)	....	....	....	....

Working Note: *Calculation of Cash Sales, Collection from Debtors, Cash Purchases and Payments to Suppliers.*

Particulars	Jan.	Feb.	Mar.	Apr.	May	Jun.	Jul.
A. No. of Units Sold	....	....	....	....	....	....	....
B. Selling Price per unit	....	....	....	....	....	....	....
C. Total Sales (A × B)	....	....	....	....	....	....	....
D. *Less:* Cash Sales	....	....	....	....	....	....	....
E. Credit Sales (C – D)	....	....	....	....	....	....	....
F. *Less:* Bad Debts	....	....	....	....	....	....	....
G. Good Debtors (E – F)	....	....	....	....	....	....	....
H. Collection from Debtors:							
In month following month of sales	....	....	....	....	....	....	....
In Second month	....	....	....	....	....	....	....
In Third month	....	....	....	....	....	....	....
I. Gross Profit on Sales (C×GP%)	....	....	....	....	....	....	....
J. Total Purchases (C – I)	....	....	....	....	....	....	....
K. *Less:* Cash Purchases	....	....	....	....	....	....	....
L. Credit Purchases (J – K)	....	....	....	....	....	....	....
M. Payment to Suppliers	....	....	....	....	....	....	....

Working Notes: When Opening and Closing Balances of Stock, Trade Debtors, Trade Creditors and Creditors for Expenses are given:

(i) Calculation of Cash Sales and Collection from Debtors

Particulars	*Jan.*	*Feb.*	*March*	*April*	*May*	*June*
A. Sales (Units)	......	......	......	......	......	......
B. Selling Price per Unit	......	......	......	......	......	......
C. Total Sales	......	......	......	......	......	......
D. *Less:* Cash Sales	......	......	......	......	......	......
E. Credit Sales	......	......	......	......	......	......
F. *Add:* Opening Trade Debtors	......	......	......	......	......	......
G. *Less:* Closing Trade Debtors	......	......	......	......	......	......
H. Collection from Debtors	......	......	......	......	......	......

(ii) Calculation of Cash Purchases and Payment to Creditors

Particulars	*Jan.* ₹	*Feb.* ₹	*March* ₹	*April* ₹	*May* ₹	*June* ₹
A. Total Sales	......	......	......	......	......	......
B. *Less:* Gross Profit	......	......	......	......	......	......
C. Cost of Goods Sold	......	......	......	......	......	......
D. *Add:* Closing Stock	......	......	......	......	......	......
E. *Less:* Opening Stock	......	......	......	......	......	......
F. *Less:* Wages & Other Direct Exp.	......	......	......	......	......	......
G. Total Purchases	......	......	......	......	......	......
H. *Less:* Cash Purchases	......	......	......	......	......	......
I. Credit Purchases	......	......	......	......	......	......
J. *Add:* Opening Trade Creditors	......	......	......	......	......	......
K. *Less:* Closing Trade Creditors	......	......	......	......	......	......
L. Payment to Creditors	......	......	......	......	......	......

(iii) Payment of Expenses (excluding Depreciation)

Particulars	*April (₹)*	*May (₹)*	*June (₹)*
Expenses (Excluding Depreciation)	......	......	......
Add: Opening Creditors for Expenses	......	......	......
Less: Closing Creditors for Expenses	......	......	......
Total Payment of Expenses	......	......	......

Illustration 19. [Calculation of the amount of Cash Sales and Collection from the Debtors]

Tulsian (1) Ltd. provides you the following information:

(a)

Month	*January*	*February*	*March*	*April*	*May*	*June*
Sales (in units)	1,000	2,000	3,000	4,000	5,000	6,000

(b) 20% of the Sales are on cash basis and the balance on credit basis.

(c) Uniform Selling Price — ₹ 20 per unit.

Required: Calculate the amount of Cash Sales and Collection from Debtors for the months, April to June in each of the following alternative cases:

Case (a) If credit period allowed to customers is 1 month.

Case (b) If credit period allowed to customers is 2 months.

Case (c) If credit period allowed to customers is 3 months.

Case (d) If 50% of Credit sales are collected in the month of Sales and the balance in the month following.

Case (e) If 50% of Credit sales are collected within one month and the balance in two months.

Case (f) If 2% of Credit sales constitute bad debt losses. 50% of the good accounts receivables are collected in the month of the sales and the rest in the next month.

Case (g) If realisation from debtors are 30% in the month of sales, 60% in the month following that and the balance in the month after that.

Case (h) If 50% of Credit sales are collected in the month following the sales, 50% of the remaining in the second month and the balance in the third month.

Solution:

CALCULATION OF CASH SALES AND CREDIT SALES

Particulars	*Jan.*	*Feb.*	*Mar.*	*Apr*	*May*	*June*
A.Sales (Units)	1,000	2,000	3,000	4,000	5,000	6,000
B.Selling Price per unit	20	20	20	20	20	20
C.Total Sales (A x B)	20,000	40,000	60,000	80,000	1,00,000	1,20,000
D.*Less*: Cash Sales @ 20%	4,000	8,000	12,000	16,000	20,000	24,000
E.Credit Sales @ 80%	16,000	32,000	48,000	64,000	80,000	96,000

Case (a)	*April* ₹	*May* ₹	*June* ₹
Cash Sales	16,000	20,000	24,000
Collection from Debtors	48,000	64,000	80,000

Case (b)	*April* ₹	*May* ₹	*June* ₹
Cash Sales	16,000	20,000	24,000
Collection from Debtors	32,000	48,000	64,000

Case (c)	*April* ₹	*May* ₹	*June* ₹
Cash Sales	16,000	20,000	24,000
Collection from Debtors	16,000	32,000	48,000

Case (d)	*April* ₹	*May* ₹	*June* ₹
Cash Sales	16,000	20,000	24,000
Collection from Debtors			
50% of the Current Month's Sales	32,000	40,000	48,000
50% of Previous Month's Sales	24,000	32,000	40,000
	56,000	72,000	88,000

Case (e)	*April* ₹	*May* ₹	*June* ₹
Cash Sales	16,000	20,000	24,000
Collection from Debtors	24,000	32,000	40,000
	16,000	24,000	32,000
	40,000	56,000	72,000

Case (f)	*April* ₹	*May* ₹	*June* ₹
Cash Sales	16,000	20,000	48,000
Collection from Debtors			
50% of Current Month's Good Receivables	31,360	39,200	47,040
50% of Previous Month's Good Receivables	23,520	31,360,	39,200
	54,880	70,560	86,240

***Working Note:** Calculation of Good Accounts Receivable*

	Jan. ₹	*Feb.* ₹	*Mar.* ₹	*Apr.* ₹	*May* ₹	*June* ₹
Credit Sales	16,000	32,000	48,000	64,000	80,000	96,000
Less: 2% Bad Debts	320	640	960	1,280	1,600	1,920
Good A/c Receivable	15,680	31,360	47,040	62,720	78,400	94,080

Case (g)	*April* ₹	*May* ₹	*June* ₹
Cash Sales	16,000	20,000	24,000
Collection from Debtors			
30% of Current Month's Sales	19,200	24,000	28,800
60% of Previous Month's Sales	28,800	38,400	48,000
10% of Previous to Previous Month's Sales	3,200	4,800	6,400
	51,200	67,200	83,200

Case (h)	*April* ₹	*May* ₹	*June* ₹
Cash Sales	16,000	20,000	24,000
Collection from Debtors			
50% of Previous Month's Sales	24,000	32,000	40,000
25% of Previous to Previous Month's Sales	8,000	12,000	16,000
25% of third Previous Month's Sales	4,000	8,000	12,000
	36,000	52,000	68,000

Illustration 20. [Calculation of the amount of Cash Sales and Collection from the Debtors]

Tulsian(2) Ltd. provides you the following information:

(a)

Month	**January**	**February**	**March**	**April**	**May**	**June**
Sales (units)	1,000	2,000	3,000	4,000	5,000	6,000
Closing Trade Debtors (₹)	16,000	40,000	64,000	88,000	1,12,000	1,36,000

(b) 20% of the sales are on Cash basis and the balance on credit sales.

(c) Uniform Selling Price — ₹ 20 per unit.

Required: Calculate the amount of Cash Sales and Collection from Debtors for the months Jan. to June.

Solution:

CALCULATION OF CASH SALES AND COLLECTION FROM TRADE DEBTORS

	Particulars	*January*	*February*	*March*	*April*	*May*	*June*
A.	Sales (Units)	1,000	2,000	3,000	4,000	5,000	6,000
B.	Selling Price per unit (₹)	20	20	20	20	20	20
C.	Total Sales (A × B)	20,000	40,000	60,000	80,000	1,00,000	1,20,000
D.	*Less:* Cash Sales (A × B)	4,000	8,000	12,000	16,000	20,000	24,000
E.	Credit Sales	16,000	32,000	48,000	64,000	80,000	96,000
F.	*Add:* Opening Debtors	—	16,000	40,000	64,000	88,000	1,12,000
G.	*Less:* Closing Debtors	16,000	40,000	64,000	88,000	1,12,000	1,36,000
H.	Collection from Debtors [E + F – G)	—	8,000	24,000	40,000	56,000	72,000

Illustration 21. [Calculation of the Amount of Cash Purchases and Payment to Creditors]

Tulsian (3) Ltd. provides you the following information:

(a)

Month	*January*	*February*	*March*	*April*	*May*	*June*	*July*
Sales (in units)	1,000	2,000	3,000	4,000	5,000	6,000	7,000

(b) 25% of the purchases are on Cash basis and balance on credit basis.

(c) Uniform Selling Price — ₹ 20 per unit. This price was fixed after adding 25% to cost.

(d) No stock remains at the end of a month.

Required: Calculate the amount of Cash Purchases and Payment to Creditors for the months, April to June in each of the following alternative cases:

Case (a) If credit period allowed by suppliers is 1 month.

Case (b) If credit period allowed by suppliers is 2 months.

Case (c) If credit period allowed by supplier is 3 months.

Case (d) If 50% of credit purchases are paid in the month of purchases and the balance in the month following.

Case (e) If 50% of credit purchases are paid within one month and the balance in two months.

Case (f) If purchases are made one month in advance and credit purchases are paid after one month.

Solution:

CALCULATION OF CASH PURCHASES AND CREDIT PURCHASES

Particulars	*Jan.*	*Feb.*	*Mar.*	*Apr.*	*May*	*June*	*July*
A. Sales (units)	1,000	2,000	3,000	4,000	5,000	6,000	7,000
B. Selling Price per unit (₹)	20	20	20	20	20	20	20
C. Total Sales (A × B)	20,000	40,000	60,000	80,000	1,00,000	1,20,000	1,40,000
D. *Less:* Gross profit @ 20%	4,000	8,000	12,000	16,000	20,000	24,000	28,000
E. Total Purchases [C – D]	16,000	32,000	48,000	64,000	80,000	96,000	1,12,000
F. *Less:* Cash Purchases @ 25%	4,000	8,000	12,000	16,000	20,000	24,000	28,000
G. Credit purchases [E – F]	12,000	24,000	36,000	48,000	60,000	72,000	84,000

Case (a)	*April*	*May*	*June*
	₹	₹	₹
Cash Purchases (25% of Current Month's Purchases)	16,000	20,000	24,000
Payment of Creditors (Preceding Month's Credit Purchases)	36,000	48,000	60,000

Case (b)	*Apr.*	*May*	*June*
	₹	₹	₹
Cash Purchases (25% of Curent Month's Purchases)	16,000	20,000	24,000
Payment to Creditors (Second Preceding Month's Credit Purchases)	24,000	36,000	48,000

Case (c)	*Apr.*	*May*	*June*
	₹	₹	₹
Cash Purchases (25% of Current Month's Purchases)	16,000	20,000	24,000
Payment to Creditors (Third Preceding Month's Credit Purchases)	12,000	24,000	36,000

Case (d)	*April*	*May*	*June*
	₹	₹	₹
Cash Purchases (25% of Current Month's Purchases	16,000	20,000	24,000
Payment to Creditors			
50% of Curent Month's Credit Purchases	24,000	30,000	36,000
50% of Preceding Month's Credit Purchases	18,000	24,000	30,000
	42,000	54,000	66,000

Case (e)	*April*	*May*	*June*
	₹	₹	₹
Cash Purchases	16,000	20,000	24,000
Payment to creditors			
50% of Preceding Month's Credit Purchases	18,000	24,000	30,000
50% of Second Preceding Month's Credit Purchases	12,000	18,000	24,000
	30,000	42,000	54,000

Case (f)	*April*	*May*	*June*
	₹	₹	₹
Cash Purchases (25% of Next Month's Purchases)	20,000	24,000	28,000
Payment to Creditors (75% of Current Month's Purchases)	48,000	60,000	72,000

Illurstration 22. [Calculation of the amount of Cash Purchases and Payments to Creditors]
Tulsian(4) Ltd. provides you the following information:

(a) Sales (in units), Closing Stock (in units) and Closing Trade Creditors.

	January	*February*	*March*	*April*	*May*	*June*	*July*
Sales (units)	1,000	2,000	3,000	4,000	5,000	6,000	7,000
Closing Stock (Units)	100	200	300	400	500	600	700
Closing Trade Creditors (₹)	11,400	28,650	45,975	62,850	79,500	96,150	1,12,800
Wages	2,400	3,000	3,600	4,800	6,000	7,200	8,400

(b) 25% of the purchases are on cash basis and the balance on credit basis.
(c) Uniform Selling Price — ₹ 20 per unit. This price was fixed after adding 25% to cost.

Required: Calculate the amount of Cash Purchases and Payment to creditors for the months Jan. to July.

Solution: **CALCULATION OF CASH PURCHASES AND PAYMENT TO TRADE CREDITORS**

Particulars	*January*	*February*	*March*	*April*	*May*	*June*	*July*
A. Sales (Units)	1,000	2,000	3,000	4,000	5,000	6,000	7,000
B. Selling Price per unit (₹)	20	20	20	20	20	20	20
C. Total Sales (A × B) (₹)	20,000	40,000	60,000	80,000	1,00,000	1,20,000	1,40,000
D. *Less:* Gross Profit @20%	4,000	8,000	12,000	16,000	20,000	24,000	28,000
E. Cost of Goods Sold (C–D)	16,000	32,000	48,000	64,000	80,000	96,000	1,12,000
F. *Add:* Closing Stock	1,600	3,200	4,800	6,400	8,000	9,600	11,200
G. *Less:* Opening Stock	—	1,600	3,200	4,800	6,400	8,000	9,600
H. *Less:* Wages	2,400	3,000	3,600	4,800	6,000	7,200	8,400
I. Total Purchases	15,200	30,600	46,000	60,800	75,600	90,400	1,05,200
J. *Less:* Cash Purchases @ 25%	3,800	7,650	11,500	15,200	18,900	22,600	26,300
K. Credit Purchases (I – J)	11,400	22,950	34,500	45,600	56,700	67,800	78,900
L. *Add:* Opening Creditors	—	11,400	28,650	45,975	62,850	79,500	96,150
M. *Less:* Closing Creditors	11,400	28,650	45,975	62,850	79,500	96,150	1,12,800
N. Payment to Creditors [K + L – M]	—	5,700	17,175	28,725	40,050	51,150	62,250

Illustration 23. [Calculation of the amount of Expenses paid]
Tulsian (5) Ltd. provides you the following information

Particulars	*March* ₹	*April* ₹	*May* ₹	*June* ₹
Budgeted Expenses	30,000	50,000	70,000	90,000

Budgeted expenses for each month include depreciation amounting to ₹.10,000.

Required: Calculate the amount of expenses paid during the months April to June in each of the following alternative cases:

Case (a) If no time lag is given
Case (b) If time lag is 1 month
Case (c) If time lag is 1/2 month.
Case (d) If time lag is 1/4 month.
Case (e) If time lag is 1/8 month.
Case (f) If time lag is 1/3 month.

Solution:

Case (a)	*April*	*May*	*June*
	₹	₹	₹
Payment of Expenses [Current Month's Expenses]	40,000	60,000	80,000

Case (b)	*April*	*May*	*June*
	₹	₹	₹
Payment of Expenses	20,000	40,000	60,000

Case (c)	*April*	*May*	*June*
	₹	₹	₹
Payment of Expenses			
1/2 of Current Month's Expenses	20,000	30,000	40,000
1/2 of previous Month's Expenses	10,000	20,000	30,000
	30,000	50,000	70,000

Case (d)	*April*	*May*	*June*
	₹	₹	₹
Payment of Expenses			
3/4 of Current Month's Expenses	30,000	45,000	60,000
1/4 of previous Month's Expenses	5,000	10,000	15,000
	35,000	55,000	75,000

Case (e)	*April*	*May*	*June*
	₹	₹	₹
Payment of Expenses			
7/8 of Current Month's Expenses	35,000	52,500	70,000
1/8 of previous Month's Expenses	2,500	5,000	7,500
	37,500	57,500	77,500

Case (f)	*April*	*May*	*June*
	₹	₹	₹
Payment of Expenses			
2/3 of Current Month's Expenses	26,666.67	40,000	53,333
1/3 of previous Month's Expenses	6,666.77	13,333	20,000
	33,333.34	53,333	73,333

Illustration 24. [Calculation of the Amount of Expenses paid]

Tulsian(6) Ltd. provides you the following information:

Particulars	*March* ₹	*April* ₹	*May* ₹	*June* ₹
Budgeted Expenses	40,000	70,000	1,30,000	1,00,000
Closing Creditors for Expenses	10,000	20,000	40,000	30,000

Budgeted Expenses for each month include depreciation amounting to ₹ 10,000.

Required: Calculate the amount of expenses paid during the months April to June.

Solution: **CALCULATION OF EXPENSES PAID**

Particulars	*April* ₹	*May* ₹	*June* ₹
A. Budgeted Expenses	70,000	1,30,000	1,00,000
B. *Less:* Depreciation	10,000	10,000	10,000
C. Cash Expenses	60,000	1,20,000	90,000
D. *Add:* Opening Creditors	10,000	20,000	40,000
E. *Less:* Closing Creditors	20,000	40,000	30,000
F. Expenses Paid	50,000	1,00,000	1,00,000

Illustration 25. Prepare Cash Budget of Tulsian(7) Ltd. for April to June 2014 from the following information:

1. Estimated Sales, Purchases and Expenses are as follows:

	Jan. ₹	Feb. ₹	March ₹	April ₹	May ₹	June ₹
Sales	2,00,000	4,00,000	6,00,000	8,00,000	10,00,000	12,00,000
Purchases	1,52,000	3,06,000	4,60,000	6,08,000	7,56,000	9,04,000
Wages	24,000	30,000	36,000	48,000	60,000	72,000
Adm. Expenses	30,000	40,000	50,000	60,000	70,000	80,000
Selling & Dist. Exp. (₹)	30,000	50,000	70,000	90,000	1,10,000	1,00,000

2. Cash Sales are 20% of total sales.
3. 50% of Credit Sales are collected within one month and the balance in two months.
4. Cash Purchases are 25% of Total Purchases.
5. 50% of Credit Purchases are paid within one month and the balance in two months.
6. No Stock remains at the end of a month.
7. Commission on Sales – 10%
8. The time lag in the payment of Wages is one third of the month and that of Adm. Expenses one month.
9. Adm. Expenses for each month include depreciation amounting to ₹ 10,000.
10. 12% ₹ 2,00,000 Debentures of ₹ 100 each were issued on 1st Jan. (Half yearly interest due on 30th June and 31st Dec.)
11. 36,000 Equity Shares of ₹ 10 each were issued on 1st May at 5% premium.
12. Cash balance at the end of March ₹ 4,00,000.

Solution: **CASH BUDGET FOR APRIL TO JUNE 2014**

Particulars	April ₹	May ₹	June ₹
A. Total Cash Available:			
Cash in hand	4,00,000	2,66,750	4,99,250
Cash Sales	1,60,000	2,00,000	2,40,000
Collection from Debtors	4,00,000	5,60,000	7,20,000
Issue of Equity Shares	—	3,78,000	—
	9,60,000	14,04,750	14,59,250
B. Total Cash Payments:			
Cash Purchases	1,52,000	1,89,000	2,26,000
Payment to Creditors for Purchases	2,87,250	4,00,500	5,11,500
Wages	44,000	56,000	68,000
Administrative Expenses	40,000	50,000	60,000
Selling and Distribution Expenses	90,000	1,10,000	1,00,000
Commission on Sales	80,000	1,00,000	1,20,000
Interest on Debentures	–	–	12,000
	6,93,250	9,05,500	10,97,500
C. Closing Balance [A – B]	2,66,750	4,99,250	3,61,750

Working Notes:

(i) Calculation of Cash Sales and Collection from Debtors

Particulars	Jan.	Feb.	March	April	May	June
A. Total Sales	2,00,000	4,00,000	6,00,000	8,00,000	10,00,000	12,00,000
B. *Less:* Cash Sales @ 20%	(40,000)	(80,000)	(1,20,000)	(1,60,000)	(2,00,000)	(2,40,000)
C. Credit Sales	1,60,000	3,20,000	4,80,000	6,40,000	8,00,000	9,60,000
D. Collection from Debtors						
50% of Previous months'		80,000	1,60,000	2,40,000	3,20,000	4,00,000
50% of Previous to Prev. Month			80,000	1,60,000	2,40,000	3,20,000
Total Collection from Debtors		80,000	2,40,000	4,00,000	5,60,000	7,20,000

(ii) Calculation of Cash Purchases and Payment to Creditors

Particulars	*Jan.* ₹	*Feb.* ₹	*March* ₹	*April* ₹	*May* ₹	*June* ₹
A. Total Purchases	1,52,000	3,06,000	4,60,000	6,08,000	7,56,000	9,04,000
B. *Less:* Cash Pur. @ 25%	(38,000)	(76,500)	(1,15,000)	(1,52,000)	(1,89,000)	(2,26,000)
C. Credit Purchases	1,14,000	2,29,500	3,45,000	4,56,000	5,67,000	6,78,000
D. Payment to Creditors						
50% of Previous Month		57,000	1,14,750	1,72,500	2,28,000	2,83,500
50% of Previous to Previous M.			57,000	1,14,750	1,72,500	2,28,000
Total Payment to Creditors		57,000	1,71,750	2,87,250	4,00,500	5,11,500

(iii) Payment of Wages	*April (₹)*	*May (₹)*	*June (₹)*
2/3rd of Current Month's	32,000	40,000	48,000
1/3rd of Previous Month's	12,000	16,000	20,000
	44,000	56,000	68,000

(iv) In the absence of any time lag Selling and Distribution Expenses and Commission on Sales are assumed to have been paid in the same month of incurrence.

Illustration 26. Prepare Cash Budget of Tulsian(8) Ltd. for April to June 2014 from the following information:

1. Sales Jan. 1,000 units. Sales are expected to be increased by 1,000 units per month.
2. Uniform Selling Price of ₹ 100 per unit was fixed after adding 25% to cost.
3. Cash sales are 25% of Net Credit Sales.
4. 2% of Accounts Receivable constitute bad debt losses. 50% of the good accounts receivable are collected in the month following the sales, 50% of the remaining in the second month and the balance in the third month.
5. Cash Purchases are 33–1/3% of Net Credit Purchases.
6. 50% of Credit Purchases are paid within one month and the balance in two months.
7. No Stock remains at the end of a month.
8. The estimated expenses are as follows:

	Jan. ₹	*Feb.* ₹	*March* ₹	*April* ₹	*May* ₹	*June* ₹
Wages	12,000	15,000	18,000	24,000	30,000	36,000
Adm. Expenses	15,000	20,000	25,000	30,000	35,000	40,000
Selling & Dist. Exp.	15,000	25,000	35,000	45,000	55,000	50,000

9. Commission on Sales – 10%
10. The time lag in the payment of Wages is one third of the month and that of Adm. Expenses one month.
11. Adm. Expenses for each month include depreciation amounting to ₹ 5,000.
12. 12% ₹ 1,00,000 Debentures of ₹ 100 each were issued on 1st Jan. (Half yearly interest due on 30th June and 31st Dec.)
13. 18,000 Equity Shares of ₹ 10 each were issued on 1st May at 5% premium.
14. Estimated Advance Tax for the Assessment Year 2015-2016 is ₹ 1,00,000. First instalment of Advance Tax is 15%.
15. Cash balance at the end of March ₹ 2,00,000.

Solution: **CASH BUDGET FOR APRIL TO JUNE 2014**

Particulars	April ₹	May ₹	June ₹
A. Total Cash Available:			
Cash in hand	2,00,000	1,17,775	2,16,825
Cash Sales	80,000	1,00,000	1,20,000
Collection from Debtors	1,76,400	2,54,800	3,33,200
Issue of Equity Shares	—	1,89,000	—
	4,56,400	6,61,575	6,70,025
B. Total Cash Payments:			
Cash Purchases	74,000	92,500	1,11,000
Payment to Creditors for Purchases	1,37,625	1,94,250	2,49,750
Wages	22,000	28,000	34,000
Administrative Expenses	20,000	25,000	30,000
Selling and Distribution Expenses	45,000	55,000	50,000
Commission on Sales	40,000	50,000	60,000
Interest on Debentures	–	–	6,000
Advance Tax	–	–	15,000
	3,38,625	4,44,750	5,55,750
C. Closing Balance [A – B]	1,17,775	2,16,825	1,14,275

Working Notes:

(i) Calculation of Cash Sales and Collection for Debtors

Particulars	Jan.	Feb.	March	April	May	June
A. Sales (Units)	1,000	2,000	3,000	4,000	5,000	6,000
B. Selling Price per Unit	100	100	100	100	100	100
C. Total Sales	1,00,000	2,00,000	3,00,000	4,00,000	5,00,000	6,00,000
D. *Less:* Cash Sales @ 20%	20,000	40,000	60,000	80,000	1,00,000	1,20,000
E. Credit Sales @ 80%	80,000	1,60,000	2,40,000	3,20,000	4,00,000	4,80,000
F. *Less:* 2% Bad Debts	1,600	3,200	4,800	6,400	8,000	9,600
G. Good A/c Receivable	78,400	1,56,800	2,35,200	3,13,600	3,92,000	4,70,400
50% of Previous Month				1,17,600	1,56,800	1,96,000
25% of Previous to Previous				39,200	58,800	78,400
25% of Third Previous Month				19,600	39,200	58,800
				1,76,400	2,54,800	3,33,200

(ii) Calculation of Cash Purchases and Payment to Creditors

Particulars	Jan. ₹	Feb. ₹	March ₹	April ₹	May ₹	June ₹
A. Total Sales	1,00,000	2,00,000	3,00,000	4,00,000	5,00,000	6,00,000
B. *Less:* Gross Profit @ 20%	(20,000)	(40,000)	(60,000)	(80,000)	(1,00,000)	(1,20,000)
C. Cost of Goods Sold	80,000	1,60,000	2,40,000	3,20,000	4,00,000	4,80,000
D. *Less:* Wages	(12,000)	(15,000)	(18,000)	(24,000)	(30,000)	(36,000)
E. Total Purchases	68,000	1,45,000	2,22,000	2,96,000	3,70,000	4,44,000
F. *Less:* Cash Purchases @25%	(17,000)	(36,250)	(55,500)	(74,000)	(92,500)	(1,11,000)
G. Credit Purchases	51,000	1,08,750	1,66,500	2,22,000	2,77,500	3,33,000
H. Payment to Creditors						
50% of Previous month				83,250	1,11,000	1,38,750
50% of Previous to previous				54,375	83,250	1,11,000
				1,37,625	1,94,250	2,49,750

(iii) *Payment of Wages*

	April (₹)	*May (₹)*	*June (₹)*
2/3rd of Current Month's	16,000	20,000	24,000
1/3rd of Previous Month's	6,000	8,000	10,000
	22,000	28,000	34,000

(iv) *In the absence of time lag in payment of Selling and Dist. expenses and commission on sales, the payment has been made in the same month.*

(v) *Depreciation being non-cash expense will not appear in the Cash Budget.*

(vi) *The first instalments of Advance Tax in case of a company assessee is payable on/before 15th June.*

Illustration 27. Prepare Cash Budget of Tulsian(9) Ltd. for April to June 2014 from the following information:

1. Sales Jan. 1,000 units. Sales are expected to be increased by 1,000 units per month.
2. Uniform Selling Price of ₹ 100 per unit was fixed after adding 25% to cost.
3. Cash sales are 25% of Net Credit Sales.
4. Cash Purchases are 33–1/3% of Net Credit Purchases.
5. The estimated Expenses, Closing Stock, Closing Trade Debtors and Closing Creditors are as follows:

	Jan. ₹	*Feb.* ₹	*March* ₹	*April* ₹	*May* ₹	*June* ₹
Wages	12,000	15,000	18,000	24,000	30,000	36,000
Adm. Expenses	15,000	20,000	25,000	30,000	35,000	40,000
Selling & Dist. Exp.	15,000	25,000	35,000	45,000	55,000	50,000
Closing Stock (Units)	100	200	300	400	500	600
Closing Trade Debtors (₹)	80,000	2,00,000	3,20,000	4,40,000	5,60,000	6,80,000
Closing Trade Creditors (₹)	5,70,000	1,43,250	2,29,875	3,14,250	3,97,500	4,80,750
Closing Creditors for Selling & Dist. Exp. (₹)	5,000	10,000	20,000	15,000	30,000	25,000

6. Commission on Sales – 10%
7. The time lag in the payment of Wages is one third of the month and that of Adm. Expenses one month.
8. Adm. Expenses for each month include depreciation amounting to ₹ 5,000.
9. 12% ₹ 1,00,000 Debentures of ₹ 100 each were issued on 1st Jan. (Half yearly interest due on 30th June and 31st Dec.)
10. 18,000 Equity Shares of ₹ 10 each were issued on 1st May at 5% premium.
11. Estimated Advance Tax for the Assessment Year 2015-2016 is ₹ 1,00,000. First instalment of Advance Tax is 15%.
12. Cash balance at the end of March ₹ 2,00,000.

Solution: **CASH BUDGET FOR APRIL TO JUNE 2014**

	Particulars	*April* ₹	*May* ₹	*June* ₹
A.	**Total Cash Available:**			
	Cash in hand	2,00,000	1,28,375	2,59,625
	Cash Sales	80,000	1,00,000	1,20,000
	Collection from Debtors	2,00,000	2,80,000	3,60,000
	Issue of Equity Shares	—	1,89,000	—
	Total Cash Available	**4,80,000**	**6,97,375**	**7,39,625**
B.	**Total Cash Payments:**			
	Cash Purchases	76,000	94,500	1,13,000
	Payment to Creditors for Purchases	1,43,625	2,00,250	2,55,750
	Wages	22,000	28,000	34,000
	Administrative Expenses	20,000	25,000	30,000
	Selling and Distribution Expenses	50,000	40,000	55,000
	Commission on Sales	40,000	50,000	60,000
	Interest on Debentures	–	–	6,000
	Advance Tax	–	–	15,000
		3,51,625	4,37,750	5,68,750
C.	**Surplus [A – B]**	**1,28,375**	**2,59,625**	**1,70,875**

Working Notes:

(i) Calculation of Cash Sales and Collection from Debtors

Particulars	*Jan.*	*Feb.*	*March*	*April*	*May*	*June*
A. Sales (Units)	1,000	2,000	3,000	4,000	5,000	6,000
B. Selling Price per Unit	100	100	100	100	100	100
C. Total Sales	1,00,000	2,00,000	3,00,000	4,00,000	5,00,000	6,00,000
D. *Less:* Cash Sales @ 20%	(20,000)	(40,000)	(60,000)	(80,000)	(1,00,000)	(1,20,000)
E. Credit Sales	80,000	1,60,000	2,40,000	3,20,000	4,00,000	4,80,000
F. *Add:* Opening Trade Debtors		80,000	2,00,000	3,20,000	4,40,000	5,60,000
G. *Less:* Closing Trade Debtors	(80,000)	(2,00,000)	(3,20,000)	(4,40,000)	(5,60,000)	(6,80,000)
H. Collection from Debtors	0	40,000	1,20,000	2,00,000	2,80,000	3,60,000

(ii) Calculation of Cash Purchases and Payment to Creditors

Particulars	*Jan.* ₹	*Feb.* ₹	*March* ₹	*April* ₹	*May* ₹	*June* ₹
A. Total Sales	1,00,000	2,00,000	3,00,000	4,00,000	5,00,000	6,00,000
B. *Less:* Gross Profit @ 20%	(20,000)	(40,000)	(60,000)	(80,000)	(1,00,000)	(1,20,000)
C. Cost of Goods Sold	80,000	1,60,000	2,40,000	3,20,000	4,00,000	4,80,000
D. *Add:* Closing Stock	8,000	16,000	24,000	32,000	40,000	48,000
E. *Less:* Opening Stock		(8,000)	(16,000)	(24,000)	(32,000)	(40,000)
F. *Less:* Wages	(12,000)	(15,000)	(18,000)	(24,000)	(30,000)	(36,000)
G. Total Purchases	76,000	1,53,000	2,30,000	3,04,000	3,78,000	4,52,000
H. *Less:* Cash Purchases @ 25%	(19,000)	(38,250)	(57,500)	(76,000)	(94,500)	(1,13,000)
I. Credit Purchases	57,000	1,14,750	1,72,500	2,28,000	2,83,500	3,39,000
J. *Add:* Opening Trade Creditors		57,000	1,43,250	2,29,875	3,14,250	3,97,500
K. *Less:* Closing Trade Creditors	(57,000)	(1,43,250)	(2,29,875)	(3,14,250)	(3,97,500)	(4,80,750)
L. Payment to Creditors	0	28,500	85,875	1,43,625	2,00,250	2,55,750

(iii) Payment of Wages

	April (₹)	*May (₹)*	*June (₹)*
2/3rd of Current Month's	16,000	20,000	24,000
1/3rd of Previous Month's	6,000	8,000	10,000
	22,000	28,000	34,000

(iv) Payment of Selling and Distribution Expenses

	April (₹)	*May (₹)*	*June (₹)*
Selling and Distribution Expenses	45,000	55,000	50,000
Add: Opening Creditors for Expenses	20,000	15,000	30,000
Less: Closing Creditors for Expenses	(15,000)	(30,000)	(25,000)
Total Payment	50,000	40,000	55,000

(v) Depreciation being non-cash expense will not appear in the Cash Budget.

(vi) The first instalments of Advance Tax in case of a company assessee is payable on/before 15th June.

Illustration 28. [Calculation of Borrowings/Sales of Securities to maintain Minimum Cash Balance]
Tulsian (10) Ltd. provides you the following information:

(a) Sales, Purchases etc.

	April ₹	*May* ₹	*June* ₹	*July* ₹	*August* ₹	*September* ₹
Cash Sales	8,000	12,000	16,000	20,000	24,000	28,000
Collection from Debtors	16,000	32,000	48,000	64,000	80,000	96,000
Cash Purchases	8,000	12,000	16,000	20,000	24,000	28,000
Payment to Creditors	12,000	24,000	36,000	48,000	60,000	72,000
Payment of Expenses	12,000	5,000	7,800	2,950	27,000	20,000

(b) The opening cash balance of ₹ 10,000 is the minimum cash balance to be maintained.

(c) Any short fall in the minimum cash balance is to be met by Bank borrowings in the multiple of ₹ 5,000 @ 12% p.a. or by sale of marketable securities in the multiple of ₹ 10,000. Bank Interest on monthly basis is payable on the first date of the subsequent month. Bank interest is payable for a minimum period of a month.

(d) Any surplus cash is to be used to repay the borrowings in the multiple of ₹ 5,000 *or* to purchase the marketable securities in the multiple of ₹ 10,000. [*Ignore Interest on securities received and paid*].

Required: Prepare the Cash Budget for April to September.

Solution: **CASH BUDGET FOR APRIL TO SEPTEMBER**

Particulars	*April* ₹	*May* ₹	*June* ₹	*July* ₹	*August* ₹	*September* ₹
A. Total Cash available:						
Opening Cash Balance	10,000	12,000	14,900	14,000	12,000	15,000
Cash Sales	8,000	12,000	16,000	20,000	24,000	28,000
Collection from Debtors	16,000	32,000	48,000	64,000	80,000	96,000
	34,000	56,000	78,900	98,000	1,16,000	1,39,000
B. Total Cash Payments:						
Cash Purchases	8,000	12,000	16,000	20,000	24,000	28,000
Payment to Creditors	12,000	24,000	36,000	48,000	60,000	72,000
Payment of Expenses	12,000	5,000	7,800	2,950	27,000	20,000
	32,000	41,000	59,800	70,950	1,11,000	1,20,000
C. Surplus (Deficit) [A – B]	2,000	15,000	19,100	27,050	5,000	19,000
Financing and Investment:						
D. Borrowings	10,000	–	–	–	–	–
E. Sales of Securities	–	–	–	–	10,000	–
F. *Less:* Repayment of Borrowings	–	–	5,000	5,000	–	–
G. *Less:* Interest on Borrowings	–	100	100	50	–	–
H. *Less:* Purchase of Securities	–	–	–	10,000	–	–
I. Closing Cash Balance [C + D + E – F – G – H]	12,000	14,900	14,000	12,000	15,000	19,000

Illustration 29. Prepare the Cash Budget for April to June 2014 if the following information is also provided in Illustration 26.

"The company maintains a minimum cash balance of ₹ 2,00,000. Any short fall in the minimum cash balance may be met by borrowing from bank or the sale of securities. The bank interest @ 12% p.a. is payable for the whole month on monthly basis. Bank borrowings can be made or repaid in the multiple of ₹ 5,000. Cash in excess of ₹ 1,10,000 is to be invested in Govt. Securities in the multiple of ₹ 10,000. Ignore interest on securities."

Solution: **CASH BUDGET FOR APRIL TO JUNE 2014**

Particulars	April ₹	May ₹	June ₹
A. Total Cash Available:			
Cash in hand	2,00,000	2,02,775	2,05,975
Cash Sales	80,000	1,00,000	1,20,000
Collection from Debtors	1,76,400	2,54,800	3,33,200
Issue of Equity Shares		1,89,000	
	4,56,400	7,46,575	6,59,175
B. Total Cash Payments:			
Cash Purchases	74,000	92,500	1,11,000
Payment to Creditors for Purchases	1,37,625	1,94,250	2,49,750
Wages	22,000	28,000	34,000
Administrative Expenses	20,000	25,000	30,000
Selling and Distribution Expenses	45,000	55,000	50,000
Commission on Sales	40,000	50,000	60,000
Interest on Debendutes	–	–	6,000
Advance Tax			15,000
	3,38,625	4,44,750	5,55,750
C. Surplus (Deficit)	1,17,775	3,01,825	1,03,425
D. *Add:* Bank Borrowings	85,000		90,000
E. *Add:* Sale of Securities		–	10,000
F. *Less:* Interest on Borrowings	–	(850)	–
G. *Less:* Repayment of Borrowings	–	(85,000)	–
H. *Less:* Purchase of Securities	–	(10,000)	–
I. Closing Balance	2,02,775	2,05,975	2,03,425

Working Notes: Same as in Illustration 26.

Illustration 30. Prepare the Cash Budget for April to October at 2014 from the information supplied by Shah Agency Trading concern.

(a) BALANCE SHEET AS ON 31ST MARCH 2014

Liabilities	₹	*Assets*		₹
Proprietor's Capital	1,00,000	Cash		20,500
Outstanding liabilities	17,000	Stock in trade		50,500
		Sundry debtors		26,000
		Furniture	25,000	
		Less : Depreciation	5,000	20,000
	1,17,000			1,17,000

(b) Estimated Sales and expenditure on salaries

Months	*Sales (₹)*	*Salaries (₹)*
April	30,000	3,000
May	52,000	3,500
June	50,000	35,000
July	75,000	4,000
August	90,000	4,000
September	35,000	3,000
October	25,000	3,000
November	25,000	3,000

(c) The other monthly expenses are : Rent ₹ 1,000, Depreciation ₹ 1,000, Misc. Expenses ₹ 500 and Commission 1% of Sales.

(d) Of the sales, 80% is on credit and 20% for cash.

(e) 70% of the credit sales are collected in one month and the balance in two months. There are no bad debt losses.
(f) Gross margin on sales an average is 30%.
(g) Purchases equal to next month's sales are made every month and they are paid during the month in which they are made.
(h) The firm maintains a minimum cash balance of ₹ 10,000.
(i) Cash deficiencies are made up by bank loans which are repaid at the earliest available opportunity and cash in excess of ₹ 15,000 is invested in securities (Interest on bank loans and securities is to be ignored).
(j) Outstanding liabilities remain unchanged.
(k) Credit Sales in February and March were equal.

Solution:

SHAH AGENCY
CASH BUDGET FOR APRIL - OCTOBER 2014

Particulars	*April* ₹	*May* ₹	*June* ₹	*July* ₹	*Aug.* ₹	*Sep.* ₹	*Oct* ₹
A. Total Cash Available:							
Opening Balance	20,500	10,000	10,000	10,000	10,000	10,000	15,000
Cash Sales	6,000	10,400	10,000	15,000	18,000	7,000	5,000
Collection from Debtors	20,000	22,800	36,320	40,480	54,000	68,400	41,200
	46,500	43,200	56,320	65,480	82,000	85,400	61,200
B. Total Cash Payments:							
Creditors	36,400	35,000	52,500	63,000	24,500	17,500	17,500
Salaries	3,000	3,500	35,000	4,000	4,000	3,000	3,000
Rent	1,000	1,000	1,000	1,000	1,000	1,000	1,000
Commission on sales (1% of sales)	300	520	500	750	900	350	250
Misc. Expenses	500	500	500	500	500	500	500
Total payments	41,200	40,520	89,500	69,250	30,900	22,350	22,250
C. Surplus/Deficiency	5,300	2,680	(33,180)	(3,770)	51,100	63,050	38,950
Financing & Investment: Borrowing to maintain minimum cash balance of ₹.10,000	4,700	7,320	43,180	13,770			
D. Repayment after Maintaining minimum Cash Balance of ₹ 10,000		—			(41,100)	(27,870)	
E. Investmont in Scourity after maintaining minimum Balance ₹ 15,000		—	—	—	—	(20,180)	(23,950)
F. Closing cash balance (C + D – E – F)	10,000	10,000	10,000	10,000	10,000	15,000	15,000

Working Notes:

(i) *Schedule of Collection from Debtors*

Particulars	*April*	*May*	*June*	*July*	*Aug.*	*Sep.*	*Oct.*
Total Sales	30,000	52,000	50,000	75,000	90,000	35,000	25,000
Cash Sales	6,000	10,400	10,000	15,000	18,000	7,000	5,000
Credit (80%)	24,000	41,600	40,000	60,000	72,000	28,000	20,000
Collection from Debtors:							
70% in one month	14,000	16,800	29,120	28,000	42,000	50,400	19,600
30% in two months	6,000	6,000	7,200	12,480	12,000	18,000	21,600
Total Collection	20,000	22,800	36,320	40,480	54,000	68,400	41,200

(ii) *Schedule of Payments to Trade Creditors*

Particulars	*April*	*May*	*June*	*July*	*Aug.*	*Sep.*	*Oct.*	*Nov.*
Sales	30,000	52,000	50,000	75,000	90,000	35,000	25,000	25,000
Purchases 70% of sales of next month	36,400	35,000	52,500	63,000	24,500	17,500	17,500	

(iii) *Assumptions*

(a) It has been assumed that collection of 70% and 30% of credit sales is effected in one month and 2 months respectively from the month of sale.

(b) Sundry Debtors of ₹ 26,000 outstanding on 31st March represent 30% of credit sales for February and 100% of credit sales for March i.e. ₹ 6,000 and ₹ 20,000 respectively. Accordingly, ₹ 6,000 February's outstanding credit sales is collected in April and ₹ 20,000 credit sales for March is collected in the ratio of 70% (₹ 14,000) and 30% (₹ 6,000) in April and May respectively.

(c) In the absence of information to compute purchases for Oct., it has been assumed that sales in November will be the same as in October, i.e. ₹ 25,000.

ADJUSTED NET INCOME METHOD (OR CASH FLOW STATEMENT METHOD)

Under this method, cash inflows and outflows are estimated usually for a year. This method is useful when the management is interested in long range planning. The cash budget prepared on the basis of this method is also called 'Cash Flow Statement'.

Meaning	The Cash Flow Statement means the statement of changes in Cash and Cash equivalents. It shows the following for the period covered by it:— 1. Net Cash flows from Operating Activities; 2. Net Cash flows from Investing Activities; 3. Net Cash flows from Financing Activities; 4. Net change in Cash and Cash Equivalents.
Objectives	Basically the purpose of Cash Flow Statement is to ascertain the reasons for the net flow (i.e. the difference between the opening and closing balance of cash & cash equivalents), and not simply the net flow which is already known. The objectives of Cash Flow Statement are as follows: 1. To ascertain the specific sources (i.e., Operating/Investing/Financing Activities) from which Cash & Cash Equivalents were generated by an enterprise; 2. To ascertain the specific uses (i.e., Operating/Investing/Financing Activities) for which Cash & Cash Equivalents were used by an enterprise; 3. To ascertain the net change in Cash & Cash Equivalents indicating the difference between total sources and total uses between the dates of two Balance Sheets.

DISTINCTION BETWEEN CASH BUDGET AND CASH FLOW STATEMENT

Cash Budget and Cash Flow Statement can be distinguished as given below:

Basis of Distinction	*Cash Budget*	*Cash Flow Statement*
1. **Time span**	It is prepared for a week, month quarter, half year or a year.	It is usually prepared for a year.
2. **Usefulness**	It is useful for short-range planning.	It is useful for long-range planning.
3. **Methods of Preparation**	It may be prepared according to any of the three method—Receipts & Payments Method, Adjusted Profit & Loss Method and Balance Sheet Method	It is prepared according to Adjusted Profit & Loss Account Method.

24.0 MASTER BUDGET

The master budget is a summary budget which incorporates all functional budgets in a capsule form and shows Budgeted Income Statement for the budget period and Budgeted Balance Sheet as at the end of the budget period. It sets out the plan of operations for all departments in considerable detail for the budget period.

The Master budget requires the approval of the Budget Committee before it is put into operation. It may happen, sometimes, that a number of master budgets have to be prepared before the final one is agreed upon. The budget generally contains details regarding sales (net), production costs, cash position, and key account balances (e.g. debtors, fixed assets, bills payable, etc.). It also shows the gross and net profits, and the important accounting ratios.

FORMAT OF BUDGETED INCOME STATEMENT

A simplest format of Budgeted Income Statement is given below:

BUDGETED INCOME STATEMENT

for the Budget period ending.....

Particulars / *Period*	*Product W (₹)*	*Product X (₹)*	*Product Y (₹)*	*Product Z (₹)*	*Total (₹)*
A Sales	....	(As per Sales budget)			....
B *Less* : Cost of Goods Sold	....	(As per Cost of Goods Sold Budget)			....
C Gross Profit (A – B)	....	....	....	....	....
D Other Operating Expenses :					
(i) Administration Costs	....	(As per Office & Adm. Costs Budget)			....
(ii) Selling Costs	....	(As Per Selling Costs Budget)			....
(iii) Distribution Costs	....	(As per Distribution Costs Budget)			....
	....	....	....	....	....
E Operating Income [C – D]	....	....	....	....	....
F Non-operating Adjustments :					
Add : Non-operating income					....
Less : Non-operating expenses					....
Less : Amortisated expenses					....
					....
G Income before tax [E ± F]					....
H Income tax					....
I Income After Tax (G – H)					....
J Appropriations out of Profits :					
(i) Dividend					....
(ii) Dividend Tax					....
(iii) Transfer to general reserve					....
(iv) Transfer to specific reserve					....
Total Appropriations					....
K Profit & Loss A/c Balance (I – J)					....

Illustration 31. Y Ltd. Provides you the following information :

	Product 'A'	*Product 'B'*
	₹	₹
Actual Cost of goods sold	1,57,100	1,47,000
Sales (in units)	8,000	5,000
Selling price per unit	30	40
Standard Cost per unit	₹ 19.50	₹ 24
Sales Manager's Commission	@ 10% on Standard Gross Profit	@ 10% on Standard Gross Profit

Other Selling expenses ₹ 22,000
Distribution Expenses ₹ 13,000
Office & Administration expenses ₹ 8,900
Income Tax @ 50%

Notes :

(i) Other Selling Expenses to be allocated to Product 'A' and Product 'B' in their sales revenue ratio.
(ii) Distribution Expenses to be allocated to Product 'A' and 'B' Product in their Sales units ratio.
(iii) Office and Administration Expenses to be allocated equally to both the products.

Required : Prepare Budgeted Income Statement.

Solution:

BUDGETED INCOME STATEMENT
for the period Ending ......

	Particulars	*Product 'A'* ₹	*Product 'B'* ₹	*Total* ₹
A.	Sales	2,40,000	2,00,000	4,40,000
B.	*Less :* Cost of Goods Sold	1,57,100	1,47,000	3,04,100
C.	Gross Profit (A – B)	82,900	53,000	1,35,900
D.	*Less :* Adm. & Selling & Dist. Expenses			
	(a) Sales Manager's Commi. Expenses	8,400*	8,000**	16,400
	(b) Other Selling Expenses @ 5% of Sales	12,000	10,000	22,000
	(c) Distribution Expenses @ ₹ 1 per unit	8,000	5,000	13,000
	(d) Office & Adm. Expenses (in 1 : 1 ratio)	4,450	4,450	8,900
		32,850	27,450	60,300
E.	Net Profit Before Tax (C – D)	50,050	25,550	75,600
F.	*Less :* Tax @ 50%			37,800
G.	Net Profit After Tax (E – F)			37,800

* 10% on [(₹ 30 – ₹ 19.50) × 8,000], ** 10% on [₹ 40 – ₹ 24) × 5,000]

FORMAT OF BUDGETED BALANCE SHEET

A simplest format of Budgeted Balance Sheet is given below:

BUDGETED BALANCE SHEET
As at ....

Items of Assets & Liabilities / *Dates*	*Last date of First Quarter* (₹)	*Last date of Second Quarter* (₹)	*Last date of Third Quarter* (₹)	*Last date of Fourth Quarter* (₹)
1. Fixed Assets	....	....	....	....
2. Current Assets :				
Cash-in-hand	....	....	....	....
Cash at bank	....	....	....	....
Stock :				
Raw-material	....	....	....	....
W.I.P.	....	....	....	....
Finished goods	....	....	....	....
Sundry debtors	....	....	....	....
Bills Receivable	....	....	....	....
Prepayments & deposits	....	....	....	....
3. Total Assets (1 + 2)	....	....	....	....
4. Share Capital	....	....	....	....

Items of Assets & Liabilities / Dates	Last date of First Quarter (₹)	Last date of Second Quarter (₹)	Last date of Third Quarter (₹)	Last date of Fourth Quarter (₹)
5. Reserves & Surplus	....	....	....	....
6. Total Shareholders' equity (4 + 5)	....	....	....	....
7. Non-current Liabilities	....	....	....	....
8. Current Liabilities & Provisions :	....	....	....	....
Sundry trade creditors	....	....	....	....
Bills Receivable	....	....	....	....
Bank Overdraft	....	....	....	....
Proposed dividend	....	....	....	....
Provision for Taxation	....	....	....	....
Other Current Liabilities	....	....	....	....
9. Total Liabilities (6 + 7 + 8)	....	....	....	....
10. Working capital (2 – 8)	....	....	....	....
11. Total Capital Employed (1 + 10) *or* (3 – 8)	....	....	....	....

Illustration 32. Z Ltd. provides you the following information :

BALANCE SHEET AS AT 31.03.2013

Liabilities	₹	*Assets*		₹
Share Capital	4,00,000	Plant & Machinery		
Retained Earnings	32,000	Original Cost	4,00,000	
Creditors	10,000	*Less* : Depreciation	1,00,000	3,00,000
Bills Payable	6,000	Stock of Raw Material		38,000
Provision for taxation	20,000	Stock of Finished goods		80,000
		Debtors		20,000
		Bills receivables		10,000
		Cash		20,000
	4,68,000			4,68,000

Additional Information :

		₹
1.	Purchase of machinery during 2013 — 2014	40,000
2.	Outstanding debtors	46,000
3.	Outstanding creditors	11,000
4.	Credit Sales	4,40,000
5.	Credit purchases	1,40,000
6.	Closing stock of raw material	52,000
7.	Closing stock of finished goods	66,900
8.	Direct labour consumed & paid	70,000
9.	Factory overheads (including depreciation for ₹ 20,000)	95,000
10.	Selling, distribution & admn. expenses	60,300
11.	Income tax is levied @ 50% and paid in the following year	
12.	*Re bills receivables :*	
	(i) to be drawn	4,000
	(ii) to be endorsed to trade creditors	1,000
	(iii) to be collected	10,000

13. ₹ *bills payables :*
    (i) to be accepted — 5,000
    (ii) to be discharged — 7,000
14. Budgeted profit for 20X1—20X2 — 75,600
15. Income-tax is to be provided @ 50%

Required : Prepare Cash Budget and Budgeted Balance Sheet.

Solution:

(a) THE CASH BUDGET
for the year ending 31st March 2014

	Particulars		₹
A.	Opening Cash Balance		20,000
B.	*Add :* (a) Receipts from Debtors *(as per Schedule I)*		4,10,000
	(b) Collection on account of B/R		10,000
C.	*Less :* Payments :		
	(a) Payment for material Purchases *(Creditors + B/P)*	1,40,000	
	(b) Direct Labour Consumed & paid	70,000	
	(c) Cash Factory Overheads *(₹ 95,000 – ₹ 20,000)*	75,000	
	(d) Selling Distribution & Adm. Expenses	60,300	
	(e) Payment of Taxes *(of last year)*	20,000	
	(f) Machinery Purchases	40,000	4,05,300
D.	Closing Cash Balance (A + B – C)		34,700

(b) THE BUDGETED BALANCE SHEET
as at 31st March 2014

Liabilities	₹	*Assets*		₹
Share Capital	4,00,000	Plant & Machinery		
Retained Earnings	69,800	Original Cost	4,40,000	
Creditors	11,000	*Less :* Depreciation	1,20,000	3,20,000
Bills Payable	4,000	Stock of Raw Materials		52,000
Provisioner for Taxation	37,800	Stock of Finished Goods		66,900
[50% of ₹ 75,600]		Debtors		46,000
		Bills Receivable		3,000
		Cash		34,700
	5,22,600			5,22,600

Working Notes :

SCHEDULE I — RECEIPTS FROM DEBTORS

		₹
A.	Opening Debtors	20,000
B.	*Add :* Credit Sales	4,40,000
C.	*Less :* (a) Bills Drawn	4,000
	(b) Closing Debtors	46,000
D.	Collection from Debtors (A + B – C)	4,10,000

SCHEDULE II — CLOSING BALANCE OF BILLS RECEIVABLE

A.	Opening Balance	10,000
B.	*Add :* Drawn during the year	4,000
C.	*Less :* (a) Endorsed to creditors	1,000
	(b) Collected	10,000
D.	Closing Balance (A + B – C)	3,000

SCHEDULE III — PAYMENT TO CREDITORS

A.	Opening Creditors	10,000
B.	*Add :* Credit Purchases	1,40,000
C.	*Less :* (a) Closing creditors	11,000
	(b) Bills accepted	5,000
	(c) B/R endorreds	1,000
D.	Payments to Creditors (A + B – C)	1,33,000

SCHEDULE IV — CLOSING BALANCE OF BILLS PAYABLE

A.	Opening Balance	6,000
B.	*Add :* Accepted during the year	5,000
C.	*Less :* Discharged during the year	7,000
D.	Closing Balance (A + B – C)	4,000

25.0 CONTROL RATIOS

Management also makes use of ratios in controlling operations. These ratios are generally known as Control Ratios. If the ratio is 100% or more, it indicates a favourable position and if the ratio is less than 100%, it indicates unfavourable position. The important control ratios are given below:

Efficiency Ratio

It is defined as *"the standard hours equivalent to the work produced expressed as a percentage of actual hours spent in production"*. Thus, this ratio shows whether actual time taken in production is more or less than the time allowed by the standard. It can be related to Overhead Efficiency Variance *or* Labour Efficiency Variance. It is calculated as follows:

$$\text{Efficiency Ratio} = \frac{\text{Standard hours for actual output (SH)}}{\text{Actual hours worked (AH)}} \times 100$$

Activity Ratio or Production Volume Ratio

It is defined as *"the standard hours equivalent to the work produced, expressed as percentage of budgeted standard hours"*. Thus this ratio shows the extent to which the production facilities have been utilised as compared with that contemplated in budgets. It can be related to Fixed Overhead Volume Variance. It is calculated as follows:

$$\text{Activity Ratio} = \frac{\text{Standard hours for actual output (SH)}}{\text{Budgeted Hours (BH)}} \times 100$$

$$= \text{Efficiency Ratio} \times \text{Capacity Ratio}$$

Capacity Ratio

It expresses actual hours worked as a percentage of the budgeted hours. It is calculated as follows:

$$\text{Capacity Ratio} = \frac{\text{Actual Hours worked (AH)}}{\text{Budgeted Hours (BH)}} \times 100 \quad or \quad \frac{\text{Activity Ratio}}{\text{Efficiency Ratio}}$$

Calender Ratio

Calender Ratio indicates the extent of actual working days availed during the budget period. It is calculated as follows:

$$\text{Calender Ratio} = \frac{\text{Actual Number of working days in the budget period}}{\text{Budgeted number of working days in the budget period}} \times 100$$

Idle Capacity Ratio

It indicates the percentage of Budgeted Capacity which is not actually utilized during the budget period. It is calculated as follows:

$$\text{Idle Capacity Ratio} = \frac{\text{Budgeted Capacity} - \text{Actual Capacity}}{\text{Budgeted Capacity}} \times 100$$

$$= 100 - \text{Capacity Ratio}$$

Standard Capacity Usage Ratio	It expresses Budgeted Hours as a percentage of the Maximum Possible Hours. It is calculated as follows: $= \frac{\text{Budgeted Hours}}{\text{Maximum Possible Hours in Budget Period}} \times 100$
Actual Usage of Maximum Capacity Ratio	It expresses Actual Hours as a percentage of the Maximum Possible Hours. It is calculated as follows: $= \frac{\text{Actual Hours}}{\text{Maximum Possible Hours in Budget Period}} \times 100$

Illustration 33.

Case (a) Budgeted Production 4,000 Units, Actual Production 3,600 Units, Standard Hours per Unit 5, Actual Working Hours 19,200. Calculate Efficiency Ratio, Activity Ratio and Capacity Ratio.

Case (b) Budgeted Production 1,00,000 Units, Actual Production 90,000 Units, Standard Output per hour 5, Actual Working Hours 19,200. Calculate Efficiency Ratio, Activity Ratio and Capacity Ratio.

Case (c) Budgeted Production 4,000 Units. The product requires 5 hours to produce. In July of 24 effective working days of 8 hours a day, 3,600 units of product were produced. The company employs 100 workers in the production department to produce the product. Calculate Efficiency Ratio, Activity Ratio and Capacity Ratio.

Case (d) Activity Ratio 90%, Efficiency Ratio 96%. Calculate Capacity Ratio.

Case (e) Activity Ratio 96%, Capacity Ratio 93.75%. Calculate Efficiency Ratio.

Case (f) Efficiency Ratio 96%, Capacity Ratio 95%. Calculate Activity Ratio.

Case (g) Capacity Ratio 96%. Calculate Idle Capacity Ratio.

Case (h) Maximum possible working hours in Budget Period 24,000 hours, Capacity Ratio 96%, Budgeted Hours 20,000. Calculate Standard Capacity Usage Ratio and Actual Usage of Maximum Capacity Ratio.

Solution:

Case (a) Actual Hours = 19,200
Budgeted Hours = 4,000 Units × 5 Hours = 20,000 Hours
Standard Hours = 3,600 Units × 5 Hours = 18,000 Hours
Efficiency Ratio = (Standard Hours for Actual Output/Actual Hours) × 100
= (18,000/19,200) × 100 = 93.75%
Activity Ratio = (Standard Hours for Actual Output/Budgeted Hours) × 100 = (18,000/20,000) × 100 = 90%
Capactity Ratio = (Actual Hours/Budgeted Hours) × 100 = (19,200/20,000) × 100 = 96%

Case (b) Actual Hours = 19,200
Budgeted Hours = 1,00,000 Units/5 = 20,000 Hours
Standard Hours = 90,000 Units/5 = 18,000 Hours
Efficiency Ratio = (Standard Hours for Actual Output/Actual Hours) × 100
= (18,000/19,200) × 100 = 93.75%
Activity Ratio = (Standard Hours for Actual Output/Budgeted Hours) × 100
= (18,000 / 20,000) × 100 = 90%
Capactity Ratio = (Actual Hours/Budgeted Hours) × 100 = (19,200/20,000) × 100 = 96%

Case (c) Actual Hours = 100 Workers × 8 Hours × 24 Days = 19,200 Hours
Budgeted Hours = 4,000 Units × 5 Hours = 20,000 Hours
Standard Hours = 3,600 × 5 Hours = 18,000 Hours
Efficiency Ratio = (Standard Hours for Actual Output/Actual Hours) × 100
= (18,000/19,200) × 100 = 93.75%
Activity Ratio = (Standard Hours for Actual Output/Budgeted Hours) × 100 = (18,000/20,000) × 100 = 90%
Capactity Ratio = (Actual Hours/Budgeted Hours) × 100 = (19,200/20,000) × 100 = 96%

Case (d) Capacity Ratio = Activity Ratio/Efficiency Ratio = 90%/96% = 93.75%

Case (e) Efficiency Ratio = Activity Ratio/Capacity Ratio = 96%/93.75% = 102.40%

Case (f) Activity Ratio = Capacity Ratio × Efficiency Ratio = 95% x 96% = 91.20%

Case (g) Idle Capacity Ratio = 100% – Capacity Ratio = 100% – 96% = 4%

Case (h) Capacity Ratio = (Actual Hours/Budgeted Hours) × 100 = (AH/20,000) × 100 = 96%
AH = 20,000 × 96% = 19,200 Hours
Standard Capacity Usage Ratio = (Budgeted Hours/Maximum possible working hours) × 100
= (20,000/24,000) × 100 = 83.33%
Actual Usage of Maximum Capacity Ratio = (Actual Hours/Maximum possible working hours) × 100
= (19,200/24,000) × 100 = 80%

Illustration 34. Tulsian Ltd. manufactures two products X and Y. Product X requires 5 hours to produce while 5 units of product Y can be produced in one hour. In July of 24 effective working days of 8 hours a day, 3000 units of X and 15,000 units of Y were produced. The company employs 100 workers in the production department to produce X and Y. There were 25 working days specified in the budget. Maximum possible working hours in July 24,000 hours

Required: Calculate (a) Efficiency Ratio, (b) Activity Ratio, (c) Capacity Ratio, (d) Calendar Ratio (e) Idle Capacity Ratio, (f) Standard Capacity Usage Ratio and (g) Actual Usage of Maximum Capacity Ratio.

Solution:

Actual Hours = 100 Workers × 8 Hours × 24 Days = 19,200 Hours.
Budgeted Hours = 100 Workers × 8 Hours × 25 Days = 20,000 Hours
Standard Hours = (3,000 × 5) + (15,000/5) = 18,000 Hours

(a) Efficiency Ratio = (Standard Hours for Actual Output/Actual Hours) × 100 = (18,000/19,200) × 100
= 93.75%

(b) Activity Ratio = (Standard Hours for Actual Output/Budgeted Hours) × 100 = (18,000/20,000) × 100 = 90%

(c) Capactity Ratio = (Actual Hours/Budgeted Hours) × 100 = (19,200/20,000) × 100 = 96%

(d) Calendar Ratio = (Actual No. of Working Days/Budgeted No. of Working Days) × 100 = (24/25) × 100 = 96%

(e) Idle Capacity Ratio = [(Budgeted Hours – Actual Hours)/Budgeted Hours] × 100
= [(20,000 – 19,200)/20,000] = 4%

(f) Standard Capacity Usage Ratio = (Budgeted Hours/Maximum possible working hours) × 100
= (20,000/ 24,000) × 100 = 83.33%

(g) Actual Usage of Maximum Capacity Ratio = (Actual Hours/Maximum possible working hours) × 100
= (19,200/24,000) × 100 = 80%

Relationships:

1 Activity Ratio = Capacity Ratio × Efficiency Ratio = 96% × 93.75% = 90%
2 Idle Capacity Ratio = 100% – Capacity Ratio = 100% – 96% = 4%

Illustration 35. Following data is available for CAS Ltd:

Standard working hours	8 hours per day of 5 days per week
Maximum capacity	100 employees
Actual working	80 employees
Actual hours expected to be worked per four week	12,800 hours
Standard hours expected to be earned per four weeks	16,000 hours
Actual hours worked in the four week period	12,000 hours
Standard hours earned in the four week period	14,000 hours

The related period is of 4 weeks. In this period there was a one special day holiday due to national event. Calculate the following ratios:

Required: Calculate (a) Efficiency Ratio, (b) Activity Ratio, (c) Capacity Ratio, (d) Calendar Ratio (e) Idle Capacity Ratio, (f) Standard Capacity Usage Ratio and (g) Actual Usage of Maximum Capacity Ratio.

Solution:

Actual Hours = 12,000 Hours (given).
Budgeted Hours = 80 Employees × 8 Hours × 5 Days × 4 Weeks = 12,800 Hours
Standard Hours = 14,000 Hours (given).
Budgeted No. of Working Days = 4 Weeks × 5 Days = 20 Days
Actual No. of Working Days = (4 Weeks × 5 Days) – 1= 19 Days

(a) Efficiency Ratio = (Standard Hours for Actual Output/Actual Hours) × 100
= (14,000/12,000) × 100 = 116.667%

(b) Activity Ratio = (Standard Hours for Actual Output / Budgeted Hours) x 100
= (14,000/12,800) × 100 = 109.375%

(c) Capacity Ratio = (Actual Hours/Budgeted Hours) × 100 = (12,000/12,800) × 100 = 93.75%

(d) Calendar Ratio = (Actual No. of Working Days/Budgeted No. of Working Days) × 100
= (19 / 20) × 100 = 95%

(e) Idle Capacity Ratio = [(Budgeted Hours - Actual Hours)/Budgeted Hours] × 100
= [(12,800 – 12,000)/12,800] = 6.25%

(f) Standard Capacity Usage Ratio = (Budgeted Hours/Maximum possible working hours) × 100
= (12,800/16,000) × 100 = 80%

(g) Actual Usage of Maximum Capacity Ratio = (Actual Hours/Maximum possible working hours) × 100
= (12,000/16,000) × 100 = 75%

Relationships:

1. Activity Ratio = Capacity Ratio × Efficiency Ratio = 93.75% × 116.667% = 109.375%
2. Idle Capacity Ratio = 100% – Capacity Ratio = 100% – 93.75% = 6.25%

Illustration 36. Based on the data given below show the calculation of:
(i) Efficiency Ratio; (ii) Production Volume Ratio; (iii) Idle Capacity Ratio.

Data	*Standard Hours of Output*	*Hours of Actual Operations*
Theoretical capacity	100	100
Theoretical capacity *less* Unavoidable lost time.	95	95
Planned activity for period	81	90
Actual Activity for period	68	85

Solution:

(i) Efficiency Ratio = (Standard Hours for Actual Output/Actual Hours) × 100
= (68/85) × 100 = 80%

(ii) Production Volume Ratio *or* Activity Ratio = (Standard Hours for Actual Output/Budgeted Hours) × 100
= (68/81) × 100 = 83.95%

(iii) Idle Capacity Ratio = [(Budgeted Hours – Actual Hours)/Budgeted Hours] × 100
= [(95 – 81)/95] × 100 = 14.74%

Illustration 37. The following data have been obtained from the records of a machine shop for an average month:

Budget	
No. of working days	25
Working hours per day	8
No. of direct workers	16
Efficiency	One standard hour per clock hour
Down time	20%
Overheads:	
Fixed	₹ 15,360
Variable	₹ 20,480

The actual data for the month of September 2013 are as under :

Overheads:	
Fixed	₹ 16,500
Variable	₹ 14,500
Net operating hours worked	1,920
Standard hours produced	2,112

There was a special holiday in September 2013

You are required to present reports to departmental Manager indicating the three cost ratios you have chosen.

Solution:

Basic Calculations :

1. Maximum Hours = Days × Working Hours per day × No. of direct workers
= 25 × 8 × 16 = 3,200
2. Budgeted Hours = 3,200 – 20% of 3,200 = 2,560

Report to Departmental Manager showing Cost Ratios:

(i) Efficiency Ratio = (Standard Hours for Actual Output/Actual Hours) × 100
= (2,112/1,920) × 100 = 110%

(ii) Activity Ratio = (Standard Hours for Actual Output/Budgeted Hours) × 100
= (2,112/2,560) × 100 = 82.50%

(iii) Calendar Ratio = (Actual No. of Working Days/Budgeted No. of Working Days) × 100
= (24/25) × 100 = 96%

(iv) Standard Capacity Usage Ratio = (Budgeted Hours/Maximum possible working hours) × 100
= (2,560/3,200) × 100 = 80%

(v) Capacity Ratio = (Actual Hours/Budgeted Hours) × 100 = (1,920/2,560) × 100 = 75%

26.0 ZERO BASE BUDGETING

Meaning	1. Zero Base Budgeting means budgeting from the beginning without any reference to any base (i.e. past budgets and actual figures). 2. **According to Peter Phyrr (known as Father of Zero Base Budgeting)** *Zero Base Budgeting may be defined as "a planning and budgeting process which requires each manager to justify his entire budget request in detail from scratch (hence zero base) and shifts the burden of proof to each manager to justify why he should spend any money at all. This approach requires that all activities be identified as decision packages which are to be evaluated by systematic analysis and ranked in order of importance".* 3. **CIMA London** *defines Zero Base Budgeting as "a method of budgeting whereby all activities are re-evaluated each time a budget is set. Discrete levels of each activity are valued and a combination chosen to match funds available".* 4. Zero Base Budgeting is defined as 'a method of budgeting which requires each cost element to be specifically justified, as though the activities to which the budget relates were being undertaken for the first time. Without approval, the budget allowance is zero.' 5. Zero Base Budgeting is so called because it requires each budget to be prepared and justified from zero, instead of simply using last year's budget as a base. Incremental level of expenditure on each activity is evaluated according to the resulting incremental benefits. Available resources are then allocated where they can be used most effectively. 6. In real terms the Zero Base Budgeting is simply an extension of the Cost Benefit Analysis Method to the area of corporate planning and budgeting. It, however, provides a number of advantages to the organizational efficiency and effectiveness.
Features	Zero Base Budgeting is based on the premise that every rupee of expenditure requires justification. Zero Base Budgeting assumes that there is no previous expenditure. 1. Each budget item (whether old or new) is to be identified and evaluated critically from the scratch each time a new budget is formulated. 2. Concentration of efforts is on **"why"** unit needs to spend and **not simply on "how much"** a unit will spend. 3. It identifies alternatives and efficient methods of utilizing limited resources in effective attainment of selected benefits. 4. Choices are made on the basis of what each unit can offer for a specific cost. 5. Individual unit's objects are linked to corporate targets.

	6. Participation of all levels in decision making. 7. Quick budget adjustments can be made if, during the operating year costs are required to maintain expenditure level.
Steps involved in the Process of Zero Base Budgeting	1. **Determining the Objectives of Budgeting:** The objective may be to effect cost reduction in Staff Overheads or it may be to drop, after careful analysis, projects which do not fit into achievement of the organizations objectives etc. 2. **Deciding on Scope of Application:** The extent to which Zero Base Budgeting is to be introduced has to be decided, i.e. whether it will be introduced in all areas of the organization's activities or only in a few selected areas on trial basis. 3. **Developing Decision Units:** Decision units for which cost-benefit analysis is proposed have to be developed so as to arrive at decisions whether they should be allowed to continue or be dropped. Each decision unit, as far as possible should be independent of other units so that it can be dropped if the cost analysis proves to be unfavourable for it. 4. **Developing Decision Packages:** A decision package for each unit should be developed. While developing a decision package, answers to the following questions would be desirable: (i) Is it necessary to perform a particular activity at all? If the answer is in the negative, there is no need to proceed further. (ii) How much has been the actual cost of the activity and what has been the actual benefit both in tangible as well as intangible forms? (iii) What should be the estimated cost of the level of activity and the estimated benefit from such activity? (iv) Should the activity be performed in the way in which it is being performed and what should be the cost? (v) If the project or activity is dropped, can the unit be replaced by an outside agency? 5. **Ranking of Decision Packages in the order of priority.** 6. **Allocation of Resources in accordance with the ranking.**
Advantages	1. It provides a systematic approach to evaluate different activities. 2. It enables management to rank the different activities in the order of priority and to allocate resources in the order of priority. 3. It enables the management to approve departmental budgets on the basis of cost-benefit analysis. No arbitrary cuts or increases in budget estimates are made. 4. It links budgets with the corporate objectives. Nothing will be allowed simply because it was being done in the past. An activity may be shelved if it does not help in achieving the goals of the enterprises. 5. It helps in identifying and eliminating the areas of wasteful expenditure and, if desired, it can also be used for suggesting alternate courses of action. 6. It facilitates the introduction and implementation of the system of MBO (i.e. 'Management by Objectives'). Thus, it can be used not only for fulfillment of the objectives of the traditional budgeting, but also for variety of other purposes. 7. Zero Base Budgeting promotes operational efficiency because it requires managers to review and justify their activities or the funds requested. 8. Since this system requires participation of all managers in the preparation of budgets, responsibility of all levels at management in successful execution of budgetary system can be ensured.

	9. It is helpful to the management in making optimum allocation of scarce resources because a unique aspect of zero base budgeting is the evaluation of both current and proposed expenditure and placing it in some order of priority.
Criticism	1. It is time consuming because it requires the development of decision units and decision packages. 2. It is difficult to define the decision units and decision packages. 3. Cost of preparing the decision packages may be very high in large firms involving large number of decision packages. 4. It requires a lot of training for managers. 5. It increases paper work. 6. It does not offer any significant control advantage where objectives are very difficult to quantify as in case of research and development,

DISTINCTION BETWEEN TRADITIONAL BUDGETING AND ZERO BASE BUDGETING

Basis of Distinction	Traditional Budgeting	Zero Base Budgeting
1. Orientation	Traditional budgeting is **Accounting Oriented**. Main stress happens to be on previous level of expenditure.	Zero base budgeting is a **Decision Oriented**.
2. Main Stress	The main stress is on **how much** a unit will spend.	The main stress is on **why** a unit needs to spend.
3. Process	It involves an adjustment to previous figures in the light of demand for inflation and new proposed programmes.	It involves critical Costs & Benefits Analysis of existing programmes and new proposed programmes, ranking the programmes and allocating the resources in the order of priority.
4. Manipulation by Manager	It **may involve** manipulation by managers in inflating their budget request so that after the cuts they still get what they want.	It **may not involve** manipulation by managers since the manager has to justify each item of expenditure in its entirely.
5. Operating Efficiency.	It **does not promote** Operating Efficiency.	It **promotes** Operating Efficiency.
6. Wasteful Activities	It **does not** identify activities involving wasteful expenditure.	It **identifies** activities involving wasteful expenditure.
7. Alternative Means	It **does not encourage** the managers to identify and evaluate alternative means of achieving the same objectives.	It **encourages** the managers to identify and evaluate alternative means of achieving the same objectives.
8. Rational Decision Making	It **does not involve** rational decision making.	It **involves** rational decision making.
9. Priorities	It **does not** fix any priority.	It **fixes** the priorities.

Basis of Distinction	Traditional Budgeting	Zero Base Budgeting
10. Inefficiencies	It **involves** carry forwarding of inefficiencies of a prior year.	It **does not involve** carry forwarding of inefficiencies of a prior year.
11. Review of Existing Activities	It does not involve the review of existing activities.	It involves the review of existing activities.

27.0 PERFORMANCE BUDGETING

Meaning	1. Performance Budgeting is a technique under which Responsibility Centres are established and the targets in terms of physical performance are set for each Responsibility Centre and then expenditures (i.e. inputs in financial terms) are linked with physical performance (i.e. output in physical terms) and performance is evaluated through Periodic Performance Reports. 2. It is a tecnique of presenting budgets for costs and revenues in terms of functions. Programmes and Activities are correlating the physical and financial aspect of the individual items comprising the budget. 3. **According to National Institute of Bank Management, Mumbai,** *Performance budgeting technique is, the process of analyzing, identifying, simplifying and crystallizing specific performance objectives of a job to be achieved over a period in the framework of the organizational objectives, the purpose and objectives of the job. The technique is characterized by its specific direction towards the business objectives of the organization. Thus, performance budgeting lays immediate stress on the achievement of specific goals over a period of time. It requires preparation of periodic performance reports. Such reports compare budget and actual data and show any existing variances.*
Features	1. The focus is on the work to be done, services to be rendered rather than resources to be spent for or acquired. 2. The emphasis is shifted from control of inputs to efficient and economic management of functions and objectives. 3. It links the inputs of the expenditure (i.e. inputs in financial terms) with the physical performance (i.e. output in physical terms). 4. The evaluation of performance is through Periodic Performance Reports.
Objectives	1. To co-ordinate the physical and financial aspects. 2. To improve the budget formulation, review and decision- making at all levels of management. 3. To facilitate better appreciation and review by controlling authorities (legislature, Board of Trustees or Governors, etc.) as presentation is more purposeful and intelligible. 4. To make more effective Performance Audit possible. 5. To measure progress towards long-term objectives which are envisaged in a development plan.

Steps in the Process of Performance Budgeting	1. Establishment of Responsibility Centres. 2. Setting of physical performance targets for each Responsibility Centre. 3. Estimating financial requirements to achieve the physical targets. 4. Measurement of Actual Performance. 5. Continuous comparison of the Actual Performance with the Budgeted performance. 6. Ascertainment of the Variances and analysis of reasons therefor. 7. Taking the Necessary Corrective Action.
Limitations	1. It is difficult to classify all programs and activities. 2. It is difficult to evaluate all performances in physical terms.
Pre-requisites	For an enterprise that wants to adopt PB, it is thus imperative that: 1. the objectives of the enterprise are spelt out in concrete terms. 2. the objectives are then translated into specific functions, programmes, activities and tasks for different levels of management within the realities of fiscal constraints ; 3. realistic and acceptable norms, yardsticks or standards and performance indicators should be evolved and expressed in quantifiable physical units. 4. a style of management based upon decentralized responsibility structure should be adopted, and 5. an accounting and reporting system should be developed to facilitates monitoring, analysis and review of actual performance in relation to budgets.

DISTINCTION BETWEEN TRADITIONAL BUDGETING AND PERFORMANCE BUDGETING

Basis of Distinction	Traditional Budgeting	Performance Budgeting
1. More Emphasis	It gives more emphasis **on the financial aspect** than the physical aspects or performance.	It gives more emphasis on the **physical aspect** (or performance) than the financial aspects. It aims at establishing a relationship between the inputs and the outputs.
2. Preparation	It is prepared with the main emphasis on items of expenditure.	It is prepared with the main emphasis on the functions (objectives) of the organization, the programmes to discharge these functions and the activities which will be involved in undertaking these programmes.

CONSIDERATION IN PERFORMANCE REPORTING

The important considerations in drawing up of reports and determining their scope are the following:

Significance	Are the facts in the reports reliable? Does it either called for action or demonstrate the effect of action? It is material enough.
Timeliness	How late can the information be and still be of use? What is the earliest moment at which it could be used if it were available? How frequently is it required?

Accuracy	How small should be an inaccuracy which does not alter the significance of the information?
Appropriateness	Is the recipient the right person to take any action that is needed? Is there any other information which is required to support the information to anyone else jointly interested?
Discrimination	Will anything be lost by omitting the item? Will any of the items gain from the omission? Is the responsibility for suppressing the item acceptable?
Presentation	Is the report clear and unbiased? Is the form of it is suitable to the subject? Is the form of it suitable to the recipient?

Conclusion: Thus, a Performance Report containing all the Accurate Required Information should be Timely Presented to the Appropriate Recipient in Clear and Unbiased Manner. There must be *neither* False Information *nor* concealment of any Material Information so as to prevent any wrong decision and action on the basis of Performance Report.

TYPES OF REPORTS

An Illustrative list of Reports which are to be prepared and submitted to management regularly at predetermined time interval is as follows:

1. Top Management	1. Balance Sheet 2. Profit & Loss Statement 3. Cash Flow Statements 4. Sales, Production, Stocks and other appropriate statistics 5. Disposition of Funds or Working Capital 6. Capital Expenditure & Forward Commitments together with progress of projects in hands 7. Control Ratios such as Gross Profit Ratio, Operating Profit Ratio, Net Profit Ratio, Return on Investment, Return on Equity, Capital Turnover, Working Capital Turnover, Debt-Equity Ratio, EPS, PE Ratio.
2. Sales Management	1. Sales Performance Report (a) Products wise (b) Territories wise (c) Individual Salesmen wise (d) Customers wise. 2. Standard Profit and Loss Product wise 3. Selling and Distribution Expenses Report (a) Products wise (b) Territories wise (c) Individual Salesmen wise (d) Customers wise. 4. Sales Promotion and Advertising Costs Report (a) Products wise (b) Territories wise (c) Individual Salesmen wise (d) Customers wise. 5. Warehousing Costs Report (a) Products wise (b) Territories wise 6. Credit Control Report Customer wise (to determine Bad Debts, Doubtful Accounts, Slow Payers and to expedite Credit Collection Program) 7. Control Ratios such as Stock Turnover Ratio, Debtors Turnover Ratio.

3. Production Management	1. Material Usage Report, Wastage Report, Scrap Report, Spoilage Report, Defective Report, Rejection Report. 2. Labour Utilization Report, Idle Time Report, Overtime Report, Labour Turnover Report. 3. Production Overheads Report. 4. Plant Utilization Report and Idle Capacity Report. 5. Variance Analysis – Material, Labour, Overheads Report. 6. Control Ratios such as Efficiency Ratio, Activity Ratio, Capacity Ratio. 7. Operating Statement Department wise.
4. Special Reports	These reports may be prepared at the request of general management or at the initiative of the management accountant. Some of the matters in respect of which such reports may be required can be: 1. Make or buy a component 2. Retain or Replace capital equipment. 3. Process further or not. 4. Expand Capacity or not. 5. Accept or Reject an Order. 6. Continue or Discontinue a Product. 7. Shut Down or Continue. 8. Equity Financing Vs. Debt Financing. 9. Debt Financing Vs. Lease Financing. 10. Special Pricing Analysis 11. Break-even Analysis 12. Taxation legislation and its effect on profits. 13. Estimates of the earning capacity of a new project.

Illustration 38. Z Ltd. had a profit plan approved for selling 5,000 units per month at an average selling price of ₹ 10 per unit. The Budgeted variable cost of production was ₹ 4 per unit and the fixed costs were budgeted at ₹ 20,000, the planned income being ₹ 10,000 per month. Due to shortage of raw materials, only 4,000 units could be produced and the cost of production increased by 50 paise per unit. The selling price was raised by ₹ 1.00 per unit. In order to improve the production process, an expenditure of ₹ 1,000 was incurred for research and development activities.

Required: Prepare a Performance Budget and a Summary Report.

Solution

Z LTD.
PERFORMANCE BUDGET

Particulars	*Original Plan* ₹	*Adjusted Plan* ₹	*Actual Position* ₹
A. Sales Revenue	50,000	40,000	44,000
B. *Less:* Variable Costs	20,000	16,000	18,000
C. Contribution [A – B]	30,000	24,000	26,000
D. *Less:* Fixed Costs	20,000	20,000	21,000
E. Net Income [C – D]	10,000	4,000	5,000

Summary Report

A.	Planned Income	₹ 10,000
B.	Selling Price Variance [4,000 × (11 – 10)]	4,000 Favourable
C.	Variable Cost Variance [4,000 × (4 – 4.50)]	2,000 (Adverse)
D.	Fixed Cost Variance (20,000 – 21,000)	1,000 (Adverse)
E.	Profit Volume Variance (1,000 × 6)	6,000 (Adverse)
F.	Total Variance	5,000 (Adverse)
G.	Actual Income [A – F]	5,000

SOLVED PROBLEMS

Problem 1. Tulsian (1) Ltd. provides you the following information:

		Product A	Product B
1	***Figures for the year 2013:***		
	Sales (₹)	2,40,000	2,00,000
	Selling Price Per unit (₹)	24	50
	Closing Stock (on FIFO basis)	74,000 @ ₹ 20	70,000 @ ₹ 20
2	***Targets for 2014:***		
	Sales Quantity Increase (Decrease)	(20%)	25%
	Selling Price Increase (Decrease)	25%	(20%)
	Closing Stock (Units)	5,700	2,500
3	***Other information:***		
	Direct Material X @ ₹ 3 Per Unit	₹ 6	₹ 12
	Direct Material Y @ ₹ 1 Per Unit	₹ 1	₹ 2
	Direct Labour in P Deptt. @ ₹ 1 Per Hour	₹.2	₹ 1
	Direct Labour in Q Deptt. @ ₹ 3 Per Hour	₹ 3	₹ 6
4	***Direct Material Stocks:***	Material X	Material Y
	Stock as on 1.1.2014	12,000 Units	2,000 Units
	Estimated Stock as on 31.12.2014	16,000 Units	4,000 Units

5 Material Prices are expected to increase by 10% and 2% inefficiency (i.e. 2% wasting allowance) is expected in the use of materials.

6 Wage Rates are expected to increase by 30% and 25% increase in labour productivity is expected.

7 The factory works for 8 hours a day, 6 days in a week and budget period is one year and during each quarter hours lost due to leave, holidays and other causes are estimated to be 124 hours.

Required: Prepare Sales Budget, Production Budget, Direct Material Usage & Purchase Budget, Man Power Budget, Direct Labour Cost Budget

Solution:

SALES BUDGET FOR THE YEAR 2014

Product A			*Product B*		
Units	*Rate (₹)*	*Amt. (₹)*	*Units*	*Rate (₹)*	*Amt. (₹)*
8,000	30	2,40,000	5,000	40	2,00,000

PRODUCTION BUDGET FOR THE YEAR 2014

	Particulars	*Product A*	*Product B*
A	Budgeted Sales	8,000	5,000
B	*Add:* Closing Stock	5,700	2,500
C	*Less:* Opening Stock	3,700	3,500
D	Units to be Produced (A + B – C)	10,000	4,000

DIRECT MATERIALS USAGE AND PURCHASE BUDGET FOR THE BUDGET YEAR 2014

Particulars	*Material X*		*Material Y*	
A. Budgeted Usage (for production) :				
For Product 'A'	(10,000 × 2)	20,000	(10,000 × 1)	10,000
For Product 'B'	(4,000 × 4)	16,000	(4,000 × 2)	8,000
Total		36,000		18,000
Add: 2% Inefficiency		720		360
		36,720		18,360
B. *Add:* Closing Stock		16,000		4,000
C. *Less:* Opening Stock		12,000		2,000
D. Budgeted Purchases (Units) [A + B – C]		40,720		20,360
E. Rate per Unit (₹)		3.3		1.1
F. Budgeted Purchases (₹) (D × E)		1,34,376		22,396

MAN POWER BUDGET SHOWING LABOUR HOURS AND NUMBER OF WORKERS

Particulars	Dept. P		Dept. Q	
A. Hours Required				
For Product 'A'	(10,000 × 2)	20,000	(10,000 × 1)	10,000
For Product 'B'	(4,000 × 1)	4,000	(4,000 × 2)	8,000
Total Hours Required		24,000		18,000
Adjustment for Increase in Efficiency (Hours × 100 / 125)		19,200		14,400
B. Hours during Budget Period		2,400		2,400
C. Budgeted No. of Workers (A/B)		8		6

Note: *Budgeted Working Hours = (8 × 6 × 52) – (24 × 4) = 2400 Hours*

DIRECT LABOUR COST BUDGET

Dept. P			Dept. Q		
Hours Required	*Rate ₹*	*Amt. ₹*	*Hours Required*	*Rate ₹*	*Amt. ₹*
16,000	1.3	20,800	8,000	3.9	31,200
3,200	1.3	4,160	6,400	3.9	24,960
		24,960			56,160

Problem 2. A manufacturing company submits the following figures for the first quarter of 20X1 :

		Product X	Product Y	Product Z
Sales in (Units) : Jan.	25,000	30,000	10,000	
	Feb.	20,000	25,000	10,000
	March	30,000	35,000	10,000
Selling Price per Unit		₹ 10	₹ 20	₹ 40
Targets for 1st Quarter of 20X2 :				
Sales quantity increase		20%	10%	10%
Selling price increase		Nil	10%	25%
Stock position on Ist Jan. 20X2				
Percentage of Jan 20X2 sales		50%	50%	50%
Stock position on 31st March 20X2		20,000	25,000	5,000
Stock position-end Jan and Feb				
Percentage of next Month's sales		50%	50%	50%

Required : Prepare the Sales and Production Budget for the 1st Quarter of 20X2.

Solution:

SALES BUDGET FOR THE 1ST QUARTER OF 20X2

Month	Product X		Product Y		Product Z	
	Units	Value @ ₹ 10 ₹	Units	Value @ ₹ 22 ₹	Units	Value @ ₹ 50 ₹
January	30,000	3,00,000	33,000	7,26,000	11,000	5,50,000
February	24,000	2,40,000	27,500	6,05,000	11,000	5,50,000
March	36,000	3,60,000	38,500	8,47,000	11,000	5,50,000
	90,000	9,00,000	99,000	21,78,000	33,000	16,50,000

PRODUCTION BUDGET FOR THE 1ST QUARTER OF 20X2

Month	*Product X Units*	*Product Y Units*	*Product Z Units*
January	27,000	30,250	11,000
February	30,000	33,000	11,000
March	38,000	44,250	10,500
	95,000	1,07,500	32,500

Working Notes :

(i) SALES FORECAST IN UNITS FOR THE IST QUARTER OF 20X2

Month	*Sales figures for the Ist Quarter of 20X1*			*Sales forecast for the Ist Quarter of 20X2*		
	Product X	*Product Y*	*Product Z*	*Product X (20% increase)*	*Product Y (10% increase)*	*Product Z (10% increase)*
January	25,000	30,000	10,000	30,000	33,000	11,000
February	20,000	25,000	10,000	24,000	27,500	11,000
March	30,000	35,000	10,000	36,000	38,500	11,000
Total	75,000	90,000	30,000	90,000	99,000	33,000
(ii) Selling price per unit	₹ 10	₹ 20	₹ 40	₹ 10 (No increase)	₹ 22 (10% increase)	₹ 50 (25% increase)
(iii) Stock position (in units) on 1.1.20X2 (50% of January 20X2 sales)				15,000	16,500	5,500
(iv) Stock (in units) on 31.1.20X2 (50% of Feb. Sales)				12,000	13,750	5,500
(v) Stock (in units) on 28.2.20X2 (50% of Mar. Sales)				18,000	19,250	5,500
(vi) Stock (in units) on 31.3.20X2				20,000	25,000	5,000

(ii) PRODUCTION BUDGET FOR THE IST QUARTER 20X2

Particulars	*January*	*February*	*March*
Product X :			
A. Closing Stock (Being 50% of following month' sales)	12,000	18,000	20,000
B. *Add* : Sales	30,000	24,000	36,000
	42,000	42,000	56,000
C. *Less* : Opening Stock (Being 50% of following month's sales)	15,000	12,000	18,000
D. Units to be produced [A + B – C]	27,000	30,000	38,000
Product Y :			
A. Closing Stock (Being 50% of following month's sales)	13,750	19,250	25,000
B. *Add* : Sales	33,000	27,500	38,500

	46,750	46,750	63,500
C. *Less* : Opening Stock (Being 50% of following month's sales)	16,500	13,750	19,250
D. Units to be produced [A + B – C]	30,250	33,000	44,250
Product Z :			
A. Closing Stock (Being 50% of following month's sales)	5,500	5,500	5,000
B. *Add* : Sales	11,000	11,000	11,000
	16,500	16,500	16,000
C. *Less* : Opening Stock (being 50% of following month's sales)	5,500	5,500	5,500
D. Units to be produced [A + B – C]	11,000	11,000	10,500

Problem 3. AC company is engaged in manufacturing two products 'X' and 'Y'. Product X uses one unit of component 'P' and two units of component 'Q'. Product 'Y' uses two units of component 'P', one unit of component 'Q' and two units of component 'R'. Component 'R' which is assembled in the factory uses one unit of component 'Q'.

Component 'P' and 'Q' are purchased from the market. The company has prepared the following forecast of sales and inventory for the next year:

Particulars	*Product 'X'*	*Product 'Y'*
Sales (in units)	80,000	1,50,000
At the end of the year	10,000	20,000
At the beginning of the year	30,000	50,000

The production of both the products and the assembling of the component 'R' will be spread out uniformly throughout the year. The company at present orders its inventory of 'P' and 'Q' in quantities equivalent to 3 months production. The company has compiled the following data related to two components:

Particulars	*P*	*Q*
Price per unit (₹)	20	8
Order placing cost per order (₹)	1,500	1,500
Carrying cost per annum	20%	20%

Required:

(a) Prepare a Budget of production and requirements of components during next year.

(b) Suggest the optimal order quantity of components 'P' and 'Q'.

Solution: **PRODUCTION BUDGET FOR PRODUCT X AND Y**

Particulars	*X Units*	*Y Units*
A. Budgeted Sales	80,000	1,50,000
B. *Add*: Ending Inventory at the end of the year	10,000	20,000
C. *Less*: Beginning inventory	30,000	50,000
D. Budgeted Production [A + B – C]	60,000	1,20,000

BUDGETED REQUIREMENTS OF COMPONENTS P, Q AND R

Particulars	*P*	*Q*	*R*
For Product X: Production 60,000 units			
P: 60,000 × 1 per unit	60,000		
Q: 60,000 × 2 per unit		1,20,000	
For Product Y: Production 1,20,000 units			
P: 1,20,000 × 2 per unit	2,40,000		

Q: 1,20,000 × 1 per unit		1,20,000	
R: 1,20,000 × 2 per unit			2,40,000
For comp R: Production 2,40,000 comp			
Q: 2,40,000 × 1 per component R		2,40,000	
Total requirements	3,00,000	4,80,000	2,40,000

(b) $$EOQ = \sqrt{\frac{2 \text{ Annual Wage} \times \text{Ordering cost per order}}{\text{Carrying cost per unit}}}$$

$$EOQ(P) = \sqrt{\frac{2 \times 3{,}00{,}000 \times 1{,}500}{20 \times 20\%}} = 15{,}000 \text{ components}$$

$$EOQ(Q) = \sqrt{\frac{2 \times 4{,}80{,}000 \times 1{,}500}{8 \times 20\%}} = 30{,}000 \text{ components}$$

Problem 4. X Ltd. has prepared the following Sales Budget for the first five months of 20X1 :

Months	*January*	*February*	*March*	*April*	*May*
Sales Units	10,800	15,600	12,200	10,400	9,800

Inventory of finished goods at the end of every month is to be equal to 25% of sales estimate for the next month. On 1st Jan., 20X1, there were 2,700 units of product on hand. There is no work in progress at the end of any month.

Every unit of product requires two types of materials in the following quantities :
Material *A* — 4 kg, Material *B* — 5 kg.

Materials equal to one half of the requirement of next month's production are to be in hand at the end of every month. This requirement was also met on 1st Jan., 20X1.

Required : Prepare the following budgets for the quarter ending 31st March, 20X1 :
(a) Production Budget (Quantitative), (b) Material Purchase Budget (Quantitative).

Solution:

PRODUCTION BUDGET
for the Quarter ended 31st March, 20X1 (Quantitative)

Particulars	*January*	*February*	*March*	*Total*
Budgeted Sales	10,800	15,600	12,200	38,600
Add : Budgeted Closing Stock	3,900[1]	3,050[2]	2,600[3]	9,550
Total	14,700	18,650	14,800	48,150
Less : Budgeted Opening Stock	2,700	3,900	3,050	9,650
Units to be produced	12,000	14,750	11,750	38,500

1. Closing Stock for January = 15,600 × 25% = 3,900
2. Closing Stock for February = 12,200 × 25% = 3,050
3. Closing Stock for March = 10,400 × 25% = 2,600

MATERIAL PURCHASE BUDGET
for the Quarter ended 31st March 20X1 (Quantitative)

Particulars	*January*	*February*	*March*	*Total*
Material A :				
Budgeted Usage	48,000	59,000	47,000	1,54,000
Add : Budgeted Closing Stock	29,500	23,500	20,500	73,500
Total	77,500	82,500	67,500	2,27,500
Less : Budgeted Opening Stock	24,000	29,500	23,500	77,000
Purchases to be made	53,500	53,000	44,000	1,50,500

Particulars	January	February	March	Total
Material B :				
Budgeted Usage	60,000	73,750	58,750	1,92,500
Add : Budgeted Closing Stock	36,875	29,375	25,625	91,875
Total	96,875	1,03,125	84,375	2,84,375
Less : Budgeted Opening Stock	30,000	36,875	29,375	96,250
Purchases to be made	66,875	66,250	55,000	1,88,125

Working Notes :

(i) *Computation of Budgeted Consumption*

Particulars	Material A		Material B	
January	(12,000* × 4)	48,000	(12,000* × 5)	60,000
February	(14,750* × 4)	59,000	(14,750* × 5)	73,750
March	(11,750* × 4)	47,000	(11,750* × 5)	58,750
Total		1,54,000		1,92,500

* These figures are taken from Production Budget.

(ii) *Computation of Production and Material required in the month of April*

	Particulars	Units
A	Sales	10,400
B	Budgeted Closing Stock (9,800 × 25%)	2,450
C	*Less :* Budgeted Opening Stock	2,600
D	Production (A + B − C)	10,250
E	Material required	
	Material A (10,250 × 4)	41,000
	Material B (10,250 × 5)	51,250

(iii) *Computation of Budgeted Closing Stock*

	Material A		Material B	
Particulars 1	Budgeted Usage 2	Budgeted Closing Stock 3 = 50% of 2	Budgeted Usage 4	Budgeted Closing Stock 5 = 50% of 4
January	59,000	29,500	73,750	36,875
February	47,000	23,500	58,250	29,125
March	41,000	20,500	51,250	25,625
Total		73,500		91,625

Problem 5. Gunjan Electronics is manufacturing for sale, four models of Television Sets. The major components viz., cabinet, high voltage transformer and the speaker are bought out by the Company. Picture Tubes for three out of the four models are purchased from other firms. Four cabinet styles (A, B, C and D), two kinds of transformers (X and Y), three kinds of speakers and three types of picture tubes are assembled in the following ways in the final product :

Model	Cabinet	Transformer	Speaker	Picture Tube
Standard	A @ ₹ 200	X @ ₹ 200	5" Cone @ ₹ 300	OWN
Deluxe	B @ ₹ 300	X @ ₹ 200	5" Cone @ ₹ 300	BEL @ ₹ 1,200
Aristocrat	C @ ₹ 500	Y @ ₹ 300	6" Cone @ ₹ 400	BEL @ ₹ 1,200
Royal	D @ ₹ 700	Y @ ₹ 300	12" Cone @ ₹ 600	TELTUBE @ ₹ 1,600

The company expects the following inventories in hand on 1st July 20X1 :
Finished Sets :

Standard 46; Deluxe 73 ; Aristrocrat 64; Royal 69.
Sub-assemblies :
Cabinet : A — 30; B — 40; C — 20; D — 25
Transformers : X — 31; Y — 17.
Speakers : 5" Cone — 27; 6" Cone — 47; 12" Cone — 18.
Picture tubes : OWN — 20; BEL 17; Teltube — 34.

The Sales Manager estimates that sales for the quarter, July—September 20X1, will be:

Model	Standard	Deluxe	Aristocrat	Royal
Quantity	200	600	500	300

The following inventory quantities have been budgeted for 30th September 20X1 :
Finished Sets : 25 in each Model
Sub-assemblies : Cabinet — 15 (each model)
Transformers — 20 (each type)
Speakers — 30 (each type)
Picture tube — OWN — 30; BEL — 40; Teltube — 20

Required : Prepare the Production and Purchase Budget for the various items stated above for the quarter July - September 20X1 :

Solution:

GUNJAN ELECTRONICS
PRODUCTION BUDGET (IN UNITS) FOR JULY TO SEPT. 20X1

Particulars	*Standard*	*Delux*	*Aristocrat*	*Royal*
A. Budgeted Sales	200	600	500	300
B. *Add :* Closing stock	25	25	25	25
C. *Less :* Opening stock	46	73	64	69
D. Units to be produced (A + B – C)	179	552	461	256

PURCHASE BUDGET [IN UNITS AND IN ₹ (IN LACS)]

Particulars	*Cabinets*				*Transformers*		*Speakers*			*Picture Tube*	
	A	*B*	*C*	*D*	*X*	*Y*	*5"*	*6"*	*12"*	*BEL*	*Tel Tube*
A. Budgeted Usage	179	552	461	256	731	717	731	461	256	1013	256
B. *Add :* Closing Stock	15	15	15	15	20	20	30	30	30	40	20
C. *Less :* Opening Stock	30	40	20	25	31	17	27	47	18	17	34
D. Units to be Purchased	164	527	456	246	720	720	734	444	268	1036	242
E. Unit Cost (₹)	200	300	500	700	200	300	300	400	600	1200	1600
F. Total Purchases	.328	1.581	2.28	1.722	1.440	2.16	2.202	1.776	1.608	12.432	3.872

Problem 6. X Ltd. manufacturing three products, has the following direct labour requirements for the products:

Operation	*Direct labour hours per unit (in minutes)*		
	Product 1	*Product 2*	*Product 3*
I	18	42	30
II	—	12	24
III	9	6	—

The factory works 8 hours per day, 6 days in a week. Each budget quarter has 13 weeks and in terms of leave, holidays and other causes, 124 hours are lost in each quarter. Operations I, II and III have the budgeted hourly rates for workers at ₹ 16, ₹ 20 and ₹ 24 respectively. The budgeted sales of the products during the quarter are :

Product 1	9,000 units
Product 2	15,000 units
Product 3	12,000 units

There were operating stocks of 5,000 units of Product 2 and 4,000 units of Product 3 and it is proposed to have closing stock at the end of the budget quarter as follows :

Product 1	1,000 units
Product 3	2,000 units

Required : Prepare a Man Power Budget for the quarter, showing for each operation : (i) Direct labour hours (ii) Direct labour cost, and (iii) Number of workers.

Solution:

MANPOWER BUDGET SHOWING FOR EACH OPERATION DIRECT LABOUR HOURS, DIRECT LABOUR COST AND NUMBER OF WORKERS FOR THE QUARTER ENDING......

Particulars	*Operation I*	*Operation II*	*Operation III*	*Total*
(i) Direct labour hrs. *[Refer to W. N. (ii)]*	15,000 hrs.	6,000 hrs.	2,500 hrs.	23,500 hrs.
(ii) Direct labour cost (₹) *[Refer to W. N. (iii)]*	2,40,000	1,20,000	60,000	4,20,000
(iii) No. of workers *[Refer to W. N. (v)]*	30 men	12 men	5 men	47 men

Working Notes :

(i) PRODUCTION BUDGET FOR THE QUARTER ENDING.....

	Particulars	*Product 1*	*Product 2*	*Product 3*
A	Budgeted Sales (units)	9,000	15,000	12,000
B	*Add :* Closing Stock (units)	1,000	—	2,000
C	*Less :* Opening Stock (units)		5,000	4,000
D	Budgeted Production [A + B – C]	10,000	10,000	10,000

(ii) BUDGETED DIRECT LABOUR HOURS REQUIRED IN EACH OPERATION FOR THE QUARTER ENDING.....

A *Product*	*B* *Budgeted Production (units)*	*C* *Direct Labour hours per unit (in minutes)*	*D = B × C/60* *Direct Labour hours required*
Operation I :			
Product 1	10,000	18 mts.	3,000 hrs.
Product 2	10,000	42 mts.	7,000 hrs.
Product 3	10,000	30 mts.	5,000 hrs.
			15,000 hrs.
Operation II :			
Product 1	10,000	—	
Product 2	10,000	12 mts.	2,000 hrs.
Product 3	10,000	24 mts.	4,000 hrs.
			6,000 hrs.

Operation III :			
Product 1	10,000	9 mts.	1,500 hrs.
Product 2	10,000	6 mts.	1,000 hrs.
Product 3	10,000	—	—
			2,500 hrs.

(iii) BUDGETED LABOUR COST FOR THE QUARTER ENDING ...

Operation	*Direct labour hours*	*Direct Labour Hourly Rate* ₹	*Direct labour cost* ₹
I	15,000	16	2,40,000
II	6,000	20	1,20,000
III	2,500	24	60,000

(iv) ***Computation of net direct labour hours available in a quarter***

A.	Total number of hours available in a quarter (13 weeks × 6 days × 8 hours)	624
B	*Less* : Estimated hours lost due to leave, etc.	124
C	Net available hours	500

(v) *No. of workers required* $= \dfrac{\text{Direct labour hours required}}{\text{Net available hours in a quarter}}$

$$\text{Operation I} = \frac{15{,}000}{500} = 30 \text{ men}$$

$$\text{Operation II} = \frac{6{,}000}{500} = 12 \text{ men}$$

$$\text{Operation III} = \frac{2{,}500}{500} = 5 \text{ men}$$

$$= 47 \text{ men}$$

Problem 7. CAS Manufacturing company takes over sales from the Selling Agents. In the first month of operation of direct sales, the following costs have been incurred. Prepare the actual percentage of selling cost on total sales, compare with the standard selling cost. Compute the variances and offer your comments about the standards, which are based on actual for the previous year, and performance of the Zonal offices.

Zonal Offices	*Sales Budget (units)*	*Standard Selling Expenses*
Eastern India (E.I.)	20,000	₹ 16,000
Western India (W.I.)	12,000	12,000
Northern India (N.I.)	6,000	8,000
Southern India (S.I.)	15,000	12,000
Central India (C.I)	10,000	10,000
Northern Western India (N.W.I)	5,000	8,000
Selling Price per unit – ₹ 25		

Actual	*E.I.*	*W.I.*	*N.I.*	*S.I.*	*C.I*	*N.W.I*
Units sold ('000 units)	19	10	5.9	17.5	9.5	5
Salesmen's salaries (₹.'000)	8	7	5	7	6	5
Sales travelling (₹.'000)	4	5	3.6	2.7	2.7	1.8
Halting charges & Bhatta (₹)	850	800	500	500	700	500
Salesmen's commission on selling prices @	1%	1.25%	1%	0.9%	1%	1%

Solution: **COMPARATIVE COST STATEMENT OF SELLING EXPENSES**

	Particulars	E.I.	W.I.	N.I.	S.I.	C.I	N.W.I
A	Standard Selling Expenses (₹)	16,000	12,000	8,000	12,000	10,000	8,000
B	Budgeted Sales (units)	20,000	12,000	6,000	15,000	10,000	5,000
C	Selling Cost p.u. ₹ (A / B)	0.80	1.00	1.3333	0.80	1.00	1.60
D	Actual Sales (units)	19,000	10,000	5,900	17,500	9,500	5,000
E	Standard Selling Cost for Actual Sales (₹) (C × D)	15,200	10,000	7,867	14,000	9,500	8,000
	Actual Selling Costs:						
	Salesmen's Salaries (₹)	8,000	7,000	5,000	7,000	6,000	5,000
	Sales Travelling	4,000	5,000	3,600	2,700	2,700	1,800
	Halting Charges etc.	850	800	500	500	700	500
	Salesmen's Commission	4,750	3,125	1,475	3,937	2,375	1,250
F.	Total Actual Selling Costs	17,600	15,925	10,575	14,137	11,775	8,550
G.	Selling Costs Variance ₹ (E) – (F)	– 2,400	– 5,925	– 2,708	– 137	– 2,275	– 550
H.	Budgeted Sales (Budgeted qty. × Budgeted Price) (₹)	5,00,000	3,00,000	1,50,000	3,75,000	2,50,000	1,25,000
I.	Budgeted Selling Expenses as a % of Budgeted Sales (A) / (H)×100	3.2	4.0	5.3	3.2	4.0	6.5
J.	Actual Sales (₹)	4,75,000	2,50,000	1,47,500	4,37,500	2,37,000	1,25,000
K.	Actual Selling Expenses as a % of Actual Sales	3.7	6.4	3.2	7.2	4.9	6.8

Comments: The above table shows that except for southern India and North – western India Zonal offices, actual sales expenses widely differ from budgeted selling expenses. However, the following points have to be noted:

(i) The standards are based on the actual expenses for the last year. Truly speaking they are not standards and, therefore, they cannot provide realistic guidance for exercising control over the selling expenses. Variances may be there because current year's conditions might have completely changed or circumstances which were applicable last year may have ceased to become applicable now.

(ii) The causes of the variances cannot be correctly spelt out in the absence of details about the "Standard selling expenses." The details of actual selling expenses have been given but the details of standard selling expenses have not been given. Salesmen's salaries is a fixed charge, variance may be there on account of increase in their salaries. Sales travelling expenses are of a semi-variable nature. Less volume of sales might have resulted in less recovery of fixed sales travelling expenses such as railway freight, hotel charges.

Problem 8 The 1st January cash balance of the CAS Gay Company is ₹ 5,000. Sales for the first four months of the year are expected to be as follows: January, ₹ 65,000; February, ₹ 54,000; March, ₹ 66,000; and April, ₹ 63,000. On January1, uncollected amounts for November and December of the previous year are ₹ 13,500 and ₹ 39,150, respectively. Collections from customers follow this pattern; 55% in the month of sale, 30% in the month following the sale, 13% in the second month following the sale, and 2% un-collectible. Materials purchases for December were ₹ 10,000. Forecast purchases for the coming year are January, ₹ 12,500; February, ₹ 16,500; March, ₹ 13,000; and April, ₹ 14,000. Purchases are usually paid by the 10th of the month following the month of purchase. Other cash expenditures of ₹ 41,000 are forecast for each month.

Required: Prepare Cash Budget for January and February

Solution:

CASH BUDGET FOR JAN. & FEB.

	Particulars	Jan (₹)	Feb (₹)
A	Opening Cash Balance	5,000	27,550
B	**Collection:**		
	Cash Sales @ 55%	35,750	29,700
	Collection pm @ 30% of sales	26,100 (39,150 × 30/45)	19,500 (65,000 × 30%)

	Collection. of 2nd Pm @ 13% of sales	11,700 (13,500 × 13/15)	11,310 (39,150 × 13/45)
	Total	78,550	88,060
C	**Payments:** Purchase of Material Misc. Expenses	 10,000 41,000	 12,500 41,000
	Total	51,000	53,500
D	Closing Cash Balance (A + B – C)	27,550	34,560

Problem 9. The budgeted level of activity of a Production Department of CAS Ltd. a manufacturing company is 5,000 hours in a period. But a technical study assumes overhead behavior mentioned below:-

Particulars	*₹ ('00) Per hr.*	*Total in ₹ ('000)*
Indirect wages (Variable Cost), Rent and Tax (Fixed Cost)	0.40	320
Consumable Supplies (Variable)	0.24	
Power Variable:		
– up to 3,600 hrs	0.25	
– for hrs above 3,600 additional cost,	0.20	
Repairs:		
– up to 2,000 hours		100
– additional each extra 500 hrs up to 4,000 hrs.		35
– additional 4,001 to 5,000 hrs		60
– additional above 5,000 hrs		70
Supervision:		
– up to 2,500 hrs		400
– additional each extra 600 hrs up to 4,900 hrs		100
– additional above 4,900 hrs		150
Depreciation:		
– up to 5,000 hrs		650
– above 5,000 hrs.		820
Clearing:		
– up to 4,000 hrs		60
– above 4,000 hrs		80
Lighting:		
– 2,100 to 3,500 hrs		120
– 3,501 hrs to 5,000 hrs		150
– above 5,000 hrs		175

Required: (a) Prepare Fixed Budget and a Flexible Budget at 70%, 85% and 110% of Budgeted Level of Activity in one statement (b) Calculate a Departmental Hourly Rate of Overhead Absorption.

Solution:

FLEXIBLE BUDGET AND FIXED BUDGET

Particulars	*Flexible Budget*			*Fixed Budget*
Capacity	70%	85%	110%	100%
A. Hours	3,500 **₹ '000**	4,250 **₹ '000**	5,500 **₹ '000**	5,000 **₹ '000**
B. Indirect wages @ ₹ 40/hr. (A × ₹ 40)	140	170	220	200

C. Rates & Taxes (Fixed)	320	320	320	320
D. Consumable supplies @ ₹ 24/hr. (A × ₹ 24)	84	102	132	120
E. Repair	205 [100 + (35 × 3)]	300 [100 + (35 × 4) + 60]	370 [100 + (35 × 4) + 60 + 70]	300 [100 + (35 × 4) + 60]
F. Supervision	600	700	950	950
G. Power	87.5 (3,500 × 25)	103 [(3,600 × 25) + (650 × 20)]	128 [(3,600 × 25) + (1,900 × 20)]	118 [(3,600 × 25) + (1,400 × 20)]
H. Depreciation	650	650	820	650
I. Clearing	60	80	80	80
J. Lighting	120	150	175	150
K. Total Cost	2,266.5	2,575	3,195	2,888
L. Rate (K/A)	647.57	605.88	580.91	577.6

Problem 10. Tulsian (2) Ltd. provides you the following information:

		Product A	Product B
1	***Figures for the year 2014:***		
	Sales (₹)	2,40,000	2,00,000
	Selling Price Per unit (₹)	24	50
	Closing Stock (on FIFO basis)	74,000 @ ₹ 20	70,000 @ ₹ 20
2	***Targets for 2015:***		
	Sales Quantity Increase (Decrease)	(20%)	25%
	Selling Price Increase (Decrease)	25%	(20%)
	Closing Stock (Units)	5,700	2,500
3	***Other information:***		
	Direct Material X @ ₹ 3 Per Unit	2 Units	4 Units
	Direct Material Y @ ₹ 1 Per Unit	1 Unit	2 units
	Direct Labour in P Deptt. @ ₹ 1 Per Hour	2 Hours	1 Hour
	Direct Labour in Q Deptt. @ ₹ 3 Per Hour	1 Hour	1 Hour
4	***Direct Material Stocks:***	Material X	Material Y
	Stock as on 1.1.2015	12,000 Units	2,000 Units
	Estimated Stock as on 31.12.2015	16,000 Units	4,000 Units
5	***Production Overheads:***	Deptt. P	Deptt. Q
	Fixed Production Overheads	₹ 48,000	₹ 14,000
	Variable Overhead Per Labour Hour	₹ 0.50	₹ 1.50

6 The factory works for 8 hours a day, 6 days in a week and budget period is one year and during each quarter hours lost due to leave, holidays and other causes are estimated to be 124 hours.

7 Administrative Expenses ₹ 11,500 to be apportioned equally to both the products.

8 Sales Manager is entitled to commission @ 10% on Standard Gross Profit.

9 Other Selling Expenses ₹ 22,000 to be apportioned to products on the basis of Sales Revenue.

10 Distribution Expenses ₹ 13,000 to be apportioned to products on the basis of Sales Quantity.

11 Tax rate 30%.

Required: Prepare Sales Budget, Production Budget, Direct Material Usage and Purchase Budget, Man Power Budget, Direct Labour Cost Budget, Production Overheads Budget, Production Cost Budget, Cost of Goods Sold Budget and Budgeted Income Statement.

Solution:

SALES BUDGET

Product A			Product B		
Units	*Rate (₹)*	*Amt. (₹)*	*Units*	*Rate (₹)*	*Amt. (₹)*
8,000	30	2,40,000	5,000	40	2,00,000

PRODUCTION BUDGET BUDGET

	Particulars	*Product A*	*Product B*
A	Budgeted Sales	8,000	5,000
B	*Add:* Closing Stock	5,700	2,500
C	*Less:* Opening Stock	3,700	3,500
D	Budgeted Production (Units) (A + B – C)	10,000	4,000

DIRECT MATERIALS USAGE AND PURCHASE BUDGET

Particulars	*Material X*	*Material Y*
A. Budgeted Usage (for production) :		
For Product 'A'	20,000	10,000
For Product 'B'	16,000	8,000
B. *Add:* Closing Stock	16,000	4,000
C. *Less:* Opening Stock	12,000	2,000
D. Budgeted Purchases (Units) [A + B – C]	40,000	20,000
E. Rate per Unit	₹ 3	₹ 1
F. Budgeted Purchases (D × E)	₹ 1,20,000	₹ 20,000

MAN POWER BUDGET SHOWING LABOUR HOURS AND NUMBER OF WORKERS

Particulars	*Dept. P*	*Dept. Q*
A. Hours Required		
For Product 'A'	20,000	10,000
For Product 'B'	4,000	4,000
Total Hours Required	24,000	14,000
B. Hours during Budget Period	2,000	2,000
C. Budgeted No. of Workers (A/B)	12	7

Note: *Budgeted Working Hours = (8 × 6 × 52) – (124 × 4) = 2000 Hours*

DIRECT LABOUR COST BUDGET

Particulars	*Dept. P*			*Dept. Q*		
	Hours Required	*Rate ₹*	*Amt. ₹*	*Hours Required*	*Rate ₹*	*Amt. ₹*
For Product 'A'	20,000	1	20,000	10,000	3	30,000
For Product 'B'	4,000	1	4,000	4,000	3	12,000
			24,000			42,000

PRODUCTION OVERHEADS COST BUDGET

Particulars	*Dept. P*	*Dept. Q*
A. Total Fixed overheads	₹ 48,000	₹ 14,000
B. Budgeted Hours	24,000	14,000
C. Fixed Overhead Rate per hour (A/B)	₹ 2.00	₹ 1.00
D. Variable Overheads Rate per hour	₹ 0.50	₹ 1.50

E. Total Overhead Rate per hour (C + D)	₹ 2.50	₹ 2.50
F. Budgeted Hours	24,000	14,000
G. Total Budgeted Production Overheads (E × F)	₹ 60,000	₹ 35,000

PRODUCTION COST BUDGET

	Particulars	*Product A (Units 10,000)*		*Product B (Units 4,000)*		
		Total (₹)	*Per unit* (₹)	*Total* (₹)	*Per unit* (₹)	*Total* (₹)
A	Direct Materials Consumed:					
	Material X	60,000	6.00	48,000	12.00	1,08,000
	Material Y	10,000	1.00	8,000	2.00	18,000
B	Direct Labour Incurred:					
	Dept.P	20,000	2.00	4,000	1.00	24,000
	Dept. Q	30,000	3.00	12,000	3.00	42,000
C	Production Overheads:					
	Fixed:					
	Dept.P	40,000	4.00	8,000	2.00	48,000
	Dept. Q	10,000	1.00	4,000	1.00	14,000
	Variable:					
	Dept.P	10,000	1.00	2,000	0.50	12,000
	Dept. Q	15,000	1.50	6,000	1.50	21,000
D	Cost of Goods Produced (A + B + C)	1,95,000	19.50	92,000	23.00	2,87,000

COST OF GOODS SOLD BUDGET

	Particulars	*Product A (Units 10,000)*		*Product B (Units 4,000)*		
		Total (₹)	*Per unit* (₹)	*Total* (₹)	*Per unit* (₹)	*Total* (₹)
A	Cost of Goods Produced (as per Production Cost Budget)	1,95,000	19.50	92,000	23.00	2,87,000
B	*Add:* Opening Stock	74,000	20.00	70,000	20.00	1,44,000
C	*Less:* Closing Stock	1,11,150	19.50	57,500	23.00	1,68,650
D	Cost of Goods Sold (A + B – C)	1,57,850		1,04,500		2,62,350

BUDGETED INCOME STATEMENT

	Particulars	*Product A*	*Product B*	*Total*
A	Sales	2,40,000	2,00,000	4,40,000
B	*Less:* Cost of Goods Sold (as per Cost of Goods Sold Budget)	1,57,850	1,04,500	2,62,350
C	Gross Profit (A – B)	82,150	95,500	1,77,650
D	*Less:* Administration and Selling & Distribution Expenses Administration Expenses (in ratio of 1 : 1)	5,750	5,750	11,500
	Sales Manager's Commission	8,400*	8,500**	16,900
	Other Selling Expenses @ 5% on Sales	12,000	10,000	22,000
	Distribution Expenses (in the ratio of 8000 : 5000 Units)	8,000	5,000	13,000
		34,150	29,250	63,400
E	Net Profit before tax (C – D)	48,000	66,250	1,14,250
F	*Less:* Tax @ 30%	14,400	19,875	34,275
G	Net Profit after tax (E – F)	33,600	46,375	79,975

*10% on [(₹ 30 – 19.50) x 8000], **10% on [(₹ 40 – ₹ 23) × 5000]

6 Standard Costing—Material Cost Variances

LEARNING OBJECTIVES

After studying this chapter, you should be able to understand:

- Is Standard Costing a method of Costing?
- Meaning of Standard
- Meaning of Standard Cost
- Meaning of Standard Costing
- Applicability of Standard Costing
- Objective of Standard Costing
- Advantages of Standard Costing
- Limitations of Standard Costing System
- Distinction between Standard Costing and Budgetary Control
- Preliminaries in Establishing a System of Standard Costing
- Types of Standards
- Setting of Standards
- Standard Hour
- Standard Cost Card/Standard Cost Sheet
- Cost Variance and Variance Analysis
- Three Distinct Group of Variances
- Material Variances
- Terms useful for Computation of Material Variances
- Direct Material Cost Variance (MCV)
- Direct Material Price Variance (MPV)
- Direct Material Usage Variance (MUV)
- Direct Material Mix Variance (MMV)
- Direct Material Yield Variance (MYV)
- Practical Steps in the Computation of Material Cost Variances

1.0 IS STANDARD COSTING A METHOD OF COSTING?

Standard Costing is one of the cost control techniques and not a method of costing like job costing, *or* process costing.

2.0 MEANING OF STANDARD

Standard means a criterion or a yardstick against which actual activity can be compared to determine the difference between the two.

3.0 MEANING OF STANDARD COST

3.1 Standard cost is the cost what should have been under a given set of operating conditions.

3.2 **According to Chartered Institute of Management Accountants (C.I.M.A.), London,** *"Standard cost is the pre-determined cost based on technical estimates for materials, labour and overhead for a selected period of time for a prescribed set of working conditions."*

FEATURES OF STANDARD COST

(a) It is a pre-determined cost which is computed before the cost is incurred (i.e. in advance of production).
(b) It is based on engineering specification of all the factors affecting cost.
(c) It is computed for a specific period of time.
(d) It is to be attained under a given set of efficient operating conditions.

DISTINCTION BETWEEN STANDARD COST AND ESTIMATED COST

Standard Cost differs from Estimated Cost in the following respects:

Basis of Distinction	Standard Cost	Estimated Cost
1. What indicates?	Standard Cost indicates **what cost should be?**	Estimated Cost indicate **what cost will be?**
2. How determined?	Standard Costs are determined on a **scientific basis.**	Estimated Costs are obtained by **adjusting past figures** to possible future changes.
3. How useful?	Standard costs are useful for **cost control.**	Estimated costs do **not** serve the purpose of **cost control.** These may be used while quoting selling price of new products etc.
4. Which firm uses?	Standard costs are used by a firm **having standard costing system** in operation.	Estimated costs are used by a firm **having historical cost system.**
5. Whether Recorded?	Standard costs are **recorded** in the regular system of accounting.	Estimated costs are **not recorded** in the regular system of accounting.

4.0 MEANING OF STANDARD COSTING

Standard Costing is one of the cost control techniques.

According to CIMA, London, *"Standard Costing is the preparation and use of standard costs, their comparison with actual costs and the analysis of variances to their causes and points of incidence."*

On the basis of above definition, the steps involved in the techniques of standard costing are as follows:

Step 1 → Fixation of realistic (i.e., attainable) standards for each element of cost, i.e. material, labour and overheads.

Step 2 → Comparison of the actual cost with the standard cost and find out the difference between the two known as variance. A variance which increases profit is called favourable and which decreases profit is called unfavourable or adverse.

Step 3 → Analysis of variances to ascertain the reasons for the variances.

Step 4 → Presentation of information to the appropriate level of management to decide upon the corrective action to be taken.

5.0 APPLICABILITY OF STANDARD COSTING

The standard costing system is suitable where:

1. A sufficient volume of standard products or components is produced.
2. Methods, operations and processes are capable of being standardised.
3. A sufficient number of costs are capable of being controlled.

Industries using process costing method like, fertilisers, cement, steel, sugar etc. may use standard costing method because such industries are producing standarised products which are repetitive in nature.

In job order industries, it is not useful to employ a full system of standard costing because in such industries each job undertaken may be different from another and setting standards for each job may prove difficult and expensive.

6.0 OBJECTIVE OF STANDARD COSTING

The main objective of Standard Costing is to control cost through variance analysis.

7.0 ADVANTAGES OF STANDARD COSTING

The main advantages of standard costing are as follows:

1. Facilitates Planning	Standard costing facilitates planning since setting up standard involves careful analysis and scrutiny of different activities of a business.
2. Facilitates Effective Delegation of Authority	Delegation of authority becomes effective since the people concerned know what they have to achieve and by what standard they will be judged.
3. Facilitates Cost Control	Standard Costs facilitates cost control by — (i) revealing exact degree of efficiency in various operations through comparison of actual figures with standard figures. (ii) revealing exact causes of deviation of actual figures from standard figures through variance analysis.
4. Facilitates Motivation	Standard costing facilitates motivation through standards which provide incentive and motivation to attain standard output of standard quality. Workers who attain standard output may be rewarded. This increases efficiency and productivity.
5. Facilitates Objective Measurement of Performance	Right person can be rewarded & promoted since performance can be judged objectively.
6. Facilitates Coordination	Standard costing facilitates co-ordination between different functions by bringing different functions such as purchasing, production, selling, accounting together while fixing standards.
7. Facilitates the use of MBE Principle	Standard costing facilitates the use of management by Exception principle since the management need to concentrate only on the areas and problems which require its attention through study of variance analysis.
8. Facilitates the Formulation of Pricing Policies	Standard costing facilitates the formulation of pricing policies for prospective orders.
9. Facilitates the Formulation of Production Policies	Standard costing facilitates the formulation of production policies for various products by providing predetermined costs of each element of cost on the basis of engineering specifications.
10. Facilitates Cost Reporting	Standard costing through variance analysis provides a ready means of interpretation of information for the management for the purpose of control and decision making. Ready reporting enhances the value of reports.

11. Reveals the areas of avoidable wastages & losses, idle capacity	Standard Costing through variance analysis reveals the areas of avoidable wastages & losses and idle capacity.
12. Facilitates Cost Audit	Standard Costing facilitates cost audit since if variances are satisfactorily explained, the accuracy of costing can be safely assumed.
13. Provides Economical means of costing	Standard costing provides economical means of costing in the sense that once the standards have been fixed some records can be kept in quantities only. This eliminates much clerical effort in pricing and balancing items on stock ledger card. The standard cost of goods produced can be calculated immediately just by multiplying the quantity by the unit standard cost.
14. Provides Uniform Valuation of Inventory	Standard costing provides uniform valuation of inventory by valuing inventory of raw-materials, work-in-progress and finished goods at standard costs and by transferring the difference between actual and standard cost to a variance account.
15. Provides Forward Looking Approach	By adoption of standard costing system, the whole concern is imbued with a dynamic forward looking mentality.
16. Provides Objective Measurement of Operational Efficiency	Standard costing through setting of standards, enables to measure the operational efficiency of workers and other materials of the staff objectively against those standards.
17. Creates Cost Consciousness	Standard costing creates cost consciousness among executives which increases efficiency and productivity.

8.0 LIMITATIONS OF STANDARD COSTING SYSTEM

The limitations of standard costing system which make it difficult to work a standard costing system successfully are given below:

1. Setting of Accurate Standards	It is difficult to fix accurate standard costs. Standards may be either too strict or too liberal. Inaccurarte and unreliable standards do more harm than benefits.
2. Revision of Standards	Standards require revision because business conditions constantly keep on charging. Revision of standards is costly and some firms ignore it.
3. Adverse Effect on Morale & Motivation	Non-achievement of unrealistic standards may have an adverse effect on the morale and motivation of the employees.
4. Unsuitability	Standard costing system is costly and unsuitable in job-order industries where the production is of a non-repetitive nature.
5. Expensive	In case of small concerns it is expensive to operate standard costing system.
6. Duplication	Where the system has not yet been fully accepted, there is duplication in recording in as much as inventory pricing etc. have to be done both at standard and actual price.

7. Difficulty in Setting Standards	Sometimes it becomes difficult to set up standard costs in view of the uncertain economic conditions, great fluctuations in prices.
8. Non Facilitate Cost Reduction	Standard costing facilitates only cost control and not cost reduction.

It may be seen that the aforesaid limitations are not so serious as to make the system unworkable. These limitations can be overcome by taking special care in the setting up of the standards and in educating the staff at different levels.

9.0 DISTINCTION BETWEEN STANDARD COSTING AND BUDGETARY CONTROL

Although basic principles of Standard Costing and Budgetary Control are same, yet they differ in the following respects:

Basis of Distinction	Standard Cost	Budgetary Control
1. Basis of Comparison	Control is effected by comparing actual figures with standard figures of actual output.	Control is effected by comparing actual figures with budgeted figures of sales, production, capital assets etc.
2. Scope	The scope of standard costing is comparatively narrow since it covers mainly production costs.	The scope of budgetary control is comparatively wide since it relates to all business operations, sales, capital and financial expenses.
3. Main Concern	It is mainly concerned with the ascertainment and control of each element of cost.	It is mainly concerned with the overall profitability and financial position of a business.
4. Projection	It includes projection of cost accounts only.	It includes projections of financial accounts as well as cost accounts.
5. Recording of Variances in Accounts	Variances (i.e. differences between actual figures and standard figures) are normally **revealed** in different cost accounts.	Variances (i.e. differences between actual figures & budgeted figures) are normally **not revealed** in different accounts.
6. Can it be operated in parts?	It **can not be** operated in parts. All items of expenditure included in cost units are to be accounted for.	It **can be** operated in parts It is possible to carryout even for a particular type of expenses say Advertising expenses, Research & Development Expenses.
7. Summary or Detailed Analysis	It involves the carrying out of detailed variance analysis in respect of each cost element in minute detail and thus facilitate in taking correcting action. Thus, it is comparatively technically improved system.	It involves budgeting and control of total expenses and revenues based on estimates. Thus, it is comparatively broad in nature.

10.0 PRELIMINARIES IN ESTABLISHING A SYSTEM OF STANDARD COSTING

1. Establishment of Cost Centres	The first step in the establishment of standard costing sytem is the establishment of cost centres with clearly defined areas of responsibility.
2. Classification and Codification of accounts	The next step in the establishment of standard costing system is the classification and codification of accounts. Classification may be by function, revenue item, etc.

11.0 TYPES OF STANDARDS

Basic Standard	Basic standard is a standard which is established for some base year and remain in use for a long period of time. Variances from basic standards indicate the trends of deviations of actual cost from the basic cost. It has no practical utility from the point of view of cost control.
Current Standard	Current Standard is a standard which is established for a limited period and is related to current conditions.
Ideal Standard	Ideal Standard is a standard which is based on perfect performance without making any allowance for unavoidable losses (e.g. Normal Idle Time, Normal Waste/Scrap/Defectives/ Spoilage etc). It is merely a theoretical standard which is unrealistic and unattainable. Variances from ideal standard generally indicate unfavourable deviations.
Expected or Practical Standard	Expected or Practical Standard is a standard which is based on expected performance after making a reasonable allowance for unavoidable losses (e.g. Normal Idle Time, Normal Waste/Scrap/Defectives/Spoilage etc.). It is realistic and attainable standard. Variances from the expected standard indicate real deviations from the attainable performance.
Normal Standard	Normal Standard is a standard which is based on average performance in the past. It is attainable under normal conditions. The main purpose of normal standard is to eliminate variations in the cost arising out of trade cycles.

12.0 SETTING OF STANDARDS

Standard cost is the key to the system of standard costing. Extreme care is required to be taken in the establishment of standards because the success of standard cost system depends on the accuracy and reliability of these standards. Standards are set for each element of cost, i.e. Material, Labour, Overhead as follows:

Standards	Who sets Standard ?	Considerable Factors
I. Direct Material Standards ***(a) Material Price Standards***	Purchase Department	1. Current Market price. 2. Market Conditions 3. Forecasts of Price Trends. 4. Discount, Packing and delivery charges etc.

(b) Material Usage Standard	Engineering Department & Production Deptt.	1. Quality of Material. 2. Quantity of Material. 3. Normal Material Losses like evaporation shrinkage,breakage etc.
II. Direct Labour Standards ***(a) Labour Rate Standard***	Personnel Department	1. Current Rates of Pay 2. Current Method of Wage Payment. 3. Forecast of wage trends.
(b) Labour Efficiency Standard	Engineering Department	1. Grade of Labour. (Skilled /semi-skilled/un-skilled) 2. Standard time for each operation 3. Most efficient method of working. 4. Normal Idle time like fatigue, tool setting etc.
III. Standard for Overheads	Engineering Department, Personnel Department, Purchase Department, Administrative Deptt. Selling & Distribution Department	1. Standard Indirect Material costs. 2. Standard Indirect Labour costs. 3. Standard Indirect Expenses 4. Standard level of activity such as Standard Hours, Standard Production (in units) 5. Fixed overheads. 6. Variable overheads.

13.0 STANDARD HOUR

Meaning	The standard hour is the quantity of output or amount which should be performed in one hour. According to C.I.M.A. London, a standard hour is a "hypothetical hour which represents the amount of work which should be performed in one hour under stated conditions."
How to Compute	Standard Hours = $\frac{\text{Actual Output}}{\text{Standard output per hour}}$ *or* = Actual Output × Standard Hours required to produce 1 unit
Practical Illustration	X Ltd. produces three types of products X, Y and Z. Production per hour should be 100 units, 200 units and 300 units respectively. Actual production during a month is 1000 units, 3,000 units and 6,000 units of X, Y and Z respectively. Production measured in standard hours will be as follows:

Product	*Actual Output* *A*	*Standard Output per hour* *B*	*Standard Hours* *C = A/B*
X	1,000	100	10
Y	3,000	200	15
Z	6,000	300	20
Total Standard hours			45

14.0 STANDARD COST CARD/STANDARD COST SHEET

Meaning	Standard Cost Card/Sheet is a record of standard material, labour and overheads costs for a particular product/service.
Contents	Standard Cost Card/Sheet shows: (a) Quantity and Price of each material item to be consumed. (b) Time and Rate of each grade of labour to be used. (c) Rate and Basis of overheads absorption. (d) Total Cost element wise.
Format	**Standard Cost Card**

Product : Component PC T – 101 — *Date of Fixing Standard : 9th Aug. 2008*
Unit : Dozen — *Date of Revision : ....*

	Rate ₹	Total ₹
Direct Materials :		
8 units of Material X	30	240
12 units of Material Y	50	600
Total		**840**
Direct Labour :		
Skilled 12 hours	100	1200
Unskilled 8 hours	40	320
Total		**1520**
Factory Overhead :		
Machine Hour Rate I. 12 hrs.	30	360
II. 8 hrs.	50	400
Total		**760**

Cost Summary

Direct Materials	₹ 840
Direct Labour	₹ 1,520
Factory Overheads	₹ 760
Standard cost per unit	₹ 3,120

15.0 COST VARIANCE AND VARIANCE ANALYSIS

Meaning of Variance	Difference between standard and actual is known as variance.
Meaning of Cost Variance	Cost Variance is the *"difference between a standard cost and the comparable actual cost incurred during a period."* **C.I.M.A. London.**
Meaning of Variance Analysis	Variance Analysis is the process of analysing variances by sub-dividing the total variance in such a way that management can assign responsibility for any deviation from standard performance. **According to C.I.M.A., London,** variance analysis is *"the process of computing the amount of variance and isolating the cause of variance between actual and standard."* An important aspect of variance analysis is the need to separate controllable from uncontrollable variances. A detailed analysis of controllable variances helps the management to ascertain (a) the amount of variance (b) the cause of variance (c) the persons responsible for its occurence and (d) corrective action to be taken.

<table>
<tr><td>Favourable and Unfavourable Variances</td><td>(a) Where the actual cost is less than standard cost, the difference is known as 'favourable' or 'credit' variance.
(b) Where the actual cost is more than standard cost, the difference is known as 'unfavourable', 'adverse' or 'debit' variance.
(c) In other words, any variance which increases the actual profit is favourable variance and any variance which decreases the actual profit is unfavourable variance/Adverse variance.
(d) Favourable variance will be designated by (F) and Adverse variance by (A).</td></tr>
<tr><td>Controllable and Uncontrollable Variances</td><td>(a) Variance is said to be a controllable variance if it can be controlled by the departmental head. For example, excess usage of material is usually the responsibility of the foreman concerned. However, if the excessive usage is due to material being defective, the responsibility may rest with the Inspection Department for non-detection of the defects.
(b) Variance is said to be a uncontrollable variance, if it can not be controlled by departmental head. For example, change in the market price of materials, general increase in the labour rates, increase in the rates of power or insurance premium, etc. are not within the control of the management of the company. Responsibility for uncontrollable variances cannot be assigned to any person or department. If the uncontrollable variances are of significant nature and are persistent, the standard may need revision.
(c) Importance of Distinction : The division of variances into controllable and uncontrollable is extremely important because the management is required to place more emphasis on controllable variance since variances require investigation and possibly corrective action. This follows the well known "principle of exception" whereby only deviations from efficient performance are investigated.</td></tr>
<tr><td>Method Variance</td><td>Method Variance is that part of Revision variance which arises due to the use of methods other than those specified. According to C.I.M.A., London Methods Variance is "the difference between the standard cost of a product or operation produced or performed by the normal method and the standard cost of a product or operation produced or performed by the alternative method actually employed."</td></tr>
<tr><td>Revision Variance</td><td>Revision Variance represents the difference between the orginal standard cost and the revised standard cost on account of unavoidable changes in prices of various factors like wages, materials etc.
Thus :
Revision Variance = Original Standard Cost of Actual Output − Revised Standard Cost of Actual Output
It arises when an interim adjustment of a standard cost is made without adjusting the budget. It can be further analysed to reflect revision due to price of materials, labour and overhead rates and changes in methods.</td></tr>
</table>

16.0 THREE DISTINCT GROUP OF VARIANCES

The three distinct groups of variances that arise in Standard Costing are as follows:

1. Variances of Efficiency	(a) These are the variances which arise due to efficiency or inefficiency in the use of materials or labour. (b) These are ascertained by comparing Actual Quantities with Standard Quantities of Material and Labour Hours.
2. Variances of Price Rates	These are the variances which arise due to difference between Actual Rate and Standard Rate of Material, Labour and Overheads.
3. Variances due to Volume	These are the variances which arise due to difference between Actual Activity and Standard Level of Activity.

These can be summarized as under:

Element	Variances of Efficiency	Variances of Price	Variances of Volume
Material	Usage, Mix, Yield	Price	—
Labour	Efficiency, idle time	Rate of pay	Revision
Variable Overheads	Efficiency	Expenditure	Revision
Fixed Overheads	Efficiency	Expenditure	Revision, Capacity, Calendar
Sales	Quantity, Mix	Price	

Material Variances have been discussed in this chapter and other Variances have been discussed in following chapters.

17.0 MATERIAL VARIANCES

Material Variances mainly arise due to the efficiency or inefficiency in the use of materials and / or change in Actual Price and Standard Price of materials. These can be summarized as follows:

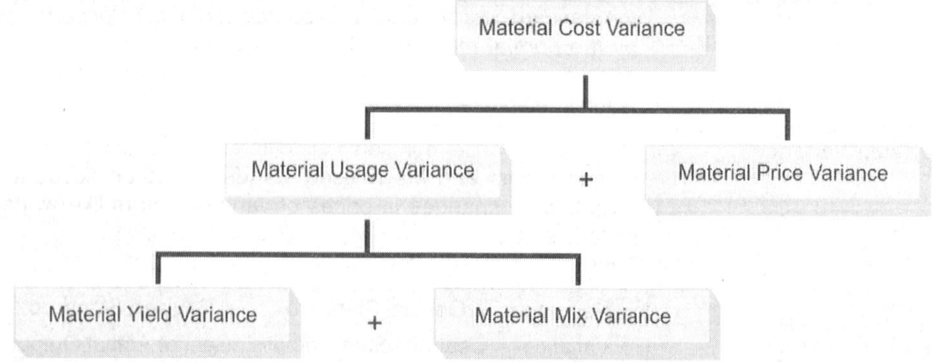

18.0 TERMS USEFUL FOR COMPUTATION OF MATERIAL VARIANCES

One must know the following terms before knowing how to compute Material Variances:

1. Standard Quantity for Actual Output	(a) It represents the Quantity of Material which should have been consumed to produce Actual Output as per standard. (b) It is calculated as follows: $= \frac{\text{Standard Quantity of Material}}{\text{Standard Output}} \times \text{Actual Output}$ *Or,* = Standard Quantity of Material required per Unit of Output × Actual Output
2. Standard Cost of Standard Quantity for Actual Output	(a) It represents the Standard Cost of Standard Quantity for Actual Output. (b) It is calculated as follows: = Standard Quantity of Material for Actual Output × Standard Price = SQ × SP
3. Standard Cost of Actual Quantity for Actual Output	(a) It represents the Standard Cost of Actual Quantity for Actual Output. (b) It is calculated as follows: = Actual Quantity of Material × Standard Price = AQ × SP
4. Revised Quantity	(a) It represents the Total Actual Quantity of all Materials in a Standard Material Mix Ratio. (b) It is calculated by dividing the Total Actual Quantity of all Materials in a Standard Mix Ratio as follows: $= \frac{\text{Standard Quantity of one Material}}{\text{Total Standard Quantity of All Materials}} \times \text{Total Actual Quantity of All Materials}$
5. Standard Cost of Revised Quantity	(a) It represents the Standard Cost of Revised Quantity. (b) It is calculated as follows: = Revised Quantity × Standard Price = RQ × SP
6. Standard Yield	(a) It represents the yield (i.e. Output) which should have been obtained from Actual Quantity of all Materials. (b) It is calculated as follows: $= \frac{\text{Standard Output}}{\text{Total Standard Quantity of All Materials}} \times \text{Total Actual Quantity of All Materials}$
7. Average Standard Price	(a) It represents Standard Material Cost per Unit of Standard Output. (b) It is calculated as follows: $= \frac{\text{Standard Cost of Standard Quantity of All Materials for Actual Output}}{\text{Standard Output}}$

Illustration 1. Tulsian Ltd. (1) provides you the following information:

	Standard		*Actual*	
	Quantity	*Unit Price*	*Quantity*	*Unit Price*
Material 'A'	30 Kg.	₹ 20	44 Kg.	₹ 25
Material 'B'	20 Kg.	₹ 10	66 Kg.	₹ 5
Output	45 Kg.		90 Kg.	

Required: Calculate (a) Standard Quantity for Actual Output (b) Standard Cost of Standard Quantity for Actual Output (c) Standard Cost of Actual Quantity for Actual Output (d) Revised Quantity (e) Standard Cost of Revised Quantity (f) Standard Yield (g) Average Standard Price

Solution:

(a) Standard Quantity for Actual Output = $\frac{\text{Standard Quantity of Material}}{\text{Standard Output}} \times$ Actual Output

Material A = $\frac{30}{45} \times 90 = 60$ kg., Material B = $\frac{20}{45} \times 90 = 40$ kg.

(b) Standard Cost of Standard Quantity for Actual Output = SQ × SP
Material A = (60 kg. × ₹ 20) = ₹ 1,200, Material B = (40 kg. × ₹ 10) = ₹ 400

(c) Standard Cost of Actual Quantity for Actual Output = AQ × SP
Material A = (44 kg. × ₹ 20) = ₹ 880, Material B = (66 kg. × ₹ 10) = ₹ 660

(d) Revised Quantity = $\frac{\text{Standard Quantity of one Material}}{\text{Total Standard Quantity of All Materials}} \times$ Total Actual Quantity of All Materials

Material A = $\frac{60}{100} \times 110 = 66$ kg., Material B = $\frac{40}{100} \times 110 = 44$ kg.

(e) Standard Cost of Revised Quantity = RQ × SP
Material A = (66 kg. × ₹ 20) = ₹ 1,320, Material B = (44 kg. × ₹ 10) = ₹ 440

(f) Standard Yield = $\frac{\text{Standard Output}}{\text{Total Standard Quantity of All Materials}} \times$ Total Actual Quantity of All Materials

$= \frac{90}{100} \times 110 = 99$ kg.

(g) Average Standard Price = $\frac{\text{Standard Cost of Standard Quantity of All Material for Actual Output}}{\text{Standard Output}}$

$= \frac{(60 \text{ kg.} \times 20) + (40 \text{ kg.} \times 10)}{90 \text{ kg.}}$ = ₹ 17.78 (Appx.)

19.0 DIRECT MATERIAL COST VARIANCE (MCV)

Meaning	Material Cost Variance (MCV) is the difference between the Standard Cost of Direct Materials specified for the output achieved and the Actual Cost of Direct Materials consumed.
How to Calculate	Material Cost Variance (MCV) is calculated as follows: MCV = Standard Cost of Standard Quantity of Materials for Actual Output ***minus*** Actual Cost of Actual Quantity of Materials consumed for Actual Output *or* = (Standard Quantity for Actual Output × Standard Price) – (Actual Quantity × Actual Price) *or* = (SQ × SP) – (AQ × AP) **Note:** *Standard Quantity of Material for Actual Output is calculated as follows:*

	$= \frac{\text{Standard Qty of Material}}{\text{Standard Output}} \times \text{Actual Output}$ *or* = Standard Qty of Material required per unit × Actual Output.
Nature	(a) **Favourable (F)** if the effect of the variance is to **increase** the profit (*i.e. where actual cost is less than the standard cost.*) (b) **Adverse (A)** if the effect of the variance is to **decrease** the profit (*i.e. where actual cost is more than the standard cost.*)
Why arises?	MCV may arise due to: (a) change in price of material, *or* (b) change in quantity of material, *or* (c) change in price and quantity of material
Division	MCV may be further divided into: (a) Material Price Variance (MPV), and (b) Material Usage Variance (MUV)

Illustration 2. Calculate Material Cost Variance from the following information:

	Standard	***Actual***
Output	100 units	200 units
Quanity of Material required per unit of output	2 kg per unit	3 kg per unit
Price	₹ 4 per kg	₹ 3 per kg

Solution:

Step 1 → Standard Qty for Actual Output (SQ) = 200 × 2 = 400 kg.

Step 2 → Actual Qty for Actual Output (AQ) = 200 × 3 = 600 kg.

Step 3 → MCV = (SQ × SP) — (AQ × AP) = (400 × ₹ 4) – (600 × ₹ 3) = ₹ 200 (A)

Illustration 3. Calculate Material Cost Variance from the following information:

Standard:	Material for 100 units	300 kg.
	Cost of Materials	₹.1,500
Actual:	Material Purchased for 800 units	3,000 kg
	Cost of Materials	₹ 18,000
	Closing Stock of Material	500 kg

Solution:

Step 1 → Standard Qty for Actual Output (SQ) = $\frac{300 \text{ kg}}{100 \text{ units}} \times 800 \text{ units} = 2{,}400 \text{ kg}$

Step 2 → Actual Qty for Actual Output (AQ) = 3,000 kg – 500 kg = 2,500 kg.

Step 3 → Standard Price (SP) = $\frac{1{,}500}{300 \text{ kg}} = ₹\ 5$

Step 4 → Actual Price (AP) = $\frac{18{,}000}{3{,}000 \text{ kg}} = ₹\ 6$

Step 5 → Material Cost Variance (MCV) = (SQ × SP) – (AQ × AP)
= (2,400 × ₹ 5) – (2,500 × ₹ 6) = ₹ 3,000 (A)

20.0 DIRECT MATERIAL PRICE VARIANCE (MPV)

Meaning	Direct Material Price Variance (MPV) is that portion of the material cost variance which is due to the difference between the standard price specified and the actual price paid.
How to Calculate	Material Price Variance (MPV) is calculated as follows: MPV = (Standard Price – Actual Price) × Actual Quantity *or* = (SP – AP) × AQ

Nature	(a) **Favourable (F)** if the effect of variance is to increase the profit (i.e. where AP < SP) (b) **Adverse (A)** if the effect of variance is to decrease the profit (i.e. where AP > SP)
Why arises?	MPV may arise due to: 1. Change in the market prices of materials. 2. Change in the quantity of materials, thereby leading to lower/higher quantity discount. 3. Not availing cash discounts, when standards set took into account such discounts 4. Change in the delivery costs. 5. Purchase of a substitute material on account of non-availability of the material specified. 6. Off-season purchasing for certain seasonal products like jute, cotton etc. 7. Change in the rates of excise duty, purchase tax, etc. 8. Failure to purchase the specified quality, thereby resulting in a different price being paid.

Illustration 4. Calculate Material Price Variance in Illustration 2.

Solution:

AQ = 200 × 3 = 600 kg

Material Price Variance = (SP – AP) × AQ = (₹ 4 – ₹ 3) × 600 = ₹ 600 (Favourable)

21.0 DIRECT MATERIAL USAGE VARIANCE (MUV)

Meaning	Direct Material Usage Variance (MUV) is that portion of the material cost variance which is due to the difference between the standard quantity specified and the actual quantity consumed.
How to Calculate	Material Usage Variance (MUV) is calculated as follows: MUV = (Standard Quantity for Actual Output – Actual Quantity) × Standard Price *or* = (SQ – AQ) × SP
Nature	(a) **Favourable (F)** if the effect of variance is to increase the profit (i.e. where AQ < SQ) (b) **Adverse (A)** if the effect of variance is to decrease the profit (i.e. where AQ > SQ)
Why arises?	MUV may arise due to: 1. Use of non-standard materials. 2. Use of non-standard material mixture. 3. Use of substitute materials. 4. Inefficiency in the use of materials. 5. Change in the quality of materials. 6. Change in the design or specification of the product. 7. Change in method of production 8. Yield from materials in excess of or less than standard yield. 9. Pilferage. 10. Defect in plant and machinery.
Division	MUV may be further divided into: (a) Material Mix Variance (MMV), and (b) Material Yield Variance (MYV).

Illustration 5. Calculate Material Usage Variance in Illustration 2:

Solution:

SQ = 200 × 2 = 400 Kg

AQ = 200 × 3 = 600 Kg

Material Usage Variance = (SQ – AQ) × SP = (400 kg – 600 kg) × ₹ 4 = ₹ 800 (Adverse)

Illustration 6. Tulsian Ltd. provides you the following information.

The standard material cost of producing 100 units has been predetermined as 200 kg @ ₹ 4 per kg. In a particular cost period the actual data was as follows:

Actual Output	200 units
Opening Stock of Materials	300 kg at Standard Price
Purchase of Materials	700 kg for ₹ 2,100
Closing Stock of Materials	400 kg.

Required: Calculate all Material Cost Variances if method used for the issue of material is (a) FIFO (b) LIFO (c) Weighted Average.

Solution:

Step 1 → Standard Qty for Actual Output = $\frac{\text{Standard Qty}}{\text{Standard Output}}$ × Actual Output = $\frac{200}{100}$ × 200 = 400 kg

Step 2 → Actual Qty for Actual Output = Opening Stock + Purchases – Closing Stock
= 300 kg + 700 kg – 400 kg = 600 kg

Step 3 → Actual Cost of Actual Qty and Actual Price per kg

(i) Under FIFO Method: (300 × ₹ 4) + (300 × ₹ 3) = ₹ 2,100
Actual Price = ₹ 2,100/600 = ₹ 3.50

(ii) Under LIFO Method: 600 × ₹ 3 = ₹ 1,800
Actual Price = ₹ 1,800/600 = ₹ 3

(iii) Under Weighted Average Method:

$$\frac{(300 \times \text{Rs } 4) + (700 \times \text{Rs } 3)}{1{,}000} \times 600 = \text{Rs } 1{,}980$$

Actual Price per kg = ₹ 1,980/600 = ₹ 3.30

Step 4 → Material Price Variance = (SP – AP) × AQ
Under FIFO Method: MPV = (₹ 4 – ₹ 3.50) × 600 = ₹ 300 (F)
Under LIFO Method: MPV = (₹ 4 – ₹ 3) × 600 = ₹ 600 (F)
Under Weighted Average Method: MPV = (₹ 4 – ₹ 3.30) × 600
= ₹ 420 (F)

Step 5 → Material Usage Variance = (SQ – AQ) × SP = (400 – 600) × ₹ 4 = ₹ 800(A)

Step 6 → Material Cost Variance = (SQ × SP) – (AQ × AP)
Under FIFO Method: MCV = (400 × ₹ 4) – (600 × ₹ 3.50)
= ₹ 1,600 – ₹ 2,100 = ₹ 500(A)
Under LIFO Method: MCV = (400 × ₹ 4) – (600 × ₹ 3)
= ₹ 1,600 – ₹ 1,800 = ₹ 200(A)
Under Weighted Average Method: MCV = (400 × ₹ 4) – (600 × ₹ 3.30)
= ₹ 1,600 – ₹ 1,980 = ₹ 380(A)

22.0 DIRECT MATERIAL MIX VARIANCE (MMV)

Meaning	Direct Material Mix Variance (MMV) is that portion of the material usage variance which is due to the difference between standard and actual composition of materials.
How to Calculate	Material Mix Variance (MMV) is calculated as follows: MMV = Standard Cost of Revised Qty of Actual Materials consumed ***minus*** Standard Cost of Actual Qty of Materials Consumed

	or = (RSQ × SP) – (AQ × SP) or = (RSQ – AQ) × SP **Note:** Revised Standard Quantity (RSQ) is calculated by dividing the total actual quantities of all materials in a standard material mix ratio as follows: $$RSQ = \frac{\text{Standard Qty of one material}}{\text{Total Standard Quantities of all materials}} \times \text{Total Actual Quantities of all materials}$$
Nature	(a) **Favourable (F)** if the effect of the variance is to increase the profit (i.e. where AQ<RSQ) (b) **Adverse (A)** if the effect of the variance is to decrease the profit (i.e. where AQ>RSQ)
Why arises?	MMV arises only when the actual two or more materials are mixed in a ratio different from the standard material mix ratio. Change from Standard mix may be due to the non-availability of one or more components of material mix.

Illustration 7. Calculate Material Mix Variance from the following information:

	Standard		*Actual*	
	Qty	*Price per kg.*	*Qty*	*Price per kg.*
Material 'A'	40 kg	₹ 12	1,250 kg	₹ 10
Material'B'	60 kg	₹ 9	850 kg	₹ 12
Output	85 kg		1,700 kg	

Solution:

Step 1 → Revised Standard Quantity (RSQ)

Material 'A' = $\frac{40}{100} \times 2100 = 840\,kg$, Material 'B' = $\frac{60}{100} \times 2100 = 1260\,kg$

Step 2 → Material Mix Variance (MMV) = (RSQ – AQ) × SP

Material 'A' = (840 – 1,250) × ₹ 12 = ₹ 4,920 (A)

Material 'B' = (1,260 – 850) × ₹ 9 = ₹ 3,690 (F)

MMV = ₹ 1,230 (A)

23.0 DIRECT MATERIAL YIELD VARIANCE (MYV)

Meaning	MYV is that portion of the material usage variance which is due to the difference between standard yield specified for actual quantity used and actual yield obtained. The standard yield is the output expected to be obtained from the actual usage of materials. MYV is an output variance which represents a gain or loss on output in terms of finished production.
How to Calculate	Material Yield Variance (MYV) is calculated as follows: MYV = (Actual Yield — Standard yield) × Average Standards Output Price **Notes:** (i) Standard Yield for Actual Input $$= \frac{\text{Standard Output}}{\text{Total SQ of all Materials}} \times \text{Total AQ of all Materials}$$

	(ii) Average Standard Output Price (ASOP) $ASOP = \frac{\text{Standard Cost of Standard Qty of all materials for Actual Output}}{\text{Standard Output}}$ *or* $= \frac{SQ \times SP}{\text{Standard Output}}$
Nature	(a) **Favourable (F)** if the effect of the variance is to increase the profit (i.e. where AY>SY) (b) **Adverse (A)** if the effect of the variance is to decrease the profit (i.e. where AY<SY)
Why Arises	MYV arises only when the actual loss as % of total actual input differs from the standard loss as % of total standard input.

Illustration 8. Calculate Material Yield Variance in Illustration 7.

Solution:

Step 1 → Standard Yield for Actual Input = $\frac{85}{100} \times 2100 = 1785$ kg

Step 2 → Average Standard Output Price (ASOP) = $\frac{(40 \times 12) + (60 \times 9)}{85} = \frac{1020}{85} = 12$

Step 3 → Material Yield Variance (MYV) = (Actual Yield – Standard Yield) × ASOP

= (1700 kg – 1785 kg) × 12 = ₹ 1,020 (A)

24.0 PRACTICAL STEPS IN THE COMPUTATION OF MATERIAL COST VARIANCES

Step 1: *Prepare a **10 Column Table** of Basic Calculations as follows:*

TABLE OF BASIC CALCULATIONS FOR THE COMPUTATION OF MATERIAL COST VARIANCES

Type of Material	*SQ for AO*	*SP*	*SQ × SP (1)*	*AQ*	*AP*	*AQ × AP (2)*	*AQ × SP (3)*	*RQ*	*RQ × SP (4)*
Material A	....	......	....	......	....	....	....	....	....
Material B	....	......	....	......	....	....	....	....	....
Input	....			......					
Less : Loss	....			......					
	....		....	......		....	....		....

Note: RQ = Revised Quantity = Actual Quantity in Standard Material Mix Ratio

Step 2: *Calculate Material Cost Variances as follows:*

Material Cost Variance (1 – 2) = (SQ × SP) – (AQ × AP)

Material A = ₹ .... – ₹ .... = ₹ ....

Material B = ₹ .... – ₹ .... = ₹ ....

MCV = ₹ ....

Material Price Variance (3 – 2) = (AQ × SP) – (AQ × AP)

Material A = ₹ .... – ₹ .... = ₹ ....

Material B = ₹ .... – ₹ .... = ₹ ....

MPV = ₹ ....

Material Usage Variance (1 – 3) = (SQ × SP) – (AQ × SP)

Material A = ₹ .... – ₹ .... = ₹ ....

Material B = ₹ .... – ₹ .... = ₹ ....

MUV = ₹ ....

Material Mix Variance (4 – 3) = (RQ × SP) – (AQ × SP)

Material A = ₹ .... – ₹ .... = ₹ ....

Material B = ₹ .... – ₹ .... = ₹ ....

MMV = ₹ ....

Material Yield Variance =(Actual Yield – Standard Yield) × Average Standard Price

$$\text{Standard Yield} = \frac{\text{Standard Output}}{\text{Total Standard Qty. of all Materials}} \times \text{Total Actual Qty. of all Materials}$$

$$\text{Average Standard Price} = \frac{\text{Total (SQ} \times \text{SR)}}{\text{Standard Output}} = ₹ \text{ ....}$$

***Alternatively*, MYV (1 – 4) = (SQ × SP) – (RQ × SP)**

= ₹ .... – ₹ .... = ₹ ....

COMPREHENSIVE ILLUSTRATIONS

Illustration 9. Calculate all the Material Cost Variances from the following information provided by Tulsian Ltd.:

	Standard		*Actual*	
	Qty.	*Unit Price*	*Qty.*	*Unit Price*
Material 'A'	30 kg	₹ 20	44 kg	₹ 25
Material 'B'	20 kg	₹ 10	66 kg	₹ 5
Output	45 kg		90 kg.	

Solution:

Basic Calculations:

	Material 'A'	*Material 'B"*	*Total*
Standard Quantity for Actual Output (SQ)	$\frac{30}{45} \times 90 = 60$	$\frac{20}{45} \times 90 = 40$	100
Actual Quantity (AQ)	= 44	= 66	110
Revised Quantity (RQ)	$\frac{60}{100} \times 110 = 66$	$\frac{40}{100} \times 110 = 44$	110

BASIC CALCULATIONS FOR THE COMPUTATION OF MATERIAL COST VARIANCES

Type of Material	*SQ for AO*	*SP*	*SQ × SP (1)*	*AQ*	*AP*	*AQ × AP (2)*	*AQ × SP (3)*	*RQ*	*RQ × SP (4)*
Material									
A	60	20	1,200	44	25	1,100	880	66	1,320
B	40	10	400	66	5	330	660	44	440
Input	100			110					
Less : Loss	10			20					
	90		1,600	90		1,430	1,540		1,760

Material Cost Variance (1 – 2) = (SQ × SP) – (AQ × AP)

Material A = ₹ 1,200 – ₹ 1,100 = ₹ 100 (F)

Material B = ₹ 400 – ₹ 330 = ₹ 70 (F)

MCV = ₹ 170 (F)

Material Price Variance (3 – 2) = (AQ × SP) – (AQ × AP)
Material A = ₹ 880 – ₹ 1100 = ₹ 220 (A)
Material B = ₹ 660 – ₹ 330 = ₹ 330 (F)
MPV = ₹ 110 (F)

Material Usage Variance (1 – 3) = (SQ × SP) – (AQ × SP)
Material A = ₹ 1200 – ₹ 880 = ₹ 320 (F)
Material B = ₹ 400 – ₹ 660 = ₹ 260 (A)
MUV = ₹ 60 (F)

Material Mix Variance (4 – 3) = (RQ × SP) – (AQ × SP)
Material A = ₹ 1320 – ₹ 880 = ₹ 440 (F)
Material B = ₹ 440 – ₹ 660 = ₹ 220 (A)
MMV = ₹ 220 (F)

Material Yield Variance = (Actual Yield – Standard Yield) × Average Standard Price

$$= \left(90\text{kg} - \frac{90\text{ kg}}{100\text{ kg}} \times 110\text{ kg}\right) \times \frac{1600}{90} = \text{Rs } 160\text{ (A)}$$

Alternatively, MYV (1 – 4) = (SQ × SP) – (RQ × SP) = ₹ 1600 – ₹ 1760 = ₹ 160 (A)

Verification:
1. MCV = MPV + MUV = ₹ 110 (F) + ₹ 60 (F) = ₹ 170 (F)
2. MUV = MMV + MYV = ₹ 220 (F) + ₹ 160 (A) = 60 (F)

Illustration 10. The Standard material cost for a normal mix of one tonne of chemical X is based on

Chemical	*Usage (kg.)*	*Price per kg.*
A	240	6
B	400	12
C	640	10

During a month, 6.25 tonnes of X were produced from:

Chemical	*Consumption Tonnes*	*Cost ₹*
A	1.6	11,200
B	2.4	30,000
C	4.5	47,250

Required: Analyse the Variances.

Solution:

Basic Calculations :

1. Standard Qty. of Material 'A' (SQ) = 240 × 6.25 = 1500 kg
2. Standard Qty. of Material 'B' (SQ) = 400 × 6.25 = 2500 kg
3. Standard Qty. of Material 'C' (SQ) = 640 × 6.25 = 4000 kg
4. Total Standard Input = 1500 + 2500 + 4000 = 8000 kg
5. Total Actual Input = 1600 + 2400 + 4500 = 8500 kg
6. Revised Qty. of Material 'A' (RQ) = $\frac{1500}{8000} \times 8500 = 1593.75$
7. Revised Qty. of Material 'B' (RQ) = $\frac{2500}{8000} \times 8500 = 2656.25$
8. Revised Qty. of Material 'C' (RQ) = $\frac{4000}{8000} \times 8500 = 4250.00$

BASIC CALCULATIONS FOR THE COMPUTATION OF MATERIAL COST VARIANCES

Type of Material	*SQ for AO*	*SP*	*SQ × SP (1)*	*AQ*	*AP*	*AQ × AP (2)*	*AQ × SP (3)*	*RQ*	*RQ × SP (4)*
A	1500	6.00	9,000	1600	7.00	11,200	9,600	1593.75	9562.50
B	2500	12.00	30,000	2400	12.50	30,000	28,800	2656.25	31875.00
C	4000	10.00	40,000	4500	10.50	47,250	45,000	4250.00	42500.00
Input	8000			8500					
Less : Loss	1750			2250					
	6250		79,000	6250		88,450	83,400		83937.50

Material Cost Variance (1 – 2) = (SQ × SP) – (AQ × AP)
= ₹ 79,000 – ₹ 88,450 = ₹ 9,450 (A)

Material Price Variance (3 – 2) = (AQ × SP) – (AQ × AP)
Material A = ₹ 9,600 – ₹ 11,200 = ₹ 1,600 (A)
Material B = ₹ 28,800 – ₹ 30,000 = ₹ 1,200 (A)
Material C = ₹ 45,000 – ₹ 47,250 = ₹ 2,250 (A)
MPV = ₹ 5,050 (A)

Material Usage Variance (1 – 3) = (SQ × SP) – (AQ × SP)
Material A = ₹ 9,000 – ₹ 9,600 = ₹ 600 (A)
Material B = ₹ 30.000 – ₹ 28,800 = ₹ 1,200 (F)
Material C = ₹ 40,000 – ₹ 45,000 = ₹ 5,000 (A)
MUV = ₹ 4400 (A)

Material Mix Variance (4 – 3) = (RQ × SP) – (AQ × SP)
Material A = ₹ 9,562.50– ₹ 9,600 = ₹ 37.50 (A)
Material B = ₹ 31,875 – ₹ 28,800 = ₹ 3,075 (F)
Material C = ₹ 42,500 – ₹ 45,000 = ₹ 2,500(A)
MMV = ₹ 537.50 (F)

Material Yield Variance = (Actual Yield – Standard Yield) × Average Standard Price

$$= \left(6250 - \frac{6250}{8000} \times 8500\right) \times \frac{79000}{6250} = \text{Rs. } 4{,}937.50 \text{ (A)}$$

Alternatively, MYV (1 – 4) = (SQ × SP) – (RQ × SP) = ₹ 79,000 – ₹ 83,937.50 = ₹ 4937.50(A)

Verification:
1. MCV = MPV + MUV = ₹ 5,050 (A) + ₹ 4,400 (A) = ₹ 9,450 (A)
2. MUV = MMV + MYV = ₹ 537.50 (F) + ₹ 4,937.50 (A) = ₹ 4,400 (A)

Illustration 11 [Calculation of Material Cost Variance when FIFO Method is used].
Eskay Ltd. produces an article by blending two basic raw materials. The following standards have been set up for raw materials :

Material	*Standard Mix*	*Standard Price kg.*
A	40%	₹ 4.00
B	60%	₹ 3.00

The standard loss in processing is 15%. During September the company produced 1,700 kg. of finished output. The position of stock and purchases for the month of September is as under :

Material	*Stock on September kg.*	*Stock on 30th September kg.*	*Purchases during September*	
			kg.	*Cost ₹*
A	35	5	800	3,400
B	40	50	1,200	3,000

Required: Calculate the following variances :
(a) Materials Price Variance; (b) Materials Usage Variance; (c) Materials Yield Variance; (d) Materials Mix Variance; (e) Total Materials Cost Variance.

Assume first in first out method for the issue of material. The opening stock is to be valued at standard price.

Solution:

Basic calculations :

1. Standard Quantity of Material 'A' for Actual Output (SQ) = $\frac{40}{85} \times 1700 = 800$ kg.
2. Standard Quantity of material 'B' for Actual Output (SQ) = $\frac{60}{85} \times 1700 = 1200$ kg.
3. Total Standard Input = 800 kg + 1200 kg = 2000 kg
4. Actual Price of Material 'A' (AP) = ₹ 3400/800 = ₹ 4.25
5. Actual Price of Material 'B' (AP) = ₹ 3000/1200 = ₹ 2.50
6. Actual Quantity of Material 'A' for Actual Output (AQ)
   = Opening Stock + Purchases – Closing Stock
   = 35 kg + 800 kg - 5 kg. = 830 kg (i.e. 35 kg. @ ₹ 4 and 795 kg @ 4.25)
7. Actual Quantity of Material 'B' for Actual Output (AQ)
   = 40 kg + 1200 kg - 50 kg = 1190 kg (i.e. 40 kg. @ ₹ 3 and 1150 kg @ ₹ 2.50)
8. Total Actual Input = 830 kg + 1190 kg. = 2020 kg
9. Actual Cost of Material 'A' (AQ × AP) = (35 × ₹ 4) + (795 × ₹ 4.25) = ₹ 3,518.75
10. Actual cost of Material 'B' (AQ × AP) = (40 × ₹ 3) + (1150 × ₹ 2.50) = ₹ 2,995.00
11. Revised Quantity of Material 'A' for Actual Output (RQ) = $\frac{40}{100} \times 2020 = 808$ kg.
12. Revised Quantity of Material 'B' for Actual Output (RQ) = $\frac{60}{100} \times 2020 = 1212$ kg.

BASIC CALCULATIONS FOR THE COMPUTATION OF MATERIAL COST VARIANCES

Type of Material	*SQ for AO*	*SP*	*SQ × SP (1)*	*AQ*	*AP*	*AQ × AP (2)*	*AQ × SP (3)*	*RQ*	*RQ × SP (4)*
A	800	4.00	3,200	830		3518.75	3,320	808	3,232
B	1200	3.00	3,600	1190		2995.00	3,570	1212	3,636
Input	2000			2020					
Less : Loss	300			320					
	1700		6,800	1700		6513.75	6,890		6,868

Material Cost Variance (1 – 2) = (SQ × SP) – (AQ × AP) = ₹ 6800 – ₹ 6513.75
= ₹ 286.25 (F)

Material Price Variance (3 – 2) = (AQ × SP) – (AQ × AP)
Material A = ₹ 3,320 – ₹ 3,518.75 = ₹ 198.75 (A)
Material B = ₹ 3,570 – ₹ 2,995 = ₹ 575 (F)
MPV = ₹ 376.25 (F)

Material Usage Variance (1 – 3) = (SQ × SP) – (AQ × SP)
Material A = ₹ 3,200 – ₹ 3,320 = ₹ 120 (A)
Material B = ₹ 3,600 – ₹ 3,570 = ₹ 30 (F)
MUV = ₹ 90 (A)

Material Mix Variance (4 – 3) = (RQ × SP) – (AQ × SP)
Material A = ₹ 3,232 – ₹ 3,320 = ₹ 88 (A)
Material B = ₹ 3,636 – ₹ 3,570 = ₹ 66 (F)
MMV = ₹ 22 (A)

Material Yield Variance = (Actual Yield – Standard Yield) × Average Standard Price

$$= \left(1700 - \frac{1700}{2000} \times 2020\right) \times \frac{6800}{1700} = 68 \text{ (A)}$$

Alternatively, MYV (1 – 4) = (SQ × SP) – (RQ × SP) = ₹ 6800 – ₹ 6868 = ₹ 68 (A)

Verification: 1. MCV = MPV + MUV = ₹ 376.25 (F) + ₹ 90 (A) = ₹ 286.25 (F)

2. MUV = MMV + MYV = ₹ 22 (A) + ₹ 68 (A) = ₹ 90 (A)

Illustration 12 [Calculation of Material Cost Variance when LIFO Method is used].

The standard material cost of producing 200 units of textiles has been pre determined as 20 kgs of A @ ₹ 30 per kg and 10 kg of B @ ₹ 150 per kg. Actually 300 units of textiles were produced. The position of stock and purchases was as under:

Material	*Opening Stock*		*Purchases*		*Closing Stock*
	kg	*Price/kg*	*kg*	*Cost*	*kg*
A	4	₹ 25	30	₹ 960	1
B	5	₹ 140	6	₹ 930	2

Stock of Material is valued on LIFO basis. Weight of each unit is 100 gram.

Required: Calculate all the Material Cost Variances.

Solution:

Basic Calculations :

1. Standard Qty of A (SQ) $= \frac{20}{200} \times 300 = 30$ kg
2. Standard Qty. of B (SQ) $= \frac{10}{200} \times 300 = 15$ kg
3. Total Standard Input = 30 kg + 15 kg = 45 kg
4. Actual Qty. of A (AQ) = 4 kg + 30 kg – 1 kg = 33 kg
5. Actual Qty of B (AQ) = 5 kg + 6 kg – 2 kg = 9 kg
6. Total Actual Input = 33 kg + 9 kg = 42 kg
7. Revised Qty of A (RQ) $= \frac{30}{45} \times 42 = 28$ kg
8. Revised Qty of B (RQ) $= \frac{15}{45} \times 42 = 14$ kg
9. Actual Cost of A consumed = (30 × ₹ 32) + (3 × ₹ 25) = ₹ 1,035
10 Actual Cost of B Consumed = (6 × ₹ 155) + (3 × ₹ 140) = ₹ 1,350

BASIC CALCULATION FOR THE COMPUTATION OF MATERIAL COST VARIANCES

Type of Material	*SQ for AO*	*SP*	*SQ × SP (1)*	*AQ*	*AP*	*AQ × AP (2)*	*AQ × SP (3)*	*RQ*	*RQ × SP (4)*
A	30	30	900	33		1,035	990	28	840
B	15	150	2,250	9		1,350	1,350	14	2,100
Input	45			42					
Less : Loss	15			12					
Output	30		3,150	30		2,385	2,340		2,940

Material Cost Variance (1 – 2) = (SQ × SP) – (AQ × AP) =₹ 3150 – ₹ 2385 = ₹ 765 (F)

Material Price Variance (3 – 2) = (AQ × SP) – (AQ × AP)

Material A = ₹ 990 – ₹ 1035 = ₹ 45 (A)
Material B = ₹ 1350 – ₹ 1350 = 0
MPV = ₹ 45 (A)

Material Usage Variance (1 – 3) = (SQ × SP) – (AQ × SP)
Material A = ₹ 900 – ₹ 990 = ₹ 90 (A)
Material B = ₹ 2250 – ₹ 1350 = ₹ 900 (F)
MUV = ₹ 810 (F)

Material Mix Variance (4 – 3) = (RQ × SP) – (AQ × SP)
Material A = ₹ 840 – ₹ 990 = ₹ 150 (A)
Material B = ₹ 2100 – ₹ 1350 = ₹ 750 (F)
MMV = ₹ 600 (F)

Material Yield Variance = (Actual Yield – Standard Yield) × Average Standard Price

$$= \left(30 - \frac{30}{45} \times 42\right) \times \frac{3150}{30} = 210 \text{ (F)}$$

Alternatively, MYV (1 – 4) = (SQ × SP) – (RQ × SP) = ₹ 3150 – ₹ 2940 = ₹ 210 (F)

Verification:
1. MCV = MPV + MUV = ₹ 45 (A) + ₹ 810 (F) = ₹ 765 (F)
2. MUV = MMV + MYV = ₹ 600 (F) + ₹ 210 (F) = ₹ 810 (F)

Illustration 13 [Calculation of Material Cost Variances when output is produced in batches].
S.V. Ltd., manufactures BXE by mixing three raw materials. For every batch of 100 kgs. of BXE, 125 kgs. of raw materials are used. In April 60 batches were prepared to produce an output of 5,600 kgs. of BXE. The standard and actual particulars for April are as under:

Raw material	*Standard*		*Actual*		*Quantity of Raw Materials Purchased*
	Mix %	*Price Per kg* ₹	*Mix* %	*Price Per kg* ₹	*kg.*
A	50	20	60	21	5,000
B	30	10	20	8	2,000
C	20	5	20	6	1,200

Required: Calculate all Material variances.

Solution:

Basic Calculations :

1. Total Standard Input required $= \frac{125}{100} \times 5{,}600 = 7{,}000$ kg.
2. Standard Quantity of Material 'A' for Actual Output (SQ) $= \frac{50}{100} \times 7{,}000 = 3{,}500$ kg.
3. Standard Quantity of Material 'B' for Actual Output (SQ) $= \frac{30}{100} \times 7{,}000 = 2{,}100$ kg.
4. Standard Quantity of Material 'C' for Actual Output (SQ) $= \frac{20}{100} \times 7{,}000 = 1{,}400$ kg.
5. Total Actual Input Consumed = 60 × 125 kg. = 7500 kg
6. Actual Quantity of Material 'A' for Actual Output (AQ) $= \frac{60}{100} \times 7{,}500 = 4{,}500$ kg.
7. Actual Quantity of Material 'B' for Actual Output (AQ) $= \frac{20}{100} \times 7{,}500 = 1{,}500$ kg.
8. Actual Quantity of Material 'C' for Actual Output (AQ) $= \frac{20}{100} \times 7{,}500 = 1{,}500$ kg.
9. Revised Quantity of Material 'A' for Actual Output (RQ) $= \frac{50}{100} \times 7{,}500 = 3{,}750$ kg.

10. Revised Quantity of Material 'B' for Actual Output (RQ) $= \frac{30}{100} \times 7,500 = 2,250$ kg.

11. Revised Quantity of Material 'C' for Actual Output (RQ) $= \frac{20}{100} \times 7,500 = 1,500$ kg.

BASIC CALCULATIONS FOR THE COMPUTATION OF MATERIAL COST VARIANCES

Type of Material	*SQ for AO*	*SP*	*SQ × SP (1)*	*AQ*	*AP*	*AQ × AP (2)*	*AQ × SP (3)*	*RQ*	*RQ × SP (4)*
A	3500	20	70,000	4500	21	94,500	90,000	3750	75,000
B	2100	10	21,000	1500	8	12,000	15,000	2250	22,500
C	1400	5	7,000	1500	6	9,000	7,500	1500	7,500
Input	7000			7500					
Less : Loss	1400			1900					
	5600		98,000	5600		1,15,500	1,12,500		1,05,000

Material Cost Variance (1 – 2) = (SQ × SP) – (AQ × AP)
= ₹ 98,000 – ₹ 1,15,500 = ₹ 17,500 (A)

Material Price Variance (3 – 2) = (AQ × SP) – (AQ × AP)
Material A = ₹ 90,000 – ₹ 94,500 = ₹ 4,500 (A)
Material B = ₹ 15,000 – ₹ 12,000 = ₹ 3,000 (F)
Material C = ₹ 7,500 – ₹ 9,000 = ₹ 1,500 (A)
MPV = ₹ 3,000 (A)

Material Usage Variance (1 – 3) = (SQ × SP) – (AQ × SP)
Material A = ₹ 70,000 – ₹ 90,000 = ₹ 20,000 (A)
Material B = ₹ 21,000 – ₹ 15,000 = ₹ 6,000 (F)
Material C = ₹ 7,000 – ₹ 7,500 = ₹ 500 (A)
MUV = ₹ 14,500 (A)

Material Mix Variance (4 – 3) = (RQ × SP) – (AQ × SP)
Material A = ₹ 75,000 – ₹ 90,000 = ₹ 15,000 (A)
Material B = ₹ 22,500 – ₹ 15,000 = ₹ 7,500 (F)
Material C = ₹ 7,500 – ₹ 7,500 = ₹ 0
MMV = ₹ 7,500 (A)

Material Yield Variance = (Actual Yield – Standard Yield) × Average Standard Price

$$= \left(5,600 - \frac{5,600}{7,000} \times 7,500\right) \times \frac{98,000}{5,600} = 7,000\ (A)$$

Alternatively, MYV (1 – 4) = (SQ × SP) – (RQ × SP) = ₹ 98,000 – ₹ 1,05,000 = ₹ 7,000 (A)

Verification:
1. MCV = MPV + MUV = ₹ 3,000 (A) + ₹ 14,500 (A) = ₹ 17,500 (A)
2. MUV = MMV + MYV = ₹ 7,500 (A) + ₹ 7,000 (A) = ₹ 14,500 (A)

Illustration 14. A company, manufacturing, a special type of facing tile 12" × 8" × 1/2" uses system of Standard Costing. The standard mix of the compound used for making the tiles is :
1200 kg. Material A @ ₹ 3 per kg.
500 kg. Material B @ ₹ 6 per kg.
800 kg. Material C @ ₹ 7 per kg.

The compound should produce 12,000 square feet of tiles of 1/2" thickness. During a period in which 90,000 tiles of the standard size were produced, the material usage (in tonnes) and material costs were as under :

Material	*Tonnes*	*Amount (₹)*
A	7	22,400
B	3	19,500
C	5	37,500

Required: Compute all the Material Cost Variances.

Solution:

Basic Calculations :

1. Area of one tile = $\frac{12'' \times 8''}{144} = \frac{96}{144}$ square feet

2. No. of tiles in 12,000 sq. ft. : $\frac{12000}{\frac{96}{144}}$ *or* 12000 × 144/96 = 18000 Tiles

3. Standard Qty. of Material for Actual Output (SQ)

A	*B*	*C*
$= \frac{1,200}{18,000} \times 90,000$	$= \frac{500}{18,000} \times 90,000$	$= \frac{800}{18,000} \times 90,000$
= 6,000	= 2,500	= 4,000

4. Total Standard Input = 6,000 kg + 2,500 kg + 4,000 kg = 12,500 kg

5. Total Actual Input = 7,000 kg + 3,000 kg + 5,000 kg = 15,000 kg

6. Revised Qty. (RQ)

A	*B*	*C*
$= \frac{6,000}{12,500} \times 15,000$	$= \frac{2,500}{12,500} \times 15,000$	$= \frac{4,000}{12,500} \times 15,000$
=7,200	= 3,000	= 4,800

BASIC CALCULATIONS FOR THE COMPUTATION OF MATERIAL COST VARIANCES

Type of Material	*SQ for AO*	*SP*	*SQ × SP (1)*	*AQ*	*AP*	*AQ × AP (2)*	*AQ × SP (3)*	*RQ*	*RQ × SP (4)*
A	6,000	3.00	18,000	7,000	3.20	22,400	21,000	7,200	21,600
B	2,500	6.00	15,000	3,000	6.50	19,500	18,000	3,000	18,000
C	4,000	7.00	28,000	5,000	7.50	37,500	35,000	4,800	33,600
Input	12500			15,000					
			61,000			79,400	74,000		73,200

Material Cost Variance (1 – 2) = (SQ × SP) – (AQ × AP) = ₹ 61,000 – ₹ 79,400 = ₹ 18,400 (A)

Material Price Variance (3 – 2) = (AQ × SP) – (AQ × AP)

Material A = ₹ 21,000 – ₹ 22,400 = ₹ 1,400 (A)

Material B = ₹ 18,000 – ₹ 19,500 = ₹ 1,500 (A)

Material C = ₹ 35,000 – ₹ 37,500 = ₹ 2,500 (A)

MPV = ₹ 5,400 (A)

Material Usage Variance (1 – 3) = (SQ × SP) – (AQ × SP)

Material A = ₹ 18,000 – ₹ 21,000 = ₹ 3,000 (A)

Material B = ₹ 15,000 – ₹ 18,000 = ₹ 3,000 (A)

Material C = ₹ 28,000 – ₹ 35,000 = ₹ 7,000 (A)

MUV = ₹ 13,000 (A)

Material Mix Variance (4 – 3) = (RQ × SP) – (AQ × SP)

Material A = ₹ 21,600 – ₹ 21,000 = ₹ 600 (F)

Material B = ₹ 18,000 – ₹ 18,000 = 0

Meterial C = ₹ 33,600 – ₹ 35,000 = ₹ 1,400 (A)

MMV = ₹ 800 (A)

Material Yield Variance = (Actual Yield – Standard Yield) × Average Standard Price

$$= \left(90{,}000 - \frac{90{,}000}{12{,}500} \times 15000\right) \times \frac{61000}{90000} = ₹\ 12{,}200\ (A)$$

Alternatively, MYV (1 – 4) = (SQ × SP) – (RQ × SP) = ₹ 61,000 – ₹ 73,200 = ₹ 12,200 (A)

Verification:
1. MCV = MPV + MUV = ₹ 5,400 (A) + ₹ 13,000 (A) = ₹ 18,400 (A)
2. MUV = MMV + MYV = ₹ 800 (A) + ₹ 12,200 (A) = ₹ 13,000 (A)

Illustration 15 [Calculation of Material Cost Variances where there is WIP].

Calculate all the material cost variances from the following information provided by BHARAT Ltd.:

	Standard		*Actual*	
	Qty. (kg.)	*Unit Price (₹)*	*Qty. (kg.)*	*Unit Price (₹)*
Material 'A'	60 kg	20	44 kg	25
Material 'B'	40 kg	10	66 kg	5
Standard Processing Loss	10 kg			

Actual data relating to finished goods and work-in-progress :

	Opening Stock	*Closing Stock*
Work-in-progress (Materials fully supplied but 40% converted)	5	10 kg
Finished Goods	20 kg	10 kg

Actual Sales of Finished Goods — 95 kg.

Solution:

Basic Calculations :

1. Units completed = Sales + Closing Stock – Opening Stock
   = 95 kg + 10 kg – 20 kg = 85 kg
2. No. of equivalent units of Actual Output for material cost purposes :

	Units	*Degree of Completion*	*Equivalent units*
A. Completed Units	85	100%	85
B. *Add :* Closing WIP	10	100%	10
C. *Less :* Opening WIP	5	100%	5
			90 kg

3.

	Material 'A'	*Material 'B"*	*Total*
Standard Quantity for Actual Output (SQ)	$\frac{60}{90} \times 90 = 60$	$\frac{40}{90} \times 90 = 40$	100
Actual Quantity (AQ)	= 44	= 66	110
Revised Quantity (RQ)	$\frac{60}{100} \times 110 = 66$	$\frac{40}{100} \times 110 = 44$	110

BASIC CALCULATIONS FOR THE COMPUTATION OF MATERIAL COST VARIANCES

Type of Material	*SQ for AO*	*SP*	*SQ × SP (1)*	*AQ*	*AP*	*AQ × AP (2)*	*AQ × SP (3)*	*RQ*	*RQ × SP (4)*
A	60	20	1,200	44	25	1,100	880	66	1,320
B	40	10	400	66	5	330	660	44	440
Input	100			110					
Less : Loss	10			20					
	90		1,600	90		1,430	1,540		1,760

Material Cost Variance (1 – 2) = (SQ × SP) – (AQ × AP) = ₹ 1600 – ₹ 1430 = ₹ 170 (F)

Material Price Variance (3 – 2) = (AQ × SP) – (AQ × AP)

Material A = ₹ 880 – ₹ 1100 = ₹ 220 (A)

Material B = ₹ 660 – ₹ 330 = ₹ 330 (F)

MPV = ₹ 110 (F)

Material Usage Variance (1 – 3) = (SQ × SP) – (AQ × SP)

Material A = ₹ 1200 – ₹ 880 = ₹ 320 (F)

Material B = ₹ 400 – ₹ 660 = ₹ 260 (A)

MUV = ₹ 60 (F)

Material Mix Variance (4 – 3) = (RQ × SP) – (AQ × SP)

Material A = ₹ 1320 – ₹ 880 = ₹ 440 (F)

Material B = ₹ 440 – ₹ 660 = ₹ 220 (A)

MMV = ₹ 220 (F)

Material Yield Variance = (Actual Yield – Standard Yield) × Average Standard Price

$$= \left(90\text{kg} - \frac{90\text{ kg}}{100\text{ kg}} \times 110\text{ kg}\right) \times \frac{1600}{90} = \text{Rs } 160\text{ (A)}$$

Alternatively, MYV (1 – 4) = (SQ × SP) – (RQ × SP) = ₹ 1600 – ₹ 1760 = ₹ 160 (A)

Verification:

1. MCV = MPV + MUV = ₹ 110 (F) + ₹ 60 (F) = ₹ 170 (F)
2. MUV = MMV + MYV = ₹ 220 (F) + ₹ 160 (A) = 60 (F)

SOLVED PROBLEMS

Problem 1. Tulsian Ltd. provides you the following information:

	Standard		*Actual*	
	Qty. (kg.)	*Price (₹)*	*Qty. (kg.)*	*Price (₹)*
Material 'A'	60	20	44	25
Material 'B'	40	?	66	5

Required: Calculate the Standard Price of Material 'B' in each of the following alternative cases :

Case (a) If Material Cost Variance is ₹ 170 (Fav)
Case (b) If Material Usage Variance is ₹ 70 (Adv.)
Case (c) If Material Yield Variance is ₹ 160 (Adv.)
Case (d) If Material Mix Variance is ₹ 110 (Fav)
Case (e) If Material Price Variance is ₹ 220 (Adv)

Solution:

Let the Standard Price of Material 'B' be '*x*'

Revised Quantity for Actual Mix : Mat. A = $\frac{60}{100}$ × 110 = 66, Mat. B = $\frac{40}{100}$ × 110 = 44

BASIC CALCULATIONS FOR THE COMPUTATION OF LABOUR COST VARIANCES

Type of Material	*SQ for AO*	*SP*	*SQ × SP (1)*	*AQ*	*AP*	*AQ × AP (2)*	*AQ × SP (3)*	*RQ*	*RQ × SP (4)*
A	60	20	1200	44	25	1,100	880	66	1320
B	40	*x*	40 *x*	66	5	330	66 *x*	44	44 *x*
			1200 + 40 *x*			1,430	880 + 66 *x*		1320 + 44*x*

Case (a) Material Cost Variance (1 – 2) = (SQ × SP) – (AQ × AP)
₹ 170 (Fav) = (1,200 + 40 x) – 1,430
1,200 + 40 x = 1,430 + 170 = 1,600
x = (1600 – 1200)/40 = ₹ 10 per kg.

Case (b) Material Usage Variance (1 – 3) = (SQ × SP) – (AQ × SP)
– ₹ 70 = ₹ 1200 + 40 x – (880 + 66 x)
– ₹ 70 = ₹ 320 – 26 x
x = (320 + 70)/26 = ₹ 15 per kg

Case (c) Material Yield Variance (1 – 4) = (SQ × SP) – (RQ × SP)
– ₹ 160 = (1200 + 40 x) – (1320 + 44 x)
– ₹ 160 = – ₹ 120 – 4 x
x = (160 – 120)/4 = ₹ 10 per kg

Case (d) Material Mix Variance (4 – 3) = RQ × SP – AQ × SP
+ ₹ 110 = ₹ 1320 + 44 x – (880 + 66 x)
+ ₹ 110 = ₹ 440 – 22 x
x = (440 – 110)/22 = ₹ 15 per kg

Case (e) Material Price Variance (3 – 2) = (AQ × SP) – (AQ × AP)
– ₹ 220 = ₹ 880 + 66 x – ₹ 1430
– ₹ 220 = ₹ – 550 + 66 x
x = (550 – 220)/66 = ₹ 5 per kg

Problem 2. Compute the missing data indicated by the question marks from the following :

	A ₹	*B* ₹
Standard Price per Unit	12	15
Actual Price per Unit	15	20
Standard Input (kgs.)	50	?
Actual Input (kgs.)	?	70
Material Price Variance	?	?
Material Usage Variance	?	300 Adverse
Material Cost Variance	?	?

Material Mix Variance for both material together was ₹ 45 adverse.

Solution:

Basic Calculations :

1. Standard Input of 'B'
   Material Usage Variance = SP(SQ – AQ)
   – ₹ 300 = 15(SQ – 70)
   SQ = 50 kg
2. Actual Input of 'A'
   Let Actual input of 'A' be x

Type of Material	*SQ for AO*	*SP*	*SQ × SP (1)*	*AQ*	*AP*	*AQ × AP (2)*	*AQ × SP (3)*	*RQ*	*RQ × SP (4)*
A	50	12	600	x	15	15 x	12 x	35 + x/2	420 + 6 x
B	50	15	750	70	20	1400	1050	35 + x/2	525 + 7.5 x
			1350	70 + x		1400 + 15x	1050 + 12x		945 + 13.5 x

Material Mix Variance (4 – 3) = (RQ × SP) – (AQ × SP)
– 45 = (945 + 13.5 x) – (1050 + 12 x)
– 45 = – ₹ 105 + 1.5 x
x = 60/1.50 = 40 kg.

BASIC CALCULATIONS FOR THE COMPUTATION OF MATERIAL COST VARIANCES

Type of Material	SQ for AO	SP	SQ × SP (1)	AQ	AP	AQ × AP (2)	AQ × SP (3)	RQ	RQ × SP (4)
A	50	12	600	40	15	600	480	55	660
B	50	15	750	70	20	1400	1,050	55	825
	100		1,350	110		2,000	1,530		1,485

		Material 'A' (₹)	Material 'B' (₹)	Total (₹)
A. Material Cost Variance	(1 – 2)	—	650 (A)	650 (A)
B. Material Usage Variance	(1 – 3)	120 (F)	300 (A)	180 (A)
C. Material Yield Variance	(1 – 4)	60 (A)	75 (A)	135 (A)
D. Material Mix Variance	(4 – 3)	180 (F)	225 (A)	45 (A)
E. Material Price Variance	(3 – 2)	120 (A)	350 (A)	470 (A)

Verification :

1. Material Cost Variance = Material Usage Variance + Material Price Variance
= ₹ 180(A) + ₹ 470(A) = ₹ 650(A)

Problem 3. One kilogram of product' K' requires two chemicals A and B. The following were the details of product 'K' for the month of June.

(a) Standard mix chemical 'A' 50% and chemical 'B' 50%.
(b) Standard price per kilogram of chemical 'A' ₹ 12 and chemical 'B' ₹ 15.
(c) Actual input of chemical 'B' 70 kilograms.
(d) Actual price per kilogram of chemical 'A' ₹ 15.
(e) Standard normal loss 10% of total input.
(f) Materials cost variance total ₹ 650 adverse.
(g) Materials yield variance total ₹ 135 adverse.
(h) Actual output 90 kg.

You are required to calculate : (i) Materials Mix Variance Total, (ii) Materials Usage Variance Total, (iii) Materials Price Variance Total, (iv) Actual loss of actual input, (v) Actual input of Chemical 'A', (vi) Actual price per kilogram of Chemical 'B'.

Solution:

Basic Calculations :

1. Cost of Standard Mix of Input = SQ × SP
Chemical A = 50 × 12.00 = 600
Chemical B = 50 × 15.00 = 750
1,350

2. Total Actual Input

Material Yield Variance = (Actual Yield – Standard Yield) × Average Standard Price

$$-135 = \left(90\text{kg} - \frac{90\text{ kg}}{100\text{ kg}} \times X\right) \times \frac{1350}{90}$$

$$\frac{-135 \times 90}{1350} = \frac{900\text{ kg} - 90X}{100}$$

$$-900\text{ kg} = 9000\text{ kg} - 90X$$

$$90X = 9900\text{ kg}$$

$$X = 9900\text{ kg}/90 = 110\text{ kg}$$

3. Actual Input of chemical 'A' = 110 kg – Actual Input of chemical 'B' = 110 kg – 70 kg = 40 kg

4. Actual Cost of Actual Input = (AQ × AP)
Material Cost Variance = (SQ × SP) – (AQ × AP)
₹ 650 (A) = ₹ 1350 – (AQ × AP)
AQ × AP = ₹ 1350 + ₹ 650 = ₹ 2,000

5. Actual Cost of chemical 'B' = Total AQ × AP – Actual Cost of chemical 'A'
= ₹ 2,000 – (40 × ₹ 15) = ₹ 1,400

6. Actual Price per kg. of chemical 'B' = ₹ 1,400/70 = ₹ 20 per kg.

BASIC CALCULATIONS FOR THE COMPUTATION OF MATERIAL COST VARIANCES

Type of Material	*SQ for AO*	*SP*	*SQ × SP (1)*	*AQ*	*AP*	*AQ × AP (2)*	*AQ × SP (3)*	*RQ*	*RQ × SP (4)*
A	50	12	600	40	15	600	480	55	660
B	50	15	750	70	20	1,400	1,050	55	825
Input	100			110					
Less: Loss	10			20					
	90		1,350	90		2,000	1,530		1,485

		Material 'A' (₹)	Material 'B' (₹)	Total (₹)
A. Material Cost Variance	(1 – 2)	—	650 (A)	650 (A)
B. Material Usage Variance	(1 – 3)	120 (F)	300 (A)	180 (A)
C. Material Yield Variance	(1 – 4)	60 (A)	75 (A)	135 (A)
D. Material Mix Variance	(4 – 3)	180 (F)	225 (A)	45 (A)
E. Material Price Variance	(3 – 2)	120 (A)	350 (A)	470 (A)

Verification :

1. Material Cost Variance = Material Usage Variance + Material Price Variance
= ₹ 180 (A) + ₹ 470 (A) = ₹ 650 (A)
2. Material Usage Variance = Material Yield Variance + Material Mix Variance
= ₹ 135 (A) + ₹ 45 (A) = ₹ 180 (A)

Specific answers to specific questions asked for :

(i) Material Mix Variance = ₹ 45 (A)
(ii) Material Usage Variance = ₹ 180 (A)
(iii) Material Price Variance = ₹ 470 (A)
(iv) Actual Loss of Actual Input = Actual Input – Actual Output
= 110 kg. – 90 kg. = 20 kg.
(v) Actual input of chemical 'A' = 40 kg.
(vi) Actual Price per kg. of chemical 'B' = ₹ 20

Problem 4.

UV Ltd. presents the following information for November :

Budgeted production of product P = 200 units.

Standard consumption of Raw materials = 2 kg. per unit of P.

Standard price of material A = ₹ 6 per kg.

Actually, 250 units of P were produced and material A was purchased at ₹ 8 per kg and consumed at 1.8 kg per unit of P. Calculate the material cost variances.

Solution:

Actual production of P	=	250 units	
Standard quantity of A for actual production = 2 × 250	=	500 kg.	(SQ)
Actual quantity of A for actual production = 1.8 × 250	=	450 kg.	(AQ)
Standard price / kg. of A	=	₹ 6	(SP)
Actual price / kg. of A	=	₹ 8	(AP)

(1) Total Material Cost Variance = (Standard Price × Standard Quantity)
– (Actual Price × Actual Quantity)
= (6 × 500) – (8 × 450) = ₹ 3,000 – ₹ 3,600 = ₹ 600 (A)

(2) Material Price Variance = (Standard Price – Actual Price) × Actual quantity
= (6 – 8) × 450 = ₹ 900 (A)

(3) Material Usage Variance = (Standard Quantity – Actual Quantity) × Standard Price
= (500 – 450) × 6 = ₹ 300 (F)

7 Standard Costing — Labour Cost Variance

LEARNING OBJECTIVES

After studying this chapter, you should be able to understand:

- Labour Variances
- Terms Useful for Computation of Labour Variances
- Direct Labour Cost Variance (LCV)
- Direct Labour Rate Variance (LRV)
- Direct Labour Efficiency Variance (LEV)
- Direct Labour Mix Variance (LMV)
- Direct Labour Yield Variance (LYV)
- Idle Time Variance (ITV)
- Direct Labour Revised Efficiency Variance [Or Labour Sub-Efficiency Variance]
- Practical Steps in the Computation of Labour Cost Variances when There is no Idle Time
- Practical Steps in the Computation of Labour Cost Variances when There is Idle Time

1.0 LABOUR VARIANCES

Labour Variances mainly arise due to the efficiency or inefficiency in the use of Labour Hours and / or change in Actual Rate and Standard Rate of Labour. These can be summarized as follows:

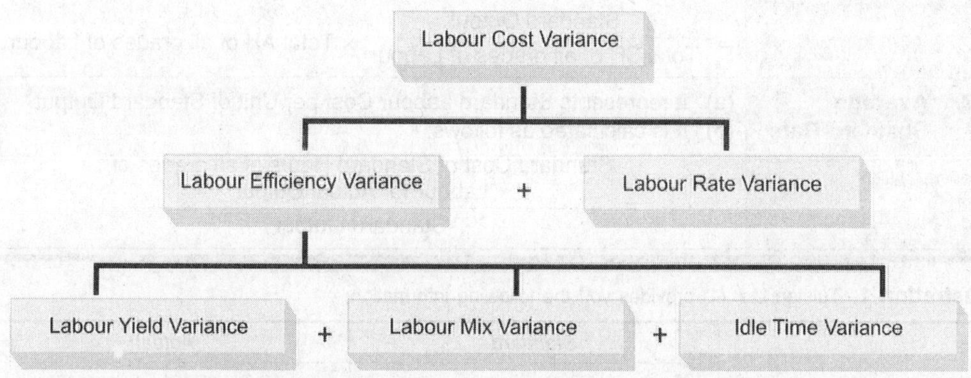

2.0 TERMS USEFUL FOR COMPUTATION OF LABOUR VARIANCES

One must know the following terms before knowing how to compute Labour Variances:

1. Standard Hours for Actual Output	(a) It represents the Labour Hours which should have been used to produce Actual Output as per standard.

	(b) It is calculated as follows: $= \frac{\text{Standard Hours}}{\text{Standard Output}} \times \text{Actual Output}$ *Or,* = Standard Labour Hours required per Unit × Actual Output
2. Standard Cost of Standard Hours for Actual Output	(a) It represents the Standard Cost of Standard Labour Hours for Actual Output. (b) It is calculated as follows: = Standard Hours for Actual Output x Standard Rate = SH × SR
3. Standard Cost of Actual Hours for Actual Output	(a) It represents the Standard Cost of Actual Labour Hours for Actual Output. (b) It is calculated as follows: = Actual Hours × Standard Rate = AH x SR
4. Revised Hours	(a) It represents the Total Actual Hours of all grades of Labour in a Standard Labour Mix Ratio. (b) It is calculated by dividing the Total Actual Hours of all grades of Labour in a Standard Mix Ratio as follows: $= \frac{\text{SH of one grade of Labour}}{\text{Total SH of all grades of Labour}} \times \text{Total AH of all grades of Labour}$
5. Standard Cost of Revised Hours	(a) It represents the Standard Cost of Revised Labour Hours. (b) It is calculated as follows: = Revised Hours × Standard Rate = RH × SR
6. Standard Yield	(a) It represents the yield (i.e. Output) which should have been obtained from Actual Hours of all grades of Labour. (b) It is calculated as follows: $= \frac{\text{Standard Output}}{\text{Total SH of all grades of Labour}} \times \text{Total AH of all grades of Labour}$
7. Average Standard Rate	(a) It represents Standard Labour Cost per Unit of Standard Output. (b) It is calculated as follows: $= \frac{\text{Standard Cost of Standard Hours of all grades of Labour for Actual Output}}{\text{Standard Output}}$

Illustration 1. Tulsian Ltd. (1) provides you the following information:

	Standard		*Actual*	
	Hours	*Rate/Hour*	*Hours*	*Rate/Hour*
Labour 'A'	30	₹ 20	44	₹ 25
Labour 'B'	20	₹ 10	66	₹ 5
Output	45 kg.		90 Kg.	

Required: Calculate (a) Standard Hours for Actual Output (b) Standard Cost of Standard Hours for Actual Output (c) Standard Cost of Actual Hours for Actual Output (d) Revised Hours (e) Standard Cost of Revised Hours (f) Standard Yield (g) Average Standard Rate

Solution:

(a) Standard Hours for Actual Output = $\frac{\text{Standard Hours of Labour}}{\text{Standard Output}}$ × Actual Output

Labour A = $\frac{30}{45}$ × 90 = 60, Labour B = $\frac{20}{45}$ × 90 = 40

(b) Standard Cost of Standard Hours for Actual Output = SH × SR
Labour A = (60 × ₹ 20) = ₹ 1,200, Labour B = (40 × ₹ 10) = ₹ 400

(c) Standard Cost of Actual Hours for Actual Output = AH x SR
Labour A = (44 × ₹ 20) = ₹ 880, Labour B = (66 × ₹ 10) = ₹ 660

(d) Revised Hours = $\frac{\text{SH of one grade of Labour}}{\text{Total SH of all grades of Labour}}$ × Total AH of all grades of Labour

Labour A = $\frac{60}{100}$ × 110 = 66, Labour B = $\frac{40}{100}$ × 110 = 44

(e) Standard Cost of Revised Hours = RH × SR
Labour A = (66 × ₹ 20) = ₹ 1,320, Labour B = (44 × ₹ 10) = ₹ 440

(f) Standard Yield = $\frac{\text{Standard Output}}{\text{Total SH of all grades of Labour}}$ × Total AH of all grades of Labour

= $\frac{90}{100}$ × 110 = 99 Hours

(g) Average Standard Rate = $\frac{\text{Standard Cost of Standard Hours of All Labour for Actual Output}}{\text{Standard Output}}$

= $\frac{(60 \times 20) + (40 \times 10)}{90 \text{ kg.}}$ = ₹ 17.78 (Appx.)

3.0 DIRECT LABOUR COST VARIANCE (LCV)

Meaning	Labour Cost Variance (LCV) is the difference between the Standard Cost of Direct Labour Hours specified for the output achieved and the Actual Cost of Direct Labour Hours expended.
How to Calculate	Labour Cost Variance (LCV) is calculated as follows: LCV = Standard Cost of Standard Labour Hours for Actual Output ***minus*** Actual Cost of Actual Labour Hours expended for Actual Output *or* = (Standard Hours for Actual Output × Standard Rate) – (Actual Hours × Actual Rate) *or* = (SH × SR) – (AH × AR) **Note:** *Standard Labour Hours for Actual Output is calculated as follows:* = $\frac{\text{Standard Labour Hours}}{\text{Standard Output}}$ × Actual Output *or* = Standard Labour Hours required per unit × Actual Output.
Nature	(a) **Favourable (F)** if the effect of the variance is to **increase** the profit (*i.e. where the actual cost is less than the standard cost.*) (b) **Adverse (A)** if the effect of the variance is to **decrease** the profit (*i.e. where actual cost is more than the standard cost.*)
Why arises?	LCV may arise due to: (a) change in Rate of Labour, *or* (b) change in Labour Hours, *or* (c) change in Rate and Labour hours
Division	LCV may further be divided into: (a) Labour Rate Variance (LRV), and (b) Labour Efficiency Variance (LEV)

Illustration 2. Calculate Labour Cost Variance from the following information:

	Standard	***Actual***
Output 100 units	200 units	
Labour hours required per unit of output	2 hours per unit	3 hours per unit
Rate	₹ 4 per hour	₹ 3 per hour

Solution:

Step 1 → Standard Hours for Actual Output (SH) = 200 × 2 = 400 hours.

Step 2 → Actual hours for Actual Output (AH) = 200 × 3 = 600 hours.

Step 3 → LCV = (SH × SR) — (AH × AR) = (400 × ₹ 4) – (600 × ₹ 3) = ₹ 200 (A)

Illustration 3. Calculate Labour Cost Variance from the following information:

Standard :	Labour hours for 100 units	300 hours
	Cost of Labour	₹ 1500
Actual :	Labour hours for 800 units	2500 hours
	Cost of Labour	₹ 15,000

Solution:

Step 1 → Standard hours for Actual Output (SH) = $\frac{300\text{hours}}{100\text{units}} \times 800\text{units}$ = 2400 hours

Step 2 → Actual Hours for Actual Output (AH) = 2500 hours.

Step 3 → Standard Rate (SR) = $\frac{1500}{300\,\text{hours}}$ = ₹ 5

Step 4 → Actual Rate (AR) = $\frac{15{,}000}{2500\,\text{hours}}$ = ₹ 6

Step 5 → Labour Cost Variance (LCV) = (SH × SR) – (AH × AR)
= (2400 × ₹ 5) – (2500 × ₹ 6) = ₹ 3,000 (A)

4.0 DIRECT LABOUR RATE VARIANCE (LRV)

Meaning	Direct Labour Rate Variance (LRV) is that portion of the labour cost variance which is due to the difference between the standard rate specified and the actual rate paid.
How to Calculate	Labour Rate Variance (LRV) is calculated as follows: LRV = (Standard Rate – Actual Rate) × Actual Hours *or* = (SR – AR) × AH
Nature	(a) **Favourable (F)** if the effect of variance is to increase the profit (i.e. where AR<SR) (b) **Adverse (A)** if the effect of variance is to decrease the profit (i.e. where AR>SR)
Why arises?	LRV may arise due to: 1. Change in the basic wage rates. 2. Change in the method of wage payment. 3. Use of grades of labour different from the standard grade specified due to non-availability of the labour grade specified or any other reason. 4. Unscheduled Overtime.

Illustration 4. Calculate Labour Rate Variance in Illustration 2.

Solution:

AH = 200 × 3 = 600 hours

Labour Rate Variance = (SR – AR) × AH = (₹ 4 – ₹ 3) × 600 = ₹ 600 (Favourable)

5.0 DIRECT LABOUR EFFICIENCY VARIANCE (LEV)

Meaning	Direct Labour Efficiency Variance (LEV) is that portion of the labour cost variance which is due to the difference between the standard hours specified for actual output and the actual hours expended.
How to Calculate	Labour Efficiency Variance (LEV) is calculated as follows: LEV = (Standard Hours for Actual Output – Actual Hours) × Standard Rate *or* = (SH – AH) × SR
Nature	(a) **Favourable (F)** if the effect of variance is to increase the profit (i.e. where AH<SH) (b) **Adverse (A)** if the effect of variance is to decrease the profit (i.e. where AH>SH)
Why arises?	LEV may arise due to: 1. Use of non-standard grade of workers. 2. Use of standard grade of workers but workers are inefficient. 3. Use of defective method of operation. 4. Use of defective or non-standard materials. 5. Use of defective tools and plant and machinery. 6. Poor working conditions e.g., inadequate lighting and ventilation, exercise heating etc. 7. Incompetent supervision.
Division	LEV may be further divided into: (a) Labour Mix Variance (LMV), and (b) Labour Yield Variance (LYV).

Illustration 5. Calculate Labour Efficiency Variance in Illustration 2:

Solution:

SH = 200 × 2 = 400 Hours., AH = 200 × 3 = 600 Hours

Labour Efficiency Variance = (SH – AH) × SR = (400 hours – 600 hours) × ₹ 4 = ₹ 800 (Adverse)

Illustration 6. Tulsian Ltd. provides you the following information.

The standard material cost of producing 100 units has been predetermined as 200 hours @ ₹ 4 per hours. In a particular cost period the actual data was as follows:

Actual Output	200 units
Labours Hours	600 hours for ₹ 1,800

Required: Calculate all labour cost variances.

Solution:

Step 1 → Standard Hours for Actual Output $= \dfrac{\text{Standard Hours}}{\text{Standard Output}} \times \text{Actual Output}$

$= \dfrac{200}{100} \times 200 = 400$ units

Step 2 → Actual Hours for Actual Output = 600 hours

Step 3 → Actual Labour Rate ₹ 1,800/600 = ₹ 3

Step 4 → Labour Rate Variance = (SR – AR) × AH = (₹ 4 – ₹ 3) × 600 = ₹ 600 (F)

Step 5 → Labour Efficiency Variance = (SH – AH) × SR = (400 – 600) × ₹ 4 = ₹ 800(A)

Step 6 → Labour Cost Variance = (SH – SR) – (AH × AR) = (400 × ₹ 4) – (600 × ₹ 3)

= ₹ 1,600 – ₹ 1,800 = ₹ 200(A)

6.0 DIRECT LABOUR MIX VARIANCE (LMV) [OR GANG COMPOSITON VARIANCE]

Meaning	Direct Labour Mix Variance (LMV) is that portion of the Labour Efficiency Variance which is due to the difference between standard and actual composition of labour.
How to Calculate	Labour Mix Variance (LMV) is calculated as follows: LMV = Standard Cost of Revised Labour Hours ***minus*** Standard Cost of Actual Labour Hours expended *or,* = (RH × SR) – (AH × SR) *or,* = (RH – AH) × SR **Note:** Revised Standard Hours (RSH) are calculated by dividing the total actual hours of all grades of labour in a standard labour mix ratio as follows: $RH = \frac{\text{Standard Hours of one grade of labour}}{\text{Total Standard Hours of all grades of labour}} \times \text{Total Actual Hours of all grades of labour}$
Nature	(a) **Favourable (F)** if the effect of the variance is to increase the profit (i.e. where AH<RSH) (b) **Adverse (A)** if the effect of the variance is to decrease the profit (i.e. where AH>RSH)
Why arises?	LMV arises only when the actual two or more grades of labour are mixed in a ratio different from the standard labour mix ratio. Change from Standard mix may be due to the non-availability of one or more grades of labour mix.

Illustration 7. Calculate Labour Mix Variance from the following information:

	Standard		*Actual*	
	Hours	*Rate per hour*	*Hours*	*Rate per hour*
Labour 'A'	40	₹ 12	1250 hours	₹.10
Labour'B'	60	₹ 9	850 hours	₹ 12
	Standard Output 85 kg		Actual Output 1700 kg	

Solution:

Step 1 → Revised Standard Hours (RSH) = $\frac{\text{Standard Hours of one grade}}{\text{Total Standard Hours}} \times \text{Total Actual Hours}$

Labour 'A' = $\frac{40}{100} \times 2100 = 840\,hours$, Labour 'B' = $\frac{60}{100} \times 2100 = 1260\,Hours$

Step 2 → Labour Mix Variance (LMV) = (RH – AH) × SR

Labour 'A' = (840 – 1250) × ₹ 12 = ₹ 4,920 (A)

Labour 'B' = (1260 – 850) × ₹ 9 = ₹ 3,690 (F)

LMV = ₹ 1,230 (A)

7.0 DIRECT LABOUR YIELD VARIANCE (LYV)

Meaning	Direct Labour Yield Variance (LYV) is that portion of the Labour Efficiency Variance which is due to the difference between standard yield specified

	for actual hours used and actual yield obtained. The standard yield is the output expected to be obtained from the actual usage of labour. LYV is an output variance which represents a gain or loss on output in terms of finished production.
How to Calculate	Labour Yield Variance (LYV) is calculated as follows: LYV = (Actual Yield — Standard yield) × Average Standard Output Rate **Notes:** (i) Standard Yield for Actual Hours $= \frac{\text{Standard Output for Total Standard Hours}}{\text{Total Standard Labour Hours of all grades for Actual output}}$ × Total Actual Productive Labour Hours of all grades (ii) Average Standard Output Rate (ASOR) $= \frac{\text{Standard Cost of Standard Hours of all grades of labour for Actual Output}}{\text{Standard Output for Total Standard Hours}}$ *or* $= \frac{\text{Total (SH} \times \text{SR)}}{\text{Standard Output}}$
Nature	(a) **Favourable (F)** if the effect of the variance is to increase the profit (i.e. where AY > SY) (b) **Adverse (A)** if the effect of the variance is to decrease the profit (i.e. where AY < SY)

Illustration 8. Calculate Labour Yield Variance in Illustration 7.

Solution:

Step 1 → Standard Yield for Actual Input = $\frac{85}{100} \times 2100$ = 1785 hours

Step 2 → Average Standard Output Rate (ASOR) = $\frac{(40 \times 12)+(60 \times 9)}{85} = \frac{1020}{85}$ = ₹ 12

Step 3 → Labour Yield Variance (LYV) = (Actual Yield – Standard Yield) × ASOR
= (1700 hours – 1785 hours) × ₹ 12
= ₹ 1,020 (A)

8.0 IDLE TIME VARIANCE (ITV)

Meaning	Idle Time Variance (ITV) is that portion of Labour Efficiency Variance which is due to abnormal idle time such as time lost due to power failure, machinery break-down, strike etc. It arises due to the difference between Actual Labour Hours worked and Actual Labour Hours paid.
How to calculate	Idle Time Variance (ITV) is calculated as follows: ITV = (Actual Hours worked – Actual Hours paid) × Standard Rate ITV = Idle Hours × Standard Rate *or,* = IH × SR
Nature	Idle Time Variance is always adverse or unfavourable because idle hours represent a loss.

Illustration 9. A manufacturing department of a company employing 100 workers produced 1040 units in a 42 hours week despite 5% of the time paid was lost due to an abnormal reason. The standard wage rate per hour was ₹ 6 but the actual wage rate per hour was ₹ 8. The standard output is 25 units per hour in a department employing 100 workers. Calculate Idle Time Variance.

Solution:

Idle Time Variance = Idle Hours × Standard Rate
= [5% of (100 × 42)] × ₹ 6 = ₹ 1,260 (A)

9.0 DIRECT LABOUR REVISED EFFICIENCY VARIANCE [OR LABOUR SUB-EFFICIENCY VARIANCE]

Meaning	Direct Labour Revised Efficiency Variance is that portion of labour efficiency variance which arises due to factors other than those which give rise to idle time variance and labour mix variance.
How to calculate	Direct Labour Revised Efficiency Variance is calculated as follows: LREV = (Standard Hours for Actual Output – Actual Productive Hours) × Standard Rate *or,* = (SH – APH) × SR **Note:** APH = Actual Hours – Idle Hours
Nature	(a) **Favourable (F)** if the effect of the variance is to increase the profit (i.e. where APH < SH). (b) **Adverse (A)** if the effect of the variance is to decrease the profit (i.e. where APH > SH)

Illustration 10. Using the information given in Illustration 9, calculate Labour Revised Efficiency Variance.

Solution:

Step 1 → SH = $\frac{100}{25} \times 1{,}040$ = 4,160

Step 2 → APH = Actual Hours – Idle Hours
= (100 × 42) – 5%(100 × 42)
= 3,990 Hours

Step 3 → Labour Revised Efficiency Variance (LREV) = (SH – APH) × SR
= (4,160 – 3,990) × ₹ 6
= ₹ 1,020 (F)

10.0 PRACTICAL STEPS IN THE COMPUTATION OF LABOUR COST VARIANCES WHEN THERE IS NO IDLE TIME

Step 1: *Prepare a **10 Column Table** of Basic Calculations as follows:*

TABLE OF BASIC CALCULATIONS FOR THE COMPUTATION OF LABOUR COST VARIANCES

Type of Labour	*SH for AO*	*SR*	*SH x SR (1)*	*AH*	*AR*	*AH x AR (2)*	*AH x SR (3)*	*RH*	*RH x SR (4)*
Skilled	....	....	....	....	....	....	....	....	....
Semi-skilled	....	....	....	....	....	....	....	....	....
	....		....	....		....	....	....	....

Note: RH = Revised Hours = Actual Hours in Standard Labour Mix Ratio

Step 2: *Calculate Labour Cost Variances as follows:*

Labour Cost Variance (1 – 2) = (SH × SR) – (AH × AR)
= ₹ .... – ₹ .... = ₹ ....

Labour Rate Variance (3 – 2) = (AH × SR) – (AH × AR)
Skilled = ₹ .... – ₹ .... = ₹ ....
Semi-skilled = ₹ .... – ₹ .... = ₹ ....
LRV = ₹ ....

Labour Efficiency Variance (1 – 3) = (SH × SR) – (AH × SR)
Skilled = ₹ .... – ₹ .... = ₹ ....
Semi-skilled = ₹ .... – ₹ .... = ₹ ....
LEV = ₹ ....

Labour Mix Variance (4 – 3) = (RH × SR) – (AH × SR)

Skilled = ₹ .... – ₹ .... = ₹ ....

Semi-skilled = ₹ .... – ₹ .... = ₹ ....

LMV = ₹ ....

Labour Yield Variance = (Actual Yield – Standard Yield) × Average Standard Output Rate

$$\text{Standard Yield} = \frac{\text{Standard Output}}{\text{Total SH of all grades Labour}} \times \text{Total AH of all grades Labour}$$

$$\text{Average Standard Output Rate} = \frac{\text{Total (SH} \times \text{SR)}}{\text{Standard Output}} = ₹\ ....$$

***Alternatively*, LYV (1 – 4) = (SH × SR) – (RH × SR)**

= ₹ .... – ₹ .... = ₹ ....

11.0 PRACTICAL STEPS IN THE COMPUTATION OF LABOUR COST VARIANCES WHEN THERE IS IDLE TIME

Step 1: *Prepare a **12 Column Table** of Basic Calculations as follows:*

TABLE OF BASIC CALCULATIONS FOR THE COMPUTATION OF LABOUR COST VARIANCES

Type of Labour	*SH for AO*	*SR*	*SH × SR (1)*	*AH*	*AR*	*AH×AR (2)*	*AH×SR (3)*	*APH*	*APH × SR (4)*	*RPH*	*RPH × SR (5)*
Skilled	....	....	....	....	....	....	....	....	....	....	....
Semi-skilled	....	....	....	....	....	....	....	....	....	....	....
	....		....	....		....	....		....		....

Notes:

(i) APH = Actual Productive Hours = AH – Idle Time,

(ii) RPH = Revised Productive Hours = Actual Productive Hours in Standard Labour Mix Ratio

Step 2: *Calculate Labour Cost Variances as follows:*

Labour Cost Variance (1 – 2) = (SH × SR) – (AH × AR)

= ₹ .... – ₹ .... = ₹ ....

Labour Rate Variance (3 – 2) = (AH × SR) – (AH × AR)

Skilled = ₹ .... – ₹ .... = ₹ ....

Semi-skilled = ₹ .... – ₹ .... = ₹ ....

LRV = ₹ ....

Labour Efficiency Variance (1 – 3) = (SH × SR) – (AH × SR)

Skilled = ₹ .... – ₹ .... = ₹ ....

Semi-skilled = ₹ .... – ₹ .... = ₹ ....

LEV = ₹ ....

Labour Mix Variance (5 – 4) = (RPH × SR) – (APH × SR)

Skilled = ₹ .... – ₹ .... = ₹ ....

Semi-skilled = ₹ .... – ₹ .... = ₹ ....

LMV = ₹ ....

Labour Yield Variance = (Actual Yield – Standard Yield) × Average Standard Output Rate

$$\text{Standard Yield} = \frac{\text{Standard Output}}{\text{Total SH of all grades Labour}} \times \text{Total AH of all grades Labour}$$

$$\text{Average Standard Output Rate} = \frac{\text{Total (SH} \times \text{SR)}}{\text{Standard Output}} = ₹\ ....$$

***Alternatively*, LYV (1 – 5) = (SH × SR) – (RPH × SR)**

= ₹ .... – ₹ .... = ₹ ....

Idle Time Variance (4 – 3) = (APH × SR) – (AH × SR)

Skilled = ₹ .... – ₹ .... = ₹ ....

Semi-skilled = ₹ .... – ₹ .... = ₹ ....

ITV = ₹ .... (Adverse)

Labour Revised Efficiency Variance (1 – 4) = (SH × SR) – (APH × SR)

Skilled = ₹ .... – ₹ .... = ₹ ....

Semi-skilled = ₹ .... – ₹ .... = ₹ ....

LREV = ₹ ....

Verification: LEV = LMV + LYV + ITV *or* LEV = ITV + LREV

COMPREHENSIVE ILLUSTRATIOINS

Illustration 11. Calculate all the Labour Cost Variances from the following information provided by Tulsian Ltd.

	Standard		*Actual*	
	Hours	*Rate Per Hour (₹)*	*Hours*	*Rate Per Hour (₹)*
Skilled	90	20	44	25
Semi-skilled	60	10	66	5
	Output 135 kg		Output 90 kg	

Solution:

Basic Calculations:

Labour	*SH for Actual Output*	*AH*	*Revised Hours (RH)*
Skilled	$\frac{90}{135} \times 90 = 60$	44	$\frac{60}{100} \times 110 = 66$
Semi-skilled	$\frac{60}{135} \times 90 = 40$	66	$\frac{40}{100} \times 110 = 44$
		110	110

BASIC CALCULATIONS FOR THE COMPUTATION OF LABOUR COST VARIANCES

Type of Labour	*SH for AO*	*SR*	*SH × SR (1)*	*AH*	*AR*	*AH × AR (2)*	*AH × SR (3)*	*RH*	*RH × SR (4)*
Skilled	60	20	1,200	44	25	1,100	880	66	1,320
Semi-skilled	40	10	400	66	5	330	660	44	440
	100		1,600	110		1,430	1,540		1,760

Labour Cost Variance (1 – 2) = (SH × SR) – (AH × AR)
= ₹ 1,600 – ₹ 1,430 = ₹ 170 (F)

Labour Rate Variance (3 – 2) = (AH × SR) – (AH × AR)

Skilled = ₹ 880 – ₹ 1,100 = ₹ 220 (A)

Semi-skilled = ₹ 660 – ₹ 330 = ₹ 330 (F)

LRV = ₹ 110 (F)

Labour Efficiency Variance (1 – 3) = (SH × SR) – (AH × SR)

Skilled = ₹ 1200 – ₹ 880 = ₹ 320 (F)

Semi-skilled = ₹ 400 – ₹ 660 = ₹ 260 (A)

LEV = ₹ 60 (F)

Labour Mix Variance (4 – 3) = (RH × SR) – (AH × SR)

Skilled = ₹ 1,320 – ₹ 880 = ₹ 440 (F)

Semi-skilled = ₹ 440 – ₹ 660 = ₹ 220 (A)

LMV = ₹ 220 (F)

Labour Yield Variance = (Actual Yield – Standard Yield) × Average Standard Output Rate

$$= \left(90 - \frac{90}{100} \times 110\right) \times \frac{₹\ 1,600}{90} = ₹\ 160\ (A)$$

Alternatively, LYV (1 – 4) = (SH × SR) – (RH × SR) = ₹ 1600 – 1760

= ₹ 160(A)

Verification: 1. LCV = LRV + LEV = ₹ 110 (F) + ₹ 60(F)

= ₹ 170 (F)

2. LEV = LMV + LYV = ₹ 220 (F) + ₹ 160 (A)

= ₹ 60 (F)

Illustration 12. Calculate all the labour cost variances from the following information provided by Tulsian Ltd :

Labour	***Standard***		***Actual***	
	No. of Workers	*Hourly Wage rate*	*No. of Workers*	*Hourly Wage rate*
Skilled	72	20	44	25
Semi-skilled	48	10	66	5

In a normal working week of 40 hours, the gang is expected to produce 108 kg of output but during the week ended 31st March the gang produced 90 kg of output.

Solution: *Basic Calculations :*

Type of Labour	*SH for Actual Output*	*Actual Hours (AH)*	*Revised Hours (RH)*
Skilled	$\frac{72 \times 40}{108} \times 90 = 2400$	44 × 40 = 1,760	$\frac{2,400}{4,000} \times 4,400 = 2,640$
Unskilled	$\frac{48 \times 40}{108} \times 90 = 1,600$	66 × 40 = 2,640	$\frac{1,600}{4,000} \times 4,400 = 1,760$
	4,000	4,400	4,400

BASIC CALCULATIONS FOR THE COMPUTATION OF LABOUR COST VARIANCES

Type of Labour	*SH for AO*	*SR*	*SH × SR (1)*	*AH*	*AR*	*AH × AR (2)*	*AH × SR (3)*	*RH*	*RH × SR (4)*
Skilled	2,400	20	48,000	1,760	25	44,000	35,200	2,640	52,800
Semi-skilled	1,600	10	16,000	2,640	5	13,200	26,400	1,760	17,600
	4,000		64,000	4,400		57,200	61,600		70,400

Labour Cost Variance (1– 2) = (SH × SR) – (AH × AR)

= ₹ 64,000 – ₹ 57,200 = ₹ 6,800 (F)

Labour Rate Variance (3 – 2) = (AH × SR) – (AH × AR)

Skilled = ₹ 35,200 – ₹ 44,000 = ₹ 8,800 (A)

Unskilled = ₹ 26,400 – ₹ 13,200 = ₹ 13,200 (F)

LRV = ₹ 4,400 (F)

Labour Efficiency Variance (1 – 3) = (SH × SR) – (AH × SR)

Skilled = ₹ 48,000 – ₹ 35,200 = ₹ 12,800 (F)

Unskilled = ₹ 16,000 – ₹ 26,400 = ₹ 10,400 (A)

LMV = ₹ 2,400 (F)

Labour Mix Variance (4 – 3) = (RSH × SR) – (AH × SR)

Skilled = ₹ 52,800 – ₹ 35,200 = ₹ 17,600 (F)

Unskilled = ₹ 17,600 – ₹ 26,400 = ₹ 8,800 (A)

LMV = ₹ 8,800 (F)

Labour Yield Variance = (Actual Yield – Standard Yield) × Average Standard Output Rate

$$= [₹\ 90 - (\frac{90}{4000} \times 4400)] \times \frac{64,000}{90} = ₹\ 6,400 (A)$$

Alternatively, LYV (1 – 4) = (SH × SR) – (RSH × SR) = ₹ 64,000 – ₹ 70,400 = ₹ 6,400 (A)

Verification:
1. LCV = LRV + LEV = ₹ 4400 (F) + ₹ 2,400 (F) = ₹ 6,800 (F)
2. LEV = LMV + LYV = ₹ 8,800 (F) + ₹ 6,400 (A) = ₹ 2,400 (F)

Illustration 13. The details regarding composition and the weekly wage rate of labour force engaged on a job scheduled to be completed in 30 weeks are as follows:

Category of Workers	***Standard***		***Actual***	
	No. of Labourers	*Weekly wage Rate*	*No. of Labourers*	*Weekly wage Rate*
Skilled	75	60	70	70
Semi-skilled	45	40	30	50
Unskilled	60	30	80	20

The work is actually completed in 32 weeks. Calculate the various labour cost variances.

Solution: *Basic Calculations :*

Type of Labour	*Standard Weeks (SH)*	*Actual Weeks (AH)*	*Revised Weeks (AH)*
Skilled	75 × 30 = 2,250	70 × 32 = 2,240	$\frac{2,250}{5,400} \times 5,760 = 2,400$
Semi-skilled	45 × 30 = 1,350	30 × 32 = 960	$\frac{1,350}{5,400} \times 5,760 = 1,440$
Unskilled	60 × 30 = 1,800	80 × 32 = 2,560	$\frac{1,800}{5,400} \times 5,760 = 1,920$
	5,400	5,760	5,760

BASIC CALCULATIONS FOR THE COMPUTATION OF LABOUR COST VARIANCES

Type of Labour	*SH for AO*	*SR*	*SH × SR (1)*	*AH*	*AR*	*AH × AR (2)*	*AH × SR (3)*	*RH*	*RH × SR (4)*
Skilled	2,250	60	1,35,000	2,240	70	1,56,800	1,34,400	2,400	1,44,000
Semi-skilled	1,350	40	54,000	960	50	48,000	38,400	1,440	57,600
Unskilled	1,800	30	54,000	2,560	20	51,200	76,800	1,920	57,600
	5,400		2,43,000	5,760		2,56,000	2,49,600	5,760	2,59,200

Labour Cost Variance (1 – 2) = (SH × SR) – (AH × AR)

= ₹ 2,43,000 – ₹ 2,56,000 = ₹ 13,000 (A)

Labour Rate Variance (3 – 2)	=	(AH × SR) – (AH × AR)		
Skilled	=	₹ 1,34,400 – ₹ 1,56,800	=	₹ 22,400 (A)
Semi-skilled	=	₹ 38,400 – ₹ 48,000	=	₹ 9,600 (A)
Unskilled	=	₹ 76,800 – ₹ 51,200	=	₹ 25,600 (F)
		LRV	=	₹ 6,400 (A)
Labour Efficiency Variance (1 – 3)	=	(SH × SR) – (AH × SR)		
Skilled	=	₹ 1,35,000 – ₹ 1,34,400	=	₹ 600 (F)
Semi-skilled	=	₹ 54,000 – ₹ 38,400	=	₹ 15,600 (F)
Unskilled	=	₹ 54,000 – ₹ 76,800	=	₹ 22,800 (A)
		LEV	=	₹ 6,600 (A)
Labour Mix Variance (4 – 3)	=	(RSH × SR) – (AH × SR)		
Skilled	=	₹ 1,44,000 – ₹ 1,34,400	=	₹ 9,600 (F)
Semi-skilled	=	₹ 57,600 – ₹ 38,400	=	₹ 19,200 (F)
Unskilled	=	₹ 57,600 – ₹ 76,800	=	₹ 19,200 (A)
		LMV	=	₹ 9,600 (F)

Labour Yield Variance = (Total Standard Weeks – Total Actual Weeks) × Average Standard Rate

$$= (5,400 - 5,760) \times \frac{₹\ 2,43,000}{5,400} = ₹\ 16,200\ (A)$$

Alternatively, LYV (1 – 4) = (SH × SR) – (RSH × SR)

= ₹ 2,43,000 – ₹ 2,59,200 = ₹ 16,200 (A)

Verification:
1. LCV = LRV + LEV = ₹ 6400 (A) + ₹ 6600 (A) = ₹ 13,000 (A)
2. LEV = LMV + LYV = ₹ 9600 (F) + ₹ 16200 (A) = ₹ 6,600 (A)

Illustration 14. A gang of workers normally consists of 30 men, 15 women and 10 boys. They are paid at standard hourly rates as under :

Men ₹ 8, Women ₹ 6, Boys ₹ 4,

In a normal working week of 40 hours, the gang is expected to produce, 2,000 units of output.

During the week ended 31st December the gang consisted of 40 men, 10 women and 5 boys. The actual wages paid were @ ₹ 7, ₹ 6.50 and ₹ 3, respectively. 4 hours were lost due to abnormal idle time and 1,600 units were produced.

Required: Calculate (i) Wage Variance, (ii) Wage Rate Variance, (iii) Labour Efficiency Variance, (iv) Gang Composition Variance (i.e. Labour Mix Variance) and (v) Labour Idle Time Variance (vi) Labour Yield Variance.

Solution:

	Men	*Women*	*Boys*	*Total*
Standard Hours for Actual output (SH)	$\frac{30 \times 40}{2000} \times 1600 = 960$	$\frac{15 \times 40}{2000} \times 1600 = 480$	$\frac{10 \times 40}{2000} \times 1600 = 320$	1760
Actual Hours for Actual Output	40 × 40 = 1600	10 × 40 = 400	5 × 40 = 200	2200
Idle Hours	40 × 4 = 160	10 × 4 = 40	5 × 4 = 20	220
Actual Productive Hours (APH)	1440	360	180	1980
Revised Productive Hours	$\frac{960}{1760} \times 1980 = 1080$	$\frac{480}{1760} \times 1980 = 540$	$\frac{320}{1760} \times 1980 = 360$	

BASIC CALCULATIONS FOR THE COMPUTATION OF LABOUR COST VARIANCES

Type of Labour	*SH for AO*	*SR ₹*	*SH × SR (1)*	*AH*	*AR ₹*	*AH × AR (2)*	*AH × SR (3)*	*APH*	*APH × SR (4)*	*RPH*	*RPH × SR (5)*
Men	960	8	7680	1600	7.00	11200	12800	1440	11520	1080	8,640
Women	480	6	2880	400	6.50	2600	2400	360	2160	540	3,240
Boys	320	4	1280	200	3.00	600	800	180	720	360	1,440
	1,760		11,840	2,200		14,400	16000	1,980	14,400	1,980	13,320

Labour Cost Variance (1 – 2) = (SH × SR) – (AH × AR) = ₹ 11,840 – ₹ 14,400 = ₹ 2,560 (A)

Labour Rate Variance (3 – 2) = (AH × SR) – (AH × AR)

Men = ₹ 12,800 – ₹ 11,200 = ₹ 1,600 (F)
Women = ₹ 2,400 – ₹ 2,600 = ₹ 200 (A)
Boys = ₹ 800 – ₹ 600 = ₹ 200 (F)
LRV = ₹ 1,600 (F)

Labour Efficiency Variance (1 – 3) = (SH × SR) – (AH × SR)

Men = ₹ 7,680 – ₹ 12,800 = ₹ 5,120 (A)
Women = ₹ 2,880 – ₹ 2400 = ₹ 480 (F)
Boys = ₹ 1,280 – ₹ 800 = ₹ 480 (F)
LEV = ₹ 4,160 (A)

Labour Mix Variance (5 – 4) = (RPH × SR) – (APH × SR)

Men = ₹ 8,640 – ₹ 11,520 = ₹ 2,880 (A)
Women = ₹ 3,240 – ₹ 2,160 = ₹ 1,080 (F)
Boys = ₹ 1,440 – ₹ 720 = ₹ 720 (F)
LMV = ₹.1,080 (A)

Labour Yield Variance = (Actual Yield – Standard Yield) × Average Standard Output Rate

$$= \left(₹\ 1600 - \frac{1600}{1760} \times 1980\right) \times \frac{11,840}{1600} = ₹\ 1,480\,(A)$$

Alternatively, LYV (1 – 5) = (SH × SR) – (RPH × SR)
= ₹ 11,840 – ₹ 13,320 = ₹ 1,480 (A)

Idle Time Variance (4 – 3) = (APH × SR) – (AH × SR)

Men = ₹ 11,520 – ₹ 12,800 = ₹ 1,280 (A)
Women = ₹ 2,160 – ₹ 2,400 = ₹ 240 (A)
Boys = ₹ 720 – ₹ 800 = ₹ 80 (A)
ITV = ₹ 1,600 (A)

Verification:

1. LCV = LRV + LEV = ₹ 1600 (F) + ₹ 4,160 (A) = ₹ 2,560 (A)
2. LEV = LMV + LYV + ITV
= ₹ 1,080 (A) + ₹ 1,480 (A) + 1,600 (A) = ₹ 4,160 (A)

Illustration 15. The standard labour complement and the actual labour complement engaged in a week for a job are as under :

	Skilled Workers	*Semi-Skilled Workers*	*Unskilled Workers*
A. Standard number of workers in the gang	32	12	6
B. Standard wage rate per hour (₹)	3	2	1
C. Actual number of workers employed in the gang during the week	28	18	4
D. Actual wage rate per hour (₹)	4	3	2

During the 40 hour working week the gang produced 1,800 standard labour hours of work.

Required: Calculate Labour Cost Variances.

Solution:

	Skilled	*Semi-skilled*	*Unskilled*	*Total*
Total Hours	32 × 40 = 1280	12 × 40 = 480	6 × 40 = 240	2000
Standard Hours	$\frac{1280}{2000}\times1800=1152$	$\frac{480}{2000}\times1800=432$	$\frac{240}{2000}\times1800=216$	1800
Revised Hours	$\frac{1152}{1800}\times2000=1280$	$\frac{432}{1800}\times2000=480$	$\frac{216}{1800}\times2000=240$	2000

BASIC CALCULATIONS FOR THE COMPUTATION OF LABOUR COST VARIANCES

Type of Labour	*SH for AO*	*SR*	*SH × SR (1)*	*AH*	*AR*	*AH × AR (2)*	*AH × SR (3)*	*RH*	*RH × SR (4)*
Skilled	1,152	3	3,456	1,120	4	4,480	3,360	1,280	3,840
Semi-skilled	432	2	864	720	3	2,160	1,440	480	960
Unskilled	216	1	216	160	2	320	160	240	240
	1,800		4,536	2,000		6,960	4,960	2,000	5,040

Labour Cost Variance (1 – 2) = (SH × SR) – (AH × AR)
= ₹ 4,536 – ₹ 6,960 = ₹ 2,424 (A)

Labour Rate Variance (3 – 2) = (AH × SR) – (AH × AR)
Skilled = ₹ 3,360 – ₹ 4480 = ₹ 1,120 (A)
Semi–Skilled = ₹ 1,440 – ₹ 2,160 = ₹ 720 (A)
Unskilled = ₹ 160 – ₹ 320 = ₹ 160 (A)
LRV = ₹ 2,000 (A)

Labour Efficiency Variance (1 – 3) = (SH × SR) – (AH × SR)
Skilled = ₹ 3,456 – ₹ 3,360 = ₹ 96 (F)
Semi-skilled = ₹ 864 – ₹ 1,440 = ₹ 576 (A)
Unskilled = ₹ 216 – ₹ 160 = ₹ 56 (F)
LEV = ₹ 424 (A)

Labour Mix Variance (4 – 3) = (RSH × SR) – (AH × SR)
Skilled = ₹ 3840 – ₹ 3360 = ₹ 480 (F)
Semiskilled = ₹ 960 – ₹ 1440 = ₹ 480 (A)
Unskilled = ₹ 240 – ₹ 160 = ₹ 80 (F)
LMV = ₹ 80 (F)

Labour Yield Variance = (Total Standard Hours – Total Actual Hours) × Average Standard Rate

$$= (1800 - 2000) \times \frac{4,536}{1800} = ₹\ 504\ (A)$$

Alternatively, LYV (1 – 4) = (SH × SR) – (RSH × SR) = (₹ 4,536 – ₹ 5040) = ₹ 504 (A)

Verification:

1. LCV = LRV + LEV = ₹ 2000(A) + 424(A) = ₹ 2424 (A)
2. LUV = LMV + LYV = ₹ 80 (F) + ₹ 504 (A) = ₹ 424 (A)

Illustration 16. The standard output of product 'EXE' is 25 units per hour in manufacturing department of a company employing 100 workers. The standard wage rate per labour hour is ₹ 6

In a 42 hours week, the department produced 1,040 units of 'EXE' despite 5% of the time paid was lost due to an abnormal reason. The hourly wage rate actually paid were ₹ 6.20, ₹ 6 and ₹ 5.70 respectively to 10, 30 and 60 of the workers. Compute Labour Cost Variance, Labour Efficiency Variance, Labour Yield Variance, Idle Time Variance and Labour Rate Variance.

Solution:

Basic Calculations :

1. Standard Labour Hours for 25 units = 100 hours
2. Standard Labour Hours for 1,040 units (SH) = $\frac{100}{25} \times 1{,}040 = 4{,}160$
3. Actual Labour Paid = 42 × 100 = 4,200 hours
4. Idle Time = 5% of 4,200 = 210 hours
5. Actual Productive Hours = 4,200 – 210 = 3,990 hours
6. Actual Wages Paid = [(10 × 42) × ₹ 6.20] + [(30 × 42) × ₹ 6] + [(60 × 42) × ₹ 5.70]
   = ₹ 2,604 + ₹ 7,560 + ₹ 14,364 = ₹ 24,528

BASIC CALCULATIONS FOR THE COMPUTATION OF LABOUR COST VARIANCES

SH for AO	*SR*	*SH× SR (1)*	*AH*	*AR*	*AH× AR (2)*	*AH× SR (3)*	*APH*	*APH× SR (4)*
4,160	6	24,960	4,200	5.84	24,528	25,200	3,990	23,940

Labour Cost Variance (1 – 2) = (SH × SR) – (AH × AR)
= ₹ 24,960 – ₹ 24,528 = ₹ 432 (F)

Labour Rate Variance (3 – 2) = (AH × SR) – (AH × AR)
= ₹ 25,200 – ₹ 24,528 = ₹ 672 (F)

Labour Efficiency Variance (1 – 3) = (SH × SR) – (AH × SR)
= ₹ 24,960 – ₹ 25,200 = ₹ 240 (A)

Labour Idle Time Variance (4 – 3) = (APH × SR) – (AH × SR)
= ₹ 23,940 – ₹ 25,200 = ₹ 1,260 (A)

Labour Yield Variance (1 – 4) = (SH × SR) – (APH × SR)
= ₹ 24,960 – ₹ 23,940 = ₹ 1,020 (F)

Alternatively, LYV = (Actual Yield – Standard yield) × Average Standard Output Rate

$$= \left(1040 - \frac{1040}{4160} \times 3990\right) \times \frac{24{,}960}{1040} = 1020\,(F)$$

Verification:

1. LCV = LRV + LEV = ₹ 672 (F) + ₹ 240 (A) = ₹ 432 (F)
2. LEV = LITV + LYV = ₹ 1260 (A) + ₹ 1020 (F) = ₹ 240 (A)

Illustration 17. Calculate all the labour cost variances from the following information provided by Tulsian Ltd.

	Standard		***Actual***	
	No, of Workers	*Hourly Wage Rate*	*No. of Workers*	*Hourly Wage Rate*
Skilled	72	20	44	25
Unskilled	48	10	66	5

In a normal working week of 40 hours, the gang is expected to produce 108 kg of output :

Actual data relating to finished goods and work-in-progress :

	Opening Stock	*Closing Stock*
Work-in-progress	5 kg [Materials fully supplied but 40% converted]	10 kg [Materials fully supplied but 80% converted]
Finished Goods	20 kg	10 kg
Actual sales of Finished Goods —	94 kg	

Solution:

Basic Calculations :

1. Units completed = Sales + Closing Stock - Opening Stock
   = 94 kg + 10 kg – 20 kg = 84 kg

2. No. of equivalent units of actual output for labour cost purposes :

	Units	*Degree of Completion*	*Equivalent Units*
A. Completed units	84	100%	84
B. *Add :* Closing WIP	10	80%	8
C. *Less :* Opening WIP	5	40%	2
			90 kg

3. Calculation of Standard Hours, Actual Hours and Revised Hours

Type of Labour	*SH for Actual Output*	*Actual Hours (AH)*	*Revised Hours (RH)*
Skilled	$\frac{72 \times 40}{108} \times 90 = 2400$	44 × 40 = 1,760	$\frac{2,400}{4,000} \times 4,400 = 2,640$
Unskilled	$\frac{48 \times 40}{108} \times 90 = 1,600$	66 × 40 = 2,640	$\frac{1,600}{4,000} \times 4,400 = 1,760$
	4,000	4,400	4,400

BASIC CALCULATIONS FOR THE COMPUTATION OF LABOUR COST VARIANCES

Type of Labour	*SH for AO*	*SR*	*SH × SR (1)*	*AH*	*AR*	*AH × AR (2)*	*AH × SR (3)*	*RH*	*RH × SR (4)*
Skilled	2400	20	48,000	1,760	25	44,000	35,200	2,640	52,800
Semi-skilled	1600	10	16,000	2,640	5	13,200	26,400	1,760	17,600
	4000		64,000	4,400		57,200	61,600	4,400	70,400

Labour Cost Variance (1– 2) = (SH × SR) – (AH × AR)
= ₹ 64,000 – ₹ 57,200 = ₹ 6,800 (F)

Labour Rate Variance (3 – 2) = (AH × SR) – (AH × AR)
Skilled = ₹ 35,200 – ₹ 44,000 = ₹ 8,800 (A)
Unskilled = ₹ 26,400 – ₹ 13,200 = ₹ 13,200 (F)
LRV = ₹ 4,400 (F)

Labour Efficiency Variance (1 – 3) = (SH × SR) – (AH × SR)
Skilled = ₹ 48,000 – ₹ 35,200 = ₹ 12,800 (F)
Unskilled = ₹ 16,000 – ₹ 26,400 = ₹ 10,400 (A)
LMV = ₹ 2,400 (F)

Labour Mix Variance (4 – 3) = (RSH × SR) – (AH × SR)
Skilled = ₹ 52,800 – ₹ 35,200 = ₹ 17,600 (F)
Unskilled = ₹ 17,600 – ₹ 26,400 = ₹ 8,800 (A)
LMV = ₹ 8,800 (F)

Labour Yield Variance = (Actual Yield – Standard Yield) × Average Standard Rate

$$=[₹\ 90 - (\frac{90}{4000} \times 4400)] \times \frac{64,000}{90} = 6,400\,(A)$$

Alternatively, LYV (1 – 4) = (SH × SR) – (RSH × SR) = ₹ 64,000 – ₹ 70,400 = ₹ 6,400 (A)

Verification:
1. LCV = LRV + LEV = ₹ 4400 (F) + ₹ 2,400 (F) = ₹ 6,800 (F)
2. LEV = LMV + LYV = ₹ 8,800 (F) + ₹ 6,400 (A) = ₹ 2,400 (F)

SOLVED PROBLEMS

Problem 1. Tulsian Ltd. provides you the following information

Type of Labour	Standard		Actual	
	Hours	*Rate per hour (₹)*	*Hours*	*Rate per hour (₹)*
Skilled Labour	60	20	44	25
Unskilled Labour	40	?	66	5

Required: Calculate the Standard Wage Rate of unskilled labour in each of the following alternative cases:

Case (a) If Labour Cost Variance is ₹ 170 (Fav)
Case (b) If Labour Efficiency Variance is ₹ 70 (Adv)
Case (c) If Labour Yield Variance is ₹ 160 (Adv)
Case (d) If Labour Mix Variance is ₹ 110 (Fav)
Case (e) If Labour Rate Variance is ₹ 220 (Adv).

Solution:

Let the Standard Wage Rate of unskilled labour be '*x*'

Revised Hours for Actual Mix $= \frac{\text{Standard hours}}{\text{Total Standard hours}} \times \text{Total Actual Hours}$

Skilled Labour $= \frac{60}{100} \times 110 = 66 \text{ hrs.}$

Unskilled Labour $= \frac{40}{100} \times 110 = 44 \text{ hrs.}$

BASIC CALCULATIONS FOR THE COMPUTATION OF LABOUR COST VARIANCES

Type of Labour	*SH for AO*	*SR*	*SH × SR (1)*	*AH*	*AR*	*AH × AR (2)*	*AH × SR (3)*	*RH*	*RH × SR (4)*
Skilled	60	20	1200	44	25	1100	880	66	1320
Unskilled	40	*x*	40 *x*	66	5	330	66 *x*	44	44 *x*
	100			110					
			1200 + 40 *x*			1,430	880 + 66 *x*		1320 + 44 *x*

Case (a) Labour Cost Variance (1 – 2) = (SH × SR) – (AH × AR)
+ ₹ 170 = 1200 + 40 *X* – 1430
1200 + 40 X = 1430 + 170 = 1600
x = (1600 – 1200)/40 = ₹ 10 per hour

Case (b) Labour Efficiency Variance (1– 3) = (SH × SR) – (AH × SR)
– ₹ 70 = ₹ 1200 + 40*x* – (880 + 66 *x*)
– ₹ 70 = ₹ 320 – 26*x*
x = (320 + 70)/26 = ₹ 15 per hour

Case (c) Labour Yield Variance (1 – 4) = (SH × SR) – (RH × SR)
– ₹ 160 = (1200 + 40*x*) – (1320 + 44*x*)
– ₹ 160 = – ₹ 120 – 4*x*
x = (₹ 160 – ₹ 120)/4 = ₹ 10 per hour

Case (d) Labour Mix Variance (4 – 3) = (RH × SR) – (AH × SR)
₹ 110 = (1320 + 44*x*) – (880 + 66*x*)
₹ 110 = ₹ 440 – 22*x*
x = (440 – 110)/22 = ₹ 15 per hour

Case (e) Labour Rate Variance (3 – 2) = (AH × SR) – (AH × AR)
– ₹ 220 = (880 + 66x) – 1430
– ₹ 220 = – ₹ 550 + 66x
x = (₹ 550 – ₹ 220)/66 = ₹ 5 per hour

Problem 2. Compute the missing data indicated by question marks from the following :

Particulars	*Labour - Grade A*	*Labour - Grade B*
Standard Wage Rate per hour	₹ 12.	₹ 15
Actual Wage Rate per hour	₹ 15	₹ 20
Standard Hours	50	?
Actual Hours	?	70
Labour Rate Variance	?	?
Labour Efficiency Variance	?	₹ 300 (Adv)
Labour Cost Variance	?	?
Labour Mix Variance for both together was ₹ 45 adverse.		

Solution: *Basic Calculations :*

1. Standard Hours of Labour Grade 'B'
   Labour Efficiency Variance = SR (SH – AH)
   – ₹ 300 = 15 (SH – 70)
   300/15 = SH – 70
   SH = 70 – 20 = 50 hours

2. Actual Hours of Labour Grade 'A' — Let actual labour grade 'A' be x

Type of Labour	*SH for AO*	*SR*	*SH × SR (1)*	*AH*	*AR*	*AH × AR (2)*	*AH × SR (3)*	*RH*	*RH × SR (4)*
A	50	12	600	x	15	15x	12x	35 + x/2	420 + 6x
B	50	15	750	70	20	1400	1050	35 + x/2	525 + 7.5x
				70 + x		1400 + 15x	1050 + 12x		945 + 13.5x

Labour Mix Variance = (RH × SR) – (AH × SR)
– ₹ 45 = (945 + 13.5x) – (1050 +12x)
– ₹ 45 = – ₹ 105 + 1.5x
x = 60/1.50 = 40 Hours

BASIC CALCULATIONS FOR THE COMPUTATION OF LABOUR COST VARIANCES

Type of Labour	*SH for AO*	*SR*	*SH × SR (1)*	*AH*	*AR*	*AH × AR (2)*	*AH × SR (3)*	*RH*	*RH × SR (4)*
A	50	12	600	40	15	600	480	55	660
B	50	15	750	70	20	1,400	1,050	55	825
	100		1,350	110		2,000	1,530		1,485

		A	**B**	**Total**
A. Labour Cost Variance	(1 – 2)	Nil	650 (A)	650 (A)
B. Labour Efficiency Variance	(1 – 3)	120 (F)	300 (A)	180 (A)
C. Labour Yield Variance	(1 – 4)	60 (A)	75 (A)	135 (A)
D. Labour Mix Variance	(4 – 3)	180 (F)	225 (A)	45 (A)
E. Labour Rate Variance	(3 – 2)	120 (A)	350 (A)	470 (A)

Verification:

Labour Cost Variance = Labour Efficiency Variance + Labour Rate Variance
= ₹ 180 (A) + ₹ 470 (A) = ₹ 650 (A)

Problem 3, From the following data of A and Co. Ltd. relating to budgeted and actual performance for the month of March, compute the Direct Material and Direct Labour Cost Variances :

Budgeted data for March :

Units to be manufactured	1,50,000
Units of direct Material required (based on Standard Rates)	4,95,000
Planned Purchases of Raw Materials (units)	5,40,000
Average Unit Cost of Direct Material	₹ 8
Direct Labour Hours per unit of finished goods	3/4 hr.
Direct Labour Cost (total)	₹ 29,92,500
Actual data at the end of March :	
Units actually manufactured	1,60,000
Direct Material Cost (purchase cost based on units actually issued)	43,41,900
Direct Material Cost (purchase cost based on units actually purchased)	45,10,000
Average Unit Cost of Direct Material	₹ 8.20
Total Direct Labour Hours for March	1,25,000
Total Direct Labour Cost for March	33,75,000

Solution:

Basic Calculations :

1. Standard Units of Direct Material required per unit of output = 4,95,000/1,50,000 = 3.30 units
2. Standard Hours for Actual output = 160,000 × 3/4 = 1,20,000 Hours
3. Total Actual Quantity of Direct Materials used = 43,41,900/8.20 = 5,29,500 units
4. Standard Quantity for Actual Output = 1,60,000 × 3.3 = 5,28,000 units
5. Standard Direct Labour Cost per hour = $\dfrac{29{,}92{,}500}{1{,}50{,}000 \times 3/4} = \dfrac{29{,}92{,}500}{1{,}12{,}500} = 26.60$
6. Actual Direct Labour Cost per hour = 33,75,000/1,25,000 = ₹ 27

BASIC CALCULATIONS FOR THE COMPUTATION OF MATERIAL COST VARIANCES

SQ for AO	*SP*	*SQ × SP* (1)	*AQ*	*AP*	*AQ × AP* (2)	*AQ × SP* (3)
5,28,000	8	42,24,000	5,29,500	8.20	43,41,900	42,36,000

A Material Cost Variance	(1 – 2) = ₹	1,17,900 (A)
B Material Usage Variance	(1 – 3) = ₹	12,000 (A)
C Material Price Variance	(3 – 2) = ₹	1,05,900 (A)

Verification :

Material Cost Variance = Material Usage Variance + Material Price Variance
= ₹ 12,000 (A) + ₹ 1,05,900 (A) = 1,17,900 (A)

BASIC CALCULATIONS FOR THE COMPUTATION OF LABOUR COST VARIANCES

SH for AO	*SR*	*SH× SR* (1)	*AH*	*AR*	*AH× AR* (2)	*AH× SR* (3)
1,20,000	26.60	31,92,000	1,25,000	27	33,75,000	33,25,000

A Labour Cost Variance	(1 – 2) = ₹	1,83,000 (A)
B Labour Efficiency Variance	(1 – 3) = ₹	1,33,000 (A)
C Labour Rate Variance	(3 – 2) = ₹	50,000 (A)

Verification:

Labour Cost Variance = Labour Efficiency Variance + Labour Rate Variance
= ₹ 1,33,000 (A) + ₹ 50,000 (A) = ₹ 1,83,000 (A)

Problem 4. From the particulars given below, compute : Material Price Variance, Material Usage Variance, Labour Rate Variance, Idle Time Variance and Labour Efficiency Variance with full working details:

1 tonne of material input yields a standard output of 1,00,000 units. The standard price of material is ₹ 20 per kg. Number of employees engaged is 200. The standard wage rate per employee per day is ₹ 6. The standard daily output per employee is 100 units. The actual quantity of material used is 10 tonnes and the actual price paid is ₹ 21 per kg. Actual output obtained is 9,00,000 units. Actual number of days worked is 50 and actual rate of wages paid is ₹ 6.50 per day. Idle time paid for and included in above time is 1/2 day.

Solution:

(i) *Calculation of Material Cost Variances*

Standard Quantity for Actual Output (SQ) = $\frac{1{,}000 \text{ kg}}{1{,}00{,}000} \times 9{,}00{,}000 = 9{,}000$ kg

BASIC CALCULATIONS FOR THE COMPUTATION OF MATERIAL COST VARIANCES

SQ for AO	*SP*	*SQ × SP* (1)	*AQ*	*AP*	*AQ × AP* (2)	*AQ × SP* (3)
9,000	20	1,80,000	10,000	21	2,10,000	2,00,000

A Material Cost Variance (1 – 2) = ₹ 1,80,000 – ₹ 2,10,000 = ₹ 30,000 (A)

B Material Usage Variance (1 – 3) = ₹ 1,80,000 – ₹ 2,00,000 = ₹ 20,000 (A)

C Material Price Variance (3 – 2) = ₹ 2,00,000 – ₹ 2,10,000 = ₹ 10,000 (A)

D Material Yield Variance = (Actual Yield – Standard yield) × Average Standard Price

$$= (9{,}000 \text{ kg} - \frac{9000}{9000} \times 10000) \times \frac{1{,}80{,}000}{9{,}000} = 20{,}000 \text{(A)}$$

Verification :

Material Cost Variance = Material Usage Variance + Material Price Variance

= ₹ 20,000 (A) + ₹ 10,000 (A) = ₹ 30,000 (A)

(ii) *Calculation of Labour Cost Variances*

Standard hours for Actual output (SH) = $\frac{1}{100} \times 9{,}00{,}000 = 9{,}000$ man days

Idle Hours = 200 men × 1/2 day = 100 Man days

Actual Productive Hours (APH) = (200 × 50) – 100 = 9,900 Man days

BASIC CALCULATIONS FOR THE COMPUTATION OF LABOUR COST VARIANCES

SH for AO	*SR*	*SH × SR* (1)	*AH*	*AR*	*AH × AH* (2)	*AH × SR* (3)	*APH*	*APH × SR* (4)
9,000	6.00	54,000	10,000	6.50	65,000	60,000	9,900	59,400

A Labour Cost Variance (1 – 2) = ₹ 54,000 – ₹ 65,000 = ₹ 11,000 (A)

B Labour Efficiency Variance (1 – 3) = ₹ 54,000 – ₹ 60,000 = ₹ 6,000 (A)

C Labour Yield Variance (1 – 4) = ₹ 54,000 – ₹ 59,400 = ₹ 5,400 (A)

D Idle Time Variance (4 – 3) = ₹ 59,400 – ₹ 60,000 = ₹ 600 (A)

E Labour Rate Variance (3 – 2) = ₹ 60,000 – ₹ 65,000 = ₹ 5,000 (A)

Verification :

1. Labour Cost Variance = Labour Efficiency Variance + Labour Rate Variance

   = ₹ 6,000 (A) + ₹ 5,000 (A) = ₹ 11,000 (A)

2. Labour Efficiency Variance = Labour Yield Variance + Idle Time Variance

   = ₹ 5,400 (A) + ₹ 600 (A) = ₹ 6,000 (A)

Labour Yield Variance = (Actual Yield – Standard Yield) × Average Standard Output Rate

$$= (9{,}00{,}000 \text{ units} - \frac{100 \times 200 \times 50}{50} \times 49.5) \times \frac{54{,}000}{9{,}00{,}000} = ₹\ 5{,}400\text{(A)}$$

8 Standard Costing — Overhead Variances

LEARNING OBJECTIVES

After studying this chapter, you should be able to understand:

- Meaning of Overhead
- Meaning of Overhead Variances
- Classification of Overhead Variances
- Terms useful for Computation of Overheads Variances
- Overhead Cost Variance
- Variable Overhead Cost Variance
- Variable Overhead Efficiency Variance
- Variable Overhead Expenditure Variance
- Fixed Overhead Cost Variance
- Fixed Overhead Expenditure Variance
- Fixed Overhead Volume Variance
- Fixed Overhead Efficiency Variance
- Fixed Overhead Capacity Variance
- Fixed Overhead Calender Variance
- Revised Fixed Overhead Capacity Variance
- Computation of Variable Overhead Variances
- Computation of Fixed Overhead Variance when the Actual Number of Working days are equal to the Budgeted Number of working days
- Computation of Fixed Overhead Variances when the Actual Number of working days are different from the Budgeted Number of working days

1.0 MEANING OF OVERHEAD

Overhead is the aggregate of Indirect Material Cost, Indirect Labour Cost and Indirect Expenses.

Overhead = Total Indirect Cost

or, = Indirect Material Cost + Indirect Labour Cost + Indirect Expenses

2.0 MEANING OF OVERHEAD VARIANCES

Overhead variances indicate under or over absorption of overhead. Favourable Overhead variances indicate over absorption of overheads and Adverse Overhead Variances indicate under absorption of overheads. Overhead Variances arise due to the difference between absorbed overheads and actual Overheads incurred. The absorbed overheads are the overheads which are charged to each unit of production on the basis of a pre-determined overhead rate (also known as Standard Overhead Recovery Rate or Standard Overhead Absorption Rate or Standard Burden Rate). Pre-determined Overhead Rate is calculated by dividing Budgeted Overheads by the Normal Capacity Level. Normal capacity level may be in terms of machine hours/labour hours/units. Since actual overheads can be known only at the time of finalisation of expense accounts at the end of accounting period, the overheads are charged to each unit of production on the basis of Pre-determined Overhead Rate.

Use of Overhead Rate (Per hour or per unit) Overhead variances may be calculated using Overhead Rate per hour or Overhead Rate per unit of output.

3.0 CLASSIFICATION OF OVERHEAD VARIANCES

Overhead variances may be classified as follows:

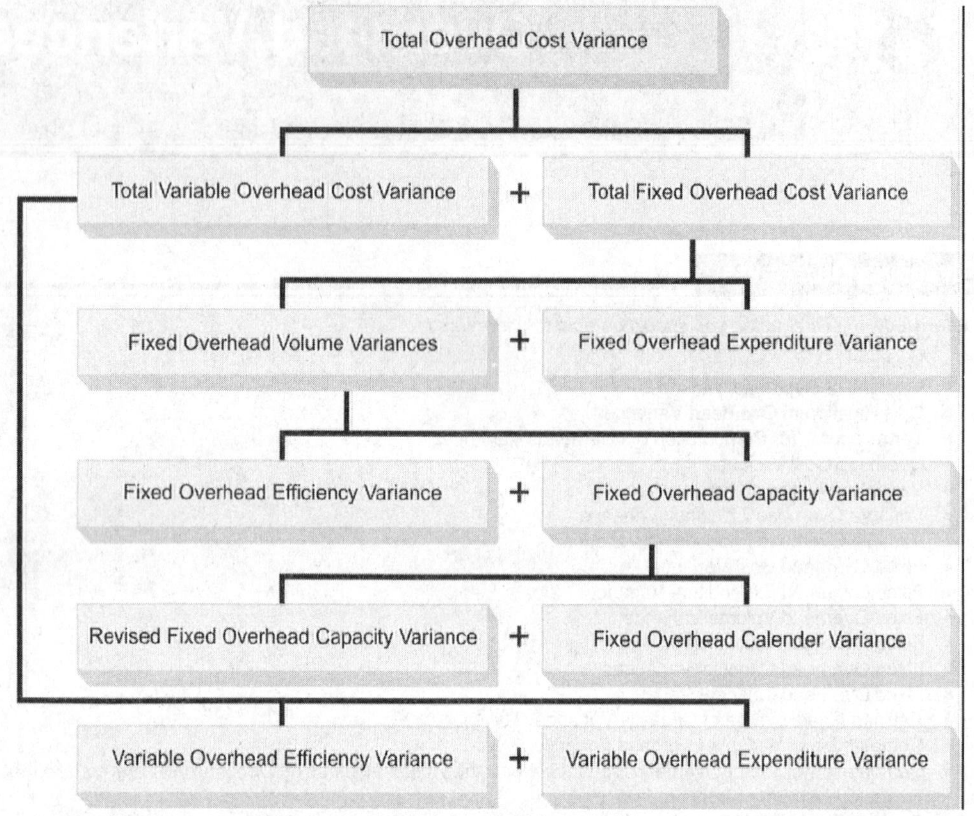

Let us discuss these variances one by one.

4.0 TERMS USEFUL FOR COMPUTATION OF OVERHEADS VARIANCES

One must know the following terms before knowing how to compute Overhead Variances:

1. **Standard Fixed Overhead Absorption Rate** ***Or*** **Standard Fixed Overhead Recovery Rate**	(a) It represents the rate at which the Fixed Overheads are charged to Production. (b) It is calculated as follows: $\text{SFOR} = \frac{\text{Budgeted Fixed Overheads}}{\text{Normal Volume Activity in terms of Output or Hours}}$
2. **Standard Variable Overhead Absorption Rate** ***Or*** **Standard Variable Overhead Recovery Rate**	(a) It represents the rate at which the Variable Overheads are charged to Production. (b) It is calculated as follows: $\text{SVOR} = \frac{\text{Budgeted Variable Overheads}}{\text{Normal Volume Activity in terms of Output or Hours}}$

3. Standard Hours for Actual Output	(a) These represent the hours which should have been taken to produce Actual Output Units as per standard. (b) These are calculated as follows: SH = Actual Output x Standard Hours per Unit *Or,* SH = Actual Output / Standard Output per Hour
4. Absorbed Overheads *Or* Recovered Overheads	(a) These represent the Overheads charged to **Standard Hours for Actual Output** on the basis of Standard Overhead Absorption/ Recovery Rate. (b) These are calculated as follows: = Standard Hours x Standard Overhead Absorption Rate per Hour *Or,* = Actual Output x Standard Overhead Absorption Rate per Output
5. Standard Overheads	(a) These represent the product of Actual Hours and Standard Overhead Absorption Rate. (b) These are calculated as follows: = Actual Hours x Standard Overhead Absorption Rate per Hour *Or,* = Standard Output for Actual Hours × Standard Overhead Absorption Rate per Output
6. Budgeted Overheads	(a) These represent the amount of Overheads for Budgeted Hours during the Budgeted Number of Working Days. (b) These are calculated as follows: = Budgeted Hours x Standard Overhead Absorption Rate per Hour *Or,* = Budgeted Output x Standard Overhead Absorption Rate per Output
7. Revised Budgeted Hours	(a) These represent the Budgeted Hours during the Actual Number of Working Days. (b) These are calculated as follows: $= \frac{\text{Budgeted Hours}}{\text{Budgeted No. of Working Days}} \times \text{Actual No. of Working Days}$
8. Revised Budgeted Overheads	(a) These represent the amount of Overheads for Revised Budgeted Hours during the Actual Number of Working Days. (b) These are calculated as follows: = Revised Budgeted Hours x Standard Overhead Absorption Rate per Hour *Or,* = Revised Budgeted Output x Standard Overhead Absorption Rate per Output
9. Actual Overheads	(a) These represent the Overheads actually incurred. (b) These are usually given in question. If not given, these are calculated as follows: = Actual Hours x Actual Overhead Rate per Hour *Or,* = Actual Output x Actual Overhead Rate per Output

Illustration 1. Tulsian (1) Ltd. provides you the following information:

	Budget	Actual
Number of Working Days	25	26
Output (Units)	15,000	16,250
Hours	30,000	33,000
Fixed Overheads	₹ 45,000	₹ 50,000
Variable Overheads	₹ 60,000	₹ 68,000

Required: Calculate (a) Standard Fixed Overhead Absorption Rate per Hour (b) Standard Variable Overhead Absorption Rate per Hour (c) Standard Hours for Actual Output (d) Absorbed Fixed Overheads (e) Absorbed Variable Overheads (f) Standard Fixed Overheads (g) Standard Variable Overheads (h) Original Budgeted Fixed Overheads (i) Revised Budgeted Hours (j) Revised Budgeted Fixed Overheads

Solution:

(a) Standard Fixed Overhead Absorption Rate (SFOR) $= \dfrac{\text{Budgeted Fixed Overheads}}{\text{Budgeted Hours}}$

$= \dfrac{45{,}000}{30{,}000} =$ ₹ 1.50 per Hour

(b) Standard Variable Overhead Absorption Rate (SVOR) $= \dfrac{\text{Budgeted Variable Overheads}}{\text{Budgeted Hours}}$

$= \dfrac{60{,}000}{30{,}000} =$ ₹ 2 per Hour

(c) Standard Hours for Actual Output (SH) $= \dfrac{\text{Budgeted Hours}}{\text{Budgeted Output}} \times \text{Actual Output}$

$= \dfrac{30{,}000}{15{,}000} \times 16{,}250 = 32{,}500$

(d) Absorbed Fixed Overheads = SH × SFOR = 32,500 × ₹ 1.50 = ₹ 48,750

(e) Absorbed Variable Overheads = SH × SVOR = 32,500 × ₹ 2 = ₹ 65,000

(f) Standard Fixed Overheads = AH × SFOR = 33,000 × ₹ 1.50 = ₹ 49,500

(g) Standard Variable Overheads = AH × SVOR = 33,000 × ₹ 2 = ₹ 66,000

(h) Original Budgeted Fixed Overheads = Original BH × SFOR = 30,000 × ₹ 1.50 = ₹ 45,000

(i) Revised Budgeted Hours $= \dfrac{\text{Original Budgeted Hours}}{\text{Budgeted Number of Working Days}} \times \text{Actual Number of Working Days}$

$= \dfrac{30{,}000}{25} \times 26 = 31{,}200$

(j) Revised Budgeted Fixed Overheads = Revised BH x SFOR = 31,200 x ₹ 1.50 = ₹ 46,800

5.0 OVERHEAD COST VARIANCE

Meaning	Overhead Cost Variance is the difference between Total Standard Overhead Absorbed and Total Actual Overhead Incurred. It indicates under or over absorption of overheads.
How to Calculate	Overhead Cost Variance = Absorbed OH – Actual OH Incurred *or,* = [(Standard Hours for Actual Output × Standard OH Rate per hour) – Actual OH Incurred] *or,* = (SH × SOR) – (AH × AOR) **Notes:** (i) Standard Hours for Actual Output (SH) $= \dfrac{\text{Budgeted Hours}}{\text{Budgeted Output}} \times \text{Actual Output}$ (ii) Standard Overhead Rate per Hour (SOR) $= \dfrac{\text{Budgeted Overheads}}{\text{Budgeted Hours}}$
Division	Overhead Cost Variance may further be divided into Fixed Overhead Variances and Variable Overhead Variances.

Illustration 2. Tulsian Ltd. provides you the following information:

	Budget	*Actual*
Output (units)	15,000	16,250
Hours	30,000	33,000
Overhead	₹ 1,05,000	₹ 1,18,000

Required: Calculate Overhead Cost Variance when: (a) When Overhead Rate per hour is used (b) When Overhead Rate per unit is used

Solution:

(a) When Overhead Rate per hour is used

Step 1: *Standard Hours for Actual Output (SH)*

$$SH = \frac{\text{Budgeted Hours}}{\text{Budgeted Output}} \times \text{Actual Output} = \frac{30{,}000}{15{,}000} \times 16{,}250 = 32{,}500$$

Step 2: *Standard Overhead Rate per Hour (SOR)*

$$SOR = \frac{\text{Budgeted Overhead}}{\text{Budgeted Hour}} = \frac{1{,}05{,}000}{30{,}000} = ₹\ 3.50 \text{ per hour}$$

Step 3: *Total Overhead Cost Variance = Absorbed Overhead – Actual Overhead*

= (SH x SOR) – (AH x AOR)

= (32,500 x ₹ 3.50) – ₹ 1,18,000 = ₹ 4,250 (A)

(b) When Overhead Rate per unit is used

Step 1: Standard Output for Actual Hours (SO)

$$SO = \frac{\text{Budgeted Output}}{\text{Budgeted Hours}} \times \text{Actual Hours} = \frac{15{,}000}{30{,}000} \times 33{,}000 = 16{,}500$$

Step 2: *Standard Overhead Rate per Hour (SOR)*

$$SOR = \frac{\text{Budgeted Overheads}}{\text{Budgeted Output}} = \frac{1{,}05{,}000}{15{,}000} = \text{Rs } 7 \text{ per unit}$$

Step 3: *Total Overhead Cost Variance* = *Absorbed Overhead – Actual Overhead*

= (AO x SOR) – (AO x AOR)

= (16,250 x ₹ 7) – ₹ 1,18,000 = ₹ 4,250 (A)

6.0 VARIABLE OVERHEAD COST VARIANCE

Meaning	Variable Overhead Cost Variance is the difference between Absorbed Variable Overhead and Actual Variable Overhead incurred. It indicates under *or* over absorption of variable overheads.
How to Calculate	Variable Overhead Cost Variance = Absorbed Variable Overhead – Actual Variable Overhead Incurred *or* = [(Standard Hours for Actual Output × Standard Variable Overhead Rate per hour) – Actual Variable Overhead Incurred] *or,* = (SH x SVOR) – (AH x AVOR) **Notes:** (i) Standard Hours for Actual Output (SH) $SH = \frac{\text{Budgeted Hours}}{\text{Budgeted Output}} \times \text{Actual Output}$ (ii) Standard Variable Overhead Rate per Hour (SVOR) $SVOR = \frac{\text{Budgeted Variable Overheads}}{\text{Budgeted Hours}}$
Division	Variable Overhead Cost Variance may further be divided into Variable Overhead Efficiency Variance and Variable Overhead Expenditure Variance.

Illustration 3. Tulsian Ltd. provides you the following information:

	Budget	*Actual*
Output (units)	15,000	16,250
Hours	30,000	33,000
Variable Overheads	₹ 60,000	₹ 68,000

Required: Calculate Variable Overhead Cost Variance.

Solution:

Step 1: *Standard Hours for Actual Output (SH)*

$$SH = \frac{\text{Budgeted Hours}}{\text{Budgeted Output}} \times \text{Actual Output} = \frac{30{,}000}{15{,}000} \times 16{,}250 = 32{,}500$$

Step 2: *Standard Variable Overhead Rate per hour (SVOR)*

$$SVOR = \frac{\text{Budgeted Variable Overhead}}{\text{Budgeted Hours}} = \frac{60{,}000}{30{,}000} = \text{Rs 2 per hour}$$

Step 3: *Variable Overhead Cost Variance*

= *Absorbed Variable Overheads – Actual Variable Overhead Incurred*

= (SH × SVOR) – (AH × AVOR)

= (32,500 × ₹ 2) – (₹ 68,000) = ₹ 3,000 (A)

7.0 VARIABLE OVERHEAD EFFICIENCY VARIANCE

Meaning	Variable Overhead Efficiency Variance is that portion of Total Variable Overhead Cost Variance which arises due to the difference between Standard Hours for Actual Output (SH) and Actual Hours (AH).
How to Calculate	Variable Overhead Efficiency Variance = Absorbed Variable Overhead – Standard Variable Overhead *or,* = (Standard Hours for Actual Output x Standard Variable Overhead Rate) ***Minus*** (Actual Hours x Standard Variable Overhead Rate) *or,* = (SH × SVOR) – (AH × SVOR) *or,* = (SH – AH) × SVOR

Illustration 4. Calculate Variable Overhead Efficiency Variance in Illustration 3.

Solution: Variable Overhead Efficiency Variance = Absorbed Variable Overhead – Standard Variable Overhead

= (SH × SVOR) – (AH × SVOR)

= (32,500 × ₹ 2) – (33,000 × ₹ 2) = ₹ 1,000 (A)

8.0 VARIABLE OVERHEAD EXPENDITURE VARIANCE

Meaning	Variable Overhead Expenditure Variance is that portion of Total Variable Overhead Cost Variance which arises due to the difference between Standard Variable Overhead allowed and Actual Variable Overhead incurred. It indicates under or over spending of variable overheads.
How to calculate	Variable Overhead Expenditure Variance = Standard Variable Overhead – Actual Variable Overhead incured or, = (Actual Hours × Standard Variable Overhead Rate) ***Minus*** (Actual Hours × Actual Variable Overhead Rate) or, = (AH × SVOR) – (AH × AVOR) or, = AH × (SVOR – AVOR)

Illustration 5. Calculate Variable Overhead Expenditure Variance in Illustration 3.

Solution:

Variable Overhead Expenditure Variance = Standard Variable Overhead – Actual Variable Overhead Incurred
= (AH x SVOR) – Actual Variable Overhead Incurred
= (33,000 x ₹ 2) – ₹ 68,000 = ₹ 2,000 (A)

9.0 FIXED OVERHEAD COST VARIANCE

Meaning	Fixed Overhead Cost Variance is the difference between Total Standard Fixed Overhead absorbed and Total Actual Fixed Overhead Incurred. It indicates under or over absorption of fixed overheads.
How to Calculate	Fixed Overhead Cost Variance = Absorbed Fixed Overhead – Actual Fixed Overhead Incurred *or,* = [(Standard Hours for Actual Output × Standard Fixed OH Rate per hour) – Actual Fixed Overhead Incurred] *or,* = (SH x SFOR) – (AH x AFOR) **Notes:** (i) Standard Hours for Actual Output (SH) $SH = \frac{\text{Budgeted Hours}}{\text{Budgeted Output}} \times \text{Actual Output}$ (ii) Standard Fixed Overhead Rate per Hour (SFOR) $SFOR = \frac{\text{Budgeted Fixed Overhead}}{\text{Budgeted Hours}}$
Division	Fixed Overhead Cost Variance may further be divided into Fixed Overhead Expenditure Variance and Fixed Overhead Volume Variance.

Illustration 6. Tulsian Ltd. provided you the following information:

	Budget	*Actual*
Output (units)	15,000	16,250
Hours	30,000	33,000
Fixed Overhead	₹ 45,000	₹ 50,000

Required: Calculate Fixed Overhead Cost Variance.

Solution:

Step 1: *Standard Hours for Actual Output (SH)*

$$SH = \frac{\text{Budgeted Hours}}{\text{Budgeted Output}} \times \text{Actual Output} = \frac{30,000}{15,000} \times 16,250 = 32,500$$

Step 2: *Standard Fixed Overhead Rate per hour (SFOR)*

$$SFOR = \frac{\text{Budgeted Fixed Overheads}}{\text{Budgeted Hours}} = \frac{45,000}{30,000} = 1.50 \text{ per hour}$$

Step 3: Total Fixed Overhead Cost Variance = Absorbed Fixed Overheads – Actual Fixed Overhead
= (SH x SFOR) – (AH x AFOR)
= (32,500 x ₹ 1.50) – ₹ 50,000
= ₹ 48,750 – ₹ 50,000
= ₹ 1,250 (A)

10.0 FIXED OVERHEAD EXPENDITURE VARIANCE

Meaning	Fixed Overhead Expenditure Variance is that portion of Total Fixed Overhead Cost Variance which arises due to the difference between Budgeted Fixed Overhead and Actual Fixed Overheads. It indicates under or over spending of Fixed Overheads.
How to calculate	Fixed Overhead Expenditure Variance = Budgeted Fixed Overhead – Actual Fixed Overhead = (Budgeted Hours × Standard Fixed Overhead Rate) ***Minus*** (Actual Hours x Actual Fixed Overhead Rate) = (BH × SFOR) – (AH × AFOR)
Why arises	It may arise due to: (a) Improper use of Available Facilities (b) Improperly set standards (c) Seasonal Conditions

Illustration 7. Calculate Fixed Overhead Expenditure Variance in Illustration 6.

Solution: Fixed Overhead Expenditure Variance = Budgeted Fixed Overhead – Actual Fixed Overhead
= (BH x SFOR) – Actual Fixed Overhead
= (30,000 x ₹ 1.50) – ₹ 50,000
= ₹ 45,000 – ₹ 50,000 = ₹ 5,000 (A)

11.0 FIXED OVERHEAD VOLUME VARIANCE (FOVV)

Meaning	Fixed Overhead Volume Variance is that portion of Total Fixed Overhead Cost Variance which arises due to the difference between Standard Hours for Actual Output (SH) and Budgeted Hours (BH). Adverse Fixed Overhead Volume Variance indicates unabsorbed portion of Fixed Overheads because of underutilisation of Capacity.
How to Calculate	Fixed Overhead Volume Variance = Absorbed Fixed Overhead – Budgeted Fixed Overhead *or,* = (Standard Hours for Actual Output x Standard Fixed Overhead Rate) ***Minus*** (Budgeted Hours x Standard Fixed Overhead Rate) *or,* = (SH x SFOR) – (BH x SFOR) *or,* = (SH – BH) x SFOR
Division	Fixed Overhead Volume Variance may further be divided into Fixed Overhead Efficiency Variance and Fixed Overhead Capacity Variance.
Why arises	It may arise due to: (a) Poor Supervision (b) Poor Scheduling of Production Processes (c) Poor Working Conditions (d) Improperly set Standards (e) Shortage of Material (f) Shortage of Labour (g) Shortage of Power (h) Machine Break Down (i) Slump in Customer's Demand

Illustration 8. Calculate Fixed Overhead Volume Variance in Illustration 6.

Solution: Fixed Overhead Volume Variance = Absorbed Fixed Overhead – Budgeted Fixed Overhead
= (SH × SFOR) – (BH × SFOR)
= (32,500 × ₹ 1.50) – (30,000 × ₹ 1.50)
= ₹ 3,750 (F)

12.0 FIXED OVERHEAD EFFICIENCY VARIANCE (FOEV)

Meaning	Fixed Overhead Efficiency Variance is that portion of Fixed Overhead Volume Variance which arises due to the difference between Standard Hours for Actual Output (SH) and Actual Hours (AH). It indicates the increased or reduced output arising from efficiency above or below the standard which is expected.
How to calculate	Fixed Overhead Efficiency Variance is calculated as follows: Fixed Overhead Efficiency Variance = Absorbed Fixed Overhead – Standard Fixed Overhead *or,* = (Standard Hours for Actual Output x Standard Fixed Overhead Rate) ***Minus*** (Actual Hours – Standard Fixed Overhead Rate) *or,* = (SH × SFOR) – (AH × SFOR) *or,* = (SH – AH) × SFOR
Why arises	It may arise due to: (a) Poor Supervision (b) Poor Scheduling of Production Processes (c) Poor Working Conditions (d) Improperly set Standards

Illustration 9. Calculate Fixed Overhead Efficiency Variance in Illustration 6.

Solution: Fixed Overhead Efficiency Variance = Absorbed Fixed Overhead – Standard Fixed Overhead
= (SH × SFOR) – (AH × SFOR)
= (32,500 × ₹ 1.50) – (33,000 × ₹ 1.50) = ₹ 750 (A)

13.0 FIXED OVERHEAD CAPACITY VARIANCE (FOCV)

Meaning	Fixed Overhead Capacity Variance is that portion of Fixed Overhead Volume Variance which arises due to the difference between Actual Hours (AH) and Budgeted Hours (BH). It indicates working at higher or lower capacity usage than the standard.
How to Calculate	Fixed Overhead Capacity Variance = Standard Fixed Overhead – Budgeted Fixed Overhead *or,* = (Actual Hours × Standard Fixed Overhead Rate) – (Budgeted Hours × Standard Fixed Overhead Rate) *or,* = (AH × SFOR) – (BH × SFOR) *or,* = (AH – BH) × SFOR
Why arises	It may arise due to: (a) Shortage of Material (b) Shortage of Labour (c) Shortage of Power (d) Machine Break Down (e) Slump in Customer's Demand

Illustration 10. Calculate Fixed Overhead Capacity Variance in Illustration 6.

Solution: Fixed Overhead Capacity Variance = Standard Fixed Overhead – Budgeted Fixed Overhead
= (AH × SFOR) – (BH × SFOR)
= (33,000 × ₹ 1.50) – (30,000 × ₹ 1.50) = ₹ 4,500 (F)

14.0 FIXED OVERHEAD CALENDER VARIANCE (FOCV)

Meaning	Fixed Overhead Calender Variance is that portion of Fixed Overhead Volume Variance which arises due to the difference between the Actual Number of Working Days and the Budgeted Number of Working Days. In other words, it indicates the difference between Revised Budgeted Fixed Overheads and Original Budgeted Fixed Overheads.
How to Calculate	Fixed Overhead Calender Variance = Revised Budgeted Fixed Overheads – Original Budgeted Overheads *or,* = (Revised Budgeted Hours × Standard Fixed Overhead Rate) ***Minus*** (Original Budgeted Hours × Standard Fixed Overhead Rate) *or,* = (RBH × SFOR) – (BH × SFOR) *or,* = (RBH – BH) × SFOR *or,* = (Actual No. of Working Days – Budgeted Number of Working Days) × Standard Fixed Overhead Rate **Note:** Revised Budgeted Hours = $\frac{\text{Budgeted Hours}}{\text{Budgeted No. of Working Days}}$ × Actual No. of Working Days

Illustration 11. Tulsian Ltd. provides you the following information:

	Budget	*Actual*
Output (units)	15,000	16,250
Hours	30,000	33,000
Fixed Overhead	₹ 45,000	₹ 50,000
No. of Working Days	25	26

Required: Calculate Fixed Overhead Calender Variance.

Solution:

Method I:

Step 1: Revised Budgeted Hours

$$= \frac{\text{Budgeted Hours}}{\text{Budgeted No. of Working Days}} \times \text{Actual No. of Working Days}$$

$$= \frac{30,000}{25} \times 26 = 31,200$$

Step 2: Fixed Overhead Calender Variance = Revised Budgeted Overhead – Original Budgeted Overhead
= (RBH × SFOR) – (BH × SFOR)
= (31,200 × ₹ 1.50) – (30,000 × ₹ 1.50) = ₹ 1,800 (F)

Method II:

Step 1: Standard Fixed Overhead Rate per day

$$= \frac{\text{Budgeted Fixed Overheads}}{\text{Budgeted No. of Working Days}} = \frac{45,000}{25} = 1,800 \text{ per day}$$

Step 2: Fixed Overhead Calender Variance
= (Actual No. of Working Days – Budgeted No. of Working Days) × SFOR per day
= (26 – 25) × ₹ 1,800 = ₹ 1,800 (F)

15.0 REVISED FIXED OVERHEAD CAPACITY VARIANCE

When Overhead Calender Variance is calculated, Fixed Overhead Capacity Variance is to be calculated as follows:

Revised Overhead Capacity Variance
= Standard Fixed Overhead – Revised Budgeted Overhead
= (Actual Hours – Revised Budgeted Hours) × Standard Fixed Overhead Rate
or = (AH – RBH) × SFOR

Illustration 12. Calculate Revised Overhead Capacity Variance in Illustration 11.

Solution: Revised Overhead Capacity Variance = Standard Fixed Overhead – Revised Budgeted Overhead
= (AH × SFOR) – (RBH × SFOR)
= (33,000 × ₹ 1.50) – (31,200 × ₹ 1.50)
= ₹ 2,700 (F)

16.0 COMPUTATION OF VARIABLE OVERHEAD VARIANCES

Basic Calculations for Variable Overhead Variances

1. Absorbed Overheads (SH x SR) =	₹ ……..
2. Standard Overheads (AH x SR) =	₹ ……..
3. Actual Overheads	₹ ……..

Computation of Variances

A. Variable Overheads Efficiency Variance (1 – 2) = ₹ …….. – ₹ …….. = ₹ ……..
B. Variable Overheads Expenditure Variance (2 – 3) = ₹ …….. – ₹ …….. = ₹ ……..
C. Total Variable Overheads Variance (A + B) = ₹ ……..

17.0 COMPUTATION OF FIXED OVERHEAD VARIANCES WHEN THE ACTUAL NUMBER OF WORKING DAYS ARE EQUAL TO THE BUDGETED NUMBER OF WORKING DAYS

Basic Calculations for Fixed Overhead Variances

1. Absorbed Overheads (SH x SR) =	₹ ……..
2. Standard Overheads (AH x SR) =	₹ ……..
3. Budgeted Overheads (BH x SR) =	₹ ……..
4. Actual Overheads	₹ ……..

Computation of Variances

A. Fixed Overheads Efficiency Variance (1 – 2) = ₹ …….. – ₹ …….. = ₹ ……..
B. Fixed Overheads Capacity Variance (2 – 3) = ₹ …….. – ₹ …….. = ₹ ……..
C. Total Fixed Overheads Volume Variance (A + B) = ₹ ……..
D. Fixed Overheads Expenditure Variance (3 – 4) = ₹ …….. – ₹ …….. = ₹ ……..
E. Total Fixed Overheads Variance (C + D) = ₹ ……..

18.0 COMPUTATION OF FIXED OVERHEAD VARIANCES WHEN THE ACTUAL NUMBER OF WORKING DAYS ARE DIFFERENT FROM THE BUDGETED NUMBER OF WORKING DAYS

Basic Calculations for Fixed Overhead Variances

1. Absorbed Overheads (SH x SR) =	₹ ……..
2. Standard Overheads (AH x SR) =	₹ ……..

3. Revised Budgeted Overheads (RBH x SR) =	₹ ....
4. Budgeted Overheads (BH x SR) =	₹ ....
5. Actual Overheads	₹ ....

Computation of Variances

A. Fixed Overheads Efficiency Variance (1 – 2) = ₹ .... – ₹ .... = ₹ ....
B. Fixed Overheads Capacity Variance (2 – 3) = ₹ .... – ₹ .... = ₹ ....
C. Fixed Overheads Calendar Variance (3 – 4) = ₹ .... – ₹ .... = ₹ ....
D. Total Fixed Overheads Volume Variance (A + B + C) = ₹ ....
E. Fixed Overheads Expenditure Variance (4 – 5) = ₹ .... – ₹ .... = ₹ ....
F. Total Fixed Overheads Variance (D + E) = ₹ ....

Illustration 13. From the following information compute all Overhead Variances:

	Fixed	*Variable*
Absorbed Overheads	₹ 48,750	₹ 65,000
Standard Overheads	₹ 49,500	₹ 66,000
Budgeted Overheads	₹ 45,000	₹ 60,000
Actual Overheads	₹ 50,000	₹ 68,000

Solution: **BASIC CALCULATIONS FOR VARIABLE OVERHEAD VARIANCES**

1. Absorbed Overheads (SH x SR) =	₹ 65,000
2. Standard Overheads (AH x SR) =	₹ 66,000
3. Actual Overheads	₹ 68,000

Computation of Variances

A. Variable Overheads Efficiency Variance (1 – 2) = ₹ 65,000 – ₹ 66,000 = ₹ 1,000 (A)
B. Variable Overheads Expenditure Variance (2 – 3) = ₹ 66,000 – ₹ 68,000 = ₹ 2,000 (A)
C. Total Variable Overheads Variance (A + B) = ₹ 3,000 (A)

BASIC CALCULATIONS FOR FIXED OVERHEAD VARIANCES

1. Absorbed Overheads (SH × SR) =	₹ 48,750
2. Standard Overheads (AH × SR) =	₹ 49,500
3. Budgeted Overheads (BH × SR) =	₹ 45,000
4. Actual Overheads	₹ 50,000

Computation of Variances

A. Fixed Overheads Efficiency Variance (1 – 2) = ₹ 48,750 – ₹ 49,500 = ₹ 750 (A)
B. Fixed Overheads Capacity Variance (2 – 3) = ₹ 49,500 – ₹ 45,000 = ₹ 4,500 (F)
C. Total Fixed Overheads Volume Variance (A + B) = ₹ 3,750 (F)
D. Fixed Overheads Expenditure Variance (3 – 4) = ₹ 45,000 – ₹ 50,000 = ₹ 5,000 (A)
E. Total Fixed Overheads Variance (C + D) = ₹ 1,250 (A)

Illustration 14. Calculate all the Overhead Variances from the following information provided by Bharat Tulsian Ltd.

	Budget	*Actual*
Fixed Overheads	₹ 30,000	₹ 30,690
Variable Overheads	₹ 10,000	₹ 8,910
Hours	10,000	9,900
Output	5,000	4,500

Solution:

Basic Calculations:

1. Standard Hours for Actual Output (SH) = $\frac{10,000}{5,000} \times 4,500$ = 9,000 hours

2. Standard Fixed Overhead Rate per Hour = $\frac{30,000}{10,000}$ = ₹ 3 per hour

3. Standard Variable Overhead Rate per Hour = $\frac{10,000}{10,000}$ = ₹ 1 per hour

BASIC CALCULATIONS FOR VARIABLE OVERHEAD VARIANCES

1. Absorbed Overheads (SH x SR) =	₹ 9,000
2. Standard Overheads (AH x SR) =	₹ 9,900
3. Actual Overheads =	₹ 8,910

Computation of Variances

A. Variable Overheads Efficiency Variance (1 – 2) = ₹ 9,000 – ₹ 9,900 = ₹ 900 (A)
B. Variable Overheads Expenditure Variance (2 – 3) = ₹ 9,900 – ₹ 8,910 = ₹ 990 (F)
C. Total Variable Overheads Variance (A + B) = ₹ 90 (F)

BASIC CALCULATIONS FOR FIXED OVERHEAD VARIANCES

1. Absorbed Overheads (SH x SR) =	₹ 27,000
2. Standard Overheads (AH x SR) =	₹ 29,700
3. Budgeted Overheads (BH x SR) =	₹ 30,000
4. Actual Overheads =	₹ 30,690

Computation of Variances

A. Fixed Overheads Efficiency Variance (1 – 2) = ₹ 27,000 – ₹ 29,700 = ₹ 2,700 (A)
B. Fixed Overheads Capacity Variance (2 – 3) = ₹ 29,700 – ₹ 30,000 = ₹ 300 (A)
C. Total Fixed Overheads Volume Variance (A + B) = ₹ 3,000 (A)
D. Fixed Overheads Expenditure Variance (3 – 4) = ₹ 30,000 – ₹ 30,690 = ₹ 690 (A)
E. Total Fixed Overheads Variance (C + D) = ₹ 3,690 (A)

Illustration 15. Calculate all the overhead variances from the following information provided by Tushar Tulsion Ltd:

	Budget	*Actual*
No. of Working days	25	25
Working hours per day	8	9
No. of Workers	150	132
Output per man-hour (in units)	1/2	1/2.2
Fixed Overheads	₹ 90,000	₹ 92,070
Variable Overheads	₹ 30,000	₹ 26,730

Solution:

1. Budgeted Hours (BH) = 25 × 8 × 150 = 30,000 hours
2. Budgeted Output = 25 × 8 × 150 × 1/2 = 15,000 units
3. Actual Hours (AH) = 25 × 9 × 132 = 29,700 hours
4. Actual Output = 25 × 9 × 132 × 1/2.2 = 13,500 units
5. Standard Hours (SH) = $\frac{\text{Budgeted Hours}}{\text{Budgeted Output}}$ × Actual Output = $\frac{30,000}{15,000}$ × 13,500 = 27,000 hours

6. Standard Fixed Overhead Rate per Hour = $\frac{90,000}{30,000}$ = ₹ 3 per hour

7. Standard Variable Overhead Rate per Hour = $\frac{30,000}{30,000}$ = ₹ 1 per hour

BASIC CALCULATIONS FOR VARIABLE OVERHEAD VARIANCES

1. Absorbed Overheads (SH x SR) =	₹ 27,000
2. Standard Overheads (AH x SR) =	₹ 29,700
3. Actual Overheads =	₹ 26,730

Computation of Variances

A. Variable Overheads Efficiency Variance (1 – 2) = ₹ 27,000 – ₹ 29,700 = ₹ 2,700 (A)
B. Variable Overheads Expenditure Variance (2 – 3) = ₹ 29,700 – ₹ 26,730 = ₹ 2,970 (F)

C. Total Variable Overheads Variance (A + B) = ₹ 270 (F)

BASIC CALCULATIONS FOR FIXED OVERHEAD VARIANCES

1. Absorbed Overheads (SH x SR) =	₹ 81,000
2. Standard Overheads (AH x SR) =	₹ 89,100
3. Budgeted Overheads (BH x SR) =	₹ 90,000
4. Actual Overheads =	₹ 92,070

Computation of Variances

A. Fixed Overheads Efficiency Variance (1 – 2) = ₹ 81,000 – ₹ 89,100 = ₹ 8,100 (A)
B. Fixed Overheads Capacity Variance (2 – 3) = ₹ 89,100 – ₹ 90,000 = ₹ 900 (A)

C. Total Fixed Overheads Volume Variance (A + B) = ₹ 9,000 (A)
D. Fixed Overheads Expenditure Variance (3 – 4) = ₹ 90,000 – ₹ 92,070 = ₹ 2,070 (A)

E. Total Fixed Overheads Variance (C + D) = ₹ 11,070 (A)

Illustration 16. If in the preceding Illustration 15 the actual number of working days were 26, then compute all the Overhead Variances (including Overhead Calendar Variance).

Solution:

1. Budgeted Hours (BH) = 25 × 8 × 150 = 30,000 hours
2. Budgeted Output = 25 × 8 × 150 × 1/2 = 15,000 units
3. Actual Hours (AH) = 26 × 9 × 132 = 30,888 hours
4. Actual Output = 26 × 9 × 132 × 1/2.2 = 14,040 units
5. Standard Hours (SH) = $\frac{\text{Budgeted Hours}}{\text{Budgeted Output}}$ × Actual Output = $\frac{30,000}{15,000}$ ×14,040 = 28,080 hours
6. Standard Fixed Overhead Rate per Hour (SR) = $\frac{90,000}{30,000}$ = ₹ 3 per hour
7. Standard Variable Overhead Rate per Hour (SR) = $\frac{30,000}{30,000}$ = ₹ 1 per hour
8. Revised Budgeted Hours (R.B.H.) = 26 × 8 × 150 = 31,200 hours

BASIC CALCULATIONS FOR VARIABLE OVERHEAD VARIANCES

1. Absorbed Overheads (SH x SR) =	₹ 28,080
2. Standard Overheads (AH x SR) =	₹ 30,888
3. Actual Overheads = s	₹ 26,730

Computation of Variances

A. Variable Overheads Efficiency Variance (1 – 2) = ₹ 28,080 – ₹ 30,888 = ₹ 2,808 (A)
B. Variable Overheads Expenditure Variance (2 – 3) = ₹ 30,888 – ₹ 26,730 = ₹ 4,158 (F)

C. Total Variable Overheads Variance (A + B) = ₹ 1,350 (F)

BASIC CALCULATIONS FOR FIXED OVERHEAD VARIANCES

1. Absorbed Overheads (SH x SR) =	₹ 84,240
2. Standard Overheads (AH x SR) =	₹ 92,664
3. Revised Budgeted Overheads (RBH x SR) =	₹ 93,600
4. Budgeted Overheads (BH x SR) =	₹ 90,000
5. Actual Overheads	₹ 92,070

Computation of Variances

A. Fixed Overheads Efficiency Variance (1 – 2) = ₹.84,240 – ₹.92,664 = ₹ 8,424 (A)
B. Fixed Overheads Capacity Variance (2 – 3) = ₹ 92,664 – ₹ 93,600 = ₹ 936 (A)
C. Fixed Overheads Calendar Variance (3 – 4) = ₹ 93,600 – ₹.90,000 = ₹ 3,600 (F)
D. Total Fixed Overheads Volume Variance (A + B + C) = ₹ 5,760 (A)
E. Fixed Overheads Expenditure Variance (4 – 5) = ₹ 90,000 – ₹ 92,070 = ₹ 2,070 (A)

F. Total Fixed Overheads Variance (D + E) = ₹ 7,830 (A)

Illustration 17. Calculate all Fixed Overhead Variances from the following:

	Budget	*Actual*
No. of Working Days per Month	20	22
Man Hours per Day	8,000	8,400
Output per Man Hour in Units	1.0	1.2
Standard Overhead Rate per Man Hour	₹ 2	
Actual Fixed Expenses per Month		₹ 3,25,000

Solution:

1. Actual Hours Worked = 8,400 Hours x 22 Days = 1,84,800 Hours
2. Actual Output = 8,400 Hours x 22 Days x 1.2 Units per Hour = 2,21,760 Units
3. Standard Hours for Actual Output = 2,21,760 Units x 1 Hour = 2,21,760 Hours
4. Budgeted Hours in Budgeted Days = 8,000 Hours x 20 Days = 1,60,000 Hours
5. Budgeted Overheads = 8,000 Hours x 20 Days x ₹ 2 per Hour = ₹ 3,20,000
6. Revised Budgeted Hours in Actual Working Days = 8,000 x 22 Days = 1,76,000 Hours

BASIC CALCULATIONS FOR FIXED OVERHEAD VARIANCES

1. Absorbed Overheads (SH x SR) =	₹ 4,43,520
2. Standard Overheads (AH x SR) =	₹ 3,69,600
3. Revised Budgeted Overheads (RBH x SR) =	₹ 3,52,000
4. Budgeted Overheads (BH x SR) =	₹ 3,20,000
5. Actual Overheads	₹ 3,25,000

Computation of Variances

A. Fixed Overheads Efficiency Variance (1 – 2) = ₹ 4,43,520 – ₹ 3,69,600 = ₹ 73,920 (F)
B. Fixed Overheads Capacity Variance (2 – 3) = ₹ 3,69,600 – ₹ 3,52,000 = ₹ 17,600 (F)
C. Fixed Overheads Calendar Variance (3 – 4) = ₹ 3,52,000 – ₹ 3,20,000 = ₹ 32,000 (F)

D. Total Fixed Overheads Volume Variance (A + B + C) = ₹ 1,23,520 (F)

E. Fixed Overheads Expenditure Variance (4 – 5) = ₹ 3,20,000 – ₹ 3,25,000 = ₹ 5,000 (A)

F. Total Fixed Overheads Variance (D + E) = ₹ 1,18,520 (F)

Illustration 18. Tulsian Ltd. provides you the following information:

Standard Overhead Absorption Rate per Hour	₹ 3
Standard Overhead Absorption Rate per Unit	₹ 18
Budgeted Production	7,500 Units
Actual Production	7,610 Units
Actual Overheads	₹ 1,45,360 out of which ₹ 45,360 were Fixed
Actual Hours	46,830

Overheads are based on the following Flexible Budget:

Production (Units)	6,000	6,750	8,250
Total Overheads	1,17,000	1,26,000	1,44,000

Required: Calculate all Overhead Variances.

Solution:

1. Variable Overhead Rate per Unit $= \dfrac{\text{Difference in Total Overheads at Two Levels}}{\text{Difference in Output at Two Levels}}$

$$= \frac{1{,}44{,}000 - 1{,}26{,}000}{8{,}250 - 6{,}750} = \frac{18{,}000}{1{,}500} = ₹\ 12$$

2. Fixed Overhead = ₹ 1,44,000 – (8,250 x ₹ 12) = ₹ 45,000

3. Standard Time per Unit $= \dfrac{\text{Standard Overhead Rate per Unit}}{\text{Standard Overhead Rate per Hour}} = \dfrac{18}{3} = 6$ Hours

4. Budgeted Hours = 7,500 x 6 = 45,000 Hours

5. Standard Fixed Overhead Rate per Hour $= \dfrac{\text{Fixed Overheads}}{\text{Budgeted Hours}} = \dfrac{45{,}000}{45{,}000} =$ ₹ 1 per Hour

6. Standard Variable Overhead Rate per Hour $= \dfrac{\text{Variable Overheads}}{\text{Budgeted Hours}}$

$$= \frac{(7{,}500 \times 12)}{45{,}000} = ₹\ 2 \text{ per Hour}$$

7. Standard Hours for Actual Output = 7,610 x 6 = 45,660

BASIC CALCULATIONS FOR VARIABLE OVERHEAD VARIANCES

1. Absorbed Overheads (SH x SR) =	₹ 91,320
2. Standard Overheads (AH x SR) =	₹ 93,660
3. Actual Overheads =	₹ 1,00,000

Computation of Variances

A. Variable Overheads Efficiency Variance (1 – 2) = ₹ 91,320 – ₹ 93,660 = ₹ 2,340 (A)
B. Variable Overheads Expenditure Variance (2 – 3) = ₹ 93,660 – ₹ 1,00,000 = ₹ 6,340 (A)
C. Total Variable Overheads Variance (A + B) = ₹ 8,680 (A)

BASIC CALCULATIONS FOR FIXED OVERHEAD VARIANCES

1. Absorbed Overheads (SH x SR) =	₹ 45,660
2. Standard Overheads (AH x SR) =	₹ 46,830
3. Budgeted Overheads (BH x SR) =	₹ 45,000
4. Actual Overheads =	₹ 45,360

Computation of Variances

A. Fixed Overheads Efficiency Variance (1 – 2) = ₹ 45,660 – ₹ 46,830 = ₹ 1,170 (A)
B. Fixed Overheads Capacity Variance (2 – 3) = ₹ 46,830 – ₹ 45,000 = ₹ 1,830 (F)
C. Total Fixed Overheads Volume Variance (A + B) = ₹ 660 (F)
D. Fixed Overheads Expenditure Variance (3 – 4) = ₹ 45,000 – ₹ 45,360 = ₹ 360 (A)
E. Total Fixed Overheads Variance (C + D) = ₹ 300 (F)

Illustration 19. From the following information of CAS Ltd. compute all Overhead Variances:

	Budget	*Actual*
Indirect Material	₹ 0.40 per Hour	₹ 0.50 per Hour
Indirect Labour	₹ 0.60 per Hour	₹ 0.60 per Hour
Maintenance	₹ 0.40 per Hour	₹ 0.45 per Hour
Power	₹ 0.30 per Hour	₹ 0.32 per Hour
Sundries	₹ 0.30 per Hour	₹ 0.29 per Hour
Fixed Overhead	₹ 240	₹ 250
Output	9,600 Units	12,160 Units
Hours	120	156

Solution:

1. Budgeted Variable Overheads = 120 Hours x (₹ 0.40 + ₹ 0.60 + ₹ 0.40 + ₹ 0.30 + ₹ 0.30) = ₹ 240
2. Actual Variable Overheads = 156 Hours x (₹ 0.50 + ₹ 0.60 + ₹ 0.45 + ₹ 0.32 + ₹ 0.29) = ₹ 337
3. Standard Hours for Actual Output (SH) = $\frac{\text{Budgeted Hours}}{\text{Budgeted Output}} \times \text{Actual Output}$

$$= \frac{120}{9,600} \times 12,160 = 152$$

BASIC CALCULATIONS FOR VARIABLE OVERHEAD VARIANCES

1. Absorbed Overheads (SH x SR) =	₹ 304
2. Standard Overheads (AH x SR) =	₹ 312
3. Actual Overheads =	₹ 337

Computation of Variances

A. Variable Overheads Efficiency Variance (1 – 2) = ₹ 304 – ₹ 312 = ₹ 8 (A)
B. Variable Overheads Expenditure Variance (2 – 3) = ₹ 312 – ₹ 337 = ₹ 25 (A)
C. Total Variable Overheads Variance (A + B) = ₹ 33 (A)

BASIC CALCULATIONS FOR FIXED OVERHEAD VARIANCES

1. Absorbed Overheads (SH x SR) =	₹ 304
2. Standard Overheads (AH x SR) =	₹ 312
3. Budgeted Overheads (BH x SR) =	₹ 240
4. Actual Overheads =	₹ 250

Computation of Variances

A. Fixed Overheads Efficiency Variance (1 – 2) = ₹ 304 – ₹ 312 = ₹ 8 (A)
B. Fixed Overheads Capacity Variance (2 – 3) = ₹ 312 – ₹ 240 = ₹ 72 (F)
C. Total Fixed Overheads Volume Variance (A + B) = ₹ 64 (F)
D. Fixed Overheads Expenditure Variance (3 – 4) = ₹ 240 – ₹ 250 = ₹ 10 (A)
E. Total Fixed Overheads Variance (C + D) = ₹ 54 (F)

Illustration 20. Calculate all the overhead variances from the following information provided by Tulsian Ltd.

(a) *Budgeted and Actual Data :*

	Budget	*Actual*
Fixed Overheads	₹ 28,500	₹ 29,340
Variable Overheads	8,800	7,830
Semi-variable Overheads	2,700	2,430
Hours	10,000	9,900
Output	5,000	?

(b) *Actual Opening Stock and Closing Stock:*

	Opening Stock	*Closing Stock*
Work-in-progress	50 units (Materials fully supplied but 40% converted)	100 units (Materials fully supplied but 80% converted)
Finished Goods	200 units	100 units

(c) *Actual Sales of Finished Goods* — 4,540 units

(d) Semi-variable overhead consists of five-ninth fixed expenses and four-ninth variable.

Solution:

Basic Calculations:

1. Budgeted Fixed Overheads = ₹ 28,500 + (2,700 × 5/9) = ₹ 30,000
2. Budgeted Variable Overheads = ₹ 8,800 + (2,700 × 4/9) = ₹ 10,000
3. Standard Fixed Overhead Rate per Hour = ₹ 30,000/10,000 = ₹ 3 per hour
4. Standard Variable Overhead Rate per Hour = ₹ 10,000/10,000 = ₹ 1 per hour
5. Actual Fixed Overheads = ₹ 29,340 + (2,430 × 5/9) = ₹ 30,690
6. Actual Variable Overheads = ₹ 7,830 + (2,430 × 4/9) = ₹ 8,910
7. Output Completed = Sales + Closing Stock of finished goods – Opening Stock of finished goods
   = 4,540 + 100 – 200 = 4,440 units
8. *Calculation of No. of equivalent output for overhead purposes*

	No. of Units	*Degree of completion*	*Equivalent units*
Output completed	4,440	100%	4,440
Add: Closing W/P	100	80%	80
Less: Opening W/P	50	40%	20
			4,500 units

9. Standard Hours for Actual Output (SH) = $\frac{10,000}{5,000} \times 4,500 = 9,000$ Hours

Now, the solution is same as in Illustration 14

Illustration 21. Calculate all the overheads variances from following information provided by Jalan Ltd:

(a) *Budgeted and Actual Data:*

	Budget for the Year 2014	*Actual for April 2014*
No. of working days	300	26
Working hours per day	8	9
No. of Workers	150	132
Output per man-hour in units	1/2	?
Fixed Overheads	10,26,000	88,020
Variable Overheads	3,16,800	23,490
Semi-variable Overheads	97,200	7,290

(b) *Actual Opening Stock and Closing Stock :*

	Opening	Closing
Work-in-progress	150 units (Materials fully supplied but 40% converted)	300 units (Materials fully supplied but 80% converted)
Finished Goods	600 units	300 units

(c) *Actual Sales of Finished Goods* — 14160 units

(d) Semi-variable Overhead consists of five-ninth fixed expenses and four-ninth variable.

Solution:

Basic Calculations:

1. Budgeted Fixed Overhead for 1 month $= \left[\frac{10,26,000}{12} + \left(\frac{97,200}{12} \times \frac{5}{9}\right)\right]$

   $= ₹\ 85,500 + ₹\ 4,500 = ₹\ 90,000$

2. Budgeted Variable Overhead for 1 month $= \left[\frac{3,16,800}{12} + \left(\frac{97,200}{12} \times \frac{4}{9}\right)\right]$

   $= ₹\ 26,400 + ₹\ 3,600 = ₹\ 30,000$

3. Budgeted Hours for 1 month $= \frac{300}{12} \times 8 \times 150 = 30,000$ hours
4. Budgeted output for 1 month $= \frac{300}{12} \times 8 \times 150 \times ½ = 15,000$ hours
5. Standard Fixed Overheads Rate per Hour = ₹ 90,000/30,000 = ₹ 3 per hour
6. Standard Variable Overhead Rate per Hour = ₹ 30,000/30,000 = ₹ 1 per hour
7. Revised Budgeted Hours = 26 × 8 × 150 = 31,200 hours
8. Actual Hours = 26 × 9 × 132 = 30,888 hours
9. Actual Fixed Overheads = ₹ 88,020 + (7,290 × 5/9) = ₹ 92,070
10. Actual Variable Overheads = ₹ 23,490 + (7,290 × 4/9) = ₹ 26,730
11. Actual Output Completed = 14,160 + 300 – 600 = 13,860 units
12. *Calculation of No. of Equivalent Output for Overhead Purpose*

	No. of Units	*Degree of Completion*	*Equivalent Units*
Output completed	13,860	100%	13,860
Add : Closing W/P	300	80%	240
Less : Opening W/P	150	40%	60
			14,040

13. Standard Hours for equivalent output (SH) $= \frac{30,000}{15,000} \times 14,040 = 28,080$ hours

Now, the solution is same as in Illustration 16

SOLVED PROBLEMS

Problem 1. In Department A the following data is submitted for the week ended 31st October:

Standard Output for 40 hours per week	1,400 units
Standard Fixed Overhead	₹ 1,400
Actual Output	1,200 units
Actual Hours Worked	32 hours
Actual Fixed Overhead	₹ 1,500

Required: Prepare a Statement of Variances.

Solution:

Basic Calculations:

1. Standard Hours for Actual Output (SH) $\frac{40}{1,400} \times 1,200 = 34.286$
2. Standard Overhead Rate (SR) = $\frac{1,400}{40}$ = ₹ 35 per hour
3. Actual Overhead Rate (AR) = $\frac{1,500}{32}$ = ₹ 46.875

BASIC CALCULATIONS FOR FIXED OVERHEAD VARIANCES

1. Absorbed Overheads (SH x SR) =	₹ 1,200
2. Standard Overheads (AH x SR) =	₹ 1,120
3. Budgeted Overheads (BH x SR) =	₹ 1,400
4. Actual Overheads =	₹ 1,500

Computation of Variances

A. Fixed Overheads Efficiency Variance (1 – 2) = ₹ 1,200 – ₹ 1,120 = ₹ 80 (F)
B. Fixed Overheads Capacity Variance (2 – 3) = ₹ 1,120 – ₹ 1,400 = ₹ 280 (A)
C. Total Fixed Overheads Volume Variance (A + B) = ₹ 200 (A)
D. Fixed Overheads Expenditure Variance (3 – 4) = ₹ 1,400 – ₹ 1,500 = ₹ 100 (A)
E. Total Fixed Overheads Variance (C + D) = ₹ 300 (A)

Problem 2. The following information is available from the records of a factory:

	Budget	*Actual*
Fixed overhead for June	₹ 10,000	₹ 12,000
Production in June (units)	2,000	2,100
Standard time per unit (hours)	10	
Actual hours worked in June		22,000

Required: Compute Fixed Overhead Cost Variance, Expenditure Variance, Volume Variance, Capacity Variance, Efficiency Variance.

Solution:

Basic Calculations:

1. Standard Hours for Actual output (SH) = 2100 × 10 = 21,000
2. Standard Overhead Rate (SR) = ₹ 10,000/20,000 = ₹ 0.50 per hour
3. Actual Overhead Rate (AR) = ₹ 12,000/22,000 = ₹ 0.545 per hour

BASIC CALCULATIONS FOR FIXED OVERHEAD VARIANCES

1. Absorbed Overheads (SH x SR) =	₹ 10,500
2. Standard Overheads (AH x SR) =	₹ 11,000
3. Budgeted Overheads (BH x SR) =	₹ 10,000
4. Actual Overheads =	₹ 12,000

Computation of Variances

A. Fixed Overheads Efficiency Variance (1 – 2) = ₹ 10,500 – ₹ 11,000 = ₹ 500 (A)
B. Fixed Overheads Capacity Variance (2 – 3) = ₹ 11,000 – ₹ 10,000 = ₹ 1,000 (F)
C. Total Fixed Overheads Volume Variance (A + B) = ₹ 500 (F)
D. Fixed Overheads Expenditure Variance (3 – 4) = ₹ 10,000 – ₹ 12,000 = ₹ 2,000 (A)
E. Total Fixed Overheads Variance (C + D) = ₹ 1,500 (A)

Problem 3. The following budget was prepared for the overhead of Department X:

Budget for period	
Fixed Overhead	₹ 5,600
Variable Overhead	₹ 10,400
Machine Hours	1,600
Standard Hours of Production	1,600
After the period the actual results were :	
Total Overhead	₹ 17,400
Machine Hours	1,630
Standard Hours Produced	1,590

Required: Calculate the overhead variances for the period.

Solution:

Basic Calculations:

1. Standard Variable Overhead Rate = $\frac{10,400}{1600}$ = ₹ 6.50
2. Standard Fixed Overhead Rate = $\frac{5,600}{1600}$ = ₹ 3.50
3. **Assumption:** Actual Variable Overheads have been incurred at Standard Variable Overhead Rate (i.e., ₹ 6.50 per hour)

BASIC CALCULATIONS FOR VARIABLE OVERHEAD VARIANCES

1. Absorbed Overheads (SH x SR) =	₹ 10,335
2. Standard Overheads (AH x SR) =	₹ 10,595
3. Actual Overheads =	₹ 10,595

Computation of Variances

A. Variable Overheads Efficiency Variance (1 – 2) = ₹ 10,335 – ₹ 10,595 = ₹ 260 (A)
B. Variable Overheads Expenditure Variance (2 – 3) = ₹ 10,595 – ₹ 10,595 = ₹ 0
C. Total Variable Overheads Variance (A + B) = ₹ 260 (A)

BASIC CALCULATIONS FOR FIXED OVERHEAD VARIANCES

1. Absorbed Overheads (SH x SR) =	₹ 5,565
2. Standard Overheads (AH x SR) =	₹ 5,705
3. Budgeted Overheads (BH x SR) =	₹ 5,600
4. Actual Overheads =	₹ 6,805

Computation of Variances

A. Fixed Overheads Efficiency Variance (1 – 2) = ₹ 5,565 – ₹ 5,705 = ₹ 140 (A)
B. Fixed Overheads Capacity Variance (2 – 3) = ₹ 5,705 – ₹ 5,600 = ₹ 105 (F)
C. Total Fixed Overheads Volume Variance (A + B) = ₹ 35 (A)
D. Fixed Overheads Expenditure Variance (3 – 4) = ₹ 5,600 – ₹ 6,805 = ₹ 1,205 (A)
E. Total Fixed Overheads Variance (C + D) = ₹ 1,240 (A)

Problem 4. Bharat Ltd. provides you the following information:

Items	*Budget*	*Actual*
No. of Working days	20	22
Man-hours per day	8,000	8,400
Output per man-hour (in units)	1.0	0.9
Overhead Cost (₹)	1,60,000	1,68,000

Required: Calculate Overhead Variances.

Solution:

Basic Calculations:

1. Budgeted Hours (BH) = 20 × 8000 = 1,60,000
2. Budgeted Output = 20 × 8000 × 1.0 = 1,60,000 units
3. Actual Hours (AH) = 22 × 8400 = 1,84,800
4. Actual Output = 22 × 8400 × 0.9 = 1,66,320 units
5. Standard Hours (SH) = $\frac{1,60,000}{1,60,000}$ × 1,66,320 = 1,66,320
6. Standard Fixed Overhead Rate per Hour = $\frac{1,60,000}{1,60,000}$ = ₹ 1 per hour
7. Revised Budgeted Hours (RBH) = 22 × 8,000 = 1,76,000 hours

BASIC CALCULATIONS FOR FIXED OVERHEAD VARIANCES

1. Absorbed Overheads (SH x SR) =	₹ 1,66,320
2. Standard Overheads (AH x SR) =	₹ 1,84,800
3. Revised Budgeted Overheads (RBH x SR) =	₹ 1,76,000
4. Budgeted Overheads (BH x SR) =	₹ 1,60,000
5. Actual Overheads	₹ 1,68,000

Computation of Variances

A. Fixed Overheads Efficiency Variance (1 – 2) = ₹.1,66,320 – ₹ 1,84,800	= ₹ 18,480 (A)
B. Fixed Overheads Capacity Variance (2 – 3) = ₹ 1,84,800 – ₹ 1,76,000	= ₹ 8,800 (F)
C. Fixed Overheads Calendar Variance (3 – 4) = ₹ 1,76,000 – ₹.1,60,000	= ₹ 16,000 (F)
D. Total Fixed Overheads Volume Variance (A + B + C)	= ₹ 6,320 (F)
E. Fixed Overheads Expenditure Variance (4 – 5) = ₹ 1,60,000 – ₹ 1,68,000	= ₹ 8,000 (A)
F. Total Fixed Overheads Variance (D + E)	= ₹ 1,680 (A)

Problem 5. S.V. Ltd. has furnished you the following data:

	Budget	*Actual*
No. of Working Days	25	27
Production in units	20,000	22,000
Fixed Overheads	₹ 30,000	31,000

Budgeted fixed overhead rate is ₹ 1.00 per hour. In July 20X9, the actual hours worked were 31,500.

Required : Calculate the following overhead variances:

Efficiency Variance, Capacity Variance, Calendar Variance, Volume Variance, Expenditure Variance, Total Overhead Variance.

Solution:

Basic Calculations:

1. Budgeted Hours (BH) = ₹ 30,000/₹ 1 = 30,000 hours
2. Standard hours for Actual output (SH) = $\frac{30,000}{20,000}$ × 22,000 = 33,000 hours
3. Revised Budgeted Hours (RBH) = $\frac{30,000}{25}$ × 27 = 32,400 hours
4. Actual Overhead Rate = $\frac{31,000}{31,500}$ = 0.984

BASIC CALCULATIONS FOR FIXED OVERHEAD VARIANCES

1. Absorbed Overheads (SH x SR) =	₹ 33,000
2. Standard Overheads (AH x SR) =	₹ 31,500
3. Revised Budgeted Overheads (RBH x SR) =	₹ 32,400
4. Budgeted Overheads (BH x SR) =	₹ 30,000
5. Actual Overheads	₹ 31,000

Computation of Variances

A. Fixed Overheads Efficiency Variance (1 – 2) = ₹.33,000 – ₹ 31,500 = ₹ 1,500 (F)
B. Fixed Overheads Capacity Variance (2 – 3) = ₹ 31,500 – ₹ 32,400 = ₹ 900 (A)
C. Fixed Overheads Calendar Variance (3 – 4) = ₹ 32,400 – ₹.30,000 = ₹ 2,400 (F)
D. Total Fixed Overheads Volume Variance (A + B + C) = ₹ 3,000 (F)
E. Fixed Overheads Expenditure Variance (4 – 5) = ₹ 30,000 – ₹ 31,000 = ₹ 1,000 (A)
F. Total Fixed Overheads Variance (D + E) = ₹ 2,000 (F)

Problem 6. The following information was obtained from the records of a manufacturing unit using Standard Costing System:

	Budget	*Actual*
Production	4,000 Units	3,800 Units
Working Days	20	21
Fixed Overhead	₹ 40,000	₹ 39,000
Variable Overhead	₹ 12,000	₹ 12,000

Required : Calculate the following Overhead Variances :

(a) Variable Overhead Variances
(b) Fixed Overhead Variances
(i) Expenditure Variance; (ii) Volume Variance; (iii) Efficiency Variance ; (iv) Calendar Variance
(c) Also prepare a Reconciliation Statement for the Standard Fixed Expenses worked out at Standard Fixed Overhead Rate and the Actual Fixed Overhead.

Solution:

Basic Calculations:

1. Assumption: Working Hours per Day = 8 hours
2. Budgeted Hours (BH) = 20 × 8 = 160 hours
3. Standard Hours for Actual Output (SH) = $\frac{160}{4,000} \times 3,800 = 152$
4. Actual Hours for Actual Output (AH) = 21 × 8 = 168
5. Revised Budgeted Hours (RBH) = $\frac{160}{20} \times 21 = 168$
6. Standard Fixed Overhead Rate per Hour = ₹ $\frac{40,000}{160} = 250$
7. Standard Variable Overhead Rate per Hour = ₹ $\frac{12,000}{160} = 75$

(a) BASIC CALCULATIONS FOR VARIABLE OVERHEAD VARIANCES

1. Absorbed Overheads (SH x SR) =	₹ 11,400
2. Standard Overheads (AH x SR) =	₹ 12,600
3. Actual Overheads =	₹ 12,000

Computation of Variances

A. Variable Overheads Efficiency Variance (1 – 2) = ₹ 11,400 – ₹ 12,600 = ₹ 1,200 (A)
B. Variable Overheads Expenditure Variance (2 – 3) = ₹ 12,600 – ₹ 12,000 = ₹ 600 (F)
C. Total Variable Overheads Variance (A + B) = ₹ 600 (A)

(b) BASIC CALCULATIONS FOR FIXED OVERHEAD VARIANCES

1. Absorbed Overheads (SH x SR) =	₹ 38,000
2. Standard Overheads (AH x SR) =	₹ 42,000
3. Revised Budgeted Overheads (RBH x SR) =	₹ 42,000
4. Budgeted Overheads (BH x SR) =	₹ 40,000
5. Actual Overheads	₹ 39,000

Computation of Variances

A. Fixed Overheads Efficiency Variance (1 – 2) = ₹.38,000 – ₹.42,000 = ₹ 4,000 (A)
B. Fixed Overheads Capacity Variance (2 – 3) = ₹ 42,000 – ₹ 42,000 = Nil
C. Fixed Overheads Calendar Variance (3 – 4) = ₹ 42,000 – ₹.40,000 = ₹ 2,000 (F)
D. Total Fixed Overheads Volume Variance (A + B + C) = ₹ 2,000 (A)
E. Fixed Overheads Expenditure Variance (4 – 5) = ₹ 40,000 – ₹ 39,000 = ₹ 1,000 (F)
F. Total Fixed Overheads Variance (D + E) = ₹ 1,000 (A)

(c) RECONCILIATION STATEMENT

	₹
A. Standard Fixed Expenses [152 × ₹ 250]	38,000
B. *Less :* Fixed Overhead Expenditure Variance	1,000 (F)
C. *Less :* Fixed Overhead Calendar Variance	2,000 (F)
D. *Add :* Fixed Overhead Efficiency Variance	4,000 (A)
E. Actual Fixed Overheads	39,000

Problem 7. In a factory the standard units of production of the year were fixed at 12,000 units and overhead expenditures were estimated to be:

Fixed ₹ 12,000 Variable ₹ 6,000
Semi-variable ₹ 1,800

Actual production during April of the year was 800 units. Each month has 20 working days. During the month in question there was one statutory holiday. The actual overheads amounted to:

Fixed ₹ 1,190 Variable ₹ 480
Semi-variable ₹ 192

Semi-variable charges are considered to include 60 per cent expenses of fixed nature and 40 per cent of variable character.

Required: Calculate all the Overhead Variances.

Solution:

Assumption: 8 Working Hours a day

1. Budgeted Hours for a month (BH) = 20 × 8 = 160
2. Budgeted Fixed Overheads for a month = $\frac{12{,}000 + 60\% \text{ of } 1{,}800}{12} = \frac{13{,}080}{12}$ = ₹ 1,090
3. Standard Fixed Overhead Rate = $\frac{1{,}090}{160}$ = ₹ 6.8125 per hour
4. Budgeted Variable Overheads for a month = $\frac{6{,}000 + 40\% \text{ of } 1{,}800}{12} = \frac{6{,}720}{12} = 560$
5. Standard Variable Overhead Rate = $\frac{560}{160}$ = ₹ 3.5 per hour
6. Standard Hours for Actual Output (SH) = $\frac{160}{1{,}000} \times 800 = 128$ hours

7. Actual Hours (AH) = 19 x 8 = 152 Hours
8. Actual Fixed Overheads = ₹ 1,190 + 60% of ₹ 192 = ₹ 1,305.20
9. Actual Variable Overheads = 480 + 40% of ₹ 192 = ₹ 556.80
10. Revised Budgeted Hours for Actual Working Days (RBH) = 19 × 8 = 152 hours

BASIC CALCULATIONS FOR VARIABLE OVERHEAD VARIANCES

1. Absorbed Overheads (SH x SR) =	₹ 448
2. Standard Overheads (AH x SR) =	₹ 532
3. Actual Overheads =	₹ 556.80

Computation of Variances

A. Variable Overheads Efficiency Variance (1 – 2) = ₹ 448 – ₹ 532 = ₹ 84 (A)
B. Variable Overheads Expenditure Variance (2 – 3) = ₹ 532 – ₹ 556.80 = ₹ 24.80 (A)
C. Total Variable Overheads Variance (A + B) = ₹ 108.80 (A)

BASIC CALCULATIONS FOR FIXED OVERHEAD VARIANCES

1. Absorbed Overheads (SH x SR) =	₹ 872
2. Standard Overheads (AH x SR) =	₹ 1,035.50
3. Revised Budgeted Overheads (RBH x SR) =	₹ 1,035.50
4. Budgeted Overheads (BH x SR) =	₹ 1,090
5. Actual Overheads	₹ 1,305.20

Computation of Variances

A. Fixed Overheads Efficiency Variance (1 – 2) = ₹.872 – ₹ 1,035.50 = ₹ 163.50 (A)
B. Fixed Overheads Capacity Variance (2 – 3) = ₹ 1,035.50 – ₹ 1,035.50 = Nil
C. Fixed Overheads Calendar Variance (3 – 4) = ₹ 1,035.50 – ₹.1,090 = ₹ 54.50 (A)
D. Total Fixed Overheads Volume Variance (A + B + C) = ₹ 218 (A)
E. Fixed Overheads Expenditure Variance (4 – 5) = ₹ 1,090 – ₹ 1,305.20 = ₹ 215.20 (A)
F. Total Fixed Overheads Variance (D + E) = ₹ 433.20(A)

Problem 8.

(a) The Budget for a period indicates :
Fixed Works Overhead ₹ 50,000
Variable Works Overhead ₹ 1,50,000
Normal Activity 100%
During the period the actual activity was only 70% of the normal load for a total expenditure of ₹ 1,50,000. What are the budget and volume variances?

(b) Determine the Budget and Capacity Variances from the following data :
Estimated Factory Overhead ₹ 25,000, Actual Overhead Expenses ₹ 26,500
Estimated Direct Labour Hours ₹ 5,000, Applied Overhead Expenses ₹ 22,500.

Solution:

Part (a)

1. Standard Fixed Overheads for Actual Activity = 70% of ₹ 50,000 = ₹ 35,000
2. Standard Variable Overheads for Actual Activity = 70% of ₹ 1,50,000 = ₹ 1,05,000
3. Actual Fixed Overhead = ₹ 1,50,000 – ₹ 1,05,000 = ₹ 45,000

Note: It has been assumed that Actual Variable Overheads same as Standard Variable Overheads.

BASIC CALCULATIONS FOR VARIABLE OVERHEAD VARIANCES

1. Absorbed Overheads (SH x SR) =	₹ 1,05,000
2. Standard Overheads (AH x SR) =	₹ 1,05,000
3. Actual Overheads =	₹ 1,05,000

Computation of Variances

A. Variable Overheads Efficiency Variance (1 – 2) = ₹. 1,05,000 – ₹ 1,05,000 = Nil

B. Variable Overheads Expenditure Variance (2 – 3) = ₹ 1,05,000 – ₹ 1,05,000 = Nil

C. Total Variable Overheads Variance (A + B) = Nil

BASIC CALCULATIONS FOR FIXED OVERHEAD VARIANCES

1. Absorbed Overheads (SH x SR) =	₹ 35,000
2. Standard Overheads (AH x SR) =	₹ 35,000
3. Budgeted Overheads (BH x SR) =	₹ 50,000
4. Actual Overheads =	₹ 45,000

Computation of Variances

A. Fixed Overheads Efficiency Variance (1 – 2) = ₹ 35,000 – ₹ 35,000 = Nil

B. Fixed Overheads Capacity Variance (2 – 3) = ₹ 35,000 – ₹ 50,000 = ₹ 15,000 (A)

C. Total Fixed Overheads Volume Variance (A + B) = ₹ 15,000 (A)

D. Fixed Overheads Expenditure Variance (3 – 4) = ₹ 50,000 – ₹ 45,000 = ₹ 5,000 (F)

E. Total Fixed Overheads Variance (C + D) = ₹ 10,000 (A)

Part (b)

BASIC CALCULATIONS FOR FIXED OVERHEAD VARIANCES

1. Absorbed Overheads (SH x SR) =	₹ 22,500
2. Standard Overheads (AH x SR) =	₹ 22,500
3. Budgeted Overheads (BH x SR) =	₹ 25,000
4. Actual Overheads =	₹ 26,500

Computation of Variances

A. Fixed Overheads Efficiency Variance (1 – 2) = ₹ 22,500 – ₹ 22,500 = Nil

B. Fixed Overheads Capacity Variance (2 – 3) = ₹ 22,500 – ₹ 25,000 = ₹ 2,500 (A)

C. Total Fixed Overheads Volume Variance (A + B) = ₹ 2,500 (A)

D. Fixed Overheads Expenditure Variance (3 – 4) = ₹ 25,000 – ₹ 26,500 = ₹ 1,500 (A)

E. Total Fixed Overheads Variance (C + D) = ₹ 4,000 (A)

SOLVED PROBLEMS II

Problem 9. Calculate the missing information in each of the following alternative cases :

	Case (a)	*Case (b)*	*Case (c)*	*Case (d)*	*Case (e)*	*Case (f)*
Fixed Overhead Efficiency Variance (A)	200	?	1,200	300	?	500
Fixed Overhead Capacity Variance (A)	?	200	?	400	800	?
Fixed Overhead Volume Variance (A)	300	?	?	?	?	800
Fixed Overhead Expenditure Variance (A)	?	500	500	500	200	200
Fixed Overhead Cost Variance (A)	?	800	?	?	?	?
Variable Overhead Efficiency Variance (A)	?	800	?	800	500	?
Variable Overhead Expenditure Variance (A)	400	?	100	?	1,000	2,000
Variable Overhead Cost Variance (A)	900	?	500	?	?	?
Total Overhead Cost Variance (A)	1,500	2,000	2,500	3,000	3,500	4,000

Note: (A) = Adverse

Solution:

Fixed Overhead Efficiency Variance (A)	200	100	1,200	300	1,000	500
Fixed Overhead Capacity Variance (A)	100	200	300	400	800	300
Fixed Overhead Volume Variance (A)	300	300	1,500	700	1,800	800
Fixed Overhead Expenditure Variance (A)	300	500	500	500	200	200
Fixed Overhead Cost Variance (A)	600	800	2,000	1,200	2,000	1,000
Variable Overhead Efficiency Variance (A)	500	800	400	800	500	1,000
Variable Overhead Expenditure Variance (A)	400	400	100	1,000	1,000	2,000
Variable Overhead Cost Variance (A)	900	1,200	500	1,800	1,500	3,000
Total Overhead Cost Variance (A)	1,500	2,000	2,500	3,000	3,500	4,000

Problem 10. X Limited uses Absorption Costing Principle for its variance analysis. The flexible budget for Production Overhead for the company, which makes one product shows a budget monthly expenditure of ₹ 72,000 for an output of 3,000 tonnes and of ₹ 1,08,000 for an output of 7,000 tonnes. The Standard Overhead Absorption rate for absorption purpose is ₹ 18 per tonne. During the month of April, the Company incurred Overhead Expenditure of ₹ 1,05,750 (₹ 52,000 Variable and ₹ 53,750 fixed) for an output of 5,500 tonnes. You are required to calculate the following:

(i) Budgeted variable overhead cost per tonne,
(ii) Total budgeted fixed cost per month,
(iii) Budgeted output per month on which the standard overhead rate is based,
(iv) Budgeted overhead allowance for the actual output in April,
(v) The total overhead absorbed for the month of April,
(vi) Variable production overhead expenditure variance for the month of April,
(vii) Fixed production overhead expenditure variance for the month of April,
(viii) Fixed production overhead volume variance for the month of April.

Solution:

1. Budgeted Variable Overhead Cost per tonne $= \dfrac{\text{Change in Overhead}}{\text{Change in Activity}}$

$$= \frac{₹\ 1{,}08{,}000 - 72{,}000}{7{,}000 - 3000}$$

$$= \frac{₹\ 36{,}000}{4000} = ₹\ 9 \text{ per tonne}$$

2. Total Budgeted Fixed Cost p.m. = Total Budgeted Overhead – Total Variable Overhead
= ₹ 1,08,000 – (7000 × ₹ 9) = ₹ 1,08,000 – ₹ 63,000 = ₹ 45,000
3. Budgeted Output per month on which the Standard Overhead rate is based (BO)

$$BO = \frac{\text{Total Budget Fixed Overhead}}{\text{Standard Fixed Overhead Rate}} = \frac{₹\ 45{,}000}{(18-9)} = 5{,}000 \text{ tonnes}$$

4. Budgeted Overhead Allowance for the Actual Output = (5500 × ₹ 9.00) + ₹ 45,000 = ₹ 94,500
5. Total Overhead Absorbed = 5500 × ₹ 18 = ₹ 99,000
6. In the absence of any information regarding hours, it has been assumed that actual hours are same as standard hours and hence, the standard output is same as actual output.

BASIC CALCULATIONS FOR VARIABLE OVERHEAD VARIANCES

1. Absorbed Overheads (SH x SR) =	₹ 49,500
2. Standard Overheads (AH x SR) =	₹ 49,500
3. Actual Overheads =	₹ 52,000

Computation of Variances

A. Variable Overheads Efficiency Variance (1 – 2) = ₹ 49,500 – ₹ 49,500 = Nil
B. Variable Overheads Expenditure Variance (2 – 3) = ₹ 49,500 – ₹ 52,000 = ₹ 2,500 (A)
C. Total Variable Overheads Variance (A + B) = ₹ 2,500 (A)

BASIC CALCULATIONS FOR FIXED OVERHEAD VARIANCES

1. Absorbed Overheads (SH x SR) =	₹ 49,500
2. Standard Overheads (AH x SR) =	₹ 49,500
3. Budgeted Overheads (BH x SR) =	₹ 45,000
4. Actual Overheads =	₹ 53,750

Computation of Variances

A. Fixed Overheads Efficiency Variance (1 – 2) = ₹ 49,500 – ₹ 49,500 = Nil

B. Fixed Overheads Capacity Variance (2 – 3) = ₹ 49,500 – ₹ 45,000 = ₹ 4,500 (F)

C. Total Fixed Overheads Volume Variance (A + B) = ₹ 4,500 (F)

D. Fixed Overheads Expenditure Variance (3 – 4) = ₹ 45,000 – ₹ 53,750 = ₹ 8,750 (A)

E. Total Fixed Overheads Variance (C + D) = ₹ 4,250 (A)

Problem 11. A Cost Accountant of a Company has given the following information regarding the fixed overheads for February 20X1:

(a) Overheads Cost Variance ₹ 1,400 adverse.
(b) Overheads Volume Variance ₹ 1,000 adverse.
(c) Budgeted hours for February 20X1, 1,200 hours.
(d) Budgeted Overheads for February 20X1, ₹ 6,000.
(e) Actual rate of recovery of overheads ₹ 8 per hour.

You are required to assist him in computing the following for February 20X1 :

(a) Overheads Expenditure Variance, (b) Actual Overheads incurred, (c) Actual Hours for actual production, (d) Overheads Capacity Variance, (e) Standard Hours for actual production.

Solution: Let Standard Hours for Actual Output (SH) be 'x' and Actual Hours (AH) be 'y'. With the given data, the Table shall appear as under :

BASIC CALCULATIONS FOR FIXED OVERHEAD VARIANCES

1. Absorbed Overheads (SH x SR) =	₹ 5x
2. Standard Overheads (AH x SR) =	₹ 5y
3. Budgeted Overheads (BH x SR) =	₹ 6,000
4. Actual Overheads =	₹ 8y

Computation of Variances

A. Fixed Overheads Efficiency Variance (1 – 2) = ₹ 5x – ₹ 5y

B. Fixed Overheads Capacity Variance (2 – 3) = ₹ 5y – ₹ 6,000

C. Total Fixed Overheads Volume Variance (A + B) = [(5x – 5y) + (5y – ₹ 6,000)] = ₹ 1,000 (A)

D. Fixed Overheads Expenditure Variance (3 – 4) = ₹ 6,000 – ₹ 8y = ₹ 1,400 (A) – ₹ 1,000 (A)
= ₹ 400 (A)

E. Total Fixed Overheads Variance (C + D) = 1,400 (A)

1. Fixed Overheads Expenditure Variance = Fixed OH Cost Variance – Fixed OH Volume Variance
= ₹ 1,400 (A) – ₹ 1,000 (A) = ₹ 400 (A)

2. Actual Hours (y): 6000 – 8 y = 400 (A)
8 y = 6000 + 400 = 6,400
y = 6400/8 = 800 Hours

3. Actual Overheads incurred (AH × AR) = 800 × ₹ 8 = ₹ 6,400

4. Fixed Overheads Capacity Variance = 5 y – 6000 = (5 × 800) – 6,000 = ₹ 2,000 (A)

5. Fixed Overheads Efficiency Variance = Fixed OH Volume Variance – Fixed OH Capacity Variance
= ₹ 1,000 (A) – ₹ 2,000 (A) = ₹ 1,000 (F)

6. Standard Hours for actual production
Fixed Overhead efficiency variance = 5 x – 5 y = ₹ 1000 (F)
5 x – (5 × 800) = ₹ 1,000 (F)
5 x = 5000/5 = 1,000 hours

Problem 12.

(i) The following standard and actual data in respect of chemical X is made available to you from the records of Naulakha Chemicals Ltd.:

Standard Data			**Total**
Materials	₹	₹	
450 kg	of material A @ ₹ 20 per kg	9,000	
360 kg	of material B @ ₹ 10 per kg	3,600	12,600
810 kg			
	Labour: @ per hour		
	2,400 skilled hours ₹ 2		4,800
	1,200 unskilled hours ₹ 1		1,200
90 kg	Normal loss		—
720 kg	Total		18,600
Actual Data:			
Material		₹	
450 kg	of material A @ 19 per kg	8,550	—
360 kg	of material B @ ₹ 11 per kg	3,960	12,510
810 kg			
	Labour: @ per hour		
	2,400 skilled hours ₹ 2.25		5,400
	1,200 unskilled hours ₹ 1.25		1,500
50 kg	Actual loss		
760 kg	Total		19,410

You are required to compute:

(a) Material Cost variance;
(b) Material Price variance,
(c) Material Yield variance,
(d) Labour Cost variance
(e) Labour Rate variance
(f) Labour Yield variance

From the following data, calculate:

(i) Fixed Overhead Expenditure variance,
(ii) Fixed overhead Volume variance,
(iii) Fixed overhead Cost variance.

	Budgeted	*Actual*
Fixed Overheads for July	₹ 10,000	₹ 10,200
Units of Production in July	5,000	5,200
Standard Time for one unit	4 hours	—
Actual Hours worked	—	20,100 hrs.

Solution:

(a) Material Cost Variance = Std. Cost of actual output – Actual cost
= (₹ 12,600/720 kg x 760 kg) – ₹ 12,510 = ₹ 790 (A)

(b) Material Price Variance = (SP – AP) x AQ
A = (20 – 19) x 450 = ₹ 450 (F)
B = (10 – 11) x 360 = 360 (A)
Total = ₹ 90 (F)

(c) Material Yield Variance = (AY – SY) × SP = (760 – 720) × 12,600/720 = ₹ 700 (F)

(d) Labour Cost Variance = (Std. Cost of actual output – Actual cost)
= (₹ 4,800 + 1,200)/720 kg × 760 kg – (5,400 + 1500)
= ₹ 566.67 (A)

(e) Labour Rate Variance = (SR – AR) × AH
Skilled = (2 – 2.25) x 2400 = ₹ 600 (A)

Unskilled = (1–1.25) x 1200 = ₹ 300 (A)

Total = ₹ 900 (A)

(f) Labour Yield Variance = (AY – SY) × SR = (760 – 720) x ₹ 6,000/720 kg
= ₹ 333.33 (F)

(i) **Fixed Overhead Expenditure Variance**
Budgeted overhead – Actual Overhead = ₹ 10,000 – ₹ 10,200 = ₹ 200 (A)

(ii) **Fixed Overhead Volume Variance**
= Absorbed Overhead – Budgeted Overhead = (20,800 x 0.50) – 10,000 = ₹ 400 (F)

(iii) Fixed Overhead Cost Variance = Absorbed Overhead – Actual Overhead
= (20,800 × 0.50) – 10,200 = ₹ 200 (F)

Note: *Calculation of Absorbed Overhead*
Std. Hrs of actual output = 5,200 limits × 4 hrs. = 20,800 hrs
Std. Rate per hr. = ₹ 10,000/5,000 units/4 hrs. = ₹ 0.50
Absorbed overhead = 20,800 hrs. x 0.50 = ₹ 10,400

Problem 13. The standard cost card for product 'Simco' reveals:

Standard materials —	₹
2 kg of A @ ₹ 2 per kg	4.00
1 kg of B @ ₹ 6 per kg	6.00
Direct Labour (3 hours @ ₹ 6 per hour)	18.00
Variable Overhead (3 hours @ ₹ 4 per direct labour hour)	12.00
Total Standard Cost per unit	40.00

It is proposed to produce 10,000 units of 'Simco' in the month of March and budgeted costs on the information contained in the standard costs card are as follows:

Direct materials —	
A 20,000 kg @ ₹ 2 per kg	40,000
B 10,000 kg @ ₹ 6 per kg	60,000
Direct labour (30,000 hours @ ₹ 6 per hour)	1,80,000
Variable Overhead (30,000 hours @ ₹ 4 per direct labour hr)	1,20,000
Total	4,00,000

The actual results are:

Direct materials-	
A 19,000 kg @ ₹ 2.20 per kg	41,800
B 10,100 kg @ ₹ 5.60 per kg	56,560
Direct labour (28,500 hours @ ₹ 6.40 per hour)	1,82,400
Variable Overheads	1,04,000
	3,84,760

Actual production was 9,000 units.
From the above information, calculate the following variances:

(a) Material price and usage
(b) Labour wages rate and labour efficiency
(c) Variable overhead —
  (i) Total variable overhead variance
  (ii) Overhead expenditure variance.
  (iii) Overhead efficiency variance.
(d) Total Cost Variance

Solution:

(a) Material Variances

(i) Material Price Variance = (SP – AP) x AQ
A = (2 – 2.20) x 19,000 = ₹ 3,800 (A)
B = (6 – 5.60) x 10,100 = ₹ 4,040 (F)
MPV = ₹ 240 (F)

(ii) Material Usage Variance = (SQ – AQ) x SP
A = (18,000 – 19,000) x 2 = ₹ 2,000 (A)
B = (9,000 – 10,100) x 6 = ₹ 6,600 (A)
MUV = ₹ 8,600 (A)

(iii) Material Cost Variance = MPV + PUV = ₹ 240 (F) + ₹ 8,600 (A) = ₹ 8,360 (A)

(b) Labour Variances

(i) Labour Rate Variance = (SR – AR) x AH = (6 – 6.40) x 28,500 = ₹ 11,400 (A)
(ii) Labour Efficiency Variance = (SH – AH) x SR = (27,000 – 28,500) x 6 = ₹ 9,000 (A)
(iii) Labour Cost Variance = LRV + LEV = 11,400 (A) + 9,000 (A) = ₹ 20,400 (A)

(c) Variable Overhead Variances

Total Variable Overhead Variance
= (St. hrs. for actual production x St. overhead rate) – Actual variable overhead
= (27,000* x 4) – 1,04,000 = ₹ 4,000 (F)
*9,000 units @ 3 hours per unit = 27,000 standard hours for actual production

(i) Overhead Expenditure Variance = (Budgeted overhead – Actual variable overhead)
= (28,500 x 4) – 1,04,000 = ₹ 10,000 (F)

(ii) Overhead Efficiency Variance
= (Standard hours for actual production – Actual hours) x Standard overhead rate
= (27,000 – 28,500) x 4 = ₹ 6,000 (A)

Total Cost Variance = Total standard Cost – Total Actual Cost
= (9,000 units x ₹ 40) – ₹ 3,84,760 = ₹ 24,760 (A)

Problem 14. XYZ Ltd. operates a standard costing system. In connection with the weekly cost report for the Shop 5 you have been informed :

(i) That the standard costs per hour of the shop based on normal week of 40 hours work are :

	₹ per hour
Wages	18
Variable expenses	5
Fixed expenses	25
	48

Standard output in units per hour is 2.

(ii) That the following information has been recorded in respect of the week ended March 17, 20X1. Hours worked 36; Non Productive hours (waiting for work) 4; Total Hours paid for 40; Output (units) 85; Actual wages paid (₹) 740; Actual variable expenses ₹ 240; Actual fixed expenses (₹) 1,000.

Required : Compute the variances relating to Shop 5 for the week.

Solution:

(i) *Calculation of Labour Cost Variances*

$$\text{Standard Hours for Actual Output (SH)} = \frac{40}{40 \times 2} \times 85 = 42.5 \text{ Hours}$$

Revised Prdouctive Hours (RPH) = 40 – 4 = 36 Hours

BASIC CALCULATIONS FOR THE COMPUTATION OF LABOUR COST VARIANCES

SH for AO	SR	SH x SR (1)	AH	AR	AH x AR (2)	AH x SR (3)	RPH	RPH x SR (4)
42.5	18	765	40		740	720	36	648

A. Labour Cost Variance (1 – 2) = ₹ 25 (F)
B. Labour Efficiency Variance (1 – 4) = ₹ 117 (F)
C. Labour Idle Time Variance (4 – 3) = ₹ 72 (A)
D. Labour Rate Variance (3 – 2) = ₹ 20 (A)

Verification:

Labour Cost Variance = Labour Efficiency Variance + Labour Idle Time Variance + Labour Rate Variance
= ₹ 117 (F) + ₹ 72 (A) + ₹ 20 (A) = ₹ 25 (F)

(ii) *Calculation of Overhead Variances*

BASIC CALCULATIONS FOR VARIABLE OVERHEAD VARIANCES

1. Absorbed Overheads (SH x SR) =	₹ 212. 50
2. Standard Overheads (AH x SR) =	₹ 180.00
3. Actual Overheads =	₹ 240.00

Computation of Variances

A. Variable Overheads Efficiency Variance (1 – 2) = ₹ 212.50 – ₹ 180 = ₹ 32.50(F)
B. Variable Overheads Expenditure Variance (2 – 3) = ₹ 180 – ₹ 240 = ₹ 60 (A)
C. Total Variable Overheads Variance (A + B) = ₹ 27.50 (A)

BASIC CALCULATIONS FOR FIXED OVERHEAD VARIANCES

1. Absorbed Overheads (SH x SR) =	₹ 1062.50
2. Standard Overheads (AH x SR) =	₹ 900.00
3. Budgeted Overheads (BH x SR) =	₹ 1,000.00
4. Actual Overheads =	₹ 1,000.00

Computation of Variances

A. Fixed Overheads Efficiency Variance (1 – 2) = ₹ 1062.50 – ₹ 900 = 162.50 (F)
B. Fixed Overheads Capacity Variance (2 – 3) = ₹ 900 – ₹ 1,000 = ₹ 100 (A)
C. Total Fixed Overheads Volume Variance (A + B) = ₹ 62.50 (F)
D. Fixed Overheads Expenditure Variance (3 – 4) = ₹ 1,000 – ₹ 1,000 = Nil
E. Total Fixed Overheads Variance (C + D) = ₹ 62.50 (F)

Problem 15. X Ltd., operates a system of standard costs. Following information is available:

Actuals:	₹
Materials consumed (3,600 units at ₹ 52.50 per unit)	1,89,000
Direct wages	22,100
Fixed Expenses	1,88,000
Variable Expenses	62,000

Output during the period was 3,500 units of finished product. For the above period, the standard production capacity was 4,800 units and the break-up of standard cost per unit was as under:

	₹
Materials (one unit @ ₹ 50 per unit)	50
Direct Wages	6
Fixed Expenses	40
Variable Expenses	20
Total Standard cost per unit	116

The standard wage per unit is based on 9,600 hours for the above period at a rate of ₹ 3.00 per hour. 6,400 hours were actually worked during the above period, and in addition, wages for 400 hours were paid to compensate for idle time due to breakdown of a machine, and overall wage rate was ₹ 3.25 per hour.

Required: Compute the following variances with appropriate workings:

(a) Direct Material Cost Variance; (b) Material Price Variance; (c) Material Usage Variance; (d) Direct Labour Cost Variance; (e) Wage Rate Variance; (f) Labour Efficiency Variance; (g) Idle Time Variance; (h) Variable Expenses Variance; (I) Fixed Expenses Expenditure Variance; (j) Fixed Expenses Volume Variance; (k) Fixed Expenses Capacity Variance; (l) Fixed Expenses Efficiency Variance; (m) Total Cost Variance.

Solution: Parts — (a) (b) & (c)

Standard Quantity for Actual Output (SQ) = 3500 × 1 = 3500

BASIC CALCULATIONS FOR THE COMPUTATION OF MATERIAL COST VARIANCES

SQ for AO	SP	SQ × SP (1)	AQ	AP	AQ × AP (2)	AQ × SP (3)
3,500	50	1,75,000	3,600	52.50	1,89,000	1,80,000

A. Material Cost Variance (1 – 2) = ₹ 1,75,000 – ₹ 1,89,000 = ₹ 14,000 (A)
B. Material Usage Variance (1 – 3) = ₹ 1,75,000 – ₹ 1,80,000 = ₹ 5,000 (A)
C. Material Price Variance (3 – 2) = ₹ 1,80,000 – ₹ 1,89,000 = ₹ 9,000 (A)

Verification:

1. Material Cost Variance = Material Usage Variance + Material Price Variance
   = ₹ 5,000 (A) + ₹ 9,000 (A) = ₹ 14,000 (A)

Parts — (d), (e), (f), (g)

Standard hours per unit = ₹ 6/₹ 3 = 2 Hours

Standard Hours for Actual output = 3500 x 2 = 7000 Hours

Actual Productive Hours (APH) = 6,400

BASIC CALCULATIONS FOR THE COMPUTATION OF LABOUR COST VARIANCES

SH for AO	SR	SH x SR (1)	AH	AR	AH x AR (2)	AH x SR (3)	APH	APH x SR (4)
7,000	3	21,000	6,800	3.25	22,100	20,400	6,400	19,200

A. Labour Cost Variance (1– 2) = ₹ 21,000 – ₹ 22,100 = ₹.1,100 (A)
B. Labour Efficiency Variance (1– 3) = ₹ 21,000 – ₹ 20,400 = ₹ 600 (F)
C. Idle Time Variance (4 – 3) = ₹ 19,200 – ₹ 20,400 = ₹ 1,200 (A)
D. Labour Rate Variance (3 – 2) = ₹ 20,400 – ₹ 22,100 = ₹ 1,700 (A)

Verification:

Labour Cost Variance = Labour Efficiency Variance + Labour Rate Variance
= ₹ 600 (F) + ₹ 1,700 (A) = ₹ 1,100

Parts — (h), (i), (k) & (l)

Standard Fixed Overhead Rate per hour = ₹ 40/2 = ₹ 20 per hour

BASIC CALCULATIONS FOR VARIABLE OVERHEAD VARIANCES

1. Absorbed Overheads (SH x SR) =	₹ 70,000
2. Standard Overheads (AH x SR) =	₹ 68,000
3. Actual Overheads =	₹ 62,000

Computation of Variances

A. Variable Overheads Efficiency Variance (1 – 2) = ₹ 70,000 – ₹ 68,000 = 2,000 (F)
B. Variable Overheads Expenditure Variance (2 – 3) = ₹ 68,000 – ₹ 62,000 = ₹ 6,000 (F)
C. Total Variable Overheads Variance (A + B) = ₹ 8,000 (F)

BASIC CALCULATIONS FOR FIXED OVERHEAD VARIANCES

1. Absorbed Overheads (SH x SR) =	₹ 1,40,000
2. Standard Overheads (AH x SR) =	₹ 1,36,000
3. Budgeted Overheads (BH x SR) =	₹ 1,92,000
4. Actual Overheads =	₹ 1,88,000

Computation of Variances

A. Fixed Overheads Efficiency Variance (1 – 2) = ₹ 1,40,000 – ₹ 1,36,000 = 4,000 (F)
B. Fixed Overheads Capacity Variance (2 – 3) = ₹ 1,36,000 – ₹ 1,92,000 = ₹ 56,000 (A)
C. Total Fixed Overheads Volume Variance (A + B) = ₹ 52,000 (A)
D. Fixed Overheads Expenditure Variance (3 – 4) = ₹ 1,92,000 – ₹ 1,88,000 = ₹ 4,000 (F)
E. Total Fixed Overheads Variance (C + D) = ₹ 48,000 (A)

Part — (m)

Total Cost Variance = Total Standard cost – Total actual Cost

Total Cost Variance = (3,500 x ₹ 116) – ₹ 4,61,100 = ₹ 55,100 (A)

or, = Direct Material Cost Variance + Direct Labour Cost Variance + Variable Expenses Variance + Fixed Expenses Variance
= ₹ 14,000 (A) + ₹ 1,100 (A) + ₹ 8,000 (F) + ₹ 48,000 (A)

Problem 16. The Standard Cost Sheet per unit for the product produced by Modern Manufactures is worked out on this basis :
Direct Materials 1.3 tons @ ₹ 4.00 per ton
Direct Labour 2.9 hours @ ₹ 2.30 per hour
Factory Overhead 2.9 hours @ ₹ 2.00 per hour
Normal Capacity is 2,00,000 direct labour hours per month.

The Factory Overhead rate is arrived at on the basis of a Fixed Overhead of ₹ 1,00,000 per month and a Variable Overhead of ₹ 1.50 per direct labour hour. In the month of May, 50,000 units of the product were started and completed. An investigation of the raw material inventory account reveals that 78,000 tons of raw material were transferred into and used by the factory during May. These goods cost ₹ 4.20 per ton. 1,50,000 hours of Direct Labour were spent during May at a cost of ₹ 2.50 per hour. Factory Overhead for the month amounted to ₹ 3,40,000 out of which ₹ 1,02,000 was fixed.

Required: Compute and identify all variances under Material, Labour and Overhead as favourable or adverse. Identify one or more departments in the company who might be held responsible for each variance.

Solution:

(i) *Calculation of Material Cost Variances*
Standard Material for Actual Output = 50,000 × 1.3 = 65,000 tons

BASIC CALCULATIONS FOR THE COMPUTATION OF MATERIAL COST VARIANCES

SQ for AO	*SP*	*SQ × SP (1)*	*AQ*	*AP*	*AQ × AP (2)*	*AQ × SP (3)*
65,000	4.00	2,60,000	78,000	4.20	3,27,600	3,12,000

A Material Cost Variance (1 – 2) = ₹ 67,600 (A)
B Material Usage Variance (1 – 3) = ₹ 52,000 (A)
C Material Price Variance (3 – 2) = ₹ 15,600 (A)

Verification:

Material Cost Variance = Material Usage Variance + Material Price Variance
= ₹ 52,000 (A) + ₹ 15,600 (A) = ₹ 67,600

(ii) *Calculation of Labour Cost Variances*
Standard hours for Actual Output = 50,000 × 2.9 = 1,45,000

BASIC CALCULATIONS FOR THE COMPUTATION OF LABOUR COST VARIANCES

SH for AO	*SR*	*SH × SR (1)*	*AH*	*AR*	*AH × AR (2)*	*AH × SR (3)*
1,45,000	2.30	3,33,500	1,50,000	2.50	3,75,000	3,45,000

A Labour Cost Variance (1 – 2) = ₹ 41,500 (A)
B Labour Efficiency Variance (1 – 3) = ₹ 11,500 (A)
C Labour Rate Variance (3 – 2) = ₹ 30,000 (A)

Verification:

Labour Cost Variance = Labour Efficiency Variance + Labour Rate Variance
= ₹ 11,500 (A) + ₹ 30,000 (A) = ₹ 41,500

(iii) *Calculation of Overhead Cost Variances*

BASIC CALCULATIONS FOR VARIABLE OVERHEAD VARIANCES

1. Absorbed Overheads (SH x SR) =	₹ 2,17,500
2. Standard Overheads (AH x SR) =	₹ 2,25,000
3. Actual Overheads =	₹ 2,38,000

Computation of Variances

A. Variable Overheads Efficiency Variance (1 – 2) = ₹ 2,17,500 – ₹ 2,25,000 = 7,500 (A)
B. Variable Overheads Expenditure Variance (2 – 3) = ₹ 2,25,000 – ₹ 2,38,000 = ₹ 13,000 (A)
C. Total Variable Overheads Variance (A + B) = ₹ 20,500 (A)

BASIC CALCULATIONS FOR FIXED OVERHEAD VARIANCES

1. Absorbed Overheads (SH x SR) =	₹ 72,500
2. Standard Overheads (AH x SR) =	₹ 75,000
3. Budgeted Overheads (BH x SR) =	₹ 1,00,000
4. Actual Overheads =	₹ 1,02,000

Computation of Variances

A. Fixed Overheads Efficiency Variance (1 – 2) = ₹ 72,500 – ₹ 75,000 = ₹ 2,500 (A)
B. Fixed Overheads Capacity Variance (2 – 3) = ₹ 75,000 – ₹ 1,00,000 = ₹ 25,000 (A)
C. Total Fixed Overheads Volume Variance (A + B) = ₹ 27,500 (A)
D. Fixed Overheads Expenditure Variance (3 – 4) = ₹ 1,00,000 – ₹ 1,02,000 = ₹ 2,000 (A)
E. Total Fixed Overheads Variance (C + D) = ₹ 29,500 (A)

Identification of department(s) who might be held responsible for each variance :

Name of the Variance	*Name of the Department*
1. Material Price variance	Purchase Department
2. Material Usage variance	Production Department/Factory Foreman
3. Labour Rate Variance	Personnel Dept./Management Policy
4. Labour Efficiency variance	Production Dept./Factory Foreman
5. Overhead variances	Production Dept./Factory Foreman mainly

Problem 17. Mahendra Ltd.. are the manufacturers of a standard product P. The standard cost card reveals the following information of the month of December 20X1.

	Per unit
Direct Material 2 kg. @ ₹ 6 per kg.	₹ 12
Direct Labour : 5 hours @ ₹ 4 per hr.	20
Overhead : 5 hours @ ₹ 2 per hr.	10
Standard Cost	42

Overhead Rate ₹ 2 per hour, the budgeted overhead being ₹ 4,000 for 2,000 budgeted hours.
The following are the other details:

Direct Material	:	Opening Stock 800 kg. @ ₹ 6 per kg.
Purchases	:	1,000 kg. @ ₹ 7 per kg.
Issued to Production	:	900 kg. as per FIFO method
Direct Labour	:	1,850 hrs. @ ₹ 4.40 per hour
Overheads	:	₹ 4,200

During the month 360 units were completed and 40 units were in process. The incomplete units are 100% completed regarding materials but only 50% complete as regards labour and overhead. 300 units were sold at ₹ 60 per unit during the month,.

Required: Calculate all the variances.

Solution:

(i) *Calculation of Material Cost Variances*

1. Equivalent units of output = 360 + 100% of 40 = 400
2. Standard Quantity of Material for Actual output = 400 × 2 = 800
3. Actual Cost of Material Consumed (AQ × AP) = (800 × ₹ 6) + 100 × ₹ 7) = ₹ 5,500

BASIC CALCULATIONS FOR THE COMPUTATION FOR MATERIAL COST VARIANCES

SQ for AO	*SP*	*SQ× SP (1)*	*AQ*	*AP*	*AQ× AP (2)*	*AQ× SP (3)*
800	6	4,800	900	6.1111	5,500	5,400

A Material Cost Variance (1 – 2) = ₹ 4,800 – ₹ 5,500 = ₹ 700 (A)
B Material Usage Variance (1 – 3) = ₹ 4,800 – ₹ 5,400 = ₹ 600 (A)
C Material Price Variance (3 – 2) = ₹ 5,400 – ₹ 5,500 = ₹ 100 (A)

Verification:

1. Material Cost Variance = Material Usage Variance + Material Price Variance
= ₹ 600 (A) + ₹ 100 (A) = ₹ 700 (A)

(ii) *Calculation of Labour Cost Variances*

1. Equivalent units of output for Labour = 360 + 50% of 40 = 380
2. Standard Hours for Actual Output = 380 × 5 = 1,900

BASIC CALCULATIONS FOR THE COMPUTATION OF LABOUR COST VARIANCES

SH for AO	*SR*	*SH× SR (1)*	*AH*	*AR*	*AH× AR (2)*	*AH× SR (3)*
1,900	4	7,600	1,850	4.40	8,140	7,400

A Labour Cost Variance (1 – 2) = ₹ 7,600 – ₹ 8,140 = ₹ 540 (A)
B Labour Efficiency Variance (1 – 3) = ₹ 7,600 – ₹ 7,400 = ₹ 200 (F)
C Labour Rate Variance (3 – 2) = ₹ 7,400 – ₹ 8,140 = ₹ 740 (A)

Verification:

Labour Cost Variance = Labour Efficiency Variance + Labour Rate Variance
= 200 (F) + ₹ 740 (A) = ₹ 540 (A)

(iii) *Calculation of Overhead Cost Variances*

BASIC CALCULATIONS FOR FIXED OVERHEAD VARIANCES

1. Absorbed Overheads (SH x SR) =	₹ 3,800
2. Standard Overheads (AH x SR) =	₹ 3,700
3. Budgeted Overheads (BH x SR) =	₹ 4,000
4. Actual Overheads =	₹ 4,200

Computation of Variances

A. Fixed Overheads Efficiency Variance (1 – 2) = ₹ 3,800 – ₹ 3,700 = ₹ 100 (F)
B. Fixed Overheads Capacity Variance (2 – 3) = ₹ 3,700 – ₹ 4,000 = ₹ 300 (A)
C. Total Fixed Overheads Volume Variance (A + B) = ₹ 200 (A)
D. Fixed Overheads Expenditure Variance (3 – 4) = ₹ 4,000 – ₹ 4,200 = ₹ 200 (A)
E. Total Fixed Overheads Variance (C + D) = 400 (A)

Problem 18. An engineering company manufactures a single product whose standard cost structure is as follows:

	₹
Direct Material 2.4 kgs. @ ₹ 30 per kg.	72.00
Direct Labour 6 Hours @ ₹ 4 per hour	24.00
Factory Overhead 6 Hours @ ₹ 0.75 per hour	4.50
Total	100.50

The factory overhead is based on the following flexible budget :

	80%	90%	100%	110%
Production (Units)	6,000	6,750	7,500	8,250
	₹	₹	₹	₹
Variable Overheads	18,000	20,250	22,500	24,750
Fixed Overheads	11,250	11,250	11,250	11,250
	29,250	31,500	33,750	36,000

Actual data for the month of January 20X1

Budgeted production	:	7,500 units
Materials used	:	19,240 kgs. @ ₹ 31 per kg.
Direct labour	:	46,830 Hours @ ₹ 4.20 per hour
Actual factory overhead	:	₹ 36,340
Production completed	:	7,620 units

Details of Work-in-progress :

Opening	:	120 units, materials fully supplied, 50% converted.
Closing	:	100 units, materials fully supplied, 50% converted.

Required: Determine and analyse :

(i) Material cost variances,; (ii) Labour cost variances; (iii) Overhead cost variances.

Solution:

CALCULATION OF NO. OF EQUIVALENT UNITS OF OUTPUT

Particulars	*No. of Units*	*For Material*		*For Labour & Overhead*	
		Degree of Completion	*Eq. Units*	*Degree of Completion*	*Eq. Units*
Production Completed	7,620	100%	7,620	100%	7,620
Add : Closing WIP	100	100%	100	50%	50
Less : Opening WIP	120	100%	120	50%	60
			7,600		7,610

(i) *Calculation of Material Cost Variances*

Standard Quantity of Material for Actual output = 7,600 × 2.4 = 18,240 kg.

BASIC CALCULATIONS FOR THE COMPUTATION OF MATERIAL COST VARIANCES

SQ for AO	*SP*	*SQ × SP* *(1)*	*AQ*	*AP*	*AQ × AP* *(2)*	*AQ × SP* *(3)*
18,24030	5,47,200	19,240	31.00	5,96,440	5,77,200	

A Material Cost Variance (1 – 2) = ₹ 49,240 (A)

B Material Usage Variance (1 – 3) = ₹ 30,000 (A)

C Material Price Variance (3 – 2) = ₹ 19,240 (A)

Verification:

Material Cost Variance = Material Usage Variance + Material Price Variance
= ₹ 30,000 (A) + ₹ 19,240 (A) = ₹ 49,240 (A)

(ii) *Calculation of Labour Cost Variances*

Standard Hours for Actual Output = 7,610 × 6 = 45,660

BASIC CALCULATIONS FOR THE COMPUTATION OF LABOUR COST VARIANCES

SH for AO	*SR*	*SH × SR* *(1)*	*AH*	*AR*	*AH × AR* *(2)*	*AH × SR* *(3)*
45,660	4	1,82,640	46,830	4.20	1,96,686	1,87,320

A Labour Cost Variance (1 – 2) = ₹ 14,046 (A)

B Labour Efficiency Variance (1 – 3) = ₹ 4,680 (A)

C Labour Rate Variance (3 – 2) = ₹ 9,366 (A)

Verification:

Labour Cost Variance = Labour Efficiency Variance + Labour Rate Variance
= ₹ 4,680 (A) + ₹ 9,366 (A) = ₹ 14,046 (A)

(iii) *Calculation of Overhead Cost Variances*

Standard Fixed Overhead Rate per hour = $\frac{11,250}{7,500 \times 6}$ = ₹ 0.25 per hour

Standard Variable Overhead Rate per hour = $\frac{22,500}{7,500 \times 6}$ = ₹ 0.50 per hour

Assumption : Actual Variable Overhead Rate per hour = Standard Variable Overhead Rate per hour

BASIC CALCULATIONS FOR VARIABLE OVERHEAD VARIANCES

1. Absorbed Overheads (SH x SR) =	₹ 22,830
2. Standard Overheads (AH x SR) =	₹.23,415
3. Actual Overheads =	₹ 23,415

Computation of Variances

A. Variable Overheads Efficiency Variance (1 – 2) = ₹ 22,830 – ₹ 23,415 = 585 (A)
B. Variable Overheads Expenditure Variance (2 – 3) = ₹ 23,415 – ₹ 23,415 = Nil
C. Total Variable Overheads Variance (A + B) = ₹ 585 (A)

BASIC CALCULATIONS FOR FIXED OVERHEAD VARIANCES

1. Absorbed Overheads (SH x SR) =	₹ 11,415
2. Standard Overheads (AH x SR) =	₹ 11,707.50
3. Budgeted Overheads (BH x SR) =	₹ 11,250
4. Actual Overheads =	₹ 12,925

Computation of Variances

A. Fixed Overheads Efficiency Variance (1 – 2) = ₹ 11,415 – ₹ 11,707.50 = ₹ 292.50 (A)
B. Fixed Overheads Capacity Variance (2 – 3) = ₹ 11,707.50 – ₹ 11,250 = ₹ 457.50 (F)
C. Total Fixed Overheads Volume Variance (A + B) = ₹ 165 (F)
D. Fixed Overheads Expenditure Variance (3 – 4) = ₹ 11,250 – ₹ 12,925 = ₹ 1,675 (A)
E. Total Fixed Overheads Variance (C + D) = ₹ 1,510 (A)

Problem 19. Budgeted and standard data for a product include the following :

Direct Labour 10 employees work for a 45 hour week. Standard rate of pay is ₹ 4 per hour. Output per hour is 40 kg. of product. Budgeted fixed overhead is ₹ 2,70,000 p.a. Budgeted output is 90,000 kg. p.a. A 50 week year is operated.

Direct Materials

Material	*Quantity*	*Price per kg.*
A	60 kg.	₹ 2.00
B	40 kg.	₹ 1.00
C	100 kg.	₹ 1.40

From this standard mix, 180 kg. of product are expected.

Actual data for the first week in April were :

Hours worked	45
Rate of pay	₹ 4 per hour
Overhead incurred	₹ 5,400
Output	1,980 kg.

Production and consumption of materials were :

Material	Quantity	Price per kg.
A	700 kgs.	₹ 1.80
B	440 kgs	₹ 1.10
C	1,120 kgs	₹ 1.30

Required : Calculate all Material, Labour and Overhead Variances.

Solution:

Basic Calculation for Material Cost Variances :

1. Standard Quantity of 'A' for Actual output = (660/1,980) × 1,980 = 660 kg
2. Standard Quantity of 'B' for Actual output = (440/1,980) × 1,980 = 440 kg
3. Standard Quantity of 'C' for Actual output = (1,100/1,980) × 1,980 = 1,100 kg
4. Total Standard Input = 660 + 440 + 1,100 = 2,200 kg.
5. Total Actual Input = 700 + 440 + 1,120 = 2,260 kg.
6. Revised Qty. of 'A' = (660/2,200) × 2,260 = 678
7. Revised Qty. of 'B' = (440/2,200) × 2,260 = 452
8. Revised Qty. of 'C' = (1,100/2,200) × 2,260 = 1,130

BASIC CALCULATIONS FOR THE COMPUTATION OF MATERIAL COST VARIANCES

Type of Material	*SQ for AO*	*SP*	*SQ × SP (1)*	*AQ*	*AP*	*AQ × AP (2)*	*AQ × SP (3)*	*RQ*	*RQ × SP (4)*
A	660	2.00	1,320	700	1.80	1,260	1,400	678	1,356
B	440	1.00	440	440	1.10	484	440	452	452
C	1,100	1.40	1,540	1,120	1.30	1,456	1,568	1,130	1,582
Input	2,200			2,260					
Less: Loss	220			280					
	1,980		3,300	1,980		3,200	3,408		3,390

			Material 'A'	**Material 'B'**	**Material 'C'**	**Total**
A	Material Cost Variance	(1 – 2)	60 (F)	44 (A)	84 (F)	100 (F)
B	Material Usage Variance	(1 – 3)	80 (A)	Nil	28 (A)	108 (A)
C	Material Yield Variance	(1 – 4)	36 (A)	12 (A)	42 (A)	90 (A)
D	Material Mix Variance	(4 – 3)	44 (A)	12 (F)	14 (F)	18 (A)
E	Material Price Variance	(3 – 2)	140 (F)	44 (A)	112 (F)	208 (F)

Verification:

1. Material Cost Variance = Material Usage Variance + Material Price Variance
   = ₹, 108 (A) + 208 (F) = ₹ 100 (F)
2. Material Usage Variance = Material Yield Variance + Material Mix Variance
   = ₹ 90 (A) + ₹ 18 (A) = ₹ 108 (A)

Note : *Alternative formula for Material Yield Variance :*

$$= \frac{\text{Total (SQ × SP)}}{\text{Standard Output for Standard Input}} \times \text{(Actual Output – Standard Output for Actual Input)}$$

$$= \frac{₹\ 3{,}300}{1{,}980} \times \left(1980 - \frac{1980}{2200} \times 2260\right) = ₹\ 1.667 \times 54 = ₹\ 90\ (A)$$

Basic Calculation for Labour Cost Variances:

1. Standard Clock Hours for Actual Output = 1980/40 = 49.5 hours
2. Standard Labour Hours for Actual Output = 49.50 × 10 = 495 hours
3. Actual Labour Hours = 45 × 10 = 450 hours

BASIC CALCULATIONS FOR THE COMPUTATION OF LABOUR COST VARIANCES

SH for AO	*SR*	*SH × SR (1)*	*AH*	*AR*	*AH × AR (2)*	*AH × SR (3)*
495	4	1,980	450	4	1,800	1,800

A	Labour Cost Variance	(1 – 2) = ₹ 1,980 – ₹ 1,800 = ₹ 180 (F)
B	Labour Efficiency Variance	(1 – 3) = ₹ 1,980 – ₹ 1,800 = ₹ 180 (F)
C	Labour Rate Variance	(3 – 2) = ₹ 1,800 – ₹ 1,800 = Nil

Basic Calculation for Overhead Cost Variances :

1. Budgeted Hours for a week = $\frac{90,000}{40} \times \frac{1}{50} \times 10$ = 450 *or* 45 × 10 = 450
2. Budgeted Fixed Overhead for a week = ₹ 2,70,000/50 = ₹ 5,400
3. Standard Fixed Overhead Rate per hour = ₹ 2,70,000/(10 × 45 × 50) = ₹ 12 per hour

BASIC CALCULATIONS FOR FIXED OVERHEAD VARIANCES

1. Absorbed Overheads (SH x SR) =	₹ 5,940
2. Standard Overheads (AH x SR) =	₹ 5,400
3. Budgeted Overheads (BH x SR) =	₹ 5,400
4. Actual Overheads =	₹ 5,400

Computation of Variances

A. Fixed Overheads Efficiency Variance (1 – 2) = ₹ 5,940 – ₹ 5,400 = ₹ 540 (F)
B. Fixed Overheads Capacity Variance (2 – 3) = ₹ 5,400 – ₹ 5,400 = Nil
C. Total Fixed Overheads Volume Variance (A + B) = ₹ 540 (F)
D. Fixed Overheads Expenditure Variance (3 – 4) = ₹ 5,400 – ₹ 5,400 = Nil
E. Total Fixed Overheads Variance (C + D) = ₹ 540 (F)

9 Standard Costing — Sales Variances

Learning Objectives

After studying this chapter, you should be able to understand:

- Sales Variances
- Terms useful for Computation of Sales Variances on Turnover Basis
- Total Sales Value Variance (SVV)
- Sales Price Variance (SPV)
- Sales Volume Variance (SVV)
- Sales Mix Variance (SMV)
- Sales Sub-Volume Variance (SSVV) or Sales Quantity Variance (SQV)
- Practical Steps in the Computation of Sales Variances (On Sales Value Basis)
- Terms useful for Computation of Sales Variances on Margin Basis
- Total Sales Margin Variance (SMV)
- Sales Margin Price Variance (SMPV)
- Sales Margin Volume Variance (SMVV)
- Sales Margin Mix Variance
- Sales Margin Sub-Volume Variance
- Practical Steps in the Computation of Sales Variances (On Sales Margin Basis)
- How to Reconcile Standard Profit with Actual Profit
- Alternative Formulae used for Calculating Sales Variances (Based on Margin)

1.0 SALES VARIANCES

The sales variances affect the budgeted profit due to changes in Sales Revenue i.e. Changes caused by *either* a Change in Selling Prices *or* Sales Quantities.

Sales Variances may be calculated according to any of the following two methods:

1. Turnover (or Value) Method.
2. Margin (or Profit) Method.

The following chart shows the various main and sub-variances of sales.

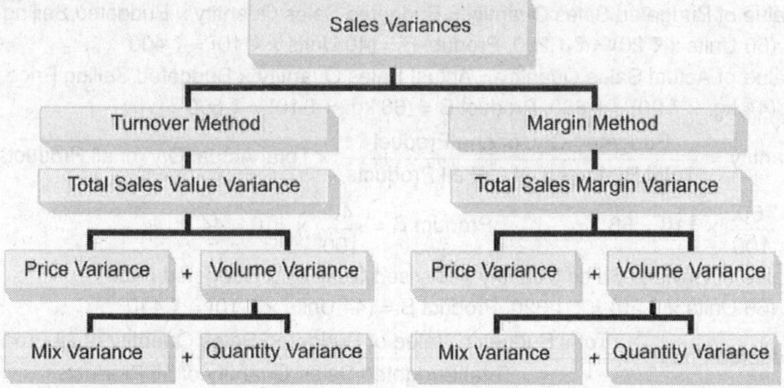

2.0 TERMS USEFUL FOR COMPUTATION OF SALES VARIANCES ON TURNOVER BASIS

One must know the following terms before knowing how to compute Sales Variances on turnover basis:

1. Budgeted Value of Budgeted Sales Quantity	(a) It represents the Budgeted Value of Budgeted Sales Quantity. (b) It is calculated as follows: = Budgeted Sales Quantity × Budgeted Selling Price = BQ × BP
2. Budgeted Value of Actual Sales Quantity	(a) It represents the Budgeted Value of Actual Sales Quantity. (b) It is calculated as follows: = Actual Sales Quantity × Budgeted Selling Price = AQ × BP
3. Revised Quantity	(a) It represents the Total Actual Quantity of all Products in a Budgeted Sales Mix Ratio. (b) It is calculated by dividing the Total Actual Sales Quantity of all Products in a Budgeted Mix Ratio as follows: $= \frac{\text{Budgeted Qty. of one Product}}{\text{Total Budgeted Qty. of all Products}} \times \text{Total Actual Qty. of all Products}$
4. Budgeted Value of Revised Sales Quantity	(a) It represents the Budgeted Value of Revised Sales Quantity. (b) It is calculated as follows: = Revised Sales Quantity × Budgeted Price = RQ × BP
5. Average Budgeted Price	(a) It represents the Budgeted Price per Unit of Budgeted Sales Quantity. (b) It is calculated as follows: $= \frac{\text{Total Budgeted Value of Budgeted Sales Quantity of all Products}}{\text{Total Budgeted Sales Quantity of all Products}}$

Illustration 1. Tulsian Ltd. (1) provides you the following information:

	Budget		***Actual***	
	Sales Quantity	*Unit Price*	*Sales Quantity*	*Unit Price*
Product 'A'	60 Units	₹ 20	44 Units	₹ 25
Product 'B'	40 Units	₹ 10	66 Units	₹ 5

Required: Calculate (a) Budgeted Value of Budgeted Sales Quantity (b) Budgeted Value of Actual Sales Quantity (c) Revised Quantity (d) Budgeted Value of Revised Sales Quantity (e) Average Budgeted Price.

Solution:

(a) Budgeted Value of Budgeted Sales Quantity = Budgeted Sales Quantity × Budgeted Selling Price
Product A = (60 Units x ₹ 20) = ₹ 1,200, Product B = (40 Units × ₹ 10) = ₹ 400

(b) Budgeted Value of Actual Sales Quantity = Actual Sales Quantity × Budgeted Selling Price
Product A = (44 kg. × ₹ 20) = ₹ 880, Product B = (66 kg. × ₹ 10) = ₹ 660

(c) Revised Quantity = $\frac{\text{Budgeted Qty. of one Product}}{\text{Total Budgeted Qty. of all Products}} \times \text{Total Actual Qty. of all Products}$

Product A = $\frac{60}{100} \times 110 = 66$, Product B = $\frac{40}{100} \times 110 = 44$

(d) Budgeted Value of Revised Sales Quantity = Revised Quantity × Budgeted Price
Product A = (66 Units × ₹ 20) = ₹ 1,320, Product B = (44 Units × ₹ 10) = ₹ 440

(e) Average Budgeted Price $= \frac{\text{Total Budgeted Value of Budgeted Sales Quantity of all Products}}{\text{Total Budgeted Sales Quantity of all Products}}$

$= \frac{(60 \times 20) + (40 \times 10)}{100 \text{ Units}} = ₹\ 16$

SALES VARIANCES ON TURNOVER BASIS
[Assuming that All Products are homogenous and not hetrogeneous]

3.0 TOTAL SALES VALUE VARIANCE (SVV)

Meaning	Sales Value Variance (SVV) is the difference between the Actual Value of Actual Sales Quantity and the Budgeted Value of Budgeted Sales Quantity.
How to Calculate	SVV = Actual Value of Actual Sales Quantity. ***minus*** Budgeted Value of Budgeted Sales Quantity *or* = (Actual Sales Quantity × Actual Selling Price) – (Budgeted Sales Quantity × Budgeted Selling Price) *or* = (AQ × AP) – (BQ × BP)
Nature	(a) **Favourable (F)** if the effect of the variance is to **increase the profit** (*i.e. where Actual Sales Value is more than the Budgeted Sales Value.*) (b) **Adverse (A)** if the effect of the variance is to **decrease** the profit (*i.e. where Actual Sales Value is less than the Budgeted Sales Value.*)
Why arises?	SVV may arise due to: (a) change in selling price of product, *or* (b) change in quantity of product, *or* (c) change in selling price and quantity of product.
Division	SVV may further be divided into: (a) Sales Price Variance (SPV), and (b) Sales Volume Variance (SVV)

Illustration 2. Calculate Sales Value Variance from the following information:

Budgeted Sales: 400 units @ ₹ 4

Actual Sales: 400 units @ ₹ 4 and 200 units @ ₹ 2

Solution: SVV = (AQ × AP) – (BQ × BP) = [(400 × ₹ 4) + (200 × ₹ 2)] – (400 × ₹ 4) = ₹ 400 (F)

4.0 SALES PRICE VARIANCE (SPV)

Meaning	Sales Price Variance (SPV) is that portion of the Sales Value Variance which arises due to the difference between the Actual Selling Price and the Budgeted Selling Price.
How to Calculate	SPV = (Actual Quantity × Actual Price) – (Actual Quantity × Budgeted Price) *or* = (AP – BP) × AQ
Nature	(a) **Favourable (F)** if the effect of variance is to **increase the profit** (*i.e. where AP > BP*) (b) **Adverse (A)** if the effect of variance is to **decrease the profit** (*i.e. where AP < BP*)
Why arises?	SPV may arise due to: 1. Change in the market prices of products. 2. Change in the quantity of products, thereby leading to lower/higher quantity discount. 3. Not giving cash discounts, when standards set took into account such discounts 4. Change in the delivery costs.

	5. Sale of a substitute material on account of non-availability of the product specified. 6. Off-season sale for certain seasonal value added like jute, cotton etc. 7. Change in the rates of excise duty, value added tax, etc. 8. Failure to supply the specified quality, thereby resulting in a different price being received.

Illustration 3. Calculate Sales Price Variance in Illustration 2.

Solution: Sales Price Variance = (AQ × AP) – (AQ × BP) = [(400 × ₹ 4) + (200 × ₹ 2)] – (600 × ₹ 4)
= ₹ 2,000 – 2,400 = ₹ 400 (A)

5.0 SALES VOLUME VARIANCE (SVV)

Meaning	Sales Volume Variance (SVV) is that portion of the Sales Value Variance which arises due to the difference between the Actual Sales Quantity Sold and the Budgeted Sales Quantity Specified.
How to Calculate	SVV = (Actual Quantity – Budgeted Quantity) × Budgeted Price *or* = (AQ – BQ) × BP
Nature	(a) **Favourable (F)** if the effect of variance is to **increase the profit** (*i.e. where AQ > BQ*) (b) **Adverse (A)** if the effect of variance is to **decrease the profit** (*i.e. where AQ < BQ*)
Why arises?	SVV may arise due to: 1. Use of non-standard products. 2. Use of non-standard Sales Mixture. 3. Pilferage. 4. Change in the design or specification of the product. 5. Change in the quality of products. 6. Use of substitute products.
Division	SVV may further be divided into: (a) Sales Mix Variance (SMV), and (b) Sales Sub-Volume Variance (SSVV) or Sales Quantity Variance (SQV)

Illustration 4. Calculate Sales Volume Variance in Illustration 2:

Solution: Sales Volume Variance = (AQ – BQ) × BP = (600 – 400) × ₹ 4 = ₹ 800 (F)

6.0 SALES MIX VARIANCE (SMV)

Meaning	Sales Mix Variance (SMV) is that portion of the Sales Volume variance which arises due to the difference between Actual and Budgeted Composition of products sold.
How to Calculate	SMV = Budgeted Value of Actual Sales Quantity – Budgeted Value of Revised Sales Quantity or = (AQ × BP) – (RQ × BP) or = (AQ – RQ) × BP **Note:** Revised Sales Quantity (RQ) is calculated by dividing the Total of Actual Sales Quantities of all products in a Budgeted Sales Mix ratio as follows: $= \frac{\text{Budgeted Qty of one product}}{\text{Total Budgeted Qty of all products}} \times \text{Total Actual Sales Qty of all Products}$

Nature	(a) **Favourable (F)** if the effect of the variance is to **increase the profit** (*i.e. where AQ > RQ*) (b) **Adverse (A)** if the effect of the variance is to **decrease the profit** (*i.e. where AQ < RQ*)
Why arises?	SMV arises only when the actual two or more products are mixed in a ratio different from the Budgeted Sales Mix ratio. Change from Budgeted Mix may be due to the non-availability of one or more components of Sales Mix.

Illustration 5. Calculate Sales Mix Variance from the following information:

Product	*Budgeted*		*Actual*	
	Qty	*Price*	*Qty*	*Price*
Product 'A'	800	₹ 12	1000	₹.10
Product 'B'	1200	₹ 10	700	₹ 12

Solution:

Step 1: Revised Quantity (RQ)

$$\text{Product 'A'} = \frac{800}{2000} \times 1700 = 680\text{, Product 'B'} = \frac{1200}{2000} \times 1700 = 1020$$

Step 2: Sales Mix Variance (SMV) = (AQ – RQ) × BP

Product 'A' = (1000 – 680) × ₹ 12 = ₹ 3,840 (F)

Product 'B' = (700 – 1020) × ₹ 10 = ₹ 3,200 (A)

SMV = ₹ 640 (F)

7.0 SALES SUB VOLUME VARIANCE (SSVV) OR SALES QUANTITY VARIANCE

Meaning	Sales Sub Volume Variance (SSVV) is that portion of the Sales Volume Variance which arises due to the difference between Total Actual Sales Quantity of all products and Total Budgeted Sales Quantity of all products.
How to Calculate	SSVV = (Total Actual Sales Qty. – Total Budgeted Sales Qty.) × Average Budgeted Price *or,* = (Total AQ – Total BQ) × ABP **Note:** $\text{ABP} = \frac{\text{Total Budgeted Value of Budgeted Sales Quantity of all products}}{\text{Total Budgeted Sales Quantity of all products}}$ *or* $= \frac{\text{Total (BQ} \times \text{BP)}}{\text{Total BQ}}$ *Alternatively,* SSVV = (Revised Quantity – Budgeted Quantity) × Budgeted Price *or*, = (RQ – BQ) × BP
Nature	(a) **Favourable (F)** if the effect of the variance is to **increase the profit** (*i.e. where RQ > BQ*) (b) **Adverse (A)** if the effect of the variance is to **decrease the profit** (*i.e. where RQ < BQ*)

Illustration 6. Calculate Sales Sub Volume Variance in Illustration 5.

Solution:

Step 1: Average Budgeted Price (ABP) $= \frac{(800 \times 12) + (1200 \times 10)}{2000} = \frac{21600}{2000} = 10.80$

Step 2: Sales Sub Volume Variance (SSVV) = (Total AQ – Total BQ.) × ABP

= (1700 – 2000) × ₹ 10.80 = ₹ 3,240 (A)

8.0 PRACTICAL STEPS IN THE COMPUTATION OF SALES VARIANCES (ON SALES VALUE BASIS)

Step 1: *Prepare a* ***10 Column Table*** *of Basic Calculations as follows:*

TABLE OF BASIC CALCULATIONS FOR THE COMPUTATION OF SALES VARIANCES (ON SALES VALUE BASIS)

Type of Material	*BQ*	*BP*	*BQ × SP (1)*	*AQ*	*AP*	*AQ × AP (2)*	*AQ × BP (3)*	*RQ*	*RQ × BP (4)*
Product A	....	....	....	....	....	....	....	....	....
Product B	....	....	....	....	....	....	....	....	....

Note: RQ = Revised Quantity = Actual Quantity in Budgeted Sales Mix Ratio

Step 2: *Calculate Sales Value Variances as follows:*

Sales Value Variance (2 – 1) = (AQ × AP) – (BQ × BP)

Product A = ₹ .... – ₹ .... = ₹ ....

Product B = ₹ .... – ₹ .... = ₹ ....

SVV = ₹ ....

Sales Price Variance (2 – 3) = (AQ × AP) – (AQ × BP)

Product A = ₹ .... – ₹ .... = ₹ ....

Product B = ₹ .... – ₹ .... = ₹ ....

SPV = ₹ ....

Sales Volume Variance (3 – 1) = (AQ × BP) – (BQ × BP)

Product A = ₹ .... – ₹ .... = ₹ ....

Product B = ₹ .... – ₹ .... = ₹ ....

SVV = ₹ ....

Sales Mix Variance (3 – 4) = (AQ × BP) – (RQ × BP)

Product A = ₹ .... – ₹ .... = ₹ ....

Product B = ₹ .... – ₹ .... = ₹ ....

SMV = ₹ ....

Sales Sub-Volume Variance = (Total AQ – Total BQ) × Average Budgeted Price

$$\text{Average Budgeted Price} = \frac{\text{Total (BQ × BP)}}{\text{BQ}} = ₹ \text{ ....}$$

***Alternatively*, SSVV (4 – 1) = (RQ × BP) – (BQ × BP)**

= ₹ .... – ₹ .... = ₹ ....

COMPREHENSIVE ILLUSTRATION

Illustration 7. Calculate all the Sales Variances on Sales Value basis from the following information provided by Bharat Tulsian Ltd.:

Product	*Budgeted Sales Quantity Units*	*Budgeted Selling Price per Unit ₹*	*Actual Sales Quantity Units*	*Actual Selling Price per Unit ₹*
A	60	20	44	25
B	40	10	66	5

Solution:

Basic Calculations:

1. Total Budgeted Sales Quantity = 60 + 40 = 100
2. Total Actual Sales Quantity = 44 + 66 = 110
3. Revised Quantity of Product A (RQ) = $\frac{60}{100} \times 110 = 66$
4. Revised Quantity of Product B (RQ) = $\frac{40}{100} \times 110 = 44$

BASIC CALCULATIONS FOR THE COMPUTATION OF SALES VARIANCES (ON SALES VALUE BASIS)

Type of Product	*BQ*	*BP*	*BQ × BP* (1)	*AQ*	*AP*	*AQ × AP* (2)	*AQ × BP* (3)	*RQ*	*RQ × BP* (4)
A	60	20	1,200	44	25	1,100	880	66	1,320
B	40	10	400	66	5	330	660	44	440
Total	100		1,600	110		1,430	1,540		1,760

Sales Value Variance (2 – 1) = (AQ × AP) – (BQ × BP)
= ₹ 1,430 – ₹ 1,600 = ₹ 170 (A)

Sales Price Variance (2 – 3) = (AQ × AP) – (AQ × BP)
Product A = ₹ 1,100 – ₹ 880 = ₹ 220 (F)
Product B = ₹ 330 – ₹ 660 = ₹ 330 (A)
SPV = ₹ 110 (A)

Sales Volume Variance (3 – 1) = (AQ × BP) – (BQ × BP)
Product A = ₹ 880 – ₹ 1200 = ₹ 320 (A)
Product B = ₹ 660 – ₹ 400 = ₹ 260 (F)
SVV = ₹ 60 (A)

Sales Mix Variance (3 – 4) = (AQ × BP) – (RQ × BP)
Product A = ₹ 880 – ₹ 1,320 = ₹ 440 (A)
Product B = ₹ 660 – ₹ 440 = ₹ 220 (F)
SMV = ₹ 220 (A)

Sales Sub-Volume Variance = (AQ – BQ) × Average Budgeted Price
= $(110 - 100) \times \frac{1,600}{100} = 160$ (F)

Alternatively, SSVV (4 – 1) = (RQ × BP) – (BQ × BP) = 1760 – ₹ 1600 = ₹ 160(F)

Verification: 1. SVV = SPV + SVV = ₹ 110 (A) + ₹ 60(A) = ₹ 170 (A)
2. SVV = SMV + SSVV = ₹ 220 (A) + ₹ 160 (F) = ₹.60 (A)

SALES VARIANCES ON MARGIN BASIS
[Assuming that All Products are homogenous and not hetrogeneous]

The purpose of measuring the variances on Margin Basis is to identify the effect of changes in sale quantities and selling prices on the profits of the company. Where a company deals in multiple products, the variances between budgeted sales and actual sales may arise due to the following reasons:

(a) Changes in Unit Price.
(b) Changes in Physical Volume of each product sold. This is quantity variance.
(c) Changes in the Physical Volume of the more profitable or less profitable products. This is mix variance.

Actual Performance may differ from Budgeted Performance due to:

1. Difference between Actual and Budgeted Unit Sale Price.
2. Difference between Actual and Budgeted Unit Cost.

3. Difference between Actual Total Quantity and Budgeted Total Quantity.
4. Difference between Actual Quantity of the constituents of Sales and Budgeted Quantity.
5. Direct Substitution of Products.

The sales management should consider particularly the interaction of more than one variable in making decisions. *For example*, decrease in selling price coupled with a favourable product quantity variance may help to assess the price elasticity of demand.

9.0 TERMS USEFUL FOR COMPUTATION OF SALES VARIANCES ON MARGIN BASIS

One must know the following terms before knowing how to compute Sales Variances on margin basis:

1. Budgeted Margin	(a) It represents the difference between Budgeted Selling Price and Standard Cost. (a) It is calculated as follows: = Budgeted Selling Price – Standard Cost
2. Actual Margin	(b) It represents the difference between Actual Selling Price and Standard Cost. (b) It is calculated as follows: = Actual Selling Price – Standard Cost
3. Budgeted Margin of Budgeted Sales Quantity	(a) It represents the Budgeted Margin of Budgeted Sales Quantity. (b) It is calculated as follows: = Budgeted Sales Quantity × Budgeted Margin = BQ x BM
4. Budgeted Margin of Actual Sales Quantity	(a) It represents the Budgeted Margin of Actual Sales Quantity. (b) It is calculated as follows: = Actual Sales Quantity × Budgeted Margin = AQ x BM
5. Revised Quantity	(a) It represents the Total Actual Quantity of all Products in a Budgeted Sales Mix Ratio. (b) It is calculated by dividing the Total Actual Sales Quantity of all Products in a Budgeted Mix Ratio as follows: $= \frac{\text{Budgeted Qty. of one Product}}{\text{Total Budgeted Qty. of all Products}} \times \text{Total Actual Qty. of all Products}$
6. Budgeted Margin of Revised Sales Quantity	(a) It represents the Budgeted Margin of Revised Sales Quantity. (d) It is calculated as follows: = Revised Sales Quantity × Budgeted Margin = RQ × BM
7. Average Budgeted Margin	(c) It represents the Budgeted Price per Unit of Budgeted Sales Quantity. (d) It is calculated as follows: $= \frac{\text{Total Budgeted Margin of Budgeted Sales Quantity of all Products}}{\text{Total Budgeted Sales Quantity of all Products}}$

Illustration 8. Tulsian Ltd. (1) provides you the following information:

	Budget		*Actual*			*Standard*
	Quantity	*Unit Price*	*Quantity*	*Unit Price*	*Unit Cost*	*Unit Cost*
Product 'A'	60 Units	₹ 20	44 Units	₹ 25	₹ 16	₹ 15
Product 'B'	40 Units	₹ 10	66 Units	₹ 5	₹ 5	₹ 4

Required: Calculate (a) Budgeted Margin (b) Actual Margin (c) Budgeted Margin of Budgeted Sales Quantity (d) Budgeted Margin of Actual Sales Quantity (e) Revised Quantity (f) Budgeted Margin of Revised Sales Quantity (g) Average Budgeted Margin.

Solution:

(a) Budgeted Margin = Budgeted Selling Price – Standard Cost

Product A = ₹ 20 – ₹ 15 = ₹ 5, Product B = ₹ 10 – ₹ 4 = ₹ 6

(b) Actual Margin = Actual Selling Price – Standard Cost

Product A = ₹ 25 – ₹ 16 = ₹ 9, Product B = ₹ 5 – ₹ 5 = ₹ 0

(c) Budgeted Margin of Budgeted Sales Quantity = Budgeted Sales Quantity × Budgeted Margin

Product A = (60 Units × ₹ 5) = ₹ 300, Product B = (40 Units × ₹ 6) = ₹ 240

(d) Budgeted Margin of Actual Sales Quantity = Actual Sales Quantity x Budgeted Margin

Product A = (44 kg. × ₹ 5) = ₹ 220, Product B = (66 kg. × ₹ 6) = ₹ 396

(e) Revised Quantity = $\frac{\text{Budgeted Qty. of one Product}}{\text{Total Budgeted Qty. of all Products}}$ × Total Actual Qty. of all Products

Product A = $\frac{60}{100} \times 110 = 66$, Product B = $\frac{40}{100} \times 110 = 44$

(f) Budgeted Margin of Revised Sales Quantity = Revised Quantity × Budgeted Price

Product A = (66 Units × ₹ 5) = ₹ 330, Product B = (44 Units × ₹ 6) = ₹ 264

(g) Average Budgeted Margin $= \frac{\text{Total Budgeted Margin of Budgeted Sales Quantity of all Products}}{\text{Total Budgeted Sales Quantity of all Products}}$

$= \frac{(60 \times 5) + (40 \times 6)}{100 \text{ Units}}$ = ₹ 5.4

10.0 TOTAL SALES MARGIN VARIANCE (SMV)

Meaning	Sales Margin Variance (SMV) is the difference between the Actual Margin of Actual Sales Quantity and the Budgeted Margin of Budgeted Sales Quantity.
How to Calculate	SMV = Actual Margin of Actual Sales Quantity – Budgeted Margin of Budgeted Sales Quantity *or,* = (Actual Sales Quantity × Actual Margin) – (Budgeted Sales Quantity × Budgeted Margin) *or,* = (AQ × AM) – (BQ × BM) **Note:** BM = Budgeted Selling Price – Standard Cost AM = Actual Selling Price – Standard Cost

Illustration 9. Calculate Total Sales Margin Variance from the following information:

	Budget	*Actual*
Sales Quantity	400 units	600 units
Selling Price per unit	₹.4	₹.3
Cost per unit	₹.1.50	₹.1.25

Solution:

Step 1: Budgeted Margin (BM) = ₹ 4 – ₹ 1.50 = ₹ 2.50

Step 2: Actual Margin (AM) = ₹ 3 – ₹ 1.50 = ₹ 1.50

Step 3: Sales Margin Variance = (AQ × AM) – (BQ × BM)

= (600 × ₹ 1.50) – (400 x ₹ 2.50) = ₹ 100 (A)

11.0 SALES MARGIN PRICE VARIANCE (SMPV)

Meaning	Sales Margin Price Variance (SMPV) is that portion of the Total Sales Margin Variance which arises due to the difference between the Actual Margin and Budgeted Margin.
How to Calculate	SMPV = (Actual Margin – Budgeted Margin) × Actual Quantity *or,* = (AM – BM) × AQ

Note: Sales Price Variance *remains* the same under Turnover Method and Margin Method.

Illustration 10. Calculate Sales Margin Price Variance in Illustration 9.

Solution: Sales Margin Price Variance = (AM – BM) × AQ = (₹ 1.50 – ₹ 2.50) × 600 = ₹ 600 (A)

12.0 SALES MARGIN VOLUME VARIANCE (SMVV)

Meaning	Sales Margin Volume Variance (SMVV) is that portion of the Total Sales Margin Variance which arises due to the difference between Actual Sales Quantity sold and Budgeted Sales Quantity specified.
How to calculate	SMVV = (Actual Quantity – Budgeted Quantity) × Budgeted Margin *or,* = (AQ – BQ) × BM
Division	Sales Margin Volume Variance may further be divided into: (a) Sales Margin Mix Variance and (b) Sales Margin Sub-Volume Variance.

Illustrarion 11. Calculate Sales Margin Volume Variance in Illustration 9.

Solution: Sales Margin Volume Variance = (AQ – BQ) × BM = (600 – 400) × ₹.2.50 = ₹.500 (F)

13.0 SALES MARGIN MIX VARIANCE

Meaning	Sales Margin Mix Variance (SMMV) is that portion of the Sales Margin Volume Variance which arises due to the difference between Actual and Budgeted Composition of products sold.
How to Calculate	SMMV= Budgeted Margin of Actual Sales Quantity ***minus*** Budgeted Margin of Revised Sales Quantity *or,* = (AQ × BM) – (RQ × BM) *or,* = (AQ – RQ) × BM **Note:** Revised Sales Quantity (RQ) is calculated by dividing the total of actual sales quantities of all products in a Budgeted Sales Mix ratio as follows: $= \frac{\text{Budgetd Qty of one product}}{\text{Total Budgeted Qty of all product}} \times \text{Total Actual Sales Qty of all Products}$

Illustration 12. Calculate Sales Margin Mix Variance from the following information:

Product	*Budget*			*Actual*		
	Qty	*Price*	*Cost*	*Qty*	*Price*	*Cost*
Product A	800	₹.12	₹.9	1000	₹.10	₹.6
Product B	1200	₹.10	₹.6	700	₹.12	₹.9

Solution:

Step 1: Revised Quantity (RQ)

Product 'A' = $\frac{800}{2000} \times 1700 = 680$ Product 'B' = $\frac{1200}{2000} \times 1700 = 1020$

Step 2: BM : Product 'A' = ₹.12 – ₹.9 = ₹ 3, Product 'B' = ₹.10 – ₹.6 = ₹.4

Step 3: Sales Margin Mix Variance = (AQ – RQ) × BM

Product 'A' = (1000 – 680) × ₹.3 = ₹.960 (F)

Product 'B' = (700 – 1020) × ₹.4 = ₹.1,280 (A)

SMMV = ₹.320 (A)

14.0 SALES MARGIN SUB–VOLUME VARIANCE/SALES QUANTITY VARIANCE

Meaning	Sales Margin Sub-Volume Variance is that portion of Sales Margin Volume Variance which arises due to the difference between Total Actual Sales Quantity of all products and Total Budgeted Sales Quantity of all products.
How to Calculate	SMSVV = (Total Actual Sales Quantity – Total Budgeted Sales Quantity) × Average Budgeted Margin Per Unit *or,* = (Total AQ – Total BQ) × ABM **Note:** Average Budgeted Margin per unit (ABM) ABM = $\frac{\text{Total Budgeted Margin of Budgeted Sales Qty of all products}}{\text{Total Budgeted Sales Qty of all products}}$ *or* = $\frac{\text{Total (BQ} \times \text{BM)}}{\text{Total BQ}}$ ***Alternatively,*** SMSVV = (Revised Quantity – Budgeted Quantity) × Budgeted Margin per unit. *or* = (RQ – BQ) × BM

Illustration 13. Calculate Sales Margin Sub-Volume Variance in Illustration 12.

Solution:

Step 1: Average Budgeted Margin (ABM) = $\frac{\text{Total (BQ} \times \text{BM)}}{\text{Total BQ}} = \frac{(800 \times 3)+(1200 \times 4)}{2000}$ = ₹.3.60

Step 2: Sales Margin Sub-Volume Variance (SMSVV)

= (Total Actual Qty – Total Budgeted Qty) × ABM = (1,700 – 2,000) × ₹.3.60 = ₹ 1,080 (A)

15.0 PRACTICAL STEPS IN THE COMPUTATION OF SALES VARIANCES (ON SALES MARGIN BASIS)

Step 1: *Prepare a **10 Column Table** of Basic Calculations as follows:*

TABLE OF BASIC CALCULATIONS FOR THE COMPUTATION OF SALES VARIANCES (ON SALES MARGIN BASIS)

Type of Product	*BQ*	*BM*	*BQ × BM (1)*	*AQ*	*AM*	*AQ × AM (2)*	*AQ × BM (3)*	*RQ*	*RQ × BM (4)*
Product A	....	....	....	....	....	....	....	....	....
Product B	....	....	....	....	....	....	....	....	....

Notes:

(i) BM = Budgeted Margin = Budgeted Selling Price – Standard Cost,

(ii) AM = Actual Margin = Actual Selling Price – Standard Cost,

(iii) RQ = Revised Quantity = Actual Quantity in Budgeted Sales Mix Ratio

Step 2: *Calculate Sales Margin Variances as follows:*

Sales Margin Variance (2 – 1) = (AQ × AM) – (BQ × BM)

Product A = ₹ .... – ₹ .... = ₹ ....
Product B = ₹ .... – ₹ .... = ₹ ....
SMV = ₹ ....

Sales Margin Price Variance (2 – 3) = (AQ × AM) – (AQ × BM)

Product A = ₹ .... – ₹ .... = ₹ ....
Product B = ₹ .... – ₹ .... = ₹ ....
SMPV = ₹ ....

Sales Margin Volume Variance (3 – 1) = (AQ × BM) – (BQ × BM)

Product A = ₹ .... – ₹ .... = ₹ ....
Product B = ₹ .... – ₹ .... = ₹ ....
SMVV = ₹ ....

Sales Margin Mix Variance (3 – 4) = (AQ × BM) – (RQ × BM)

Product A = ₹ .... – ₹ .... = ₹ ....
Product B = ₹ .... – ₹ .... = ₹ ....
SMMV = ₹ ....

Sales Margin Sub-Volume Variance = (Total AQ – Total BQ) × Average Budgeted Margin

$$\text{Average Budgeted Margin} = \frac{\text{Total (BQ} \times \text{BM)}}{\text{BQ}} = ₹ \text{ ....}$$

***Alternatively*, SMSVV (4 – 1) = (RQ × BM) – (BQ × BM)**

= ₹ .... – ₹ .... = ₹ ....

16.0 HOW TO RECONCILE STANDARD PROFIT WITH ACTUAL PROFIT

STATEMENT RECONCILING THE STANDARD PROFIT WITH ACTUAL PROFIT

			₹
A.	Budgeted Profit		
	Product A [BQ × BM]	.....	
	Product B [BQ × BM]	.....	.....
B.	*Add*: Fav. Sales Margin Volume Variance		.....
C.	Standard Profit [A + B]		.....
D.	*Less*: Adverse Sales Price Variance	.....	
	Adverse Cost Variance: Product 'A' AQ × (Standard Cost – Actual Cost)	.....	
	Product 'B' AQ × (Standard Cost – Actual Cost)	.....	.....
E.	Actual Profit [C – D]		.....

Verification : Actual Profit = AQ × AM

COMPREHENSIVE ILLUSTRATION

Illustration 14. Calculate all the Sales Variances on Sales Margin basis from the following information provided by Tushar Tulsian Ltd.:

Product	*Budgeted Sales Quantity Units*	*Budgeted Selling Price per Unit ₹*	*Standard Cost per Unit ₹*	*Actual Sales Quantity Units*	*Actual Selling Price per Unit ₹*	*Actual Cost per Unit ₹*
A	60	20	15	44	25	16
B	40	10	4	66	5	5

Also Reconcile the Standard Profit with Actual Profit.

Solution:

Basic Calculations:

1. Budgeted Margin Per Unit (BM) = Budgeted Selling Price Per Unit – Standard Cost Per Unit
   Product A = ₹ 20 – ₹ 15 = ₹ 5
   Product B = ₹ 10 – ₹ 4 = ₹ 6

2. Actual Margin Per Unit (AM) = Actual Selling Price per Unit – Standard Cost per Unit
   Product A = ₹ 25 – ₹ 15 = ₹ 10
   Product B = ₹ 5 – ₹ 4 = ₹ 1

BASIC CALCULATIONS FOR THE COMPUTATION OF SALES VARIANCES (ON SALES MARGIN BASIS)

Type of Product	*BQ*	*BM*	*BQ × BM (1)*	*AQ*	*AM*	*AQ × AM (2)*	*AQ × BM (3)*	*RQ*	*RQ × BM (4)*
A	60	5	300	44	10	440	220	66	330
B	40	6	240	66	1	66	396	44	264
Total	100		540	110		506	616		594

Sales Margin (Profit) Variance (2 – 1) = (AQ × AM) – (BQ × BM)
= ₹ 506 – ₹ 540 = ₹ 34 (A)

Sales Margin Price Variance (2 – 3) = (AQ × AM) – (AQ × BM)
Product A = ₹ 440 – ₹ 220 = ₹ 220 (F)
Product B = ₹ 66 – ₹ 396 = ₹ 330 (A)
SMPV = ₹ 110 (A)

Sales Margin Volume Variance (3 – 1) = (AQ × BM) – (BQ × BM)
Product A = ₹ 220 – ₹ 300 = ₹ 80(A)
Product B = ₹ 396 – ₹ 240 = ₹ 156 (F)
SMVV = ₹ 76 (F)

Sales Margin Mix Variance (3 – 4) = (AQ × BM) – (RQ × BM)
Product A = ₹ 220 – ₹ 330 = Rs110 (A)
Product B = ₹ 396 – ₹ 264 = ₹ 132 (F)
SMMV = ₹ 22 (F)

Sales Margin Sub-Volume Variance = (AQ – BQ) × Average Budgeted Margin

$$= (110 - 100) \times \frac{540}{100} = 54\ (F)$$

Alternatively, SMSVV (4 – 1) = (RQ × BM) – (BQ × BM) = ₹ 594 – ₹ 540 = ₹ 54 (F)

Verification: 1. SMV = SMPV + SMVV = ₹ 110 (A) + ₹ 76 (F) = ₹ 34 (A)
2. SMVV = SMMV + SMSVV = ₹ 22(F) + 54 (F) = ₹ 76 (F)

STATEMENT RECONCILING THE STANDARD PROFIT WITH ACTUAL PROFIT

	₹	₹
A. Budgeted Profit		
Product A [60 × ₹ 5]	300	
Product B [40 × ₹ 6]	240	540
B. *Add*: Fav. Sales Margin Volume Variance		76
C. Standard Profit [A + B]		616
D. *Less*: Adverse Sales Price Variance	110	
Adverse Cost Variance: Product 'A' 44 × (₹ 15 – ₹ 16)	44	
Product 'B' 66 × (₹ 4 – ₹ 5)	66	220
E. Actual Profit [C – D]		396

Verification : Actual Profit = [44 × (₹ 25 – ₹ 16] + [66 × (₹ 5 – 5)] = ₹ 396

17.0 ALTERNATIVE FORMULAE USED FOR CALCULATING SALES VARIANCES (BASED ON MARGIN)

Sales Variance	*Formula*
1. *Sales Margin Variance*	= Actual Profit – Budgeted Profit
2. *Sales Margin Price Variance*	= Actual Profit – Standard Profit
3. *Sales Margin Volume Variance*	= Standard Profit – Budgeted Profit

4. *Sales Margin Mix Variance*	=	Standard Profit – Revised Standard Profit
5. *Sales Margin Sub-Volume Variance* *or* *Sales Margin Quantity Variance*	=	Revised Standard Profit – Budgeted Profit *Where,* Actual Profit = AQ × AM Budgeted Profit = BQ × BM Standard Profit = AQ × BM Revised Standard Profit = RQ × BM

Illustration 15. From the following information, Calculate all Sales Variances:

Actual Profit	₹ 5,200	Standard Profit	₹ 7,800
Budgeted Profit	₹ 7,200	Revised Standard Profit	₹ 6,120

Solution:

Total Sales Margin Variance = Actual Profit – Budgeted Profit
= ₹ 5,200 – ₹ 7,200 = ₹ 2,000 (A)

Total Sales Margin Price Variance = Actual Profit – Standard Profit
= ₹ 5,200 – ₹ 7,800 = ₹ 2,600 (A)

Total Sales Margin Volume Variance = Standard Profit – Budgeted Profit
= ₹ 7,800 – ₹ 7,200 = ₹ 600 (F)

Total Sales Margin Mix Variance = Standard Profit – Revised Standard Profit
= ₹ 7,800 – ₹ 6,120 = ₹ 1,680 (F)

Total Sales Margin Sub-Volume Variance = Revised Standard Profit – Budgeted Profit
= ₹ 6,120 – ₹ 7,200 = ₹ 1,080 (A)

SOLVED PROBLEMS

Problem 1. Calculate all the Sales Variances (a) On Sales Value Basis (b) On Sales Margin Basis from the following information provided by Bharat Tushar Ltd. :

(a) *BUDGETED DATA*:

Product	*Sales (₹)*	*Selling Price per Unit (₹)*	*Standard Contribution Margin per Unit (₹)*
A	1,200	20	5
B	400	10	6

(b) *ACTUAL DATA :*

Product	*Sales (₹)*	*Cost per Unit (₹)*	*Opening Stock units*	*Closing Stock units*	*Production units*
A	1100	16	20	10	34
B	330	5	10	20	76

Also reconcile the Actual Profit with the Standard Profit.

Solution:

Basic Calculations :

1. Actual Sales Quantity of 'A' = Production + Opening Stock – Closing Stock = 34 + 20 – 10 = 44
2. Actual Sales Quantity of 'B' = 76 + 10 – 20 = 66 units
3. Total Actual Sales Quantity = 44 + 66 = 110 units
4. Total Budgeted Sales Quantity = 60 + 40 =100 units

5. Revised Quantity of Product 'A' (RQ) = $\frac{60}{100} \times 110 = 66$ units
6. Revised Quantity of Product 'B' (RQ) = $\frac{40}{100} \times 110 = 44$ units
7. Budgeted Sales Quantity of 'A' = ₹ 1200/₹ 20 = 60 units
8. Budgeted Sales Quantity of 'B' = ₹ 400/₹ 10 = 40 units
9. Standard Cost of 'A' = ₹ 20 – ₹ 5 = ₹ 15
10. Standard Cost of 'A' = ₹ 10 – ₹ 6 = ₹ 4
11. Actual Selling Price of 'A' = ₹ 1100/44 = ₹ 25
12. Actual Selling Margin of 'B' = ₹ 330/66 = ₹ 5
13. Actual Margin of 'A' = ₹ 25 – ₹ 15 = ₹ 10
14. Actual Margin of 'B' = ₹ 5 – ₹ 4 = ₹ 1

Now, the rest of the solution is same as given in Illustration 7 and 14.

Problem 2. The Sales Manager of a company engaged in the manufacture and sale of three products A, B and C gives you the following information for the month of October :

BUDGETED SALES :

Product	*Units Sold*	*Selling Price per Unit* ₹	*Standard Contribution Margin per Unit*
A	2,000	12	6
B	2,000	8	4
C	2,000	5	1

Actual Sales :

A. 1,500 units for ₹ 15,000, B. 2,500 units for ₹ 17,500, C. 3,500 units for ₹ 21,000

You are required to calculate (i) The Sales Price Variance; (ii) The Sales Volume Variance; (iii) The Sales Quantity Variance; (iv) The Sales Mix Variance.

Solution:

BASIC CALCULATIONS FOR THE COMPUTATION OF SALES VARIANCES (ON SALES VALUE BASIS)

Type of Product	*BQ*	*BP*	*BQ × BP* (1)	*AQ*	*AP*	*AQ × AP* (2)	*AQ × BP* (3)	*RQ*	*RQ × BP* (4)
A	2,000	12	24,000	1,500		15,000	18,000	2,500	30,000
B	2,000	8	16,000	2,500		17,500	20,000	2,500	20,000
C	2,000	5	10,000	3,500		21,000	17,500	2,500	12,500
	6,000		50,000	7,500		53,500	55,500		62,500

Sales Value Variance (2 – 1) = (AQ × AP) – (BQ × BP)
= ₹ 53,500 – ₹ 50,000 = ₹ 3,500 (F)

Sales Price Variance (2 – 3) = (AQ × AP) – (AQ × BP)
Product A = ₹ 15,000 – ₹ 18,000 = ₹ 3,000 (A)
Product B = ₹ 17,500 – ₹ 20,000 = ₹ 2,500 (A)
Product C = ₹ 21,000 – ₹ 17,500 = ₹ 3,500 (F)
SPV = ₹ 2,000(A)

Sales Volume Variance (3 – 1) = (AQ × BP) – (BQ × BP)
Product A = ₹ 18,000 – ₹ 24,000 = ₹ 6,000 (A)
Product B = ₹ 20,000 – ₹ 16,000 = ₹ 4,000 (F)
Product C = ₹ 17,500 – ₹ 10,000 = ₹ 7,500 (F)
SVV = ₹ 5,500 (F)

Sales Mix Variance (3 – 4) = (AQ × BP) – (RQ × BP)

Product A = ₹ 18,000 – ₹ 30,000 = ₹ 12,000 (A)

Product B = ₹ 20,000 – ₹ 20,000 = Nil

Product C = ₹ 17,500 – ₹ 12,500 = ₹ 5,000 (F)

SMV = ₹ 7,000 (A)

Sales Sub-Volume Variance = (Actual Qty. – Budgeted Qty) × Average Budgeted Price

$$= (7{,}500 - 6{,}000) \times \frac{50{,}000}{6{,}000} = 12{,}500\,(F)$$

Alternatively, SSVV (4 – 1) = (RQ × BP) – (BQ × BP) = ₹ 62,500 – ₹ 50,000 = ₹ 12,500 (F)

Verification: 1. SVV = SPV + SVV = ₹.2,000 (A) + ₹.5,500 (F) = ₹ 3500 (F)

2. SVV = SMV + SSVV = ₹.7,000 (A) + ₹.12,500 (F) = ₹.5,500(F)

Calculation of Standard Margin and Actual Margin:

	SP	*AP*	*SC*	*SM*	*AM*
A	12	10	6	6	4
B	8	7	4	4	3
C	5	6	4	1	2

BASIC CALCULATIONS FOR THE COMPUTATION OF SALES VARIANCES (ON MARGIN BASIS)

Type of Product	*BQ*	*BM*	*BQ × BM (1)*	*AQ*	*AM*	*AQ × AM (2)*	*AQ × BM (3)*	*RQ*	*RQ × BM (4)*
A	2,000	6	12,000	1,500	4	6,000	9,000	2,500	15,000
B	2,000	4	8,000	2,500	3	7,500	10,000	2,500	10,000
C	2,000	1	2,000	3,500	2	7,000	3,500	2,500	2,500
	6,000		22,000			20,500	22,500		27,500

Sales Margin (Profit) Variance (2 – 1) = (AQ × AM) – (BQ × BM)

= ₹ 20,500 – ₹ 22,000 = ₹ 1,500 (A)

Sales Margin Price Variance (2 – 3) = (AQ × AM) – (AQ × BM)

Product A = ₹ 6,000 – ₹ 9,000 = ₹ 3,000 (A)

Product B = ₹ 7,500 – ₹ 10,000 = ₹ 2,500 (A)

Product C = ₹ 7,000 – ₹ 3,500 = ₹ 3,500 (F)

SMPV = ₹ 2,000 (A)

Sales Margin Volume Variance (3 – 1) = (AQ × BM) – (BQ × BM)

Product A = ₹ 9,000 – ₹ 12,000 = ₹ 3,000 (A)

Product B = ₹ 10,000 – ₹ 8,000 = ₹ 2,000 (F)

Product C = ₹ 3,500 – ₹ 2,000 = ₹ 1500 (F)

SMVV = ₹ 500 (F)

Sales Margin Mix Variance (3 – 4) = (AQ × BM) – (RBQ × BM)

Product A = ₹ 9,000 – ₹ 15,000 = ₹ 6,000 (A)

Product B = ₹ 10,000 – ₹ 10,000 = NIL

Product C = ₹ 3,500 – ₹ 2,500 = ₹ 1,000 (F)

SMMV = ₹ 5,000 (A)

Sales Margin Sub-Volume Variance = (AQ – BQ) × Average Standard Margin

$$= (7{,}500 - 6{,}000) \times \frac{22{,}000}{6{,}000} = 5{,}500\,(F)$$

Alternatively, SMSVV (1–4) = (RQ × BM) – (BQ × BM) = ₹ 27,500 – ₹ 22,000 = ₹ 5,500 (F)

Verification: 1. SMV = SMPV + SMVV = ₹ 2,000 (A) + ₹.500 (F) = ₹ 1,500 (A)

2. SMVV = SMMV + SMSVV = ₹ 5,000(A) + 5,500 (F) = ₹ 500 (F)

Problem 3. Super Computers Manufactures and sells three related PC models:

1. PC — Sold mostly to college students
2. Portable PC— Smaller version of PC positioned as home computer
3. Super PC — Sold mostly to business executives
4. Budgeted and Actual Data :

Particulars	*Budgeted*				*Actual*	
	Selling Price per unit ₹	*Variable Cost/unit* ₹	*Sales volume in units*	*Contribution margin/unit* ₹	*Variable Cost/unit* ₹	*Sales volume in units*
PC	24,000	14,000	7,000	12,000	10,000	8,250
Portable PC	16,000	10,000	1,000	5,000	8,000	1,650
Super PC	1,00,000	60,000	2,000	20,000	50,000	1,100
Total:			10,000			11,000

Required: Compute Sales Variances

Solution

(i) Computation of Sales Variances

Basic Calculations:

(i) BM = Budgeted Margin = Budgeted Selling Price – Standard Cost
For PC = ₹ 24,000 – ₹ 14,000 = ₹ 10,000 and similarly for others.

(ii) AM = Actual Margin = Actual Selling Price – Standard Cost
For PC = ₹ 22,000 – ₹ 14,000 = ₹ 8,000 and similarly for others.

(iii) RQ = Revised Quantity = Total Actual Quantity (11,000) in Budgeted Sales Mix Ratio i.e. 7:1:2
For PC = 11,000 x 7/10 = 7,700 and similarly for others.

BASIC CALCULATIONS FOR THE COMPUTATION OF SALES VARIANCES ***[₹ In '000']***

Type of Product	*BQ*	*BM*	*BQ × BM (1)*	*AQ*	*AM*	*AQ × AM (2)*	*AQ × BM (3)*	*RQ*	*RQ × BM (4)*
PC	7,000	10	70,000	8,250	8.00	66,000	82,500	7,700	77,000
Portable PC	1,000	6	6,000	1,650	3.00	4,950	9,900	1,100	6,600
Super PC	2,000	40	80,000	1,100	10.00	11,000	44,000	2,200	88,000
	10,000		**1,56,000**	**11,000**		**81,950**	**1,36,400**	**1,100**	**1,71,600**

Step 2: *Calculate Sales Margin Variances as follows:*

Sales Margin Variance (2 – 1) = (AQ × AM) – (BQ × BM)

PC = ₹ 66,000 – ₹ 70,000 – ₹ 4,000 (A)
Portable PC = ₹ 4,950 – ₹ 6,000. = ₹ 1,050 (A)
Super PC = ₹ 11,000 – ₹ 80,000 = ₹ 69,000 (A)
SMV = ₹ 74,050 (A)

Sales Margin Price Variance (2 – 3) = (AQ × AM) – (AQ × BM)

PC = ₹ 66,000 – ₹ 82,500 = ₹ 16,500 (A)
Portable PC = ₹ 4,950 – ₹ 9,900 = ₹ 4,950 (A)
Super PC = ₹ 11,000 – ₹ 44,000 = ₹ 33,000 (A)
SMPV = ₹ 54,450 (A)

Sales Margin Volume Variance (3 – 1) = (AQ × BM) – (BQ × BM)

PC = ₹ 82,500 – ₹ 70,000 = ₹ 12,500 (F)
Portable PC = ₹ 9,900 – ₹ 6,000 = ₹ 3,900 (F)
Super PC = ₹ 44,000 – ₹ 80,000 = ₹ 36,000 (A)
SMVV = ₹ 19,600 (A)

Sales Margin Mix Variance (3 – 4) = (AQ × BM) – (RQ × BM)

PC = ₹ 82,500 – ₹ 77,000 = ₹ 5,500 (F)
Portable PC = ₹ 9,900 – ₹ 6,600 = ₹ 3,300 (F)
Super PC = ₹ 44,000 – ₹ 88,000 = ₹ 44,000 (A)
SMMV = ₹ 35,200 (A)

Sales Margin Sub-Volume Variance = **(Total AQ – Total BQ) × Average Budgeted Margin**
= (11,000 – 10,000) x ₹ 15.6 = ₹ 15,600 (F)

Note: Average Budgeted Margin = $\frac{\text{Total (BQ × BM)}}{\text{BQ}}$

$= \frac{(10 \times 7{,}000) + (6 \times 1{,}000) + (40 \times 2{,}000)}{7{,}000 + 1{,}000 + 2{,}000}$ = ₹ 15.6

***Alternatively,* SMSVV (4 – 1) = (RQ × BM) – (BQ × BM)**

PC = ₹ 77,000 – ₹ 70,000 = ₹ 7,000 (F)
Portable PC = ₹ 6,600 – ₹ 6,000 = ₹ 600 (F)
Super PC = ₹ 88,000 – ₹ 80,000 = ₹ 8,000 (F)
SMSVV = ₹ 15,600 (F)

Problem 4. Tulsian Ltd. provides you the following information:

Product	*Budgeted Sales Qty. kg.*	*Budgeted Selling price per unit ₹*	*Actual Sales Qty. kg.*	*Actual Selling price per unit ₹*
A	60	20	44	25
B	40	?	66	5

Calculate the Budgeted Selling Price of Product 'B' in each of the following alternative cases:

Case (a) If Sales Value Variance is ₹ 170 (Adv.)
Case (b) If Sales Volume Variance is ₹ 70 (Fav.)
Case (c) If Sale Sub-volume Variance is ₹ 160 (Fav.)
Case (d) If Sales Mix Variance is ₹ 110 (Adv.)
Case (e) If Sales Price Variance is ₹ 220 (Fav.)

Solution: Let the Budgeted Selling Price of Product 'B' be *x*,

Revised Quantity for Actual Mix : A : $\frac{60}{100} \times 110 = 66$ kg. B : $\frac{40}{100} \times 110 = 44$ kg.

BASIC CALCULATIONS FOR THE COMPUTATION OF SALES VARIANCES (ON SALES VALUE BASIS)

Type of Product	*BQ*	*BP*	*BQ × BP (1)*	*AQ*	*AP*	*AQ × AP (2)*	*AQ × BP (3)*	*RQ*	*RQ × BP (4)*
A	60	20	1,200	44	25	1,100	880	66	1,320
B	40	*x*	40*x*	66	5	330	66*x*	44	44*x*
	100		1,200 + 40*x*	110		1,430	880+66*x*	110	1,320+44*x*

Case (a) Sales Value Variance (2 – 1) = (AQ × AP) – (BQ × BP)

– ₹ 170 = 1,430 – (1,200 + 40 *x*)

1200 + 40 *x* = 1,430 + 170 = 1,600

x = (1,600 – 1,200)/40 = ₹ 10 per kg.

Case (b) Sales Volume Variance (3 – 1) = (AQ × BP) – (BQ × BP)

₹ 70 = (880 + 66 *x*) – (₹ 1,200 + 40 *x*)

₹ 70 = – ₹ 320 + 26 *x*

x = (320 + 70)/26 = ₹ 15 per kg.

Case (c) Sales Sub-volume Variance (4 – 1) = (RQ × BP) – (BQ × BP)

₹ 160 = (1,320 + 44 *x*) – (1,200 + 40 *x*)

₹ 160 = + ₹ 120 + 4 *x*

x = (₹ 160 – ₹ 120)/4 = ₹ 10 per kg.

Case (d) Sales Mix Variance (3 – 4) = (AQ × BP) – (RQ × BP)

– ₹ 110 = (880 + 66 *x*) – (1,320 + 44 *x*)

– ₹ 110 = – 440 + 22 *x*

x = (440 – 110)/22 = ₹ 15 per kg.

Case (e) Sales Price Variance (2 – 3) = (AQ × AP) – (AQ × BP)

₹ 220 = 1,430 – (880 + 66 *x*)

₹ 220 = + 550 – 66 *x*

x = (550 – 220)/66 = ₹ 5 per kg.

Problem 5. Compute the missing data indicated by the question from the following :

	Product A	*Product B*
Budgeted Sales Quantity (units)	?	400
Actual Sales Quantity (units)	500	?
Budgeted Selling Price per Unit	₹ 12	₹ 15
Actual Selling Price per Unit	₹ 15	₹ 20
Sales Price Variance	?	?
Sales Volume Variance	₹ 1200 (F)	?
Sales Value Variance	?	?

Sales Mix Variance for Both the Products Together was ₹ 450 (F).
"F" Denotes Favourable.

Solution:

Basic Calculations:

1. *Budgeted Quantity of Product 'A'*

Sales Volume Variance = SP (AQ – BQ)

₹ 1,200 = ₹ 12 (500 – BQ) = 12 BQ – 6,000

BQ = (6,000 – 1,200)/12 = 400 units

2. *Actual Quantity of Product 'B'*

Let Actual Quantity of Product 'B' be *x*

Type of Product	*BQ*	*BP*	*BQ × BP* (1)	*AQ*	*AP*	*AQ × AP* (2)	*AQ × BP* (3)	*RQ*	*RQ × BP* (4)
A	400	12	4,800	500	15	7500	6000	250+*x*/2	3000+6*x*
B	400	15	6,000	*x*	20	20*x*	15*x*	250+*x*/2	3750+7.5*x*
	800		10,800			7500+20*x*	6000+15*x*	500+*x*	6750+13.5*x*

Sales Mix Variance (3 – 4) = (AQ × BP) – (RQ × BP)

₹ 450 = (6000 + 15 *x*) – (6750 + 13.5 *x*)

1.5 *x* = 1200

x = 1200/1.5 = 800 units

BASIC CALCULATIONS FOR THE COMPUTATION OF SALES VARIANCES (ON SALES VALUE BASIS)

Type of Product	*BQ*	*BP*	*BQ × BP* (1)	*AQ*	*AP*	*AQ × AP* (2)	*AQ × BP* (3)	*RQ*	*RQ × BP* (4)
A	400	12	4,800	500	15	7,500	6,000	650	7,800
B	400	15	6,000	800	20	16,000	12,000	650	9,750
	800		10,800	1,300		23,500	18,000	1,300	17,550

		Product 'A'	Product 'B'	Total
A. Sales Value Variance	(2 – 1)	2,700 (F)	10,000 (F)	12,700 (F)
B. Sales Volume Variance	(3 – 1)	1,200 (F)	6,000 (F)	7,200 (F)
C. Sales Sub-volume Variance	(4 – 1)	3,000 (F)	3,750 (F)	6,750 (F)
D. Sales Mix Variance	(3 – 4)	1,800 (A)	2,250 (F)	450 (F)
E. Sales Price Variance	(2 – 3)	1,500 (F)	4,000 (F)	5,500 (F)

Verification:

1. Sales Value Variance = Sales Volume Variance + Sales Price Variance
   = ₹ 7,200 (F) + ₹ 5,500 (F) = ₹ 12,700 (F)
2. Sales Volume Variance = Sales Sub-volume Variance + Sales Mix Variance
   = ₹ 6,750 (F) + ₹ 450 (F) = ₹ 7,200 (F)

10 Standard Costing — Miscellaneous Variances

LEARNING OBJECTIVES

After studying this chapter, you should be able to understand:

- Standard Cost Card/Standard Cost Sheet
- Standard Cost for Actual Output, Flexible Budget, Original Budget and Variances
- Budgeted Profit, Standard Profit and Actual Profit
- How to Reconcile the Actual Profit With the Standard Profit
- Format of Statement Reconciling the Actual Profit With the Standard Profit
- Market Size Variance
- Market Share Variance
- Quality Cost Variance
- Planning Variance
- Operational Variances
- Budget Variance
- Revision Variance
- Method Variance
- Substitution Variance
- Investigation of Variances
- Variance Reports
- Accounting Procedure for Standard Cost
- How to Dispose off Variances in a Standard Costing System?
- Behavioural Aspects of Standard Costing

1.0 STANDARD COST CARD/STANDARD COST SHEET

Meaning	Standard Cost Card/Sheet is a record of standard material, labour and overheads costs for a particular product/service.
Contents	Standard Cost Card/Sheet shows: (a) Quantity and Price of each material item to be consumed. (b) Time and Rate of each grade of labour to be used. (c) Rate and Basis of overheads absorption. (d) Total Cost element wise.
Format	**Standard Cost Card**

Product : Component PC T – 101 — *Date of fixing standard : 9th Aug. 2008*
Unit : Dozen — *Date of revision : ....*

	Rate ₹	*Total* ₹
Direct Materials :		
8 units of Material X	30	240

	12 units of material Y	50	600
	Total	**840**	
	Direct Labour :		
	Skilled 12 hours	100	1200
	Unskilled 8 hours	40	320
	Total	**1520**	
	Factory Overhead :		
	Machine hour rate I. 12 hrs.	30	360
	II. 8 hrs.	50	400
		Total	**760**

COST SUMMARY

Direct Materials	₹ 840
Direct Labour	₹ 1,520
Factory Overheads	₹ 760
Standard cost per unit	₹ 3,120

Illustration 1. Tulsian Ltd. manufactures a product "XYZ" and provides you the following information :

Standard and Budgeted Data :

Direct Material: 2 kg. @ ₹ 20 per kg

Direct Labour: 20 Hours @ ₹ 2 per hour

Budgeted Output 10,000 units. Budgeted Overheads ₹ 2,80,000 (including ₹ 2,00,000 Fixed Overheads). Profit 20% of selling price.

Required: Prepare Standard Cost Sheet per unit.

Solution: **STANDARD COST SHEET PER UNIT**

	Particulars	₹
A	Direct Material: (2 kg. × ₹ 20 per kg)	40
B	Direct Labour: (20 Hours × ₹ 2 per hour)	40
C	Variable Overhead (20 × ₹ 0.40)	8
D	Fixed Overhead (20 × ₹ 1.00)	20
E	Total Cost (A + B + C + D)	108
F	*Add :* Profit @ 20% on Sales or 25% on Cost	27
G	Selling Price [E + F]	135

Working Notes:

(i) Budgeted Hours = Budgeted output × Labour Hours per unit
= 10,000 × 20 = 2,00,000 Hours

(ii) Variable Overhead Rate Per hour = ₹ 80,000/2,00,000 = ₹ 0.40 per hour

(iii) Fixed Overhead Rate per hour = ₹ 2,00,000/2,00,000 = ₹ 1.00 per hour

Illustration 2. The CEO of your Company has given the following Master Budget for a recent month:

	₹
Production and Sales Units	10,000
Sales	8,00,000
Direct Material	2,00,000
Direct Wages	3,00,000
Variable Overhead	1,00,000
Fixed Overhead	1,00,000
Total Cost	7,00,000
Net Surplus	1,00,000

Require: Prepare Standard Cost Sheet per unit.

Solution **STANDARD COST SHEET PER UNIT**

	Particulars	₹
A	Direct Material	20
B	Direct Labour	30
C	Variable Overhead	10
D	Fixed Overhead	10
E	Total Cost (A + B + C + D)	70
F	*Add* : Profit	10
G	Selling Price [E + F]	80

Illustration 3. The CEO of your Company has been given the following statement showing the results for a recent month:

(a) Actual Data:

Particulars	Actual
Production and Sales Units	9,000
Sales	7,00,000
Direct Material	1,84,000
Direct Wages	2,62,000
Variable Overhead	94,000
Fixed Overhead	98,000
Net Surplus	62,000

(b) Variances:

Particulars	Favourable (₹)	Adverse (₹)
Material Price Variance	12,000	
Material Usage Variance		16,000
Labour Rate Variance	2,000	
Labour Efficiency Variance	6,000	
Variable Overhead Efficiency Variance	2,000	
Variable Overhead Expenditure Variance		6,000
Fixed Overhead Efficiency Variance	2,000	
Fixed Overhead Capacity Variance		12,000
Fixed Overhead Expenditure Variance	2,000	
Sales Price Variance		20,000
Sales Margin Volume Variance		10,000

Require: Prepare Standard Cost Sheet per unit.

Solution: **STANDARD COST SHEET PER UNIT**

Particulars A	Actual (₹) B	Variance (₹) C	Standard Cost for 9,000 Units (₹) D = B ± C	Standard Cost per Unit (₹) E = D / 9,000
A Direct Material	1,84,000	(4,000)	1,80,000	20
B Direct Labour	2,62,000	8,000	2,70,000	30
C Variable Overhead	94,000	(4,000)	90,000	10
D Fixed Overhead	98,000	(8,000)	90,000	10
E Total Cost (A + B + C + D)	6,38,000		6,30,000	70
F *Add* : Profit	62,000		90,000	10
G Sales [E + F]	7,00,000	(20,000)	7,20,000	80

2.0 STANDARD COST FOR ACTUAL OUTPUT, FLEXIBLE BUDGET, ORIGINAL BUDGET AND VARIANCES

Standard Cost for Actual Output	Standard Cost for Actual Output represents **Absorbed Cost** for Actual Output. It is calculated as follows: = Actual Output × Standard Cost Per Unit
Flexible Budget	Flexible Budget for Actual Output represents **Budgeted Cost** for Actual Output. It is calculated as follows: = (Actual Output × Standard Variable Cost Per Unit) + Budgeted Fixed Overheads
Original Budget	Original Budget represents **Budgeted Cost for Budgeted Output**. It is calculated as follows: = Budgeted Output × Standard Cost Per Unit
Variances	Variances represent the differences between Standard Cost for Actual Output and Actual Cost for Actual Output.

2.1 Difference between Standard Cost for Actual Output and Flexible Budget for Actual Output

Standard Cost for Actual Output includes only Absorbed Fixed Overheads (i.e. Actual Output × Standard Fixed Overhead Rate per Unit) but **Flexible Budget for Actual Output** includes total Budgeted Fixed Overheads.

Illustration 4. Tulsian Ltd. manufactures a product "XYZ" and provides you the following information:

(a) *Standard and Budgeted Data :*
Direct Material: 2 kg. @ ₹ 20 per kg
Direct Labour: 20 Hours @ ₹ 2 per hour
Budgeted Output 10,000 units. Budgeted Overheads ₹ 2,80,000 (including ₹ 2,00,000 Fixed Overheads). Profit 20% of selling price.

(b) *Actual Data* — Direct Materials (16,500 units) ₹ 3,96,000; Direct Labour (1,70,000 Hours) ₹ 3,46,800, Variable Overheads ₹ 60,000, Fixed Overheads ₹ 1,84,000; Sales (8,000 units) ₹ 11,20,000. No. opening and closing stocks.

Required: Prepare (a) Statement showing Total Standard Cost for Actual Output; (b) Original Budget for the Budget Period; (c) Flexible Budget for Actual Output; (d) Statement showing Variances.

Solution:

(a) (b) (c) (d) TOTAL STANDARD COST FOR ACTUAL OUTPUT, ORIGINAL BUDGET, FLEXIBLE BUDGET AND VARIANCES

Particulars *A*	*Standard Cost Per unit* *B* ₹	*Total Standard Cost for 8,000 units* *C = 8,000 × B*	*Original Budget for 10,000 units* *D = 10,000 × B* ₹	*Flexible Budget for 8,000 units* *E* ₹	*Actual for 8,000 Units* *F* ₹	*Variances* *G = C − F* ₹
Direct Material	40	3,20,000	4,00,000	3,20,000	3,96,000	−76,000
Direct Labour	40	3,20,000	4,00,000	3,20,000	3,46,800	−26,800
Variable Overhead	8	64,000	80,000	64,000	60,000	+4,000
Fixed Overhead	20	1,60,000	2,00,000	2,00,000	1,84,000	−24,000
Total Cost	108	8,64,000	10,80,000	9,04,000	9,86,800	−1,22,800
Profit	27	2,16,000	2,70,000	1,76,000	1,33,200	+82,800
Sales	135	10,80,000	13,50,000	10,80,000	11,20,000	− 40,000

3.0 BUDGETED PROFIT, STANDARD PROFIT AND ACTUAL PROFIT

Budgeted Profit	Budgeted Profit represents Budgeted Margin on Budgeted Output. It is calculated as follows: Budgeted Profit = Budgeted Output × Budgeted Margin per Unit
Standard Profit	Standard Profit represents Budgeted Margin on Actual Output. It is calculated as follows: 1. Standard Profit = Actual Output × Budgeted Margin per Unit 2. Standard Profit = Budgeted Profit ± Sales Margin Volume Variance
Actual Profit	Actual Profit represents Actual Margin on Actual Output. It is calculated as follows: 1. Actual Profit = Actual Sales – Actual Cost 2. Actual Profit = Actual Output × Actual Margin per Unit 3. Actual Profit = Standard Profit ± Sales Price Variance ± Material, Labour & Overhead Cost Variances

Illustration 5. Taking the same information as given in Illustration 4, calculate Budgeted Profit, Standard Profit and Actual Profit

Solution:

Budgeted Profit = Budgeted Output × Budgeted Margin per Unit = 10,000 Units × ₹ 27 = ₹ 2,70,000

Standard Profit = Actual Output × Budgeted Margin per Unit = 8,000 Units × ₹ 27 = ₹ 2,16,000

Actual Profit = Actual Sales – Actual Cost

= ₹ 11,20,000 – (₹ 3,96,000 + ₹ 3,46,800 + ₹ 60,000 + ₹ 1,84,000) = ₹ 1,33,200

4.0 HOW TO RECONCILE THE ACTUAL PROFIT WITH THE STANDARD PROFIT

To Reconcile the Actual Profit with the Standard Profit the following Practical Steps should be followed:

Step 1: *Calculate Budgeted Profit (i.e. Budgeted Output × Budgeted Margin per Unit)*

Step 2: *Calculate Standard Profit (i.e. Budgeted Profit ± Sales Margin Volume Variance)*

Step 3: *Make Adjustment for Sales Price Variance*

Step 4: *Make Adjustment for Material, Labour & Overhead Cost Variances*

Step 5: *Calculate Actual Profit (i.e. Standard Profit ± Sales Price Variance ± MLO Cost Variances)*

5.0 FORMAT OF STATEMENT RECONCILING THE ACTUAL PROFIT WITH THE STANDARD PROFIT

			₹
A. Budgeted Profit			.....
B. *Add :* Favourable Sales margin Volume Variance *OR* *Less :* Adverse Sales Margin Volume Variance			.....
C. Standard Profit [A + B]			.....
D. *Add :* Favourable Sales Price Variance *OR* *Less :* Adverse Sales Price Variance			.....
E. Profit before Adjustment for Cost Variances [C ± D]			.....
F. Adjustment of Cost Variances :			
	Favourable	*Adverse*	
Material Yield Variance			
Material Mix Variance			
Material Price Variance			
Labour Yield Variance			

Labour Mix Variance			
Labour Idle Time Variance			
Labour Rate Variance			
Fixed Overhead Efficiency Variance			
Fixed Overhead Capacity Variance			
Fixed Overhead Calendar Variance			
Fixed Overhead Expenditure Variance			
Variable Overhead Efficiency Variance			
Variable Overhead Expenditure Variance	.....	.....	.....
G. Actual Profit (E – F)			.....

Illustration 6. Tulsian (1) Ltd. manufactures a product XYZ and provides you the following information:

(a) *Actual Data* — Direct Materials (16,500 units) ₹ 3,96,000; Direct Labour (1,70,000 Hours) ₹ 3,46,800, Variable Overheads ₹ 60,000, Fixed Overheads ₹ 1,84,000; Sales (8,000 units) ₹ 11,20,000. No. opening and closing stocks.

(b) *Variances :*

	Favourable ₹	*Adverse* ₹
Material Price Variance		66,000
Material Usage Variance		10,000
Labour Rate Variance		6,800
Labour Sub-Efficiency Variance		12,000
Idle Time Variance		8,000
Variable Overhead Efficiency Variance		2,400
Variable Overhead Expenditure Variance	6,400	
Fixed Overhead Efficiency Variance		6,000
Fixed Overhead Capacity Variance		34,000
Fixed Overhead Expenditure Variance	16,000	
Sales Price Variance	40,000	
Sales Margin Volume Variance		54,000

(c) Budgeted Output 10,000 units

Required:

(a) Prepare a Statement showing total standard cost for actual output.
(b) Prepare a Standard Cost Sheet.
(c) Prepare Original Budget for budgeted output.
(d) Reconcile the Actual Profit with the Standard Profit.

Solution:

STATEMENT SHOWING TOTAL AND PER UNIT STANDARD COST AND ORIGINAL BUDGET

Particulars A	*Actual for 8000 units* B	*Variances* C	*Standard for 8000 units* D = B ± C	*Standard Cost Sheet per unit* E = D/8,000	*Original Budget for 10000 units* F = E × 10,000
Direct Material	3,96,000	– 76,000	3,20,000	40	4,00,000
Direct Labour	3,46,800	– 26,800	3,20,000	40	4,00,000
Variable Overhead	60,000	+ 4,000	64,000	8	80,000
Fixed Overhead	1,84,000	– 24,000	1,60,000	20	2,00,000
Total Cost	9,86,800	– 1,22,800	8,64,000	108	10,80,000
Net Profit	1,33,200	+ 82,800	2,16,000	27	2,70,000
Sales	11,20,000	– 40,000	10,80,000	135	13,50,000

STATEMENT RECONCILING THE ACTUAL PROFIT WITH THE STANDARD PROFIT

	₹
A. Budgeted Profit (10000 @ ₹ 27)	2,70,000
B. *Less :* Adverse Sales Margin Volume Variance [₹ 27 × (8,000 – 10,000)]	–54,000
C. Standard Profit (A – B)	2,16,000

D. *Add :* Sales Price Variance [8,000 (₹ 135 – ₹ 140)]			+ 40,000
E. Profit before adjustment of cost variances (C + D)			2,56,000
F. Adjustment of Cost Variances :			
	Favourable ₹	*Adverse* ₹	
Material Price Variance		66,000	
Material Usage Variance		10,000	
Labour Rate Variance		6,800	
Labour Sub-Efficiency Variance		12,000	
Idle Time Variance		8,000	
Variable Overhead Efficiency Variance		2,400	
Variable Overhead Expenditure Variance	6,400		
Fixed Overhead Efficiency Variance		6,000	
Fixed Overhead Capacity Variance		34,000	
Fixed Overhead Expenditure Variance	16,000		
	22,400	1,45,200	–1,22,800
G Actual Profit (E – F)			1,33,200

Working Note: *Calculation of Budgeted output*

Sales Margin Volume Variance = Budgeted Margin per unit × (Budgeted Qty. – Actual Qty.)

₹ 54,000 = ₹ 27 (Budgeted Qty. – 8000)

$$\text{Budgeted Quantity} = \frac{54,000}{27} + 8,000 = 10,000$$

Illustration 7. Tulsian (2) Ltd. manufactures a product XYZ and provides you the following information:

(a) *Budgeted Data*— Direct Materials ₹ 4,00,000; Direct Labour ₹ 4,00,000; Variable Overheads ₹ 80,000; Fixed Overheads ₹ 2,00,000; Sales (10,000 units) ₹ 13,50,000; No. opening and closing stock.

(b)

	Favourable ₹	*Adverse* ₹
Material Price Variance		66,000
Material Usage Variance		10,000
Labour Rate Variance		6,800
Labour Sub-Efficiency Variance		12,000
Idle Time Variance		8,000
Variable Overhead Efficiency Variance		2,400
Variable Overhead Expenditure Variance	6,400	
Fixed Overhead Efficiency Variance		6,000
Fixed Overhead Capacity Variance		34,000
Fixed Overhead Expenditure Variance	16,000	
Sales Price Variance	40,000	
Sales Margin Volume Variance		54,000

Required: (a) Prepare a Standard Cost Sheet; (b) Prepare a statement showing Total Standard Cost for Actual Output; (c) Prepare Actual Cost Sheet; (d) Reconcile the Actual Profit with the Standard Profit.

Solution:

STATEMENT SHOWING STANDARD COST SHEET, TOTAL STANDARD COST FOR ACTUAL OUTPUT AND ACTUAL COST SHEET.

Particulars	*Original Budget for 10,000 units*	*Standard Cost per unit*	*Standard Cost for 8000 units*	*Variance*	*Actual for 8000 units*
A	*B*	*C = B/10000*	*D = C × 8000*	*E*	*F = D ± E*
Direct Material	4,00,000	40	3,20,000	– 76,000	3,96,000
Direct Labour	4,00,000	40	3,20,000	– 26,800	3,46,800
Variable Overhead	80,000	8	64,000	+ 4,000	60,000
Fixed Overhead	2,00,000	20	1,60,000	– 24,000	1,84,000
Total Cost	10,80,000	108	8,64,000	–1,22,800	9,86,800
Net Profit	2,70,000	27	2,16,000	– 82,800	1,33,200
Sales	13,50,000	135	10,80,000	+ 40,000	11,20,000

Statement Reconciling the Actual Profit with the Standard Profit

			₹
A. Budgeted Profit (10000 @ ₹ 27)			2,70,000
B. *Less :* Adverse Sales Margin Volume Variance [₹ 27 5 (8,000 – 10,000)]			–54,000
C. Standard Profit (A – B)			2,16,000
D. *Add :* Sales Price Variance [8,000 (₹ 135 – ₹ 140)]			+ 40,000
E. Profit before adjustment of cost variances (C + D)			2,56,000
F. Adjustment of Cost Variances :	*Favourable* ₹	*Adverse* ₹	
Material Price Variance		66,000	
Material Usage Variance		10,000	
Labour Rate Variance		6,800	
Labour Sub-Efficiency Variance		12,000	
Idle Time Variance		8,000	
Variable Overhead Efficiency Variance		2,400	
Variable Overhead Expenditure Variance	6,400		
Fixed Overhead Efficiency Variance		6,000	
Fixed Overhead Capacity Variance		34,000	
Fixed Overhead Expenditure Variance	16,000		
	22,400	1,45,200	–1,22,800
G. Actual Profit (E - F)			1,33,200

Working Note: *Calculation of Actual Output*

Sales Margin volume variance = Budgeted Margin per unit × (Budgeted Qty. – Actual Qty.)

₹ 54,000 = 27 × (10,000 – Actual Qty.)

$$\text{Actual Qty.} = 10{,}000 - \frac{54{,}000}{27}$$

Actual Qty. = 10,000 – 2,000 = 8,000 units

Illustration 8. In a company operating on a standard costing system, for a given four week period budgeted sales were 10,000 units at ₹ 50 per unit, actual sales were 9,000 units at ₹ 51.25 per unit. Costs relating to that period were as follows :

	Budget ₹	*Actual* ₹
Materials	2,50,000	2,57,400
Wages	75,000	70,875
Fixed Overheads	20,000	18,810
Variable Overheads	10,000	9,250
Semi Variable Overheads	2,700	2,430
Standard Hours	50,000	40,500

(i) The standard material content of each unit is estimated at 25 kg. @ ₹ 1 per kg. Actual figures were 26 kg at ₹ 1.10 per kg.

(ii) The standard wages per unit are 5 hours @ ₹ 7.50 per unit, actual wages were 4.5 hours @ ₹ 7.875 per unit.

(iii) Semi Variable Overhead consists of five-ninths fixed expenses and four-ninths variable.

(iv) There were no opening stocks and the whole production for the period was sold.

(v) The four week period was a normal period.

Required : (a) Compute the variances in Sales, Materials, Labour and Overheads due to all possible causes; and (b) with the help of such a computation draw a statement reconciling the actual profit for the period with the standard profit.

Solution:

(a) (i) *Calculation of Material Cost Variances*

Standard Qty. of Material for Actual output = 9,000 × 25 = 2,25,000 kg.

Actual Qty of Material for Actual Output = 9,000 × 26 = 2,34,000

STATEMENT SHOWING THE BASIC CALCULATIONS FOR THE COMPUTATION OF MATERIAL COST VARIANCES

SQ for AO	*SP*	*SQ × SP* (1)	*AQ*	*AP*	*AQ × AP* (2)	*AQ × SP* (3)
2,25,000	1.00	2,25,000	2,34,000	1.10	2,57,400	2,34,000

A Material Cost Variance (1 – 2) = ₹ 2,25,000 – ₹ 2,57,400 = ₹ 32,400 (A)
B Material Usage Variance (1 – 3) = ₹ 2,25,000 – ₹ 2,34,000 = ₹ 9,000 (A)
C Material Price Variance (3 – 2) = ₹ 2,34,000 – ₹ 2,57,400 = ₹ 23,400 (A)

Verification:

Material Cost Variance = Material Usage Variance + Material Price Variance
= ₹ 9,000 (A) + ₹ 23,400 (A) = ₹ 32,400 (A)

(a) (ii) *Calculation of Labour Cost Variances*

Standard Hours for Actual output = 9,000 × 5 = 45,000
Actual Hours for Actual output = 9,000 × 4.5 = 40,500
Standard Rate per Hour = ₹ 7.50/5 = ₹ 1.50
Actual Rate per Hour = ₹ 7.875/4.5 = ₹ 1.75

STATEMENT SHOWING THE BASIC CALCULATIONS FOR THE COMPUTATION OF LABOUR COST VARIANCES

SQ for AO	*SR*	*SH × SR* (1)	*AH*	*AR*	*AH × AR* (2)	*AH × SR* (3)
45,000	1.50	67,500	40,500	1.75	70,875	60,750

A Labour Cost Variance (1 – 2) = ₹ 67,500 – ₹ 70,875 = ₹ 3,375 (A)
B Labour Efficiency Variance (1 – 3) = ₹ 67,500 – ₹ 60,750 = ₹ 6,750 (F)
C Labour Rate Variance (3 – 2) = ₹ 60,750 – ₹ 70,875 = ₹ 10,125 (A)

Verification :

Labour Cost Variance = Labour Efficiency Variance + Labour Rate Variance
= ₹ 6,750 (F) + ₹ 10,125 (A) = ₹ 3,375 (A)

(a) (iii) *Calculation of Overhead Cost Variances*

$$\text{Standard Fixed Overhead Rate per hour} = \frac{20{,}000 + 5/9\text{th of } 2{,}700}{50{,}000} = ₹\ 0.43$$

$$\text{Standard Variable Overhead Rate per hour} = \frac{10{,}000 + 4/9\text{th of } 2{,}700}{50{,}000} = ₹\ 0.224$$

Actual Fixed overheads = ₹ 18,810 + 5/9th of ₹ 2,430 = ₹ 20,160
Actual Variable overheads = ₹ 9,250 + 4/9th of ₹ 2,430 = ₹ 10,330

BASIC CALCULATIONS FOR VARIABLE OVERHEAD VARIANCES

1. Absorbed Overheads (SH × SR) =	₹ 10,080
2. Standard Overheads (AH × SR) =	₹ 9,072
3. Actual Overheads =	₹ 10,330

Computation of Variances

A. Variable Overheads Efficiency Variance (1 – 2) = ₹ 10,080 – ₹ 9,072 = ₹ 1,008 (F)
B. Variable Overheads Expenditure Variance (2 – 3) = ₹ 9,072 – ₹ 10,330 = ₹ 1,258 (A)
C. Total Variable Overheads Variance (A + B) = ₹ 250 (A)

BASIC CALCULATIONS FOR FIXED OVERHEAD VARIANCES

1. Absorbed Overheads (SH × SR) =	₹ 19,350
2. Standard Overheads (AH × SR) =	₹ 17,415
3. Budgeted Overheads (BH × SR) =	₹ 21,500
4. Actual Overheads =	₹ 20,160

Computation of Variances

A. Fixed Overheads Efficiency Variance (1 – 2) = ₹ 19,350 – ₹ 17,415 = ₹ 1,935 (F)
B. Fixed Overheads Capacity Variance (2 – 3) = ₹ 17,415 – ₹ 21,500 = ₹ 4,085 (A)
C. Total Fixed Overheads Volume Variance (A + B) = ₹ 2,150 (A)
D. Fixed Overheads Expenditure Variance (3 – 4) = ₹ 21,500 – ₹ 20,160 = ₹ 1,340 (F)
E. Total Fixed Overheads Variance (C + D) = ₹ 810 (A)

(a) (iv) *Calculation of Sales Variances*

STATEMENT SHOWING THE BASIC CALCULATIONS FOR THE COMPUTATION OF SALES VARIANCES

BQ	*BM*	*BQ × BM* (1)	*AQ*	*AM*	*AQ × AM* (2)	*AQ × BM* (3)
10,000	14.23	1,42,300	9,000	15.48	1,39,320	1,28,070

A Sales Margin Value Variance (2 – 1) = ₹ 2,980 (A)
B Sales Margin Volume Variance (3 – 1) = ₹ 14,230 (A)
C Sales Margin Price Variance (2 – 3) = ₹ 11,250 (F)

Verification:

Sales Margin Value Variance = Sales Margin Volume Variance + Sales Margin Price Variance
= ₹ 14,230 (A) + ₹ 11,250 (F) = ₹ 2,980 (A)

(b) STATEMENT RECONCILING THE ACTUAL PROFIT WITH THE STANDARD PROFIT

	Particulars			₹
A.	Budgeted Profit			1,42,300
B.	*Less :* Adv. Sales Volume Variance (on margin basis)			14,230
C.	Standard Profit (A – B)			1,28,070
D.	*Add :* Fav. Sales Price Variance			11,250
				1,39,320
E.	*Adjustment for cost variances :*	*Fav.*	*Adv.*	
	Material Usage Variance		9,000	
	Material Price Variance		23,400	
	Labour Efficiency Variance	6,750		
	Labour Rate Variance		10,125	
	Fixed Overhead Efficiency Variance	1,935		
	Fixed Overhead Capacity Variance		4,085	
	Fixed Overhead Expenditure Variance	1,340		
	Variable Overhead Efficiency Variance	1,008		
	Variable Overhead Expenditure Variance		1,258	
		11,033	47,868	36,835
F.	Actual Profit (D – E)			1,02,485

Working Note : *(i) Calculation of Budgeted Profit and Actual Profit*

		Budget	*Per unit*	*Actual*
A.	Sales	5,00,000	50.00	4,61,250
B.	*Less* : Costs :			
	Materials	2,50,000	25.00	2,57,400
	Wages	75,000	7.50	70,875
	Fixed overhead	20,000	2.00	18,810
	Variable overhead	10,000	1.00	9,250
	Semi-Variable overhead	2,700	.27	2,430
		3,57,700	35.77	3,58,765
C.	Profit	1,42,300	14.23	1,02,485

(ii) Actual Margin = Actual Selling Price - Standard Cost = ₹ 51.25 – ₹ 35.77 = ₹ 15.48

Illustration 9. The following information is available from the records of X Ltd. which produces only one product:

BUDGETED INCOME STATEMENT : JANUARY

	₹	₹	₹
Sales Revenue : 20,000 units @ ₹ 5			1,00,000
Production Costs :			
Budgeted Production 20,000 units			
Direct Materials :			
A (10,000 kg. @ ₹ 0.30)	3,000		
B (10,000 kg. @ ₹ 0.70)	7,000	10,000	
Direct Labour :			
Skilled (9,000 Hrs. @ ₹ 3.00)	27,000		
Unskilled (5,200 Hrs @ ₹ 2.50)	13,000	40,000	
Production Overhead :			
Fixed	20,000		
Variable (20,000 units @ ₹ 0.50)	10,000	30,000	80,000
Add : Opening Stock (1,000 Units @ ₹ 4.00)			4,000
Less : Closing Stock (1,000 Units @ ₹ 4.00)			4,000
Budgeted Profit			20,000

During January production and sales were both above budget and the following income statement was prepared:

INCOME STATEMENT : JANUARY

	₹	₹	₹
Sales Revenue :			
14,000 units @ ₹ 5.00			70,000
8,000 units @ ₹ 4.75			38,000
			1,08,000
Direct Materials :			
A (16,000 kg. @ ₹ 0.20)	3,200		
B (10,000 kg. @ ₹ 0.80)	8,000	11,200	
Direct Labour :			
Skilled (13,000 Hrs. @ ₹ 2.95)	38,350		
Unskilled (6,300 Hrs. @ ₹ 2.60)	16,380	54,730	
Overhead Costs :			
Fixed		18,020	
Variable (24,000 units @ ₹ 0.625)		15,000	
Add : Opening Stock (1,000 units @ ₹ 4)		4,000	
Less : Closing Stock (3,000 units @ ₹ 4)		12,000	90,950
Cost of Goods Sold			
Actual Profit			17,050

During the period 1,000 abnormal idle hours for skilled labour due to machine breakdown was reported. In the above statement, stock is valued at standard cost of ₹ 4 per unit.

Required: Prepare a standard costing statement analysing the differences between the budget and the actual performance. In your analysis include calculations of the sales volume and sales price variances; direct material price, mix, yield and usage variance; direct labour rate, idle time and efficiency variances; overhead expenditure and volume variances :

Solution:

STATEMENT RECONCILING THE ACTUAL PROFIT WITH THE BUDGETED PROFIT

	Reference of Working Note	Variance Amount Fav. ₹	Variance Amount Adv. ₹	₹
A. Budgeted Profit (as per Budgeted income statement)			20,000	
B. *Add :* Favourable Sales Volume Margin variance	(iv)			2,000
C. Standard Profit (A + B)				22,000
D. *Less :* Adverse Sales Margin Price Variance				2,000
E. *Less :* Profit before adjustment of cost variances				20,000
F. Cost Variances :				
Material :				
— Price	(i)	600	—	
— Mix	(i)	1,200	—	
— Yield	(i)	—	1,000	
Labour :				
— Rate	(ii)	20	—	
— Efficiency	(ii)	—	3,750	
— Idle time	(ii)	—	3,000	
Variable Overhead :				
— Efficiency	(iii)		887	
— Idle Time	(iii)	—	705	
— Expenditure	(iii)	—	1,408	
Fixed Overhead :				
— Expenditure	(iii)	1,980	—	
— Volume	(iii)	4,000	—	
		7,800	10,750	2,950
G. Actual Profit (E - F)				17,050

Working Notes:

(i) *Calculation of Material Cost Variances*

Standard Output = Sales + Closing Stock - Opening Stock = 22,000 + 3,000 – 1,000 = 24,000

Standard Quantity of Material 'A' for Actual output (SQ) = $\frac{10,000}{20,000} \times 24,000 = 12,000$ kg

Standard Quantity of Material 'B' for Actual output (SQ) = $\frac{10,000}{20,000} \times 24,000 = 12,000$ kg

Total Standard Input = 12,000 kg + 12,000 kg = 24,000 kg

Total Actual Input = 16,000 kg + 10,000 kg = 26,000 kg

Revised Quantity of Material 'A' for Actual output (RQ) = $\frac{12,000}{24,000} \times 26,000 = 13,000$ kg

Revised Quantity of Material 'B' for Actual output (RQ) = $\frac{12,000}{24,000} \times 26,000 = 13,000$ kg

STATEMENT SHOWING THE BASIC CALCULATIONS FOR THE COMPUTATION OF MATERIAL COST VARIANCES

Type of Material	*SQ for AO*	*SP*	*SQ × SP* (1)	*AQ*	*AP*	*AQ × AP* (2)	*AQ × SP* (3)	*RQ*	*RQ × SP* (4)
A	12,000	0.30	3,600	16,000	0.20	3,200	4,800	13,000	3,900
B	12,000	0.70	8,400	10,000	0.80	8,000	7,000	13,000	9,100
Input	24,000			26,000					
Less : Loss	—			2,000					
	24,000		12,000	24,000		11,200	11,800		13,000

			Material 'A'	Material 'B'	Total
A	Material Cost Variance	(1 – 2)	400 (F)	400 (F)	800 (F)
B	Material Usage Variance	(1 – 3)	1,200 (A)	1,400 (F)	200 (F)
C	Material Yield Variance	(1 – 4)	300 (A)	700 (A)	1,000 (A)
D	Material Mix Variance	(4 – 3)	900 (A)	2,100 (F)	1,200 (F)
E	Material Price Variance	(3 – 2)	1,600 (F)	1,000 (A)	600 (F)

Verification:

1. Material Cost Variance = Material Usage Variance + Material Price Variance
   = ₹ 200 (F) + ₹ 600 (F) = ₹ 800 (F)
2. Material Usage Variance = Material Yield Variance + Material Mix Variance
   = ₹ 1,000 (A) + ₹ 1,200 (F) = ₹ 200 (F)

Note : *Alternative formula for Material Yield Variance*

$$= \frac{\text{Total (SQ} \times \text{SP)}}{\text{Standard Input}} \times \text{(Standard Input – Actual Input)}$$

$$= \frac{12{,}000}{24{,}000} \times (24{,}000 - 26{,}000) = ₹\ 1{,}000\ \text{(A)}$$

(ii) *Calculation of Labour Cost Variances*

Standard hours of skilled labour for Actual output (SH) = $\frac{9{,}000}{20{,}000} \times 24{,}000 = 10{,}800$ hrs.

Standard hours of unskilled labour for actual output (SH) = $\frac{5{,}200}{20{,}000} \times 24{,}000 = 6{,}240$ hrs.

Total Standard Hours = 10,800 + 6,240 = 17,040 Hours

Total Actual Hours = 13,000 + 6,300 = 19,300 Hours

Revised Hours of skilled labour (RH) = $\frac{10{,}800}{17{,}040} \times 19{,}300 = 12{,}232$

Revised Hours of unskilled labour (RH) = $\frac{6{,}240}{17{,}040} \times 19{,}300 = 7{,}068$

Idle time for skilled labour = 1000 Hours

Actual Productive Hours (APH) of skilled labour = 13,000 – 1,000 = 12,000

Actual Productive Hours (APH) of unskilled labour = 6,300 – 0 = 6,300

STATEMENT SHOWING THE BASIC CALCULATIONS FOR THE COMPUTATION OF LABOUR COST VARIANCES

Type of Labour	*SH for AO*	*SR*	*SH × SR* (1)	*AH*	*AR*	*AH × AR* (2)	*AH × SR* (3)	*APH*	*APH × SR* (4)
Skilled	10,800	3.00	32,400	13,000	2.95	38,350	39,000	12,000	36,000
Unskilled	6,240	2.50	15,600	6,300	2.60	16,380	15,750	6,300	15,750
	17,040			19,300					
			48,000			54,730	54,750		51,750

			Skilled	Unskilled	Total
A	Labour Cost Variance	(1 – 2)	5,950 (A)	780 (A)	6,730 (A)
B	Labour Efficiency Variance	(1 – 4)	3,600 (A)	150 (A)	3,750 (A)
C	Idle Time Variance (Idle Hours × SR) 1,000 × ₹ 3				3,000 (A)
D	Labour Rate Variance	(3 – 2)	650 (F)	630 (A)	20 (F)

Verification:

Labour Cost Variance = Labour Efficiency Variance + Idle Time Variance + Labour Rate Variance
= ₹ 3,750 (A) + ₹ 3,000 (A) + ₹ 20 (F) = ₹ 6,730 (A)

(iii) *Calculation of Overhead Variances*

$$\text{Standard Fixed Overhead Rate per hour} = \frac{\text{Budgeted Fixed Overhead}}{\text{Budgeted Hours}}$$

$$\text{Standard Variable Overhead Rate per hour} = \frac{20{,}000}{14{,}200} = ₹\ 1.4085$$

$$\text{Standard Variable Overhead Rate per hour} = \frac{\text{Budgeted Fixed Overhead}}{\text{Budgeted Hours}}$$

$$\text{Standard Variable Overhead Rate per hour} = \frac{10{,}000}{14{,}200} = ₹\ 0.7042$$

STATEMENT SHOWING THE BASIC CALCULATIONS FOR THE COMPUTATION OF OVERHEAD VARIANCES

Name of Overhead	*SH for AO*	*SR*	*SH × SR (1)*	*AH*	*AR*	*AH × AR (2)*	*AH × SR (3)*	*BH*	*BH × SR (4)*	*APH*	*APH × SR (5)*
Fixed	17040	1.4085	24000	19300		18020	27183	14200	20000	18300	25,775
Variable	17040	0.7042	12000	19300		15000	13592	14200	10000	18300	12,887

A Fixed Overheads Efficiency Variance (1 – 5) = ₹ 24,000 – ₹ 25,775 = ₹ 1,775 (A)
B Fixed Overheads Idle Time Variance (5 – 3) = ₹ 25,775 – ₹ 27,183 = ₹ 1,408 (A)
C Fixed Overheads Capacity Variance (3 – 4) = ₹ 27,183 – ₹ 20,000 = ₹ 7,183 (F)
D Fixed Overheads Expenditure Variance (4 – 2) = ₹ 20,000 – ₹ 18,020 = ₹ 1,980 (F)
E Variable Overheads Efficiency Variance (1 – 5) = ₹ 12,000 – ₹ 12,887 = ₹ 887 (A)
F Variable Overheads Idle Time Variance (5 – 3) = ₹ 12,887 – ₹ 13,592 = ₹ 705 (A)
G Variable Overheads Expenditure Variance (3 – 2) = ₹ 13,592 – ₹ 15,000 = ₹ 1,408 (A)
H Total Overhead Cost Variance (A + B + C + D + E + F + G) = ₹ 2,980 (F)

Verification:

1. Fixed Overheads Volume Variance = Fixed Overheads Efficiency Variance + Fixed Overheads Idle Time Variance + Fixed Overheads Capacity Variance = ₹ 1,775 (A) + ₹ 1,408 (A) + ₹ 7,183 (F) = ₹ 4,000 (F)
2. Total Fixed Overheads Cost Variance = Fixed Overheads Volume Variance + Fixed Overheads Expenditure Variance = ₹ 4,000 (F) + ₹ 1,980 (F) = ₹ 5,980 (F)
3. Total Variable Overhead Cost Variance = Variable Overheads Efficiency Variance + Variable Overheads Idle Time Variance + Variable Overhead Expenditure Variance = ₹ 887 (A) + ₹ 705 (A) + ₹ 1,408 (A) = ₹ 3,000 (A)
4. Total Overheads Cost Variance = Total Fixed Overheads Cost Variance + Total Variable Overhead Cost Variance = ₹ 5,980 (F) + ₹ 3,000 (A) = ₹ 2,980 (F)

(iv) *Calculation of Sales Margin Variances*

$$\text{Standard Cost per unit} = \frac{80{,}000}{20{,}000} = ₹\ 4 \text{ per unit}$$

Standard Margin per unit = Standard Selling Price – Standard Cost
= ₹ 5 – ₹ 4 = ₹ 1

$$\text{Actual selling Price per unit} = \frac{(14{,}000 \times 5) + (8000 \times 4.75)}{22{,}000} = ₹\ 4.9091$$

Actual Margin per unit = Actual Selling Price – Standard Cost
= ₹ 4.9091 – ₹ 4.00 = ₹ 0.9091

STATEMENT SHOWING THE BASIC CALCULATIONS FOR THE COMPUTATION OF SALES VARIANCES

BQ	*BM*	*BQ × BM* (1)	*AQ*	*AM*	*AQ × AM* (2)	*AQ × BM* (3)
20,000	1	20,000	22,000	.9091	20,000	22,000

A Sales Margin Value Variance (2 – 1) = Nil
B Sales Margin Volume Variance (3 – 1) = ₹ 2,000 (F)
C Sales Margin Price Variance (2 – 3) = ₹ 2,000 (A)

Verification:

Sales Margin Value Variance = Sales Margin Volume Variance + Sales Margin Price Variance
= ₹ 2,000 (F) + ₹ 2,000 (A) = Nil

6.0 MARKET SIZE VARIANCE

Meaning	Market Size Variance arises due to the difference between the company's Budgeted Market Share of Actual Industry Sales Volume in Units and Budgeted Market Share of Budgeted Industry Sales Volume in Units.
Computation	(Budgeted Market Share Percentage) × (Actual Industry Sales Volume in Units – Budgeted Industry Sales Volume in Units) × Budgeted Average Contribution Margin per Unit **Note:** Budgeted Average Contribution Margin per Unit = $\frac{\text{Total (BQ × BM)}}{\text{Total BQ}}$

7.0 MARKET SHARE VARIANCE

Meaning	Market Share Variance arises due to the difference between the company's Actual Share of Actual Industry Sales Volume in Units and Budgeted Share of Actual Industry Sales Volume in Units.
Computation	(Actual Market Share Percentage – Budgeted Market Share Percentage) × (Actual Industry Sales Volume in Units) × (Budgeted Average Contribution Margin per Unit) **Note:** Actual Market Share Percentage = $\frac{\text{Actual Sales of the Company}}{\text{Actual Sales of the Industry}}$
Applicability	It is applicable when Actual Size of a product or product group is known.
Interpretation	It indicates whether the Market Share has decreased or increased or remained constant.

Illustration 10. Tulsian Ltd. provides you the following information:

1. Budgeted and Actual Data for 2014:

Particulars	*Budgeted*			*Actual*		
	Selling Price per kg. ₹	*Variable Cost/kg.* ₹	*Sales volume in kgs.*	*Contribution margin / kg.* ₹	*Variable Cost / kg.* ₹	*Sales volume in kgs.*
Product A	20	15	60	9	16	44
Product B	10	4	40	0	5	66

2. Tulsian Ltd. derived its total unit sales budget for 2014 from the internal management estimate of a 20% market share.
3. Industry sales forecast by computer manufacturers association was of 500 Kgs. but at the end of the year the association reported actual industry sales of 687.50 Kgs.

Required: Compute the Market Size and Market Share Variances.

Solution:

Market Size Variance:

(Budgeted Market Share Percentage)

×

(Actual Industry Sales Volume in Units – Budgeted Industry Sales Volume in Units)

×

Budgeted Average Contribution Margin per Unit

= 0.20 × (687.50 Kgs. – 500 Kgs.) × ₹ 5.40 = ₹ 202.50 (F)

Market Share Variance:

(Actual Market Share Percentage – Budgeted Market Share Percentage)

×

(Actual Industry Sales Volume in Units) X (Budgeted Average Contribution Margin per Unit)

= (0.16 – 0.20) × 687.50 Kg × ₹.5.40 = ₹ 148.50 (A)

Note: Actual Market Share Percentage $= \frac{\text{Actual Sales of Company (Kgs.)}}{\text{Actual Industry Sales (Kgs.)}} \times 100$

$= \frac{\text{110 Kgs.}}{\text{687.50 Kg.}} \times 100 = 16\%$

Illustration 11. Super computers manufactures and sells three related PC models:

1. PC — Sold mostly to college students
2. Portable PC— Smaller version of PC positioned as home computer
3. Super PC — Sold mostly to business executives
4. Budgeted and Actual Data for 2014:

Particulars	*Budgeted*				*Actual*	
	Selling Price per unit ₹	*Variable Cost/unit* ₹	*Sales volume in units*	*Contribution margin /unit* ₹	*Variable Cost/unit* ₹	*Sales volume in units*
PC	24,000	14,000	7,000	12,000	10,000	8,250
Portable PC	16,000	10,000	1,000	5,000	8,000	1,650
Super PC	1,00,000	60,000	2,000	20,000	50,000	1,100
Total:			10,000			11,000

5. Super computers derived its total unit sales budget for 2014 from the internal management estimate of a 20% market share.
6. Industry sales forecast by computer manufacturers association was of 50,000 units but at the end of the year the association reported actual industry sales of 68,750 units.

Required:

(a) Compute Sales Variances.
(b) Compute the Market Size and Market Share Variances.
(c) Comment on your results.

Solution:

(a) Computation of Sales Variances

Basic Calculations:

(i) BM = Budgeted Margin = Budgeted Selling Price – Standard Cost
For PC = ₹ 24,000 – ₹ 14,000 = ₹ 10,000 and similarly for others.

(ii) AM = Actual Margin = Actual Selling Price – Standard Cost
For PC = ₹ 22,000 – ₹ 14,000 = ₹ 8,000 and similarly for others.

(iii) RQ = Revised Quantity = Total Actual Quantity (11,000) in Budgeted Sales Mix Ratio i.e. 7:1:2
For PC = 11,000 × 7/10 = 7,700 and similarly for others.

[₹ In '000']

Type of Product	*BQ*	*BM*	*BQ × BM (1)*	*AQ*	*AM*	*AQ × AM (2)*	*AQ × BM (3)*	*RQ*	*RQ × BM (4)*
PC	7,000	10	70,000	8,250	8.00	66,000	82,500	7,700	77,000
Portable PC	1,000	6	6,000	1,650	3.00	4,950	9,900	1,100	6,600
Super PC	2,000	40	80,000	1,100	10.00	11,000	44,000	2,200	88,000
	10,000		**1,56,000**	**11,000**		**81,950**	**1,36,400**	**1,100**	**1,71,600**

Step 2: *Calculate Sales Margin Variances as follows*:

Sales Margin Variance (2 – 1) = (AQ × AM) – (BQ × BM)

PC = ₹ 66,000 – ₹ 70,000 = ₹ 4,000 (A)
Portable PC = ₹ 4,950 – ₹ 6,000. = ₹ 1,050 (A)
Super PC = ₹ 11,000 – ₹ 80,000 = ₹ 69,000 (A)
SMV = ₹ 74,050 (A)

Sales Margin Price Variance (2 – 3) = (AQ × AM) – (AQ × BM)

PC = ₹ 66,000 – ₹ 82,500 = ₹ 16,500 (A)
Portable PC = ₹ 4,950 – ₹ 9,900 = ₹ 4,950 (A)
Super PC = ₹ 11,000 – ₹ 44,000 = ₹ 33,000 (A)
SMPV = ₹ 54,450 (A)

Sales Margin Volume Variance (3 – 1) = (A Q × BM) – (BQ × BM)

PC = ₹ 82,500 – ₹ 70,000 = ₹ 12,500 (F)
Portable PC = ₹ 9,900 – ₹ 6,000 = ₹ 3,900 (F)
Super PC = ₹ 44 – ₹ 80,000 = ₹ 36,000 (A)
SMVV = ₹ 19,600 (A)

Sales Margin Mix Variance (3 – 4) = (AQ × BM) – (RQ × BM)

PC = ₹ 82,500 – ₹ 77,000 = ₹ 5,500 (F)
Portable PC = ₹ 9,900 – ₹ 6,600 = ₹ 3,300 (F)
Super PC = ₹ 44,000 – ₹ 88,000 = ₹ 44,000 (A)
SMMV = ₹ 35,200 (A)

Sales Margin Sub-Volume Variance = (Total AQ – Total BQ) × Average Budgeted Margin

= (11,000 – 10,000) × ₹ 15.6 = ₹ 15,600 (F)

Note: Average Budgeted Margin = $\frac{\text{Total (BQ × BM)}}{\text{BQ}}$

$= \frac{(10 \times 7{,}000) + (6 \times 1{,}000) + (40 \times 2{,}000)}{7{,}000 + 1{,}000 + 2{,}000}$ = ₹ 15.6

Alternatively, **SMSVV (4 – 1) = (RQ × BM) – (BQ × BM)**

PC = ₹ 77,000 – ₹ 70,000 = ₹ 7,000 (F)
Portable PC = ₹ 6,600 – ₹ 6,000 = ₹ 600 (F)
Super PC = ₹ 88,000 – ₹ 80,000 = ₹ 8,000 (F)
SMSVV = ₹ 15,600 (F)

(b) Computation of the Market Size and Market Share Variances

1. Market Size Variance:
(Budgeted Market Share Percentage)
×
(Actual Industry Sales Volume in Units – Budgeted Industry Sales Volume in Units)
×
Budgeted Average Contribution Margin per Unit = 0.20 × (68,750 units – 50,000 units) × ₹ 15.60
= ₹ 58,500 (F)

2. Market Share Variance:
(Actual Market Share Percentage – Budgeted Market Share Percentage)
×
(Actual Industry Sales Volume in Units) × (Budgeted Average Contribution Margin per Unit)
= (0.16 – 0.20) × 68,750 units × ₹.15.60
= ₹.42,900 (A)

Note: Actual market share percentage = $\frac{\text{Actual Sales of 3 PC models}}{\text{Actual Industry Sales}} \times 100 = \frac{\text{11,000 Units}}{\text{68,750 Units}} \times 100 = 16\%$

(c) Comment on above results

1. Favourable sales quantity variance of ₹ 1.56 crores was because of growth in industry as a whole. However, the firm could not retain the budgeted market share of 20%. As a result the benefit of increased market size i.e. ₹.5.85 crores is partly offset by loss due to fall in market share i.e. ₹.4.29 crores.
2. Increase in the percentage sale of computers below-average budgeted margins and a decrease in the percentage sale of computers above-average budgeted margins had resulted in the reduction of operating profit by ₹.3.52 crores.
3. As a result of above, the operating profit of 'Super Computers' had been adversely affected by ₹.1.96 crores due to sales variances.

8.0 QUALITY COST VARIANCE

Meaning	Quality Cost Variance represents the difference between Actual Quality Cost and Budgeted Quality Cost. It is the aggregate of Material Cost Variance, Material Scrap Variance and Material Rework Cost Variance.
Computation	It is computed as follows: = Material Cost Variance + Material Scrap Variance + Material Rework Cost Variance **Notes:** (i) Material Scrap Variance = (SQ of Scrap × SP of Scrap) – (AQ of Scrap × AP of Scrap) (ii) Material Rework Cost Variance = (SQ of Rework × SC of Rework) – (AQ of Rework × AC of Rework)

Illustration 12. To produce 1,000 units of product X, the standard materials input is 1,200 units at a standard price of ₹ 6 per unit. The standard allows for rejects at the rate of 25% of input; it is estimated that one-third of total rejects can be reworked at an additional standard cost of ₹ 2 per unit. Scrapped units can be sold for 50 p each.

During the period just ended, 19,500 units of X were produced. 24,000 units of material were issued to production, at the standard cost of ₹ 6 per unit; 7,000 units were rejected on initial inspection and of these, 2,500 were reworked, at a cost of ₹ 5,100. The remainder were sold as scrap for 50 paise per unit.

Required: Calculate the relevant variances.

Solution:

The standard cost of product X is as follows :

	Units	*Price*	*Cost*
Material	1,200	₹ 6	₹ 7,200
Rejection (25% of 1,200)	300		
	900		
Reworked (1/3 × 25% × 1200)	100	2	200
	1,000		7,400
Less : Scrap Proceeds from 200 units i.e. (200 × 0.50)			100
Net Processing Cost			7,300

The standard yield for the process is 5/6 of input
Material cost Variance is :

Material	24,000	6	1,44,000
Rejection	7,000		

	17,000	
Reworked	2,500	5,100
	19,500	1,49,100
Less : Scrap Proceeds [(7,000 – 2,500) × .50]	—	2,250
Actual	19,500	1,46,850

	SQ	*SP*	*SQ × SP* (1)	*AQ*	*AP*	*AQ × AP* (2)
Material	23,400	6.00	1,40,400	24,000	6.00	1,44,000
Scrap	3,900	0.50	1,950	4,500	0.50	2,250
Rework	1,950	2.00	3,900	2,500	2.04	5,100

A Material Cost Variance (1 – 2) = ₹ 1,40,400 – ₹ 1,44,000 = ₹ 3,600 (A)
B Material Scrap Variance (1 – 2) = ₹ 1,950 – ₹ 2,250 = ₹ 300 (A)
C Material Rework Cost Variance (1 – 2) = ₹ 3,900 – ₹ 5,100 = ₹ 1,200 (A)
D Quality Cost Variance (A + B + C) = ₹ 3,600 (A) + ₹ 300 (F) + ₹ 1,200 (A) = ₹ 4,500 (A)

9.0 PLANNING VARIANCE

Meaning	1. Planning Variance represents the difference between Original Cost (as per original plan) and Revised Cost (as per revised plan). 2. It tests management's forecasting ability. 3. It can be further analyzed to reflect controllable and uncontrollable variances.
Computation	It is computed as follows: = Original Standard (as per original plan) – Revised Standard (as per revised plan)

Illustration 13. Country preserves product jams, marmalade and preserves. All products are produced in a similar fashion : the fruits are low temperature cooked in a vacuum process and then blended with glucose syrup with added citric acid and pectin to help setting. Margins are tight and the firm operates a system of standard costing for each batch of jam.

The Standard cost data for a batch of raspberry jam are :

Fruit extract	400 kg	@ ₹ 0.16 per kg
Glucose syrup	700 kg.	@ ₹ 0.10 per kg
Pectin	99 kg.	@ ₹ 0.332 per kg.
Citric acid	1 kg.	@ ₹ 2.00 per kg.
Labour	18 hrs	@ ₹ 3.25 per hour

Standard processing loss 3%

The summer of 20X1 proved disastrous for the raspberry crop with a late frost and cool, cloudy conditions at the ripening period, resulting in a low national yield. As a consequence normal prices in the trade were ₹ 0.19 per kg. for fruit extract although good buying could achieve some savings. The impact of exchange rates on imports of sugar has caused the price of syrup to increase by 20%.

The actual results for the batch were:

Fruit extract	428 kg.	@ ₹ 0.18 per kg
Glucose syrup	742 kg.	@ ₹ 0.12 per kg
Pectin	125 kg.	@ ₹ 0.328 per kg
Citric acid	1 kg.	@ ₹ 0.95 kg
Labour	20 hrs	@ ₹ 3.00 per hour

Actual output was 1,164 kg. raspberry jam.

You are required to: (a) calculate the ingredientss planning variances that are deemed uncontrollable; (b) calculate the ingredients operating variances that are deemed controllable; (c) calculate the mixture and yield variance; and (d) calculate the total variance for the batch :

Solution: **STATEMENT SHOWING ORIGINAL AND REVISED DATA**

Original Standard			*Revised Standard*		
400 × ₹ 0.16	=	₹ 64.000	400 × ₹ 0.19	=	76.000
700 × ₹ 0.10	=	₹ 70.000	700 × ₹ 0.12	=	84.000
99 × ₹ 0.332	=	₹ 32.868	99 × ₹ 0.332	=	32.868
1 × ₹ 2.00	=	₹ 2.000	1 × ₹ 2.0	=	2.000
1,200		168.868	1200		194.868
	Labour	58.500		Labour	58.500
1,200		227.368	1,200		253.368
36	Loss 3%		36	Loss 3%	
1,164			1,164		

(a) Planning Variance = Original Cost – Revised Cost
Fruit Extract = 64 – 76 = ₹ 12 (A)
Glucose Syrup = 70 – 84 = ₹ 14 (A)
Total = 227.368 – ₹ 253.368 = ₹ 26.00 (A)

(b) & (c) STATEMENT SHOWING THE BASIC CALCULATIONS FOR THE COMPUTATION OF MATERIAL COST VARIANCES

Type of Material	*SQ for AO*	*SP*	*SQ × SP (1)*	*AQ*	*AP*	*AQ × AP (2)*	*AQ × SP (3)*	*RQ*	*RQ × SP (4)*
A	400	.19	76	428	0.18	77.04	81.32	432.00	82.08
B	700	.12	84	742	0.12	89.04	89.04	756.00	90.72
C	99	.332	32.868	125	0.328	41.00	41.50	106.92	35.497
D	1	2.00	2	1	0.95	0.95	2.00	1.079	2.160
Input	1200			1296					
Less : Loss	36			132					
	1164		194.868	1164		208.03	213.86		210.457

		Material 'A'	Material 'B'	Material 'C'	Material 'D'	Total
A Material Cost Variance	(1 – 2)	1.04 (A)	5.04 (A)	8.132 (A)	1.05 (F)	13.162 (A)
B Material Usage Variance	(1 – 3)	5.32 (A)	5.04 (A)	8.632 (A)	Nil	18.992 (A)
C Material Yield Variance	(1 – 4)	6.08 (A)	6.72 (A)	2.629 (A)	0.16 (A)	15.589 (A)
D Material Mix Variance	(4 – 3)	0.76 (F)	1.68 (F)	6.003 (A)	0.16 (F)	3.403 (A)
E Material Price Variance	(3 – 2)	4.28 (F)	Nil	0.50 (F)	1.05 (F)	5.830 (F)

Verification:

1. Material Cost Variance = Material Usage Variance + Material Price Variance
 = ₹ 18.992 (A) + ₹ 5.83 (F) = ₹ 13.162 (A)
2. Material Usage Variance = Material Yield Variance + Material Mix Variance
 = ₹ 15.589 (A) + ₹ 3.403 (A) = ₹ 18.992 (A)

 Labour Cost Variance = (SH × SR) – (AH × AR) = (18 × ₹ 3.25) – (20 × ₹ 3) = ₹ 1.50 (A)
 Total Cost Variance = Original Standard Cost – Actual Cost = ₹ 227.368 – (₹ 208.03 + ₹ 60)
 = ₹ 40.662 (A)

(d) Total Variance = Planning Variance + Usage Variance + Price Variance + Labour Operating Variance
 = (26) + (18.992) + 5.83 + (1.50) = 40.662 (A)

10.0 OPERATIONAL VARIANCES

Meaning	Operational Variances indicate management's current level of operating efficiency.
Computation	It is computed as follows: = Actual – Standard (or Revised Standard)

11.0 BUDGET VARIANCE

Meaning	1. Budget Variance represents the difference between Budgeted Cost and Actual Cost. 2. It is computed on the basis of Fixed Budgeting System.
Computation	It is computed as follows: = Budgeted Cost – Actual Cost

12.0 REVISION VARIANCE

Meaning	It arises when an interim adjustment of standard cost is made without adjusting the budget. It represents the difference between the original standard cost and the revised standard cost on account of unavoidable changes in prices of various factors like materials, wages.
Computation	It is computed as follows: = Original Standard Cost of Actual Output – Revised Standard Cost Actual Output
Division	It can further be analyzed to reflect revisions due to price of materials, labour and overhead rates and changes in methods.

13.0 METHOD VARIANCE

Meaning	It is that part of revision variance which arises due to the use of methods other than those specified. **According to C.I.M.A., London** *Methods Variance is "the difference between the Standard Cost of a product or operation produced or performed by the normal method and the standard cost of a product or operation produced or performed by the alternative method actually employed".*
Computation	It is computed as follows: = Standard Cost under specified method – Standard Cost under method actually employed

14.0 SUBSTITUTION VARIANCE

Meaning	It arises due to the substitution of one grade of labour by another grade of labour. It represents the difference between the actual hours at standard rate of standard worker and the actual hours at standard rate of actual worker.
Computation	= (AH × SR of Standard Worker) – (AH × SR of Actual Worker)

15.0 INVESTIGATION OF VARIANCES

To decide whether to investigate the Variances or not, the Cost of Investigation should be compared with the Cost of No Investigation. In this regard the following steps are suggested:

Step 1: *Ascertain the Probability of the process being in control.*
Step 2: *Ascertain the Probability of the process being out of control.*
Step 3: *Ascertain the Cost of Investigation*
Step 4: *Ascertain the Cost of Correction if Investigation is undertaken and process is found out of control.*

Step 5: *Ascertain the Cost of Correction if No Investigation is undertaken and process is found out of control.*

Step 6: *Investigation should be undertaken if the Cost of No Investigation exceeds the Cost of Investigation.*

Or

Investigation should not be undertaken if the Cost of Investigation exceeds the Cost of No Investigation.

Illustration 14. Tulsian Ltd. using a detailed system of standard costing finds that the cost of investigation of variances is ₹ 40,000. If after investigation an out of control situation is discovered, the cost of correction is ₹ 60,000. If no investigation is made, the present value of extra cost involved is ₹ 3,00,000. The probability of the process being in control is 0.82.

You are required to advise: (a) Whether investigation of the variances should be undertaken or not; (b) the probability at which it is desirable to institute investigation into variances.

Solution:

Part (a)

Situation	*Probability*	*Effective cost if Investigation is undertaken*	*Effective cost if Investigation is not undertaken*
Process under control	0.82	40000 × 0.82 = 32,800	Nil
Process out of control	0.18	1,00,000 × 0.18 = 18,000	3,00,000 × 0.18 = 54,000
		50,800	54,000
Total	1.00		

Decision: Investigation of the variances should be undertaken since the cost of no investigation exceeds the cost of investigation.

Part (b) **Let the probability of Process being under control be *x***

Process under control	x	40000 x	Nil
Process out of control	$1 - x$	1,00,000 $(1 - x)$	3,00,000 $(1 - x)$
Total		1,00,000 – 60,000 x	3,00,000 – 3,00,000 x

Equating both the costs:

$$1{,}00{,}000 - 60{,}000\,x = 3{,}00{,}000 - 3{,}00{,}000\,x$$
$$2{,}40{,}000\,x = 2{,}00{,}000$$
$$x = 2{,}00{,}000/2{,}40{,}000 = 0.833$$

Decision: If the probability of process being in control is below .833, the investigation should be instituted since in that case the cost of not investigating will be greater than the cost of investigation.

Illustration 15. X Ltd. uses a Standard Costing system in its factory. Unfavourable Variances in a process have been about ₹ 2,000 a month. If the cause of variance can be found out, and if that cause is correctible, it will take two months to correct it. The correction, if made would be effective for two months. Investigation of variance will cost ₹ 1,000. Correcting the cause, if a cause is found, will cost ₹ 500. Management believes the probability of finding a correctible cause is 0.6.

Required:

(a) Would you recommend launching an Investigation ?
(b) What is the minimum probability of finding a correctible cause that would justify an investigation ?

Solution:

(a) It is given that correction of cause of variance would be effective for two months. Thus, the ensuing benefit will be :

Benefit : [₹ 2,000 5 2]	₹ 4,000
Less: Cost of correcting the cause	₹ 500
Benefit	3,500
Probability	0.60
Expected value of benefit (3,500 × 0.60)	₹ 2,100

Less: Cost of Investigation	1,000
Net value of benefit	1,100

As there is positive net value, the investigation should be launched.

(b) It has been asked in the question to compute the minimum probability of finding correctible cause that would justify the investigation. In other words, break even probability is to be found out.

Benefit × Probability – Cost = 0

₹ 3,500 × p – ₹ 1,000 = 0

p = ₹ 1,000/₹ 3,500 *or* 0.2857

16.0 VARIANCE REPORTS

The main purpose of standard costing is cost control. To achieve this purpose, the variances should be analysed according to their causes. Analysis should be timely so that much time is not lost in taking corrective action wherever needed. Computation of variances and their reporting is not the final step towards the control of various elements of cost. It infact demands an analysis of variances from the side of the executives, to ascertain the correct reasons for their occurance. After knowing the exact reasons, it becomes their responsibility to take necessary steps so as to stop the re-occurance of adverse variances in future. To enhance the utility of such a reporting system it is necessary that such a system of reporting should not only be prompt but should also facilitate the concerned managerial level to take necessary steps. Variance reports should be prepared after keeping in view its ultimate use and its periodicity. Such reports should highlight the essential cost deviations and possibilities for their improvements. In fact the variance reports should give due regard to the following points:-

(i) What the cost performance should have been?
(ii) How does the actual cost performance differ from standard cost performance?
(iii) What are the causes of variances?
(iv) Reporting should be based on the principle of management by exception.

STANDARD COST REPORTS

For control purposes the following two Standard Cost Reports may be prepared:

(a) Standard Costing Profit & Loss statement: A Standard Costing Profit and Loss Statement shows the variance of each type under each element of cost department wise and is illustrated as below:

STANDARD COSTING PROFIT AND LOSS REPORT FOR THE MONTH ________ 20______

Particulars			*Total*	*Dept. A*	*Dept. B*	*Dept. C*
A. Sales Value			.....	.....	.....	.....
B. *Less* : Standard Cost of Sales			.....	.....	.....	.....
C. Standard Profit			.....	.....	.....	.....
D. Adjustment of Cost Variances:						
	Favourable	*Adverse*				
Material Yield Variance						
Material Mix Variance						
Material Price Variance						
Labour Yield Variance						
Labour Mix Variance						
Labour Idle Time Variance						
Labour Rate Variance						
Fixed Overhead Efficiency Variance						
Fixed Overhead Capacity Variance						
Fixed Overhead Calendar Variance						
Fixed Overhead Expenditure Variance						
Variable Overhead Efficiency Variance						
Variable Overhead Expenditure Variance	.....	.....	.....	.....	.....	.....
E. Actual Profit (C ± D)			.....	.....	.....	.....

(b) Material Usage Variance Report: This report is sent to the heads of departments for necessary corrective action as illustrated below:

MATERIAL USAGE VARIANCE REPORT - DEPT. A MONTH_________20_________

Material	*Standard requirement* Kg.	*Actual consumption* Kg.	*This month's variance*		*Cumulative variance*	
			Qty.	Value	Qty.	Value
A	6,000	5,500	500	500	2,000	2,000
B	9,000	10,000	(1,000)	(500)	1,000	500
C	20,500	20,000	500	1,000	2,500	(5,000)
D	5,000	4,750	250	125	375	190
						(2,310)

17.0 ACCOUNTING PROCEDURE FOR STANDARD COST

The standard cost operations can be recorded in the books of account by using Partial Plan or Single Plan.

1. PARTIAL PLAN

The features of Partial Plan are as follows:

1. Analysis of the variance is done after the end of the month. This method is simple in operation because variances are analysed after the end of month but may present difficulties if the firm makes a variety of products.
2. It uses current standards in which the inventory will be valued at current standard cost figure.
3. Work-in-progress Account is charged at the actual cost of production for the month and is credited with the standard cost of the month's production of finished product.
4. The closing balance of work-in-progress is also shown at standard cost.
5. The closing balance after making the credit entries represents the variance from standard for the month.
6. Material Stocks are carried at Actual Cost.
7. The work-in-progress and finished goods are valued at standard cost.
8. Material Price Variance is computed on material used in finished goods and work-in-progress.
9. It is suitable where simple analysis of variance is sufficient at the end of the period.

Illustration 16. The following information is available from the records of CAS Ltd. which follows the Partial Plan of accounting for Standard Costs for October:

Material purchased 10,000 pieces at ₹ 11 ₹ 1,10,000
Materials consumed 9,500 pieces at ₹ 11 ₹ 1,04,500
Actual wages paid 2,475 hours at ₹ 35 ₹ 86,625
Actual factory expenses incurred ₹ 1,70,000 (Budgeted ₹ 1,65,000)
Units produced: 900 units and sold at ₹ 60 per unit.
The standard rates and prices are as under:
Direct Materials ₹ 10 per unit
Standard Input 10 pieces per unit
Direct Labour Rate ₹ 30 per hour
Standard Requirement 2.5 hours per unit
Overheads ₹ 60 per labour hour

Required: (a) Prepare Standard Cost Sheet (b) Calculate the Variances, (c) Show the Journal Entries to record the transactions, (d) Show Journal Entry for disposal of variances, (e) Prepare Material Control Account and WIP Control Account.

Solution:

(a) STANDARD COST SHEET

Cost	*SQ*	*SR*	*Standard Cost (₹)*
Direct material	9,000	10	90,000
Direct labour	2,250	30	67,500
Overheads	2,250	60	1,35,000
			2,92,500

(b) CALCULATION OF VARIANCES

Material Price Variance = AQ (SP – AP) = 9,500 Pcs. (₹ 10 – ₹.11) = ₹ 9,500 (A)
Material Usage Variance = SR (SQ – AQ) = ₹ 10 (9,000 pcs. – 9,500 pcs.) = ₹ 5,000 (A)
Labour Rate Variance = AH (SR – AR) = 2,475 hrs. (₹ 30 – ₹ 35) = ₹ 12,375 (A)
Labour efficiency variance = SR (SH – AH) = ₹ 30 (2,250 hrs. – 2,475 hrs.) = ₹ 6,750 (A)

Overhead variances:

1. Absorbed Overheads (SH × SR) = (2,250 × ₹ 60)	₹ 1,35,000
2. Standard Overheads (AH × SR) = (2,475 Hrs. × ₹ 60)	₹ 1,48,500
3. Budgeted Overheads	₹ 1,65,000
4. Actual Overheads	₹ 1,70,000

Efficiency Variance: (1 – 2) ₹ 13,500 (A)
Capacity Variance: (2 – 3) ₹.16,500 (A) (idle time)
Expense Variance: (3 – 4) ₹ 5,000 (A)
Total Variance: (1 – 4) ₹ 35,000 (A)

(c) JOURNAL ENTRIES TO RECORD THE TRANSACTIONS

Particulars		*Dr. (₹)*	*Cr. (₹)*
Material Control A/c	Dr	1,10,000	
To General Ledger Adjustment A/c			1,10,000
(Being the purchase value of 10,000 pieces of materials at ₹ 11 each)			
Work-in-Progress A/c	Dr.	1,04,500	
To Material Control A/c			1,04,500
(Being the cost of 9,500 pieces of materials actually issued to production at the actual price of ₹ 11 each)			
Work-in-Progress A/c	Dr.	86,625	
To Wages Control A/c			86,625
(Being the actual amount of direct wages paid for 2,475 hours at ₹ 35 per hour)			
Work-in-Progress A/c	Dr.	1,70,000	
To Overhead Expense Control A/c			1,70,000
(Being the actual overhead expenses incurred)			
Finished Stock Control A/c	Dr.	2,92,500	
To Work-in-Progress A/c			2,92,500
(Being the standard cost of production transferred to finished goods account)			
Cost of Sales A/c	Dr.	2,92,500	
To Finished Stock Control A/c			2,92,500
(Being the standard cost of goods sold transferred to Cost of Sales A/c)			

After the basic transactions are posted, the materials control account will show the actual value of stock of material in hand and the work-in-progress account will show a balance representing the cumulative variances on all the accounts and closing balance of work-in-progress at standard cost. The variances have already been analysed in Para (b) above and they will be carried to the respective accounts pending investigation before being finally disposed off. In this Illustration we have assumed that there is no closing balance of work-in-progress.

(d) JOURNAL ENTRY FOR DISPOSAL OF VARIANCES

Particulars		Dr. (₹)	Cr. (₹)
Material Price Variance A/c	Dr.	9,500	
Material Usage Variance A/c	Dr.	5,000	
Labour Rate Variance A/c	Dr.	12,375	
Labour Efficiency Variance A/c	Dr.	6,750	
Overhead Efficiency Variance A/c	Dr.	13,500	
Overhead Capacity Variance A/c	Dr.	16,500	
Overhead Expense Variance A/c	Dr.	5,000	
To Work-in-progress A/c			68,625

(e)

Dr. **MATERIAL CONTROL ACCOUNT** Cr.

Particulars	₹	Particulars	₹
To Opening balance	—	By Work-in-Progress A/c	1,04,500
To General Ledger Adjustment A/c	1,10,000	By Balance c/d	5,500
	1,10,000		1,10,000

Dr. **WORK-IN-PROGRESS CONTROL ACCOUNT** Cr.

Particulars	₹	Particulars	₹
To Opening balance	—	By Finished Stock Control A/c	2,92,500
To Material control A/c	1,04,500	By Material Price Variance A/c	9,500
To Wages control A/c	86,625	By Material Usage Variance A/c	5,000
To Overheads control A/c	1,70,000	By Labour Rate Variance A/c	12,375
		By Labour Efficiency Variance A/c	6,750
		By Overhead Efficiency Variance A/c	13,500
		By Overhead Capacity Variance A/c	16,500
		By Overhead Expense Variance A/c	5,000
	3,61,125		3,61,125

2. SINGLE PLAN

(a) Features: The features of Single Plan are as follows:

1. Analysis of variances is done from the original documents like invoices, labour sheets, etc., and this method of analysis is known as analysis at source.
2. It envisages the posting of all items in the debit side of the work-in-progress account at the standard cost leaving the credit side to represent the standard cost of finished production and work-in-progress.
3. It enables the ascertainment of variances as and when the transaction is posted to Work-in-progress Account.
4. Its installation requires more planning so that effective documentation at each stage is introduced for proper recording and analysis of variance since the single plan system contemplates the analysis of variances at source. Thus for example, the issue of bill of materials to the stores enables the storekeeper to calculate the standard value of materials. If any material is requisitioned beyond the standard, he can mark the same for material usage variance account. In the production department, as and when the finished output is recorded, the standard waste and actual waste can be compared and necessary entries can be made by the shop supervisors for posting the excessive usage to appropriate variance accounts.
5. Material Stocks are carried at Standard Cost.
6. The work-in-progress and finished goods are valued at standard cost.
7. It uses Current Standards.
8. Material Price Variance is computed on the material quantity purchased.

9. It is preferred if frequent detailed analysis of variance is desired, as (a) the comparison of actual with standard cost of each operation or operator or (b) the daily reporting of standard cost of excess material used.

(b) Accounting Entries under Single Plan: So far as materials are concerned, material price variances are recorded at the time of receipt of the material and the material quantity variances are recorded as far as possible when excess materials are used. The entries will be as illustrated below:

1. Dr. Material Control A/c *(with the Actual Purchases at Standard Cost)*
   Dr. or Cr. Material Price Variance A/c
   (With Material Price Variance at the time of Purchases)
   Cr. Creditors A/c *(with the Actual Purchases at Actual Cost)*
2. Dr. Work-in-progress Control A/c *(with the Standard Cost of Standard Quantity)*
   Dr. or Cr. Material Usage Variances A/c *(With Material Usage Variance at the time of Issue)*
   Cr. Material Control A/c *(with the Standard Cost of Actual Quantity)*
3. Dr. Wages Control A/c *(With Wages at Standard Rate)*
   Dr./Cr. Labour Rate Variances A/c *(With Labour Rate Variance at the time of Payment)*
   Cr. Cash *(With Wages at Actual Rate)*
4. Dr. Work-in-progress Control A/c *(With Overhead at Standard Rate)*
   Dr. or Cr. Overhead Expense Variances A/c *(With Overhead Expense Variance)*
   Cr. Overhead Expense Control A/c. *(With Overhead at Actual Rate)*

17.3 Distinction between Partial Plan and Single Plan

Basis of Distinction	Partial Plan	Single Plan
1. When Analysis done	Analysis is done at the end of month.	Analysis is done from source document.
2. WIP Account	It is debited with Actual Cost.	It is debited with Standard Cost.
3. Stock of Material	It is carried at Actual Cost.	It is carried at Standard Cost.
4. Material Price Variance	It is computed on Material Quantity Consumed.	It is computed on Material Quantity Purchased.

17.4 Similarities between Partial Plan and Single Plan

1. Both use Current Standards.
2. Stock of WIP and Finished Goods are valued at Standard Cost.

Note: Dual Plan of Standard Costing helps to convert standards into actuals by using the ratios.

Illustration 17. The following information is available from the records of CAS Ltd. which follows the Single Plan of accounting for Standard Costs for October:

STANDARD COST SHEET PER UNIT

Particulars		₹
Direct Material 3 pcs. @ ₹ 21.50		64.50
Direct Labour:		
Dept. A: 2 hrs @ ₹ 17.5	35	
Dept. B: 4 hrs. @ ₹ 15.0	60	95
Overheads :		
Dept. A: 2 hrs. @ ₹ 5	10	
Dept. B: 4 hrs. @ ₹ 10	40	50
		209.50

Other information:
Materials purchased and consumed: 8,600 pcs. @ ₹ 250 each
Labour time spent: Dept. A. 5,200 hours, Dept. B. 12,000 hours. There is no change in labour rates.
Actual factory overheads are: Dept. A. ₹ 30,000, Dept B. ₹ 1,25,000
Units produced: Dept. A. 28,000, Dept. B. 28,000
Budgeted overheads: Dept. A. ₹ 30,000, Dept. B. ₹ 1,20,000

Required: (a) Prepare Standard Cost Sheet (b) Calculate the Variances, (c) Show the Journal Entries to record the transactions, (d) Prepare the necessary Ledger Accounts

Solution

(a) Standard Cost Sheet

(i) Material price variance: 8,600 pcs. (₹ 21.50 – ₹ 25) = ₹ 30,100 (A)
(ii) Material usage variance: ₹ 21.50 (8,400 Pcs. – 8,600 Pcs.) = ₹ 4,300 (A)
[Standard requirement of materials = 2,800 units produced × 3 pcs. per unit = 8,400 pcs.]
(iii) Labour efficiency variance:
Dept. A: Standard time required = 2,800 pcs. × 2 hrs. = 5,600 hours.
Dept. B: Standard time required = 2,800 pcs. × 4 hrs. = 11,200 hours.

(b) Calculation of Variances:

Dept. A: 17.50 (5,600 – 5,200) = ₹ 7,000 (F)
Dept. B: 15 (11,200 – 12,000) = ₹ 12,000 (A)

OVERHEADS VARIANCES

Particulars	*Dept. A (₹)*	*Dept. B (₹)*	*Total (₹)*
1. Charged to Production:			
Dept. A. 5,600 × 5	28,000		
Dept. B. 11,200 × 10		1,12,000	1,40,000
2. Actual Hours at Standard Rate :			
Dept. A. 5,200 × 5	26,000		
Dept. B. 12,000 × 10		1,20,000	1,46,000
3. Budgeted Overheads	30,000	1,20,000	1,50,000
4. Actual Expenses	30,000	1,25,000	1,55,000
Efficiency variance: (1 – 2)	2,000 (F)	8,000 (A)	6,000 (A)
Capacity variance: (2 – 3)	4,000 (A)	—	4,000 (A)
Expense variance: (3 – 4)	—	5,000 (A)	5,000 (A)
Total variance: (1 – 4)	2,000 (A)	13,000 (A)	15,000 (A)

(c) JOURNAL ENTRIES TO RECORD THE TRANSACTIONS

	Particulars		*Dr. (₹)*	*Cr. (₹)*
(i)	Material Control A/c	Dr.	1,84,900	
	Material Price Variance A/c	Dr.	30,100	
	To Creditors A/c			2,15,000
(ii)	Work-in-Progress Dept. A. A/c	Dr.	1,80,600	
	Material Usage Variance A/c	Dr.	4,300	
	To Material Control A/c			1,84,900
(iii)	Work-in-progress Dept. A. A/c	Dr.	98,000	
	To Wages Control A/c			98,000
(iv)	Wages Control A/c	Dr.	7,000	
	To Labour Efficiency Variance Dept A A/c			7,000
(v)	Work-in-Progress Dept. B A/c.	Dr.	1,68,000	
	Labour Efficiency Variance Dept. B A/c	Dr.	12,000	
	To Wages Control A/c			1,80,000

	Particulars		Dr. (₹)	Cr. (₹)
(vi)	Work-in-Progress Dept. A A/c	Dr.	28,000	
	Overhead Capacity Variance Dept. A. A/c	Dr.	4,000	
	To Overhead Efficiency Variance Dept. A. A/c			2,000
	To Overhead Expense Control Dept. A A/c			30,000
(vii)	Work-in-Progress Dept. B A/c	Dr.	1,12,000	
	Overhead Efficiency Variance A/c	Dr.	8,000	
	Overhead Expenses Variance A/c	Dr.	5,000	
	To Overhead Control Dept. B A/c			1,25,000
(viii)	Work-in-Progress Dept. B A/c	Dr.	3,06,600	
	To Work-in-Progress Dept. A A/c			3,06,600
	(Being the transfer at standard cost of finished Production of Department A to Department B for processing in Department B)			
(ix)	Finished Stock control A/c		5,86,600	
	To Work-in-Progress Dept. B A/c	Dr.		5,86,600

(d) Necessary Ledger Accounts

Dr. **MATERIAL CONTROL ACCOUNT** Cr.

Particulars	₹	Particulars	₹
To Creditors	1,84,900	By Work-in-Progress (Dept. A) A/c	1,80,600
		By Material usage variance A/c	4,300
	1,84,900		1,84,900

Dr. **WAGES CONTROL ACCOUNT** Cr.

Particulars	₹	Particulars	₹
To Cash (or Wages payable A/c)	2,71,000	By Work-in-Progress (Dept. A) A/c	98,000
To Labour efficiency Variance (Dept, A) A/c	7,000	By Work-in-Progress (Dept. B) A/c	1,68,000
		By Labour efficiency variance (Dept. B) A/c	12,000
	2,78,000		2,78,00

Dr. **WORK-IN-PROGRESS (DEPT. A) CONTROL ACCOUNT** Cr.

Particulars	₹	Particulars	₹
To Material Control A/c	1,80,600	By Work-in-Progress (Dept. B) A/c	3,06,600
To Wages Control A/c	98,000		
To Overhead Control (Dept. A) A/c	28,000		
	3,06,600		3,06,600

Dr. **WORK-IN-PROGRESS (DEPT. B) CONTROL ACCOUNT** Cr.

Particulars	₹	Particulars	₹
To Work-in-Progress (Dept. A) A/c	3,06,600	By Finished Stock Control A/c	5,86,600
To Wages Control A/c	1,68,000		
To Overhead Control (Dept. B) A/c	1,12,000		
	5,86,600		5,86,600

Dr. **OVERHEAD EXPENSE CONTROL (DEPT. A) ACCOUNT** Cr.

Particulars	₹	Particulars	₹
To Cash	30,000	By Work-in-Progress (Dept. A) A/c	28,000
To Overhead Efficiency Variance A/c	2,000	By Overhead Capacity Variance A/c	4,000
	32,000		32,000

Dr. **MATERIAL PRICE VARIANCE ACCOUNT** Cr.

Particulars	₹	Particulars	₹
To Creditros	30,100	By Costing P & L A/c	30,100
	30,100		30,100

Dr. **MATERIAL USAGE VARIANCE ACCOUNT** Cr.

Particulars	₹	Particulars	₹
To Material Control A/c	4,300	By Costing P & L A/c	4,300
	4,300		4,300

Dr. **LABOUR EFFICIENCY VARIANCE ACCOUNT** Cr.

Particulars	₹	Particulars	₹
To Wages Control A/c	12,000	By Wages Control A/c (Efficiency of Dept. B) By Costing P & L A/c	7,000 5,000
	12,000		12,000

Dr. **OVERHEAD EFFICIENCY VARIANCE ACCOUNT** Cr.

Particulars	₹	Particulars	₹
To Overhead Expenses Control (Dept. B) A/c	8,000	By Overhead Exp. Control (Dept. A) A/c By Costing P & L A/c	 2,000 6,000
	8,000		8,000

Dr. **OVERHEAD CAPACITY VARIANCE ACCOUNT** Cr.

Particulars	₹	Particulars	₹
To Overhead Expenses Control (Dept. A) A/c	4,000	By Costing P & L A/c	4,000
	4,000		4,000

Dr. **OVERHEAD EXPENSES VARIANCE ACCOUNT** Cr.

Particulars	₹	Particulars	₹
To Overhead Expenses Control (Dept. B) A/c	5,000	By Costing P & L A/c	5,000
	5,000		5,000

Dr. **CREDITORS ACCOUNT** Cr.

Particulars	₹	Particulars	₹
To Balance	2,15,000	By Material Control A/c By Material Variance A/c	1,84,900 30,100
	2,15,000		2,15,000

Dr. **OVERHEAD EXPENSES CONTROL (DEPT 'B') ACCOUNT** Cr.

Particulars	₹	*Particulars*	₹
To Cash	1,25,000	By Work-in-Progress Dept. A A/c	1,12,000
		By Overhead Efficiency Variance (Dept. B) A/c	8,000
		By Overhead Expenses Variance (Dept. B) A/c	5,000
	1,25,000		1,25,000

Dr. **FINISHED STOCK CONTROL ACCOUNT** Cr.

Particulars	₹	*Particulars*	₹
To Work-in-Progress Dept. B A/c	5,86,600	By Balance c/d	5,86,600
	5,86,600		5,86,600

18.0 HOW TO DISPOSE OFF VARIANCES IN A STANDARD COSTING SYSTEM?

There is no unanimity of opinion among Cost Accountants regarding the disposition of Variances. Following three Methods are commonly used for disposition of Variances:

1. Transfer to Profit & Loss Account Method

Accounting Treatment	All Variances are transferred to Profit & Loss Account.
Disclosure of Cost of Sales, Stock of WIP, Stock of Finished Goods	These are shown at **Standard Cost**.
Suitability	This Method is suitable where all the Variances arise due to efficiency **factors within the control** of management.

2. Pro-rata Distribution of Variances Method

Accounting Treatment	All the Cost Variances are distributed over the Cost of Sales, Stock of WIP, and Stock of Finished Goods on some equitable basis (*say units or values*).
Disclosure of Cost of Sales, Stock of WIP, Stock of Finished Goods	These are shown at **Actual Cost**.
Suitability	This Method is suitable where all the Variances arise due to **reasons beyond the control** of management.

3. Mixed Method

Accounting Treatment	(a) All Controllable Variances (*say Quantity Variances*) are transferred to Profit & Loss Account. (b) All Uncontrollable Variances (*say Price Variances*) are distributed over the Cost of Sales, Stock of WIP, and Stock of Finished Goods on some equitable basis (*say units or values*).

Disclosure of Cost of Sales, Stock of WIP, Stock of Finished Goods	(a) These are shown at Standard Cost if the Variances are Controllable. (b) These are shown at Actual Cost if the Variances are Uncontrollable.
Suitability	This Method is suitable where all the Variances can be segregated into Controllable Variances and Uncontrollable Variances.

19.0 BEHAVIOURAL ASPECTS OF STANDARD COSTING

1. Projection of Fixed Overheads and Estimated Selling Price in a Standard Cost Sheet is a circular exercise with no added value.	In an award winning article, "**Cost/Management Accounting the 21st Century Paradigm**", published in Management Accounting (USA), December 1995, William L Ferrara argues that while preparing a Standard Cost Sheet, one of the objectives of which is to assist management in pricing products, a professional cannot project fixed overheads until and unless he is aware of the production quantum to be effected. The forecast of future production can only be made if a tentative selling price of the product is known because, in a competitive market, it is the selling price which decides the sale quantity and therefore the production volume. The authors contend that in case the selling price is known at the time of projecting fixed overheads then the re computation of the same is a valueless exercise.
2. Traditional Costing tools like Standard Costing induce a static behavior in the employees.	It is argued that the use of standard costing renders employees static and curbs innovation and that companies following traditional standard costing find it difficult to improve upon standards because of severe resistance from employees who are convinced that the established best practice cannot be improved further.
3. Fear of Adverse Variances forces managers to give undue importance to material price, labour rate and efficiency and capacity utilization. These concepts are detrimental to the modern day world class manufacturing environment characterized by concepts of JIT and TQM.	Just-in-Time (JIT) Policy requires purchase of small quantities of raw material, increase in the number of set ups and minimal importance to capacity utilization. Policies like JIT result in increased adverse variances related to raw material prices, labour efficiency and production volume. It is argued that the fear of such adverse variances affects goal congruence and forces managers to behave against their company's policies.
4. Traditional Costing does not provide the management with what is the allowable cost; rather it emphasizes on the standard or actual costs.	It is argued that techniques like Target costing are much more motivating when compared to Traditional costing since the former encourages the use of concepts like value engineering and value analysis.

SOLVED PROBLEMS

Problem 1. The Managing Director of your company has been given the following statement showing the results for a recent month :

	Month ending 31st October		
	Master Budget	*Actual*	*Variance*
Units produced and sold	10,000	9,000	(1,000)
Sales	₹ 40,000	₹ 35,000	₹ (5,000)
Direct Material	10,000	9,200	800
Direct Wages	15,000	13,100	1,900
Variable Overhead	5,000	4,700	300
Fixed Overhead	5,000	4,900	100
	35,000	31,900	3,100
Net Surplus	5,000	3,100	(1,900)

Figures in parentheses indicate adverse variances.

The standard costs of the product are as follows :

	Per unit
Direct material (1 kg @ ₹ 1 per kg)	₹ 1.00
Direct Wages (1 hour @ ₹ 1.50)	₹ 1.50
Variable Overhead (1 hour @ ₹ 0.50)	₹ 0.50

Actual results for the month showed that 9,800 kg of material were used and 8,800 labour hours were recorded.

Required:

(a) Prepare a flexible budget for the month and compare with the actual results; and

(b) Calculate the variances which have arisen.

Solution:

(a) STATEMENT SHOWING FLEXIBLE BUDGET FOR THE MONTH AND ITS COMPARISON WITH ACTUAL

	Particulars	*Master Budget For 10,000* ₹	*Flexible Budget Per unit* ₹	*Flexible Budget For 9,000* ₹	*Actual For 9,000* ₹	*Variance* ₹
A	Sales	40,000	4.00	36,000	35,000	1,000 (A)
B	Direct Material	10,000	1.00	9,000	9,200	200 (A)
C	Direct Wages	15,000	1.50	13,500	13,100	400 (F)
D	Variance Overhead	5,000	0.50	4,500	4,700	200 (A)
E	Total Variable Cost	30,000	3.00	27,000	27,000	—
F	Contribution (A – B)	10,000	1.00	9,000	8,000	1,000 (A)
G	Fixed Overhead	5,000	0.50	5,000	4,900	100 (F)
H	Net Surplus	5,000	0.50	4,000	3,100	900 (A)

(b) Calculation of Variances

BASIC CALCULATIONS FOR THE COMPUTATION OF MATERIAL COST VARIANCES

SQ for AO	*SP*	*SQ × SP* (1)	*AQ*	*AP*	*AQ × AP* (2)	*AQ × SP* (3)
9,000	1.00	9,000	9,800		9,200	9,800

A. Material Cost Variance (1 – 2) = ₹ 9,000 – ₹ 9,200 = ₹ 200 (A)
B. Material Usage Variance (1 – 3) = ₹ 9,000 – ₹ 9,800 = ₹ 800 (A)
C. Material Price Variance (3 – 2) = ₹ 9,800 – ₹ 9,200 = ₹ 600 (F)

Verification:

Material Cost Variance = Material Usage Variance + Material Price Variance
= ₹ 800 (A) + ₹ 600 (F) = ₹ 200 (A)

BASIC CALCULATIONS FOR THE COMPUTATION OF LABOUR COST VARIANCES

SH for AO	*SR*	*SH × SR* (1)	*AH*	*AR*	*AH × AR* (2)	*AH × SR* (3)
9,000	1.50	13,500	8,800		13,100	13,200

A. Labour Cost Variance (1 – 2) = ₹ 13,500 – ₹ 13,100 = ₹ 400 (F)
B. Labour Efficiency Variance (1 – 3) = ₹ 13,500 – ₹ 13,200 = ₹ 300 (F)
C. Labour Rate Variance (3 – 2) = ₹ 13,200 – ₹ 13,100 = ₹ 100 (F)

Verification :

Labour Cost Variance = Labour Efficiency Variance + Labour Rate Variance
= ₹ 300 (F) + (₹ 100 (F) = ₹ 400 (F)

BASIC CALCULATIONS FOR VARIABLE OVERHEAD VARIANCES

1. Absorbed Overheads (SH x SR)	= ₹ 4,500
2. Standard Overheads (AH x SR)	= ₹ 4,400
3. Actual Overheads	= ₹ 4,700

COMPUTATION OF VARIANCES

A. Variable Overheads Efficiency Variance (1 – 2) = ₹ 4,500 – ₹ 4,400 = ₹ 100 (F)
B. Variable Overheads Expenditure Variance (2 – 3) = ₹ 4,400 – ₹ 4,700 = ₹ 300 (A)

C. Total Variable Overheads Variance (A + B) = ₹ 200 (A)

BASIC CALCULATIONS FOR FIXED OVERHEAD VARIANCES

1. Absorbed Overheads (SH x SR)	= ₹ 4,500
2. Standard Overheads (AH x SR)	= ₹ 4,400
3. Budgeted Overheads (BH x SR)	= ₹ 5,000
4. Actual Overheads	= ₹ 4,900

COMPUTATION OF VARIANCES

A. Fixed Overheads Efficiency Variance (1 – 2) = ₹ 4,500 – ₹ 4,400 = ₹ 100 (F)
B. Fixed Overheads Capacity Variance (2 – 3) = ₹ 4,400 – ₹ 5,000 = ₹ 600 (A)
C. Total Fixed Overheads Volume Variance (A + B) = ₹ 500 (A)
D. Fixed Overheads Expenditure Variance (3 – 4) = ₹ 5,000 – ₹ 4,900 = ₹ 100 (F)

E. Total Fixed Overheads Variance (C + D) = ₹ 400 (A)

Note:

Actual Sales Margin = Actual Sales – Standard Cost of Actual Sales
= ₹ 35,000 – (9,000 × ₹ 3.50) = ₹ 3,500

BASIC CALCULATIONS FOR THE COMPUTATION OF SALES VARIANCES

BQ	*BM*	*BQ × BM* (1)	*AQ*	*AM*	*AQ × AM* (2)	*AQ × BM* (3)
10,000	0.50	5,000	9,000	0.3889	3,500	4,500

A	Sales Margin Value Variance	(2 – 1) = ₹ 5,000 – ₹ 3,500 = ₹ 1,500 (A)
B	Sales Margin Volume Variance	(3 – 1) = ₹ 5,000 – ₹ 4,500 = ₹ 500 (A)
E	Sales Margin Price Variance	(2 – 3) = ₹ 3,500 – ₹ 4,500 = ₹ 1,000 (A)

Verification:

Sales Margin Value Variance = Sales Margin Volume Variance + Sales Margin Price Variance
= ₹ 500 (A) + ₹ 1,000 (A) = ₹ 1,500 (A)

Problem 2. JS Limited used a full standard cost system with raw materials inventory carried at standard. The following data was taken from the records of the company for the year :

	₹
Opening raw materials inventory	300
Closing raw materials inventory	250
Net Purchases	410
Material Price variance	10 A
Materials usage variance	20 A
Direct Labour cost (Actuals)	900
Direct Labour cost at standard	840
Actual overhead cost incurred	875
Overheads cost variance	45 F
Opening work-in-progress inventory	120
Closing work-in-progress inventory	140
Cost of goods sold reported	2,240
Opening Finished Goods Inventory	360

Note: 'F' denotes favourable and 'A' denotes adverse.

You are required to compute : (1) Raw Material purchases at standard; (2) Raw Materials consumed at actuals; (3) Raw Materials consumed at standard; (4) Labour cost variance; (5) Standard overhead costs; (6) Total manufacturing cost at standard; (7) Cost of goods manufactured; (8) Cost of products sold to customers; (9) Closing finished goods inventory.

Solution:

1. Raw Material Purchases at Standard = Net Raw Material Purchases + Material Price Variance
   = ₹ 410 (– ₹ 10) = ₹ 400
2. Raw Materials consumed (at actuals)= Opening Inventory + Purchases at Standard – Closing Inventory
   = ₹ 300 + ₹ 400 – ₹ 250 = ₹ 450
3. Raw Materials consumed at standard = Raw Materials Consumed at Actuals + Usage Variance
   = ₹ 450 + (– ₹ 20) = ₹ 430
4. Labour Cost Variance = Standard Labour Cost – Actual Labour Cost
   – ₹ 840 – ₹ 900 – ₹ 60 (Adverse)
5. Standard Overhead Costs= Actual Overhead Costs Incurred + Overhead Cost Variance
   = ₹ 875 + ₹ 45 = ₹ 920
6. Total Manufacturing Cost at Standard

	₹
Raw Material	430
Labour	840
Overhead	920
	2,190

7. Cost of goods Manufactured (at Standard)
   = Opening WIP + Manufacturing Cost at Standard – Closing WIP
   = ₹ 120 + ₹ 2,190 – ₹ 140 = ₹ 2,170
8. Cost of products sold to Customers (at standard)
   = Cost of goods sold reported + Cost Variances
   = ₹ 2,240 + ₹ (–20 – 10 – 60) + ₹ 45 = ₹ 2,195
9. Closing finished goods inventory (at Standard)
   = Opening Finished Goods Inventory + Cost of Goods manufactured
   – Cost of products sold to Customers
   = ₹ 360 + ₹ 2,170 – ₹ 2,195 = ₹ 335.

11 Transfer Pricing

Learning Objectives

After studying this chapter, you should be able to understand:

- Why there is Need of Transfer Pricing?
- What is meant by the Transfer Price?
- What is the rationale for Transfer Pricing?
- What are the Objectives of setting Transfer Pricing Mechanism?
- What are the different Methods/Approaches for setting Transfer Price?
- Market Based Transfer Price
- What should be the Policy if Market Prices are at Distress Level?
- Cost – Based Transfer Price
- Negotiated Transfer Price
- Dual Prices
- Disadvantages of using Transfer Pricing Method
- Conflict Between a Division and the Company
- Multinational Transfer Pricing

1.0 WHY THERE IS NEED OF TRANSFER PRICING?

The whole organisation can be divided into a number of divisions, the performance of each division can be measured in terms of both the income earned and the costs which are incurred. In profit centred divisional approach, the manager of each division is responsible for costs, incomes and profits of his division. Further he is given freedom to make all decisions affecting his division. In such a decentralised organisation there may be transfer of goods from one division to another division. In these cases management uses **transfer price** to integrate the efforts of the division and to evaluate their performance.

The price charged for transfer of goods of one division to another division is the purchase cost to receiving division and revenue of supplying division. It means that the transfer price fixed will affect the profitability of both divisions.

2.0 WHAT IS MEANT BY THE TRANSFER PRICE?

Transfer price is the internal **pricing mechanism** of the organisation under which one division of an organisation charges for a product or service transferred to another division of the same organisation thereby forming basis for allocation of combined revenue among the various divisions.

3.0 WHAT IS THE RATIONALE FOR TRANSFER PRICING?

The **rationale for transfer pricing** is that divisional manager while making decision has only to decide how the decision will affect their division's performance and not to see how the decision will affect the company as a whole. If there is well designed transfer pricing system then **maximising the divisional profit** will lead to **maximisation of the overall company's profit.**

4.0 WHAT ARE THE OBJECTIVES OF SETTING TRANSFER PRICING MECHANISM?

The main objectives of intra-company transfer pricing are as follows:

1. To analyse the profit performance of each profit centre.
2. To optimise the maximum utilisation of plant capacity.
3. To optimise the allocation of financial resources.
4. To allow goal congruence to take place i.e. objective of the department is in align with the organisation's objective.

5.0 WHAT ARE THE DIFFERENT METHODS/APPROACHES FOR SETTING TRANSFER PRICE?

The different methods/approaches for setting transfer price are as follows:-

1. Market – Based Transfer Prices
2. Cost – Based Transfer Prices
3. Negotiated Transfer Prices
4. Dual Prices

6.0 MARKET BASED TRANSFER PRICE

6.1 What is Market – Based Transfer Price?

Market – Based Transfer Price is the method under which the transfer prices of goods/services transferred to other divisions are based on market prices. Since market prices will, by and large be determined by demand and supply in the long run, it is claimed that profits which result under this method, will provide a good indicator of the overall efficiency of the various divisions.

6.2 What are the situations under which market based transfer price lead to optimal decision?

The market based transfer price lead to optimal decision under the following conditions:

1. Perfectly Competitive Market	The market for intermediate product is perfectly competitive i.e. the selling division can sell its output in the external market as much as it can at stated price hence there exist no idle capacity for selling division. Similarly buying division can buy as much output as it can at stated price from the external market.
2. No Additional Costs or Benefits in External Market	There are no additional costs or benefits to the company as a whole from buying or selling in the external market. *For example* there is no selling or ordering cost.
3. Minimal Interdependence	Interdependencies among divisions are minimal.

6.3 What are the Merits of Market – Based Transfer Prices?

(i) Such a competitive market provides an incentive to efficient production.

(ii) Since market prices will, by and large be determined by demand and supply in the long run, it is claimed that Profits which results under this method, will provide a good indicator of the overall efficiency of the various units.

(iii) Competitive market prices provide reliable measures of divisional income because these prices are established independently rather than by individuals who have an interest in the results.

6.4 What are the Limitations of Market – Based Transfer Prices?

1. Imperfections in the Market	Unfortunately, competitive markets with well defined prices rarely exist. Therefore imperfections in the market do not lead to optimal decision in market – based transfer prices.
2. Difficulty in obtaining just market prices	Sometimes it is difficult to obtain at all any market price for those vary products which are manufactured only for internal consumption.
3. Difficulty in determining the elements of selling and distribution expenses	Such as commission, discounts, advertisement and sales promotion etc., so that necessary adjustment may be made in the market price to provide benefit of these expenses, to the profit centre, receiving the goods.

6.5 WHAT SHOULD BE THE POLICY IF MARKET PRICES ARE AT DISTRESS LEVEL?

When there is excess supply in the market then it that case price may fall to the significant level. However, if this drop is temporary then low market prices are called distress prices. As long as distress prices are above variable cost it may be used in respect of transfer pricing. But if it falls below variable cost then selling division should stop selling the product and buying division should buy it from outside.

7.0 COST – BASED TRANSFER PRICE

7.1 What is Cost – based Transfer Price Method ?

There are many cost – based transfer price methods like:

Full Cost	1. **Transfer Price:** Goods or Services are transferred at their **full cost** of production. Full Cost means cost of production plus expenses like selling and distribution,administration, research and development cost etc. It includes both variable and fixed cost. 2. **Merits: (a)** Supplying unit is allowed to recover the full cost of the goods/services transferred. (b) Supplying unit is free to earn profit on outside sale. 3. **Demerits: (a)** Supplying unit is not allowed to make any profit on transfers to other units of the organisation. (b)The problem involved in the full cost method is how to allocate fixed cost. If fixed cost is to be allocated then the problem is whether it should be allocated on the basis of actual production or standard production. So there are many problems involved in it.

Full Cost *plus* Mark up	1. **Transfer Price:** Goods or Services are transferred at their **full cost of production plus some mark-up.** Full Cost means cost of production plus expenses like selling and distribution,administration, research and development cost etc. The markup added to full cost is either expressed as a percentage of full cost or of capital employed. Selling expenses here are recovered by the supplying unit without incurring them, specially when the goods/services are transferred internally. Mark up is added to provide a return for unallocated corporate level costs and investments deemed to be supporting product production. 2. **Merits: (a)** Supplying unit is allowed to recover the full cost of the goods/services transferred. (b) Supplying unit is free to earn profit on internal as well as outside sale. 3. **Demerit:** Selling expenses here are recovered by the supplying unit without incurring them, specially when the goods/services are transferred internally. To overcome this defect either the use of standard cost plus or actual cost plus are preferred.
Variable Cost	1. **Transfer Price:** Goods or Services are transferred at their variable costs(excluding Variable Selling Costs which are not to be incurred on internal demand) of production. 2. **Suitability:** It is useful for those units where the responsibility of profit performance is centralized. This method is especially useful when the Supplying Division has idle capacity which is more than internal demand. 3. **Demerit:** It is difficult to measure the performance of each profit centre.
Variable Cost *plus* Mark up	In addition to variable cost some mark up is added for any exigencies.
Standard Cost	1. **Transfer Price:** Goods or Services are transferred at their **standard cost** of production. Any difference between actual and standard cost viz., variances are usually absorbed by the supplying unit. In some cases, variances are transferred to the user unit as well. This will result in the inventory being carried at identical standard cost by both the supplying and receiving units. This will result in the inventory being carried at identical standard cost by both the supplying and receiving units. 2. **Suitability:** It is useful for those units where the responsibility of profit performance is centralized and where more cost controls are required. 3. **Demerit:** It is difficult to measure the performance of each profit centre.

7.2 When Cost – based transfer price method is appropriate?

Cost – based transfer price is appropriate when market prices are unavailable, inappropriate or too costly to obtain.

7.3 What are the limitations of using Cost – Based Transfer pricing method?

The limitations of Cost – Based Transfer pricing method are as follows:

1. Price based on cost are not equilibrium prices since cost based prices are not determined from demand and supply conditions. Therefore at a given price there may be excess demand or excess supply.
2. Divisions are profit centres and not cost centres. Therefore Cost – based transfer pricing mechanism do not support the objective of maximisation of division profit.
3. This method assumes that cost of a product can be calculated accurately. But this does not always happen. Even activity based costing which result in computation of more accurate cost but still it is only an estimate.

4. It does not provide any incentive to control cost, since cost can be recovered. But solution to this problem can be obtained by using standard cost method.
5. Cost – based approach is not a good approach when an organisation does not have idle capacity since cost – based approach shall not consider the opportunity loss.

8.0 NEGOTIATED TRANSFER PRICE

8.1 What is Negotiated Transfer Price?

Negotiated transfer price results from the bargaining process between the selling and the buying division of the organisation. Each division is finally responsible for the transfer price it negotiates. However such transfer prices may reflect the negotiating skills of the two divisions rather than economic consideration.

Here it is important to understand the range within which the two divisions negotiate. Here the concept of **Minimum Transfer Price** and **Maximum Transfer Price** come into existence. Prices are negotiated between Minimum Transfer Price and the Maximum Transfer Price.

8.2 Minimum Transfer Price

Meaning Minimum Transfer Price is the price below which the supplying division will not transfer the good to the buying division.

How to Calculate It is generally calculated as follows:

Situation	*Minimum Transfer Price*
(i) Where there exists no idle capacity or where there is perfectly competitive market [.i.e.Production Capacity of Supplying Division (18000)=External Demand of Product of Supplying Division(18000)]	Variable Cost (excluding Variable Selling Cost) per unit + Contribution loss per unit
(ii) Where there exists idle capacity but such capacity is less than or equal to internal demand. [.i.e.(Production Capacity of Supplying Division(20000)-External Demand of Product of Supplying Division(18000)< Internal Demand(5000)]	= Variable Cost per unit – Variable Selling Cost per unit + $\frac{\text{(Units not available for sale due to transfer to Buying Division)}}{\text{Units Required by Buying Division}}$ × Contribution per unit
(iii) When there exists idle capacity but it is more than internal demand or when no market exists for intermediate product. [.i.e.(Production Capacity of Supplying Division(25000)-External Demand of Product of Supplying Division(18000)> Internal Demand(5000)]	= Variable Cost (excluding Variable Selling Cost) per unit

Minimum Transfer Price = Incremental cost per unit incurred up to the point of transfer + Opportunity Cost per unit to the supplying division.

8.3 What is Maximum Transfer Price?

Meaning	The Maximum Transfer Price is a price above which the buying division will not accept the internal transfer.
How to Calculate	= Price of Outside Supply per unit – Additional cost to be incurred by buying division to make the intermediate product usable

8.4 Whether the Internal Transfer or Outside Supply is profitable?

Situation	*Whether Internal Transfer or Outside Supply profitable*
1. When Maximum Transfer Price > Minimum Transfer Price	Internal transfer is more profitable than outside supply.
2. When Maximum Transfer Price < Minimum Transfer Price	Outside supply is more profitable than Internal transfer. As a general rule, it should be avoided in the interest of the organisation.

8.5 Merit of Negotiated Transfer Price

The buying division may be tempted to purchase from outside source if the outside prices are lower than the internal division's price. In order to avoid any reduction in overall profits of the company, the top management may impose restriction on the external purchase/sale of goods.

8.6 Considerable Factors for effective system of intra company transfer pricing

In order to have an effective system of intra company transfer pricing; the following points should be kept in view:

1. Prices of all transfers in and out of a profit centre should be determined by negotiation between the buyer and the seller.
2. Negotiations should have access to full data on alternative sources and markets and to public and private information about market prices.
3. Buyers and sellers should be completely free to deal outside the company.

9.0 DUAL PRICES

9.1 What is Dual Pricing Method?

Under this method, two method of transfer pricing are used in respect of transfer from one division to another. *For example* when transfer price for selling division is market price and transfer price for buying division is full cost. In this case difference is balanced by using Control Account.

Suppose Selling Division transfers the product at market price i.e. ₹ 160 per unit and buying division receive the product at full cost price i.e. ₹ 120 then the journal entry in respect of this transaction will be passed in the following manner:

Buying Division A/c	Dr. ₹	120	
Control A/c	Dr. ₹	40	
To Selling Division A/c			₹ 160

10.0 DISADVANTAGES OF USING TRANSFER PRICING METHOD

The disadvantages of using Transfer Pricing Method are as follows:

1. The essence of decentralization is reflected in the freedom to make decisions. Under such a set up it is expected that the top management should not interfere with the decision making process of its subordinates heading different units. In other words, management of decentralized units is given autonomy with regard to decision making. In this system top management is expected to preserve 'autonomy in decision making'. The management of such organisation also expects that each division should not only achieve its own objective necessary for evaluating the performance but should also achieve the objective of goal Congruence. In case of failure of a division to achieve the objective of 'goal congruence' the management of the organisation may dictate their 'transfer price'. Such interference of management of the organisation is usually the main basis of conflict between a division and the organisation as a whole.
2. Division may compete with each other and take decision to increase their profit at the expense of other division or the organisation as a whole.
3. The conflict is aggravated if the management advocates the transfer of goods and services at cost. As such the transfer price will not reflect a good picture about the performance of the transferring division. The profitability of the transferring division will not be known by the use of such a transfer price.
4. Each division appreciates the transfer of its goods/services at usual selling price/market price so as to arrive at the correct return/profitability figure, used for measuring the performance. There is no incentive to the transferring division if goods and services are transferred at variable cost.
5. Lack of co – ordination
6. Lack of Co – operation.
7. It may also lead to reduction in overall company's profit.
8. Top management may lose control.

11.0 CONFLICT BETWEEN A DIVISION AND THE COMPANY

1. Usually a conflict between a division of the company and the company as a whole is faced by the management of decentralized units when products or services are exchanged among different divisions of the company. Such a conflict becomes more significant in the case of those concerns where profitability is used as a criteria for evaluating the performance of each division.
2. The essence of decentralization is reflected in the freedom to make decisions. Under such a set up it is expected that the top management should not interfere with the decision making process of its subordinates heading different units. In other words, management of decentralized units is given autonomy with regard to decision making. In this system top management is expected to preserve 'autonomy in decision making'. The management of such companies also expects that each division should not only achieve its own objective necessary for evaluating the performance but should also achieve the objective of goal Congruence.
3. In case of failure of a division to achieve the objective of 'goal congruence' the management of the company may dictate their 'transfer price'. Such interference of management of the company is usually the main basis of conflict between a division and the company as a whole.
4. Further this conflict is aggravated if the management advocates the transfer of goods and services at cost. As such the transfer price will not reflect a good picture about the performance of the transferring division. The profitability of the transferring division will not be known by the use of such a transfer price.
5. Each division appreciates the transfer of its goods/services at usual selling price/market price so as to arrive at the correct return/profitability figure, used for measuring the performance. There is no incentive to the transferring division if goods and services are transferred at variable cost.

12.0 MULTINATIONAL TRANSFER PRICING

1. In multinational companies transfer pricing policies affect not only the motivation of managers but also worldwide income taxes, import duties, and tariffs.
2. Supplying division in a high-income-tax-rate country transfers its products to a division in a low-income-tax-rate country at low transfer price to recognize most of the profit in low-income-tax-rate country to minimize taxes and vice versa.
   For example, Nike might prefer to make its profits in a country, with its maximum corporate tax rate of 8%, rather than in some other place where the rate is 30%.
3. Sometimes import duties offset income tax effects. Most countries base import duties on the price paid for an item, whether bought from an outside company or transferred from another division. Therefore, low transfer prices generally lead to low import duties.
   For example a product maufactured by a Swiss Company with an 8% income tax rate is transferred to its Indian division with a 30% income tax rate. In addition, suppose India imposes an import duty equal to 20% of the price of the item and that Swiss Company cannot deduct this import duty for tax purposes. Suppose the full unit cost of a **product** is ₹ 100, and the variable cost is ₹ 60. If tax authorities allow either variable- or full-cost transfer prices, which should Swiss Company choose?
   Effect of Transferring at ₹ 100 instead of at ₹ 60
   A. Lower Income Taxes on Lower Income of Indian division = 30% of ₹ 40 = ₹ 12
   B. Less: Higher Import duty paid by Indian division on higher transfer price =20% of ₹ 40 = ₹ 8
   C. **Less:** Income Taxes on Income of Swiss division = 8% of ₹ 40 = ₹ 3.20
   D. Net saving from transferring at ₹ 100 instead of ₹ 60 = ₹ 12 – ₹ 8 – ₹ 3.20 = ₹ 0.80
4. Financial restricitions imposed by some governments may be avoided by an effective use of transfer price. For example, in case a country restricts the amount of dividend paid to foreign owners, it may be easier for a company to get cash from a foreign division in form of payments for poduct transferred rather than cash dividend.

   In summary, transfer pricing is more complex in a multinational company than it is in a domestic company. Multinational companies try to achieve more objectives through transferpricing policies.

12.1 Potential for Maximization of Income by a multinational through the use of transfer pricing mechanism

Potential for Maximization of Income by a multinational through the use of transfer pricing mechanism is based on the successful implementation of the following steps:

(i) Transfer pricing may be set relatively higher for affiliates in relatively hightax countries that purchase inputs from affiliates located in relatively low-tax countries.

(ii) Transfer prices to affiliates in countries which are subject to import duties for goods or services purchase may be set low so as to avoid host country taxes.

(iii) Transfer prices to an affiliate in a country that is encountering relatively high inflation may be set relatively high to avoid some of the adverse effects of local currency devaluation that are related to the high inflation.

(iv) Transfer prices may be set high for goods and services purchased by an affiliate operating in a country that has imposed restriction on the repatriation of income to foreign companies.

(v) Transfer prices may be set low for an affiliate that is trying to establish a competitive advantage over a local company either to break into a market or to establish a higher share of the company's business.

Illustration 1

BHARAT TULSIAN Ltd. has 2 divisions namely A & B. Both divisions have full autonomy over their operating decisions. Division A produces Product P and Division B produces Product Q.

Product P may be used for producing Product Q with little alteration.

Division A provides the following information:

Demand of Product P in external market: 18000 units @ ₹ 30 per unit

Variable Cost (including Variable Selling Cost of ₹ 2 per unit) : ₹ 20 per unit

Division B provides the following information:

Division B requires 5000 units of Product P to be used in production of Product Q.

However, Division B has to incur ₹ 5 per unit as additional cost to make Product P useable for the production of Product Q . Independent supply of Product R is available in the market which is refined form of ProductP at a price of ₹ 32 and on which no further alteration is required and it can be directly used for the production of Product Q.

Required: Calculate minimum and the maxium transfer price and state whether internal transfer is profitable or not in each of the following alternative cases:

Case (a) If the production capacity of Division A is limited to 25,000 units of Product P.

Case (b) If the production capacity of Division A is limited to 20,000 units of Product P.

Case (c) If the production capacity of Division A is limited to 18,000 units of Product P.

Case (d) If the production capacity of Division A is limited to 25,000 units of Product P and Production facilities of Division A can be rented out at (i) ₹ 1,50,000 or (ii) ₹ 2,30,000

Case (e) If the production capacity of Division A is limited to 20,000 units of Product P and Production facilities of Division A can be rented out at (i) ₹ 1,50,000 or (ii) ₹ 2,30,000

Case (f) If the production capacity of Division A is limited to 18,000 units of Product P and Production facilities of Division A can be rented out at (i) ₹ 1,50,000 or (ii) ₹ 2,30,000

Solution

Case (a) Minimum Transfer Price = Variable Cost (excluding Variable Selling Cost) per unit

= (20 – 2) = 18

Maximum Transfer Price = Supply Price of Product R – Additional Cost to be incurred in making Product P useable

= ₹.32 – ₹.5 = ₹ 27

Recommendation: Internal transfer is more profitable than outside supply, since Minimum Transfer Price is lower than Maximum Transfer Price.

Case (b) Minimum Transfer Price = Variable Cost (excluding Variable Selling Cost) + Contribution foregone per unit

$$= 18 + \frac{\text{Units not available for sale due to transfer to Division B}}{\text{Units Required by Division B}} \times \text{Contibution per unit}$$

$$= 18 + \frac{3000}{5000} \times 10 = ₹\ 18 + ₹\ 6 = ₹\ 24$$

Maximum Transfer Price = Supply Price of Product R – Additional Cost to be incurred in making Product P useable

= ₹ 32 – ₹ 5 = ₹ 27

Recommendation: Internal transfer is more profitable than outside supply, since Minimum Transfer Price is lower than Maximum Transfer Price.

Case (c) Minimum Transfer Price = Variable Cost (excluding Variable Selling Cost) + Contribution foregone per unit

$$= 18 + \frac{\text{Units not available for sale due to transfer to Division B}}{\text{Units Required by Division B}} \times \text{Contibution per unit}$$

$$= 18 + \frac{5000}{5000} \times 10 = ₹\,18 + ₹.10 = ₹\,28$$

Maximum Transfer Price = Supply Price of Product R – Additional Cost to be incurred in making Product P useable

$$= ₹\,32 - ₹\,5 = ₹\,27$$

Recommendation: Outside supply is more profitable than Internal transfer, since Minimum Transfer Price is higher than Maximum Transfer Price.

Case (d) Minimum Transfer Price= Variable Cost (excluding Variable Selling Cost) per unit

= (20 – 2) = 18

Maximum Transfer Price = Supply Price of Product R – Additional Cost to be incurred in making Product P useable

= ₹ 32 – ₹ 5 = ₹ 27

Internal transfer is more profitable than outside supply, since Minimum Transfer Price is lower than Maximum Transfer Price.

Now to see whether internal transfer/external sale or renting out is profitable in each of the following cases:

Case (i)

Particulars		*Internal Transfer/ External Sale*	*Renting out*
Cost Involved in making Units	(5,000 x ₹ 23)	(1,15,000)	
Cost involved in Purchasing	Product R (5,000 x ₹.32)		(1,60,000)
Contribution from Sale of	Product P (18,000 x ₹.10)	1,80,000	
Income due to renting out	of Production facilities		1,50,000
	Total	65,000	(10,000)

Recommendation: Internal transfer is more profitable than Renting out since there are more Cash Inflows in Internal Transfer.

Case (ii)

Particulars		*Internal Transfer/ External Sale*	*Renting out*
Cost Involved in making Units	(5,000 x ₹ 23)	(1,15,000)	
Cost involved in Purchasing	Product R (5,000 x ₹.32)		(1,60,000)
Contribution from Sale of	Product P (18,000 x ₹.10)	1,80,000	
Income due to renting out	of Production facilities		2,30,000
	Total	65,000	70,000

Recommendation: Renting Out is more profitable than Internal Transfer Since there are more Cash Inflows in Renting out.

Case (e) Minimum Transfer Price= Variable Cost (excluding Variable Selling Cost) + Contribution foregone per unit

$$= 18 + \frac{\text{Units not available for sale due to transfer to Division B}}{\text{Units Required by Division B}} \times \text{Contibution per unit}$$

$$= 18 + \frac{3000}{5000} \times 10 = ₹\,18 + ₹\,6 = ₹\,24$$

Maximum Transfer Price = Supply Price of Product R – Additional Cost to be incurred in making Product P useable

$$= ₹\,32 - ₹\,5 = ₹\,27$$

Internal transfer is more profitable than outside supply, since
Minimum Transfer Price is lower than Maximum Transfer Price.

Now to see whether internal transfer/external sale or renting out is profitable in each of the following cases:

Case (i)

Particulars		Internal Transfer/ External Sale	Renting out
Cost Involved in making Units	(5,000 x ₹ 23)	(1,15,000)	
Cost involved in Purchasing	Product R (5,000 x ₹.32)		(1,60,000)
Contribution from Sale of	Product P (15,000 x ₹.10)	(1,50,000)	
Income due to renting out	of Production facilities		1,50,000
	Total	35,000	(10,000)

Recommendation: Internal transfer is more profitable than Renting out since there are more Cash Inflows in Internal Transfer.

Case (ii)

Particulars		Internal Transfer/ External Sale	Renting out
Cost Involved in making Units	(5,000 x ₹ 23)	(1,15,000)	
Cost involved in Purchasing	Product R (5,000 x ₹.32)		(1,60,000)
Contribution from Sale of	Product P (15,000 x ₹.10)	1,50,000	
Income due to renting out	of Production facilities		2,30,000
	Total	35,000	70,000

Recommendation: Renting Out is more profitable than Internal Transfer Since there are more Cash Inflows in Renting out.

Case(f) Minimum Transfer Price = Variable Cost (excluding Variable Selling Cost) + Contribution foregone per unit

$$= 18 + \frac{\text{Units not available for sale due to transfer to Division B}}{\text{Units Required by Division B}} \times \text{Contibution per unit}$$

$$= 18 + \frac{5000}{5000} \times 10 = ₹\,18 + ₹\,10 = ₹\,28$$

Maximum Transfer Price = Supply Price of Product R – Additional Cost to be Incurred In making Product P useable

$$= ₹.32 - ₹.5 = ₹\,27$$

Outside Supply is more profitable than Internal Transfer, since
Minimum Transfer Price is higher than Maximum Transfer Price.

Now to see whether External Sale of Product P or renting out is profitable in each of the following cases:

Case (i)

Particulars		Internal Transfer/ External Sale	Renting out
Contribution from Sale of	Product P (18,000 x ₹.10)	1,80,000	
Income due to renting out	of Production facilities		1,50,000
	Total	1,80,000	1,50,000

Recommendation: External Sale is more profitable than Renting out since there are so more Cash Inflows in External Sale.

Case (ii)

Particulars		*Internal Transfer/ External Sale*	*Renting out*
Contribution from Sale of	Product P (18,000 x ₹.10)	1,80,000	
Income due to renting out	of Production facilities		2,30,000
	Total	1,80,000	2,30,000

Recommendation: Renting Out is more profitable than External Sale Since there are more Cash Inflows in Renting out.

Illustration 2

TUSHAR TULSIAN Ltd. has two divisions namely A & B functioning autonomously. Division A produces Product P and Division B produces Product Q. Product P is used in the production of Product Q.

Particulars	*Division A*		*Division B*	
	Units	*Price*	*Units*	*Price*
Sales demand of Product in External Market	3000 7000 10000	30 25 20	3000 7000 10000	100 90 80
Variable Cost Per unit	₹ 15			
Additional Processing Cost Per unit			₹ 40	
Production capacity	10000			
Fixed Cost	₹ 50,000		₹ 150,000	

One unit of Product P is required for producing one unit of Product Q.
Outside Supply of Product P is available at the following prices:

Quantity	*Price*
0 – 3000	30
3001 – 7000	25
7001 – 10000	20

Required:

(i) Determine the operating level for both the divisions which will maximise their profits assuming no internal transfer and prepare the profitability statement at that level.

(ii) Determine the operating level which will maximise the profit of the organisation as a whole (i.e. internal transfer can take place) and prepare the profitability statement and comment whether it is the same operating level which maximise the division's profit.

(iii) Recommend the transfer price between A & B which will be favourable for both the divisions and prepare the profitability statement on that transfer price.

Solution

(i) OPERATING LEVEL FOR DIVISION A

Units	*Price*	*Total Revenue*	*Excess Revenue*	*Marginal Revenue per unit*
3000	30	90000	—	—
7000	25	175000	85000	21.25 (85000/4000)
10000	20	200000	25000	8.33 (25000/3000)

When price is ₹.25 then Marginal Revenue (i.e. ₹.21.25) is greater than Marginal Cost (i.e. ₹ 15) therefore it is beneficial to operate at a price of ₹ 25.

When price is ₹ 20 then Marginal Revenue (i.e. ₹ 8.33) is lower than Marginal Cost (i.e. ₹ 15) therefore it is not beneficial to operate at a price of ₹ 20.

PROFITABILITY STATEMENT OF DIVISION A

Particulars	₹
A. Sales (7,000 x ₹ 25)	1,75,000
B. *Less*: Variable Cost (7,000 x ₹ 15)	1,05,000
C. Contribution (A – B)	70,000
D. *Less*: Fixed Cost	50,000
E. Profit (C – D)	20,000

OPERATING LEVEL FOR DIVISION B

Units	*Price*	*Additional Processing Cost*	*Total Revenue Subject to Cost of Product P*	*Excess Revenue*	*Marginal Revenue per unit*
3000	100	40	1,80,000	—	—
7000	90	40	3,50,000	1,70,000	42.50
10000	80	40	4,00,000	50,000	16.67

Marginal Revenue (i.e. 42.5) at a price of ₹ 90 is higher than all outside supply price therefore it is better to operate at this price.

Marginal Revenue (i.e. 16.67) at a price of ₹ 80 is lower than all outside supply price therefore it is not advisable to operate at this price.

Supply required = 7000 units

Purchasing cost if purchased at ₹ 25 per unit is 7000 × ₹ 25 = ₹ 1,75,000

Purchasing Cost if 7001 units are purchased at a cost of 7001 × ₹ 20 = 1,40,020.

Hence Division B would purchase 7001 units at a cost of ₹ 1,40,020.

PROFITABILITY STATEMENT OF DIVISION B

Particulars	₹
A. Sales (7,000 × ₹ 90)	6,30,000
B. *Less*: Additional Processing Cost (7,000 × ₹ 40)	2,80,000
C. *Less*: Outside Purchasing Cost	1,40,020
D. Contribution (A – B – C)	2,09,980
E. *Less*: Fixed Cost	1,50,000
F. Profit (D – E)	59,980

(ii) OPTION (A) IF DIVISION A PRODUCES 10000 UNITS OF PRODUCT P AND TRANSFER ALL UNITS TO DIVISION B

Particulars	₹
Contribution forgone by Division A	(70,000)
Additional Variable cost incurred (10000*₹ 15)	(1,50,000)
Additional Revenue to Division B	50,000
Cost Savings	1,40,020
Total Decrease in Contribution	29,980

OPTION (B) IF DIVISION A PRODUCES 10000 UNITS AND SOLD 3000 UNITS IN OUTSIDE MARKET AND TRANSFER 7000 UNITS TO DIVISION B

Particulars	₹
Contribution forgone by A [₹ 70,000 – 3000 × ₹ (30 – 15)]	(25,000)
Additional Variable Cost incurred (7000 × ₹ 15)	(1,05,000)
Additional Revenue to Division B	0
Cost Savings	1,40,020
Total increase in contribution	10,020

OPTION (C) IF DIVISION A PRODUCES 10000 UNITS AND SOLD 7000 UNITS IN OUTSIDE MARKET AND TRANSFER 3000 UNITS TO DIVISION B

Particulars	₹
Contribution forgone by A	0
Additional Variable Cost incurred (3000 x ₹ 15)	(45,000)
Additional Purchasing Cost (4000 x ₹ 25)	(1,00,000)
Additional Revenue to Division B	0
Cost Savings	1,40,020
Total decrease in contribution	(4,980)

Therefore only option B is preferable since it will maximise the organisation's total profit.

PROFITABILITY STATEMENT OF DIVISION A, DIVISION B AND THE ORGANISATION AS A WHOLE UNDER OPTION B

Particulars	*Division A*	*Division B*	*Total*
A. External Revenue	90,000	6,30,000	7,20,000
B. Internal Revenue	1,05,000		
C. Total (A + B)	1,95,000	6,30,000	7,20,000
D. *Less*: Variable Cost/Additional Processing Cost	1,50,000	2,80,000	43,000
E. *Less*: Internal transfer Cost	1,05,000		
F. Contribution (C – D – E)	45,000	2,45,000	2,90,000
G. *Less*: Fixed Cost	50,000	1,50,000	2,00,000
H. Profit (Loss) (F – G)	(5000)	95,000	90,000

From above it can be seen that operating level which maximise the organisation's profit is different from the level which maximises the division's objective. Hence the top management should interfere in the autonomy of the divisions so the organisation could achieve goal congruency otherwise if the divisions are allowed to maximise their profit it will lead to goal displacement and not goal congruency.

(iii) Since the level at which organisation's profit is maximised is different from the level at which division profit is maximised. Now goal congruency can be achieved through setting appropriate transfer price.

Division A Profit if organisation profit is not maximised	20,000
Division B Profit if organisation profit is not maximised	59,980
Total	79,980
Division A Profit if organisation profit is maximised	(5000)
Division B Profit if organisation profit is not maximised	95,000
Total	90,000
Increase in Profit	10,020

Now this increase in profit can be shared between A & B in some ratio. Let it be the ratio of profit if organisation's profit is not maximised . Hence the ratio is 20,000 : 59,980

So A's share of excess profit =[(10,020 x 20,000)/ 79,980] = 2505
B's share of excess profit = [(10,020 x 59,980)/79,980] = 7515
Total A's Profit = 20,000 + 2505 = 22,505
Increase in Profit required = 22,505 + Loss = 22505 + 5000 = 27,505
Hence increase in contribution required per unit = 27,505/7000 = 3.93
So Transfer Price would be Variable cost + Additional contribution per unit = 15 + 3.93 = 18.93

Profitability Statement of Division A, Division B and the organisation at a transfer price of ₹.18.93 per unit

Particulars	*Division A*	*Division B*	*Total*
A. External Revenue	90,000	6,30,000	7,20,000
B. Internal Revenue	1,32,510		
C. Total (A + B)	2,22,510	6,30,000	7,20,000
D. *Less*: Variable Cost/Additional Processing Cost	(1,50,000)	(2,80,000)	4,30,000
E. *Less*: Internal transfer Cost		(1,32,510)	
F. Contribution (C – D – E)	72,510	2,17,490	2,90,000
G. *Less:* Fixed Cost	(50,000)	(1,50,000)	(2,00,000)
H. Profit (F – G)	22,510	67,490	90,000

Illustration 3

CAS Ltd. manufactures foam, carpets and upholstery in the three divisions. Its operating statement for 2010-2011 showing the performance of these divisions drawn for the use of management is reproduced below:

(Rupees in '000)

Particulars	*Manufacturing Divisions*			*Total*
	Foam	*Carpets*	*Upholstery*	
A. Sales Revenue	1,600	1,200	1,200	4,000
B. *Less:* Manufacturing Costs :				
Variable	1,200	700	680	2,580
Fixed (Traceable)	—	100	20	120
	1,200	800	700	2,700
C. Gross Profit [A – B]	400	400	500	1300
D. Expenses :				
Administration	134	116	172	422
Selling	202	210	232	644
	336	326	404	1,066 (B)
E. Net Income [C – D]	64	74	96	234
Division's Ranking	3rd	2nd	1st	

(A) Sales include foam tansferred to the Upholstery division at its manufacturing cost of ₹ 2,00,000.

(B) Common expenses of ₹ 1,30,000 and ₹ 1,00,000 on account of administration and selling respectively stand apportioned to these divisions at 10% of Gross Profit in case of administration and 2.5% of Sales in case of selling expenses. Rest of ₹ 8,36,000 of the expenses are traceable to respective divisions.

The manager of the foam division is not satisfied with the above approach of presenting operating performance. In his opinion his division is best among all the divisions. He requests the management for preparation of revised operating statement using contribution approach and showing internal transfer at market price.

You are required to :

(a) Draw the revised operating statement using contribution approach and pricing the internal transfer at market price.

(b) Compute relevant ratios to show comparative profitability of these divisions and rank them in the light of your answer at (a) above. Further, offer your comments on the contention of the manager of foam division.

(c) State why the contribution approach and pricing of internal transfers at market price are more appropriate in realistic assessment of the performance of various divisions.

Solution

(a) **REVISED OPERATING STATEMENT USING CONTRIBUTION APPROACH**

(₹ '000)

	Particulars	*Foam*	*Carpets*	*Upholstery*	*Total*
A	Sales revenue	1,680	1,200	1,200	4,080
B	*Less :* Variable manufacturing costs:	1,200	700	760	2,660
C	Contribution [A – B]	480	500	440	1,420
D	*Traceable Costs :*				
	Fixed manufacturing costs	—	100	20	120
	Administration expenses	94	76	122	292
	Selling expenses	162	180	202	544
	Total	256	356	344	956
E	Operating income : [C – D]	224	144	96	464
F	*Less:* Common expenses (₹ 130 + ₹ 100)				230
G	Net Income of the company [E – F]				234

Working Notes:

(i) ***Computation of Sales Revenue of Foam division***

	(₹ '000)
Sales of foam division to outside customers (₹ 1,600 – ₹ 200)	1,400
Less : Variable manufacturing costs (₹ 1200 – ₹ 200)	(1,000)
Mark-up on outside sale	400
Percentage of mark-up (₹ 400/₹ 1000) × 100 = 40%	
Transfer Price of foam to upholstery division	280
Sales of foam division to outside customers	1,400
Total	1,680

(ii) ***Variable Mfg. costs of Upholstery Division in (₹ '000)***

(₹ 680 ₹ 200 + ₹ 280) – ₹ 760

(iii) ***Computation of Traceable Administration Expenses***

(₹ '000)

Particulars	*Foam*	*Carpets*	*Upholstery*	*Total*
A. Given Administration Expenses	134	116	172	422
B. *Less :* Common Expenses (10% of Gross Profit)	(40)	(40)	(50)	(130)
C. Traceable Administration Expenses	94	76	122	292

(iv) Traceable Selling Expenses

(₹ '000)

Particulars	*Foam*	*Carpets*	*Upholstery*	*Total*
A. Given Selling Expenses	202	210	232	644
B. *Less* : Common Expenses (2.5% of Sales)	(40	(30)	(30)	(100)
C. Traceable Selling Expenses [A – B]	162	180	202	544

(b) COMPARATIVE PROFITABILITY & RANKING STATEMENT (BASED ON CONTRIBUTION APPROACH RELEVANT RATIOS CALCULATED BY USING FIGURES OF (A) PART)

(₹ '000)

Particulars	*Foam*	*Carpets*	*Upholstery*
Contribution Margin Ratio (in %)	28.57 (₹ 480/1680) x 100	41.67 (₹ 500/1200)× 100	36.67 (₹ 440/1200) × 100
Ranking	III	I	II
Net Contribution Ratio (in %) or (Operating income ratio)	13.33 (₹ 224/1,680) x 100	12 (₹144/1200) × 100	8 (₹ 96/1200) × 100
Ranking	I	II	III

Comment: The Manager of Foam Division, appears to be correct in raising objection over the approach used for presenting operating performance of three divisions for the year 2010-2011%. His division is the best among all, on the basis of (Net Contribution/Sales) ratio which is the highest inspite of its contribution margin ratio to be the lowest.

(c) The use of contribution approach for reporting is more realistic for assessing the performance of various divisions as it considers variable and traceable costs only and avoids common costs while finding out profitability. This approach enables the management to rightly interpret the information. Further pricing of internal transfers at market price will give due credit to specific profit centre i.e. transferor.

Illustration 4

A Company has two Divisions, Division 'A' and Division 'B'. Division 'A' has a Budget of selling 2,00,000 nos. of a particular component 'x' to fetch a return of 20% on the average assets employed. The following particulars of Division 'A' are also known:

Fixed Overhead	₹ 5 lakhs
Variable Cost	₹. 1 per unit
Average Assets:	
Sundry Debtors	₹ 2 lakhs
Inventories	₹ 5 lakhs
Plant & Equipments	₹ 5 lakhs

However, there is constraint in Marketing and only 1,50,000 units of the component 'x' be directly sold to the proposed price.

It has been gathered that the balance 50,000 units of component 'x' can be taken up by Division 'B' Division 'A' wants a price of ₹ 4 per unit of 'x' but Division 'B' is prepared to pay ₹ 2 per unit of 'x'.

Division 'A' has another option in hand, which is to produce only 1,50,000 units of component 'x'. This will reduce the holding of assets by ₹ 2 lakhs and fixed overhead by ₹ 25,000.

Required: Advise the most profitable course of action for Dlvlslon 'A'.

Solution

EVALUATION OF BOTH OPTIONS

Particulars	Option-1 (Sell 1,50,00 units in market and transfer 50,000 units to ₹	Option-2 Sell only 1,50,000 units in market Div. B) ₹
Sales Revenue (1,50,000 units of component 'x' @ ₹ 4,70 per unit)	7,05,000	7,05,000
Unit of component 'x' transferred to Div. B @ ₹ 2 per unit (Under Option - 1 only)	1,00,000	
A. Total Revenue:	8,05,000	7,05,000
B. *Less:* Costs incurred:		
Fixed overhead	5,00,000	4,75,000
Variable overhead	2,00,000	1,50,000
Total Costs:	7,00,000	6,25,000
C. Profit [A – B]	1,05,000	80,000
D. Capital Employed (D)	12,00,000	10,00,000
E. Return on Capital Employed [(C)/(D)] × 100	8.75%	8%

Since the return on capital employed under option – 1 is more than that under option – 2, therefore option – 1 is preferred over option-2. Selection of this option also gives an extra profit of ₹ 25,000.

Working Notes:

(i) Profit = 20% return on the average assets employed.
= 20% × ₹ 12,00,000 = ₹ 2,40,000

(ii) Desired Revenue (on the sale of 2,00,000 units of component 'x')
= Fixed cost + variable cost + profit
= ₹ 5,00,000 + ₹ 2,00,000 + ₹ 2,40,000 = ₹ 9,40,000

(iii) Selling Price per unit = Desired revenue/No, of units to be sold of component x
= ₹ 9,40,000/2,00,000 units = ₹ 4.70 per unit

Illustration 5

A company is organized on decentralized lines, with each manufacturing division operating as a separate profit centre. Each division manager has full authority to decide on sale of division's output to outsiders or to other divisions. Division AB manufactures a single standardized product. Some output is sold externally and remaining is transferred to division XY where it is a subassembly in the manufacture of the division product. The unit cost of division AB product and division XY is as follows:

	Division AB (₹)	*Division XY (₹)*
Transfer from division AB to XY	–	42.00
Direct Material	6.00	35.00
Direct Labour	3.00	4.50
Direct expenses	3.00	–
Variable manufacturing overheads	3.00	18.00
Fixed manufacturing overheads	6.00	18.00
Variable selling and packing expenses	3.00	2.50
	24.00	120.00

Division AB sold 40,000 units annually at the standard price of ₹ 45 in external market. In additions to the external sales, 10,000 units are transferred annually to division XY at internal price of ₹ 42 per unit. Variable selling and packing expenses are not incurred by supplying division- for the internal transfer of the product. Division XY incorporates the transferred goods into more advance product. The manager of division XY disagrees with the basis used to set the transfer price. He argues that transfer price should be made at variable cost since he claims that his division is taking output that division AB should be unable to sell at price ₹ 45.

He also submitted a report of the relationship between selling price and demand to support of his disagreement, the report of customer demand at various selling prices for division AB and for division XY is as follows:

Division AB			
Selling Price per unit (₹)	30	45	60
Demand (Units)	60,000	40,000	20,000
Division XY			
Selling Price per unit (₹)	120	135	150
Demand (Units)	15,000	10,000	5,000

The company has sufficient capacity to meet demand at various selling prices. Internal transfer demanded units will be decided by XY division.

Required:

(i) To calculate divisional profitability and overall profitability of company if division AB transfers demanded units to XY at price of ₹ 42.

(ii) To calculate divisional profitability and overall profitability of company if division AB transfers demanded units to XY at variable cost.

(iii) In place of internal transfers, AB division can sell 10,000 units of their product in new external market without effecting existing market, at price ₹ 32 per unit and XY division can purchase these units at the rate of ₹ 31 in open market. Calculate company's profit by following above strategies.

Solution

(i) AB SELLS PRODUCT AT EXTERNAL MARKET

A. Selling Price (₹)	30	45	60
B. *Less:* Variable Cost	18	18	18
C. Contribution (per unit) [A – B]	12	27	42
D. Demands (units)	60,000	40,000	20,000
E. Total Contribution [C × D]	7,20,000	10,80,000	8,40,000

Optimal output is 40,000 units at a selling price of ₹ 45

AB TRANSFER AT ₹ 42 TO XY DIVISION THEN CONTRIBUTION OF XY

A. Selling Price (₹)	120	135	150
B. *Less:* Variable Cost V+TP (42 + 60)	102	102	102
C. Contribution (per unit) [A – B]	18	33	48
D. Demands (units)	15,000	10,000	5,000
E. Total Contribution [C × D]	2,70,000	3,30,000	2,40,000

Manager will choose out put level 10,000 units at a selling price of ₹ 135.

OVERALL PROFIT WHEN TRANSFER MADE AT ₹ 42

A. Division AB contribution on 10,000 units [42 – (18 – 3)]	2,70,000
B. Division XY contribution 10,000 (135 – 102)	3,30,000
C. Total Contribution [A + B]	6,00,000
D. Division AB contribution from external market sale	10,80,000
E. Total Profit [C + D]	16,80,000

(ii) AB TRANSFER AT VARIABLE COST

A. Selling Price (₹)	120	135	150
B. *Less:* Variable Cost (15+60)	75	75	75
C. Contribution (per unit) [A – B]	45	60	75
D. Demands (units)	15,000	10,000	5,000
E. Total Contribution [C – D]	6,75,000	6,00,000	3,75,000

Optimal is 15,000 units at the rate of 120 per unit.
If AB transfer at Variable cost (₹ 15) then no contribution will be generated by AB division

XY division choose 15,000 units level gives contribution (15,000 × 45)	= 6,75,000
Division AB contribution from external market sale	= 10,80,000
Total Contribution	= 17,55,000

(iii) CONTRIBUTION AB DIVISION BY SELLING 10,000 UNITS TO NEW EXTERNAL MARKET AT ₹ 32 AND XY DIVISION PURCHASING AT ₹ 31.

A. Contribution (32 – 18) × 10,000	=	1,40,000
B. XY Contribution [135 – (31 + 60)]	=	4,40,000
C. Division AB contribution from external market sale	=	10,80,000
D. Total Contribution [A + B + C]	=	16,60,000

Illustration 6

A large business consultancy firm is organized into several divisions. One of the divisions is the Information Technology (IT) division which provides consultancy services to its clients as well as to the other divisions of the firm. The consultants in the IT divisions always work in a team of three professional consultants on each day of consulting assignment. The external clients are charged a fee at the rate of ₹ 4,500 for each consulting day. The fee represents the cost *plus* 150% profit mark up. The break up of cost involved in the consultancy fee is estimated at 80% as being variable and the balance is fixed.

The textiles division of the consultancy firm which has undertaken a big assignment requires the services of two teams of IT consultants to work five days in a week for a period of 48 weeks. While the director of the textiles division intends to negotiate the transfer price for the consultancy work, the director of IT division proposes to charge the textiles division at ₹ 4,500 per consulting day.

In respect of the consulting work of the textiles division. IT division will be able to reduce the variable costs by ₹ 200 per consulting day. This is possible in all cases of internal consignations because of the use of specialized equipment.

You are required to explain the implications and set transfer prices per consulting day at which the IT division can provide consultancy services to the textiles division such that the profit of the business consultancy firm as a whole is maximized in each of the following scenarios:

(i) Every team of the IT division is fully engaged during the 48 week period in providing consultancy services to external clients and that the IT division has no spare capacity of consultancy teams to take up the textiles division assignment

(ii) IT division will be able to spare only one team of consultants to provide services to the textiles division during the 48 week period and all other teams are fully engaged in providing services to external clients.

(iii) A new external client has come forward to pay IT division a total fee of ₹ 15,84,000 for engaging the services of two teams of consultants during the aforesaid period of 48 weeks.

Solution

Transfer Price is ₹ 4,500 for each consulting day.

Profit mark-up = 150%

Let cost = x

$$\text{Profit} = x \times \frac{150}{100} = 1.5x$$

$$\text{Cost + Profit} = \text{Transfer Price}$$

$$\Rightarrow \quad x + 1.5x = 4{,}500$$

$$\Rightarrow \quad 2.5x = 4{,}500$$

$$\Rightarrow \quad x = 4{,}500/2.5 = 1{,}800$$

$$\therefore \quad \text{Cost} = ₹\ 1{,}800$$

$$\text{and Profit} = 1.5x = 1.5 \times 1.800 = ₹\ 2{,}700$$

$$\text{Variable Cost (80\%)} = ₹\ 1{,}800 \times 80\% = ₹\ 1{,}440$$

$$\text{Fixed Cost (20\%)} = ₹\ 1{,}800 \times 20\% = ₹\ 360.$$

Scenario (i)

Every consultancy team is fully engaged. There is no idle time or spare capacity. Hence, transfer price = Marginal cost *plus* opportunity cost

Marginal Cost	= ₹ 1,440
Saving for internal work	= ₹ 200
Net Marginal Cost	= ₹ 1,240

Opportunity Cost is the lost contribution.

Lost Contribution = Contribution from external client
= Fee charged from external client – Variable cost
= ₹ (4,500 – 1,440) = ₹ 3,060.

∴ Transfer Price = ₹ 1,240 + 3,060
= ₹ 4,300 per consulting day per team.

Scenario (ii):

One team is idle. Idle time has no opportunity cost. Variable cost for internal work is ₹ 1,240 per consulting day. Second team is busy. Hence opportunity cost is relevant in case of second team. Hence charge of second team is ₹ 4,300 per consulting day per team.

Average of charge of two teams= ₹ (1,240 + 4,300) / 2
= ₹ 2,770 per consulting day per team.

Scenario (iii):

New client offers a fee of ₹ 15,84,000	
Duration: 5 days of 48 weeks × 2 teams	= 480 days
Fee per day 15,84,000/480	= ₹ 3,300
Variable Cost	= ₹ 1,440
Contribution ₹ (3,300 – 1,440)	= ₹ 1,860
Fee for consulting day for internal work:	
Variable cost	= ₹ 1,240
Contribution lost	= ₹ 1,860
Fee to be charged	= ₹ 3,100 per consulting day per team.

Illustration 7

Two divisions of a company, both manufacturing the same product with same grade and quality are located at two distant places A and B. The annual output of the division at A is 6,000 tonnes (80% capacity) and that of division B is 7,500 tonnes (60% capacity). The basic raw material used is available locally at both the places, but limited to 3,000 tonnes per annum @ ₹ 900 per tonne at division A and 8,000 tonnes per annum @ ₹ 1,000 per tonne at division B. Any additional requirement will have to be purchased from other markets at a rate of ₹ 1,150 per tonne. *F.O.R.* at either division. Variable costs at each division are constant per tonne of output. For every 100 tonnes of output, 80 tonnes of basic raw material is required.

The details of other annual variable and fixed costs of the divisions are as under:

	Division A ₹ in lakhs	*Division B ₹ in lakhs*
Other Variable Cost (excluding raw material)	78.00	96.00
Fixed cost	50.00	60.00

You are Required to

(a) determine for each tonne of output, the raw material cost, other variable cost and total cost, in respect of each division, give details of workings:

(b) determine the quantity of production that could be transferred between the two divisions, if the company desires to fully utilise the available local supplies of raw material to reduce cost of production, keeping the total production of both the divisions put together, the same as at present;

(c) determine the revised schedule of production at both the divisions based on the answer to (b) above and identify the cost saving.

Solution

	Division A	*Division B*
(a) **Output and Cost details**		
(i) Output	6,000 T	7,500 T
(ii) Raw Materials Cost:		
Raw Material required for 80% output:	4,800 T	6,000 T
Locally available supplies	3,000 T	8,000 T
So this raw material will be made available as follows:		
(a) Local Supply	3,000 T	6,000 T
(b) From Other "Market	1,800 T	Nil
Total Cost of Material		
(a) 3,000 T × ₹ 900	₹ 27,00,000	
1,800 T × ₹ 1150	20,70,000	
(b) 6,000 T × ₹ 1,000	47,70,000	₹ 60,00,000
(iii) Raw Material Cost per tonne		
(a) ₹ 47,70,000 ÷ 6,000 T	₹ 795.00	
(b) ₹ 60,00,000 ÷ 7,500 T		₹ 800
(iv) Other Variable Cost (excluding Material)	₹ 1,300.00	
(₹ 78,00,000 ÷ 6,000 tonne)		
(₹ 96,00,000 ÷ 7,500 tonne)		₹ 1,280
(v) Fixed Cost		
(₹ 50,00,000 ÷ 6,000 tonne)	₹ 833.33	
(₹ 60,00,000 ÷ 7,500 tonne)		₹ 800
(vi) Total Cost/Tonne of output	₹ 2,928.33	₹ 2,880
(b) (i) Maximum Output *i.e.* 100% Capacity	7,500 T	12,500 T
(ii) (a) Material Cost with local supplier per tonne of output		
₹ 900 × 80%	₹ 720	
₹ 1,000 × 80%		₹ 800
(b) Material Cost with outside supplier		
₹ 1,150 × 80%	₹ 920	₹ 920
(iii) Total Variable Cost per tonne of output	1,300	1,280
(iv) Total Variable Cost per tonne of output		
– Local Material used	2,020	2,080
– Outside Material used	2,220	2,200
(v) *Ranking*		
Division A Local Supply	I	
Division B Local Supply	II	

Division B Outside Supply III
Division A Outside Supply IV

Based on the above, the revised schedule between the Divisions will be as follows:

Particulars		*Output*	
		Existing	*Revised*
Division A			
Materials from Local Supplier [3,000 T ÷ 0.80]	3,750		3,750 T
Material from Outside [1,800 ÷ 0.80]	2,250 T	6,000 T	
Division B			
Material from Local Supplier [6,000 T ÷ 0.80]		7,500 T	9,750 T
Total Output		13,500 T	13,500 T

(c) Total Cost as per Revised Schedule

(₹ *in lakhs*)

Particulars	*Division A*	*Division B*	*Total*
3,750 T @ ₹ 2,020	75.75		75.75
9.750 T @ ₹ 2,080		202.80	202.80
Fixed Cost	50.00	60.00	110.00
	125.75	262.80	388.55
Total Costs per Existing Schedule			
6.000 T × ₹ 2,928.33	175.70		
7,500 T × ₹ 2,880.00		216.00	391.70

Net Cost Savings = ₹ 391.70 lakhs – ₹ 388.55 lakhs = ₹ 3.15 lakhs.

Illustration 8

M/s Foamstar have two divisions—Foam and Star. Foam manufacturers an intermediate product for which there Is no intermediate external market. Star incorporates this intermediate product into the final product which it sells. One unit of the intermediate product is used in the production of the final product The expected units of the final product which Star division estimates it can sell at various selling prices are as follows:

Net Selling Price ₹	*Quantity Sold* (*Units*)
1,000	10,000
900	20,000
800	30,000
700	40,000
600	50,000
500	60,000

The costs of each division are as follows:

	Foam	*Star*
Variable cost per unit (₹)	110	70
Fixed costs per annum (₹)	60,00,000	90,00,000

The transfer price is ₹ 350 for the intermediate product and is determined on a full cost-*plus* basis.

You are required to:

(a) Prepare profit statements for each division and the company as a whole for the various selling prices.
(b) State which selling price maximise profit for the Star division and the company as a whole and comment on why the latter selling price is not selected by Star division.
(c) State which transfer pricing policy will maximise the company's profit under a divisional organisation.

Solution

(a) STATEMENT OF CONTRIBUTION FOR EACH DIVISION AND THE COMPANY AS A WHOLE:

FOAM DIVISION

(₹ *in lakhs*)

Output Levels (Units)	*Total Revenue*	*Variable Cost*	*Total Contribution*	*Fixed Cost*	*Profit*
10,000	35	11	24	60	(36)
20,000	70	22	48	60	(12)
30,000	105	33	72	60	12
40,000	140	44	96	60	36
50,000	175	55	120	60	60
60,000	210	66	144	60	84

STAR DIVISION

(₹ *in lakhs*)

Output (Units)	*Total Revenue*	*Variable Cost*	*Cost of Transfer*	*Total Contribution*	*Fixed Cost*	*Profit*
10,000	100	7	35	58	90	(32)
20,000	180	14	70	96	90	6
30,000	240	21	105	114	90	24
40,000	280	28	140	112	90	22
50,000	300	35	175	90	90	Nil
60,000	300	42	210	48	90	(42)

THE COMPANY

(₹ *in lakhs*)

Output Level (Units)	*Total Revenue*	*Divisional Variable Cost*	*Total Contribution*	*Total Fixed cost*	*Total Profit*
30,000	100	18	82	150	(68)
20,000	180	36	144	150	(6)
30,000	240	54	186	150	36
40,000	280	72	208	150	58
50,000	300	90	210	150	60
60,000	300	108	192	150	42

(b) Based on the tables and calculations. Star Division should select the selling price of ₹ 800 per unit. At this price, it will show maximum contribution of ₹ 114 lakhs and a profit of ₹ 24 lakhs.

For company as a whole, maximum contribution of ₹ 210 lakhs will be realised at a selling price of ₹ 600 per unit. At this point, the profit will be ₹ 60 lakhs. If Star Division selects this price, its contribution will go down to ₹ 90 lakhs. *i.e.*, reduction of ₹ 24 lakhs and hence it will be reluctant to do so.

(c) The market for the intermediate product may be imperfect or perhaps no market may exist. If the supplying division has no capacity constraints, the correct transfer price is the marginal cost of the supplying division for that output at which marginal cost equals the sum of the receiving divisions' net marginal revenue from converging the intermediate product and the marginal revenue from any sale of the intermediate product on the external market.

Foam's marginal cost is ₹ 110 per unit at all levels of production. For Star marginal revenues are as follows:

Output (units)		*Revenue less Variable cost of Star (₹ in lakh)*		*Marginal Revenue per arm*
Cumulative	*Marginal*	*Cumulative*	*Marginal*	
10,000	10,000	100 − 7 = 93	93	₹ 930
20,000	10,000	380 − 14 = 166	73	730
30,000	10,000	240 − 21 = 219	53	530
40,000	10,000	280 − 28 = 252	33	330
50,000	10,000	300 − 35 = 265	13	130
60,000	10,000	300 − 42 = 258	(7)	(70)

It is obvious that at output level of 50,000 units Star's marginal revenue is ₹ 130, which approximates Foam's marginal cost of ₹ 110. It is assumed both the divisions have no other products to make. Foam must earn at best ₹ 1,15.00,000 (*i.e.,* ₹ 110 × 50,000 + ₹ 60,00,000) to breakeven. This is *the lower limit.* Star must recover at best ₹ 1,25,00,000 (i.e., 50,000 × ₹ 70 + ₹ 90,00,000). Thus after recovering ₹ 1,25,00,000, surplus with Star will be ₹ 3,00,00,000 − ₹ 3,25,00,000 = ₹ 1,75,00,000.

Therefore, transfer price will be between following two limits:

(a) ₹ 1,15,00,000 ÷ 50,000 = ₹ 230 per unit; and

(b) ₹ 1,75,00,000 ÷ 50,000 = ₹ 350 per unit.

However, to motivate Foam Division, it is necessary to distribute ₹ 1,75,00,000 in both the divisions. If profit is distributed among both the divisions equally then transfer price should be ₹ 290, *i.e., average* ₹ 230 arid ₹ 350. This transfer price of ₹ 290 will present the best compromise between the two divisions, presuming that equal investments are made in both the divisions.

Illustration 9

AB Cycles Ltd. has 2 divisions, A and B which manufacture bicycle. Division A produces bicycle frame and Division B assembles rest of the bicycle on the frame. There is a market for sub-assembly and the final product. Each division has been treated as a profit centre. The transfer price has been set at the long-run average market price. The following data are available to each division:

Estimated selling price of final product	₹ 3,000 p.u.
Long run average market price of sub-assembly	₹ 2,000 p.u.
Incremental cost of completing sub-assembly in division B	₹ 1,500 p.u.
Incremental cost in Division A	₹ 1,200 p.u.

Required:

(i) If Division A's maximum capacity is 1,000 p.m. and sales to the intermediate are now 800 units, should 200 units be transferred to B on long-term average price basis.

(ii) What would be the transfer price, if manager of Division B should be kept motivated?

(iii) If outside market increases to 1,000 units, should Division A continue to transfer 200 units to Division B or sell entire production to outside market?

Solution

(i) In this case there are two options available:

(a)	Sell at the sub assembly stage (after completion of Div, A) @	₹ 2000
	Incremental cost in Div. A	₹ 1,200
	Contribution	₹ 800
(b)	Sell at the final product stage	₹ 3,000
	Cost at Div. A and Div. B ₹ (1200 + 1500)	₹ 2,700
	Contribution	₹ 300

Therefore it is profitable to sell at the subassembly stage because of higher contribution, provided there is a market.

Hence, if there is market at intermediate stage, first priority is to sell intermediary (sub assembly). Therefore, 800 units should be sold as sale of intermediary.

The balance capacity available of (1000 – 800) = 200 units should be transferred to B and B should complete the assembly and sell as final product, since the company can earn ₹ 300 per unit for each unit of such sale.

(ii) If B Div. receives the subassembly at market price of ₹ 2,000, plus its own incremental cost of ₹ 1,500 will give total cost of ₹ 3,500, thereby yielding a loss of ₹ 3500 – ₹ 3000 = ₹ 500 per unit, whereas the company makes a profit of ₹ 300 per unit.
In order to keep the manager of Div. B motivated, the profit earned of ₹ 300 per unit should be shared between A and B. Hence transfer price will be variable cost of Div. A + 50% of profit earned in the final product = 1200 + 150 = ₹ 1,350

(iii) Both Div. A and the Company make higher contribution by selling to inter mediate market. If the market demand increases to 1,000 units, the full quantity should be sold outside as intermediary and nothing should be transferred to Div. B.

Illustration 10

Tripod Lid. has three divisions – X, Y and Z, which make products X, Y and Z respectively. For division Y, the only direct material is product X and for Z, the only direct material is product Y. Division X purchases all its raw material from outside. Direct selling overhead, representing commission to external sales agents are avoided on all internal transfers. Division Y additionally incurs ₹ 10 per unit and ₹ 8 per unit on units delivered to external customers and Z respectively. Y also incurs ₹ 6 per unit picked up from X, whereas external suppliers supply at Y's factory at the stated price of ₹ 85 per unit.

Additional information is given below:

	Figures ₹/unit		
	X	*Y*	*Z*
Direct Materials (external supplier rate)	40	85	135
Direct Labour	30	50	45
Sales Agent's commission	15	15	10
Selling Price in external market	110	170	240
Production Capacity	20,000	30,000	40,000 units
External Demand	14,000	26,000	42,000 units

Required: Discuss the range of negotiation for Managers X, Y and Z, for the number of units and the transfer price for internal transfers.

Solution

ANALYSIS OF RANGE OF NEGOTIATION FOR MANAGER OF DIVISION X

(Figures in ₹)

Particulars	*Outside Sales*		*Sales to Y (Range)*	
A. Selling Price	110	70	–	79
B. *Less:* Commission	15	–		–
C. Net Selling Price [A – B]	95	70	–	79
D. *Less:* Variable Cost	70	70	–	70
E. Contribution per unit [C – D]	25	0		9
F. Units	14,000	6,000		6,000
G. Total Contribution	3,50,000	0		54,000

ANALYSIS OF RANGE OF NEGOTIATION FOR MANAGER OF DIVISION Y

(Figures in ₹)

Particulars	*Outside Sales*			*Sale to Z*		
	From A	*From outside*		*From A*	*From outside*	
Price Range	70	79	85	70	79	85
Add: Transport	6	6	–	6	6	–
	76	85	85	76	85	85
Add: Direct Labour	50	50	50	50	50	50
	126	135	135	126	135	135
Add: Delivery cost	10	10	10	8	8	8
	136	145	145	134	143	143
Add: Sales Commission	15	15	15	–	–	–
A. Total Cost	151	160	160	134	143	143
B. Selling Price	170	170	170	135	135	135
C. Contribution [B – A]	19	10	10	±1	(–)8	(–)8

Range of Negotiations: **Manager of division X will sell 14,000 units outside at 110 ₹ per unit and earn contribution of ₹ 3.50 lakhs.**

Excess capacity of 6,000 units can be offered to Y at a price between 70 (the variable manufacturing cost at X) and ₹ 95 (the maximum amount to equal outside contribution). But Y can get the material outside @ 85. So, y will not pay to X anything above (₹ 85 – 6) = ₹ 79 to match external available price.

X will be attracted to sell to Y only in the range of 71 – 79 ₹ per unit at a volume of 6,000 units. At ₹ 70, X will be indifferent, but may offer to sell to Y to use idle capacity.

Z will not buy from Y at anything above 135. If X sells to Y at 70 per unit, Y can sell to Z at 134 and earn no contribution, only for surplus capacity and if units transferred by X to Y at ₹ 70 per unit.

	Y	Z
Provided X sells to Y at ₹ 70 per unit	Sell 4,000 units to Z at 134 (Indifferent)	Buy 4,000 units from y at 134 (attracted)
	Sell 4,000 units to Z at 135 (willingly for a contribution of ₹ 1)	Indifferent, since market price is also 135

For buying from X at 71 – 79 price range, Y will be interested in selling to Z only at prices 136 – 143, which will not interest Z.

Thus Y will sell to Z only if X sells to Y at ₹ 70 per unit and Y will supply to Z maximum 4,000 units.

Illustration 11

XYZ Ltd. has two divisions, A and B. Division A makes and sells product A, which can be sold outside as well as be used by B. A has a limitation on production capacity, that only 1,200 units can pass through its machining operations in one month. On an average, about 10% of the units that A produces are defective. It may be assumed that out of each lot that A supplies, 10% are defectives.

When A sells in the outside market, the defectives are not returned, since the transportation costs make it uneconomical for the customer. Instead, A's customers sell the defectives in the outside market at a discount.

But, when B buys product A, it has to fix it into its product, which is reputed for its quality. Therefore, B returns all the defective units to A. A can manually rework the defectives, incurring only variable labour cost and sell them outside at ₹ 150 and not having to incur any selling costs on reworked units. If A chooses not to rework, it can only scrap the material at ₹ 30 per unit. B can buy product A from outside at ₹ 200 per unit, but has to incur ₹ 10 per unit as variable transport cost. B can insist to its outside suppliers also that it will accept only good units.

A incurs a variable selling overhead only on units (other than reworked units) sold outside. The following figures are given for the month:

Variable cost of production – Dept. A (₹/unit)	120
Variable selling overhead (₹/u)	20
Selling price per unit in the outside market (₹/u)	200
Current selling price to B (₹/u)	190
Additional variable labour cost of reworking defectives (₹/u)	100
Selling price of reworked defectives (₹/u)	150
Fixed costs for the month (₹)	36,000
Maximum demand from B at present (no. of units)	630

The outside demand can be freely had upto 900 units.

Given the demand and supply conditions, you are required to present appropriate calculations for the following:

(i) Evaluation of the best strategy for A in the present condition.

(ii) If B can buy only upto 540 units and the outside demand is only 600 units, how much should A charge B to maintain the same level of profit as in (I) above?

Solution

1. (a) (i) Contribution per unit against sale to outside = ₹ (200 – 120 – 20) = ₹ 60

In case of transfer, good units and rejected units are in proportion of 9:1

In case of transfer, contribution per good unit = ₹ (190 – 120) = ₹ 70

In case of transfer, contribution per rejected unit = ₹ (150 – 120 – 100) = ₹ –70

Thus, effective contribution per unit of transfer = ₹ (70 × 0.9 –70 × 0.1) = ₹ 56

As contribution per unit against outside sale is higher, the best strategy should be to sell maximum number of unit to outside marker.

Contribution from outside market from sale of 900 units = ₹ 54,000 ₹ (900 × 60)

Contribution from transfer of 300 units to B ₹ (300 × 56) = ₹ 16,800

Total Contribution from best strategy = ₹ 70,800

(ii) If B's demand is 540 unit, total production required (540 /0.9) = 600 units.

Taking outside market demand of 600, it is within production capacity of 1200 units.

Now contribution from 600 units of outside sale ₹ (600 × 60)	= ₹ 36,000
Contribution from rejected 60 units ₹ (60 × – 70)	= ₹ (4,200)
	= ₹ 31,800

To keep same level of contribution as in (i), the contribution required from transfer of 540 unit to B (₹ 70,800 – 31,800) = ₹ 39,000

Thus, contribution required per unit ₹ 39,000/540 = ₹ 72.22

Hence price to be charged per unit against transfer to B ₹ (120 + 72.22) = ₹ 192.2

Alternative Solution:

Let x be the number of units sold outside and y be the number of units sold to B, before B returns 10% as defectives.

Then, x + y = 1,200, is the limitation on production capacity of A.

Particulars	Outside ₹	Department A to B ₹
A. Selling Prices	200	190
Variable Cost-Production	120	120
Variable Cost-Sale	20	–
B. Total Variable Cost	140	120
C. Contribution [A – B]	60	70

Contribution on x units sold outside = 60x

Out of y units to B, 10% = $\frac{1}{10}$ = 1y is returned to A. If A scraps, amount got = 30 per unit.

If reworked and sells, it gets 150 – 100 = 50 per unit.

∴ Decision to reworks all defectives, i.e. (.1) (y)

Contribution on good units of B = 0.9y × 70 = 63y

Contribution on reworked units of B = (.1) (y) × 50 = 5y

Amount of material lost on manufacture of defectives to B = 12y

(.1)(y) × 120

∴ Contribution on y gross units transferred to B = 56y

63y + 5Y – 12y

Total contribution earned by A = 60x + 56y

where x + y =1200

To maximize contribution, maximize units sold outside.

∴ 900 units – sell outside.

Balance $\frac{300}{1200}$ units (gross transfer to B, of which B gives back 30 defectives)

Contribution: ₹ 60 × 900 + ₹ 56 × 300 = ₹ 70,800

Fixed Cost = ₹ 36,000

(i) Profit = ₹ 70,800 – ₹ 36,000 = ₹ 34,800

(ii) Outside demand = 600 units

Contribution = 600 × ₹ 60 = ₹ 36,000

Balance to be got = ₹ 34,800

= ₹ 70,800

Out of ₹ 34,800, defectives of B will give

₹	3,000	60 × 50
₹	31,800	charge to B for 540 units

Contribution to be obtained from 540 units of B	=	₹ 31,800
Add: Production cost of 600 units @ 120	=	₹ 72,000
Amount changed for 540 units	=	₹ 1,03,800

∴ Price to be charged to B = $\frac{1,03,800}{540}$ = 192.22

Per good unit transferred, to maintain the same level of profit as in (a).

Illustration 12

Bearings Ltd. makes three products, A, B and C in Divisions A, Band C respectively. The following information is given:

	A	B	C	
Direct Materials (excluding material A for Divisions B and C)	4	15	20	₹/unit
Direct Labour	2	3	4	₹/unit
Variable Overhead	1	1	1	₹/unit
Selling price to outside customers	15	40	50	₹/unit
Existing Capacity	5,000	2,500	2,500	(No. of units)
Maximum External demand	3,750	5,000	4,000	(No. of units)
Additional fixed costs that would be incurred to install additional capacity	24,000	6,000	18,700	₹
Maximum Additional units that can be produced by additional capacity	5,000	1,250	2,250	(No. of units)

B and C need material A as their input. Material A is available outside at ₹ 15 per unit. Division A supplies the material free from defects. Each unit of B and C requites one unit of A as the input material.

If B purchases from outside, it has to pay ₹ 15 per unit. If B purchases from A, it has to incur in addition to the transfer price, ₹ 2 per unit as variable cost to modify it.

B has sufficient idle capacity to inspect its inputs without additional costs.

If C gets material from A, it can use it directly, but if it gets material from outside, which is at ₹ 15. it has to do one of the following:

(i) Inspect it at its own shop floor at ₹ 3 per unit

Or

(ii) Get the supplier to supply inspected products and pay the supplier ₹ 2 per unit as inspection charges.

Or

(iii) A has enough idle labour, which it can lend to C to inspect at ₹ 1 per unit even though C purchases from outside.

A has to fix a uniform transfer price for both B and C. The transfer price will not be known to outsiders and is at the discretion of the Divisional Managers.

What is the best strategy for each division and the company as a whole?

Solution

B will not pay A anything more than 13, because at 13, it will incur additional cost of ₹ 2 to modify it, 13 + 2 = 15, the outside cost.

Particulars	*A*		*B*	*C*
	Outside sale	*Transfer to B & C*		
Divisional Variable Cost of Production	7	7	19	25
Transfer from A			13	13
Modification			2	
A. Total Variable Cost of production	7	7	34	38
B. Selling Price	15	13	40	50
C. Contribution [B – A]	8	6	6	12

Option for C, Purchase all units from A @ 13: Any other option is costlier.

	A	B	C
Maximum external demand	3,750	5,000	4,000
Exiting capacity	5,000	2,500	2,500
Maximum capacity that can be added	5,000	1,250	2,250
Total maximum that can be produced	10,000	3,750	4,750
Additional fixed cost on expansion	24,000	6,000	18,700
Units that must be sold/transfer to get this amount as contribution	$\frac{24,000}{6} = 4,000$	$\frac{6,000}{6} = 1,000$	$\frac{18,700}{12} = 1,558.33$
External demand not covered by existing capacity	–	2,500	1,500
Decision	Expand make 10,000 units 3750 – outside 3,750 – B 2,500 – C	Expand make 2,500 + 1,250 = 3,750 units	Do not expand make only 2,500 units.

	A		B	C
	Outside sale	Transfer to B & C		
Units	3,750	3,750 + 2,500 = 6,250	3,750	2,500
Contribution/unit	8	6	6	12
Contribution (₹)	30,000	37,500	22,500	30,000
Total	67,500		22,500	30,000
Less: Additional Fixed Cost	(24,000)		(6,000)	–
Profit	43,500		16,500	30,000

Individual strategy is the Company's best strategy.

Illustration 13

X Ltd. has two divisions, A and B, which manufacture products A and 8 respectively. A and B are profit centres with the respective Divisional Managers being given full responsibility and credit for their performance.

The following figures are presented:

	Division A *₹ Per Unit*	*Division B* *₹ Per Unit*
Direct material cost	50	24* *(other than A)
Material A, if transferred from Division A	–	144
Material A, if purchased from outside	–	160
Direct labour	25	14
Variable production overhead	20	2
Variable selling overhead	13	26
Selling price in outside market	160	300
Selling price to B	144	–
Selling price to S Ltd.	–	250

Other Information:

To make one unit of B, one unit of component A is needed. If transferred from A, B presently takes product A at ₹.144 per unit, with A not incurring variable selling overheads on units transferred to B.

Product A is available in the outside market at ₹ 160 per unit from competitors.

B can sell its product B in the external market at ₹ 300 per unit, whereas, if it supplied to X Ltd.'s subsidiary, S Ltd., it supplies at ₹ 250 per unit, and need not incur variable selling overhead on units transferred to S Ltd. S Ltd. requires 6,000 units and stipulates a condition that either all 6,000 units be taken from B or none at all.

	A(units)	*B(units)*	
Manufacturing capacity	20,000	28,000	
Demand in external market	18,000	26,000	
S Ltd.'s demand	–	6,000	or zero

Assume that Divisions A and B will have to operate during the year.

What is the best strategy for:

(i) Department A?

(ii) Department B, given that A will use its best strategy?

(iii) For X Ltd. As a whole?

Solution

(a)

Particulars	*Div. A ₹/unit*	*B ₹/unit*	*B ₹/unit*
Direct Material (Other than A)	50	24	
Direct Labour	25	14	
Variable Overhead (Production)	20	2	
Variable Production Cost (excl. A)	95	40	40
From A		144	
From Outside			160
Variable production Cost / unit		184	200
Selling Price			
From outside	160	300	
Less: Selling Overhead	13	26	
Net Selling Price (outside)	147	274	
Net Selling Price to B	144		
Net Selling Price to S		250	
Net Selling Price (outside)	147	274	274
Less: Variable Production Cost	95	184	200
Contribution/unit (outside)	52	90	74
(Sale to B & S respectively)	144	250	250
Variable Production Cost	–95	–184	–200
Contribution/unit	49	66	50

Best Strategy for A

A = Maximise Production; Sell maximum no. of units @ 52 / unit (outside)	18,000 × 52 =	9,36,000
(To B) remaining units	2,000 × 49 =	98,000
Total Contribution for A		10,34,000

Best strategy for B:

Maximise contribution/unit by selling outside and procuring from A 90/unit Contribution × 2,000 units
Balance units can yield contribution of either 74/unit for outside or ₹ 50 / unit to S Ltd.
Production Capacity = 28,000.

Option I				*Option II*
Outside Sales		*Sales to S*		*Outside Sales x Contribution/ unit*
20,000 × 74 = 14,80,000		6,000 × 50	= 3,00,000	24,000 × 74 = 17,76,000
2,000 × 90 =1,80,000				2,000 × 90 = 1,80,000
16,60,000			3,00,000	
Total Contribution		(16,60,000 + 3,00,000)	19,60,000	19,56,000

(b) Choose Option I i.e. get 2,000 units from A, sell 6,000 units to S and 20,000 to outside. Make 28,000 units @ full capacity. Total Contribution ₹ 19,60,000.
If A and B are allowed to act independent of the group synergy,

	₹
Total Contribution	A – 10,34.000 B – 19,60,000
Total Contribution for X Ltd.	29,94,000

COST FROM X LTD.'S PERSPECTIVE

Variable Cost of production	Div A	₹ 95
	Div B	
Variable Cost of production other than A	40	40
A supplied by Division	95	
A – Variable Cost		
A purchased		160
	135	200

Option I	*Outside 26,000 units*	*Option II*	
Outside 20,000 × (274 – 135)	27,80,000	20,000 (274 – 135)	27,80,000
2,000 × (274 – 200)	148,000	6,000(274 – 200)	4,44,000
22,000			
S Ltd. 6.000 units (250 – 200)	3,00,000		
	32,28,000		32,24,000

Choose Option I
Contribution = ₹ 32,28,000 for X Ltd. as a whole
Transfer (2,000 units)

Make A transfer all output to B. Sell 6,000 units of B to S and 22,000 units to outside market. This will make X Ltd. better off by 32,28,000 – 29,94,000 = ₹ 2,34,000

(i.e. 18,000 units of A sold to outside increases contribution to A by 3 ₹ / unit and decreases contribution to B by 16 ₹ / unit Net negative effect = 13 × 18,000 = ₹ 2,34,000).

Illustration 14

Optically Ltd. makes two kinds of products, P (lenses) and Q (swimming goggles) in divisions P and Q respectively. P is an input for Q and two units of P are needed to make one unit of Q.

The following data is given to you for a period :

	P ₹/unit of P	Q ₹/unit of Q
Direct Materials	20	25 (excluding P)
Direct Labour	30	35
Variable Overhead	10	20
External Demand (units)	3,000	3,000
Capacity (units)	7,000	2,500
Selling Price ₹/unit (outside market)	100	410

If Q buys P from outside, it has the following costs:

For order quantity 2,499 or less	₹ 90 per unit for the entire quantity ordered.
For order quantity 2,500 - 5,000	₹ 80 per unit for the entire quantity ordered.
For order quantity more than 5,000	₹ 70 per unit for the entire quantity ordered.

You are required to:

(i) Evaluate the best strategies for Division P and Q.

(ii) Briefly explain the concept of goal congruence.

Solution

Opticals Ltd manufactures P(lenses) and Q (swimming goggles).

Division P has option to supply to Division Q or sell to outside market.

Division Q has option to buy from Division P or purchase from outside market.

However, both divisions have to work within their individual capacity.

Variable Cost for product P in Division P = ₹ 60.

Variable cost for product Q in Division Q (excluding 2 Nos P's) = ₹ 80.

Division P has better market price of its product P than the market price offered to Q division.

For maximizing profit of the organization :	₹
P division should optimise its profit by selling maximum units to outside market.	
Contribution per unit for sale to outside for division P	40
Contribution per unit for Div Q as follows :	
Sale price - Variable cost (excluding lenses)	330
Max Contribution per unit (if procured from P div at its variable cost i.e. ₹ 60)	210
Min Contribution per unit (if procured at ₹ 90 per unit from outside)	150
Contribution per unit at transfer price of ₹ 70 i.e. minimum market price	190

Option 1: Division Q buys 5001 units from market @ ₹ 70 and meets its capacity. Division P sells 3000 units to outside market @ ₹ 100

Sale/Transfer	Contrib. /unit	Contribution in thousand rupees		
	₹	P Div	Q Div	Total
Div P:Sale of 3000 units to outside market @ ₹ 100	40	120		120
Div Q: Sale of 2500 units with P from market @ ₹ 70	190		475	475
Less: cost of rejection of one unit of product P			−0.07	−0.07
Total		120	474.93	594.93

Option 2: Division P sells 3000 units to outside market, transfer 4000 units to div Q and Division Q buys 1000 units from outside market to work within the capacity

P Division agrees to a transfer price so that profitability of Q is not affected. To maintain the same profitability of Q, contribution required from 2000 units for Div Q is ₹ 400,000 i.e. contribution per unit ₹ 200 i.e. transfer price per unit of P is ₹ 65 per unit to make cost of lenses ₹ 130

Sale/Transfer	*Contribution /unit*	*Contribution in thousand rupees*		
	₹	*P Div*	*Q Div*	*Total*
Div P : Sale of 3000 units to outside market	40	120		120
Div P : Transfer of 4000 units to div Q at ₹ 65	5	20		20
Div Q: Sale of 2000 units with P from P div @ ₹ 65	200		400	400
Div Q : Sale of 500 units with P from market @ ₹ 90	150		75	75
Total		140	475	615

Under Option 1, both divisions worked dis-jointly without caring for capacity utilization resulting lower profitability of the organization.

Under Option 2, both divisions worked with mutual advantages for optimizing their individual profits and overall profit for the organization has gone up by effective utilization of capacity.

Product P from Division P fetches higher price from open market indicating good quality of product. Moreover, supply from P division is well assured in the long run which is the justification of establishment of two parallel divisions.

Hence, Option 2 is suggested.

(ii) Division functioning as profit centers strive to achieve maximum divisional profits, either by internal transfers or from outside purchase. This may not match with the organisation's objective of maximum overall profits. Divisions may be commercial to advice overall objects objectives, where divisional decisions are in line with the overall best for the company, and this is goal congruence. Divisions at a disadvantage may be given due weightage while appraising their performance. Goal incongruence defeats the purpose of divisional profit centre system.

Illustration 15

BUE is a group consisting of four operating companies. British Angles. British Bars, British Circles and British Dies. Dritish Dies proposes to palace a contract for a sub-assembly to be used in one of its new products and in accordance with BUE policy has to obtain quotations from any suitable company within the group and at least one oulside company.

Within the group British Angles is approached as the most suitable company and submits a quotation of ₹ 2,400. In order to do the job, however British Angles will need to sub-contract some of the work to British Bars and some to British Circles.

Arrangements between the companies for this sub-contract are as follows:

British Angles will buy from British Bars special parts at a price of ₹ 200.

British Angles wil buy from British Circles components at a price of ₹ 1,500.

To make up its components, however, British Circles must buy from British Bars standard parts at a price of ₹ 380.

British Angles total costs (including purchases from British Bars and British Circles) for the British Dies contract are ₹ 2,200.

From companies outside the group, British Dies obtain the following quotations:

- Instalment quotes ₹ 1,650.
- Detachment quotes ₹ 1,800.

1. The variable costs of each group company relating to the work for which it has quoted are:

   As a proportion of the total cost of the work it does itself (i.e. excluding parts or components bought from other group companies):

British Angles 60%
British Circles 80%
As a proportion of selling price
British Bars 75%

2. British Circles prices included a 25% profit margin on total cost (including where appropriate, any special parts purchased).
3. British Bars price of ₹ 380 is the current market price for these parts. They are in heavy demand by buyers outside the BUE group, and their supply from British Bars is severely limited.
4. Detachment will buy certain components from British Angles for their jobs at ₹ 550. In order to make these components British Angles will have to buy parts from British Circles at a price of ₹ 350. British Angles assesses that it could make profit of 33-1/3% on the cost of its own work on the Detachment contract.

Solution

	British angle ₹	*Instalment* ₹	*Detachment* ₹
Relevant cost	1,486	1,650	1,800
— Benefit to be achieved	—	—	(236)
Cost	1,486	1,650	1,564

Decision: It is better to give the contract to the British Angle, to produce the components in house.

Working Notes:

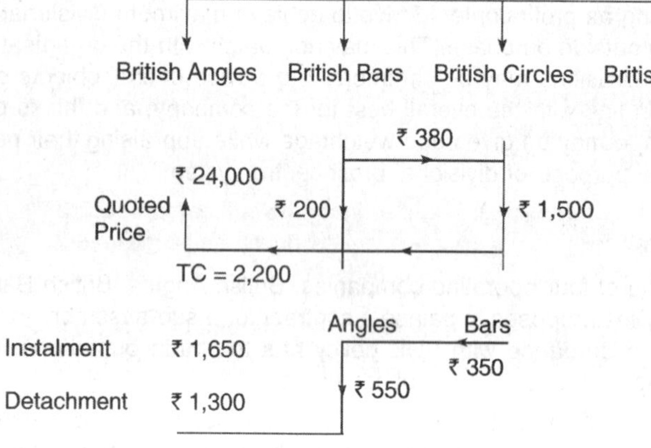

(1) STATEMENT OF RELEVANT COST (B. ANGLE)

B. Angle		*B. Circle*		*B. Bar (spare part)*		*B. Bar (busy)*
Variable cost	300	VC	656	VC	150	
Fixed cost	200	FC	164 (B.f.)			285
Own cost	500		820	Contribution	50	95
Add: Purchase		*Add*: Purchase				
B. circle	1500	B. Bar	380			
B. bar	200					
Total Cost	2200	Total Cost	1,200			
Add: Profit	200	Profit	300			
Transfer Price	₹ 2400	Transfer Price	1,500		200	380

STATEMENT OF RELEVANT COST

	Cost to be incurred	Benefit Loss	Total
B. angle	300	—	300
B. circle	656	—	656
B. Bar	150	—	150
B. Bar (Busy) 285	285	95	380
		Total Relevant Cost	1,486

STATEMENT OF COST ANALYSIS
(DETACHMENT CONTRACT)

	B. angle		B. circle
Variable cost 60%	90	Variable cost 80%	224
Fixed cost (40%)	60	Fixed cost 20%	58
Own cost	150	Own cost	280
Add: Purchase (B. circle)	350	*Add:* Purchase cost	—
Total cost	500	Total cost	280
Add: Profit	50*	*Add*: Profit	70
	550		350

* Own cost + Profit = 200

Let own cost = x

$x + 1/3x = 200$

$x = 150$

Profit = $150 \times 1/3 = 50$

Benefit to be achieved from Detachment Contract

	₹
Revenue	550
Less: Cost to be incurred (90 + 224)	(314)
Benefit	236

SOLVED PROBLEMS

PROBLEM 1

A Co. has two divisions, *viz.*, Processing and Refining. Processing Division produces 500 tonnes of product M from 1,000 tonnes of a raw material per month. Refining produces 300 tonnes of product FM from 500 tonnes of M received from the Processing Division. The cost data are:

Processing Division :

Raw materials	₹ 120 per tonne of input
Variable costs	₹ 80 per tonne of output
Fixed costs	₹ 50.000 per month

Refining Division:

Variable costs	₹ 30 per tonne of output
Fixed costs	₹ 21,000 per month.

The market price of product M is ₹ 500 per tonne and of product FM is ₹ 1,200 per tonne.

Required:

(i) Compute, the overall profit of the company for the month:

(ii) Compute the profit of each Division based on the following pricing methods:

(a) 200% of variable costs of Processing Division for M.

(b) Market price for M:

(iii) Which method will you recommend and why?

Solution. (a) **PROCESSING DIVISION**

Product M	*Total Cost*	*Output of M 500 tonnes Cost per tonne*
Raw Materials (1,000 × 120)	₹ 1,20,000	240
Processing Variable Cost (500 × 80)	40,000	80
Total Variable Cost	1,60,000	320
Fixed Costs	50,000	100
Total Cost of Processing	2,10,000	420

(i) **STATEMENT SHOWING OVERALL PROFIT OF THE COMPANY**

Sales (FM–300 × ₹ 1,200):			₹ 3,60,000
Processing Division Cost Transferred		₹ 2,10,000	
Refining Division Cost:			
Variable Costs (300 × ₹ 30)	9,000		
Fixed cost	21,000	30,000	
			(2,40,000)
Profit			1,20,000

(iii) **STATEMENT SHOWING PROFIT FROM EACH DIVISION**

Processing Division	200% of *Variable Cost of processing*	*Market Price*
Selling Price (₹ 320 × 2)	₹ 640	₹ 500
Sale (500 tonnes)	₹ 3,20,000	₹ 2,50,000
Costs	2,10,000	2,10,000
Profit	1,10,000	40,000
Refining Division		
Selling Price	₹ 1,200	₹ 1,200
Sales (300 tonnes)	₹ 3,60,000	₹ 3,60,000
Transfer Price	3,20,000	2,50,000
Cost of Refining	30,000	30,000
Profit	10,000	80,000

(iii) The transfer price based on 200% of variable cost is ₹ 640 per tonne while the market price i s ₹ 500 per tonne. If the Divisions are organised into profit centres the Refining Division is tempted to buy from the outside market.

If the Processing Division has no alternative use for its spare capacity/full capacity, its fixed costs of ₹ 50,000 will remain unrecovered. Thus, charging a price for the captive products higher than the market price will be dyfunctional.

When market price method is used Processing Division will be encouraged to reduce its costs to improve contribution. The Refining Division will also be encouraged to make product competitive.

Assuming that there is idle capacity in each Division, with the transfer price matching with the market price, both the Divisions will be eager to reap the benefit of large-scale production. Individual Division's profit will increase and so will be the overall profit of the company.

PROBLEM 2

A company Is engaged In the manufacture of edible oil. It has three divisions as under:

(i) Harvesting oil seeds and transportation thereof to the oil mill.

(ii) Oil Mill, which processes oil seeds and manufactures edible oil.

(iii) Marketing Division, which packs the edible oil in 2 kg. containers for sale at ₹ 150 each container.

The Oil Mill has a yield of 1000 kgs. of oil from 2,000 kg. of oil seeds during a period The Marketing Division has a yield of 500 cans of edible oil of 2 kg. each from every 1,000 kg. of oil. The net weight per can is 2 kg. of oil.

The cost data for each division four the period are as under:

Harvesting Division:

Variable cost per kg. of oil seed	₹ 2.50
Fixed cost per kg. of oil seed	₹, 5.00

Oil Mill Division:

Variable cost of processed edible oil	₹ 10.00 per kg.
Fixed cost of processed edible oil	₹ 7.50 per kg.

Marketing Division:

Variable cost per can of 2 kg. of oil	₹ 3.75
Fixed cost per can of 2 kg. of oil	₹ 8.75

The fixed costs are calculated on the basis of the estimated quantity of 2,000 kg. of oil seeds harvested, 1,000 kg. of processed oil and 500 cans of edible oil packed by the aforesaid divisions respectively during the period under review.

The other oil mills buy the oil seeds of same quality at ₹ 12.50 per kg. in the market. The market price of edible oil processed by the oil mill, if sold without being packed in the marketing division is ₹ 62.50 per kg. of oil.

Required:

(i) Compute the overall profit of the company of harvesting 2,000 kg. of oil seeds, processing it into edible oil and selling the same in 2 kg, cans as estimated for the period under review.

(ii) Compute the transfer prices that will be used for internal transfers from (1) Harvesting Division to Oil Mill Division and (2) from Oil Mill Division to Marketing Division under the following pricing methods:

(1) Shared contribution in relation to variable costs; and

(2) Market price.

(iii) Which transfer pricing method will each divisional manager prefer to use? ***(May 2001)***

Solution

(i) STATEMENT OF THE OVERALL PROFIT OF THE COMPANY (BY HARVESTING 2,000 KGS OF OIL SEEDS, PROCESSING IT INTO EDIBLE OIL & SELLING THESAME IN 2 KG CANS)

Particulars	*Harvesting Division*	*Oil Mill Division*	*Marketing Division*	*Total ₹*
Output of each department	2,000 Kgs. of oil seed	1,000 kgs. of oil produced	500 cans of 2 kg each	
A. Total Costs:				
Variable Cost (₹)	5,000	10,000	1,875	16,875
	(2,000 kgs × ₹ 2.50)	(1,000 kgs × ₹ 10)	(500 × ₹ 3.75)	
Fixed Cost (₹):	10,000	7,500	4,375	21,875
	(2,000 kgs. × ₹ 5)	(1,000 kgs × ₹ 7.50)	(500 × ₹ 8.75)	
Total Cost (₹)	15,000	17,500	6,250	38,750
B. Sales Revenue (₹) (500 cans × ₹.150)				75,000
C. Profit (₹) [A – B]				36,250

Working Note:

(a) Total Contribution = {Sales Revenue – Total Variable Cost}

= ₹ 75,000 – ₹ 16,875 = ₹ 58,125

(b) Amount of shared contribution in relation to variable costs:

Harvesting Division = ₹ 58,125 × $\frac{5,000}{16,875}$ = ₹ 17,222

Oil Mill Division = ₹ 58,125 × $\frac{10,000}{16,875}$ = ₹ 34,445

Marketing Division = ₹ 58,125 × $\frac{1,875}{16,875}$ = ₹ 6,458

(ii) Computation of Transfer Price (for internal transfers) under the following pricing methods:

(1) Shared contribution in relation to variable costs:

Transfer price from Harvesting Division to Oil Mill Division

= Variable cost of Harvesting Division + Shared contribution of Harvesting Division in relation to variable costs

= ₹ 5,000 + ₹ 17,222 (Refer to working note 2) = ₹.22,222

Transfer price from Oil Mill Division to Marketing Division

= Transfer price from Harvesting Division to Oil Mill Division + Variable cost of Oil Mill Division + Shared contribution of Oil Mill Division in relation to variable costs (Refer to working note 2)

= ₹ 22,222 + ₹ 10,000 + ₹ 34,445 = ₹ 66,667

(2) Market Price:

Transfer price from Harvesting Division to Oil Mill Division

= Market price of 2,000 kgs of Oil seeds transferred to Oil Mill Division

= 2,000 kgs × ₹ 12.50 = ₹ 25,000

Transfer price from Oil Mill Division to Marketing Division

= Market price of 1,000 kgs of edible oil = 1,000 kgs × ₹ 62.50 – ₹ 62,500

STATEMENT OF PROFITABILITY (UNDER DIFFERENT TRANSFER PRICES METHOD)

Particulars	*From Harvesting Division to Oil Mill Division* ₹	*From oil Mill to Marketing Division* ₹	*From Marketing Division to market (500 cans of 2 Kgs.)* ₹
Shared Contribution Method:			
A. Transfer Price:	22,222	66,667	75,000
B. *Less: Transfer Price*		22,222	66,667
C. *Less:* Variable cost	5,000	10,000	1,875
D. *Less:* Fixed cost	10,000	7,500	4,375
E. Profit [A – B – C – D]	7,222	26,945	2,083
Market Price Method:			
A. Transfer Price	25,000	62,500	75,000
B. *Less:* Transfer in price	—	25,000	62,500
C. *Less:* Variable cost	5,000	10,000	1,875
D. *Less:* Fixed cost	10,000	7,500	4,375
E. Profit [A – B – C – D]	10,000	20,000	6,250

(iii) Decision: Divisional Manager of Harvesting Division would prefer the use of market price method for transferring 2,000 kgs of oil seeds to Oil Mill Division because its usage increases the profit by ₹ 2,778 (₹ 10,000 – ₹.7,222) over the shared contribution method.

Whereas Oil Mill Divisional manager would prefer the use of shared contribution method over the market price method because its use would increase its profit by ₹ 6,945 (₹ 26,945 – ₹ 20,000). Similarly Marketing Divisional Manager would be benefited to the extent of ₹ 4,167 (₹ 6,250 – ₹ 2,083) by using market price method.

PROBLEM 3

SV Ltd. manufactures a product which is obtained basically from a series of mixing operations. The finished product is packaged in the company-made glass bottles and packed in attractive cartons.

The company is organised into two independent divisions viz. one for the manufacture of the end-product and the other for the manufacture of glass bottles. The product manufacturing division can buy all the bottle requirements from the bottle manufacturing division.

The General Manager of the bottle manufacturing division has obtained the following quotations from the outside manufacturers for the supply of empty bottles.

No. of Empty Bottles	*Total Purchase Value (₹)*
8,00,000	14,00,000
12,00,000	20,00,000

A cost analysis of the bottle manufacturing division for the manufacture of empty bottles reveals the following production costs:

No. of Empty bottles	*Total Cost (₹)*
8,00,000	10,40,000
12,00,000	14,40,000

The production cost and sales value of the end product marketed by the product manufacturing division are as under:

Volume (Bottles of end product)	*Total cost of end product (excluding cost of empty bottles)*	*Sales value (Packed in bottles)*
	₹	₹
8,00,000	64,80,000	91,20,000
12,00,000	96,80,000	1,27,80,000

There has been considerable discussion at the corporate level as to the use of proper price for transfer of empty bottles from the bottle manufacturing division to product manufacturing division. This interest is heightened because a significant portion of the Divisional General Manager's salary is in incentive bonus based on profit centre results.

As the corporate management accountant responsible for defining the proper transfer prices for the supply of empty bottles by the bottle manufacturing division to the product manufacturing division, you are required to show for the two levels of volumes of 8,00,000 and 12,00,000 bottles, the profitability by using (i) market price and (ii) shared profit relative to the costs involved basis for the determination of transfer prices. The profitability position should be furnished separately for the two divisions and the company as a whole under each method. Discuss also the effect of these methods on the profitability of the two divisions.

Solution

STATEMENT SHOWING PROFITABILITY OF TWO DIVISIONS AT TWO DIFFERENT LEVELS OF OUTPUT USING DIFFERENT TRANSFER PRICES

Particulars	*8,00,000 Bottles*	*12,00,000 Bottles*
	₹	₹
A. Sales Value (Packed Product):	91,20,000	1,27,80,000
B. *Less : Costs*		
Product Manufacturing Division	64,80,000	96,80,000
Bottle Manufacturing Division	10,40,000	14,40,000
Total Costs	75,20,000	1,11,20,000
C. Profit : [A – B]	16,00,000	16,60,000
D. Profit pro-rated to Bottle Mfg. Division and Product Mfg. Division.		
Share of Bottle Manufacturing Division:		
[16,00,000 × 10,40,000/75,20,000]	2,21,276	
[16,60,000 × 14,40,000/1,11,20,000]		2,14,964
Balance profit relates to Product Mfg. Division	13,78,724	14,45,036
	16,00,000	16,60,000
	₹	₹
Transfer Prices of Bottles		
A. Costs	10,40,000	14,40,000
B. Profit as computed above	2,21,276	2,14,964
C. Total Price [A + B]	12,61,276	16,54,964
Transfer Price per bottle	₹ 1.577	₹ 1.379

From the above computations, it is observed that shared profit relative to the cost involved is ₹ 2,21,276 (₹ 0.2766 per bottle) at 8,00,000 production level and ₹ 2,14,964 (₹ 0.179 per bottle) at

12,00,000 production level. The profit of Product Mfg. Division is ₹ 13,78,724 (₹ 1.723 per bottle) at 8,00,000 production level and ₹ 14,45,036 (₹ 1.2042 per bottle) at 12,00,000 production level.

PROFITABILITY BASED ON MARKET PRICE

No. of Bottles	8,00,000	12,00,000
Bottle Mfg. Division:	₹	₹
A. Market Price	14,00,000	20,00,000
B. *Less:* Cost	(10,40,000)	(14,40,000)
C. Profit [A – B]	3,60,000	5,60,000
Product Mfg. Division:		
A. Sales	93,20,000	1,27,80,000
B. *Less:* Bottle cost	(14,00,000)	(20,00,000)
C. *Less:* Product cost	(64.80,000)	(96,80,000)
D. Profit [A – B – C]	12,40,000	11,00,000
E. Total Profit	16,00,000	16,60,000

Production level	*Profit based on Cost (₹ Lakhs)*		*Profit based on Market Price (₹ Lakhs)*	
	Bottle Mfg. Div.	*Product Mfg. Div.*	*Bottle Mfg. Div.*	*Product Mfg. Div.*
8,00,000 bottles	2.21	13.79	3.60	12.40
12,00,000 bottles	2.15	14.45	5.60	11.00

Observations:

(i) *Market price method gives a better profitability to Bottle Mfg. Division at both the production levels.*

(ii) *Market price method gives a lower profitability to Product Mfg. Division as compared to Bottle Mfg. Division.*

(iii) *Under Cost-based method, there is a better profit at lower level of production in Bottle Mfg. Division. However in Product Mfg. Division 12,00,000 production level gives a higher profit. But in Market price method, the position is quite reverse.*

PROBLEM 4

Your company fixes the inter-divisional transfer prices for its products on the basis of cost, plus a return on investment in the division. The Budget for Division A for 2010-11 appears as under:

Investment in Division A

	₹
Fixed Assets	5,00,000
Current Assets	3,00,000
Debtors	2,00,000
Annual fixed cost of the division	8,00,000
Variable cost per unit of product	10
Budgeted volume	4,00,000 units per year
Desired ROI	28%

Required: Determine the transfer price for Division A.

Solution

Total Profit Margin [₹ 28% of (₹ 5,00,000 + ₹ 3,00,000 + ₹ 2, 00,000)] = ₹ 2,80,000

	₹
Profit margin per unit (₹ 2,80,000/4,00,000 units)	0.70
Fixed cost per unit (₹ 8,00,000/4,00,000 units)	2.00
Variable Cost per unit	10.00
Transfer Price per unit	12.70

PROBLEM 5

Division A of Better Margins Ltd. has been given a budgeted target of selling 2,00,000 components COM 21, it manufactures at a price which would fetch a return of 25% on the average assets employed by it. The following figures are relevant:

Fixed Overhead	₹ 4,00,000
Variable Cost	₹ 1 per unit
Average Assets :	
Sales Debtors	2,00,000
Stocks	6,00,000
Plant and Other Assets	4,00,000

However, the marketing department of the company finds out by a survey that the maximum number of COM 21, the market can take, at the proposed price is only 1,40,000 units.

Fortunately Division B is willing to purchase the balance 60,000 units. The Manager, Division A is willing to sell to Division B at a concessional price of ₹ 4 per unit. But the Manager, Division B is ready to pay ₹ 2.25 only per unit, as he feels he can himself make COM 21 in his Division at that price.

Rather than sell to Division B at ₹ 2.25, the Manager, Division A feels he will restrict the activity of his Division to the manufacture and sale of 1,40,000 components only. By this, he could reduce ₹ 80,000 in stocks, ₹ 1,20,000 of plant and other assets and ₹ 40,000 in selling and administration expenses.

As a Cost Accountant, you are asked to work out the various computations and show that selling 60,000 COM 21 to Division B at ₹ 2.25 per unit would be in the interest of the organisation.

Solution

Neither Selling Price *nor* Total Sales is given. Division A of Better Margins Ltd. expects a return of 25% on average assets employed i.e., ₹ 12,00,000.

Total sales will be:	₹
(a) Profit (25% of 12,00,000)	3,00,000
(b) Fixed overhead	4,00,000
(c) Variable cost (2,00,000 × ₹ 1)	2,00,000
Total Sales	9,00,000
Sales per unit (₹ 9,00,000/2,00,000 units)	₹ 4.50

Particulars	Transfer to Division B & Sale to outside parties	Sale to outside parties only
Sales (units)	2,00,000	1,40,000
	₹	₹
A. Sales Value *(1,40,000 units @ ₹ 4.50)*	6,30,000	6,30,000
(60,000 units @ ₹ 2.25)	1,35,000	Nil
	7,65,000	6,30,000
B. *Less:* Variable Costs *(₹ 1 per unit)*	2,00,000	1,40,000
C. Contribution	5,65,000	4,90,000
D. *Less:* Fixed Overheads	4,00,000	3.60,000*
E. Net Profit [C – D]	1,65,000	1,30,000
F. Average Assets employed	12,00,000	10,00,000
G. Return on Investment [(E/F) × 100%]	13.75%	13.00%

If the component is transferred to Division B as well as sold to outside parties, it is more profitable as the contribution, net profit and return on investment is more than the existing proposal. Therefore selling the components to Division B at ₹ 2.25 per unit is in the overall interest of the company.

*Reduction in selling and administration expenses (fixed in nature) by ₹ 40,000.

PROBLEM 6

Fasteners Ltd. is having production shops reckoned as cost centres. Each shop charges other shops for material supplied and services rendered.

The shops are motivated through goal congruence, autonomy and management efforts. Fastner Limited is having a welding shop and painting shop. The welding shop welds annually 75,000 purchased items with other 1,50,000 shop made parts into 12,000 assemblies. The assemblies are having variable cost of ₹ 9.50 each and are sold in market at ₹ 12 per assembly. Out of the total production, 80% is diverted to painting shop at same price ruling in the market. Welding shop incurs a fixed cost of ₹ 25,000 per annum. The painting shop is having fixed cost of ₹ 30,000 and its cost of painting including transfer price from welding shop comes to ₹ 20 per unit. This shop sells all units transferred to it by welding shop at ₹ 25 per assembly.

You are required to:

(a) Find out profit of individual cost centres and overall profitability of the concern.

(b) Recommend course of action if painting shop wishes to purchase its full requirement (at market price which is ₹ 10 per assembly) either from open market or from welding shop at market price of ₹ 10 per assembly.

Give reasons for your recommendations.

Solution

FASTNERS LIMITED

(A) PRESENT PROFITABILITY OF INDIVIDUAL SHOPS AND OVERALL PROFITABILITY

Particulars	*Welding Shop*			*Painting Shop*		
	Qty. Units	*Rate ₹*	*Value ₹*	*Qty Units*	*Rate ₹*	*Value ₹*
Sale in open market	2,400	12.00	28,800	9,600	25.00	2,40,000
Transfer to painting shop	9,600	12.00	1,15,200			
A. Total Sales:	12,000		1,44,000	9,600		2,40,000

B. *Less:* Variable Cost:	1,14,000 *(12,000 units × 9.50)*	1,92,000 (9600 units × ₹ 20)
C. Contribution: [A – B]	30,000	48,000
D. *Less:* Fixed Costs	25,000	30,000
E. Profit [C – D]	5,000	18,000

Overall Profit for the company (₹ 5,000 + ₹ 18,000) = ₹ 23,000

(b) (i) WHEN PAINTING SHOP PURCHASES ALL ITS REQUIREMENT FROM OPEN MARKET AT A PRICE OF ₹ 10 PER UNIT

Particulars	*Welding Shop*			*Painting Shop*		
	Qty. Unit	*Rate ₹*	*Value ₹*	*Qty Unit*	*Rate ₹*	*Value ₹*
A. Sale	2,400	12.00	28,800	9,600	25.00	2,40,000
B. *Less:* Variable cost	2,400	9.50	(22,800)	9,600	18.00*	(1,72,800)
C. Contribution [A – B]			6,000			67,200
D. *Less:* Fixed cost			(25,000)			(30,000)
E. Profit/(Loss)			(19,000)			37,200
F. Overall Profit for the company [₹ 37,200 – ₹ 19,000 – ₹ 18,200]						

*It is given in the question that cost of painting including transfer price from welding shop is ₹ 20 per unit. The transfer price from welding shop is ₹ 12 per unit. Therefore, the variable cost of ₹ 8 (₹ 20 — ₹ 12) is incurred by painting shop exclusively. The painting shop will be purchasing its requirement from open market at ₹ 10 per unit. Therefore, the variable cost per unit in painting shop will be ₹ 18 (₹ 10 + ₹ 8). This point should be noted carefully.

(b) (ii) WHEN ALL THE REQUIREMENTS OF PAINTING SHOP IS MET BY TRANSFER FROM WELDING SHOP AT A TRANSFER PRICE OF ₹ 10 PER UNIT

Particulars	*Welding Shop*			*Painting Shop*		
	Qty. Unit	*Rate ₹*	*Value ₹*	*Qty Unit*	*Rate ₹*	*Value ₹*
Sale in the open market	2,400	12.00	28,800	9,600	25.00	2,40,000
Transfer to Painting Shop	9,600	10.00	96,000			
Total Sales	12,000		1,24,800			
Less: Variable cost *(12,000 writs × ₹ 9.50)*			1,14,000	*(9,600 units × ₹ 18)*		1,72,800
Contribution			10,800			67,200
Less: Fixed cost			25,000			30,000
Profit/(Loss)			(14,200)			37,200

Overall Profit of the company = ₹ 37,200 – ₹ 14,200 – ₹ 23,000

For the purpose of comparison, the results of the three alternatives are summarised below:

	Welding Shop ₹	*Painting Shop* ₹
Profit under (i)	5,000	18,000
Profit/(Loss) under (b)(i)	(19,000)	37,200
Profit/(Loss) under (b)(ii)	(14,200)	37,200

		₹
The overall profit under	(a)	23,000
	b(i)	18,200
	b(ii)	23,000

Alternative (b)(ii) should be accepted due to the following reasons:

(a) It gives a maximum overall profit of ₹ 23,000. The discussion is confined to either b(i) or b(ii).

(b) Each shop is treated as a separate cost centre and not a profit centre.

(c) The policy of overall goal congruence of the company is followed.

PROBLEM 7

A boatyard is divided into three profit centres whose managers are rewarded according to results. Transactions between these profit centres are frequent.

Sales centre (S) buys and sells new boats.

If it needs to take part-exchange from a customer in order to sell a new boat, it transfers the part-exchanged boat to B at an agreed price.

Brokerage (B) buys and sells second-hand boats:

(i) in part-exchange from S (B names the price at which it can buy a comparable boat that is in a suitable condition for resale to an end-user customer, but deducts the likely cost of repairs) and

(ii) from other sources, on a normal trading basis.

Repairs (R) does repairs for

(i) B (to put boats into saleable condition) and

(ii) other customers.

The following situation arises:

S can sell to a customer for ₹ 35,000 a new boat which would cost ₹ 29,000. To do so, it needs to offer ₹ 16,000 in part-Exchange for the customer's old boat. However, the customer's boat is estimated by R to need repairs that will cost:

Materials	₹ 300
Labour	60 hours at ₹ 15 per hour

B can buy for ₹ 15,000 a boat comparable to the one being offered by the customer in part-exchange but which needs no repair. B could then sell that boat for ₹ 19,000.

Other data:

R's labour rate per hour is made up as follows:

	₹
Variable cost	6.00
Fixed cost	4.50 *(based on 20,000 budgeted hours p.a.)*
Profit	4.50
	15.00

45% of R's time is reserved for work from B

Annual fixed cost is budgeted at:

S ₹ 70,000, B ₹ 80,000

You are required, in relation to the above situation, to set out the contribution to profit for each profit centre that would result :

(i) assuming that all estimates and budgets materialised as expected,

(ii) assuming that all estimates and budgets materialised as in (i), except that the repairs undertaken by R took an extra 10 hours and ₹ 100 of materials due to a problem not noticed by B or R.

Solution

(a)(i) STATEMENT SHOWING THE CONTRIBUTION TO PROFIT FOR EACH ASSUMING THAT ALL ESTIMATES AND BUDGETS MATERIALISED AS EXPECTED.

	₹	₹	₹
Sales Centre (S)			
New Board Sold			
– Selling price			35,000
– Purchase price			29,000
Gross margin			6,000
Less: Second hand boat			
Part-exchange of old boat		(16,000)	
Broker's Price	15,000		
Less: Repairs	(1,200)	13,800	(2,200)
Contribution			3,800
Brokerage Centre (B)			
Second-hand boat sold			19,000
Less: Paid to Centre S		13,800	
Paid to Centre R		1,200	15,000
Contribution			4,000
Repair Centre (R)			
Sales to Centre B			1,200
Less: Materials		300	
Direct labour variable cost		360	660
Contribution			540

(ii) *Assuming Additional Costs*

It is noticed that all estimates and budgets are materialised except that repairs undertaken by R took an extra 10 hours and ₹ 100 of materials due to a problem not noticed by B or R.

R is responsible for giving correct repair costs and, therefore, he has to bear the additional cost:

	₹	₹
Repair Centre (R)'s contribution		540
Less: Extra cost of materials	100	
Extra D.L. variable cost (10 hrs × ₹ 6)	60	160
Revised contribution		380

However, full details are not given in the question. 'B' is a middleman passing on R's costs to S and as such should not bear additional costs. Had the item been noticed originally then S would have paid the cost and perhaps it should be passed back. This would be particularly so if R had insufficient opportunity for a complete inspection. In that case extra cost should be:

	₹
Material	100
Labour (10 hrs. × ₹ 15)	150
	250

Reduced contribution of S = ₹ 3,800 – ₹ 250 – ₹ 3,550

	₹
Original contribution of R	540
Add.: Saving in variable cost [10 hrs × (₹ 15 – ₹ 6)]	90
Increased contribution of R	630

Note: Other solutions are equally acceptable if well argued and logically justified.

PROBLEM 8

Tycon Ltd. has two manufacturing departments organized into separate profit centres known as Textile unit and Process House. The Textile unit has a production capacity of 5 lacs metres cloth per month, but at present its sales is limited to 50% to outside market and 30% to process house.

The transfer price for the year 2011 was agreed at ₹ 6 per metre. This price has been fixed in line with the external wholesale trade price on 1st January, 2011. However, the price of yarn declined, which was the raw material of textile unit, with effect, that wholesale trade price reduced to ₹ 5.60 per metre with effect from 1st June, 2011. This price was however not made applicable to the sales made to the processing house of the company. The textile unit turned down the processing house request for revision of price.

The Process house refines the cloth and packs the output known as brand Rayon in bundles of 100 metres each. The selling price of the Rayon is ₹ 825 per bundle. The process house has a potential of selling a further quantity of 1,000 bundles of Rayon provided the overall prices is reduced to ₹ 725 per bundle. In that event it can buy the additional 1,00,000 metres of cloth from textile unit, whose capacity can be fully utilised. The outside market has no further scope.

The cost data relevant to the operations are:

	Textile unit	*Process house*
	₹	₹
Raw material (per metre) on 1st June, 2011	3.00	Transfer price
Variable cost	1.20 (per metre)	80 (per bundle)
Fixed cost (per month)	4,12,000	1,00,000

You are required to:

(i) Prepare statement showing the estimated profitability for June, 2011 for Textile unit and Process house and company as a whole on the following basis:

(a) At 80% and 100% capacity utilisation of the Textile unit at the market price and the transfer price to the Processing house of ₹ 6 per metre.

(b) At 80% capacity utilisation of the Textile unit at the market price of ₹ 5.60 per metre and the transfer price to the Processing house of ₹ 6 per metre.

(c) At 100% capacity utilisation of the Textile unit at the market price of ₹ 5.60 per metre and the transfer price to the Processing house of ₹ 5.60 per metre.

(ii) Comment on the effect of the company's transfer pricing policy on the profitability of Processing house.

Solution

(1) (a) ***At 80% level (in ₹)***

Textile unit		**Process house**	
Sales (4,00,000 × 6)	24,00,000	Sales(1,50,000/100) × 825	12,37,500
Less:		*Less:*	
Raw Material (4,00,000 × 3)	(12,00,000)	Transfer Price (1,50,000 × 6)	(9,00,000)
Variable Cost (4,00,000 × 1.2)	(4,80,000)	Variable cost (1,500 × 80)	(1,20,000)
Fixed Cost	(4,12,000)	Fixed cost	(1,00,000)
Profit	3,08,000	Profit	1,17,500

Overall profit = 3,08,000 + 1,17,500 = ₹ 4,25,500

At 100% level

Sales (5,00,000 × 6)	30,00,000	Sales (2,50,000/100) × 725	18,12,500
Less:		Less	
Raw Material (5,00,000 × 3)	(15,00,000)	Transfer Price (2,50,000 × 6)	(15,00,000)
Variable Cost (5,00,000 × 1.2)	(6,00,000)	Variable cost	(2,00,000)
Fixed Cost	(4,12,000)	Fixed cost	(1,00,000)
Profit	4,88,000	Profit	12,500

Overall Profit = 4,88,000 +12,500 = ₹ 5,00,500

(b) At 80% level (market price 5.60 and transfer price 6) (in ₹)

Textile unit		**Process house**	
Sales (2,50,000 × 5.6)	14,00,000		
(1,50,000 × 6.0)	9,00,000		
	23,00,000		
Less:			
Raw Material (4,00,000 × 3)	(12,00,000)		
Variable Cost (4,00,000 × 1.2)	(4,80,000)		
Fixed Cost	(4,12,000)		
Profit	2,08,000	Profit	1,17,500

Overall Profit = 2,08,000 + 1,17,500 = ₹ 3,25,500

(c) ***Sales 100% level at (5.60) (in ₹)***

Sale (5,00,000 × 5.6)	28,00,000	Sales (2,50,000 × 725)	18,12,500
Less:		*Less:*	
Raw Material (5,00,000 × 3)	(15,00,000)	Transfer Profit (2,50,000 × 5.6)	(14,00,000)
Variable Cost (5,00,000 × 1.20)	(6,00,000)	Variable Cost (2,500 × 80)	(2,00,000)
Fixed Cost	(4,12,000)	Fixed Cost	(1,00,000)
Profit	2,88,000	Profit	1,12,500

Overall Profit = 2,88,000 + 1,12,500 = 4,00,500

(ii) Comments on the profitability of processing units:

		Transfer Price (₹)	Profit (₹)
(a)	80% capacity	6.00	1,17,500
	100% capacity	6.00	12,500
(b)	80% capacity	6.00	1,17,500
(c)	100% capacity	5.60	1,12,500

Processing house will not be interested to buy more than 1,50,000 meters from textile units.

PROBLEM 9

A large Company is organised into several manufacturing divisions. The policy of the Company is to allow the Divisional Managers to choose their sources of supply and when buying from or selling to sister divisions, to negotiate the prices just as they will for outside purchase or sales.

Division X buys all of its requirement of its main raw material R from Division Y. The full manufacturing cost of R for Division Y is ₹ 88 per kg. at normal volume.

Till recently, Division Y was willing to supply R to Division X at a transfer price of ₹ 80 per kg. The incremental cost of R for Division Y is ₹ 76 per kg. Since division Y is now operating at its full capacity, it is unable to meet the outside customers' demand for R at its market price of ₹ 100 per kg. Division Y, therefore, threatened to cut off suppliers to Division X unless the latter agrees to pay the market price for R.

Division X is resisting the pressure because its budget based on the consumption of 1,00,000 kg. per month at a price of ₹ 80 per kg. is expected to yield a profit of ₹ 25,00,000 per month and so a price increase to ₹ 100 per kg. will takings the Division X close to break-even point.

Division X has even found an outside source for a substitute material at a price of ₹ 95 per kg. Although the substitute material is slightly different from R, it would meet the needs of Division X. Alternatively, Division X is prepared to pay Division Y even the manufacturing cost of ₹ 88, per kg.

Required:

(i) Using each of the transfer price of ₹ 80, ₹ 88, ₹ 95 and ₹ 100, show with supporting calculation, the financial results as projected by the:
(a) Manager of Division X: (b) Manager of Division Y: (c) Company.

(ii) Comment on the effect of each transfer price on the performance of the Managers of Division X and Division Y.

(iii) If you were to make a decision in the matter without regard to the views of the individual Divisional Managers, where should Division X obtain its materials from and at what price.

Solution

(i) **Statement showing the impact of different transfer prices on divisional profits**

(a) *Transfer price of ₹ 80*

Division X		*Division Y*		*For the Company*	
Budgeted Profit on this price	= ₹ 25,00,000	Sales (1,00,000 × 80)	80,00,000	X Division	= 25,00,000
		Variable Cost: (1,00,000 × 76)	= 76,00,000	Y Division	= 4,00,000
		Profit	= 4,00,000	Profit of Company	29,00,000

(b) *Transfer price of ₹ 88*

Division X		*Division Y*		*For the Company*	
Budgeted Profit	= ₹ 25,00,000	Sales		*Profit form:*	
		1,00,000 × ₹ 88	= 88,00,000	X	₹ 17.00.000
Less Additional cost =		Variable Cost	–	Y	12,00,000
1,00,000 × ₹ 8	= 8,00,000	1,00,000 × ₹ 76	76,00,000		
Profit X	17,00,000	Profit of Y	12,00,000	Profit for the Co.	29,00,000

(c) *Transfer Price of ₹ 95*

Division X		*Division Y*		*For the Company*	
Budgeted	= ₹ 25,00,000	Sales 1,00,000 × ₹ 95		X	10,00,000
			= ₹ 95,00,000	Y	19,00,000
Less Additional Cost		Variable Cost			
1,00,000 × (95 – 80)	15,00,000	1,00,000 × ₹ 76 =	76,00,000		
Profit	10,00,000	Profit	19,00,000	Profit for the Co.	29,00,000

(d) *Transfer Price of ₹ 100*

Division X		*Division Y*		*For the Company*	
Budgeted Profit	= ₹ 25.00,000	Sales 1,00,000 × ₹ 100 =		*Profit from:*	
			₹ 1,00,00,000	X	₹ 5,00,000
Less Addl. Cost		*Less* Variable Cost		Y	24,00,000
1,00,000 × (₹.100–80) =	20,00,000	(1,00,000 × ₹ 76)	76,00,000	Profit for the Co.	29,00,000
	5,00,000		24,00,000		

(ii) Comments on different prices

(a) Transfer price of ₹ 80 gives good incentive to Manager of X Division, but it discourages the Manager of Y Division, because he can sell outside at ₹ 100 and thus he can show better profit if he is allowed to sell outside.

(b) Transfer price of ₹ 88 reduces the profits of Division X and boasts the performance of Division Y in comparison to existing arrangement. The decision neither increase nor decrease the company's profit.

(c) Transfer price of ₹ 95 further reduces the profit of Division X and correspondingly improve the profit of division Y. Company's profit again neither increase nor decrease due to this decision.

(d) Transfer price of ₹ 100 puts Manager of X Division to very disadvantageous position, because he is able to get the material from outside source at ₹ 95. Therefore, at this price profit of Division X are unnecessarily decreased by ₹ 5,00,000. *i.e.,* 1,00,000 × (₹ 100 – ₹ 95.00). Since Y can get ₹ 100 from outside customers, this price means loss of company's profit by ₹ 5,00,000.

(iii) *Decision in the matter.* The transfer price must motivate the concerned divisional managers maintaining the divisional autonomy. The best course will be:

(a) X Division should buy the material R from outside source at price of ₹ 95.

(b) Y Division should sell entire quantity of R to outside consumers at ₹ 100.

The decision will maximise the company's profits, as is clear from the following analysis:

Division X		*Division Y*	
Budgeted Profit	= ₹ 25,00,000	Sales 1,00,000 × ₹ 100	= ₹ 1,00,00,000
Less Additional Cost	–	*Less* V. Cost 1,00,000 × ₹ 76	= 76,00,000
1,00,000 × (₹ 95 – ₹ 80)	= 15,00,000	–	
	10,00,000		24,00,000

Company's Profit = ₹ 10,00,000 + ₹ 24,00,000 = ₹ 34,00,000.

PROBLEM 10

A Company has two Divisions, viz., LD and KD. LD operates at full capacity and KD operates at 50% capacity.

LD produces two products. LX and *LY* using the same labour force for each product. The direct wage rate per production hour is ₹ 5. During the next year, its budgeted capacity of 42,000 direct labour hcurs involves a commitment to sell 6,000 kg. of LY. The balance capacity will be used for the production of LX. Cost data are:

	LX	*LY*
	₹/Kg	*₹/Kg*
Direct Materials	36	28
Direct Wages	30	20

The Company's overheads amount to ₹ 7,56,000 per annum relating to LX and LY in proportion to other direct wages. At full capacity ₹ 4,20,000 of this overhead is variable. LD prices its products with 50% mark-up on its total costs.

KD wishes to buy 2,000 kg. of LX from LD for being processed into KX to be sold at ₹ 300 per kg. The processing materials and wage cost are ₹ 30 per kg. and the variable overheads amount to ₹ 4 per kg. The fixed costs amount to ₹ 1,00,000 per annum.

Prepare a report showing the profitability of LD and KD and the Company as a whole for each of the following transfer price methods:

(i) LD transfers LX at a price applicable to outside customers on the basis of total cost.

(ii) LD transfers LX at a price based on total costs *less* credit for selling and distribution expenses of ₹ 4 per kg. which will not be incurred in respect of the sale of KD.

(iii) LD transfers LX at a price based on marginal cost as reduced by ₹ 4 per kg. of selling and distribution expenses.

(iv) LD manufactures the quantity of LX required by KD by employing overtime payable at double the normal wage rate and transfers at marginal cost less ₹ 4 per kg. being selling and distribution costs not incurred in respect of sale to KD. LD sells the entire regular production to outside customers at the usual price.

Solution

For the budgeted level of activities and expenses of LD various costs and prices have been determined as follows:

Total Overhead per year	₹ 7,56,000	
Less: Variable Overhead	4,20,000	
Fixed Overhead per year	3,36,000	
Variable Overhead per hour	= ₹ 4,20,000/42,000	= ₹ 10 per hour
Fixed Overhead per hour	= ₹ 3,36,000/42,000	= ₹ 8 per hour

The costs and selling prices of products of LD for normal sale to outside parties will be as under:

(*₹ per kg.*)

	LX	*LY*
Direct Material	36	28
Direct Wages	30	20
Variable Overhead		
₹ 10 × 6 hrs.	60	
₹ 10 × 4 hrs		40
A. Total Variable Costs	126	88
B. Fixed Cost:		
₹ 8 × 6 hrs	48	
₹ 8 × 4 hrs		32
C. Total Costs [A + B]	174	120
D. *Add:* Mark-up 50%	87	60
E. Selling Price [C + D]	261	180

Committed production of LV of 6,000 kg. would involve labour hours of 24,000, *i.e.*, 6,000 × 4 hrs.

Balance labour hrs. for production of LX = 42,000 – 24,000 = ₹ 18,000 hrs

Production of LA = 18,000 ÷ 6 = 3,000 kg.

Cost estimate of KX, if KD purchase LX from LD at normal prices:

Cost of LX	261
Processing materials and wage costs	30
Variable overheads	4
Total Variable Costs	295

PROFIT STATEMENTS OF LD AND KD

(i) TRANSFER PRICE BASED ON TOTAL COST

LD		KD	
Sales LX 3,000 × ₹ 261	₹ 7,83,000	A. Sales KX	
LY 6,000 × ₹ 180	10,80,000	2,000 kg. × ₹ 300	₹ 6,00,000
A. Total Sales	18,63,000		
Variable Cost		Variable Cost	
LX 2,000 × ₹ 122*	2,44,000	2,000 × ₹ 295	5,90,000
1,000 × 126	1,26,000		
LY 6,000 × 88	5,28,000		
Total Variable Cost	8,98,000		
Fixed Cost	3,36,000	Fixed Cost	1,00,000
B. Total Cost	12,34,000	B. Total Cost	6,90,000
C. Profit [A – B]	6,29,000	C. Loss [A – B]	(90,000)

Total Profit for the company ₹ 6,29,000 – 90,000 = ₹ 5,39,000

*₹ 126 – ₹ 4 (selling expenses will not be incurred in case of sale to KD)

(ii) TRANSFER PRICE BASED ON TOTAL COST AFTER ADJUSTMENT FOR SELLING EXPENSES

LD			*KD*	
Sales	LX 2,000 × ₹ 257	₹ 5,14,000	Sales 2,000 × ₹ 300	₹ 6,00,000
	1,000 × 261	2,61,000		
	LY 6,000 × 180	10,80,000		
Total Sales		18,55,000	Total Costs [(6,90,000 – (4 × 2000)]	(6,82,000)
Less: Costs as above		(12,34,000)		
Profit		6,21,000	Loss	(82,000)

Total profit to the company = ₹ 6,21,000 – 82,000 = ₹ 5,39,000

@ ₹ 261 – ₹ 4, i.e., selling expenses not incurred in case of sale to KD.

(iii) TRANSFER PRICE BASED ON MARGINAL COST AFTER ADJUSTMENT FOR SELLING EXPENSES

LD			*KD*	
Sales	LX 2,000 × ₹ 122 ₹	2,44,000	Sales KX 2,000 × ₹ 300	₹ 6,00,000
	1,000 × ₹ 261	2,61,000		
	LY 6,000 × ₹ 180	10,80,000		
		15,85,000	*Less* Variable Cost:	
Less: Total Costs as above		(12,34,000)	2,000 × (122 + 30 + 4)	(3,12,000)
Profit		3,51,000	Fixed	(1,00,000)
			Total Cost	(4,12,000)
			Profit	1,88,000

Total Profit for the company = ₹ 3,51,000 + 1,88,000 = ₹ 5,39,000

(iv) MANUFACTURE OF LX BY USING OVERTIME AND TRANSFER PRICE BASED ON ADJUSTED MARGINAL COST

LD			*KD*	
Sales	LX		Sales 2,000 × ₹ 300	₹ 6,00,000
	2,000 × (₹ 126 + 30 – 4)	₹ 3,04,000		
	3,000 × ₹ 261	7,83,000		
	LY = 6,000 × ₹ 180	10,80,000		
Total Sales		21,67,000		
Variable Costs:			*Variable Cost:*	
	LX – 2,000 × ₹ 152	3,04,000	2,000 × ₹ (1 52 + 30 + 4)	3,72,000
	3,000 × 126	3,78,000		
	LY– 6,000 × ₹ 88	5,28,000		
		12,10,000		
Fixed Costs		3,36,000	Fixed Costs	1,00,000
Total Cost		15,46,000	Total	4,72,000
Profit		6,21,000	Profit	1,28,000

Total Profit for the company = ₹ 6,21,000 + 1,28,000 = ₹ 7,49,000

* For this output material required is 7,800 T, whereas 8,000 T is available from local supplier. Therefore, it should be purchased through Division B locally.

PROBLEM 11

CAS Ltd. is organised on decentralised lines, with each manufacturing division operating as a separate profit centre. Each division manager has full authority to decide on sale of the division's output to outsiders and to other divisions.

Division C has always purchased its requirements of a component from Division A. But when informed that Division A was increasing its selling price to ₹ 150, the manager of Division C decided to look at outside suppliers.

Division C can buy the component from an outside supplier for ₹ 135. But Division A refuses to lower its price in view of its need to maintain its return on the investment.

The top management has the following information :

C's annual purchase of the component	1,000 units
A's variable costs per unit	₹ 120
A's fixed cost per unit	₹ 20

Required:

(i) Will the company as a whole benefit, if Division C bought the component at ₹ 135 from an outside supplier?

(ii) If A did not produce the material for C, it could use the facilities for other activities resulting in a cash operating savings of ₹ 18,000. Should C then purchase from outside sources?

(iii) Suppose there is no alternative use of A's facilities and the market price per unit for the component drops by ₹ 20. Should C now buy from outside?

Solution

(i) THE COMPANY AS A WHOLE WILL NOT BENEFIT IF DIVISION C BOUGHT THE COMPONENT FROM AN OUTSIDE SUPPLIER AT ₹ 135/- PER UNIT

	Particulars	₹
A	Purchase cost from outside supplier (*1,000 units × ₹ 135 per unit*)	1,35,000
B	*Less* : Saving in variable cost of division A by reducing Divisions' output (*1,000 units × ₹ 120 per unit*)	(1,20,000)
C	Net Cost (benefit) to the company as a whole	15,000

Advice: *The company as a whole will not benefit, as it will be required to incur an additional cost of ₹ 15,000 if Division C bought the company from outside supplier.*

(ii) THE COMPANY WILL BE BENEFITTED IF C PURCHASED THE COMPONENT FROM A OUTSIDE SUPPLIER AND DIVISION A USES THE FACILITIES FOR OTHER ACTIVITIES

	Particulars	₹	₹
A	Purchase cost from outside supplier (*1,000 units × ₹ 135*)		1,35,000
B	*Less :* Savings in variable cost of Division A for the units purchased by Division C from outside (*1,000 units × ₹ 120 per unit*)	(1,20,000)	
C	*Less:* Cash operating saving of Division A for the use of facilities for other activities	(18,000)	(1,38,000)
D	Net benefit to the company as a whole		(3,000)

Advice: It is advisable that Division C should purchase the component from outside sources as this decision will benefit the company by ₹ 3,000.

(iii) THE COMPANY WILL BE BENEFITTED IF C PURCHASED THE COMPONENT FROM AN OUTSIDE SUPPLIER AND THERE IS NO ALTERNATIVE USE OF DIVISION A'S FACILITIES.

		₹
A	Purchase cost from outside supplier (*1,000 units × ₹ 115*)	1,15,000
B	*Less :* Saving in variable cost of Division A by reducing division's output (*1,000 units × ₹ 120*)	(1,20,000)
C	Net Benefit to the company	(5,000)

Advice: It is advisable that the Division C should buy the component from outside as this decision will benefit the company by ₹ 5,000.

PROBLEM 12

A Company is organised into two divisions. Division *X* produces a component, which is used by division *Y* in making of a final product. The final product is sold for ₹ 540 each. Division *X* has capacity to produce 2,500 units and division *Y* can purchase the entire production. The variable cost of division *X* in manufacturing each component is ₹ 256.50.

Division *X* informed that due to installation of new machines, its depreciation cost had gone up and hence wanted to increase the price of component to be supplied to division *Y* to ₹ 297, however division *Y* can buy the component from out side the market at ₹ 270 each. The variable cost of division *Y* in manufacturing the final product by using the component is ₹ 202.50 (excluding component cost).

Present the statement indicating the position of each Division and the company as whole taking each of the following situations separately:

(i) If there is no alternative use for the production facility of *X*, will the company benefit, if division *Y* buys from out side suppliers at ₹ 270 per component.

(ii) If internal facilities of *X* are not otherwise idle and the alternative use of the facilities will bring an annual cash saving of ₹ 50,625 to division *X*, should division *Y* purchase the component from outside suppliers?

(iii) If there is no alternative use for the production facilities of division *X* and the selling price for the component in the outside market drops by ₹ 20.25, should division *Y* purchase from outside supplier?

(iv) What transfer price would be fixed for the component in each of the above circumstances?

Solution

(i) WHEN COMPONENT IS PURCHASED BY DIVISION *Y* FROM OUTSIDE

	Particulars	₹
	Division Y sales (2500 × 540)	13,50,000
	Less: Cost of Purchase (2500 × 270)	(6,75,000)
	Variable Cost (2500 × 202.50)	(5,06,250)
A	Division Y Contribution	1,68,750
B	Division X Contribution	Nil
C	Total Contribution [A + B]	1,68,750

(b) WHEN COMPONENT IS PURCHASED FROM DIVISION X

	Particulars	₹
	Division *X* Sales (2500 × 297)	7,42,500
	Less: Variable Cost (2500 × 256.50)	(6,41,250)
A	Contribution of Division *X*	1,01,250
	Division *Y* Sales (2500 × 540)	13,50,000
	Less: Variable Costs:	
	Purchase Cost (2500 × 297)	(7,42,500)
	Variable Cost of division *Y* (2500 × 202.50)	(5,06,250)
B	Contribution of Division *Y*	1,01,250
C	Total Contribution [*A* + *B*]	2,02,500

Thus it will be beneficial for the company as whole to buy component from division *X*.

(ii) WHEN THERE IS ALTERNATIVE USE OF DIVISION X WITH GIVEN CASH SAVING

	Particulars	₹
A	Division *X* Contribution from alternative use of facilities	50,625
	Division *Y* Sales (2500 × 540)	13,50,000
	Less: Cost of Purchase (2500 × 270)	(6,75,000)
	Variable Cost (2500 × 202.50)	(5,06,250)
B	Division *Y* contribution	1,68,750
C	Total Contribution [*A* + *B*]	2,19,375

Thus, it is beneficial to buy the component from outside.

(iii) WHEN THERE IS NO ALTERNATIVE USE OF DIVISION X & SELLING PRICE OF COMPONENT REDUCES IN THE MARKET

	Particulars	₹
A.	Division *Y* Sales (2500 × 540)	13,50,000
B.	*Less:* Cost of Purchase (2500 × 249.75)	(6,24,375)
	Variable Cost (2500 × 202.20)	(5,06,250)
C.	Total Contribution [A – B]	2,19,375

It is beneficial to buy component from outside.

(iv) Transfer Price

(a) Where there is no alternative use of capacity of division *X*, then variable cost i.e. ₹ 256.50 per component will be charged.

(b) If facilities of division *X* can be put to alternative use then variable cost ₹ 256.50 + opportunity cost ₹ 20.25 = ₹ 276.75 will be transfer price. But in this case transfer will be profitable.

(c) If market price gets reduced to ₹ 249.75 and there is no alternative use of facilities of Division *X* the variable cost ₹ 256.50 per component should be charged. But in this case transfer will be profitable.

PROBLEM 13

Division A of CAS Ltd. a profit centre which produces three products *X*, *Y* and *Z*.

Each product has an external market.

Products	*X* ₹	*Y* ₹	*Z* ₹
External market price per unit	48	46	40
Variable cost of production in division A	33	24	28
Labour hours required per unit in division A	3	4	2

Product *Y* can be transferred to Division B, but the maximum quantity that might be required for transfer is 300 units of *Y*.

The maximum external sales are:

X 800 units Y 500 units Z 300 units

Instead of receiving transfers of product *Y* from Division A, Division B could buy similar product in the open market at a sightly cheaper price of ₹ 45 per unit.

What should the transfer price be for each unit for 300 units of *Y*, if the total labour hours available in Division A are:

(a) 3,800 hours (b) 5,600 hours

Solution

(a) **If only 3,800 hours are available in Division A (if no Internal Transfer)**

300 units of *Z* (maximum), which will take*	600 hrs.
500 units of *Y* (maximum), which will take	2,000 hrs.
400 units of *X* to use remaining hrs.	1,200 hrs.
	3,800 hrs.

***Note:** Labour hours required per unit are given in the question. If 300 units of *Y* are to be transferred to '*B*' division, then 1,200 hours will have to be used for production of *Y* instead of *X*. It means Division A will sacrifice production of 400 units of *X*, which are yielding ₹ 5 per hr. Given above is the optimum mix for Division A for 3,800 hrs. If 300 units of *Y* are to be transferred to '*B*' division with time constraint of 3,800 hours, then additional 300 units of *Y* will have to be produced sacrificing the production of 400 units of *X* which is yielding contribution.

Transfer price

	₹
(i) Variable cost of Y	24.00
Opportunity cost	
(ii) Contribution relating to 'X' forgone for producing additional units of Y (4 hrs × ₹ 5*)	20.00
	44.00

*Y takes 4 hours and in each hour production of X would have generated contribution of ₹ 5.

(b) **If 5,600 hours are available**

Maximum time required to meet external sales *(Refer to Working note 1)*	5,000 hrs.
Hours now available	5,600 hrs.

(i) It means 600 hrs can be easily used for the production of Y and transfer price will be variable cost only i.e. (600 hrs. 4 hrs) × ₹ 24 ₹ 3,600

Note: Y takes 4 hours per unit

(ii) For producing additional 150 units, production of X will be disturbed.

Variable costs		
(i) 150 units of X @ ₹ 24	₹ 3,600	
Opportunity cost		
(ii) Contribution of 'X' units		
forgone (600 hrs. × ₹ 5)	₹ 3,000*	6,600
Total Price for 300 units		10,200

Average Transfer Price should be ₹ 34 per unit (i.e. ₹ 10, 200/300)

*Contribution per hr. of X forgone.

Working Notes:

(i) *Hours required to meet maximum demand:*

External sales	*Hours/ unit*	*Total Hrs.*
(i)	(ii)	(iii) = (i) × (ii)
X 800 units	3	2,400
Y 500 units	4	2,000
Z 300 units	2	600
	Total	5,000

(ii) *Contribution per unit:*

Product	X	Y	Z
	₹	₹	₹
A. Selling price	48	46	40
B. *Less* : Variable Cost	33	24	28
C. Contribution per unit: [A – B]	15	22	12
D. Labour hours required per unit	3	4	2
E. Contribution per hour (₹): [C/D]	5	5.5	6
Ranking	III	II	I

12 Activity Based Costing

Learning Objectives

After studying this chapter, you should be able to understand:

- Meaning of Activity Based Costing
- Need for Activity based costing
- Areas in which ABC is used for decision making
- How does ABC support Corporate Strategy?
- ABC: A Decision Making Tool
- Features of the Service organisations which may create problems for the application of Activity Based Costing
- ABC System installation and operation
- Manufacturing Cost Hierarchy
- Terms used in Activity Based Costing
- Practical Steps in Activity Based Costing Approach
- Examples of Activities, Cost Drivers and Cost Driver Rates
- Traditional Approach
- Distinction between Traditional Approach and Activity Based Costing Approach
- Activity Based Cost Management (ABM)
- Activity Based Budgeting (ABB)

1.0 MEANING OF ACTIVITY BASED COSTING

Activity Based Costing (ABC) is a technique of charging overheads to cost objects (i.e., products, services, jobs, customers etc.) on the basis of benefits received from various indirect activities (i.e. ordering, setting up etc. Under ABC Approach overheads are first calculated separately for each activity and then are charged to various cost objects on the basis of activities consumed by these cost objects.

According to Cooper and Kalpan, "ABC systems calculate the costs of individual activities and assign costs to cost objects such as products and services on the basis of activities undertaken to produce each product *or* service."

CIMA, London, defines activity based costing as "*Cost attribution to cost units on the basis of benefits received from indirect activities, i.e., ordering, setting up, assuring quality etc.*"

Note: Activity based costing is not an alternative to job costing *or* process costing.

ABC is an accounting methodology that assigns costs to activities rather than products and services. It enables resources and overhead costs to be more accurately assigned to products and services that consume them when compared to traditional methods where either labour or machine hours considered as absorption basis over cost centres. In order to correctly associate costs with products and services, ABC assigns cost to activities based on their resources. It then assigns cost to 'Cost objects', such as products and customers, based on their use of activities. ABC can track the flow of activities in organization by creating a link between the activity and the cost objects.

Under activity based costing costs are accumulated for each activity as a separate cost object. The collected costs are applied to products based on the benefits received from various activities. The final product cost are built up from the costs of the specific activities undergone in the first stage the activity driven overhead cost is charged to activity based cost pools and in the second stage cost driver based rates are derived to charge cost to product lines. The cost driver rates are based on activities.

Factors contributing to the development of ABC System include:

1. Growing overhead costs because of increasingly automated production. It is said that twenty years ago rate of 200 percent to 300 percent was normal for overhead rates, now 500 to 800 percent is not uncommon.
2. Increasing market competition which necessitated more accurate product costs.
3. Increasing product diversity to secure economies of scope and increased market share

2.0 NEED FOR ACTIVITY BASED COSTING

ABC is particularly needed by organisations for product costing where:

- Production overheads are high in relation to direct costs.
- There is a great diversity in the product range.
- Products use very different amount of the overhead resources.
- Consumption of overhead resources is not primarily driven by volume

3.0 AREAS IN WHICH ABC IS USED FOR DECISION MAKING

The areas in which Activity Based Information is used for decision making are as follows:

1. Pricing of Products
2. Design and Development of New Products
3. Market Segmentation ana Distribution Channels
4. Make-or-buy decisions and outsourcing
5. Transfer Pricing
6. Plant Closed Down Decisions
7. Evaluation of offshore production
8. Capital Investment decisions
9. Product line profitability

4.0 HOW DOES ABC SUPPORT CORPORATE STRATEGY?

ABC supports corporate strategy in many ways such as:

1. ABC system can effectively support the management by furnishing data, at the operational level and strategic level. Accurate product costing will help the management to compare the profits of various customers, product lines and to decide on price strategy etc.
2. It can also encourage management to redesign the products.
3. It can change the method of evaluation of new process technologies, to reduce setup times, rationalization of plant lay out in order to reduce or lower material handling cost, improve quality etc.
4. It will report on the resource spending.
5. ABC analysis helps managers' focus their attention and energy on improving activities and the actions allow the insights from ABC to be translated into increased profits.
6. Accurate information on product costs enables better decisions to be made on pricing, marketing, product design and product mix.
7. Performance base accurate feedback can be provided to cost centre managers.

5.0 ABC: A DECISION MAKING TOOL

ABC is a useful management decision-making tool for many managerial decisions. ABC is useful in analyzing specific segments of an organization. It might include a market line, a group of products (even a single product), a customer, or an employee. The ABC is implemented in following decisions:

1. ABC is a complement to Total Quality Management (TQM). It provides quantitative data that can track the financial impact of improvements implemented as part of the TQM initiative. Amoco Performance Products, Transparent Container Co. and Fellowes Manufacturing Co. are a few companies that have utilized the ABC/TQM modeling concept to improve performance and profitability.
2. ABC helps the Wholesale distributors in the decision-making process. The expansion of line offerings has brought about difficult decisions for the distributor.
3. ABC facilitates facility and resource expansion decision. Often the basis for relocation or opening of a new distribution center is based on cost associations. Reduction in freight or other logistics costs can offset the expense of the new facility, staff or equipment. When the numbers used are enterprise-based, the return might not develop as expected. The ABC model can identify the specific cost elements being targeted, providing a much clearer picture from which management can act.
4. ABC facilitates decision support for human resources. Where activity, and therefore cost, can be associated to an individual, new levels of financial performance can be determined. This might be appropriate in cases of branch management or sales. Adding or deleting resource slots can be determined based on costs of activities as well. The added data provided through ABC can present a number of options, including outsourcing, productivity improvements through automation, and a determination of employee/revenue ratios.

In summary, activity-based costing is a management decision-making tool. It provides financial support data structured in a fashion fundamentally different from accounting data provided in the general ledger. By associating cost to the activity, a clear relationship can be established between sources of activity demand and the related costs. This association can benefit the distributor in determining where costs are being incurred, what is initiating the costs and where to apply efforts to curb inflationary costs. This can be of particular value in tracking new products or customers. It can also provide tracking of logistics costs, one of the fastest growing areas of expense to the distribution operation.

6.0 FEATURES OF THE SERVICE ORGANISATIONS WHICH MAY CREATE PROBLEMS FOR THE APPLICATION OF ACTIVITY-BASED COSTING

The following may create problem for adoption of ABC system in service organisation:

1. Facility sustaining costs (such as property, rents etc.) represent a significant portion of total costs and may only be avoidable if the organisation ceases business. It may be impossible to establish appropriate cost drivers.
2. It is often difficult to define products where they are of intangible nature. Cost objects can therefore be difficult to specify.
3. Many service organisations have not previously had a costing system and much of the information required to set up a ABC system will be non-existent. Therefore introduction of ABC may be expensive.

7.0 ABC SYSTEM INSTALLATION AND OPERATION

1. **Motives**	The motives for pursuing an ABC implementation, or at least of investigating its feasibility, must be established at the outset. Most commonly these will be: 1. **To Improve Product Costing** where a belief exists that existing methods undercost some products and overcost other; or 2. **To Identify Non-Value -Adding Activities** in the production process which might be a suitable focus for attention or elimination.

	In practice, the former is the most quoted goal, even though the latter may be more appropriate. This is especially so for firms which are highly labour intensive and which do not have a great diversity of products in their range, and where allocation of overhead based on direct labour hours may already function efficiently.
2. Practical Stages	1. **Staff Training** to secure the co-operation of the staff by educating them about the benefits and working of the ABC system. 2. **Process Specification** to identify different stages of the production process by interviewing the key numbers of personnel. 3. **Activity Definition** to identify Material Activities for which costs can be accumulated and ascertained. 4. **Activity Driver Selection** to select appropriate Activity Cost Driver which may be used to assign activity cost to cost objects. 5. **Assignment of Cost** Activity Cost Driver Rates are used to assign activity costs to cost objects on the basis of activities consumed.

8.0 MANUFACTURING COST HIERARCHY

Activities basically fall into four different categories, known as the manufacturing cost hierarchy. These categories are generally accepted today but were first identified by Cooper (1990). The categories of activities help to determine the type of activity cost driver required. The four categories of activities are as follows:

Category	Example
1. **Unit Level Activities** [i.e. Activities relating to no. of units produced]	(i) Use of Indirect Materials (ii) Inspection or Testing of every item produced or say every 100th item produced (iii) Indirect Consumables
2. **Batch Level Activities** [i.e. Activities relating to No. of Batches of units produced]	(i) Material Ordering (ii) Machine Set up Costs (iii) Inspection of Products-like first item of every batch
3. **Product Level Activities** [i.e. Activities relating to a Particular Product]	(i) Designing the Product (ii) Producing Parts to a certain specification (iii) Advertising Costs, if advertisement is for individual products
4. **Facility Level Activities** [i.e. Activities relating to organisation as a whole and not to any particular product]	(i) Maintenance of buildings (ii) Plant Security (iii) Production Manager's Salaries (iv) Advertising Campaigns promoting the company as a whole

Notes:

1. ABC will not improve the Overhead Analysis greatly if an organisation's costs are mainly made up of the first and last categories since the first and last categories above are the same as those in traditional absorption costing.
2. ABC analysis will provide a different and more accurate analysis if the organisation's costs fall mainly in the second and third categories.

9.0 TERMS USED IN ACTIVITY BASED COSTING

Activity	An activity may be defined as a particular task *or* unit of work with a specific purpose. *For Example,* placing of a purchase order, setting up of a machine, after sales service, etc.
Cost Object	It is an item for which cost measurement is required. *For example,* a product, a service, a job *or* a customer etc.
Cost Driver	It is a factor that influences the cost of an activity. It is a factor whose change causes a change in the total cost of a related cost object. Cost driver is of two types–Resource Cost Driver and Activity Cost Driver. (*i*) **Resource Cost Driver** — It is a measure of the quantity of resource consumed by an activity. *For example,* number of purchase orders placed will influence the cost of purchasing the materials. Similarly, the number of times machines are set up will influence the cost of setting up of machines. Resource cost driver is used to assign the cost of a resource to an activity *or* cost pool. (*ii*) **Activity Cost Driver** — It is a measure of the frequency and intensity of demand placed on the activities by cost objects. It is used to assign activity costs to cost objects consuming the activity.

9.1 Examples of Cost Drivers for Various Business Activities

Business Activities	Cost Drivers
1. **Purchase of Materials**	— Number of orders placed. — Number of receipts of materials. — Number of inspections.
2. **Setting up of Machines**	— Number of machine set-ups. — Number of machine hours.
3. **Customer Service**	— Number of products serviced. — Number of service calls. — Number of hours spent on servicing.
4. **Research & Development**	— Number of research projects — Number of personnel Hours on a project — Technical Complexities of project

10.0 PRACTICAL STEPS IN ACTIVITY BASED COSTING APPROACH

Practical Steps involved in Activity Based Costing Approach

Step 1 → *Identify Significant Activities*

An activity is considered to be significant when the total cost involved in the activity is significant enough to justify to give an activity a separate treatment.

***Example** — Ordering of materials, Receiving and inspection of deliveries, Production set-up, Shelf stocking, Customer support,*

Step 2 → *Calculate the Total Cost of Each Activity (i.e. Cost Pool)*

***Example** — Total cost of ordering, Total cost of receiving deliveries, Total cost of Production set-up, Total cost of shelf stocking, Total cost of customer support.*

Step 3 → *Determine the Appropriate Activity Cost Drivers for each Activity*

Cost driver is a factor that influences the cost of an activity.

Example *— No. of orders, No. of deliveries, No. of production set-ups, No. of hours of shelf-stocking per store delivery, No. of items sold.*

Step 4 → *Calculate the Activity Cost Driver Rate as follows:*

$$\text{Activity Cost Driver Rate} = \frac{\text{Total Cost of an Activity}}{\text{Activity Cost Driver Volume}}$$

Example *— Total Cost of Ordering ₹ 1,00,000, No. of Orders 1000*

$$\text{Cost per Purchase Order} = \frac{1,00,000}{1000} = ₹\ 100 \text{ per purchase order}$$

Step 5 → *Charge Activity Cost to end products, jobs and processes as follows:*

Activity Cost charged to end product

= Activity consumed × Activity Cost Driver Rate

Example *— No. of Purchase Orders for Product A and Product B are 10 and 20. Activity Cost Driver Rate is ₹ 100 per purchase order.*

Ordering cost charged to Product A = 10 × ₹ 100 = ₹ 1,000
Ordering cost charged to Product B = 20 × ₹ 100 = ₹ 2,000

11.0 EXAMPLES OF ACTIVITIES, COST DRIVERS AND COST DRIVER RATES

Activity	Cost Driver	Cost Driver Rate
1. Ordering	No. of Purchase Orders placed	= Total Ordering Costs for Purchases / No. of Purchase Orders Placed
2. Receiving	No. of Receipts of Materials	= Total Receiving Costs / No. of Receipts of Materials
3. Inspection	No. of Inspections of Materials	= Total Inspection Costs / No. of Inspections of Materials
4. Engineering	No. of Production Orders or No. of Engineering Hours	= Total Engineering Costs / No. of Production orders or No. of Engineering Hours
5. Setting up of Machines	No. of Production Runs or No. of Machine Set-ups or No. of Set-up Hours	= Total Set-up Costs / No. of Production Runs or No. of Machine set-ups or No. of set-up hours
6. Quality Control	No. of Production Runs	= Total Quality Control Costs / No. of Production Runs
7. Testing and Inspection	No. of Hours of Testing and Inspection	= Total Testing and Inspection Costs / No. of Hours of Testing and Inspection
8. Material Handling and Dispatch	No. of Orders Executed	= Total Material Handling and Dispatch Costs / No. of Orders Executed
9. Shelf Stocking	No. of hours of Shelf Stocking Time	= Total Shelf Stocking Costs / No. of Hours of Shelf Stocking Time

Activity	Cost Driver	Cost Driver Rate
10. Customer visit	No. of Customer Visits	$= \frac{\text{Total Customer Visit Costs}}{\text{No. of Customer Visits}}$
11. Customer Sales Order Processing	No. of Sales Order executed	$= \frac{\text{Total Sales Order Processing Costs}}{\text{No. of Sales Orders Executed}}$
12. Packing	No. of Sales Deliveries	$= \frac{\text{Total Packing Costs}}{\text{No. of Sales Deliveries}}$
13. Reworking	No. of Rework Units	$= \frac{\text{Total Re-work Costs}}{\text{No. of Re-work Units}}$
14. Delivery of goods to Customers	No. of Deliveries and No. of Kilometres travelled per delivery	$= \frac{\text{Total Cost of Delivery}}{\text{No. of Deliveries} \times \text{No. of kilometeries travelled per delivery}}$
15. Expedited Deliveries	No. of Expedited Deliveries	$= \frac{\text{Total Cost of Expedited Deliveries}}{\text{No. of Expedited Deliveries}}$

12.0 TRADITIONAL APPROACH

Under traditional approach, overheads are first allocated and apportioned to various production departments and service departments, then overheads of service departments are re-apportioned to production departments and then overheads of production departments are charged to the end products on some suitable basis (like machine hours, labour hours, direct wages etc.)

Thus, all overheads are absorbed (or recovered) on the basis of volume measures like Direct Labour Hours. Machine Hours under the assumption that end products consume resources in proportion to volume of production. Hence the traditional overhead absorption system over cost high volume products and under cost low volume products.

Practical Example:

		Product 'X'	*Product 'Y'*
A.	Annual Output (Units)	10,000	20,000
B.	Total Machine Hours	20,000	10,000
	Total Annual Overheads ₹ 3,00,000		

$$\text{Overhead Absorption Rate} = \frac{\text{Total Overheads}}{\text{Total Machine Hours}} = \frac{3,00,000}{30,000} = ₹\ 10 \text{ per hour}$$

C.	Overhead Cost @ ₹ 10 per machine hour	₹ 2,00,000	₹ 1,00,000
D.	Overhead Cost per unit (C/A)	₹ 20	₹ 5

13.0 DISTINCTION BETWEEN TRADITIONAL APPROACH AND ACTIVITY BASED COSTING APPROACH

Traditional Approach differs from Activity Based Costing Approach in the following respects:

Basis of Distinction	Traditional Approach	Activity Based Costing (ABC) Approach
1. Assumption	It is based on the assumption that end products consume resources in proportion to the **volume of production.**	It is based on the assumption that end products consume resources in proportion to the **volume of activities.**

Basis of Distinction	Traditional Approach	Activity Based Costing (ABC) Approach
2. Meaning	Overheads are first allocated and apportioned to various production departments and service departments, then overheads of service departments are re-apportioned to production departments and then overheads of production departments are charged to the end products on some suitable basis (like machine hours, labour hours, direct wages etc.)	Activity Based Costing is a technique of charging overheads to cost objects (*i.e.*, products, services, jobs, customers etc.) under which overheads are first calculated separately for each activity and then are charged to various cost objects on the basis of activities consumed by these cost objects.
3. Overheads Calculation	Overheads are calculated for each functional cost centres (Production and Service)	Overheads are calculated for each activity like Ordering, Setting up.
4. Basis of Overheads Absorption	Overheads are absorbed on the basis of volume measures like Direct Labour Hours, Machine Hours	Overheads are absorbed on the basis of activities consumed.
5. Accuracy	It is **not so accurate** as ABC.	It is an **accurate system** of costing because the distribution of overheads is based on cause and effect relationship.
6. Objective/ Subjective	It is **subjective** approach because it uses arbitrary bases for apportionment of overheads.	It is an **objective** approach because it uses activities as bases for distribution of overheads.
7. Control	It **does not facilitate** the control over those activities which cause fixed overheads.	It **facilitates** the control over those activities which cause fixed overheads.
8. Identification of Unnecessary activities	It **does not facilitate** the identification of unnecessary activities.	It **facilitates** the identification of unnecessary activities.
9. Costing system in highly automated plants	The conventional product cost system was in vogue when companies manufactured narrow range of products, overhead costs were relatively small and distortions arising from inappropriate overhead allocations were not significant. It used volume measures like direct labour hours or machine hours for charging overhead costs to products. In the case of a company using highly automated plant, direct labour is a small fraction of cost when compared with overheads (because of higher amount of depreciation). In	Activity Based Costing (ABC) system aims at refining the costing system used in automated plants in the following manner: 1. ABC systems trace more costs as direct costs. 2. ABC systems create homogeneous cost pools linked to different activities. 3. For each activity cost pool, ABC systems seek a cost allocation base that has a cause-and-effect relationship with costs in the cost pool.

	case where such a company is multi product, overheads which are large in proportion to direct labour are influenced by number of set up, inspection, number of purchases etc. In these circumstances, the volume based method of recovery of overheads is no longer appropriate and such a measure will report inaccurate product costs. Hence, the traditional system of costing was found to overcost high volume products and undercost low volume products.	

Illustration 1. The following and Product Nova Shaft's data for next year budget:

Activity	*Cost Driver*	*Cost Driver volume/year*	*Cost pool*
Purchasing	Purchase order	1,500	₹ 75,000
Setting	Batches produced	2,800	₹ 1,12,000
Materials handling	Materials movements	8,000	₹ 96,000
Inspection	Batches produced	2,800	₹ 70,000
Machining costs	Machine hours	50,000	₹ 1,50,000

Purchase Orders	25	Materials movements per batch	6
Output	15,000 units	Machine hours per unit	0.1
Production batch size	100 units		

Required:

(i) Calculate the budgeted overhead cost using absorption costing (absorb overhead using machine hours).
(ii) Calculate the budgeted overhead costs using activity based costing principles.
(iii) How can the company reduce the ABC for Product Nova Shaft?

Solution:

(i) Computation of Budgeted Overheads Cost using Absorption Costing

Budgeted Overheads – (₹ 75,000 + ₹ 96,000 + ₹ 1,12,000 + ₹ 70,000 + ₹ 1,50,000)
= ₹ 5,03,000

Budgeted Absorption Cost/Machine Hours = ₹ 5,03,000/50,000 = ₹ 10.06

Budgeted Machining Hours for Product Nova Shaft = 1,500

Budgeted Absorbed Overheads = 1,500 × ₹ 10.06 = ₹ 10.06 = ₹ 15,090.

(ii) Computation of the Budgeted Overheads Using Activity Based Costing

STEP 1 COMPUTE COST DRIVER COST = COST POOL/COST DRIVER VOLUME

Activity	*Cost Driver*	*Cost Pool (a)*	*Cost Driver Volume/year (b)*	*Cost Driver Rate (a)/(b)*
Purchasing	Purchase orders	₹ 75,000	1,500	₹ 50/purchase order
Setting	batches produced	₹ 112,000	2,800	₹ 40/batch
Materials handling	Material movements	₹ 96,000	8,000	₹ 12/movement
Inspection	Batches produced	₹ 70,000	2,800	₹ 25/batch
Machining	Machine hours	₹ 150,000	50,000	₹ 3/machine hour

STEP 2 COMPUTE THE VOLUME OF COST DRIVERS CONSUMED BY PRODUCT NOVA SHAFT

Purchase orders (given) = 25
Batches = 15,000 units/100 = 150
Materials movement = 150 batches × 6 = 900
Machine hours = 15,000 units × 0.1 = 1,500

STEP 3 COMPUTE THE BUDGETED OVERHEADS COST USING ACTIVITY BASED COSTING

Activity	*Cost Driver*	*Cost Driver Rate (₹)*	*Activity Based Overheads*	
Purchasing	Purchase orders	50	25 order × ₹ 50 = ₹	1,250
Setting	Batches produced	40	150 batches × ₹ 40 = ₹	6,000
Material handling	Material Movements	12	900 movement × ₹ 12 = ₹	10,800
Inspection	Batches produced	25	150 batches × ₹ 25 = ₹	3,750
Machining	Machine hours	3	1,500 hours × ₹ 3 = ₹	4,500
			₹	26,300

(iii) Ways in which the company can reduce the ABC for product Nova Shaft:

1. Reduce the number of batches by increasing the batch size which will then reduce the setting up overhead, material handling and inspection cost.
2. Reduce the number of purchase orders
3. Innovate ways of speeding up production so that the machining hours are reduced.

Illustration 2. *PCT* Ltd. produces three products X, Y and Z for which the standard cost and quantities per unit are as follows:

Particulars	*Products* X	Y	Z
Output (units)	10,000	20,000	30,000
Direct Material Cost per unit	₹ 30	₹ 20	₹ 10
Direct Labour Wages per unit (@ ₹ 20)	₹ 20	₹ 40	₹ 60
Machine Hours per unit	3	2	1
No. of Purchase Requisitions	1000	200	300
No. of Machine Set-ups	150	100	50
Production Overheads:			
Department *P* – ₹ 7,00,000			
Q – ₹ 11,00,000			

Department *P* is labour intensive and *Q* is machine intensive.
Total labour hours in Dept. *P* = 1,40,000; Total machine hours in Dept. *Q* = 1,00,000
Production overheads by activity:

Receiving and inspection	₹ 6,00,000
Production scheduling/set up	₹ 12,00,000

Required: Prepare Statement of Cost per unit under traditional absorption costing and activity based costing approaches. Also compare the result of the two methods and give your comments.

Solution:

TRADITIONAL ABSORPTION COSTING METHOD

Step 1 → Overhead Absorption Rate : $\dfrac{\text{Overheads of the department}}{\text{Hours}}$

Department $P = \dfrac{7{,}00{,}000}{1{,}40{,}000 \text{ labour hours}}$ = ₹ 5 per labour hour.

Department $Q = \dfrac{11{,}00{,}000}{1{,}00{,}000 \text{ machine hours}}$ = ₹ 11 per machine hour.

STEP 2 STATEMENT OF COST USING TRADITIONAL METHOD

Particulars	Cost per unit X ₹	Y ₹	Z ₹
Direct Materials	30	20	10
Direct Wages	20	40	60
Overheads – Dept. P			
X – 1 hr @ ₹ 5	5		
Y – 2 hrs. @ ₹ 5		10	
Z – 3 hrs @ ₹ 5			15
– Dept. Q			
X – 3 hrs @ ₹ 11	33		
Y – 2 hrs. @ ₹ 11		22	
Z – 1 hr. @ ₹ 11			11
Total Cost per unit	88	92	96

ABC METHOD

Step 1→ Cost Driver Rates = $\frac{\text{Overhead Cost of the activity}}{\text{Cost drivers}}$

Receiving and inspection = $\frac{6,00,000}{1500 \text{ batches}}$ = ₹ 400 per batch

Scheduling and set-up = $\frac{12,00,000}{300 \text{ batches}}$ = ₹ 4,000 per set-up.

STEP 2 CALCULATION OF OVERHEAD USING ABC

Particulars	X		Y		Z	
	Receiving	*Set-up*	*Receiving*	*Set-up*	*Receiving*	*Set-up*
A. *Activity Cost Driver Rate*	*400*	*4000*	*400*	*4000*	*400*	*4000*
B. *Activity Consumed*	*1000*	*150*	*200*	*100*	*300*	*50*
C. *Activity Cost assigned (A × B)*	*4,00,000*	*6,00,000*	*80,000*	*4,00,000*	*1,20,000*	*2,00,000*
D. *No. of units*	*10,000*	*10,000*	*20,000*	*20,000*	*30,000*	*30,000*
E. *Per unit (C/D)*	*40*	*60*	*4*	*20*	*4*	*6.67*

STEP 3 STATEMENT OF COST USING ABC

Particulars	Cost per unit X ₹	Y ₹	Z ₹
Direct Materials cost per unit	30	20	10
Direct Wages per unit	20	40	60
Overhead per unit – Receiving	40	4	4
– Set-up	60	20	6.67
Total Cost per unit	150	84	80.67

Comparison: Under traditional method, product Z appears quite costly as compared to activity based costing, because product Z consumers relatively more direct labour hours. On the other hand, product X shows higher cost under activity based costing than traditional method. As the *ABC* approach is considered more logical, it may be presumed that results shown by *ABC* are more accurate. If selling prices are fixed on the basis of cost, product Z would be priced higher under traditional costing and product X would be priced lower. This will result in loss of sales of product Z and loss per unit on product X, leading to a loss to the company.

Illustration 3. *ABCD* Co. Ltd. produces and sells four products *A, B, C* and *D*. These products are similar and usually in production runs of 10 units and sold in a batch of 5 units. The production details of these products are as follows:

Product	*A*	*B*	*C*	*D*
Production (Units)	100	110	120	150
Cost per unit:				
Direct material (₹)	30	40	35	45
Direct labour (₹)	25	30	30	40
Machine hour (per unit)	5	4	3	4

The production overheads during the period are as follows:

Factory works expenses	₹ 19,000
Stores receiving costs	₹ 19,800
Machine set-up costs	₹ 12,000
Cost relating to quality control	₹ 4,800
Material handling and dispatch	₹ 9,000

The cost drivers of these overheads are detailed below:

Cost	*Cost drivers*
Factory works expenses	Machine hours
Stores receiving costs	Requisitions raised
Machine set-up costs	No. of production runs
Cost relating to quality control	No. of production runs
Material handling and dispatch	No. of orders executed

The number of requisitions raised on the stores was 25 for each product and number of orders executed was 96, each order was in a batch of 5 units.

Required:

(*i*) Total Cost of each product assuming the absorption of overheads on machine hour basis;

(*ii*) Total Cost of each product assuming the absorption of overheads by using activity base costing; and

(*iii*) Show the differences between (*i*) and (*ii*) and comment.

Solution:

(*i*) **Absorption of Overheads on Machine Hour basis**

Step 1 → Overhead Rate = $\frac{\text{Total Overhead Cost}}{\text{Total Machine Hours}} = \frac{64,600}{1,900}$ = ₹ 34 per unit

STEP 2 TOTAL COST USING ABSORPTION OF OVERHEADS ON MACHINE HOUR RATE BASIS

Particulars	*A*	*B*	*C*	*D*	*Total*
A. Output (units)	100	110	120	150	480
B. Direct material (₹)	30	40	35	45	150
C. Direct labour (₹)	25	30	30	40	125
D. Machine hrs	5	4	3	4	
E. Overheads @ ₹ 34 per machine hr [D × ₹ 34]	170	136	102	136	544
F. Total Cost per unit (₹) [B + C + E]	225	206	167	221	819
G. Total Cost (₹) (A × F)	22,500	22,660	20,040	33,150	98,350

(*ii*) **Absorption of Overheads using Activity Base Costing**

Step 1→ Calculation of Cost Driver Rate

$$\text{Factory works expenses} = \frac{\text{Total expenses}}{\text{Total No. of machine Hrs}} = \frac{19{,}000}{1900} = ₹\ 10$$

$$\text{Stores receiving cost} = \frac{\text{Stores receiving cost}}{\text{No. of Stores requisition}} = \frac{19{,}800}{100} = ₹\ 198$$

$$\text{Machine setup costs} = \frac{\text{Machine set-up cost}}{\text{No. of production runs}} = \frac{12{,}000}{48} = ₹\ 250$$

$$\text{Costs relating to quality control} = \frac{\text{Cost to QC}}{\text{No. of production runs}} = \frac{4{,}800}{48} = ₹\ 100$$

$$\text{Expense relating of material} = \frac{\text{Material handling \& dispatch cost}}{\text{No. of orders executed}} = \frac{9{,}000}{96} = ₹\ 93.75$$

STEP 2 CALCULATION OF TOTAL OVERHEADS OF EACH PRODUCT USING ACTIVITY BASED COSTING

Particulars	*A*	*B*	*C*	*D*	*Total*
Output (Units)	100	110	120	150	480
No. of machine hours	500	440	360	600	1,900
No. of production runs	10	11	12	15	48
No. of stores requisition	25	25	25	25	100
No. of sales orders	20	22	24	30	96
Total factory work exp. @ ₹ 10	5,000	4,400	3,600	6,000	19,000
Total stores receiving cost @ ₹ 198	4,950	4,950	4,950	4,950	19,800
Total machine set up costs	2,500	2,750	3,000	3,750	12,000
Total cost relating to quality control	1,000	1,100	1,200	1,500	4,800
Total material handling & dispatch cost	1,875	2,062.5	2,250	2,812.5	9,000

STEP 3 STATEMENT OF TOTAL COST USING ACTIVITY BASED COSTING

Particulars	*A* Total ₹	*A* Per unit ₹	*B* Total ₹	*B* Per unit ₹	*C* Total ₹	*C* Per unit ₹	*D* Total ₹	*D* Per unit ₹
A. Direct Material	3,000	30.00	4,400	40.00	4,200	35.00	6,750	45.00
B. Direct Labour	2,500	25.00	3,300	30.00	3,600	30.00	6,000	40.00
C. Factory work exp	5,000	50.00	4,400	40.00	3,600	30.00	6,000	40.00
D. Stores receiving cost	4,950	49.50	4,950	45.00	4,950	41.25	4,950	33.00
E. Machine set-up cost	2,500	25.00	2,750	25.00	3,000	25.00	3,750	25.00
F. Cost related to quality control	1,000	10.00	1,100	10.00	1,200	10.00	1,500	10.00
G. Material handling & dispatch cost	1875	18.75	2,062.5	18.75	2,250	18.75	2,812.5	18.75
H. Total cost	20,825	208.25	22,962.50	208.75	22,800	190.00	31,762.50	211.75

(*iii*) **STATEMENT SHOWING DIFFERENCES (IN ₹)**

Particulars	*A*	*B*	*C*	*D*
Total cost under MHR	22,500	22,660	20,040	33,150
Total cost under ABC	20,825	22,962.50	22,800	31,762.50

Why difference: Because A consumes comparatively more of machine hours.

Comment — The use of activity based costing gives different product costs than what were arrived at by utilizing traditional costing. It can be argued that product costs using ABC are more precise as overheads have been identified with specific activities.

Illustration 4. An engine manufacturing company has two production departments: (*i*) Snowmobile engine and (*ii*) Boat engine and two service departments: (*i*) Maintenance and (*ii*) Factory office.

Budgeted cost data and relevant cost are as follows:

Departmental costs:	₹
Snowmobile engine	12,00,000
Boat engine	34,00,000
Factory office	6,00,000
Maintenance	4,80,000
Cost drivers:	
Factory office department:	*No. of employees*
Snowmobile engine department	2,160 employees
Boat engine department	540 employees
Maintenance department	300 employees
	3000 employees
Maintenance department:	*No. of work orders*
Snowmobile engine department	1,140 orders
Boat engine department	380 orders
Factory office department	80 orders
	1600 orders

Required:

(*i*) Compute the cost driver allocation percentage and then use these percentages to allocate the service department costs by using direct method.

(*ii*) Compute the cost driver allocation percentage and then use these percentages to allocate the service department costs by using non-reciprocal method/step method.

Solution:

STEP 1 CALCULATION OF COST DRIVER ALLOCATION PERCENTAGES

Factory office dept.	*Number of employees*	*Per cent used*
Snowmobile engine	2,160	80%
Boat engine	540	20%
Total	2,700	100%
Maintenance dept.	*Number of work orders*	
Snowmobile engine	1,140	75%
Boat engine	380	25%
Charging of	1,520	100%

STEP 2 CHARGING OF SERVICE DEPARTMENT COSTS

Particulars	*Factory office dept.* ₹	*Maintenance dept.* ₹	*Snowmobile engine* ₹	*Boat engine* ₹
Departmental Cost	6,00,000	4,80,000	12,00,000	34,00,000
Allocated Costs (₹):				
Factory Office Dept.	(6,00,000)	—	4,80,000	1,20,000
Maintenance Dept.		(4,80,000)	3,60,000	1,20,000
Total	0	0	20,40,000	36,40,000

STEP 3 CALCULATION OF COST ALLOCATION PERCENTAGES

Factory office dept	Number of employees	Per cent used
Snowmobile engine	2,160	72%
Boat engine	540	18%
Maintenance dept	300	10%
	3,000	100%
Maintenance dept	Work order	Per cent used
Snowmobile engine	1,140	75%
Boat engine	380	25%
	1,520	100%

STEP 4 CHARGING SERVICE DEPARTMENT COSTS

Particulars	Factory office dept. ₹	Maintenance dept. ₹	Snowmobile engine ₹	Boat engine ₹
Departmental costs	6,00,000	4,80,000	12,00,000	34,00,000
(a) Factory office	(6,00,000)	60,000	4,32,000	1,08,000
(c) Maintenance dept.	—	(5,40,000)	4,05,000	1,35,000
Total cost	0	0	20,37,000	36,43,000

Illustration 5. Tulsian Ltd. manufactrures products P, Q and R and provides the following information:

	P	Q	R
Direct Labour Hours Per Unit @ ₹ 20	4	12	8
Direct Material Cost Per Unit @ ₹ 10 Per Unit of Material	90	80	120
Prime Cost (₹)	5,10,000	16,00,000	56,00,000

Currently the company uses Traditional Costing Method and absorbs all Production overheads at the rate of ₹ 7 per machine hour.

The company proposes to use Activity Based Costing system and the activity analysis is as under.

	P	Q	R
Batch Size (Units)	150	500	1,000
Number of Machine Hours Per Batch	1,500	9,000	14,000
Number of Inspections Per Batch	5	4	3
Material Purchase Order Size (Units)	450	400	2,000

The Total Production Overheads are analysed as under:

Machine Set up Costs	20%
Machine Operation Costs	30%
Inspection Costs	40%
Material Procurement Costs	10%

Required:

(i) Calculate the Cost Per Unit of each product using Traditional Method of absorbing all Production Overheads on the basis of machine hours.

(ii) Calculate the Cost Per Unit of each product using Activity Based Costing Principles.

Solution:

(i) **COST PER UNIT USING TRADITIONAL COSTING METHOD**

Particulars	P	Q	R
Direct Labour Cost @ ₹ 20 for 4/ 12/ 8 Hours	80	240	160
Direct Material Cost	90	80	120
Production Overheads @ ₹ 7 for 10 / 18 /14 Hours	70	126	98
Production Cost Per unit	240	446	378

(ii) **COST PER UNIT USING ACTIVITY BASED COSTING SYSTEM**

Particulars	*P*	*Q*	*R*	
Direct Material Cost	2,40,000	12,00,000	32,000	
Direct Labour Cost @ ₹ 20 for 4/ 12/ 8 Hours	2,70,000	4,00,000	24,00,000	
Production Overheads:				
Setup Cost ₹ 11200 per set up (20: 10: 20)	2,24,000	1,12,000	2,24,000	5,60,000
Inspection Cost ₹ 5600 per inspection (100: 40: 60)	5,60,000	2,24,000	3,36,000	11,20,000
Purchase Related Costs ₹ 1000 per purchase (60: 100: 120)	60,000	1,00,000	1,20,000	2,80,000
Machine Operation Costs ₹ 2.10 per hour (3: 9: 28)	63,000	1,89,000	5,88,000	8,40,000
Total Production Cost	14,17,000	22,25,000	37,00,000	28,00,000
Production Units	3,000	5,000	20,000	
Production Cost Per unit	472.33	445	185	

Working Notes:

(i) **COST DRIVER VOLUME**

A	Direct Labour Cost	80	240	160	
B	Direct Material Cost	90	80	120	
C	Prime Cost Per Unit (A + B)	170	320	280	
D	Prime Cost (₹)	5,10,000	16,00,000	56,00,000	
E	Production Units (D / C)	3,000	5,000	20,000	
F	Batch Size (Units)	150	500	1,000	
G	No. of Batches (E / F)	20	10	20	50
H	Number of Machine Hours Per Batch	1,500	9,000	14,000	
J	Total Machine Hours (G x H)	30,000	90,000	2,80,000	4,00,000
K	Number of Inspections Per Batch	5	4	3	
L	Total Inspections (G x K)	100	40	60	200
M	Material Requirements Per unit (Material Cost / ₹ 10)	9	8	12	
N	Total Material Requirements (E x M)	27,000	40,000	2,40,000	
O	Material Purchase Order Size (Units)	450	400	2,000	
P	Total No. of Material Purchase Orders (N / O)	60	100	120	280

(ii) **Total Production Overheads** = Total Machine Hours × Overhead Absorption Rate
= 4,00,000 × ₹ 7 = ₹ 28,00,000

(iii) **COST DRIVER RATES**

Cost Driver Rates A	*Cost Pool* % B	*Overheads* ₹ C	*Cost Driver Volume* D	*Cost Driver Rate* ₹ E = C / D
Set up	20%	5,60,000	50	11,200 per setup
Inspection	40%	11,20,000	200	5,600 per inspection
Purchases	10%	2,80,000	280	1000 per purchase
Machine Hours	30%	8,40,000	4,00,000	2.10 per machine hour

Illustration 6. S.K. Store wants information about the profitability of individual product lines: Soft drinks, Fresh produce and Packaged food. S.K. Store provides the following data for the current year for each product line:

Particulars	*Soft drinks*	*Fresh Produce*	*Packaged food*
No. of Unit Sold	1,50,000	3,00,000	2,00,000
Selling Price per unit	₹ 6.00	₹ 7	₹ 6
Cost of Goods sold per unit	₹ 4.00	₹ 5	₹ 4.50
Number of Purchase Orders placed	360	840	360
Number of Deliveries received	300	2,190	660
Hours of Shelf-Stocking Time	500	4,850	2,400

S.K. Store also provides the following information for the current year

Activity	*Description of activity*	*Total Cost (₹)*	*Cost-allocation base*
Bottles returns	Returning of empty bottles	12,000	Direct tracing to soft drink line
Ordering	Placing of orders for purchases	1,56,000	1,560 purchase orders
Delivery	Physical delivery and receipt of goods	2,52,000	3,150 deliveries
Shelf stocking	Stocking of goods on store shelves and on-going restocking	1,55,000	7,750 hours of shelf-stocking time
Customer support	Assistance provided to customers including checkout	3,25,000	6,50,000 items sold

Required:

(*i*) If S.K. Store currently allocates support costs (all costs other than cost of goods sold) to product lines on the basis of cost of goods sold of each product line. Calculate the operating income and operating income as a % of revenues for each product line.

(*ii*) If S.K. Store allocates support costs (all costs other than cost of goods sold) to product lines using an activity-based costing system, calculate the operating income and operating income as a % of revenues for each product line.

(*iii*) Comment on your answers in requirements (*i*) and (*ii*).

Solution: (*i*) **Traditional Approach**

STEP 1 CALCULATION OF TOTAL SUPPORT COST (OVERHEAD)

	₹
Bottles returns	12,000
Ordering	1,56,000
Delivery	2,52,000
Shelf-stocking	1,55,000
Customer support	3,25,000
Total Support Cost	9,00,000

Step 2 → Total Cost of Goods Sold = ₹ 6,00,000 + ₹ 15,00,000 + ₹ 9,00,000 = ₹ 30,00,000.

Step 3 →Total Support Cost as a % of Cost of Goods Sold = $\frac{9,00,000}{30,00,000} \times 100 = 30\%$

STEP 4 STATEMENT OF OPERATING INCOME AND OPERATING INCOME AS A % OF REVENUES

Particulars	*Soft Drinks*	*Fresh Produce*	*Packaged Foods*	*Total*
A. No. of units sold	1,50,000	3,00,000	2,00,000	
B. Actual Selling Price per unit	₹ 6	₹ 7	₹ 6	
C. Revenues (₹) [A × B]	9,00,000	21,00,000	12,00,000	42,00,000
D. Cost of Goods Sold per unit (₹)	4	5	4.50	
E. *Less:* Cost of Goods Sold (COGS) (₹) [A × D]	6,00,000	15,00,000	9,00,000	30,00,000
F. Gross Margin (₹) [C – E]	3,00,000	6,00,000	3,00,000	12,00,000
G. *Less:* Support Cost (30% of COGS)	1,80,000	4,50,000	2,70,000	9,00,000
H. **Operating Income** [F – G]	1,20,000	1,50,000	30,000	3,00,000
I. **Operating Income as a % of Revenue** $\left(\frac{H}{C} \times 100\right)$	13.33%	7.14%	2.5%	7.14%

(*ii*) **ABC Approach**

STEP 1 CALCULATION OF COST DRIVER RATES

Activity	*Total cost (₹)*	*Cost drivers*	*Cost driver rate (₹)*
1. Ordering	1,56,000	1,560 purchase orders	100 per purchase order
2. Delivery	2,52,000	3,150 deliveries	80 per delivery
3. Shelf-stocking	1,55,000	7,750 hours	20 per stocking hours
4. Customer support	3,25,000	6,50,000 items sold	0.50 per item sold

STEP 2 STATEMENT OF OPERATING INCOME AND OPERATING INCOME AS A % OF REVENUES

Particulars	*Soft Drinks* ₹	*Fresh Produce* ₹	*Packaged Foods* ₹	*Total* ₹
A. No. of units sold	1,50,000	3,00,000	2,00,000	
B. Actual Selling Price per unit	₹ 6	₹ 7	₹ 6	
C. Revenues (₹) [A × B]	9,00,000	21,00,000	12,00,000	42,00,000
D. Cost of Goods Sold per unit (₹)	4	5	4.50	
E. *Less:* Cost of Goods Sold (COGS) (₹) [A×D]	6,00,000	15,00,000	9,00,000	30,00,000
F. Gross Margin [C – E]	3,00,000	6,00,000	3,00,000	12,00,000
G. *Less:* Support Costs:				
(*i*) Bottle Return Costs	12,000	0	0	12,000
(*ii*) Ordering Cost (360 : 840 : 360)	36,000	84,000	36,000	1,56,000
(*iii*) Delivery Cost (300 : 2,190 : 660)	24,000	1,75,200	52,800	2,52,000
(*iv*) Shelf Stocking Cost (500 : 4,850 : 2,400)	10,000	97,000	48,000	1,55,000
(*v*) Customer support cost (1,50,000 : 3,00,000 : 2,00,000)	75,000	1,50,000	1,00,000	3,25,000
	1,57,000	5,06,200	2,36,800	9,00,000
H. Operating Income (F – G)	1,43,000	93,800	63,200	3,00,000
I. Operating Income as % of Revenues	15.89%	4.47%	5.27%	7.14%

Comments : Statements prepared under traditional approach and activity based costing show different results in the form of operating income as a % of revenue. It is generally felt that allocation of support costs under activity based costing is more reliable and accurate than under traditional method. The allocation of delivery cost on the basis of number of deliveries and self stocking cost on the basis of per stocking hour, has caused substantial increase of the those costs for Fresh Produce product line. With the decrease in the share of revised support costs under *ABC* system, the operating income of Soft Drinks and Packaged Foods has increased.

14.0 ACTIVITY BASED COST MANAGEMENT (ABM)

Meaning	**Consortium for Advanced Management International (CAM)** defines ABM as : "A discipline that focuses on the management of activities as the route to improving the value received by the customer and the profit achieved by providing this value. This discipline includes Cost Driver Analysis, Activity Analysis, and Performance Measurement. Activity-Based Management depends on Activity-Based Costing as its major source of information." ABM uses the information gathered through ABC in various analysis designed to yield continuous improvement.
Difference between ABC and ABM	ABC is a supplier of improved cost information and ABM is the user of cost information supplied by ABC in carrying out Cost Driver Analysis, Activity Analysis and Performance Analysis.

Objective	The objective of ABM is to improve the value received by the customer and the profit achieved by providing this value.
Analysis under ABM	
1. Cost Driver Analysis	To identify the casual factors causing an activity to place inefficiently (e.g. Slow Processing of Customer Invoices due to lack of trained staff)
2. Activity Analysis	To identify various activities of an organisation, Activity Centres, Value-Added Activities and Non-Value Added Activities.
3. Performance Analysis	To identify the best ways to measure the performance of factors that are important to organisations in order to stimulate continuous improvement (e.g. No. of Customer Invoices processed per hour as the most appropriate performance measure to monitor timeliness in processing customer invoices.)
Activities under ABM	ABM classifies each activity as Value Added (VA) Activity or Non-Value Added (NVA) Activity:
1. Value-Added Activity	VA is an activity which enhances the value of products and services in the eyes of customers and for which the customer is usually willing to pay. *For example,* Painting a car by a car manufacturer, polishing a furniture by a furniture manufacturer.
2. Non-Value-Added Activity	NVA is an activity which does not enhance the value of products or services in the eyes of customers and for which the customer is not willing to pay. It can adversely affect costs and prices. *For example,* Storage and moving of Raw-materials, Reworking or Repairing of Products, Machine set up.
Business Applications	The goal of the ABM is to make customer needs to be satisfied while making fewer demands for resources. Current research suggests that customers have perceived needs in four areas, all of which must be satisfied simultaneously. The customers require: (i) Lower Costs (ii) Higher Quality (iii) Faster Response Time (iv) Greater Innovation. To satisfy these needs ABM is currently being used for a variety of business applications. Such as:
1. Cost Reduction	ABM helps the organisation to identify those activities where cost reduction is possible. It is particularly useful in identifying and quantifying process waste and providing vehicle for continuous process improvement through continuous cost reduction.
2. Activity Based Budgeting	ABB is a process of planning and controlling the expected activities for the organisation.
3. Business Process re-Engineering	Business process re-engineering involves examining business processes and making substantial changes to how organisation currently operates. ABM is a powerful tool for measuring business performance, determining the cost of business output and is used as a means of identifying opportunities to improve process efficiency and effectiveness. A business process consist of linked set of activities. *For example* purchasing of materials might be considered as business process consist of activities such as receiving a purchase request, identifying supplier, preparing purchase orders, mailing purchase orders and performing

	follow up. The process might be reengineered by sending the production schedule direct to the suppliers and to enter into contractual agreement to deliver materials according to the production schedule. The end result might be permanent reduction or elimination of some activities.
4. Benchmarking	Benchmarking is the process of identifying the yardstick against which the Actual performance of an Activity can be measured. Its objective is to identify the product, service or activity which need to be improved.
5. Performance Measurement	To monitor efficiency and effectiveness of activities performance measures are required. Activity performance measures consist of measures relating to costs, time, quality and innovation. *For example*, now-a days in the globalisation the goal for a company is to produce a quality product at a globally competitive price. Product quality starts with the correct design. The next stages are high quality raw material inputs, quality processing and work, and proper handling and packaging etc. The various performance measures of quality are: *Area* — *Measures* Quality of purchased component — Zero defects Quality of output — % yield Customer awareness — Orders; Number of Complaints
Benefits	1. Provides excellent basis and focus for cost reduction. 2. Provides operational management with a clear view of how to implement an Activity Based budget. 3. Provides of clear understanding of the underlying causes of business processing costs. 4. Provides excellent basis for effectiveness of management decision making. 5. Identifies key process waste elements permit management prioritisation and leverage of key resources.

15.0 ACTIVITY BASED BUDGETING (ABB)

Meaning of Activity Based Budgeting	Activity-based budgeting is a process of planning and controlling the expected activities for the organisation to derive a cost-effective budget that meets forecast workload and agreed strategic goals.
Meaning of Activity Based Budget	An activity-based budget is a quantitative expression of the expected activities of the firm, reflecting management's forecast of workload and financial and nonfinancial requirements to meet agreed strategic goals and planned changes to improve performance.
Key Elements of ABB	1. Type of Work/Activity to be performed; 2. Quantity of Work/Activity to be performed; and 3. Cost of Work/Activity to be performed.
Objective	ABB focuses on the activity/business processes. Resources required are determined on the expected activities and workload. The objective is to bring in efficiency into the system. So, in the process of budget preparation, many key questions, need to be addressed and properly answered.

SOLVED PROBLEMS I

Problem 1. A company, manufacturing two products, furnishes the following data for a year.

Products	*Annual Output (units)*	*Total Machine Hours*	*Total Number of Purchase Orders*	*Total Number of Set-ups*
A	5,000	20,000	160	20
B	60,000	1,20,000	384	44

The annual overhead are as under :

	₹
Volume related activity Costs	5,50,000
Set-up related Costs	8,20,000
Purchase related Costs	6,18,000

You are required to calculate the cost per unit of each product A and B based on :

(*i*) Traditional method of charging overheads.

(*ii*) Activity based costing method.

Solution:

(*i*) **Traditional Method**

Step 1 → **Calculation of Machine Hour Rate**

Total Overheads = ₹ 5,50,000 + ₹ 8,20,000 + ₹ 6,18,000 = ₹ 19,88,000

Total Machine Hours = 20,000 + 1,20,000 = 1,40,000

$$\text{Machine Hour Rate} = \frac{\text{Total Overheads}}{\text{Total Machine Hours}} = \frac{19{,}88{,}000}{1{,}40{,}000 \text{ hours}} = \textbf{₹ 14.20}$$

STEP 2 STATEMENT SHOWING THE COST PER UNIT

Particulars	*Products* A	*Products* B
A. Output (units)	5,000	60,000
B. Machine Hours	20,000	1,20,000
C. Overhead Cost @ ₹ 14.20 per machine hour	2,84,000	17,04,000
D. Overhead Cost per unit (C /A) ₹	**56.80**	**28.40**

(*ii*) **ABC Method**

Step 1 → **Calculation of Cost Driver Rates**

$$(i)\ \text{Machine Hour Rate} = \frac{\text{Total Overhead Cost for volume Related Activities}}{\text{Total Machine Hours}} \quad \frac{5{,}50{,}000}{1{,}40{,}000 \text{ hours}} = \textbf{₹ 3.93} \text{ (approx.)}$$

$$(ii)\ \text{Cost of one Set-up} = \frac{\text{Total Costs related to set-ups}}{\text{Total Number of set-ups}} = \frac{8{,}20{,}000}{64 \text{ set-ups}} = \textbf{₹ 12,812.50}$$

$$(iii)\ \text{Cost of one Purchase Order} = \frac{\text{Total Costs related to purchases}}{\text{Total Number of Purchases Orders}} = \frac{6{,}18{,}000}{544 \text{ orders}} = \textbf{₹ 1,136.03}$$

STEP 2 STATEMENT SHOWING THE COST PER UNIT

Particulars		*Products*	
		A	*B*
A. Machine Hours		20,000	1,20,000
B. No. of Purchase Orders		160	384
C. No. of Set-ups		20	44
D. Cost related to Volume related activities	@ ₹ 3.93	₹ 78,600	₹ 4,71,600
E. Cost related to Purchase orders	@ ₹ 1,136.03	₹ 1,81,765	₹ 4,36,235.52
F. Cost related to Set-ups	@ ₹ 12,812.50	₹ 2,56,250	₹ 5,63,750
G. Total Cost (D + E + F)		₹ 5,16,615	₹ 14,71,586
H. Annual output (units)		5,000	60,000
I. **Cost per unit** (G/H)		**₹ 103.323**	**₹ 24.526**

Problem 2. CAS Ltd. produces three products A, B and C for which the standard costs and quantities per unit are as follows:

Products	*A*	*B*	*C*
Quantity produced	10,000	20,000	30,000
Direct Material per unit (₹)	50	40	30
Direct Labour per unit (₹)	30	40	50
Labour Hours per unit	3	4	5
Machine Hours per unit	4	4	7
No. of Purchase Requisitions	1,200	1,800	2,000
No. of Set ups	240	260	300

Production Overhead split by departments — Department 1 = ₹ 11,00,000
— Department 2 = ₹ 15,00,000

Department 1 is labour intensive and Department 2 is machine intensive

Total Labour Hours in Department 1 = 1,83,333, Total Machine Hours in Department 2 = 5,00,000

Production Overhead split by activity	— Receiving/Inspecting	₹ 14,00,000
	— Production Scheduling/Machine set up	₹ 12,00,000
		₹ 26,00,000

Number of batches received/inspected = 5,000

Number of batches for scheduling and set-up = 800

You are required to:

(i) Prepare Product Cost Statement under Traditional Absorption Costing and Activity Based Costing Method.

(ii) Compare the results under two methods.

Solution: **Traditional Absorption Costing**

Step 1: Overhead Absorption Rates:

Department 1 = ₹ 11,00,000/1,83,333 = ₹ 6 per Labour Hour

Department 2 = ₹ 15,00,000/5,00,000 = ₹ 3 per Machine Hour

STEPS 2 PRODUCT COST STATEMENT UNDER TRADITIONAL METHOD

Products	*A* ₹	*B* ₹	*C* ₹
Direct Materials	50	40	30
Direct Labour	30	40	50
Overhead:			
Department 1	18	24	30
	(3 hrs. × ₹ 6)	(4 hrs. × ₹ 6)	(5 hrs. × ₹ 6)
Department 2	12	12	21
	(4 hrs. × ₹ 3)	(4 hrs. × ₹ 3)	(7 hrs. × ₹ 3)
Total Cost per unit	110	116	131

Activity Based Costing

Step 1: Cost Driver Rates:

$$\text{Receiving/inspecting} = \frac{14{,}00{,}000}{5{,}000 \text{ (No. of Batches received/inspected)}} = ₹\ 280 \text{ per requisition}$$

Production Scheduling/Machine set ups = ₹ 1,500 per set up

PRODUCT COST STATEMENT (PER UNIT) UNDER ABC SYSTEM

Products	A ₹	B ₹	C ₹
Direct Materials (₹)	50	40	30
Direct Labour (₹)	30	40	50
Overhead:			
Receiving	34*	25	19
Production scheduling	36**	20	15
Total cost per unit	150	125	114

{₹ 280 × 1,200} ÷ 10,000 units = ₹ 34*; similarly ₹ 25 and ₹ 19

(₹ 1,500 × 240) ÷ 10,000 units = ₹ 36**; similarly ₹ 20 and ₹ 15

Comparison: The two absorption methods produce different results. Product C appears to be much more expensive using the traditional method than it does with ABC, while product A is the opposite. If it is assumed that ABC is more accurate, which it may or may not be, then Product C would be overpriced under the traditional method and sales would presumably be poor as a consequence-assuming competitors supply more cheaply. Product A would be the opposite : sales would be high and it is possible that the company would unknowingly make a loss per unit on product A.

Problem 3. The following information provides details of costs, volume & cost drivers for a particular period in respect of ABC. Ltd. for product X, Y and Z

	Product X	*Product Y*	*Product Z*	*Total*
1. Production and Sales (units)	30,000	20,000	8,000	
2. Raw Material Usage (units)	5	5	11	
3. Direct Material Cost (₹)	25	20	11	12,38,000
4. Direct Labour Hours	1.33	2	1	88,000
5. Machine Hours	1.33	1	2	76,000
6. Direct Labour Cost (₹)	8	12	6	
7. Number of Production runs	3	7	20	30
8. Number of Deliveries	9	3	20	32
9. Number of Receipts (2 × 7)*	15	35	220	270
10. Number of Production Orders	15	10	25	50
11. Overhead Costs:				
Set-up				₹ 30,000
Machines				₹ 7,60,000
Receiving				₹ 4,35,000
Packing				₹ 2,50,000
Engineering				₹ 3,73,000
				₹ 18,48,000

*The company operates a just-in-time inventory policy, and receives each component once per production run.

From the above information you are required to:

(a) Compute the product costs using a traditional volume-related costing system based on the assumption that:

(i) All overheads are recovered on the basis of direct labour hours (i.e. the company's past product costing system);

(ii) The overheads of the receiving department are recovered by a materials handling overhead rate and the remaining overheads are recovered using a machine hour rate (i.e. the company current costing system).

(b) Compute Product Costs using an Activity-Based Costing System.

Solution:

(a) Computation of the Product Cost using a Traditional Costing System

(i) *When all over-heads are recovered on the basis of Direct Labour Hours (i.e. the company product costing system)*

STATEMENT SHOWING THE PRODUCT COST

Products	X ₹	Y ₹	Z ₹
Direct Labour	8	12	6
Direct Materials	25	20	11
Overheads [18,48,000/88,000]	28 (1.33 hrs. × ₹ 21)	42 (2 hrs. × ₹ 21)	21 (1 hr.. × ₹ 21)
Total	61	74	38

(ii) *When the overheads of the receiving department are recovered by a material handling overhead rate & the remaining overheads are recovered by using a machine hour rate (i.e. the company current costing system)*

STATEMENT SHOWING THE PRODUCT COST

Particulars	X ₹	Y ₹	Z ₹
Direct Labour	8	12	6
Direct Materials	25	20	11
Material Handling Overhead [4,35,000/12,38,000]	8.78 (₹ 25 × 35.14%)	7.03 (₹ 20 × 35.14%)	3.87 (₹ 11 × 35.14%)
Other Overheads [14,13,000/76,000]	24.79 (1.33 hrs × ₹ 18.59)	18.59 (1 hr. × ₹ 18.59)	37.18 (2 hrs. × ₹ 18.59)
Total cost	66.57	57.62	58.05

(b) STATEMENT SHOWING THE PRODUCT COSTS USING AN ACTIVITY BASED COSTING SYSTEM.

Products	X ₹	Y ₹	Z ₹
Direct Labour	8	12	6
Direct Materials	25	20	11
Machine Overheads	13.33 (1.33 hrs. × ₹ 10)	10 (1 hr. × ₹ 10)	20 (2 hrs. × ₹ 10)
Set-up Costs per unit	0.10 [(1,000 × 3)/30,000]	0.35 [(1,000 × 7) × 20,000]	2.50 [(1000 × 20)/8000]
Receiving Cost per unit	0.81 [(1,611 × 15)/30,000]	2.82 [1,611 × 35/20,000]	44.30 [1611 × 220/8,000]
Packing	2.34 [(7,813 × 9)/30,000]	1.17 [(7,813 × 3)/20,000]	19.53 [(7813 × 20)/8,000]
Engineering	3.73 [(7,460 × 15)/30,000]	3.73 [7,460 × 10)/30,000]	23.31 [(7460 × 25)/8,000]
Total Manufacturing Cost	53.31	50.07	126.64

Working Note:

(i) Cost per setup = ₹ 30,000/30 = ₹ 1,000

(ii) Cost per receiving order = ₹ 4,35,000/270 = ₹ 1611 (App.)

(iii) Cost per delivery = ₹ 2,50,000/32 = ₹ 7,813 (App.)

(iv) Cost per production order = ₹ 3,70,000/50 = ₹ 7,400

Problem 4. Having attended a CIMA course on Activity-Based Costing (ABC) you decide to experiment by applying the principles to the four products currently made and sold by your company. Details of the four products and relevant information are given below for one period:

Product	*A*	*B*	*C*	*D*
Output in units	120	100	80	120
Direct Material cost per unit (₹)	40	50	30	60
Direct Labour cost per unit (₹)	28	21	14	21
Machine Hours (per unit)	4	3	2	3

The four products are similar and are usually produced in production runs of 20 units and sold in batches of 10 units.

The production overhead is currently absorbed by using a machine hour rate, and the total of the production over head has been analysed as follows:

	₹
Machine department costs (rent, Business, rates, depreciation and Supervision)	10,430
Set-up costs	5,250
Stores receiving	3,600
Inspection/quality control	2,100
Material handling and dispatch	4,620

You have ascertained that the 'Cost Drivers' to be used are as listed below for the overhead costs shown:

Cost	*Cost*
Set-up costs	Number of Production Runs
Stores receiving	Requisitions Raised
Inspection/quality control	Number of Production Runs
Materials handling and dispatch	Orders Executed

The number of requisitions raised on the stores was 20 for each product and the number of orders executed was 42, each order being for a batch of 10 of a product.

Requirements:

(a) Calculate the total costs for each product if all overhead costs are absorbed on a Machine Hour Basis.

(b) Calculate the total cost of each product, using Activity-Based Costing.

(c) Calculate and list the unit product costs from your figures in (a) and (b) above, to show the differences and comment briefly on any conclusions which may be drawn which could have pricing and profit implications.

Solution:

(a) **Overheads Absorbed on Machine Hour Basis**

Step 1: Machine Hour Absorption Rate $= \dfrac{10,430 + 5,250 + 3,600 + 2,100 + 4,620}{(120 \times 4) + (100 \times 3) + (80 \times 2) + (120 \times 3)}$

$= \dfrac{26,000}{1,300} =$ ₹ 20 per machine hour

STEP 2 STATEMENT OF TOTAL COSTS BASED ON MACHINE HOUR BASIS

Particulars	*A* ₹	*B* ₹	*C* ₹	*D* ₹
Direct Material	40	50	30	60
Direct Labour	28	21	14	21
Production Overhead	80	60	40	60
Production Cost per unit	148	131	84	141
Output in units	120	100	80	120
Total Production cost	₹ 17,760	₹ 13,100	₹ 6,720	₹ 16,920

(b) Overheads Absorbed Based on ABC

Step 1: No. of Production Runs = Output in units/20 = (120 + 100 + 80 + 120)/20 = 21

Step 2: No. of Requisition Raised = No. of Products × 20 = 4 × 20 = 80

Step 3: Cost Driver Rates

	Overhead Costs ₹	*Level of Activity*	*Cost/activity*
Machine Department Costs	10,430	1,300	8.02/hour
Set-up Costs	5,250	21*	250.0/run
Stores Receiving Costs	3,600	80**	45.00/requisition
Inspection/Quality Costs	2,100	21*	100.00/run
Material Handling and Dispatch	4,620	42	110.00/order

STEP 4 STATEMENT OF TOTAL COST UNDER ABC SYSTEM

Particulars	*A* ₹	*B* ₹	*C* ₹	*D* ₹
Direct Materials	40.00	50.00	30.00	60.00
Direct Labour	28.00	21.00	14.00	21.00
Machine Dept Costs	32.09	24.07	16.05	24.07
Set-up Costs	12.50	12.50	12.50	12.50
Stores Receiving	7.50	9.00	11.25	7.50
Inspection	5.00	5.00	5.00	5.00
Material Handling	11.00	11.00	11.00	11.00
Production Cost/unit	136.09	132.57	99.80	141.07
Output in units	120	100	80	120
Total Production Costs	₹ 16,331	₹ 13,257	₹ 7,984	₹ 16,928

(c) COMPARISON OF THE TWO UNIT COSTS UNDER TRADITIONAL AND ABC SYSTEM

Product	*A* ₹	*B* ₹	*C* ₹	*D* ₹
Based on Machine Hour Rate	148.00	131.00	84.00	141.00
ABC Method	136.09	132.57	99.80	141.07
Difference	11.91	(1.57)	(15.80)	(0.07)

Problem 5. Traditional Ltd. is a manufacturer of a range of goods. The cost structure of its different products is as follows:

Particulars	*Product A*	*Product B*	*Product C*	
Direct materials	50	40	40	₹/u
Direct labour @ 10 ₹/hour	30	40	50	₹/u
Production overheads	30	40	50	₹/u
Total Cost	110	120	140	₹/u
Quantity produced	10,000	20,000	30,000	units

Traditional Ltd. was absorbing overheads on the basis of direct labour hours. A newly appointed management accountant has suggested that the company should introduce ABC system and has identified cost drivers and cost pools as follows:

Activity Cost Pool	Cost Driver	Associated Cost
Stores Receiving	Purchase Requisitions	2,96,000
Inspection	Number of Production runs	8,94,000
Dispatch	Orders Executed	2,10,000
Machine Setup	Number of setups	12,00,000

The following information is also supplied:

Details	Product A	Product B	Product C
No. of Setups	360	390	450
No. of Orders Executed	180	270	300
No. of Production runs	750	1,050	1,200
No. of Purchase Requisitions	300	450	500

You are required to calculate activity based production cost of all the three products.

Solution:

The total production overheads are ₹ 26,00,000:

Product A: 10,000 × ₹ 30 = ₹ 3,00,000

Product B: 20,000 × ₹ 40 = ₹ 8,00,000

Product C: 30,000 × ₹ 50 = ₹ 15,00,000

On the basis of ABC analysis this amount will be apportioned as follows:

STATEMENT OF ACTIVITY BASED PRODUCTION COST

Activity Cost Pool	Cost Driver	Ratio	Total Amount (₹)	A (₹)	B (₹)	C (₹)
Stores Receiving	Purchase Requisitions	6:9:10	2,96,000	71,040	1,06,560	1,18,400
Inspection	Production Runs	5:7:8	8,94.000	2,23,500	3,12,900	3,57,600
Dispatch	Orders Executed	6:9:10	2,10,000	50,400	75,600	84,000
Machine Setups	Setups	12:13:15	12,00,000	3,60,000	3,90,000	4,50,000
Total Activity Cost				7,04,940	8,85,060	10,10,000
Quantity Sold				10,000	20,000	30,000
Unit Cost				70.49	44.25	33.67
Add: Conversion Cost				80	80	90
Total				150.49	124.25	123.67

Problem 6. A company manufactures three types of products namely P, Q and R. The data relating to a period are as under:

	P	Q	R
Machine hours per unit	10	18	14
Direct labour hours per unit @ ₹ 20	4	12	8
Direct Material per unit (₹) @ ₹ 10	90	80	120
Production (units)	3,000	5,000	20,000

Currently the company uses traditional costing method and absorbs all production overheads on the basis of machine hours. The machine hour rate of overheads is ₹ 6 per hour.

The company proposes to use activity based costing system and the activity analysis is as under:

	P	Q	R
Batch Size (units)	150	500	1,000
Number of purchase orders per batch	3	10	8
Number of inspections per batch	5	4	3

The total production overheads are analysed as under:

Machine set up costs	20%
Machine operation costs	30%
Inspection costs	40%
Material procurement related costs	10%

Required:

(i) Calculate the cost per unit of each product using traditional method of absorbing all production overheads on the basis of machine hours,

(ii) Calculate the cost per unit of each product using activity based costing principles.

Solution:

(i) COST PER UNIT USING TRADITIONAL METHOD

Products	*P* ₹	*Q* ₹	*R* ₹
Direct Materials	90	80	120
Direct Labour (4:12:8 hours) × ₹ 20	80	240	160
Production Overheads (10:18:14 hours) × ₹ 6	60	108	84
Cost per unit	230	428	364

(ii) COST PER UNIT USING ACTIVITY BASED COSTING

	P	Q	R
A. Production (units)	3,000	5,000	20,000
B. Total Costs:	₹	₹	₹
Direct Materials (90:80:120)	2,70,000	4,00,000	24,00,000
Direct Labour (80:240:160)	2,40,000	12,00,000	32,00,000
Overheads:			
Machine related costs @ ₹ 1.80/hour (30,000:90,000:2,80,000)	54,000	1,62,000	5,04,000
Set-up costs @ ₹ 9600/set up (20:10:20)	1,92,000	96,000	1,92,000
inspection costs @ ₹ 4800/ inspection (100:40:60)	4,80,000	1,92,000	2,88,000
Purchase related costs @ ₹ 750 / purchase (60 : 100:160)	45,000	75,000	1,20,000
Total Costs	12,81,000	21,25,000	67,04,000
C. Costs per unit [B/A]	427.00	425.00	335.20

Working Notes:

(i) PRODUCT WISE AND COST DRIVER VOLUME

Products	*P*	*Q*	*R*	*Total*
A. Production (units)	3,000	5,000	20,000	
B. Batch Size (units)	150	500	1000	
C. Number of Batches [A ÷ B]	20	10	20	50
D. Number of Purchase Order per batch	3	10	8	
E. Total Purchase Orders [C × D]	60	100	160	320
F. Number of Inspections per batch	5	4	3	
G. Total Inspections [C × F]	100	40	60	200

(ii) TOTAL PRODUCTION OVERHEADS

A. Machine hours per unit	10	18	14
B. Production units	3,000	5,000	20,000
C. Total Machine Hours [A × B]	30,000	90,000	2,80,000

Total Machine Hours = 4,00,000

Total Production Overheads = 4,00,000 × ₹ 6 = ₹ 24,00,000.

(iii) COST DRIVER RATES:

Cost Pool (A)	*% (B)*	*Overheads ₹ (C)*	*Cost Driver Units (D)*	*Cost Driver Rate ₹ (E = C/D)*
Setup	20%	4,80,000	50	9,600 per set up
Inspection	40%	9,60,000	200	4,800 per inspection
Purchases	10%	2,40,000	320	750 per purchase
Machine hours	30%	7,20,000	4,00,000	1.80 per Machine Hour

Problem 7. During the last 20 years, KL Ltd's manufacturing operation has become increasingly automated with Computer-controlled robots replacing operators. KL currently manufactures over 100 products of varying levels of design complexity. A single plant wise overhead absorption rate, based on direct labour hours, is used to absorb overhead costs.

In the quarter ended March, KL's manufacturing overhead costs were:

	(₹ '000)
Equipment operation expenses	125
Equipment maintenance expense	25
Wages paid to technicians	85
Wages paid to Store men	35
Wages paid to despatch staff	40
	310

During the quarter, the company reviewed the Cost Accounting System and concluded that absorbing overhead costs to individual products on a labour hour absorption basis is meaningless. Overhead costs should be attributed to products using an Activity Based Costing (ABC) system and the following was identified as the most significant activities:

(i) Receiving component consignments from suppliers

(ii) Setting up equipment for production runs

(iii) Quality inspections

(iv) Despatching goods as per customer's orders.

It was further observed that in the short-term KL's overheads are 40% fixed and 60% variable. Approximately, half the variable overheads vary in relating to direct labour hours worked and half vary in relation to the number of quality inspections.

(a) Equipment operation and maintenance expenses are apportioned as:
Component stores 15%, manufacturing 70% and goods dispatch 15%

(b) Technician's wages are apportioned as:
Equipment maintenance 30%, set up equipment for production runs 40% and quality inspections 30%

During the quarter:

(i) a total of 2000 direct labour hours were worked (paid at ₹ 12 per hr.)

(ii) 980 components consignments were received from suppliers

(iii) 1020 production runs were set up

(iv) 640 quality inspections were carried out

(v) 420 orders were dispatched to customers.

KL's production during the quarter included components R, S and T. The following information is available:

	Component. R	*Component S*	*Component T*
Direct labour Hrs worked	25	480	50
Direct Material	₹ 1,200	₹ 2,900	₹ 1,800
Component Consignments Recd.	42	24	28
Production runs	16	18	12
Quality Inspections	10	8	18
Orders (goods) despatched	22	85	46
Quantity produced	560	12,800	2,400

Required:

(a) Calculate the unit cost of R, S and T components, using KL's existing cost accounting system.

(b) Explain how an ABC system would be developed using the information given. Calculate the unit cost of components R, S and T using ABC system.

Solution:

(a) **Single Factory Direct Labour Hour Overhead Rate** = $\frac{3,10,000}{2,000}$ = ₹ 155 per Direct Labour Hour

STATEMENT SHOWING THE COMPUTATION OF UNIT COST (UNDER EXISTING SYSTEM)

Particulars	*R(₹)*	*S(₹)*	*T(₹)*
A. Direct Labour Cost @ ₹ 12 per hour	300	5,760	600
B. Direct Material	1,200	2,900	1,800
C. Overheads (direct labour hours × ₹ 155 per hour)	3,875	74,400	7,750
D. Total cost [A + B + C]	5,375	83,060	10,150
E. Quantity Produced (No)	560	12,800	2,400
F. Cost per unit [D/E]	9.60	6.49	4.23

(b) ABC system involves the following stages,

1. Identifying the major activities that take place in an organisation.
2. Creating a cost pool /cost centre for each activity
3. Determining the cost driver for each activity
4. Assigning the cost of activities to cost objects (e.g. products, components, customers etc.)

The most significant activities have been identified e.g. receiving components consignments from suppliers, setting up equipment for production runs, quality inspections, and despatching orders to customers. The following shows the assignment of the costs to these activities,

Step 1: **CALCULATION OF ACTIVITY COSTS**

	Receiving supplies	*Setups*	*Quality inspection*	*Despatch*	*Total*
Equipment operation expenses	18.75	87.50		18.75	125.00
Maintenance	3.75	17.50		3.75	25.00
Technicians wages initially allocated to Maintenance (30% of ₹ 85,000= ₹ 25,500 and then reallocated on same basis on maintenance)	3.83	17.85		3.82	25.50
Balance of technicians wages allocated to setups and quality inspections		34.00	25.50		59.50
Stores wages - Receiving	35.00				35.00
Despatch wages - Despatch				40.00	40.00
	61.33	156.85	25.50	66.32	310.00

Note: Equipment operation expenses and Maintenance allocated on the basis 15%, 70% and 15% as specified in the question.

Step 2. Calculation of Cost Driver Rates.

The next stage is to identify the cost drivers for each activity and establish cost driver rates by dividing the activity costs by a measure of cost driver usage for the period. The calculations are as follows :-

Receiving supplies $\left(\frac{61,330}{980}\right)$ = ₹ 62.58 per component.

Performing set ups $\left(\frac{1,56,850}{1,020}\right)$ = ₹ 153.77 per set up

Quality inspection $\left(\frac{25,500}{640}\right)$ = ₹ 39.84 per quality inspection

Despatching goods $\left(\frac{66,320}{420}\right)$ = ₹ 157.90 per despatch

STEP 3 CALCULATION OF UNIT COST UNDER ABC SYSTEM

	R(₹)	*S(₹)*	*T(₹)*
A. Direct Labour	300	5,760	600
B. Direct Materials	1,200	2,900	1,800
C. Receiving Supplies @ ₹ 62.58	2,628.36	1,501.92	1,752.24
D. Performing Set ups @ ₹ 153.77	2,460.32	2,767.86	1,845.24
E. Quality inspections @ ₹ 39.84	398.40	318.72	717.12
F. Despatching goods @ ₹ 157.93	3,474.46	13,424.05	7,264.78
G. Total Cost [A + B + C + D + E + F]	10,461.54	26,672.55	13,979.38
H. No of units produced	560	12,800	2,400
I. Cost per unit [G/H]	18.68	2.08	5.82

Problem 8. Alpha Limited has decided to analyse the profitability of its five new customers. It buys bottled water at ₹ 90 per case and sells to retail customers at a list price of ₹ 108 per case. The data pertaining to five customers are:

Particulars	*Customers*				
	A	*B*	*C*	*D*	*E*
Cases sold	4,680	19,688	1,36,800	71,550	8,775
List Selling Price	₹ 108	₹ 108	₹ 108	₹ 108	₹ 108
Actual Selling Price	₹ 108	₹ 106.20	₹ 99	₹ 104.40	₹ 97.20
Number of Sales Orders	15	25	30	25	30
Number of Customer Visits	2	3	6	2	3
Number of Deliveries	10	30	60	40	20
Kilometres Travelled per delivery	20	6	5	10	30
Number of Expedited Deliveries	0	0	0	0	1

Its five activities and their drivers are:

Activity	*Cost Driver Rate*
Order taking	₹ 750 per sales order
Customer visits	₹ 600 per customer visit
Deliveries	₹ 5.75 per delivery km travelled
Product handling	₹ 3.75 per case sold
Expedited deliveries	₹ 2,250 per expedited delivery

Required: Compute the customer level operating income of each of five retail customers now being examined (*A, B, C, D* and *E*). Comment on the results.

Solution: **STEP 1 CALCULATION OF CUSTOMER LEVEL ACTIVITY COSTS**

Particulars	*Customers*				
	A ₹	*B* ₹	*C* ₹	*D* ₹	*E* ₹
1. Order taking costs (No. of sales orders × ₹ 750)	11,250	18,750	22,500	18,750	22,500
2. Customer visits costs (No. of customer visits × ₹ 600)	1,200	1,800	3,600	1,200	1,800
3. Delivery vehicles travel costs (Kms travelled by delivery vehicles × ₹ 5.75 per km)	1,150	1,035	1,725	2,300	3,450
4. Products handing costs (Cases sold × ₹ 3.75)	17,550	73,830	5,13,000	2,68,313	32,906
5. Cost of expedited deliveries (No. of expedited deliveries × ₹ 2,250)	—	—	—	—	2,250
Total Cost of customer level operating activities:	31,150	95,415	5,40,825	2,90,563	62,906

STEP 2 CALCULATION OF CUSTOMER LEVEL OPERATING INCOME

Particulars	*Customers*				
	A	*B*	*C*	*D*	*E*
A. Cases sold	4,680	19,688	1,36,800	71,550	8,775
	₹	₹	₹	₹	₹
B. Actual selling price	108	106.20	99	104.40	97.20
C. Cost	90	90	90	90	90
D. Sales at actual price (A × B)	5,05,440	20,90,866	1,35,43,200	74,69,820	8,52,930
E. *Less:* Cost of goods sold (A × C)	4,21,200	17,71,920	1,23,12,000	64,39,500	7,89,750
F. **Gross Margin** [D – E]	84,240	3,18,946	12,31,200	10,30,320	63,180
G. *Less:* Customer level activity costs (*as per Step 1*)	31,150	95,415	5,40,825	2,90,563	62,906
H. **Customer Level Operating Income** [F – G]	53,090	2,23,531	6,90,375	7,39,757	274

Problem 9. *RST* Limited specializes in the distribution of pharmaceutical products. It buys from the pharmaceutical companies and resales to each of the three different markets:

(*i*) General Supermarket Chains
(*ii*) Drugstore Chains
(*iii*) Chemist Shops

The following data for the month of April in respect of *RST* Limited has been reported:

	General Supermarket Chains	*Drugstore Chains*	*Chemist Shops*
Average revenue per delivery	₹ 84,975	₹ 28,875	₹ 5,445
Average cost of goods sold per delivery	₹ 82,500	₹ 27,500	₹ 4,950
Number of deliveries	330	825	2,750

In the past, *RST* Limited has used gross margin percentage to evaluate the relative profitability of its distribution channels.

The company plans to use activity-based costing for analysing the profitability of its distribution channels. The Activity analysis of RST Limited is as under :

Activity Area	*Cost Driver*
Customer purchase order processing	Purchase orders by customers
Line-item ordering	Line-items per purchase order
Store delivery	Store deliveries
Cartons dispatched to stores	Cartons dispatched to a store per delivery
Shelf-stocking at customer store	Hours of shelf-stocking

The April operating costs (other than cost of goods sold) of *RST* Limited are ₹ 8,27,970. These operating costs are assigned to five activity areas. The cost in each area and the quantity of the cost allocation basis used in that area for April are as follows:

Activity Area	*Total Costs in April*	*Total Units of Cost Allocation Base used in April*
Customer purchase order processing	₹ 2,20,000	5,500 orders
Line-item ordering	₹ 1,75,560	58,520 line items
Store delivery	₹ 1,95,250	3,905 store deliveries
Cartons dispatched to store	₹ 2,09,000	2,09,000 cartons
Shelf-stocking at customer store	₹ 28,160	1,760 hours

Other data for April include the following:

	General Supermarket Chains	*Drugstore Chains*	*Chemist Shops*
Total number of orders	385	990	4,125
Average number of line items per order	14	12	10
Total number of store deliveries	330	825	2,750
Average number of cartons shipped per store delivery	300	80	16
Average number of hours of shelf-stocking per store delivery	3	0.6	0.1

Required:

(*i*) Compute for April gross-margin percentage for each of its three distribution channels and compute *RST* Limited's operating income.

(*ii*) Compute the April rate per unit of the cost-allocation base for each of the five activity areas.

(*iii*) Compute the operating income of each distribution channel in April using the activity-based costing information. Comment on the results. What new insights are available with the activity-based cost information?

(*iv*) Describe four challenges one would face in assigning the total April operating costs of ₹ 8,27,970 to five activity areas.

Solution:

(*i*) STATEMENT OF OPERATING INCOME AND GROSS MARGIN PERCENTAGE FOR APRIL

Particulars	*General Supermarket Chains* ₹	*Drugstore Chains* ₹	*Chemist Shops* ₹	*Total* ₹
A. Revenues	2,80,41,750 (330 × ₹ 84,975)	2,38,21,875 (825 × ₹ 28,875)	1,49,73,750 (2,750 × ₹ 5,445)	6,68,37,375
B. *Less :* Cost of Goods Sold	2,72,25,000 (330 × ₹ 82,500)	2,26,87,500 (825 × ₹ 27,500)	1,36,12,500 (2,750 × ₹ 4,950)	6,35,25,000

Particulars	General Supermarket Chains ₹	Drugstore Chains ₹	Chemist Shops ₹	Total ₹
C. **Gross Margin**	8,16,750	11,34,375	13,61,250	33,12,375
D. *Less :* Other Operating Costs				8,27,970
E. **Operating Income**				24,84,405
F. Gross Margin % of revenue	2.91%	4.76%	9.09%	4.96%
G. Operating Income % of revenue				3.72%

ABC Approach

(*ii*) COMPUTATION OF RATE PER UNIT OF THE COST-ALLOCATION BASE FOR APRIL

A. Customer purchase order processing (₹ 2,20,000/5,500 orders)	₹ 40 per order
B. Line item ordering (₹ 1,75,560/58,520 line items)	₹ 3 per line item order
C. Store delivery (₹ 1,95,250/3,905 store deliveries)	₹ 50 per delivery
D. Cartons dispatched (₹ 2,09,000/2,09,000 dispatches)	₹ 1 per dispatch
E. Shelf-stocking at customer store (₹ 28,160/1,760 hours)	₹ 16 per hour

(*iii*) COMPUTATION OF OPERATING INCOME OF EACH DISTRIBUTION CHANNEL

Particulars	General Super Market Chains ₹	Drugstore Chains ₹	Chemist Shops ₹
A. Gross margin as per part (*i*)	8,16,750	11,34,375	13,61,250
B. Operating cost:			
Customer purchase order processing	15,400 (₹ 40 × 385 orders)	39,600 (₹ 40 × 990 orders)	1,65,000 (₹ 40 × 4,125 orders)
Line item ordering	16,170 (₹ 3 × 14 × 385 orders)	35,640 (₹ 3 × 12 × 990 orders)	1,23,750 (₹ 3 × 10 × 4,125 orders)
Store delivery	16,500 (₹ 50 × 330 deliveries)	41,250 (₹ 50 × 825 deliveries)	1,37,500 (₹ 50 × 2,750 deliveries)
Cartons dispatched	99,000 (₹ 1 × 300 cartons × 330 deliveries)	66,000 (₹ 1 × 80 cartons × 825 deliveries)	44,000 (₹ 1 × 16 cartons × 2,750 deliveries)
Shelf-stocking	15,840 (₹ 16 × 330 deliveries × 3 hrs.)	7,920 (₹ 16 × 825 deliveries × 0.6 hrs.)	4,400 (₹ 16 × 2,750 deliveries × 0.1 hr.)
Operating Cost	1,62,910	1,90,410	4,74,650
C. **Operating Income** (A – B)	6,53,840	9,43,965	8,86,600
D. $\frac{\text{Operating Income}}{\text{Revenue}} \times 100$	2.33%	3.96%	5.92%

Comments: The ABC shows that chemist shops use a larger amount of company resources per rupee of revenue than general supermarket chains and drugstore chains. Operating costs as a percentage of revenues for the three channels is shown below:

1. General supermarket chains (₹ 1,62,910/2,80,41,750) × 100	0.58%
2. Drug store chains (₹ 1,90, 410/₹.2,38,21,875) × 100	0.80%
3. Chemist shops (₹ 4,74,650/₹ 1,49,73,750) × 100	3.17%

(*v*) Challenges Faced in Assigning Total Operating Cost

In assigning total operating cost of ₹ 8,27,970 to different activity areas, one may face the following challenges:

(*i*) For each activity an appropriate cost driver is to be selected.

(*ii*) For each cost driver, a reliable data base is to be developed.

(*iii*) There may be certain costs that may be common for several activities. How to distribute these costs over activities may pose questions.

(*iv*) For computing cost driver rates, appropriate time period is to be selected.

13 Operating Costing (Service Costing)

LEARNING OBJECTIVES

After studying this chapter, you should be able to understand:

- What is Operating Costing?
- How to Select Cost Unit In Operating costing?
- Transport Costing
- Transport Costing Procedure
- Format of Transport Operating Cost Sheet
- Boiler House and Power House Costing
- Canteen Costing
- Hotel Costing
- Hospital Costing

1.0 WHAT IS OPERATING COSTING?

Meaning	Operating Costing is a method of ascertaining the cost of providing *or* operating a service within *or* outside the undertaking. It is also known as '*Service Costing.*' **CIMA London,** defines Operating Costing as "*that form of operation costing which applies where standardised services are rendered either by an undertaking or by a service cost centre within an undertaking.*"
Basic Features	The basic features of Operating Costing are as follows: (*a*) Services are standardised. (*b*) Investment in fixed assets is high and in working capital is low. (*c*) Major portion of the total cost is fixed cost. Hence, the cost per unit of service rendered is affected by the economies and scale of operations. Cost per unit will decrease if more units of service are rendered. *For example,* in a passenger transport company, if buses run full capacity, the cost per passenger will be lower than that if buses do not run full capacity.
Applications	Operating Costing is applied in those undertakings which are engaged in providing services rather than manufacturing of tangible products. It is generally applied in– (*a*) Road Transport, Railways, Airlines (*b*) Hotels (*c*) Hospitals (*d*) Electricity Supply Companies (*e*) Water Supply Companies (*f*) Gas Supply Companies (*g*) Cinema (*h*) Canteen

2.0 HOW TO SELECT COST UNIT IN OPERATING COSTING?

The unit for which the operating cost is to be computed should be decided after considering all the technical and other factors affecting the operating cost. The cost unit may be of two types as follows:

<table>
<tr><td rowspan="5">Simple Cost Unit</td><td colspan="2">A cost unit is said to be simple cost unit when only one cost unit is used. For Example:</td></tr>
<tr><td>Undertaking</td><td>Cost Unit</td></tr>
<tr><td>1. Transport</td><td>per kilometre</td></tr>
<tr><td>2. Canteen</td><td>per item, per meal</td></tr>
<tr><td>3. Water</td><td>per 1000 litres</td></tr>
<tr><td rowspan="7">Composite Cost Unit</td><td colspan="2">A cost unit is said to be composite cost unit when two units are merged into one. For example:</td></tr>
<tr><td>Undertaking</td><td>Cost Unit</td></tr>
<tr><td>1. Passenger Transport</td><td>per passenger - km</td></tr>
<tr><td>2. Goods Transport</td><td>per tonne - km</td></tr>
<tr><td>3. Hotel</td><td>per room per day</td></tr>
<tr><td>4. Hospital</td><td>per bed per day</td></tr>
<tr><td>5. Electricity</td><td>per kilowatt hour</td></tr>
</table>

3.0 TRANSPORT COSTING

<table>
<tr><td>Meaning</td><td>Transport costing is a method of ascertaining the cost of providing service by a transport undertaking.</td></tr>
<tr><td>Objectives</td><td>The objectives of Transport Costing are as follows:
(a) To ascertain the operating cost of running a vehicle per kilometre.
(b) To fix the rates of carriage of goods or passengers on the basis of operating costs.
(c) To fix the hire charges where vehicles are given on hire.
(d) To compare the cost of using own vehicles with that of using alternative mode of transport
(e) To determine what should be charged to departments which use internal transport facilities.</td></tr>
<tr><td>Daily Log Sheet</td><td>(a) Meaning — A log sheet is a record which is maintained for each vehicle to record the details of trips, running time, capacity, distance covered, cost of petrol/diesel, lubricants, loading and unloading time etc. on daily basis.
(b) Usefulness — A log sheet enables the management –
(i) to ascertain the operating cost
(ii) to avoid idleness of vehicle.
(iii) to prevent waste of capacity.
(iv) to exercise other controls.</td></tr>
</table>

Format

A general format of a log sheet is given below:

DAILY LOG SHEET

Vehicle No............................ Route No. ....
Date of purchase................. Driver ....
Make and specification........ Time of leaving ....
Time of returning ....

Particular of Trips

Trip No.	*From*	*To*	*Packages*		*Kilo-metre*	*Time*			*Remarks*
			Out	*Collected*		*Out*	*In*	*Hrs.*	

Supplies	**Workers' time**	**Abnormal delays**
Petrol/Diesel........	Driver................	Loading/unloading......
Oil........................	Conductor........	Traffic delays................
Grease..................	Cleaner.............	Accidents.......................

4.0 TRANSPORT COSTING PROCEDURE

Transport costing procedure involves the following practical steps:

PRACTICAL STEPS INVOLVED IN TRANSPORT COSTING PROCEDURE

Step 1 → *Select the Cost Unit as follows:*

Cost unit	*Example*
(*a*) *Simple Cost Unit*	*per kilometre, per passenger*
(*b*) *Composite Cost Unit*	*per tonne km, per passenger km*

Step 2 → *Calculate the total units of service for a particular period* (*say year, quarter, month, or week*)

1. ***Effective kilometres***
   = Distance covered one way × No. of Trips per Day × No. of Days operated in a Month × No. of Months operated in a Year
2. ***Effective Passenger kilometres*** (***in case of passenger transport***)
   = Effective Kilometres × Seating Capacity × Seating Capacity Occupancy Rate
   Note : *If seating capacity occupied in outward journey is different from inward journey, effective passenger kilometres would be calculated separately for outward and inward journey.*
3. ***Absolute tonnes km*** *= Various distances × respective load quantities carried*
4. ***Commercial tonnes km*** *= Total distance × Average load quantity carried*

Step 3 → *Calculate Total Fixed or Standing Charges* (*i.e., those do not vary with the change in the number of units of service rendered*) *for a particular period* (*say year, quarter, month or week*).

(*i*) *The full amount of an individual item of cost should be charged directly to a cost centre for which this item of cost was incurred. For example, Road Tax, Insurance, Driver's salary, Conductor's salary. Cleaner's salary, Depreciation if related to effluxion of time, Interest on capital if it is explicitly given.*

(*ii*) *The common items of cost should be apportioned to two or more cost centres on some equitable basis (say Actual Benefit, Potential Benefit & Ability to pay/*

Survey). For example, Garage Rent may be apportioned on the basis of floor area occupied.

Step 4 → *Calculate Fixed or Standing Charges per unit of service as follows:*

$$\text{Fixed/Standing Charges per unit} = \frac{\text{Total Fixed/Standing Charges (as per step 3)}}{\text{Total Units of service (as per step 2)}}$$

Step 5 → *Calculate Total Variable or Running Charges (i.e., those vary with the change in the number of units of service rendered) for a particular period. For example, Petrol or Diesel or CNG, lubricating oil, Repairs & Maintenance, Tyres and Tubes, Depreciation (if it is related to the activity level)*

Step 6 → *Calculate Variable or Running Charges per unit of service as follows:*

$$\text{Variable or Running Charges per unit} = \frac{\text{Total Variable Charges (as per step 5)}}{\text{Total Units of Service (as per step 2)}}$$

Step 7 → *Calculate Operating Cost per unit of service as follows:*

A. Fixed/Standing charges per unit	xxx
B. Variable charges per unit	xxx
C. Operating cost per unit	xxx

5.0 FORMAT OF TRANSPORT OPERATING COST SHEET

OPERATING COST SHEET

Vehicle No............................ Period ....

Cost Unit .... No. of Cost Units ....

Particulars	*Total* ₹	*Per km.* ₹
A. Fixed Costs (*or Standing Charges*):		
1. Road Tax	....	....
2. Insurance	....	....
3. Driver's wages	....	....
4. Conductor's wages	....	....
5. Cleaner's wages	....	....
6. Depreciation (if related to effuxion of time)	....	....
7. Interest on Capital	....	....
8. Garage Rent	....	....
9. Office & Administration overheads	....	....
Total (*A*)	....	....
B. Variable (Running) Costs:		
Depreciation (if related to operation)	....	....
Petrol or diesel	....	....
Lubricating Oil	....	....
Repairs and Maintenance	....	....
Tyres and tubes	....	....
Total (*B*)	....	....
C. Operating Cost (A + B)	....	....

Illustration 1. From the following information, calculate the (*a*) Effective kilometres p.a.; (*b*) Effective passenger kilometres p.a.; (*c*) Total fuel consumption; and (*d*) Total cost of fuel; (*e*) Cost of fuel per kilometre

Distance of one way route	40 kilometres
Round trips per day	3
Days operated in a month	25
Seating capacity	50 passengers

Seating Capacity occupied	80%
Fuel Consumption	1 litre per 6 kms
Rate of Fuel	₹ 15 per litre

Solution:

(*a*) Effective kilometres = Distance covered one way × No. of trips per day × No. of days operated × No. of months operated

= 40 × (3 × 2) × 25 × 12 = 72,000

(*b*) Effective passenger kilometres = Effective kilometres × Seating capacity × Seating capacity occupied

= 72,000 × 50 × 80% = 28,80,000

(*c*) Fuel Consumption = $\frac{\text{Distance Covered}}{\text{Mileage per Litre}} = \frac{72,000}{6}$ = 12,000 Litres

(*d*) Cost of Fuel = Fuel Consumption × Rate of Fuel = 12,000 × ₹ 15 = ₹ 1,80,000

(*e*) Cost of Fuel per Kilometre = $\frac{\text{Total Cost of Fuel}}{\text{Total Distance Covered}} = \frac{1,80,000}{72,000}$ = ₹ 2.50 per km.

Illustration 2. A truck starts with a load of 10 tonnes of goods from station *P*. It unloads 4 tonnes at station *Q* and rest of the goods at station *R*. It reaches back directly to station *P* after getting reloaded with 8 tonnes of goods at station *R*. The distances between *P* to *Q*, *Q* to *R* and then from *R* to *P* are 40 kms, 60 kms and 80 kms respectively.

Required: Compute 'Absolute Tonne-km' and 'Commercial Tonne-km'.

Solution:

Absolute tonnes-kms = 10 tonnes × 40 kms + 6 tonnes × 60 kms + 8 tonnes × 80 kms

= 1,400 tonnes-kms

Commercial tonnes-kms = Average load × Total kilometres travelled

= $\frac{(10 + 6 + 8)}{3}$ tonnes × 180 kms = 8 tonnes × 180 kms

= 1,440 tonnes-kms

Note: It may be noted that while calculating the Absolute tonnes-kms, the travel between any two stations is considered individually, while in the case of commercial tonne-kms, the trip is considered as a whole.

Illustration 3. From the following information, calculate the bus fare to be charged from each passenger : (*a*) Delhi to Agra; (*b*) Delhi to Bhiwani; (*c*) Delhi to Chandigarh :

(*a*)	Delhi to Agra	200 km
	Delhi to Bhiwani	120 km
	Delhi to Chandigarh	250 km
(*b*)	Effective passenger km	3,72,000

(*c*) Total Cost (excluding Conductor's commission @ 15% and Passenger Tax @ 5% of total takings) ₹ 1,48,800

(*d*) Desired Profit — 30 % on total takings.

Solution: **STATEMENT SHOWING FARE TO BE CHARGED**

	Particulars	₹
A.	Total Cost (excluding Commission & Passenger Tax)	1,48,800
B.	*Add :* Passenger Tax @ 5% of ₹ 2,97,600	14,880
C.	*Add :* Conductor's Commission @ 15% of ₹ 2,97,600	44,640
D.	Total Cost (including Commission & Passenger Tax (A + B + C)	2,08,320
E.	*Add :* Profit @ 30% of ₹ 2,97,600	89,280
F.	Total Takings (D + E)	2,97,600
G.	Effective Passenger km	3,72,000
H.	Taking per passenger km (₹ 2,97,600 / 3,72,000)	₹ 0.80
I.	Fare to be charged Delhi to Agra per passenger = 200 km × ₹ 0.80 = ₹ 160 Delhi to Bhiwani per passenger = 120 km × ₹ 0.80 = ₹ 96 Delhi to Chandigarh per passenger = 250 km × ₹ 0.80 = ₹ 200	

Working Note: *Calculation of Total Takings*

Let the Total Takings be *X*

$$X = \text{Total Cost} + \text{Profit}$$
$$X = (₹\ 1{,}48{,}800 + 0.05\,X + .15\,X) + 0.30\,X$$
$$X - .50X = ₹\ 1{,}48{,}800$$
$$X = ₹\ 1{,}48{,}800/.5 = ₹\ 2{,}97{,}600$$

Illustration 4. From the following information calculate the average cost per student in respect of students coming from a distance of : (*a*) Upto 4 kms from school and (*b*) Beyond 4 kms from school:

Operating cost of a bus	₹ 4,800
Seating capacity of each bus	60 students
Seating capacity occupied	$83\ ^1/_3\%$

Students picked up and dropped within a range up to 4 kms of distance from the school are charged half fare and fifty per cent of the students travelling in each trip are in this category. The bus makes two trips in the morning to pick up first senior students and then junior students and similarly makes two trips in the afternoon to drop first senior students and then junior students.

Solution:

A.	Operating cost of a bus	4,800
B.	No. of students on half fee basis	150
C.	Cost per student (half fee) (₹ 4800/150)	₹ 32.00
D.	Cost per student (full fee) (₹ 32 × 2)	₹ 64.00

Working Note: *Calculation of number of student per bus*

A.	Bus Capacity	50 students
B.	Half fare students (50% of 50)	25 students
C.	Full fare students (50% of 50)	25 students
D.	Full fare students as equivalent to half fare students (C × 2)	50 students
E.	Total Number of half fare students per trip (B + D)	75 students per trip
F.	Total number of half fare students for both the trips (E × 2)	150 students

Illustration 5. A truck owner provides you the following information:

Capacity of truck	10 tonnes
Distance covered each way	50 kms
No. of round trips per day	2
No. of days operated	25 days a month
Operating cost of a truck	₹ 55,000 per month

On outward trip freight is available to the extent of 90% capacity and on return 20% of capacity.
Required: Calculate (*a*) Tonne – kms per month; (*b*) Operating cost per tonne – km ; (*c*) Rate per tonne – km per trip to be charged so as to earn a profit of 50% on freight; (*d*) Freight earned per outward trip; (*e*) Freight earned per inward trip.

Solution:

(*a*) Tonne – kms per month

Outward trip tonne - kms	= 2 × (90% of 10) × 50 × 25	= 22,500
Inward trip tonne - kms	= 2 × (20% of 10) × 50 × 25	= 5,000
		27,500

(*b*) Operating cost per tonne - km = ₹ 55,000/ 27,500 = ₹ 2 per tonne km

(*c*) Rate per tonne - km = Operating cost per tonne km + Profit per tonne km
= ₹ 2 + ₹ 2 (i.e. 50% on freight or 100% of cost) = ₹ 4

(*d*) Freight earned per outward trip = (90% of 10) tonne × 50 kms × ₹ 4 = ₹ 1,800

(*e*) Freight earned per inward trip = (20% of 10) tonne × 50 kms × ₹ 4 = ₹ 400

Illustration 6. Tulsian passenger transport company provides you the following informations:

No. of buses	5
Cost of each bus	₹ 3,00,000
Estimated life	5 years
Repairs & maintenance	₹ 7,285 p.m. per bus
Driver's Salary	₹ 800 p.m. per bus
Conductor's salary	₹ 600 p.m. per bus
Garage rent	₹ 6,000 p.a.

Insurance	@ 2% p.a.
Taxes	₹ 6,000 p.a.
Road licence	₹ 600 p.a. per bus
Interest	@ 18% p.a.
km per litre of fuel	20 km
Cost of fuel	₹ 300 per 10 litres
Total capacity	50 passengers
Average capacity which is used	90%
Normal % of vehicles laid up for repair	5%
No. of round trips per day	4
Distance of route	20 km
Working days in a month	25
Manager's salary	₹ 1,000 p.m.
Accountant's salary	₹ 500 p.m.
Peon's salary	₹ 250 p.m.
Cleaner's salary	₹ 100 p.m.
Mechanic's salary	₹ 300 p.m.
Cost of tickets	₹ 10 per 1000 passenger km
Office rent	₹ 250 p.m.
Office routine expenses	₹ 500 p.m.
Cost of each tyre	₹ 3,000
Tyres to be replaced per bus	1 p.m.

Notes: (*i*) Commission @ 10% of the taking is to be paid to conductor
(*ii*) Profit @ 20% on taking is desired by the owner

Required — Calculate:
(*a*) Cost per month; (*b*) Cost per day; (*c*) Cost per trip; (*d*) Cost per km; (*e*) cost per passenger km; (*f*) Bus fare to be charged from each passenger.

Solution:

A.	Cost p.m. *[Refer to Working Note No. (i)]*	₹ 34,200
B.	No. of working days in a month	25
C.	No. of trips p.m. (25 × 4)	100
D.	km. covered p.m. (100 × 40 × 95%)	3,800
E.	Passenger km. p.m. (3800 × 50 × 90%)	1,71,000
F.	Cost per day (A/B)	₹ 1,368
G.	Cost per trip (A/C)	₹ 342
H.	Cost per km (A/D)	₹ 9.00
I.	Cost per Passenger km (A/E)	20 paise
J.	Profit desired by owner (20% on taking or 25% on cost)	5 paise
K.	Bus fare to be charged (I + J)	25 paise

Working Notes:

(*i*) STATEMENT SHOWING THE OPERATING COST PER BUS PER MONTH

	₹
A. Fixed Expenses p.m.	
(*i*) Driver's salary	800
(*ii*) Conductor's salary	600
(*iii*) Interest $\left[\frac{3,00,000 \times 18}{12 \times 100}\right]$	4,500
(*iv*) Insurance $\left[\frac{2\% \text{ of } 3,00,000}{12}\right]$	500
(*v*) Taxes $\left[\frac{6,000}{12 \times 5}\right]$	100
(*vi*) Road Licence $\left[\frac{600}{12}\right]$	50

(*vii*) Garage Rent $\left[\frac{6,000}{12 \times 5}\right]$	100
(*viii*) Cleaner's Salary $\left[\frac{100}{5}\right]$	20
(*ix*) Mechanic's Salary $\left[\frac{300}{5}\right]$	60
(*x*) Office Administration Cost	500
Total Fixed Expenses	7,230
B. Semi-Variable Expenses p.m.	
(*i*) Depreciation $\left[\frac{3,00,000}{5 \times 12}\right]$	5,000
(*ii*) Repair & Maintenance	7,285
Total Semi-Variable Expenses	12,285
C. Variable Expenses p.m.	
(*i*) Cost of Fuel	5,700
(*ii*) Cost of Tyres	3,000
(*iii*) Cost of Tickets (1,71,000 × 10/1000)	1,710
Total Variable Expenses	10,410
D. Total Operating Cost (Without Commission) (A + B + C)	29,925
E. Commission of Conductor @ 10% on takings (10% of ₹ 42,750)	4,275
F. Total Cost p.m. (D + E)	34,200
G. Owner's profit @ 20% on takings (20% of ₹ 42,750)	8,550
H. Total Takings (F + G)	42,750

(*ii*) *Calculation of Total km covered per bus*

= Distance of one round trip × No. of round trips per day × No. of days in a month × % of bus available
= (20 × 2) × 4 × 25 × 95/100 = 3,800 km

(*iii*) *Calculation of total passenger kms covered*

= Total km covered × Total capacity × % of Average Capacity
= 3,800 × 50 × 90/100 = 1,71,000 passenger km

(*iv*) *Calculation of Cost of Fuel*

(*i*) Fuel Consumption (in litres) = $\frac{\text{Total kms covered}}{\text{km run per litre}} = \frac{3800}{20}$ = 190 Ltr.

(*ii*) Cost of Fuel = Fuel Consumed (in litres) × Rate of Fuel per litre. = 190 × ₹ 30 = ₹ 5,700

(*v*) *Calculation of Share of Office & Admn. Cost*

		₹
A.	Office Rent	250
B.	Office other routine expenses	500
C.	Manager's salary	1,000
D.	Accountant's salary	500
E.	Peon's salary	250
F.	Total for 5 buses (A + B + C + D + E)	2,500
G.	For 1 bus (₹ 2,500/5)	₹ 500

(*vi*) *Calculation of Total Takings*

Let the total takings be *X*

A.	Total Operating cost (without Commission)	29,925
B.	*Add :* Conductor's Commission	10% of *X*
C.	Total Cost (including Commission)	29,925 + 10% of *X*
D.	*Add :* Profit @ 20% on takings	20% of *X*
E.	Total taking (C + D)	29,925 + 30% of *X*

X = 29,925 + 30% of *X*

$X - .30\ X = 29,925$
$.70\ X = 29,925$
$X = 29,925/.70 =$ ₹ 42,750

Illustration 7. You have been given a permit to run a bus on a route 20 km long. The bus costs you ₹ 90,000. It has to be insured @ 3% p.a. and the annual tax will be ₹ 900. Garage rent is ₹ 100 p.m. Annual repairs will be ₹ 960 and the bus is likely to last for 5 years at the end of which the scrap value is likely to be ₹ 6,000.

The driver's salary will be ₹ 110 p.m. and the conductor's ₹ 100 together with 10% of the takings as commission (to be shared equally by both). Stationery will cost ₹ 50 p.m. The manager-cum-accountant's salary will be ₹ 350 p.m.

Diesel and oil be ₹ 25 per hundred kilometers. The bus will make 3 round trips for carrying on the average 40 passengers on each trip. Assuming 15% profit on takings, calculate the bus fare to be charged from 100 passengers. The bus will work on the average 25 days in a month.

Solution: **OPERATING COST STATEMENT**

Bus No. : DL-CAP 0575
Carrying capacity : 40

Particulars	*Per annum* ₹	*Per 100 Passenger km* ₹ P.
A. **Standing Charges:**		
Depreciation [(90,000 – 6,000)/5]	16,800	
Tax	900	
Insurance	2,700	
Stationery	600	
Manager's salary	4,200	
Total	25,200	1.75
B. **Maintenance Charges:**		
Garage rent	1,200	
Repairs	960	
Total	2,160	0.15
C. **Operating *or* Running Charges:**		
Diesel and oil	9,000	
Driver's salary	1,320	
Conductor's salary	1,200	
Total	11,520	0.80
D. Grand Total (A + B + C)		2.70
E. Loading for commission & profit @ 25/75		0.90
F. Fare per passenger-km (D + E)		3.60

Working Notes:

(*i*) Number of kms. run in a month = 3 × 2 × 20 × 25 = 3,000

(*ii*) Diesel & oil = 3,000 × 25/100 = ₹ 750

(*iii*) Number of passenger-kms. per annum = 3,000 × 40 × 12 = 1,20,000 = 14,40,000

(*iv*) *Loading*— If taking is ₹ 100, 10 will have to be given as commission and 15 must remain as profit; the cost must therefore be 75. On 75 the loading must be 25 to make the taking equal to 100.

Illustration 8. Transport Company supplies the following details in respect of a truck of 5-tonne capacity

Cost of truck	₹ 90,000	Cleaner's wages	₹ 250 per month
Estimated life	10 years	Insurance	4,800 per year
Diesel, oil, grease	₹ 15 per trip each way	Tax	2,400 per year
Repairs and maintenance	500 per month	General supervision	4,800 per year
Driver's wages	500 per month	charges	

The truck carries goods to and from the city covering a distance of 50 kms each way. On outward trip freight is available to the extent of full capacity and on return 20% of capacity.

Assuming that the truck runs on an average 25 days a month, work out —

(*a*) Operating cost tonne-km.

(*b*) Rate per tonne per trip that the company should charge if a profit of 50% on freight is to be earned.

Solution: **(a) STATEMENT SHOWING OPERATING COST PER TRUCK**

Particulars		*Operating Costs*	
		Per month	*Per tonne- km*
A. Fixed Costs:	₹	₹	₹
Driver's Wages	500		
Cleaner's Wages	250		
Insurance (₹ 4,800/12)	400		
Taxes (₹ 2,400/12)	200		
General Supervision (₹ 4,800/12)	400	1,750	0.233
B. Running and Maintenance Costs:			
Diesel, Oil, Grease (₹ 15 × 2 × 25)	750		
Depreciation (90,000/10 × 12)	750		
Repairs and Maintenance	500	2,000	0.267
C. Operating Cost [A + B]		3,750	0.500

Freight Rate:	
Cost per tonne-km (₹ 3,750/7,500)	₹ 0.50
Profit per tonne-km @ 50% on freight or 100% on cost	₹ 0.50
Freight	₹ 1.00

Freight per trip-both ways 300 tonnes-kms @ ₹ 1

Assuming Truck makes only one trip a day, tonnes-kms covered in a trip would be 300 (i.e., 7,500/25)

Working Notes:

(*i*) Tonne-kms per month

Outward trip tonne-kms	5 × 50 × 25 = ₹ 6,250
Inward trip tonne-kms.	1 × 50 × 25 = ₹ 1,250
Total	7,500

(*ii*) It is assumed that the truck makes only one trip per day.

Illustration 9. Global Transport Ltd. charges ₹ 90 per tonne for its 6 tonnes truck lorry load from city '*A*' to city '*B*'. The charges for the return journey are ₹ 84 per tonne. No concession or reduction in these rates is made for any delivery of goods at intermediate station '*C*'. In January, the truck made 12 outward journeys for city '*B*' will full load out of which 2 tonnes were unloaded twice in the ways at city '*C*'. The truck carried a load of 8 tonnes in its return journey for 5 times but once caught by police and ₹ 1,200 was paid as fine. For the remaining trips the truck carried full load out of which all the goods on load were unloaded once at city '*C*'. The distance from city '*A*' to city '*C*' and city '*B*' are 140 kms and 300 kms respectively. Annual fixed costs and maintenance charges are ₹ 60,000 and ₹ 12,000 respectively. Running charges spent during January are ₹ 2,944.

Required: Calculate the cost per absolute tonne-kilometer and the profit for January.

Solution: **OPERATING COST AND PROFIT STATEMENT**
M/S GLOBAL TRANSPORT LTD.

Particulars	₹
A. Fixed costs (₹ 60,000/12)	5,000
B. Maintenance charges (₹ 12,000/12)	1,000
C. Running charges	2,944
D. Total Operating Cost (A + B + C)	8,944
E. Cost per absolute tonnes km (₹ 8,944/44,720 absolute tonnes kms)	0.20
F. Net revenue received (*Refer to Working Note iv*)	12,168
G. *Less:* Total operating cost	8,944
H. Profit [F – G]	3,224

Working Notes :

(*i*) *Tonne-km on outward journeys:*

From city A to city B : 10 journeys × 300 kms × 6 tonnes	=	18,000 tonnes-kms
From city A to city C : 2 journeys × 140 kms × 6 tonnes	=	1,680 tonnes-kms
From city C to city B : 2 journeys × 160 kms × 4 tonnes	=	1,280 tonnes-kms
	Total	20,960 tonnes-kms

(*ii*) *Tonne-km on between journeys:*

From city B to city A :

5 journeys × 300 kms × 8 tonnes	= 12,000 tonnes-kms
6 journeys × 300 kms × 6 tonnes	= 10,800 tonnes-kms
From city B to city C : 1 journey × 160 kms × 6 tonnes	= 960 tonnes-kms
Total	23,760 tonnes-kms

(*iii*) *Total absolute tonnes-kms of outward and return journeys:*

= 20,960 tonnes-kms + 23,760 tonnes-km = 44,720 tonnes-kms

(*iv*) *Net revenue received during January 20X6.*

	₹
(From city A to city B) 12 trucks × 6 tonnes × ₹ 90	6,480
(From city B to city A) 5 trucks × 8 tonnes × ₹ 84	3,360
(From city B to city A) 6 trucks × 6 tonnes × ₹ 84	3,024
(From city B to city C) 1 truck × 6 tonnes × ₹ 84	504
Total revenue:	13,368
Less: Fine paid	1,200
Net revenue received	12,168

Illustration 10. A company is considering three alternative proposals for conveyance facilities for its sales personnel who have to do considerable travelling, approximately 20,000 kilometres every year.

The proposals are as follows:

(*i*) Purchase and maintain its own fleet of cars. The average cost of a car is ₹ 1,00,000.

(*ii*) Allow the executive to use his own car and reimburse expenses at the rate of ₹ 1.60 per kilometre and also bear insurance costs.

(*iii*) Hire cars from an agency at ₹ 20,000 per year per car. The company will have to bear costs of petrol, taxes and tyres.

The following further details are available:

Petrol ₹ 0.60 per km.

Repairs and Maintenance ₹ 0.20 per km.

Tyre ₹ 0.12 per km.

Insurance ₹ 1,200 per car per annum.

Taxes ₹ 800 per car per annum.

Life of the car : 5 years with annual mileage of 20,000 kms.

Resale value : ₹ 20,000 at the end of the fifth year.

Required: Work out the relative costs of three proposals and rank them.

Solution:

	Particulars	Alternative Proposals			
		I Use of Concern's Car		II Use of Own Car	III Use of Hire Car
		₹ Per annum	₹ Per km.	₹ Per km.	₹ Per km.
A.	**Reimbursement :** of Hire Charges		—	1.60	1.0C (20,000/20,000 km)
B.	**Fixed Costs :** (Per Car Per km)				
	Taxes (p.a.)	800	—	—	0.04 (₹ 800/20,000 km)

Particulars	Alternative Proposals I Use of Concern's Car ₹ Per annum	₹ Per km.	II Use of Own Car ₹ Per km.	III Use of Hire Car ₹ Per km.
Depreciation (₹ 1,00,000 — ₹ 20,000) / 5	16,000	—	—	—
Insurance	1,200	—	0.06 (1,200/20,000 km)	—
Total	18,000	0.90	1.66	1.04
(₹ 18,000/20,000 km)				
C. **Running & Maintenance Cost :** Per Car Per km				
Petrol		0.60	—	0.60
Repairs and maintenance		0.20	—	—
Tyre		0.12	—	0.12
D. **Total Cost : (Per km) (A + B + C)**		1.82	1.66	1.76
E. **Cost for 20,000 kms**	₹ 36,400 (20,000 × ₹ 1.82)		₹ 33,200 (20,000 × ₹ 1.66)	₹ 35,200 (20,000 × ₹ 1.76)
F. **Ranking of Alternative Proposals**		III	I	II

Decision: Use of own car by Sales Executives will be the most economical proposal from the Concern's point of view. Hiring of car, for the use of Sales Executives will be the IInd best choice and maintaining a fleet of cars for its executives will be the costliest alternative.

Illustration 11. Iron ore is transported from two mines "*A*" and "*B*" and unloaded at plots in a railway station. "*A*" is at a distance of 15 kms and "*B*" is at a distance of 10 kms from the railhead plots. A fleet of lorries of 5 tonne carrying capacity is used for the transport of ore from the mines. Records reveal that the lorries averages a speed of 30 kms per hour when running and regularly take 10 minutes to unload at the railhead. At mine "*A*" loading time average 30 minute per load while at mine "*B*" loading time averages 20 minutes per load.

Driver's wages, depreciation, insurance and taxes are found to cost ₹ 9 per hour operated. Fuel, oil, tyres, repairs and maintenance cost ₹ 1.20 per km.

Required: Draw up a statement showing the cost per tonne-kilometre of carrying iron ore from each mine.

Solution: **STATEMENT SHOWING COST PER TONNE-KM**

	Particulars	Mine 'A' ₹	Mine 'B' ₹
A.	Drivers Wages, depreciation Insurance & Taxes @ ₹ 9 per hour.	$\frac{100 \times 9}{60} = 15.00$	$\frac{70 \times 9}{60} = 10.50$
B.	Fuel, Oil, Tyres, Repairs & Maintenance Cost @ ₹ 1.20 km	(15 + 15) × 1.20 = 36.00	(10 + 10) × 1.20 = 24.00
C.	Total Cost (A + B)	51.00	34.50
D.	Tonne km	75	50
E.	Cost per tonne-km (C/D)	0.68	0.69

Working Notes:

(*i*) *Calculation of Tonne km*

		A	B
A.	Distance-km	15	10
B.	Tonne	5	5
C.	Tonne-km (A × B)	75	50

(*ii*) *Calculation of Time taken per trip-(Minutes)*

A.	Running time-going	30	20
B.	Running time-returning	30	20
C.	Loading	30	20
D.	Unloading	10	10
E.	Total (A + B + C + D)	100	70

Illustration 12. In order to develop tourism, TULSIAN airlines has been given permit to operate three flights in a week between *P* and *Q* cities (both side). The airline operates a single aircraft of 150 seats capacity. The normal occupancy is estimated at 60% through out the year of 52 weeks. The one-way fare is ₹ 7,000. The cost of operation of flights are:

Fuel cost (variable)	₹ 85,500 per flight
Food served on board on non-chargeable basis	₹ 100 per passenger
Commission	5% of fare applicable for all booking
Fixed costs :	
Aircraft lease	₹ 3,00,000 per flight
Landing charges	₹ 54,000 per flight

Required: (*i*) Calculate the net operating income per flight.

(*ii*) The airline expects that its occupancy will increase to 70% if the fare is reduced by 5%. Advise whether this proposal be implemented *or* not.

Solution: (*i*) **STATEMENT SHOWING THE OPERATING INCOME PER FLIGHT**

Particulars		₹	₹
A. Fare collection (90 × 7,000)			6,30,000
B. *Less:* Variable Costs:	Fuel		85,500
	Food (90 × ₹ 100)		9,000
	Commission (5% of ₹ 6,30,000)		31,500
Total variable Costs			1,26,000
C. Contribution per flight [A – B]			5,04,000
D. *Less:* Fixed Costs:	*Lease*	3,00,000	
	Crew	54,000	3,54,000
E. Net Income per flight [C – D)			1,50,000

Note: No. of passengers = 150 × 60% = 90

(*ii*) **STATEMENT SHOWING THE EVALUATION OF PROPOSAL**

		₹
A. Fare collection [105 × (₹ 7,000 – 5% of ₹ 7000)]		6,98,250
B. *Less:* Variable costs: Fuel		85,500
	Food [105 × ₹ 100]	10,500
	Commission @ 5%	34,912.50
		1,30,912.50
C. Contribution [A – B]		5,67,337.50

Advise: There is an increase in contribution by ₹ 63,337.50. Hence the proposal is acceptable.

6.0 BOILER HOUSE AND POWER HOUSE COSTING

MEANING AND OBJECTIVES OF BOILER HOUSE COSTING

Meaning	Boiler House Costing is a method of ascertaining the cost of producing steam by a Boiler house.
Objectives	The objectives of Boiler House Costing are as follows: (*a*) To ascertain the operating cost of producing steam (*b*) To fix the rates of steams to be charged to various departments using steam (*c*) To compare the cost of producing steam with that of using alternative mode of producing steam.

MEANING AND OBJECTIVES OF POWER HOUSE COSTING

Meaning	Power House Costing is a method of ascertaining the cost of generating electricity by a power house.
Objectives	The objectives of Power House Costing are as follows: (*a*) To ascertain the operating cost of generating electricity (*b*) To fix the rates of electricity to be charged to various departments using electricity (*c*) To compare the cost of generating electricity with that of using alternative mode of generating electricity.

POWER HOUSE COSTING PROCEDURE

Power House Costing procedure involves the following practical steps:

PRACTICAL STEPS INVOLVED IN POWER HOUSE COSTING PROCEDURE

Step 1 → *Select the cost unit as follows:*

Cost Unit	*Example*
(*a*) *Simple Cost Unit*	*per kilowatt*
(*b*) *Composite Cost Unit*	*per kilowatt hour*

Step 2 → *Calculate effective units of service for a particular period as follows:*
Effective units of service = Total units generated — Units consumed by the plant it self – Normal loss (if any) in the process

Step 3 → *Calculate Total and per unit Steam Production Costs*

Step 4 → *Calculate Total and per unit Electricity Generation Costs*

FORMAT OF POWER HOUSE OPERATING COST SHEET

POWER HOUSE OPERATING COST SHEET

For the Month of .....

Steam produced.......units

Electricity generated .... units
Steam used for generation .... units

Particulars	*Total* ₹	*Per unit* ₹
Steam Production Costs:		
Direct material : Coal	......	......
: Water	......	......

Direct Labour :	Wages for coal handling	......	......
:	Wages for stoking	......	......
Overheads :	Indirect Materials – oil	......	......
:	Indirect Labour – supervision	......	......
:	Indirect Expenses – Depreciation	......	......
:	Repair & Maintenance	......	......
	Total lbs.	......	......
Total Production of Steam.....units		......	......
Steam used for generation of electricity		......	
Electricity Generation Costs:			
Cost of steam used		......	
Wages of operators		......	
Depreciation		......	......
Repairs		......	......
Supervision charges		......	......
	Total....	......	......

Illustration 13. From the following data pertaining to the current year prepare a cost sheet showing the cost of electricity generated per KWh by National Thermal Power Station.

Total units generated	20,00,000 KWh
	₹
Operating labour	1,00,000
Repairs & maintenance	1,00,000
Lubricants, spares and stores	80,000
Plant supervision	60,000
Administration overheads	40,000

Coal consumed per KWh for the year is 2.5 Kg. @ ₹ 0.02 per kg. Depreciation charges @ 5% on capital cost of ₹ 4,00,000.

Solution: **POWER HOUSE COST STATEMENT**

Total units generated 20,00,000 KWh.

Particulars	*Per annum* ₹	*Per k.w.h.* ₹
A. Fixed Costs:		
Plant supervision	60,000	
Administration overheads	40,000	
Depreciation (5% of ₹ 4,00,000 p.a.)	20,000	
Total fixed cost:	1,20,000	0.06
B. Variable Costs:		
Operating labour	1,00,000	0.05
Lubricating, spares & stores	80,000	0.04
Repairs & maintenance	1,00,000	0.05
Coal cost (*Refer to working note*)	1,00,000	0.05
Total variable cost:	3,80,000	0.19
C. Total Cost [(*A*) + (*B*)]	5,00,000	0.25

Working Note: Coal cost = 20,00,000 KWh × 2.5 kg × 0.02 per kg = ₹ 1,00,000

Illustration 14. From the following information calculate the cost of generating electricity per unit :

(*a*) Coal used 600 tonnes @ ₹ 20 per tonne.
(*b*) Freight and handling charges: 10% of value of the coal used.
(*c*) Oil : 10 tonnes @ ₹ 250 per tonne.
(*d*) Water : 25,000 litres @ ₹ 0.50 per 100 litres.
(*e*) Depreciation of steam boiler ₹ 250
(*f*) Salaries and wages of the boiler house : 5 men @ ₹ 200 each; 20 coolies @ ₹ 40 each.
(*g*) Recovery on account of sale of ashes : 100 tonnes @ ₹ 1 per tonne.
(*h*) Salaries and wages of generating stations : 25 men @ ₹ 200 each; 10 collies @ ₹ 40 each
(*i*) Repairs and maintenance of generating equipment ₹ 260.

(*j*) Depreciation on generating equipment @ 10% p.a. cost of generating equipment ₹ 25,000
(*k*) Share of administration charges : ₹ 2,865
(*l*) Total Number of units generated : 1,46,000.
(*m*) Normal loss in the process : 2,000 units generated

Solution: **OPERATING COST STATEMENT**

Materials:		
Coal used 600 tonnes @ ₹ 20 per tonne		₹ 12,000
Oil 10 tonnes @ ₹ 250 per tonne		2,500
Water 25,000 litres @ ₹ 0.50 per 100 litres		125
Wages :	₹	
Boiler House : 5 men @ ₹ 200 each	1,000	
20 coolies @ ₹ 40 each	800	1,800
Generating Station : 25 men @ ₹ 200 each	5,000	
10 cooles @ ₹ 40 each	400	5,400
Freight and handling charges : 10% of value of coal used		1,200
Prime Cost		23,025
Depreciation on steam boiler		250
Repairs and maintenance of generating equipment		260
Depreciation of generating equipment		2,500
		26,035
Less : Recovery on account of sale of ashes : 100 tonnes @ ₹ 1 per tonne		100
Works Cost		25,935
Share of administration charges		2,865
A. **Total Operating Cost**		28,800
B. Units generated	1,46,000	
Less : Normal loss	2,000	1,44,000
C. Cost of electricity generated per unit (28,800/1,44,000)		20 paise

Illustration 15. From the following information, calculate cost per therm and cost per unit of electricity generated for the month of March :

(*a*) Coal 200 Tonnes @ ₹ 0.12 per kg
(*b*) Water 4,00,000 litres @ ₹ 10 per 10,000 litres
(*c*) Oil 30 quintals @ ₹ 10,000 per 10 quintals
(*d*) Freight & Handling of coal — 10% of cost of coal
(*e*) Charges for ash disposal is ₹ 200
(*f*) *Common expenses :*

Wages and Salaries	₹ 30,000
Repair and Maintenance	₹ 3,500
Office and Administrative Cost	₹ 4,000

(*g*)

	Steam Producing Plant	*Electricity Generating Plant*
Cost	₹ 62,000	₹ 2,50,000
Residual Value	₹ 2,000	₹ 10,000
Life	10 yrs.	10 yrs.
Wages and Salaries (Ratio)	2	1
Office and Administrative Cost (Ratio)	3	5
Repair and Maintenance (Ratio)	2	5
Total Production	1,00,000	10,00,000
Production used by plant itself	—	10%
Steam used for generation	80%	—

Solution: **STATEMENT SHOWING COST PER THERM**

	Particulars	₹
	Coal 200 tons (200 × ₹ 120)	24,000
	Oil 30 quintals (30 × ₹ 1,000)	30,000
	Water 4,00,000 Lt. (4,00,000 × ₹ .001)	400
	Freight & Handling Charges @ 10% of cost of coal	2,400
	Charges for ash disposal	200
	Wages & Salaries of employees	20,000
	Share of Office & Adm. Cost	1,500
	Repairs & Maintenance	1,000
	Depreciation [(₹ 62,000 – ₹ 2,000)/10 yrs/12]	500
A.	Cost of 1,00,000 production	80,000
B.	*Less :* 1/5 allocated to heating 20,000 Therm	16,000
C.	Used for generation of electricity (80,000 Therm)	64,000
D.	Cost per Therm (₹ 64,000/80,000)	80 Paise

STATEMENT SHOWING COST PER UNIT OF ELECTRICITY GENERATION

	Particulars	*Units*	₹
A.	Cost of 80,000 Therm @ 80 paise		64,000
B.	Wages & Salaries		10,000
C.	Share of Office & Adm. Cost		2,500
D.	Repair & Maintenance		2,500
E.	Depreciation [(₹ 2,50,000 – ₹ 10,000)/10/12]		2,000
F.	Cost of 10,00,000 units	10,00,000	81,000
G.	Electricity used in generating the electricity	1,00,000	—
H.	Total Cost of 9,00,000 units	9,00,000	81,000
I.	Cost Per Unit (₹ 81,000/9,00,000)		9 Paise.

7.0 CANTEEN COSTING

Meaning	Canteen Costing is a method of ascertaining the cost of providing meals *or* dishes of different types.
Objectives	The objectives of Canteen Costing are as follows: (*a*) To ascertain the cost of producing meals *or* dishes (*b*) To fix the rates of meals/dishes to be charged.
Procedure	Canteen Costing procedure involves the following practical steps: **PRACTICAL STEPS INVOLVED IN CANTEEN COSTING PROCEDURE** **Step 1 →** *Select the cost unit which is usually cost per meal* **Step 2 →** *Calculate Total fixed/standing charges allocated and apportioned to canteen* **Step 3 →** *Calculate total and per unit variable charges (like provisions, e.g., fruits, vegetables, flour, maida, spices, oil etc)* **Step 4 →** *Calculate Cost per meal*

FORMAT OF CANTEEN OPERATING COST SHEET

CANTEEN OPERATING COST SHEET
for the month..........

Particulars	*Total* ₹	*Per unit* ₹
Provisions:		
Wheat flour	......	......
Bread	......	......
Vegetable	......	......
Milk	......	......
Cream	......	......
Cold drinks	......	......
Eggs	......	......
Tea and Coffee	.....	......
Wages and Salaries:		
Wages of Cooks	......	......
Wages of Kitchen Assistants	......	......
Wages of Waiters	......	......
Salary of Supervisor	......	......
Services:		
Gas (LPG)	......	......
Power and lighting	......	......
Water	......	......
Consumable Stores:		
Crockery and Glassware	......	......
Cleaning Materials	......	......
Miscelleneous:		
Rent	......	......
Insurance	......	......
Depreciation	......	......
Total	......	......
Profit	......	......
Sales	......	......

Illustration 16. RAM JI KA DHABA serves fixed lunch/dinner thali to its customers and provides you the following information for the month of April :

	₹
Wheat flour	9,000
Vegetables	4,500
Oil	3,600
Spices etc.	900
Wages of cook	3,000
Wages of Kitchen assistant	2,400
Wages of waiter	1,500
Gas 1,500	
Water	300
Power & lighting	750
Crockery	225
Cleaning materials	150
Rent	2,175
No. of thalies served (including 60 thalies served to Drivers & Conductors)	1,560
Profit margin	$33\frac{1}{3}$% on sales

It is the policy to serve drivers & conductors free of charge.

Required: Calculate the selling price to be charged for each thali.

Solution:

RAM JI KA DHABA
THALI OPERATING COST SHEET
for the month April — *No. of Thalies 1500*

Particulars	*Total* ₹	*Per unit* ₹
Provisions:		
Wheat flour	9,000	6.00
Vegetable	4,500	3.00
Oil	3,600	2.40
Spices etc.	900	.60
Wages and Salaries:		
Wages of Cook	3,000	2.00
Wages of Kitchen Assistants	2,400	1.60
Wages of Waiter	1,500	1.00
Services:		
Gas (LPG)	1,500	1.00
Power and lighting	750	.50
Water	300	.20
Consumable Stores:		
Crockery and glassware	225	.15
Cleaning materials	150	.10
Miscellaneous:		
Rent	2,175	1.45
A Total Cost	30,000	20
B Profit @ $33\frac{1}{3}$ % on sales *or* 50% on Cost	15,000	10
C Sales [A + B]	45,000	30

Note: Cost of 60 thalies served to Drivers and Conductors has been treated as normal loss and hence no. of thalies has been taken as 1500 (i.e., 1560 – 60) so as to inflate the cost per thali.

8.0 HOTEL COSTING

Meaning	Hotel Costing is a method of ascertaining the cost of providing services by a hotel.
Objectives	The objectives of Hotel Costing are as follows: (a) To ascertain the operating cost of running a hotel. (b) To fix the room rent per day on the basis of operating costs. (c) To fix the hire charges of banquet hall.
Hotel Costing Procedure	Hotel Costing Procedure involves the following practical steps: **PRACTICAL STEPS INVOLVED IN HOTEL COSTING PROCEDURE** **Step 1:** *Select the Cost Unit as follows:* *(a) Per Room Per Day* *(b) Per Bed Per Day* **Step 2:** *Calculate the Total Room Days for a particular period (say year, quarter, month or week)* ***Effective Room Days*** *= No. of Rooms × Occupancy Rate × No. of days* **Step 3:** *Calculate Total Fixed Costs for a particular period (For Example, Salary of Permanent Staff, Depreciation on Hotel Building & Furniture)* **Step 4:** *Calculate Fixed Costs per room day as follows:* *Fixed Costs per room day* $= \frac{\text{Total Fixed Costs (as per Step 3)}}{\text{Total No. of Room Days (as per Step 2)}}$

Step 5: *Calculate Total Variable Costs (For Example, Cost of Free Tea and Coffee in the Room, Cost of Complementary Breakfast, Cost of Toilet and Bathroom Supplies, Laundry Cost of Bed Sheets and Towels)*

Step 6: *Calculate Variable Costs per room day as follows:*

Variable Costs per room day

$$= \frac{\text{Total Variable Costs (as per step 5)}}{\text{Total No. of Room Days (as per step 2)}}$$

Step 7: *Calculate Operating Cost per room day as follows:*

A. Fixed Costs per room day	xxx
B. Variable Costs per room day	xxx
C. Operating Cost per room day	xxx

Format of Hotel Operating Cost Sheet

OPERATING COST SHEET

Particulars	*Total* ₹	*Per Room Day* ₹
A. Fixed Costs (or Standing Charges):		
1. Staff Salaries	......	......
2. Room Attendant's Wages	......	......
3. Lighting, Heating & Power	......	......
4. Repairs & Maintenance	......	......
5. License Fees	......	......
6. Interior Decorating & Furnishing	......	......
7. Depreciation on Hotel Building & Furniture	......	......
Total (A)	......	......
B. Variable Costs :		
1. Cost of Free Tea and Coffee in the Room	......	......
2. Cost of Complementary Breakfast	......	......
3. Cost of Toilet and Bathroom Supplies	......	......
4. Laundry Cost of Bed Sheets and Towels	......	......
Total (B)	......	......
Operating Cost (A + B)	......	......

Illustration 17. From the following information, calculate room days of a Hotel:

Number of Rooms	300
Occupancy Rate	90%
No. of days in a month	30
No. of working months in a year	7

Solution:

Room Days = Number of Rooms × Occupancy Rate × No. of Days in a month × No. of Working Months in a Year
= 300 × 90% × 30 × 7 = 56,700

Illustration 18. From the following information, calculate what rent should be charged for each type of suits :

Single Room Days	51,300
Double Room Days	22,800
Three Room Days	9,300
Total Room Rent Receipts	₹ 62,46,000

Rent of single room to be fixed as 2/3rd of double room suite of which rent is 3/4 of the rent of three room suite.

Solution:

(i) 2 Double Room Suite = 3 Single Room
1 Double Room Suite = 3/2 Single Room

(ii) 3 Three Room Suite = 4 Double Room Suite
1 Three Room Suite = 4/3 Double Room Suite

or, 1 Three Room Suite = 4/3 × 3/2 = 2 Single Room Suite
Thus, Ratio is 1 : 3/2 : 2 = (1 × 51,300) : (3/2 × 22,800) : (2 × 9,300)
= 51,300 + 34,200 + 18,600 = 1,04,100

A.	Total Room Rent Receipts	₹ 62,46,000
B.	Total Single Room Days	1,04,100
C.	Rent per Single Room (A/B)	₹ 60
D.	Rent per Double Room Suite (₹ 60 × 3/2)	₹ 90
E.	Rent for Three Room Suite (₹ 60 × 2)	₹ 120

Illustration 19. From the following information relating to a hotel, calculate the room rent to be charged to give a profit of 25% on cost excluding interest

(i) Salaries of staff : ₹ 1,02,200 p.a.
(ii) Wages of the room attendant : ₹ 4 per day
There is a room attendant for each room. He is paid wages only when the room is occupied.
(iii) Lighting, Heating and Power
(a) The normal lighting expenses for each room for the whole month is ₹ 100 when occupied.
(b) Power is used only in winter and the charges are ₹ 40 p.m. for a room, when occupied.
(iv) Repairs to buildings : ₹ 10,000 p.a.
(v) Licence etc : ₹ 4,800 p.a.
(vi) Sundries : ₹ 6,600 p.a.
(vii) Interior decoration and furnishing : ₹ 10,000 p.a.
(viii) Depreciation @ 5% is to be charged on buildings costing ₹ 4,00,000 and 10% on equipments.
(ix) Interest to be charged @ 20% on investment in buildings and equipments amounting to ₹ 5,00,000.
(x) There are 100 rooms in the hotel 80% of the rooms are generally occupied in summer and 30% in winter. The period of summer and winter may be considered to be of 6 month in each case : A month may be assumed of 30 days.

Solution: OPERATING COST STATEMENT SHOWING ROOM RENT PER DAY

(Room-Days : 19,800)

	Particulars		*Per annum*
A.	**Total Cost**		
	Staff Salaries		1,02,200
	Room Attendant's wages [Refer to Working Note (ii)]		79,200
	Lighting, Heating and Power [Refer to Working Note (iii)]		73,200
	Repair to buildings		10,000
	Licence etc.		4,800
	Sundries		6,600
	Interior Decoration and Furnishing		10,000
	Depreciation on :		
	Building @ 5% on ₹ 4,00,000	₹ 20,000	
	Other Equipments @ 10% (5,00,000 – 4,00,000)	₹ 10,000	30,000
	Interest on Investments (20% on ₹ 5,00,000)		1,00,000
	Total Cost		4,16,000
B.	Profit @ 25% on cost excluding interest (i.e. 25% on ₹ 3,16,000)		79,000
C.	Total Rent to be charged for all rooms (A + B)		4,95,000
D.	Room-days		19,800
E.	Room Rent per day (C/D)		25

Working Notes :

(i) *Calculation of Room Days :*

Summer : 100 rooms × 80/100 × 6 months × 30 days	=	14,400
Winter : 100 rooms × 30/100 × 6 months × 30 days	=	5,400
Total		19,800

(ii) *Calculation of Room Attendants' Wages :*

Summer : ₹ 4 × 100 rooms × 80% × 6 months × 30 days	=	₹ 57,600
Winter : ₹ 4 × 100 rooms × 30% × 6 months × 30 days	=	21,600
Total		79,200

(iii) *Calculation of Lighting, Heating and Power :*

Lighting :

Summer : ₹ 100 × 100 rooms × 80% × 6 months	=	₹ 48,000
Winter : ₹ 100 × 100 rooms × 30% × 6 months	=	18,000
Power :		
Winter : ₹ 40 × 100 rooms × 30% × 6 months	=	7,200
Total		73,200

Illustration 20. From the following informations, calculate what rent should be charged for each type of suits.

	Summer Season for 7 Months			*Winter Season for 5 Months*		
	1 Room	*2 Rooms*	*3 Rooms*	*1 Room*	*2 Rooms*	*3 Rooms*
No. of Rooms	100	50	25	100	50	25
Occupancy Rate	90%	80%	60%	45%	40%	40%
Wages of Room Attendant per Day	₹ 2	₹ 3	₹ 4	₹ 3	₹ 4.50	₹ 6
Lighting p.m. per room	₹ 45	₹ 60	₹ 90	₹ 45	₹ 60	₹ 90
Power p.m.per room	₹ 18	₹ 30	₹ 36	₹ 9	₹ 9	₹ 9

Detail of Annual Expenses :

(a) Staff Salaries ₹ 1,76,000
(b) Repair and Maintenance ₹ 30,000
(c) Linen etc. ₹ 45,000
(d) Interior Decoration Costs ₹ 60,000
(e) Sundry Expenses ₹ 47,730
(f) *Details of Investments and Rates of Depreciation :*
 (a) Building ₹ 20 lacs, Rate of Depreciation 5%
 (b) Furniture and Fixtures ₹ 7.5 lacs, Rate of Depreciation 10%
(g) Interest @ 18% p.a. on the Total fixed Investments to be charged as part of cost.
(h) Desired Profit is 20% on Rent Receipts
(i) Rent of single room to be fixed as 2/3rd of double room suite of which rent is 3/4 the of the rent of three room suite.

Solution: **STATEMENT SHOWING RENT PER ROOM TO BE CHARGED**

Particulars		₹
Staff Salaries		1,76,000
Room Attendant's Salary		1,18,350
Lighting Charges		75,225
Power Charges		26,895
Repairs & Maintenance		30,000
Linen etc.		45,000
Interior Decoration & Provision		60,000
Salaries		47,730
Depreciation on :		
— Building	₹ 1,00,000	
— Furniture & Fixture	₹ 75,000	1,75,000
Interest @ 18% on ₹ 27,50,000		4,95,000
A. Total cost		12,49,200
B. Profit @ 25% on Cost		3,12,300
C. Total Rent Receipts (A + B)		15,61,500
D. Total Single Room Days		52,050
E. Rent per Single Room (C/D)		₹ 30
F. Rent for Double Room Suite (₹ 30 ✖ 3/2)		₹ 45
G. Rent for Three Room Suite (₹ 30 ✖ 2)		₹ 60

Working Notes :

(i) **CALCULATION OF ROOM DAYS, ROOM ATTENDANTS SALARY, LIGHT AND POWER**

Particulars	*Summer Season for 7 Months*			*Winter Season for 5 Months*			*Total*
	Single Room	*Double Room*	*Three Room*	*Single Room*	*Double Room*	*Three Room*	
1. No. of Rooms	100	50	25	100	50	25	
2. Occupancy Rate	90%	80%	60%	45%	40%	40%	
3. No. of Days in a month	30	30	30	30	30	30	
4. No. of months	7	7	7	5	5	5	
5. Room Days (1 × 2 × 3 × 4)	18,900	8,400	3,150	6,750	3,000	1,500	
6. Room Attendant's Wages per room per day	₹ 2	₹ 3	₹ 4	₹ 3	₹ 4.50	₹ 6	
7. Total Room Attendant's Salary (5 × 6)	37,800	25,200	12,600	20,250	13,500	9,000	1,18,350
8. Lighting per room per day	₹ 1.50	₹ 2	₹ 3	₹ 1.50	₹ 2	₹ 3	
9. Total Light Charges (5 × 8)	₹ 28,350	₹ 16,800	₹ 9,450	₹ 10,125	₹ 6,000	₹ 4,500	75,225
10. Power per room per day	₹ 0.60	₹ 1	₹ 1.20	₹ 0.30	₹ 0.30	₹ 0.30	
11. Total Power charges (5 × 10)	₹ 11,340	₹ 8,400	₹ 3,780	₹ 2,025	₹ 900	450	26,895

(ii) *Calculation of Single Room Days*

2 Double Room Suite = 3 Single Room
1 Double Room Suite = 3/2 Single Room
3 Three Room Suite = 4 Double Room Suite
1 Three Room Suite = 4/3 Double Room Suite
or, 1 Three Room Suite = 4/3 × 3/2 = 2 Single Room Suites
Thus, Ratio is 1 : 3/2 : 2 = 1 × 25,650 + 1.5 × 11,400 + 2 × 4,650 = 52,050

Verification:

	Single Room	*Double Room*	*Three Room*	*Total*
1. Total Days	25,650	11,400	4,650	52,050 Single Room Days
2. Rent per Day	₹ 30	₹ 45	₹ 60	
3. Total Rent (1 x 2)	₹ 7,69,500	₹ 5,13,000	₹ 2,79,000	₹ 15,61,500

9.0 HOSPITAL COSTING

Meaning	Hospital Costing is a method of ascertaining the cost of providing services by a hospital.
Objectives	The objectives of Hospital Costing are as follows: (a) To ascertain the operating cost of running a Hospital. (b) To fix the room rent per day/bed on the basis of operating costs.
Hospital Costing Procedure	Hospital Costing Procedure involves the following practical steps: **PRACTICAL STEPS INVOLVED IN HOSPITAL COSTING PROCEDURE** **Step 1:** *Select the Cost Unit as follows:* *(a) Per Patient Per Day* *(b) Per Bed Per Day*

Step 2: *Calculate the total Patient Days for a particular period (say year, quarter, month or week)*

***Effective Patient days** = No. of Beds × Occupancy Rate × No. of days*

Step 3: *Calculate Total Fixed Costs for a particular period (For Example, Salary of Permanent Staff, Depreciation on Hospital Building & Furniture)*

Step 4: *Calculate Fixed Costs per patient days as follows:*

Fixed Costs per patient day

$$= \frac{\text{Total Costs (as per step 3)}}{\text{Total No. of Patient days (as per step 2)}}$$

Step 5: *Calculate Total Variable Costs. (For Example, Cost of Free Food Supply, Cost of Toilet and Bathroom Supplies, Laundry Cost of Bed Sheets and Towels)*

Step 6: *Calculate Variable Costs per patient day as follows:*

Variable Costs per patient day

$$= \frac{\text{Total Variable Costs (as per step 5)}}{\text{Total No. of Patient days (as per step 2)}}$$

Step 7: *Calculate Operating Cost per patient day as follows:*

A.	*Fixed Costs per patient day*	*xxx*
B.	*Variable Costs per patient day*	*xxx*
C.	*Operating Cost per patient day*	*xxx*

Format of Hotel Operating Cost Sheet

OPERATING COST SHEET

Particulars	*Total* ₹	*Per Room Day* ₹
A. Fixed Costs (or Standing Charges):		
1. Staff Salaries (Permanent Doctors, Supervisors, Nurses, Ward Boys, etc.)	....	....
2. Room Attendant's Wages	....	....
3. Lighting, Heating & Power	....	....
4. Repairs & Maintenance	....	....
5. Rent	....	....
6. License Fees	....	....
7. General Administrating Expenses	....	....
8. Depreciation on Hospital Building & Furniture	....	....
Total (A)	....	....
B. Variable Costs :		
1. Cost of Free Food Supply	....	....
2. Cost of Toilet and Bathroom Supplies	....	....
3. Laundry Cost of Bed Sheets and Towels	....	....
Total (B)	....	....
Operating Cost (A + B)	....	....

Illustration 21. From the following information, calculate Patient Days:

	General Ward	*Semi-Deluxe Ward*	*Deluxe Ward*
Number of Wards	10	20	30
Number of Beds in each Ward	30	2	1
Occupancy Rate for 200 Days	100%	80%	60%
Occupancy Rate for rest of the year	80%	60%	40%

But in General Ward there were occasions when beds are full, extra beds are hired at a charge of ₹ 100 per bed. The total hire charges for the extra beds incurred for the whole year amounted to ₹ 20,000.

The rent of Semi-Deluxe Ward Bed is to be fixed at 3 times of the General Ward Bed and that of Deluxe Ward Bed as twice of Semi-Deluxe Ward Bed.

Solution: **CALCULATION OF PATIENT DAYS**

Ward	*No. of Wards*	*No. of Beds*	*Occupancy Rate*		*Occupancy*			*Weight of Rent*	*Patient Days*
			For 200 Days	For 165 Days	For 200 Days	For 165 Days	Total		
General	10	30	100%	80%	60,000	39,600	99,600	1	99,600
Additional General	—	200 (₹ 20,000 /₹ 100)	100%	100%	40,000	33,000	73,000	1	73,000
Semi-Deluxe	20	2	80%	60%	6,400	3,960	10,360	3	31,080
Deluxe	30	1	60%	40%	3,600	1,980	5,580	6	33,480
Total									2,37,160

Illustration 22. Along with the following information in previous Illustration 21 calculate the Rent to be charged for each Bed Day for different types of Wards:

Total Operating Cost (excluding Building Rent @ 5% on Total Takings): ₹1,778.70 Lakhs
Desired Profit: 20% on Total Takings

Solution:

Let the Total Takings be x

x = Total Operating Cost + Profit = (₹ 1,778.70 Lakhs + 0.05x) + 0.20x

₹ 1,778.70 Lakhs / 0.75 = ₹ 2,371.60 Lakhs

Rent to be charged for General Ward Bed $= \dfrac{\text{Total Takings}}{\text{No. of Patient Days}}$

$= \dfrac{\text{2,371.60 Lakhs}}{\text{2.37160 Lakhs}}$ = ₹ 1,000 per bed per day

Rent to be charged for Semi-Deluxe Ward Bed = ₹ 1,000 × 3 = ₹ 3,000 per bed per day

Rent to be charged for Deluxe Ward Bed = ₹ 1,000 × 6 = ₹ 6,000 per bed per day

Illustration 23. Roop Nagar Hospital runs an intensive Medical Care Unit. For this purpose, it has hired a building at a rent of ₹ 5,000 p.m. with the understanding that it would bear the repairs and maintenance charges also.

The unit consists of 25 beds and 5 more beds can be comfortably accommodated when occasion demands. The permanent staff attached to the unit are as follows :

1 Supervisor, at a salary of ₹ 1,000 p.m.
2 Nurses, each at a salary of ₹ 600 p.m.
1 Ward boy, at a salary of ₹ 300 p.m.

Though the unit was open for the patients all the 365 days in a year, scrutiny of accounts revealed that only for 120 days in the year, the unit had the 100% occupacy rate and for another 80 days it had on an average 80% occupacy rate. But there were occasions when the beds were full, extra beds were hired from outside at a charge of ₹ 5 per bed per day and this did not come to more than 5 beds extra above the normal capacity on any one day. The total hire charges for the extra beds incurred for the whole year amounted to ₹ 2,000.

The unit engaged expert doctors from outside to attend on the patients and the fees were paid on the basis of the number of patients attended and time spent by them and on an average worked out to ₹ 10,000 p.m. in 20X1.

The other expenses for the year were as under :

	₹
Repairs and Maintenance	14,450
Food supplied to patients	44,000
Monitor and other services for them	12,500
Laundry charges for their bed linen	28,000
Medicines supplied	73,500
General administration charges allocated to the unit	49,550

(i) If the unit recovered an over all amount of ₹ 100 per day on an average from each patient, what is the profit per patient made by the unit in 20X1 ?

(ii) The unit wants to work on a budget for the year 20X2, but the number of patients requiring intensive medical care is a very uncertain factor. Assuming that same revenue and expenses prevail in 20X2, in the first instance, work out the number of patient-days required by the unit to break even.

Solution:

ROOP NAGAR HOSPITAL
INTENSIVE MEDICAL CARE UNIT
(I) STATEMENT SHOWING OPERATING COST & PROFIT

	Particulars	*P.A.* ₹	*Per patient-Day* ₹
A.	**Fixed Expenses :**		
	(a) Rent (₹ 5,000 x 12)	60,000	
	(b) Salaries *[Refer to Working Note (i)]*	30,000	
	(c) Repair & Maintenance	14,450	
	(d) Gen-Adm. Charges	49,550	
		1,54,000	30.80
B.	**Variable Expenses :**		
	(a) Hire charges for extra beds	2,000	
	(b) Fees Paid to expert doctors	1,20,000	
	(c) Food	44,000	
	(d) Monitor & Other like services	12,500	
	(e) Laundry Charges	28,000	
	(f) Medicines	73,500	
		2,80,000	56.00
C.	Total Operating Cost (A + B)	4,34,000	86.80
D.	Average Charges recovered from patient	5,00,000	100.00
E.	Profit per Patient-Day (D – C)	66,000	13.20
F.	Contribution per Patient-Day (D – B)	2,20,000	44.00

(ii) Break Even Point = Fixed Cost ÷ Contribution per Patient Day
(in Patient-Days) = ₹ 1,54,000 ÷ ₹ 44 = ₹ 3,500 Patient–Days

Working Notes :

(i) *Calculation of Salaries*

Supervisors (1 × ₹ 1,000 × 12)	= ₹	12,000
Nurses (2 × ₹ 600 × 12)	= ₹	14,400
Ward boy (1 × ₹ 300 × 12)	= ₹	3,600
	₹	30,000

(ii) Patient-Days = (120 × 25) + (80 × 20) + (2000/5) = 3,000 + 1,600 + 400 = 5,000 Patient - Days

SOLVED POBLEMS I

Problem 1. The Union Transport Company has been given a 20 kilometre long route to ply a bus. The bus costs the company ₹ 1,00,000. It has been insured at 3% per annum. The annual Road Tax amounts to ₹ 2,000. Garage rent is ₹ 400 per month. Annual repair is estimated to cost ₹ 2,360 and the bus is likely to last for five years.

The salary of the driver and the conductor is ₹ 600 per month and ₹ 200 per month respectively in addition to 10% of takings as commission to be shared equally by them. The manager's salary is ₹ 1,400 per month and stationery will cost ₹ 100 per month. Petrol and oil will cost ₹ 50 per 100 kilometres. The bus will make three round trips per day carrying on an average 40 passengers in each trip. Assuming 15% profit on takings and that the bus will ply on an average 25 days in a month, prepare operating cost statement on a full year basis and also calculate the bus fare to be charged from each passenger per kilometer.

Solution: **UNION TRANSPORT COMPANY STATEMENT OPERATING COST OF THE BUS PER ANNUM**

	Particulars	₹
A.	**Fixed Charges:**	
	Manager's Salary (₹ 1,400 × 12)	16,800
	Driver's Salary (₹ 600 × 12)	7,200
	Conductor's Salary (₹ 200 × 12)	2,400
	Road Tax	2,000
	Insurance (3% of ₹ 1,00,000)	3,000
	Garage Rent (₹ 400 × 12)	4,800
	Stationery (₹ 100 × 12)	1,200
	Depreciation (₹ 1,00,000/5 years)	20,000
		57,400
B.	**Maintenance Costs:**	
	Repairs	2,360
C.	**Running Charges:**	
	Petrol and Oil (36,000 km/100) × ₹ 50	18,000
D.	**Total Cost :** (A + B + C)	77,760
E.	*Add :* 10 per cent of takings for Commission of Driver and Conductor and 15 per cent for desired profit i.e. 25 per cent on takings *or* 33 $^1/_3$ per cent of Total Cost	25,920
F.	Total Takings (D + E)	1,03,680

Calculation of bus fare to be charged

A.	Effective km (20 km × 2 × 3 × 25 × 12)	36,000 km
B.	Effective passenger kilometres : (36,000 × 40)	14,40,000 Passenger km
C.	Total takings	₹ 1,03,680
D.	Rate to be charged per kilometre from each passenger (₹ 1,03,680/14,40,000)	₹ 0.072

Working Note : *Calculation of distance covered*

= 20 km × 2 × 3 × 25 × 12 = 36,000 km per annum.

Problem 2. Shankar has been promised a contract to run a tourist car on a 20 km long route for the chief executive of a multinational firm. He buys a car costing ₹ 1,50,000. The annual cost of insurance and taxes are ₹ 4,500 and ₹ 900 respectively. He has to pay ₹ 500 per month for a garage where he keeps the car when it is not in use. The annual repair costs are estimated at ₹ 4,000. The car is estimated to have a life of 10 years at the end of which the scrap value is likely to be ₹ 50,000.

He hires a driver who is to be paid ₹ 300 per month *plus* 10% of the takings as commission. Other incidental expenses are estimated at ₹ 200 per month.

Petrol and oil will cost ₹ 100 per 100 kms. The car will make 4 round trips each day. Assuming that a profit of 15% on takings is desired and that the car will be on the road for 25 days on an average per month, what should he charge per round-trip?

Solution: **STATEMENT OF OPERATING COST**

	Particulars	*Per Annum* ₹	*Per Month* ₹
A.	**Standing Charges:**		
	Depreciation [(₹ 1,50,000 – ₹ 50,000)/10]	10,000	
	Insurance	4,500	
	Taxes	900	
	Garage (₹ 500 × 12)	6,000	
	Annual Repairs	4,000	
	Driver's Salary (₹ 300 × 12)	3,600	
	Incidental Expenses (₹ 200 × 12)	2,400	
		31,400	2,616.67
B.	**Variable Expenses:**		
	Petrol and Oil: (4,000 kms × 100)/100)		4,000.00
C.	**Total Cost** (without commission)		6,616.67

Let x be the total takings per month

Driver's commission = 10% of $x = \frac{10}{100} x = \frac{x}{10}$

Profit = 15% of $x = \frac{15}{100} x = \frac{3x}{20}$

Total takings per month = Total Cost + Driver's Commission + Profit

or, $x = ₹\ 6{,}616.67 + \frac{x}{10} + \frac{3x}{20}$

or, $x - 3x/20 - x/10 = ₹\ 6{,}616.67$

or, $\frac{20x - 3x - 2x}{20} = 6{,}616.67$

or, $15x/20 = ₹\ 6{,}616.67$

or, $x = \frac{6{,}616.67 \times 20}{15} = ₹\ 8{,}822.22$

Total number of round trips per month : 25 days × 4 round trips per day = 100

Hence, the charge per round trip = $\frac{8{,}822.22}{100} = ₹\ 88.22$

Working Note: *Calculation of Effective kms.*

Effective km per month = Distance of trips × No. of trips per day × No. of working days
= 20 km × (4 × 2) × 25 = 4000 kms.

Problem 3. A factory which uses a large amount of coal is situated between two collieries *X* and *Y*, the former being 5 kilometres and the latter 10 kilometres distant from the factory. A fleet of lorries of 5-tonne carying capacity is used for the collection of coal from the pitheads. The lorries average a speed of 20 kilometres per hour when running and regularly take 10 minutes in the factory premises to unload. At colliery *X* loading time averages 30 minutes per load, and at colliery *Y* 20 minutes per load.

Driver's wages, licences, insurance depreciation, garage and similar charges are noticed to cost ₹ 6 per hour operated. Fuel, oil, tyres, repairs and similar charges are noticed cost 60 paise per kilometre run.

Required: Draw up a statement showing the cost per tonne-kilometre of carrying coal from each colliery. If the coal is of equal quality and price at pithead, from which colliery should the purchases be made?

Solution: **STATEMENT SHOWING COST PER TONNE-KILOMETRE**

Particulars	*Colliery X*	*Colliery Y*
Time taken per trip	1 hour 10 minutes	1 hour 30 minutes
Fixed cost per trip @ ₹ 6 per hour	₹ 7.00	9.00
Running cost per trip @ 60 paise per km	6.00	12.00
Cost per trip	13.00	21.00
Tonne-kms**	25	50
Cost per tonne-kilometre	0.52	0.42
Cost per tonne	(i.e. 0.52 × 5) 2.60	(i.e. 0.42 × 10) 4.20
* It consists of :	Colliery *X*	Colliery *Y*
To and fro travelling time	30 minutes	60 minutes
Loading time	30 minutes	20 minutes
Unloading time	10 minutes	10 minutes
Total	70 minutes	90 minutes
Tonne-kms :	Colliery *X*	Colliery *Y*
Journey from colliery	5 tonnes × 5 kms = 25	5 tonnes × 10 kms = 50
Journey to colliery	0 × 5 = 0	0 × 10 = 0
** Total tonne-kms	25	50

Advice: In spite of the fact the cost per tonne-kilometre is lower in the case of colliery *Y*, it is preferable to purchase from colliery *X* since it involves a lesser distance and hence a lower cost per tonne.

Problem 4. Mr. Jaidka owns a fleet of taxis and the following information is available from the records maintained by him:

(*i*) Number of taxis	10	(*vii*)	Garage Rent	₹ 600 p.m.
(*ii*) Cost of each taxi	₹ 20,000	(*viii*)	Insurance Premium	5% p.a.
(*iii*) Salary of Manager	₹ 600 p.m.	(*ix*)	Annual Tax	₹ 600 per taxi
(*iv*) Salary of Accountant	₹ 500 p.m.	(*x*)	Driver's Salary	₹ 200 p.m. per taxi
(*v*) Salary of Cleaner	₹ 200 p.m.	(*xi*)	Annual Repair	₹ 1,000 per taxi
(*vi*) Salary of Mechanic	₹ 400 p.m.			

Total life of a taxi is about 2,00,000 kms. A taxi runs in all 3,000 kms in a month of which 30% it runs empty. Petrol consumption is one litre for 10 kms @ ₹ 25.00 per litre.

Oil and other sundries are ₹ 5 per 100 kms.

Required: Prepare Operating Cost Sheet.

Solution: **OPERATING COST SHEET**

Particulars	*Amount Per Month* ₹	*Cost Per km* ₹
A. Fixed Expenses : (for the whole fleet)		
Salary of Manager	600.00	
Salary of Accountant	500.00	
Salary of Cleaner	200.00	
Salary of Mechanic	400.00	
Garage Rent	600.00	
Insurance Premium [(5% on ₹ 2,00,000)/12]	833.33	
Driver's Salary (₹ 200 × 10)	2,000.00	
Tax [(600 × 10)/12]	500.00	
Depreciation (2,00,000 × 3,000/2,00,000)	3,000.00	
Repairs (1,000 × 10/12)	833.33	
Total	9466.66	
Fixed Expenses per km [₹ 9,466.66/21000]		0.451
B. Variable Expenses per Taxi:		
Petrol $\left[\frac{300 \times 25}{2100}\right]$		3.571
Oil & other Sundries $\left[\frac{5 \times 3,000}{100 \times 2100}\right]$		0.071
C. **Total Cost per kilometre**		4.093

Working Notes:

(*i*) Effective km. per taxi = 3000 – 30% of 3000 = 2,100 K.M.

(*ii*) Consumption of Petrol (in Litres) per taxi = $\frac{3,000 \times 1}{10}$ = 300 litres

Problem 5. Mr. *X* owns a bus which runs according to the following schedule :

(*i*) Delhi to Chandigarh and back, the same day.
Distance covered : 150 kms one way.
Number of days run each month : 8
Seating capacity occupied : 90%

(*ii*) Delhi to Agra and back, the same day.
Distance covered : 120 kms one way.
Number of days run each month : 10
Seating capacity occupied : 85%

(*iii*) Delhi to Jaipur and back, the same day.
Distance covered : 270 kms one way.
Number of days run each month : 6
Seating capacity occupied : 100%

(iv) Following are the other details :

Cost of the bus	₹ 6,00,000
Salary of the driver	₹ 2,800 p.m.
Salary of the conductor	₹ 2,200 p.m.
Salary of the part time Accountant	₹ 200 p.m.
Insurance of the bus	₹ 4,800 p.a.
Diesel consumption 4 kms per litre at	₹ 6 per litre
Road Tax	₹ 1,500 p.a.
Lubricant Oil	₹ 10 per 100 kms
Permit fee	₹ 315 p.m.
Repairs and maintenance	₹ 1,000 p.m.
Depreciation of the bus	@ 20% p.a.
Seating capacity of the bus	50 persons.

Passenger tax is 20% of the total takings.

Required: Calculate the bus fare to be charged from each passenger to earn a profit of 30% on total takings. The fares are to be indicated per passenger for the journeys:

(i) Delhi to Chandigarh
(ii) Delhi to Agra
(iii) Delhi to Jaipur.

Solution:

OPERATING COST STATEMENT

	Particulars		₹	₹
A.	**Fixed Costs :**			
	Salary of Driver		2,800	
	Salary of Conductor		2,200	
	Salary of the part-time Accountant		200	
	Depreciation $\left[6,00,000 \times \frac{20}{100} \times \frac{1}{12}\right]$		10,000	
	Insurance (₹ 4,800 × 1/12)		400	
	Road Tax (₹ 1,500 × 1/12)		125	
	Repairs and Maintenance		1,000	
	Permit Fee		315	
	Total Fixed Expenses			17,040
B.	**Variable Costs:**			
	Diesel $\frac{8,040 \text{ kms}}{4 \text{ kms}}$ × ₹ 6 *[(Refer to Working Note (i)]*			12,060
	Lubricant Oil $\frac{8,040 \text{ kms}}{100 \text{ kms}}$ × ₹ 10 *[(Refer to Working Note (i)]*			804
C.	**Total Cost per month** (A + B)			29,904
D.	*Add :* Profit and passenger tax together accounts for 50% of total takings p.m. *or* 100% of cost			29,904
E.	Total Takings (C + D)			59,808
F.	Effecting Passenger km *[(Refer to Working Note (ii)]*			3,72,000
G.	Rate per passenger km (₹ 59,808/3,72,000)			.161
H.	**Fare to be charged**			
	Delhi to Chandigarh, per passenger	(150 kms × 0.161)		₹ 24.15
	Delhi to Agra, per passenger	(120 kms × 0.161)		₹ 19.32
	Delhi to Jaipur, per passenger	(270 kms × 0.161)		₹ 43.47

Working Notes :

(*i*) *Calculation of Total Running kms per month:*

Particulars	*km. per Trip*	*Trips per Day*	*Days per Month*	*km. per Month*
Delhi to Chandigarh	150	2	8	2,400
Delhi to Agra	120	2	10	2,400
Delhi to Jaipur	270	2	6	3,240
				8,040

(*ii*) *Calculation of Passenger kms per month:*

Particulars	*A Seats Available*	*B Capacity Utilised %*	*C Seats Occupied Month*	*D km. per month*	*E = C × D Passenger kms. Per Month*
Delhi to Chandigarh & back	50	90	45	2400	1,08,000
Delhi to Agra & back	50	85	42.50	2400	1,02,000
Delhi to Jaipur & back	50	100	50	3240	1,62,000
					3,72,000

Problem 6. SMC is a public school having five buses each plying in different directions for the transport of its school students. In view of a large number of students availing of the bus service, the buses work two shifts daily both in the morning and in the afternoon. The buses are garaged in the school. The work-load of the students has been so arranged that in the morning the first trip picks up the senior students and the second trip plying an hour later picks up the junior students. Similarly, in the afternoon the first trip drops the junior students and an hour later the second trip takes the senior students home.

The distance travelled by each bus one way is 8 km. The school works 25 days in a month and remains closed for vacation in May, June and December. Bus fee, however, is payable by the students for all the 12 months of the year. The details of expenses for a year are as under :

Driver's salary	₹ 450 per month per driver
Cleaner's salary (one cleaner employed for all the five buses)	₹ 350 per month.
License fee, taxes etc.	₹ 860 per bus per annum
Insurance	₹ 1,000 per bus per annum
Repairs & maintenance	₹ 3,500 per bus per annum
Purchase price of bus (Life 12 years)	₹ 1,50,000 each
Scrap value	₹ 30,000
Diesel cost	₹ 2.00 per litre

Each bus gives an average mileage of 4 kms per litre of diesel.
Seating capacity of each bus is 50 students.
The seating capacity is fully occupied during the whole year.

Students picked up and dropped within a range upto 4 kms of distance from the school are charged half fare and fifty per cent of the students travelling in each trip are in this category. Ignore interest. Since the charges are to be based on average cost,

Required:

(*i*) Prepare a statement showing the expenses of operating a single bus and the fleet of five buses for a year.

(*ii*) Work out the average cost per student per month in respect of —

(*A*) Students coming from a distance of upto 4 kms from the school and

(*B*) Students coming from a distance beyond 4 kms from the school.

Solution: **OPERATING COST STATEMENT**

	Particulars	*Rate* ₹	*Per Bus p.a.* ₹	*Fleet of 5 Buses p.a.* ₹
	Driver's salary	450 p.m.	5,400	27,000
	Cleaner's salary	350 p.m.	840	4,200
	Licence fee, taxes etc.	860 p.a.	860	4,300
	Insurance	1,000 p.a.	1,000	5,000
	Repairs & maintenance	3,500 p.a.	3,500	17,500
	Depreciation	10,000 p.a.	10,000	50,000
	Diesel *[Refer to Working Note (i)]*		7,200	36,000
A.	Total		28,800	1,44,000
B.	Cost per month (A/12)		2,400	12,000
C.	No. of students on half fee basis [See Note (*ii*)]		150	750
D.	Cost per student (half fee) (B/C)		16.00	16.00
E.	Cost per student (Full fee) (₹ 16 × 2)		32.00	32.00

Working Notes:

(*i*) *Calculation of Diesel Cost per bus*

A.	Distance per trip	8 km
B.	No. of trips per day	8
C.	No. of working days per month	25
D.	No. of working months per year	9
E.	Distance covered p.a. (8 × 8 × 25 × 9)	14,400 km
F.	Mileage per Litre	4 km
G.	Diesel Consumption (14,400/4)	3,600 Ltr.
H.	Cost of Diesel (3600 × ₹ 2)	₹ 7200

(*ii*) *Calculation of number of students per bus*

A.	Bus capacity	50 students
B.	Half fare 50%, i.e.,	25 students
C.	Full fare 50%, i.e.,	25 students
D.	Full fare students as equivalent to half fare students i.e.	50 students
E.	Total number of half fare students per trip [B + D]	75 students per trip
F.	Total number of half fare students per trip in two trips. (75 × 2)	150 students

Problem 7. From the following particulars relating to a four wheeled Tempo, you are required to compute the cost per running kilometre.

Value of Tempo	₹ 50,000
Estimated life of Tempo	2,00,000 kms
Estimated annual kilometres	20,000 kms
No. of kilometres per litre of petrol	5 kms
Driver's wage per month	₹ 750
Cost of petrol per litre	₹ 3.50
Repairs and maintenance per km	₹ 1.00
Tyre allocations per kilometre	₹ 0.32
Annual expenses :	
Road Licence fees	₹ 1,350
Insurance	1/2%
Garage rent	₹ 3,000
Supervision and salaries	₹ 2,400

You are required to charge interest @ 10% p.a. on the cost of the vehicle.

Solution: **STATEMENT SHOWING THE COMPUTATION OF COST PER RUNNING KM**

Particulars	*P.A.* ₹	*Per km* ₹
A. Fixed Costs :		
(*a*) Driver wages (₹ 750 × 12)	9,000	.4500
(*b*) Road licence fee	1,350	.0675
(*c*) Insurance (1/2% of ₹ 50,000)	250	.0125

		₹	₹
(*d*)	Garage rent	3,000	.1500
(*e*)	Supervision & salaries	2,400	.1200
(*f*)	Interest (10% of ₹ 50,000)	5,000	.2500
(*g*)	Depreciation (50,000 × 20,000/2,00,000)	5,000	.2500
		26,000	1.30
B.	**Running & Maintenance Costs:**		
(*a*)	Repair & Maintenance	20,000	1.00
(*b*)	Tyre	6,400	.32
(*c*)	Petrol	14,000	.70
		40,400	2.02
C.	**Total Cost (A + B)**	**66,400**	**3.32**

Working Notes:

(*i*) Total Consumption of petrol = 20,000/5 = 4000 Lts.

(*ii*) Total Cost of Petrol = 4000 × ₹ 3.50 = ₹ 14,000

Problem 8. The 'Kangaroo Transport Ltd.' operates a fleet of lorries. The records for lorry L-14, reveal the following information for September :

Days maintained	30	Total hours operated	300
Days operated	25	Total kms covered	2,500
Days idle	5	Total tonnage carried	200
		(4 tonne = load per trip, return journey empty)	

The following further information is made available :

A. *Operating Cost for the Month :*
Petrol ₹ 400; Oil ₹ 170; Grease ₹ 90; Wages to Driver ₹ 550; Wages to Khalasi ₹ 350

B. *Maintenance Costs for the Month :*
Repairs ₹ 170, Overhaul ₹ 60; Tyres ₹ 150; Garage charges ₹ 100.

C. *Fixed cost for the Month Based on the Estimates for the year :*
Insurance ₹ 50; Licence, Tax etc. ₹ 80; interest ₹ 40; Other overheads ₹ 190

D. *Capital Costs :*
Cost of acquisition of ₹ 54,000
Residual value at the end of 5 years life is ₹ 36,000

Required: Prepare a cost Sheet and Performance Statement showing :
(*a*) Cost per day maintained; (*b*) Cost per day operated; (*c*) Cost per kilometer; (*d*) Cost per hour; (*e*) Cost per commercial tonne-kms.

Solution:

On the basis of the above data and other information given, the Vehicle Cost Sheet and Performance Statement can be prepared as follows :

VEHICLES COST SHEET AND PERFORMANCE STATEMENT

Vehicle : Lorry No. L-14 Month : September

A. MONTHLY CHARGES

(*a*) *Wages & Running Costs*	₹	(*b*) *Maintenance Charges*	₹	(*c*) *Proportionate Fixed Charges*	₹
Petrol	400	Repairs	170	Insurance	50
Oil	170	Overhaul	60	Depreciation	300
Grease	90	Tyres	150	Licence, Tax etc.	80
Wages to Driver	550	Garage Charges	100	Interest	40
Wages to Khalasi	350			Other Overheads	190
	1,560		480		660

B. PERFORMANCE STATEMENT

	Particulars	This Month	Last Month	Average of Last year
(a)	Performance Data :			
	Days maintained		30	
	Days operated		25	
	Days idle		5	
	Total hours operated		300	
	Total kms covered		2,500	
	Total trips (200/4)		50	
	Total commercial tonne-kms		5,000	
(b)	Cost Efficiency :			
	Total monthly charges (a) + (b) + (c)		₹ 2,700.00	
	(i) Cost per day maintained (₹ 2700/30)		90.00	
	(ii) Cost per day operated (₹ 2700/25)		108.00	
	(iii) Cost per km (₹ 2,700/2500)		1.08	
	(iv) Cost per hour (₹ 2,700/300)		9.00	
	(v) Cost per commercial tonne-km (₹ 2700/5000)		0.54	

Working Notes:

(i) Km per loaded journey per day = 2500/(25 × 2) = 50 km

(ii) Commercial tonne kms per month = 50 km × 4 tonne × 25 days = 5000 Tonne-kms

(iii) Depreciation per month = $\frac{54,000 - 36,000}{5 \times 12}$ = ₹ 18,000/60 = ₹ 300

Problem 9. Prakash Automobiles distributes its goods to a regional dealer using a single lorry. The dealer's premises is 40 kilometres away by road. The lorry has a capacity of 10 tonnes and makes the journey twice a day fully loaded on the outward journeys and empty on return journeys. The following information is available for a four weekly period during the year :

Petrol consumption	8 kilometres per litre
Petrol cost	₹ 13 per litre
Oil	₹ 100 per week
Driver's wages	₹ 400 per week
Repairs	₹ 100 per week
Garage rent	₹ 150 per week
Cost of Lorry (excluding tyres)	₹ 4,50,000
Life of Lorry	80,000 kilometres
Insurance	₹ 6,500 per annum
Cost of Tyres	₹ 6,250
Life of Tyres	25,000 kilometres
Estimated sale value of lorry at the end of its life	₹ 50,000
Vehicle Licence cost	₹ 1,300 per annum
Other overhead cost	₹ 41,600 per annum

The Lorry operates on a five day week.

Required :

(a) A statement to show the total cost of operating the vehicle for the four weekly period analysed into running costs and fixed costs.

(b) Calculate the vehicle cost per kilometre and per tonne kilometre.

Solution:(a) STATEMENT OF OPERATING COST OF THE VEHICLE (FOR THE FOUR WEEKLY PERIOD)

		₹
A.	**Running and Maintenance Costs :**	
	Petrol Cost (400 × ₹ 13)	5,200
	Oil Expenses (₹ 100 × 4)	400
	Driver's Wages (₹ 400 × 4)	1,600
	Repairs (₹ 100 × 4)	400
	Tyre Cost (₹ 6,250 × 3200/25,000)	800
	Depreciation (₹ 4,50,000 – ₹ 50,000)/80000) × 3200	16,000
	Total Running Cost	24,400

		₹
B.	**Fixed Costs :**	
	Garage Rent (₹ 150 × 4)	600
	Insurance (₹ 6,500 × 4/52)	500
	Licence Cost (₹ 1,300 × 4/52)	100
	Other Overhead (₹ 41,600 × 4/52)	3,200
	Total Fixed Cost	4,400
C.	**Total Cost (A + B)**	28,800

(*b*) 1. Cost per kilometre : $\frac{28,800}{3,200}$ = ₹ 9

2. Cost per tonne kilometre = $\frac{28,800}{1,600 \text{ km} \times 10 \text{ tonne}}$ = ₹ 1.80

Working Notes :

(*i*) Effective km = (2 × 40) km × 2 trips × 20 days = 3200 km
(*ii*) Effective tonnes km = 40 km × 2 trips × 20 days × 10 tonne = 16,000 tonne km
(*iii*) Consumption of petrol = 3200 km/8 Ltr. = 400 Ltrs.

Problem 10. A chemical factory runs its boiler on furnace oil obtained from Indian Oil and Bharat Petroleum, whose depots are situated at a distance of 12 and 8 miles from the factory site. Transportation of Furnace Oil is made by the Company's own tank lorries of 5 tonnes capacity each. Onward trips are made only on full load and the lorries return empty. The filling in time takes an average 40 minutes for Indian Oil and 30 minutes for Bharat Petroleum. But the emptying time in the factory is only 40 minutes for all. From the records available, it is seen that the average speed of the company's lorries works out to 24 miles per hour. The varying operating charges average 60 paise per mile covered and fixed charges give an incidence of ₹ 7.50 per hour of operation.

Requried: Calculate the cost per tonne mile for each source.

Solution: **STATEMENT SHOWING THE COST PER-TONNE MILE OF CARRYING FURNANCE OIL FROM INDIAN OIL AND BHARAT PETROLEUM DEPOTS TO CHEMICAL FACTORY**

	Particulars	*Indian Oil* ₹	*Bharat Petroleum* ₹
A.	Variable cost of operating *[Refer to Working Note (i)]*	14.40	9.60
B.	Fixed charges *[Refer to Working Note (ii)]*	17.50	13.75
C.	Total cost (A + B)	31.90	23.35
D.	Tonne-mile	60	40
E.	Cost per tonne-mile: (C/D)	53 Paise (Approx)	58 Paise (Approx)

Working Notes:

	Particulars	*Indian Oil*	*Bharat Petroleum*
(*i*)	Variable Costs :		
	Distance of oil depots from chemical factory :	12 miles	8 miles
	Mileage covered under on trip by a lorry .	24 miles	16 miles
	Variable cost of operation @ 60 paise per mile.	₹ 14.40	₹ 9.60
(*ii*)	Fixed Charges :		
A.	Running time of lorries	60 minutes	40 minutes
B.	Filling in time	40 minutes	30 minutes
C.	Emptying time	40 minutes	40 minutes
D.	Total time (A + B + C)	140 minutes	110 minutes
E.	Fixed charges @ ₹ 7.50 per hour	₹ 17.50	₹ 13.75
(*iii*)	Total effective tonnes-mile	(12 miles × 5 tonnes) = 60	(8 miles × 5 tonnes) = 40

Problem 11. EPS is a public School having 25 buses each plying in different directions for the transport of its school students. In view of large number of students availing of the bus service, the buses work two shifts daily both in the morning and the afternoon. The buses are garaged in the school. The workload of the students has been so arranged that in the morning, the first trip picks up senior students and the second trip plying an hour later picks up junior students. Similarly, in the afternoon, the first trip takes the junior students and an hour later the second trip takes the senior students home.

The distance travelled by each bus, one way is 16 km. The school works 24 days in a month and remains closed for vacation in May and June. The bus fee, however, is payable by the students for all the 12 months in a year.

The details of expenses for the year 20X5-20X6 are as under:

Driver's salary-payable for the 12 months	₹ 5,000 per month per driver
Cleaner's salary payable for all the 12 months	₹ 3,000 per month per cleaner
(One cleaner has been employed for every five buses)	
Licence fees, taxes etc.	₹ 2,300 per bus per annum
Insurance premium	₹ 15,600 per bus per annum
Repairs and maintenance	₹ 16,400 per bus per annum
Purchase price of the bus	₹ 16,50,000 each
Life of the bus	16 years
Scrap value	₹ 1,50,000
Diesel cost	₹ 18.50 per litre

Each bus given an average of 10 km per litre diesel. The seating capacity of each bus is 60 students. The seating capacity is fully occupied during the whole year.

The school follows differential bus fee based on distance travelled as under:

Students picked up and dropped within the range of distance from the school	*Bus fee*	*Percentage of students availing this facility*
4 km	25% of full	15%
8 km	50% of full	30%
16 km	Full	55%

Ignore interest. Since the bus fee has to be based on average cost, you are required to:

(*i*) Prepare a statement showing the expenses of operating a single bus and fleet of 25 buses for a year.

(*ii*) Work out average cost per student per month in respect of:

(*a*) Students coming from a distance of upto 4 km from the school:

(*b*) Students coming from a distance of upto 8 km from the school; and

(*c*) Students coming from a distance of upto 16 km from the school.

Solution:

(*i*) **OPERATING COST STATEMENT**

Particulars	*For 25 buses p.a.* ₹
Driver's salary	15,00,000
Cleaner's salary	1,80,000
Licence fee, taxes etc.	57,500
Insurance	3,90,000
Depreciation	23,43,750
Diesel *[Refer to Working Note (i)]*	14,20,800
Repairs and maintenance	4,10,000
Total cost for 25 buses.	63,02,050
Cost per bus per annum [₹ 63,02,050/25 buses]	2,52,082

(*ii*) **Average cost per student per month in respect of students coming from a distance of:**

(*a*)	4 km from the school $\left(\dfrac{2,52,082}{354 \text{ students} \times 12 \text{ months}}\right)$	₹ 59.34
(*b*)	8 km from the school (₹ 59.34 × 2)	₹ 118.68
(*c*)	16 km from the school (₹ 59.34 × 4)	₹ 237.36

Working Notes:

(*i*) *Calculation of diesel cost per bus:*

No. of trips made by a bus each day	4
Distance travelled in one trip both ways (16 km × 2)	32 km
Distance travelled per day by a bus (32 km × 4 shifts)	128 km
Distance travelled during a month (128 km × 24 days)	3,072 km
Distance travelled per year (3,072 km × 10 months)	30,720 km
No. of liters of diesel required per bus per year (30,720 km/10 km)	3,072 litre
Cost of diesel per year (3,072 liters × ₹ 18.50) × 25 buses	₹ 14,20,800

(*ii*) *Calculation of number of students per bus:*

Bus capacity of 2 trips	120 students
25% fare students (15% × 120 students)	18 students
50% fare 30% students (equivalent to 25% fare students)	72 students
Full fare 55% students (equivalent to 25% fare students)	264 students
Total 25% fare students (18 + 72 + 264)	354 students

ALTERNATIVE METHOD FOR CALCULATING AVERAGE COST PER STUDENT

	4 km	8 km	16 km
Bus Fee Ratio	1	2	4
Student Ratio	0.15	0.30	0.55
Weighted Ratio	0.15 +	0.60 +	2.20 = 2.95

A. Weighted No. of Students per bus p.a. = 120 × 12 × 2.95 = 4248

B.	Cost per Bus p.a.	₹ 2,52,082	
C.	Average cost per student (4 km) [B/A]	₹ 59.34	(Approx)
D.	Average cost per student (8 km (C × 2)	₹ 118.68	
E.	Average cost per student (16 km (C × 4)	₹ 237.36	

Problem 12. A transport company has a fleet of three trucks of 10 tonnes capacity each plying in different directions for transport of customer's goods. The trucks run loaded with goods and return empty. The distance travelled, number of trips made and the load carried per day by each truck are as under:

Truck No.	*One way Distance Km.*	*No. of trips per day*	*Load carried per trip / day tonnes*
1	16	4	6
2	40	2	9
3	30	3	8

The analysis of maintenance cost and the total distance travelled during the last two years is as under:

Year	*Total Distance travelled*	*Maintenance Cost ₹*
1	1,60,200	46,050
2	1,56,700	45,175

The following are the details of expenses for the year under review:

Diesel	: ₹ 10 per litre. Each litre gives 4 km per litre of diesel on an average.
Driver's salary	: ₹ 2,000 per month
Licence and taxes	: ₹ 5,000 per annum per truck
Insurance	: ₹ 5,000 per annum for all the three vehicles

Purchase Price per truck : ₹ 3,00,000 Life 10 years. Scrap value at the end of life is ₹ 10,000.
Oil and sundries : ₹ 25 per 100 km run.
General Overhead : ₹ 11,084 per annum.

The vehicle operated 24 days per month on an average.

Required:

(i) Prepare an Annual Cost Statement covering the fleet of three vehicles.
(ii) Calculate the cost per km. run.
(iii) Determine the freight rate per tonne km. to yield a profit of 10% on freight.

Solution:

(i) ANNUAL COST STATEMENT OF THREE VEHICLES

Particulars	₹
A. Diesel [(1,34,784 kms/4km) × ₹ 10)]	3,36,960
B. Oil and sundries [(1,34,784 kms/100 kms) × ₹ 25]	33,696
C. Maintenance [(1,34,784 kms × 0.25P) + ₹ 6,000)]	39,696
D. Driver's salary [(₹ 2,000 × 12 months) × 3 trucks]	72,000
E. Licence and taxes	15,000
F. Insurance	5,000
G. Depreciation [(₹ 2,90,000/10 years) × 3 trucks]	87,000
H. General overhead	11,084
I. Total Annual Cost	6,00,436

(ii) Cost per kilometer run = $\frac{\text{Total annual cost of vehicles}}{\text{Total kilometre travelled annually}} = \frac{6,00,436}{1,34,784} = 4.4548$

(iii) Freight rate per tonne km (to yield a profit of 10% on freight)

Cost per tonne km. = $\frac{\text{Total annual cost of three vehicles}}{\text{Total effective tonnes kms. per annum}} = \frac{6,00,436}{5,25,312} = 1.143$

Freight rate per tonne km. [₹ 1.143 × 10/9] = ₹ 1.27

Working Notes:

(i) **TOTAL KILOMETRE TRAVELLED & TONNES KM (LOAD CARRIED) BY THREE TRUCKS IN ONE YEAR**

Truck number	*One way distance in kms*	*No. of trips*	*Total distance covered in km. per day*	*Load carried per trip / day in tonnes*	*Total effective tonnes km.*
1	16	4	128	6	384
2	40	2	160	9	720
3	30	3	180	8	720
Total			468		1824

Total kilometre travelled by three trucks in one year (468 kms × 24 days × 12 months) — 1,34,784

Total effective tonnes kilometre of load carried by three trucks during one year (1,824 tonnes km × 24 days × 12 months) — 5,25,312

(ii) **Fixed and variable component of maintenance cost:**

Variable maintenance cost per km. $= \frac{\text{Difference in maintenance cost}}{\text{Difference in distance travelled}}$

$= \frac{46,050 - 45,175}{160,200 \text{ kms} - 1,56,700 \text{ kms.}} = ₹\ 0.25$

Fixed maintenance cost = Total maintenance cost – Variable maintenance cost

= ₹ 46,050 – 1,60,200 kms × 0.25 = ₹ 6,000

14 Just in Time (JIT)

Learning Objectives

After studying this chapter, you should be able to understand:

- Meaning, Characteristics, Advantages and Steps in JIT
- Description of Just-in-time Systems
- Impact of JIT System
- JIT Cost Allocation Differences
- Performance Measurements in a JIT System
- Backflushing in a JIT System

1.0 MEANING, CHARACTERISTICS, ADVANTAGES AND STEPS IN JIT

Meaning	JIT system involves (a) Installing a system of receiveing **requisite quantity** of products/spare parts/materials of **required quality** from its suppliers on the **exact date and at the exact time** and **at the exact place** and thereby reducing inventory carrying costs (b) Reducing the machine setup time so as to make even small production runs economical and thereby reducing (i) the amount of WIP inventory & inventory carrying costs(ii) the amount of defective products & scrap costs (iii) Product Obsolescence.
Characteristic	1. A characteristic of the **JIT** system is its continuous focus on eliminating all types of wastes (whether of Raw- Materials, WIP, Finished Goods, Time) from a system. Raw materials inventory is reduced because suppliers deliver only small quantities of parts as and when they are needed. Work-in process inventory drops because the conversion to machine cells and the use of kanban cards greatly reduces the need to pile up inventory between machines. Finally, finished goods inventory drops because inventory is produced only when there are orders in hand from customers (though finished goods inventories are also allowed to build if a company experiences high seasonal sales). 2. It converts most of the overhead costs to direct costs because a machine cell is designed to produce either a single product or a single component that goes into a similar product line.and all the costs generated by the machine cell are charged directly to the only product it produces.
Competitive Advantages	1. Stocks of raw materials and finished goods are eliminated, and as a result stock holding costs are avoided.

	2. JIT aims at elimination of non-value added activities and elimination of cost in this direction will improve competitive advantage. 3. It affords flexibility to customer requirements where the company can manufacture customized products and the competitive advantage is thereby improved. 4. It focuses the direction of performance based production of high quality product. 5. It minimizes waiting times and transportation costs.
Other Advantages improving an organisation 's Profitability	1. Immediate detection of defective goods being manufactured so thatearly correction is ensured with least scrapping. 2. Eliminates/reduces WIP between machines within working cell. 3. Overheads costs in the form of rentals for inventory, insurance, main tenance costs etc. are reduced. 4. Higher product quality ensured by the JIT approach leads to higher premium in the selling price. 5. Detection of problem areas due to better pdn/scrap reporting/labour tracing and inventory accuracy lead to reduction in costs by improvement.
Inventory Costs Reduced though JIT	1. Oppourtunity cost of funds used in inventory investment 2. Cost of inventory that becomes obsolete over time 3. Cost of rent for inventory storage facilities 4. Cost of all equipment used in the warehouse 5. Cost of warehouse utilities 6. Cost of warehouse employees 7. Cost of insurance needed to cover the possible loss of inventory
Steps in JIT	1. Evaluate supplier by purchase staff with regards to quality,timely delivery of supply and reliability. 2. Visit supplier's site and inspect quality of supply there to ensure quality and time etc 3. Install a system so that it receives **requisite quantity** of products/spare parts/materials of **required quality** from its suppliers on the **exact date and at the exact time** when they are needed and **at the exact place** where they are needed. 4. Reduce the machine setup time so as to make even small production runs economical 5. Use Kanban Card (which authorizes production of the right quantity by its feeder machine ensures 'pulling' the production process) and group machines into working cells (i.e.small cluster of machines which can be run by a single machine operator) 6. Train employees how to operate a multitude of different machines, perform limited maintenance on the machines without having to call in the maintenance staff, spot product errors, understand how the entire system flows, and when to halt the production process to fix problems 7. Make a single consolidated monthly payment to each supplier on the basis of theoretical finished production quantity(finished products quantity X No. of parts listed on the bill of materials), which is also adjusted for scrap during the production process

2.0 DESCRIPTION OF JUST-IN-TIME SYSTEMS

A complete JIT system begins with production, includes deliveries to a company's production facilities, continues through the manufacturing plant, and even includes the types of transactions processed by the accounting system.

(i) Install a system so that it receives **requisite quantity** of products/spare parts/materials of **required quality** from its suppliers on the **exact date and at the exact time** when they are needed and **at the exact place** where they are needed. This step reduces the amount of raw-materials inventory and thereby reducing inventory carrying costs

(ii) Reduce the machine setup time so as to make even small production runs economical .JIT system focuses on making a video tape of a typical set up. A team of industrial engineers and machine users examines this tape, spotting and gradually eliminating the need for long production runs to reduce setup cost per unit . This step reduces:

(a) the amount of work-in-process and thereby reducing inventory carrying costs

(b) Defective Products and thereby reducing scrap costs

(c) Product Obsolescence.

(iii) The **two ways to reduce excessive work-in-process inventory and defective parts** are:

(a) To Use Kanban Card," which is a notification card that a downstream machine sends to each machine that feeds it parts, authorizing the production of just enough components to fulfill the production requirements being authorized in turn by the next machine further downstream. This is also known as a "pull" system, since kanbans are initiated at the *end* of the production process, pulling work authorizations through the production system. With this approach, there is no way for work-in-process inventory to build up in the production system, since it can be created only with a kanban authorization.

(b) to group machines into working cells. A working cell is a small cluster of machines which can be run by a single machine operator. This individual machine operator takes each output part from machine to machine within the cell; and thus there is no way for work-in-process to build up between machines. Also, this operator can immediately identify defective output which otherwise is difficult for each machine of the cell. This configuration has the additional benefit of lower maintenance costs since the smaller machines used in a machine cell are generally much simpler than the large, automated machinery they replace.

Both kanbans and machine cells should be used together—they are not mutually exclusive. This step reduces product defect rates, and investments in work-in-process inventory.

(iv) Train employees how to operate a multitude of different machines, perform limited maintenance on the machines without having to call in the maintenance staff, spot product errors, understand how the entire system flows, and when to halt the production process to fix problems. This usually results in a reconfiguration of the compensation system as well, because the focus of attention shifts away from performance based to high production volumes and in the direction of performance based to high product quality.

(v) The quick response capabilities of a JIT system allows the cost accountant to omit a large amount of the variance reporting that was previously an important central job function . A major result of having an empowered workforce is that employees are allowed to stop their machines when they see a problem, and either fix it on the spot or immediately call in a repair team. In either case the result is immediate resolution of the bulk of performance problems. This one step has a profound impact on much of the manufacturing variance analysis. Historically, cost accountants compile all kinds of variance information at the end of each month, investigate problems in detail, and then present a formal problem analysis report to management a few weeks after the end of the month. However, because the production staff resolved the underlying issues within a few minutes of their occurence, the variance report becomes a complete waste of time. Management no longer cares what happened a month in the past because it is presently dealing with current problems that will not appear on cost accountant reports for weeks to come.

(vi) Finally, the massive changes caused by a JIT system also requires several alterations in the supporting accounting systems.

(a) making a single consolidated monthly payment to each supplier because the suppliers deliver parts directly to the production operation and there is no receiving paperwork,

(b) paying suppliers on the basis of theoretical finished production quantity(finished products quant ity X No. of parts listed on the bill of materials), which is also adjusted for scrap during the production process

Thus,the company relies solely on its internal production records to complete payments.

3.0 IMPACT OF JIT SYSTEM

A characteristic of the **JIT** system is its continuous focus on eliminating all types of wastes(whether of Raw- Materials,WIP,Finished Goods,Time) from a system..

Impact of JIT on Overhead Costs	Overhead Costs decline due to: (a) Elimination of some storage costs(that is due to reduction in the storage space due to reduction of all types of inventory), (b) Conversion of some overhead costs into direct costs (e.g.the depreciation, maintenance, labour and utility costs of each machine cell can be charged directly to a product)
Impact of JIT on Other Costs	Reduction of all types of inventory(whether of Raw Materials, WIP, Finished Goods,) and reduced capital requirement of JIT systems have a significant impact on the levels of fixed assets, working capital, and inventory needed to run a business, which in turn reduces the associated overhead costs charged to products. 1. Due to Reduction of all types of inventory, there is a reduction in the level of working capital and inventory-related costs.Some of these inventory-related costs are: Oppourtunity cost of funds used in inventory investment Cost of inventory that becomes obsolete over time Cost of rent for inventory storage facilities Cost of all equipment used in the warehouse Cost of warehouse utilities Cost of warehouse employees Cost of insurance needed to cover the possible loss of inventory Cost of taxes on the inventory 2. A company can also reduce its investment in capital assets by replacing a few large machines with a larger number of much smaller machines to have shorter production runs
Impact of JIT on Product Prices	The impact of a JIT system on product pricing is primarily driven by customers' perceived need for higher product quality and reliable delivery times, as well as the presence of competitors with JIT system, the same installation, and operational base. It may be possible to increase prices substantially If (a) customers are highly sensitive to two factors i .e. product quality & timely delivery,and (b) therabsence of competitors with JIT system, the same installation, and operational base.

4.0 JIT COST ALLOCATION DIFFERENCES

The chief difference between the types of cost allocations under JIT and traditional environment is that of converting most of the overhead costs to direct costs. The primary reason for this change is the machine cell. Because a machine cell is designed to produce either a single product or a single component that goes into a similar product line. Therefore all the costs generated by the machine cell can be charged directly to the only product it produces Specifically, the costs that can now be charged directly to product are:

Depreciation	The depreciation cost of each machine in a machine cell can be charged directly to a product if It is possible to depreciate a machine based on its actual use
Power Cost	The power cost of each machine in a machine cell can be charged directly to a product if the power used by the machine in a cell can be separately metered.
Material Handling Cost	Most materials handling costs in a JIT system are eliminated since machine operators move parts around within their machine cells. Only materials handling costs between cells should be charged to an overhead cost pool for allocation.
Operating Supplies	The cost of operating supplies of each machine in a machine cell can be charged directly to a product since it can be separately tracked by individual machine cell.
Repairs and Maintenance	The Repairs and maintenance cost of each machine in a machine cell can be charged directly to a product . Only Repairs and maintenance cost on the facility is still charged to an overhead cost pool.
Supervision	The supervision cost of each machine in a machine cell can be charged directly to a product if it can be split among the cells supervised. But the cost of general facility management as well as of any support staff, must still be charged to an overhead cost pool. Thus,higher proportion of overhead cost pool are allocated to machine cells as direct costs and only a smaller proportion(such as building occupancy costs, insurance, and tax)is charged to an overhead cost pool for allocation . A typical overhead allocation pool under the traditional system can easily include 75% of all costs incurred, whereas this figure can be dropped to less than 25% of total costs by switching to a JIT system. With such a higher proportion of direct costs associated with each product, managers then have much more relevant information about the true cost of each product manufactured.

5.0 PERFORMANCE MEASUREMENTS IN A JIT SYSTEM

Many of the performance measurement measures used under a traditional accounting system are not useful in a JIT environment, while new measures can be implemented that take advantage of the unique characteristics of this system.

5.1 Performance Measurements used under a Traditional System but not useful under a JIT System

1. Machine Utilization	JIT system focuses on machine cells which tend to be smaller and less costly than the highly automated (and expensive) juggernauts used in more traditional systems, so there is less need to justify the investment in these smaller machines by proving that they have been heavily used. In short, machine utilization measurements can be discarded under JIT environment

2. Piece Rate tracking for each Employee	JIT system focuses on producing only what is needed, on the quality of output & the number of employee suggestions for improving the system,
3. Direct Labour Efficiency	JIT system focuses only on the quality of the products manufactured and not on how fast an employee works. Labour tracking is a non-value-added activity, which JIT system strives to avoid .

5.2 Performance Measurements useful under a JIT system

Installing a JIT system does not mean that there should be a complete elimination of variance or operational measures .There are still several measures that are highly relevant to operations. Some of them are :

1. Setup time reduction	The shortest possible setup intervals are crucial for the success of short production runs, so this is a major JIT measurement.
2. Cost of quality	One focus of JIT is on creating high-quality products and on avoiding quality costs(which comprises defect control costs, failure costs, and the cost of lost sales) as far as possible
3. Scrap	One focus of JIT is on avoiding scrap costs as far as possible
4. Customer complaints	One focus of JIT is on solving product problems of customers immediately.
5. Customer service	One focus of JIT is on providing the highest possible degree of customer service(Timely Delivery, Full Delivery,No Return due to poor quality).
6. Ideas generated	A JIT system works best when employees pitch in with hundreds of suggestions for improvements that, when taken in total, result in a vastly improved, efficient operation. The amount of idea generation going on can be measured by the number of ideas per worker, the number of ideas suggested in total, the number of ideas implemented, or the proportion of ideas suggested that are implemented.
7. Inventory turnover	JIT systems emphasize the extraordinarily high inventory turnover for raw materials, work in process, and finished goods. The turnover levels of such well-known JIT companies as Toyata have been known to exceed 70 per year, as opposed to the levels of 2 to 10 per year that are more common for companies with other types of manufacturing systems.

Conclusion: *All the JIT measures just listed is that they are not financial in nature (with the exception of the cost of quality)—they are operational measures that focus attention on the nuts-and-bolts details of creating and running a JIT system. A cost accountant involved in the calculation and reporting of these measures may feel that this is quite a departure from the more traditional cost variance measures, but the end result will be a much more efficient JIT process that churns out and delivers high-quality products.*

6.0 BACKFLUSHING IN A JIT SYSTEM

Meaning	Backflushing requires no data entry of any kind until a finished product is completed. At that time the total amount finished is entered into the computer system, which multiplies it by all the components listed in the bill of materials for each item produced. This yields a lengthy list of components that should have been used in the production process and which is subtracted from the opening inventory balance to arrive at the amount of closing inventory. . Back the entire production process. Given the large transaction volumes associated with JIT, this is an ideal solution to the problem.
Problems	Problems with backflushing that must be corrected before it will work properly are as follows: 1. **Production Reporting** The total production figure entered into the system must be absolutely correct, or else the wrong component types and quantities will be subtracted from stock. This problem aries when there is high turnover or a low level of training to the production staff that records this information. 2. **Scrap Reporting** All abnormal scrap must be diligently tracked and recorded; otherwise these materials will fall outside the blackflushing system and will not be charged to inventory. Since scrap can occur anywhere in a production process, a lack of attention by any of the production staff can result in an inaccurate inventory. This problem aries when there is high turnover or a low level of training to the production staff that records this information. 3. **Lot Tracing** Lot tracing is impossible under the backflushing system. It is required when a manufacturer need to keep records of which production lots were used to create a product in case all the items in a lot must be recalled. Only a picking system can adequately record this information. Some computer system allow picking and backflushing system to coexist, so that pick transactions for lot tracing purpose can still be entered in the computer. Lot tracing may then still be possible if the right software is available; however, this feature is generally present only on high-end systems. 4. **Inventory Accuracy** The inventory balance may be too high at all times because the backflushing transaction that relievs inventory usually does so only once a day, during which time other inventory is sent to the production process; this makes it difficult to maintain an accurate set of inventory records in the warehouse.

Conclusion: *Of all the issues noted here, the worst is a situation where the production staff is clearly incapable of providing sufficiently accurate scrap or production reporting for the backflushing system. If there is an easily traceble cause, such as less capable workers on a particular shift, moving a few reliable employees into these positions can provide immediate relief from the problem. It may even be possible to have an experienced shift supervisor to collect this information. However, where this is not possible for whatever reason, computer system users experience backflushing garbage in, garbage out (GIGO)—entering inaccurate information rapidly eliminates any degree of accuracy in the inventory records, requiring many physical inventory counts to correct the problem. Consequently, the success of a backflushing system is directly related to a company's willingness to invest in a well-paid, experienced well-educated production staff that undergoes little turnover.*

Illustration 1

X Video Company sells package of blank video tapes to its customer. It purchases video tapes from Y Tape Company @ Rs140 a packet. Y Tape Company pays all freight to X Video Company. No incoming inspection is necessary because Y Tape Company has a superb reputation for delivery of quality merchandise. Annual demand of X Video Company is 13,000 packages. X Video Co. requires 15% annual return on investment. The purchase order lead time is two weeks. The purchase order is passed through Internet and it costs Rs2 per order. The relevant insurance, material handling etc Rs3.10 per package per year. X Video Company has to decide whether or not to shift to JIT purchasing. Y Tape Company agrees to deliver 100 packages of video tapes 130 times per year (5 times every two weeks) instead of existing delivery system of 1,000 packages 13 times a year with additional amount of Rs0.02 per package. X Video Co. incurs no stock out under its current purchasing policy. It is estimated X Video Co. incurs stock out cost on 50 video tape packages under a JIT purchasing policy. In the event of a stock out, X Video Co. has to rush order tape packages which costs Rs4 per package. Comment whether X Video Company should implement JIT purchasing system.

Z Co. also supplies video tapes. It agrees to supply @ Rs13.60 per package under JIT delivery system. If video tape purchased from Z Co., relevant carrying cost would be Rs3 per package against Rs3.10 in case of purchasing from Y Tape Co. However Z Co. doesn't enjoy so sterling a reputation for quality. X Video Co. anticipates following negative aspects of purchasing tapes from Z Co.

- ***To incur additional inspection cost of 5 paisa per package.***
  Average stock out of 360 tapes packages per year would occur, largely resulting form late deliveries. Z Co. cannot rush order at short notice. X Video Co. anticipates lost contribution margin per package of Rs8 from stock out.
- ***Customer would likely return 2% of all packages due to poor quality of the tape and to handle this return an additional cost of ₹ 25 per package would be incurred:***

Required: Comment whether X Video Co should place order to Z Co

Solution

(i) COMPARATIVE STATEMENT OF COST FOR PURCHASING FROM Y CO LTD UNDER CURRENT POLICY & JIT

Particulars	*Current Policy ₹*	*JIT ₹*
Purchasing Cost	18,20,000 (13,000 × 140)	18,20,260 (13,000 × 140.02)
Ordering Cost	26.00 (2×13 orders)	260.00 (2×130 orders)
Opportunity Carrying Cost	10,500.00 (1/2×1000×140×15%)	1,050.15 (1/2×100×140.02×15%)
Other Carrying Cost (Insurance, material handling etc)	1,550.00 (1/2×1000×3.10)	155.00
Stock out cost		200(4 × 50)
Total Relevant Cost	18,32,076	18,21,925.15

Comments: As may be seen from above, the relevant cost under the JIT purchasing policy is lower than the cost incurred under the existing system. Hence, a JIT purchasing policy should be adopted by the company.

(ii) STATEMENT OF COST FOR PURCHASING FROM Z CO LTD.

Particulars	₹
Purchasing cost (13,000 × 13.60)	1,76,800
Ordering Cost (2 × 130 orders)	260
Opportunity Carrying	102
Cost (1/2 × 100 × 13.60 × 15%)	
Other Carrying Cost (1/2 × 100 × 3.00)	150
Stock out Cost (8 × 360)	2,880
Inspection Cost (13,000 × .05)	650
Customer Return Cost (13,000 × 2% × 25)	6,500
Total Relevant Cost	1,87,342

Comments: The comparative costs are as follows:
Under Current Policy: ₹ 18,32,076.00
Under Purchase Under JIT: ₹ 18,21,925.10
Under Purchase from Z Co Ltd: ₹ 1,87,342.00
Packages should be bought from Z Co as it is the cheapest.

Illustration 2

X Ltd. has decided to adopt JIT policy for materials. The following effects of JIT policy are identified:-

(a) Capital Expenditure ₹ 6,00,000.
(b) The new facilities will require a cash operating cost ₹ 48,000 per annum.
(c) Raw Material Stockholding will be reduced from ₹ 28 lakhs to ₹ 8 lakhs.
(d) The Company can earn 15% on its long-term investments.
(e) The Company can avoid rental expenditure on storage facilities amounting to ₹ 30,000 per annum. Property Taxes and insurance amounting to ₹ 12,000 will be saved due to JIT Programme.
(f) Presently tnere are 7 workers in the Stores Department at a Salary of ₹ 3,000 each per month. After implementing JIT Scheme, only 2 workers will be required in this Department. Of the balance 5 workers, 3 will be transferred to other departments, while 2 workers employment only 2 are terminated.
(g) Due to receipt of smaller lots of Raw Materials, there will be some disruption of producnon. The Costs of Stock-out will be ₹ 3,40,000 in the first year only. This Stock-out Costs can be brought down to nil from the second year onwards.

Required: Determine the financial impact of the JIT policy. Is it advisable for the company to implementing JIT system?

Solution

STATEMENT OF COST & BENEFITS

Particulars	₹
A. **Benefits:**	
Interest on working capital released [(28,00,000 – 8,00,000) × 15%]	3,00,000
Rental Expenditure	30,000
Savings in property tax	12,000
Savings in salary (2 × 3,000 × 12)	72,000
	4,14,000

Particulars	₹
B. Expenses:	
Interest on capital cost (6,00,000 × 15%)	90,000
Cash operating cost	48,000
Stock out cost	3,40,000
	4,78,000
C. Net Benefit [A–B]	(64,000)

Decision: Its better to follow JIT Policy for the future year though loss exist in first year but such loss would not exist for the subsequent year because there is no stock out cost for the subsequent years.

Illustration 3

Rosen Manufacturing Corporation produces office furniture and sells it wholesale to furniture distributors. Rosen's management is reviewing a proposal to purchase a Just-in-time inventory (J!T) system to better serve its customers. The JIT system will include a computer system and materials handling equipment. The decision will be based on wheather the new JIT system is cost effective to the organization for the next Three years.

The computer system, including hardware and software, will initially cost ₹ 12,50,000. Materials handline equipment will cost ₹ 4,50,000. Both groups of equipment will have a three-years useful life for tax reporting of depreciation (straight-line) calculated assuming a Nil terminal disposal value. At the end of the three years, the newly acquired materials-handling equipment is expected to be sold for ₹ 1,50,000. The computer system will have a Nil terminal disposal value at the end of three years.

1. ***Due to the service improvement resulting from this new JIT system, Rosen will realize a ₹ 8,00,000 revenue increase to continue to grow by 10% per year thereafter.***
2. ***The contribution margin is 50%.***
3. ***Annual material-ordering costs will increase ₹ 50,000 due to a greater level of purchase orders.***
4. ***There will be a one-time decrease in working capital investment of ₹ 1,50,000 at the end of the first year, (ii) There will be a 20% savings in warehouse rent due to less space being needed. The current annual rent is ₹ 3,00,000.***

Required: Prepare an analysis of the after tax effects for the purchase of the JIT system at Rosen using the net present value method for evaluating capital expenditures. Be sure to Show all of your compulations & Determine whether Rosen should purchase the jit system. Explain your answer. Rosen uses an after-tax required rate of return of 10% and is subject to an income tax rate of 50%. Assume that all cash flows occur at year-end for tax purposes except for any initial purchase amounts.

Solution

STATEMENT OF NPV (NET PRESENT VALUE)

Particulars	1st year ₹	2nd Year ₹	3rd Year ₹
Sales	8,00,000	8,80,000	9,98,000
Contribution (50% of sales)	4,00,000	4,40,000	4,84,000
Warehouse rent	60,000	60,000	60,000
Ordering cost	(50,000)	(50,000)	(50,000)
Cash inflow	4,10,000	4,50,000	4,94,000
Cash inflow (after tax)	2,05,000	2,25,000	2,47,000

Add: Tax saving on Dep. [50%(₹ 17,00,000/3)]	2,83,333	2,83,333	2,83,333
Cashflow	4,88,333	5,08,333	5,30,333
PVF@10%	0.909	0.826	0.751
	4,43,895	4,19,883	3,98,280

Required:

PV of Cash Inflow = 4,43,895 + 4,19,883 + 3,98,280 = ₹ 12,62,058

PV of Cash outflow = ₹ 17,00,000 – PV of Capital Gain [i.e., (50% of ₹ 75,000) × 0.751]
– Benefit of Release of WC (i.e., ₹ 23,655) = ₹ 16,20,020

NPV = ₹ 12,62,058 – ₹ 16,20,020 = (₹ 3,57,962)

Decision: It is not advisable to apply JIT analysis.

Illustration 4

X Ltd. is considering JIT implementationi in 2003. The Company's annual demand for Product XJ-200, a surgical scalpel, is 20,0,00 units. If company implements JIT, the purchase price of the scalpal is expected to increase from ₹ 10 to ₹ 10.05 because of frequent deliveries by Merrison Manufacturing, Inc. Morrison enjoys a sterling reputation for quality and reliability. Ordering costs will remain at ₹ 5 per order. However, the annual pumber of orders placed will be 200 instead of the current 20. As a result of frequent ordering. Company's order size will decrease proportionally. Company's required rate of return on Investment is 20%. Other carrying Costs (insurance, materials handling and so on) will remain at ₹ 4.50 per unit. Currently Hardesty has no stock out costs. Lower inventory levels from implementing JIT will lead to ₹ 3 per unit stock out costs on 100 units during the year.

Required: Calculate the estimated dollar savings (Loss) for X Ltd. from the adoption of JITpurchasing.

Solution

STATEMENT OF COMPARATIVE COST (RELEVANT COST)

Particulars	*Present System* ₹	*JIT System* ₹
Purchase Cost	2,00,000 (10 × 20,000)	2,01,000 (10.05 × 20,000)
Ordering Cost	100 (5 × 20)	1,000 (50 × 200)
Storage Cost	2,250 (4.50 × 500)	220 (4.5 × 50)
Stock out Cost	—	300 (3 × 100)
Opportunify Cost	1,000	100.50
	2,03,350	2,02,625.50

Decision: It is better to implement Just In Time due to cost saving ₹ 724.50 (2,03,350 – 2,02,625.50)

Working Note:

Particulars	*Present*	*JIT Analysis*
Purchase cost	10	10.05
Order	20	200
Required (unit)	20,000	20,000
Order size	1,000	100
Average stock	1/2 × 1,000 = 500	1/2 × 100 = 50
Carrying cost	4.5	4.5
Working capital blocked	5,000 (500 × 10)	502.5 (50 × 10.05)
Qpp. cost on WC blocked	1,000 (5,000 × 20%)	100.50 (502.5 × 20%)

Illustration 5

X Ltd. is an automotive supplier that uses automatic turning machines to manufacture precision parts from steel bars. The company's inventory of raw steel averages ₹ 6,00,000. John, President, and Helen company's controller, are concerned about the costs of carrying inventory. The steel suppliers is willing to supply steel in smaller lots at no additional charge. Helen identified the following effects of adopting a JIT inventory program to virtually eliminate steel inventory.

- ***Without scheduling any overtime, lost sales due to stock outs would increase by 35,000 units per year. However, by incurring overtime premiums of ₹ 40,000 per year, the increase in lost sales could be reduced to 20,000 units. This would be the maximum amount of overtime that would be feasible for company.***
- ***Two warehouses currently used for steel bar storage would no longer be needed. Margo rents one warehouse from another company, under a cancelableJeasing arrangement, at an annual cost of ₹ 60,000. The other warehouse is owned by company and contains 12,000 square feet. Three-fourths of the space in the owned warehouse could be rented for ₹ 1.50 per square foot per year. Insurance and properly tax costs totaling ₹ 14,000 per year would be eliminated.***

Long-term capital investments by company are expected to Produce an annual rate of return of 20%. Company Budgeted income statement for the year ending December 31,2013 (in thousands) is as follows:

Particulars	₹
A. Revenues (900,000 units)	10,800
B. *Less:* Cost of goods sold:	
Variable costs	(4,050)
Fixed Costs	(1,450)
C. Gross Margin [*A – B*]	5,300
D. *Less:* Marketing and distribution costs:	
Variable costs	(900)
Fixed Costs	(1,500)
E. Operating income [*C – D*]	2,900

Required: Calculate the estimated savings (loss) for the company that would result in 2013 from required the adoption of the JIT inventory-control method.

Solution

STATEMENT OF COMPARATIVE COST

Particulars	*Present (₹)*	*JIT(₹)*
Stock out cost	—	1,70,000
Ware house rent	60,000	—
Rent	—	(12,000 × 3/4 × 1.50) (13,500)
Insurance & property tax costs	14,000	
Opportunity cost on working capital (6,00,000 × 20%)	1,20,000	
	1,94,000	1,56,500
Benefit firm JIT		37,500

Recommendation: It is better to follow JIT.

Working note: *Contribution from regular sales*

		(₹ in lakhs)
Revenue		108.00
— Variable cost	40.50	
— Variable cost	9.00	49.50
Contribution		58.50
Quantity		9,00,000
Contribution p.u.		₹ 6.50

Working note

	Present	JIT
Lost sale	NIL	35,000
After incurring ₹ 40,000 as premium		
(a) Sale	35,000 units	15,000 units
(b) Lost sale		20.000 units
Contribution lost	—	20,000 units × ₹ 6.50 = ₹ 1,30,000

Present: No change in situation after incurring ₹ 40,000 as premium. No lost sales

JIT: Lost sales = 35,000

After incurring ₹ 40,000 as premium — Actual sales 15,000 units; Lost sales 20,000 units

Total Stock out cost = ₹ 40,000 + ₹ 1,30,000 (Premium + Cont Lost) = ₹ 1,70,000

Contribution on 15000 units to be achieved in present situation as well as in just in time situation but in just in time system we have to incur extra cost of ₹ 40,000.

Illustration 6

X Ltd. has an annual turnover of ₹ 6,00,00,000 from a range of products, Material costs and conveision costs account for 30% and 25% of turnover, respectively. Other information relating to the company is as follows:

(i) Stock values are currently at a constant level, being:

Raw materials stock: 10% of the material element of annual turnover.

(a) Work in Progress: 15% of the material element of annual turnover together with a proportionate element of conversion costs in annual turnover allowing for 60% completion of work in progress as to conversion cost and 100% completion for material. The Ratio is constant for all products.

(b) Finished goods stock: 12% of the material element of annual turnover together with a proportionate element of conversion cost in Annual turnover.

(ii) Holding and acquisition costs of materials comprise fixed costs of ₹ 2,00,000 per annum plus variable costs of ₹ 0.10 per ₹ of Stock held.

(iii) Movement and control costs of work in progress comprise fixed costs of ₹ 2,80,000 per annum plus variable costs of ₹ 0.05 per ₹ of material value of work-in-progress.

(iv) Holding and control costs of finished goods comprise fixed costs of ₹ 3,60,000 per annum plus variable costs of ₹ 0.02 per ₹ of finished goods (material cost + Conversion cost)

(v) Financial charges due to the impact of stock holding on working capital requirement are incurred at 20% per annum on the value of stocks held.

X Ltd. is considering a number of changes due to following JIT Policy, which it is estimated will affect stock levels and costs as follows:

1. Raw Material Stock: Negotiate delivery from suppliers on a just in time basis. Stock levels will be reduced to 20% of the present level. Fixed costs of holding and acquiring

stock will be reduced to 20% of the presen level and variable costs to ₹ 0.07 per ₹ of stock held.

2. ***Work in Progress: Convert the layout of the production area into a dedicated cell format for each product type instead of the existing system which comprises groups of similar machines to which each product type must be taken. Work in progress volume will be reduced to 20% of the present level with the same stage completion as at present .Fixed costs of movement and control will be reduced to 40% of the present level and variable costs to ₹ 0.03 per ₹ of material value of work in progress.***
3. ***Finished Goods Stock: Improved control of the flow of each product type from the production area will enable stocks to be reduced to 25% of the present level. Fixed costs of holding and control will be reduced to 40% of the present level and variable costs to ₹ 0.01 per ₹ of finished goods held. Evaluate the Proposal.***

Solution

STATEMENT OF COMPARATIVE COST

Particulars	Present System ₹		JIT System ₹	
Opportunit Cost (W.N. 2)	1,96,200			4,32,000
Storage cost:				
Raw material:				
Fixed	2,00,000	40,000		
Variable	(0.01 × 18,00,000)	1,80,000	(0.07 × 3.60,000)	25,200
Fixed		2,80,000		1,12,000
Variable	(0.05 × 27,00,000)	1,35,000	(5,40,000 × 0.03)	16,200
Finished goods:				
Fixed	3,60,000			1,44,000
Variable	(39,60,000 × 0.02)	79,200	(0.01 x 9.90,000)	9,900
Total cost	31,96,200			7,79,300

Decision: It is better to apply Just In Time approach due to cost saving.

Working Notes:

(i) Material = ₹ 600 lakh × 30%

(ii) Conversion cost = 600 lakh × 25% = ₹ 150 lakhs

2. STATEMENT OF CAPITAL BLOCKED

Particulars	Present ₹		JIT ₹	
Raw-material	(180 × 10%)	18 lakh		3.6 lakhs
WIP				
Material	(150% of 180 × 100%)	27		5.4 lakhs
Conversion	(15% of 150 × 60%)	13.5		2.7 lakhs
Finished Goods:				
Material	(12% of 180)	21.6 lakhs		5.4 lakhs
Conversion Cost	(12% of 150)	18 lakhs		4.5 lakhs
Total Average Investment		98.1 lakhs		21.6 lakhs
Opportunity Cost	(98.1 × 20%)	19.62 lakhs	(21.6 × 20%)	4.32 lakh

15 Target Costing

Learning Objectives

After studying this chapter, you should be able to understand:

- Meaning, Objective, Advantages, Process, Stages, Features, Problems of Target Costing
- How to Implement a Target Costing System
- Impact of Target Costing on Profitability
- Value Engineering
- Cost Accountant's Role in a Target Costing Environment
- Most Useful Situations for Target Costing
- Target Costing Control Points

1.0 MEANING, OBJECTIVE, ADVANTAGES, PROCESS, STAGES, FEATURES PROBLEMS OF TARGET COSTING

Meaning	Target Costing is a cost management technique which aims to design & produce a product with specified functionality and quality at expected cost not exceeding the target cost to ensure the target margin and target level of customer satisfaction at target selling price.
Objective	1. The objective of Target Costing is to produce and sell products that will ensure the target margin. 2. The objective of Target Costing is to design a product with expected cost not exceeding the target cost but also meeting target level of customer satisfaction.
Advantages	1. The main advantage is that it is deployed during a product's design and planning stage so that it can have maximum impact in determining the level of locked-in costs. 2. It tries to eliminate those product functions that add cost but do not increase selling price. 3. It designs a product with expected cost less than or equal to target cost but also meeting target level of customer satisfaction. 4. The design teams continuously tries to develop a product design costing less than target cost with the help of— (i) Value Engineering (ii) Reverse Engineering 5. **Target costing may assist control of costs and pricing of product.** (i) Target costing considers the price that ought to be charged by a company to achieve a given market share.

	(ii) Target costing takes life cycle costs in to consideration. (iii) If there is a gap between the target cost and expected cost, ways and means of reducing or eliminating it are explored. (iv) The target cost may be used for controlling costs by comparison. 6. It reinforces top-to-bottom commitment to process and product innovation, and is aimed at identifying issues to be resolved, in order to achieve some competitive advantage. 7. It helps to create a company's competitive future with market-driven management for designing and manufacturing products that meet the price required for market success. 8. It uses management control systems to support and reinforce manufacturing strategies and to identify market opportunities that can be converted into real savings to achieve the best value rather than simply the lowest cost. 9. It is an important part of a comprehensive management process aimed at helping an organization to survive in an increasingly competitive environment.
Target Costing Process	It involves following stages: **Stage1:** *Determine the Target Price which customers will be prepared to pay for the product with specified functionality and quality.* **Stage 2:** *Deduct a Target Profit margin from Target Price to determine Target Cost. Note: The target profit margin depends on the planned return on the investment for organization as a whole and profit on selling price.* **Stage 3:** *Estimate the Actual Cost of the product.* **Stage 4:** *If the Actual Cost exceeds Target Cost, investigate ways of driving down Actual Cost to Target Cost with the help of Techniques like Value Engineering and Reverse Engineering.*
Target Price	Target Price is the price which customers will be prepared to pay for the product with specified functionality and quality.
Target Margin	Target Margin is the margin which the management desires to achieve.
Target Costs	1. Target Cost is the difference between Estimated Selling Price of a proposed product and the Target Margin. 2. Target Selling Price – Target Profit
How differ from Standard Costing	Under Target Costing first Target Selling Price and Target Margin are estimated and then Target Cost is determined whereas under Standard costing first Standard Costs (Engineered Costs) and Mark-up are determined and then Desired Selling Price is ascertained.
Stages to the Methodology	1. **Planning Phase:** Under this phase, competitors products are to be analyzed, with regard to price, quality, service and support, delivery and technology. The features which consumers would like to have like consumer value etc. are established. The competitive advantage which a company can have is established. 2. **Development Phase:** Under this Phase the most competitive product in the market is selected and studied with respect to requirements of material, manufacturing process along with competitor's cost structure. The firm should also develop estimates of internal cost structure based on internal cost of similar products being produced by the company. If

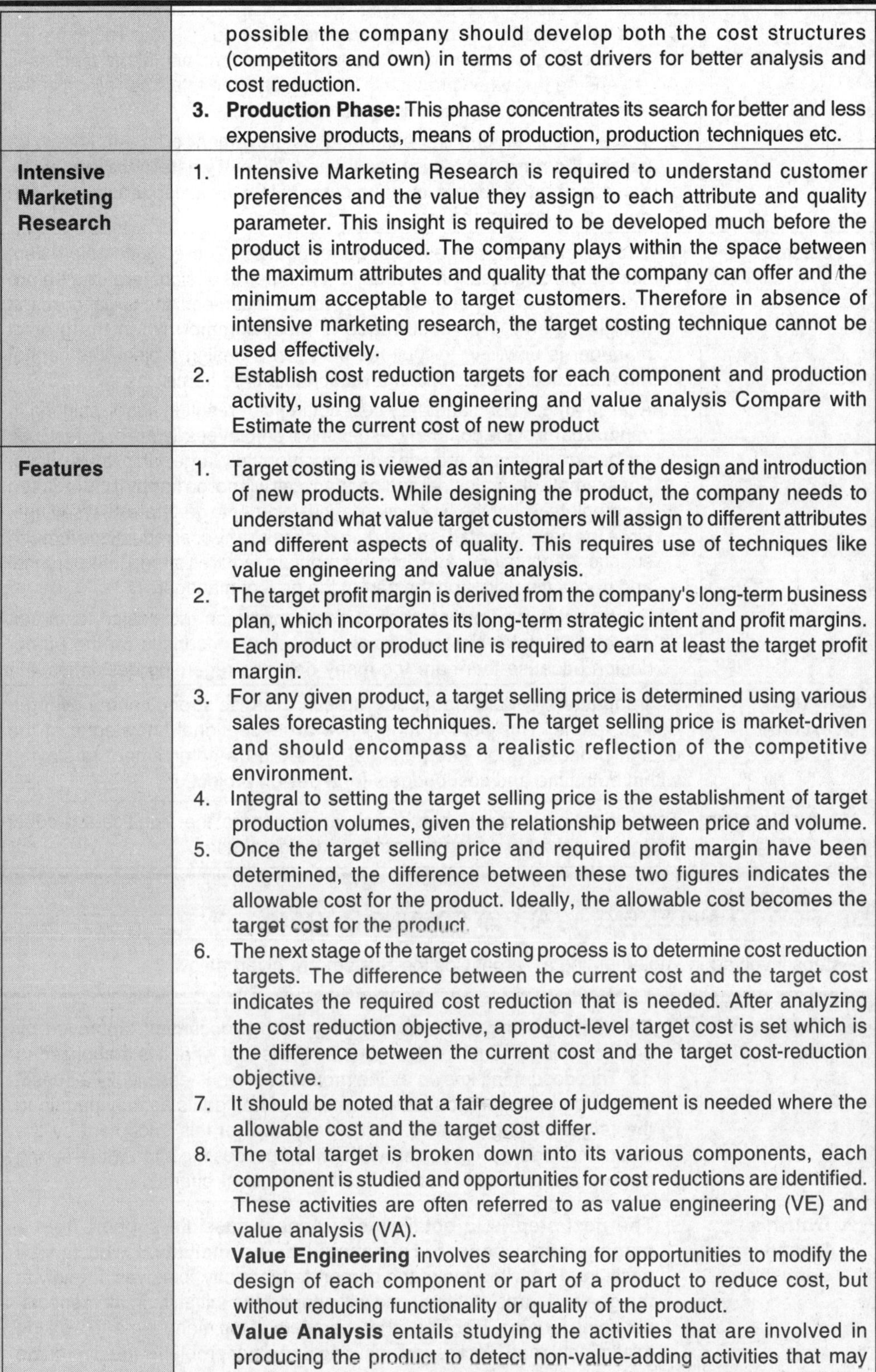

	possible the company should develop both the cost structures (competitors and own) in terms of cost drivers for better analysis and cost reduction. 3. **Production Phase:** This phase concentrates its search for better and less expensive products, means of production, production techniques etc.
Intensive Marketing Research	1. Intensive Marketing Research is required to understand customer preferences and the value they assign to each attribute and quality parameter. This insight is required to be developed much before the product is introduced. The company plays within the space between the maximum attributes and quality that the company can offer and the minimum acceptable to target customers. Therefore in absence of intensive marketing research, the target costing technique cannot be used effectively. 2. Establish cost reduction targets for each component and production activity, using value engineering and value analysis Compare with Estimate the current cost of new product
Features	1. Target costing is viewed as an integral part of the design and introduction of new products. While designing the product, the company needs to understand what value target customers will assign to different attributes and different aspects of quality. This requires use of techniques like value engineering and value analysis. 2. The target profit margin is derived from the company's long-term business plan, which incorporates its long-term strategic intent and profit margins. Each product or product line is required to earn at least the target profit margin. 3. For any given product, a target selling price is determined using various sales forecasting techniques. The target selling price is market-driven and should encompass a realistic reflection of the competitive environment. 4. Integral to setting the target selling price is the establishment of target production volumes, given the relationship between price and volume. 5. Once the target selling price and required profit margin have been determined, the difference between these two figures indicates the allowable cost for the product. Ideally, the allowable cost becomes the target cost for the product. 6. The next stage of the target costing process is to determine cost reduction targets. The difference between the current cost and the target cost indicates the required cost reduction that is needed. After analyzing the cost reduction objective, a product-level target cost is set which is the difference between the current cost and the target cost-reduction objective. 7. It should be noted that a fair degree of judgement is needed where the allowable cost and the target cost differ. 8. The total target is broken down into its various components, each component is studied and opportunities for cost reductions are identified. These activities are often referred to as value engineering (VE) and value analysis (VA). **Value Engineering** involves searching for opportunities to modify the design of each component or part of a product to reduce cost, but without reducing functionality or quality of the product. **Value Analysis** entails studying the activities that are involved in producing the product to detect non-value-adding activities that may

	be eliminated or minimized to save costs, but without reducing the functionality or quality of the product. Overall, the aim of the process is to ensure that when production commences, the total cost will meet the target, and profit goals will be achieved. 9. There is also an ongoing continuous improvement program, known as **Kaizen Costing** that focuses on the reduction of waste in the production process, thereby further lowering costs below the initial targets specified during the design phase.
Problems	1. The development process can be lengthened to a considerable extent since the design team may require a number of design iterations before it can devise a sufficiently low-cost product that meets the target cost and margin criteria. This occurrence is most common when the project manager is unwilling to "pull the plug" on a design project that cannot meet its costing goals within a reasonable time frame. 2. A large amount of mandatory cost cutting can result in finger-pointing in various parts of the company, especially if employees in one area feel they are being called on to provide a disproportionately large part of the savings. For example, the industrial engineering staff will not be happy if it is required to completely alter the production layout in order to generate cost savings, while the purchase staff is not required to make any cost reductions through supplier negotiations. Avoiding this problem requires strong interpersonal and negotiation skills on the part of the project manager. 3. Representatives from number of departments on the design team can sometimes make it more difficult to reach a consensus on the proper design because there are too many opinions regarding design issues.
How to overcome Problems	A strong team leader is required who can exercise strong control over the design teams. This person must have an exceptional knowledge of the design process, good interpersonal skills, and a commitment to staying within both time and cost budgets for a design project.
Useful Situation	Target costing is most useful in situations where the significant product costs are locked in during the product design phase.

2.0 HOW TO IMPLEMENT A TARGET COSTING SYSTEM

The steps involved in implementing a Target Costing System are given below:

1. Create a Project Charter	The target costing effort should begin with a document, approved by senior management that describes its goals and what it is authorized to do. This document, known as the project charter, is essentially a subset of the corporate mission statement and related goals as they pertain to the target costing initiative. Written approval of this document by the senior management group provides the target costing effort with a strong basis of support and direction in all subsequent efforts.
2. Obtain a Management sponsor	The next step is to obtain the strongest possible support from a management sponsor. This should be an individual who is well positioned near the top of the corporate hierarchy, believes strongly in the goals of target costing, and will support the initiative in all respects-obtaining funding, lobbying other members of top management, working to eliminate road blocks, and ensuring that other problems are overcome in timely manner. This person is central to the success of target costing.

3. Obtain a Budget	The target costing program requires funds to ensure that one or more well-staffed design teams can complete target costing tasks. The funding should be based on a formal allocation of money through the corporate budget, rather than a parsimonious sub-allocation grudgingly granted by one or more departments. In the first case the funds are unreservedly given to the target costing effort, whereas in the latter case, they can be suddenly withdrawn by a department manager who is not fully persuaded of the need for target costing or who suddenly finds a need for the money elsewhere.
4. Assign a Strong Team Manager	Because the typical target costing program involves so many people with different backgrounds and represents so many parts of a company, it can be difficult to weld the group together into a smoothly functioning team focused on key objectives. The best way to ensure that the team functions properly is to assign to the effort a strong team manager skilled in dealing with management, the use of project tools, and working with a diverse group of people. This manager should be a full-time employee, so that his or her complete attention can be directed toward the welfare of the project.
5. Enroll Full-Time Participants	A target costing team member puts the greatest effort into the program when he or she is focused only on target costing. Thus, it is essential that as many members of the team as possible be devoted to it full-time rather than also trying to fulfil other commitment elsewhere in the company at the same time. This may call for the replacement of these individuals in the departments they are leaving so that there are no emergencies requiring their sudden withdrawal back to their "home" departments to deal with other work problems. It may even be necessary to permanently assign them to a target costing program, providing them with a single focus on ensuring the success of the target costing program because their livelihood are now tied to it.
6. Use Project Management Tools	Target costing can be a highly complex effort especially for high-cost products with many features and components. To ensure that the project stays on track, the team should use all available project management tools, such as Microsoft Project (for tracking the completion of specific tasks), a company database containing various types of costing information, and a variety of product design tools. All these items require assured access to many corporate database, as well as a budget for whatever computing equipment is needed to access this data. The main focus of the step described in this section is to ensure the fullest possible support for target costing by all available means-management, money and staff. Only when all these elements are in place and concentrated on the goals at hand does a target costing program have the greatest chance for success.

3.0 IMPACT OF TARGET COSTING ON PROFITABILITY

Target costing can have a startlingly large positive impact on profitability, depending on the commitment of management to its use, the constant involvement of cost accountants in all phases of a product's life cycle, and the type of strategy a company follows. Target costing improves profitability in two ways:

First	**It places such a detailed continuing emphasis on product costs throughout the life cycle of every product that it is unlikely that a company will experience runaway costs;** also, the management team is completely aware of costing issues since it receives regular reports from the cost accounting members of all design teams.
Second	**It improves profitability through precise targeting of the correct prices at which the company feels it can field a profitable product in the marketplace that will sell in a robust manner.** This is opposed to the more common cost-plus approach under which a company builds a product, determines its cost, tacks on a profit and then does not understand why its resoundingly high price does not attract buyers. Thus, target costing results not only in better cost control but also in better price control. Target costing is really part of a larger concept called concurrent engineering, which requires participants from many departments to work together on project teams rather than having separate departments handle new product design only after they have been handed off from the preceding department in the design chain. Clustering representatives from many departments together on a single design team can be quite a struggle, especially for older companies that have a history of conflict between departments. Consequently, only the most involved, prolonged support by all members of the senior management group can ensure that target costing and the greater concept of concurrent engineering, will result in significant profitability improvements. The review of product costs under the target costing methodology is not reserved just for the period up to the completion of design work on a new product. On the contrary, there are always opportunities to control costs after the design phase is completed, though these opportunities are fewer than during the design phase. Therefore, cost accountants should not be pulled from a design team once the final drawings have left the engineering department. Instead, they should regularly monitor actual component costs and compare them to planned costs, warning management whenever significant adverse variances arise. Also, cost accountants should take a lead role in the continuing review of supplier costs to see if they can be reduced, perhaps by visiting supplier facilities, as well as constantly reviewing existing product designs to see if they can be improved, and by targeting for elimination waste or spoilage on the production floor. Therefore, the cost accounting staff must be involved in all phases of a product's life cycle if a company is to realize profitability improvements from target costing to the fullest extent. A company's strategy can also has its impact on profitability. If it constantly issues a stream of new products, or if its existing product lines is subject to severe pricing pressure, it must make target costing a central part of its strategy so that the correct price points are used for products and actual costs match those originally planned. However, there are other strategies, such as growth by geographical expansion of the current product line (as is practiced by retail stores) or growth by acquisition, where there is no particular need for target costing-these companies make their money in other ways than by a focused concentration on product features and costs. For them, there may still be a role for target costing, but it is strictly limited by the reduced need for new products. If the issues presented here are properly dealt with by a management team, it should find that target costing is one of the best accounting methods available for improving profitability. It is indeed one of the most pro-active systems found in the entire range of accounting knowledge.

4.0 VALUE ENGINEERING

Meaning	**Value Engineering** involves searching for opportunities to modify the design of each component or part of a product to reduce cost, but without reducing functionality or quality of the product.
Issues that are dealt with during a Value Engineering Review	1. **Can we eliminate functions from the production process?** This involves a detailed review of the entire manufacturing process to see if there are any steps, such as interim quality reviews, that add no value to the product. By eliminating them, one can take their associated direct or overhead costs out of the product cost. However, these functions were originally put in for a reason, so the engineering team must be careful to develop work-around steps that eliminate the need for the original functions. 2. **Can we eliminate some durability or reliability?** It is possible to design an excessive degree of sturdiness into a product. For example, a vacuum cleaner can be designed to withstand a 1-ton impact, although there is only the most vanishing chance that such an impact will ever occur; designing it to withstand an impact of 100 pounds may account for 99.999% of all probable impacts, while also eliminating a great deal of structural material from the design. However, this concept can be taken too far, resulting in a visible reduction in durability or reliability, so any designs that have had their structural integrity reduced must be thoroughly tested to ensure that they meet all design standards. 3. **Can we minimize the design?** This involves the creation of a design that uses fewer parts or has fewer features. This approach is based on the assumption that a minimal design is easier to manufacture and assemble. Also, with fewer parts to purchase, less procurement overhead is associated with the product. However, reducing a product to extremes, perhaps from dozens of components to just a few molded or prefabricated arts, can result in excessively high costs for these few remaining parts, since they may be so complex or custom made in nature that it would be less expensive to settle for a few extra standard parts that are more easily and cheaply obtained. 4. **Can we design the product better for the manufacturing process?** Also known as design for manufacture and assembly (DFMA), this involves the creation of a product design that can be created in only a specific manner. For example, a toner cartridge for a laser printer is designed so that it can be successfully inserted into the printer only when the sides of the cartridge are correctly aligned with the printer opening; all other attempts to insert the cartridge will fail. When used for the assembly of an entire product, this approach ensures that a product is not incorrectly manufactured or assembled, which would call for a costly disassembly or (even worse) product recalls from customers who have already received defective goods. 5. **Can we substitute parts?** This approach encourages the search for less expensive components or materials that can replace more expensive parts currently used in a product design. It is becoming an increasingly valid approach since new materials are being developed every year. However, sometimes the use of a different material impacts the types of materials that can be

used elsewhere in the product, which may result in cost increases in these other areas, for a net increase in costs. Thus, any parts substitution must be accompanied by a review of related changes elsewhere in the design. This step is also known as component parts analysis and involves one extra activity-tracking the intentions of suppliers to continue producing parts in the future; if parts will not be available, they must be eliminated from the product design.

6. **Can we combine steps?**
A detailed review of all the processes associated with a product sometimes reveals that some steps can be consolidated, which may mean that one can be eliminated (as noted earlier) or that several can be accomplished by one person, rather than having people in widely disparate parts of the production process perform them. This is also known as process centering. By combining steps in this manner, we can eliminate some of the transfer and queue time from the production process, which in turn reduces the chance that parts will be damaged during these transfers.

7. **Is there a better way?**
Though this step sounds rather vague, it really strikes at the core of the cost reduction issue—the other value engineering steps previously mentioned focus on incremental improvements to the existing design or production process, whereas this one is a more general attempt to start from scratch and build a new product or process that is not based in any way on preexisting ideas. Improvements resulting from this step lend to have the largest favourable impact on cost reductions but can also be the most difficult for the organization to adopt, especially if it has used other designs or systems for the production of earlier models. Another approach to value engineering is to call on the services of a company's suppliers to assist in the cost reduction effort. These organizations are particularly suited to contribute information concerning enhanced types of technology of materials, since they may specialize in areas that a company has no information about. They may have also conducted extensive value engineering for the components they manufacture, resulting in advanced designs that a company may be able to incorporate into its new products. Suppliers may have also redesigned their production processes, or can be assisted by a company's engineers in doing so, producing cost reductions or decreased production waste that can be translated into lower component costs for the company. A mix of all the value engineering steps noted above must be applied to each product design to ensure that the maximum permissible cost is safely reached. Also, even if a minimal amount of value engineering is needed to reach a cost goal, one should conduct the full range of value engineering analysis anyway, since this can result in further cost reductions that improve the margin of the product or allow management the option of reducing the product's price, thereby creating a problem for competitors who sell higher-priced products. Another term mentioned in the earlier explanation of the target costing process is "kaizen costing." This is a Japanese term for a number of cost reduction steps that can be used subsequent to issuing a new product design to the factory floor. Some of the activities in the kaizen costing methodology include the elimination of waste in the production, assembly, and distribution processes, as

	well as the elimination of work steps in any of these areas. Though these points are also covered in the value engineering phase of target costing, the initial value engineering may not uncover all possible cost savings. Thus, kaizen costing is really designed to repeat many of the value engineering steps for as long as a product is produced, constantly refining the process and thereby stripping out extra costs. The cost reductions resulting from kaizen costing are much smaller than those achieved with value engineering but are still worth the effort since competitive pressures are likely to force down the price of a product over time, and any possible cost savings allow a company to still attain its targeted profit margins while continuing to reduce cost.

5.0 COST ACCOUNTANT'S ROLE IN A TARGET COSTING ENVIRONMENT

1. To Provide Cost Estimates	The cost accountant should be able to provide for the other members of the design team a running series of cost estimates based on initial designs sketch, activities based costing reviews of production processes, and "best guess" costing information from suppliers based on estimated production volumes. Essentially in the earliest stages of a design, the cost accountant works with vague costing information and so must be able to provide estimates within a high-low range costs, gradually tightening this estimated cost range as more information becomes available.
2. Responsibility for any Capital Budgeting Requests	The cost accountant should also be responsible for any capital budgeting requests generated by the design team since he or she has the knowledge of the capital budgeting process, how to fill out the required forms, and precisely what types of equipment are needed for the anticipated product design. The cost accountant also becomes the key contact on the design team for answers to any questions from the finance staff regarding issues or uncertainties in the capital budgeting proposal.
3. Cost-Benefit Trade-Offs	The cost accountant should work with the design team to help it understand the nature of various costs (such as cost allocations based on an activity-based costing system), as well as the cost-benefit trade-offs of using different design or cost operations in the new product.
4. Responsibility for tracking the gap between the current cost of a product design and the target cost	The cost accountant is responsible for tracking the gap between the current cost of a product design and the target cost that is the design team's goal, providing an itemization of where cost savings have already been achieved and where there has not been a sufficient degree of progress.
5. Comparison	Finally, the cost accountant must continue to compare a product's actual cost to the target cost after the design is completed, and for as long as the company sells the product. This is a necessary step because management must know immediately if costs are increasing beyond budgeted levels and why these increases are occurring.

5.1 Qualities of a Cost Accountant

The cost accountant must—

1. Know what are the features of company products
2. Know what are the components of company products
3. Know how to create an activity based costing system to evaluate related production costs, or at least interpret such costing data developed by someone else.
4. Work well in a team environment, proactively assisting other members of the team in constantly evaluating the costs of new design concepts.
5. Have good analytical and presentation skills, since the ongoing costing results must be continually presented not only to other members of the team but also to the members of the milestone review committee.

   Thus, the best cost accountant for this position is an outgoing person with several years of experience within a company or industry.

6.0 MOST USEFUL SITUATIONS FOR TARGET COSTING

Target costing is most useful in situations where the significant product costs are locked in during the product design phase. This is the case for most manufactured products, but few services. In the services area, such as consulting, the bulk of all activities can be reconfigured for cost reduction during the "production" phase, which is when services are being provided directly to the customer. In the services environment the "design team" is still present but is more commonly concerned with streamlining the activities conducted by the employees providing the service, which can continue to be enhanced at any time, not just when the initial services process is being laid out.

For example, design team can lay out the floor plan of a fast-food restaurant, with the objective of creating an arrangement that allows employees to cover the shortest possible distances while preparing food and serving customers; this is similar to the design of a new product. However, unlike a product design, this layout can be readily altered at any time if the design team can arrive at a better layout, so that the restaurant staff can continue to experience high levels of productivity improvement even after the initial design and layout of the facility. In this situation costs are not locked in during the design phase, so there is less need for target costing.

Another situation where target costing results in less value is the production of raw materials, such as chemicals. In this case there are no design features for a design team to labour over; instead, the industrial engineering staff tries to create the most efficient possible production process, which has little to do with cost reduction through the improvement of customer value by creating a product with a high ratio of features to costs.

7.0 TARGET COSTING CONTROL POINTS

A target costing program eventually results in major cost reductions if design teams are given an unlimited amount of time to carry out a multitude of design iterations. However, there comes a point where the cost of maintaining the design team exceeds the savings to be garnered from additional iterations. Also, most product must be released within a reasonably short time frame or they will miss the appropriate market window when they can beat the delivery of competing products to the market. To avoid both these cost and time delays, we use milestones as the principal control point over the course of a target costing program.

Several milestone reviews should be incorporated into a target costing program. Each one should include a thorough analysis of the progress of the design team since the last review, such as a comparison of the current cost of a design with its target cost. The main issue here is that the amount of cost yet to be worked out of a product must shrink, on a dollar or percentage basis, after each successive milestone review, or else management has the right to cancel the design project. For example, there may be a standard allowable cost variance of 12% for the first milestone meeting, 10% at the next meeting, and so on until the target cost must be reached by a specific future milestone data. If a design team cannot quite reach its target cost, but comes close, the management team should be required to make a "go/no go" decision at that time which overrides the cost target and sends the design into production, allows time of additional design iterations, or terminates the project. A milestone can be based on a time budget (e.g., one per month) or on the points in the design process at which specific activities are completed. For example, a milestone review can occur as soon as each successive design iteration is completed, when the conceptual drawings are finished, when the working model has been created, or when the production pilot has been run. In the last-mentioned case, there are many more steps that the management group can build into the milestone review process so that cost analysis become a nearly continual part of the target costing regime.

Illustration 1

A company has the capacity of production of 80,000 units and presently sells 20,000 units at ₹.100 each. The demand is sensitive to selling price and it has been observed that every reduction of ₹.10 in selling price the demand is doubled.

Required: (a) What should be the target cost at full capacity if profit margin on sale is taken as 25%? (b) What should be the cost reduction scheme if at present 40% of cost is variable with same % of profit? (c) If Rate of Return is 15%, what will be maximum investment at full capacity?

Solution

(a) SELLING PRICE AT FULL CAPACITY

Selling Price/unit	*Demand*
100	20,000
90	40,000
80	80,000 = Full capacity

Therefore, **Target Cost per unit** = ₹ 80 – 25% of sales = ₹ 80 – ₹ 20 = ₹ 60 per unit

(b) Present Total Cost = ₹ 100 – 25% = ₹ 75

Present Variable Cost Per Unit = 40% of cost *i.e.* 75 = ₹ 30

Present Fixed Cost per unit = ₹ 75 – ₹ 30 = ₹ 45

Total Estimated Cost at full capacity = Fixed Cost + Variable Cost

= (80000 × ₹ 45) + (80000 × ₹ 40) = ₹ 60 lakhs

Therefore, Required Cost reduction following value engineering = ₹ 60 lakhs – ₹ 48 lakhs

= ₹ 12 lakhs

(c) Maximum Investment at full capacity

Profit before tax = ₹ 20 × 80,000 units = ₹ 16 lakhs

Investment = (PBI/ROCE) = 16 lakhs/15% = ₹ 106.67 Lakhs

Illustration 2

Sterling Enterprises has prepared a draft budget for the next year as follows:

Quantity	10,000 units
Selling Price per unit	30
Variable Costs per unit:	
Direct Materials	8
Direct Labour	6

Variable Overheads (2 hrs × ₹ 0.50)	1
Contribution per unit	15
Budgeted Contribution	1,50,000
Budgeted Fixed costs	1,40,000
Budgeted Profit	10,000

The Board of Directors is dissatisfied with this budget, and asks a working party to come up with an alternate budget with higher target profit figures. The working party reports back with the following suggestions that will lead to a budgeted profit of ₹ 25,000. The company should spend ₹ 28,500 on advertising, & the target sales price up to ₹ 32 per unit. It is expected that the sales volume will also rise, inspite of the price rise, to 12,000 units. In order to achieve the extra production capacity, however, the work force must be able to reduce the time taken to make each unit of the product. It is proposed to offer a pay and productivity deal in which the wage rate per hour is increased to ₹ 4. The hourly rate for variable overhead will be unaffected.

Required: Ascertain the target labour time required to achieve the target profit.

Solution

CALCULATION OF TARGET LABOUR TIME

Particulars	₹
Target Profit	25,000
Add: Fixed cost	1,40,000
Add: Additional Advertisement	28,500
A. Total Contribution	1,93,500
B. Required Sales volume	12,000
Contribution per unit [A/B]	16.125
Target Selling Price/unit	32.000
Less: Contribution/unit	16.125
Target Variable Cost per unit	15.875
Less: Material Cost per unit	8.000
Labour and Variable Overheads	7.875
Labour: = 4*X* and Variable Overhead = 0.5*X*	
4.5*x* = 7.875	
x (hr.) = 7.875/4.5 = 1.75	
Target Labour Time 1.75	
Present 2.00	
Time reduction. 0.25 hr	

Illustration 3

IBM Ltd. manufactures and sells computers peripherals to several retail outlets throughout the country. Amar is the manager of the printer division. Its two largest-selling printers are P1 & P2.

The manufacturing cost of each printer is calculated using IBM's activity based costing system. IBM has one direct manufacturing cost category (direct materials) and the following five indirect manufacturing cost pools.

Indirect Manufacturing Cost Pool	*Allocation Base*	*Allocation Rate (₹)*
1. Materials handling	No. of Parts	₹ 1.20 per part
2. Assembly management	Hours of assembly time	₹ 40 per hour of assembly time
3. Machine insertion of parts per machine inserted part.	No. of machine inserted parts	₹ 0.70
4. Manual insertion of parts	No. of manually inserted parts	₹ 2.10 per manually inserted part
5. Quality testing per testing	Hours of quality testing time	₹ 25 per testing hour.

Product characteristics of P1 and P2 are as follows:

Product	*P1*	*P2*
Direct materials costs	₹ 407.50	₹ 292.10
Number of parts	85.00	46.00
Hours of assembly time	3.20	1.90
Number of machine—inserted parts	48.00	31.00
Number of manually inserted parts	36.00	15.00
Hours of quality testing time	1.40	1.10

A foreign competitor has introduced products very similar to P1 and P2. Given their announced selling prices, to maintain the company's market share and profits. Amar estimated the P1 to have manufacturing cost of approximately ₹ 680 and P2 to have a manufacturing cost of approximately ₹ 390. he calls a meeting of product designers and manufacturing personnel at the printer division. They all agreed to have the ₹ 680 and ₹ 390 figures become target costs for designed version of P1 and P2 respectively. Product designers examine alternative ways of designing printer with comparable performance but lower costs. They come up with the following revised designs for P1 and P2 (termed P1– REV and P2 – REV, respectively)

Particulars	*P1 - REV*	*P2 - REV*
Direct materials cost	₹ 381.20	₹ 263.10
Number of parts	71	39
Hours of assembly time	2.1	1.6
Number of machine - inserted parts	59	29
Number of manually - inserted parts	12	10
Hours of quality testing time	1.2	0.9

Required:

(a) Compute the present costs of products P1 and P2 using ABC system.

(b) Compute the manufacturing costs of P1 - REV and P2 - REV. How do they compare with the ₹ 680 and ₹ 390 target costs?

Solution

STATEMENT OF PRESENT COST OF P_1 AND P_2

Particulars	*P1* *₹/unit*	*P2* *₹/unit*
Material	407.5	292.1
Overhead : Material handling	85 × 1.2 = 102	46 × 1.2 = 55.2
Assembly Management	40 × 3.2 = 128	40 × 1.9 = 76
Machine insertion	48 × 0.7 = 33.6	31 × 0.7 = 21.7
Manual insertion	36 × 2.1 = 75.6	25 × 2.1= 31.5
Quality testing	1.4 × 25 = 35	1.1 × 25 = 27.5
Present Cost	781.70	504.00

STATEMENT OF REVISED COST

Direct Material	381.20	263.10
Material handling	(71 × 1.2) = 85.2	(39 × 1.2) = 46.8
Assembly Management	(21 × 40) = 84.0	(1.6 × 40) = 64.0
Machine Inspection	(59 × 0.7) = 41.3	(29 × 0.7) = 20.30
Manual Inspection	(12 × 2.10) = 25.2	(10 × 2.10) = 21.00
Quality Testing	(1.2 × 25) = 30.00	(0.9 × 25) = 22.50
Revised Cost	646.90	437.70
Target Cost	680.00	390.00
Whether the company achieves Target Cost	**Achieved**	**Not Achieved**
Whether Further Reduction in Activities required	**Not Required**	**Required**

Illustration 4

X Ltd. is developing a high speed modem:

(a) Given the following information. Compute Cost Reduction Target.

Expected market price	***₹ 500***
Required return on sales	***20%***
Product life	***3 years***
Current feasible cost	***₹ 7,50,00,000***
Expected average annual sales	***50,000 units***

(b) If X Ltd. believes that it can reduce the cost of the modem by not more than 18% ,is it a feasible to introduce the product ?

Solution

(a) STATEMENT OF COST REDUCTION TARGET

Particulars	*₹ (in lakhs)*
Sales Value (N.R.V) (500 × 50,000 × 3)	750
Required return on sales	150
Target cost	600
Current feasible cost	750
Cost reduction target	150

(b) Revised Feasible Cost (7,50,00,000 × 82%)	615
Target cost	600
Cost still to be reduced	15

Advice: It is not feasible to introduce that product since its Revised Feasible Cost is still higher than its Target Cost.

Illustration 5

X Limited undertakes market research for clients. A typical study takes three months and uses two types of staff as follows:

Type of staff used	*Proportion of variable costs incurred in*			
	Month 1	*Month* 2	*Month* 3	*Total*
Research	40%	—	60%	100%
Tabulating	—	—	100%	100%

Research staff and tabulating staff account for 80 per cent and 20 per cent respectively of the variable costs of a study.

When quoting a price for a study X Ltd. adds the following contribution on the estimated variable cost: Research Staff 112.50 percent of Variable Cost. Tabulating Staff 50 percent of VC. In April X Ltd. started work on orders of ₹ 30,000 & In May ₹ 40,000 & In June ₹ 23,000. For calculation of monthly income the value of an order is divided on the basis of first month 34 percent, second month 6 per cent and third month 60 per cent. X Ltd. target contribution is 10 per cent above fixed cost which is ₹ 16,000 per month.

Required: Calculate the value of additional orders which should be received, by X Ltd. for work to start in June to achieve the target contribution in June.

Solution

STATEMENT OF CONTRIBUTION TO BE ACHIEVED IN JUNE

Particulars	₹
For April order (₹ 30,000 × 26%)	7,800
For May order (₹ 40,000 × 6%)	2,400
For June order (₹ 23,000 × 18%)	4,140
Present Cntribution	14,340
Target Cost (₹ 16,000 + ₹ 1600)	17,600
Deficit	3,260

Working Notes:

(i) Let the variable cost of study be ₹ 100, then VC of Research Staff = ₹ 80 and VC of Tabulating Staff = ₹ 20

Research Staff = (₹ 80 + 1.125% × ₹ 80)	= 170
Tabulating Staff = (₹ 20 + 50% × ₹ 20)	= 30
Total Selling Price	200

It indicates overall margin in 50% on sales over 3 months

(ii) STATEMENT OF ALLOCATION OF INCOME

Month	*I*	*II*	*III*	*Total*
A. Sales Value	68	12	120	200
B. Variable Cost:				
Research Staff	32	—	48	80
Tabulating Staff	—	—	20	20
	32	Nil	68	100
C. Profit [A – B]	36	12	52	100
D. % of Selling Price of ₹ 200	18%	6%	26%	50%

Illustration 6

Toshiba manufactures on brand of personal computers called Toshiba. Following is the profitability statement for Toshiba personal computer:

	Amount (₹) For 75,000 units	*Amount (₹) per unit*
Revenues (A)	30,00,00,000	4,000
Cost of Goods Sold:		
Direct Materials Cost	13,80,00,000	1,840
Direct Manufacturing Labour Costs	1,92,00,000	256
Direct Machining Costs (Fixed)	2,28,00,000	304
Manufacturing Overheads cost	2,40,00,000	320
Cost of Goods Sold(B)	20,40,00,000	2,720
R&D Costs	1,08,00,000	144
Design Cost of Product and Processor	1,20,00,000	160
Marketing Costs	3,00,00,000	400
Distribution Costs	72,00,000	96
Customer Service Costs	60,00,000	60
Operating Costs (C)	6,60,00,000	880
Full Product Costs (D = B + C)	27,00,00,000	3,600
Operating Income (A – D)	3,00,00,000	400

Required: Compute the target cost. Also Compute difference between Target and Allocable Cost.

Solution

STATEMENT OF TARGET COST AND DIFFERENCE

Particulars	₹
Present selling price (30,00,00,000/75000)	4,000
Cost per unit	3,600
Profit (i.e. 10% of Sale)	400
Revised selling price	3,200
Less: Profit (3200 × 10%)	(320)
Target Cost	2,880
Difference per unit = ₹ 3,600 – ₹ 2,880	₹.720

Illustration 7

Toshiba's value engineering team focus their cost-reduction efforts on analyzing the Toshiba design. Their goal is to design a high-quality, highly reliable machine with fewer features that meets customers price expectations and achievers target cost.

Toshiba is discontinued in its place. Toshiba introduced Toshiba II. Toshiba II has fewer components than Toshiba and is easier to manufacture and test. The following tables compare the direct costs and the manufacturing overhead costs and cost drivers of Toshiba and Toshiba II. In place of the 75,000 Toshiba units manufactured and sold in 2013, Toshiba expects to make and sell 1,00,000 Toshiba II units in 2014 on account of the reduction in prices.

Direct Cost Category	*Cost per unit in ₹*		*Explanation of Costs for Toshiba II*
	Toshiba	*Toshiba II*	
1. Direct Materials	1,840	1,540	The Toshiba II design will use a simplified main printed circuit board, fewer components and no audio features.
2. Direct Manufacturing	256	212	Toshiba II will require less labour and assembly time.
3. Direct Maching Costs	304	228	Toshiba can use the machine capacity to produce Toshiba II. The new design will enable Toshiba to manufacture each unit of Toshiba II in less time than a unit of Toshiba.

Cost Driver	*Quantity of Cost Driver*	*Explanation for quantity of Cost Driver Toshiba*	*Quantity of Cost Driver for Toshiba II*	*Explanation for Quantity Driver Used by Toshiba II*
1. Number of Orders	22,500	Toshiba places 50 orders for each of the 450 components in Toshiba Cost per order ₹ 160	21,250	Toshiba will place 50 orders for each of the 425 components in Toshiba II
2. Testing Hours	22,50,000	Toshiba required 30 testing hours p.u. Cost per testing hour is ₹ 8.	15,00,000	Toshiba II is easier to test and will require 15 testing hours per unit.
3. Units Reworked	6,000	The rework rate is 8% of the units manufactures. The rework cost ₹ 400 per unit reworked.	6,500	Toshiba II will have a lower rework rate of 6.5% because it is is easier to manufacture.

Further there is a change in the non-manufacturing cost as follows:

R & D	***80,00,000***
Design of Product & Process cost	***1,20,00,000***
Marketing Costs	***3,60,00,000***
Distribution Costs	***1,00,00,000***
Customer-Service Costs	***60,00,000***

Following further information has been provided:

(i) No opening closing inventory.

(ii) Manufacturing Overhead Cost = Ordering and Receiving cost + Testing and inspection Cost + Rework Cost.

(iii) Toshiba expects its competitors to lower the prices of PCs that compete against Toshiba by 15%. Toshiba's management belives that it must respond aggressively by reducing Toshiba's price by 20%.

Required: Determine whether Toshiba achieves the target cost?

Solution

STATEMENT OF REVISED COST

Particulars	*Cost per unit*	*Total Cost*
Material (1540 × 100000)	1540	15,40,00,000
Labour (212 × 100000)	212	2,12,00,000
Machining Cost (228 × 100000)	228	2,28,00,000
Manufacturing Cost	180	1,80,00,000
Others (80 + 120 + 360 + 600 + 60)	720	7,20,00,000
	2,880	28,80,00,000
Quantity		1,00,000
Cost per unit		2,880
Target Cost		2,880

Decision: With application of value engineering technique, company can achieve the target cost.

Working Note: *Calculation of Manufacturing Overhead Cost*

Ordering Cost (22,500 x 160), (21,250 x 160)	36,00,000	34,00,000
Testing Cost (22,50,000 x 8), (15,00,000 x 8)	1,80,00,000	1,20,00,000
Rework Cost (75,000 x 8% x 400) (1,00,000 x 6.5% x 400)	24,00,000	26,00,000
	2,40,00,000	1,80,00,000
Quantity	75,000 units	1,00,000 units
Cost/unit	320	180

Illustration 8

You are the manager of a paper mill (XYZ Ltd.) and have recently come across a particular type of paper, which is being sold at a substantially lower rate (by another company-ABC Ltd) than the price charged by your own mill.The value chain for one use of one tone of such paper for ABC Ltd. Is as follows:

ABC LTD → Merchant → Printer → Customer

ABC Ltd. Sells this particular paper to the merchant at the rate of ₹ 1,466 per tone. ABC Ltd. pays for the freight which amounts to ₹ 30 per tone. Average returns and allowances amount to 4% of sales and approximately equals ₹ 60 per tone.

The value chain of your company, through which the paper reaches the ultimate customer is similar to the one of ABC Ltd. However your mill does not sell directly to the merchant, the latter receiving the paper from a huge distribution center maintained by your company at Haryana. Shipment costs from the mill to the Distribution Centre amount to ₹ 11 per tone while the operation costs in the Distribution centre have been estimated to be ₹ 25 per tone. The return on investment required by the Distribution Centre for the investment madde amount to an estimated ₹ 58 per tone.

Required: Compute the "Mill manufacturing Target Cost" for this particular paper for your company. You may assume that the return on the investment expected by your company equals ₹ 120 per tone of such paper.

Solution

STATEMENT OF TARGET COST

Particulars		₹
A. Gross Selling Price		1,466
B. Expenses to be incurred to generate Sale:		
(a) Freight	30	
(b) Return & Allowances	60	90
C. Net Realizable Value (A – B)		1,376
D. Desired Profit		120
E. Total Target Cost (C – D)		1,256
F. Distribution Expenses		94
G. Target Manufacturing Cost (E – F)		1,162

Illustration 9

X Ltd. has sales of 100 units at a price of ₹ 200 per unit and profit of ₹ 40.00 lakhs in the current year. Due to strff competition, the company has to reduce its price of product next year 5% to achieve same volume target of sales. The cost structure and profit for the current year is given as below:

	₹ Lakhs
Direct Materials	60
Direct Wages	45
Variatle Factory overheads	20
Fixed Overheads including sales and admin expenses	35
Total Cost	160

To achieve the target cost of maintain the same profit, the company is evaluating the proposal to reduce labour cost and fixed factory overheads. A vendor supplying machine for suitable for the company's operation has offered an advanced technology semi-auto machine of ₹ 20 lakhs as replacement of old machine of worth ₹ 5 lakhs. The vendor is agreable to take back the old machine at ₹ 2.70 lakhs only. Company' s policy is to charge depreciation @ 10% on WDV. The maintenance charge of the existing machine is ₹ 1.20 lakhs per annum whereas there will be warranty of services free of cost for the new machine first two years. There are ten (10) supervisors whose salary is ₹ 1.50 lakhs per annum.

The new machine having conveyor belt is expected to help in cost cutting measures in the following ways:

(i) Improving productivity of workers by 20%.

(ii) Cut down material wastage by 1.0%

(iii) Elimination of services of supervision because of auto facilities of the machine.

(iv) Saving in packaging cost by ₹ 1.5 lakhs.

Required: Assuming cost of capital to be 15% calculate how many supervisors are to be removed from the production activities to achieve the target cost.

Solution

Due to cut in price of product, sales value will decrease by ₹ 10.00 lakhs.

For maintaining same profit margins i.e. ₹ 40 lakhs, cost has to be down by ₹ 10.00 lakhs. With improvement of labour productivity, wages will be (45/1.20) = ₹ 37.50.

Particulars	₹ Lakhs
Reduction in wages	7.50
Elimination of Wastage of Materials	0.60
Saving in Packaging Cost	1.50
Saving in Maintenance Cost	1.20
Loss in disposal of selling of old machine	(2.30)
Difference in Depreciation	(1.50)
Cost of capital investment	(3.00)
Effective cost reduction	4.00
Additional reduction required for Target Cost [₹ 10 lakhs – ₹ 4 lakhs]	6.00

Hence, No of supervisions to be eliminated = ₹ 6,00,000/₹ 1,50,000 = 4

16 Total Quality Management (TQM)

Learning Objectives

After studying this chapter, you should be able to understand:

- Meaning, Core Concepts and Benefits of Total Quality Management (TQM)
- Critical Success Factors for Implementation of TQM or Six C's of TQM
- Cost of Quality Report
- The Praise Six-step Quality Improvement Process
- Difficulties Experienced at Each Step of The Praise Six-steps
- How to Overcome Total Quality Paralysis
- 'Four Ps' of Quality Improvement
- A Three-point Action Plan for the Choice of Projects and the Implementation of the Process
- Stages in Operationalising TQM
- Control: the Missing Link of TQM

1.0 MEANING, CORE CONCEPTS AND BENEFITS OF TOTAL QUALITY MANAGEMENT (TQM)

Meaning	TQM is a **continuous process** of quality improvement where **commitment** come from top management to bring TQM **culture** in the entire organization by making 'quality' a part of everyone's job with the **cooperation** and involvement of all Employees & **control** procedures with a view to **focus on customer** by delivering products or services of consistent high quality in a timely fashion and thereby reducing the costs associated with scraps, spoilage & defectives.	
Three Core Concepts	1. **Quality Control (QC)**	It is concerned with the past, and deals with data obtained from previous production which allow action to be taken to stop the production of defective units.
	2. **Quality Assurance (QA)**	It deals with the present, and concerns the putting in place of systems to prevent defects from occurring. QA is responsible for systems which prevent departures from budgeted costs and corrective mechanisms to prevent future departures from budgeted costs.
	3. **Quality Management (QM)**	It is concerned with the future, and manages people in a process of continuous

		improvement to the products and services offered by the organization. QM uses the skills and participation of the workforce to reduce the costs of production of goods and services.
Benefits	1. There will be increased awareness of quality culture in the organization. 2. It will lead to commitment to continuous improvement. 3. It will focus on customer satisfaction. 4. A greater emphasis on team work will be achieved. 5. TQM seeks to increase customer satisfaction by finding the factors that limit current performance.	
Cost of Quality	In a manufacturing environment the cost of quality might be viewed as the sum of the costs associated with scrap, reworks, warranty claims and inspection expenses. The fundamental principles of TQM focus on a process of continuous improvement which enhances the satisfaction of customer requirements by changing the attitude of the workforce. The reduction of waste is made implicit in each worker's task. This suggests the elimination of all non-value-adding processes, processes which include all control functions - monitoring, inspecting, progress chasing, even auditing - which would now be replaced by self-auditing as part of the change in corporate culture	

2.0 CRITICAL SUCCESS FACTORS FOR IMPLEMENTATION OF TQM OR SIX C'S OF TQM

1. Commitment	If a TQM culture is to be developed, total commitment must come from top management. It is not sufficient to delegate 'quality' issues to a single person. Steps necessary to provide an environment for changing attitudes and breaking down barriers to quality improvement must be provided. Quality expectation must be made clear from top management along with the support and training required for its achievement.
2. Culture	Training lies at the centre of effecting a change in culture and attitudes. Negative perceptions must be changed to encourage individual contributions and to make 'quality' a part of everyone's job. Appropriate training and education to everyone to understand the aim of TQM
3. Continuous Improvement	TQM should be recognized as a continuous process and not merely a one-time programme. It is not a "one time programme". There is always room for improvement, however small. Though the goal is zero defect, the methodology is one of continuous improvement.
4. Cooperation	TQM visualizes Total Employee Involvement. The on-the-job experience of all employees must be fully utilized. Employee involvement and cooperation should be sought in the development of improvement strategies and associated performance measures. Everyone in the organisation should be involved
5. Customer Focus	The needs of external customers (in receipt of the final products or services) and also the internal customers (people who receive and

	supply goods, services) should be the prime focus. Perfect service with zero defectives with satisfaction to end user whether external customer or internal customer.
6. Control	Documentation, procedures and awareness of current best practices are essential if TQM implementations are to function appropriately. Unless, control procedures are in place, improvements cannot be measured nor monitored nor deficiencies corrected. Rewards and performance measurements should be renewed

3.0 COST OF QUALITY REPORT

Meaning	A cost of quality report indicates the total cost to the organization of producing products or services that do not conform with quality requirements.
Purpose	(a) The report draws management's decision to the possibility of reducing total quality costs by a wise allocation of costs among the four quality categories. (b) The investments in these costs should be composed with the benefits arising from such expenditure. (c) Increase in preventive maintenance costs reduces breakdown maintenance as well as internal and external failure costs. Analyzed through four categories— 1. **Preventive Costs** Preventive maintenance, training. Costs incurred in preventing the production of products that do not conform to specification. **Example**—Preventive Maintenance Cost, Quality Planning Training, Extra costs of acquiring high quality of raw materials. 2. **Appraisal Costs** Testify inspection, Breakdown maintenance. Costs incurred to ensure that materials and products meet quality conformance standards. **Example**—Inspection of Material Purchased, Inspecting Finished Goods, WIP, Quality Audits, Field Tests. 3. **Internal Failure Costs (before delivery to customer)** Cost incurred with materials and products that fail to meet quality standards. Cost incurred before the product is dispatched to customers. **Example**—Cost of Scrap, Repair, down time and work stoppage caused by defects, downgraded units. 4. **External Failure Costs** Cost incurred when products or services fail to satisfy customer demands after they have been delivered. **Example**—Specifications loss (Warranty Replacement), Repairs of returned products, Cost of handling customer complaints.

4.0 THE PRAISE SIX-STEP QUALITY IMPROVEMENT PROCESS

The Praise Six-Step Quality Improvement Process consists of following Activities:

Step	Activity	Elements
1	**Problem identification**	Areas of customer dissatisfaction Absence of competitive advantage Complacency regarding present arrangements

2	**Ranking**	Prioritize problems and opportunities by I perceived importance, and I ease of measurement and solution
3	**Analysis**	Ask 'Why ?' to identify possible causes Keep asking 'Why ?' to move beyond the symptoms and to avoid jumping to premature conclusions Ask 'What ?' to consider potential implications Ask 'How much ?' to quantify cause and effect
4	**Innovation**	Use creative thinking to generate potential solutions Operationalize these solutions by identifying — barriers to implementation, — available enablers, and — people whole co-operation must be sought
5	**Solution**	Implement the preferred solution Take appropriate action to bring about the required changes Reinforce with training and documentation back-up.
6	**Evaluation**	Monitor the effectiveness of actions Establish and interpret performance indicators to track progress towards objectives Identify the potential for further improvements—and return to step 1

5.0 DIFFICULTIES EXPERIENCED AT EACH STEP OF THE PRAISE SIX-STEPS

At Step 1	The symptoms or observed effects of a problem may be readily apparent, but it may be more difficult to identify a measurable improvement opportunity. Attempts to identify problems broadly as 'communication', 'organisation', 'morale' or 'productivity' should be resisted - much more specific target areas are required to allow a focus on precisely what is wrong.
At Step 2	It may not be possible to achieve consensus at step 2 because of the pet projects of a minority of the team members. Multi-voting may therefore be necessary to provide a focus in a democratic manner.
At Step 3	Lateral thinking may be helpful at step 3 to encourage a wide-ranging discussion and to avoid a blinkered approach to the nature of the problem. The required objective is the identification of the root cause and this is unlikely to be one that promotes a quick-fix solution.
At Step 4	'Innovation' and 'creativity' are the keywords at step 4 to encourage a multitude of suggested solutions. These may then be evaluated in terms of the extent to which they may be converted into operating plans which achieve the required objectives. A systematic evaluation of positive and negative aspects of each strategy is essential - but remember, no matter how sophisticated the analysis, the final solution is only as good as the original list from which it is chosen.
At Step 5	The implementation of the solution at step 5 may require a great deal of diplomacy, especially in divisions or departments resistant to change. Possible side-effects must be identified and the whole process smoothed through with the co-operation of the workforce at all levels, efficient internal communication, training programmes where appropriate, and feedback throughout.

At Step 6	The evaluation at step 6 may indicate the trouble-free implementation of a strategy which has solved 100 per cent of the problem. More likely it will not! As part of the drive for continuous improvement in quality, several other areas capable of improvement will emerge. As such, step 6 is not the last stage in the process but the first stage in a renewed process. The new problems emerging here provide fresh improvement opportunities ready for restatement at step 1 and prioritisation at step 2. Central to the whole PRAISE system are both quality control—the search for continuous improvements in quality - and total employee involvement - the co-operation and commitment of employees. This dual approach provides a single focus—the customer—whose increased satisfaction remains the primary goal of the procedure. A number of essential requirements emerge, therefore, for successful implementation, which may be described as the six Cs of TQM.

6.0 HOW TO OVERCOME TOTAL QUALITY PARALYSIS

A quality improvement process like the PRAISE system restricts the adoption of sub- optimum quick-fix solutions and increases the participants' awareness of barriers to change.

However, it does not overcome completely some of the behavioral difficulties associated with individual motivation and group dynamics. The problem is not one of an awareness of the usefulness of TQM but rather the ability to do something about it - the inertia associated with total quality paralysis. Some fundamental requirements in getting started are:

1. A clear commitment, from the top, to TQM ideals. Without this, all else fails. It is not sufficient to delegate 'quality' issues to a single person, since this will not provide an appropriate environment for changing attitudes and behaviour and breaking down the barriers to quality improvement. The aim is to develop a TQM culture so that quality improvement becomes a normal part of everyone's job. This expectation must be made clear, and whatever support and training is necessary to its achievement must be provided.
2. Managers must be provided with the skills, tools and techniques to pursue systematic improvement. Training should be practical, avoiding unnecessary abstractions and keeping management jargon to a minimum. It may even be necessary to avoid the acronym 'TQM' itself, because of the barriers associated with buzzwords, reverting to reference instead to the phrase 'quality improvement process'.
3. The general awareness of improvement opportunities must be improved through the creation of a database documenting the status quo and covering those things that the organisation currently does well, as well as its deficiencies. Such a database should contain answers to questions like these:
   (a) Where do we make errors?
   (b) Where do we create waste?
   (c) What should we do that we currently make no attempt to do?

7.0 'FOUR PS' OF QUALITY IMPROVEMENT

Ideally; the quality improvement process should be a vehicle for positive and constructive movement within an organization. We must, however, be aware of the destructive potential of the process. Failure to observe the fundamental principles associated with the 'four Ps' of quality improvement may so severely damage motivation that the organization is unable to recover fully. Those four Ps are :

1. People	**It will quickly become apparent that some individuals are not ideally suited to the participatory process. Lack of enthusiasm will be apparent from a generally negative approach and a tendency to have pre-arranged meeting which coincide with the meetings of TQM teams.** Where these individuals are charged with the responsibility for driving group success then progress will be slow or negligible. Quality improvement teams may have to be abandoned largely for associated reasons before they are allowed to grind to a halt.
2. Process	**The rhetoric and inflexibility of a strict Deming approach will often have a demotivating effect on group activity.** It is essential to approach problem-solving practically and to regard the formal process as a system designed to prevent participants from jumping to conclusions. As such it will provide a means to facilitate the generation of alternatives while ensuring that important discussion stages are not omitted.
3. Problem	**Experience suggest that the least successful groups are those approaching problems that are deemed to be too large to provide meaningful solutions within a finite time period.** Problems need to be approached in bite-sized chunks, with teams tackling solvable problems with a direct economic impact, allowing for immediate feedback together with a recognition of the contribution made by individual participants. For example, while 'communications' and 'morale' are frequently cited as key problem areas, they are too broad to provide successful quality improvement targets. Smaller aspects of these issues must be identified.
4. Preparation	**A training in the workings of Deming-like processes is an inadequate preparation for the efficient implementation of a quality improvement process.** Additional courses on creative thinking and statistical processes are needed in order to give participants a greater appreciation of the diversity of the process. This training must quickly be extended beyond the immediate accounting circle to include employees at supervisory levels and below who are involved at the data input stage.

8.0 A THREE-POINT ACTION PLAN FOR THE CHOICE OF PROJECTS AND THE IMPLEMENTATION OF THE PROCESS

A three-point action plan for the choice of projects and the implementation of the process is as follows:

1. Bite-sized chunks	It is tempting to seek a large cherry to pluck, but big improvement opportunities are inevitably complex and require extensive inter-departmental co-operation. The choice of a relatively small problem in the first instance provides a greater chance of success.
2. A solvable problem	The problem selected should not be trivial, but it should be one with a potential impact and a clear improvement opportunity. Measurable progress towards implementation should be accomplished within three or four months (or less if possible) in order to maintain the motivation of participants and advertise the success of the improvement process itself.

3. Recognition of Participants	The successful projects and team members should receive appropriate recognition throughout the enterprise, at the very least being 'mentioned in despatches' via company newsletters. Prominent individuals should be rewarded for their efforts both as personal recognition and as encouragement to others. The precise nature of the reward may be recognition itself, although in some situations material, but usually nonmonetary, prizes may also be appropriate. The implementation of TQM processes can provide long-lasting benefits as long as the achievement of quality goals is not in conflict with other objectives. This might be the case, where, for instance. — bonuses are based on the volume of output alone; or — retrenchments result from the increased efficiency associated with the quality improvement process. By overcoming the initial obstacles, a TQM process can provide us with an additional tool to improve competitiveness and ensure long-term survival.

9.0 STAGES IN OPERATIONALISING TQM

The Stages In Operationalising TQM are as follows:

Stage 1	**Who is the Customer?** A team approach was adopted to generate priorities in the identification of customers and critical issues in the provision of decision-support information. This provided a structured, group decision-making process for reaching consensus through the assignment of ranked priorities together with an environment conducive to the development of creative suggestions. The nominal group technique discussed earlier was employed. A multi-voting technique was employed to priortise the list of customers and provide a focus of services. The ranking or perceived customer importance reveals the priority customers for management accounting services as : 1. manager; 2. engineers; and 3. leading hands.
Stage 2	**What does the Customer expect from us?** Managers having been identified as the priority group in receipt of accounting output, a second brainstorming session was used to generate a comprehensive list of their perceived expectations from the accounting function. Multi-voting was again used to identify the relative importance of these expectations, providing a ranking of 12 accounting functions : 1. compliance with procedures; 2. focus on problems; 3. performance reviews; 4. provision of budget information; 5. assessment of proposals; 6. payment of salaries;

	7. tax advice; 8. management processes advice; 9. information forecasting; 10. commercial training; 11. information-processing skills; and 12. professional advice.
Stage 3	**What are the Customer's decision-making requirements?** Brainstorming revealed a list of 18 processes perceived to be major elements of the service provided by management accountants : 1. pay people (wages and salaries); 2. pay accounts (vendors and contractors); 3. keep the books of account; 4. budget; 5. forecast; 6. audit; 7. conduct business-impact analyses; 8. manage authorisation procedures; 9. issue guidelines; 10. maintain a library of procedures; 11. analyse performance; 12. manage licences; 13. contribute to meetings; 14. manage property; 15. carry out strategic planning; 16. train others; 17. evaluate insurance requirements; and 18. produce ad hoc reports; Combining management perceptions of customer expectations and the importance of the various functions, we find four processes clearly ranked as the key areas of importance to managers : 1. performance analysis; 2. ad hoc reporting; 3. strategic planning; and 4. contribution to meetings. This series of steps, therefore, establishes managers as the priority customers for management accounting reporting and procedures, while performance analysis is the priority consideration in their use of management accounting information. Typically, management accountants focus on the analysis of total performance in cost centres, using cost-per-unit comparisons and calculations of variance to generate plans. Where the focus is on quality improvement, the overriding need is to stay close to the customers and follow their suggestions. In this way, a decision-support system can be developed, incorporating both financial and non-financial information, which provides a flexible reporting system meeting user requirements. In order to do this properly, we need to know :

	— the nature of the decisions being made; — the nature of the decision-making process; and — the degree to which information requirements are being met. A survey of users is required to provide this information, but critical issues can be identified and prioritized in advance, in order to refine the necessary survey questions.	
Stage 4	**What problem areas do we perceive in the decision-making process?** Once again using brainstorming and multi-voting, the team ranked the characteristics of an accounting information system thought most desireable from a decision-making point of view, as follows : 1. Relevance. A targeted decision-making process. 2. Congruence. Consistency with the long-term strategy of the business. 3. Comprehensibility. Systems should be readily understandable and, therefore, readily usable, by customers. 4. Linkage to non-financial indicators. Systems need to reflect the monetary impact of physical parameters. 5. Timelines. Systems should be on-time and on-line. These characteristics were perceived as being areas of weakness where the greatest impact could be achieved through the implementation of improvements. It is instructive to consider some of the actual situtations that might be associated with improvements in these areas.	
	Lack of Relevance	If line managers ignore most of the data reported to them by traditional cost accounting systems and treat head office cost analysis with disdain, they may prefer to perform their own specific cost investigations to determine the cause of deviations from plan, seeing management accounting reports as irrelevant and technically unrealistic. These informal systems may incorporate superior information which would be of benefit to all and which would be better incorporated within a global management information system. The solution: develop formal and informal reporting mechanism targeted to the needs of the user.
	Lack of Congruence	Where the management accounting system focuses entirely on the measurement of costs, then it is not surprising that employees adopt a similar focus. Where the plant level emphasis is on production and productivity, a detailed analysis of process performance evaluation may reveal that the pursuit of efficiency measures is not necessarily consistent with the stated strategic goals of the organisation as a whole. For example, a reputation for industry leadership and innovation might be aided by a strategy of rapid asset replacement. Where divisional performance - and management rewards - are based on ROI-type indicators, a short-term perspective might be adopted, inconsistent with corporate strategy. But the revaluation of old assets, no longer depreciable, through inflation indices, might promote their replacement with new, more efficient assets.

	The solution: develop a robust process to ensure that the accounting department's performance analysis is linked to strategic direction.
Lack of Comprehe-nsibility	If management accountants believe that they prepare detailed financial reports for their managers to enable them to report to the managing director at the monthly board meeting, and the managing director declares that he or she is cognisant with all the relevant reported material for informal sources well in advance of the meeting, then clearly the customer for existing management accounting reports is not the managing director. Where such reports do not embrace the full extent of information generators, and fail to target a designated customer, there is room for a distinct improvement in the service offered. This may derive from more timely reporting, the provision of non-financial indicators, new performance measures, or a complete reformatting of the reporting process. The solution: generate accounting information systems of a format and content suitable to meet user requirements.
Absence of a link to non-financial indicators	The focus of management accounting must move beyond financial summary, measures of manufacturing operations if it is to maintain its central evaluation and control role. If a corporate goal of rapid internal growth is being pursued through a strategy of introducing automated production processes requiring less direct labour, then products using automated machinery intensely will be under-costed if direct labour hours are used to allocate manufacturing overhead costs for products. A more flexible allocation procedure should be adopted incorporating non-financial indicators, such as inspection and set-up times, in order to provide a 'fairer' distribution. In the absence of a 'right' answer, corporate strategy might serve to provide more guidance. Perseverance with an allocation on the basis of direct labour penalises those products reliant on manual operations and provides an incentive to automate, consistent with the corporate strategy. The solution: generate a concise group of non-financial indicators which reflect the overall performance of the company.
Lack of Timeliness	Suppose that the management accounting team prides itself on producing its monthly operating report on the eighth working day of the following month. An unexpected equipment failure means that it is unable to meet its accustomed deadline until the fifteenth working day. The team receives no complaints or enquiries during the interim on timeliness. The following month it produces, but does not distribute, the report. There is no response from the customer. The team continues this practice for the next three months until an internal memo indicates that the customer no longer wishes to receive the report - it is now surplus to

		requirements. In this case, the relevance of the whole reporting process is questionable and a close look at the distribution list of any given report, if not the existence of the report itself, is advisable. The solution: generate reports in a form and time-envelope which meets the needs of the target customer.
Stage 5	**How do we compare with other organizations? What can we gain from benchmarking?** Detailed and systematic internal deliberatios allow the accounting team to develop a clear idea of their own strengths and weaknesses and of the areas of most significant deficiency. The benchmarking exercise at stage 5 of the TQM review process allows us to see how other similar companies are coping with similar problems and opportunities. Stage 1 to 5 provide an information base developed without reference to the key player - the customer. This is rectified at stage 6 with a survey of representative customers which embraces their views on perceived problem areas.	
Stage 6	**What does the Customer think?** Respondents to the survey were encouraged to talk freely about their attitudes towards accounting information services, within a semi-structured outline covering: 1. the nature of decisions made; 2. the use made of existing formal reports; 3. the preferred format (graphical, tabular or narrative) for formal reporting; 4. other information sources employed; 5. information, currently unavailable, which would aid decision-making; and 6. non-financial indicators used in performance appraisal. Attitudes to the management reporting process were particularly illuminating, and directly applicable to other organisations. Monthly variance reports as a means of control were viewed as pointless by : — senior management, conscious of inevitable process fluctuations during the year; and — junior management, who viewed budgets as unrealistic and no major constraint on their spending. However, formal reports were generally perceived as having four positive features. They were seen as useful in: — highlighting and reinforcing the existence of large variances, especially when close to the budget setting period; — reporting unanticipated items associated with unexpected and late accruals, end of month 'adjustements', and misallocations to inappropriate accounts; — providing information which might change priorities, and — communicating a degree of analysis not available through on-lines systems. However, a number of criticisms of content were widespread. The reports were considered to: — place too much emphasis on the reporting of unfavourable variances constituting insignificantly small monetary amounts rather than focusing on an explanation of large expenditures actually incurred;	

<table>
<tr><td></td><td>
— expend too much energy chasing inconsequential items representing minor out-of-budget fluctuations, rather than focusing on wrongly trended items (even where in-budget);
— show an unrealistic concern with comparison of actual versus budgeted outcomes where unfavourable variances were in fact inevitable and symptomatic of inflexible budgeting and time shifts; and
— report too many items for their own sake rather than to satisfy particular objectives or meet the requirements of particular individuals.
Unsatisfied needs embraced three major areas :
1. Ease of access to labour information to facilitate :
(a) the quantification and explanation of severe downturns in maintenance productivity;
(b) the distinction between normal and overtime hours on maintenance jobs, replacing inadequate composite hourly rates;
(c) accounting for non-productive hours per worker resulting from the adoption of a more participatory style of management;
2. predictive models concerning :
(a) early warning of massive deteriorations;
(b) forecasts of monthly maintenance expenditures;
(c) relationships between breakdown and scheduled maintenance expenditures;
(d) the impact of performance of safety training;
(e) probability-based analysis of risk to facilitate the management of maintenance expenditure; and
3. trend information, ideally weekly and on-line, covering :
(a) downtime and cost of breakdowns;
(b) operating supplies;
(c) maintenance materials;
(d) purchased services; and
(e) statistical process control.
</td></tr>
<tr><td>Stage 7</td><td>Identification of improvement opportunities</td></tr>
<tr><td>Stage 8</td><td>Quality improvement process → New strategies → Elimination of deficiencies Solutions</td></tr>
<tr><td></td><td>
The outcomes of the customer survey, benchmarking and internal analysis, provides the raw material for stage 7 and 8 of the review process : the identification of improvement opportunities and the implementation of a formal improvement process.
Table 1 depicts the framework for the six-step analysis, identified by the acronym 'PRAISE'. The successful adoption of this sequence of steps demands discipline and commitment. The goal of quality improvement is paramount and guides the actions of the change team throughout.
</td></tr>
</table>

10.0 CONTROL: THE MISSING LINK OF TQM

The fundamental principles of TQM focus on a process of continuous improvement which enhances the satisfaction of customer requirements by changing the attitude of the workforce. The reduction of waste is made implicit in each worker's task. This suggests the elimination of all non-value-adding processes, processes which include all control functions - monitoring, inspecting, progress chasing, even auditing - which would now be replaced by self-auditing as part of the change in corporate culture. Such extreme expectations are unrealistic. A control function, properly defined, is essential and can contribute to the achievement of TQM objectives. The development of TQM provides a vehicle for the accounting function to achieve control, continuous improvement and maximum efficiency by ensuring that all of the processes carried out by that function are both in control and capable. Such movements will have a dramatic effect on the accounting function and may well redefine the audit function. The basic requirement of accounting control is that a process is capable of meeting customer requirements, whether they are those of the directors, the shareholders, or the law. Techniques which have historically been used to achieve this control include procedures and audit, but these have major flaws. If we are not appropriately focused, it is possible that the process is never going to be capable of meeting customer requirements, no matter how complex the levels of audit or procedure adopted. Further, there will be no focus for the documentation of flaws and their subsequent reversal. Qualitative and non-financial data, vital for control, may not be subject to the same strict standards of measurement as financial and technical data. Their role in the quality programme may, therefore, be underestimated.

Documentation of the activities to be performed in the accounting function is an essential first step in identifying the dimensions of processes and the interrelationships between tasks, Table 2 details eight basic processes which may be identified in the accounting function, each covering multiple activities and crossing task boundries. A narrow control function is apparent in each process, but this is effectively just the checking or audit component of controllership. The controllership function interacts with the TQM process to impact upon the other six dimensions to provide timely and relevant information to decision-makers and to monitor compliance with corporate expectations where policies, procedures, ethical behaviour and professional conduct are concerned.

The quality manual is usually the major document controlling the implementation of the quality process. It defines the basic philosophy of the organisation, the structure and responsibilities of managers and departments and the relationship between them. It also contains the methods to be used to ensure quality, including the composition of teams, and the audit procedures to be adopted.

The definition of the process, inputs and outputs gives a framework for the writing of procedures and standard methods while also providing a focus for improvement opportunities. Underpinning both is a control and audit process, defining the way that the system is to be checked.

For every process within the accounting organisation, a policy and procedure is established in accordance with industry best practice and communicated throughout the organisation. Its objective is to satisfy customer requirements and to identify improvement opportunities which allow the continuous extention of the customer service provided. The writing of procedures and standard methods is a fundamental step in pursuing excellence of process. Procedures are concerned with the properties of the system that we are trying to influence (controlled parameters). Standard working methods are concerned with the process variables that are being manipulated in order to influence the system (control points).

Thus, if we want to control the water level in a bath, the level is the controlled parameter, and the tap and plug are the control points.

Table: DIMENSIONS OF THE ACCOUNTING FUNCTION

	Process	*Activity*
1	Planning	Strategic planning Operating planning Forecasts

	Process	Activity
2	Book-keeping	Costing Inventory accounting Project accounting Fixed capital Maintenance system
3	Discharging liabilities	Payroll Accounts receivable Accounts payable Cashier Contracts administration
4	Reporting	Corporate reporting Statutory reporting Management reporting
5	Business support	Project or opportunity evaluation Cost improvement Tax advice or guidance Operating centres
6	Corporate services	Tax Insurance Legal
7	Functional administration	Technology management Personnel management Non-accounting procedures TQM Agreements
8	Controllership	Accounting guidelines Accounting procedures Accounting policy and standards Internal audits External audits

By providing a sound control environment, which supports business decisions with appropriate measurement and analysis, the controllership function pursues complete customer satisfaction. The aim is to achieve acknowledged industry leadership for excellence of process, personnel and service. Underpinning this aim is an audit process that ensures that all of the above are in place and operating. The audit process is partly external, but largely internal, consisting of a control check system that monitors the critical processes of the system. Depending on the breakdown consequences and risk of failure, additional control points can be introduced into the process chain.

Thus, the system allows not only for control, but also for continuous improvement. The monitoring of the data around a process will allow modifications which make it in control and capable. As changes or improvements are made they are documented and the system updated so that everyone uses the current best method.

The clear definition and documentation of procedures facilitates job flexibility, making control easier and increasing the level of productivity in the accounting department. Thus, a good control system facilitates continuous improvement by focusing on customer needs, identifying priorities, and relating processes to one another. Variation and inaccuracy is caused by poor control and incompatible systems. A quality system is therefore essential to reduce these problems.

The application of the PRAISE quality improvement process to the timeliness problem provides an excellent example of service improvement, one which observes the fundamental quality principles of waste elimination and doing things right the first time. Traditionally, a consolidated profit figure has been produced by midday on the fifth working day of the month. Ideally, month-end closing would always be completed on the first working day of the new month, providing more relevant information for decision-making at board level and allowing more efficient use of accounting resources.

By identifying the barriers which prevent the generation of on-time data, a procedure can be implemented to generate a substantial reduction in the completion time for the earlyclosing process. Careful documentation of the network of tasks allows performance information (embracing financial cost data, technical and non-financial data) to be available at the beginning of the second working day, allowing a full executive performance review to take place before the end of that day. By focusing on further small improvements in procedure, completion might eventually approach the first-day ideal.

Documentation of key data on processes is the first, and arguably the most important, step in the procedure. By charting processes for each activity, establishing time barriers, constraints, priorities, degrees of difficulty and expected improvement times, a critical database is established. Small, dedicated problem-solving teams are charged with developing solutions for task improvements, with the success of the process demonstrated by the dramatic daily improvement apparent at month end.

Illustration 1

X Ltd. manufactures a single product, the estimated costs of which are as follows:

Direct Materials ₹ 10 each

Direct Wages 8 hours at ₹ 0.50 per hour

Overhead absorption rate ₹ 1.75 per .hour. (50% fixed overhead included)

During this period 1,000 units will be produced and sold as follow:

900 units of first at	***₹ 30 each***
50 units of second at	***₹ 20 each***
50 units of third at	***₹ 10 each***

Present information to management showing the loss due to the production of inferior units.

By reprocessing the inferior units taking the full reprocessing time of a further 8 hours and adding further material Costing ₹ 4 per unit these, "seconds" and "thirds" can be converted into firsts. Present information to the management.

Solution

STATEMENT OF PROFIT /LOSS

Particulars	*I*	*II*	*III*	*Total*
Units	900	50	50	1,000
A. Sales	₹ 27,000	₹ 1,000	₹ 500	₹ 28,500
B. Variable Costs:	₹	₹	₹	₹
Material	9,000	500	500	10,000
Labour	3,600(900 × 4)	200(50 × 4)	200(50 × 4)	4,000
Variable Overheads	6,300(900 × 7)	350(50 × 7)	350(50 × 7)	7,000
(1.75 × 50% × 8)	18,900	1050	1050	21,000
C. Contribution [A – B]	8,100	(50)	(550)	7,500
D. Less: Fixed Costs				7,000
E. Profit				500

STATEMENT SHOWING INCREMENTAL PROFIT

Particulars	*II(₹)*	*III(₹)*	*Total (₹)*
A. Increment Revenue	(10 × 50)500	(50 × 20)1,000	1,500
B. *Less:* Incremental Costs:			
Material	(200)	(200)	(400)
Labour	(200)	(200)	(400)
Variable Overheads	(350)	(350)	(700)
C. Net Benefit [A – B]	250	250	—

Decision: It is better to convert only third category goods due to incremental benefit of ₹ 250.

Illustration 2

The budget estimates of a company using sophisticated high speed machines based on a normal working of 50,000 machine hours during 2014 are as under:

Particulars	*Amount (₹)*
Sales (1,00,000 units)	100
Raw Materials	20
Direct wages	20
Factory Overheads: Variable	10
Fixed	10
Selling & Distribution Overheads: Variable	5
Fixed	5
Administration Overheads: Fixed	10
Total costs	80
Profit	20

Since the demand for the company's product is high, the possibilities of increasing the production are explored by the budget committee. The Technical Director stated that maintenance has not been given due importance in the budget and that if preventive maintenance is introduced, the breakdown repair costs and the hours lost due to breakdown can be reduced and consequently production can be increased.

In support of this, he presented the following data, showing how injection of more and more funds on preventive maintenance will bring down the break down repair costs and reduce or eliminate the machine stoppages due to breakdown:

Proposed exp. on Preventive Maintenance ₹	*Exp. estimated to be incurred on Breakdown Repairs* ₹	*Machine hours saved* ₹
19,200	1,92,000	Nil
38,400	1,53,600	800
76,800	1,15,200	1,600
1,53,600	76,800 2,400	
3,07,200	57,6,00	3,200
6,14,400	—	4,000

Using differential and contribution concept, advice the management up to what level breakdown hours can be reduced to increase production and maximise profits of the company consistent with minimum costs.

Solution

STATEMENT OF COST

Particulars		*Amount (₹ In lakh)*
Revenue		100
Variable cost	₹	
Material	20	
Labour	20	
Variable overhead	10	
Variable overhead	5	55
Contribution		45
Hours		50,000
Contribution per hour ₹ (45,00,000 + 50,000)		₹ 90

STATEMENT OF INCREMENTAL BENEFIT

S. No.	*Preventive Machine Cost*	*Extra Cost (a)*	*Breakdown Cost*	*Saving in Breakdown (b)*	*Contribution Saving (c) on Hrs*	*Net Benefit (b) + (c) – (a)*
1.	19,200	—	1,92,000	—	—	—
2.	38,400	19,200	1,53,600	38,400	(90 × 800)7,200	9,200
3.	76,800	38,400	1,15,200	38,100	(90 × 800)72,000	72,000
4.	1,53,600	76,800	76,800	38,400	72,000	33,600
5.	3,07,200	1,53,600	57,600	19,200	72,000	(62,400)
6.	6,14,400	3,07,200	—	57,600	72,000	(1,77,600)

Decision: It is better to select 4th level to operate preventive maintenance system show that the company can achieve incremental benefit of ₹ 1,96,800.

Illustration 3

A company manufactures a component on batches of 2000 each. Each component is tested before being sent to the agents for sales. Each components can be tested at the factory at a cost of ₹ 25. If any component is found to be defective, it can be rectified by spending ₹ 200. In view of the large demand for the components and the sophisticated system of manufactures, a proposal came up that the practice of pre-testing of the components be dispensed with to save costs. In that event, any defective component is received back from the customer under warranty, the cost of rectification and redispatch will be ₹ 400 per component.

Required: States at what percentage of manufacture of components will the company find it cheaper to pre-test each component.

Solution

Testing Cost = ₹ 25 × 2,000 = ₹ 50,000

Rectification Cost = 200, Rectification cost = 400 (without test)

Let x be defective units

Then $$Tc_1 = Tc_{11}$$

or $$50{,}000 + 200x = \text{nil} + 400x$$

or $$x = \frac{50{,}000 - \text{nil}}{400 - 200} = \frac{50{,}000}{200} = 250 \text{ units}$$

STATEMENT OF RANGE

Level (defectives)	*Preference*
0–249	without test
250	In difference
250	with test

Illustration 4

Carlon Ltd. makes and sells a single product, the unit specifications are as follows:-

Direct Materials X	***8 sq mm at ₹ 40 per sq mm***
Machine Time	***0.6 Running hours***
Machine cost per gross hour	***₹ 400***
Selling price	***₹ 1,000***

Carlon Ltd. requires to fulfill orders for 5,000 product units per period. There are no stocks of product units at the beginning or end of the period under review. The stock level of material X remains unchanged throughout the period.

Carlon Ltd. is planning to implement a Quality Management Programme (QMP) the following additional information regarding costs and revenues are given as of now and after implementation of Quality Management Programme.

Before the Implementation of QMP	*After the Implementation*
1. 5% of incoming material from suppliers scrapped due to poor receipt and storage organization	1. Reduced to 3%.
2. 4% of materials X input to the machine process is wasted due to processing problems.	2. Reduced to 2.5%
3. Inspection and Storage of Material X costs ₹ 1 per square meter purchased.	3. No change in the unit rate.
4. Inspection during the production cycle, calibration checks on inspection equipment vendor rating and other checks cost ₹ 2,50,000 per period.	4. Reduction of 40% of the existing cost,
5. Production Qty. is increased to allow for the downgrading of 12.5% of the production units at the final inspection stage. Down graded units are sold as seconds at a discount of 30% of the standard selling price.	5. Reduction to 7.5%
6. Production Quantity is increased to allow for return from customers (these are replaced free of charge) due to specification failure and account for 5% of units actually delivered to customer.	6. Reduction to 2.5%
7. Product liability other claims by customers is estimated at 3% of sales revenue from standard product sale.	7. Reduction to 1%
8. Machine idle time is 20% of Gross machine hrs. used (i.e. running hour = 80% of gross/ hrs.)	8. Reduction to 12.5%
9. Sundry costs of Administration, Selling and Distribution total. ₹ 6,00,000 per period.	9. Reduction by 10% of the existing
10. Prevention programme costs ₹ 2,00,000	10. Increase to ₹ 6.00,000

The Total Quality Management Programme will have a reduction in Machine Run Time required per product unit to 0.5 hr.

(a) Prepare summaries showing the calculation of (i) Total production units (pre inspection), (ii) Purchase of Materials X (Square meters), (iii) Gross Machine Hours.

In each case, the figures are required for the situation both before and after the implementation of the Quality Management Programme so that orders for 5,000 products can be fulfilled.

(b) Prepare Profit and Loss Account for Carlon Ltd. for the period showing the profit earned both before and after the implementation of the total Quality programme.

[C.A. (May 2005)]

Solution

STATEMENT OF FINISHED GOODS REQUIRED

Present Situation	*Quantity*	*After TQM*	*Quantity*
Gross Production (5250/87.5%)	6,000	Production (5124/92.5%)	5,541
Less: Defective @12.5%	750	Defective @7.5%	415
Gross delivery	5,250	Gross delivery	5,125
Specification loss @5%	250	Specification loss @2.5%	125
Invoiced Sale/Actual delivered	5,000	Sale/Actual delivered	5,000

STATEMENT OF RAW MATERIAL REQUIRED

Particulars	*Present (Qty.)*	*TQM (Qty.)*
Purchase	52,632	46,871
Less: Storage	2,632	1,406
Issued to production	50,000	45,465
Less: Processing loss	2,002	1,137
Net required finished goods	6,000 × 8 = 48,000	5,541 × 8 = 44,328

STATEMENT OF MACHINE HOURS REQUIRED

Particulars	*Present*	*TQM*
Gross machine hour	4,500	3,167
Loss	900	396
Effective machine hours	3,600(0.6 × 6,000)	2,771(0.5 × 5,541)

STATEMENT OF COMPARATIVE PROFIT/LOSS

Particulars	*Present (₹)*	*TQM (₹)*
Sale	50,00,000 (5,000 × 1,000)	50,00,000 (5,000 × 1,000)
Sale on down grading loss	52,500(700 × 750)	2,91,200(700 × 416)
Less: Cost of Material	21,05,280(52,632 × 40)	18,74,840(46,871 × 40)
Storage	52,632 (52,632 × 1)	46,871 (46,871 × 1)
Fixed cost	2,50,000	1,50,000
Product liability	1,50,000	50,000
Sundry cost	6,00,000	5,40,000
Preventive cost	2,00,000	6,00,000
Machine cost	18,00,000 (400 × 4,500)	12,66,800 (400 × 3,167)
Profit	3,67,088	7,62,689

Decision: It is better to implement the TQM profit because saving in cost is sufficient to convert the extra cost of preventive maintenance system.

Illustration 5

X Ltd. convert synthetic slabs into components AX and BX for use in the car industry. It is planning a quality management programme at a cost of ₹ 2,50,000. The following information relates to the costs incurred by X Ltd. Both before and after the implementation of the quality management programme:

1. ***Synthetic Slabs Synthetic slabs cost ₹ 40 per hundred. On average 2.5% of synthetic slabs received are returned to the supplier as scrap because of deterioration in stores. The supplier allows a credit of ₹.1 per hundred slabs for such returns. In addition, on receipt in stores, checks to ensure that the slabs received conform to specification costs ₹.14,000 per annum.***

   A move to a just in time purchasing system will eliminate the holding of stocks of synthetic slabs. This has been negotiated with the supplier who will deliver slabs of guaranteed design specification for ₹ 44 per hundred units, eliminating all stockholding costs.
2. ***Curing/moulding Process The synthetic slabs arc issued to a curing/moulding process, which has variable conversion costs of ₹ 20 per hundred slabs input. This process produce sub-components A and B, which have the same cost structure. Loss of 10% of input to the process because of incorrect temperature control during the process are sold as scrap at ₹ 5 per hundred units. The quality programme will rectify the temperature control problem thus reducing losses to 1% of input to the process.***
3. ***Finishing Process The finishing process has a bank of machines which perform additional operations on type A and B sub-components as required and converts them into final components AX and BX are ₹ 15 and ₹ 25 per hundred units respectively. At the end of the finishing process 15% of units are found to be defective. Defective units are sold for scrap at ₹ 10 per hundred units. The quality programme will convert the finishing process into two dedicated cell, one for each of components types AX and BX. The dedicated cell variable costs per hundred sub-components A and B processed will be ₹ 12 and ₹ 20, respectively. Defective units of components AX and BX are expected to fall to 2.5% of the input to each cell. Defective components will be sold as scrap as at present.***
4. ***Finished Goods A finished goods stock of components AX and BX of 15,000 and 30,000 units respectively is held throughout the year in order to allow for customer demand fluctuations and free replacement of units returned by customers due to specification faults. Customers returns are currently 2.5% of components delivered to customers. Variable stock holding costs are ₹.15 per thousand components units.***

   The proposed dedicated cell layout of the finishing process will eliminate the need to hold stocks of finished components, other than sufficient to allow for the free replacement of those found to be defective in customer hands. This stock level will be set at one month's free replacement to customers which is estimated at 500 and 1000 units for types AX and BX respectively. Variable stockholding costs will remain at ₹.15 per thousand components units.
5. ***Quantitative Data Some preliminary work has already been carried out in calculating the number of units of synthetic salbs, subcomponents A and B and components AX and BX which will be required both before and after the implementation of the quality management programme, making use of the information in the question. Table 1 summarises the relevant figures.***

Table 1

Particulars Type	Existing Situation A/AX (units)	Existing Situation Type B/BX (units)	Amended Situation Type A/AX (units)	Amended Situation TypeB/BX (units)
Sales	8,00,000	12,00,000	800,000	12,00,000
Customer returns	20,000	30,000	6,000	12,000
Finished goods Delivered(Gross)	8,20,000	12,30,000	8,06,000	12,12,000
Finished process loss(Defective)	1,44,706	2,17,059	20,667	31,077
Input to finishing process	9,64,706	14,47,059	8,26,667	12,43,077
	↓	↓	↓	↓
	24,11,765		20,69,744	
Curing/moulding losses	2,67,974		20,907	
Input to curing/moulding	26,79,739		20,90,651	
Stores losses	68,711		—	
Purchase of Synthetic slabs	27,48,450		20,90,651	

Required: Evaluate and Present a statement showing the net financial benefit or loss per annum of implementing the quality management programme, using the information in the question and the data in Table 1. (All relevant working must be shown).

Solution

STATEMENT OF FINISHED GOODS

Particulars	*Existing Situation*	*Amended Situation*
Purchase	27,48,450	20,90,651
—Store loss (2.5%)	(68,711)	—
Issue to production	26,79,739	20,90,651
Less: Loss (process)	(2,67,974)	(20,907)
Gross Finished goods	24,11,765	20,69,744

	A	*B*	*A*	*B*
	9,64,706	14,47,059	8,26,667	12,43,077
Defective	(1,44,706)	(2,17,051)	(20,667)	(31,077)
Gross Figure	8,20,000	12,30,000	8,06,000	12,12,000
Less: Specific loss	(20,000)	(30,000)	(6,000)	(12,000)
	8,00,000	12,00,000	8,00,000	12,00,000

STATEMENT OF COMPARATIVE COST

Particulars	*Present(₹)*	*TOM (₹)*
A. Net Purchase Cost		
Purchase Cost	10,99,380	9,19,886
	(27,48,450 × 0.4)	(20,90,651 × 0.44)
Less: Credit	(687)	—
	(68,711 × 1/100)	—
Inspection cost	14,000	—
	11,12,693	9,19,886
B. Net Processing Cost:	5,35,948	4,18,130
	(26,79,736 × 20%)	(20,90,651 × 20)
Less: Scrap	(13,399)	(1,045)
	(2,67,974 × 5%)	(20,907 × 5%)
	5,22,549	4,17,085
C. Net Final Finishing cost		
AX	1,40,706	99,200
	(9,64,706 × 15%)	(8,26,667 × 12%)
BX	3,61,765	2,48,615
	(14,47,059 × 25%)	(12,43,077 x 20%)
Less: Scrap	(36,177)	
	(3,61.765 × 10%)	
	4,70,294	3,42,841
D. Stock Holding Cost	6750	225
	(45,000 × 15%)	(1,500 × 15%)
E. Total Cost (A+B + C + D)	21,12,286	16,79,837
F. Further Cost	—	2,50,000
G. Total Cost	21,12,2,286	19,29,837
Cost Saving (Present – TQM)		1,82,449

Hence, it is better to implement the quality management programme due to net cost saving ₹ 1,82,449.

Illustration 6

Burdoy Pic has a dedicated set of production facilities for component X. A just-in-time system is in place such that no stock of materials, Work-in-progress or finished goods are held.

At the beginning of period 1, the planned information relating to the production of component X through the dedicated facilities is as follows:

1. ***Each unit of component X has input materials: 3 units of material A at ₹.18 per unit and 2 units of material B at ₹ 9 per unit.***
2. ***Variable cost per unit of component X (excluding materials) is ₹ 15 per unit worked on.***
3. ***Fixed costs of the dedicated facilities for the period ₹.1,62,000.***
4. ***It is anticipated that 10% of the units of X worked on irTthe process will be defective and will be scrapped.***

It is estimated that customers will require replacement (free of charge) of faulty units of components X at the rate of 2% of the quantity invoiced to them in fulfillment of orders.

Burdoy pic is pursuing a total quality management philosophy. Consequently all losses will be treated as abnormal in recognition of a zero defect policy and will be valued at variable cost of production.

Actual results for each period 1 to 3 for component X are shown in table given below. No changes have occurred from the planned price levels for materials, variable overhead or fixed overhead costs.

Actual free replacements of component X to customers were 170 units and 40 units in periods 2 and 3 respectively. Other data relating to periods 2 and 3 is shown in Table given below. Burdoy plc authorized additional expenditure during periods 2 and 3 as follows:

Period 2: Equipment accuracy checks of ₹ 10,000 and staff training of ₹ 5,000.

Period 3: Equipment accuracy checks of ₹ 10,000 plus ₹ 5,000 of inspection costs; also staff training costs of ₹ 5,000 plus ₹ 3,000 on extra planned maintenance of equipment.

Required:

(a) Prepare an analysis of the relevant figures provided in table given below to show that the period 1 actual results were achieved at the planned level in respect, of (i) Quantities and losses and (ii) Unit cost levels for materials and variable costs.

(b) Use your analysis from (a) in order to calculate the value of the planned level of each of internal and external failure costs for period 1.

(c) Prepare an analysis for Each of period 2 and 3 which reconciles the number of components invoiced to customers with those worked on in the production process. The analysis should show the changes from the planned quantity of process losses and changes from the planned quantity of replacement of faulty components in customer hands.

(d) Prepare a cost analysis for each of periods 2 and 3, which shows actual internal failure costs, external failure costs, appraisal costs and prevention costs.

Table

ACTUAL STATISTICS FOR COMPONENT X

Particulars	*Period 1*	*Period 2*	*Period 3*
Invoices to customers (units)	5,400	5,500	5,450
Worked on in the process (units)	6,120	6,200	5,780
Total Costs:			
Materials A and B (₹)	4,40,640	4,46,400	4,15,160
Variable cost of production (₹) (excluding materials cost)	91,800	93,000	86,700
Fixed Cost (₹)	1,62,000	1,77,000	1,85,000

Solution

STATEMENT OF RECONCILIATION (PERIOD 1)

Particulars	*Qty.*
Worked	6,120
Downgrade loss @ 10%	612
Gross goods delivered @ 102%	5,508
Less: Specific Loss @ 2	108
Invoice 100%	5,400

STATEMENT OF COST

Particulars	Standard Cost (₹)	Actual (₹)
Material ₹ (3 × 18 + 9 × 2)	(72 × 6120) = 4,40,640	4,40,640
Other Variable Cost (₹ 15 p.u.)	6120 × 15 = 91,800	91,800
	5,32,440	5,32,440

FOR THE PERIOD I, ACTUAL RESULTS WERE ACHIEVED AS PER BUDGET IN RESPECT OF QUANTITY LOSSES AND COST

Particulars	I (₹)	II (₹)	III (₹)
Previous maintenance	–	5,000	8,000
Breakdown maintenance	–	10,000	15,000
Internal failure	53,244 (612 × 87)	46,110 (530 × 87)	25,230 (290 × 87)
External failure	9,396 (108 × 87)	14,790 (170 × 87)	3,480 (40 × 87)
	62,640	75,000	51,710

STATEMENT OF RECONCILIATION (PERIOD '2')

Particulars	Standard	Actual	Difference
Worked on	6,200	6,200	
Less: down graded	(620)	(530) (B.f.)	90F
Gross delivered	5,580	5,570	
—Free replacement @ 2%	(110)	(170) (given)	60A
Net Invoice no.	5,470	5,500	30F

STATEMENT OF RECONCILIATION (PERIOD '3')

Particulars	Standard	Actual	Difference
Worked on	5,780	5,780	
Less: Down grade	(578)	(290) (B.f.)	288F
Gross delivered	5,202	5,490	
—Free replacement @ 2%	(110)	(40)	(62A)
Net Invoice	5,100	5,450	350F

COST OF QUALITY REPORT

Particular	Period 2	Period 3
Preventive maintenance	5,000	8,000
Appraisal cost	10,000	15,000
Internal failure (4,46,400 + 93,000/6,200)	46,110 (530 × 87)	25,230 (290 × 87)
External failure (4,46,400 + 9,300/6,200)	14,790(170 × 87)	3,480(40 × 87)

Illustration 7

X Ltd. makes printed cloth in two operations, weaving and printing. Direct material costs are Wellesley's only variable costs. The demand for Wellesley's cloth is very strong. Wellesley can sell whatever output Quantity produces at ₹ 1,250 per roll to a distributor who markets, distributes and provides customer service for the product.

	Weaving	*Printing*
Monthly capacity	10,000 rolls	15,000 rolls
Monthly production	9,500 rolls	8,550 rolls
Direct materials costs per roll of cloth		
Processed at each operation	₹ 500	₹ 100
Fixed operating costs	₹ 28,50,000	₹ 4,27,500
FIXED OPERATING COSTS PER ROLL		
(₹ 28,50,000/9,500; ₹ 4,27,500/8,550)	₹ 300 per roll	₹ 50 per roll

X Ltd. can start only 10,000 rolls of cloth in the Weaving Department because of capacity constraints of the weaving machines. If the weaving operation produces defective cloth, the cloth must be scrapped and yield zero net disposal value. Of the 10,000 rolls of cloth started at the weaving operation, 500 rolls (5%) are scrapped. Scrap costs per roll, based on total (fixed and variable) manufacturing costs per roll incurred up to the end of the weaving opera ration, equal ₹ 785 per roll as follows:

Direct materials costs per roll (variable)	₹ 500
Fixed operating costs per roll (₹ 2,850/10,000 rolls)	285
Total manufacturing costs per roll in Weaving Department	₹ 785

The good rolls from the Weaving Department (called gray cloth) are sent to the Printing Department of the 9,500 good rolls started at the printing operation, 950 rolls (10%) are scrapped and yield zero net disposal value Scrap costs, based on total (fixed and variable) manufacturing costs per unit incurred up to the end of the printing operation, equal ₹ 930 per roll calculated as follows:

Total Manufacturing costs per roll in Weaving Department	***₹ 785***
Printing Department manufacturing costs	
Direct materials costs per roll (variable)	***₹ 100***
Fixed operating costs per roll (₹ 4,27,500 /9.500 rolls)	***45***
Total manufacturing costs per roll in Printing Department	***145***
Total manufacturing costs per roll	***₹ 930***

The Wellesley Corporation total monthly sale of printed cloth equal the Printing Department's output.

Required: Each requirement refers only to the preceding data. There is no connection between the requirements.

1. ***The printing Department is considering buying 5,000 additional rolls of gray cloth from an outside supplier at ₹ 900 per roll. The Printing Department manager is concerned theft the cost of purchasing the gray cloth is much higher than Wellesley cost of manufacturing it.The quality of the grey cloth acquired from outside is very similar to that manufactures in house.***

   The Printing Department expects that 10% of the rolls obtained from the outside supplier will be defective in the process of printing. Show your calculations.
2. ***Wellesley engineers have developed a method that would lower the Printing Department's scrap rate to 6% at the printing operation. Implementing the new method***

would cost ₹ 3,50,000 per month. Should Wellesley implement the change? Show your calculations.

3. ***The design engineering team has proposed a modification that would lower the Weaving Department's scrap rate to 3%. The modification would cost the company ₹ 1,75,000 per month. Should X Ltd. implement the change? Show your calculations.***

Solution

(1) STATEMENT OF COST & BENEFIT

Particulars	₹
Incremental revenue ₹ 1250 × (5,000 – 500)	56,25,000
Less: Incremental cost (5,000 × ₹ 900) = 45,00,000	
Less: Maintenance cost (5,000 × ₹ 100) = 5,00,000	50,00,000
Net Benefits	6,25,000

Decision: It is better to purchase 5000 additional grey cloth due to incremental benefit of ₹ 6,25,000. Further, we can say that fixed cost has no influence over the decision due to utilization of capacity.

(2) STATEMENT OF COST & BENEFIT

Particulars	₹
Incremental Revenue (380 × ₹ 1250)	4,75,000
Less: Extra Cost	3,50,000
Net Benefit	1,25,000

(3) STATEMENT OF COST & BENEFIT

Particulars	₹
A. Incremental	
B. Revenue (180 × ₹ 1250)	2,25,000
Less: Incremental Cost	
Material (200 × ₹ 100) = 20,000	
Extra cost = 1,75,000	1,95,000
C. Net Benefit	30,000

Working Note:

Particulars	*Present Weaving*	*I Weaving*	*II Weaving*
Input	10,000	10,000	10,000
Loss	500	500	300
Good Rolls (Grey cloth)	9,500	9,500	9,700
	Print	**Print**	**Print**
Input	9,500	9,500	9,700
Loss	950	570	970
Output	8,550	8,930	8,730
Incremental units	380	180	

Illustration 8

X Ltd. manufactures and sells 20,000 copiers each year. The variable and fixed costs of rework and repair are as follows:

	Variable Costs	*Fixed Costs*	*Total Costs*
Rework cost per hour	₹ 40	₹ 60	₹ 100
Repair costs			
Customers support costs per hour	20	30	50
Transportion costs per load	180	60	240
Warranty repair costs per hour	45	65	110

The company's engineers are currently working to solve the problem of copies being too light or too dark. They propose changing the lens of the Copier. The new lens will cost ₹ 50 more than the old lens. Each copier uses one lens. The company uses a one-year time horizon for this decision, because it plans to introduce a new copier at the end of the year. The company believes that even as it improve quality, it will not be able to save any of the fixed costs of rework or repair.

By changing the lens, The company expects that it will (1) Save 12,000 hours of rework, (2) Save 800 hours of customers support, (3) Move 200 fewer loads, (4) Save 8,000 hours of repair, and (5) Sell 100 additional copiers for a total contribution margin of ₹ 6,00,000.

Required: Should the company change to the new lens? Show your calculations.

Solution

STATEMENT OF COMPARATIVE COST BENEFIT
SAVING IN COST

Particulars		₹
Rework (hr) cost	(1,200 × ₹ 440)	4,80,000
Customer support	(800 × ₹ 20)	16,000
Load	(200 × ₹ 180)	36,000
Repair	(800 × ₹ 45)	3,60,000
Additional contribution (100 Copies × ₹ 6,000)		6,00,000
Saving in costs		14,92,000
[Extra cost (₹ 50 × 20,000)]		10,00,000
Net Benefit		4,92,000

Decision: It is better to introduce new lens. The additional cost of lens on addition copier bas been already analyzed in arriving at figure of contribution $6,000. Hence, there is no need to consider again.

Illustration 9

X Ltd. uses multicolor molding to make plastic lamps. The molding operation has a capacity or 2,00,000 units per year. The demand for lamps is very strong. The company will be able to sell whatever output quantities it can produce at ₹ 40 per lamp.

The company can start only 2,00,000 units into production in the Molding Department because of capacity constraints on the molding machines. If a defective unit is produced at the molding operation, it must be scrapped and the net disposal value of scrap is zero. Of the 2,00,0,00 units started at the molding operation 30,000 units (15%) are scrapped. Scrap costs, based oh total (fixed and variable) manufacturing costs incurred up to molding operation equal ₹ 25 per unit as follows:

Particulars	*Amount (₹)*
Direct materials (variable)	₹ 16 per unit
Direct manufacturing labor, Setup labor And materials handling labor (variable)	3 per unit
Equipment, rent and other allocated overhead, including Inspection and testing costs on scrapped parts (Fixed)	6 per unit
Total	₹ 25 per unit

The conpany designers have determined that adding a different type of material to the existing direct materials would reduce scrap to zero, but it would increase the variable costs by ₹ 4 per lamp In the Molding Department.

Required: Should The company use the new material? Show your calculations.

Solution

STATEMENT OF INCREMENTAL PROFIT

Particulars	₹
Incremental revenue (30,000 × ₹ 40)	12,00,000
Less: Additional material (2,00,000) × ₹ 4	(8,00,000)
Net Profit	4,00,000

Decision: Its is better to introduce new material manufacturing cost on 30,000 units.

Note: Output = 2,00,000 – 30,000 = 1,70,000.

Illustration 10

X Ltd. manufactures a sells industrial grinders. The following table presents financial information pertaining to quality in 2013 and 2014 (in thousands):

Year	*2014*	*2013*
Revenue	₹ 12,500	₹ 10,000
Inspection of Production	85	110
Scrap	200	250
Design engineering	240	100
Cost of returned goods	145	60
Product-testing equipment	50	50
Customers support	30	40
Rework costs	135	160
Preventive equipment maintenance	90	35
Product liability claims	100	200
Incoming materials inspection	40	20
Breakdown maintenance	40	90
Product testing labor	75	220
Training	120	45
Warranty repair	200	300
Supplier evaluation	50	20

Solution

A: STATEMENT OF COST OF QUALITY REPORT

Particulars	*2013* ₹	*2014* ₹
Revenue	10,000	12,500
A: Preventive:		
Design Engg.	100	240
Preventive maintenance	35	90
Training cost	45	120
Supplier evaluation	20	50
	200	500
As percentage of Revenue	2%	2%

B: BREAKDOWN MAINTENANCE COST

Particulars	₹	₹
Inspection cost	110	85
Product testing	50	50
Incoming material inspection	40	20
Breakdown maintenance	90	40
Product testing	220	75
490	290	
As percentage of Revenue	4.9%	2.32%

C: INTERNAL FAILURE COST

Particulars	*2013* ₹	*2014* ₹
Scrap	250	200
Rework cost	160	135
	410	335
As percentage of Revenue	4.1%	2.68%

D: EXTERNAL FAILURE COST

Particulars	₹	₹
Cost of return goods	60	145
Customer support	40	30
Warrantee	300	200
Product liability claim	200	100
	600	475
As percentage of Revenue	6%	3.8%

Decision: A preventive maintenance cost has been increased, hence, loss in case of breakdown maintenance. Internal as well as external maintenance cost can be decreased.

Illustration 11

A Company manufactures a single product, which requires two components. The Company purchases one of the components from two suppliers: X Ltd. and Y Ltd. The price quoted by X Ltd. Is ₹ 180 per hundred units of the components and it is found that on an average 3% of the total receipts from this Supplier is defective. The corresponding quotation from Y Ltd is ₹ 174 per hundred units, but the defective would go up to 5%. If the defectives are not detected, they are utilized in production causing a damage of ₹ 180 per 100 units of the component.

Preventive Maintenance: A

- ***Supplier evaluation cost***
- ***Extra Inspection cost***
  Extra Maintenance Cost
  Design Cost

Breakdown maintenance: B (Appraised cost)

- ***Normal Inspection cost of material, machine and labour Internal Failure Cost: C***
- ***Cost of downgraded units***
- ***Cost of verification work***
- ***(Repair/Rework)***

External Failure: D

- ***Cost of Specification cost goods (Pre-replacement goods)***
- ***Warranty cost***
- ***Customers support cost***
- ***Product liability claim (Penalty cost)***

The Company intends to introduce a system of inspection for the components on receipt. The inspection cost is estimated at ₹ 24 per 100 units of the components. Such as inspection will be able to detect only 90% of the defective components received. No payment will be made for components found to be defective in inspection.

Required:

1. ***Advise whether inspection at the point of receipt is justified?***
2. ***Which of the two suppliers should be asked to supply? Assume total requirement is 10,000 units of the components.***

Solution

STATEMENT OF COMPARATIVE COST
(WITHOUT INSPECTION)

Particulars	*X Limited*	*Y Limited*
Requirement (Units)	10,000	10,000
Defective @ 3% / 5%	(300)	(500)
Good Unit/s	9,700	9,500
Purchase Units	18,000 (180/100 × 10,000)	17,400 (174/100 × 10,000)
Damage Cost	540 (180/100 × 300)	900 (180/100 × 500)
Total Cost	18,540	18,300
Cost per good unit	1,911 (18,540/9,700)	1,926 (18,300/9,500)

STATEMENT OF COMPARATIVE COST
(WITH INSPECTION)

If inspection	*X Limited*	*Y Limited*
Quantity requirement (Units)	10,000	10,000
Defective Exist (Units)	300 (3% × 10,000)	500
Defective traced (Units)	270 (90% × 300)	450
Defective not traced (Units)	30(300 – 270)	50
Purchase Cost	(180/100 × 9,730) = ₹ 17,514	(174 × 100 × 9,550) = ₹ 16,617
Inspection Cost	(24/100 × 10,000) = ₹ 2,400	(24/100 × 10,000) = ₹ 2,400
Damage Cost	(180/100 × 30) = 754	(180/100 × 50) = ₹ 50
Total Cost	₹ 19,968	₹ 19,107
Units	9,700	9,500
Cost per unit	₹ 2.05	₹ 2.011

Therefore, it will be better not to introduce inspection activity because inspection cost is higher than the cost of damage. Further we can say it is better to purchase from X Limited supplier.

Illustration 12

X Ltd. manufactures phamiaccutical products in two departments: Mixing and Table Making. Additional information on the two departments follows. Each tablet contains 0.5 gram of direct materials.

Particulars	*Mixing*	*Tablet Making*
Capacity per hour	150 grams	200 tablets
Monthly capacity (2,000 hours available In each of mixing and tablet making)	3,00,000 grams	4,00,000 tablets
Monthly production	2,00,000 grams	3,90,000 tablets
Fixed operating costs (excluding direct materials)	₹ 16,000	₹ 39,000
Fixed operating costs per tablet (₹ 16,000 / 2,00,000; ₹ 39,000 / 3,90,000)	₹ 0.08 per gram	₹ 0.10 per tablet

The Mixing Departments makes 200,000 grams of direct materials mixture (enough to make 400,000 tablets) because the Tablet-Making Departments has only enough capacity to process 400,000 tablets All direct materials) costs are incurred in the Mixing Department, Aardee incurs ₹ 1,56,000 in direct materials costs. The tablet-Making Department manufactures orjly 3,90,000 tablet from the 2,00,000 grams of mixture processed; 2.5% of the direct materials mixture is lost in the tablet-making process. Each tablet sells for ₹ 1. All costs other than direct materials costs are fixed costs. The following requirements refer only to the preceding data. There is no connection between the requirements.

Required:

1. ***An outside contractor makes the following offer. If the company will supply the contractor with 10,000 grams of mixture, the contractor will manufacture 19,500 tablets for X Ltd. following for the normal 2.5% loss during the tablet-making process at ₹ 0.12 per tablet. Should the company accept the company's offer? Show your calculations.***
2. ***Another company offers to prepare 20,000 grams of mixture a month from-direct materials X Ltd. supplies. The company will charge ₹ 0.07 per gram of mixture. Should X Ltd. accept the company's offer? Show your calculations.***
3. ***X Ltd. engineers have devised a method'that would improve quality in the tablet-making operation, the estimate that the 10,000 tablets currently being lost would be saved. The modification would cost ₹ 7,000 per month. Should X. Ltd. implement the new method? Show your calculation.***

4. Suppose that X Ltd. also loses 10,000 grams of mixture in itss mixing operation. These losses can be reduced to zero if the company is willing to spend ₹ 9,000 per month in quality-improvement methods. Should X Ltd. adopt the quality improvement method? Show your calculations.

Solution

(i) **STATEMENT OF COST AND BENEFIT**

Particulars	₹
Incremental Revenue (19500 × 1)	19,500
Less: Incremental Cost (156000 × 19500/30900)	(7,800)
Less: Throughout Contribution	11,700
Processing Charges (0.12 × 19500)	(2,340)
Net Benefit	9,360

It is better to accept the offer.

(ii) Its not better to do mixing work on sub contract basis because

(a) Spare capacity already exists in mixing department

(b) It does not provide any extra through put contribution

(iii) **STATEMENT OF COST AND BENEFIT**

Particulars	₹
Incremental Revenue	10,000
Incremental Cost (irrelevant)	—
Incremental benefit	10,000
Extra Cost	(7,000)
Net Benefit	3,000

(iv) Due to occurrence of loss of 10,000 grams of mixture in mixing department the company will have to incur extra cost of ₹ 7,800 = (1,56,000/2,00,000 × 10,000). Such loss can be reduced to zero by incurring extra cost of ₹ 9,000 which is not beneficial to the company.

Illustration 13

ABC Ltd. initiated a quality improvement program at the beginning of the year. Efforts were made to reduce the number of defective units produced. By the end of the year, reports from the production manager revealed that scrap and rework had both decreased. Though pleased with the sucess, the President of the company wanted some assessment of the finanical impact of the improvements. To make this assessment the following financial data were collected for the current and preceding year:

	Preceding Year (2001-2002) ₹	*Current Year (2002-2003)* ₹
Sales	1,00,00,000	1,00,00,000
Scrap	4,00,000	3,00,000
Rework	6,00,000	4,00,000
Product inspection	1,00,000	1,25,000
Product warranty	8,00,000	6,00,000
Quantity training	40,000	80,000
Materials inspection	60,000	40,000

Required:

(a) (i) Classify the costs as prevention, appraisal, internal failure or external failure.

(ii) Compute the profit that has increased because of quality improvements.

(iii) A Company has forecast sales and cost of sales for the coming year as ₹ 25 lakhs and ₹ 18 lakhs respectively.

The inventory turnover has been taken as 9 times per year. In case the inventory turnover increases to 12 times and the short term interest rate on working capital is taken as 10% what will be saving in cost?

Solution

(a) (i) **Cost classified:**

Prevention costs: quality training

Appraisal costs: Product inspection and materials inspection

Enternal failure costs: Scrap and rework

External failure cost: warranty

(ii) **Increase in Profit**

Preceding year-Total quality costs, 2001-2002: ₹ 20,00,000:

Current year-Total quality costs: ₹ 15,45,000:

Profit has increased by ₹ 4,55,000.

(iii) **Saving in Cost** $= \frac{1800,000}{9} \times \frac{10}{100} - \frac{1800,000}{12} \times \frac{10}{100} = \text{Rs. } 5,000.$

Illustration 14

X Limited buys compon ents which it uses in manufacturing solar water heater. Presently, each component is subject to a thorough inspection process on delivery. Because of high cost involved in such inspection, it now considers not inspecting at all. Records show that the components are of acceptable standardU6% of the time. If costs ₹ 800 to inspect a component and another ₹ 800 to put right any defect found at that stage. If the component is not inspected and is then found to be faulty at the finished goods stage, the cost of rework is ₹ 3,200.

Required: Advice the company whether or not the company should change its policy as considered above. Please show your workings.

Solution

The possible outcomes are	*Cost (₹)*	*Chance (%)*
(i) Inspect and find no problems	800	90
(ii) Inspect and find problems	1600	10
(iii) Do not inspect and no problem exist	0	90
(iv) Do not inspect and problems do exist	3200	10

The expected value of the cost of each policy is then:

Inspect 0.9 × ₹ 800 + 0.1 × ₹ 1600 = ₹ 880

Do not inspect 0.9 × ₹ 0 + 0.1 × ₹ 3200 = ₹ 320

Thus over a long period of time, a policy of not carrying out an inspection would result in a saving in cost of ₹ 560 per component, restricted to quantitative analysis, therefore this is correct policy to adopt.

However in the real environment of present day business world, the requirement for a quality product and continual improvement is essential. The above quantitative analysis is simply a mathematical exercise and tjirowsjittle light on the decision maker's choice of policy. It would rather be more useful to ask the supplier some basic questions regarding his quantity management in order to be assured of tlhe outcome (iii) above and make a fundamental change in the matter of inspection policy.

Illustration 15

X Ltd. carries is a transporting company at transports goods from one place to another. It measures quality of service in terms of: (i) Time required to transport goods, (ii) On-time delivery, (iii) Number of lost or damaged cartons.

To improve its business prospects and performance, the Company is seriously considering to install a scheduling and tracking system, which involves an annual outlay of ₹ 1.50,000 besides equipments costing ₹ 2,00,000 needed for installation of the system.The Company proposes to utilize the proceeds of the fixed deposit maturing next month to purchase the equirjrrjpnt.The rate of interest at present on depost is 10%. The Company furnishes the following about its present and anticipated future performance.

Particulars and On-time delivery%	***Current at 85%***	***Expected at 95%***
Varaible costs per carton lost or damaged	***₹ 50***	***₹ 50***
Fixed Costs per carton lost	***₹ 30***	***₹ 30***
Number of cartoons lost or damaged	***3,000***	***1,000***

The company expects that each percent point increase in on-time performance will result in revenue increase of ₹ 18,000 per annum. Contribution margin of 45% is required. Should X Ltd. acquire and install the new system?

Solution

Relevant Costs	₹	*Relevant Benefits*	₹
Annual Costs of new system (given)	1,50,000	Contribution Earned (18,000 × 10 × 45%)	81,000
Interest lost on Capital (2,00,000 × 10%)	20,000	Savings in Variable Costs	
Fixed Costs (not Relevant)	Nil	(3,000 – 1,000) × ₹ 50	1,00,000
Net benefit(balancing Figure)	11,000		
Total	1,81,000	Total	1,81,000

Decision: The system may be implemented.

17 Throughput Accounting and Theory of Constraints

LEARNING OBJECTIVES

After studying this chapter, you should be able to understand:

Throughput Accounting (TA)

Theory of Constraints

1.0 THROUGHPUT ACCOUNTING (TA)

Meaning	Throughput Accounting (TA) is a method of performance measurement which relates production and other costs to throughput (i.e. usage of key resources by various products.) It recognizes the interdependencies of modern production processes. For any given product, customer or supplier, it is a tool to measure the contribution per unit of constrained resource.
Assumption	It assumes that a manager has a given set of resources available. These comprise the existing buildings, capital equipment and labour force. Using these resources, purchased materials and components must be processed to generate sales revenue. To achieve this, maximum amount of throughput is required with the financial definition.
Throughput	= SALES REVENUE – DIRECT MATERIALS COST
Contribution	The cost of all other is deemed at least time related rather than fixed. Here labour & variable overhead are considered as fixed items as it is found in maximum organization now a day technique known, as "labour is not a unit variable cost". Therefore only variable cost in production is material.
Factors Affecting	Throughput is influenced by : – Selling price – Direct purchase price – Usage of direct materials – Volume of throughput.
Constraints	Constraints on throughput might include : – the existence of an uncompetitive selling price – the need to deliver on time to particular customers – the lack of product quality and reliability – the lack of reliable materials suppliers – the existence of shortage of production resources.

Duty of Management	It becomes management's duty to eliminate these constraints. Shortage of resources are usually termed bottlenecks, and their elimination often only moves a problem from one location to another. Thus the careful planning to minimize and eliminate all bottlenecks becomes very important.

2.0 THEORY OF CONSTRAINTS

Introduction	Theory of Constraints (TOC) was developed by Goldratt and Core (1986) in USA and it was inducted into an accounting system in the UK where it is known as Throughput Accounting (TA).It is based on the principle that profits are expanded by increasing the throughput of the plant i.e. rate at which raw material are turned into sales.. This approach advocates that bottleneck resources/ activities should be fully utilized while non bottleneck resources/ activities should not be utilized to 100% of their capacity since it would result in increase in inventory.
Meaning	1. The Theory of Constraint(TOC) focuses its attention on constraints and bottlenecks within the organisation which hinder speedy production. 2. It describes methods to maximize operating income under bottleneck situation. The objective of TOC is to increase throughput contribution while decreasing investments and operating costs. TOC considers a short run time and assumes that operating costs are fixed costs.
Objective	The main objective is to maximize the rate of manufacturing output i.e. the throughput of the organisation. This requires to examine the bottlenecks and constraints. It describes methods to maximize operating income under bottleneck situation. The objective of TOC is to increase throughput contribution while decreasing investments and operating costs. TOC considers a short – run time and assumes that operating costs are fixed costs. The important concept behind TOC is that the production rate of the entire factory is set at the pace of the bottleneck resource. Hence, in order to achieve the best result TOC emphasises the importance of removing bottlenecks or limiting factor.
Bottleneck	A bottleneck is an activity within the organisation where the demand for that resource is more than its capacity to supply.
Constraint	A constraint is a situational factor which makes the achievement of objectives/ throughput more difficult then it would otherwise be. Constraints may take several forms such as lack of skilled employees, lack of customers orders or the need to achieve a high level of quality product output.
Is a bottleneck always a constraint?	A bottleneck is always a constraint but a constraint need not be a bottleneck. Let the customers due date performance i.e. meeting the delivery schedule for customers orders is the major constraint in the organisation. The bottleneck in such a case may be certain machine in the factory. Throughput thus related directly to the ability to cope with the constraint and to manage the bottleneck. This focus on throughput forced management to examine both the constraints and the bottleneck in order to increase throughput.
Assumption	Raw materials are the only variable cost. Labour & Variable overheads are considered as fixed cost.

Procedure	**Step 1:** *Find the Total Requirement of Resources = S of units × Resource required per unit. Compute it for each department separately.* **Step 2:** *Throughput Accounting Ratio (TA ratio) = (Capacity Required, Capacity Available) × 100 for each department. (noting mention go by normal capacity)* **Step 3:** *The highest among the TA ratio will be considered as the bottleneck factor. So the problem is now converted into many product none limiting factor situation.*
Three Key Measurements	1. **Throughput Contribution** (i.e., Rate at which system generates profit through sales) = Selling Price – Direct Materials Cost of the goods sold. 2. **Investments** = Sum of Materials Costs in Direct Materials, Work – in – process, and Finished Goods Inventories; R & D costs; and Costs of equipment and Buildings. 3. **Operating Costs** equal all costs of operations (other than direct materials) incurred to earn throughput contribution. Operating Costs include salaries and wages, rent utilities, and depreciation.

Illustration 1

A company produces 3 products A, B and C. The following information is available for a period.

	Production		
	A	*B*	*C*
Contribution (Sales – Direct Materials)	₹ 24	₹ 20	₹ 12
Machine hours required per unit:			
Machine 1	12	4	2
Machine 2	18	6	3
Machine 3	6	2	1
Estimated Sales Demand	200	200	200

It is given that machine capacity is limited to 3,200 hours for each machine, you are required to analyze the above information and apply TOC process to remove the constraint.

Solution

Step 1: Calculation of TA Ratio

PRODUCTION

	A	*B*	*C*	*Total*	*Capacity Machine*	*TA ratio*
Demand (units)	200	200	200			
Hrs. required in Dept.:						
Machine 1	2,400	800	400	3,600	3,200	112.5%
Machine 2	3,600	1,200	600	5,400	3,200	**168.75%**
Machine 3	1,200	400	200	1,800	3,200	56.25%

Therefore, Machine 2 is the bottleneck

Step 2: Through put Contribution per unit of bottleneck & Ranking the Product

Particulars	*A*	*B*	*C*
Throughput Contribution	24	20	12
Machine 2 Hours per unit	18	6	3
Contribution per Machine 2 Hours	1.33	3.33	4
Ranking	III	II	I

Step 3: Identification of Product Mix

	Hrs. in Machine 2	*Units of Product*
Available	3,200	—
Less: Used for Rank I C (200 × 3)	600	200 units
Less: Used for Rank II B (200 × 6)	1,200	200 units
Less: Balance used for Rank III A	1,400	77.77 or 77 units

Illustration 2

The following data is to be used to answer questions (a), (b) and (c) below.

CAS Ltd. plc manufactures four products. The unit cost, selling price and bottleneck resource details per unit are as follows:

	Product W ₹	*Product X* ₹	*Product Y* ₹	*Product Z* ₹
Selling price	56	67	89	96
Materials	22	31	38	46
Labour	15	20	18	24
Variable overhead	12	15	18	15
Fixed overhead	4	2	8	7
	Minutes	Minutes	Minutes	Minutes
Bottleneck Resource Time	10	10	15	15

(a) Assuming the labour is a unit variable cost, if the products are ranked according to their contribution , the most profitable product is:

(A) W *(B) X*

(C) Y *(D) Z*

(b) Assuming that labour is a unit variable cost, if budgeted unit sales are in the ratio W: 2; X: 3; Y:3; Z:4 and monthly fixed costs are budgeted to be ₹ 15,000, the number of units of W that would be sold at the budgeted breakeven point is nearest to:

(A) 106 units ***(B) 142 units.***

(C) 212 units ***(D) 283 units***

(c) If the company adopted throughput accounting and the products were ranked according to 'product return per minute', the highest ranked product would be:

(A) W ***(B) X***

(C) Y ***(D) Z***

Solution

CALCULATION OF CONTRIBUTION PER UNIT OF KEY FACTOR AND RANKING

Particulars	*W*	*X*	*Y*	*Z*
A. Sales Price	56	67	89	96
B. *Less:* Material	(22)	(31)	(38)	(46)
Labour	(15)	(20)	(18)	(24)
Variable Overheads	(12)	(15)	(18)	(15)
C. Contribution	7	1	15	11
D. Limiting Factor	10	10	15	15
E. Contribution/unit (C/D)	0.7	0.1	1.0	7.3
F. Ranking	III	IV	I	II

(c)

Product	*Contribution per unit*	*Mix*	*Total*
W	7	2	14
X	1	3	3
Y	15	3	45
Z	11	4	44
		12	106

Fixed cost = 15,000

BEP = 15,000/(106/12) = 1,698.11 *i.e.* 1,699 units

Sales of W = 1,699 × 2/12 = 283 units

Sales of X = 1,699 × (3/12) = 424.75

Sales of Y = 1,699 × 3/12 = 424.75

Sales of Z = 1,699 × 4/12 = 566.33

(d)

Particulars	*W*	*X*	*Y*	*Z*
A. Sales	56	67	89	96
B. *Less:* Material	22	31	38	46
C. Through put Contribution per unit	34	36	51	50
D. Bottleneck Minutes /unit	10	10	15	15
E. Through Contribution/min (A / B)	3.4	3.6	3.4	3.33
Ranking	II	I	II	III

Illustration 3

X Ltd. manufactures filing cabinets in two operations: machining and finishing. It provides the following information:

	Machining	*Finishing*
Annual capacity	1,00,000 units	80,000 units
Annual production	80,000 units	80,000 units
Fixed operating costs (Excluding direct materials)	₹ 6,40,000	₹ 4,00,000
Fixed operating costs pet unit produced (₹ 6,40,000/80,000); (₹ 4,00,000/80,000)	₹.9 per unit	₹ 5 per unit

Each cabinet sells for ₹ 72 and has direct materials costs of ₹ 32 incurred at the start of the machining operation. Mayfield has no other variable costs. The company can sell whatever output it produces. The following requirements refer only to the preceding data, there is no connection between the requirements.

(i) The company is considering using some modern jigs and tools in the finishing operation that would increase annual finishing output by 1.000 units. The annual cost of these jigs and tools, is ₹ 30,000. Should the company acquire these tools? Show your calculations.

(ii) An outside contractor offers to do the finishing operation for 12,000 units at ₹ 10 per unit, double the ₹ 5 per unit that it costs the company to do the finishing in-house. Should accept the subcontractors offer? Show your Calculations.

(iii) Y Ltd. offeres for machining operation 4,000 units at ₹ 4 per unit, half the ₹ 8 per unit that it costs. Mayfield to do the machining in-house. Should X Ltd. accept the subcontractor's offer? Show your calculations.

(iv) If X Ltd. produces 2,000 defective units at the machining operation. What is the cost to X Ltd. of defctive items produced? Explain your answer briefly.

(v) If X Ltd. produceds 2,000 defective units at the finishing operation. What is the ccst to X Ltd. of the defective items produced? Explain your answer briefly.

Solution

STATEMENF OF COST BENEFIT

Particulars	₹
Incremental Revenue (70 × 1000)	72,000
Less: Material Cost (machining) (32 × 1000)	(32,000)
Through put Contribution	40,000
Less: Extra cost	(30,000)
Net benefit	10,000

It is better to process additional 1000 units in finishing department due to the following reasons:

(i) Spare capacity exist in receiving Department. It provides as an extra net benefit ₹ 10,000 to the company.

(ii) It is not advisable to incur extra cost ₹ 5,000 in machining department to increase the capacity due to the following.

(a) Spare capacity already exist in machining department.

(b) No other alternative should be used to utilize the existing spare capacity as well as extra capacity due to capacity constraint in the succeeding department, Finished Goods Department.

(ii) STATEMENT OF INCREMENTAL PROFIT

Particulars	₹
Incremental Revenue 12,000 × 72	8,64,000
Less: Incremental cost (Dept. I) 1200 × 32	3,84,000
Through put contribution	4,80,000
Less: Payment to outsiders	1,20,000
Net Profit	3,60,000

It is better to accept the offer as it can be processed in Machine without any change in existing cost (only material cost to be termed as relevant cost).

Payment to outsider for Department II work along with the material cost to be covered with incremental revenue ajid providing net benefit to the company of ₹ 3,60,000.

(iv) It is not better to sub contract the machining operation because spare capacity already exists in Department I and material cost is irrelevant cost and further, we can say that existing fixed cost remains constants.

(v) The cost of defective = Extra material cost in machine department = 2,000 × 32 = ₹ 64,000.

(vi) Due defective unit existing in finishing Department II, we can't process 8200 units in this department due to capacity constraints. The loss of revenue is loss to the company which may be termed as cost of defective = 2,000 × 72 = ₹ 1,44,000.

Illustration 4

X Ltd. produces three products X, Y and Z. The capacity of the plant is restricted by process alpha. Process alpha is expected to be operational for eight hours per day and can produce 1,200 units of X per hour or 1,500 units of Y per hour or 600 units of Z per hour. Selling prices and material costs for each product are as follows:

Product	*Selling Price ₹ per unit*	*Material Cost ₹ per unit*	*Throughput contribution ₹ per unit*
X	150	70	80
Y	120	40	80
X	300	100	200

Conversion costs are ₹ 7,20,000 per day.

Calculate profit finding if X = 6000, *Y* = 4,500, *Z* = 4,200.

Solution

(I) STATEMENT OF PROFIT

Throughput Contribution:	₹
X [6,000 × 80]	4,80,000
Y [4,500 × 80]	3,60,000
Z [200 × 200]	2,40,000
Total throughput contribution	10,80,000
Less: Conversion Cost	(7,20,000)
Profit	3,60,000

(II) STATEMENT OF EFFICIENCY

Product	*Budget output*	*Budgeted Hrs*	*Output*	*Std. hrs for actual output*	*Actual firs for acutal output*
X	1,200	1	6,000		5
Y	1,500	1	4,500	3	
Z	600	1	1,200	2	8
				10	

∴ Efficiency of process = Standard Hours for Actual output/Actual hours for Actual output = 10Hrs/8Hrs = 1.25

(III) STATEMENT OF TA RATIO FOR EACH PRODUCT

Manufacturing	*X*	*Y*	*Z*
Throughput contribution	7,68,000(9,600 × 80)	9,60,000(12,000 × 80)	9,60,000(4,800 × 200)
per day (a) ₹	7,20,000	7,20,000	7,20,000
Conversion cost/day (b)	1.06	1.33	1.33
Ranking	III	I	II

In case of demand restriction, it is better to produce either product Y or Z and resource can be diverted to product X.

Illustration 5

CAS Ltd. produces 4 products using 3 different machines. Machine capacity is limited to 3,000 hours for each machine. The following information is available for February, 2014:

Particulars	*A*	*B*	*C*	*D*
Contribution (Sales-direct material) ₹	1,500	1,200	1,000	600
Machine Hours Required/Unit:				
Machine 1	10	6	2	1
Machine 2	10	9	3	1.5
Machines 3	10	3	1	0.5
Estimated Demand (units)	200	200	200	200

From the above information you are required to identify the bottleneck activity and allocate the machine time.

Solution

STATEMENT OF RANKING

Particulars	*A*	*B*	*C*	*D*
Revised Contribution per unit	1,500	1,200	1,000	600
Machine hrs on Machine (2 P.u.)	10	9	3	1.5
Revised contribution per machine hrs	150	133.3	332.3	400
Ranking	III	IV	II	I

STATEMENT OF OPTIMUM PRODUCT MIX

Particulars	*Qty*	*M1*	*M2*	*M3*
D	200	200	300	100
C	200	400	600	200
A	200	2,000	2,000	2,000
B	11.11	400(BF)	100(BF)	700(BF)
		3,000	3,000	3,000
Possible Unit		66.66	11.11	233.33

	M1	M2	M3
O/B	400/6	100/9	700/3
Spare	333.33	Nil	666.66
	[400 – (11.11 × 6)]	X	[700 – (11.11 × 3)]

Illustration 6

Z Ltd produces a single product X, which passes through three different processes. A, B and C. The throughput per hour of the three processes is 12, 10 and 15 units of X respectively. The company works an 8 hour day, 6 days a week, 48 weeks a year. The selling price of X is ₹ 150 per unit and its material cost is ₹ 30 per unit. Conversion costs are planned to be ₹ 24,000 per week.

Required:

(a) ***Determine the throughput accounting (TA) ratio per day.***

(b) ***Calculate how much the company could spend on equipment to improve the throughput of process B if it wished to recover its cost in the following time periods:***
(i) 2 years, (ii) 12 weeks

(c) ***Calculate the revised TA ratio if this money is spent.***

Solution

Z LTD. (a) (i)

	Process A ₹	*Process B* ₹	*Process C* ₹
Throughput per hour (units)	12	10	15
Throughput per day (units)	96	80	120
Throughput contribution per unit	SP—Material cost = ₹ (150 – 30) = ₹ 120		
Throughput accounting ratio = (contribution/day) ÷ (Conversion cost/day)			
(₹ 120 x 80 units of B) ÷ (₹ 24,000 + 6) = 2.4			

(b) (i) Gain of bottleneck at process B is eliminated = 96 – 80 of 16 units per day.
Gain over two years = 16 units × 6 days × 48 weeks × 2 × ₹ 120 = ₹ 11,05,920. Therefore, ₹ 11 lakh could be spent if the cost were to be recovered in 2 years.

(ii) In this alternative case of 12 week
Gain will be16 × 6 × 12 × ₹ 120 = ₹ 1,38,240.
Therefore ₹ 1.38 lakh could be spent if the costs were to be recovered over 12 weeks.

(c) TA ratio = (96 units × ₹ 120) ÷ 4,000 = 2.88.

Illustration 7

A Company manufactures two products using its maximum capacity of 30,000 machine hours. The price and cost data relating to the two products are as under:

	Product A	*Product B*
Selling price	₹/unit 400	560
Material Cost	₹/unit 160	200
Variable conversion cost	₹/unit 40	120
Maximum sales potential (units)	75,000	35,000
Production per machine hours (units)	3.125	2.5

Total Fixed overheads ₹ 84 lacs

As the company uses just-in-time system, the stocks of work-in-process and finished goods are negligible.

Required:

(i) Determine the optimal product mix using marginal costing.

(ii) Calculate the throughput accounting ratio for each product and rank the products for manufacture,

(iii) Based on the concept of throughput accounting. Compute the product mix to yield maximum profit. For this purpose, use the total variable costs as calculated on the basis of the product mix obtained by using the marginal costing method in (i) above.

Solution

(i.) Optimal product mix using marginal costing:

REQUIREMENT OF MACHINE HOURS FOR THE MAXIMUM SALES POTENTIAL

Product	*Maximum sales Units*	*Production/Machine hour*	*Machine hours needed*
A	75,000	3.125	24,000
B	35,000	2.50	14,000
		Total	38,000

With 30,000 hours available, shortage = 8,000 hours

CONTRIBUTION BY KEY FACTOR (MACHINE HOUR) AND RANKING

Products			*A* ₹	*B* ₹
Selling Price per unit			400	560
Variable Costs per unit:	A	B		
Materials	160	200		
Conversion	40	120	200	320
Contribution per unit			200	240
Production: units per hour			3.125	2.50
Contribution per hour			₹ 625	₹ 600
Rank (Based on Marginal Contribution)			I	II

Machine Hours required per unit of output: A 1/3.125 = 0.32: B 1/2.50 = 0.40.
Optimal product mix using marginal costing:
A 75,000 (max, sales potential) × 0.32 = 24,000 hours
B 15,000 (Constrained by hours) × 0.40 = 6000 balance hrs.
Total available machine hours = 30,000
Contribution from this product mix = A, 75,000 × ₹ 200 + B, 15,000 × ₹ 240 = ₹ 1,86,00,000
With fixed overheads of ₹ 84,00,000, Profit = ₹ 1,02,00,000.

(ii) Ranking products based on throughput accounting ratio:

(a) Ranking by return per factory hour:

PRODUCT

Selling price	₹/unit	**400**	560
Material Cost	₹/unit	**160**	200
Return	₹/unit	**240**	360
Hours required	Per unit	0.32	0.40
Return per hour		₹ 750	₹ 900
Rank		II	I

(b) Since under this method, all costs other than material and components are treated as fixed costs, the total of fixed costs (as per the question) = Conversion costs + Fixed costs = A 75,000 x ₹ 40 + B 35,000 x ₹ 120 + ₹ 84,00,000 = ₹ 1,32,00,000.

Fixed costs per bottleneck hour = ₹ 1,32,00,000 – 30,000 hrs = ₹ 440.

(c) Throughput accounting ratio (value added per time period/conversion cost per time period):

	A	*B*
₹ 750/₹ 440: ₹ 900/₹ 440	1.70	2.05
Rank	II	I

(iii) Product mix based on throughput accounting ratio:

Cost Driver	*Quantity of Cost Driver*	*Explanation for quantity of Cost Driver Toshiba*	*Quantity of Cost Driver for Toshiba II*	*Explanation for Quantity Driver Used by Toshiba II*
B	35,000	14,000	1,26,00,000	16,000
A	50,000	16,000	1,20,00,000	Nil
			2,46,00,000	
Less: total fixed costs			1,32,00,000	
Operational profit			₹ 1,14,00,000	
Limited by available machine hours.				

Illustration 8

X Ltd. manufactures automated industrial trolleys known as TRLs. Each TRL sells for ₹ 2,000 and material cost per unit is ₹ 600. Labour and variable overhead are ₹ 5,500 and ₹ 8,000 per week respectively. Fixed production costs are ₹ 4,50,000 per annum and marketing and administrative costs are ₹ 2,65,000 per annum.

The trolleys are made on three different machines. Machine X makes the four frame panels required for each TRL. Its maximum output is 180 frame panels per week. Machine X is old and unreliable and it breaks down from time to time-it is estimated that, on average, between 15 and 20 hours of production are lost per month. Machine Y can manufacture parts for 52 TRLs per week and machine Z, which is old but reasonably liable can process and assemble SOTRLs per week.

The company has recently introduced a just-in time (JIT) system and it is company policy to hold little work-in-progress and no finished goods stock from week to week. The company operates a 40 hour week, 48 weeks a year (12 months x 4 weeks) but cannot meet demand. The demand for the next year is predicted to be as follows and this is expected to be typical of the demand for the next four years.

	Units per week		*Units per week*
January	30	July	48
February	30	August	45
March	33	September	42
April	36	October	40
May	39	November	33
June	44	December	30

The production manger has suggested that the company replaces machine Z with machine G which can process 45 TRLs per week. The maintenance manager is keen to spend ₹ 1,00,000 on a major overhaul of ma-jchine X as he says this will make it 100% reliable.

Required: Calculate the throughput accounting ratio (defined below) for the key resource for an average hour next year.

Throughout accounting ratio = return per factory hour/Cost per factory hour.

Where return per factory hour = Sales price – material cost/time on key resource.

Solution

Key resource:

Particulars	Machine X Output	Machine Y Output	Machine Z Output
Up to 5 hour production time lost per week (=1/8 of maximum weekly production time)	7/8 × 180/4 = 39 TRLS		
Machine Y		52 TRLS	
Machine Z			30TRLS
Key resource id therefore Machine Z time			₹
Selling price			2,000
Material Cost			(600)
			1400

Time on Key resource = 40 hours per week /J30TRLS = 1.333 hours per TRL
Return per factory hour 1400/1.333 = ₹ 1,050.

COST PER FACTORY HOUR

Particulars	₹
Labour	5500
Variable overhead	8000
Fixed production costs [4,50,000/48 weeks]	9,375
	22,875

Cost per factory hour = ₹ 22,875/40 = ₹ 571.88
Throughput accounting ratio = ₹ 1050/571.88 = 1.84

Illustration 9

X Ltd. is a food processing company that produces pre-prepared meals for sale to consumers though a number of different supermarkets. The company specializes in three particular pre-prepared meals and has invested significantly in modern manufacturing process to ensure a high quality product. The company is very aware of the importance of training and retaining high quality staff in all areas of the company and, in order to ensure their production employees' commitment to the company, the employees are guaranteed a weekly salary that is equivalent to their normal working hours paid at their normal hourly rate of ₹ 7 per hour.

The meals are produced in batches of 100 units. Costs and selling prices per batch are as follows, X Ltd. has adopted throughput accounting for its short-term decisions.

Meal	*TR ₹ batch*	*PN ₹ batch*	*BE ₹ batch*
Selling price	340	450	270
Ingredient K (₹ 5/Kg)	150	120	90
Ingredient L(₹ 10/Kg)	70	90	40
Ingredient M (₹ 15/Kg)	30	75	45
Labour (₹ 7/hour)	21	28	42
Factory Costs absorbed	20	80	40

Required: X Ltd. is preparing its production plans for the next three months and has estimated the "maximum demand from its customers to be as follows.

	Batches
TR	***500***
PN	***400***
BE	***350***

These maximums demand are amended figures because a customer has just delayed its jequest for a TSfge order and X Ltd. has unusually got some spare capacity over the next three months. However, these demand maximums do include a contract for the delivery of 50 batches of each to an important costomer. If this minimum contract is not satisfied then X Ltd. will have to pay a substantial financial penalty for non-delivery.

The production director is concerned at hearing news that two of the ingredients used are expected to be in short supply for the next three months. X Ltd. does not hold inventory of these ingredients and although there are no supply problems for ingredient K, the supplies of ingredients L and M are expected to be limited to.

	Kilos
Ingredient L	***7,000***
Ingredient M	***3,000***

The production director has researched the problem and found that ingredient V can be used as a direct substitute for ingredient M. It also costs the same as ingredient M. There is an unlimited supply of ingredient V.

Required: Prepare calculations to determine the production mix that will maximise the profit X Ltd. during the next three months.

Solution

If resources are limiting factors, then contribution is maximised by earning the biggest possible contribution per unit of limiting factor.

ASCERTAIN WHETHER MATERIAL L IS THE LIMITING FACTOR

Product	*TR*	*PN*	*BE*	*Total*
Kgs of L per batch (kg)	7	9	4	
Kgs of L needed to meet sales demand	3,500 (500 × 7)	3,600 (9 × 400)	1,400 (4 × 350)	8,500
Kgs available				7,000
Shortfall				1,500

CALCULATION CONTRIBUTION PER UNIT OF SCARCE RESOURCE AND RANK INGREDIENTS

Product	*TR*	*PN*	*BE*
Contribution per batch (₹)	90	165	95
Kgs per batch	7	9	4
Contribution per kg (₹)	12.86	18.33	23.75
Ranking	3	2	1

DETERMINE THE OPTIMUM PRODUCT MIX

Product	*Demand Batches*	*Ingredient L required kgs*	*Ingredient L available kgs**	*Batches produced*
			7,000	
BE	350 (× 4)	1,400	(1,400)	350
			5600	
PN	400 (× 9)	3,600	(3,600)	400
			2,000	
TR	500 (× 7)	3,500	(1,995)	285
			5	

*Demand includes a requirement to produce 50 batches as a minimum

18 Product Life Cycle Costing

LEARNING OBJECTIVES

After studying this chapter, you should be able to understand:

- Product Life Cycle-Meaning, Phases, Stages
- Meaning, Objective, Benefits and three Stages in Product Life Cycle Costing

1.0 MEANING, OBJECTIVE, BENEFITS AND THREE STAGES IN PRODUCT LIFE CYCLE COSTING

<table>
<tr><td>Meaning</td><td colspan="2">Life Cycle Costing estimates, tracks and accumulates the costs over a product's entire life cycle from its inception to abandonment or from the initial R & D stage till the final customer servicing and support of the product with a view to determine whether the profits earned during the manufacturing phase will cover the costs incurred during pre and post manufacturing stages.</td></tr>
<tr><td>Features</td><td colspan="2">1. It involves tracing & accumulation of costs and revenues of each product over several calendar periods throughout the entire life cycle.
2. It traces research and design and development costs etc., incurred to individual products over their entire life cycles, so that the total magnitude of these costs for each individual product can be reported and compared with product revenues generated in later periods.
3. It ensures that costs for each individual product can be reported and compared with product revenues generated in later periods. Hence the costs are made more visible.</td></tr>
<tr><td>Objective</td><td colspan="2">The objective is to determine whether the profits earned during the manufacturing phase will cover the costs incurred during pre and post manufacturing stages.</td></tr>
<tr><td rowspan="5">Costs included in Product Life Cycle Cost</td><td colspan="2">The costs are included in different stages of the product life cycle.</td></tr>
<tr><td>Development Phase</td><td>R & D cost/ Design cost.</td></tr>
<tr><td>Introduction Phase</td><td>Promotional cost/ Capacity costs.</td></tr>
<tr><td>Growth/Maturity Phase</td><td>Manufacturing cost/ Distribution costs/ Product support cost.</td></tr>
<tr><td>Decline/Replacement Phase</td><td>Plants reused/ sold/ scrapped/ related costs.</td></tr>
</table>

Benefits	1. **Earlier actions** The product life cycle costing results in earlier actions to generate revenue or to lower costs than otherwise might be considered. There are a number of factors that need to the managed in order to maximize return on a product. 2. **Better Decisions** A more accurate and realistic assessment of revenues and costs, at least within a particular life cycle stage facilitates Better decisions. 3. **Long-term rewarding** Product life cycle thinking can promote long-term rewarding in contrast to short-term profitability rewarding. 4. **Cost Effectiveness** It provides an overall framework for considering total incremental costs over the entire life span of a product, which in turn facilitates analysis of parts of the whole where cost effectiveness might be improved.
Importance	Product life cycle costing is important for the following reasons: 1. **To identify significant non-production costs** (like costs associated with R & D, design, marketing, distribution and customer service) for target pricing, value engineering and cost management. For example, a poorly designed software package may involve higher costs on marketing, distribution and after sales service. 2. **To identify the significant pre-manufacturing costs** (like R & D and design) to decide whether the costly R & D and design activities should be undertaken. 3. **To identify significant material and labour costs** expected to be incurred due to adoption of a particular design in order to decide whether this design should be adopted or not. For example, the adoption of a certain design will determine the product's material and labour inputs to be incurred during the manufacturing stage. A complicated design may lead to greater expenditure on material and labour costs every time the product is produced. 4. Life cycle budgeting highlights costs throughout the product life cycle and facilitates value engineering at the design stage before costs are locked in. 5. Total life-cycle costing approach accumulates product costs over the value chain. It is a process of managing all costs along the value chain starting from product's design, development, manufacturing, marketing, service and finally disposal.
Three Stages	1. Planning and Design Stage 2. Manufacturing Stage 3. Service and Abandonment Stage Approximately 80% of the product's costs are committed during planning and design stage as at this stage product designers determine the product's design and the production process. In contrast, majority of the costs are incurred in the manufacturing stage but these were already locked-in at planning and design stage and are difficult to alter. Cost management can be most effective at planning and design stage and not at manufacturing stage where product designs and processes have already been determined and costs have been committed.

Different from Traditional Costing	Life cycle costing is different to traditional cost accounting system which report cost object profitability on a calendar basis i.e. monthly, quarterly and annually. In contrast life cycle costing involves tracing cost and revenues on product by product bases over several calendar periods. Costs and revenue can be analyzed by time period, but the emphasis is on cost revenue accumulation over the entire life cycle of each product. Now, we will discuss life cycle costing for products.

2.0 PRODUCT LIFE CYCLE-MEANING, PHASES, STAGES

(a) Meaning	Each product has a life cycle. The life cycle of a product vary from a few months to several years. For example, in the case of cameras, photocopying machines etc. the life is more than 100 years. Whereas in the case of black and white T.V./V.C.R. it was for few years only. Product life cycle is thus a pattern of expenditure, sale level, revenue and profit over the period from new idea generation to the deletion of product from product range.
(b) Phases of Product Life Cycle	
1. Introduction	During introductory phase, a product is launched into the market. Its customers are innovators. Competition is almost negligible and profits are non-existent.
2. Growth	Under growth phase, sales and profits rise, at a rapid pace. Competitors enter the market often in large numbers. As a result of competition, profits starts declining near the end of the growth phase.
3. Maturity	During the phase of maturity sales continue to increase, but at a decreasing rate. When sales level off, profits of both producers and middlemen decline. The main reason is intense price competition, some firms extend their product lines with new models.
4. Decline	Decline in sales volume characterizes this last phase of the product life cycle. The need or demand for product disappears. Availability of better and less costly substitutes in the market accounts for the arrival of this phase.
(c) Characteristics	The major characteristics of product life-cycle concept are as follows : **1.** The products have finite lives and pass through the cycle of development, introduction, growth, maturity, decline and deletion at varying speeds. **2.** Product cost, revenue and profit patterns tend to follow predictable courses through the product life cycle. Profits first appear during the growth phase and after stabilizing during the maturity phase, decline thereafter to the point of deletion. **3.** Profit per unit varies as products move through their life cycles. **4.** Each phase of the product life-cycle poses different threats and opportunities that give rise to different strategic actions.

	5. Products require different functional emphasis in each phase-such as an R&D emphasis in the development phase and a cost control emphasis in the decline phase. 6. Finding new uses or new users or getting the present uses to increase their consumption, this may extend the life of the product.
(d) Stages of Product Life Cycle	
1. Market Research	Before any investment is made the investor must believe that what the company proposes to make can be sold at a price which will permit a profit to be made. This usually means that market research will establish what product the customer wants, how much he is prepared to pay for it and how many he will buy.
2. Specification	When market research has established what is to be made, it will be necessary to turn the general statement of requirements into a detailed specification which will tell the designer and manufacturing engineer precisely what is required. The design specification will give such details as required life, maximum permissible maintenance costs, maximum permissible manufacturing cost, the number required, the delivery date, the required performance of the product.
3. Design	With a precise specification, the designers can produce the drawings and process schedules which define the geometry of the product and some of the manufacturing processes.
4. Prototype manufacture	From the drawings it will be possible to manufacture a small number of the product. These prototypes will be used to develop the product and eventually to demonstrate that it meets the requirements of the specification.
5. Development	When a product has been made for the first time, it is necessary to prove that it meets the requirements of the specification. In fact, when a product is first made it rarely meets the requirements of the specification and changes have to be made until it does. This period of testing and changing is 'development'. **Development can be very expensive and often generates a large negative cash flow before any products have been sold and hence, before any positive cash flows have been generated.**
6. Tooling	When a product is shown to meet the requirements of the specification and if calculations suggest that it will be profitable, the decision will be made to make it to sell. This is not a decision that will be taken lightly because, in many cases, the decision to make a product for sale is commitment to tool up for production. Tooling up for production can mean building a production line costing several lakhs of rupees, building expensive jigs, buying special purpose machine tools or, in some other say, making a very large initial investment.
7. Manufacture	The manufacture of a product involves the purchase of the raw materials, the purchase of bought out components, the use of labour to make and assemble the product, and the use of supervisory labour.

8. Selling	When the product is fit to sell and available, it may be necessary to spend money on a campaign to sell the product
9. Distribution	In the process of selling the product, it must be distributed to the sales outlets and to the customers.
10. Product support	When the product has been bought, the customer will expect it to be supported. The manufacturer or supplier will have to make sure that spares and expert servicing are available for the life of the product. The manufacturer or the supplier may even have to offer free servicing and parts replacement during the early life of the product.
11. Decommis-sioning or Replacement	When a manufacturing product comes to an end, the plant used to build the product must be re-used, sold, scrapped, or decommissioned in away that is acceptable to society.

Illustration 1

CAS Ltd. is considering the purchase of a new machine for ₹ 7,00,000. It feels quite confident that it can sell the goods produced by the machine so as to yield an annual cash surplus of ₹ 2,00,000. There is however some uncertainly as to the machine's working life. A recently publish Trade Association Survey shows that members of the Association have between them owned 250 of these machines and have found the lives of the machines vary as under:

No. of year of Machine life	3	4	5	6	7	Total
No. of machines having given life	20	50	100	70	10	250

Assuming a discount rate of 10% the net present value for each different machine life is as follows:

Machine life	3	4	5	6	7
NPV (₹)	(2,02,000)	(66,000)	58,000	1,72,000	2,74,000

You are required to advice whether the company should purchase a new machine or not.

Solution

Computation of NPV of an asset considering the prob. of life of machine

Year	***Probability (a)***	***NPV (₹) (b)***	***Expected Value (₹) (a x b)***
3	20/250	(2,02,000)	(16,160)
4	50/250	(66,000)	(13,200)
5	100/250	58,000	23,200
6	70/250	1,72,000	48,160
7	10/250	2,74,000	10,960
			52,960

Therefore, Assets should be purchased.

Illustration 2

X Ltd. makes digital watches. Company is preparing/product life-cycle budget for a new watch MX3. Development on the new watch is to start shortly. Estimates for MX3 are as follows:

Life- cycle units manufactured and sold	400,000
Selling price per watch	₹ 40
Life-cycle costs:	
R&D and desigrt-etfsts	₹ 1,000,000
Manufacturing	
Variable cost per watch	₹ 15
Variable cost per batch	₹ 600
Watches per batch	500
Fixed costs	₹ 1,800,000
Marketing	
Variable cost per watch	₹ 3.20
Fixed costs	₹ 1,000,000
Distribution	
Variable cost per batch	₹ 280
Watches per batch	160
Fixed costs	₹ 7,20,000
Customer-service cost per watch	₹ 1.50
Ignore the time value of money.	

Required:

(i) Calculate the budgeted life-cycle operating income for the new watch.

(ii) What percentage of the budgeted total product life-cycle costs will be incurred by the end of the R&D and design stages?

(iii) X Ltd's market research department estimates that reducing MX3's price by ₹ 3 will increase life-cycle unit sales by 10%. If unit sales increase by 10% destin plans to increase manufacturing and distribution batch sizes by 10% as well. Assume that all variable costs per watch variable costs per batch, and fixed costs will remain the same. Should X Ltd. reduce MXSVprice by ₹ 3? Show your calculations.

Solution

STATEMENT OF CYCLE COST

(A) Revenue (4,00,000 × 40)	1,60,00.000
(B) Cost:	
Cost Pre-Mgr	
Research & design	10,00,000
Mgr Cost	
Variable Cost (15 × 400000)	60,00,000
Other (600 × 400000/500)	4,80,000
Fixed Cost	18,00,000
Post Mgr Cost	
Variable Cost (3.2 × 400000)	12,80,000
Fixed Cost	10,00,000
Variable Cost (280 × 400000/160)	7,00,000
Fixed Cost	7,20,000
Customer Service (1.5 × 400000)	6,00,000
Total costs (B)	1,35,80,000
Net Benefit (A – B)	**24,20,000**

19 Balanced Score Card

LEARNING OBJECTIVES

After studying this chapter, you should be able to understand:

Meaning, Objective and Perspectives of Balance Score Card

1.0 MEANING, OBJECTIVE AND PERSPECTIVES OF BALANCED SCORE CARD

<table>
<tr><td>Meaning</td><td colspan="3">Balanced Scorecard is an approach which provides information relating to financial and non-financial measures from four different perspectives(i.e. Customer Perspective, Internal Business Perspective, Innovation & Learning Perspective, Financial Perspective) to management to assist in strategy formulation and implementation .</td></tr>
<tr><td>Objective</td><td colspan="3">The objective of Balanced Scorecard is to provide a comprehensive framework for translating the company's strategic objectives into a coherent set of financial and non-financial performance measures.</td></tr>
<tr><td>Perspectives/ Elements/ Components</td><td colspan="3">The central idea of the Balanced Scorecard is that managers should develop the measures on which they manage the business from four different perspectives. An ideal Balanced score card combines financial measures of past performance with measures of the firm's drivers of future performance. The following perspectives are evaluated:
1. Customer Perspective: It considers performance measures of Price,Delivery,Quality,Support.
2. Internal Business Perspective: It considers performance measures of Efficiency of manufacturing Process, Sales penetration, New Product introduction.
3. Innovation & Learning Perspective: It considers performance measures of Technology Leadership, Cost Leadership, Market Leadership, Research & Development
4. Financial Perspective: It considers performance measures of Sales, Cost of Sales, Profitability, Prosperity.</td></tr>
<tr><td rowspan="3">Goals and Performance for each Perspective</td><td rowspan="3">1. Customer Perspective</td><td>Goals</td><td>Performance Measures</td></tr>
<tr><td>Price</td><td>Competitive price</td></tr>
<tr><td>Delivery</td><td>Number of on time delivery, lead time receipt of order to delivery to from customer.</td></tr>
</table>

		Quality	Own quality relative to industry standards, number of defects or defect level.
		Support	Response time, customer satisfaction survey
	2. Internal Business	**Goals**	**Performance Measures**
		Efficiency of manufacturing process	Manufacturing cycle time
		Sales penetration	Sales plan, Increase in number of customer in a unit of time.
		New Product introduction	Rate of new product introduction
	3. Innovation & Learning Perspective	**Goals**	**Performance Measures**
		Technology Leadership	Performance of product, use of technology
		Cost Leadership	Manufacture overhead per quarter
		Market Leadership	Market share in all major markets
		Research And Development	Number of new products, Patents
	4. Financial Perspective	**Goals**	**Performance Measures**
		Sales	Revenue and profit growth
		Cost of Sales	Extent in remain fixed or decreased each year
		Profitability	Return on capital employed
		Prosperity	Cash flows
Why Balanced Scorecards sometimes fail to provide for the desired results	1. The use of non financial measures leads managers to think that they have a Balanced Scorecard already working for strategic purposes. 2. Senior executives misguidedly delegate the responsibility of the Scorecard implementation to middle level managers. 3. Company's try to copy measures and strategies used by the best companies rather than developing their own measures suited for the environment under which they function. 4. There are times when Balanced Scorecards are thought to be meant for reporting purposes only. This notion does not allow a Business to use the Scorecard to manage Business in a new and more effective way. 5. If efforts are made to negotiate targets rather than to build consensus since an approach to establish targets through negotiation defeats the very purpose of balanced score card (i.e.the components and targets should flow from strategy).		

Whether a Balanced Scorecard is useful for external reporting	It is a matter of debate whether a Balanced Scorecard is useful for external reporting. Critics argue that if the Scorecard is indeed a relevant driver of long term performance, shouldn't the information generated be of interest to the investment community? However, it has been noticed that the Scorecard does not translate easily to the investment community for the simple reason that it makes sense for individual business units and different individual projects rather than the company as a whole. Most companies have different divisions with their own mission and strategy and hence these individual scorecards cannot be aggregated into an overall corporate scorecard. However, in case the company somehow manages to overcome such a problem and indeed use its Scorecard for external reporting, it may end up passing sensitive information to its competitors which may end up being detrimental to the company in the long run. However, with changes in the thinking process of the investment community, such strategic reporting could well be accepted in the near future.
Responsibility	The responsibility to devise and implement a Balanced Scorecard should be that of the managers working with the business. Since every company is different, it shall need to work out for itself the various financial and non - financial measures, which need to be focussed upon for its own development. Since the Balanced Scorecard is recommended as a management tool used both for internal and external reporting purposes, it is again the manager's responsibility to decide as to what information needs to be disclosed and how any problems of confidentiality can best be overcome.

Conclusion: *According to Kaplan and Norton, the ultimate result of using the Balanced Scorecard approach should be an improved long-term financial performance. Since the scorecard gives equal importance to the relevant non—financial measures, it should discourage the short termism that leads to cuts in spending on new product development, human resource development etc which are ultimately detrimental for the future prospects of the company.*

"In many organisations, initiatives to introduce balanced score card failed because efforts were made to negotiate targets rather than to build consensus."

Components to be included in the balanced score card must flow from strategy since Balanced score card is an approach which provides information to management to assist in strategy implementation. is necessary that managers should agree to the components and targets because in absence of a consensus, managers may not commit to the targets established by the top management / the board of directors. Moreover, the functions are interdependent and results in one functional area/perspective (e.g. innovation and learning) have direct bearing on the results in other functional area / perspective (e.g. customer perspective). Therefore, it is not sufficient that individual managers agree to their targets. Successful implementation requires that the top management builds an overall consensus on the components and targets of the balanced score card. Negotiation undermines the fundamental principle that the components and targets should flow from strategy. As a result, an approach to establish targets through negotiation defeats the very purpose of balanced score card.

20 Value Chain Analysis

LEARNING OBJECTIVES

After studying this chapter, you should be able to understand:

- Meaning, Objective, Benefits Etc. of Value Chain Analysis
- Distinction Between 'Traditional Management Accounting' and 'Value Chain Analysis
- Three Strategic Frameworks for Value Chain Analysis
- Limitations of Value Chain Analysis
- Organisational and Managerial Accounting Challenges

1.0 MEANING, OBJECTIVE, BENEFITS ETC. OF VALUE CHAIN ANALYSIS

Meaning	Value Chain Analysis is a continuous process of identifying Value Chain (i.e. a linked set of value creating activities from the basic raw materials and components sources to the ultimate end use of the product or service delivered to the customer) which will yield the maximum competitive advantage and applying the organization's resources to each linked process so as to achieve cost effectiveness.
Objective	The objective of value chain is to serve as means of increasing the customer satisfaction in terms of cost efficiency, quality and delivery and managing costs effectively.
Six Business Functions	1. Research and Development 2. Design 3. Production 4. Marketing 5. Distribution and 6. Customer service.
Benefits	1. Value Chain Analysis helps the organizations to better understand which segments, distribution channels, price points. product differentiation. selling prepositions and value chain configuration will yield them the greatest competitive advantage. 2. It helps managers in deciding how to apply the organization's valuable physical and human resources to each linked process so as to achieve cost effectiveness.

<table>
<tr><td></td><td colspan="2">3. Value analysis facilitates cost reduction in the following manner:
• By identifying and removing unnecessary components in a product which had utility earlier.
• By introducing component substitution at a lesser cost without affecting the quality of the product.
• By simplifying the product design.
• By introducing alternative methods with less cost but improved efficiency.
4. Value chain analysis offers an excellent opportunity to integrate strategic planning with management accounting to guide the firm to growth and survival.</td></tr>
<tr><td>Methodology</td><td colspan="2">1. The firm should identify the industry value chain and then assign costs, revenues and assets to value activities.
2. Diagnose the cost drivers regulating each value activity.
3. Develop sustainable cost advantage either by controlling cost drivers better than competitors or by reconfiguring the chain value.</td></tr>
<tr><td>Industry Value Chain</td><td colspan="2">The industry value chain starts with the value-creating processes of suppliers, who provide the basic raw materials and components. It continues with the value creating processes of different classes of buyers or end-use consumers, and culminates in the disposal and recycling of materials.</td></tr>
<tr><td rowspan="4">Competitive Advantage</td><td>Meaning</td><td>Competitive advantage for a company means not just matching or surpassing their competitors, but discovering what the customers want and then profitably satisfying, and even exceeding, their expectations. Competitive advantage with regard to products and services can be achieved through low cost advantage and/or differentiation advantage.</td></tr>
<tr><td>Low Cost Advantage</td><td>Low Cost Advantage means offering equivalent customer value for a lower price. Relative Cost Advantage enables a business to do one of the two things ; price its product or services lower than its competitors' in order to gain market share and still maintain current profitability; or match with the price of competing products or services and increase its profitability</td></tr>
<tr><td>Differentiation Advantage</td><td>Differentiation Advantage means offering better customer value for an equivalent price</td></tr>
<tr><td colspan="2">Steps: To assess Competitive Advantage following Steps are required:</td></tr>
<tr><td></td><td>(i) Internal Cost Analysis</td><td>To determine the sources of profitability and the relative cost positions of internal value-creating processes, Steps involved in Internal Cost Analysis are:
1. Identify the firm's value-creating processes
2. Determine the portion of the total cost of the product or service attributable to each value creating process
3. Identify the cost drivers for each value-creating process</td></tr>
</table>

		4. Identify the links between processes 5. Evaluate the opportunities for achieving relative cost advantage
	(ii) Internal Differentiation Analysis	To understand the sources of differentiation (including the cost) within internal value-creating processes; Steps involved in Internal Differentiation Analysis are: 1. Identify the customers' value-creating processes 2. Evaluate differentiation strategies for enhancing customer value 3. Determine the best sustainable differentiation strategies
	(iii) Vertical Linkage Analysis	to understand the relationships and associated costs among external suppliers and customers in order to maximize the value delivered to customers and to minimize cost. Vertical linkage analysis is a much broader application of internal cost and differentiation analysis that includes all upstream and downstream value-creating processes throughout the industry. Vertical linkage analysis considers all links from the source of raw materials to the disposal and/or recycling of the product. Vertical linkage can reveal which activities are the most (and least) critical to competitive advantage (or disadvantage). Steps involved in Vertical Linkage Analysis are: 1. Identify the industry's value chain and assign costs, revenues and assets to value creating processes 2. Diagnose the cost drivers for each value-creating process 3. Evaluate the opportunities for sustainable competitive advantage These types of analysis are not mutually exclusive
Primary Activities	Primary activities are directly involved in transforming inputs into outputs and delivery and after-sales support to output. In other words they include: (a) material handling and warehousing (b) transforming inputs into final product (c) order processing and distribution (d) communication, pricing and channel management, and (e) installation, repair and parts replacement.	
Support Activities	Support activities are the activities which support primary activities. They are handled by the organization's staff functions and include the following: 1. **Procurement** – purchasing of raw materials, supplies and other consumable items as well as assets. 2. **Technology Development** – know-how, procedures and technological inputs needed in every value chain activity. 3. **Human resource management** – selection, promotion and placement, appraisal, rewards; management development; and labour/employee relations.	

<table>
<tr><td></td><td colspan="2">Firm infrastructure—general management, planning, finance, accounting, legal, government affairs and quality management.</td></tr>
<tr><td>Role of The Management Accountant</td><td colspan="2">The management accountant in the past were considered an expert on cost analysis; cost estimation; cost behaviour; standard costing; profitability analysis by product, customer or distribution channel; profit variance analysis; and financial analysis. Today, management accountants are expected to make use of activity-based costing, benchmarking, re-engineering, target costing, life-cycle costing, economic value analysis, total quality management and value chain analysis for decision making.

Value chain analysis requires a team effort. Management accountants of today has to collaborate with engineering, production, marketing, distribution and service professionals to focus on the strengths, weaknesses, opportunities and threats identified in the value chain analysis results.

By championing the use of value chain analysis, the management accountant enhances the firm's value and demonstrates the value of the finance staff to the firm's growth and survival.</td></tr>
<tr><td rowspan="5">National Competitive Advantage</td><td colspan="2">Finding innovative ways to perform value-creating activities helps firms to improve their overall performance and achieve competitive advantage: Global competition, cites following four major factors that influences national competitive advantage:</td></tr>
<tr><td>Factor Conditions</td><td>The nation's position in factors of production, such as skilled labour or infrastructure, necessary to compete in a given industry</td></tr>
<tr><td>Demand Conditions</td><td>The nature of domestic demand for the industry's product or service</td></tr>
<tr><td>Related and Supporting Industries</td><td>The presence or absence in the nation of supplier industries and related industries that are internationally competitive</td></tr>
<tr><td>Firm Strategy, Structure and Rivalry</td><td>The conditions in the nation governing how companies are created, organised and managed and the nature of domestic rivalry. Geographic scope can allow firms to gain substantial competitive advantages by sharing or co-ordinating similar value activities in different places.</td></tr>
</table>

2.0 DISTINCTION BETWEEN 'TRADITIONAL MANAGEMENT ACCOUNTING' AND 'VALUE CHAIN ANALYSIS

Traditional management accounting focuses on internal information. It often places excessive emphasis on manufacturing costs. It also assumes that cost reduction must be found in the "value-added" process i.e. selling price less the cost of raw material. The value chain analysis approach encompasses external and internal data, uses appropriate cost drivers for all major value-creating processes, exploits linkages throughout the value chain, and provides continuous monitoring of a firm's strategic competitive advantages.

Basic of Comparison	*Traditional Management Accounting*	*Value Chain Analysis in the Strategic Framework*
Focus	It focuses on internal information	It focuses on external informations.
Perspective	Value Added	Entire set of linked activities from suppliers to end-use customers
Cost Driver Concept	3. It applies Single cost driver (cost is function of volume)at the overall firm level (cost-volume-profit analysis)	3.It applies Multiple cost drivers-Structural drivers (e.g. scale, scope, experience, technology and complexity)&Executional Drivers (e.g. participative management and plant layout) A set of unique cost drivers for each value activity
Cost Containment	"It assumes that cost reduction must be found in the value added process	It views cost containment as a function of the cost drivers regulating each value activity. It exploits linkages throughout the value chain i.e. within firm, with suppliers and customers.
Insights for Strategic Decisions	Some What Limited	It Identifies cost drivers at the individualactivity level, and develop cost/ differentiation advantage either by controlling those drivers better than competitors or by reconfiguring the value chain

3.0 THREE STRATEGIC FRAMEWORKS FOR VALUE CHAIN ANALYSIS

Value chain analysis requires a strategic framework or focus for organising internal and external information, for analysing information, and for summarising findings and recommendations. Because value chain analysis is still evolving, no uniform practices have yet been established. However, borrowing recent concepts from strategists and organization experts, three useful strategic frameworks for value chain analysis are :

1. Industry Structure Analysis	Michael Porter developed a five factors model as a way to organise information about an industry structure to evaluate its potential attractiveness. Under this model, the profitability of an industry or market - measured by the long-term return on investment of the average firm - depends largely on five factors that influence profitability **1. Bargaining power of buyers** **2. Bargaining power of suppliers** **3. Threat of substitute products or services** **4. Threat of new entrants** **5. Intensity of competition**
2. Core Competencies Analysis	Organisations need to be viewed not only as a portfolio of products or services, but also as a portfolio of core competencies. Core competencies are created by superior integration of technological,

	physical and human resources. They represent distinctive skills as well as intangible, invisible, intellectual assets and cultural capabilities. Cultural capabilities refer to the ability to manage change, the ability to learn and teamworking. Organisations should be viewed as a bundle of a few core competencies, each supported by several individual skills. They are the lingua franca that allows managers to translate insights and experience from one business setting into another. Core competence-based diversification reduces risk and investment and increases the opportunities for transferring learning and best practice across business units. For instance, Microsoft's only factory asset is its human imagination. This company has excelled in inventing new ways of using information technology for a wide variety of end users. A core competence is identified by the following tests: — Can it be leveraged? - does it provide potential access to a wide variety of markets? — Does it enhance customer value? - does it make a significant contribution to the perceived customer benefits of the end product? — Can it be imitated? - does it reduce the threat of imitation by competitors? Applying the value chain approach to core competencies for competitive advantage includes the following **Four Steps:** 1. ***Validate core competencies in current businesses*** 2. ***Export or leverage competencies to the value chains of other existing businesses*** 3. ***Use core competencies to reconfigure the value chains of existing businesses*** 4. ***Use core competencies to create new value chains***
3. Segmentation Analysis	If the nature and intensity of Porter's five forces or the core competencies vary for various segments of an industry, then the structural characteristics of different industry segments need to be examined. This analysis will reveal the competitive advantages or disadvantages of different segments. A firm may use this information to decide to exit the segment, to enter a segment, reconfigure one or more segments, or embark on cost reduction/ differentiation programs. Using the value chain approach for segmentation analysis, Grant (1991) recommended **five Steps:** 1. ***Identify segmentation variables and categories*** 2. ***Construct a segmentation matrix*** 3. ***Analyse segment attractiveness*** 4. ***Identify key success factors for each segment*** 5. ***Analyse attractiveness of broad versus narrow segment scope***

4.0 LIMITATIONS OF VALUE CHAIN ANALYSIS

Value chain analysis is neither an exact science nor it is easy. It is more "art" than preparing precise accounting reports. There are several limitations to the implementation and interpretation of value chain analysis.

1. **the internal data on costs, revenues and assets used for value chain analysis are derived from one period's financial information.** For longterm strategic decision-making,

changes in cost structures, market prices and capital investments from one period to the next may alter the implications of value chain analysis. Organisations, should ensure that the value chain analysis is valid for future periods.

Otherwise, the value chain analysis must be repeated under new conditions. Identifying stages in an industry's value chain is limited by the ability to locate at least one firm that participates in a specific stage. Breaking a value stage into two or more stages when an outside firm does not compete in these stages is strictly judgement.

2. **It is difficult to find the çosts, revenues and assets for each value chain activity** There is much experimentation underway that may provide better approaches. Having at least one firm operate in each value chain activity helps to identify external prices for goods and services transferred between value chains. For intermediate products or services with no external or competitive market information, transfer prices must be estimated on the basis of the best information available. Isolating cost drivers for each value-creating activity, identifying value chain linkages across activities, and computing supplier and customer profit margins present serious challenges.

3. **The use of full cost assumes that the full capacity of the value chain activity's facilities is used to derive the costs.** Plant and manufacturing personnel and vendors of equipment are good sources for capacity information. They can also be helpful in estimating the current or replacement cost of the assets. Independent companies, for valuation services for assets must exist.

   Despite the calculational difficulties, experience indicates that performing value chain analysis can yield firms invaluable information for their competitive situation, cost structure, and linkages with suppliers and customers.

5.0 ORGANISATIONAL AND MANAGERIAL ACCOUNTING CHALLENGES

1. The most significant challenge for senior management and management accountants is to recognise that the traditional, functional, internally oriented information system is inadequate for the firm engaged in global competition.
2. Another challenge for management accountants is to bring the importance of customer value to the forefront of managements strategic thinking. For many managers and firms, this requires a great deal of education and awareness. Management accountants should take the initiative to bring the value chain message to major players in the firm. Seminars, articles, value chain examples and company-specific applications are useful to illustrate the advantages of value chain analysis.
3. Although value chain analysis requires expertise in internal operations and information, it demands a great deal of external information. Management accountants must seek relevant financial and non-financial information from sources outside the organisation. Management accountants must integrate databases and potential sources of timely information on competitive forces confronting the business. This calls for innovation and creativity in gathering and analysing information for management decisions.

   Designing internal and external information systems to assist managers in planning, monitoring and improving value-creating processes is another challenge facing management accountants. Information technology is improving daily but existing information systems are slow to change. Management accountants should solicit support from all senior managers for allocating resources to develop and improve value chain-oriented information systems.
4. Value chain analysis requires the cooperation of all managers involved in value chain processes, including engineers, designers, production managers, marketing managers and distribution managers. Leadership from the CEO is vital to successful cooperation of managers. The management accountant should ensure that the CEO is committed to value chain analysis and the organisational changes necessary for its successful implementation. For many service companies, Porter's value chain model emphasising manufacturing firms may appear inappropriate. However, every organisation (banks, hospitals,

airlines,professional firms) has a variety of primary and support value-creating activities to which value chain analysis applies. For example, a publishing company might have the following primary activities; information acquisition, editorial, production, distribution, sales and service. Support activities include new product and business development, technology assessment and development, human resource management and firm infrastructure. If strategy is seen as the pursuit of competitive advantage, the link between the formulation of service strategy and operational service delivery is vital.

21 Miscellaneous Advanced Issues in Costing

LEARNING OBJECTIVES

After studying this chapter, you should be able to understand:

- Manufacturing Resources Planning (MRP)
- Manufacturing Resources Planning (MRP- II)
- Enterprise Resource Planning
- Business Process Re-engineering [BPR]
- Value Engineering [Value Analysis]
- Computer-aided Manufacturing
- Synchronous Manufacturing
- Benchmarking
- Down Sizing
- Tear-down Analysis [Reverse Engineering]
- Shut Down & Divestment

1.0 MANUFACTURING RESOURCES PLANNING (MRP)

Meaning	MRP is a production scheduling system which specifies: 1. When what quantity of finished products should be produced on the basis of **The Master Production Schedule.** 2. What quantity of sub-assemblies, components and materials is required for each finished product as per **The Bill of Material File.** **3.** **Inventory** of ub-assemblies, components and materials in hand as per **The Inventory File.** **4.** The sequence of operations required to manufacture components, sub-assemblies and finished products as per **The Routing File.** **5.** The production time of sub-assemblies and components produced internally and lead times for externally acquired items as per**The Master Parts File.**
Aims	1. To determine for final products (what should be produced and at what time). 2. To ascertain the required units of production of sub-assemblies. 3. To determine the requirement for materials based on an up-to-date bill of materials file (BOM). 4. To compute inventories of Raw Material, WIP & Finished products, Batch Sizes and manufacturing and packaging lead times.

	5. To Control inventory by ordering bought-in components and raw materials in relation to the orders received or forecast rather than the more usual practice of ordering from stock-level indicators.
Benefits	Detailed forecast of the inventory position is highlighted period by period.
Data requirements	Data requirements to operate material requirement Planning system are as follows: 1. **The Master Production Schedule:** This schedule specifies the quantity of each finished unit of products to be produced, and the time at which each unit will be required. 2. **The Bill of Material File:** The bill of material file specifies the sub-assemblies, components and materials required for each finished product. 3. **The Inventory File:** This file maintains details of items in hand for each sub-assemblies, components and materials required for each finished products. 4. **The Routing File:** This file specifies the sequence of operations required to manufacture components, sub-assemblies and finished products. 5. **The Master Parts File:** This file contains information on the production time of subassemblies and components produced internally and lead times for externally acquired items.
Method of Operation	A material requirements planning (MRP) system is a computer based inventory information system which is used to plan and control raw material and component parts inventories. Like all computer-based information system, MRP systems can be divided into following: 1. Pre-requisite information 2. System input 3. System processing. 4. System output
Pre-requisite Information and System Input	1. **The Master Production Schedule (MPS)** File states the production goal, generally for a week time, in terms of desired units of production. MRP system first focuses on the forecasted units of production and timing of finished goods demand and the determines the demand for materials, components and sub-assemblies at each stages of production. This makes MRP a push system in which once the scheduled production starts, the output of each department is pushed through the system to the next department for processing or into inventory to be retrieved later. 2. **The Bill of Materials (BOM)** File contains information about how the production of the finished goods is undertaken. A bill of material structure is used: (a) To assess all of the raw materials and component parts required to complete a product and (b) to describe the multiple levels of assembly or manufacturing necessary to complete a unit of finished product. 3. **The Inventory Records Files of the MRP** system defines current levels of finished goods, raw materials, and component parts inventory at the beginning of some planning period. During the planning period, the organization may receive units of raw materials, components parts, sub-assemblies, and even finished goods inventory from suppliers,

	vendors, and subcontractors. These planned inventory receipts and delivery lead times are included in the inventory records file so that their addition can be appropriately considered in the time bucket of their arrival.
Pre-requisites for successful operation	1. **Strict adherence to the Schedule:** The successful operation of MRP system requires a strict adherence to the latest production and purchasing schedules. Workers must be educated to understand the importance of schedule adherence, and controls should be in place to ensure this adherence. 2. **Accurate Data Base:** Data accuracy is vital to the system. If a plan is based on inaccurate data it may be impossible to adhere to the schedule. For example, if the bill of materials file is not updated to reflect any changes in product composition it will be impossible to adhere to the schedule.

2.0 MANUFACTURING RESOURCES PLANNING (MRP- II)

Meaning	When the scope of MRP-1 is developed further which includes 1. Planning of raw material 2. Planning of component & sub- assemblies 3. Compute the other resources e.g. machine or labour capacity 4. to create a full integrated plan for management, then it is known as Manufacturing resources planning (MRP - 2) MRPII (also written MRP-2) adds the MRP schedule into a capacity planning system and then builds the information into a production schedule. It is also seen as a link between strategic planning and manufacturing control.
Sequence of Events	From that document, 1. A manufacturing plan is developed based upon inputs from purchasing & production. 2. Adjustments may be necessary to allow for production rates. 3. Possible inventory levels in seasonal trades & the size of the workforce. 4. The manufacturing plan leads into a detailed master production schedule which is akin to the original philosophy of MRP already outlined. 5. If correctly applied, MRPII provides a common data base for the different function units such as manufacturing, purchasing and finance within a firm.

3.0 ENTERPRISE RESOURCE PLANNING

Meaning	Enterprise resource planning (ERP) software is a single integrated software that runs off a single database which attempts to integrate all departments and functions (like Manufacturing, Selling and Distribution, Payables, Receivables, Inventory etc.) across the enterprise into a single computer system so that various departments can more easily &quickly share information and communicate with each other.
Benefits of ERP	1. ERP bridges the information gap across the organization. 2. Better Purchase Management

	3. Better Production Management (Automatic control of quality, improved production planning, productivity enhancements). 4. Better inventory Management 5. Better Sales Management 6. Better Distribution Management 7. Better After Sales Service Management 8. Better Finance Management 9. E-commerce 10. Quick response to change in market condition. 11. Competitive edge by improving business process 12. It allows automatic induction of latest technologies like Electronic Fund Transfer (EFT), Electronic Data Interchange (EDI), Internet, Intranet, Video Conferencing, E-commerce etc. 13. ERP eliminates most business problems like material shortage, productivity enhancements, customer service, cash management etc. 14. It provides business intelligence tools.

4.0 BUSINESS PROCESS RE-ENGINEERING [BPR]

Meaning	1. Business Process Re-engineering involves redesigning the business processes by improving the current methods of performing business processes and introducing new methods of performing business processes by focusing on (a) simplification, (b) cost reduction, (c) improved quality and (d) enhanced customer satisfaction 2. BPR involves radical and dramatic changes in process by abandoning current practices and reinventing completely new methods of performing business processes.
Features	A Business Process Re-engineering consists of a collection of activities that are linked together in a coordinated & sequential manner to achieve goal & objective.
Aim	The aim of business process re-engineering is to improve the key business process in an organization by focusing on (a) simplification, (b) cost reduction, (c) improved quality and (d) enhanced customer satisfaction
Example	***Example 1:*** Material handling activity may consist of: (a) scheduling production, (b) storing materials, (c) processing purchase orders, (d) inspecting materials and (e) paying suppliers Material handling activity can be re-engineered into—

	Sending production schedule directly to nominated suppliers and entering into contractual agreements to deliver the materials in accordance with production schedule along with quality check before delivery. Thus, elimination of non-value activities like (storing, purchasing and inspecting activities) ***Example 2:*** Move from Traditional plant layout to Just in time product layout

5.0 VALUE ENGINEERING [VALUE ANALYSIS]

Meaning	**Value Engineering** involves (i) Identifying improved product designs that reduces the product's costs without sacrificing functionality/quality(ii) Eliminating unnecessary Non-Value added activities that increase the product's cost and for which customers are not prepared to pay extra. 1. **Value Engineering** involves searching for opportunities to modify the design of each component or part of a product to reduce cost, but without reducing functionality or quality of the product. 2. It is a systematic interdisciplinary examination of factors affecting the cost of a product or service in order to devise means of achieving the specified purpose at the required standard quality and reliability at target cost. 3. It requires the use of functional analysis. 4. It involves decomposing the product into its many elements or attributes.
Aim	The aim of value engineering is to achieve the assigned target cost by - (i) Identifying improved product designs that reduced the product's costs without sacrificing functionality. (ii) Eliminating unnecessary Non-Value added activities that increase the product's cost and for which customers are not prepared to pay extra.
Example	In case of automobiles, there are many functions consisting of style, comfort, reliability, quality, operability and many others.
Process	1. A value for each element is determined which reflects the amount the customer is prepared to pay. 2. The total of values of each function gives the estimated selling price from which the target profit is deducted to arrive at target cost. 3. The cost of each function of a product is compared with the benefits perceived by the customers. 4. If the cost exceeds the benefit to customer, then the function should be eliminated, modified to reduce its costs or enhanced in terms of value so that value exceeds the cost. 5. Also by focusing on the product's functions, the design team will often consider components that perform same function in other products, thereby using standard components and reducing costs.
Issues that are dealt with during a Value Engineering Review	1. **Can we eliminate functions from the production process?** This involves a detailed review of the entire manufacturing process to see if there are any steps, such as interim quality reviews, that add no value to the product. By eliminating them, one can take their associated direct or overhead costs out of the product cost. However, these functions

were originally put in for a reason, so the engineering team must be careful to develop work-around steps that eliminate the need for the original functions.

2. **Can we eliminate some durability or reliability?** It is possible to design an excessive degree of sturdiness into a product. For example, a vacuum cleaner can be designed to withstand a 1-ton impact, although there is only the most vanishing chance that such an impact will ever occur; designing it to withstand an impact of 100 pounds may account for 99.999% of all probable impacts, while also eliminating a great deal of structural material from the design. However, this concept can be taken too far, resulting in a visible reduction in durability or reliability, so any designs that have had their structural integrity reduced must be thoroughly tested to ensure that they meet all design standards.
3. **Can we minimize the design?** This involves the creation of a design that uses fewer parts or has fewer features. This approach is based on the assumption that a minimal design is easier to manufacture and assemble. Also, with fewer parts to purchase, less procurement overhead is associated with the product. However, reducing a product to extremes, perhaps from dozens of components to just a few molded or prefabricated arts, can result in excessively high costs for these few remaining parts, since they may be so complex or custom made in nature that it would be less expensive to settle for a few extra standard parts that are more easily and cheaply obtained.
4. **Can we design the product better for the manufacturing process?** Also known as design for manufacture and assembly (DFMA), this involves the creation of a product design that can be created in only a specific manner. For example, a toner cartridge for a laser printer is designed so that it can be successfully inserted into the printer only when the sides of the cartridge are correctly aligned with the printer opening; all other attempts to insert the cartridge will fail. When used for the assembly of an entire product, this approach ensures that a product is not incorrectly manufactured or assembled, which would call for a costly disassembly or (even worse) product recalls from customers who have already received defective goods.
5. **Can we substitute parts?** This approach encourages the search for less expensive components or materials that can replace more expensive parts currently used in a product design. It is becoming an increasingly valid approach since new materials are being developed every year. However, sometimes the use of a different material impacts the types of materials that can be used elsewhere in the product, which may result in cost increases in these other areas, for a net increase in costs. Thus, any parts substitution must be accompanied by a review of related changes elsewhere in the design. This step is also known as component parts analysis and involves one extra activity-tracking the intentions of suppliers to continue producing parts in the future; if parts will not be available, they must be eliminated from the product design.
6. **Can we combine steps?** A detailed review of all the processes associated with a product sometimes reveals that some steps can be consolidated, which may mean that one can be eliminated (as noted earlier) or that several can be accomplished by one person, rather than having people in widely disparate parts of the production process

perform them. This is also known as process centering. By combining steps in this manner, we can eliminate some of the transfer and queue time from the production process, which in turn reduces the chance that parts will be damaged during these transfers.

7. **Is there a better way?** Though this step sounds rather vague, it really strikes at the core of the cost reduction issue-the other value engineering steps previously mentioned focus on incremental improvements to the existing design or production process, whereas this one is a more general attempt to start from scratch and build a new product or process that is not based in any way on preexisting ideas. Improvements resulting from this step lend to have the largest favourable impact on cost reductions but can also be the most difficult for the organization to adopt, especially if it has used other designs or systems for the production of earlier models. Another approach to value engineering is to call on the services of a company's suppliers to assist in the cost reduction effort. These organizations are particularly suited to contribute information concerning enhanced types of technology of materials, since they may specialize in areas that a company has no information about. They may have also conducted extensive value engineering for the components they manufacture, resulting in advanced designs that a company may be able to incorporate into its new products. Suppliers may have also redesigned their production processes, or can be assisted by a company's engineers in doing so, producing cost reductions or decreased production waste that can be translated into lower component costs for the company. A mix of all the value engineering steps noted above must be applied to each product design to ensure that the maximum permissible cost is safely reached. Also, even if a minimal amount of value engineering is needed to reach a cost goal, one should conduct the full range of value engineering analysis anyway, since this can result in further cost reductions that improve the margin of the product or allow management the option of reducing the product's price, thereby creating a problem for competitors who sell higher-priced products. Another term mentioned in the earlier explanation of the target costing process is "kaizen costing." This is a Japanese term for a number of cost reduction steps that can be used subsequent to issuing a new product design to the factory floor. Some of the activities in the kaizen costing methodology include the elimination of waste in the production, assembly, and distribution processes, as well as the elimination of work steps in any of these areas. Though these points are also covered in the value engineering phase of target costing, the initial value engineering may not uncover all possible cost savings. Thus, kaizen costing is really designed to repeat many of the value engineering steps for as long as a product is produced, constantly refining the process and thereby stripping out extra costs. The cost reductions resulting from kaizen costing are much smaller than those achieved with value engineering but are still worth the effort since competitive pressures are likely to force down the price of a product over time, and any possible cost savings allow a company to still attain its targeted profit margins while continuing to reduce cost.

Illustration 1

ABC electronics makes audio player model "AB 100". It has 80 components. ABC sells 10,000 units each month at ₹ 3,000 per unit. The cost of manufacturing is ₹ 2,000 per unit or ₹ 200 lakh per month for the production of 10,000 units. Monthly manufacturing costs incurred are as follows:

	(₹ Lakhs)
Direct material costs	100.00
Direct manufacturing labour costs	20.00
Machining costs	20.00
Testing costs	25.00
Rework costs	15.00
Ordering costs	0.20
Engineering costs	19.80
	200.00

Labour is paid on piece rate basis, therefore, ABC corasiders direct manufacturing labour cost as variable cost. The following additional information is available for "AB 100":

1. ***Testing and inspection time per unit is 2 hours.***
2. ***10 per cent of "AB 100" manufactured are reworked.***
3. ***It currently takes 1 hour to manufacture each unit of "AB 100".***
4. ***ABC places two orders per month for each component. Each component is supplied by a different supplier.***

ABC has identifies activity cost pools and cost drivers for each activity. The cost per unit of the cost driver for each activity cost pool is as follows:

Manufacturing Activity	*Description of Activity*	*Cost Driver*	*Cost per unit of Cost driver*
1. Machining Costs	Machining components	Mach. Hours	₹ 200
2. Testing costs	Testing components and finished products (each hours unit of AB 100 is tested individually)	Capacity Testing	₹ 125
3. Rework costs	Correcting and fixing errors and defects	Units of AB100 reworked	₹ 1,500 per unit
4. Ordering Cost	Ordering of components	No. of orders	₹ 125 per order
5. Eng. Costs	Designing & managing of products and Processes hour.	Engineering hours	₹ 1,980 per engineering

Over long-run horizon, each of the overhead costs described above vary with chosen cost drivers. In response to competitive pressure ABC must reduce the price of its product to ₹ 2,600 and to reduce the cost by ai least ₹ 400 per unit. ABC does not anticipate increase in sales due to price "reduction. However if it does not be able to minimum the current sales level.

Cost reduction on the existing model is almost impossible. Therefore ABC has decided to replace AB 100 by a new model 'AB 200' which is a modified version of AB 100. The expected effect of design modifications is as follows:

1. ***The number of component will be reduced to 50.***
2. ***Direct material costs to be lower by ₹ 200 per unit.***
3. ***Direct manufacturing labour cots to be lower by ₹ 20 per unit.***
4. ***Machining time required to be lower by 20 per cent.***
5. ***Testing time required to be lower by 20 per cent.***
6. ***Rework to decline to 5 per cent.***
7. ***Machining capacity and engineering hours capacity to remain the same.***

ABC currently outsourcers the rework on defective units.

Required:

(a) Compare the manufacturing cost per unit of 'AB 100; and 'AB 200'.

(b) Determine the immediate effect of design change and pricing decision on the operating income of ABC.

Ignore income tax. Assume that the cost per unit of each cost driver for 'AB 100' continues to apply to 'AB 200'.

Solution

(a) STATEMENT SHOWING THE MANUFACTURING COST

Particulars	*Present AB-100* ₹	*AB-200* ₹
Material (₹ 1,00,00,000/10,000)	1,000	800
Labour	(20,00,000/10,000)200	180
Machining cost	(20,00,000/10,000)200	160
Testing cost:	250	200
Rework cost	150	75
Ordering cost	2	1.25
Eng. cost	198	I98
	2,000	1,614.25

Working Note (i)

Particulars	*Present*	*Revised*
	1 Hr × 10,000 = 10,000 hours	0.8 Hr × 10,000 = 8,000 Hours
Labour	10,000 Hr × 200 = 2,00,000/10,000 = ₹ 200	8000 Hr × 200 16,00,000/10,000=160

Working Note (ii)

Particulars	*Present*	*Revised*
Testing	2 Hr × 10,000 × 125/10,000 = ₹ 250	1.6 × 10,000 × 125/10,000 = ₹ 200
Rework	1,000 defective × ₹ 1500 = ₹ 15,00,000	(10,000 x 5%) x ₹ 1500 = ₹ 7,50,000
4. Ordering cost	160 orders × 125/10,000 = ₹ 2	100 order x 125/10,000 = ₹ 1.25

(b) The following factors may have immediate effect.

(i) Material Cost (ii) Labour Cost and (iii) Ordering cost.

Due to reduction of component and due to a learning procedure following factors may not have immediate effect:

(i) Machine cost: (reduction of setting of time on production time)
(ii) Testing cost: (reduction of testing time applicationof TOM system)
(iii) Rework cost: (with application preventive, maintenance system)

6.0 COMPUTER-AIDED MANUFACTURING

Meaning	Computer–Aided Manufacturing (CAM) involves carrying out the manufacturing process by a range of machinery which are linked together with a single integrated computer software with the help of Computer Numerical Control (CNC) and robotics with a view to achieve the goal of high speed & accuracy.CNC machines are programmable machine tools.
Elements	Maximum elements of CAM are Computer Numerical Control (CNC) and robotics. CNC machines are programmable machine tools. These are capable of performing a number of machining tasks, e.g. cutting, grinding, moulding, bending etc.
How works	1. A program stores all the existing manufacturing activities and set-up instructions for a particular machine or group of machines 2. Programme provides facility of changing its configuration in a matter of seconds via the keyboard; changes to existing configurations and new configurations are easily accommodated.
Benefits	1. CNC offers great flexibility, and 2. CNC reduces set-up times. 3. CNC machines are able to repeat the same operation continuously in identical manner, with high accuracy level.
Example	The car producer found that the time taken to completely retool car body panel jigs in their intelligent body assembly system (IBAS) fell from 12 months to less than 3 months by reprogramming the process machinery by computer and using computerized jig robots.

7.0 SYNCHRONOUS MANUFACTURING

Meaning	The concept of 'synchronous manufacturing' was started in 1984. It has been defined as an all-encompassing manufacturing management philosophy that includes a consistent set of principles, procedures, and techniques where every action is evaluated in terms of the common global goal of the organisation to focus on those areas of operations where there exist potential global improvements
Seven Principles	A set of seven 'principles' are associated with synchronous manufacturing: 1. Do not focus on balance idle capacities; focus on synchronizing the production flow. 2. The marginal value of time at a bottleneck resource is equal to the throughput rate of the products processed by the bottleneck. 3. The marginal value of time at a non-bottleneck resource is negligible. 4. The level of tilization of a non-bottleneck resource is controlled by other constraints within the system. 5. Resources must be utilized, not simply activated. 6. A transfer batch may not, and many times should not, be equal to the process batch. 7. A process batch should be variable both along its route and over time.

	According to synchronous manufacturing principles 2 and 3, the return on improvements at a bottleneck resource is very high. But the return on improvement made at non-bottlenecks is marginal at best.
Focus	The synchronous manufacturing philosophy required managers to focus on those areas of operations where there exist potential global improvements.

8.0 BENCHMARKING

Meaning	Benchmarking is the process of identifying and learning from the best practices anywhere in the world so as to find out how the product, service or activity can be improved and ensure that the improvements are implemented.
Objective	The objective is to find out how the product, service or activity can be improved and ensure that the improvements are implemented.
Benefit	It is a powerful tool for continuous improvement in performance.
Stages in Process of Benchmarking	The process of benchmarking requires a Company to identify the areas i.e. processes, activity etc. which are central to its business and then selects the **top-performing companies in** those areas. **Stage 1: Planning** (a) Determining the benchmarking goal statement. (b) Identification of best practice. (c) Establishment of the benchmarking or process improvement team. (d) Defining the relevant benchmarking measurement. **Stage 2: Collection of data and information** **Stage 3: Analysis of findings based on data collected in stage 2.** **Stage 4: Formulation and implementation of recommendations** **Stage 5: Constant monitoring and reviewing**
Types of Bench Marking	1. **Competitive benchmarking:** It involves the comparison of competitors products, processes and business results with own. 2. **Strategic benchmarking:** It is similar to the process benchmarking in nature but differs in its scope and depth. 3. **Global benchmarking:** It is a benchmarking through which distinction in international culture, business processes and trade practices across companies are bridged and their ramification for business process improvement are understood and utilized. 4. **Process benchmarking:** It involves the comparison of an organisation critical business processes and operations against best practice organization that performs similar work or deliver similar services 5. **Functional Benchmarking or Generic Benchmarking:** This type of benchmarking is used when organizations look to benchmark with partners drawn from different business sectors or areas of activity to find ways of improving similar functions or work processes. 6. **Internal Benchmarking:** It involves seeking partners from within the same organization, for example, from business units located in different areas.

	7. **External Benchmarking:** It involves seeking help of outside organisations that are known to be best in class. External benchmarking provides opportunities of learning from those who are at the leading edge, although it must be remembered that not every best practice solution can be transferred to others.
Benchmarking Code of Conduct	To contribute to efficient, effective and ethical bench marking, individuals agree for themselves and their organisation to be abided by the following principles for the benchmarking with other organisations. Suggested benchmarking code of conduct: 1. Principle of legality 2. Principle of exchange 3. Principle of confidentiality 4. Principle of use 5. Principle of first party contact 6. Principle of third party contact 7. Principle of preparation

Illustration 2

Explain briefly stages involved in the process of Bench marking.

Solution

Process of Benchmarking: The process of benchmarking requires a Company to identify the areas i.e. processes, activity etc. which are central to its business and then selects the top-performing companies in those areas.

The benchmarking process is comprised of following stages. These stages are:

Stage 1. Planning:

(i) **Determination of benchmarking goal statement:** This requires identification of areas to be benchmarked. In practice, one should start with the identification of those areas which have to be really good to be really successful.

(ii) **Identification of best performance:** Once the benchmarked goal statement are defined, the step is seeking the best of the breed of best of the best.

(iii) **Establishment of the benchmarking or process improvement team:** Ideally this should include the persons who are most knowledgeable about the internal operations and will be directly affected by changes due to benchmarking.

(iv) **Defining the relevant benchmarking measurement:** Relevant measures will not include the measures used by the organisation today but they will be refined measures that comprehend the true performance differences.

Stage 2. Collection of data and information:

The data gathering for benchmarking could be done through national/international clearing houses, mail surveys, suppliers, company visits, telephone, interviews etc. In recent years national and international clearing houses have been set up.

Stage 3. Analyzing the findings as per Stage (2) requires following:

1. Review the findings and produce tables, charts and graphs to support the analysts.
2. Identify gaps in performance between our organization and better performers.
3. Seek explanations for the gaps in performance. The performance gaps can be positive, negative or zero.

4. Ensure that comparisons are meaningful and credible.
5. Communicate the findings to those who are affected.
6. Identify realistic opportunities for improvements.

Stage 4. Making Recommendations requires –

(i) Deciding the feasibility of making the improvements in the light of the conditions that apply within own organisation.
(ii) Agreement of the improvements that are likely to be feasible.
(iii) Producing a report on the Benchmarking in which the recommendations are included.
(iv) Obtaining the support of key stakeholder groups for making the changes needed.
(v) Developing action plan(s) for implementation.

Stage 5. Monitoring and Reviewing which involves –

1. Evaluating the benchmarking process undertaken and the results of the improvements against objectives and success criteria plus overall efficiency and effectiveness.
2. Documenting the lessons learnt and make them available to others.
3. Periodically re-considering the benchmarks

Illustration 3

Relevant information with regard to the operation of the sales order department of X Ltd. is as follows.

- ***A team of staff deals with existing customers in respect of problems with orders of with prospective customers enquiring about potential orders.***
- ***The processing of orders requires communication with the production and dispatch functions of the company.***
- ***The nature of the business in such that there's some dispatching of part orders to customers Sales literature is sent out to existing and prospective customers by means of a monthly mail shot.***

The activity malrix below sholvs Lhe budget for ihc siiles order department.

ACTIVITY COST MATRIX-SALES ORDER DEPARTMENT

Cost element	*Total Cost*	*Customer negotiations*	*Processing of Home*	*Orders Export*	*Implemen-ting Dispatches*	*Sales Literature*	*General gdmin*
	₹ '000	₹ '000	₹ '000	₹ '000	₹ '000	₹ '000	₹ '000
Salaries	500	80	160	100	90	20	50
Stores/supplies	90	16	6	8	60		
IT	70	10	30	20	10		
Sundry Costs	80	8	10	6	20	10	26
Total	740	98	216	132	128	90	76
Volume of Activity	2,000 Customers	3,000 Negotiations	5,000 Order	1,200 Orders	11,500 Dispatches		

X Ltd. has decided to acquire additional computer software with internet links in order to improve the effectiveness of the sales order department. The cost to the company of this initiative is estimated at ₹ 2,30,000 pa.

If the proposed changes are implemented. There will be cost and volume changes to activities in the sales order department and it is estimated that the following activity cost matrix will result.

ACTIVITY COST MATRIX-SALES ORDER DEPARTMENT AFTER THE PROPOSED CHANGES

Cost element	*Total Cost*	*Customer negotiations*	*Processing of Home*	*Orders Export*	*Implemen-ting Dispatches*	*Sales Literature*	*General gdmin*
	₹ '000	₹ '000	₹ '000	₹ '000	₹ '000	₹ '000	₹ '000
Salaries	450	72	144	90	81	18	45
Stores/supplies	54	–	16	6	8	24	—
IT	300	40	120	80	40	20	—
Sundry Costs	106	16	11	10	33	10	26
Total	910	128	291	186	162	72	71
Volume of Activity	2,600 Customers	6,000 Negotiations	5,500 Order	2,000 Orders	18,750 Dispatches		

Recent industry average statistics for sales order department activities in business of similar size, customer mix and product mix are as follows.

Particulars	₹
Cost per customer per year	₹ 300
Cost per home order processed	₹ 50
Cost per export order processed	₹ 60
Cost per dispatch	₹ 8
Sales literature cost per customer	₹ 35
Average number of orders per customer per year	4.1
Average number ot dispatches per order	3.3

Solution

STATEMENT OF BENCH MARKING

Particulars	*Present* ₹ *(a)*	*Industry Average* ₹ *(b)*	*Revised* ₹ *(c)*	*Inter firm* ₹ *(a and c)*	*Intra firm* ₹ ₹
Cost per customer	370(7,40,000/2,000)	300	350(9,10,000/2,600)	70 A	20 F
Costperhome	43.2(2,16,000/500)	50	52.9(2,91,000/5,500)	6.8 F	9.7A
order process	110(1,32,000/1,200)	60	93(1,86,000/2,000)	50 A	17 A
Cost per dispatch	11.13(1,28,000/11,500)	8	8.64(1,62,000/18,750)	3.13A	2.49A
Sales literature cost per customer	45(90,000/2,000)	35	27.69(72,000/2,600)	10 A	17.31 A
Av. no. of dispatch per order	1.85(11,500/6,200)	3.3	2.5(18,750/7,500)	1.446F	0.65A
Order per customer	3.1(6,200/200)	4.1	2.88(7,500/2,600)	1.0A	0.22A

9.0 DOWN SIZING

Down sizing means that if any present activity or service does not provide target profit or provide loss, we have the following two options—

Option 1: Either to reduce the present level of activity.
Option 2: Sub-contract the existing activity to outside agency.

10.0 TEAR-DOWN ANALYSIS [REVERSE ENGINEERING]

Meaning	It involves examining competitor's products in order to identify opportunities for product improvement and cost reduction with a view to incorporate relative advantage of competitor's product to the product design.
Objective	The objective is to incorporate relative advantage of competitor's product to the product design.

11.0 SHUT DOWN & DIVESTMENT

11.1 Introduction

Very often it becomes necessary for a firm to temporarily close down the factory due to trade recession with a view to reopening it in the future. In such cases, the decision should be based on the marginal cost analysis. If the products are making a contribution towards fixed expenses or in other words if selling price is above the marginal cost, it is preferable to continue because the losses are minimized. By suspending the manufacture, certain fixed expenses can be avoided and certain extra fixed expenses may be incurred depending up on the nature of the industry, say, for example, extra cost incurred in protecting the machinery. So the decision is based on as to whether the contribution is more than the difference between the fixed expenses incurred in normal operation and the fixed expenses incurred when the plant is shut down. In other words, the shut down point is calculated by using the formula:

11.2 Decision Making in Relation to Shut Down

1. Shut down point = {(Total fixed cost – Shut down costs) ÷ Contribution per unit} *Decision Making in Relation to Shut Down Vs. Continue*

In case of decision rendering closure or shut down we consider the following points:

1. Current profit situation has to be maintained, So by analyzing the proposal of shut down or outsourcing if the current income is reduced then shut down will not be allowed unless the product or factory has reached at the end of its life cycle.
2. In case of outsourcing proposal we can also apply the differential cost concept i.e. saving in cost must be greater than or equal to out-sourcing fees payment. Here saving in cost i.e. cash inflow is computed from the concept of relevant cost i.e. by closing down we are saving variable cost of production, and discretionary fixed cost or shut down cost. This cash inflow further may be classified into two parts:
    1. Saving in variable cost per time period i.e. CIF per annum.
    2. One time cash inflow following shut down i.e. sale of machine, sale of current stock of material etc.

Total CIF or saving following shut down = one time CIF + CIF p.a. × life span of the proposal of outsourcing.

If this total is greater than total outsourcing fees then shutdown will take place other production will be continue.

11.3 Divestment Strategy

Meaning	Divestment involves a strategy of selling off or shedding business operations to divert the resources, so released, for other purposes. Selling off a business segment or product division is one of the frequent forms of divestment strategy. It may also include selling off or giving up the control over a subsidiary where by the wholly owned subsidiaries may be floated as independently quoted companies.

Reason	1. In case of a firm having an opportunity to get more profitable product or segment but have resource constrain, it may selling off it's unprofitable or less profitable division and utilised the recourse so released. Cost Benefit Analysis & Capita Budgeting Method are the useful tool for analysing this type of situation. 2. In case of purchase of new business, it may be found that some of the part of the acquired business is not upto the mark. In such type of situation disposal of the unwanted part of the business is more desirable than hold it. 3. In case where any business segment or product or subsidiary is pull down the profit of the whole organisation, it is better to cut down of that operation of the product or business segment or subsidiary. 4. If managing of the organisation is very constrained, it is good to dispose off the unwanted and undesirable activity of the organisation, which involve large management skill. So that it can concentrated on the core activities of the organisation. 5. In the situation where the firm suffering from loss, selling off or divestment policy is one suitable option to exit in the current position and to go for turn around strategy.

22 Responsibility Accounting

Learning Objectives

After studying this chapter, you should be able to understand:

- Meaning of Responsibility Accounting
- Pre-requisities for Responsibility Accounting
- Advantages of Responsibility Accounting
- Divisional Performance Measurement
- How to measure the Performance of A Division
- Non-Financial Measures of Performance

1.0 MEANING OF RESPONSIBILITY ACCOUNTING

Respnsibility Accounting is a system of accounting under which is:

1. The costs and revenues are accumulated, classified, measured and reported for each responsibility centre (which is under the control of a manager who has direct responsibility for its performance).
2. The performance is evaluated by comparing the actual with those budgeted through Periodic Performance Reports.
3. The variances are analysed as to fix the responsibility and to take the necessary corrective action.

   The basic idea of responsibility accounting is that a manager should be held responsible only for those items over which he can exercise a significant degree of control.

2.0 PRE-REQUISITIES FOR RESPONSIBILITY ACCOUNTING

1. There should be ***clear allocation of authority and responsibility.***
2. There should be ***active participation of managers*** of responsibility centres in the preporation of budgets.
3. There should be ***fixed and practically attainable targets*** of performance.
4. There shoud be a ***system of collecting actual and accurate information*** on timely basis.
5. There should be a ***system of timely evaluation of performance*** through Performance Report.
6. There should be a ***system of taking the necessary corrective action*** (if any) timely.

3.0 ADVANTAGES OF RESPONSIBILITY ACCOUNTING

The main advantages of responsibility accounting are as follows:

1. It facilitates *effective budgeting* through active participation of managers in the preparation of budgets.
2. It facilitates the *effective delegation* of authority through creation of various responsibility centres.
3. It facilitates the *effective evaluation* of performace through prompt and timely performace reports.
4. It faciliates the *principle of management by objective (MBO)* through evaluation of performace on the basis of already set goals.
5. It facilitates the *principles of management by exception (MBE)* by enabling the management to focus on significance matters on the basis of variance analysis.
6. It facilitates the *effective control and decision making* through prompt and timely performance reporting.
7. It *increases the morale* of managers because of:
   (a) active participation in the preparation of budgets
   (b) linkage of rewards to performace
   (c) exclusion of those items which are beyond their control
   (d) autonomy in planning and decision-making of their centres.
8. It facilitates the optimum utilization of organisation's resources (i.e. Capital, Human etc.) by various managers. and thereby improves overall profitability.
9. It facilates the *effective communication* of goals, objectives etc. through budgets to all the managers.
10. It develops an atmosphere of cost-consciousness and profit mindedness.

4.0 DIVISIONAL PERFORMANCE MEASUREMENT

4.1 Meaning and Objective

Divisions are the creation of decentralized organization structure. Divisionalisation is suitable to high diversified companies which produce and sell a wide variety of products over various locations. The main objectives of divisionalisation are:

1. To improve the quality and speed of Decision-making process
2. To make free top management from detailed involvement in day-to day routine operations and to enable them to concentrate on important policy matters (say formulation of strategies)
3. To improve the accountability within the organization
4. To motivate the managers to perform better by linking rewards with performance
5. To improve the morale and job satisfaction of managers by providing autonomy

4.2 Advantages of Divisionalisation

The main advantages of divisionalisation are as follows:

1. It improves the quality and speed of Decision-making process
2. It makes free top management from detailed involvement in day-to day routine operations and to enable them to concentrate on important policy matters (*say formulation of strategies*)
3. It improves the accountability within the organization
4. It motivates the managers to perform better by linking rewards within performance
5. It improves the morale and job satisfaction of managers by providing autonomy

4.3 Dangers of Divisionalisation

The main dangers of divisionalisation are as follows:

1. Managers may focus on improving their own division's performance at the cost of organization as a whole.
2. There may be conflict over transfer pricing matters, allocation of common costs and common assets.
3. There may be lack of co-operation and co-ordination among various divisions.
4. It is more expansive to initiate and maintain divisional organization.

5.0 HOW TO MEASURE THE PERFORMANCE OF A DIVISION

Both financial and non-financial measures are used to measure the performance of division. The main financial measures to measure the performance of a division are as follows:

1. Direct Profit	Direct Profit is defined as the difference between divisional scales and divisional direct costs. Division Direct Profit = Divisional Sales – Divisional Direct costs **Limitation** – Some direct costs which are not controllable by the divisional manager (say division manager's salary) are included.
2. Controllable Profit	Controllable Profit is defined as the difference between divisional sales and divisional controllable costs. Divisional Controllable Profit = Divisional Sales – Divisional Controllable Costs.
3. Contribution Margin	Contribution Margin is defined as the difference between Divisional Sales and Divisional Variable Costs Divisional Contribution Margin = Divisional Sales – Divisional Variable Costs **Limitation** – Some fixed costs which are controllable by divisional manager are also excluded.
4. Net Profit	Net Profit is defined as the difference between Divisional Revenue and Divisional Expenses Divisional Net Profit = Divisional Revenue – Divisional Expenses ***Advantages:*** Profit measure is suitable where divisional manager has no control and capital investment or capital investment is insignificant. ***Limitations:*** 1. Some costs which are not controllable by the manager (e.g., Apportioned Overheads) are also included. 2. Division manager may increase the profit at the cost of organisation as a whole.
5. Return on Investment (ROI)	ROI is defined as the ratio of Net Operating Income to Net Operating Assets. $\text{RoI} = \frac{\text{Net Operating Income(EBIY)}}{\text{Net Operating Assets}}$ *or,* = Profit Margin on Sales × Assets Turnover *or,* $= \frac{\text{Net Operating Income}}{\text{Net Sales}} \times \frac{\text{Net Sales}}{\text{Net Operating Assets}}$

How to Improve ROI

RoI can be improved by:

(a) increasing sales volume or selling price, or,

(b) decreasing operating costs, or

(c) decreasing investment in operating assets, or

(d) any combination of above factors.

Advantages of Return on Investment:

The Return on investment is a very important concept in the field of operational management and the financial management. Its managerial uses included the following:

(i) It is measure of overall profitability of an enterprise.

(ii) It can be used to measure and compare the performance of various divisions with an enterprise.

(iii) It can be used to compare the performance of various enterprises within an industry.

(iv) it can be used for evaluating investment Decisions (or Capital Budgeting Decisions or Capital expenditure Decisions) investment Decision in a decision to invest in long-term assets. Other thing remaining the same, the projects yielding higher Rate of Return on investment may be selected.

(v) It can be used for planning the capital structure. Capital Structure Decision is a decision to decide upon the proportion of various sources of long-term funds, viz., long-term debts, preference shares, equity funds (including retained earnings). A financial manager should not take the financial risk by employing the funds carrying fixed financial charges if he is not in position to generate a Rate of Return on investment greater than the Rate of Fixed Financial Charges.

(vi) It can be used for determining the price of product/contract. The price of a product/contract should be fixed in such as way that a reasonable rate of return on investment is obtained after recovering the operating cost of that product/contract.

(vii) It directs the divisional manager to use the investment in assets very efficiently and effectively.

(viii) It assists the top management in allocation of organisation's resources.

Limitations of Return of Investment:

The major limitation of LoI are as follows:

(i) It ignores the importance of non-financial performance measures relating to such area as market share, development of product, delivery of product, development of personal, quality, employee relations.

(ii) What should be included in the definition of Investment? i.e., whether total assets or total assets less current liability, at what value (book value, realizable value, or replacement value) *fixed assets should be included*? Whether intangible assets should be included or not. Whether non-operating assets (such as capital work-in-progress, Advance for purchase of capital assets) should be included or not.

(iii) It may distort the allocation of resources unless the cost of capital is also taken into consideration.

	(iv) There is also a problem as to: How to collocate common assets (e.g., Building, Central Research Laboratory) to various divisions?
6. Residual Income (RI) Method	Residual Income is defined as the difference between the Net Income of Division and Required Minimum Rate of Return on Investment in the division. Residual income = Net Income of Division – (Investment in Division × Required Minimum Rate of Return) ***Advantages*** 1. Positive Residual income indicates that there is scope for expansion of that division. 2. It permits the use of different rates of return for different type of assets. ***Limitations*** 1. It is difficult to define the minimum rate of return. 2. It does not facilitate the inter division comparison since it is an absolute measure.

Illustration 1

TULSIAN Ltd having there divisions provided you the following information:

	Division X	*Division Y*
Investments	₹ 5 lacs	₹ 10 lac
Sales	₹ 10 lacs	₹ 20 lacs
Variable Costs	30%	40%
Direct Operating Fixed Costs		
– Controllable	₹ 1.50 lacs	₹ 3.00 lacs
– Un-controllable	₹ 0.50 lacs	₹ 1.00 lacs
Indirect Operating Fixed Costs (Un-controllable)	₹ 3.00 lacs	₹ 5.50 lacs

Required: Which is the most profitable division:

(a) using Division Direct Profit as the criterion

(b) using Division Controllable Profit as the criterion

(c) using Division Contribution Margin as the criterion

(d) using Division Net Profit as the criterion

(e) using Return on Investment (RoI) as the criterion

(f) using Residual Income (RI) as the criterion (assume company's minimum rate of return being 15%).

Solution

Particulars	*Division X*	*Division Y*
A. Sales	₹ 10 lacs	₹ 20 lacs
B. *Less:* Variable costs	₹ 3 lacs	₹ 8 lacs
C. Contribution Margin [*A – B*]	₹ 7 lacs	₹ 12 lacs
D. *Less:* Direct Controllable Fixed Costs	₹ 1.50 lacs	₹ 3 lacs

Particulars	Division X	Division Y
E. Contrallable Profit	₹ 5.50 lacs	₹ 9 lacs
F. *Less:* Direct Uncontrollable Fixed Costs	₹ 0.50 lac	₹ 1 lacs
G. Direct Profit	₹ 5.00 lacs	₹ 8 lacs
H. *Less:* Indirect Uncontrollable Fixed Costs	₹ 3.00 lacs	₹ 5.5 lacs
I. Net Profit or Operating Profit margin	₹ 2.00 lacs	₹ 2.5 lacs

Case (a) Division *Y* since its Direct Profit is higher than that of division *X*.

Case (b) Division *Y* since its Controllable Profit is higher than that of division *X*.

Case (c) Division *Y* since its Contribution Margin is higher than that of division *X*.

Case (d) Division *Y* since its Net Profit is higher than that of division *X*.

Case (e) $\text{RoI (Division } X) = \frac{\text{Operating Margin}}{\text{Investment}} \times 100 = \frac{₹\ 2 \text{ lacs}}{₹\ 5 \text{ lacs}} \times 100 = 40\%$

$\text{RoI (Division } Y) = \frac{\text{Operating Margin}}{\text{Investment}} \times 100 = \frac{₹\ 2.5 \text{ lacs}}{₹\ 10 \text{ lacs}} \times 100 = 25\%$

Division *X* is more profitable since its ROI is higher than that of division *Y*.

Case (f) Residual Income = Operating Margin – (Investment × Minimum Rate of Return)

RI (Division *X*) = ₹ 2.00 lacs – (₹ 5 lacs × 15%) = ₹ 1.25 lacs

RI (Division *Y*) = ₹ 2.50 lacs – (₹ 10 lacs × 15%) = ₹ 1.00 lacs

Division X is more profitable since its Residual Income is higher than that of Division *Y*.

6.0 NON-FINANCIAL MEASURES OF PERFORMANCE

To judge the total contribution of a divisional manager to the long term success of the organization, non-financial measures (qualitative measures) relating to such areas as market share development of product, delivery of product, development of personnel, quality, employee relations should also be considered in addition to financial measures of performance.

Illustration 2 (Responsibility Accounting)

In a cotton textile mill, the spinning superintendent, weaving superintendent and the processing superintendent report to the Mill Manager who alongwith the Chief Engineer reports to Director (Technical). The sales manager alongwith publicity manager reports to Director (Marketing) who alongwith the Director (Technical) reports to the Managing Director. The following data have been extracted from the books for a particular period.

	Budget	*Variances*
Travelling expenses	₹ 40,000	₹ 2,000 A
Publicity Department Salaries and Administration	1,20,000	10,000 A
Sales Commission	2,50,000	10,000 F
Spinning Department Labour	8,00,000	40,000 A
Weaving Department Labour	6,00,000	20,000 A
Raw Materials	28,00,000	1,20,000 A
Process House Material	7,00,000	60,000 F
Maintenance Stores	2,00,000	10,000 F
Processing Department Labour	5,00,000	12,000 A
Maintenance Department Labour	2,60,000	5,000 F
Utilities — Spinning Department	1,50,000	15,000 A
— Weaving Department	2,00,000	10,000 F

— Processing Department	3,00,000	50,000 A
— Maintenance Department	50,000	10,000 A
Weaving Materials	1,00,000	5,000 A
Sales Department Salaries and Administration	1,00,000	5,000 F
Publicity expenses	2,00,000	2,000 F
Director (Technical) Office Salaries and Administration	1,75,000	25,000 A
Director (Marketing) Office Salaries and Administration	2,00,000	10,000 F
Managing Director's Office Salaries and Administration	2,50,000	20,000 A
Mill Manager's Salaries and Administration	1,00,000	5,000 A
Sales	1,00,00,000	12,00,000 A

A = Adverse; F = Favourable

Required: Prepare Responsibility Accounting Reports for the Managing Director, Director (Marketing). Director (Technical) and Mill Manager.

Solution

1. RESPONSIBILITY ACCOUNTING REPORTS FOR MILL MANAGER

Particulars	*Budget* ₹	*Actual* ₹	*Variance* ₹
A. Spinning Superintendent:			
Raw Materials	28,00,000	29,20,000	1,20,000 (A)
Labour	8,00,000	8,40,000	40,000 (A)
Utilities	1,50,000	1,65,000	15,000 (A)
Total A	37,50,000	39,25,000	1,75,000 (A)
B. Weaving Superintendent:			
Materials	1,00,000	1,05,000	5,000 (A)
Labour	6,00,000	6,20,000	20,000 (A)
Utilities	2,00,000	1,90,000	10,000 (F)
Total B	9,00,000	9,15,000	15,000 (A)
C. Processing Superintendent			
Raw Materials	7,00,000	6,40,000	60,000 (F)
Labour	5,00,000	5,12,000	12,000 (A)
Utilities	3,00,000	3,50,000	50,000 (A)
Total	15,00,000	15,02,000	2,000 (A)
D. Mill Manager's Salaries and Admn.	1,00,000	1,05,000	5,000 (A)
Total for Mill Manager (A + B + C + D)	62,50,000	64,47,000	1,97,000(A)

2. RESPONSIBILITY ACCOUNTING REPORTS FOR CHIEF ENGINEER

Particulars	*Budget* ₹	*Actual* ₹	*Variance* ₹
Maintenance Stores	2,00,000	1,90,000	10,000 (F)
Maintenance Labour	2,60,000	2,55,000	5,000 (F)
Maintenance Utilities	50,000	60,000	10,000 (A)
Total for Chief Engineer	5,10,000	5,05,000	5,000 (F)

3. RESPONSIBILITY ACCOUNTING REPORTS FOR DIRECTOR TECHNICAL

Particulars	*Budget* ₹	*Actual* ₹	*Variance* ₹
Mill Manager	62,50,000	64,47,000	1,97,000 (A)
Chief Engineer	5,10,000	5,05,000	5,000 (F)
Office Salary and Admn.	1,75,000	2,00,000	25,000 (A)
Total for Director (Technical)	69,35,000	71,52,000	2,17,000 (A)

4. RESPONSIBILITY ACCOUNTING REPORTS FOR DIRECTOR MARKETING

Particulars	*Budget* ₹	*Actual* ₹	*Variance* ₹
A. *Sales Manager*			
Income-Sales	1,00,00,000	88,00,000	12,00,000 (A)
Expenditure-Travelling	40,000	42,000	2,000 (A)
Sales Commission	2,50,000	2,40,000	10,000 (F)
Salary and Admn.	1,00,000	95,000	5,000 (F)
Total X	3,90,000	3,77,000	13,000 (F)
B. *Publicity Manager*			
Salary and Admn.	1,20,000	1,30,000	10,000 (A)
Publicity Expenses	2,00,000	1,98,000	2,000 (F)
Total for B	3,20,000	3,28,000	8,000 (A)
C. *Director Marketing*			
Sales Manager (Income)	10,00,000	88,00,000	12,00,000 (A)
Sales Manager Expenses	3,90,000	3,77,000	13,000 (F)
Publicity Manager	3,20,000	3,28,000	8,000 (A)
Office Salary and Admn.	2,00,000	1,90,000	10,000 (F)
Total Expenses	9,10,000	8,95,000	15,000 (F)

5. RESPONSIBILITY ACCOUNTING REPORTS FOR MANAGING DIRECTOR

Particulars	*Budget* ₹	*Actual* ₹	*Variance* ₹
Mg. Dir.'s office staff	2,50,000	2,70,000	20,000 (A)
Director Marketing	9,10,000	8,95,000	15,000 (F)
Director Technical	69,35,000	71.52.000	2,17,000 (A)
Total Expenses	80,95,000	83,17,000	2,22,000 (A)
Director-Marketing			
Sales	1,00,00,000	88,00,000	12,00,000 (A)
Profit	19,05,000	7,83,000	14,22,000 (A)

23 Cost Control and Cost Reduction

LEARNING OBJECTIVES

After studying this chapter, you should be able to understand:

- Cost Control
- Cost Reduction
- Distinction between Cost Control and Cost Reduction
- Application of Cost Control in Material Cost
- Programmes for Cost Reduction
- Value Analysis

1.0 COST CONTROL

Meaning	1. Cost Control is defined as the "*the guidance and regulations by executives action of the cost of operating and undertaking*". 2. Cost Control implies that cost should not exceed the budgeted or standard limits. If it exceeds, investigation is necessary.
Objective	Its main objective is to control the Cost so as not to exceed the budgeted or standard limits.
Assumption	It assumes the existence of standards.
Nature	It is a preventive function. Costs are optimized before they are incurred.
Process	The process of Cost Control involves: 1. Setting Standards. 2. Measuring Actual Performance. 3. Comparing Actual Performance with standards and finding variances. 4. Ascertaining the causes of variances. 5. Taking necessary corrective action.
Techniques	The various techniques of Cost Control include: 1. ABC Analysis 2. Economic Order Quantity (EOQ) 3. Stock Levels, Minimum Level, Maximum Level, Recorder Level, Re-order Quantity. 4. Inventory Turnover Ratio and review of Slow and Non-moving items. 5. Time and Motion Study. 6. Job Evaluation and Merit Rating. 7. Standard Costing. 8. Budgetary Control.

2.0 COST REDUCTION

Meaning	1. Cost Reduction is defined as "*the achievement of real and permanent reduction in the unit cost of goods manufactured or services rendered without impairing their suitability for the use intended.*" 2. Cost reduction means waste reduction, expenses reduction and increased production. It, therefore, continuously attempts to achieve genuine savings in cost of production, administration, selling and distribution.
Objective	Its main objective is to achieve real and permanent reduction in the unit cost of goods manufactured or services rendered without impairing their suitability for the use intended.
Assumption	It assumes the existence of concealed potential savings in the standards. It does not accept a standard or budget as or fined. It rather challenges the standards / budgets continuously to make improvement in them.
Nature	It is a corrective function.
Techniques	The various techniques of Cost Reduction include: 1. Inventory Control Techniques (such as EOQ). 2. Labour Control Techniques (such as Time and Motion Study). 3. Production Planning and Control (such as Economic Batch Quantity). 4. Quality Control Techniques (such as Statistical Quality Control Techniques). 5. Value Analysis. 6. Improvement in Product Design. 7. Substitute Material Utilization. 8. Operational Research. 9. Market Research. 10. Standardization and Simplification.

3.0 DISTINCTION BETWEEN COST CONTROL AND COST REDUCTION

Basis of Distinction	Cost Control	Cost Reduction
Meaning	Cost Control is defined as the "the guidance and regulations by executives action of the cost of operating and undertaking." Cost Control implies that cost should not exceed the budgeted or standard limits. If it exceeds, investigation is necessary.	Cost Reduction is defined as "the achievement of real and permanent reduction in the unit cost of goods manufactured or services rendered without impairing their suitability for the use intended." Cost reduction means waste reduction, expenses reduction and increased production.
Objective	Its main objective is to control the Cost so as not to exceed the budgeted or standard limits.	Its main objective is to achieve real and permanent reduction in the unit cost of goods manufactured or services rendered without impairing their suitability for the use intended.
Assumption	It assumes the existence of standards.	It assumes the existence of concealed potential savings in the standards.

Nature	It is a preventive function. Costs are optimized before they are incurred.	It is a corrective function.
What Represents	Cost Control represents the efforts.	Cost reduction is a continuous attempt towards improvement. Cost Reduction represents achievement.

4.0 APPLICATION OF COST CONTROL IN MATERIAL COST

Materials Cost is the price paid and the cost incurred by an organization in procuring materials for production. If material cost is effectively controlled we must have a proper system of material control and the following are the essential requirements of such a control:

1. Proper Co-ordination	There should be proper co-ordination of all departments involved *viz.* Purchasing, Receiving, Inspection, Storage, Production, Cost and Finance.
2. Proper Purchase System	There should be proper purchase system to ensure the procurement of materials and stores of the required quality at minimum cost from a reliable source.
3. Proper Storage System	There should be proper storage system to ensure a place for everything and everything in its place and avoidance of losses during storage and minimum storage cost.
4. Proper Issue System	There should be proper system for the issue of materials to ensure the delivery of materials of the required quality in the required quantity at the required time upon requisition to the department making requisition.
5. Perpetual Inventory System	There should be perpetual inventory system so as to determine the quantity and value of each item of materials in stock at any point of time.
6. Continuous Stock Taking System	There should be continuous stock taking system so as to ensure accuracy of perpetual inventory records.
7. Internal Check System	These should be internal check system so that all transactions concerning materials are automatically checked.
8. Proper Budgetary Control System	There should be proper budgetary control system to ensure economy in purchasing and usage of materials and stores.
9. Proper Forms	There should be use of proper forms with regard to Purchase Requisition, Purchase Order, Material Received Note, Material Requisition, Bill of Materials, Material Returned Note, Material Transfer Note, Bin Card, Stores Card etc.
10. Proper Accounting System	There should be proper accounting system so as to determine the cost of materials at time of receipt and consumption.

11. Proper Reporting System	These should be proper reporting system to ensure regular reporting to the management regarding– (a) Materials purchased (b) Materials issued (c) Materials in hand (d) Slow-moving and obsolete stock etc.

5.0 PROGRAMMES FOR COST REDUCTION

The possibilities of reducing the cost of a product are the applications of cost reduction methods. The lines of approach in laying out a cost reduction plan are suggested below:

1. Product Design	Cost reduction starts with the design of the product. The impact of any economy or cost reduction effected in Product design (being first step in manufacturing of a product) will be felt through out the manufacturing life of the product. Efficient designing for a new product or improving the design for an existing product, reduces cost in the following manner :- **(i) Material Cost:** By using cheaper substitute, by obtaining higher yield (i.e. output). **(ii) Labour Cost:** By reducing time of operation and by increasing productivity labour cost can be reduced. (iii) Cost of gigs, tools and fixtures are to be minimized. (iv) Standardization and simplification in variety increases productivity and reduces costs.
2. Organization	An efficient cost reduction programme should consider the following points relating to organization with a view to reducing costs: (i) Definition of each function and responsibility. (ii) Proper assignment of task and delegation of responsibility to avoid overlapping (iii) A suitable channel of communication between various management level. (iv) Encouragement to employees for cost reduction suggestion. (v) Co-operation and closed relationship between the various executives. (vi) Removal of doubts and fiction.
3. Factory Lay Out Equipment	An efficient cost reduction programme should study the factory layout and the utilization of the existing equipment to determine whether there is any scope of cost reduction by elimination of wastage of men, materials and maximum utilization of the facilities available. The necessity for replacement of Plants, introduction of new techniques or expansion of facilities should be considered and various alternatives explored with a view to reducing costs.
4. Production Plan Programme and Method	Production control ensures proper planning of work by installing and efficient procedure and programme ordering correct machine and proper utilization of materials, manpower and resources so that there is no waste of time and money due to wait for components, men, material etc. An efficient cost reduction programme should examine the following points relating to production control:

	(i) Whether wastage of manpower and material is kept to the minimum (ii) Whether there is any scope for reducing idle capacity. (iii) Whether the procedures for the control of stores and maintenance services are efficient. (iv) Whether labour wastage may be reduced and productivity increased by eliminating faulty production method, plant layout and designs or introducing incentive schemes. (v) Whether there is scope for reduction of overhead, whether a budgetary control system is in operation to ensure the control over overhead costs.

6.0 VALUE ANALYSIS

1. Meaning	Value Analysis is one of the important tools of modern management in the area of cost reduction. It is also known by other names such as Value Engineering, Value Control and Product Research. Value analysis is the process of systematic analysis and evaluation of various techniques and functions with a view to improve organizational performance. It aims at reducing and controlling the cost of a product from the point of view of its value by analyzing the value currently received. It investigates into the economic attributes of value analysis, believes in a planned action to improve performance and thereby, generates higher value in a product and ultimately causes reduction in its cost. The meaning of the term value may vary from person to person, time to time and place to place. However, in the context of cost reduction and control it refers to the 'use value'.
2. Advantages	The reduction in the costs of a product and thus increasing the profitability of a concern is the main advantage of value analysis.
3. Application	The benefits of value analysis are being derived in many industries, *e.g.,* engineering, building construction and the oil industry. It is being applied to components of a product, finished product and also be methods of packaging.
4. Steps involved in value analysis	**Step 1:** *Identification of the problem;* **Step2:** *Collecting information about the function, design, material, labour, overhead costs, etc. of the product and finding out the availability of the competitive products in the market, and* **Step 3:** *Exploring and evaluating alternatives and developing them.*

Illustration. CAS Ltd. is manufacturing and selling two products Splash and Flash at selling price of ₹ 3 and ₹ 4 respectively. The following sales strategy has been outlined for the year:

(i) Sales planned for year will be ₹ 7.20 lakhs in the case of Splash and ₹ 3.50 lakhs in the case of Flash.
(ii) To meet competition, the selling price of Splash will be reduced by 20% and that of Flash by 12 ½ %.
(iii) Break- even is planned at 60% of the total sales of each product.
(iv) Profit for the year to be achieved is planned as ₹ 69,120 in the case of Splash and ₹ 17,500 in the case of Flash. This would be possible by launching a cost reduction programme and reducing the present annual fixed expenses of ₹ 1,35,000 allocated as ₹ 1,08,000 to Splash and ₹ 27,000 to Flash.

Required:

(a) Calculate the total number of units of Splash and Flash to be sold during the year and Number of units to be sold of Splash and Flash to break-even.

(b) Calculate the reduction in fixed expenses product-wise that is envisaged by the Cost Reduction Programme

Solution:

CALCULATION OF NO. OF UNITS TO BE SOLD AND BEP (UNITS)

	Particulars	*Splash*	*Flash*
A	Sales (₹)	7,20,000	3,50,000
B	Selling Price / Unit (Revised)	2.4 (80% of 3)	3.5 (87.5% of 4)
C	Sales Units (A / B)	3,00,000	1,00,000
D	BEP (%)	60%	60%
E	BEP (Units) (C × D)	1,80,000	60,000

CALCULATION OF REDUCTION IN FIXED EXPENSES PRODUCT-WISE

	Particulars	*Splash*	*Flash*
A	Margin of Safety (MS) [Sales Units × (100 – BEP%) × Selling Price]	2,88,000 (3,00,000 × 40% × 2.4)	1,40,000 (1,00,000 × 40% × 3.5)
B	Profit (given)	69,120	17,500
C	Previous Fixed cost (given)	1,08,000	27,000
D	New P/V Ratio [(Profit / MS) × 100]	24%	12.5%
E	Break- Even Sales [Sales Units × BEP% × Selling Price]	4,32,000 (3,00,000 × 60% × 2.4)	2,10,000 (1,00,000 × 60% × 3.5)
F	Revised Fixed Cost (BES × P/V Ratio)	1,03,680	26,250
G	Reduction in Fixed cost (C – E)	4,320	750

24 Uniform Costing

Learning Objectives

After studying this chapter, you should be able to understand:

- Meaning of Uniform Costing
- Objectives of Uniform Costing
- Essential Prerequisites for the installation of uniform costing system in an industry
- Points on which Uniformity is essential before introducing Uniform Costing
- Advantages of Uniform Costing
- Limitations of Uniform Costing
- Uniform Cost Manual

1.0 MEANING OF UNIFORM COSTING

Uniform Costing is not a distinct method of costing. Rather it is the practice of using the same costing principles and/or practices by a number of firms [whether or not under the same management] in the same industry. It helps in inter firm comparison, fixation of prices, cost control, cost reduction and in seeking tax relief or protection from government.

Infect when several undertakings start using the same costing principles and / or practices, they are said to be following uniform costing. The basic idea behind uniform costing is that the different concerns in an industry should adopt a common method of costing and apply uniformly the same principles and techniques for better cost comparison and common good.

Its introduction helps the firms to submit reliable cost data to price fixing bodies to determine the average cost and fixing the fair selling prices of various products. It adoption helps mutually in cost control and cost reduction.

Thus, Adherence to the same costing methods and procedures specially when there can be two or more options is the characteristic feature of a uniform system of costing.

2.0 OBJECTIVES OF UNIFORM COSTING

The main objectives of Uniform Costing are as follows:

1. To bring standardization and uniformity in the operation of participating units.
2. To facilitate the comparison of costs and performances of different units in the same industry; it provides objective basis.
3. To improve production capacity level and labour efficiency by comparing the production costs of different units with each other.
4. To eliminate unhealthy competition among the different units of an industry.
5. To reduce production, administration, selling and distribution costs, and to exercise control on fixed costs.
6. To provide relevant cost information/data to the Government for fixing and regulating prices of the products.

3.0 ESSENTIAL PREREQUISITES FOR THE INSTALLATION OF UNIFORM COSTING SYSTEM IN AN INDUSTRY

A successful system of uniform costing requires the following essential requisites for its installation.

1. The firms in the industry should be *willing* to share /furnish relevant data/information.
2. A spirit of *cooperation and mutual trust* should prevail among the participating firms.
3. *Mutual exchange* of ideas, methods used, special achievements made, research and know-how etc. should be *frequent*.
4. Bigger firms should take the lead towards sharing their experience and know-how with the smaller firms to enable the latter to improve their performance.
5. Uniformity must be established with regard to several points before the introduction of uniform costing in an industry. In fact, uniformity should be with regard to following points:
   (a) Size of the various units covered by uniform costing.
   (b) Production methods.
   (c) Accounting methods, principles, and procedures used.

4.0 POINTS ON WHICH UNIFORMITY IS ESSENTIAL BEFORE INTRODUCING UNIFORM COSTING:

The points in respect of which uniformity is required to be established before the introduction of uniform costing in an industry are as follows:

(i) **Uniformity in the size of various units where uniform costing is to be introduced:**
The size of units should be more or less the same which are to be brought under uniform costing. Units differing in size should be classified in a number of categories according to their size. Since the cost structure in an organisation in influenced by its size, the classification of units based on their size would make the cost statements of these units more comparable.

(ii) **Uniformity in the Production Method:**
All units in an industry should use uniform methods of production.

(iii) **Uniformity in the Accounting Method, Principles and Procedures.**
In fact, the uniformity should be achieved in respect of following:

1. Stages of production at which costs are to be measured.
2. Methods of valuing inventory of WIP & Finished Goods.
3. Cost unit and Cost Centres
4. Classification of costs and its components.
5. Grouping of expenses
6. Principles to be followed while determining direct & indirect expenses and variable & fixed expenses.
7. Method of pricing material issues.
8. Treatment of material losses life waste, scrap, defectives & spoilage.
9. Methods of remunerating and providing incentives to labour.
10. Treatment of notional expenses (like Interest on Owned Capital, Rent of Owner Premises)
11. Basis of apportionment of overheads.
12. Basis of Reapportionment of overheads of Service Deptt. to Production Deptt.
13. Treatment of Under/over absorption of overheads.
14. Basis apportionment of joint costs.
15. Treatment of By-products
16. Standardization of cost statements reports and their submission schedule.

5.0 ADVANTAGES OF UNIFORM COSTING:

Saving of efforts of an individual firm	The management of an individual firm/unit will be saved of the botheration of developing and introducing a costing system of their own.
Facilitates Adoption	Since the system is devised by manual consultation and after considering the difficulties and circumstances prevailing in the various undertakings, therefore it is readily adopted and successfully implemented.
Facilitates Comparison	It facilitates comparison of cost figures of various firms. Such a comparison enables the firms to identify their weak and strong points and control costs effectively and efficiently.
Reveals Standing of Firm	The availability of cost data of other firms in the industry enables each firm to know its standing in the industry.
Benefit of R&D	The benefits of research and development of bigger firms are made available to smaller firms at no cost.
Reduces Labour Turnover	The introduction of a uniform costing reduces labour turnover since it requires the introduction of a uniform wage system in all the firms in the industry.
Facilitates Negotiation with Govt. Agencies	It helps trade associations in negotiating with the government in trade matters, particularly, when an industry seeks any assistance or concession from the government in matters of subsidies, exports, taxation, duties and price determination, etc.
Facilitates Price Fixation	Uniform costing is of great help in price fixation. Unhealthy competition is avoided between the firms in the same industry in framing policies and submitting tenders.
Helps Govt. in Regulating the Prices of Production	It helps the government also in regulating the prices of essential and important items such as bread, flour, sugar, cement and steel etc.

6.0 LIMITATIONS OF UNIFORM COSTING

Difficulty in Adoption	Due to the differing circumstances in which firms operate, it is difficult to have uniform standards, methods and procedures of costing. This renders the adoption of uniform costing difficult.
Hesitation in Disclosure	Adoption of a uniform costing system requires various firms to disclose their cost and other data. Some of the firms do not like this and are thus hesitant towards the use of this costing system.
Only for Big Firms	Small firms feels that uniform costing system is meant only for large and medium size firms and thus they cannot afford it.

6.0 UNIFORM COST MANUAL

Meaning	Uniform Cost Manual is a written document, which may be in the form of a booklet or bulletin, containing the principles, methods and procedures for the ascertainment and control of cost of uniform costing. It is necessary for the successful operation of uniform costing system. Such a manual provides guidelines to the participating firms to organise their cost accounting system on a uniform basis.
Features	1. It includes statement of objectives and purpose of the system, scope of the system, advantages and extent of co-operation necessary. 2. It contains the general principles of accounting, nature coding, terminology to be followed, classification and description of accounts. This section also includes details of stock control, labour and overhead cost collection and control. 3. Essential cost data and various ratios to be computed for comparison of performance and efficiency in the operation of the participating units. 4. Mode, format and time for presenting cost data and reports to the management. 5. It provides necessary guidelines about the treatment of depreciation, interest on capital, wastage, scrap, by-product, etc.

Section–B
OPERATIONS RESEARCH

1 Linear Programming – Formulation

PRACTICAL STEPS INVOLVED IN THE FORMULATION OF LP PROBLEM

The practical steps involved in the formation of linear programming problem are as follows:

Step 1→ *Identify the **Decision Variables** of interest to the decision maker and express them as x_1, x_2, x_3 ....*

Step 2→ *Ascertain the **Objective** of the decision maker whether he wants to minimize or to maximize.*

Step 3→ *Ascertain the **cost** (in case of minimization problem) or the **profit** (in case of maximization problem) per unit of each of the decision variables.*

Step 4→ *Ascertain the **constraints** representing the maximum availability or minimum commitment or equality and represent them as less than or equal to (≤) type inequality or greater than or equal to (≥) type inequality or 'equal to' (=) type equality respectively.*

Step 5→ *Put **non-negativity restriction** as under:*

$x_j \geq 0$; *j = 1, 2 ....n (non-negativity restriction)*

Step 6→ *Now **formulate the LP problem as under**:*

Maximize (or Minimize) $Z = c_1x_1 + c_2x_2 .....c_nx_n$

Subject to constraints:

$a_{11}x_1 + a_{12}x_2 ,....a_{1n}x_n \leq b_1$ *(Maximum availability)*

$a_{21}x_1 + a_{22}x_2 ,....a_{2n}x_n \geq b_2$ *(Minimum commitment)*

$a_{31}x_1 + a_{32}x_2 ,....a_{3n}x_n = b_3$ *(Equality)*

$a_{m1}x_1 + a_{m2}x_2 ,....a_{mn}x_n \lesseqgtr b_m$

$x_1; x_2 .... x_n \geq 0$ *(Non-negativity restriction)*

where,

x_j = *Decision Variables i.e. quantity of jth variable of interest to the decision maker.*

c_j = *Constant representing per unit contribution (in case of Maximization Problem) or Cost (in case of Minimization Problem) of the jth decision variable.*

a_{ij} = *Constant representing exchange coefficients of the jth decision variable in the ith constant.*

b_i = *Constant representing i^{th} constraint requirement or availability.*

PROBLEM 1.1

A firm produces three products A, B and C. It uses two types of raw materials I and II of which 5,000 and 7,500 units respectively are available. The raw material requirements per unit of the products are given below:

Raw Material	*Requirement per unit of Product*		
	A	*B*	*C*
I	3	4	5
II	5	3	5

The labour time for each unit of product A is twice that of Product B and three times that of Product C. The entire labour force of the firm can produce the equivalent of 3,000 units. The minimum demand of the three products is 600, 650 and 500 units respectively. Also the ratios of the number of units produced must be equal to 2 : 3 : 4. Assuming the profits per unit of A, B and C as ₹ 50, 50 and 80 respectively.

Required: Formulate the problem as a linear programming model in order to determine the number of units of each product, which will maximize the profit.

Solution

Let X_1, X_2 and X_3 be the units produced & sold of Product A, B and C respectively.

The labour time for each unit of Product A is twice that of Product B and three times that Product C. Also the entire labour force can produce the equivalent of 3000 units.

$$x_1 + \frac{x_2}{2} + \frac{x_3}{3} \leq 3000$$

or $$6x_1 + 3x_2 + 2x_3 \leq 18000$$

Since the ratios of the number of units produced must be equal to 2 :3 :4, therefore,

$$\frac{1}{2}x_1 = \frac{1}{3}x_2, \text{ and } \frac{1}{3}x_2 = \frac{1}{4}x_3$$

or $$3x_1 = 2x_2 \text{ and } 4x_2 = 3x_3 \quad \text{...(v)}$$

Since the objective of the firm is to maximize the profit, therefore, the objective function is given by–

Maximise $$Z = 50x_1 + 50x_2 + 80x_3$$

Subject to the constraints

$$3x_1 + 4x_2 + 5x_3 \leq 5000 \text{ [Maximum Raw-Material I]}$$

$$5x_1 + 3x_2 + 5x_3 \leq 7500 \text{ [Maximum Raw-Material II]}$$

$$6x_1 + 3x_2 + 2x_3 \leq 18000 \text{ [Maximum Labour Time]}$$

$$3x_1 = 2x_2 \text{ and } 4x_2 = 3x_3 \text{ [Ratio of No. of units Produced]}$$

$$x_1 \geq 600, x_2 \geq 650 \text{ and } x_3 \geq 500 \text{ [Minimum Demand for Products]}$$

PROBLEM 1.2

In a chemical industry two products A and B are made involving two operations The production of B also results in a by-product C. The product A can be sold at a profit of ₹ 3 per unit and B at a profit of ₹ 8 per unit. The by-product C has a profit of ₹, 2 per unit. Forecasts show that upto 5 units of C can be sold. **The company gets 3 units of C for each unit of B produced.** The manufacturing times are 3 hours per unit for A on each the operation one and two and 4 hours and 5 hours per unit for B on operation one and two respectively. Because the product C results from producing B, no time is used in producing C. The available times are 18 hours and 21 hours of operation one and two respectively. The company desires to know that how much A and B should be produced keeping C in mind to make the highest profit. Formulate LPP model for this problem.

Solution

Let x_1 x_2, x_3 be the number of units produced & sold of products A, B, and C respectively.

In first operation, A takes 3 hours of manufacturer's time and B takes 4 hours of manufacturer's time Therefore, total number of hours required in first operation becomes,

$$3x_1 + 4x_2$$

Further, the company gets three units of by product C for every unit of product B produced, therefore

$$x_3 = 3x_2$$

Now, the allocation problem of the industry can be finally put in the following linear programming problem:

Maximise $Z = 3x_1 + 8x_2 + 2x_3$

Subject to the constraints

$3x_1 + 4x_2 \leq 18$ [Maximum Hours in First Operation]

$3x_1 + 5x_2 \leq 21$ [Maximum Hours in Second Operation]

$x_3 \leq 5,$ [Maximum Sales units of Product C]

$x_3 = 3x_2$ [Ratio of Product C to Product B]

$x_1, x_2, x_3 \leq 0$ [Non-Negativity]

PROBLEM 1.3

A firm buys castings of P and Q type of parts and sells them as finished product after machining, boring and polishing. The purchasing cost for castings are ₹ 3 and ₹ 4 each for parts P and Q and selling prices are ₹ 8 and ₹ 10 respectively. The per hour capacity of machines used for machining, boring and polishing for two products is given below:

Capacity (per hour)	*P*	*Q*
Machining	30	50
Boring	30	45
Polishing	45	30

The running costs for machining, boring and polishing are ₹ 30, ₹, 22.5 and ₹ 22.5 per hour respectively.

Formulate the linear programming problem to find out the product mix to maximize the profit.

Solution

Let the firm buy x units of castings of P and y units of castings of Q which are sold as finished product after machining , boring and polishing. According to the given data, the capacity constraints of machining, boring and polishing machines on per hour basis have been formulated as below:

$\frac{x}{30} + \frac{y}{50} \leq 1$ *or* $50x + 30y \leq 1500$ (*Machining Constraint*) ...(i)

$\frac{x}{30} + \frac{y}{45} \leq 1$ *or* $45x + 30y \leq 1350$ (*Boring Constraint*) ...(ii)

$\frac{x}{45} + \frac{y}{30} \leq 1$ *or* $30x + 45y \leq 1350$ (*Polishing Constraint*) ...(iii)

Calculation of Total Cost and Profit per unit

	Cost/per unit	
	Castings of P type	*Castings of Q type*
Machining	₹.30/30 = ₹ 1.00	₹.30/50 = ₹ 0.60
Boring	₹ 22.5/30 = ₹ 0.75	₹ .22.5/45 = ₹ 0.50
Polishing	₹ 22.5/45 = ₹ 0.50	₹ 22.5/30 = ₹ 0.75
Purchasing Cost	₹ 3.00	₹ 4.00
Total Cost	₹ 5.25	₹ 5.85
Sale Price	₹ 8.00	₹ 10.00
Profit	₹ 2.75	₹ 4.15

The required product mix to maximise the profit of the firm will be given by the following relation:

Maximise $Z = 2.75x + 4.15\,y$

Subject to the Constraints

$$50\,x + 30\,y \leq 1500$$
$$45x + 30y \leq 1350$$
$$30\,x + 45\,y \leq 1350$$

where x, y, ≥ 0

PROBLEM 1.4

A manufacturer produces three products Y_1, Y_2, Y_3 from three raw materials X_1, X_2, X_3. The cost of raw materials X_1, X_2 and X_3 is ₹ 30, ₹ 50 and ₹ 120 per kg respectively and they are available in a limited quantity viz 20 kg of X_1, 15 kg of X_2 and 10 kg of X_3. The selling price of Y_1, Y_2 and Y_3 is ₹ 90, ₹ 100 and ₹ 120 per kg respectively. In order to produce 1 kg of Y_1, ½ kg of X_1, ¼ kg of X_2 and ¼ kg of X_3 are required. Similarly to produce 1 kg of Y_2, 3/7 kg of X_1, 2/7 kg of X_2 and 2/7 kg of X_3 and to produce 1 kg of Y_3, 2/3 kg of X_2 and 1/3 kg of X_3 will be required.

Formulate the linear programming problem to maximize the profit.

Solution

The information given in the question can be presented of the following tabular form.

Products	*Raw material (in kg) required to produce one kg of product* X_1	X_2	X_3	*Selling Price (per kg)*
Y_1	1/2	1/4	1/4	₹ 90
Y_2	3/7	2/7	2/7	₹ 100
Y_3	—	2/3	1/3	₹ 120
Cost of raw material (per kg)	₹ 30	₹ 50	₹ 120	
Availability of raw material	20 kg	15 kg	10 kg	

From the above table, the cost of producing 1 kg of Y_1, Y_2 and Y_3 can be calculated as given below:

Cost to produce 1 kg of Y_1 = ½ ₹ 30 + ¼ ₹ 50 + ¼ ₹ 120
= ₹ 15 + ₹ 12.50 + ₹ 30 = ₹ 57.50

∴ Profit per kg of Y_1 = ₹ 90 – ₹ 57.50 = ₹ 32.50

Similarly, Cost to produce 1 kg of Y_2 = 3/7 ₹ 30 + 2/7 ₹ 50 + 2/7 ₹ 120
= 1/7(₹ 90 + ₹ 100 + ₹ 240)
= ₹ 430/7 = ₹ 61.43

Profit per kg of Y_2 = ₹.100 – ₹.61.43 = ₹.38.57

and cost to produce 1 kg of Y_3 = 2/3 ₹.50 + 1/3 ₹.120 = ₹.220/3 = ₹.73.33

Profit per kg of Y_3 = ₹.120 – ₹.73.33 = ₹.46.67

Let the manufacturer produce y_1, y_2 and y_3 units of the products Y_1, Y_2 and Y_3 respectively.

Since the manufacturer wants to maximise the profit, the objective function is given by

Maximise $Z = 32.50\ Y_1 + 38.57\ Y_2 + 46.67\ Y_3$

Subject to the constraints

$$\tfrac{1}{2} Y_1 + 3/7\ Y_2 \le 20 \text{ or } 7\ Y_1 + 6\ Y_2 \le 280$$

$$\tfrac{1}{4} Y_1 + 2/7\ Y_2 + 2/3\ Y_3 \le 15 \text{ or } 21\ Y_1 + 24\ Y_2 + 56\ Y_3 \le 1260$$

$$\tfrac{1}{4} Y_1 + 2/7\ Y_2 + 1/3\ Y_3 \le 10 \text{ or } 21\ Y_1 + 24\ Y_2 + 28\ Y_3 \le 840$$

where Y_1, Y_2 and $Y_3 \ge 0$

PROBLEM 1.5

An agriculturist has a farm with 125 acres. He produces Radish, Muttar and Potato. Whatever he raises is fully sold in the market. He gets ₹ 5 for Radish per kg. ₹.4 for Muttar per kg. and ₹ 5. For Potato per kg. The average yield is 1,500 kg. of Radish per acre, 1,800 kg. of Muttar per acre and 1,200 kg. of Potato per acre. To produce each 100 kg. of Radish and Muttar and to produce each 80 kg. of Potato, a sum of ₹ 12.50 has to be used for manure. Labour required for each acre to raise the crop is 6 man days for Radish and Potato each and 5 man days for Muttar. A total of 500 man days of labour at a rate of ₹ 40 per man day are available.

Formulate this as a Linear Programming model to maximize the Agriculturist's total profit.

Solution

Let x_1, x_2 and x_3 be the number of acres allotted for cultivating radish, mutter and potato respectively.

Sales Revenue/acre (Radish) = ₹ 5 × 1500 = ₹ 7,500

Sales Revenue/acre (Matter) = ₹ 4 × 1800 = ₹ = 7,200

Sales Revenue/acre (Patato) = ₹ 5 × 1200 = ₹ 6,000

Now, the selling price, manure cost, labour cost and profit per acre of land for will be as fallows:

Per acre	Radish	Muttar	Potato
A. Selling Price	₹ 7,500	₹ 7,200	₹ 6,000
B. Manure Cost	$\frac{\text{Rs. } 12.50 \times 1500}{100}$ = ₹ 187.50	$\frac{\text{Rs. } 12.50 \times 1800}{100}$ = ₹ 225	$\frac{\text{Rs. } 12.50 \times 1200}{80}$ = ₹ 187.50
C. Labour Cost	₹.40 × 6 = ₹.240	₹.40 × 5 = ₹.200	₹.40 × 6 = ₹ 240
D. Profit [A – B – C]	= ₹.7,072.50	= ₹.6,775	= ₹ 5,572.50

Since, the agriculturist wants to maximise the total profit, hence the objective function of the problem is given by:

Maximise $Z = 7072.5x_1 + 6775x_2 + 5572.5x_3$

Subject to following constraints:

$x_1 + x_2 + x_3 \leq 125$ [Maximum Land Area]

$6x_1 + 5x_2 + 6x_3 \leq 500$ [Maximum Man Days]

where x_1, x_2 and $x_3 \geq 0$

PROBLEM 1.6

Three grades of coal A, B and C contains phosphorus and ash as impurities. In a particular industrial process, **fuel up to 100 ton (maximum) is required which could contain ash not more than 3% and phosphorus not more than .03%.** It is desired to maximize the profit while satisfying these conditions. There is an unlimited supply of each grade. The percentage of impurities and the profits of each grade are as follows:

Coal	*Phosphorus (%)*	*Ash (%)*	*Profit in ₹ (per ton)*
A	.02	3.0	12.00
B	.04	2.0	15.00
C	.03	5.0	14.00

You are required to formulate the Linear-programming (LP) model.

Solution

Let X_1, X_2 and X_3 respectively be the amounts in tons of grades A, B, and C used. The constraints are

(i) Phosphorus content must not exceed 0.03%

$$.02\,X_1 + .04\,X_2 + 0.03\,X_3 \leq .03\,(X_1 + X_2 + X_3)$$

$$2\,X_1 + 4\,X_2 + 3\,X_3 \leq 3\,(X_1 + X_2 + X_3)\ or - X_1 + X_2 \leq 0$$

(ii) Ash content must not exceed 3%

$$3\,X_1 + 2\,X_2 + 5\,X_3 \leq 3(X_1 + X_2 + X_3)\ or - X_2 + 2\,X_3 \leq 0$$

(iii) Total quantity of fuel required is not more than 100 tons. $X_1 + X_2 + X_3 \leq 100$

The Mathematical formulation of the problem is

Maximize $Z = 12\,X_1 + 15\,X_2 + 14X_3$

Subject to the constraints:

$$-X_1 + X_2 \leq 0$$

$$-X_2 + X_3 \leq 0$$

$$X_1 + X_2 + X_3 \leq 100$$

$$X_1, X_2, X_3 > 0$$

PROBLEM 1.7

An oil refinery can blend three grades of crude oil to produce quality A and quality B petrol. Two possible blending processes are available. For each production run, the older process uses 5 units of crude Q, 7 units of crude P and 2 units of crude R and produces 9 units of A and 7 units of B. The newer process uses 3 units of crude Q, 9 unit of crude P and 4 units of crude R to produce 5 units of A and 9 units of B.

Because of prior contract commitments, the refinery must produce at least 500 units of A and at least 300 units of B for the next month. It has 1,500 units of crude Q, 1,900 units of crude P and 1,000 of crude R. For each unit of A, refinery receives ₹ 60 while for each unit of B, it receives ₹ 90.

Formulate the problem as linear programming model so as to maximize the revenue.

Solution

Maximize $Z = 60(9x_1 + 5x_2) + 90(7x_1 + 9x_2) = 1170x_1 + 1110x_2$

Subject to $9x_1 + 5x_2 \geq 500$ commitment for A

$7x_1 + 9x_2 \leq 300$ commitment for B

$5x_1 + 3x_2 \leq 1500$ availability of Q

$7x_1 + 9x_2 \leq 1900$ availability of P

$2x_1 + 4x_2 \leq 1000$ availability of R

and $x_1 \geq 0,\ x_2 \geq 0.$

PROBLEM 1.8

A refinery makes 3 grades of petrol (A, B, C) from 3 crude oils (d, e, f,). Crude can be used in any grade but the others must satisfy the following specifications

Grade	Specification	Selling price per litre
A	Not less than 50% crude d Not more than 25% crude e.	16
B	Not less than 25% crude d Not more than 50% crude e	13
C	No specifications	11

There are capacity limitations on the amounts of the three crude elements that can be used.

Crude	Capacity	Price/litre
d	2,50,000	19
e	2,50,000	11
f	1,50,000	13

Build a LPP to produce the maximum profit.

Solution

Let there be x_1 litres of d in A

x_2 litres of e in A

x_3 litres of f in A

y_1 litres of d in B

y_2 litres of e in B

y_3 litres of f in B

z_1 litres of d in C

z_2 litres of e in C

z_3 litres of f in C

Calculation of Profit per Litre in each Grade

	x_1	x_2	x_3	y_1	y_2	y_3	z_1	z_2	z_3
Selling Price	16	16	16	13	13	13	11	11	11
Cost	19	11	13	19	11	13	19	11	13
Profit	-3	5	3	-6	2	0	-8	0	-2

Since the objective is to maximize profit, the objective function is given by —

Maximize $Z = -3x_1 + 5x_2 + 3x_3 - 6y_1 + 2y_2 - 8z_1 - 2z_3$

Subject to constraints:

$$\frac{x_1}{x_1 + x_2 + x_3} \geq \frac{1}{2} \quad \text{i.e.} - x_1 + x_2 + x_3 \leq 0$$

$$\frac{x_1}{x_1 + x_2 + x_3} \geq \frac{1}{4} \quad \text{i.e.} - x_1 + 3x_2 - x_3 \leq 0$$

$$\frac{y_1}{y_1 + y_2 + y_3} \geq \frac{1}{4} \quad \text{i.e.} - 3y_1 + y_2 + y_3 \leq 0$$

$$\frac{y_1}{y_1 + y_2 + y_3} \geq \frac{1}{4} \quad \text{i.e.} - y_1 + y_2 - y_3 \leq 0$$

$$x_1 + y_1 + z_1 \leq 2{,}50{,}000$$

$$x_2 + y_2 + z_2 \leq 2{,}50{,}000$$

$$x_3 + y_3 + z_3 \leq 1{,}50{,}000$$

PROBLEM 1.9

A Mutual Fund Company has ₹ 20 lakhs available for investment in Government Bonds, Blue Chip Stocks, Speculative Stocks and Short-term Bank Deposits. The annual expected return and risk factor are given below:

Type of Investment	*Annual Expected Return %*	*Risk Factor (0 to 100)*
Government Bonds	14	12
Blue Chip Stocks	19	24
Speculative Stocks	23	48
Short-term Deposits	12	6

Mutual fund is required to keep at least 10% of funds in short-term deposits and not to exceed an average risk factor of 42, Speculative stocks must be at most 20 percent of the total amount invested.

Govt. Bonds must be at least 10% of Total Investment. Mutual Fund will not accept on Average Rate of Return below 15%.

How should mutual fund invest the funds so as to maximize its total expected annual return ? Formulate this as a Linear Programming Problem. Do not solve it.

Solution

Let x_1 x_2, x_3 and x_4 denote the amount of funds to be invested in Government Bonds, Blue chip Stocks, Speculative Stocks and Short term Deposits respectively. Let Z denote the Total Expected Return.

The average risk factor is given by—

$$\frac{12x_1 + 24x_2 + 48x_3 + 6x_4}{x_1 + x_2 + x_3 + x_4}$$

$$x_1 \geq 0.10\,(x_1 + x_2 + x_3 + x_4)$$

Since the average risk factor for Mutual Fund should not exceed 42, we get the following . constraint

$$\frac{12x_1 + 24x_2 + 48x_3 + 6x_4}{x_1 + x_2 + x_3 + x_4} \le 42$$

or $12\,x_1 + 24\,x_2 + 48\,x_3 + 6\,x_4 \le 42\ \ (x_1 + x_2 + x_3 + x_4)$

or $30x_1 - 18x_2 + 6x_3 - 36x_4 \le 0$

Further, speculative stock must be at most 20 per cent of the total amount invested, hence

$$x_3 \le 0.20\,(x_1 + x_2 + x_3 + x_4)$$

or $-0.2\,x_1 - 0.2\,x_2 + 0.8\,x_3 - 0.2\,x_4 \le 0$

For Minimum Average Rate of Return

$$0.14x_1 + 0.19x_2 + 0.23x_3 + 0.12x_4 \ge 0.15\,(x_1 + x_2 + x_3 + x_4)$$

$$-0.01x_1 + 0.04x_2 + 0.08x_3 + 0.03x_4 \ge 0 \text{ (Minimum Average Rate of Return)}$$

For Minimum Govt. Bonds

$$x_1 \ge 0.10\,(x_1 + x_2 + x_3 + x_4)$$

$$0.9x_1 - 0.1x_2 - 0.1x_3 - 0.1x_4 \ge 0$$

Since, the objective is to maximise the total expected annual return, the objective function for Mutual Fund is given by:

Maximise $Z = 0.14\,x_1 + 0.19\,x_2 + 0.23\,x_3 + 0.12\,x_4$

Subject to the constraints:

$$x_1 + x_2 + x_3 + x_4 \le 20{,}00{,}000 \text{ [Maximum Total Investment]}$$

$$x_4 \ge 2{,}00{,}000 \text{ [Minimum Short-term Deposit]}$$

$$-30x_1 - 18x_2 + 6\,x_3 - 36\,x_4 \le 0 \text{ [Maximum Average Risk Factor]}$$

$$-0.2\,x_1 - 0.2\,x_2 + 0.8\,x_3 - 0.2\,x_4 \le 0 \text{ [Maximum Speculative Stocks]}$$

$$0.9x_1 - 0.1x_2 - 0.3x_3 - 0.1x_4 \ge 0 \text{ [Maximum Govt. Bonds Investments]}$$

$$-0.01x_1 + 0.04x_2 + 0.08x_3 + 0.03x_4 \ge 0 \text{ (Minimum Average Rate of Return)}$$

where $x_1 \ge 0,\ x_2 \ge 0,\ x_3 \ge 0$ *and* $x_4 \ge 0$

PROBLEM 1.10

An investor has money making activities A_1, A_2, A_3 and A_4. He has only ₹ 1 lakh to invest. In order to avoid excessive investment, no more than 50% of the total investment can be placed in Activity A_2 and for Activity A_3. Activity A_1 is very conservative, while Activity A_4 is speculative. To avoid excessive speculation at least ₹ 1 must be invested in Activity A_1 for every ₹ 3 invested in Activity A_4. The data on the return on investment are as follows:

Activity	*Anticipated return On investment (%)*
A_1	10
A_2	12
A_3	14
A_4	16

Investor wishes to know how much to invest in each activity to maximize the total return on the investment.

Solution

Let x_1, x_2, x_3 and x_4 represent the percentages of the total fund invested in securities A_1, A_2, A_3 and A_4 respectively. Since the objective of the investor is to maximize total return on the investment,

Let x_1, x_2 and x_3 be the number of acres allotted for cultivating radish, mutter and potato respectively.

Sales Revenue/acre (Radish) = ₹ 5 × 1500 = ₹ 7,500

Sales Revenue/acre (Matter) = ₹ 4 × 1800 = ₹ 7,200

Sales Revenue/acre (Patato) = ₹ 5 × 1200 = ₹ 6,000

Now, the selling price, manure cost, labour cost and profit per acre of land for will be as fallows:

Per acre	*Radish*	*Muttar*	*Potato*
A. Selling Price	₹ 7,500	₹ 7,200	₹ 6,000
B. Manure Cost	$\frac{\text{Rs. } 12.50 \times 1500}{100}$ = ₹ 187.50	$\frac{\text{Rs. } 12.50 \times 1800}{100}$ = ₹ 225	$\frac{\text{Rs. } 12.50 \times 1200}{80}$ = ₹ 187.50
C. Labour Cost	₹.40 × 6 = ₹.240	₹.40 × 5 = ₹.200	₹.40 × 6 = ₹ 240
D. Profit [A – B – C]	= ₹.7,072.50	= ₹.6,775	= ₹ 5,572.50

Since, the agriculturist wants to maximise the total profit, hence the objective function of the problem is given by:

Maximise $Z = 7072.5x_1 + 6775x_2 + 5572.5x_3$

Subject to following constraints:

$x_1 + x_2 + x_3 \leq 125$ [Maximum Land Area]

$6x_1 + 5x_2 + 6x_3 \leq 500$ [Maximum Man Days]

where x_1, x_2 *and* $x_3 \geq 0$

Z = 10% (rupees invested in A_1) + 12% (rupees invested in A_2)

+ 14% (rupees invested in A_3) + 16% (rupees invested in A_4).

$= 0.10\ x_1 + 0.12\ x_2 + 0.14\ x_3 + 0.16\ x_4$

Since total money invested in activities is ₹ 1 lakh,

$$x_1 + x_2 + x_3 + x_4 \leq 1,00,000$$

Also money invested in activity A_2 and activity A_3 is less than or equal to 50% of money invested in four activities, therefore,

$$x_2 + x_3 \leq 0.50\ (x_1 + x_2 + x_3 + x_4)$$

or, $$-0.5x_1 + 0.5x_2 + 0.5x_3 - 0.5x_4 \leq 0$$

or, $$-x_1 + x_2 + x_3 - x_4 \leq 0$$

Further, the money invested in activity A_1 being greater than or equal to one-third of the money invested in activity A_4,

$$x_1 \geq 1/3x_4 \text{ or } 3x_1 - x_4 \geq 0$$

Thus, the appropriate mathematical formulation of the LP problem is:

Maximize $Z = 0.10x_1 + 0.12x_2 + 0.14x_3 + 0.16x_4$

Subject to the constraints:

$x_1 + x_2 + x_3 + x_4 \leq 1{,}00{,}000$ (Funds Constraint)

$-x_1 + x_2 + x_3 - x_4 \leq 0$ (Maximum Constraint)

$3x_1 - x_4 \geq 0$ (Minimum Constraint)

$x_1, x_2, x_3 \geq 0$ (Non-Negativity Constraint)

PROBLEM 1.11

A leading Chartered Accountant is attempting to determine a 'best' investment portfolio and is considering six alternative investment proposals. The following table indicates point estimates for the price per share, the annual growth rate in the price per share, the annual dividend per share and a measure of the risk associated with each investment.

PORTFOLIO DATA

	Shares under consideration					
	A	*B*	*C*	*D*	*E*	*F*
Current price per share (₹)	80	100	160	120	150	200
Projected annual growth rate	0.08	0.07	0.10	0.12	0.09	0.15
Projected annual dividend per share (₹)	4.00	4.50	7.50	5.50	5.75	0.00
Projected risk in return	0.05	0.03	0.10	0.20	0.06	0.08

1. The total amount available for investment is ₹ 25 lakhs and the following conditions are required to be satisfied.
2. The maximum rupee amount to be invested in alternative F is ₹ 2,50,000.
3. No more than ₹ 5,00,000 should be invested in alternatives A and B combined.
4. Total weighted risk should not be greater than 0.10, where

$$\text{Total weighted risk} = \frac{\text{(Amount invested in alternative) (risk of alternative)}}{\text{Total amount invested in all the alternatives}}$$

5. For the sake of diversity, at least 100 shares of each stock should be purchased.
6. At least 10 percent of the total investment should be in alternatives A and B combined.
7. Dividends for the year should be at least ₹ 10,000.

Rupees return per share of stock is defined as price per share one year hence less current price per share PLUS dividend per share. If the objective is to maximise total rupee return, formulate the linear Programming model for determining the optimal number of shares to be purchased in each of the shares under consideration. You may assume that the time horizon for the investment is one year. The formulated LP problem is not required to be solved.

SOLUTION

Let x_1, x_2, x_3, x_4, x_5 and x_6 denote the number of shares to be purchased in each of the six investment proposals A, B, C, D, E and F.

Rupee return per share = Price per share one year hence
Less Current price per share
Plus dividend per share
= Current price per share ✖ Projected annual growth rate
(i.e. Project growth for each share)
Plus dividend per share.

Thus, we get following table of data.

Investment alternatives	A	B	C	D	E	F
No. of shares purchased	x_1	x_2	x_3	x_4	x_5	x_6
Projected growth for each share (₹)	6.40	7.00	16.00	14.40	13.50	30.00
Projected annual dividend per share (₹)	4.00	4.50	7.50	5.50	5.75	0.00
Rupee return per share	10.40	11.50	23.50	19.90	19.25	30.00

The objective of the Chartered Accountant is to maximise the total rupee return, the objective function of the linear programming problem is given by:

Maximise $Z = 10.40x_1 + 11.50x_2 + 23.50x_3 + 19.90x_4 + 19.25x_5 + 30x_6$

Various constraints are as follows:

Since the total amount available for investment is ₹ 25 lakhs, hence

(I) $80x_1 + 100x_2 + 160x_3 + 120x_4 + 150x_5 + 200x_6 \leq 25,00,000$

(II) $200x_6 \leq 2,50,000$ [from condition (i)]

(III) $80x_1 + 100x_2 \leq 5,00,000$ [from condition (ii)]

(IV) As per condition (iii) of the problem

≤ 0.10

or $4x_1 + 3x_2 + 16x_3 + 24x_4 + 9x_5 + 16x_6 \leq 8x_1\ 10x_2 + 16x_3 + 12x_4 + 15x_5 + 20x_6$

or $-4x_1 - 7x_2 + 0x_3 + 12x_4 - 6x_5 - 4x_6 \leq 0$

(V) Also $x_i \geq 100$, i = 1, 2, 3, 4, 5, 6 ...[from condition (iv)]

(VI) $80x_1 + 100x_2 \geq 0.10\,(80x_1 + 100x_2 + 160x_3 + 120x_4 + 150x_5 + 200x_6)$

[from condition (v)]

on simplification, we get

$80x_1 + 100x_2 \geq 8x_1 + 10x_2 + 16x_3 + 12x_4 + 15x_5 + 20x_6$

or $72x_1 + 90x_2 - 16x_3 - 12x_4 - 15x_5 - 20x_6 \geq 0$

(VII) $4x_1 + 4.5x_2 + 7.5x_3 + 5.5x_4 + 5.75x_5 \geq 10,000$ [from condition (vi)]

Combining all the constraints from I...VII, the linear programming problem becomes

Maximise $Z = 10.40x_1 + 11.50x_2 + 23.50x_3 + 19.90x_4 + 19.25x_5 + 30x_6$

Subject to the constraints:

$80x_1 + 100x_2 + 160x_3 + 120x_4 + 150x_5 + 200x_6 \leq 25,00,000$ (Maximum Funds)

$200x_6 \leq 2,50,000$ (Max. Investment in Proposal F)

$80x_1 + 100x_1 \leq 5,00,000$ (Max. Investment in Proposal A & B)

$-4x_1 - 7x_2 + 0x_3 + 12x_4 - 6x_5 - 4x_6 \leq 0$ (Maximum Risk)

$xi, x_2, x_3, x_4, x_5, x_6, \geq 100$ (Minimum No. of Shares)

$72x_1 + 90x_2 - 16x_3 - 12x_4 - 15x_5 - 20x_6 \geq 0$ (Minimum Investment in Proposal A & B)

$4x_1 + 4.5x_2 + 7.5x_3 + 5.50x_4 + 5.75x_5 + 0x_6 \geq 10,000$ (Minimum Dividend)

PROBLEM 1.12

An advertising firm desires to reach two types of audiences - customers with annual income of more than ₹ 40,000 (target audience A) and customers with annual income of less than ₹ 40,000 (target audience B), The total advertising budget is ₹ 2,00,000. One programme of T.V. advertising costs ₹ 50,000 and one programme of Radio advertising costs ₹ 20,000. Contract conditions ordinarily require that there should be at least 3 programmes on T.V. and the number of programmes on Radio must not exceed 5. Survey indicates that a single T.V. programme reaches 7,50,000 customers in target audience A and 1,50,000 in target audience B. One Radio programme reaches 40,000 customers in target audience A and 2,60,000 in target audience B.

Formulate this as a linear programming problem and determine the media mix to maximize the total reach using graphic method.

Solution

Let x_1 be the number of programmes of T.V. advertising and X_2 denote the number of programmes of radio advertising.

Since the advertising firm desires to determine the media mix to maximise the total reach, the objective function is given by

Maximise $Z = (7,50,000+1,50,000)\ x_1 + (40,000+2,60,000)\ x_2$

Subject to the constraints

$5\ x_1 + 2\ x_2 < 20$ [Maximum Adv. Budget]

$x_1 \geq 3$, [Minimum T.V. Programmes]

$x_2 \leq 5$ [Maximum Radio Programmes]

where $x_2, x_2 > 0$

Point of intersection for lines $x_1 = 3$ and $5x_1 + 2x_2 = 20$ is P(3, 5/2).

Similarly, lines $x_2 = 5$ and $5x_1 + 2x_2 = 20$ intersect at point (2, 5).

Line $x_1 = 0$ meets $5x_1 + 2x_2 = 20$ at point (0, 10)

Line $x_2 = 0$ meets $5x_1 + 2x_2 = 20$ at point Q(4, 0)

The graphical solution for the problem is given below:

The feasible region is given by the shaded area PQR, and the feasible points are *P*(3,5/2), *Q*(3, 0) and *R*(4, 0).

Value of the objective function Z at P(3, 5/2) Is

$$9,00,000 \times 3 + 3,00,000 \times 5/2 = 27,00,000 + 7,50,000 = 34,50,000$$

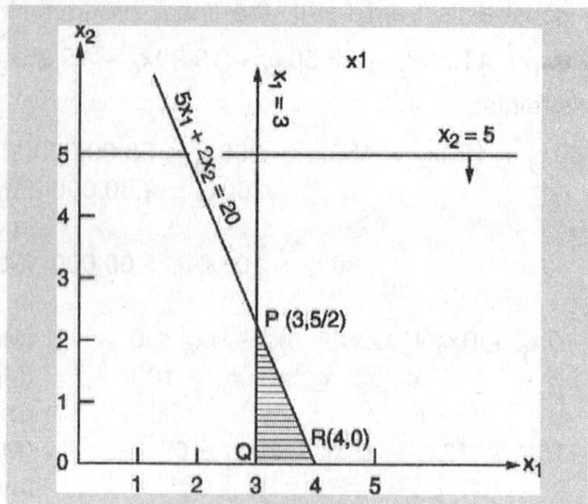

Fig. 1.1

Value of Z at Q(3, 0) is

$$9{,}00{,}000 \times 3 = 27{,}00{,}000$$

and value of Z at R(4, 0) is given by

$$9{,}00{,}000 \times 4 = 36{,}00{,}000$$

It can be seen that the value of Z is maximum at point R (4, 0). Thus, the solution to the given problem is:

$x_1 = 4$, $x_2 = 0$ and Maximum Z = 36,00,000.

In other words, the advertising firm should give 4 programmes on TV and no programme on Radio in order to achieve a maximum reach of 36,00,000 customers.

PROBLEM 1.13

Bharat Advertisers Ltd. is preparing a proposal for an advertising campaign for a client who are manufacturers of law products. An optimal allocation of advertising funds to maximise the total number of exposures has to be made for the client. The characteristics of the three alternative publications are shown in the following table.

	Home Beautiful	*Home and Garden*	*Law Care*
	₹	₹	₹
Cost Per Advertisement	12,000	16,000	900 0
Maximum no. of advertisements	12	24	12
Minimum no. of advertisements	3	6	2
Characteristics			
Homeowner	80%	70%	20%
Income : ₹ 10,000 or more	70%	80%	60%
Occupation : Gardener	15%	20%	40%
Audience size	1,00,000	50,000	2,00,000

The relative importance of the three characteristics are:

Homeowner, 0.4; income 0.2; gardener, 0.4. The advertising budget is ₹ 4,00,000. Formulate the LPP to find the most effective number of exposures in each magazine.

Solution

Let us first calculate, effective exposure

Media *A*	*Effectiveness Coefficient* *B*	*Audience Size* *C*	*Effective Exposure* *D = B 5 C*
1	0.80 (0.4) + 0.70 (0.2) + 0.15 (0.4) = 0.52	1,00,000	52,000
2	0.70 (0.4) + 0.80 (0.2) + 0.20 (0.4) = 0.52	50,000	26,000
3	0.20 (0.4) + 0.60 (0.2) + 0.40 (0.4) = 0.36	2,00,000	72,000

Let x_1, x_2 and x_3 represent the number of advertisement inserted in the three media 1, 2 and 3 respectively.

Since the objective is to maximize the effective exposure, the objective function is given by:

Maximize $Z = 52{,}000x_1 + 26{,}000x_2 + 72{,}000x_3$

Subject to:

$12{,}000x_1 + 16{,}000x_2 + 9{,}000x_3 \leq 4{,}00{,}000$ (Budget Amount constraint)

$x_1 \geq 3$ (Minimum No. of Advertisement in Home Beautiful constraint)

$x_2 \geq 6$ (Minimum No. of Advertisement in Home and Garden constraint)

$x_3 \geq 2$ (Minimum No. of Advertisement in Law Care constraint)

$x_1 \leq 12$ (Maximum Number of Advertisement in Home Beautiful constraint)

$x_2 \leq 24$ (Maximum Number of Advertisement in Home and Garden constraint)

$x_3 \leq 12$ (Maximum Number of Advertisement in Law Care constraint)

PROBLEM 1.14

The ABC Company, manufacturers of 'ZOLO', a leading brand of hair dye, are planning the media-mix for the next year within their and budget of ₹ 1,00,000. The characteristics of target audience for 'ZOLO' and weightages for each are as follows:

	Characteristics	*Weightage (%)*
Age	Over 35 years	50
Monthly income	Over ₹ 1,200	40
Education	Graduate and above	10

The audience characteristics for the three magazines under consideration are given below:

	Characteristic	*Magazine X(%)*	*Magazine Y(%)*	*Magazine Z(%)*
Age	Over 35 years	50	30	45
Monthly Income	Over ₹ 1,200	70	60	55
Education	Graduate and above	60	50	50

The cost per insertion and the readership for the three magazines are as follows:

Magazine	*Cost per insertion (₹)*	*Readership (in 000's)*
X (Monthly)	4,000	170
Y (Fortnightly)	3,500	220
Z (Monthly)	5,000	160

Also at least 2 insertions are necessary in X and Y to create an impact, whilst minimum 3 insertions will be required in case of Z.

Formulate a Linear Programming Model for the given problem to maximize the expected effective exposure.

Solution

Let x_1, x_2 and x_3 represent the number of advertisement inserted in the three magazines X, Y and Z respectively. In order to formulate the objective function, we shall first calculate the effectiveness coefficients as follows:

Media	*Effectiveness Coefficient*
Magazine X	0.50 5 0.50 + 0.70 5 0.40 + 0.60 5 0.10 = 0.59
Magazine Y	0.30 5 0.50 + 0.60 5 0.40 + 0.50 5 0.10 = 0.44
Magazine Z	0.45 5 0.50 + 0.55 5 0.40 + 0.50 5 0.10 = 0.495

The effective exposures for all the three media employed can be computed as follows:

Effective exposure = Effectiveness coefficient × Audience size, where effectiveness coefficient is a weighted average of audience characteristics. Thus effective exposure for

Magazine (X) = 0.59 × 170,000 = 1,00,300

Magazine (Y) = 0.44 × 220,000 = 96,800

Magazine (Z) = 0.495 × 160,000 = 79,200

Now the objective function and constraints of the linear programming model can be written as:

$$\text{Maximize } Z = 1{,}00{,}300x_1 + 96{,}800x_2 + 79{,}200x_3$$

Subject to the constraints:

$4{,}000x_1 + 3{,}500x_2 + 5{,}000x_3 \leq 1{,}00{,}000$ (Budget constraint)

$x_1 \geq 2,\ x_2 \geq 2,\ x_3 \geq 3$ (Minimum number of advertisements allowed constraints)

$x_1 \geq 0,\ x_2 \geq 0,\ x_3 \geq 0$ (Non-Negetivity constraints)

PROBLEM 1.15

Computer Company produces three types of models, which are first required to be machined and then assembled. The time (in hours) for these operations for each model is given below:

Model	*Machine Time*	*Assembly Time*
PIII	20	5
P II	15	4
Celeron	12	3

The total available machine time and assembly time are 1,000 hours and 1,500 hours respectively. The selling price and other variable costs for three models are:

	PIII	PII	Celeron
Selling Price (₹)	3,000	5,000	15,000
Labour, Material and other Variable Costs (₹)	2,000	4,000	8,000

The company has taken a loan of ₹ 50,000 from a Nationalised Bank, which is required to be repaid on 1.4.2011. In addition, the company has borrowed ₹ 1,00,000 from XYZ Cooperative Bank. However, this bank has given its consent to renew the loan.

The Balance Sheet of the company as on 31.3.2011 is as follows:

Liabilities	₹	*Assets*	₹
Equity Share Capital	1,00,000	Land	80,000
Capital reserve	20,000	Buildings	50,000
Profit & Loss Account	30,000	Plant & Machinery	1,00,000
Long-term Loan	2,00,000	Furniture etc.	20,000
Loan from XYZ Cooperative Bank	1,00,000	Vehicles	40,000
		Cash	2,10,000
Loan from National Bank	50,000		
	5,00,000		5,00,000

The company is required to pay a sum of ₹ 15,000 towards the salary. Interest on long-term loan is to be paid every month @ 18% per annum. Interest on loan from XYZ Cooperative and Nationalised Banks may be taken as ₹ 1,500 per month. The company has already promised to deliver three P III, Two P II and five Celeron Type of Computer to M/s ABC Ltd. next month. The level of operation in the company is subject to the availability of cash next month.

The Company Manager is willing to know that how many units of each model must be manufactured next month, so as to maximize the profit.

Required: Formulate a linear programming problem for the above.

Solution

Let X_1, X_2 and X_3 denote the number of P Hi, P II and Celeron computers respectively to be manufactured in the company. The following data is given:

	PIII	PII	Celeron
Selling Price per unit (₹)	3,000	5,000	15,000
Labour, Material & Other variable cost per unit (₹)	2,000	4,000	8,000
Profit per unit (₹)	1,000	1,000	7,000

Calculation of cash availability for the next month from the balance sheet:

Cash balance (₹ 2,10,000)

Loan to repay to Nationalized bank (₹ 50,000)

Interest on loan from XYZ cooperative bank and Nationalized bank (₹ 1500)

Interest on long term loans $\left[\dfrac{0.18 \times 2,00,000}{12}\right] = \text{Rs. } 3,000$

Salary to staff (₹ 15,000)

Or, Cash availability = ₹ 2,10,000 – (₹ 50,000 + ₹ 1,500 + ₹ 3,000 + ₹ 15,000)

= ₹ 1,40,500

Since the company wants to maximize the profit, hence the objective function is given by:

Maximize Z = $1000X_1 + 1000X_2 + 7000X_3$ – (₹ 15,000 + ₹ 3,000, + ₹ 1,500) Subject to the constraints:

$20X_1 + 15X_2 + 12X_3 < 1000$ (Machine Time Restriction)

$5X_1 + 4X_2 + 3X_3 < 1500$ (Assembly Time Restriction)

$2000X_1 + 4000X_2 + 8000X_3 <$ ₹ 1,40,500 (Cash Requirements & Availability)

$X_1 \geq 3$, $X_2 > 2$, $X_3 > 5$ (Minimum Deliveries)

X_1, X_2 and $X_3 \geq 0$

PROBLEM 1.16 [Capital Mix Problem]

The most recent audited summarised Balance Sheet of Stop and Shop Financial Services is given below:

Balance Sheet as on March 31, 20X1

Liabilities	*(₹ in lakhs)*	*Assets*	*(₹ in lakhs)*
Equity Share Capital	65	**Fixed Assets:**	
Reserves & Surplus	110	— Assets on Leave	
Term Loan from IFCI	80	(original cost: ₹ 550 lakhs)	375
Public Deposits	150	— Other Fixed Assets	50
Bank Borrowings	147	Investments (on wholly owned	
Other Current Liabilities	50	subsidiaries)	20
		Current Assets:	
		— Stock on Hire	80
		— Receivables	30
		— Other Current Assets	35
		Miscellaneous expenditure	
		(not written off)	12
	602		**602**

The company intends to enhance its investment in the lease portfolio by another ₹ 1,000 lakhs. For this purpose it would like to raise a mix of debt and equity in such a way that the overall cost of raising additional funds is minimised. The following constraints apply to the way the funds can be mobilised:

1. Total debt divided by net owned funds, cannot exceed 10.
2. Amount borrowed from financial institutions cannot exceed 25% of the net worth.
3. Maximum amount of bank borrowings cannot exceed three times the net owned funds.
4. The company would like to keep the total public deposit limited to 40% of the total debt.

The post-tax costs of the different sources of finance are as follows :

Equity	:	25%
Term Loans	:	8.5%
Public Deposits	:	7%
Bank Borrowings	:	10%

Formulate the funding problem as a LPP.

Note: (a) Total Debt = Term Loans from Financial Institutions + Public Deposits + Bank Borrowings
(b) Net Worth = Equity Share Capital + Reserve & Surplus
(c) Net Owned Funds= Net Worth – Miscellaneous Expenditures

Solution

Let x_1, x_2, x_3 and x_4 be the quantum of additional funds (all figures here are in lakhs) raised by way of additional equity, additional term loans, additional public deposits and additional bank borrowings respectively. The objective function to minimise the cost of additional funds raised by the company is as follows:

Minimize $Z = 0.25x_1 + 0.085x_2 + 0.07x_3 + 0.1x_4$

subject to the following constraints:

(1) $$\frac{\text{Total debt}}{\text{Net owned funds}} \leq 10$$

or $$\frac{(\text{Existing debt} + \text{Additional debt})}{(\text{Equity share capital} + \text{Reserves \& Surplus})} \leq 10$$

or $$\frac{(80 + 150 + 147 + x_2 + x_3 + x_4)}{(65 + 110 + x_1) - 12} \leq 10$$

or $$\frac{x_2 + x_3 + x_4 + 377}{(x_1 + 163)} \leq 10$$

or $x_2 + x_3 + x_4 + 377 \leq 10x_1 + 1630$

or $-10\,x_1 + x_2 + x_3 + x_4 \leq 1253$

(2) Amount borrowed (financial institutions) $\leq$ 25% of net worth

or (Existing long term loan from financial institutions + Additional loan) $\leq$ 25% (Existing Equity Capital + Reserves & Surplus + Addl. Equity Capital)

or $(80 + x_2) \leq 0.25\,(175 + x_1)$

$(80 + x_2) \leq 1/4\,(175 + x_1)$

PROBLEM 1.17

The costs and selling prices per unit of two products manufacturing by a company are as under:

Product	*A (₹)*	*B (₹)*
Selling Price	500	450
Variable costs:		
Direct Materials @ ₹ 25 per kg.	100	100
Direct Labour @ ₹ 20 per hour	80	40
Painting @ ₹ 30 per hour	30	60
Variable overheads	190	175
Fixed Costs @₹ 17.50/D.LHr.	70	35
Total Costs	470	410
Profit	30	40

In any month the maximum availability of inputs is limited to the following:

Direct Materials	480 kg.
Direct Labour hours	400 hours
Painting hours	200 hours

Required:

(I) Formulate a linear programme to determine the production plan which maximizes the profits by using graphical approach.

(ii) State the optimal product mix and the monthly profit derived from your solution in (i) above.

If the company can sell the painting time at ₹ 40 per hour as a separate service, show what modification will be required in the formulation of the linear programming problem. You are requi'ed to re-formulate the problem but not to solve.

Solution

Contribution Analysis

Products	*A* (₹)	*B* (₹)
A. Selling Price	500	450
B. Variable Costs:		
Direct Materials	100	100
Direct Labour	80	40
Painting	30	60
Variable Overheads	190	115
Total Variable Costs	400	375
C. Contribution (A – B)	100	175
Direct Material per unit	100/25 = 4 kg.	100/25 = 4 kg.
Direct Labour hour per unit	80/20 = 4 hours	40/20 = 2 hours
Painting hour per unit	30/30 = 1 hour	60/30 = 2 hours

Let A be the units to be produced of Product A and B be the units to be produced of Product B.

LP Problem formulation:

Max Z = 100A + 75B   Maximisation of contribution

Subject to:

$4A + 4B \leq 480$ Raw material constraint

$4A + 2B \leq 400$ Direct Labour hour constraint

$A + 2B \leq 200$ Painting hour constraint

$A, B \geq 0$ Non negativity constraint

Raw Material Constraint: Put B = 0, A = 120

Put A = 0, B = 120

Direct Labour Constraint: Put B = 0, A = 100

Put A = 0, B = 200

Painting Constraint: Put B = 0, A = 200

Put A = 0, B = 100

The graphical representation will be as under:

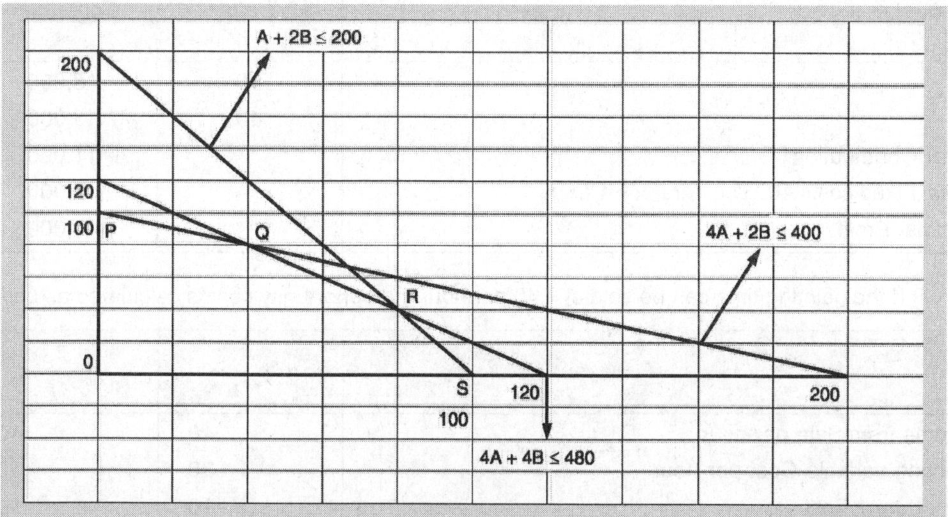

Fig.1.2

Q Intersects $4A + 2B = 400$ ...(1)

and $4A + 4B = 480$ ...(2)

Subtracting (2) from (1), we get $-2B = -80$

$\Rightarrow$ $B = 80/2 = 40$

Putting value of B in (1). we get $4A + 2 \times 40 = 400$

$\Rightarrow$ $A = \dfrac{400 - 80}{4} = 80$

R Intersects $4A + 4B = 480$ ...(3)

and $A + 26 = 200$ ...(4)

Multiplying (4) by (2) and then subtracting from (3), we get

$2A = 80$

$\Rightarrow$ $A = 40$

Putting the value of A in (4), we get $2B = 200 - 40$

$\Rightarrow$ $B = 80.$

Evaluation of Corner Points:

Point	*Products*		*Contribution*		*Total Contribution*
	A	B	A (₹) 100 perunit	B (₹) 75 per unit	₹
P	0	100	0	7,500	7,500
Q	80	40	8,000	3,000	11,000
R	40	80	4,000	6,000	10,000
S	100	0	10,000	0	10,000

Optimal Product Mix is Q

Product	*Units*	*Contribution* ₹
A	80	8,000
B	40	3,000
Total Contribution		11,000
Less: Fixed costs 400 D.L. Mrs. × ₹ 17.50		7,000
Optimal Profit		4,000

(iii) If the painting time can be sold at ₹ 40 per hour the opportunity cost is calculated as under:

	A (₹)	*B* (₹)
Income from Sale per hour	40	40
Painting variable Cost per hour	30	30
Opportunity Cost	10	10
Painting hours per unit	1	2
Opportunity Cost	10	20
Revised Contribution	100 – 10 = 90	75 – 20 = 55

Hence, modification is required in the objective function.

Re-formulated problem will be:

Z Max.	90A + 55B	Maximisation of contribution Subject to:
	$4A + 4B \leq 480$	Raw Material constraint
	$4A + 2B \leq 400$	Direct Labour hour constraint
	$A + 2B \leq 200$	Painting hour constraint
	$A, B \geq 0$	Non-negativity constraint

PROBLEM 1.18

Transport Ltd. provides tourist vehicles of 3 types - 20-seater vans, 8-seater big cars and 5-seater small cars. These seating capacities are excluding the drivers. The company has 4 vehicles of the 20-seater van type, 10 vehicles of the 8-seatcr big car types and 20 vehicles of the 5-seater small car types. These vehicles have to be used to transport employees of their client company from their residences to their offices and back. All the residences are in the same housing colony. The offices are at two different places, one is the Head Office and the other is the Branch. Each vehicle plies only one round trip per day, if residence to office in the morning and office to residence in the evening. Each day, 180 officials need to be transported in Route I (from residence to Head Office and back) and 40 officials need to be transported in Route II (from Residence to Branch office and back). The cost per round trip for each type of vehicle along each route is given below.

You are required to formulate the information as a linear programming problem, with the objective of minimising the total cost of [hiring vehicles] for the client company, subject to the constraints mentioned above, (only formulation is required. Solution is not needed).

	20-Seater Vans	8-Seater Big Cars	*Figs. – ₹/round trip* 5-seater Small Cars
Route I— Residence —Head Office and Back	600	400	300
Route II— Residence—Branch Office and Back	500	300	200

Solution

(a) Type	I 20 – Seater vans	II 8 – Sealer Big cars	III 5 – Seater Small cars	Total no. of Passengers
Route I Residence H.O. Residence	600	400	300	180
Route II Residence Br. Residence	500	300	200	40
No. of Vehicles	4	10	20	
Max. Capacity	80	80	100	220
				260
No. of Passengers				

Let i be the ith route,

and j be the type of vehicle, so that

S_{11} = no. of vans (vehicles on Route I, Type I)

S_{12} = no. of 8 seater cars on Route I

S_{13} = no. of 5 seater cars on Route I

S_{21} = no. of vans — on Route II

S_{22} = no. of 8 seater cars on Route II

S_{23} = no. of 5 seater cars on Route II

LPP

Minimise Cost $Z = 600\ S_{11} + 400\ S_{12} + 300\ S_{13} + 500\ S_{21} + 300\ S_{22} + 200\ S_{23}$

Subject to

$20\ S_{11} + 8\ S_{12} + 5\ S_{13} = 180$

$20\ S_{21} + 8\ S_{22} + 5\ S_{23} = 40$

$S_{11} + S_{21} \leq 4$

$S_{21} + S_{22} \leq 10$

$S_{31} + S_{32} \leq 20$

All $Sij \geq 0$

PROBLEM 1.19

The following matrix gives the unit cost of transporting a product from production plants P_1, P_2 and P_3 to destinations. D_1, D_2 and D_3. Plants P_1, P_2 and P_3 have a maximum production of 65, 24 and 111 units respectively and destinations D_1, D_2 and D_3 must receive at least 60, 65 and 75 units respectively:

To *From*	D_1	D_2	D_3	*Supply*
P_1	400	600	800	65
P_2	1,000	1,200	1,400	24
P_3	500	900	700	111
Demand	60	65	75	200

You are required to formulate the above as a linear programming problem. (Only formulation is needed. Please do not solve).

Solution

Let p_i, d_j, be the variable to denote the number of units of product from the ith plant to this jth destination, so that

$$P_1\, d_1 = \text{transport from plant } P_1 \text{ to } D_1$$

$$P_2\, d_2 = \text{transport from plant } P_2 \text{ to } D_2 \text{ etc.}$$

Objective function

$$\text{Minimize } Z = 400\, p_1d_1 + 600\, p_1d_2 + 800\, p_1d_3 + 1000\, p_2d_1 + 1200\, p_2d_2 + 1400\, p_2d_3 + 500\, p_3d_1 + 900\, p_3d_2 + 700\, p_3d_3.$$

Subject to:

$$\left.\begin{aligned} p_1d_1 + p_1d_2 + p_1d_3 &\le 65 \\ p_2d_1 + p_2d_2 + p_2d_3 &\le 24 \\ p_3d_1 + p_3d_2 + p_3d_3 &\le 111 \end{aligned}\right\} \text{(Plant constraints)}$$

and

$$\left.\begin{aligned} p_1d_1 + p_2d_1 + p_3d_1 &\le 60 \\ p_1d_2 + p_2d_2 + p_3d_2 &\le 65 \\ p_1d_3 + p_2d_3 + p_3d_3 &\le 75 \end{aligned}\right\} \text{(destination constraints)}$$

all $p_1d_1 \ge 0$

PROBLEM 1.20 [Transportation Problem]

A company is to subcontract work on four assemblies. The five subcontractors have agreed to submit a bid price on each assembly type and a limit on the total number of assemblies (if any combination) for which they are willing to contract. These bids, the contract times, and time requirements for assemblies are given in the following matrix.

		Subcontractor					
		A	***B***	***C***	***D***	***E***	***Assemblies Required***
	1	10	11	12	13	14	500
	2	11	12	11	10	9	300
Assembly	3	12	13	8	9	10	300
	4	13	8	9	10	11	400
Contract Limits		250	280	330	360	380	

Formulate the LP model.

Solution

Let x_{11} be Assembly 1 to Subcontractor A, x_{12} be assembly to Subcontractor B and so on.

		Subcontractor					
		A	***B***	***C***	***D***	***E***	***Assemblies Required***
	1	10 x_{11}	11 x_{12}	12 x_{13}	13 x_{14}	14 x_{15}	500
Assembly	2	11 x_{21}	12 x_{22}	11 x_{23}	10 x_{24}	9 x_{25}	300
	3	12 x_{31}	13 x_{32}	8 x_{33}	9 x_{34}	10 x_{35}	300
	4	13 x_{41}	8 x_{42}	9 x_{43}	10 x_{44}	11 x_{45}	400
Contract Limits		250	280	330	360	380	

It is a minimization problem since the objective is to minimize the cost of sub-contract price of the assembly. Hence, objective function is given by—

$$\text{Minimum} \quad Z = 10x_{11} + 11x_{12} + 12x_{13} + 13x_{14} + 14x_{15}$$
$$+ 11x_{21} + 12x_{22} + 11x_{23} + 10x_{24} + 9x_{25}$$
$$+ 12x_{31} + 13x_{32} + 8x_{33} + 9x_{34} + 10x_{35}$$
$$+ 13x_{41} + 8x_{42} + 9x_{43} + 10x_{44} + 11x_{45}$$

Subject to the following constraints:

$x_{11} + x_{21} + x_{31} + x_{41} \leq 250$ (No. of Contract limits)

$x_{12} + x_{22} + x_{32} + x_{42} \leq 280$ (No. of Contract limits)

$x_{13} + x_{23} + x_{33} + x_{43} \leq 330$ (No. of Contract limits)

$x_{14} + x_{24} + x_{34} + x_{44} \leq 360$ (No. of Contract limits)

$x_{15} + x_{25} + x_{35} + x_{45} \leq 380$ (No. of Contract limits)

$x_{11} + x_{12} + x_{13} + x_{14} + x_{15} \leq 500$ (No. of Assemblies required)

$x_{21} + x_{22} + x_{23} + x_{24} + x_{25} \leq 300$ (No. of Assemblies required)

$x_{31} + x_{32} + x_{33} + x_{34} + x_{35} \leq 300$ (No. of Assemblies required)

$x_{41} + x_{42} + x_{43} + x_{44} + x_{45} \leq 400$ (No. of Assemblies required)

$x_{ij} \geq 0$ for all i and j (Non-Negativity constraint)

PROBLEM 1.21

North-East Aircraft Company, which operates out of a central terminal, has 8 aircraft of Type I, 15 aircraft of Type II, and 12 aircraft of Type III available for today's flights. The tonnage capacities (in thousands of tons) are 4.5 for Type I, 7 for Type II and 4 for Type III.

The company dispatches its planes to cities A and B. Tonnage requirements (in thousands of tons) are 20 at city A and 30 at city B; excess tonnage capacity supplied to a city has no value. A plane can fly once only during the day.

The cost of sending a plane from the terminal to each city is given by the following table:

	Type I	*Type II*	*Type III*
City A	23	5	1.4
City B	58	10	3.8

Formulate the LP model to minimise the air-transportation cost.

Solution

Let x_{11} be the I planes coming to A, x_{12} the II plane coming to A; and so on.

		Aircraft Type			
		I	*II*	*III*	
		8	15	12	(Nos.)
		4.5	7	4	(Capacity in tons)
	Tons A(20)	x_{11}	x_{12}	x_{13}	Cost matrix
		23	5	1.4	
Requirements	B(30)	x_{21}	x_{22}	x_{23}	(Cost of sending a plane)
		58	10	3.8	

Min. Z = $23x_{11} + 5x_{12} + 1.4x_{13} + 58x_{21} + 10x_{22} + 3.8x_{23}$

$4.5x_{11} + 7x_{12} + 4x_{13} \geq 20$

$4.5x_{21} + 7x_{22} + 4x_{23} \geq 30$

$x_{21} + x_{11} \leq 8$

$x_{22} + x_{12} \leq 15$

$x_{23} + x_{72} \leq 12$

$xij \geq 0$

PROBLEM 1.22 [Assignment Problem]

A company has two grades of inspectors, 1 and 2 to undertake quality control inspection. At least 3,500 pieces must be inspected in an 8 hour day. Grade 1 inspector can check 50 pieces in an hour with an accuracy of 95%. Grade 2 inspector checks 25 pieces an hour with an accuracy of 90%.

The daily wages of grade 1 inspectors are ₹ 6 per hour while those of grade 2 inspectors are ₹ 5 per hour. Any error made by an inspector costs ₹ 4 per piece to the company. If there are, in all, 20 grade 1 inspectors and 25 grade 2 inspectors in the company, find the optimal assignment of inspectors that minimizes the daily inspection cost. Formulate the LP problem.

Solution

Let x_1 and x_2 be the number of grade 1 and 2 inspectors

Calculation of Inspection Cost of Inspectors

	Grade 1 (x_1)	Grade 2 (x_2)
A. Wage rate per hour	₹ 6	₹ 5
B. Inspection error cost per piece	₹ 4	₹ 4
C. Probability of Inspection Error	5%	10%
D. No. of pieces checked per hour	50	25
E. Cost of Inspection Error per hour [B 5 C 5 D]	₹ 10	₹ 10
F. Total Inspection cost per hour [A + E]	₹ 16	₹ 15
G. Total Inspection cost per day [F 5 8]	₹ 128	₹ 120

The above inspection problem can now be formulated in an appropriate mathematical from as follows:

Minimize (Daily inspection cost) $Z = 128x_1 + 120x_2$

Subject to the constraints:

$400x_1 + 200x_2 \geq 3500$ (Inspection pieces constraint)

$x_1 \leq 20$ (Grade 1 inspectors constraint)

$x_2 \leq 25$ (Grade 2 inspectors constraint)

$x_1, x_2 \geq 0$ (Non-Negetivity constraint)

PROBLEM 1.23 [Trim Problem]

The Fine Paper Company produces rolls of paper used in cash registers. Each roll of paper is 500 ft. in length and can be produced in widths of 1, 2, 3 and 5 inch. The company's production process results in 500' rolls that are 12 inches in width. Thus, the company must cut its 12 inch roll to the desired widths. It has six basic cutting alternatives as follows:

Cutting Alternative	*No . of Rolls*				*Waste (inches)*
	1"	*2"*	*3"*	*5"*	
1	6	3	0	0	0
2	0	3	2	0	0
3	1	1	1	1	1
4	0	0	2	1	1
5	5	2	1	0	1
6	4	2	1	0	1

The minimum demand requirements for the four rolls are as follows:

Roll Width (inches)	*Demand Requirements (Rolls)*
1	6000
2	4000
3	3000
5	2000

The company wishes to minimise the wastes generated by its production process, while meeting its demand requirements. Formulate the LP model.

Solution

Let x_j be the number of times cutting alternative (j = 1, 2, ... 6) is employed.

Since the objective is to minimize the waste generated, the objective function is given by—

Minimise (waste produced) $Z = 1x_3 + 1x_4 + 1x_5 + 1x_6$

Subject to constraints:

$6x_1 + 1x_3 + 5x_5 + 4x_6 \geq 6000$ (Minimum Demand Requirement of 1" Roll)

$3x_1 + 3x_2 + 1x_3 + 4x_5 + 2x_6 \geq 4000$ (Minimum Demand Requirement of 2" Roll)

$2x_2 + 1x_3 + 2x_4 + 1x_5 + 1x_6 \geq 3000$ (Minimum Demand Requirement of 3" Roll)

$1x_3 + 1x_4 \geq 2000$ (Minimum Demand Requirement of 5" Roll)

$x_j \geq 0$, for all j (Non-Negativity constraint)

PROBLEM 1.24 [Job Schedulings]

A big hospital has the following minimal daily requirements of doctors:

Period	**Clocktime (24 hours.)**	**No. of doctors required**
1	6 a.m. - 10 a.m.	72
2	10 a.m. - 2 p.m.	77
3	2 p.m. - 6 p.m.	85
4	6 p.m. - 10 p.m.	68
5	10 p.m. - 2 a.m.	25
6	2 a.m. - 6 a.m.	23

Doctors report to the hospital at the beginning of each period and work for 8 consecutive hours. Formulate this problem as a linear programming problem to minimise the total number of doctors to meet the needs of the hospital throughout the day.

Solution

Let x_1 represent the number of doctors required at starting period *k* (*k* = 1, 2, ..., 6). Then the objective function and constraints can be written as:

Minimise (total number of doctors)

$$Z = x_1 + x_2 + x_3 + x_4 + x_5 + x_6$$

Subject to the constraints:

(i) $\begin{pmatrix}\text{Number of doctors}\\\text{starting period 1}\end{pmatrix} + \begin{pmatrix}\text{Number of doctors that started}\\\text{at period 6 and still on duty}\end{pmatrix} \geq 72$

or, $x_1 + x_6 \geq 72$

(ii) $\begin{pmatrix}\text{Number of doctors}\\\text{starting period 2}\end{pmatrix} + \begin{pmatrix}\text{Number of doctors that started}\\\text{at period 1 and still on duty}\end{pmatrix} \geq 77$

or, $x_2 + x_1 \geq 77$

(iii) $\begin{pmatrix}\text{Number of doctors}\\\text{starting period 3}\end{pmatrix} + \begin{pmatrix}\text{Number of doctors that started}\\\text{at period 2 and still on duty}\end{pmatrix} \geq 85$

or, $x_3 + x_2 \geq 85$

(iv) $\begin{pmatrix}\text{Number of doctors}\\\text{starting period 4}\end{pmatrix} + \begin{pmatrix}\text{Number of doctors that started}\\\text{at period 3 and still on duty}\end{pmatrix} \geq 68$

or, $x_4 + x_3 \geq 68$

(v) $\begin{pmatrix}\text{Number of doctors}\\\text{starting period 5}\end{pmatrix} + \begin{pmatrix}\text{Number of doctors that started}\\\text{at period 4 and still on duty}\end{pmatrix} \geq 25$

or, $x_5 + x_4 \geq 25$

(vi) $\begin{pmatrix}\text{Number of doctors}\\\text{starting period 6}\end{pmatrix} + \begin{pmatrix}\text{Number of doctors that started}\\\text{at period 5 and still on duty}\end{pmatrix} \geq 23$

or, $x_6 + x_5 \geq 23$

Alternative Solution:

Minimize $Z = x_1 + x_2 + x_3 + x_4 + x_5 + x_6$

Subject to constraints:

$x_1 + x_2 \geq 72$

$x_2 + x_3 \geq 77$

$x_3 + x_4 \geq 85$

$x_4 + x_5 \geq 68$

$x_5 + x_6 \geq 25$

$x_6 + x_1 \geq 23$

$x_1 \geq 0,\ x_2 \geq 0,\ x_3 \geq 0,\ x_4 \geq 0,\ x_5 \geq 0,\ x_6 \geq 0,$

Note: There also exist other alternative solutions.

MISCELLENEOUS SOLVED PROBLEMS

PROBLEM 1.25

Piyush is an aspiring freshman at Delhi University. He realizes that "all work and no play make Piyush a dull boy." As a result, Piyush wants to apportion his available time of about 10 hours a day between work and play. He estimates that play is twice as much fun as work. He also wants to study at least as much as he plays. However, he realizes that if he is going to get all his homework assignments done, he cannot play more than 4 hours a day. How should Piyush allocate his time to miximize his pleasure from both work and play?

Solution

Let x_1 = play hours per day, x_2 = work hours per day

Maximize $Z = 2x_1 + x_2$

Subject to,

$x_1 + x_2 \leq 10$ [Maximum Total Time constraint]

$x_1 + x_2 \leq 0$ [Minimum Work Hours constraint]

$x_1 \leq 4$ [Maximum Play Hours constraint]

$x_1, x_2 \geq 0$ [Non negativity constraint]

PROBLEM 1.26

An assembly line consisting of three consecutive stations produces two radio models: HiFi-1 and HiFi-2. The following table porvides the assembly times for the three workstations.

Workstation	*Minutes per unit*	
	HiFi-1	*HiFi-2*
1	6	4
2	5	5
3	4	6

The daily maintenance for stations 1, 2, and 3 consumes 10%, 14%, and 12%, respectively, of the maximum 480 minutes available for each station each day. Determine the optimal product mix that will minimize the idle (or unused) time in the three workstations.

Solution

Let x_1 = Number of HiFi 1 units, x_2 = Number of HiFi 2 units

Minimize $Z = 1267.2 - (15x_1 + 15x_2)$

As, Total Minutes per unit of HiFi 1 = 6 + 5 + 4 = 15 minutes &

Total Minutes per unit of HiFi 2 = 4 + 5 + 6 = 15 minutes

Total Available Time = 432 + 412.8 + 422.4 = 1267.2 minutes

Subject to,

$6x_1 + 4x_2 \leq 432$ Ist constraint [480 – 10% of 480] [Time constraint]

$5x_1 + 5x_2 \leq 412.8$ IInd constraint [480 – 14% of 480] [Time constraint]

$4x_1 + 6x_2 \leq 422.4$ IIIrd constraint [480 – 12% of 480] [Time constraint]

$x_1, x_2 \geq 0$ [Non negativity constraint]

PROBLEM 1.27

A city will undetake five urban renewal housing projects over the next five years. Each project has a different starting year and a different duration. The following table provides the basic data of the situation:

	Year 1	*Year 2*	*Year 3*	*Year 4*	*Year 5*	*Cost (million $)*	*Annual income (million $)*
Project 1	Start		End			5.0	.05
Project 2		Start			End	8.0	.07
Project 3	Start				End	15.0	.15
Project 4			Start	End		1.2	.02
Budget (million $)	3.0	6.0	7.0	7.0	7.0		

Projects 1 and 4 must be finished completely within their durations. The remaining two projects can be finished partially within budget limitations, if necessary. However, each project must be at least 25% completed within its duration. At the end of each year, the completed section of a project is immediately occupied by tenants and a proportional amount of income is realized.

Solution

Let x_{11} = Portion of project 1 completed in year 1
x_{12} = Portion of project 1 competed in year 2
x_{13} = Portion of project 1 completed in year 3 [Project End]
x_{22} = Portion of project 2 completed in year 2 [As Project 2 starts in year 2]
x_{23} = Portion of project 2 completed in year 3
x_{24} = Portion of project 2 completed in year 4
x_{25} = Portion of project 2 completed in year 5
x_{31} = Portion of project 3 completed in year 1
x_{32} = Portion of project 3 completed in year 2
x_{33} = Portion of project 3 completed in year 3
x_{34} = Portion of project 3 completed in year 4
x_{35} = Portion of project 3 completed in year 5
x_{43} = Portion of project 4 completed in year 3 [As project 4 starts in year 3]
x_{44} = Portion of project 4 completed in year 4 [Project End]

Note: Year 5 will not be considered, for revenue for revenue come in next year and we are considering 5 year horizon. Now optimum function of project 1 is

Year 2 Year 3 Year 4 Year 5

$$[x_{11} \times 0.05] + [(x_{11} + x_{12})\ 0.05] + [(x_{11} + x_{12} + x_{13})\ 0.05] + [(x_{11} + x_{12} + x_{13})\ 0.05]$$

i.e. $$0.05\ [x_{11} + (x_{11} + x_{12}) + (x_{11} + x_{12} + x_{13}) + (x_{11} + x_{12} + x_{13})]$$

$$= 0.05(4x_{11} + 3x_{12} + 2x_{13})$$

Similarly for project 2, 3 and 4

$$0.07\ (3x_{22} + 2x_{23} + x_{24})$$

$$0.15\ (4x_{31} + 3x_{32} + 2x_{33} + x_{34})$$

$0.02\ (2x_{43} + x_{44})$ respectively

$$\text{Maximize } Z = 0.05\ (4x_{11} + 3x_{12} + 2x_{13}) + 0.07\ (3x_{22} + 2x_{23} + x_{24}) + 0.15\ (4x_{31} + 3x_{32} + 2x_{33} + x_{34}) + 0.02\ (2x_{43} + x_{44})$$

Subject to

$x_{11} + x_{12} + x_{13} = 1$ I[st] constraint [Project 1 to be completed at given time]

$x_{43} + x_{44} = 1$ IInd constraint [Project 4 to be completed at given time]

$x_{22} + x_{23} + x_{24} + x_{25} \geq 0.25$ IIIrd constraint [Minimum completion constraint]

$x_{22} + x_{23} + x_{24} + x_{25} \leq 1$ IVth constraint

$x_{31} + x_{32} + x_{33} + x_{34} + x_{35} \geq 0.25$ V[th] constraint [Minimum completion constraint]

$x_{31} + x_{32} + x_{33} + x_{34} + x_{35} \leq 1$ VIth constraint

$5x_1 + 15x_{31} \leq 3$ VIIth constraint [Budget constraint]

$5x_{12} + 8x_{22} + 15x_{32} \leq 6$ VIIIth constraint [Budget constraint]

$5x_{13} + 8x_{23} + 15x_{33} + 1.2x_{43} \leq 7$ IXth constraint [Budget constraint]

$8x_{24} + 15x_{34} + 1.2x_{44} \leq 7$ X[th] constraint [Budget constraint]

$8x_{25} + 15x_{35} \leq 7$ XIth constraint [Budget constraints]

$x_{11}, x_{12}, x_{13}; x_{22}, x_{23}, x_{24}; x_{31}, x_{32}, x_{33}, x_{34}; x_{43}, x_{44} \geq 0$ [Non negativity constraint]

PROBLEM 1.28

Prarthna Mittal owns 800 acres of undeveloped land on a scenic lake in the heart of the Ozark Mountains. In the past, little or no regulation was imposed upon new developments around the lake. The lake shores are now dotted with vacation homes, and septic tanks, most of them improperly installed, are in extensive use. Over the years, seepage from the septic tanks led to severe water pollution. To curb further degradation of the lake, county officials have approved stringent ordinances applicable to all future developments: (1) Only single, double, and triple-family homes can be constructed, with single-family homes accounting for at least 50% of the total. (2) To limit the number of septic tanks, minimum lot sizes of 2, 3, and 4 acres are required for single, double, and triple-family homes, respectively. (3) Recreation areas of 1 acre each must be established at the rate of one area per 200 families. (4) To preserve the ecology of the lake, underground water may not be pumped out for house or garden use. The president of Realco is studying the possiblity of developing the 800-acre property. The new development will include single, double, and triple-family homes. It is estimated that 15% of the acreage will be allocated to streets and utility easements. Realco estimates the returns from the different housing units as follows:

Housing unit	*Single*	*Double*	*Triple*
Net return per unit (₹)	10,000	12,000	15,000

The cost of connecting water service to the area is proportionate to the number of units constructed. However, the county charges a minimum of ₹ 100,000 for the project. Additionally, the expansion of the water system beyond its present capacity is limited to 200,000 gallons per day during peak periods. The following data summarize the water service connection cost as well as the water consumption, assuming an average size family:

Housing unit	*Single*	*Double*	*Triple*	*Recreation*
Water service connection cost per unit (₹)	1000	1200	1400	800
Water consumption per unit (gal/day)	400	600	840	450

Develop an optimal plan for Prarthna Mittal.

Solution

Let x_1 = Single Family Home
x_2 = Double Family Home
x_3 = Triple Family Home
x_4 = Recreation Area

Now,

$$(10,000 - 1000)x_1 + (12,000 - 1200)x_2 + (15000 - 1400)x_3 - 800\,x_4$$

i.e. Maximize $Z = 9000x_1 + 10,800x_2 + 13,600x_3 - 800x_4$

Subject to

$2x_1 + 3x_2 + 4x_3 + x_4 \leq 680$ Ist constraint as [800 – 15% of 800] [size constraint]

$x_1 \geq \frac{1}{2}(x_1 + x_2 + x_3)$... [at least 50% of total constraint]

$\Rightarrow$ $0.5x_1 - 0.5x_2 - 0.5x_3 \geq 0$ IInd constraint

$x_4 \geq \frac{x_1 + 2x_2 + 3x_3}{200}$ [Recreation area per family constraint]

$\Rightarrow$ $200x_4 - x_1 - 2x_2 - 3x_2 \geq 0$ IIIrd constraint

$400x_1 + 600x_2 + 840x_3 + 450x_4 \leq 2,00,000$ IVth constraint [water capacity constraint]

$x_1, x_2, x_3, x_4 \geq 0$ [Non negativity constraint]

PROBLEM 1.29

Investor Piyush Jindal has ₹ 10,000 to invest in four projects. The following table gives the cash flow for the four investments.

Project	*Cash flow (₹ 1000) at the start of*				
	Year 1	*Year 2*	*Year 3*	*Year 4*	*Year 5*
1	–1.00	0.50	0.30	1.80	1.20
2	–1.00	0.60	0.20	1.50	1.30
3	0.00	–1.00	0.80	1.90	0.80
4	–1.00	0.40	0.60	1.80	0.95

The information in the table can be interpreted as follows: For project 1, ₹ 1.00 invested at the start of year 1 will yield ₹ 50 at the start of year 2, ₹ .30 at the start of year 3, ₹ 1.80 at the start of year 4, and ₹ 1.20 at the start of year 5. The remaining entries can be interpreted similarly. The entry 0.00 indicates that no transaction is taking place. Doe has the additional option of investing in a bank account that earns 6.5% annually. All funds accumulated at the end of one year can be reinvested in the following year. Formulate the problem as a linear program to determine the optimal allocation of funds to investment opportunities.

Solution

Let x_1 = Amount invested in project 1 in beginning of year 1
x_2 = Amount invested in project 2 in beginning of year 1
x_3 = Amount invested in project 3 in beginning of year 2
x_4 = Amount invested in project 4 in beginning of year 1

y_1 = Amount invested in Bank in beginning of year 1
y_2 = Amount invested in Bank in beginning of year 2
y_3 = Amount invested in Bank in beginning of year 3
y_4 = Amount invested in Bank in beginning of year 4
y_5 = Amount invested in Bank at the end of year 4

Maximize $Z = Y_5$

Subject to

$x_1 + x_2 + x_4 + y_1 \leq 10{,}000$ I[st] constraint [Budget constraint]
$0.5x_1 + 0.6x_2 - x_3 + 0.4x_4 + 1.065y_1 - y_2 = 0$ IInd constraint [Budget constraint]
$0.3x_1 + 0.2x_2 + 0.8x_3 + 0.6x_4 + 1.065y_2 - y_3 = 0$ IIIrd constraint [Budget constraint]
$1.8x_1 + 1.5x_2 + 1.9x_3 + 1.8x_4 + 1.065y_3 - y_4 = 0$ IVth constraint [Budget constraint]
$1.2x_1 + 1.3x_2 + 0.8x_3 + 0.95x_4 + 1.065y_4 - y_5 = 0$ V[th] constraint [Budget constraint]
$x_1, x_2, x_3, x_4; y_1, y_2, y_3, y_4 \geq 0$ [Non negativity constraint]

PROBLEM 1.30

TULSIAN Construction can bid on two 1-year projects. The following table provides the quarterly cash flow (in millions of dollars) for the two projects.

Project	Cash flow (in millions of ₹) at				
	1/1/11	*4/1/11*	*7/1/11*	*10/1/11*	*12/31/011*
I	–1.0	–3.1	–1.5	1.8	5.0
2	–3.0	–2.5	1.5	1.8	2.8

TULSIAN has cash funds of ₹ 1 million at the beginning of each quarter and may borrow at most ₹ 1 million at a 10% nominal annual interest rate. Any borrowed money must be returned at the end of the quarter. Surplus cash can earn quarterly interest at an 8% nominal annual rate. Net accumulation at the end of one quarter is invested in the next quarter.

Assume that TULSIAN is allowed partial or full participation in the two projects. Determine the level of participation that will maximize the net cash accumulated on 31.12.2011.

Solution

Let x_1 = Degree of participation in project 1
x_2 = Degree of participation in project 2
b_1 = Borrowings in beginning of quarter 1
b_2 = Borrowings in beginning of quarter 2
b_3 = Borrowings in beginning of quarter 3
b_4 = Borrowings in beginning of quarter 4
S_1 = Surplus in beginning of quarter 1
S_2 = Surplus in beginning of quarter 2
S_3 = Surplus in beginning of quarter 3
S_4 = Surplus in beginning of quarter 4
S_5 = Surplus in beginning of quarter 4

Maximize S_5

Subject to

$x_1 + 3x_2 + S_1 - b_1 = 1$ I[st] constraint [Budget constraint]
as $[x_1 + 3x_2 + S_1 = 1 - b_1]$
$3.1x_1 + 2.5x_2 + 1.025b_1 - b_2 - 1.02\,S_1 + S_2 = 1$ IInd constraint [Budget constraint]
$[\text{as } 3.1x_1 + 2.5x_2 + 1.025b_1 - 1.02\,S_1 + S_2 = 1 + b_1]$

$1.5x_1 - 1.5x_2 + 1.025b_3 - 1.02\ S_2 - b_3 + S_3 = 1$ IIIrd constraint [Budget constraint]
$-1.8x_1 - 1.8x_2 + 1.025b_3 - 1.02S_3 - b_4 + S_4 = 1$ IVth constrain [Budget constraint]
$5x_1 - 2.8x_2 + 1.025b_4 - 1.02S_4 + S_5 = 0$ V[th] constraint [Budget constraint]
$b_1 \le 1, b_2 \le 1, b_3 \le 1, b_4 \le 1$ VIth constraint [As borrowings can not be more than 1]
$x_1, x_2, b_1, b_2, b_3, b_4, S_1, S_2, S_3, S_4, S_5 \ge 0$ [Non negativity constraint]

PROBLEM 1.31

A business executive has the option to invest money in two plans: Plan A guarantees that each dollar invested will earn ₹ .70 a year later, and plan B guarantees that each rupee invested will earn ₹ 2 after 2 years. In plan A, investments can be made annually, and in plan B, investments are allowed for periods that are multiples of two years only. How should the executive invest ₹ 100,000 to maximize the earnings at the end of 3 years?

Solution

Let A_1 = Amount Invested in plan A in beginning of year 1
A_2 = Amount Invested in plan A in beginning of year 2
A_3 = Amount Invested in plan A in beginning of year 3
A_4 = Amount Invested in plan A in beginning of year 3
B_1 = Amount Invested in plan B in beginning of year 1
B_2 = Amount Invested in plan B in beginning of year 2

Maximize A_4

$A_1 + B_1 = 1{,}00{,}000$ I[st] constraint [Budget constraint]
$-1.70A_1 + A_2 + B_2 = 0$ IInd constraint [Budget constraint]
$-1.70A_2 + A_3 - 3B_1 = 0$ IIIrd constraint [Budget constraint]
$1.70A_3 - A_4 + 3B_2 = 0$ IVth constraint [Budget constraint]
$A_1, A_2, A_3, A_4, B_1, B_2 \ge 0$ [Non negativity constraint]

PROBLEM 1.32

TUSHAR Manufacturing Company has contracted to deliver home windows over the next 6 months. The demands for each month are 100, 250, 190, 140, 220 and 110 units, respectively. Production cost per window varies from month to month depending on the cost of labor, material, and utilities. Acme estimates the production cost per window over the next 6 months to be \$50, \$45, \$55, \$48, \$52, and \$50, respectively. To take advantage of the fluctuations in manufacturing cost, Acme may elect to produce more than is needed in a given month and hold the excess units for delivery in later months. This, however, will incur storage costs at the rate of \$8 per window per month assessed on end-of-month inventory. Develop a linear program to determine the optimum production schedule.

Solution

Let x_1 = No. of units produced in 1st month
x_2 = No. of units produced in 2nd month
x_3 = No. of units produced in 3rd month
x_4 = No. of units produced in 4th month
x_5 = No. of units produced in 5th month
x_6 = No. of units produced in 6th month
S_1 = Inventory at the end of 1st month
S_2 = Inventory at the end of 2nd month
S_3 = Inventory at the end of 3rd month
S_4 = Inventory at the end of 4th month
S_5 = Inventory at the end of 5th month

Minimize $Z = 50x_1 + 45x_2 + 55x_3 + 48x_4 + 52x_5 + 50x_6 + 8S_1 + 8S_2 + 8S_3 + 8S_4 + 8S_5$

Subject to,

$x_1 - S_1 = 100$ Ist constraint [Demand constraint]

$x_2 + S_1 - S_2 = 250$ IInd constraint [Demand constraint]

$x_3 + S_2 - S_3 = 190$ IIIrd constraint [Demand constraint]

$x_4 + S_3 - S_4 = 140$ IVth constraint [Demand constraint]

$x_5 + S_4 - S_5 = 220$ Vth constraint [Demand constraint]

$x_6 + S_5 = 110$ VIth constraint [Demand constraint]

$x_1, x_2, x_3, x_4, x_5, x_6, S_1, S_2, S_3, S_4, S_5 \geq 0$ [Non negativity constraint]

PROBLEM 1.33

A company will manufacture a product for the next four months: March, April, May and June. The demands for each month are 520, 720, 520 and 620 units, respectively. The company has a steady workforce of 10 employees but can meet fluctuating production needs by hiring and firing temporary workers, if necessary. The extra costs of hiring and firing in any month are ₹ 200 and ₹ 400 per worker, respectively. A permanent worker can produce 12 units per month, and a temporary worker, lacking comparable experience, only produce 10 units per month. The company can produce more than needed in any month and carry the surplus over to a succeeding month at a holding cost of ₹ 50 per unit per month. Develop an optimal hiring/firing policy for the company over the four-month planning horizon.

Solution

Let H_1 = Hired labour in month of March

H_2 = Hired labour in month of April

H_3 = Hired labour in month of May

H_4 = Hired labour in month of June

F_2 = Fired labour in month of April

F_3 = Fired labour in month of May

F_4 = Fired labour in month of June

S_1 = Inventory in month of March

S_2 = Inventory in month of April

S_3 = Inventory in month of May

Minimize $Z = 200(H_1 + H_2 + H_3 + H_4) + 400(F_2 + F_3 + F_4) + 50(S_1 + S_2 + S_3)$

Subject to

$10H_1 - S_1 = 400$ Ist constraint [Demand for month of March constraint]

as $10H_1 + (12 \times 10) - S_1 = 520$

$\Rightarrow 10H_1 - S_1 = 520 - 120 = 400$

Similary

$10H_2 + 10(H_1 - F_2) + S_1 - S_2 = 600$ IInd constraint [Demand for month of April constraint]

$10H_3 + 10(H_2 + H_1 - F_2 - F_3) + S_2 - S_3 = 400$ IIIrd constraint

[Demand for the month of May constraint]

$10H_4 + 10(H_3 + H_2 + H_1 - F_2 - F_3 - F_4) + S_3 = 500$

[Demand for the month of June constraint]

$H_1, H_2, H_3, H_4, F_2, F_3, F_4, S_1, S_2, S_3 \geq 0$ [Non negativity constraint]

PROBLEM 1.34

A firm wants to reach two types of customers: House holds having ₹ 5 lakhs or more of annual family income and those having income of less than ₹ 5 lakhs. The first category purchases twice as much as the second group. One unit of TV advertisement reaches 2,000 families of first group and 8000 families of second group and costs ₹ 20,000 while advertisements in a magazine costs ₹ 12,000 and reaches 6,000 and 3,000 families respectively. Not more than 12 advertisements can be given in the magazine and at least 6 TV advertisements have to be given. The advertisement budget is ₹ 1,80,000. Assume that every contracted family purchases the company product. The firm wants to maximize its sales. Formulate the above problem as a linear programming model.

Solution

Determination of Revenue Function

Let,

No. of T.V advertisement to be given x_1

No. of magazine advertisement to be given x_2

As T.V advertisement reaches 2000 families of first group and 8000 families of second group. Therefore effective reach $[(2000 \times 2) + 8000] = 12000$.

In case of magazine advertisement

$= 6000 \times 2 + 3000 = 15000.$

Therefore Maximise $Z = 12000x_1 + 15000x_2$

Subject to

$x_2 \leq 12$ Ist constraint [Maximum no. of Magazine Advertisement constaint]

$x_1 \geq 6$ IInd constraint [Minimum no. of T.V Advertisement constraint]

$20{,}000\ x_1 + 12{,}000x_2 \leq 1{,}80{,}000$ IIIrd constraint [Budget constraint]

$x_1, x_2 \geq 0$ Non negativity constraint.

PROBLEM 1.35

Industrial design company has been awarded a contract to design a label for a new medicine produced by a pharmaceutical company. The company estimates that 150 hours will be required to complete the project. The firm's three graphic designers available with the company for this project are Leena a senior designer and team leader; Rahul, a senior designer and Sarah, a junior designer. Because Leena has worked on several projects for the company, and that she must be assigned 40% of the total number of hours assigned to the two senior designers. To provide label designing experience for Sarah, she must be assigned at least 15% of the total project time. However, the number of hours assigned to Sarah must not exceed 25% of the total number of hours assigned to the two senior designers. Due to other projects commitments, leena has a maximum of 50 hours available to work on the project.

Hourly wage rate are ₹ 1,500 for Leena, ₹ 1,250 for Rahul and ₹ 900 for Sarah.

Formulate a linear programme problem to determine number of hours each graphic designer should be assigned for the project to minimize the total cost.

Solution

Let x_1 = Work hours of Leena

x_2 = Work hours of Rahul

x_3 = Work hours of Sarah

Minimize $Z = 1500x_1 + 1250x_2 + 900x_3$

Subject to,

$x_1 + x_2 + x_3 = 150$ Ist constraint [Total hours constraint]

also $x_1 \geq \frac{2}{5}[x_1 + x_2]$ [Leena should work 40% i.e. (2/5) of works of senior managers]

i.e. $5x_1 - 2x_1 - 2x_2 \geq 0$

$\Rightarrow$ $3x_1 - 2x_2 \geq 0$ IInd constraint

also, $x_3 \geq \frac{15}{100}(x_1 + x_2 + x_3)$ [Sarah should work at least 15%]

i.e. $100x_3 - 15x_1 - 15x_2 - 15x_3 \geq 0$

$\Rightarrow$ $-15x_1 - 15x_2 + 85x_3 \geq 0$ IIIrd constraint

$x_3 \leq \frac{1}{4}(x_1 + x_2)$ [Sarah can work maximum 25%. i.e. 1/4 of work of senior managers]

i.e. $4x_3 - x_1 - x_2 \leq 0$

$\Rightarrow$ $-x_1 - x_2 + 4x_3 \leq 0$ IVth constraint

$x_1 \leq 50$ Vth constraint [Leena can work maximum 50 hours]

$x_1, x_2, x_3 \geq 0$ [Non negativity constraint]

PROBLEM 1.36

A complete unit of certain product consists of 4 units of component A, 3 units of component B and 2 units of component C. The three components (A, B and C) are manufactured from two different raw materials of which 500 units and 800 units, respectively are available. Four departments are engaged in the production process. The following table gives the raw material requirement per production run and the resulting units of each component. The objective is to determine the number of production runs for each department which will maximise the total number of complete units of the final product. Formulate the problem as a linear programming problem:

	Input per run (units)		*Output per run (units)*		
Deptd.	*Raw material 1*	*Raw material 2*	*Component A*	*Component B*	*Component C*
1	6	4	5	3	3
2	3	7	4	7	6
3	1	6	6	2	5
4	2	5	7	3	2

Solution

Let y be the number of find units

x_1 = No. of production run in deptt. 1

x_2 = No. of production run in deptt. 2

x_3 = No. of production run in deptt. 3

x_4 = No. of production run in deptt. 4

Maximise Z = y

Subject to constraint

$6x_1 + 3x_2 + x_3 + 2x_4 \leq 500$ [Raw material 1 constraint]

$4x_1 + 7x_2 + 6x_3 + 5x_4 \leq 800$ [Raw material 2 constraint]

$$\frac{5x_1 + 4x_2 + 6x_3 + 7x_4}{4} \geq y$$

$5x_1 + 4x_2 + 6x_3 + 7xy - 4y \geq 0$ (Component units of A constraint)

$$\frac{3x_1 + 7x_2 + 2x_3 + 3x_4}{3} \geq y$$

$3x_1 + 7x_2 + 2x_3 + 3x_4 - 3y \geq 0$ (Component units of B constraint)

$$\frac{3x_1 + 6x_2 + 5x_3 + 2x_4}{2} \geq y$$

$3x_1 + 6x_2 + 5x_3 + 2x_4 - 2y \geq 0$ (Component units of C constraint)

$x_1, x_2, x_3, x_4, y \geq 0$ (Non negativity constraint).

PROBLEM 1.37

The PQR stone company sells stone secure feam any of three adjacent quaries. The stone sold by the company must conform to the following specifications:

Material X equal to 30%
Material Y equal to or less than 40%
Material Z between 30% and 40%

Stone from quarry A costs ₹ 100 per tonne and has the following properties:

Material X – 20%

Material Y – 60%

Material Z – 20%

Stone from quarry B costs ₹ 120 per tonne and has the following properties:

Material X – 20%
Material Y – 30%
Material Z – 30%

Stone from quarry C costs ₹ 150 per tonne and has the following properties:

Material X – 10%
Material Y – 40%
Material Z – 50%

From what quarries should PQR stone company secure rock in order to minimise the cost per tonne of rock.

Solution

Let,

x_1 = Proportion of tonne of rock to be secured from quarry A
x_2 = Proportion of tonne of rock to be secured from quarry B
x_3 = Proportion of tonne of rock to be secured from quarry C

Minimise $Z = 100x_1 + 120x_2 + 150x_3$

Subject to constraints

$0.20x_1 + 0.40x_2 + 0.10x_3 = 0.30$ [Material X constraint]
$0.60x_1 + 0.30x_2 + 0.40x_3 \leq 0.40$ [Material Y constraint]
$0.20x_1 + 0.30x_2 + 0.50x_3 \geq 0.30$ [Minimum material 2 constraint]
$0.20x_1 + 0.30x_2 + 0.50x_3 \leq 0.40$ [Maximum material 2 contraint]
$x_1 + x_2 + x_3 = 1$
$x_1, x_2, x_3 \geq 0$ [Non negativity constraint]

2 Linear Programming – Graphical Method

PRACTICAL STEPS INVOLVED IN SOLVING LPP BY GRAPHICAL METHOD

The practical steps involved in solving linear programming problems by Graphical Method are given below:

Step 1 → *Consider each inequality constraint as equation.*

Step 2 → *Take one variable (say x) in a given equation equal to zero and find the value of other variable (say y) by solving that equation to get one co-ordinate [say (0, y)] for that equation.*

Step 3 → *Take the second variable (say y) as zero in the said equation and find the value of first variable (say x) to get another co-ordinate [say (x, 0)] for that equation.*

Step 4 → *Plot both the co-ordinates so obtained [i.e., (0, y) and (x, 0)] on the graph and join them by a straight line. This straight line shows that any point on that line satisfies the equality and any point below or above that line shows inequality. Shade the feasible region which may be either convex to the origin in case of less than type of inequality (<) or opposite to the origin in case of more than type of inequality (>).*

Step 5 → *Repeat Steps 2 to 4 for other constraints.*

Step 6 → *Find the common shaded feasible region and mark the co-ordinates of its corner points.*

Step 7 → *Put the co-ordinates of each of such vertex in the Objective Function. Choose that vertex which achieves the most optimal solution (i.e., in the case of Maximisation, the vertex that gives the maximum value of 'Z' & in case of Minimisation the vertex that gives the minimum value of 'Z). Solution can be obtained in the following manner:*

Vertex No.	*Co-ordinates of vertices of Common shaded feasible region*	*Value of Z*
1	(x_1, y_1)	$Z_1 =$ .....
2	(x_2, y_2)	$Z_2 =$ .....
3	(x_3, y_3)	$Z_3 =$ .....
4 & so on	(x_4, y_4)	$Z_4 =$ .....

Step 8 → Optimal Solution:

Type of Problem	*Optimal Solution*
(a) In case of Maximisation Problem	The vertex which gives the maximum value of Z is the optimal solution.
(b) In case of Minimisation Problem	The vertex which gives the minimum value of Z is the optimal solution.

PROBLEM 2.1

Sky Ltd. has two products Cloud and Wind. To produce one unit of Cloud, 2 units of material X and 4 units of material Y are required. To produce one unit of Wind, 3 units of material X and 2 units of material Y are required. As the raw material X is in short supply so not more than 16 units of material X can be used. Atleast 16 units of material Y must be used in order to meet the committed sales of Cloud and Wind. Cost per unit of material X and material Y are ₹ 2.50 and ₹ 0.25 respectively. The selling price per unit of cloud and wind are ₹ 12 and ₹ 16 respectively.

You are required:

(i) To formulate mathematical model.

(ii) To solve it for maximum contribution (Graphically).

Solution

Calculation of Contribution per Unit of each Product

Particulars		*Cloud* (₹)		*Wind* (₹)
A Selling price per unit		12.00		16.00
B *Less* : cost per unit				
(i) Material X	(₹ 2.50 × 2)	5.00	(₹ 2.50 × 3)	7.50
(ii) Material Y	(₹ 0.25 × 4)	1.00	(₹ 0.25 × 2)	0.50
Total (i) + (ii)		6.00		8.00
C Contribution (A – B)		6.00		8.00

Part (i)

Since the objective is to maximise the profit, the objective function is given by:

Maximise $Z = 6x + 8y$

Subject to constraints:

$2x + 3y \leq 16$ (Maximum material X constraint) ...(i)

$4x + 2y \geq 16$ (Minimum material Y constraint) ...(ii)

$x, y \geq 0$ (Non-Negativity constraint)

Part (ii)

Step 1: Finding the vertex for each constraint by treating the constraint of inequality nature as equality.

Constraint (i) in limiting form $2x + 3y = 16$

When $x = 0, y = \frac{16}{3}$

When $y = 0$, $x = \frac{16}{2} = 6$

Thus, the vertices are $(0, \frac{16}{3})$ & (8, 0)

Constraint (ii) in limiting form $4x + 2y = 16$

When $x = 0$, $y = \frac{16}{2}$

When $y = 0$, $x = \frac{16}{4} = 4$

Thus, the vertices are (0, 8) & (4, 0)

Step 2: Plotting both the co-ordinates of the 1st constraint on the graph and joining them by straight line and shading the feasible region which is convex to origin in case of less than type of inequality. Similarly drawing straight line and shading feasible region for other constraint.

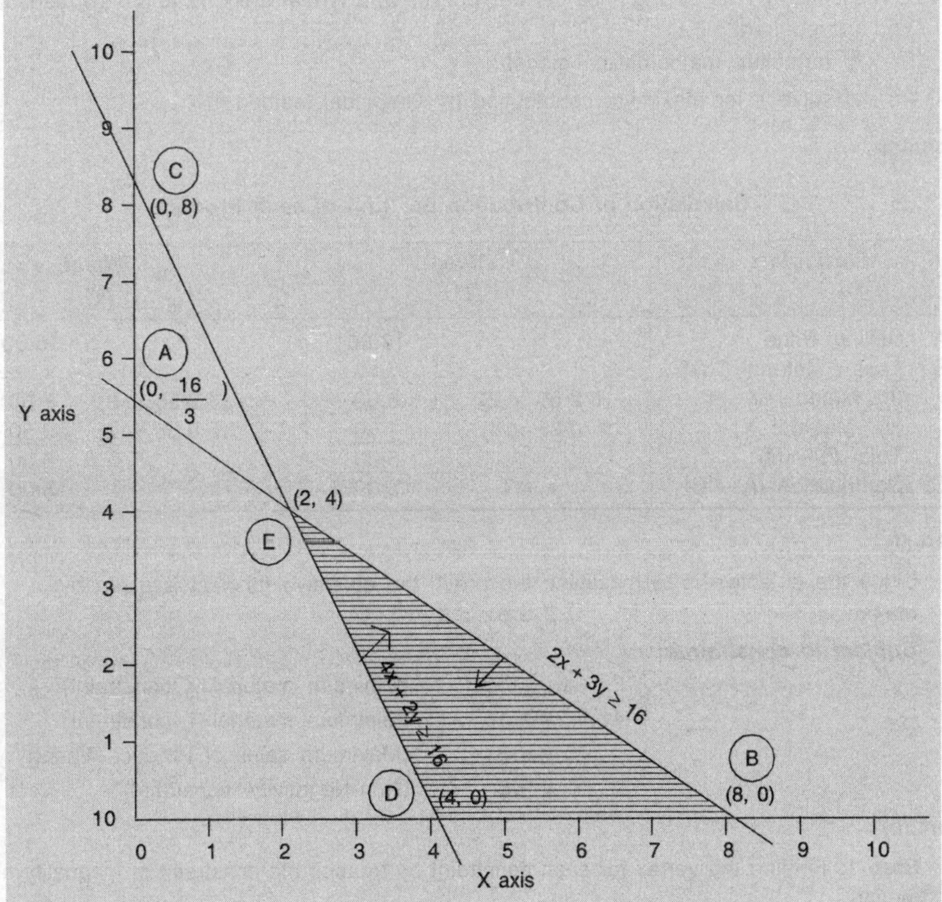

Step 3: Reading the co-ordinates of the vertices of common shaded feasible region and putting the co-ordinates of each of such vertex in the objective function. Selecting those vertices which achieve the most optimal solution (i.e. in case of maximisation vertices which give the maximum value of Z).

Set No.	Co-ordinates of vertices of Common shaded feasible region	Value of Z
1	E (2, 4)	$Z_1 = 6 \times 2 + 8 \times 4 = 44$
2	B (8, 0)	$Z_2 = 6 \times 8 + 8 \times 0 = 48$
3	D (4, 0)	$Z_3 = 6 \times 4 + 8 \times 0 = 24$

Optimal Solution: Thus, set no. 2 gives the max. value of 2 with $x = 8$ and $y = 0$.

PROBLEM 2.2

Seed Ltd has two products Rice and Wheat. To produce one unit of Rice 2 units of material X and 4 units of material Y are required. To produce one unit of Wheat 3 units of material X and 2 units of material Y are required. Atleast 16 units of each material must be used in order to meet committed sales of Rice and Wheat. Due to moderate marketing facilities not more than 8 units of product wheat can be sold. Cost per unit of material X and material Y are ₹ 2.50 and ₹ 0.25 respectively. The selling price per unit of Rice and Wheat are ₹ 12 and ₹ 16 respectively.

You are required:

(i) to formulate mathematical model.

(ii) to solve it for maximum contribution by Graphical method.

Solution

Calculation of Contribution per Unit of each Product

	Particulars	Rice (₹)		Wheat (₹)	
A	Selling Price		12.00		16.00
B	*Less :* Material Cost				
	(i) Material X	(₹ 2.50 × 2)	5.00	(₹ 2.50 × 3)	7.50
	(ii) Material Y	(₹ 0.25 × 4)	1.00	(₹ 0.25 × 2)	0.50
	Total (i) + (ii)		6.00		8.00
C	Contribution (A – B)		6.00		8.00

Part (i)

Since the objective is to maximise the profit, the objective function is given by:

Maximise $Z = 6x + 8y$

Subject to constraints:

$2x + 3y \geq 16$ (Minimum material X constraint) ...(i)

$4x + 2y \geq 16$ (Minimum material Y constraint) ...(ii)

$y \leq 8$ (Maximum sales of Product Wheat) ...(iii)

$x, y \geq 0$ (Non-Negativity constraint)

Part (ii)

Step 1: Finding the vertex for each constraint by treating the constraint of inequality nature as equality.

Constraint (i) in limiting form $2x + 3y = 16$

When $x = 0$, $y = \frac{16}{3}$

When $y = 0$, $x = 8$

Thus, the vertices are $(0, \frac{16}{3})$ & (8, 0)

Constraint (ii) in limiting form $4x + 2y = 16$

When $x = 0,\ y = 8$

When $y = 0,\ y = 4$

Thus, the vertices are (0, 8) & (4, 0)

Step 2: Plotting both the co-ordinates of the 1st constraint on the graph and joining them by straight line and shading the feasible region which is opposite to origin in case of more than type of inequality. Similarly drawing straight line and shading feasible region for other constraints.

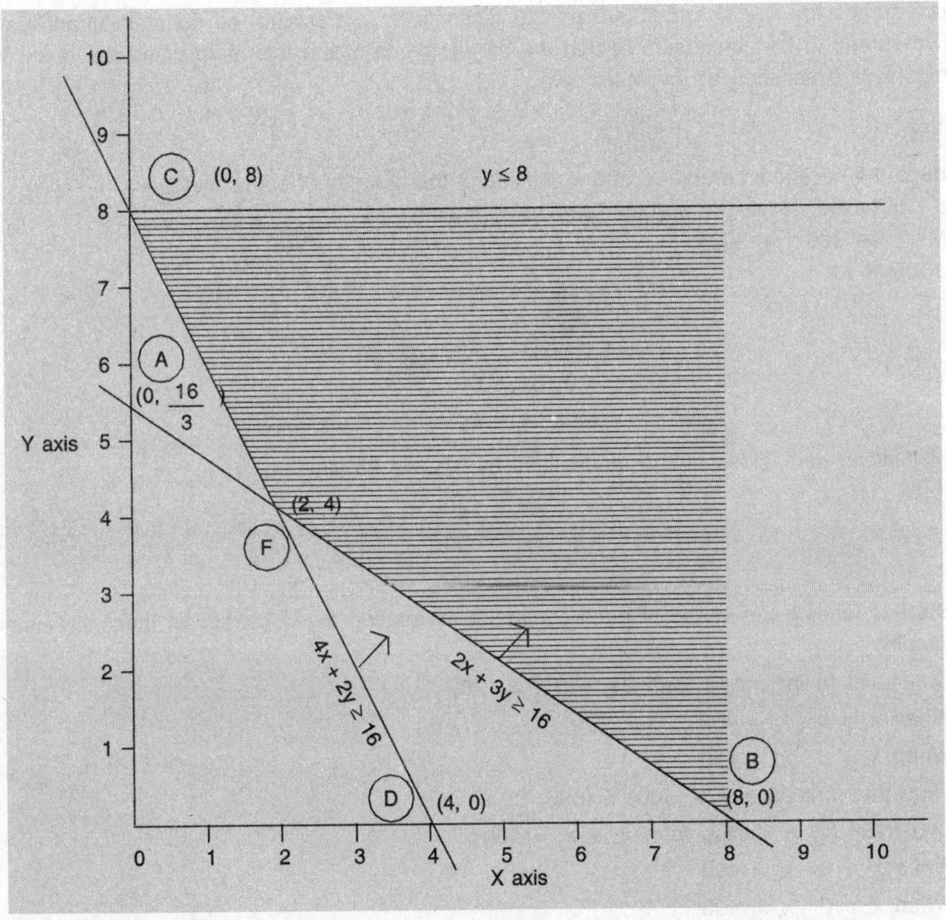

Step 3: Reading the co-ordinates of the vertices of common shaded feasible region and putting the co-ordinates of each of such vertex in the objective function. Selecting those vertices which achieve the most optimal solution (i.e. in case of maximisation vertices which give the maximum value of Z).

Set No.	Co-ordinates of vertices of Common shaded feasible region	Value of Z
1	C (0, 8)	$Z_1 = 6 \times 0 + 8 \times 8 = 64$
2	F (2, 4)	$Z_2 = 6 \times 2 + 8 \times 4 = 44$
3	B (8, 0)	$Z_2 = 6 \times 8 + 8 \times 0 = 48$

The solution of this problem is **unbounded.**

PROBLEM 2.3

A company buying scrap metal has two types of scrap available to them. The first type of scrap has 20% of metal A, 10% of impurity and 20% of metal B by weight. The second type of scrap has 30% of metal A, 10% of impurity and 15% of metal B by weight. The company requires at least 120 kg of metal A, at most 40 kg. of impurity and at least 90 kg of metal B. The price for the two scraps are ₹ 200 and ₹ 300 per kg respectively. Determine the optimum quantities of the two scraps to be purchased so that the requirements of the two metals and the restriction on impurity are satisfied at minimum cost.

Solution

Introduce the decision variable x_1 and x_2 indicating the quantity of scrap metal (in kg.) to be purchased. Now, the problem can be formulated as –

Minimise $200x_1 + 300x_2$

subject to:

$$0.2x_1 + 0.3x_2 \geq 120$$
$$0.1x_1 + 0.1x_2 \leq 40$$
$$0.2x_1 + 0.15x_2 \geq 90$$
$$x_1, x_2 \geq 0$$

Multiplying both sides of the inequalities by 10, we obtain

$$2x_1 + 3x_2 \geq 1200$$
$$x_1 + x_2 \leq 400$$
$$2x_1 + 1.5x_2 \geq 900$$

Step 1: Finding the vertex of each constraint by treating the constraint of inequality nature as equality.

Constraint (i) in limiting form $2x_1 + 3x_2 = 1200$

When $x_1 = 0$ $x_2 = 400$

When $x_2 = 0$ $x_1 = 600$

Thus the vertices are (0, 400) & (600, 0).

Constraint (ii) in limiting form $x_1 + x_2 = 400$

When $x_1 = 0$ $x_2 = 400$

When $x_2 = 0$ $x_1 = 400$

Thus the vertices are (0, 400) & (400, 0).

Constraint (iii) in limiting form $2x_1 + 1.5x_2 = 900$

When $x_1 = 0$ $x_2 = 600$

When $x_2 = 0$ $x_1 = 450$

Thus the vertices are (0, 600) & (450, 0)

Step 2: Plotting the co-ordinates of 1st constraint on the graph and joining them by a straight line, and shading the feasible region. Similarly drawing a straight line and shading feasible region for other constraints.

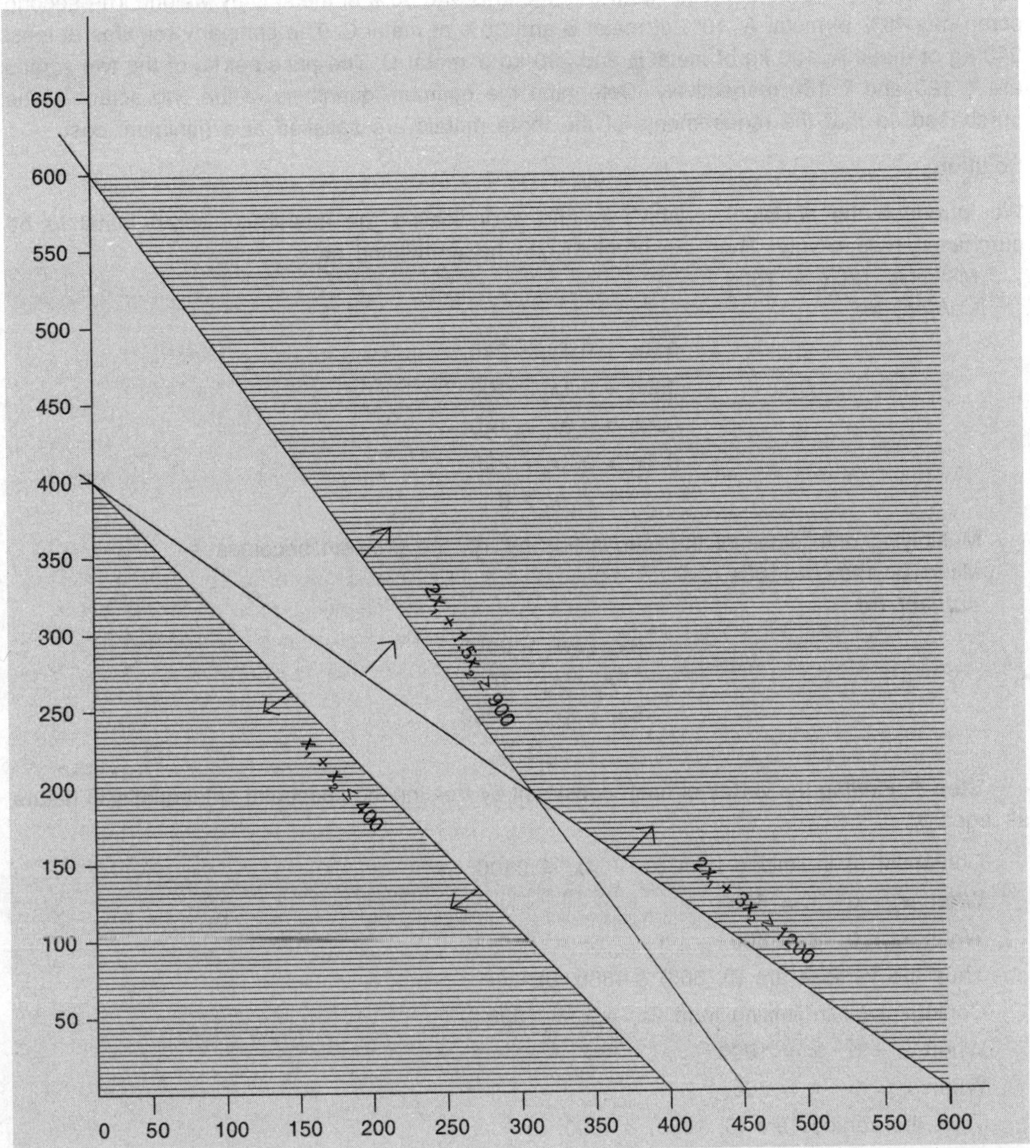

Step 3: There exists **no feasible solution** for this problem since there is no common shaded feasible region.

PROBLEM 2.4

A company buying scrap metal has two types of scrap metals available to him. The first type of scrap metal has 30% of metal A, 20% of metal B and 50% of metal C by weight. The second scrap has 40% of metal A, 10% of metal B and 30% of metal C. The company requires at least 240 kg of metal A, 100 kg of metal B and 290 kg of metal C. The price per kg of the two scraps are ₹ 120 and ₹ 160 respectively. Determine the optimum quantities of the two scraps to be purchased so that the requirements of the three metals are satisfied at a minimum cost.

Solution

We introduce the decision variables x_1 and x_2 indicating the amount of scrap metal to be purchased respectively. Then the problem can be formulated as

Minimise $120x_1 + 160x_2$

subject to:

$$0.3x_1 + 0.4x_2 \geq 240$$
$$0.2x_1 + 0.1x_2 \geq 100$$
$$0.2x_1 + 0.3x_2 \geq 120$$
$$0.5x_1 + 0.3x_2 \geq 290$$
$$x_1, x_2 \geq 0$$

Multiplying both sides of the inequalities by 10, the problem becomes —

Minimise $120x_1 + 160x_2$

subject to:

$$3x_1 + 4x_2 \geq 2400$$
$$2x_1 + x_2 \geq 1000$$
$$5x_1 + 3x_2 \geq 2900$$
$$x_1, x_2 \geq 0$$

Step 1: Finding the vertex of each constraint by treating the constraint of inequality in nature as equality.

Constraint (i) in limiting form $3x_1 + 4x_2 = 2400$

When $x_1 = 0$ $x_2 = 600$

When $x_2 = 0$ $x_1 = 800$

Thus the vertices are (0, 600) & (800, 0)

Constraint (ii) in limiting form $2x_1 + x_2 = 1000$

When $x_1 = 0$ $x_2 = 1000$

When $x_2 = 0$ $x_1 = 500$

Thus the vertices are (0, 1000) & (500, 0)

Constraint (iii) in limiting form $5x_1 + 3x_2 = 2900$

When $x_1 = 0$ $x_2 = 966.67$

When $x_2 = 0$ $x_1 = 580$

Thus the vertices are (0, 966.67) & (580, 0)

Step 2: Plotting the co-ordinates of 1st constraint on the graph and joining them by a straight line, and shading the feasible region. Similarly drawing a straight line and shading feasible region for other constraints.

Step 3: Reading the co-ordinates of the vertices of the common shaded feasible region & putting the co-ordinates of each of such vertex in the objective function. Selecting those vertices which achieve the most optimal solution (i.e. in case of minimisation vertices which give the minimum value of Z).

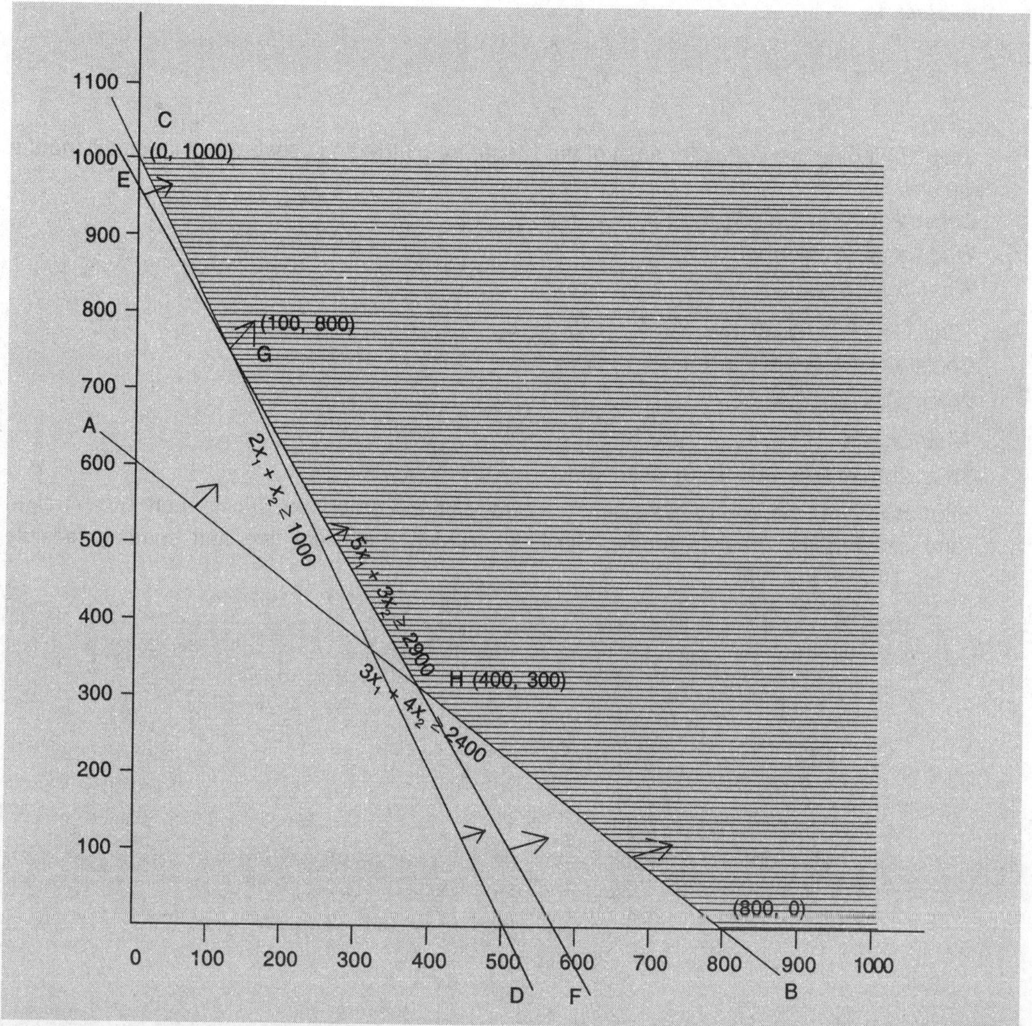

Set No.	Co-ordinates of vertices of Common shaded feasible region	Value of Z
1	C (0, 1000)	$Z_1 + 120 \times 0 + 160 \times 1000 = 1,60,000$
2	G (100, 800)	$Z_2 = 120 \times 100 + 160 \times 800 = 1,40,000$
3	H (400, 300)	$Z_3 = 120 \times 400 + 160 \times 300 = 96,000$
4	B (800, 0)	$Z_4 = 120 \times 800 + 160 \times 0 = 96,000$

Optimal Solution: Thus at both sets i.e. set No. 3 and 4, value of Z is minimum, at $x_1 = 400$ and $x_2 = 300$ or $x_1 = 800$ and $x_2 = 0$.

PROBLEM 2.5

Solve graphically the following linear programming problems:

Maximise $3x_1 + 2x_2$

subject to:

$$x_1 - x_2 \leq 1$$
$$x_1 + x_2 \geq 3$$
$$x_1, x_2 \geq 0$$

Step 1: Finding the vertex for each of the constraint by treating constraint of inequality nature as equality.

Constraint (I) in limiting form $x_1 - x_2 = 1$

When $x_1 = 0$ $x_2 = -1$

When $x_2 = 0$ $x_1 = 1$

Thus the vertices are (0, –1) & (1, 0)

Constraint (ii) in limiting form $x_1 + x_2 = 3$

When $x_1 = 0$ $x_2 = 3$

When $x_2 = 0$ $x_1 = 3$

Thus the vertices are (0, 3) & (3, 0).

Step 2: Plotting the co-ordinates of 1st constraint on the graph and joining them by a straight line, and shading the feasible region. Similarly drawing a straight line and shading feasible region for other constraint.

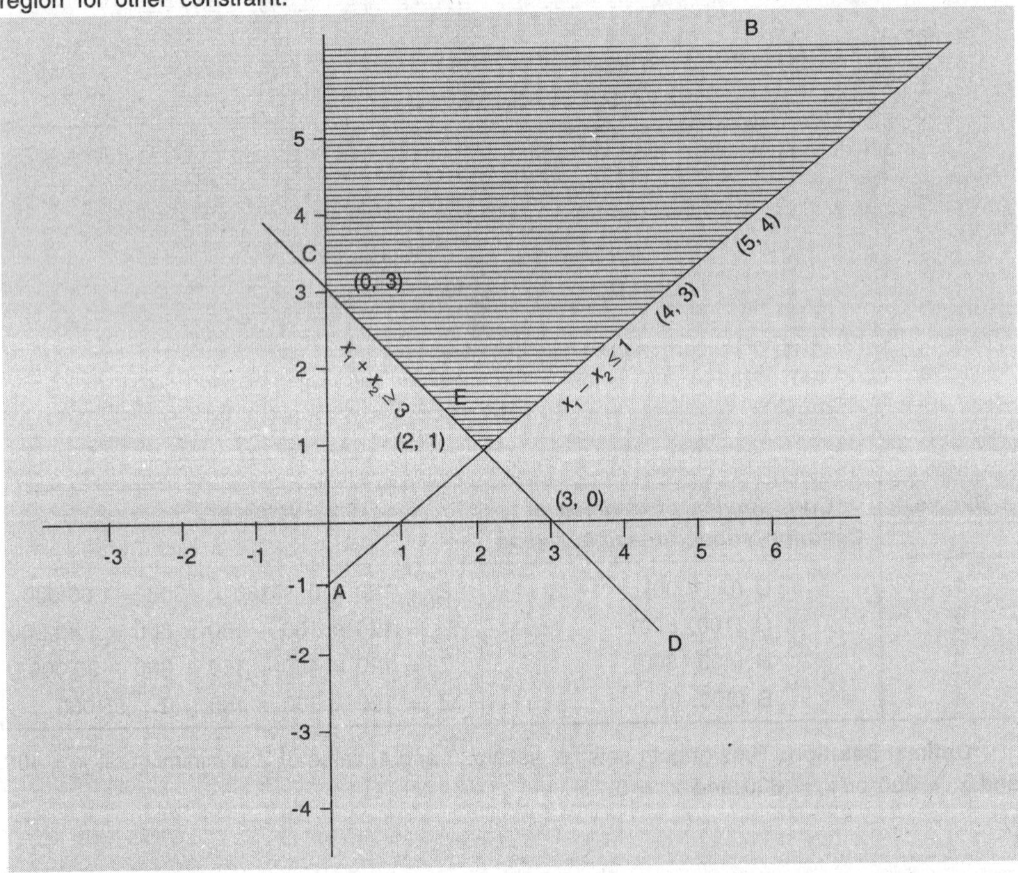

Step 3: Reading the co-ordinates of the vertices of the common shading feasible region & putting the co-ordinates of each of such vertex in the objective function. Selecting those vertices which achieve the most optimal solution (i.e. in case of maxmisation vertices which give the maximum value of Z).

Set No.	*Co-ordinates of vertices of Common shaded feasible region*	*Value of Z*
1	(0, 3)	$Z_2 = 3 \times 0 + 2 \times 3 = 6$
2	(2, 1)	$Z_1 = 3 \times 2 + 2 \times 1 = 8$
3	(4, 3)	$Z_3 = 3 \times 4 + 2 \times 3 = 18$
4	(5, 4)	$Z_4 = 3 \times 5 + 2 \times 4 = 23$

It seems from solution that solution is **unbounded**. As we take, higher values, Z proportionately increases. But this type of problem does not exist in actual practice.

PROBLEM 2.6

A local travel agent is planning a charter trip to a major island resort. The eight day seven-night package includes the fare for round-trip travel, surface transportation, board and lodging and selected tour options. The charter trip is restricted to 200 persons and past experience indicates that there will not be any problem for getting 200 persons. The problem for the travel agent is to determine the number of Deluxe, Standard, and Economy tour packages to offer for this charter. These three plans each differ according to seating and service for the flight, quality of accommodations, meal plans and tour options. The following table summarises the estimated prices for the three packages and the corresponding expenses for the travel agent. The travel agent has hired an aircraft for the flat fee of ₹ 2,00,000 for the entire trip.

Price and Costs for Tour Packages per Person

Tour Plan (₹)	*Price (₹)*	*Resort Costs (₹)*	*Meals & other Expenses*
Deluxe	10,000	3,000	4,750
Standard	7,000	2,200	2,500
Economy	6,500	1,900	2,200

In planning the trip, the following considerations must be taken into account:

(i) At least 10 per cent of the packages must be of the deluxe type.

(ii) At least 35 percent but not more than 70 percent must be of the standard type.

(iii) At least 30 percent must be of the economy type.

(iv) The maximum number of deluxe packages available in any aircraft is restricted to 60.

(v) The resort desires that at least 120 of the tourists should be on the deluxe and standard packages together.

The travel agent wishes to determine the number of packages to offer in each type so as to maximise the total profit.

(a) Formulate the above as a linear programming problem.

(b) Restate the above linear programming problem in terms of two decision variables, taking advantage of the fact that 200 packages will be sold.

(c) Find the optimum solution using graphical methods for the restated linear programming problem and interpret your results.

Solution

Let x_1, x_2, x_3 denote the number of Deluxe, Standard and Economy tour packages to be offered to 200 persons that will maximise the profit. It other words, the total number of tours of three types offered by the concern is restricted to 200 only to maximise its profits.

The contribution (per person) arising out of each type of tour package offered is as follows:

Packages Offered	*Price (₹) (1)*	*Resort costs (₹) (2)*	*Meals & Other Expenses (₹) (3)*	*Net profit (₹) (4)=(1) – [(2)+(3)]*
Deluxe	10,000	3,000	4,750	2,250
Standard	7,000	2,200	2,500	2,300
Economy	6,500	1,900	2,200	2,400

The travel agent has to pay the flat fee of ₹ 2,00,000 for the chartered aircraft for the entire trip. Consequently the objective function (profit function) will be:

Maximise Z = ₹ $2{,}250x_1$ + ₹ $2{,}300x_2$ + ₹ $2{,}400x_3$ – ₹ 2,00,000

Part (a)

Condition (1): $x_1 + x_2 + x_3 \le 200$

Condition (2): $x_1 \ge \frac{10}{100}(x_1 + x_2 + x_1)$

or, $x_1 \ge \frac{1}{10}(x_1 + x_1 + x_1)$

or, $9x_1 - x_2 - x_3 \ge 0$

Condition (3): $x_2 \ge \frac{35}{100}(x_1 + x_2 + x_3)$

or, $-35x_1 + 65x_2 - 35x_3 \ge 0$

Condition (4): $x_2 \le \frac{70}{100}(x_1 + x_2 + x_3)$

or, $-70x_1 + 30x_2 - 70x_3 \le 0$

Condition (5): $x_3 \ge \frac{30}{100}(x_1 + x_2 + x_3)$

or, $-30x_1 - 30x_2 + 70x_3 \ge 0$

Condition (6): $x_1 \le 60$

Condition (7): $x_1 + x_2 \ge 120$

Now, the linear problem is:

Maximize Z = $2{,}250x_1 + 2{,}300x_2 + 2{,}400x_3 - 2{,}00{,}000$

Subject to contraints:

$x_1 + x_2 + x_3 \le 200$ (Seat availability constraint)

$9x_1 - x_2 - x_3 \ge 0$ (Minimum number of Delux type)

$-35x_1 + 65x_2 - 35x_3 \ge 0$ (Minimum number of Standard type)

$-70x_1 + 30x_2 - 70x_3 \le 0$ (Maximum number of Standard type)

$-30x_1 - 30x_2 + 70x_3 \ge 0$ (Minimum number of Economy type)

$x_1 \le 60$ (Maximum seat available for Delux type)

$x_1 + x_2 \ge 120$ (Toursit constraint)

$x_1, x_2, x_3 \ge 0$ (Non-Negativity constraint)

Part (b)

Since the value of $x_1 + x_2 + x_3 = 200$, the value of x_3 will be equal to $200 - x_1 - x_2$ and substituting the value of x_3, the LP model will be formulated as under

Maximise $Z = 2{,}250x_1 + 2{,}300x_2 + 2{,}400\ (200 - x_1 - x_2) - 2{,}00{,}000$

or $Z = 2{,}250x_1 + 2{,}300x_2 + 4{,}80{,}000 - 2{,}400x_1 + 2400x_2 - 2{,}00{,}000$

$Z = -150x_1 - 100x_2 + 2{,}80{,}000$

Subject to constraints:

$x_1 \geq 20$ (i.e. 10% of 200) (Minimum number of Delux type)

$x_2 \geq 70$ (i.e. 35% of 200) (Minimum number of Standard type)

$x_2 \leq 140$ (i.e. 70% of 200) (Maximum number of Standard type)

$x_1 \leq 60$ (i.e. 70% of 200) (Maximum seat available for Delux type)

$x_1 + x_2 \geq 120$ (Tourist constraint)

$x_3 \geq 60$ (Minimum no. of Economy type)

$-x - x_2 + 200 \geq 60$

or, $-x - x_2 \geq -140$

or, $x_1 + x_2 \leq 140$

$x_1 + x_2 \geq 0$ (Non-Negativity constraint)

Part (c)

Step 1: Finding the vertex of each constraint by treating the constraint of inequality nature as equality.

Constraint (v) in limiting form $x_1 + x_2 = 120$

when $x_1 = 0$ $x_2 = 120$

when $x_2 = 0$ $x_1 = 120$

Thus the vertices are (0, 120) & (120, 0)

Constraint (vii) in limiting form $x_1 + x_2 = 140$

when $x_1 = 0$ $x_2 = 140$

when $x_2 = 0$ $x_1 = 140$

Thus the vertices are (0, 140) & (140, 0)

Step 2: Plotting the co-ordinates of 1st constraint on the graph and joining them by a straight line, and shading the feasible region. Similarly drawing a straight line and shading feasible region for other constraints. (Graph on next page)

Step 3: Reading the co-ordinates of the vertices of the common shaded feasible region & putting the co-ordinates of each of such vertex in the objective function. Selecting those vertices which achieve the most optimal solution (i.e. in case of maxmisation vertices which give the maximum value of Z).

Point	***Co-ordinates of the corner points of the feasible region (values of x_1 and x_2)***	***Values of the objective function $Z = -150x_1 - 100x_2 + 2{,}80{,}000$***
A	(50, 70)	₹ 2,65,500
B	(60,70)	₹ 2,64,000
C	(60, 80)	₹ 2,63,000
D	(20,120)	₹ 2,65,000
E	(20,100)	₹ 2,67,000

The maximum profit is attained at the point E, whose coordinates are (20, 100)

Interpretation: The profit of the objective function stated under (a) becomes maximum i.e. ₹ 2,67,000 when

x_1 = 20; x_2 = 100 and x_3 = 80 {∴ $x_3 = 200 - (x_1 + x_2) = 200 - (20 + 100)$}

i.e. the travel agent should offer 20 Deluxe, 100 Standard and 80 Economy tour packages so as to get the maximum profit of ₹ 2,67,000.

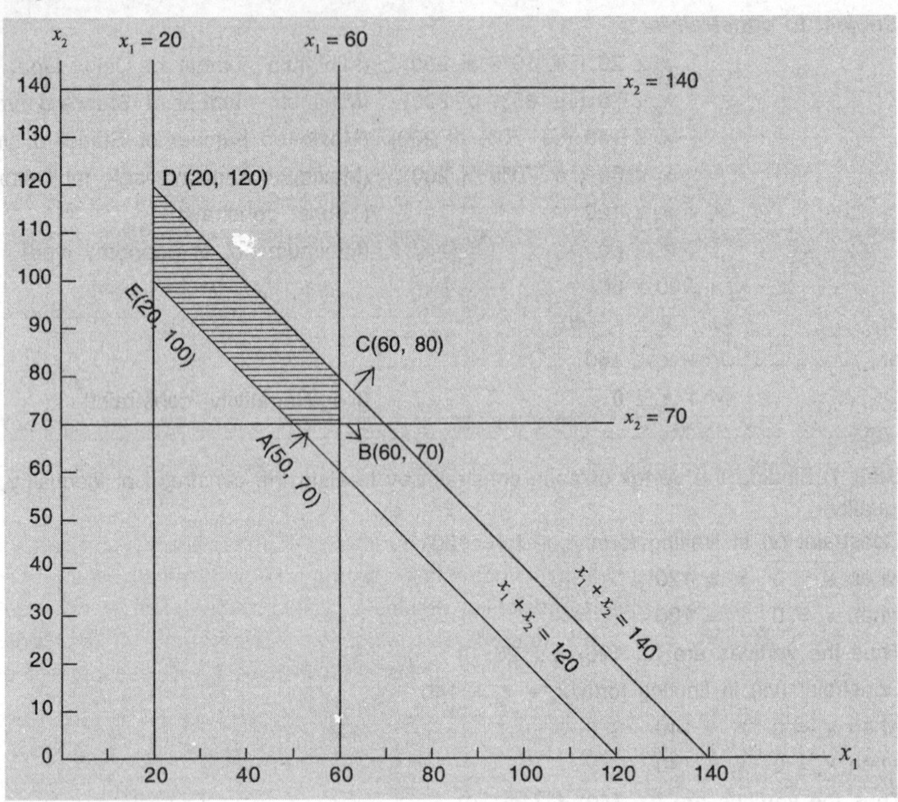

PROBLEM 2.7

Semicond is an electronics company manufacturing tape recorders and radios. Its per unit labour costs, raw material costs and selling prices are given in Table 1. An extract form from its balance sheet on 31.3.20X1 is shown in Table 2. Its current asset/current liability ratio (called the current ratio) is 2.

Table 1 : Cost Information

Items	*Products*	
	Tape Recorder ₹	***Radio*** ₹
Selling Price	1,000	900
Labour Cost	500	350
Raw Material Cost	300	400

Table 2 : Extract from Balance Sheet as on 31.3.20X1

	Current Liabilities ₹	*Current Assets* ₹
Cash		1,00,000
*Accounts Receivable		30,000
**Inventory		70,000
Short-Term Bank Borrowing	1,00,000	

* Accounts receivable is amount due from customers.

** 100 units of raw material used for tape recorder and 100 units of raw material used for radio.

Semicond must determine how many tape recorders and radios should be produced during April 20X1. Demand is large enough to ensure that all goods produced will be sold. All sales are on credit and payment for goods sold in April 20X1 will not be received until 31.5.20X1. During April 20X1, it will collect ₹ 20,000 in accounts receivable and it must pay off ₹ 10,000. On 30.4.20X1 it will receive a shipment of raw material worth ₹ 20,000, which will be paid for on May 31, 20X1. The management has decided that the cash balance on April 30, 20X1 must be at least ₹ 40,000. Also its banker requires that the ratio of current assets to current liabilities as on April 30, 20X1 be at least 2. In order to maximise the contribution to profit for April 20X1 production it has to find the product mix for April 20X1. Assume that labour costs (wages) monthly rent (₹ 10,000) are paid in the month in which they are incurred.

Formulate this as a Linear Programming Problem and graphically solve it.

Solution

Let x_1 = Number of tape recorders to be produced

x_2 = Number of tape radios to be produced

Since the objective is to maximise, the objective function is given by —

Maximise $Z = 200x_1 + 150x_2$

Condition (1) Regarding funds available for production

$500x_1 + 350x_2 \leq 60,000$

Calculation of Funds Available for Production

A	Balance of cash		1,00,000
B	*Add :* Collection from Debtors		20,000
C	*Less :* Payment of Bank Loan	10,000	
	Payment of monthly rent	10,000	20,000
D	Balance (A + B – C)		1,00,000
E	Minimum Balance required		40,000
F	Funds available (D – E)		60,000

Condition (2) Regarding Maximum Raw Material

$x_1 \leq 100$ (i.e. $\frac{30,000}{300}$)

$x_2 \leq 100$ (i.e. $\frac{30,000}{300}$)

Condition (3) Ragarding Ratio of Current Assets to Current Liabilities

Calculation of Current Assets

A Cash available	100,000
B *Less* : Utilised for Production	$(800x_1 + 750x_2)$
C *Add* : (i) Sales Revenue	$1000x_1 + 900x_2$
(ii) Stock	70,000
(iii) Debtors	10,000
(iv) New Stock	20,000
D Current Assets (A – B + C)	$2,00,000 + 200x_1 + 150x_2$

Calculation of Current Liabilities

A Bank loan (1,00,000 – 10,000)	90,000
B Liabilities due to supplies	20,000
C Current Liability (A + B)	1,10,000

$$\text{Current Ratio} = \frac{\text{Current Assets}}{\text{Current Liabilities}}$$

$$\frac{2,00,000 + 200x_1 + 150x_2}{1,10,000} \geq 2$$

$$2,000,000 + 200x_1 + 150x_2 \geq 2,20,000$$

or $$200x_1 + 150x_2 \geq 20,000$$

Now, LP problem can be shown below:

Maximise $Z = 200x_1 + 150x_2$

Subject to constraints:

$500x_1 + 350x_2 \leq 60,000$	(Funds availability constraints)
$x_1 \leq 100$	(Maximum Raw material available for Tape recorder)
$x_2 \leq 100$	(Maximum Raw material available for Radio)
$200x_1 + 150x_2 \geq 20,000$	(Current Ratio constraint)
$x_1, x_2 \geq 0$	(Non-Negativity constraint)

Step 1: Finding the vertex of each constraint by treating the constraint of inequility value as equality

Constraint (i) in limiting form $500x_1 + 350x_2 = 60,000$

when $x_1 = 0$ $x_2 = 171.43$

when $x_2 = 0$ $x_1 = 120$

Thus the vertices are (0, 171.43) & (120, 0)

Constraint (iv) in limiting form $200x_1 + 150x_2 = 20,000$

when $x_1 = 0$ $x_2 = 133.33$

when $x_2 = 0$ $x_1 = 100$

Thus the vertices are (0, 133.33) & (100, 0)

Step 2: Plotting the co-ordinates of 1st constraint on the graph and joining them by a straight line, and shading the feasible region. Similarly drawing a straight line and shading feasible region for other constraints.

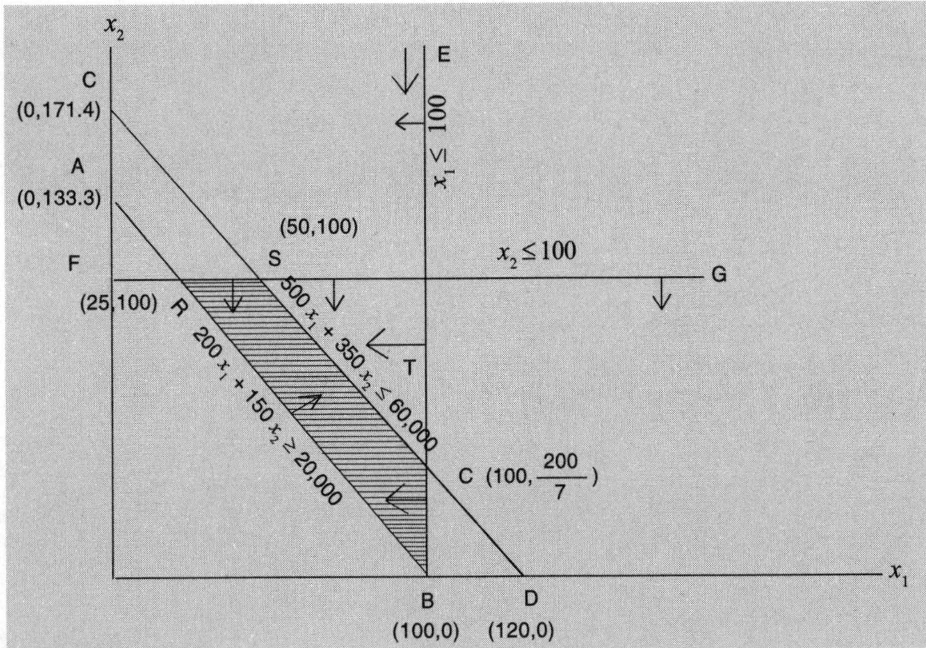

Step 3: Reading the co-ordinates of the vertices of the common shaded feasible region & putting the co-ordinates of each of such vertex in the objective function. Selecting those vertices which achieve the most optimal solution (i.e. in case of maxmisation vertices which give the maximum value of Z).

Set No.	***Co-ordinates of vertex of Common shaded region***	***Value of Z***
1	R (25, 100)	$Z_1 = 200 \times 25 + 150 \times 100 = 20{,}000$
2	S (50, 100)	$Z_2 = 200 \times 50 + 150 \times 100 = 25{,}000$
3	T (100, 200/7)	$Z_3 = 200 \times 100 + 150 \times 200/7 = 24{,}285.70$
4	D (100, 0)	$Z_4 = 200 \times 100 + 150 \times 0 = 20{,}000$

Optimal Solution: Thus, Set No. 2 gives the maximum value of Z (i.e. ₹ 25,000) at $x_1 = 50$ & $x_2 = 100$.

3 Linear Programming – Simplex Method

PRACTICAL STEPS INVOLVED IN SOLVING MAXIMISATION PROBLEMS (WHERE ALL CONSTRAINTS HAVE "≤" TYPE INEQUALITIES

Step 1→ Non-Negative Slack Variables—*Add Non-negative Slack Variables (say S_1, S_2 etc.) in each constraint to convert inequalities into equations. A Slack Variable indicates under-utilisation of capacity of the constraint; hence, its contribution to Objective Function is assumed to be zero (or negative, if given). This Slack Variable is also called as Basic Variable. Other variables are called Non-basic Variables.*

Step 2→ Value of Basic Variable—*Assuming the value of each Non-basic Variable equal to 'zero' (i.e. assuming that no performance has taken place), calculate the value of each Basic Variable from the equations.*

Step 3→ Value of Z—*Find the value of 'Z' by putting the value of each basic and non-basic variable in the Objective Function.*

Step 4→ Initial Simplex Table—*Draw the Initial Simplex Table as follows:*

Contribution per unit		$C_j \rightarrow$	C_1	C_2	0	0	Replacement
C_i	Variables	Quantity	x_1	x_2	S_1	S_2	Ratio Qty/value of key column
C_1	S_1	....	....	....	1	0	
C_2	S_2	....	....	....	0	1	
Total Contribution	Z_j	0	0*	0	....	....	
Opportunity Cost	$(C_j\text{-}Z_j)$		C_1	C_2	0	0	

* **Note:** *The value in the Z_j Row for x_1 variable is computed by the formula = $C_1x_1 + C_2x_1$. The values in the Z_j Row in the column for other variables are computed by the same formula as stated.*

Step 5→ *Key Column* – *Mark the Column having **maximum positive value** in $(C_j - Z_j)$ row by ↑ sign representing the Opportunity Cost or Loss of not introducing one unit of the variable of that column. This Column is also known as Key Column. This column indicates the selection of **incoming variable** in the Next Simplex Table.*

Step 6→ ***Replacement Ratio***–*Find out Replacement Ratio (also known as Key Ratio) by dividing value in the Quantity Column of each row by corresponding Key Column value. Replacement Ratio represents how much quantum of variable can be produced based on that row taking the Key Column value.*

Step 7→ ***Key Row***—*Mark the Row having* ***minimum non-negative*** *Replacement Ratio by → sign. Minimum Replacement Ratio ensures that no basic variable will ever be negative. (This can be verified by putting higher Replacement Ratio in all constraints). This Row is known as Key Row. This row indicates the selection of* ***outgoing variable*** *from the Current Simplex Table.*

Step 8→ ***Key Element***—*Encircle the* ***element at the intersection*** *of Key Row and Key Column. This value is known as Key Element or Pivot Element.*

Step 9→ *Replace the outgoing variable by the incoming variable with its contribution per unit, i.e., C_i in the first Column for Contribution Per Unit.*

Step 10→ *New Values of Key Row—Calculate the New Values of the Key Row as under:*

$$\text{New Values of Key Row} = \frac{\text{Old Values of Key Row}}{\text{Key Element}}$$

Step 11→ **New Values of Non-Key Row—***Calculate the New Values of Other Rows (i.e. Non-Key Rows) as under:*

A	Old Values						
B	New values of Key Row						
C	Key Column Element						
D	Product of B&C						
E	New Values (A–D)						

Step 12→ *Draw another Simplex Table based on new values of each row.*

Step 13→ *Repeat Steps 4 to 12 till all values in $(C_i - Z_j)$ row becomes zero or negative which indicates that any further introduction of additional unit of the variable having negative value in $(C_i - Z_j)$ row will have negative contribution towards Objective Function [no effect in case of zero in $(C_i - Z_j)$ row]. This is also known as condition for optimal solution.*

Step 14→ **Optimal Solution—***Find Optimal Solution from the Final Simplex Table, i.e., the value of Z and quantity of Non-basic Variables.*

$$\text{Value of } Z = C_i .(\text{Qty of } x_i) + C_j\ (\text{Qty of } x_j)$$

PROBLEM 3.1

Use simplex method to solve the following L P problem:

Max Z. = $6x_1 + 8x_2$

Subject to Constraints:

$$2x_1 + 3x_2 \leq 16$$
$$4x_1 + 2x_2 \leq 16$$

Solution

Step 1→ Formulation of LP problem after introducing slack variables:

Max. Z = $6x_1 + 8x_2 + 0S_1 + 0S_2$

Subject to constraints:

$$2x_1 + 3x_2 + S_1 = 16$$

$$4x_1 + 2x_2 + S_2 = 16$$

$$x_1, x_2, S_1, S_2 \geq 0$$

Step 2→ Preparing Initial Simplex Table:

Simplex Table I

Contribution per unit C_i →			6	8	0	0	Replacement Ratio
↓ C_i	Variable	Qty	x_1	x_2	S_1	S_2	Qty/Value of Key Column
0	S_1	16	2	[3]	1	0	$\frac{16}{3} = 5.33$ ←
0	S_2	16	4	2	0	1	$\frac{16}{2} = 8$
Total Contribution (Z_j)			0	0	0	0	
Opportunity Loss ($C_i - Z_j$)			6	8	0	0	
				↑ Key Column	↓ Key Element		Kew Row ←

Hence, the outgoing variable is S_1 and the incoming variable is x_2

Step 3→ Replacing the outgoing variable (S_1) by incoming variable (x_2) together with its contribution per unit.

Step 4→ Calculating the new values of Key Row as under:

$$\text{New Values of Key Row} = \frac{\text{Old Values of Key Row}}{\text{Key Element}}$$

$$= \frac{16}{3} \quad \frac{2}{3} \quad \frac{3}{3} \quad \frac{1}{3} \quad \frac{0}{3}$$

Step 5→ Calculating the new values of other Rows (i.e. Non-key Row) as under:

A	Old Values	16	4	2	0	1
B	New Values of Key Row	$\frac{16}{3}$	$\frac{2}{3}$	1	$\frac{1}{3}$	0
C	Key Column Element	2	2	2	2	2
D	Product of B & C	$\frac{32}{3}$	$\frac{4}{3}$	2	$\frac{2}{3}$	0
E	New Values (A – D)	$\frac{16}{3}$	$\frac{8}{3}$	0	$-\frac{2}{3}$	1

Step 6→ Preparing Second Simplex Table

Simplex Table II

Contribution per unit C_i →			6	8	0	0	Replacement Ratio
C_i ↓	Variable	Qty	x_1	x_2	S_1	S_2	Qty/Value of Key Column
8	x_2	$\frac{16}{3}$	$\frac{2}{3}$	1	$\frac{1}{3}$	0	$\frac{16/3}{2/3} = 8$
0	S_2	$\frac{16}{3}$	$\boxed{\frac{8}{3}}$ ←	0	$-\frac{2}{3}$	1	$\frac{16/3}{8/3} = 2$ ←
Total Contribution (Z_j)			5.33	8	$\frac{8}{3}$	0	
Opportunity Loss ($C_i - Z_j$)			– 67	0	$-\frac{8}{3}$	0	
			↑ Key Column	Key Element			Key Row

Step 7→ Replacing the outgoing variable (S_2) by incoming variable (x_1) together with its contribution per unit.

Step 8→ Calculating the new values of Key Row as under:

$$\text{New Values of Key Row} = \frac{\text{Old Values of Key Row}}{\text{Key Element}}$$

$$= \frac{16/3}{8/3} \quad \frac{8/3}{8/3} \quad \frac{0}{8/3} \quad \frac{-2/3}{8/3} \quad \frac{1}{8/3}$$

$$= \quad 2 \quad 1 \quad 0 \quad -\frac{1}{4} \quad \frac{2}{3}$$

Step 9→ Calculation of the New Values of Non Key Rows as under:

A	Old Values	$\frac{16}{3}$	$\frac{2}{3}$	1	$\frac{1}{3}$	0
B	New Values of Key Row	2	1	0	$\frac{-1}{4}$	$\frac{3}{8}$
C	Key Column Element	$\frac{2}{3}$	$\frac{2}{3}$	$\frac{2}{3}$	$\frac{2}{3}$	$\frac{2}{3}$
D	Product of B & C	$\frac{4}{3}$	$\frac{2}{3}$	0	$\frac{1}{-6}$	$\frac{1}{4}$
E	New Values (A – D)	4	0	1	$\frac{1}{2}$	$-\frac{1}{4}$

Step 10→ Preparing Simplex Table III

Simplex Table III

Contribution per unit C_i →			6	8	0	0
↓ C_i	Variable	Quantity	x_1	x_2	S_1	S_2
8	x_2	4	0	1	$\frac{1}{2}$	$-\frac{1}{4}$
6	x_1	2	1	0	$-\frac{1}{4}$	$\frac{3}{8}$
Total Contribution (Z_j)		44	6	8	2.5	.25
Opportunity Loss ($C_i - Z_j$)0			0	–2.5	–.25	

Optimal Solution : Since, the values of $C_i - Z_j$ are ≤ 0, the solution is optimal at $x_1 = 2$ and $x_2 = 4$. The optimal value of Z = 2 × 6 + 4 × 8 = ₹ 44.

PRACTICAL STEPS INVOLVED IN SOLVING MINIMISATION PROBLEMS (WHERE ALL CONSTRAINTS HAVE "≥" TYPE INEQUALITIES).

Step 1→ *Deduct Non-negative Surplus Variables (say S_1, S_2, etc.) (also known as Basic Variables) in each constraint to convert inequalities into equations. Suppose the values of Surplus Variables exceed the values of Non-basic Variables; in such case, the total of Left Hand Side of the equation will become negative which is false; hence, we also add Non-negative Artificial Variables (say A_1, A_2, etc.) (also known as Basic Variables) in each constraint to satisfy the equations. We assume that the conribution of each Artificial Variable towards the Objective Function is infinitely large, say 'M'.*

Step 2→ *Assuming the value of each Non-basic Variable and Surplus Variable equal to 'zero', calculate the value of each Artificial Variable from the equations.*

Step 3→ *Find the value of 'Z' by putting the value of each basic and non-basic variable in the Objective Function.*

Step 4→ *Draw the Initial Simplex Table as given below:*

Contribution per unit	C_i →		C_1	C_2	0	0	M	M	Replacement
(C_i)	Variables	Quantity	x_1	x_2	S_1	S_2	A_1	A_2	Ratio Qty/Value of column
M	A_1	....	....	....	–1	0	1	0	
M	A_2	....	....	....	0	–1	0	1	
Total Contribution	Z_j	....	....	....	M	M	M	M	
Opportunity Cost ($C_i - Z_j$)			.....	....	–M	–M	0	0	

Note: *The value in the Z_j row for x_1 variable is computed by the formula = $C_1.x_1 + C_2.x_1$. In otherwords, all the values in Z_j Row and ($C_i - Z_j$) Row are computed in the same manner as in the case of Maximisation Problems.*

Step 5→ ***Key Column*** – *Mark the Column having* ***Minimum Value*** *in $(C_i - Z_j)$ row by ↑ sign representing the Opportunity Cost or Loss of not introducing one unit of the variable of that column. This Column is also known as Key Column. This column indicates the selection of* ***incoming variable*** *in the Next Simplex Table.*

Step 6→ ***Replacement Ratio*** – *Find out the Replacement Ratio (also known as Key Ratio) by dividing value in the Quantity Column of each row by corresponding Key Column value. Replacement Ratio represents how much quantum of variables can be produced based on that row taking the Key Column value.*

Step 7→ ***Key Row*** – *Mark the Row having* ***Minimum Non-Negative*** *Replacement Ratio by → sign. Minimum Replacement Ratio ensures that no basic variable will ever be negative. (This can be verified by putting higher Replacement Ratio in all constraints). This Row is known as Key Row. This row indicates the selection of* ***outgoing variable*** *from the current simplex table.*

Step 8→ ***Key Element*** – *Encircle the* ***element at the intersection*** *of Key Row and key column. This value is known as Key Element or Pivot Element.*

Step 9→ *Replace the outgoing variable by the incoming variable together with its contribution per unit.*

Step 10→ *Calculate the New Values of the Key Row as under:*

$$\text{New values of key row} = \frac{\text{Old Value of Key Row}}{\text{Key Element}}$$

Step 11→ *Calculate the New Values of other rows (i.e. Non-key rows) as under:*

A Old Values				
B New Values of Key Row				
C Key Column Element				
D Product of B & C				
E New Values (A – D)				

Step 12→ *Draw another Simplex Table based on new values of each row.*

Step 13→ *Repeat Steps 4 to 12 till all values in $(C_i - Z_j)$ row becomes zero or positive which indicates that any further introduction of additional unit of the variable having positive value in $(C_i - Z_j)$ row will have negative contribution towards Objective Function [no effect in case of zero in $(C_i - Z_j)$ row]. This is also known as condition for optimal solution.*

Step 14→ *Find Optimal Solution from the Final Simplex Table, i.e., the values of Z and quantity of Non-basic Variables.*

PROBLEM 3.2

Use Simplex Method to solve the following LP problem:

Minimize $Z = 3x_1 + 2.5x_2$

Subject to constraints:

$$2x_1 + 4x_2 \geq 40$$
$$-5x_1 - 2x_2 \leq -50$$
$$x_1, x_2 \geq 0$$

Solution

Step 1→ Formulation of LP problem after introducing Slack and Artificial Variables:

Minimize $3x_1 + 2.5x_2 - 0S_1 - 0S_2 + MA_1 + MA_2$

Subject to constraints:

$$2x_1 + 4x_2 - S_1 + A_1 = 40$$
$$5x_1 + 2x_2 - S_2 + A_2 = 50$$

Step 2→ Preparing Initial Simplex Table I

Simplex Table I

Contribution per unit	$C_i \to$		3	2.5	0	0	M	M	Replacement
↓ C_i	Variable	Quantity	x_1	x_2	S_1	S_2	A_1	A_2	Ratio Qty/Value of Key Column
M	A_1	40	2	4	–1	0	1	0	$\frac{40}{2}$=20
M	A_2	50	[5] ←	2	0	–1	0	1	$\frac{50}{2}$=25 ←
Total Contribution (Z_j)		90M	7M	6M	–M	–M	M	M	
Opportunity Loss ($C_i - Z_j$)			3–7M	2.5–6M	M	M	0	0	

Key Column   Key Element   Key Row

Step 3→ Replacing the outgoing variable (A_2) by incoming variable (x_1) together with its contribution per unit.

Step 4→ Calculating the New Values of Key Row as under:

$$\text{New Value of Key Row} = \frac{\text{Old Value of Key Row}}{\text{Key Element}}$$

$$= \frac{50}{5} \quad \frac{5}{5} \quad \frac{2}{5} \quad \frac{0}{5} \quad -\frac{1}{5} \quad \frac{0}{5} \quad \frac{1}{5}$$

$$= 10 \quad 1 \quad \frac{2}{5} \quad 0 \quad -\frac{1}{5} \quad 0 \quad \frac{1}{5}$$

Step 5→ Calculation of the New Values of other Non Key Row:

A	Old Values	40	2	4	–1	0	1	0
B	New Values of Key Row	10	1	$\frac{2}{5}$	0	$-\frac{1}{5}$	0	$\frac{1}{5}$
C	Key Column Element	2	2	2	2	2	2	2
D	Product of B & C	20	2	$\frac{4}{5}$	0	$-\frac{2}{5}$	0	$\frac{2}{5}$
E	New Values (A – D)	20	0	$\frac{16}{5}$	–1	$\frac{2}{5}$	1	$-\frac{2}{5}$

Step 6→ Preparing Second Simplex Table II.

Simplex Table II

Contribution per unit	$C_j \rightarrow$		3	2.5	0	0	M	M	Replacement
↓ C_i	Variable	Quantity	x_1	x_2	S_1	S_2	A_1	A_2	Ratio Qty/Value of Key Column
M	A_1	20	0	$\boxed{\frac{16}{5}}$ ←	–1	$\frac{2}{5}$	1	$-\frac{2}{5}$	$\frac{20}{16/5} = 20$ ←
3	x_1	10	1	$\frac{2}{5}$	0	$-\frac{1}{5}$	0	$\frac{1}{5}$	$\frac{10}{2/5} = 25$
Total Contribution	(Z_j)	20M+30	3	$\frac{16M+6}{5}$	–M	$\frac{2M}{5} - \frac{3}{5}$	M	$-\frac{2}{5}M + \frac{3}{5}$	
Opportunity Loss $(C_j - Z_j)$			0	$25 - \frac{16M+6}{5}$ ↑	M	$\frac{3}{5} - \frac{2M}{5}$	0	$M + \frac{2}{5}M - \frac{3}{5}$	

Key Coloumn Key Element Key Row

Step 7→ Replacing the outgoing variable (A_1) by incoming variable (x_2) together with its contribution per unit.

Step 8→ Calculating the New Values of Key Row as under:

$$\text{New Value of Key Row} = \frac{\text{Old Value of Key Row}}{\text{Key Element}}$$

$$= \frac{20}{16/5} \quad \frac{0}{16/5} \quad \frac{16/5}{16/5} \quad \frac{-1}{16/5} \quad \frac{2/5}{16/5} \quad \frac{1}{16/5} \quad \frac{-2/5}{16/5}$$

$$= 6.5 \quad 0 \quad 1 \quad -\frac{5}{16} \quad \frac{1}{8} \quad \frac{5}{16} \quad -\frac{1}{8}$$

Step 9→ Calculation of the New Values of Non Key Row:

A	Old Values	10	1	$\frac{2}{5}$	0	$-\frac{1}{5}$	0	$\frac{1}{5}$
B	New Values of Key Row	6.25	0	1	$-\frac{5}{16}$	$\frac{1}{8}$	$\frac{5}{16}$	$-\frac{1}{8}$
C	Key Column Element	$\frac{2}{5}$	$\frac{2}{5}$	$\frac{2}{5}$	$\frac{2}{5}$	$\frac{2}{5}$	$\frac{2}{5}$	$\frac{2}{5}$
D	Product of B & C	$\frac{20}{8}$	0	$\frac{2}{5}$	$-\frac{1}{8}$	$\frac{2}{40}$	$\frac{1}{8}$	$-\frac{2}{40}$
E	New Values (A – D)	7.5	1	0	$\frac{1}{8}$	$-\frac{1}{4}$	$-\frac{1}{8}$	$\frac{1}{4}$

Step 10→ Preparing Simplex Table III.

Simplex Table III

Contribution per unit C_i →			3	2.5	0	0	M	M
↓ C_i	Variable	Quantity	x_1	x_2	S_1	S_2	A_1	A_2
2.5	x_2	6.25	0	1	$-\frac{5}{16}$	$\frac{1}{8}$	$\frac{5}{16}$	$-\frac{1}{8}$
3	x_1	7.5	1	0	$\frac{1}{8}$	$-\frac{1}{4}$	$-\frac{1}{8}$	$\frac{1}{4}$
Total Contribution(Z_j)		38.125	3	2-5	-.40625	-.4375	.40625	.4375
Opportunity Loss (C_j–Z_j)			0	0	.40625	.4375	M-.40625	M-.4375

Optimal Solution: Since all $C_i - Z_j$ are ≥ 0, the table provides the optimal solution, i.e. $x_1 = 7.5$, and $x_2 = 6.25$. The optimal value of Z = 7.5 × 3 + 6.25 × 2.5 = 38.125.

PRACTICAL STEPS INVOLVED IN SOLVING MAXIMISATION PROBLEMS (WHERE ANY CONSTRAINT HAS "≥" OR "=" SIGN).

Step 1→

(a) ***Add*** *Non-negative Slack Variables in case of constraints having "≤" sign as usual in case of Maximisation Problems.*

(b) ***Deduct*** *Surplus Variables (say S_1, S_2) and Artificial Variables (say A_1, S_1) in case of constraints having "≥" sign as in case of Minimisation Problems.*

(c) ***Add*** *Artificial Variables (say A_1, S_1) in case of constraints having "=" sign. However, the contribution of Artificial Variables will be deducted in the Objective Function.*

Step 2→ *Follow steps 2 to 14 (given on Page 3.1 & 3.2) as usual in case of Maximisation Problems to obtain the Solution to the given problem.*

PROBLEM 3.3

Use Simplex Method to solve the following LP Problem:

Maximize Z = $30x_1 + 20x_2$

Subject to constraints:

$$-x_1 - x_2 \geq -8$$
$$-6x_1 - 4x_2 \leq -12$$
$$5x_1 + 8x_2 = 20$$
$$x_1, x_2 \geq 0$$

Solution

Step 1→ Formulation of LP problem after introducing slack and artificial variables:

Max. Z = $30x_1 + 20x_2 + 0S_1 + 0S_2 - MA_1 - MA_2$

Subject to constraints:

$$x_1 + x_2 + S_1 = 8$$
$$6x_1 + 4x_2 - S_2 + A_1 = 12$$
$$5x_1 + 8x_2 + A_2 = 20$$

Step 2→ Preparing Initial Simplex Table I:

Simplex Table I

Contribution per unit C_j →		30	20	0	0	–M	–M	Replacement	
↓ C_i	Variable	Quantity	x_1	x_2	S_1	S_2	A_1	A_2	Ratio Qty/Value of Key Column
0	S_1	8	1	1	1	0	0	0	$\frac{8}{1} = 8$
–M	A_1	12	6	4	0	–1	1	0	$\frac{12}{4} = 3$
–M	A_2	20	5	[8] ←	0	0	0	1	$\frac{20}{8} = 2.50$ ←
Total Contribution(Z_j)		–32M	–11M	–12M	0	M	–M	–M	
Opportunity Loss (C_j–Z_j)			30+11M	20+12M	0	0	0	0	

↑ Key Coloumn — Key Element — Key Row

Hence the outgoing variable is A_2 and the incoming variable is x_2.

Step 3→ Replacing the outgoing variable (A_2) by incoming variable (x_2) together with its contribution per unit.

Step 4→ Calculating the New Values of Key Row as under:

$$\text{New Values of Key Row} = \frac{\text{Old Value of Key Row}}{\text{Key Element}}$$

$$= \frac{20}{8} \quad \frac{5}{8} \quad \frac{1}{8} \quad \frac{0}{8} \quad \frac{0}{8} \quad \frac{0}{8} \quad \frac{1}{8}$$

Step 5→ Calculation of the New Values of Other Non Key Rows:

I[st] Non Key Row:

A	Old Values	8	1	1	1	0	0	0
B	New Values of Key Row	2.50	$\frac{5}{8}$	1	0	0	0	$\frac{1}{8}$
C	Key Column Element	1	1	1	1	1	1	1
D	Product of B & C	2.50	$\frac{5}{8}$	1	0	0	0	$\frac{1}{8}$
E	New Values (A – D)	5.50	$\frac{3}{8}$	0	1	0	0	$-\frac{1}{8}$

IInd Non Key Row:

A	Old Values	12	6	4	0	–1	1	0
B	New Values of Key Row	2.50	$\frac{5}{8}$	1	0	0	0	$\frac{1}{8}$
C	Key Column Element	4	4	4	4	4	4	4
D	Product of B & C	10	2.50	4	0	0	0	.50
E	New Values (A – B)	2	3.50	0	0	–1	1	$-\frac{1}{2}$

Step 6→ Preparing Second Simplex Table II.

Simplex Table II

Contribution per unit C_j →			30	20	0	0	–M	–M	Replacement
↓ C_i	Variable	Quantity	x_1	x_2	S_1	S_2	A_1	A_2	Ratio Qty/Value of Key Column
0	S_1	5.50	$\frac{3}{8}$	0	1	0	0	$-\frac{1}{8}$	$\frac{55}{3/8} = 14.67$
–M	A_1	2	**3.50** ←	0	0	–1	–1	$\frac{1}{-2}$	$\frac{2}{35} = 5.71$ ←
20	x_2	2.50	$\frac{5}{8}$	1	0	0	0	$\frac{1}{8}$	$\frac{2.5}{5/8} = 4$
Total Contribution(Z_j)		50-2M	12.50-3.50M	20	0	M	M	M+2.50	
Opportunity Loss	(C_j–Z_j)		17.50+3.50M	0	0	–M	0	–2.50	
			↑ Key Coloumn		Key Element				Key Row

Hence, the outgoing variable is A_1 and the incoming variable is x_1.

Step 7→ Calculating the New Values of Key Row as under:

$$\text{New Values of Key Row} = \frac{\text{Old Values of Key Row}}{\text{Key Element}}$$

$$= \frac{4}{7} \quad 1 \quad 0 \quad 0 \quad -\frac{2}{7} \quad -\frac{2}{7} \quad -\frac{1}{7}$$

Step 8→ Calculation of the New Values of Non Key Rows:

I[st] Non Key Row:

A	Old Values	5.50	$\frac{3}{8}$	0	1	0	0	$-\frac{1}{8}$
B	New Values of Key Row	$\frac{4}{7}$	1	0	0	$-\frac{2}{7}$	$-\frac{2}{7}$	$-\frac{1}{7}$
C	Key Column Element	$\frac{3}{8}$	$\frac{3}{8}$	$\frac{3}{8}$	$\frac{3}{8}$	$\frac{3}{8}$	$\frac{3}{8}$	$\frac{3}{8}$
D	Product of B & C	$\frac{3}{14}$	$\frac{3}{8}$	0	0	$-\frac{3}{28}$	$-\frac{3}{28}$	$-\frac{3}{56}$
E	New Values (A – D)	$\frac{74}{14}$	0	0	1	$\frac{3}{28}$	$\frac{3}{28}$	$-\frac{1}{14}$

IInd Non key Row:

A	Old Values	2.50	$\frac{5}{8}$	1	0	0	0	$\frac{1}{8}$
B	New Values of Key Row	$\frac{4}{7}$	1	0	0	$-\frac{2}{7}$	$-\frac{2}{7}$	$-\frac{1}{7}$
C	Key Column Element	$\frac{5}{8}$	$\frac{5}{8}$	$\frac{5}{8}$	$\frac{5}{8}$	$\frac{5}{8}$	$\frac{5}{8}$	$\frac{5}{8}$
D	Product of B & C	$\frac{5}{14}$	$\frac{5}{8}$	0	0	$-\frac{5}{28}$	$-\frac{5}{28}$	$-\frac{5}{56}$
E	New Values (A – D)	$\frac{30}{14}$	0	1	0	$\frac{5}{28}$	$\frac{5}{28}$	$\frac{3}{14}$

Step 9→ Preparing Simplex Table III.

Simplex Table III

Contribution per unit C_i →			30	20	0	0	–M	–M	Replacement
↓ C_i	Current Variable	Quantity	x_1	x_2	S_1	S_2	A_1	A_2	Ratio Qty/Value of Key Column
0	S_1	$\frac{37}{7}$	0	0	1	$\frac{3}{28}$	$\frac{3}{28}$	$-\frac{1}{14}$	$\frac{37/7}{3/28}=\frac{148}{3}$
30	x_1	$\frac{4}{7}$	1	0	0	$-\frac{2}{7}$	$-\frac{2}{7}$	$-\frac{1}{7}$	$\frac{4/7}{-2/7}=\frac{148}{3}$
20	x_2	$\frac{15}{7}$	0	1	0	$\boxed{\frac{5}{28}}$ ← Key Element	$\frac{5}{28}$	$\frac{3}{14}$	$\frac{15/7}{5/28}=12$ ← Key Row
Total Contribution (Z_j)		60	30	20	0	$-\frac{20}{28}$	$-\frac{20}{28}$	0	
Opportunity Loss ($C_j - Z_j$)			0	0	0	$\frac{20}{28}$ ↑ Key Coloumn	$-M+\frac{20}{28}$	–M	

Key Coloumn Key Element Key Row

Hence, the outgoing variable is x_2 and the incoming variable is S_2.

Step 10→ Replacing the outgoing variable (x_2) by incoming variable (S_2) together with its contribution per unit.

Step 11→ Calculating the New Values of Key Row as under:

$$\text{New Values of Key Row} = \frac{\text{Old Values of Key Row}}{\text{Key Element}}$$

$$= 12 \quad 0 \quad \frac{28}{5} \quad 0 \quad 1 \quad 1 \quad \frac{6}{5}$$

Step 12→ Calculation of the New Values of Non Key Rows:

Ist Non Key Row:

A	Old Values	$\frac{37}{7}$	0	0	1	$\frac{3}{28}$	$\frac{3}{28}$	$-\frac{1}{14}$
B	New Values of Key Row	12	0	$\frac{28}{5}$	0	1	1	$\frac{6}{5}$
C	Key Column Element	$\frac{3}{28}$	$\frac{3}{28}$	$\frac{3}{28}$	$\frac{3}{28}$	$\frac{3}{28}$	$\frac{3}{28}$	$\frac{3}{28}$
D	Product of B & C	$\frac{9}{7}$	0	0	$\frac{3}{5}$	$\frac{3}{28}$	$\frac{3}{28}$	$\frac{3}{70}$
E	New Values (A – D)	4	0	0	$\frac{2}{5}$	0	0	$-\frac{4}{35}$

IInd Non Key Row:

A	Old Values	$\frac{4}{7}$	1	0	0	$-\frac{2}{7}$	$-\frac{2}{7}$	$\frac{1}{7}$
B	New Values of Key Row	12	0	$\frac{28}{5}$	0	1	1	$\frac{6}{5}$
C	Key Column Element	$-\frac{2}{7}$	$-\frac{2}{7}$	$-\frac{2}{7}$	$-\frac{2}{7}$	$-\frac{2}{7}$	$-\frac{2}{7}$	$-\frac{2}{7}$
D	Product of B & C	$-\frac{24}{7}$	0	$-\frac{8}{5}$	0	$-\frac{2}{7}$	$-\frac{2}{7}$	$-\frac{12}{35}$
E	New Values (A – D)	4	1	$\frac{8}{5}$	0	0	0	$\frac{17}{35}$

Step 13→ Preparing Simplex Table IV.

Simplex Table IV

Contribution per unit C_j →			30	20	0	0	–M	–M
↓ C_i	Variable	Quantity	x_1	x_2	S_1	S_2	A_1	A_2
0	S_1	4	0	0	$\frac{2}{5}$	0	0	$-\frac{4}{35}$
30	x_1	4	1	$\frac{8}{5}$	0	0	0	$\frac{17}{35}$
0	S_2	12	0	$\frac{28}{5}$	0	1	1	$\frac{6}{5}$
Total Contribution(Z_j)		120	30	48	0	0	0	$\frac{102}{7}$
Opportunity Loss ($C_j - Z_j$)			0	–28	0	0	–M	$-M - \frac{102}{7}$

Optimal Solution: Since all $C_j - Z_j$ are ≤ 0 the solution is optimum at $x_1 = 4$ and $x_2 = 0$. Thus, the value of Z = 4 × 30 = 120.

PRACTICAL STEPS INVOLVED IN SOLVING MINIMISATION PROBLEMS (WHERE ANY CONSTRAINT HAS "≤" SIGN OR "=" SIGN)

Step 1→

(a) ***Deduct*** *Non-negative Surplus Variables and* ***Add*** *Artificial Variables in case of constraints having "≥" sign as usual in case of Minimisation Problems.*

(b) ***Add*** *Surplus Variables and Artificial Variables in case of constraints having "≤" sign as in case of Maximisation Problems.*

(c) ***Add*** *Artificial Variables in case of constraints having "=" sign.*

***Step 2→** Follow Steps 2 to 14 (given on Page 3.5 and 3.6) as usual in case of Minimisation Problems to obtain the Solution to the given problem.*

PROBLEM 3.4

Use Simplex Method to solve the following LP problem:

Minimize $Z = 30x_1 + 20x_2$

Subject to constraints:

$$-x_1 - x_2 \geq -8$$
$$-6x_1 - 4x_2 \leq -12$$
$$5x_1 + 8x_2 = 20$$
$$x_1, x_2 \geq 0$$

Solution

Step 1→ Formulation of problem after introducing slack variables:

$$-x_1 - x_2 \geq -8 \text{ or } x_1 + x_2 \leq 8$$
$$-6x_1 - 4x_2 \leq -12 \text{ or } 6x_1 + 4x_2 \geq 12$$

Minimize $Z = 30x_1 + 20x_2 - 0S_1 - 0S_2 + MA_1 + MA_2$

Subject to constraints:

$$x_1 + x_2 + S_1 = 8$$
$$6x_1 + 4x_2 - S_2 + A_1 = 12$$
$$5x_1 + 8x_2 + A_2 = 20$$

Step 2→ Preparing Initial Simplex Table I:

Simplex Table I

Contribution per unit C_j →			30	20	0	0	−M	−M	Replacement
↓ C_i	Variable	Quantity	x_1	x_2	S_1	S_2	A_1	A_2	Ratio Qty/Value of Key Column
0	S_1	8	1	1	1	0	0	0	$\frac{8}{1} = 8$
M	A_1	12	6	4	0	−1	1	0	$\frac{12}{4} = 3$
M	A_2	20	5	[8] ←	0	0	0	1	$\frac{28}{8} = 2.5$ ←
Total Contribution (Z_j)			11M	12M	0	−M	M	M	
Opportunity Loss ($C_j - Z_j$)			30−11M	20−12M	0	M	0	0	

↑ Key column — Key Element — Key Row

Step 3→ Replacing the outgoing variable (A_2) by incoming variable (x_2) together with its contribution per unit.

Step 4→ Calculating the New Values of Key Row as under:

$$\text{New Values of Key Row} = \frac{\text{Old Value of Key Row}}{\text{Key Element}}$$

$$= \frac{20}{8} \quad \frac{5}{8} \quad \frac{1}{8} \quad \frac{0}{8} \quad \frac{0}{8} \quad \frac{0}{8} \quad \frac{1}{8}$$

$$= 2.5 \quad .625 \quad 1 \quad 0 \quad 0 \quad 0 \quad .125$$

Step 5→ Calculation of the New Values of Non Key Rows:

I[st] Non Key Row:

A Old Values	8	1	1	1	0	0	0
B New Values of Key Row	2.5	.625	1	0	0	0	.125
C Key Column Element	1	1	1	1	1	1	1
D Product of B & C	2.5	.625	1	0	0	0	.125
E New Values (A – D)	5.5	.375	0	1	0	0	–.125

IInd Non Key Row:

A Old Values	12	6	4	0	–1	1	0
B New Values of Key Row	2.5	.625	1	0	0	0	.125
C Key Column Element	4	4	4	4	4	4	4
D Product of B & C	10	2.5	4	0	0	0	.5
E New Values (A – D)	2	3.5	0	0	–1	1	–.5

Step 6→ Preparing Second Simplex Table II.

Simplex Table II

Contribution per unit C_j →			30	20	0	0	–M	–M	Replacement
↓ C_i	Variable	Quantity	x_1	x_2	S_1	S_2	A_1	A_2	Ratio Qty/Value of Key Column
20	x_2	2.5	.625	1	0	0	0	.125	$\frac{2.5}{.625} = 4$
0	S_1	5.5	.375	0	1	0	0	–.125	$\frac{5.5}{.375} = 14.67$
M	A_1	2	[3.5] ←	0	0	–1	1	–.5	$\frac{2}{3.5} = .57$ ←
Total Contribution (Z_j)			12.5+3.5M	20	0	–M	M	.32-.5M	
Opportunity Loss (C_j – Z_j)			17.5-3.5M	0	0	M	0	1.5M-.32	
			↑ Key Column		Key Element				Key Row

Step 7→ Replacing the outgoing variable (A_1) by incoming variable (x_1) together with its contribution per unit.

Step 8→ Calculating the New Values of Key Row as under:

$$\text{New Values of Key Row} = \frac{\text{Old Value of Key Row}}{\text{Key Element}}$$

$$= \frac{2}{3.5} \quad \frac{3.5}{3.5} \quad \frac{0}{3.5} \quad \frac{0}{3.5} \quad \frac{-1}{3.5} \quad \frac{1}{35} \quad \frac{-5}{3.5}$$

$$= .571 \quad 1 \quad 0 \quad 0 \quad .28 \quad -.28 \quad -.14$$

Step 9→ Calculation of the new value of Non Key Rows:

Ist Non Key Row:

A	Old Values	2.5	.625	1	0	0	0	.125
B	New Values of Key Row	.571	1	0	0	-.28	.28	–.14
C	Key Column Element	.625	.625	.625	.625	.625	.625	.625
D	Product of B & C	.356	.625	0	0	–0.175	.175	–.0875
E	New values (A – D)	2.14	0	1	0	.175	–.175	.2125

IInd Non Key Row:

A	Old Values	5.5	.375	0	1	0	0	–.125
B	New Values of Key Row	.571	1	0	0	–.28	.28	–.14
C	Key Column Element	.375	.375	.375	.375	.375	.375	.375
D	Product of B & C	.21	.375	0	0	–.105	.105	–.0525
E	New values (A – D)	5.285	0	0	1	.105	–.105	–.0725

Step 10→ Preparing Simplex Table III.

Simplex Table III

Contribution per unit C_i →			30	20	0	0	–M	–M	
↓ C_i	Variable	Quantity	x_1	x_2	S_1	S_2	A_1	A_2	
30	x_1	.571	1	0	0	–.28	.28	–.14	
20	x_2	2.14	0	1	0	.175	–.175	.2125	
0	S_1	5.285	0	0	1	.105	–.105	–0.0725	
Total Contribution (Z_j)			30	20	0	–5	5	0	
Opportunity Loss ($C_i - Z_j$)			0	0	0	5	M–5	M	

Optimal Solution: Since all $C_i - Z_j$ are ≥ 0, the table provides the optimal solution, i.e. x_1 = .571 and x_2 = 2.14. The optimal value of Z = (.571 × 30) + (2.14 × 20) = 59.93.

PRACTICAL STEPS INVOLVED IN FORMULATING DUAL PROBLEM FROM THE PRIMAL PROBLEM

The practical steps involved in formulating dual problem from the primal problem are as follows:

Step 1→ *Ensure that in case of a maximization problem all constraints are of '≤' type or in case of a minimization problem, all constraints are of '≥' type.*

If not, adopt the following procedure:

In case of Maximisation Problem

Sign used in Constraints	*Procedure*
1. '≤' type	No change is required.
2. '≥' type	Convert the '≥' type inequality into '≤' type by changing the signs of all values appearing on left hand side and right hand side, (*e.g.* '+' sign into '–' sign, '–' sign into '+' sign).
3. '=' type	(a) Convert equality into two inequalities - one having '≥' sign and the other having '≤' sign. (b) Convert '≥' type inequality into ≤ type inequality by the changing the sign of all values.

In case of Minimization Problem

Sign used in Constraints	*Procedure*
1. '≤' type	Convert '≤' type inequality into '≥' type by changing the signs of all values appearing on left hand side and right hand side. (*e.g.* '+' sign into '–' sign, '–' sign into '+' sign).
2. '≥' type	No change in required.
3. '=' type	(a) Convert equality into two inequalities - one having '≥' sign and the other having '≤' sign. (b) Convert '≤' type inequality into '≥' type by changing the sign of all values.

Step 2→ *Restate the primal problem after taking Step 1.*

Step 3→ ***Change of Objective*** *– If the primal problem is a maximization problem, the dual problem will be a minimization problem. If the primal problem is a minimization problem, the dual problem will be a maximization problem.*

Step 4→ ***Number of Decision Variables in Dual Problem*** *– The number of decision variables in the dual problem is equal to the number of constraints in the primal problem.*

Step 5→ ***Coefficient of Decision Variables in Objective Function Dual Problem*** *– The constraints of the primal problem which appear on the right hand side of the constraints of the primal problem become the coefficients of the decision variables in objective function of the dual problem.*

Step 6→ ***Numbers of Constraints in Dual Problem*** – *The number of constraints in the decision problem is equal to the number of variables in the primal problem.*

Step 7→ *The coefficients of the constraints of the primal problem which appear from left to right are placed from top to bottom in the consraints of the dual problem.*

Step 8→ ***Change of Type of Constraint*** – *If the primal problem has 'less than or equal to' (≤) type constraints, the dual problem will have 'greater than or equal to' (≥) type constraints. If the primal problem has 'greater than or equal to' (≥) type constraints, the dual problem will have 'less than or equal to' (≤) type constraints.*

Step 9→ ***Right hand Side of the Constraints of Dual Problem*** – *The coefficients of objective function of the primal problem appear on the right hand side of the constraints of the dual problem.*

Step 10→ *Non-negativity restriction will also apply to decision variables of dual problem.*

TUTORIAL NOTES:

(i) *The maximum value of the objective function of the primal problem is the minimum value of the objective function of the dual problem.*

(ii) *If the primal problem is in the standard form, the solution of the dual problem can be obtained by multiplying the values of the slack variables in the final Simplex Table by the values ($C_i - Z_j$) appearing on the right hand side of the constraints of the primal problem.*

(iii) *The value of dual variable is referred to as the shadow price or imputed price of a resource. This is the highest price the manufacturer would be willing to pay for the resource. The shadow price of a resource is the unit price that is equal to the increase in profit to be realised by one additional unit of the resource.*

PROBLEM 3.5

Find the dual of the following problem:

Maximize $Z = 30x_1 + 20x_2$

Subject to constraints:

$-x_1 - x_2 \geq -8$ I

$-6x_1 - 4x_2 \leq -12$ II

$5x_1 + 8x_2 = 20$ III

$x_1, x_2 \geq 0$

Solution

Step 1→ *Restating Equality III as two inequalities:*

$5x_1 + 8x_2 \leq 20$ IV

$5x_1 + 8x_2 \geq 20$ V

Step 2→ *Converting '≥' type inequality into '≤' type*

$x_1 + x_2 \leq 8$

$-5x_1 - 8x_2 \leq -20$

Step 3→ *Now, restating the primal as below:*

Maximize $Z = 30x_1 + 20x_2$

Subject to constraints:

$x_1 + x_2 \leq 8$

$$- 6x_1 - 4x_2 \leq -12$$
$$- 5x_1 - 8x_2 \leq -20$$
$$5x_1 + 8x_2 \leq 20$$
$$x_1, x_2 \geq 0$$

Step 4→ *Now formulating the dual as below:*

Minimize **$Z = 8y_1 - 12y_2 - 20y_3 + 20y_4$**

Subject to constraints:

$$y_1 - 6y_2 - 5y_3 + 5y_4 \geq 30$$
$$y_1 - 4y_2 - 8y_3 + 8y_4 \geq 20$$
$$y_1 \text{ to } y_4 \geq 0 \text{ (non negativity constraint)}$$

PROBLEM 3.6

Find the dual of the following problem:

Minimize $Z = 30x_1 + 20x_2$

Subject to constraints:

$$-x_1 - x_2 \geq -8 \quad \text{I}$$
$$-6x_1 - 4x_2 \leq -12 \quad \text{II}$$
$$5x_1 + 8x_2 = 20 \quad \text{III}$$
$$x_1, x_2 \geq 0$$

Solution

Step 1→ *Restating equality III as two inequalities:*

$$5x_1 + 8x_2 \leq 20 \quad \text{IV}$$
$$5x_1 + 8x_2 \geq 20 \quad \text{V}$$

Step 2→ *Converting '≤' type inequality into '≥' type*

$$6x_1 + 4x_2 \geq 12$$
$$-5x_1 - 8x_2 \geq -20$$

Step 3→ *Now, Restating the primal as below:*

Minimize $Z = 30x_1 + 20x_2$

Subject to constraints:

$$- x_1 - x_2 \geq - 8$$
$$6x_1 + 4x_2 \geq 12$$
$$- 5x_1 - 8x_2 \geq -20$$
$$5x_1 - 8x_2 \geq 20$$
$$x_1, x_2 \geq 0$$

Step 4→ *Now the dual will be formulated as below:*

Maximize $Z = - 8y_1 + 12y_2 - 20y_3 + 20y_4$

Subject to constraints:

$$- y_1 + 6y_2 - 5y_3 + 5y_4 \leq 30$$
$$- y_1 + 4y_2 - 8y_3 + 8y_4 \leq 20$$
$$y_1 \text{ to } y_4 \geq 0 \text{ (Non-negativity constraint)}$$

4 Assignment Problems

PRACTICAL STEPS INVOLVED IN SOLVING MINIMISATION PROBLEMS

Step 1 → ***Dummy Row/Column:*** *See whether Number of Rows are equal to Number of Column. If yes, problem is balanced one; if not, then add a Dummy Row or Column to make the problem a balanced one by alloting zero value or specific value (if any given) to each cell of the Dummy Row or Column, as the case may be.*

Step 2 → ***Row Subtraction:*** *Subtract the minimum element of each row from all elements of that row.*

Note: *If there is zero in each row,there is no need for row substraction.*

Step 3 → ***Column Subtraction:*** *Subtract the minimum element of each column from all elements of that column.*

Note: *If there is zero in each column, there is no need for column substraction.*

Step 4 → ***Minimum No. of Horizontal and/or Vertical Lines:*** *Draw minimum number of Horizontal and/or Vertical Lines to cover all zeros.*

To draw minimum number of lines the following procedure may be followed:

1. *Select a row containing exactly one uncovered zero and draw a vertical line through the column containing this zero and repeat the process till no such row is left.*
2. *Select a column containing exactly one uncovered zero and draw a horizontal line through the row containing the zero and repeat the process till no such column is left.*

Step 5 → ***Subtraction/Addition of Minimum Uncovered Element:*** *If the total lines covering all zeros are equal to the size of the matrix of the Table, we have got the optimal solution; if not,* ***subtract*** *the minimum uncovered element from all uncovered elements and* ***add*** *this element to all elements at the intersection point of the lines covering zeros.*

Step 6 → ***Repeat Steps 4 and 5*** *till minimum number of lines covering all zeros is equal to the size of the matrix of the Table.*

Step 7 → ***Assignment:*** *Select a row containing exactly one unmarked zero and surround it by '□'and draw a vertical line through the column containing this zero. Repeat this process till no such row is left; then select a column containing exactly one unmarked zero and surround it by '□' and draw a horizontal line through the row containing this zero and repeat this process till no such column is left.*

Note: *If there are more than one unmarked zero in any row or column, it indicates that an alternative solution exists. In this case, select any one arbitrarily and pass two lines horizontally and vertically.*

Step 8 → *Add up the value attributable to the allocation which shall be the minimum value.*

Step 9 → ***Alternate Solution:*** *If there are more than one unmarked zero in any row or column, select the other one (i.e., other than the one selected in Step 7) and pass two lines horizontally and vertically. Add up the value attributable to the allocation which shall be the minimum value.*

PROBLEM 4.1

To stimulate interest and provide an atmosphere for intellectual discussion, a finance faculty in a management school decides to hold special seminars on four contemporary topics - leasing, portfolio management, private mutual funds, swaps, and options. Such seminars should be held once per week in the afternoons. However, scheduling these seminars (one for each topic, and not more than one seminar per afternoon) has to be done carefully so that the number of students unable to attend is kept to a minimum. A careful study indicates that the number of students who cannot attend a particular seminar on a specific day is as follows:

	Leasing	*Portfolio Management*	*Private Mutual funds*	*Swaps and Options*
Monday	50	40	60	20
Tuesday	40	30	40	30
Wednesday	60	20	30	20
Thursday	30	30	20	30
Friday	10	20	10	30

Required: Find an optimal schedule of the seminars. Also find out the total number of students who will be missing at least one seminar.

Solution

Step 1 → Introducing a dummy topic to make the problem balanced one by alloting zero students.

	Leasing	*Portfolio Management*	*Private Mutual funds*	*Swaps and Options*	*Dummy*
Monday	50	40	60	20	0
Tuesday	40	30	40	30	0
Wednesday	60	20	30	20	0
Thursday	30	30	20	30	0
Friday	10	20	10	30	0

Step 2 → ***Column Subtraction:*** Subtracting the minimum element of each column from all elements of that column. Since there is zero in each row, there is no need for row subtraction. Drawing minimum number of lines to cover all zeros.

	Leasing	*Portfolio Management*	*Private Mutual funds*	*Swaps and Options*	*Dummy*
Monday	40	20	50	0	0
Tuesday	30	10	30	10	0
Wednesday	50	0	20	0	0
Thursday	20	10	10	10	0
Friday	0	0	0	10	0

Since the number of lines (4) ≠ order of matrix (5), we will have to take step to increase the number of zeros.

Step 3 → Subtracting the minimum uncovered element (10 in this case) from all uncovered elements and adding it to all elements at the intersection point of the above lines and then drawing minimum number of lines to cover all zeros.

	Leasing	*Portfolio Management*	*Private Mutual funds*	*Swaps and Options*	*Dummy*
Monday	30	20	40	0	0
Tuesday	20	10	20	10	0
Wednesday	40	0	10	0	0
Thursday	10	10	0	10	0
Friday	0	10	0	20	10

Since number of lines drawn (5) = order of matrix (5), the above matrix will provide the optimal solution.

Step 4 → ***Assignment:*** Selecting a row containing exactly one unmarked zero and surrounding it by '□' and draw a vertical line through the column containing this zero. Repeating this process till no such row is left : then selecting a column containing exactly one unmarked zero and surrounding it by '□' and drawing a horizontal line through the row containing this zero and repeating the process till no such column is left.

	Leasing	*Portfolio Management*	*Private Mutual funds*	*Swaps and Options*	*Dummy*
Monday	30	20	40	[0]	0
Tuesday	20	10	20	10	[0]
Wednesday	40	[0]	10	0	0
Thursday	10	10	[0]	10	0
Friday	[0]	10	0	20	10

Step 5 → Computing minimum number of Students:

Day	*Seminar*	*No. of Students*
Monday :	Swaps and options	20
Tuesday :	No seminar	0
Wednesday :	Portfolio Management	20
Thursday :	Pvt. Mutual funds	20
Friday :	Leasing	10
		70

Thus, the total number of students who will be missing at least one seminar = 70

PROBLEM 4.2

A factory is going to modify of a plant layout to install four new machines M1, M2, M3 and M4. There are 5 vacant place J, K, L, M and available. Because of limite space machine M2 cannot be placed at L and M3 cannot be placed at J. The cost of locating machine to place in Rupees is shown below:

(₹)

	J	K	L	M	N
M1	18	22	30	20	22
M2	24	18	–	20	18
M3	–	22	28	22	14
M4	28	16	24	14	16

Required: Determine the optimal assignment schedule in such a manner that the total cost are kept at a minimum,

Solution

Dummy machine (M5) is inserted to make it a balanced cost matrix and assume its installation cos to zero. Cost of install at cell M3 (J) and M2 (L) is very high marked as é.

	J	K	L	M	N
M1	18	22	30	20	22
M2	24	18	é	20	18
M3	é	22	28	22	14
M4	28	16	24	14	16
M5 (Dummy)	0	0	0	0	0

Step 1 → *Subtract the minimum element of each row from each element of that row*

	J	K	L	M	N
M1	0	4	12	2	4
M2	6	0	é	2	0
M3	é	8	14	8	0
M4	14	2	10	0	2
M5 (Dummy)	0	0	0	0	0

Step 2 → *Subtract the minimum element of each column from each element of that column*

	J	K	L	M	N
M1	0	4	12	2	4
M2	6	0	é	2	0
M3	é	8	14	8	0
M4	14	2	10	0	2
M5 (Dummy)	0	0	0	0	0

Step 3 → *Draw lines to connect the zero as under:*

	J	*K*	*L*	*M*	*N*
M1	0	4	12	2	4
M2	6	0	é	2	0
M3	é	8	14	8	0
M4	14	2	10	0	2
M5 (Dummy)	0	0	0	0	0

There are five lines which are equal to the order of the matrix. Hence the solution is optimal. We may proceed to make the assignment as under:

	J	*K*	*L*	*M*	*N*
M1	[0]	4	12	2	4
M2	6	[0]	é	2	0
M3	é	8	14	8	[0]
M4	14	2	10	[0]	2
M5 (Dummy)	0	0	[0]	0	0

The following is the assignment which keeps the total cost at minimum:

Machines	*Location*	*Cost ₹*
M1	J	18
M2	K	18
M3	N	14
M4	M	14
M5 (Dummy)	L	0
Total		64

PROBLEM 4.3

Five swimmers are eligible to compete in a relay team which is to consist of four swimmers swimming four different swimming styles; back stroke, breast stroke, free style and butterfly. The time taken for the five swimmers—Anand, Bhaskar, Chandru, Dorai and Easwar—to cover a distance of 100 meters in various swimming styles are given below in minutes: seconds. Anand swims the back stroke in 1 : 09, the breast stroke in 1 : 15, and has never competed in the free style or butterfly. Bhaskar is a free style specialist averaging 1 : 01 for the 100 meters but can also swim the breast stroke in 1 : 16 and butterfly in 1 : 20. Chandru swims all styles - back stroke 1 : 10, butterfly 1 : 12, free style 1 : 05, and breast stroke 1 : 20. Dorai swims only the butterfly 1 : 11 while Easwar swims the back stroke 1 : 20, the breast stroke 1 : 16, the free style 1 : 06 and the butterfly 1 : 10. Which swimmer should be assigned to which swimming style? Who will not be in the relay?

Solution

Step 1 → Let us first create the assignment matrix with time expressed in seconds and Introducing a dummy to make the problem a balanced one by alloting zero.

	Back Stroke	*Breast Stroke*	*Free style*	*Butterfly*	*Dummy*
Anand	69	75	—	—	0
Bhaskar	—	76	61	80	0
Chandru	70	80	65	72	0
Dorai	—	—	—	71	0
Easwar	80	76	66	70	0

Step 2 → ***Column Subtraction:*** Subtracting the minimum element of each column from all elements of that column. Since there is zero in each row, there is no need for row subtraction. Drawing minimum number of Lines to cover all zeros.

	Back Stroke	*Breast Stroke*	*Free style*	*Butterfly*	*Dummy*
Anand	0	0	—	—	0
Bhaskar	—	1	0	10	0
Chandru	1	5	4	2	0
Dorai	—	—	—	1	0
Easwar	11	1	5	0	0

Since the number of lines (4) ≠ order of matrix (5), we will have to take step to increase the number of zeros.

Step 3 → Subtracting the minimum uncovered element (1 in this case) from all uncovered elements and adding it to all elements at the intersection point of the above lines and then drawing minimum numbers of lines to cover all zeros.

	Back Stroke	*Breast Stroke*	*Free style*	*Butterfly*	*Dummy*
Anand	0	0	—	—	1
Bhaskar	—	1	0	10	1
Chandru	0	4	3	1	0
Dorai	—	—	—	0	0
Easwar	11	1	5	0	1

Since the number of lines drawn (5) = the order of the matrix (5), the above matrix will provide the optimal solution.

Step 4 → *Assignment:* Selecting a row containing exactly one unmarked zero and surrounding it by '□' and draw a vertical line through the column containing this zero. Repeating this process till no such row is left; then selecting a column containing exactly one unmarked zero and surrounding it by '□' and draw a horizontal line through the row containing this zero and repeating the process till no such column is left.

	Back Stroke	*Breast Stroke*	*Free style*	*Butterfly*	*Dummy*
Anand	0	[0]	—	—	1
Bhaskar	0	1	[0]	10	1
Chandru	[0]	4	3	1	0
Dorai	—	—	—	0	[0]
Easwar	11	1	5	[0]	1

Step 5 → Computing minimum time:

	Time
Anand will be in Breast Stroke	75 seconds
Bhaskar will be in Free stroke	61 seconds
Chandru will be in Back stroke	70 seconds
Dorai will not participate (dummy)	00 seconds
Easwar will be in Butterfly	70 seconds
Total minimum time in the relay	276 (or 4 minutes 36 sec.)

Dorai will be out of the relay.

PROBLEM 4.4

Four Operators O_1, O_2, O_3 and O_4 are available to a manager who has to get four jobs J_1, J_2, J_3 and J_4 done by assigning one job to each operator. Given the time needed by different operators for different jobs in the matrix below:

	J_1	J_2	J_3	J_4
O_1	12	10	10	8
O_2	14	12	15	11
O_3	6	10	16	4
O_4	8	10	9	7

(i) How should manager assign the jobs so that the total time needed for all four jobs is minimum?

(ii) If job J_2 is not to be assigned to operator O_2, what should be the assignment over how much additional total time will be required?

Solution

Step 1 → *Row subtraction:* Subtracting the minimum element of each row from all elements of that row.

Operators	Job			
	J_1	J_2	J_3	J_4
O_1	4	2	2	0
O_2	3	1	4	0
O_3	2	6	12	0
O_4	1	3	2	0

Step 2 → *Column Subtraction:* Subtracting the minimum element of each column from all element of that column and drawing minimum number of lines to cover all zeros.

Operators	Job			
	J_1	J_2	J_3	J_4
O_1	3	1	0	0
O_2	2	0	2	0
O_3	1	5	10	0
O_4	0	2	0	0

Since the number of lines drawn (4) = order of matrix (4), the above matrix will provide the optimal solution.

Step 3 → *Assignment:* Selecting a row containing exactly one unmarked zero and surrounding it by '□' and draw a vertical line through the column containing this zero. Repeating this process till no such row is left; they selecting a column containing exactly one unmarked zero and surrounding it by '□' and draw a horizontal line through the row containing this zero and repeating the process till no such column is left.

Operators	Job			
	J_1	J_2	J_3	J_4
O_1	3	1	[0]	0
O_2	2	[0]	2	0
O_3	1	5	10	[0]
O_4	[0]	2	0	0

Step 4 → Computing the Minimum Time:

	Time
Operator O_1 is assigned to Job J_3	10
Operator O_2 is assigned to Job J_2	12
Operator O_3 is assigned to Job J_4	4
Operator O_4 is assigned to Job J_1	8
Total	34

(ii) Step 1 → If Job J_2 is not be assigned to operator O_2 then put a '–' in the cell to obtain the following matrix.

Operators	Job			
	J_1	J_2	J_3	J_4
O_1	12	10	10	8
O_2	14	—	15	11
O_3	6	10	16	4
O_4	8	10	9	7

Step 2 → ***Row Subtraction:*** Subtracting the minimum element of each row from all elements of that row.

Operators	Job			
	J_1	J_2	J_3	J_4
O_1	4	2	2	0
O_2	3	—	4	0
O_3	2	6	12	0
O_4	1	3	2	0

Step 3 → ***Column Subtraction:*** Subtracting the minimum element of each column from all elements of that column and drawing minimum number of lines to cover all zeros.

Operators	Job			
	J_1	J_2	J_3	J_4
O_1	3	0	0	0
O_2	2	—	2	0
O_3	1	4	10	0
O_4	0	1	0	0

Since the number of lines = 3 and order of matrix = 4, we will have to take step to increase the number of zeros.

Step 4 → Subtracting the minimum uncovered element (1 in this case) from all uncovered elements and adding it to all elements at the intersection point of the above lines and then drawing minimum number of lines to cover all zeros.

Operators	Job			
	J_1	J_2	J_3	J_4
O_1	3	0	0	1
O_2	1	—	1	0
O_3	0	3	9	0
O_4	0	1	0	1

Since the number of lines drawn (4) = order of matrix (4), the above matrix will provide the optimal solution.

Step 5 → ***Assignment:*** Selecting a row containing exactly one unmarked zero and surrounding it by '□' and draw a vertical line through the column containing this zero. Repeating this process till no such row is left; then selecting a column containing exactly one unmarked zero and surrounding it by '□' and draw a horizontal line through the row containing this zero and repeating the process till no such column is left.

Operators	Job			
	J_1	J_2	J_3	J_4
O_1	3	[0]	0	1
O_2	1	—	1	[0]
O_3	[0]	3	9	0
O_4	0	1	[0]	1

Step 6 → Computing minimum Time:

	Time
Operator O_1 is assigned Job J_2	10
Operator O_2 is assigned Job J_4	11
Operator O_3 is assigned Job J_1	6
Operator O_4 is assigned Job J_3	9
Total	36

Additional Total Time Required = 36 – 34 = 2 units of time.

PROBLEM 4.5 [Assignments of Job to Typists]

A solicitor firm employs typists on hourly piece basis for their daily work. There are five typists for service and their charges and speeds are different. According to an earlier understanding only one job is given to one typist and the typist is paid for full hours even if he works for a fraction of an hour. Find the least cost allocation for the following data:

Typist	*Rate per hour (₹)*	*No. of pages Typed/hour*	*Job*	*No. of Pages*
A	5	12	P	199
B	6	14	Q	175
C	3	8	R	145
D	4	10	S	298
E	4	11	T	178

Solution

Step 1 → The following matrix gives the cost incurred if the typist (i = A, B, C, D, E) executes the job (j = P, Q, R, S, T) which is calculated by following formula:

$$= \frac{\text{Total No. of Pages}}{\text{No. of pages typed/hour}} \text{ (Rounded off to next integer) } \quad \text{Rate per hour (₹)}$$

Typist	*Job*				
	P	*Q*	*R*	*S*	*T*
A	85	75	65	125	75
B	90	78	66	132	78
C	75	66	57	114	69
D	80	72	60	120	72
E	76	64	56	112	68

Step 2 → ***Row Subtraction:*** Subtracting the minimum element of each row from all elements of that row.

	Job				
Typist	*P*	*Q*	*R*	*S*	*T*
A	20	10	0	60	10
B	24	12	0	66	12
C	18	9	0	57	12
D	20	12	0	60	12
E	20	8	0	56	12

Step 3 → ***Column Subtraction:*** Subtracting the minimum element of each column from all the elements of that column and then drawing the minimum number of lines to cover all zeros.

	Job				
Typist	*P*	*Q*	*R*	*S*	*T*
A	2	2	0	4	0
B	6	4	0	10	2
C	0	1	0	1	2
D	2	4	0	4	2
E	2	0	0	0	2

Since the number of lines = 4 and order of matrix = 5, we will have to take step to increase the number of zeros.

Step 4 → Subtracting the minimum uncovered element (2 in this case) from all uncovered elements and adding it to all elements at the intersection point of the above lines and then drawing minimum number of lines to cover all zeros.

	Job				
Typist	*P*	*Q*	*R*	*S*	*T*
A	2	2	2	4	0
B	4	2	0	8	0
C	0	1	2	1	2
D	0	2	0	2	0
E	2	0	2	0	2

Since number of lines = 4 and order of matrix = 5, we will have to take step to increase the number of zeros.

Step 5 → Subtracting the minimum uncovered element (1 in this case) from all uncovered elements and adding it to all elements at the intersection point of the above lines and then drawing the minimum number of lines to cover all zeros.

	Job				
Typist	*P*	*Q*	*R*	*S*	*T*
A	2	1	2	3	0
B	4	1	0	7	0
C	0	0	2	0	2
D	0	1	0	1	0
E	3	0	3	0	3

Step 6 → *Assignment:* Selecting a row containing exactly one unmarked zero and surrounding it by '□' and draw a vertical line thorough the column containing this zero. Repeating this process till no such row is left; then selecting a column containing exactly one unmarked zero and surrounding it by '□' and draw a horizontal line through the row containing this zero and repeating the process till no such column is left.

Typist	*Job*				
	P	*Q*	*R*	*S*	*T*
A	2	1	2	3	[0]
B	4	1	[0]	7	0
C	0	[0]	2	0	2
D	[0]	1	0	1	0
E	3	0	3	[0]	3

Step 7 → Computing minimum cost:

Typist	*Job*		*Cost (₹)*
A	T	:	75
B	R	:	66
C	Q	:	66
D	P	:	80
E	S	:	112
	Total	₹	399

Alternate Solution:

Typist	*Job*				
	P	*Q*	*R*	*S*	*T*
A	2	1	2	3	[0]
B	4	1	[0]	7	0
C	0	0	2	[0]	2
D	[0]	1	0	1	0
E	3	[0]	3	0	3

Minimum cost:

Typist	*Job*	*Cost (₹)*
A	T	75
B	R	66
C	S	114
D	P	80
E	Q	64
	Total	399

PROBLEM 4.6 [Assignment of Rooms]

Welldone Company has taken the third floor of a multistoreyed building for rent with a view to locate one of their zonal offices. There are five main rooms in this floor to be assigned to five managers. Each room has its own advantages and disadvantages. Some have windows, some are closer to the washrooms or to the canteen or secretarial pool. The rooms are of all different sizes and shapes. Each of the five manages were asked to rank their room preferences amongst the rooms 301, 302, 303, 304 and 305. Their preferences were recorded in a table as indicated below.

Manager				
M_1	M_2	M_3	M_4	M_5
302	302	303	302	301
303	304	301	305	302
304	305	304	304	304
	301	305	303	
		302		

Most of the managers did not list all the five rooms since they were not satisified with some of these rooms and they have left off these from the list. Assuming that their preferences can be quantified by numbers, find out as to which manager should be assigned to which rooms so that their total preference ranking is a minimum.

Solution

Step 1 → Formulating the preference ranking assignment problem.

Rooms No.	*Managers*				
	M_1	M_2	M_3	M_4	M_5
301	—	4	2	—	1
302	1	1	5	1	2
303	2	—	1	4	—
304	3	2	3	3	3
305	—	3	4	2	—

Step 2 → ***Row Subtraction:*** Subtracting the minimum element of each row from all elements of that row. Since there is zero in each column, there is no need for column subtraction. Drawing the minimum number of lines to cover all zeros.

Rooms No.	*Managers*				
	M_1	M_2	M_3	M_4	M_5
301	—	3	1	—	0
302	0	0	4	0	1
303	1	—	0	3	—
304	1	0	1	1	1
305	—	1	2	0	—

Since number of lines = 5 and order of matrix = 5, the above matrix will provide the optimal solution.

Step 3 → ***Assignment:*** Selecting a row containing exactly one unmarked zero and surrounding it by '□' and draw a vertical line thorough the column containing this zero. Repeating this process till no such row is left; then selecting a column containing exactly one unmarked zero and surrounding it by '□' and draw a horizontal line through the row containing this zero and repeating the process till no such column is left.

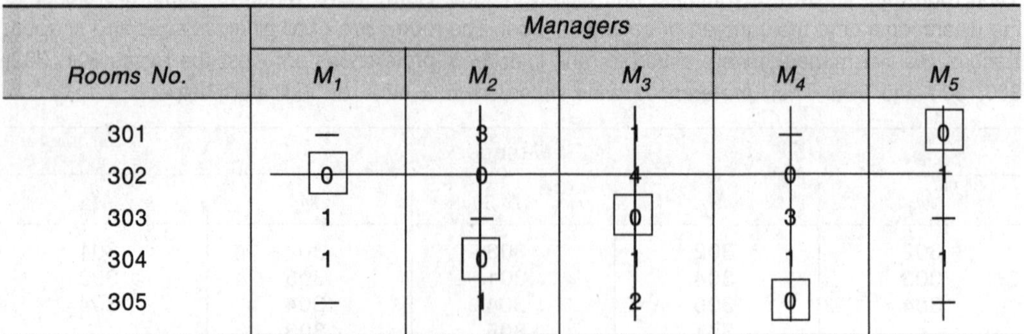

Rooms No.	Managers				
	M_1	M_2	M_3	M_4	M_5
301	—	3	1	—	[0]
302	[0]	0	4	0	1
303	1	—	[0]	3	—
304	1	[0]	1	1	1
305	—	1	2	[0]	—

Step 4 → Computing minimum ranking

The assignment is given below:

			Ranking
M_1	→	Room No 302	1
M_2	→	Room No 304	2
M_3	→	Room No 303	1
M_4	→	Room No 305	2
M_5	→	Room No 301	1
			7

Thus, the total minimum ranking is 7.

PROBLEM 4.7

A machine operator processes five types of items on his machine each week, and must choose a sequences for them. The set-up cost per change depends on the item presently on the machine and the set-up to be made, according to the following table:

For item	To item				
	A	B	C	D	E
A	—	4	7	3	4
B	4	—	6	3	4
C	7	6	—	7	5
D	3	3	7	—	7
E	4	4	5	7	—

If he processes each type of item once and only once each week, how should he sequence the items on his machine in order to minimize the total set-up cost?

Solution

Step 1 → *Row Subtraction:* Subtracting the minimum element of each row from all elements of that row.

For item	To item A	B	C	D	E
A	—	1	4	0	1
B	1	—	3	0	1
C	2	1	—	2	0
D	0	0	4	—	4
E	0	0	1	3	—

Step 2 → *Column Subtraction:* Subtracting the minimum element of each column from all elements of that column and drawing minimum number of lines to cover all zeros.

For item	To item A	B	C	D	E
A	—	1	3	0	1
B	1	—	2	0	1
C	2	1	—	2	0
D	0	0	3	—	4
E	0	0	0	3	—

Since number of lines = 4 and order of matrix = 5, we will have to take step to increase the number of zeros.

Step 3 → Subtracting the minimum uncovered element (1 in this case) from all the uncovered elements and adding it to all the elements at the intersection point of the above lines and drawing minimum number of Lines to cover all zeros.

For item	To item A	B	C	D	E
A	—	0	2	0	0
B	0	—	1	0	0
C	2	1	—	3	0
D	0	0	3	—	4
E	0	0	0	4	—

Since the number of lines (5) = order of matrix (5), the above matrix will provide Optimal Solution.

Step 4 → *Assignment:* Selecting a row containing exactly one unmarked zero and surrounding it by '□' and draw a vertical line through the column containing this zero. Repeating this process till no such row is left; then selecting a column containing exactly one unmarked zero and surrounding it by '□' and draw a horizontal line through the row containing this zero and repeating the process till no such column is left.

For item	To item				
	A	*B*	*C*	*D*	*E*
A	—	0	2	[0]	0
B	[0]	—	1	0	0
C	2	1	—	3	[0]
D	0	[0]	3	—	4
E	0	0	[0]	4	—

Step 5 → Computing Minimum Set-up cost

Item	*Item*	*Cost (₹)*
A	D	3
B	A	4
C	E	5
D	B	3
E	C	5
	Total	**20**

Alternative Solution:

For item	To item				
	A	*B*	*C*	*D*	*E*
A	—	[0]	2	0	0
B	0	—	1	[0]	0
C	2	1	—	3	[0]
D	[0]	0	3	—	4
E	0	0	[0]	4	—

Minimum Set-up cost:

Item	*Item*	*Cost (₹)*
A	B	4
B	D	3
C	E	5
D	A	3
E	C	5
	Total	20

PROBLEM 4.8

A large engineering workshop has five shops. Hitherto, they have been fabricating five different types of components, one in each shop. Fabrication of one of these components is to be discontinued. Since the firm will follow the policy one shop-one component, one of the shops will be closed down. Data on the number of units to be manufactured and the unit costs are given below. Recommend an optimal plan as to which component should be produced in which shop and which of the shops be closed down. [Matrix elements are cost of fabrication in Rupees per unit.]

		C_1	C_2	C_3	C_4
S	S_1	6	7	5	8
H	S_2	7	6	5	9
O	S_3	8	7	6	9
P	S_4	8	9	4	8
S	S_5	9	8	6	7
Number of units (000)		8	6	4	5

Solution

This is an Assignment Problem, since each shop will produce only one component.

Because the number of units of the components differ the total cost of fabrication has to be taken into account instead of just the unit cost.

Total cost = Unit cost × No. of units.

Step 1 → Since there are five shops but only four components, a dummy component C_5 [with 0 costs] has to be included to balance the AP.

	C_1	C_2	C_3	C_4	C_5
S_1	48	42	20	40	0
S_2	56	36	20	45	0
S_3	64	42	24	45	0
S_4	64	54	16	40	0
S_5	72	48	24	35	0

Step 2 → ***Column Subtraction:*** Subtracting the minimum element of each column from all elements of that column and drawing the minimum number of lines to cover all zeros.

	C_1	C_2	C_3	C_4	C_5
S_1	0	6	4	5	0
S_2	8	0	4	10	0
S_3	16	6	8	10	0
S_4	16	18	0	5	0
S_5	24	12	8	0	0

Since number of lines drawn (5) = order of matrix = (5), the above matrix will provide optimal solution.

Step 3 → ***Assignment:*** Selecting a row containing exactly one unmarked zero and surrounding it by '☐' and draw a vertical line through the column containing this zero. Repeating this process till no such row is left; then selecting a column containing exactly one unmarked zero and surrounding it by '□' and draw a horizontal line through the row containing this zero and repeating the process till no such column is left.

	C_1	C_2	C_3	C_4	C_5
S_1	0	6	4	5	0
S_2	8	0	4	10	0
S_3	16	6	8	10	0
S_4	16	18	0	5	0
S_5	24	12	8	0	0

Step 4 → Computing the Minimum:

Shop	*Component*	*Cost (₹ 000)*
S_1	C_1	48
S_2	C_2	36
S_3	C_5	0 Shop to be closed down
S_4	C_3	16
S_5	C_4	35
	Total cost	135

PROBLEM 4.9 [Flight Scheduling]

Sohil Airlines, operating seven days a week, serves three cities A, B, and C according to the schedule shown in the following table. The layover cost per stop is roughly proportional to the square of the layover time. How should planes be assigned the flights so as to minimize the total layover cost?

Flight No. and Index	*From*	*Departure*	*To*	*Arrival*
A_1 B	A	09 A.M.	B	Noon
A_2 B	A	10 A.M.	B	01 P.M.
A_3 B	A	03 P.M.	B	06 P.M.
A_4 C	A	08 P.M.	C	Midnight
A_5 C	A	10 P.M.	C	02 A.M.
B_1 A	B	04 A.M.	A	07 A.M.
B_2 A	B	11 A.M.	A	02 P.M.
B_3 A	B	03 P.M.	A	06 P.M.
C_1 A	C	07 A.M.	A	11 A.M.
C_2 A	C	03 P.M.	A	07 P.M.

Solution

Assumption:

1. Any plane flying from a station must come back within 24 hours for scheduled trip.
2. Any plane starting from A for B must avail the next opportunity to come back to A.
3. It is not possible for any plane to make more than 2 trips, i.e., going and coming back.
4. Five planes will be operating on the line.

Step 1 → Let us first consider the cost matrix associated with the flights connecting A and C. Any plane through C_1A must return back to C by evening route A_4C or A_5C. At station A the layover for A_4C is 9 hours (11 A.M.–8 P.M.) while at station C, the layover for C_1A is 7 hours (Midnight–7 A.M.). Thus, the layover cost for route C_1A - A_4C is $9^2 + 7^2 = 130$ units. Similarly, the other route costs can be computed and the following cost matrix is obtained:

Table 1

	A_4 C	A_5 C
C_1A	130	146
C_2A	226	178

Step 2 → We now consider the cost associated with the flights connecting A and B. Any plane through the route A_1B cannot return by B_2A, because reaching B at noon, the plane has to return back the next day at 11 A.M. Thus we may consider the cost associated with this flight to be very high say M, to avoid this possibility. The costs for other trips between A and B are easily computed, and the following cost matrix is obtained:

Table 2

	B_1 A	B_2 A	B_3 A
A_1B	260	M	234
A_2B	234	M	260
A_3B	164	290	M

Finding optimal solution for Table 1

Step 3 → ***Row Subtraction:*** Subtracting the minimum element of each row from all elements of that row and drawing a minimum number of lines to cover all zeros.

	A_4 C	A_5 C
C_1A	0	16
C_2A	48	0

Since number of lines (2), = order of matrix = (2), the above matrix will provide optimal solution for table 1.

Step 4 → ***Assignment:*** Selecting a row containing exactly one unmarked zero and surrounding it by '□' and draw a vertical line thorough the column containing this zero. Repeating this process till no such row is left; then selecting a column containing exactly one unmarked zero and surrounding it by '□' and draw a horizontal line through the row containing this zero and repeating the process till no such column is left.

	A_4C	A_5C
C_1A	0	16
C_2A	48	0

Finding Solution for Table 2

Step 1 → *Row Subtraction:* Subtracting the minimum element of each row from all elements of that row and drawing the minimum number of lines to cover all zeros.

	$B_1 A$	$B_2 A$	$B_3 A$
A_1B	26	M	0
A_2B	0	M	26
A_3B	0	126	M

Since number of lines = 2, and order of matrix = 3, we will have to take step to increase the number of zeros.

Step 2 → Subtracting the minimum uncovered element (26 in this case) from all uncovered elements and adding it to all elements at the intersection point of the above lines and drawing a minimum number of lines to cover all zeros.

	$B_1 A$	$B_2 A$	$B_3 A$
A_1B	52	M	0
A_2B	0	M	0
A_3B	0	100	M

Since number of lines (3), = order of matrix (3), the above matrix will provide optimal solution for Table 2.

Step 3 → *Assignment:* Subtracting a row containing exactly one unmarked zero and surrounding it by '□' and draw a vertical line thorough the column containing this zero. Repeating this process till no such row is left; then selecting a column containing exactly one unmarked zero and surrounding it by '□' and draw a horizontal line through the row containing this zero and repeating the process till no such column is left.

	$B_1 A$	$B_2 A$	$B_3 A$
A_1B	52	M	0
A_2B	0	M	0
A_3B	0	0	M

Step 4 → So, Optimal Route Schedule for 5 planes is as follows:

Plane No.	*Departure Route*	*Arrival Route*
1	A_1B	B_3A
2	A_2B	B_1A
3	A_3B	B_2A
4	C_1A	A_4C
5	C_2A	A_5C

PROBLEM 4.10 [Flight Scheduling]

XYZ airline operating 7 days a week has given the following time-table. Crews must have a minimum layover of 5 hours between flights. Obtain the pairing flights that minimizes layover time away from home. For any given pairing the crew will be based at the city that results in the smaller layover.

Chennai-Mumbai			*Mumbai-Chennai*		
Flight Number	*Depart.*	*Arrive*	*Flight Number*	*Depart.*	*Arrive*
A_1	6 AM	8 AM	B_1	8 AM	10 AM
A_2	8 AM	10 AM	B_2	9 AM	11 AM
A_3	2 PM	4 PM	B_3	2 PM	4 PM
A_4	8 PM	10 PM	B_4	7 PM	9 PM

Solution

Step 1 → *Formulation of Assignment Problem:*

To begin with, let us first assume that the crew is based at Chennai. The flight A_1, which starts from Chennai at 6 AM, reaches Mumbai at 8 AM. The schedule time for the flight at Mumbai is 8 AM. Since the minimum layover time for crew is 5 hours, this flight can depart only on the next day i.e. the layover time will be 24 hours. Similarly, layover times for other flights are also calculated and given in the following tables.

Table 1: Layover Time in hours at Mumbai

Flight No.	B_1	B_2	B_3	B_4
A_1	24	25	6	11
A_2	22	23	28	9
A_3	16	17	22	27
A_4	10	11	16	21

Table 2: Layover Time in hours at Chennai

Flight No.	B_1	B_2	B_3	B_4
A_1	20	19	14	9
A_2	22	21	16	11
A_3	28	27	22	17
A_4	10	9	28	23

Now since the crew can be based at either of the places, minimum layover times can be obtained for different flight numbers by selecting the corresponding lower value out of the above two tables. The resulting table is given below:

Table 3: Minimum Layover Time between Flights

Flight No.	*Flight No.*			
	B_1	B_2	B_3	B_4
A_1	20	19	6	9
A_2	22	21	16	9
A_3	16	17	22	17
A_4	10	9	16	21

Step 2 → Subtracting the minimum element of each row from all the elements of that row, we get the following matrix. Since there is a zero in each column, there is no need to perform column reduction and drawing the minimum number of lines to cover all zeros.

Flight No.	Flight No.			
	B_1	B_2	B_3	B_4
A_1	14	13	0	3
A_2	13	12	7	0
A_3	0	1	6	1
A_4	1	0	7	12

Since the minimum number of lines to cover all zeros is four which is equal to the order of the matrix, the above table will give the optimal solution.

Step 3 → *Assignment:* Subtracting a row containing exactly one unmarked zero and surrounding it by '□' & draw a vertical line thorough the column containing this zero. Repeating this process till no such row is left; then selecting a column containing exactly one unmarked zero and surrounding it by '□' and draw a horizontal line through the row containing this zero and repeating the process till no such column is left.

Flight No.	Flight No.			
	B_1	B_2	B_3	B_4
A_1	14	13	[0]	3
A_2	13	12	7	[0]
A_3	[0]	1	6	1
A_4	1	[0]	7	12

Step 4 → Computing the Minimum Layover Time :

From Flight No.	*To Flight No.*	*Layover time*
A_1	B_3	6
A_2	B_4	9
A_3	B_1	16
A_4	B_2	9
		40 hours

PROBLEM 4.11 [Flight Scheduling]

A trip from Madras to Bangalore takes six hours by bus. A typical time table of the bus service in both directions is given below:

Departure from Madras	*Route Number*	*Arrival at Bangalore*	*Arrival at Madras*	*Route Number*	*Departure from Bangalore*
06.00	a	12.00	11.30	1	05.30
07.30	b	13.30	15.00	2	09.00
11.30	c	17.30	21.00	3	15.00
19.00	d	1.00	00.30	4	18.30
00.30	e	06.30	06.00	5	00.00

The cost of providing this service by the transport company depends upon the time spent by the bus crew (driver and conductor) away from their places in addition to service times. There are five crews. There is a constraint that every crew should be provided with more than 4 hours of rest before the return trip again and should not wait for more than 24 hours of rest before the return trip again. The company has residential facilities for the crew of Madras as well as at Bangalore. Find which line of service be connected with which other line so as to reduce the waiting time to the minimum.

Solution

Step 1 → *Formulation of Assignment Problem:* As the service time is constant for each line it does not appear directly in the computation. If the entire crew resides at Madras then the waiting times in hours at Bangalore for different route connections are given in the following Table :

Table 1 : Layover Time in Hours at Bangalore

Route	*1*	*2*	*3*	*4*	*5*
a	17.5	21	—	6.5	12
b	16	19.5	—	5	10.5
c	12	15.5	21.5	—	6.5
d	4.5	8	14	17.5	23
e	23	—	8.5	12	17.5

If Route a is combined with Route 1, the crew after arriving at Bangalore at 12 Noon start at 5.30 next morning. Thus the waiting time is 17.5 hours. Some of the assignments are infeasible. Route 3 leaves Bangalore at 15.00 hours. Thus the crew of Route a reaching Bangalore at 12 Noon are unable to take the minimum stipulated rest of four hours if they are asked to leave by Route 3. Hence a_3 is an infeasible assignment. Similarly other infeasible assignments have been markd with '–'.

Similarly, if the crew are assumed to reside at Bangalore then the waiting times of the crew in hours at Madras for different route combinations are given in Table 2.

Table 2 : Layover Time in hours at Madras

Route	*1*	*2*	*3*	*4*	*5*
a	18.5	15	9	5.5	24
b	20	16.5	10.5	7	-
c	24	20.5	14.5	11	5.5
d	7.5	-	22	18.5	13
e	13	9.5	-	24	18.5

As the crew can be asked to reside either at Madras or at Bangalore, minimum waiting time from the above operation can be computed for different route combination by choosing the minimum of the two waiting times. This is presented in Table 5. The asterisk marked waiting times indicates that the crew are based at Madras, otherwise they are based at Bangalore.

Table 3 : Minimum Layover Time in Hours

Route	*1*	*2*	*3*	*4*	*5*
a	17.5	15	9	5.5	12
b	16	16.5	10.5	5	10.5
c	12	15.5	14.5	11	5.5
d	4.5	8	14	17.5	13
e	13	9.5	8.5	12	17.5

Step 2 → *Row Subtraction:* Subtracting the minimum element of each row from all the elements of that row.

Route	*1*	*2*	*3*	*4*	*5*
a	12.00	9.5	3.5	0	6.5
b	11.00	11.5	5.5	0	5.5
c	6.5	10.00	9.0	5.5	0
d	0	3.5	9.5	13.0	8.5
e	4.5	1.0	0	3.5	9.0

Step 3 → *Column Subtraction:* Subtracting the minimum element of each column of the above matrix from all the elements of that column and then drawing the minimum number of line to cover all zeros.

Route	*1*	*2*	*3*	*4*	*5*
a	12.00	8.5	3.5	0	6.5
b	11.00	10.5	5.5	0	5.5
c	6.5	9.0	9.0	5.5	0
d	0	2.5	9.5	13.0	8.5
e	4.5	0	0	3.5	9.0

Since number of lines drawn (4) and order of matrix (5), we will have to take the step to increase the no. of zeros.

Step 4 → Subtracting the minimum uncovered element (3.5 in this case) from all the uncovered elements and adding to the elements at the intersection points and then drawing the minimum number of lines to cover all zeros.

Route	*1*	*2*	*3*	*4*	*5*
a	8.5	5.0	0	0	3.0
b	7.5	7.0	2.0	0	2
c	6.5	9.0	9.0	9.0	0
d	0	2.5	9.5	16.5	8.5
e	4.5	0	0	7.0	9.0

Since number of lines drawn (5) = order of matrix (5), the above matrix will provide the optimal solution.

Step 5 → *Assignment:* Subtracting a row containing exactly one unmarked zero and surrounding it by '☐' and draw a vertical line thorough the column containing this zero. Repeating this process till no such row is left; then selecting a column containing exactly one unmarked zero and surrounding it by '☐' and draw a horizontal line through the row containing this zero and repeating the process till no such column is left.

Route	*1*	*2*	*3*	*4*	*5*
a	8.5	5.0	[0]	[0]	3.0
b	7.5	7.0	2.0	0	2
c	6.5	9.0	9.0	9.0	[0]
d	[0]	2.5	9.5	16.5	8.5
e	4.5	[0]	0	7.0	9.0

Step 6 → Computing the Minimum Layover Time

Route to be Paired	Residence of the Crew	Waiting time
a – 3	Bangalore	9
b – 4	Madras	5
c – 5	Bangalore	5.5
d – 1	Madras	4.5
e – 2	Bangalore	9.5

The minimum total waiting time is thus 33.5 hours.

PRACTICAL STEPS INVOLVED IN SOLVING MAXIMISATION PROBLEMS

Step 1 → ***Dummy/Row/Column*** *See whether Number of Rows are equal to Number of Columns. If yes, problem is a balanced one; if not, then add a Dummy Row or Column to make the problem a balanced one by alloting zero value or specific value (if any given) to each cell of the Dummy Row or Column, as the case may be.*

Step 2 → *Derive* ***Profit Matrix*** *by deducting Cost from Revenue.*

Step 3 → *Derive* ***Loss Matrix*** *by deducting all elements from the largest element.*

Step 4 → *Follow the same Steps 2 to 9 as involved in solving Minimisation Problems.*

PROBLEM 4.12

Imagine yourself to be the Executive Director of a 5-star Hotel which has four banquet halls that can be used for all functions including weddings. The halls were all about the same size but the facilities in each hall differed. During a heavy marriage season, 4 parties approached you to reserve a hall for the marriage to be celebrated on the same day. These marriage parties were told that the first choice among these 4 halls would cost ₹ 10,000 for the day. They were also required to indicate the second, third and fourth preferences and the price that they would be willing to pay. Marriage party A & D indicated that they won't be interested in Halls 3 & 4. Other particulars are given in the following table:

Marriage Party	Revenue per Hall			
	1	2	3	4
A	10,000	9,000	X	X
B	8,000	10,000	8,000	5,000
C	7,000	10,000	6,000	8,000
D	10,000	8,000	X	X

Where *X* indicated that the party does not want that hall.

Required: Decide on an allocation that will maximise the revenue to your hotel.

Solution

Step 1 → Deriving loss matrix by deducting all events from the largest element (10,000)

Marriage Party	Loss Matrix/Hall			
	1	2	3	4
A	0	1000	X	X
B	2000	0	2000	5000
C	3000	0	4000	2000
D	0	2000	X	X

Step 2 → ***Column Subtraction:*** Subtracting the minimum element of each column from all elements of that column and drawing the minimum number of lines to cover all zeros.

Marriage Party	Loss Matrix/Hall 1	2	3	4
A	0	1000	X	X
B	2000	0	0	3000
C	3000	0	2000	0
D	0	2000	X	X

Since Number of Lines = 3 and Order of Matrix = 4, the above matrix will provide the optimal solution.

Step 3 → Subtracting the minimum uncovered element (1000 in this case) from all uncovered elements and adding it to all elements at the intersection points of the above lines and drawing the minimum number of lines to cover all zeros.

Marriage Party	Loss Matrix/Hall 1	2	3	4
A	0	0	X	X
B	3000	0	0	3000
C	4000	0	2000	0
D	0	1000	X	X

Since number of lines (4) = order of matrix (4), the above matrix will provide the optimal solution.

Step 4 → ***Assignment:*** Selecting a row containing exactly one unmarked zero and surrounding it by '□' and draw a vertical line thorough the column containing this zero. Repeating this process till no such row is left; then selecting a column containing exactly one unmarked zero and surrounding it by '□' and draw a horizontal line through the row containing this zero and repeating the process till no such column is left.

Marriage Party	Loss matrix/Hall 1	2	3	4
A	0	[0]	X	X
B	3000	0	[0]	3000
C	4000	0	2000	[0]
D	[0]	1000	X	X

Step 5 → Computing maximum:

		Revenue
Marriage Party	A – Hall 2	9,000
Marriage Party	B – Hall 3	8,000
Marriage Party	C – Hall 4	8,000
Marriage Party	D – Hall 1	10,000
	Total	35,000

PROBLEM 4.13 [Assignment of Batting Positions]

The captain of a cricket team has to allot five middle batting positions to five batsmen. The average runs scored by each batsman at these positions are as follows:

	Batting positions				
Batsman	*I*	*II*	*III*	*IV*	*V*
P	40	40	35	25	50
Q	42	30	16	25	27
R	50	48	40	60	50
S	20	19	20	18	25
T	58	60	59	55	53

(i) Find the assignment of batsmen to positions, which would give the maximum number of runs.

(ii) If another batsman 'U' with the following average runs in batting positions as given below:

Batting position:	I	II	III	IV	V
Average runs:	45	52	38	50	49

Is added to the team, should he be included to play in the team ? If so, who will be replaced by him?

Solution

Step 1 → Deriving Loss Matrix by deducting all elements from the largest element (60).

	Batting positions				
Batsman	*I*	*II*	*III*	*IV*	*V*
P	20	20	25	35	10
Q	18	30	44	35	33
R	10	12	20	0	10
S	40	41	40	42	35
T	2	0	1	5	7

Step 2 → *Row Subtraction:* Subtracting the minimum element of each row from all elements of that row.

	Batting positions				
Batsman	*I*	*II*	*III*	*IV*	*V*
P	10	10	15	25	0
Q	0	12	26	17	15
R	10	12	20	0	10
S	5	6	5	7	0
T	2	0	1	5	7

Step 3 → *Column Subtraction:* Subtracting the minimum element of each column from all elements of that column and drawing minimum number of lines to cover all zeros.

	Batting positions				
Batsman	*I*	*II*	*III*	*IV*	*V*
P	10	10	14	25	0
Q	0	12	25	17	15
R	10	12	19	0	10
S	5	6	4	7	0
T	2	0	0	5	7

Since number of lines = 4 and order of matrix = 5, we will have to take step to increase the number of zeros.

Step 4 → Subtracting the minimum uncovered element (in this case 4) from all uncovered elements and adding it to all elements at the intersection point of the above lines and drawing minimum number of lines to cover all zeros.

	Batting positions				
Batsman	*I*	*II*	*III*	*IV*	*V*
P	6	6	10	25	0
Q	0	12	25	21	19
R	6	8	15	0	10
S	1	2	0	7	0
T	2	0	0	9	11

Since the number of lines drawn (5) = order of matrix (5), the above matrix will provide the optimal solution.

Step 5 → *Assignment:* Selecting a row containing exactly one unmarked zero and surrounding it by '□' and draw a vertical line thorough the column containing this zero. Repeating this process till no such row is left; then selecting a column containing exactly one unmarked zero and surrounding it by '□' and draw a horizontal line through the row containing this zero and repeating the process till no such column is left.

	Batting positions				
Batsman	*I*	*II*	*III*	*IV*	*V*
P	6	6	10	25	[0]
Q	[0]	12	25	21	19
R	6	8	15	[0]	10
S	1	2	[0]	7	0
T	2	[0]	0	9	11

Step 6 → Computing Maximum Runs:

Batsman	*Batting positions*	*Runs*
P	V	50
Q	I	42
R	IV	60
S	III	20
T	II	60
	Total	232

Part (ii)

Step 1 → Including Batsman U in Initial Table. **Introducing a Dummy batting position** to make the problem a balanced one by alloting zero.

	Batting positions					
Batsman	*I*	*II*	*III*	*IV*	*V*	*VI*
P	40	40	35	25	50	0
Q	42	30	16	25	27	0
R	50	48	40	60	50	0
S	20	19	20	18	25	0
T	58	60	59	55	53	0
U	45	52	38	50	49	0

Step 2 → Deriving Loss Matrix by deducting all elements from the largest element (60).

	Batting positions					
Batsman	*I*	*II*	*III*	*IV*	*V*	*VI*
P	20	20	25	35	10	60
Q	18	30	44	35	33	60
R	10	12	20	0	10	60
S	40	41	40	42	35	60
T	2	0	1	5	7	60
U	15	8	22	10	11	60

Step 3 → ***Row Subtraction:*** Subtracting the minimum element of each row from all elements of that row.

	Batting positions					
Batsman	*I*	*II*	*III*	*IV*	*V*	*VI*
P	10	10	15	25	0	50
Q	0	12	26	17	15	42
R	10	12	20	0	10	60
S	5	6	5	7	0	25
T	2	0	1	5	7	60
U	7	0	14	2	3	52

Step 4 → *Column Subtraction:* Subtracting the minimum element of each column from all element of that column and drawing minimum number of Lines to cover all zeros.

	Batting positions					
Batsman	*I*	*II*	*III*	*IV*	*V*	*VI*
P	10	10	14	25	0	25
Q	0	12	25	17	15	17
R	10	12	19	0	10	35
S	5	6	4	7	0	0
T	2	0	0	5	7	35
U	7	0	13	2	3	27

Since number of lines (6) = order of matrix (6), the above matrix will provide the optimal solution.

Step 5 → *Assignment:* Selecting a row containing exactly one unmarked zero and surrounding it by '□' and draw a vertical line through the column containing this zero. Repeating this process till no such row is left; then selecting a column containing exactly one unmarked zero and surrounding it by '□' and draw a horizontal line through the row containing this zero and repeating the process till no such column is left.

	Batting positions					
Batsman	*I*	*II*	*III*	*IV*	*V*	*VI*
P	10	10	14	25	[0]	25
Q	[0]	12	25	17	15	17
R	10	12	19	[0]	10	35
S	5	6	4	7	0	[0]
T	2	0	[0]	5	7	35
U	7	[0]	13	2	3	17

Step 6 → Computing Maximum Runs:

Batsman	*Batting Positions*	*Runs*
P	V	50
Q	I	42
R	IV	60
S	VI (dummy)	-
T	III	59
U	II	52
	Total	263

∴ Batsman S will be replaced by Batsman U.

PROBLEM 4.14 [Assignment of New Methods]

A production manager wants to assign one of the five new methods to each of the four operations. The following table summarises the weekly output in units:

Operator	Weekly Output				
	M_1	M_2	M_3	M_4	M_5
A	4	6	11	16	9
B	5	8	16	19	9
C	9	13	21	21	13
D	6	6	9	11	7

Cost per unit in ₹ 10, Selling Price per unit ₹ 35. Find the maximum profit per month.

Solution

Note: Since Profit per unit (₹ 25 i.e., ₹ 35 – ₹ 10) is same the given problem can be solved using minimization technique.

Step 1 → Introducing a Dummy Operator to make the problem a balanced one by alloting zero output.

Operator	Methods				
	M_1	M_2	M_3	M_4	M_5
A	4	6	11	16	9
B	5	8	16	19	9
C	9	13	21	21	13
D	6	6	9	11	7
Dummy	0	0	0	0	0

Step 2 → Deriving Loss Matrix by subtracting all elements from the largest element (21).

Operator	Methods				
	M_1	M_2	M_3	M_4	M_5
A	17	15	10	5	12
B	16	13	5	2	12
C	12	8	0	0	8
D	15	15	12	10	14
Dummy	21	21	21	21	21

Step 3 → *Row Subtraction:* Subtracting the minimum element of each row from all elements of that row and then drawing the minimum number of lines to cover all zeros.

Operator	Methods				
	M_1	M_2	M_3	M_4	M_5
A	12	10	5	0	7
B	14	11	3	0	10
C	12	8	0	0	8
D	5	5	2	0	4
Dummy	0	0	0	0	0

Since number of lines = 3 and order of matrix = 5, we will have to take step to increase the number of zeros.

Step 4 → Subtracting the minimum uncovered element (4 in this case) from all uncovered elements and adding it to all elements at the intersection point of the above lines and drawing minimum number of lines to cover all zeros.

Operator	Methods				
	M_1	M_2	M_3	M_4	M_5
A	8	6	5	0	3
B	10	7	3	0	6
C	8	4	0	0	4
D	1	1	2	0	0
Dummy	0	0	4	4	0

Since the number of lines = 4 and order of matrix = 5, we will have to take step to increase the number of zeros.

Step 5 → Subtracting the minimum uncovered element (3 in this case) from all uncovered elements and adding it to all elements at the intersection point of the above lines and drawing minimum number of lines to cover all zeros.

Operator	Methods				
	M_1	M_2	M_3	M_4	M_5
A	5	3	2	0	0
B	7	4	0	0	3
C	8	4	0	0	3
D	1	1	2	3	0
Dummy	0	0	4	7	0

Since the number of lines = 4 and order of matrix = 5, we will have to take step to increase the number of zeros.

Step 6 → Subtracting the minimum uncovered elements (1 in this case) from all uncovered elements and adding it to all elements at the intersection point of the above lines and drawing minimum number of lines to cover all zeros.

Operator	Methods				
	M_1	M_2	M_3	M_4	M_5
A	4	2	2	0	0
B	6	3	0	0	3
C	7	3	0	3	4
D	0	0	2	3	0
Dummy	0	0	5	8	1

Since number of lines (5) = order of matrix (5), the above matrix will provide optimal Solution.

Step 7 → ***Assignment:*** Selecting a row containing exactly one unmarked zero and surrounding it by '□' and draw a vertical line thorough the column containing this zero. Repeating this process till no such row is left; then selecting a column containing exactly one unmarked zero and surrounding it by '□' and draw a horizontal line through the row containing this zero and repeating the process till no such column is left.

Operator	Methods M_1	M_2	M_3	M_4	M_5
A	4	2	2	0	[0]
B	6	3	0	[0]	3
C	7	3	[0]	3	4
D	[0]	0	2	3	0
Dummy	0	[0]	5	8	1

Step 8 → Computing Optimal Output per month and Maximum Profit:

Operators	Methods	Units Per week	Units Per month
A	M_5	9	36
B	M_4	19	76
C	M_3	21	84
D	M_1	6	24
Dummy	M_2	0	0
	Total Output	55	220

Total sales Revenue for the month @ ₹ 35 per unit	7,700
Less: Total Production Cost for the month @ ₹ 10 per unit	(2,200)
Maximum Profit	5,500

Alternative Solution:

Operator	Methods M_1	M_2	M_3	M_4	M_5
A	4	2	2	0	[0]
B	6	3	0	[0]	3
C	7	3	[0]	3	4
D	0	[0]	2	3	0
Dummy	[0]	0	5	8	1

Operators	Methods	Units Per week	Units Per month
A	M_5	9	36
B	M_4	19	76
C	M_3	21	84
D	M_2	6	24
Dummy	M_1	0	0
	Total Output	55	220

Total sales Revenue for the month @ ₹ 35 per unit	7,700
Less: Total Production Cost for the month @ ₹ 10 per unit	(2,200)
Maximum Profit	5,500

PROBLEM 4.15

The cost matrix giving selling cost per unit of a product by salesman A, B, C and D in regions R_1, R_2, R_3 and R_4 is given below:

	A	B	C	D
R_1	4	12	16	8
R_2	20	28	32	24
R_3	36	44	48	40
R_4	52	60	64	56

(i) Assign one salesman to one region to minimise the selling cost.

(ii) If the selling price of the product is ₹ 2000 per unit and variable cost excluding the selling cost given in the table is ₹ 100 per unit, find the assignment that would maximise the contribution.

(iii) What other conclusion can you make form the above?

Solution

4	12	16	8
20	28	32	24
36	44	48	40
52	60	64	56

Subtracting minimum element – each row.

0	8	12	4
0	8	12	4
0	8	12	4
0	8	12	4

Subtracting minimum element – each column.

0	0	0	0
0	0	0	0
0	0	0	0
0	0	0	0

Minimum no. of lines to cover all zeros = 4 = order of matrix. Hence optional assignment is possible.

Minimum cost = 4 + 28 + 56 = 136.

$= AR_1 + BR_2 + CR_3 + DR_4$

Since all zeros, the are 24 solution to the assignment problem

Viz.	A	B	C	D	
	R_1	R_2	R_3	R_4	
	R_2	R_3	R_4	R_1	
	R_3	R_4	R_1	R_2	
	R_4	R_1	R_2	R_3	
	R_1	R_3	R_4	R_2	etc.

A can be assigned in 4 ways, B in 3 ways for each of A's 4 ways.

(ii) SP – VC = 100 ₹

	A	*B*	*C*	*D*
R_1	96	88	84	92
R_2	80	72	68	76
R_3	64	56	52	60
R_4	48	40	36	44

Subtracting the highest term

0	8	12	4
16	24	28	20
32	40	44	36
48	56	60	52

Subtracting minimum term of each row

0	8	12	4
0	8	12	4
0	8	12	4
0	8	12	4

Which is the same as the earlier matrix

Maximum contribution = ₹ (96 + 72 + 52 + 44) = ₹ 264.

Alternative Solution:

Maximization of contribution is same as minimizing cost. Hence, same assignments as in (i) will be optional solution

Maximum Contribution ₹ (400 – 136) = ₹ 264

(iii) (a) The relative cost of assigning person i to region r does not change by addition or subtraction of a constant from either a row, or column or all elements of the matrix.

(b) Minimizing cost is the same as maximizing contribution. Hence, the assignment solution will be same applying point (i) above.

(c) Many zero's represent many feasible least cost assignment. Here, all zeros mean maximum permutation of a 4 × 4 matrix, viz. 4 × 3 × 2 × 1 = 24 solutions are possible.

PROBLEM 4.16 [Assignment of Machines]

A company is faced with the problem of assigning 4 machines to 6 different jobs (one machine to one job only). The profits are estimated as follows:

Job	Machine			
	A	*B*	*C*	*D*
1	3	6	2	6
2	7	1	4	4
3	3	8	5	8
4	6	4	3	7
5	5	2	4	3
6	5	7	6	4

Required: Solve the problem to maximize the total profits.

Solution

Step 1 → Introducing Dummy machines to make the problem a balanced one by alloting zero profit.

	A	*B*	*C*	*D*	*E*	*F*
1	3	6	2	6	0	0
2	7	1	4	4	0	0
3	3	8	5	8	0	0
4	6	4	3	7	0	0
5	5	2	4	3	0	0
6	5	7	6	4	0	0

Step 2 → Derive Loss Matrix by deducting all elements from the largest element (8)

	A	*B*	*C*	*D*	*E*	*F*
1	5	2	6	2	8	8
2	1	7	4	4	8	8
3	5	0	3	0	8	8
4	2	4	5	1	8	8
5	3	6	4	5	8	8
6	3	1	2	4	8	8

Step 3 → *Row Subtraction:* Subtracting the minimum element of each row from all elements of that row.

	A	*B*	*C*	*D*	*E*	*F*
1	3	0	4	0	6	6
2	0	6	3	3	7	7
3	5	0	3	0	8	8
4	1	3	4	0	7	7
5	0	3	1	2	5	5
6	2	0	1	3	7	7

Step 4 → *Column Subtraction:* Subtracting the minimum element of each column from all elements of that column and drawing minimum number of lines to cover all zeros.

	A	B	C	D	E	F
1	3	0	3	0	1	1
2	0	6	2	3	2	2
3	5	0	2	0	3	3
4	1	3	3	0	2	2
5	0	3	0	2	0	0
6	2	0	0	3	2	2

Since number of lines = 5 and order of matrix = 6, we will have to take step to increase the number of zeros.

Step 5 → Subtracting the minimum uncovered element (1 in this case) from all uncovered elements and adding it to all elements at the intersection point of the above lines and drawing minimum number of Lines to cover all zeros.

	A	B	C	D	E	F
1	3	0	3	0	0	0
2	0	6	2	3	1	1
3	5	0	2	0	2	2
4	1	3	3	0	1	1
5	1	4	1	3	0	0
6	2	0	0	3	1	1

Since number of lines (6), = order of matrix (6), the above matrix will provide Optimal Solution.

Step 6 → *Assignment:* Selecting a row containing exactly one unmarked zero and surrounding it by '□' and draw a vertical line thorough the column containing this zero. Repeating this process till no such row is left; then selecting a column containing exactly one unmarked zero and surrounding it by '□' and draw a horizontal line through the row containing this zero and repeating the process till no such column is left.

	A	B	C	D	E	F
1	3	0	3	0	0	0
2	0	6	2	3	1	1
3	5	0	2	0	2	2
4	1	3	3	0	1	1
5	1	4	1	3	0	0
6	2	0	0	3	1	1

Step 7 → Computing Maximum Profit:

Job	*Machine*	*Profit (₹)*
1	E	0
2	A	7
3	B	8
4	D	7
5	F	0
6	C	6
	Total	28

Alternative Solution:

	A	*B*	*C*	*D*	*E*	*F*
1	3	0	3	0	0	[0]
2	[0]	6	2	3	1	1
3	5	[0]	2	0	2	2
4	1	3	3	[0]	1	1
5	1	4	1	3	[0]	0
6	2	0	[0]	3	1	1

Computing Maximum Profit:

Job	*Machine*	*Profit (₹)*
1	F	0
2	A	7
3	B	8
4	D	7
5	E	0
6	C	6
	Total	28

PROBLEM 4.17 [Assignment of Production]

A firm is contemplating the introduction of three products 1, 2 and 3, in it's plants A, B and C. Only a single product is decided to be introduced in each of the plants. The unit cost of producing ith product in jth plants, is given in the following matrix:

	Plant		
Product	*A*	*B*	*C*
1	8	12	—
2	10	6	4
3	7	6	6

(i) How should the products be assigned so that the total unit cost is minimised?

(ii) If the quantity of different products is as follows, then what assignment shall minimise the aggregate production cost?

Product	*Quantity (in units)*
1	2,000
2	2,000
3	10,000

(iii) It is expected that the selling prices of the products produced by different plants would be different; as shown in the following table:

	Plant		
Product	*A*	*B*	*C*
1	15	18	—
2	18	16	10
3	12	10	8

Assuming that the quantities mentioned in (ii) above would be produced and sold, how should the products be assigned to the plants to obtain maximum profits ?

Solution

Part (i)

Step 1 → *Row Subtraction:* Subtracting the minimum element of each row from all elements of that row. Since there is zero in each column, there is no need for column subtraction. Drawing minimum number of lines to cover all zeros.

	Plant		
Product	*A*	*B*	*C*
1	0	4	—
2	6	2	0
3	1	0	0

Since number of lines (3) = order of matrix (3), the above matrix will provide the optimal Solution.

Step 2 → *Assignment:* Selecting a row containing exactly one unmarked zero and surrounding it by '□' and draw a vertical line thorough the column containing this zero. Repeating this process till no such row is left; then selecting a column containing exactly one unmarked zero and surrounding it by '□' and draw a horizontal line through the row containing this zero and repeating the process till no such column is left.

	Plant		
Product	*A*	*B*	*C*
1	[0]	4	—
2	6	2	[0]
3	1	[0]	0

Step 3 → Computing Minimum Unit Cost:

Products	*Plants*	*Units Cost (₹)*
1	A	8
2	C	4
3	B	6
	Total	18

Part (ii)

Step 1 → Deriving Total Production Cost Matrix by multiplying Quantity Matrix by Unit Cost Matrix.

	Plant		
Product	*A*	*B*	*C*
1	16,000	24,000	—
2	20,000	12,000	8,000
3	70,000	60,000	60,000

Step 2 → ***Row Subtraction:*** Subtracting the minimum element of each row from all elements of that row. Since there is zero in column, there is no need for column subtraction. Drawing minimum number of lines to cover all zeros.

	Plant		
Product	*A*	*B*	*C*
1	0	8,000	—
2	12,000	4,000	0
3	10,000	0	0

Since number of lines (3) and order of matrix (3), the above matrix will provide the optimal solution.

Step 3 → ***Assignment:*** Selecting a row containing exactly one unmarked zero and surrounding it by '☐' and draw a vertical line thorough the column containing this zero. Repeating this process till no such row is left; then selecting a column containing exactly one unmarked zero and surrounding it by '☐' and draw a horizontal line through the row containing this zero and repeating the process till no such column is left.

	Plant		
Product	*A*	*B*	*C*
1	[0]	8,000	—
2	12,000	4,000	[0]
3	10,000	[0]	0

Step 4 → Computing Minimum Cost

Products	Plants	Units Cost (₹)
1	A	16,000
2	C	8,000
3	B	60,000
	Total	84,000

Part (iii)

Step 1 → Deriving Sales Matrix by following formula:
Sale = Units Selling Price Per Unit

	Plant		
Product	A	B	C
1	30,000	36,000	—
2	36,000	32,000	20,000
3	1,20,000	1,00,000	80,000

Step 2 → Deriving Profit Matrix by deducting Cost from revenue by the following formula:
Profit = Total Sales − Total Cost

	Plant		
Product	A	B	C
1	14,000	8,000	—
2	16,000	20,000	12,000
3	50,000	40,000	20,000

Step 3 → Deriving Loss Matrix by deducting all elements from the largest element (50,000).

	Plant		
Product	A	B	C
1	36,000	42,000	—
2	34,000	30,000	38,000
3	0	10,000	30,000

Step 4 → *Row Subtraction:* Subtracting the minimum element of each row from all elements of that row.

	Plant		
Product	A	B	C
1	0	6,000	—
2	4,000	0	8,000
3	0	10,000	30,000

Step 5 → *Column Subtraction:* Subtracting minimum element of each column from all elements of that column and drawing minimum number of Lines to cover all zeros.

	Plant		
Product	*A*	*B*	*C*
1	0	6,000	—
2	4,000	0	0
3	0	10,000	22,000

Since number of lines = 2 and order of matrix = 3, we will have to take step to increase the number of zeros.

Step 6 → Subtracting the minimum uncovered element (6,000 in this case) from all uncovered elements and adding it to all elements at the intersection point of the above lines and drawing minimum number of lines to cover all zeros.

	Plant		
Product	*A*	*B*	*C*
1	0	0	—
2	10,000	0	0
3	0	4,000	16,000

Since number of lines (3) and order of matrix (3), the above matrix will provide the optimal solution..

Step 7 → *Assignment:* Selecting a row containing exactly one unmarked zero and surrounding it by '□' and draw a vertical line thorough the column containing this zero. Repeating this process till no such row is left; then selecting a column containing exactly one unmarked zero and surrounding it by '□' and draw a horizontal line through the row containing this zero and repeating the process till no such column is left.

	Plant		
Product	*A*	*B*	*C*
1	0	0	—
2	10,000	0	0
3	0	4,000	16,000

Step 7 → Computing Maximum Profit:

Products	*Plants*	*Profit (₹)*
1	B	8,000
2	C	12,000
3	A	50,000
	Total	70,000

PROBLEM 4.18 [Assignment of Sales Territory]

A manufacturing company has four zones A, B, C, D and four sales engineers P, Q, R, S respectively for assignment. Since the zones are not equally rich in sales potential, therefore it is estimated that a particular engineer operating in a particular zone will bring the following sales:

Zone A	:	4,20,000
Zone B	:	3,36,000
Zone C	:	2,94,000
Zone D	:	4,62,000

The engineers are having different sales ability. Working under the same conditions, their yearly sales are proportional to 14, 9, 11 and 8 respectively. The criteria of maximum expected total sales is to be met by assigning the best engineer to the richest zone, the next best to the second richest zone and so on.

Required: Find the optimum assignment and the maximum sales.

Solution

Step 1 → Deriving Revenue Matrix.

Sales Engineer	*Proportion*	*Index taking B as base*
P	14	1
Q	9	$\frac{9}{14}$
R	11	$\frac{11}{14}$
S	8	$\frac{8}{14}$

The problem here is to find the optimum assignment in thefollowing sales table so as to maximise the total sales of the company.

Territory Engineer	*Zones (Sales in thousands of rupees)*			
	I	*II*	*III*	*IV*
P	$420 \times 1 = 420$	$336 \times 1 = 336$	$294 \times 1 = 294$	$462 \times 1 = 462$
Q	$420 \times \frac{9}{14} = 270$	$336 \times \frac{9}{14} = 216$	$294 \times \frac{9}{14} = 189$	$462 \times \frac{9}{14} = 297$
R	$420 \times \frac{11}{14} = 330$	$336 \times \frac{11}{14} = 264$	$294 \times \frac{11}{14} = 231$	$462 \times \frac{11}{14} = 363$
S	$420 \times \frac{8}{14} = 240$	$336 \times \frac{8}{14} = 192$	$294 \times \frac{8}{14} = 168$	$462 \times \frac{8}{14} = 264$

Step 2 → Deriving Loss Matrix by deducting all elements from the largest element (462).

Sales Engineer	Zones (Loss in thousands of rupees)			
	A	***B***	***C***	***D***
P	42	126	168	0
Q	192	246	273	165
R	132	198	231	99
S	222	270	294	198

Step 3 → ***Row Subtraction:*** Subtracting the minimum element of each row from all elements of that row.

Sales Engineer	Zones (Loss in thousands of rupees)			
	A	***B***	***C***	***D***
P	42	126	168	0
Q	27	81	108	0
R	33	99	132	0
S	24	72	96	0

Step 4 → ***Column Subtraction:*** Subtracting the minimum element of each column from all elements of that column and drawing minimum number of lines to cover all zeros.

Sales Engineer	Zones (Loss in thousands of rupees)			
	A	*B*	*C*	*D*
P	18	54	72	0
Q	3	9	12	0
R	9	27	36	0
S	0	0	0	0

Since number of lines = 2 and order of matrix = 4, we will have to take step to increase the number of zeros.

Step 5 → Subtracting the minimum uncovered element (in this case 3) from all uncovered elements and adding it to all elements at the intersection point of the above lines and drawing minimum number of lines to cover all zeros.

Sales Engineer	Zones (Loss in thousands of rupees)			
	A	*B*	*C*	*D*
P	15	51	69	0
Q	0	6	9	0
R	6	24	33	0
S	0	0	0	3

Since number of lines = 3 and order of matrix = 4, we will have to take step to increase the number of zeros.

Step 6 → Subtracting the minimum uncovered element (in this case 6) from all uncovered elements and adding it to all elements at the intersection point of the above lines and drawing minimum number of lines to cover all zeros.

Sales Engineer	Zones (Loss in thousands of rupees)			
	A	B	C	D
P	15	45	63	0
Q	0	0	3	0
R	6	18	27	0
S	6	0	0	9

Since number of lines = 3 and order of matrix = 4, we will have to take step to increase the number of zeros.

Step 7 → Subtracting the minimum uncovered element (in this case 6) from all uncovered elements and adding it to all elements at the intersection point of the above lines and drawing minimum number of lines to cover all zeros.

Sales Engineer	Zones (Loss in thousands of rupees)			
	A	B	C	D
P	9	39	57	0
Q	0	0	3	6
R	0	12	21	0
S	6	0	0	15

Since the minimum number of lines drawn to cover all the zeros is 4 which is equal to the order of the matrix. Hence, the above table will give the optimum assignment.

Step 8 → ***Assignment:*** Selecting a row containing exactly one unmarked zero and surrounding it by '▯' and draw a vertical line thorough the column containing this zero. Repeating this process till no such row is left; then selecting a column containing exactly one unmarked zero and surrounding it by '▯' and draw a horizontal line through the row containing this zero and repeating the process till no such column is left.

Sales Engineer	Zones (Loss in thousands of rupees)			
	A	B	C	D
P	9	39	57	[0]
Q	0	[0]	3	6
R	[0]	12	21	0
S	6	0	[0]	15

Step 9 → Computing the Maximum Sales:

Engineers	Zones	Sales (in ₹)
P	D	4,62,000
Q	B	2,16,000
R	A	3,30,000
S	C	1,68,000
		11,76,000

It can be seen from the above assignments that the best engineer P is assigned to the richest zone D, the next best engineer R is assigned to second richest zone A, the next best engineer Q is assigned to zone B and so on. Hence, the optimum assignment matches the company's criteria of achieving the maximum expected total sales.

PROBLEM 4.19 [Preparation of Production and Profit Matrix]

A firm produces four products. There are four operators who are capable of producing any of these four products. The processing time varies from operator to operator. The firm records 8 hours a day and allows 30 minutes for lunch. The processing time in minutes and the profit for each of the products are given below:

Operators	*Products*			
	A	*B*	*C*	*D*
1	15	9	10	6
2	10	6	9	6
3	25	15	15	9
4	15	9	10	10
Profit (₹) per unit	8	6	5	4

Find the optimal assignment of products to operators.

Solution

Step 1 → *Deriving Production Matrix:* The firm records 8 hours a day and allows 30 minutes for lunch, hence the net working time available per day is 7 hours and 30 minutes i.e. 450 minutes. The number of units of each product which could be produced in 450 minutes by the four operators is calculated in the table given below by using the formula (i.e. 450 Minutes/Processing time).

Operators	*Products*			
	A	*B*	*C*	*D*
1	30	50	45	75
2	45	75	50	75
3	18	30	30	50
4	30	50	45	45
Profit per unit	8	6	5	4

Step 2 → Deriving Profit Matrix by multiplying output by profit per unit

Operators	*Profit matrix in ₹ of Products*			
	A	*B*	*C*	*D*
1	240	300	225	300
2	360	450	250	300
3	144	180	150	200
4	240	300	225	180

Step 3 → Deriving Loss Matrix by deducting all the elements from the largest element (450)

Operators	*Loss matrix in ₹ of Products*			
	A	*B*	*C*	*D*
1	210	150	225	150
2	90	0	200	150
3	306	270	300	250
4	210	150	225	270

Step 4 → ***Row Subtraction:*** Subtracting the minimum element of each row from all elements of that row.

Operators	*Loss matrix in ₹ of Products*			
	A	*B*	*C*	*D*
1	60	0	75	0
2	90	0	200	150
3	56	20	50	0
4	60	0	75	120

Step 5 → ***Column Subtraction:*** Subtracting the minimum element of each column from all elements of that column and drawing minimum number of lines to cover all zeros.

Operators	*Loss matrix in ₹ of Products*			
	A	*B*	*C*	*D*
1	4	0	25	0
2	34	0	150	150
3	0	20	0	0
4	4	0	25	120

Since number of lines = 3 and order of matrix = 4, we will have to take step to increase the number of zeros.

Step 6 → Subtracting the minimum uncovered element (in this case 4) from all uncovered elements and adding it to all elements at the intersection point of the above lines and drawing minimum number of lines to cover all zeros.

Operators	*Loss matrix in ₹ of Products*			
	A	*B*	*C*	*D*
1	0	0	21	0
2	30	0	146	150
3	0	24	0	4
4	0	0	21	120

Step 7 → ***Assignment:*** Selecting a row containing exactly one unmarked zero and surrounding it by '□' and draw a vertical line thorough the column containing this zero. Repeating this process till no such row is left; then selecting a column containing exactly one unmarked zero and surrounding it by '□' and draw a horizontal line through the row containing this zero and repeating the process till no such column is left.

Operators	Loss matrix in ₹ of Products			
	A	*B*	*C*	*D*
1	0	0	21	[0]
2	30	[0]	146	150
3	0	24	[0]	4
4	[0]	0	21	120

Step 8 → Computing the Maximum Profit:

Operator	*Product*	*Profit (₹)*
1	D	300
2	B	450
3	C	150
4	A	240
	Total	₹ 1,140

5 Transportation Problems

PRACTICAL STEPS INVOLVED IN SOLVING TRANSPORTATION PROBLEMS OF MINIMIZATION TYPE

Step 1 → ***Dummy Origin/Destination:*** *See whether Total Requirements are equal to Total Availability; if yes, go to Step 2; if not, introduce a Dummy Origin/Destination, as the case may be, to make the problem a balanced one, taking Transportation Cost per unit as zero for each Cell of Dummy Origin/Destination or as otherwise indicated.*

↓

Step 2 → ***Initial Feasible Solution:*** *Find Initial Feasible Solution by following either the Least Cost Method (or LCM) or North-West Corner Method (or NWCM) or Vogel's Approximation Method (or VAM), (Refer to page 5.2, 5.3 and 5.4).*
Note: *Unless otherwise stated, Use VAM.*

↓

Step 3 → ***Introduction of Infinitely Small Quantity 'e':*** *After obtaining the Initial Feasible Solution Table, see whether Total Number of Allocations are equal to "m + n - 1",; if yes, go to Step 4; if not, introduce an infinitely small quantity 'e' to the Least Cost Independent Cell. (i.e., for which no Loop can be formed).*
Note : *Introduce as many number of 'e' as the total number of allocated cells falls below "m + n -1".*

↓

Step 4 → ***Optimality Test:*** *Carry out the Optimality Test on the Initial Solution Table to find out the optimal solution. (Refer to page 5.27).*

Step 5 → ***Minimum Cost:*** *Calculate the Total Minimum Cost =* $\Sigma (X_{ij} \; C_{ij})$,
where, X *= Units Allocated to a Cell;*
C *= Shipping Cost per Unit of a Cell;*
i *= Row Number;*
j *= Column Number*

FINDING INITIAL (OR BASIC) FEASIBLE SOLUTION

In general, any basic feasible solution of a transportation problem with **m origins** (such as factories) and **n destinations** (such as warehouses) should have *'m + n - 1'* non zero basic variables.

A transport problem is said to be a degenerate transport problem if it has a basic feasible solution with number of non zero basic variables less than $m + n - 1$.

According to Mustafit, "A degenerate basic feasible solution in a transportation problem exists if and only if some partial sum of availabilities (row) is equal to a partial sum of requirements (column)".

Initial feasible solution can be obtained by any of the following three methods:

Method I	:	Least Cost Method (or LCM)
Method II	:	North-West Corner Method (or NWCM)
Method III	:	Vogel's Approximation Method (or VAM)

Let us discuss these methods one by one as under:

METHOD I : Least Cost Method (or LCM)

The practical steps involved in the Least Cost Method are given below:

Step 1 → *Make maximum possible Allocation to the* ***Least Cost Cell*** *depending upon the demand/supply for the Column/Row containing that Cell. In case of Tie in the Least Cost Cells, make allocation to the Cell by which maximum demand or capacity is exhausted.*

↓

Step 2 → *Make allocation to the* ***Second Lowest Cost Cell*** *depending upon the remaining demand/supply for the Row/Column containing that Cell.*

↓

Step 3 → *Repeat the above Steps till all Rim Requirements are exhausted, i.e., entire demand and supply is exhausted.*

PROBLEM 5.1 [Introduction of Dummy Origin in Case of Contribution Matrix]

Find the basic feasible solution by Least Cost Method.

	W_1	W_2	W_3	W_4	*Supplies*
F_1	48	60	56	58	140
F_2	45	55	53	60	260
F_3	50	65	60	62	360
Demand	200	320	250	210	

Note: Cell entries are the unit contributions.

Solution

Step 1→ Introducing a Dummy factory with zero profit per unit as the total demand is not equal to total supply in order to make the problem balanced one.

	W_1	W_2	W_3	W_4	Supplies
F_1	48	60	56	58	140
F_2	45	55	53	60	260
F_3	50	65	60	62	360
F_4	0	0	0	0	220
Demand	200	320	250	210	

Step 2→ Deriving Loss Matrix by deducting each element from the maximum element (i.e. 65) in order to use minimisation technique and finding initial feasible solution by LCM.

	W_1	W_2	W_3	W_4	Supplies
F_1	17	5	9 [140]	7	140
F_2	20	10	12 [90]	5 [170]	260
F_3	15	0 [320]	5	3 [40]	360
F_4	65 [200]	65	65 [20]	65	220
Demand	200	320	250	210	

METHOD II : North-West Corner Method (or NWCM)

The practical steps involved in the North-West Corner Method are given below:

Step 1→ *Make maximum possible* ***allocation to the Upper-Left Corner Cell*** *(also known as North-West Corner Cell) in the First Row depending upon the availability of supply for that Row and demand requirement for the Column containing that Cell.*
Note: *Unit transportation cost is completely ignored.*

↓

Step 2→ *Move to the* ***Next Cell of the First Row*** *depending upon remaining supply for that Row and the demand requirement for the next Column. Go on till the Row total is exhausted.*

↓

Step 3→ *Move to the the next Row and make allocation to the Cell below the Cell of the preceding Row in which the last allocation was made and follow Steps 1 and 2.*

↓

Step 4→ *Follow Steps 1 to 3 till all Rim requirements are exhausted, i.e., the entire demand and supply is exhausted.*

PROBLEM 5.2 [Introduction of Dummy Origin in Case of Contribution Matrix]

Find initial feasible solution by North West Corner Method in Problem 5.1.

Solution

Initial Feasible Solution by North West Corner Method (NWCM)

	W_1	W_2	W_3	W_4	*Supplies*
F_1	17 [140]	5	9	7	140
F_2	20 [60]	10 [200]	12	5	260
F_3	15	0 [120]	5 [240]	3	360
F_4	65	65	65 [10]	65 [210]	220
Demand	200	320	250	210	

METHOD III : Vogel's Approximation Method (or VAM)

The practical steps involved in Vogel's Approximation Method (*or VAM*) are given below:

Step 1 → ***Row Difference:*** *Find the difference between Smallest and Second Smallest element of each Row, representing the Opportunity Cost of not making the allocation to the Smallest Element Cell, and write the difference on the right-hand side of the concerned Row. In case of tie between two smallest elements, the difference should be taken as zero.*

↓

Step 2 → ***Column Difference:*** *Find the difference between Smallest and Second Smallest element of each column, representing the Opportunity Cost of not making the allocation to the Smallest Element Cell, and write the difference below the concerned Column. In case of tie between two smallest elements, the difference should be taken as zero.*

↓

Step 3 → ***Largest Difference:*** *Mark the Largest Difference amongst all Differences by an arrow indicating the allocation to be made to the row/column having largest difference. Allocate maximum possible quantity to the Least Cost Cell of the Selected row/column depending upon the quantity available. In case of tie between the Differences, select the row or column having least cost cell. However, in case of tie even in case of Least Cost, make allocation to that Cell by which maximum requirements are exhausted.*

↓

Step 4 → *Shade the Row/Column whose availability or requirement is exhausted so that it shall not be considered for any further allocation.*

↓

Step 5 → *Repeat Step 1 and 4 till entire demand and supply is exhausted.*

↓

Step 6 → *Draw the Initial Feasible Solution Table obtained after the above steps.*

PROBLEM 5.3 [Introduction of Dummy Origin in Case of Contribution Matrix]

Find initial feasible solution by VAM in Problem 5.1.

Solution

Initial Feasible Solution by Vogel's Approximation Method (VAM)

	W_1	W_2	W_3	W_4	Supplies	D_1	D_2	D_3	D_4	D_5
F_1	17	5	9 [140]	7	140	2	2	8	8	—
F_2	20	10	12 [50]	5 [210]	260	5	7	8	8	8
F_3	15	0 [320]	5 [40]	3	360	3	2	10	—	—
F_4	65 [200]	65	65 [20]	65	220	0	0	0	0	0
Dem.	200	320	250	210						
D_1	2	5	4	2						
D_2	2	—	4	2						
D_3	2	—	4	—						
D_4	3	—	3	—						
D_5	45	—	53	—						

(Figures in brackets are the allocations shown in the boxed corners of the cells.)

INTRODUCING AN INFINITELY SMALL QUANTITY 'e' IN CASE THE TOTAL NUMBER OF ALLOCATION IS LESS THAN "M + N - 1"

PROBLEM 5.4 [Case when Total Number of Allocations < M + N - 1]

Find the initial basic feasible solution by VAM. Is the number of allocation equal to 'M + N – 1'? If no, how will you deal with this situation?

	W_1	W_2	W_3	W_4	Supplies
F_1	1	2	4	4	6
F_2	4	3	2	0	8
F_3	0	2	2	1	10
Demand	4	6	8	6	

Note: Cell entries are the unit transportation costs.

Solution

Initial Feasible Solution by Vogel's Approximation Method

	W_1	W_2	W_3	W_4	*Supplies*	D_1	D_2	D_3
F_1	1	2 (6)	4	4	6	1	1	2
F_2	4	3	2 (2)	0 (6)	8	2	1	1
F_3	0 (4)	2	2 (6)	1	10	1	2	0
Dem.	4	6	8	6				
D_1	1	0	0	1				
D_2	1	0	0	—				
D_3	—	0	0	—				

Since Allocations are 5 which is less than m + n – 1 (i.e. 4 + 3 – 1 = 6), an infinitestimally small allocation e is placed in the least cost and independent cell in such a way that no loop can be formed by the allocated cells (includes the one in which *e* to be allocated)

There are two least cost cells (1, 1) & (3, 4)

Suppose, *e* is allocated in cell (3, 4)

	W_1	W_2	W_3	W_4
F_1	1	2 (6)	4	4
F_2	4	3	2 (2)	0 (6)
F_3	0 (4)	2	2 (6)	1 (e)

Since loop can be formed after allocating '*e*' in the cell (3, 4), '*e*' should not be allocated here.

Let us allocate '*e*' in the cell (1, 1)

	W_1	W_2	W_3	W_4	*Supplies*
F_1	1 (e)	2 (6)	4	4	6
F_2	4	3	2 (2)	0 (6)	8
F_3	0 (4)	2	2 (6)	1	10
	4	6	8	6	

APPLICATION OF OPTIMALITY TEST

The practical steps involved in Optimality Test are given below :

Step 1 → ***U_i & V_j:*** *Compute "U_i" and "V_j" for all Rows and Columns respectively on the basis of Allocated Cells such that $C_{ij} = U_i + V_j$ after taking any U_i or $V_j = 0$, where C_{ij} = Shipping Cost per unit of Occupied Cell;*
i = Row Number;
j = Column Number;
U_i = Shipping Cost per unit of Supplying Station; and
V_j = Shipping Cost per unit of Receiving Station
Note: *While taking any U_i or $V_j = 0$, that row or column which is having maximum allocated cells, should preferably be selected.*

↓

Step 2 → ***Opportunity Cost for Unallocated Cells:*** *Compute Opportunity Cost, (say OC), for Unallocated Cells where OC = $C_{ij} - (U_{ij} + V_{ij})$.*

↓

Step 3 → ***Loop:*** *If 'OC' of each cell is either positive or zero, Initial Feasible Solution is the Optimal Solution. However, if 'OC' for any Cell is negative, Initial Feasible Solution is not optimal. In that case, Find Closed Loop (explained on page 5.9) for the Cell having negative 'OC' and transfer entire quantity from the Allocated Cell having minimum quantity, that is covered by that Loop amongst all Allocated Cells covered by that Loop, to the Unallocated Cell having negative 'OC' (the procedure to transfer the quantity has been explained on page 5.9).*
Note: *The above procedure will be followed even in case 'OC' of any Unallocated Cell is "zero" and 'OC' of other Unallocated Cells is positive to get Alternate Solution.*

↓

Step 4 → ***Infinitely Small Quantity 'e':*** *See whether total number of allocated cells after Step 3 is equal to "m + n −1"; if yes, go to step 5, if not introduce an Infinitely small quantity 'e' to the Least Cost Independent Cell, i.e., for which no Loop can be formed.*
Note: *Introduce as many number of 'e' as the total number of Allocated Cells falls below "m + n − 1".*

↓

Step 5 → *Repeat Steps 1 to 4 till 'OC' of all Unallocated Cells is positive.*

PROBLEM 5.5 [When the Number of Allocation is Less Than 'm + n - 1']

Test the following initial solution for optimality

	W_1	W_2	W_3	W_4	Supplies
F_1	1 (e)	2 (6)	4	4	6
F_2	4	3	2 (2)	0 (6)	8
F_3	0 (4)	2	2 (6)	1	10
Demand	4	6	8	6	

Note: Cell entries are transportation costs per unit.

Solution

Step 1 → : *Calculation of U_i and V_i on the basis of costs of allocated cells*

	W_1	W_2	W_3	W_4	U_i
F_1	1	2			$U_0 = 0$
F_2			2	0	$U_1 = -1$
F_3	0		2		$U_2 = -1$
V_j	$V_0 = 1$	$V_1 = 2$	$V_2 = 3$	$V_3 = 1$	

Step 2 → *C_{ij} Matrix of Costs for unallocated cells*

	W_1	W_2	W_3	W_4
F_1			4	4
F_2	4	3		
F_3		2		1

Step 3 → *$U_i + V_j$ Matrix for unallocated Cells*

	W_1	W_2	W_3	W_4
F_1			3	1
F_2	0	1		
F_3		1		0

Step 4 → *Δ_{ij} Matrix where $\Delta_{ij} = C_{ij} - (U_i + V_j)$*

	W_1	W_2	W_3	W_4
F_1			1	3
F_2	4	2		
F_3		1		1

Step 5 → *Since all Δ_{ij} are positive the above solution is optimal. The optimal solution is given below:*

Factory	*Warehouse*	*Qty.*	*Cost per Unit*	*Total cost*
F_1	W_3	6	2	12
F_2	W_3	2	2	4
F_2	W_4	6	0	0
F_3	W_1	4	0	0
F_3	W_3	6	2	12
				28

LOOPING AND REALLOCATION MATRIX

The practical steps involved in the Looping are given below:

Step 1 → ***Most Negative Opportunity Cost Cell:*** *Put a 'Tick' mark in the most negative Opportunity Cost Cell.*
In case of tie, any one may be selected arbitraily, preferably select that one with which corners points are minimum.

↓

Step 2 → ***Draw Loop:*** *Draw at least four lines in the form of a rectangle covering at least four Cells out of which One Cell will be the ticked Cell and the rest will be the Allocated Cells. This is called 'Loop'. In other words all the corners (except the starting corner which lies in most negative unallocated cell) of the Loop will lie in the allocated cells.*

↓

Step 3 → ***Putting '+' & '–' Signs:*** *Put '+' sign on ticked cell and '–' sign on the next allocated corner cell covered by the loop and '+' sign on the next to next allocated corner cell covered by the loop and so on.*
In other words, '+' or '–' sign should be put in each allocated corner cell in alternative order.

↓

Step 4 → ***Transfer of Entire Quantity:*** *Transfer the entire quantity from the Least Allocated Cell (i.e. cell having the least quantity) which has '–', to the Cells containing '+' and deduct the transferred quantity from the other cell containing '–'.*
Note: *A Loop can even contain more than Four Cells; however, Number will always remain 'even'. In that case, one Cell will be the Unallocated Cell having most negative Opportunity Cost and the Others will be the Allocated Cells.*

PROBLEM 5.6 [When there is a Tie between the Two Most Negative Cells]

Prepare a reallocation matrix from the following information:

Initial Allocation Matrix

	1	2	3	4
A	3		6	1
B		4		
C		6		
D				5
E	10	e		

Δ_{ij} (Cell Evaluation) Matrix

	1	2	3	4
A		16		
B	20		35	–8
C	40		20	7
D	13	18	33	
E			10	–8

Solution

Step 1 →Ticking one of the most negative cells (B, 4) and (E, 4) of cell evaluation matrix from where looping is to be started and putting θ quantity therein and drawing lines in such a way that turning point of the line is in the allocated cells. Let us first tick (B, 4) cell.

	1	2	3	4
A	3+		6	1–
B		4–		+
C		6		
D				5
E	10–	e+		

Step 2 → Calculating new quantity of each corner of the loop after subtracting from and adding to 1 quantity (being the least one in negative corner cells) to each of the loop corner quantity.

Corner (B, 4) = 0 + 1 = 0
Corner (A, 4) = 1 – 1 = 0
Corner (A, 1) = 3 + 1 = 4
Corner (E, 1) = 10 – 1= 9
Corner (E, 2) = e + 1 = 1
Corner (B, 2) = 4 – 1 = 3

Step 3 → Now Reallocation Matrix becomes as under:

	1	2	3	4
A	4		6	
B		3		1
C		6		
D				5
E	9	1		

Alternative Solution: Let us tick (E, 4) cell.

Step 1 → Ticking the another most negative cell (E, 4) of cell evaluation matrix from where looping is to be started and putting θ quantity therein and drawing lines in such a way that turning point of the line is in the allocated cells.

	1	2	3	4
A	3+		6	1–
B		4		
C		6		
D				5
E	10–	e		θ +

Step 2 → Calculating new quantity of each corner of the loop after subtracting from and adding to 1 quantity (being the least one in negative corner cells) to each of the loop corner quantity.

Corner (E, 4) = 0 + 1 = 0
Corner (A, 4) = 1 – 1 = 0
Corner (A, 1) = 3 + 1 = 4
Corner (E, 1) = 10 – 1 = 9

Step 3 → Now Reallocation Matrix becomes as under:

	1	2	3	4
A	4		6	
B		4		
C		6		
D				5
E	9	e		1

PROBLEM 5.7 [Use of High Cost Where there is Restriction on Transfer]

Solve the following transportation problem:

GODOWNS

		1	*2*	*3*	*4*	*5*	*6*	*Stock Available*
FACTORY	1	7	5	7	7	5	3	60
	2	9	11	6	11	—	5	20
	3	11	10	6	2	2	8	90
	4	9	10	9	6	9	12	50
Demand		60	20	40	20	40	40	

Note: It is not possible to transport any quantity from factory 2 to godown 5.

Required: State whether the solution derived by you is unique.

Solution

Step 1 → Finding Initial Feasible Solution by following the Vogel's Approximation Method (or VAM).

Factory	*Godowns* 1	2	3	4	5	6	*Availability*	*Diff.*
1	7	5 [20]	7	7	5	3 [40]	60/40/0	2/4/0
2	9 [10]	11	6 [10]	11	∞	5	20/10/0	1/3
3	11	10	6 [30]	2 [20]	2 [40]	8	90/70/30/0	0/4/2/5
4	9 [50]	10	9	6	9	12	50/0	3/0
Demand	60 50 0	20 0	40 10 0	20 0	40 0	40 0		
Diff.	2	5	0/1	4	3	2		

Step 2 → Since the total number of allocations is less than "M + N – 1" allocations, let us introduce an infinitely small quantity 'e' to the least cost independent cell to make the total number of allocations equal to "M + N – 1" allocations.

Let us calculate "U_i's" and "V_j's" for all rows and columns respectively on the basis of allocated cells such that $C_{ij} = U_i + V_j$ assuming $U_1 = 0$,

Let us calculate Δ_{ij} (Opportunity Cost), for unallocated cells where $\Delta_{ij} = C_{ij} - (U_{ij} + V_{ij})$.

U_i & V_j Matrix

						U_i
	5				3	–2
9		6			5 (e)	0
		6	2	2		0
9						0
V_j 9	7	6	2	2	5	

C_{ij} Matrix for Unallocated Cells

7		7	7	5	
	11		11	∞	
11	10				8
	10	9	6	9	12

$U_i + V_j$ Matrix for Unallocated cells

						U_i
7		4	0	0		-2
	7		2			0
9	7				5	0
	7	6	2	2	5	0
V_j 9	7	6	2	2	5	

$\Delta_{ij} = C_{ij} - (U_i + V_j)$ Matrix

0		3	7	5	
	4		9		
2	3				3
	3	3	4	7	7

Step 3 → Since all Δ_{ij} are positive, the above solution is optimal. The optimal solution is given below:

Factory	*to Godown*	*Unit*	*Cost*	*Value (₹)*
1	2	20	5	100
1	6	40	3	120
2	1	10	9	90
2	3	10	6	60
3	3	30	6	180
3	4	20	2	40
3	5	40	2	80
4	1	50	9	450
			Total cost ₹	1120

Note: Since one of Δ_{ij} is zero, the above solution is not unique. Hence an alternative solution exists. The alternative solution can be found by taking any cell with zero Δ_{ij} as the basic cell.

Students may find that the alternate solution is as given below:

Factory	*to Godown*	*Unit*	*Cost*	*Value (₹)*
1	1	10	7	70
1	2	20	5	100
1	6	30	3	90
2	3	10	6	60
2	6	10	5	50
3	3	30	6	180
3	5	40	2	80
3	4	20	2	40
4	1	50	9	450
			Total Cost	₹ 1120

PROBLEM 5.8

Consider the following data for the transportation problem:

	Destination			
Factory	*(1)*	*(2)*	*(3)*	*Supply to be exhausted*
A	5	1	7	10
B	6	4	6	80
C	3	2	5	15
Demand	75	20	50	

Since there is not enough supply, some of the demands at the three destinations may not be satisfied. For the unsatisfied demands, let the penalty costs be rupees 1, 2 and 3 for destinations (1), (2) and (3) respectively.

Find the optimal allocation that minimizes the transportation and penalty costs

Solution

Step 1 → *Formulating the Transportation Problem.*

Since demand (= 75 + 20 + 50 = 145) is greater than supply (= 10 + 80 + 15 = 105) by 40 units, the given problem is an unbalanced one. We introduce a dummy factory with a supply of 40 units. It is given that for the unsatisfied demands, the penalty cost is rupees 1, 2 and 3 for destinations (1), (2) and (3) respectively. Hence, the transportation problem becomes:

Factory	*Destination* (1)	(2)	(3)	*Supply to be exhausted*
A	5	1	7	10
B	6	4	6	80
C	3	2	5	15
Dummy	1	2	3	40
Demand	75	20	50	

Step 2 → Finding Initial Feasible Solution by following the Vogel's Approximation Method (or VAM).

Factory	*Destination* (1)	(2)	(3)	*Supply*	*Differences*
A	5	1 [10]	7	10/0	4 - -
B	6 [20]	4 [10]	6 [50]	80/70/50/0	2 2 2
C	3 [15]	2	5	15/0	1 1 1
Dummy	1 [40]	2	3	40/0	11 -
Demand	75/35/20/0	20/10/0	50/0		
Difference	2	1	2		
	2	0	2		
	3	2	1		

Step 3 → *Optimality Test:* Since the total number of allocations is equal to "M+N–1" allocations, the initial solution is straight away tested for optimality.

Let us calculate "Ui's" and "Vj's" for all rows and columns respectively on the basis of allocated cells such that $C_{ij} = U_i + V_j$ assuming $U_1 = 0$,

Let us calculate Δ_{ij} (Opportunity Cost), for unallocated cells where $\Delta_{ij} = C_{ij} - (U_{ij} + V_{ij})$.

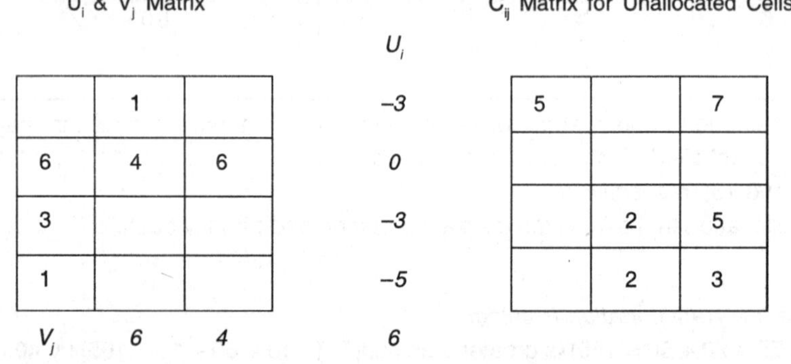

U_i & V_j Matrix

			U_i
	1		–3
6	4	6	0
3			–3
1			–5
V_j 6	4		6

C_{ij} Matrix for Unallocated Cells

5		7
	2	5
	2	3

$U_i + V_j$ Matrix of unallocated cells U_i

			U_i
3		3	−3
			0
	1	3	−3
	−1	1	−5
V_j	6	4	6

$\Delta_{ij} = C_{ij} - (U_i + V_j)$ Matrix

2		4
	1	2
	3	2

Step 4 → Since all Δ_{ij} are positive, the above solution is optimal. The optimal solution is given below:

Factory	Destination	Units	Cost	Total Cost	
A	(2)	10	₹ 1	₹ 10	Transportation cost
B	(1)	20	₹ 6	₹ 120	
B	(2)	10	₹ 4	₹ 40	
B	(3)	50	₹ 6	₹ 300	
C	(1)	15	₹ 3	₹ 45	
Dummy	(1)	40	₹ 1	₹ 40	Penalty cost
				₹ 555	

PROBLEM 5.9 [How to deal with cost in fractions and fixed price for destinations]

A company produces a small component for all industrial products and distributes it to five wholesalers at a fixed price of Rs.2.50 per unit. Sales forecasts indicate that monthly deliveries will be 3,000, 3,000, 10,000, 5,000 and 4,000 units to wholesalers 1, 2, 3, 4 and 5 respectively. The monthly production capabilities are 5,000, 10,000, 12,500 at plants 1, 2 and 3 respectively. The direct costs of production of each unit are ₹ 1.00, ₹ 0.90 and ₹ 0.80 at plants 1, 2 and 3 respectively. The transportation costs of shipping a unit from a plant to a wholesaler are given below:

		Wholesaler				
		1	2	3	4	5
	1	0.05	0.07	0.10	0.15	0.15
Plant	2	0.08	0.06	0.09	0.12	0.14
	3	0.10	0.09	0.08	0.10	0.15

Find how many components each plant supplies to each wholesaler in order to maximize profit.

Solution

Since the total capacity of plants is more than the supply to the wholesalers by a quantity 27500 units – 25000 units = 2500 units, so the problem is an unbalanced transportation problem. Introduce a dummy wholesaler supplying 2500 units such that the transportation costs plus the production cost from various plants to this destination are assumed to be zero. Also, the direct costs of production of each unit are given as ₹ 1, ₹ 0.90 and ₹ 0.80 at plants 1, 2 and 3 respectively. The modified balanced transportation problem is now obtained as follows:

		1	2	3	4	5	Dummy	Capacity
	1	1.05	1.07	1.10	1.15	1.15	0	5000
Plant	2	0.98	0.96	0.99	1.02	1.04	0	10000
	3	0.90	0.89	0.88	0.90	0.95	0	12500
		3000	3000	10000	5000	4000	2500	

For simplicity in computations multiply all direct cost *plus* transportation costs in the above table by 100, and consider 100 units = 1 unit of items. Hence, the simplified cost table becomes:

		1	2	3	4	5	Dummy	Capacity
	1	105	107	110	115	115	0	50
Plant	2	98	96	99	102	104	0	100
	3	90	89	88	90	95	0	125
Supply		30	30	100	50	40	25	3

Let us now apply Vogel's Approximation method to find the initial basic feasible solution.

Plant	Wholesaler 1	2	3	4	5	Dummy	Capacity	Difference
1	105 [25]	107	110	115	115	0 [25]	50/25/0	105/2/2/2/5/10
2	98 [5]	96 [30]	99 [25]	102	104 [40]	0	100/70/4/5/5	96/2/2/2/1/6
3	90	89	88 [75]	90 [50]	95	0	125/75/0	88/1/–
Supply	30/25/0	30/0	100/25/0	50/0	40/0	25/0		
Diff.	8	7	11	12	9	0		
	8	7	11	12	9	–		
	8	7	11	–	9	–		
	7	11	11	–	11	–		
	7	–	11		11			

The initial basic feasible solution as obtained by VAM is given below:

Plant	Wholesaler 1	2	3	4	5	Capacity	Difference
1	105 [25]	107	110	115	115	0 [25]	50
2	98 [5]	96 [30]	99 [25]	120	104 [40]	0	100
3	99	98	88 [75]	90 [50]	95	0	120
Supply		30	30	100	50	40	25

We now apply the optimally test to find whether the initial solution found above is optimal or not. The number of allocations is 8 which is equal to the required m + n – 1 (=8) allocations. Also, these allocations are independent. Hence, both the conditions of optimality test are satisfied.

Let us now introduce $u'_{i's}$, (1 = 1, 2, 3) and $v_{j's}$, (j = 1, 2, 3, ... 6) such that $\Delta_{ij} = c_{ij} - (u_i + v_j)$ for allocated cells. We assume that $u_2 = 0$ and remaining ui'_s, v_js and Δ_{ij}'s are calculated as below:

Plant	Wholesaler 1	2	3	4	5	Dummy	u_i's
1	[25] 105	4 107	4 110	7 115	4 115	[25] 0	7
2	[5] 98	[30] 96	[25] 99	[1] 102	[40] 104	7 0	0
3	3 90	4 89	[75] 88	[50] 90	2 95	18 0	−11
v_j	98	96	99	101	104	−7	

Since all Δ_{ij}'s for non-basic cells are positive, therefore, the solution obtained above is an optimal one. The allocation of plant to wholesaler and their (transportation cost + direct production cost) is given below:

Plant		Warehouse	No. of units	Cost per unit (₹)	Total cost ₹
1	→	1	2500	1.05	2625
2	→	1	500	0.98	490
2	→	2	3000	0.96	2880
2	→	3	2500	0.99	2475
2	→	5	4000	0.104	4160
3	→	3	7500	0.88	6600
3	→	4	5000	0.90	4500
					23730

Since the company distributes the component at a fixed price of Rs.2.50 per unit to all five wholesalers, the profit is given by

Profit = ₹ 2.50 × 22500 − ₹ 23,730 = ₹ 56,250 − ₹ 23,730 = ₹ 32,520

(**Note:** The problem has been solved using the cost matrix. However, it can be solved using the profit matrix first and then converting it to minimization problem).

PROBLEM 5.10

The following table shows all the necessary information on the available supply to each warehouse, the requirement of each market and the unit transportation cost from each warehouse to each market:

		Market I	II	III	IV	Supply
Warehouse	A	5	2	4	3	22
	B	4	8	1	6	15
	C	4	6	7	5	8
Requirement		7	12	17	9	

The shipping clerk has worked out the following schedule from his experience:

12 Units from A to II

1 Unit from A to III

9 Units from A to IV

15 Units from B to III

7 Units from C to I and

1 Unit from C to III.

You are required to answer the following:

(i) Check and see if the clerk has the optimal schedule;

(ii) Find the optimal schedule and minimum total shipping cost; and

(iii) If the clerk is approached by a carrier of route C to II, who offers to reduce his rate in the hope of getting some business, by how much should the rate be reduced before the clerk should consider giving him an order?

Solution

(i) The shipping clerk has worked out the following schedule as initial solution:

		Market				
		I	*II*	*III*	*IV*	*Supply*
Warehouse	A	5	12 2	1 4	9 3	22
	B	4	8	15 1	6	15
	C	7 4	6	1 7	5	8
Requirement		7	12	17	9	

The initial solution is tested for optimality. The total number of independent allocations is 6 which is equal to the desired (m + n – 1) allocations. We introduce u_i's (I = 1, 2, 3) and v_j's (j = 1, 2, 3, 4) such that $\Delta_{ij} = c_{ij} - (u_i + v_j)$. Let us assume $u_i = 0$, remaining u_1's and v_1's are calculated as below:

	I	II	III	IV	u_i
A	4 5	12 2	1 +θ 4	9 –θ 3	0
B	6 4	9 8	15 1	6 6	–3
C	7 4	1 6	1 –θ 7	–1 θ 5	3
v_j	1	2	4	3	

Since one of the Δ_{ij}'s is negative, the schedule worked out by the clerk is not the optimal solution.

(ii) Introduce in the cell with -ve Δ_{ij} [i.e. the cell (C, IV)], an assignment θ. The value of θ and the reallocated solution as obtained from above is given below. The value of u_i's, v_j's are also calculated.

$$\theta = \min(9 - \theta = 0 \ \& \ 1 - \theta = 0) = 1$$

	I	II	III	IV	u_i
A	3 5	12 2	2 4	8 3	0
B	5 4	9 8	15 1	6 6	–3
C	7 4	2 6	1 7	1 5	2
v_j	2	2	4	3	

Since all Δ_{ij}'s for non basic cells are positive, the solution as calculated in the above table is optimal solution. The supply of units from each warehouse to markets, along with the transportation cost is given below:

Warehouse	*Market*	*Units unit(₹)*	*Cost per Cost(₹)*	*Total*
A	II	12	2	24
A	III	2	4	8
A	IV	8	3	24
B	III	15	1	15
C	I	7	4	28
C	IV	1	5	5
		Minimum Total Shipping Cost		= 104

(iii) If the clerk wants to consider the carrier of route C to II for giving an order, then his transportation cost must be less than the cost of carrier of routes C to I and C to IV i.e. his transportation cost should be at the most ₹ 3 per unit. If the carrier C to II brings down his cost to ₹ 3, he will get an order for 1 unit, and the schedule will be:

Warehouse	*Market*	*Units unit(₹)*	*Cost per Cost(₹)*	*Total*
A	II	11	2	22
A	III	2	4	8
A	IV	9	3	27
B	III	15	1	15
C	I	7	4	28
C	II	1	3	3
		Minimum Total Shipping Cost		= 103

and the Total Shipping Cost will be ₹ 103

PROBLEM 5.11

A particular product is manufactured in factories A, B, C and D; and is sold at centres 1, 2 and 3. The cost in ₹ of product per unit and capacity in kg per unit time of each plant is given below:

Factory	*Cost (₹) per unit*	*Capacity (kg) per unit*
A	12	100
B	15	20
C	11	60
D	13	80

The sale price in ₹ per unit and the demand in kg per unit time are as follows:

Sales centre	*Sale Price (₹) per unit*	*Demand (kg) per unit*
1	15	120
2	14	140
3	16	60

Required: Find the optimal sales distribution.

Solution

Step 1 → Deriving profit matrix by equation (i.e. Selling Price – Cost) and Introducing a Dummy factory with zero profit per unit as the total demand is not equal to total supply in order to make the problem balanced one.

Factory	*Sales Centres*			*Capacity (kg) per unit*
	1	*2*	*3*	
A	3	2	4	100
B	0	−1	1	20
C	4	3	5	60
D	2	1	3	80
Dummy	0	0	0	60
Demand (kg)	120	140	60	320

Step 2 → Deriving Loss Matrix by deducting each element from the maximum element (i.e. 5) in order to use minimisation technique and Finding Initial Feasible Solution by VAM.

Factory	*Sales Centre*			*Capacity*	*Difference*
	1	*2*	*3*		
A	2 [100]	3	1	100/0	1 1 -
B	5	6 [20]	4	20/0	1 1 1
C	1	2	0 [60]	60/0	1 - -
D	3 [20]	4 [60]	2	80/60/0	1 1 1
Dummy	5	5 [60]	5	60/0	0 0 0
Demand	120/20/0	140/120/60/0		60/0	
Difference	1	1	1		
	1	1	—		
	2	1	—		

Step 3 → Since the total number of allocations is less than "M + N – 1" allocations, let us introduce an infinitely small quantity 'e' to the least cost independent cell to make the total number of allocations equal to "M + N – 1" allocations.

Let us calculate "U_i's" and "V_j's" for all rows and columns respectively on the basis of allocated cells such that $C_{ij} = U_i + V_j$ assuming $U_1 = 0$,

Let us calculate Δ_{ij} (Opportunity Cost), for unallocated cells where $\Delta_{ij} = C_{ij} - (U_{ij} + V_{ij})$.

U_i & V_j Matrix

			U_i
2		e 1	3
	6		6
		0	2
3	4		4
	5		5
V_j: –1	0	–2	

C_{ij} Matrix for Unallocated cells

	3	
5		4
1	2	
		2
5		5

$U_i + V_j$ Matrix

			U_i
	3		3
5		4	6
1	2		2
		2	4
4		3	5
V_j: –1	0	–2	

$\Delta_{ij} = C_{ij} - (U_i + V_j)$ Matrix

	0	
0		0
0	0	
		0
1		2

Step 4 → Since all Δ_{ij} are positive, the above solution is optimal. The optimal solution is given below:

From Factory	To Sales Centre	Quantity	Profit per unit (₹)	Total Profit (₹)	
A	1	100	3	300	
B	2	20	–1	–20	
C	3	60	5	300	
D	1	20	2	40	
D	2	60	1	60	
Dummy	2	60	0	0	
			Total Profit =	680	

***Note:** Since some of Δ_{ij} are zero, the above solution is not unique. Hence an alternative solution exists. The alternative solution can be found by taking any cell with zero Δ_{ij} as the basic cell.*

PROBLEM 5.12

A company has four factories situated in four different locations in the country and four sales agencies located in four other locations in the country. The cost of production (₹ per unit), the sale price (₹ per unit), shipping cost (₹ per unit) in the cells of matrix, monthly capacities and monthly requirements are given below:

Factory	*Sales Agency*				*Monthly Capacity (Units)*	*Cost of Production*
	1	*2*	*3*	*4*		
A	7	5	6	4	10	10
B	3	5	4	2	15	15
C	4	6	4	5	20	16
D	8	7	6	5	15	15
Monthly Requirements (Units)	8	12	18	22		
Sales Price	20	22	25	18		

Find the monthly production and distribution schedule which will maximize profit.

Solution

Step 1 →Deriving Profit Matrix below by equation:

Profit = Sales Price – Cost of Production – Shipping Cost

Factory	*Sales Agency*				*Monthly Capacity (units)*
	1	*2*	*3*	*4*	
A	3	7	9	4	10
B	2	2	6	1	15
C	0	0	5	–3	20
D	–3	0	4	–2	15
Monthly Requirements	8	12	18	22	

Step 2 → Deriving Loss Matrix by deducting each element from the maximum element (i.e. 9) in order to use minimisation technique and Finding Initial Feasible Solution VAM.

Factory	*Sales Agency*				*Monthly Capacity*	*Difference*
	1	2	3	4		
A	6	2	[10] 0	5	10/0	2/3-
B	7	7	3	[15] 8	15/0	4/0/0-
C	[2] 9	9	[18] 4	12	20/2/0	5/0/0/0
D	[6] 12	[2] 9	5	[7] 11	15/13/6/0	4/2/2/2
Monthly Requirement	8/6/0	12/2/0	18/0	22/7		
Difference	1/2/2/3	5/2/2/0	3 - - -	3/4/4/1		

Step 3 → Since the total number of allocations is equal to "M + N – 1" allocations, the initial solution is straight away tested for optimality.

Let us calculate "U_i's" and "V_j's" for all rows and columns respectively on the basis of allocated cells such that $C_{ij} = U_i + V_j$ assuming $U_3 = 0$,

Let us calculate Δ_{ij} (Opportunity Cost), for unallocated cells where $\Delta_{ij} = C_{ij} - (U_{ij} + V_{ij})$.

U_i & V_j Matrix

				U_i
	2			−7
			8	−3
9		4		−3
12	9		11	0
12	*9*	*7*	*11*	V_j

C_{ij} Matrix for Unallocated cells

6		0	5
7	7	3	
	9		12
		5	

$U_i + V_j$ Matrix

				U_i
5		0	4	−7
9	6	4		−3
	6		8	−3
		7		0
12	*9*	*7*	*11*	V_j

$\Delta_{ij} = C_{ij} - (U_i + V_j)$ Matrix

1		0	1
−2	5	−1	
	3		4
		−2	

Step 4 → Since all Δ_{ij} are not positive, the above solution is not optimal. Let us place a small allocation θ in the cell with most negative Δ_{ij} and form a loop including this cell and test the solution for optimality. Next improved solution as obtained from above is shown below which is tested for optimality. The value of "U_i's", "V_j's" and Δ_{ij} are also calculated.

Looping Matrix

	10		
			15
2+		18−	
−6	2	θ +	

Reallocation Matrix

	10		
			15
8		12	
θ	2	6	7

U_i & V_j Matrix

				U_i
	2			−7
			8	−3
9		4		−1
	9	5	11	0
10	*9*	*5*	*11*	V_j

C_{ij} Matrix for Unallocated cells

6		0	5
7	7	3	
	9		12
12			

$U_i + V_j$ Matrix

				U_i
3		−2	4	−7
7	6	2		−3
	8		10	−1
10				0
V_j: 10	9	5	11	

$\Delta_{ij} = C_{ij} - (U_i + V_j)$ Matrix

3		2	1
	0	1	1
	1		2
	2		

Step 5 → Since all Δ_{ij} are positive, the above solution is optimal. The optimal solution is given below:

Factory	*Sales Agency*	*Profit*
A	2	10 x Rs 7 = ₹ 70
B	4	15 x Rs 1 = ₹ 15
C	1	8 x Rs 0 = ₹ 0
C	3	12 x Rs 5 = ₹ 60
D	2	2 x Rs 0 = ₹ 0
D	3	6 x Rs 4 = ₹ 24
D	4	7 x Rs −2 = ₹ −14
	Total	= ₹ 155

Note: Since one of Δ_{ij} is zero, the above solution is not unique. Hence an alternative solution exists. The alternative solution can be found by taking cell with zero Δ_{ij} as the basic cell.

PROBLEM 5.13

ABC Enterprises is having three plants manufacturing dry-cells, located at different locations. Production cost differs from plant to plant. There are five sales offices of the company located in different regions of the country. The sales prices can differ from region to region. The shipping cost from each plant to each sales office and other data are given by following table:

Production Data Table

Production cost per unit	*Max. Capacity in No. of units*	*Plant No.*
20	150	1
22	200	2
18	125	3

Shipping Costs Table

	Sales Office 1	*Sales Office 2*	*Sales Office 3*	*Sales Office 4*	*Sales Office 5*
Plant 1	1	1	5	9	4
Plant 2	9	7	8	3	6
Plant 3	4	5	3	2	7

Demand & Sales Prices

	Sales Office 1	Sales Office 2	Sales Office 3	Sales Office 4	Sales Office 5
Demand	80	100	75	45	125
Sales Price	30	32	31	34	29

Find the production and distribution schedule most profitable to the company.

Solution

Step 1 → Deriving the Profit Matrix by equation (i.e. Profit = Selling Price – Cost of Production – Shipping Cost) and Introducing a Dummy Sales Office with zero profit per unit as the total demand is not equal to total supply in order to make the problem balanced one.

9	11	6	5	5	0	150
–1	3	1	9	1	0	200
8	9	10	14	4	0	125
80	100	75	45	125	50	475

Step 2 → Deriving Loss Matrix by deducting each element from the maximum element (i.e. 14) in order to use minimisation technique and finding the initial feasible solution by VAM.

Plant	*Sales Centre* 1	2	3	4	5	6	*Capacity*	*Difference*
1	(50) 5	(100) 3	8	9	9	14	150	2 2 2 4 - -
2	15	11	13	(45) 5	(105) 13	(50) 14	200	6 2 2 2 1 1
3	(30) 6	5	(75) 4	0	(20) 10	14	125	1 1 1 4 4 4
Demand	80	100	75	45	125	50		
Diff.	1	2	4	5	1	0		
	1	2	4	-	1	0		
	1	2	-	-	1	0		
	1	-	-	-	1	0		
	9	-	-	-	3	0		
	-	-	-	-	3	0		

Step 3 → Since the total number of allocations is equal to "M + N – 1" allocations, the initial solution is straightaway tested for optimality.

Let us calculate "U_i's" and "V_j's" for all rows and columns respectively on the basis of allocated cells such that $C_{ij} = U_i + V_j$ assuming $U_3 = 0$,

Let us calculate Δ_{ij} (Opportunity Cost), for unallocated cells where $\Delta_{ij} = C_{ij} - (U_{ij} + V_{ij})$.

U_i & V_j Matrix

						U_i
5	3					–4
			5	13	14	0
6		4		10		–3
9	7	7	5	13	14	V_j

C_{ij} Matrix for Unallocated cells

		8	9	9	14
15	11	13			
	5		0		14

$U_i + V_j$ Matrix

						U_i
		3	1	9	10	−4
9	7	7				0
	4		2		11	−3
V_j 9	7	7	5	13	14	

$\Delta_{ij} = C_{ij} - (U_i + V_j)$ Matrix

		5	8	0	4
6	4	6			
	1		-2		3

Step 4 → Since all Δ_{ij} are not positive, the above solution is not optimal. Let us place a small allocation θ in the cell with most negative Δ_{ij} and form a loop including this cell and test the solution for optimality. Next improved solution as obtained from above is shown below which is tested for optimality. The value of "U_i's", "V_j's" and Δ_{ij} are also calculated.

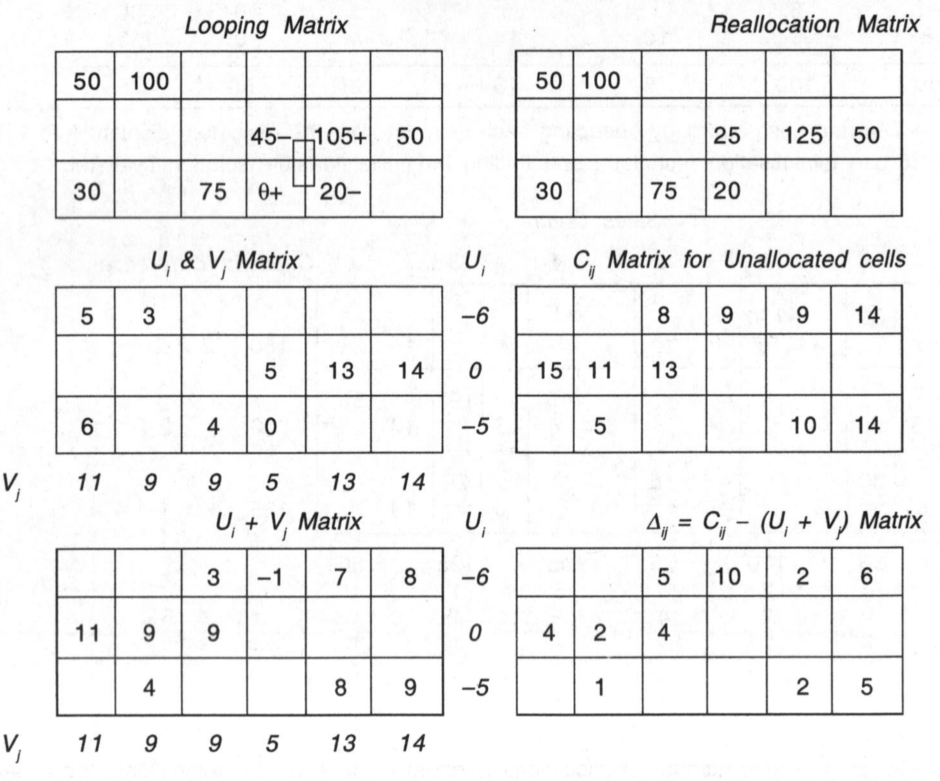

Looping Matrix

50	100				
			45–	105+	50
30		75	θ+	20–	

Reallocation Matrix

50	100				
			25	125	50
30		75	20		

U_i & V_j Matrix

						U_i
5	3					−6
			5	13	14	0
6		4	0			−5
V_j 11	9	9	5	13	14	

C_{ij} Matrix for Unallocated cells

		8	9	9	14
15	11	13			
	5			10	14

$U_i + V_j$ Matrix

						U_i
		3	−1	7	8	−6
11	9	9				0
	4			8	9	−5
V_j 11	9	9	5	13	14	

$\Delta_{ij} = C_{ij} - (U_i + V_j)$ Matrix

		5	10	2	6
4	2	4			
	1			2	5

Step 5 → Since all Δ_{ij} are positive, the above solution is optimal. The optimal solution is given below:

Plant	Sales Office	Units	Profit per unit	Profit
1	1	50	9	450
1	2	100	11	1100
2	4	25	9	225
2	5	125	1	125
2	Dummy	50	0	0
3	1	30	8	240
3	3	75	10	750
3	4	20	14	280
			Total	3,170

PROBLEM 5.14 [Maximizing Billing of Assignment]

A leading firm has three auditors. Each auditor can work upto 160 hours during the next month, during which time three projects must be completed. Project 1 will take 130 hours, project 2 will take 140 hours, the project 3 will take 160 hours. The amount per hour that can be billed for assigning each auditor to each project is given below:

Auditor	Project 1 ₹	Project 2 ₹	Project 3 ₹
1	1,200	1,500	1,900
2	1,400	1,300	1,200
3	1,600	1,400	1,500

Required: Formulate this as a transportation problem and find the optimal solution. Also find out the maximum total billings during the next month.

Solution

Step 1 → Introducing a Dummy Project with zero amount per unit as the total hours required is not equal to total hours available in order to make the problem balanced one and divide by Rupees by 100 to ease computations.

Auditor	Project 1 ₹	Project 2 ₹	Project 3 ₹	Dummy ₹	Time available (hours)
1	12	15	19	0	160
2	14	13	12	0	160
3	16	14	15	0	160
Time required (hrs)	130	140	160	50	480

Step 2 → Deriving Loss Matrix by deducting each element from the maximum element (i.e. 19) in order to use minimisation technique and Finding Initial Feasible Solution VAM.

Auditor	Project 1	Project 2	Project 3	Dummy	Time available	Difference
1	7	4	0 [160]	19	160/0	4/-/-/-
2	5	6 [110]	7	19 [50]	160/50/0	1/1/13/13
3	3 [130]	5 [30]	4	19	160/30/0	1/2/14/-
Time Required	130/0	140/110/0	160/0	50/0		
Difference	2/2/-/-	1/1/1/1	4/-/-	0/0/0		

Step 3 → Since the total number of allocations is less than "M + N – 1" allocati[...] introduce an infinitely small quantity 'e' to the least cost independent cell to mak[...] number of allocations equal to "M + N – 1" allocations.

Let us calculate "U_i's" and "V_j's" for all rows and columns respectively on [...] allocated cells such that $C_{ij} = U_i + V_j$ assuming $U_1 = 0$,

Let us calculate Δ_{ij} (Opportunity Cost), for unallocated cells where $\Delta_{ij} = C_{ij} - (U_{ij} + V_{ij})$.

U_i & V_j Matrix

				U_i
		0	19	−4
	6		19	1
		e		
3	5	4		0
V_j 3	5	4	18	

C_{ij} Matrix for Unallocated cells

7	4		19
5		7	
			19

$U_i + V_j$ Matrix

-1	1		14	−4
4		5		1
			18	0
3	5	4	18	

$\Delta_{ij} = C_{ij} - (U_i + V_j)$ Matrix

8	3		5
1		2	
			1

Step 4 → Since all Δ_{ij} are positive, the above solution is optimal. The optimal solution is given below:

Auditor	*Project*	*Billing amount (₹)*
1	3	160 × ₹ 1900 = 3,04,000
2	2	110 × ₹ 1300 = 1,43,000
3	1	130 × ₹ 1600 = 2,08,000
3	2	30 × ₹ 1400 = 42,000
	Total billing	= 6,97,000

PROBLEM 5.15

A company has four factories F_1, F_2, F_3 and F_4 manufacturing the same product. Production and raw material costs differ from factory to factory, and are given in the following table in the first two rows. The transportation costs from the factories to sales depots S_1, S_2, S_3 are also given.

The last two columns in the table give the sale price and the total requirement at each depot. The production capacity of each factory is given in the last row.

	F_1	F_2	F_3	F_4	*Sales Price per unit*	*Requirements in units*
Production cost/unit	15	18	14	13		
Raw material cost/unit	10	9	12	9		
S_1	3	9	5	4	34	80
ransportation S_2	1	7	4	5	32	120
ost per unit : S_3	5	8	3	6	31	150
	10	150	50	100		

Determine the most profitable production and distribution schedule and the corresponding . The surplus production should be taken to yield zero profit.

Solution

Step 1 → Deriving the profit matrix below by the following equation:

Profit = Sales Price – Product Cost – Raw Material Cost – Transportation Cost.

	F_1	F_2	F_3	F_4	
S_1	6	–2	3	8	80
S_2	6	–2	2	5	120
S_3	1	–4	2	3	150
	10	150	50	100	

Step 2 → Introducing a Dummy factory with zero profit per unit as the total demand is not equal to total supply in order to make the problem balanced one.

	F_1	F_2	F_3	F_4	*Dummy*	
S_1	6	–2	3	8	0	80
S_2	6	–2	2	5	0	120
S_3	1	-4	2	3	0	150
	10	150	50	100	40	

Step 3 → Deriving Loss Matrix by deducting each element from the maximum element (i.e. 8) in order to use minimisation technique.

	F_1	F_2	F_3	F_4	*Dummy*	
S_1	2	10	5	0	8	80
S_2	2	10	6	3	8	120
S_3	7	12	6	5	8	150
	10	150	50	100	40	

Step 4 → Finding Initial Feasible Solution by following the Vogel's Approximation Method (or VAM).

							Diff
	2	10	5	0 [80]	8	80/0	2
	2 [10]	10 [40]	6 [50]	3 [20]	8	120/110/90/40/0	1/3*/2*/2
	7	12 [110]	6	5	8 [40]	150/110/0	1/1/2/4*
Av.	10/0	150/40/0	50/0	100/20/0	40/0		
	0/5	0/2	1/0	3/2*	0/0		

Step 5 → Since the total number of allocations is equal to "M + N – 1" allocations, the initial solution is straight away tested for optimality.

Let us calculate "U_i's" and "V_j's" for all rows and columns respectively on the basis of allocated cells such that $C_{ij} = U_i + V_j$ assuming $U_1 = 0$,

Let us calculate Δ_{ij} (Opportunity Cost), for unallocated cells where $\Delta_{ij} = C_{ij} - (U_{ij} + V_{ij})$.

U_i & V_j Matrix

						U_i
				0		−3
	2	10	6	3		0
		12			8	2
V_j	2	10	6	3	6	

C_{ij} Matrix for Unallocated cells

2	10	5		8
				8
7		6	5	

$U_i + V_j$ Matrix

						U_i
	−1	7	3		3	−3
					6	0
	4		8	5		2
V_j	2	10	6	3	6	

$\Delta_{ij} = C_{ij} - (U_i + V_j)$ Matrix

3	3	2		5
				2
3		-2	0	

Step 6 → Since all Δ_{ij} are not positive, the above solution is not optimal. Let us place a small allocation θ in the cell with most negative Δ_{ij} and form a loop including this cell and test the solution for optimality. Next improved solution as obtained from above is shown below which is tested for optimality. The value of "U_i's", "V_j's" and Δ_{ij} are also calculated.

Looping Matrix

			80	
10	40+	50–	20	
	110–	θ+		40

Reallocation Matrix

			80	
10	90		20	
	60	50		40

U_i & V_j Matrix

						U_i
				0		−3
	2	10		3		0
		12	6		8	2
V_j	2	10	4	3	6	

C_{ij} Matrix for Unallocated cells

2	10	5		8
		6		8
7			5	

$U_i + V_j$ Matrix

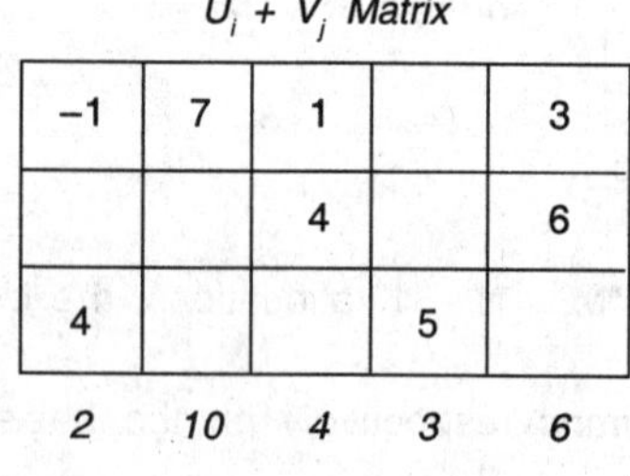

						U_i
	−1	7	1		3	−3
			4		6	0
	4			5		2
V_j	2	10	4	3	6	

$\Delta_{ij} = C_{ij} - (U_i + V_j)$ Matrix

3	3	4		5
		2		2
3			0	

Step 6 → Since all Δ_{ij} are positive, the above solution is optimal. The optimal solution is given below:

Sales Department	*Factory*	*Qty*	*Profit per Unit (₹)*	*Total Profit (₹)*
S_1	F_4	80	8	640
S_2	F_1	10	6	60
S_2	F_2	90	–2	–180
S_2	F_4	20	5	100
S_3	F_2	60	–4	–240
S_3	F_3	50	2	100
			Total	480

Note: Since one of Δ_{ij} is zero, the above solution is not unique. Hence an alternative solution exists. The alternative solution can be found by taking cell with zero Δ_{ij} as the basic cell.

PROBLEM 5.16 [Portfolio Problem]

XYZ and Co. provided the following data seeking your advice on optimum investment strategy:

Investment Made at the Beginning of year	*Net Return Data (in Paise) of Selected Investments*				*Amount Available*
	P	*Q*	*R*	*S*	*(Lacs)*
1	95	80	70	60	70
2	75	65	60	50	40
3	70	45	50	40	90
4	60	40	40	30	30
Maximum Investment (Lacs)	40	50	60	60	—

The following additional information are also provided :

— P, Q, R and S represent the selected investments.

— The company has decided to have four years investment plan.

— The policy of the company is that amount invested in any year will remain so until the end of the fourth year.

— The values (Paise) in the table represent net return on investment of one Rupee till the end of the planning horizon (for example, a Rupee invested in Investment P at the beginning of year I will grow to ₹ 1.95 by the end of the fourth year, yielding a return of 95 paise).

Using the above, determine the optimum investment strategy.

Solution

Step 1 → Introducing a Dummy Investment with zero return per unit as the total demand is not equal to total supply in order to make the problem balanced one.

Year	*Net Return data (in paise) of investment*					*Amount Available*
	P	*Q*	*R*	*S*	*Dummy*	
1	95	80	70	60	0	70
2	75	65	60	50	0	40
3	70	45	50	40	0	90
4	60	40	40	30	0	30
Maximum Investment	40	50	60	60	20	

Step 2 → Deriving Loss Matrix by deducting each element from the maximum element (i.e. 95) in order to use minimisation technique and then finding Initial Feasible Solution by VAM.

Year	*P*	*Q*	*R*	*S*	*Dummy*	*Amount available*	*Difference*
	Loss Matrix-Investment type						
1	0 [40]	15 [30]	25	35	95	70/30/0	15/10 —
2	20	30 [20]	35 [20]	45	95	40/20/0	10/5/5/10
3	25	50	45 [40]	55 [50]	95	90/50/0	20/5/5/ 10/40
4	35	55	55	65 [10]	95 [20]	30/20/0	20/0/ 0/10/30
Maximum Investment	40/0	50/20/0	60/40/0	60/10/0	20/0		
Difference	20 — — —	15 15 20 —	10 10 10 10	10 10 10 10	0 0 0 0		

(Figures in brackets denote allocations.)

Step 3 → Since the total number of allocations is equal to "M + N – 1" allocations, the initial solution is straight away tested for optimality.

Let us calculate "U_i's" and "V_j's" for all rows and columns respectively on the basis of allocated cells such that $C_{ij} = U_i + V_j$ assuming $U_4 = 0$,

Let us calculate Δ_{ij} (Opportunity Cost), for unallocated cells where $\Delta_{ij} = C_{ij} - (U_{ij} + V_{ij})$.

U_i & V_j Matrix

					U_i
0	15				*–35*
	30	35			*–20*
		45	55		*–10*
			65	95	*0*
35	*50*	*55*	*65*	*95*	V_j

C_{ij} Matrix for Unallocated cells

		25	35	95
20			45	95
25	50			95
35	55	55		

$U_i + V_j$ Matrix

					U_i
		20	30	60	*–35*
15			45	75	*–20*
25	40			85	*–10*
35	50	55			*0*
35	*50*	*55*	*65*	*95*	V_j

$\Delta_{ij} = C_{ij} - (U_i + V_j)$ Matrix

		5	5	35
5			0	20
0	10			10
0	5	0		

Step 4 → Since all Δ_{ij} are positive, the above solution is optimal. The optimal solution is given below:

Year A	*Investment* Strategies B	*Investment* C	*Return* D	*Total Return* E = C D
1	P	40	0.95	38
1	Q	30	0.80	24
2	Q	20	0.65	13
2	R	20	0.60	12
3	R	40	0.50	20
3	S	50	0.40	20
4	S	10	0.30	3
				130

Note: Since some of Δ_{ij} are zero, the above solution is not unique. Hence the alternative solution exist. The alternative solution can be found by taking any cell with zero Δ_{ij} as the basic cell.

PROBLEM 5.17 [Portfolio Problem]

A company wishes to determine an investment strategy for each of the next four years. Five investment types have been selected, investment capital has been allocated for each of the coming four years, and maximum investment levels have been established for each investment type. An assumption is that amounts invested in any year will remain invested until the end of the planning horizon of four years. The following table summarises the data for this problem. The values in the body of the table represent net return on investment of one rupee upto the end of the planning horizon. For example, a rupee invested in investment type B at the beginning of year 1 will grow to ₹ 1.90 by the end of the fourth year, yielding a net return of ₹ 0.90.

Investment made At the beginning Of year	*Investment Type* A	B *NET*	C *RETURN*	D *DATA*	E	*Rupees available (in 000's)*
1	0.80	0.90	0.60	0.75	1.00	500
2	0.55	0.65	0.40	0.60	0.50	600
3	0.30	0.25	0.30	0.50	0.20	750
4	0.15	0.12	0.25	0.35	0.10	800
Maximum Rupees Investment (in 000's)	750	600	500	800	1,000	

The objective in this problem is to determine the amount to be invested at the beginning of each year in an investment type so as to maximise the net rupee return for the four-year period.

Solve the above transportation problem and get an optimal solution. Also calculate the net return on investment for the planning horizon of four year period.

Solution

Step 1 → **Introducing a Dummy Variable with zero net rupee return as the total amount available is not equal to total investment in order to make the problem balanced one and expressing the Net Return Data in Paise.**

Years	*Net Return Data (₹)*					*Available ₹ (in 000's)*
	A	*B*	*C*	*D*	*E*	
1	80	90		75	100	500
2	55	65	40	60	50	600
3	30	25	30	50	20	750
4	15	12	25	35	10	800
Dummy	0	0	0	0	0	1000
Maximum rupees Investment in ('000)	750	600	500	800	1000	3650

Step 2 → **Deriving Loss Matrix by deducting each element from the maximum element (i.e. 1.00) in order to use minimisation technique.**

Years	*Net Return Data (₹)*					*Available ₹ (in 000's)*
	A	*B*	*C*	*D*	*E*	
1	20	10	40	25	0	500
2	45	35	60	40	50	600
3	70	75	70	50	80	750
4	85	88	75	65	90	800
Dummy	100	100	100	100	100	1000
Maximum rupees Investment in ('000)	750	600	500	800	1000	3650

Step 3 → Finding Initial Feasible Solution VAM.

Years	A	B	C	D	E	₹ available (000's)	Difference				
1	20	10	40 [500]	25	0	500/0	10	-	-	-	-
2	45	35 [600]	60	40	50	600/0	5	5	-	-	-
3	70	75	70	50 [750]	80	750/0	20	20	20	-	-
4	85 [250]	88	75 [500]	65 [50]	90	800/750	10	10	10	10	10
Dummy	100 [500]	100	100	100	100 [500]	1000/500/00	0	0	0	0	
Maximum Rupee investment in ('000)	750/ 500/0	600/0	1000/0	800/ 50/0	500/ 500/0						

Differences				
25	25	20	15	50
25	40	10	10	30
15	-	5	15	10
15	-	25	35	10
15	-	25	-	10

Step 4 → Since the total number of allocations is less than "M + N – 1" allocations, let us introduce an infinitely small quantity 'e' to the least cost independent cell to make the total number of allocations equal to "M + N – 1" allocations.

Let us calculate "U_i's" and "V_j's" for all rows and columns respectively on the basis of allocated cells such that $C_{ij} = U_i + V_j$ assuming $U_1 = 0$,

Let us calculate Δ_{ij} (Opportunity Cost), for unallocated cells where $\Delta_{ij} = C_{ij} - (U_{ij} + V_{ij})$.

U_i & V_j Matrix (e placed in the cell with 10)

						U_i
		10			0	*–85*
		35				*–60*
				50		*–15*
	85		75	65		*0*
	100				100	*15*
V_j	*85*	*95*	*75*	*65*	*85*	

C_{ij} Matrix for Unallocated cells

20		40	25	
45		60	40	50
70	75	70		80
	88			90
	100	100	100	

$U_i + V_j$ Matrix

						U_i
	0		–10	–20		*–85*
	25		15	5	25	*–60*
	70	80	60		70	*–15*
		95			85	*0*
		110	90	80		*15*
V_j	*85*	*95*	*75*	*65*	*85*	

$\Delta_{ij} = C_{ij} - (U_i + V_j)$ Matrix

20		50	45	
20		45	35	25
0	–5	10		10
	–7			5
	–10	10	20	

Step 5 → Since all Δ_{ij} are not positive, the above solution is not optimal. Let us place a small allocation θ in the cell with most negative Δ_{ij} and form a loop including this cell and test the solution for optimality. Next improved solution as obtained from above is shown below which is tested for optimality. The value of "U_i's", "V_j's" and Δ_{ij} are also calculated.

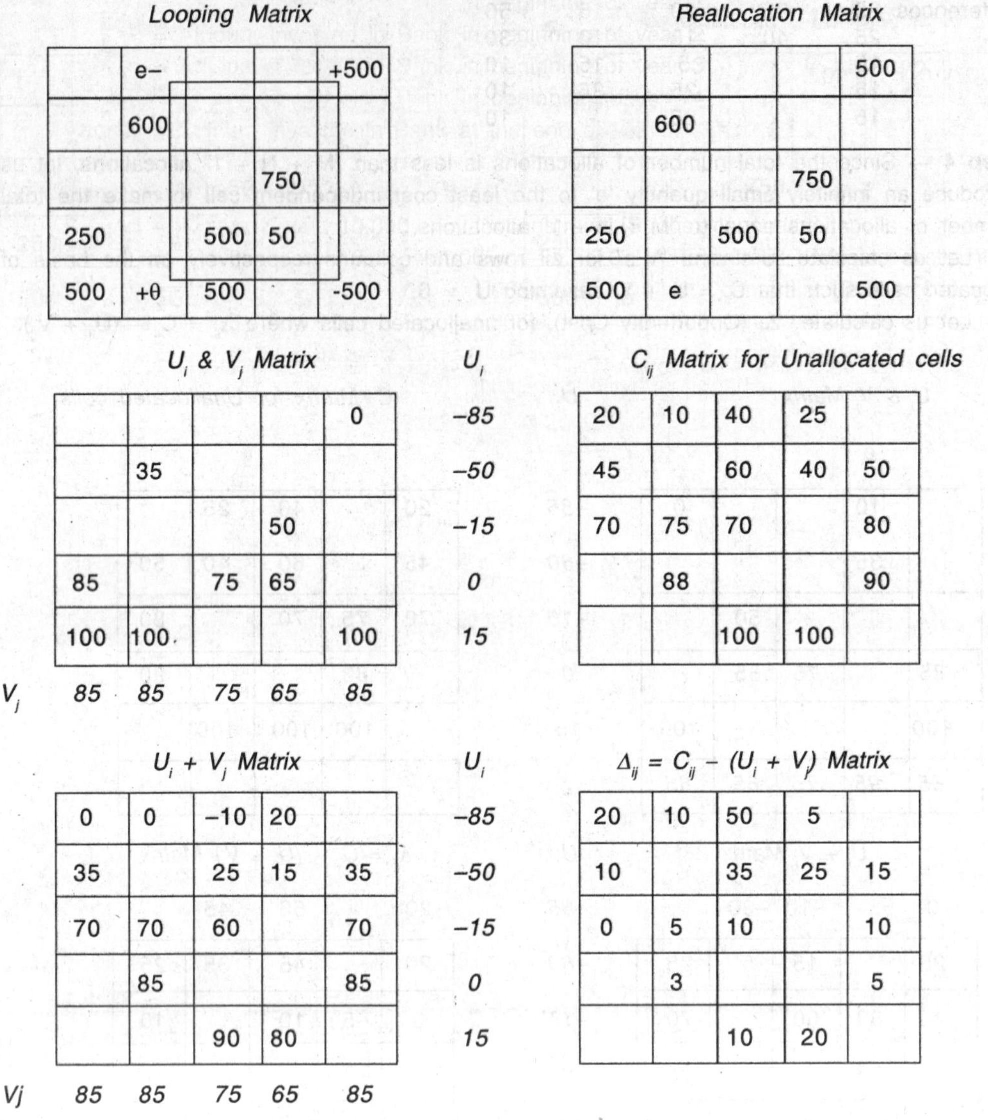

Looping Matrix

	e–			+500
	600			
			750	
250		500	50	
500	+θ	500		-500

Reallocation Matrix

				500
	600			
			750	
250		500	50	
500	e			500

U_i & V_j Matrix

					U_i
				0	*–85*
	35				*–50*
			50		*–15*
85		75	65		*0*
100	100			100	*15*
85	*85*	*75*	*65*	*85*	V_j

C_{ij} Matrix for Unallocated cells

20	10	40	25	
45		60	40	50
70	75	70		80
	88			90
		100	100	

$U_i + V_j$ Matrix

					U_i
0	0	–10	20		*–85*
35		25	15	35	*–50*
70	70	60		70	*–15*
	85			85	*0*
		90	80		*15*
85	*85*	*75*	*65*	*85*	*Vj*

$\Delta_{ij} = C_{ij} - (U_i + V_j)$ Matrix

20	10	50	5	
10		35	25	15
0	5	10		10
	3			5
		10	20	

Step 6 → Since all Δ_{ij} are positive, the above solution is optimal. The optimal solution is given below:

In the year	*Investment type*	*Amount (in 000's)*	*Net Return per ₹*	*Total Return*
1	E	500	1.00	500.0
2	B	600	.65	390.0
3	D	750	.50	375.0
4	A	250	.15	37.5
4	C	500	.25	125.0
4	D	50	.35	17.5
			Total	1,445.0

Note: Since one of Δ_{ij} is zero, the above solution is not unique. Hence an alternative solution exists. The alternative solution can be found by taking cell with zero Δ_{ij} as the basic cell.

6 Critical Path Method – Drawing Network

NETWORK (OR ARROW DIAGRAM)

A network is a graphical representation of inter-relationship of the various activities of a project. While drawing network, the following rules must be kept in mind.

1. An activity cannot occur untill all activities leading to it are complete.
2. No activity can start untill its tail event is reached.

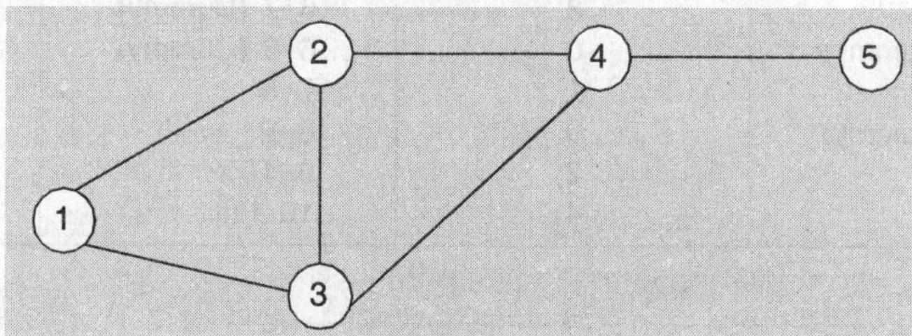

Activity	*Head Event*	*Tail Event*
1 – 2	2 (Burst Event)	1 (Burst Event)
1 – 3	3 (Merge Event)	1 (Burst Event)
2 – 3	3 (Merge Event)	2 (Burst Event)
2 – 4	4 (Merge Event)	2 (Burst Event)
3 – 4	4 (Merge Event)	3
4 – 5	5	4

The aforesaid graphical representation showing the inter-relationships of the various activities of a project is called '**Network**'.

WORKING METHODOLOGY OF CRITICAL PATH ANALYSIS

The working methodology of Critical Path Analysis (CPA) which includes both CPM and PERT, consists of following five steps:

Step 1: *Analyse and breakdown the project in terms of specific activities and/or events.*
Step 2: *Determine the interdependence and sequence of specific activities and prepare a network.*
Step 3: *Assign estimate of time, cost or both to all the activities of the network.*
Step 4: *Identify the longest or critical path through the network.*
Step 5: *Monitor, evaluate and control the progress of the project by replanning, rescheduling and reassignment of resources.*

CONVENTIONS FOLLOWED IN DRAWING NETWORK

The conventions followed in drawing a network are as follows:

1. Draw the arrow directing from left to right, that is, time and progress of the project flows from left to right.
2. As far as possible avoid drawing arrows that cross each other. Where ever crossing of arrows is unavoidable, bridging may be done.
3. An activity is always bounded by two events, called the start event and the end event. No event should hang loosely on the network.
4. Each node should be numbered without ambiguity. The numbers are assigned to events in such a way that the number assigned to the ending event of an activity is greater than the number assigned to the beginning event of that activity.

PROBLEM 6.1

Draw a network from the following activity and find a critical path and duration of project.

Activity	*Duration (Days)*	*Activity*	*Duration (Days)*
1–2	3	5–6	7
1–3	8	6–7 (Dummy)	0
2–4 (Dummy)	0	6–8 (Dummy)	0
2–7	1	7–9	5
3–4 (Dummy)	0	8–9	6
3–8	2	9–10	8
4–5	4	10-11	9

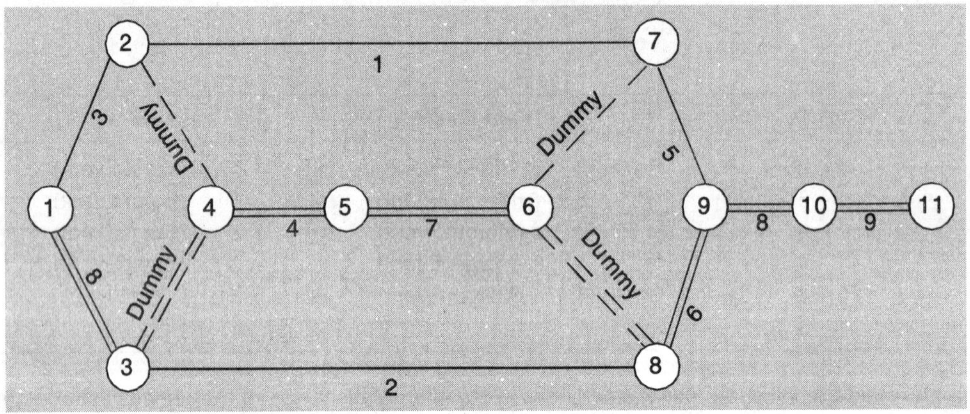

Solution

Various Paths	*Duration of Paths*
1 – 2 – 7 – 9 – 10 – 11	(3 + 1 + 5 + 8 + 9) = 26
1 – 2 – 4 – 5 – 6 – 7 – 9 – 10 – 11	(3 + 0 + 4 + 7 + 0 + 5 + 8 + 9) = 36
1 – 2 – 4 – 5 – 6 – 8 – 9 – 10 – 11	(3 + 0 + 4 + 7 + 0 + 6 + 8 + 9) = 37
1 – 3 – 8 – 9 – 10 – 11	(8 + 2 + 6 + 8 + 9) = 33
1 – 3 – 4 – 5 – 6 – 7 – 9 – 10 – 11	(8 + 0 + 4 + 7 + 0 + 5 + 8 + 9) = 41
1 – 3 – 4 – 5 – 6 – 8 – 9 – 10 – 11	(8 + 0 + 4 + 7 + 0 + 6 + 8 + 9) = 42

Hence the critical path is 1 – 3 – 4 – 5 – 6 – 8 – 9 – 10 – 11 with duration of 42 days.

PROBLEM 6.2

Draw a network for the following activity and find a critical path and total project duration.

Activity	*Duration (Days)*	*Activity*	*Duration (Days)*
1–2	3.3	4–5	11
2–3	6.7	5–6 (Dummy)	0
2–4	3.0	5–7	4.0
3–4 (Dummy)	0	6–7	6.0
3–6	7.7		

Solution

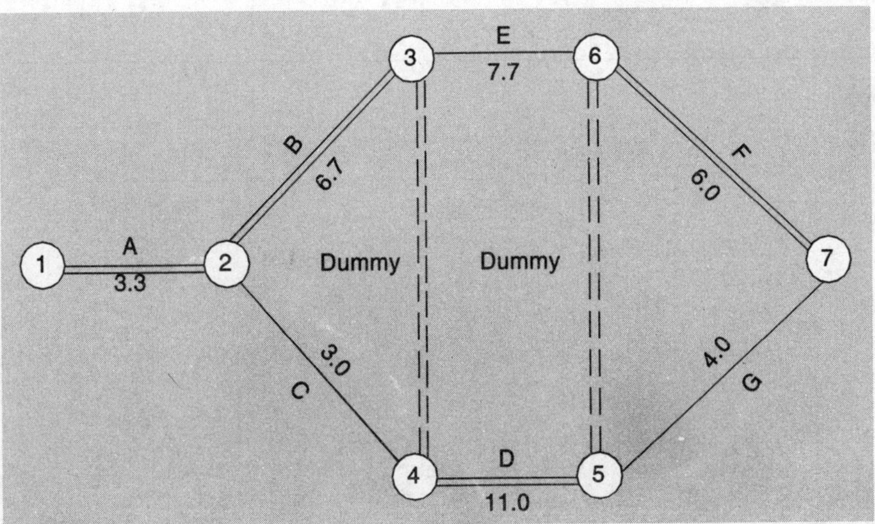

Various Paths	*Duration of Paths*
1 – 2 – 3 – 4 – 5 – 6 – 7	[3.3 + 6.7 + 0 + 11 + 0 + 6] = 27 days
1 – 2 – 3 – 6 – 7	[3.3 + 6.7 + 7.7 + 6] = 23.7 days
1 – 2 – 3 – 4 – 5 – 7	[3.3 + 6.7 + 0 + 11 + 4] = 25 days
1 – 2 – 4 – 5 – 6 – 7	[3.3 + 3 + 11 + 0 + 6] = 23.3 days
1 – 2 – 4 – 5 – 7	[3.3 + 3 + 11 + 4] = 21.3 days

Thus, the critical path is 1-2-3-4-5-6-7 or A-B-D-F and the expected project completion time is 27 days.

PROBLEM 6.3

Construct a PERT Diagram from the following information, and determine the critical path.

Activity	*Immediate Predecessor*	*Duration (Days)*
A	—	2
B	A	4
C	A	6
D	B	8
E	C	6
F	C	10
G	E	10
H	F	14
I	G,H	8
J	G, H	12
K	I	4
L	J	10

Solution

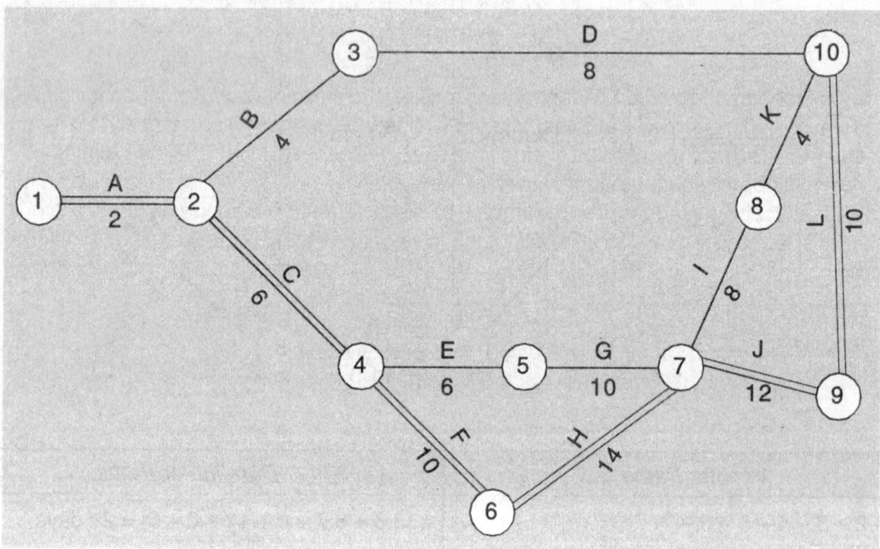

Various Paths	*Duration of Paths*
1 – 2 – 3 – 10	2 + 4 + 8 = 14
1 – 2 – 4 – 5 – 7 – 8 – 10	2 + 6 + 6 + 10 + 8 + 4 = 36
1 – 2 – 4 – 5 – 7 – 9 – 10	2 + 6 + 6 + 10 + 12 + 10 = 46
1 – 2 – 4 – 6 – 7 – 8 – 10	2 + 6 + 10 + 14 + 8 + 4 = 44
1 – 2 – 4 – 6 – 7 – 9 – 10	2 + 6 + 10 + 14 + 12 + 10 = 54

Hence the critical path is 1 – 2 – 4 – 6 – 7 – 9 – 10 i.e. (A – C – F – H – J – L) with project duration of 54 days.

PROBLEM 6.4

Draw a network from the following activity and find a critical path and duration of project.

Activity	*Immediate Predecessor*	*Duration (Days)*
A	—	3
B	—	8
C	A, B	4
D	B	2
E	A	1
F	C	7
G	E, F	5
H	D, F	6
I	G, H	8
J	I	9

Solution

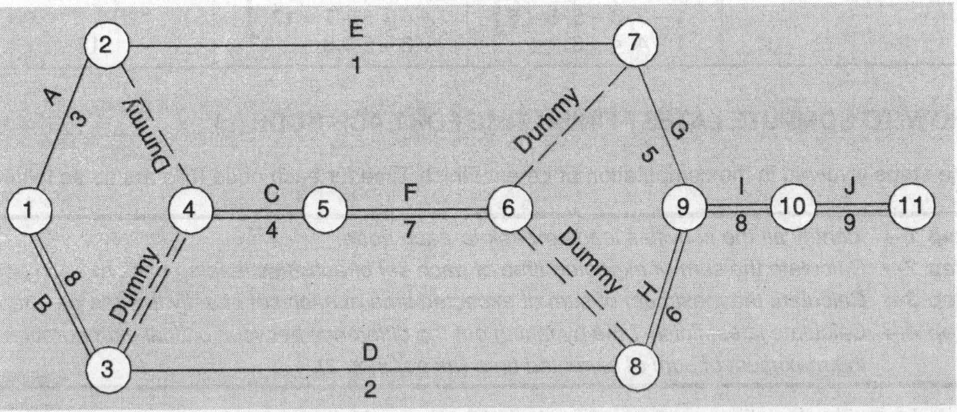

Various Paths	*Duration of Paths*
1 – 2 – 7 – 9 – 10 – 11	(3 + 1 + 5 + 8 + 9) = 26
1 – 2 – 4 – 5 – 6 – 7 – 9 – 10 – 11	(3 + 0 + 4 + 7 + 0 + 5 + 8 + 9) = 36
1 – 2 – 4 – 5 – 6 – 8 – 9 – 10 – 11	(3 + 0 + 4 + 7 + 0 + 6 + 8 + 9) = 37
1 – 3 – 8 – 9 – 10 – 11	(8 + 2 + 6 + 8 + 9) = 33
1 – 3 – 4 – 5 – 6 – 7 – 9 – 10 – 11	(8 + 0 + 4 + 7 + 0 + 5 + 8 + 9) = 41
1 – 3 – 4 – 5 – 6 – 8 – 9 – 10 – 11	(8 + 0 + 4 + 7 + 0 + 6 + 8 + 9) = 42

Hence the critical path is 1 – 3 – 4 – 5 – 6 – 8 – 9 – 10 – 11 (B – C – F – H – I – J) with duration of 42 days.

HOW TO COMPUTE EARLIEST START TIME FOR EACH NODE (E)

The steps involved in the computation of Earliest Start Time for each node (E) are as follows:

Step 1→ *Identify all the activities leading to each node.*
Step 2→ *Calculate the sum of expected Time of each set of activities leading to each node.*
Step 3→ *Calculate the maximum of the sum of expected time of each set of activities (as per step 2).*

The aforesaid calculations may be presented in the form of following table:

Table Showing the Computation of Earliest Start Time (E)

Node	*Activities leading to Node*	*Sum of Expected time*	*ES (being the Maximum of expected time)*
1	–	0	0
2	1 – 2	2	2
3	1 – 3	4	4
4	1 – 4	3	3
5	1 – 2, 2 – 5	2 + 1 = 3	
	1 – 3, 3 – 5	4 + 6 = 10	10
6	1 – 2, 2 – 5, 5 – 6	2 + 1 + 7 = 10	
	1 – 3, 3 – 5, 5 – 6	4 + 6 + 7 = 17	
	1 – 4, 4 – 6	3 + 5 = 8	17

HOW TO COMPUTE LATEST FINISH TIME FOR EACH NODE (L)

The steps involved in the computation of Latest Finish Time for each node (LF) are as as follows:

Step 1→ *Identify all the activities leading back to each node.*
Step 2→ *Calculate the sum of expected time of each set of activities leading back to each node.*
Step 3→ *Calculate the maximum of sum of expected time of each set of activities (as per step 2).*
Step 4→ *Calculate latest finish Time by taking out the difference between critical path duration and the maximum of sum of expected time (as per step 3).*

The aforesaid calculations may be presented in the form of following table:

Table Showing the Computation of Latest Finish Time (L)

Node (1)	*Activities leading back to Node* (2)	*Sum of Expected time* (3)	*Max. of sum of Expected time* (4)	*LF (17 - Col. 4)* (5)
6	–	0	0	17
5	6 – 5	7	7	10
4	6 – 4	5	5	12
3	6 – 5, 5 – 3	7 + 6 = 13	13	4
2	6 – 5, 5 – 2	7 + 1 = 8	8	9
1	6 – 5, 5 – 2, 2 – 1	7 + 1 + 2 = 10		
	6 – 5, 5 – 3, 3 – 1	7 + 6 + 4 = 17		
	6 – 4, 4 – 1	5 + 3 = 8	17	0

PROBLEM 6.5

The monthly maintenance work in a machine shop consists of 10 steps A to J. The inter-relationship between them are identified by event numbers:

Steps	*Event Numbers*	*Duration (Days)*
A	1–2	3
B	2–3	5
C	2–4	8
D	3–5	4
E	3–6	2
F	4–6	9
G	4–7	3
H	5–8	12
I	6–8	10
J	7–8	6

(a) Draw a Network.
(b) Compute early and late start and finish time for each activity.
(c) How much slack does Activity (3–5), Activity (4–6) and Activity (7–8) have?
(d) Identify the critical path and critical activities.
(e) If Activity (2–3) takes 8 days instead of 5 days what will be the project completion time ?
(f) Identify the activities that have a free slack.

Solution

(a) **Network**

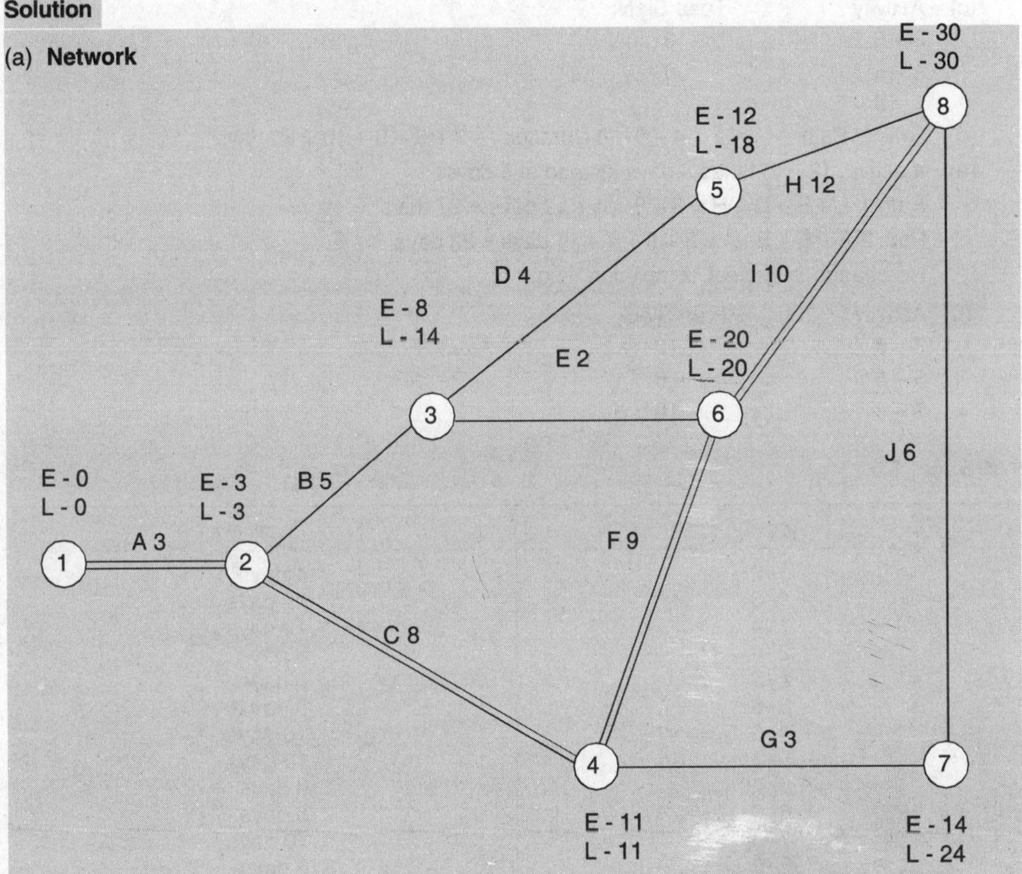

Various Paths	*Duration of Paths*
1 – 2 – 3 – 5 – 8	(3 + 5 + 4 + 12) = 24
1 – 2 – 3 – 6 – 8	(3 + 5 + 2 + 10) = 20
1 – 2 – 4 – 6 – 8	(3 + 8 + 9 + 10) = 30
1 – 2 – 4 – 7 – 8	(3 + 8 + 3 + 6) = 20

Hence the critical path is 1 – 2 – 4 – 6 – 8 (A – C – F – I) with duration of 30 days.

(b) Early and Late Start & Finish Time

	1	*2*	*3*	*4*	*5*	*6*	*7*	*8*	*9*	*10*	*11*
	i-j	*D*	*ES*	*LF*	*EF*	*LS*	*Total float*	*HES*	*Free float*	*TES*	*IF*
					(2 + 3)	*(4 – 2)*	*(6 – 3)*		*(7 – 8)*		*(9 – 10)*
A	1 – 2	3	0	3	3	0	0	0	0	0	0
B	2 – 3	5	3	14	8	9	6	6	0	0	0
C	2 – 4	8	3	11	11	3	0	0	0	0	0
D	3 – 5	4	8	18	12	14	6	6	0	6	0
E	3 – 6	2	8	20	10	18	10	0	10	6	4
F	4 – 6	9	11	20	20	11	0	0	0	0	0
G	4 – 7	3	11	24	14	21	10	10	0	0	0
H	5 – 8	12	12	30	24	18	6	0	6	6	0
I	6 – 8	10	20	30	30	20	0	0	0	0	0
J	7 – 8	6	14	30	20	24	10	0	10	10	0

(c)

Activity	Total Slack
3 – 5	6
4 – 6	0
7 – 8	10

(d) Critical Path — 1 – 2 – 4 – 6 – 8 Duration — 3 + 8 + 9 + 10 = 30 days

(e) If activity (2 – 3) takes 8 days instead of 5 days

Path 1 A – B – D – H = 3 + 8 + 4 + 12 days = 27 days

Path 2 A – B – E – I = 3 + 8 + 4 + 10 days = 23 days

No change in project completion time.

(f)

Activity	Free Slack
3 – 6	10
5 – 8	6
7 – 8	10

PROBLEM 6.6

Activity	*Duration*
1–2	4 days
1–3	12 days
1–4	10 days
2–4	8 days
2–5	6 days
3–6	8 days
4–6	10 days
5–7	10 days
6–7	0 days
6–8	8 days
7–8	10 days
8–9	6 days

With the help of the activities given above draw a network. Determine its critical path, earliest start time, earliest finish time, latest start time, latest finish time, total float, free float and independent float.

Solution

The network based on the activities is as follows:

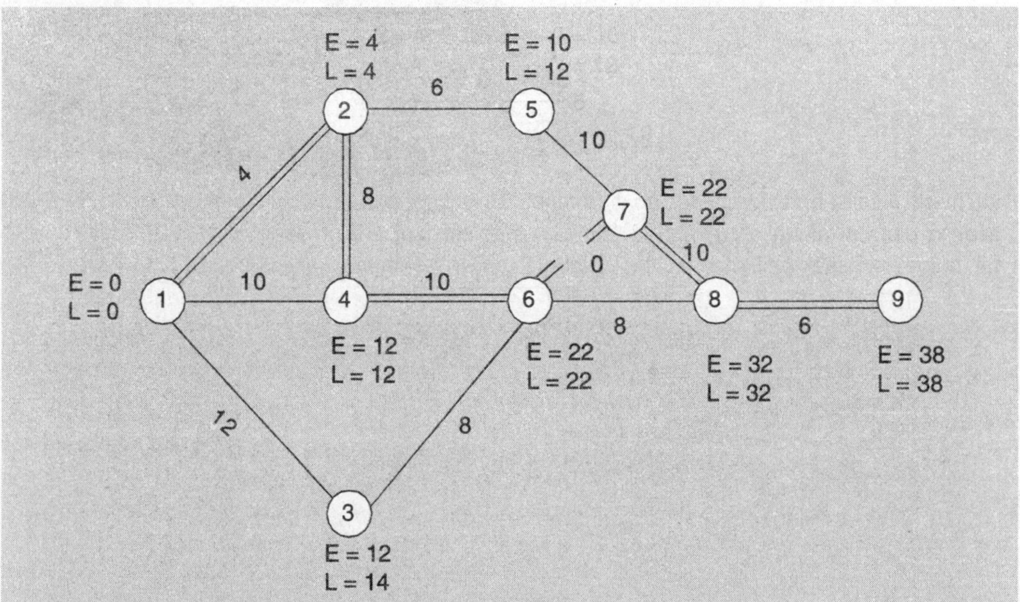

The time estimates and floats are calculated as below:

1 Activity	2 D	3 ES	4 LF	5=(2+3) EF	6=4–2 LS	7=(6–3) Total Float	8 HES	9=(7–8) Free Float	10 TES	11=(9–10) IF
1 - 2	4	0	4	4	0	0	0	0	0	0
1 - 3	12	0	14	12	2	2	2	0	0	0
1 - 4	10	0	12	10	2	2	0	2	0	2
2 - 4	8	4	12	12	4	0	0	0	0	0
2 - 5	6	4	12	10	6	2	2	0	0	0
3 - 6	8	12	22	20	14	2	0	2	2	0
4 - 6	10	12	22	22	12	0	0	0	0	0
5 - 7	10	10	22	20	12	2	0	2	2	0
6 - 7	0	22	22	22	22	0	0	0	0	0
6 - 8	8	22	32	30	24	2	0	2	0	2
7 - 8	10	22	32	32	22	0	0	0	0	0
8 - 9	6	32	38	38	32	0	0	0	0	0

Critical Path is represented by 1 - 2 - 4 - 6 - 7 - 8 - 9.

7 PERT

PRACTICAL STEPS INVOLVED IN SOLVING PERT PROBLEMS

The practical steps involved in solving PERT problems are given below:

Step 1→ *Prepare a table showing Expected Duration and Variance for each activity of the project:*

Activity		*Estimated Duration*			*Standard Deviation*	*Variance*
		Optmistic	*Pessimistic*	*Most Likely Expected*		
$i - j$	t_o	t_p	t_m	t_e	σ	σ^2

Where, Expected Duration $(t_e) = \dfrac{(t_0 + t_p + 4t_m)}{6}$

Standard Deviation $(\sigma) = \dfrac{(t_p - t_0)}{6}$

Variances (σ^2) = Square of standard deviation

Step 2→ *Draw a Project Network of Activities (or Jobs) based upon Expected Duration of the Activities.*

Step 3→ *Find out the Critical Path.*

Step 4→ *Find out the Total Expected Duration of the Project based upon the Network. This is also the Average Duration (or $\bar{X}$) of the Project.*

Step 5→ *Find out the Standard Deviation of the Project by following formula:*

$\sigma = \sqrt{(\textit{Sum of Variances of Critical Path Activities})}$

Step 6→ *Calculate the Probability of completing the Project, if required, within a particular time period, say X, as follows:*

(i) *Calculate the value of Z as follows:*

$$Z = \frac{X - \bar{X}}{\sigma} \quad \text{or} \quad Z = \frac{T_1 - T_2}{\sigma} \quad \text{where, } X = T_1 = \text{Expected Duration}$$

$$\bar{X} = T_2 = \text{Critical Path Duration}$$

(ii) *Find out the Probability for the value of Z from the Normal Variate Table as follows:*

If the value of Z is positive $P = 0.50 +$ *Probability for Z from the Table.*
If the value of Z is negative $P = 0.50 -$ *Probability for Z from the Table.*

Step 7→ *Calculate the Expected Time of completion of the Project at a given probability, if required, as follows:*

(i) *Find out the value of Z from the Normal Variate Table for the given Probability after deducting 0.50 from the Probability.*

(ii) *Put the value of Z in the formula given in Step 6 and find out the value of X, i.e. the Expected Time of completion of the Project at the given Probability.*

PROBLEM 7.1

Tulsian Ltd., has undertaken a project which has an expected duration of 15 days with a variance of 9 days.

Calculate:

(a) The probability that the project will be completed on or before 12 days.
(b) The probability that the project will be completed on or before 18 days.
(c) The probability that the project will not be completed on or before 12 days.
(d) The probability that the project will not be completed on or before 18 days.
(e) The probability that the project will be completed in not less than 3 days earlier than expected.
(f) The probability that the project will be completed in not more than 3 days later than expected.
(g) The probability that the project will take more than 12 days, but not more than 18 days.
(h) The probability that the project will be completed not before 12 days but before 18 days.
(i) The probability that the company has to pay a maximum penalty of ₹ 15,000 if there is a penalty of ₹ 5,000 per day if duration of project extend beyond expected duration.
(j) The probability that the company has to pay a minimum penalty of ₹ 20,000 if there is penalty of ₹ 5,000 per day if duration extend beyond expected duration.

Solution

(a) $Z = \frac{X - \bar{X}}{\sigma} = \frac{12-5}{3} = -1 \ (\sigma^2 = 9 \text{ or } \sigma = 3)$

Area lying between $Z = 0$ and $Z = -1$ is equal to 0.3413
Hence $P(x \leq 12) = 0.50 - 0.3413 = .1587$ or 15.87%

(b) $Z = \frac{X - \bar{X}}{\sigma} = \frac{18-15}{3} = 1$

Area lying between $Z = 0$ and $Z = 1$ is equal to 0.3413
Hence $P(x \leq 18) = .50 + .3413 = .8413$ or 84.13%

(c) $P(x > 12) = 1 - P(x \leq 12) = 1 - .1587 = 84.13$ or 84.13%

(d) $P(x > 18) = 1 - P(x \leq 18) = 1 - .8413 = .1587$ or 15.87%

(e) Same solution as given in Case (a).

(f) Same solution as given in Case (b).

(g) $P(12 < x \leq 18) = .8413 - .1587 = .6826$ or 68.26%

(h) $Z = \frac{11-15}{3} = 1.33$

$P(x \leq 11) = .50 - .4082 = .0918$

$Z = \frac{17-15}{3} = .667$

Area lying between $Z = 0$ and $Z = .667$ is equal to .2486

$P(x \leq 17) = .5 + .2486 = .7486$

$P(11 < x \leq 17) = .7486 - .0918 = .6568$ *or* 65.68%

(i) $P(x \leq 18) = .8413$

$P(x \leq 15) = .5000$

$P(15 < x \leq 18) = .8413 - .5000 = .3413$ *or* 34.13%

(j) $P(x \leq 18) = .8413$

$P(x > 18) = 1 - .8413 = .1587$ *or* 15.87%

PROBLEM 7.2

A project has the following activities and characteristics.

Activity	*Estimated Duration in Weeks*		
i – j	*Optimistic*	*Most Likely*	*Pessimistic*
1 – 2	1	1	7
1 – 3	1	4	7
1 – 4	2	2	8
2 – 5	1	1	1
3 – 5	2	5	14
4 – 6	2	5	8
5 – 6	3	6	15

Required:

(a) Find expected time and variance.

(b) Draw the project network.

(c) Find total float.

(d) Find expected project length and activities on the critical path.

(e) Determine the variance and Standard Deviation of critical path.

(f) Determine the probability that project will be completed:

(i) At least 3 weeks earlier than expected;

(ii) Not more than 3 weeks than expected;

(g) If the project due date is 18 weeks, what is probability of meeting and non-meeting the due date at 90% level?

(h) Within how many weeks would you expect the project to be completed with probability of 0.99?

(i) Find the event variances. (For both Tail and Head Event)

(j) The contract specifies a ₹ 5,000 per week penalty for each week the completion of the project extends beyond 17 weeks. What is the probability that this company will have to pay a maximum penalty of ₹ 15,000.

Solution

(a) Expected duration on the basis of the assumption that the activity follows beta distribution, has been calculated with the help of the following formulae:

Activity	$t_e = \dfrac{t_0 + 4t_m + t_p}{6}$	$Variance = \left(\dfrac{t_p - t_0}{6}\right)^2$
1 – 2	$\dfrac{1+4\times1+7}{6} = 2$	$\left(\dfrac{7-1}{6}\right)^2 = 1$
1 – 3	$\dfrac{1+4\times4+7}{6} = 4$	$\left(\dfrac{7-1}{6}\right)^2 = 1$
1 – 4	$\dfrac{2+4\times2+8}{6} = 3$	$\left(\dfrac{8-2}{6}\right)^2 = 1$
2 – 5	$\dfrac{1+4\times1+1}{6} = 1$	$\left(\dfrac{1-1}{6}\right)^2 = 0$
3 – 5	$\dfrac{2+4\times4+14}{6} = 6$	$\left(\dfrac{14-2}{6}\right)^2 = 4$
4 – 6	$\dfrac{2+4\times5+8}{6} = 6$	$\left(\dfrac{8-2}{6}\right)^2 = 1$
5 – 6	$\dfrac{3+4\times6+15}{6} = 7$	$\left(\dfrac{15-3}{6}\right)^2 = 4$

Activity 1	*Duration* 2	*ES* 3	*LF* 4	*EF* 5 = 2 + 3	*LS* 6 = 4 – 2	*TF* 7 = 6 – 3
1 - 2	2	0	9	2	7	7
1 - 3	4	0	4	4	0	0
1 - 4	3	0	12	3	9	9
2 - 5	1	2	10	3	9	7
3 - 5	6	4	10	10	4	0
4 - 6	5	3	17	8	12	9
5 - 6	7	10	17	17	10	0

(b) The network is drawn as follows:

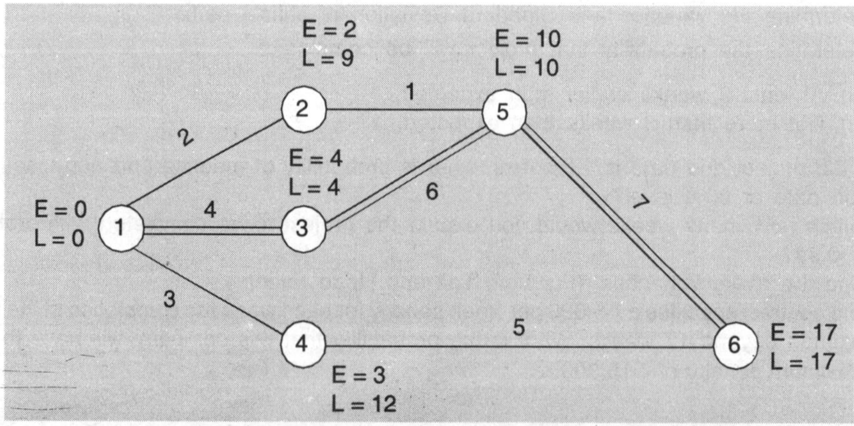

Various Paths	*Duration of Paths*
1 – 2 – 5 – 6	2 + 1 + 7 = 10
1 – 3 – 5 – 6	4 + 6 + 7 = 17
1 – 4 – 6	3 + 5 = 8

Hence the critical Path is 1 – 3 – 5 – 6 with duration of 17 weeks.

(c) Expected Project Length = 17 weeks

(d) Activities on Critical Path are 1 – 3, 3 – 5 & 5 – 6

(e) Variance and Standard Deviation of critical path

Activity	*Variance* $= \left(\frac{t_p - t_0}{6}\right)^2$
1 – 3	$\left(\frac{7-1}{6}\right)^2 = 1$
3 – 5	$\left(\frac{14-2}{6}\right)^2 = 4$
5 – 6	$\left(\frac{15-3}{6}\right)^2 = 4$
	$V_t\ (\sigma^2) \quad = 9$

S. D. $(\sigma) = \sqrt{\sigma^2} = \sqrt{9} = 3$

(f) (i) $$Z = \frac{X - \bar{X}}{\sigma}$$

where, X = Actual Duration = 14 and $\bar{X}$ = CPM Duration = 17

$$Z = \frac{14-17}{3} = -1$$

Area between $Z = 0$ and $Z = -1$ is equal to .34

Probability of 14 or less weeks = .50 – .34 = .16 or 16%

(ii) $$Z = \frac{20-17}{3} = 1$$

Area between $Z = 0$ and $Z = 1$ is equal to .34

= Probability of 20 or less weeks = 50 + .34 = .84 = 84%

(g) $$Z = \frac{18-17}{3} = \frac{1}{3} = .33$$

Area between $Z = 0$ and $Z = .33$ is equal to .13

Probability of meeting due date = .50 + .13 = .63 or 63%

Probability of not meeting due date is 100 – 63% = 37%

(h) Value of Z with 99% is 3 (from the Z table)

$$\frac{X-17}{3} = 3$$

X – 17 = 9

X = 17 + 9 = 26 weeks

Note: At critical activities, all kinds of floats (whether TF/FF/IF) and slacks (whether HES/TES) shall always be zero.

(i) **Calculation of Event variances for Earliest Time TE**

Event	*Activities on the Largest Path Leading to event No. 1, 2 .....6*	*Max. of Sum of variances of such activities*
1	None	0
2	1 – 2	1
3	1 – 3	1
4	1 – 4	1
5	1 – 2, 2 – 5, V = 1 + 0 = 1 1 – 3, 3 – 5 V = 1 + 4 = 5	5
6	1 – 3, 3 – 5, 5 – 6, V = 1 + 4 + 4 = 9 1 – 2, 2 – 5, 5 – 6, V = 1 + 0 + 4 = 5 1 – 4, 4 – 6, V = 1 + 1 = 2	9

Calculation of Event variances for Latest Time TL

Event	*Activities on Largest Path From it to last event 6 Of these activities*	*Sum of variances*
1	1 – 3, 3 – 5, 5 – 6	9
2	2 – 5, 5 – 6	4
3	3 – 5, 5 – 6	8
4	4 – 6	1
5	5 – 6	4
6	None	0

(j) $P(x \leq 17) = .50$

$P(x \leq 20) = P\left(Z = \dfrac{20-17}{3}\right)$ or $P(Z \leq 1) = .84$

$P(P7 < x \leq 20) = .84 - .50 = .34$ or 34%

PROBLEM 7.3

The following information is given:

Activity	(1–2)	(2–3)	(2–4)	(3–5)	(4–6)	(5–6)	(5–7)	(6–7)
Pessimistic time (in weeks)	3	9	6	8	8	0	5	8
Most likely time (in weeks)	3	6	4	6	6	0	4	5
Optimistic time (in weeks)	3	3	2	4	4	0	3	2

Required:

Draw the Network diagram for the above. Calculate :

(i) Variance to each activity.

(ii) Critical path and expected project length.

(iii) The probability that the project will be completed in 23 weeks.

Given that :

Z Value :	1.90	1.91	1.92	1.93	1.94
Probability :	0.9713	0.9719	0.9726	0.9732	0.9738

Solution

The required network is drawn below:

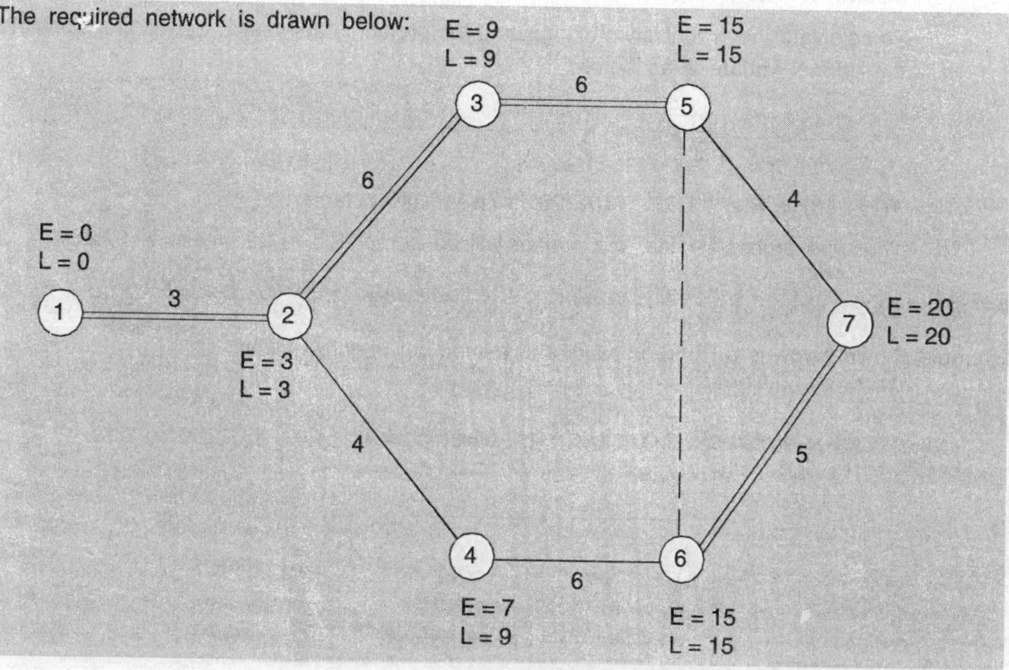

The expected time marked in the above network diagram for various activities is calculated in the table below:

Activities	*Optimistic* (t_o)	*Time(in weeks) Most likely* (t_m)	*Pessimistic* (t_p)	*Expected time (weeks)* $t_e = \frac{t_o + 4t_m + t_p}{6}$	*Variance* $v_t = \left(\frac{t_p - t_o}{6}\right)^2$
1–2	3	3	3	3	0
2–3	3	6	9	6	1
2–4	2	4	6	4	4/9
3–5	4	6	8	6	4/9
4–6	4	6	8	6	4/9
5–6	0	0	0	0	0
5–7	3	4	5	4	1/9
6–7	2	5	8	5	1

Various Paths	*Duration of Paths*
1 – 2 – 3 – 5 – 7 – 10	3 + 6 + 6 + 4 = 19
1 – 2 – 3 – 5 – 6 – 7	3 + 6 + 6 + 0 + 5 = 20
1 – 2 – 4 – 6 – 7	3 + 4 + 6 + 5 = 18

Hence the critical path is 1 – 2 – 3 – 5 – 6 – 7 with duration of 20 weeks.

(i) Variance of each of the activities has been calculated in the last column of the above table.

(ii) Critical path is given by 1 – 2 – 3 – 5 – 6 – 7 and the expected project length is 20 weeks.

(iii) Variance of the critical path = σ^2 = 0 + 1 + 4/9 + 0 + 1 = 22/9 = 2.444

Mean = x = 20 weeks

To calculate the probability of completing the project in 23 weeks, we will first calculate the normal variate Z as below:

$$Z = \frac{D - \bar{x}}{\sigma} = \frac{23 - 20}{\sqrt{2.444}} = 1.92$$

$P(x \leq 23) = P(z \leq 1.92) = 0.9726$ (from the given table)

Thus the probability that the project will be completed in 23 weeks is 97.26%.

PROBLEM 7.4

Example shown below is a PERT network and related set of activity time:

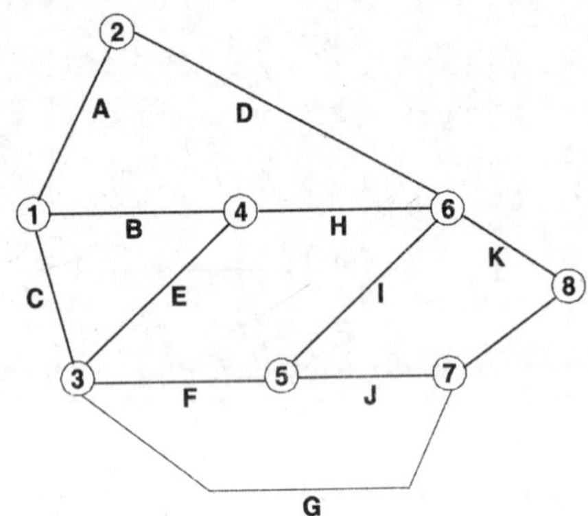

i-j	A	B	C	D	E	F	G	H	I	J	K	L
t_o	10	12	8	4	0	12	6	9	4	0	5	9
t_m	13	15	11	7	0	18	12	12	6	0	8	12
t_p	22	18	20	16	0	36	18	27	8	0	11	33

Required:

(a) Determine the expected completion time of each activity.

(b) Determine the earliest expected completion time, the latest expected completion time and float of each activity.

(c) What is the total project completion time, and what are activities on the critical path?

(d) Determine S.D. of expected completion time for only those activities on the critical path.

(e) Determine the probability that the project will be completed within 41 weeks.

Solution

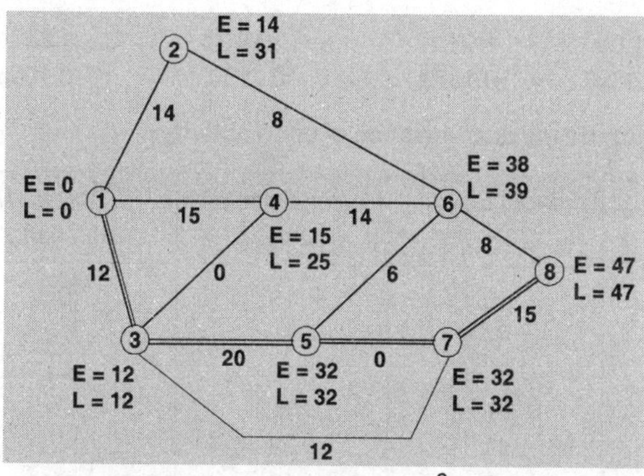

$$t_e = \frac{t_p + 4t_m + t_o}{6}; V_t = \left(\frac{t_p - t_o}{6}\right)^2$$

1 i-j	t_o	$4t_m$	t_p	2 t_e	3 ES	4 LF	5=3+2 EF	6=4-2 LS	7=6-3 TF	V_t	S.D.
1–2	10	52	22	14	0	31	14	17	17		
1–3	8	44	20	12	0	12	12	0	0	4	2
1–4	12	60	18	15	0	25	15	10	10		
2–6	4	28	16	8	14	39	22	31	17		
3–4	0	0	0	0	12	25	12	25	13		
3–5	12	72	36	20	12	32	32	12	0	16	4
3–7	6	48	18	12	12	32	24	20	8		
4–6	9	48	27	14	15	39	29	25	10		
5–6	4	24	8	6	32	39	38	33	1		
5–7	0	0	0	0	32	32	32	32	0	0	0
6–8	5	32	11	8	38	47	46	39	1		
7–8	9	48	33	15	32	47	47	32	0	16	4
									$\Sigma V_t = 36$		

Hence S.D. of the critical path $= \sqrt{36} = 6$, $Z = \dfrac{41 - 47}{6} = -1$,

Probability of completing critical path in 41 weeks = 0.159.

PROBLEM 7.5

A project consists of seven activities and the time estimates of the activities are furnished as under:

Activity	*Optimistic Days*	*Most likely Days*	*Pessimistic Days*
1-2	4	10	16
1-3	3	6	9
1-4	4	7	16
2-5	5	5	5
3-5	8	11	32
4-6	4	10	16
5-6	2	5	8

(i) Draw the network diagram. (ii) Identify the critical path and its duration. (iii) What is the probability that the project will be completed in 5 days earlier than the critical path duration? (iv) What project duration will provide 95% confidence level of completion ($Z_{0.95} = 1.65$)?

Given

Z	11.00	1.09	1.18	1.25	1.33
Probability	0.1587	0.1379	0.7190	0.1056	0.0918

(c) Calculation of expected time and variance of each activity:

Activity	*Optimistic Days*	*Most likely Days*	*Pessimistic Days*	*Expected Duration*	*Varian*
1-2	4	10	16	10	4
1-3	3	6	9	6	1
1-4	4	7	16	8	4
2-5	5	5	5	5	0
3-5	8	11	32	14	16
4-6	4	10	16	10	4
5-6	2	5	8	5	1

Paper-5: Cost Management

The network diagram is as under:

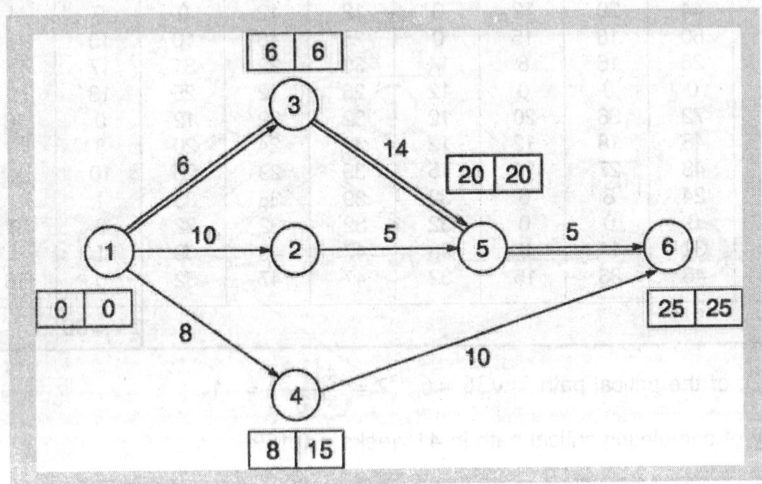

Critical Path:	1–3		3–5		5–6
Duration (days)	6		14		5 = 25 days
Standard deviation:	1	+	16	+	1 = 18
					$\sqrt{18} = 4.24$

Probability that the project will be completed five days earlier:

$$Z = \frac{20 - 25}{4.24} = -1.18.$$

According to probability values given in the question probability is 11.9%

To obtain 95% confidence level:

$$1.65 = \frac{X - 25}{4.24}$$

$$X - 25 = 6.996$$

$$X = 32 \text{ days}$$

PROBLEM 7.6

An Engineering Project has the following activities whose time estimates are listed below:

Activity	*Estimated duration (in months)*		
	Optimistic	*Most likely*	*Pessimistic*
1-2	2	2	14
1-3	2	8	14
1-4	4	4	16
3-5	4	10	28
4-6	4	10	16
5-6	6	12	30

(i) Draw the project network and find the critical path.

(ii) Find the expected duration and variance for each activity. What is the expected project length?

(iii) Calculate the variance and standard deviation of the project length.

(iv) What is the probability that the project will be completed at least eight months earlier than expected time?

(v) If the project due date is 38 months, what is the probability of not meeting the due date?

Given:

Z:	0.50	0.67	1.00	1.33	2.00
Prob.:	0.3085	0.2514	0.1587	0.0918	0.0228

(Nov 2001)

Solution

The earliest and latest expected time for each event is calculated by considering the expected time of each activity as shown in the table below:

Activity $(i - j)$	t_o	t_m	t_p	$t_e = (t_o + 4t_m + t_p)/6$	$\sigma^2 = \left(\frac{t_p - t_o}{6}\right)^2$
1-2	2	2	14	4	4
1-3	2	8	14	8	4
1-4	4	4	16	6	4
2-5	2	2	2	2	0
3-5	4	10	28	12	16
4-6	4	10	16	10	4
5-6	6	12	30	14	16

(a) The project network is drawn below:

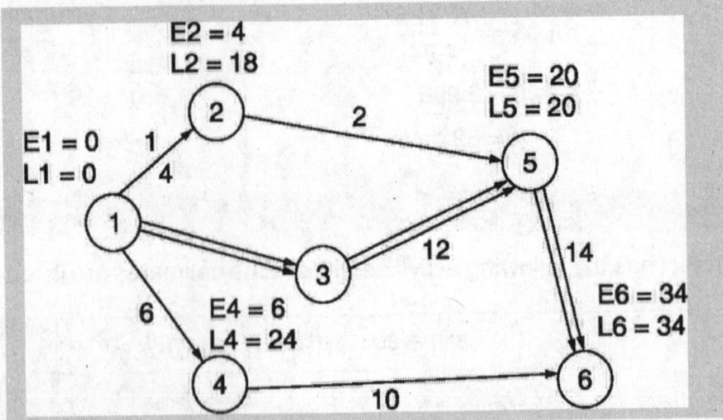

(i) Critical Path is: 1 – 3 – 5 – 6

(ii) The expected duration and variance of each activity is shown in the table above.
The expected project length is the sum of the duration of critical activities. Hence,
Expected project Length = 8 + 12 + 14 = 34 months

(iii) Variance of the project length Is the sum of the variances of critical activities,
Variance of project length = σ^2 * 4 + 16 + 18 = 38 months

Therefore, Standard Deviation = $\sigma = \sqrt{36} = 6$

(iv) Probability that the project will be completed at least 8 months earlier than the expected time of 34 months is given by

$$\text{Probability}\left[Z \leq \frac{T_s - T_e}{\sigma_e} = \frac{(34-8)-34}{6}\right] = \text{Prob. } [Z \leq -1.33]$$

But Z = –1.33 from the normal distribution table is 0.0918.

Students may please note that the values for the Prob. for a Z value correspond to the shaded area as shown In the diagram below:

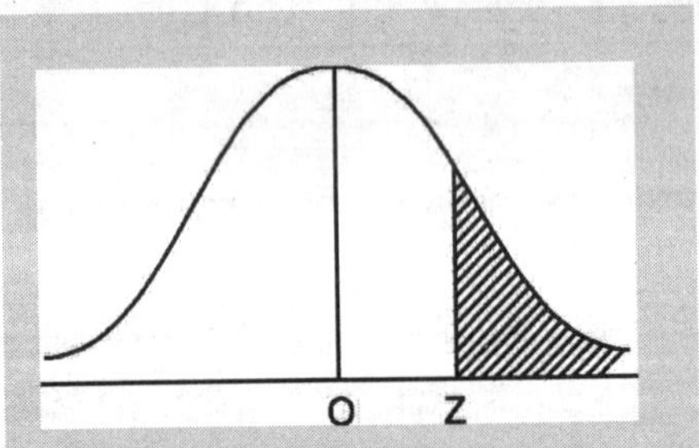

Thus, the probability of completing the project within 26 months is 9.18%.

(v) If the project due date is 38 months, then the probability of not meeting the due date is given by

$$\text{Prob.}\left[Z > \frac{T_s - T_e}{\sigma_e} = \frac{(38-34)}{6}\right] = \text{Prob. } [Z > 0.67]$$

But Z = 0.67 from the normal distribution is 0.2514.
Thus, the probability of not meeting the due date is 25.14%.

8 Crashing,Resource and Smoothing

PROBLEM 8.1

A project has the following time schedule.

Activity	*Time in months*	*Activity*	*Time in months*
1-2	2	3-7	5
1-3	2	4-6	3
1-4	1	5-8	1
2-5	4	6-9	5
3-6	8	7-8	4
		8-9	3

Required:

(i) Construct PERT Network and compute, (a) Total float for each activity, (b) Critical path and its duration.

(iii) Also find the minimum number of cranes the project must have for its activities 2 – 5, 3 – 7 and 8 – 9 without delaying the project. Then, is any change required in PERT Network? If so, indicate the same.

Solution

Table Showing the Calculation of Total Float

Activity (1)	*Duration (2)*	*ES (3)*	*LS (4)*	*EF (5 = 2 + 3)*	*LF (6 = 4 – 2)*	*TF (7 = 6 – 3)*
1-2	2	0	7	2	5	5
1-3	2	0	2	2	0	0
1-4	1	0	7	1	6	6
2-5	4	2	11	6	7	5
3-6	8	2	10	10	2	0
3-7	5	2	8	7	3	1
4-6	3	1	10	4	7	6
5-8	1	6	12	7	11	5
6-9	5	10	15	15	10	0
7-8	4	7	12	11	8	1
8-9	3	11	15	14	12	1

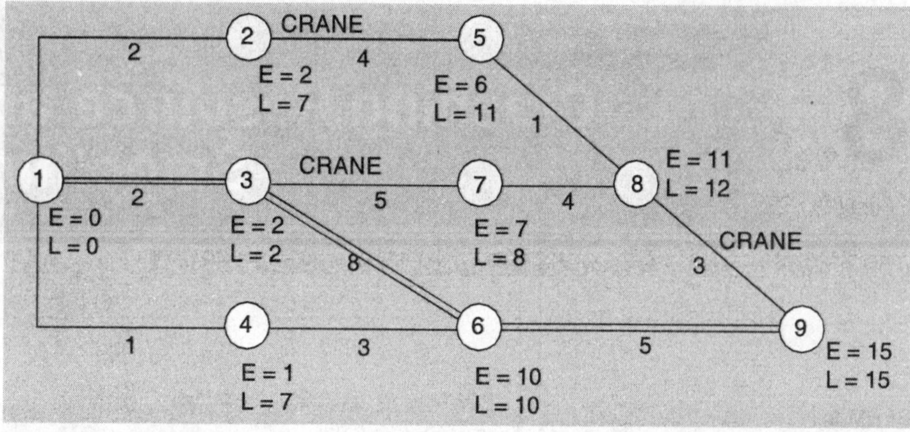

Various Paths	*Duration of Paths*
1 – 2 – 5 – 8 – 9	2 + 4 + 1 + 3 = 10
1 – 3 – 7 – 8 – 9	2 + 5 + 4 + 3 = 14
1 – 3 – 6 – 9	2 + 8 + 5 = 15
1 – 4 – 6 – 9	1 + 3 + 5 = 9

Hence the critical path is 1 – 3 – 6 – 9 with total project duration of 15 days.

Minimum No. Cranes

Finish	3 – 7	at	7	with one crane
Finish	2 – 5	at	7 + 4 = 11	with the same crane
Finish	5 – 8	at	11 + 1 = 12	without the crane
Finish	8 – 9	at	12 + 3 = 15	with the same crane.

Thus one crane is sufficient.

2 – 5, 5 – 8 and 8 – 9 start at 7, 11 and 12 respectively.

PROBLEM 8.2

The following table lists the activities of a maintenance project :

Activity	*Duration (in months)*
1–2	2
1–3	2
1–4	1
2–5	4
3–6	5
3–7	8
4–7	3
5–8	1
6–8	4
7–9	5
8–9	3

(i) Draw the project network.

(ii) Find the critical path and duration of the project.

(iii) Suppose we are required to employ a special piece of equipment on activities 1 – 3, 3 – 6, 2 – 5, 5 – 8 and 8 – 9, one at a time. Will it affect the duration of the project? Explain.

Solution

(i) The network for the given project is drawn below:

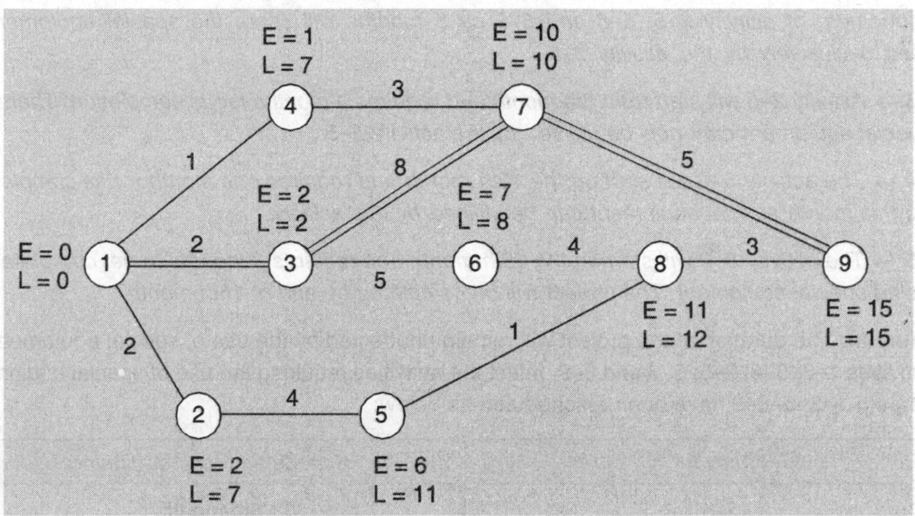

Various Paths	Duration of Paths
1 – 3 – 7 – 9	2 + 8 + 5 = 15
1 – 3 – 6 – 8 – 9	2 + 5 + 4 + 3 = 14
1 – 2 – 5 – 8 – 9	2 + 4 + 1 + 3 = 10
1 – 4 – 7 – 9	1 + 3 + 5 = 9

Hence the critical path is 1 – 3 – 7 – 9 with project duration of 15 days.

(ii) The critical path is 1 – 3 – 7 – 9 and the project duration is 15 months.

(iii) The time scaled version of the above network is drawn below :

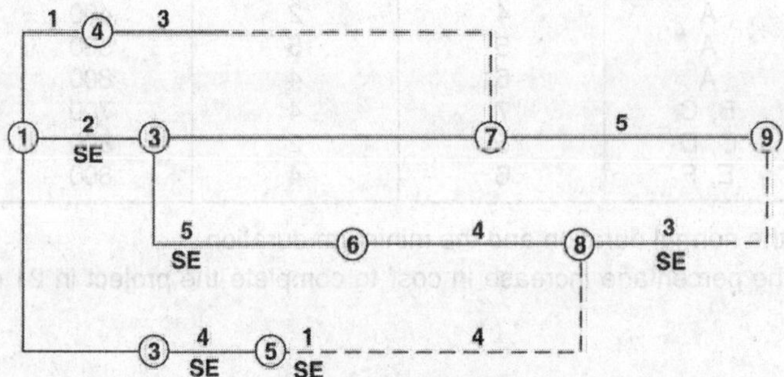

Various paths are 1 – 3 – 7 – 9 of 15 months duration.

1 – 3 – 6 – 8 – 9 of 14 months duration.

1 – 2 – 5 – 8 – 9 of 10 months duration.

1 – 4 – 7 – 9 of 9 months duration.

Special equipment (SE) is required on activities 1 – 3; 3 – 6; 2 – 5; 5 – 8 and 8 – 9.

Step 1 → *We are required to calculate new schedule of activities due to Special Equipment requirement on 1 – 3; 3 – 6; 2 – 5; 5 – 8; and 8 – 9 activities.*

Activities on the paths 1 – 4 – 7 – 9; 1 – 3 – 7 – 9 will continue as per the existing schedule.

Step 2 → *Special equipment is required from 3rd onwards on activities 3–6 and 2–5. The path 1–2–5–8–9 on which 2–5 lies has a total float of 5 months and if the activity 2–5 on this path is delayed by 5 months then during this period the activity 3–6 will be completed. Such a post-ponement of activity 2–5, 5–8 and 8–9 by 5 months will spare the special equipment to be used exclusively by the activity 3–6.*

Step 3 → *Activity 2–5 will start from 8th month and requires 4 months for its completion. Therefore the special equipment may now be utilised by the activity 2–5.*

Step 4 → *The activity 5–8 will start on the 12th month and requires one month for its completion. During this month special equipment can be utilised by this activity.*

Step 5 → *The activity 8–9 will start on the 13th month and requires 3 months to get completed by a utilising special equipment. The project will be completed by end of 15th month.*

Conclusion: The duration of the project will remain unaffected by the use of special equipment on the activities 1–3; 3–6; 2–5; 5–8 and 8–9. Infact the activities requiring the use of special equipment on the path 1–2–5–8–9 have been rescheduled as below:

Activity	*Schedule of their beginning*
2–5	8th month
5–8	12th month
8–9	13th month

PROBLEM 8.3

A small project is having seven activities. The relevant data about these activities is given below:

Activity	*Dependence*	*Normal duration (Days)*	*Crash duration (Days)*	*Normal cost (₹)*	*Crash cost (₹)*
A	—	7	5	500	900
B	A	4	2	400	600
C	A	5	5	500	500
D	A	6	4	800	1,000
E	B, C	7	4	700	1,000
F	C, D	5	2	800	1,400
G	E, F	6	4	800	1,600

(i) Find out the normal duration and the minimum duration.

(ii) What is the percentage increase in cost to complete the project in 21 days?

Solution

The required network is drawn below:

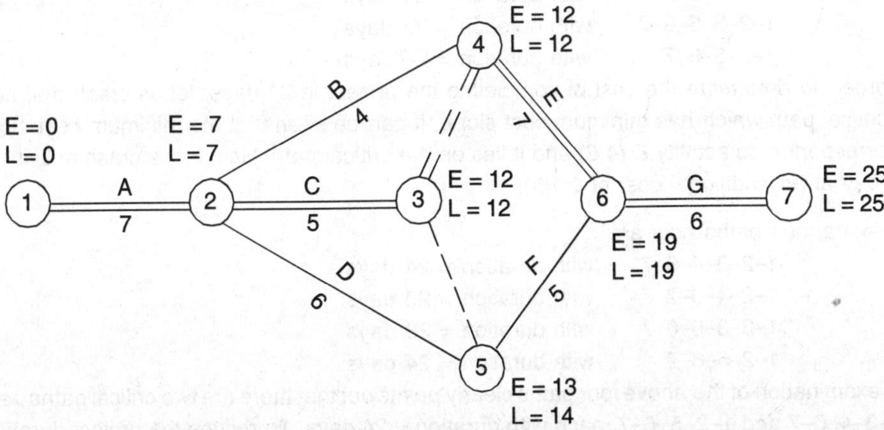

Various Paths	*Duration of Paths*
1 – 2 – 4 – 6 – 7	7 + 4 + 7 + 6 = 24
1 – 2 – 3 – 4 – 6 – 7	7 + 5 + 0 + 7 + 6 = 25
1 – 2 – 3 – 5 – 6 – 7	7 + 5 + 0 + 5 + 6 = 23
1 – 2 – 5 – 6 – 7	7 + 6 + 5 + 6 = 24

(i) **The critical path of the project is A → C → E → G or 1–2–3–4–6–7 with normal duration of 25 days.**

The minimum duration of the project is 18 days.

(ii) **The cost slope for various activities is given below:**

Activity	*Normal Duration*	*Crash duration*	*Normal cost (₹)*	*Crash cost (₹)*	*Cost slope (₹)*
A (1-2)	7	5	500	900	$\frac{900-500}{7-5}=200$
B (2-4)	4	2	400	600	$\frac{600-400}{4-2}=100$
C (2-3)	5	5	500	500	N.A.
D (2-5)	6	4	800	1000	$\frac{1000-800}{6-4}=100$
E (4-6)	7	4	700	1000	$\frac{1000-700}{7-4}=100$
F (5-6)	5	2	800	1400	$\frac{1400-800}{5-2}=200$
G (6-7)	6	4	800	1600	$\frac{1600-800}{6-4}=400$
		Total	4,500		

Step 1 → Various paths of the network are given below:

1–2–3–4–6–7 with duration = 25 days
1–2–4–6–7 with duration = 24 days
1–2–3–5–6–7 with duration = 23 days
1–2–5–6–7 with duration = 24 days

In order to determine the cost of completing the project in 21 days, let us crash that activity on the critical path which has minimum cost slope. It can be seen that the minimum cost slope of ₹ 100 corresponds to activity E (4-6) and it lies on the critical path. Hence, we crash activity E (4-6) by 1 day at an additional cost of ₹ 100.

Step 2 → Various paths now are

1–2–3–4–6–7 with duration = 24 days
1–2–4–6–7 with duration = 23 days
1–2–3–5–6–7 with duration = 23 days
1–2–5–6–7 with duration = 24 days

An examination of the above four paths clearly points out that there are two critical paths namely viz 1–2–3–4–6–7 and 1–2–5–6–7, each with duration = 24 days. To reduce the project duration by three days more, there are following possible combinations of activities.

1. Crash activities 4 – 6 on the path 1–2–3–4–6–7 and 5 – 6 on the path 1–2–5–6–7 by one day each at an addition cost of ₹ 100 + ₹ 200 = ₹ 300
2. Crash activities 4 – 6 on path 1–2–3–4–6–7 and 2 – 5 on path 1–2–5–6–7 by one day each at an additional cost of ₹ 100 + ₹ 100 = ₹. 200
3. Crash activity 1–2 by one day at an additional cost of ₹ 200.

It can be observed that the additional cost of reducing the project duration by one day in combination 2 as well as combination 3 is ₹ 200. Hence any of these two can be selected for crashing. However, since crashing activity 1–2 by 1 day reduces the duration of all the paths by 1 day, we will crash it by 1 day. The project duration becomes = 23 days at an additional cost = ₹ 200.

Step 3 → Crash activity 1 – 2 by 1 day further, it would reduce the project duration to 22 days at an additional cost = ₹ 200.

Step 4 → Activity 1 – 2 can not be crashed further. So we now select the combination of an additional cost of ₹ 100 + ₹ 100 = ₹ 200.

The project duration now becomes equal to 21 days.

Hence, in order to complete the project in 21 days, an additional cost of ₹ 100 + ₹ 200 + ₹.200 + ₹ 200 = ₹ 700 will be incurred.

The normal cost of completing the project in 25 days = ₹ 4500.

Hence, the percentage increase in cost to complete the project is 21 days

$$= \frac{\text{Rs. } 700}{\text{Rs. } 4500} \times 100 = 15.5\%$$

PROBLEM 8.4

The Arcot Machinery Company has been offered a contract to build delivery nine extruding presses to the Home Bottling Company. The contract price negotiated contingent upon meeting a specified delivery time, with a bonus offered for early delivery. The marketing department has established the following cost and time information.

Activity	Normal Time (Weeks)			Normal Cost (₹,)	CrashTime (weeks)	Crash Cost (₹)
	a	b	m			
1-2	1	5	3	5,000	1	9,000
2-3	1	7	4	8,000	3	14,000
2-4	1	5	3	4,000	2	6,000
2-5	5	11	8	5,000	7	6,000
3-6	2	6	4	3,000	2	5,000
4-6	5	7	6	2,000	4	3,600
5-7	4	6	5	10,000	4	14,000
6-7	1	5	3	7,000	1	10,600

Normal delivery time is 16 weeks for a contract price of ₹ 62,000.

On the basis of the calculated profitability for each delivery time specified in the following table, what delivery schedule do you recommend that the company should implement?

Contract Delivery Time (weeks)	*Contract Amount (₹)*
15	62,500
14	64,000
13	70,000
12	72,500

(Here a = t_o : Optimistic time, b = t_p : pessimistic time, m = t_m : Most likely time.)

Solution

Let us first calculate the expect duration of each activity.

Activity	Normal Time (weeks)			Expected duration ₹	Normal Cost (weeks)	Crash Time (₹)	Crash Cost	Cost Slope
	a	b	m					
1-2	1	5	3	3	5000	1	9000	2000
2-3	1	7	4	4	8000	3	14000	6000
2-4	1	5	3	3	4000	2	6000	2000
2-5	5	11	8	8	5000	7	6000	1000
3-6	2	6	4	4	3000	2	5000	1000
4-6	5	7	6	6	2000	4	3600	800
5-7	4	6	5	5	10000	4	14000	4000
6-7	1	5	3	3	7000	1	10600	1800

The network for the given problem is drawn below:

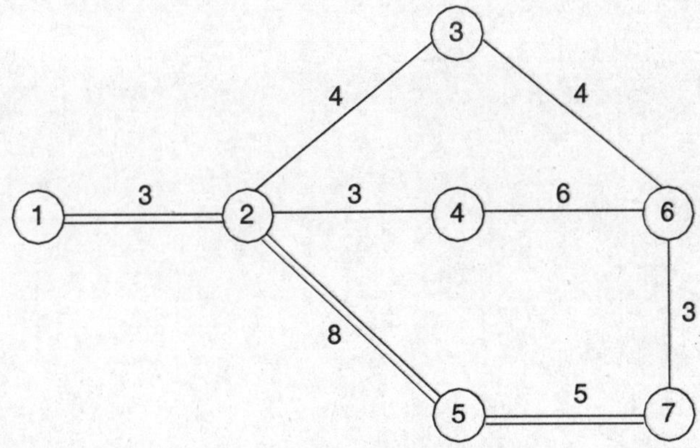

The critical path is 1-2-5-7 with total duration of 16 weeks. Cost of all activities is ₹ 44,000.

Contract price is ₹ 62,000 for normal delivery time of 16 weeks. Hence the profit is of ₹ 18000.

For calculating the most profitable delivery schedule, let us start crashing the activities on the critical path. Cost slopes for various activities are given in the above table.

Step 1 → The critical activity 2-5 has the least cost slope of ₹ 1,000, so we crash this activity by 1 day. Crashing cost is ₹ 1,000. The contract amount for delivery time of 15 weeks is ₹ 62,500

Profit = ₹ 62,500 – (₹ 44,000 + ₹ 1,000)
= ₹ 62,500 – ₹ 45,000 = ₹ 17,500

Step 2 →Now there are two critical paths viz. 1-2-4-6-7 and 1-2-5-7 with duration of 15 weeks. So we crash activity 1-2 by 1 day at crash cost of ₹ 2,000. Project duration is 14 weeks.

Profit = ₹ 65,000 – ₹ (45,000 + 2,000) = ₹ 18,000.

Step 3 → We again crash activity 1-2 by 1 day. So the project duration is 13 weeks

Profit = ₹ 70,000 – (₹ 47,000 + ₹ 2,000)
= ₹ 70,000 – ₹ 49,000 = ₹ 21,000

Step 4 → Now we crash activity 4-6 for path 1-2-4-6-7 at crash cost of ₹ 800 and activity 5-7 for path 1-2-5-7 at crash cost of ₹ 4,000. Project duration is now 12 weeks.

Profit = ₹ 72,500 – (₹ 49,000 + ₹ 4000 + ₹ 800)
= ₹ 72,500 – ₹ 53,800 = ₹ 18,700

No further crashing is possible.

From step 3, it can be seen that the profit is maximum when the project duration is 13 weeks. Hence, the company should implement at the delivery schedule of 13 weeks at a contract amount of ₹ 70,000 to gain maximum profit of ₹ 21,000.

9 Simulation

PRACTICAL STEPS IN THE SIMULATION PROCESS

Although simulations vary in complexity from situation to situation, in general one would have to go through the following steps:

Step 1→ *Define the problem or system you inteneded to simulate.*

Step 2→ *Formulate the model you intend to use.*

Step 3→ *Test the model and Compare its behaviour with the behaviour of the actual problem.*

Step 4→ *Identify and collect the data needed to test the model.*

Step 5→ *Run the Simulation*

Step 6→ *Analyze the resuls of the simulation and, if desired, change the solution you are evaluating.*

Step 7→ *Rerun the Simulation to test the new solution.*

Step 8→ *Validate the simulation; this involves increasing the chances of the inferences you may draw about the real situation from running the simulation to become valid.*

MONTE CARLO SIMULATION

The Monte Carlo method is the earliest method of simulation. It employs random numbers and is used to solve problems that depend upon probability, where physical experimentation is impractable and the creation of a mathematical formula impossible. It is a method of simulation by the sampling technique. That is, first of all, the probability distribution of the variable under consideration is determined; then a set of random numbers is used to generate a set of values that have the same distributional characteristics as the actual experience it is designed to simulate. The steps involved in carrying out Monte Carlo Simulation are:

Step 1→ *Select the measure of effectiveness of the problem, that is, what element is used to measure success in improving the system modelled. This is the element one wants to maximise or minimise. For example, this might be idle time of a service facility, or inventory shortages per period.*

Step 2→ *Identify the variables which influence the measure of effectiveness significantly. For example, the number of service facilities in operation or the number of units in inventory and so on.*

Step 3→ *Determine the proper cumulative probability distribution of each variable selected under Step (2) plot these, with the probability on the vertical axis and the values of variables on horizontal axis.*

Step 4→ *Get a set of random numbers.*

Step 5→ *Consider each random number as a decimal value of the cumulative probability distribution. With the decimal, enter the cumulative distribution plot from the vartical axis. Project this point horizontally, until it intersects cumulative probability distribution curve. Then project the point of intersection down into the vertical axis.*

Step 6→ *Record the value generated in Step (5) into the formula derived from the chosen measure of effectiveness. Solve and record the value. This value is the measure of effectiveness for that simulated value.*

Step 7→ *Repeat Steps (5) and (6) until sample is large enough for the satisfaction of the decision maker.*

PROBLEM 9.1 [Frequency Distribution of Probability Estimates]

The investment required for introducing a new product is ₹ 10,000. The probability estimates for variable cost selling price and annual sales volume are given below :

Selling price		*Variable cost*		*Annual volume*	
Value (₹)	*Probability*	*Value (₹)*	*Probability*	*Value (₹)*	*Probability*
3	0.20	1	0.20	4,000	0.20
4	0.60	2	0.50	6,000	0.50
5	0.20	3	0.30	8,000	0.30

Required: Simulate the situation by generating random number to find out selling price, variable cost and the annual sales volume. The random number schemes for the three factors are given below:

Selling price

Value	*Cumulative probability*	*Random number*
3	0.2	00-19
4	0.8	20-79
5	1.0	80-99

Variable cost

Value	*Cumulative probability*	*Random number*
1	0.2	00-19
2	0.7	20-69
3	1.0	70-99

Annual Sales volume

Value	*Cumulative probability*	*Random number*
4,000	0.2	00-19
6,000	0.7	20-69
8,000	1.0	70-99

Also prepare the frequency distribution of the Probability Estimates

Use the following sequence of Sixty random numbers (First 3 random numbers for the first trial etc.)

97, 95, 12, 02, 92, 75, 80, 67, 14, 66, 24, 72, 86, 76, 20, 55, 64, 82, 50, 02, 74, 29, 53, 08, 58, 16, 01, 51, 16, 69, 14, 55, 36, 86, 54, 35, 24, 23, 52, 39, 36, 99, 47, 41, 41, 60, 71, 41, 65, 88, 48, 44, 74, 11, 93, 10, 95, 20, 46, 36

Solution

Net Profit = (Selling price – Variable cost) Annual sales – ₹ 10,000 (being fixed cost)

Table : Simulation Work Sheet

Observation No.	Selling price		Variable cost		Annual volume		Net
	Random No.	Value (₹)	Random No.	Value (₹)	Random No.	Value (units)	Profit (₹)
1	97	5	95	3	12	4,000	–2,000
2	02	3	92	3	75	8,000	–10,000
3	80	5	67	2	14	4,000	2,000
4	66	4	24	2	72	8,000	6,000
5	86	5	76	3	20	6,000	2,000
6	55	4	64	2	82	8,000	6,000
7	50	4	2	1	74	8,000	14,000
8	29	4	53	2	08	4,000	–2,000
9	58	4	16	1	01	4,000	2,000
10	51	4	16	1	69	6,000	8,000
11	14	3	55	2	36	6,000	–4,000
12	86	5	54	2	35	6,000	8,000
13	24	4	23	2	52	6,000	2,000
14	39	4	36	2	99	8,000	6,000
15	47	4	41	2	41	6,000	2,000
16	60	4	71	3	41	6,000	–4,000
17	65	4	88	3	48	6,000	–4,000
18	44	4	74	3	11	4,000	–6,000
19	93	5	10	1	95	8,000	22,000
20	20	4	46	2	36	6,000	2,000

Total Profit = ₹ 50,000, Average Profit = ₹ 50,000/20 = ₹ 2,500

The results of 20 simulations are noted in the following table. We find that losses have occurred in some of the trials and the average profit = ₹ 2,500. The associated risk can be easily found out by taking the profitability figures and computing the associated probabilities.

Table Showing the Frequency Distribution of the Probability Estimates

Profit	Frequency	Cumulative Frequency	Probability
22,000	1	1	1/20
14,000	1	2	2/20
8,000	2	4	4/20
6,000	3	7	7/20
2,000	6	13	13/20
-2,000	2	15	15/20
-4,000	3	18	18/20
-6,000	1	19	19/20
-10,000	1	20	20/20

PROBLEM 9.2 [SIMULATING THE DEFECTED ITEMS]

The output of a production line is checked by an inspector for one or more of three different types of defects, called defects A, B and C. If defect A occurs, the item is scrapped. If defect B or C occurs, the item must be reworked. The time required to rework a B defect is 15 minutes and the time required to rework a C defect is 30 minutes. The probabilities of an A, B and C defects are .15, .20 and .10 respectively. For ten items coming off the assembly line, determine the number of items without any defects, the number scrapped and the total minutes of rework time. Use the following random numbers:

RN for defect A	48	55	91	40	93	01	83	63	47	52
RN for defect B	47	36	57	04	79	18	10	13	57	09
RN for defect C	82	95	18	96	20	8	56	11	52	03

Solution

Table I - Random Numbers Coding

Defect A			***Defect B***			***Defect C***		
Whether Defect Exists ?	***Cum. Prob.***	***Random numbers assigned***	***Whether Defect Exists ?***	***Cum. Prob.***	***Random numbers assigned***	***Whether Defect Exists ?***	***Cum. Prob.***	***Random numbers assigned***
Yes	0.15	00-14	Yes	0.20	00-19	Yes	0.10	00-09
No	1.00	15-99	No	1.00	20-99	No	1.00	10-99

Table II - Simulation Worksheet

Item No.	***RN for defect A***	***Whether defect exist or not***	***RN for defect B***	***Whether defect exist or not***	***RN for defect C***	***Whether defect exist or not***	***Which defect***	***Rework time (in minutes) exists***	***Remarks***
1	48	No	47	No	82	No	—	—	—
2	55	No	36	No	95	No	—	—	—
3	91	No	57	No	18	No	—	—	—
4	40	No	04	Yes	96	No	B	15	—
5	93	No	79	No	20	No	—	—	—
6	01	Yes	18	Yes	8	Yes	A, B, C	—	Scrap
7	83	No	10	Yes	56	No	B	15	—
8	63	No	13	Yes	11	No	B	15	—
9	47	No	57	No	52	No	—	—	—
10	52	No	09	Yes	03	Yes	B,C	15 + 30 = 45	—

During the simulated period,

No. of items without any defect = 5

No. of items scrapped = 1

No. of items required rework = 4

Total rework time required = 90 minutes

PROBLEM 9.3 [Penalty Cost for Excess & Short Output]

A company manufacturers 30 items per day. The sale of these items depends upon demand which has the following distribution:

Sales (Units)	Probability
27	0.10
28	0.15
29	0.20
30	0.35
31	0.15
32	0.05

The production cost and selling price of each unit are ₹ 40 and ₹ 50 respectively. Any unsold product is to be disposed off at a loss of ₹ 15 per unit. There is a penalty of ₹ 5 per unit if the demand is not met.

Required: Using the following random numbers estimate total profit/loss for the company for the next 10 days : 10, 99, 65, 99, 95, 01, 79, 11, 16,20

If the company decides to produce 29 items per day, what is the advantage or disadvantage to the company?

Solution

Table I - Random Number Coding

Sales (units)	*Probability*	*Cumulative Probability*	*Random numbers assigned*
27	0.10	0.10	00-09
28	0.15	0.25	10-24
29	0.20	0.45	25-44
30	0.35	0.80	45-79
31	0.15	0.95	80-94
32	0.05	1.00	95-99

Profit per unit = Selling Price per unit – Cost per unit
= ₹ 50 – ₹ 40 = ₹ 10 per unit

Table II - Simulation Work Sheet

(i) Day	*(ii)* Random number	*(iii)* Estimated sale	*(iv)* Profit/Loss per day when production = 30 items per day	*(v)* Profit/Loss per day when production = 29 items per day
1	10	28	28 × ₹ 10 – 2 × ₹ 15 = 250	28 × ₹ 10 – 1 × ₹ 15 = 265
2	99	32	30 × ₹ 10 – 2 × ₹ 5 = 290	29 × ₹ 10 – 3 × ₹ 5 = 275
3	65	30	30 × ₹ 10 = 300	29 × ₹ 10 – 1 × ₹ 5 = 285
4	99	32	30 × ₹ 10 – 2 × ₹ 5 = 290	29 × ₹ 10 – 3 × ₹ 5 = 275
5	95	32	30 × ₹ 10 – 2 × ₹ 5 = 290	29 × ₹ 10 – 3 × ₹ 5 = 275
6	01	27	27 × ₹ 10 – 3 × ₹ 15 = 225	27 × ₹ 10 – 2 × ₹ 15 = 240
7	79	30	30 × ₹ 10 = 300	29 × ₹ 10 – 1 × ₹ 5 = 285
8	11	28	28 × ₹ 10 – 2 × ₹ 15 = 250	28 × ₹ 10 – 1 × ₹ 15 = 265
9	16	28	28 × ₹ 10 – 2 × ₹ 15 = 250	28 × ₹ 10 – 1 × ₹ 15 = 265
10	20	28	28 × ₹ 10 – 2 × ₹ 15 = 250	28 × ₹ 10 – 1 × ₹ 15 = 265
Total Profit =			**₹ 2,695**	**₹ 2,695**

It is evident from this table that there is no additional profit or loss if the production is reduced to 29 items per day since the total profit remains unchanged i.e. ₹ 2,695.

PROBLEM 9.4 [Calculation of No. of Mopeds waiting in the factory and No. of Empty spaces on the Lorry]

A company manufactures around 200 mopeds. Depending upon the availability of raw materials and other conditions, the daily production has been varying from 196 mopeds to 204 mopeds, whose probability distribution is as given below :

Production/day:	196	197	198	199	200	201	202	203	204
Probability :	0.05	0.09	0.12	0.14	0.20	0.15	0.11	0.08	0.06

The finished mopeds are transported in a specially designed three storeyed lorry that can accomodate only 200 mopeds.

Required: Using the following 15 random numbers 82, 89, 78, 24, 53, 61, 18, 45, 04, 23, 50, 77, 27, 54, 10 simulate the process to find out:

(i) What will be the average number of mopeds waiting in the factory?

(ii) What will be the average number of empty space on the lorry.

Solution

Table I - Random Numbers Coding

Production per day	*Probability*	*Cumulative probability*	*Random number interval*
196	0.05	0.05	00-04
197	0.09	0.14	05-13
198	0.12	0.26	14-25
199	0.14	0.40	26-39
200	0.20	0.60	40-59
201	0.15	0.75	60-74
202	0.11	0.86	75-85
203	0.08	0.94	86-93
204	0.06	1.00	93-99

Table II - Simulation Worksheet

Random numbers *A*	*Daily production* *B*	*Capacity of lorry* *C*	*No. of Mopeds Waiting (Empty Space)* *D = B – C*	*Cumulative No. of mopeds waiting* *E*	*No. of empty spaces* *F*
82	202	200	2	2	0
89	203	200	3	5	0
78	202	200	2	7	0
24	198	200	(2)	5	0
53	200	200	0	5	0
61	201	200	1	6	0
18	198	200	(2)	4	0
45	200	200	0	4	0
04	196	200	(4)	0	0
23	198	200	(2)	0	2
50	200	200	0	0	0
77	202	200	2	2	0
27	199	200	(1)	1	0
54	200	200	0	1	2
10	197	200	(3)	-	-
				42	4

(i) Average No. of Mopeds waiting in the factory = 42/15 = 2.8 per day

(ii) Average No. of Empty spaces on the lorry = 4/15 = .267 per day

PROBLEM 9.5 [Simulating Process Time]

XYZ Scientific Equipment manufacturing company is engaged in producing different types of high class equipment for use in science laboratories. The company has two different assembly times to produce its most popular product. The processing time for each of the assembly lines is regarded as a random variable and is described by the following distributions:

Processing time (minutes)	*Assembly A_1*	*Assembly A_2*
20	0.20	0.10
21	0.40	0.15
22	0.20	0.40
23	0.15	0.25
24	0.05	0.10

Using the following random numbers, generate data on the process times for 15 units of the item and compute the expected process time for the product :

3441 7674 4349 4383 8311 1519 0236 4594 1554
0575 8900 8008 2874 2434 0993

For the purpose, read the numbers horizontally, taking the first two digits for the processing time on assembly A_1 and the last two digits for processing time on assembly A_2.

Solution

Table I : Random Number Coding

Time	*Assembly A_1*			*Assembly A_2*		
(mts.)	*Prob.*	*Cum. prob.*	*RN Interval*	*Prob.*	*Cum. Prob.*	*RN Interval*
20	0.20	0.20	00-19	0.10	0.10	00-09
21	0.40	0.60	20-59	0.15	0.25	10-24
22	0.20	0.80	60-79	0.40	0.65	25-64
23	0.15	0.95	80-94	0.25	0.90	65-89
24	0.05	1.00	95-99	0.10	1.00	90-99

The random numbers for the first unit are 34 and 41 respectively for the assemblies A1 and A2. From Table 2, we observe that the times corresponding to these are 22 and 21 minutes respectively. Thus the total time required for the unit is 43 minutes. In the same way, the times for the other 14 units are determined and shown in the last column of the table.

Table II : Simulation Worksheet

Unit	*Assembly A_1*		*Assembly A_2*		*Total time*
	R. Number	*Time*	*R. Number*	*Time*	*(mts.)*
1	34	21	41	22	43
2	76	22	74	23	45
3	43	21	49	22	43
4	43	21	83	23	44
5	83	23	11	21	44
6	15	20	19	21	41
7	02	20	36	22	42
8	45	21	94	24	45
9	15	20	54	22	42
10	05	20	75	23	43
11	89	23	00	20	43
12	80	23	08	20	43
13	28	21	74	23	44
14	24	21	34	22	43
15	09	20	93	24	44
				Total	**649**

Expected time = 649/15 = 43.27

PROBLEM 9.6

A d.p. manager estimates that the keypunch staff is idle 20% of the time and would like to take a work-sampling study that would be accurate within $\pm$ 4%. The manager wishes to have 95% confidence in the resulting study. How many observations should be taken? The demand and leadtime for a particular item have the distributions show below. Explain how the demand over the lead time could be generated using Monte Carlo simulation. Use the random numbers shown in your explanation.

Leadtime (week)	*Probability*	*Random Nos.*
2	0.25	38, 10, 41, 82
3	0.50	
4	0.25	

Demand items/week	*Probability*	*Random Nos.*
100 150 200 250 300	0.10 0.15 0.50 0.15 0.10	15, 51, 60, 30, 72 09, 40, 50, 84, 86 49, 32

Solution

$$n = \frac{Z^2 pq}{h^2} = \frac{1.96^2 \times 0.2 \times 0.8}{0.04^2} = 384 \text{ observations.}$$

Leadtime	*Cumulative Probability*	*Random Number Interval*
2	0.25	00 – 24
3	0.75	25 – 74
4	1.00	75 – 99

Therefore, leadtimes for the given random nos. are as follows in brackets: 38 (3), 10 (2), 41 (3), 82 (4).

Demand Items/week	*Cumulative Probability*	*Random Number Interval*
100	0.10	00 – 09
150	0.25	10 – 24
200	0.75	25 – 74
250	0.90	75 – 89
300	1.00	90 – 99

Therefore demands for the given random nos. are as follows in brackets : 15 (150), 51(200), 60(200), 30(200), 72(200), 02(100), 40(200), 50(200), 84(250), 76(250), 49(200), 32(200).

Leadtime	*Leadtime Demand*
3	150 + 200 + 200 = 550
2	200 + 200 = 400
3	100 + 200 + 200 = 500
4	250 + 250 + 200 + 200 = 900

PROBLEM 9.7 [Simulating the weather]

The occurrence of rain in a city on a day is dependent upon whether or not it rained on the previous day. If it rained on the previous day, the rain distribution is given by:

Event	*Probability*
No rain	0.50
1 cm. rain	0.25
2 cm. rain	0.15
3 cm. rain	0.05
4 cm. rain	0.03
5 cm. rain	0.02

If it did not rain the previous day, the rain distribution is given by :

Event	*Probability*
No rain	0.75
1 cm. rain	0.15
2 cm. rain	0.06
3 cm. rain	0.04

Simulate the city's weather for 10 days and determine by simulation the total days without rain as well as the total rainfall during the period. Use the following random numbers :

67 63 39 55 29 78 70 06 78 76

for simulation assume that for the first day of the simulation it had not rained the day before.

Solution

Table I - Random Number Coding (Rain on Previous Day)

Event	*Probability*	*Cumulative Probability*	*Random numbers assigned*
No rain	0.50	0.50	00-49
1 cm. rain	0.25	0.75	50-74
2 cm. rain	0.15	0.90	75-89
3 cm. rain	0.05	0.95	90-94
4 cm. rain	0.03	0.98	95-97
5 cm. rain	0.02	1.00	98-99

Table II - Random Number Coding (No Rain on previous day)

Event	*Probability*	*Cumulative Probability*	*Random numbers assigned*
No rain	0.75	0.75	00-74
1 cm. rain	0.15	0.90	75-89
2 cm. rain	0.06	0.96	90-95
3 cm. rain	0.04	1.00	96-99

Table III - Simulation Work Sheet

Day	*Random Numbers*	*Event*	
1	67	No rain	(from table 2)
2	63	No rain	(from table 2)
3	39	No rain	(from table 2)
4	55	No rain	(from table 2)
5	29	No rain	(from table 2)
6	78	1 cm. rain	(from table 2)
7	70	1 cm. rain	(from table 1)
8	06	No rain	(from table 1)
9	78	1 cm. rain	(from table 2)
10	76	2 cm. rain	(from table 1)

Hence, during the simulated period, it did not rain on 6 days out of 10 days. The

PROBLEM 9.8 [Simulating the Dentist's Clinic]

Dr. Strong is a dentist who schedules all her patients for 30 minutes appointments. Some of the patients take more or less than 30 minutes depending on the type of dental work to be done. The following summary shows the various categories of work, their probabilities and the time actually needed to complete the work :

Category	*Time required*	*Probability of category*
Filling	45 minutes	0.40
Crown	60 minutes	0.15
Cleaning	15 minutes	0.15
Extraction	45 minutes	0.10
Checkup	15 minutes	0.20

Simulate the dentist's clinic for four hours and determine the average waiting time for the patients as well as the idleness of the doctor. Assume that all the patients show up at the clinic at exactly their scheduled arrival time starting at 8.00 a.m. Use the following random numbers for handling the above problem :

40 82 11 34 25 66 17 79

Solution

Table I - Random Number Coding

Type	*Probability*	*Cumulative Probability*	*Random Numbers*
Filling	0.40	0.40	00-39
Crown	0.15	0.55	40-54
Cleaning	0.15	0.70	55-69
Extraction	0.10	0.80	70-79
Checkup	0.20	1.00	80-99

Table II - Simulation Work Sheet

Patient	*Scheduled Arrival*	*Random Number*	*Category*	*Service Time*
1	8.00	40	Crown	60 minutes
2	8.30	82	Checkup	15 minutes
3	9.00	11	Filling	45 minutes
4	9.30	34	Filling	45 minutes
5	10.00	25	Filling	45 minutes
6	10.30	66	Cleaning	15 minutes
7	11.00	17	Filling	45 minutes
8	11.30	79	Extraction	45 minutes

Now, let us simulate the dentist's clinic for four hours starting at 8.00 A.M.

Table showing the waiting times for the patients

A	*B*	*C*	*D*	*E = C + D*	*F = C − B*
Patient	*Arrival*	*Service Starts*	*Service Time*	*Service Ends*	*Waiting (Minutes)*
1	8.00	8.00	60 Minutes	9.00	0
2	8.30	9.00	15 Minutes	9.15	30
3	9.00	9.15	45 Minutes	10.00	15
4	9.30	10.00	45 Minutes	10.45	30
5	10.00	10.45	45 Minutes	11.30	45
6	10.30	11.30	15 Minutes	11.45	60
7	11.00	11.45	45 Minutes	12.30	45
8	11.30	12.30	45 Minutes	1.15	60
				Total	285

The average waiting time of a patient = $\frac{285}{5}$ 35.625 minutes.

The dentist was not idle during the entire simulated period.

PROBLEM 9.9

Ramu and Raju are workers on a two station assembly line. The distribution of activity times at their station is:

Time (in sec.)	10	20	30	40	50	60	70	80
Time freq. for Ramu :	4	6	10	20	40	11	5	4
Time freq. for Raju :	4	5	6	7	10	8	6	4

(a) Simulate operation of the line for 8 items using the random numbers : 06, 57, 47, 17, 43, 07, 27, 68 for Ramu and 26, 97, 76, 02, 02, 05, 16, 56 for Raju.

(b) Assuming Raju must wait until Ramu completes first item before starting work will he have to wait to process any of the other eight items. Explain your answer based upon your simulation.

Solution

Table I : Random Number Coding

For Ramu				*For Raju*			
Time in secs.	*Time frequency*	*cum. f*	*Random Number allotted*	*Frequency*	*cum. f*	*2* x cum. f*	*Random Number allotted*
10	4	4	00 - 03	4	4	8	00 - 07
20	6	10	04 - 09	5	9	18	08 - 17
30	10	20	10 - 19	6	15	30	18 - 29
40	20	40	20 - 39	7	22	44	30 - 43
50	40	80	40 - 79	10	32	64	44 - 63
60	11	91	80 - 90	8	40	80	64 - 79
70	5	96	91 - 95	6	46	92	80 - 91
80	4	100	96 - 100	4	50	100	92 - 100

*Cumulative frequencies for Raju are multiplied by 2 to make these from 100.

Table 2 : Stimulation Number Sheet

For Ramu		*For Raju*	
Random Nos.	*Processing* time*	*Random Nos.*	*Processing* time*
6	20	26	30
57	50	97	80
47	50	76	60
17	30	02	10
43	50	02	10
7	20	05	10
27	40	16	20
68	50	56	50

* This time corresponds to the time value of the random number corresponding to cumulative frequency value e.g., for Ramu in first row the random number is 6 which lies in the class of cum. freq. = 10 having time value equal to 20 sec. Similarly, processing time for Raju can be calculated.

Table 3 : Computation of Waiting time for Raju

	For Ramu		*For Raju*			
Item No.	*Processing time*	*Cum. time*	*Start time*	*Processing time*	*End. time*	*Waiting time*
1	20	20	20	30	50	—
2	50	70	70*	80	150	20
3	50	120	150	60	210	—
4	30	150	210	10	220	—
5	50	200	220	10	230	—
6	20	220	230	10	240	—
7	40	260	260*	20	280	20
8	50	310	310*	50	360	30

Thus Raju has to wait for items 2, 7 and 8.

* End time of current item of Ramu or end time of previous item of Raju whichever is higher has been taken as start time of current item for Raju.

PROBLEM 9.10

A process involves the production of a particular component which is then installed into an end product. The average production time for the component is 4 minutes and the following probability distribution has been derived from past observation :

Production time (Minutes)	*Probability*
2	0.10
3	0.25
4	0.40
5	0.10
6	0.10
7	0.05

The time taken to install a component is 3 minutes on the average with the following probability distribution:

Installation time (Minutes)	*Probability*
2	0.30
3	0.45
4	0.15
5	0.10

The system uses one operative for installation but the company is considering employing another operative on the installation process.

Required: Simulate 10 arrivals on the current system, using the following 2 digit random numbers:

20, 74, 94, 22, 90, 45, 44, 16, 04, 32, 03, 62, 61, 89, 01, 27, 49, 50, 90, 98.

Solution

Table I - Random Number Coding

Production time			*Installation time*		
Minutes	*Probability*	*R.N. allotted*	*Minutes*	*Probability*	*R.N. allotted*
2	0.10	00-09	2	0.30	00-29
3	0.25	10-34	3	0.45	30-74
4	0.40	35-74	4	0.15	75-89
5	0.10	75-84	5	0.10	90-99
6	0.10	85-94			
7	0.05	95-99			

Table II - Simulation Work Sheet

A.N.	*R.N.*	*A.T. (cum)*	*R.N.*	*Installation*			*Minutes*	
				Time	*Start*	*End*	*I.T.*	*W.T.*
1	20	3	03	2	3	5	3	—
2	74	7	62	3	7	10	2	—
3	94	13	61	3	13	16	3	—
4	22	16	89	4	16	20	—	—
5	90	22	01	2	22	24	2	—
6	45	26	27	2	26	28	2	—
7	44	30	49	3	30	33	2	—
8	16	33	50	3	33	36	—	
9	04	35	90	5	36	41	—	1
10	32	38	98	5	41	46	—	3
						Total	**14**	**4**

PROBLEM 9.11 [Monte Carlo Simulation for Inventory Decision]

A book store wishes to carry 'Ramayana' in stock. Demand is probabilistic and replenishment of stock takes 2 days (i.e. if an order is placed on March 1, it will be delivered on March 3). The probabilities of demand are given below:

Demand (daily)	0	1	2	3	4
Probability	0.05	0.10	0.3	0.45	0.10

Each time an order is placed, the store incurs an ordering cost of ₹ 10 per order. The store also incurs a carrying cost of 50 paise per book per day which is calculated on the basis of stock at the end of each day.

The manager of the book store wishes to compare two options for his inventory decision.

Option A: Order 5 books when the inventory at the beginning of the day *plus* orders outstanding is less than 8 books.

Option B: Order 8 books when the inventory at the beginning of the day *plus* orders outstanding is less than 8 books.

Currently (beginning of 1st day) the store has a stock of 8 books plus 6 books ordered two days ago and expected to arrive next day.

Required: Using Monte Carlo Simulation for 10 cycles, recommend which option the manager should choose.

The two digit random nos. are given below:

89, 34, 78, 63, 61, 81, 39, 16, 13, 73

Solution

Table I : Random Number Coding

Demand	*Prob.*	*Cum. Prob.*	*Random Nos.*
0	0.05	0.05	00-04
1	0.10	0.15	05-14
2	0.30	0.45	15-44
3	0.45	0.90	45-89
4	0.10	1.00	90-99

Stock in hand = 8 and stock on order = 6 (expected next day)

Table II : Simulation Worksheet for option 'A'

A Random Number (given)	*B Sales*	*C Op. Stock*	*D Receipt*	*E = C + D − B Closing Stock on hand*	*F Orders out-standing*	*G = C + F Opening stock + orders o/s*	*H Order quantity*
89	3	8	—	5	6	14	—
34	2	5	6	9	6	11	—
78	3	9	—	6	—	9	—
63	3	6	—	3	—	6	*5
61	3	3	—	0	5	8	*5
81	3	0	5	2	5	5	*5
39	2	2	—	0	5	7	—
16	2	0	5	3	10	10	—
13	1	3	5	7	5	8	—
73	3	7	—	4	0	7	*5

*5 books have been ordered 4 times.

∴ Ordering cost = ₹ (4 × 10) = ₹ 40

Closing stock of 10 days = (5 + 9 + 6 + 3 + 2 + 3 + 7 + 4) = 39 books.

Closing cost @ ₹ 0.5 per book/day = 39 × 0.5 = ₹ 19.5

Total cost for 10 days = ₹ (40 + 19.5) = ₹ 59.5

Table III : Simulation Worksheet for option 'B'

A Random Number (given)	B Sales	C Op. Stock	D Receipt	E = C + D - B Closing Stock on hand	F Orders out-standing	G = C + F Opening stock + orders o/s	H Order quantity
89	3	8	0	5	6	4	—
34	2	5	6	9	—	11	—
78	3	9	—	6	—	9	—
63	3	6	—	3	8	6	8
61	3	3	—	0	8	11	—
81	3	0	8	5	—	8	—
39	2	5	—	3	8	5	8
16	2	3	—	1	8	11	—
13	1	1	8	8	—	9	—
73	3	8	—	5	—	8	—

*8 books have been ordered two times when the inventory at the beginning of the day plus orders outstanding is less than 8.

∴ ordering cost = ₹ 2 ₹ 10 = ₹ 20. (1)

Closing stock of 10 days = (5 + 9+ 6 + 3 + 5 + 3 + 1 + 8 + 5) = 45 books

Carrying cost @ ₹ 0.5 per book per day

= (45 ₹ .5) = ₹ 22.50 (2)

∴ Total cost = ₹ (22.50 + 20) = ₹ 42.50

Since 'Option B' has lower cost than 'Option A', i.e., 42.50 < 59.50 the manager should choose option 'B'.

PROBLEM 9.12

The management has the following available data:

Quantity Demanded	Probability	Lead time (days)	Probability
0	0.10	2	0.20
1	0.45	3	0.65
2	0.30	4	0.15
3	0.15		

The management wants to ascertain its inventory cost if they wish to reord when the quantity on hand is 6 units and order each time a quantity of 12 units. The cost of ordering is ₹ 120, and the cost of holding the inventory per day in stock is ₹ 5 per unit. The management has found that when it runs out of stock, it cost ₹ 75 per unit. Simulate the situation for 15 days by using given random numbers.

Random No. for Sale (49, 67, 06, 30, 95, 01, 10, 70, 80, 66, 69, 76, 86, 56, 84)

Random No. for lead time (84, 79)

[Assume that opening stock is 10 units and sale is made at the beginning of day, and ordered quantity is also received at the beginning of the day and order is placed by checking opening stock at beginning of every day].

Solution

Statement showing Allocation of Random Numbers

(Demand)

Demand	*Probability*	*Cumulative Probability*	*Random Nos.*
0	0.10	0.10	0-9
1	0.45	0.55	10-54
2	0.30	0.85	55-84
3	0.15	1.00	85-99
Lead Time			
2	0.20	0.20	0-19
3	0.65	0.85	20-84
4	0.15	1.00	85-99

Table : Simulation of Demand and Lead Time for 15 Days

Day	*Stock On hand Beginning Of week*	*Demand Random No.*	*Quantity demand-ded*	*Quantity received*	*Stock on hand end of week*	*Inventory carrying costs*	*Stock Out Quantity*	*Lead Time Costs*	*Random No.*	*Lead Time period*
1	10	49	1	—	9	45				
2	9	67	2	—	7	35				
3	7	06	0	—	7	35				
4	7	30	1	—	6	30				
5	6	95	3	—	3	15			84	3
6	3	01	0	—	3	15				
7	3	10	1	—	2	10				
8	2	70	2	12	12	60				
9	12	80	2	—	10	50				
10	10	66	2	—	8	40				
11	8	69	2	—	6	30				
12	6	76	2	—	4	20			79	3
13	4	86	3	—	1	5				
14	1	56	2	—	—	—	1	75		
15	—	84	2	12	10	59				

For the simulated period of 15 days, the total inventory costs are:-

Inventory carrying costs	= ₹	440
Ordering costs (2 orders × 120)	= ₹	240
Stock-out costs (1 stock-out)	= ₹	75
Total	= ₹	755

PROBLEM 9.13

An Investment Corporation wants to study the investment projects based on three factors: market demand in units, price per unit *minus* cost per unit, and the investment required. These factors are felt to be independent of each other. In analysing a new consumer product, the corporation estimates the following probability distributions :

Annual Demand Units	*Probability*	*(Price-Cost) per unit ₹*	*Probability*	*Investment ₹*	*Required Probability*
25,000	0.05	3.00	0.10	27,50,000	0.25
30,000	0.10	5.00	0.20	30,00,000	0.50
35,000	0.20	7.00	0.40	35,00,000	0.25
40,000	0.30	9.00	0.20		
45,000	0.20	10.00	0.10		
50,000	0.10				
55,000	0.05				

Required: Using simulation process, repeat the trial 10 times, compute the return on investment for each trial taking these three factors into account. Approximately, what is the most likely return ?

Use the following random numbers for annual demand, (Price-Cost) and the investment required:

28, 57, 60, 17, 64, 20, 27, 58, 61, 30, 19, 07, 90, 02, 57,
28, 29, 83, 58, 41, 18, 67, 16, 71, 43, 68, 47, 24, 19, 97

Solution

Statement showing the Allocation of Random Numbers

Annual Demand

Events	*Probabilities Probability*	*Cumulative Number*	*Random*
25,000	0.05	0.05	0-4
30,000	0.10	0.15	5-14
35,000	0.20	0.35	15-34
40,000	0.30	0.65	35-64
45,000	0.20	0.85	65-84
50,000	0.10	0.95	85-94
55,000	0.05	1.00	95-99

Price- Cost

3.00	0.10	0.10	0.-9
5.00	0.20	0.30	10-29
7.00	0.40	0.70	30-69
9.00	0.20	0.90	70-89
10.00	0.10	1.00	90-99

Investment

27,50,000	0.25	0.25	0-24
30,00,000	0.50	0.75	25-74
35,00,000	0.25	1.00	75-99

Simulation Worksheet

Trials *A*	*Random Number for demand* *B*	*Simulated Demand* *C*	*Random No. for profit* *D*	*Simulated Profit* *E*	*Total Profit* *F = C × E*	*Random No. for investment* *G*	*Simulated Investment* *H*	*Return (in %)* *I = F/H × 100*
1	28	35,000	19	5.00	1,75,000	18	27,50,000	6.36
2	57	40,000	07	3.00	1,20,000	67	30,00,000	4.00
3	60	40,000	90	10.00	4,00,000	16	27,50,000	14.55
4	17	35,000	02	3.00	1,05,000	71	30,00,000	3.50
5	64	40,000	57	7.00	2,80,000	43	30,00,000	9.33
6	20	35,000	28	5.00	1,75,000	68	30,00,000	5.83
7	27	35,000	29	5.00	1,75,000	47	30,00,000	5.83
8	58	40,000	83	9.00	3,60,000	24	27,50,000	13.10
9	61	40,000	58	7.00	2,80,000	19	27,50,000	10.18
10	30	35,000	41	7.00	2,45,000	97	35,00,000	7.00

10 Learning Curve Theory

LEARNING OBJECTIVES

After studying this chapter, you should be able to understand:

- Learning Curve Theory
- Meaning of Learning Curve
- Meaning of Learning Curve Ratio
- Meaning of Learning Curve Equation
- Applications of Learning Curve

1.0 LEARNING CURVE THEORY

As the production quantity of a given item is doubled, the cost of the item decreases at a fixed rate. This phenomenon is the basic premise on which the theory of learning curve has been formulated. As the quantity produced doubles, the absolute amount of cost increase will be successively smaller but the rate of decrease will remain fixed. It occurs due to the following distinctive features of manufacturing environment:

(i) Better tooling methods are developed and used.
(ii) More productive equipments are designed and used to make the product.
(iii) Design bugs are detected and corrected.
(iv) Engineering changes decrease over time.
(v) Earlier teething problems are overcome.
(vi) Rejections and rework tend to diminish over time.

2.0 MEANING OF LEARNING CURVE

Learning curve is a geometrical progression, which reveals that there is steadily decreasing cost for the accomplishment of a given repetitive operation, as the identical operation is increasingly repeated. The amount of decrease will be less and less with each successive unit produced. The slope of the decision curve is expressed as a percentage. The other names given to learning curve are Experience curve, Improvement curve and Progress curve.

3.0 MEANING OF LEARNING CURVE RATIO

In the initial stage of a new product or a new process, the learning effect pattern is so regular that the rate of decline established at the outset can be used to predict labour cost well in advance. The effect of experience on cost is summarised in the learning ratio or improvement ratio:

Average labour cost of first N units
Learning curve ratio = Average labour cost of first 2N units

For example, if the average labour cost for the first 500 units is ₹ 25 and the average labour cost for the first 1,000 units is ₹ 20, the learning curve ratio is (₹ 20/25) or 80%. Since the average cost per unit of 1,000 units is ₹ 20, the average cost per unit of first 2,000 units is likely to be 80% of ₹ 20 or ₹ 16.

4.0 MEANING OF LEARNING CURVE EQUATION

Mathematicians have been able to express relationship in equations. The basic equation

$$Y_x = KX^s$$

where, X is the cumulative number of units or lots produced
Y is the cumulative average unit cost of those units X or lots.
K is the average co.. of the first unit or lots is the improvement exponent or the learning coefficient or the index of learning which is calculated as follows:
s = log of learning ratio/log 2

5.0 APPLICATIONS OF LEARNING CURVE

Some of the applications of learning curve are as follows:

1 Learning curve helps in analyzing cost-volume profit relationships during familiarisation phase of product or process to arrive at cost estimates. It helps in budgeting and profit planning.
2. It helps in pricing and consequent decision making – e.g. acceptance of an order, negotiations in establishing contract prices etc. with the advantage of the knowledge of decreasing unit cost.
3. It helps in setting standards in the learning phase.

ILLUSTRATION 1

The following information is provided by a factory manager who wants to use appropriate average learning rate on following activities:

(i) A set of very experienced people feed data into the computer for processing inventory records in the factory. The manager wishes to apply 80% learning rate on data entry and calculation of inventory.
(ii) A new type of machinery is to be installed in the factory. This is patented process and the output may take a year for full fledged production. The factory manager wants to use a learning rate on the workers at the new machine.
(iii) An operation uses contract labour. The contractor shifts people among various jobs once in two days. The labour force performs one task in 3 days. The manager wants to apply an average learning rate for these workers.

Required: Advise to the manager with reasons on the applicability of the learning curve theory on the above information.

Solution

(i) The learning curve does not apply to very experienced people for the same job, since time taken can never tend to become zero or reduce very considerably after a certain range of output. This is the limitation of the learning curve.
Data entry is a manual job so learning rate theory may be applied. Calculation of inventory is a computerized job. Learning rate applies only to manual labour.
(ii) Learning rate should not be applied to a new process which the firm has never tried before.
(iii) The workers are shifted even before completion of one unit of work. Hence learning rate will not apply.

ILLUSTRATION 2

XYZ Co. has observed that a 90% learning curve ratio applies to all labour related costs each time a new model enters production. It is anticipated that 320 units will be manufactured during 1999. Direct labour cost for the first lot of 10 units amounts to 1,000 hours at ₹ 8 per hour. Variable overhead cost is assigned to products at the rate of ₹ 2 per direct labour hour.

Required:

1. Find total labour and labour-related costs to manufacture 320 units of output.
2. Average cost of (a) the first 40 units produced (b) the first 80 units, (c) the first 100 units.
3. Incremental cost of (a) units 41-80 and (b) units 101-200.

Solution

Statement of Cost Projections on 90% Learning Curve

Cummulative Quantity	*Average time per unit*	*Cummulative time taken*	*Incremental Hours*
10	100	1,000	—
20	90	1,800	800
40	81	3,240	1,440
80	72.90	5,832	2,592
160	65.61	10,497.6	4,665.6
320	59.049	18,895.68	8,398.08

(i) **Total labour and labour related cost**

For first 320 units = 1,8895.68 x ₹ 10/hr = ₹ 1,88,956.80

(ii) (a) **Average cost of 40 units** $= \dfrac{3{,}240 \times 10 \text{ p.u.}}{40}$ = ₹ 810 per unit

(b) **Average cost of first 80 units** $= \dfrac{5{,}832 \times 10 \text{ p.u.}}{80}$ = 729 p.u

(iii) (a) **Incremental cost of units 41 – 80**

= (total time taken for 80 units – total time taken for 40 units) × 10

= (5,832 – 3,240) × 10 = ₹ 25,920

Now, the basic learning curve formula must be used to derive the average cost of the first 100 units and the incremental cost of units 101 – 200.

We have,

$$Y = ax^b$$

Here,

$$A = 1000$$
$$X = 10$$

and

$$b = \frac{\text{logarithm of learning ratio}}{\text{logarithm of 2}}$$

$$= \frac{\log 90\%}{\log 2} = \frac{\log \frac{9}{10}}{\log 2} = \frac{\log 9 - \log 10}{\log 2}$$

$$= \frac{0.9542 - 1}{0.3010} = -0.15216$$

Now,

$$A = 1000$$
$$Y = ax^b$$

Taking log on both sides

$\log Y = \log ax^b$

$\log Y = \log 1000 + b \log 10$

$\log Y = 3 \times 1 + (-0.15216) \times 1$

= Antilog 2.84784

= (7031 + 1 3) = 7044

Hence, Average Time for first 100 units = 70.4 hours

Therefore, Average cost per unit of first 100 units = 70.4 × 10 = ₹ 70.4 P.U.

(i.e. first 10 lots)

Due to 90% learning curve

Average Time taken for 200 units = 70.44 × 90% = 63.396 hrs/unit

Therefore, total time taken = 63.396 × 200 hrs = 12,679.20 hours

Therefore, total cost = 12,679.20 × 10 = ₹ 1,26,792

Therefore, incremental cost = ₹ 1,26,792 – ₹ 70,400 = ₹ 56,392

ILLUSTRATION 3

Bharat Tulsian Ltd has observed that learning curve applies to all labour related cost, each time a new unit enter into production. It is anticipated that 400 units will be manufactured during the current year. Direct labour hours for the first lot of 5 units is 80 hours. Material cost is ₹ 10 per unit and labour cost per hour is ₹ 2. Variable cost of manufacturing is ₹ 1 per direct labour hour.

Calculate the cost of producing 400 units in each of the following alternative cases:

Case (a) *Learning Curve Rate is 90% and it applies when cumulative production volume becomes double.*

Case (b) *Learning Curve Rate is 90% and it applies when cumulative production volume becomes 1.5 times.*

Case (c) *Learning Curve Rate is 80% and it applies when cumulative production volume becomes double.*

Case (d) *Learning Curve Rate is 80% and it applies when cumulative production volume becomes 2.5 times.*

Solution

Labour hours required for the first unit = $\frac{80 \text{ hours}}{5}$ = 16 hours.

Comulative average labour hour of 400 units.

$$Y_x = Kx^s$$

$$K = 16 \text{ hours}$$

$$X = 400$$

$$S = \frac{\log(0.90)}{\log(2)}$$

$$\log(0.9) = \log\left(\frac{9}{10}\right) = \log 9 - \log 10$$

$$= 0.9542 - 1.0000 = -0.0458$$

$$S = \frac{-0.0458}{0.3010} = -0.1522$$

$$Y_x = 16(400)^{-0.1522}$$

Taking log of both sides

$$\log Y_x = \log(16)(400)^{-0.1522}$$
$$= \log 16 - 0.1522 \log 400$$
$$= 1.2041 - 0.1522(\log 10 \times 4)$$
$$= 1.2041 - 0.1522\ (\log 100 + \log 4)$$
$$= 1.2041 - 0.1522\ (2 + 0.6021)$$
$$= 1.2041 - 0.1522\ (2.6021)$$
$$= 1.2041 - 0.3960 = 0.8081$$
$$\log Y_x = 0.8081$$
$$Yx = \text{Antilog}\ (0.8081)$$
$$Yx = 6.428 \text{ hours}$$
$$\text{Total hours} = 6.428 \times 400 = 2571.20 \text{ hours.}$$

Statement showing the Cost of producing 400 units

Particulars	₹
Direct Material (₹ 10 × 400)	4,000.00
Direct labour (2571.20 × ₹ 2)	5,142.40
Variable cost (2,571.20 × ₹ 1)	2,571.20
	11,713.60

Case (b) Comulative Average Labour Hours for 400 units

$$Y_x = Kx^s$$
$$K = 16 \text{ hours}$$
$$X = 400$$
$$S = \frac{\log(0.90)}{\log(1.5)}$$
$$S = \frac{-0.0458}{0.1761} = -0.2601$$
$$Y_x = 16(400) - 0.2601$$

Taking log of both sides

$$= \log 16 - 0.2601 \log 400$$
$$= 1.2041 - 0.2601\ (2.6021)$$
$$= 1.2041 - 0.6768 = 0.5273$$
$$\log Y_x = 0.5273$$
$$Y_x = \text{Antilog}\ (0.5273)$$
$$Y_x = 3.367$$
$$\text{Total hours} = 3.367 \times 400 = 1{,}346.80 \text{ hours}$$

Statement showing the cost of producing 400 units.

Particluars	₹
Direct Material (₹ 400 × ₹ 10)	4,000.00
Direct labour (1,346.80 × ₹ 2)	2,693.60
Variable Cast (1,346.80 × ₹ 1)	1,346.80
	8,040.40

Case (c) Cummulative Average Labour Hour of 400 units

$$Y_x = Kx^s$$
$$K = 16 \text{ hours}$$
$$X = 400$$
$$S = \frac{\log(0.80)}{\log(2)}$$
$$= \log(0.80) = \log\left(\frac{8}{10}\right) = \log 8 - \log 10$$
$$= 0.9031 - 1.0000 = -0.0969$$
$$S = \frac{-0.0969}{\log(2)} = \frac{-0.0969}{0.3010} = -0.3219$$
$$Y_x = 16(400)^{-0.3219}$$

Taking log of both sides

$$\log Y_x = \log 16 - 0.3219(\log 400)$$
$$= 1.2041 - 0.3219\ (2.6021)$$
$$= 1.2041 - 0.8376$$
$$\log Y_x = 0.3665$$
$$Y_x = 2.325$$
$$\text{Total hours} = 2.325 \times 400 = 930 \text{ hours}$$

Statement showing the Cost of producing 400 units.

Particluars	₹
Direct Matarial (400 × ₹ 10)	4,000
Direct Labour (930 × ₹ 2)	1,860
Variable Lost (930 × ₹ 1)	930
	6,790

Case (d) Cumulative average labour hours of 400 units

$$Y_x = Kx^s$$
$$K = 16 \text{ hours}$$
$$X = 400$$
$$S = \frac{\log(0.80)}{\log(2.5)}$$
$$= \frac{-0.0969}{0.3979} = -0.2435$$
$$Y_x = 16(400)^{-0.2435}$$

Taking log of both sides

$$\log Y_x = \log 16 - 0.2435 \log (400)$$
$$= 1.2041 - 0.2435\ (2.6021)$$
$$= 1.2041 - 0.6336$$
$$\log Y_x = 0.5705$$
$$Y_x = \text{Antilog } (0.5705) \Rightarrow Y_x = 3.72 \text{ hours}$$
$$\text{Total hours} = 3.72 \text{ hours} \times 400 = 1488 \text{ hours}$$

Statement showing the Cost of Producing 400 units

Particluars	₹
Direct Material (400 × ₹ 10)	4,000
Direct Labour (1,488 × ₹ 2)	2,976
Variable Cost (1,488 × ₹ 1)	1,488
	8,464

ILLUSTRATION 4

Tushar Tulsian Ltd. invent a new product '*Kx*'. It is to be processed in 3 departments, i.e., Department A, B and respectively. The cost of producing first 100 units are given below:

Particluars	₹
Direct Material (100 × ₹ 8)	800
Direct Labour:	
Department A (100 × 2 hour × 5)	1,000
Department B (100 × 3 hour × 10)	3,000
Department C (100 × 2 hour × 10)	2,000
Variable Costs:	
Department A (200 hour × 2)	400
Department B (300 hour × 3)	900
Department C (200 hour × 4)	800
Total	8,100

These units are sold in market and obtained good response. Units are to be produced in a batch of 100 units. The company receives the further order for 200 units. What minimum price should the company quote considering the following:

(1) Department A is highly automated and learning curve effect does not take place there.
(2) Department B requires highly skilled labour so learning curve effect will take place there at a rate of 80%.
(3) Department C requires semi-skilled labour so learning curve effect will take place there at a rate of 90%.
(4) Company desires to earn a profit of 20% on quotation price.

Solution

Labour Hours at Department B

Average cumulative hours for producing 300 units in lot of 100.

$$Y_x = Kx^s$$

$$K = 300 \text{ hour}$$

$$X = 3$$

$$S = \frac{\log(0.80)}{\log(2)} = \frac{-0.0969}{0.3010} = -0.3219$$

$$Y_x = 300 \times 3^{-0.3219}$$

$$\log Yx = \log 300 - 0.3219 \log 3$$

$$= 2.4771 - 0.3219\ (0.4771)$$

$$= 2.4771 - 0.1536$$

$$= 2.3235$$

$$Yx = \text{Antilog}\ (2.3235) = 210.62 \text{ hours}$$

Total Hours = 210.62 hours × 3 = 631.86 hours

Incremented hours for 200 units = 631.86 hours – 300 hours

= 331.86 hours

Labours Hours of Department C

Average cumulative hours for producing 300 units in lot of 100 units.

$$Yx = Kxs$$

$$K = 200$$

$$X = 3$$

$$S = \frac{\log(0.90)}{\log 2} = \frac{-0.0458}{0.3010} = -0.1522$$

$$Y_x = 200 \times 3^{-0.1522}$$

$$\log Y_x = \log(200) - 0.1522 \log 3$$

$$= 2.3010 - 0.1522\ (0.4771)$$

$$= 2.3010 - 0.0726$$

$$= 2.2284$$

$$Y_x = \text{Antilog}\ (2.2284)$$

$$Y_x = 169.20$$

Total Hours = 169.20 × 3 = 507.60

Incremented Hours = 507.60 hours – 200 hours = 307.60 hours

Statement showing the Minimum Price to be quoted for the order

Particulars		₹
Direct Material (200 × ₹ 8)		1,600.00
Direct Labour:		
Department A (200 × 2 hours × ₹ 5)	2,000.00	
Department B (331.86 hours × ₹ 10)	3,318.60	
Department C (307.60 hours × ₹ 10)	3,076.00	8,394.60
Variable Cost:		
Department A (400 hours × ₹ 2)	800.00	
Department B (331.86 hours × ₹ 3)	995.58	
Department C (307.60 hours × ₹ 4)	1,230.40	3,025.98
Total cost		13,020.58
Add: Profit margin @ 25% on cost		3,255.145
Minimum Quotation Price		16,275.725

ILLUSTRATION 5

Calculate the expected average unit cost of making,

(a) 4 machines; (b) 8 machines

Using the data below:

Data:

Direct labour needed to make first machine 1,000 hours

Learning curve = 90%

Direct labour cost ₹ 15 per hour

Direct materials cost ₹ 1,50,000 per machine.

Fixed cost for either size orders ₹ 60,000.

Solution

Statement of Learning Curve

Cummulative Quantity	*Average time per unit*	*Cummulative time taken*	*Incremental Hours*
1	1,000	1,000	—
	900	1,900	900
4	810	3,240	1,340
8	729	5,832	2,592

Statement showing Expected Average Cost per unit

Particulars	*First 4 Machines (₹)*	*First 8 Machines (₹)*
Material	6,00,000	12,00,000
Labour	48,600	87,480
Fixed Cost	60,000	60,000
Total Cost	7,08,600	13,47,480
Average Cost per unit	177150	1,68,435

ILLUSTRATION 6

XYZ & Co. has given the following data:

80% Average – Time Curve

Cumulative Units (X)	*Average Hours*	*Total Hours*	*Marginal*
1	100	100	100
	80	**160**	60
	?	?	?
4	64	56	?

Required: Fill in the blanks.

Solution:

Know

$$Y = ax^b$$

Where Y = average time per unit

a = total time for the first unit

x = the cumulative no. of units manufactured

b = the learning curve

Now,

The learning coefficient, b, is determined as follows

$$b = \frac{\log 80\%}{\log 2} = \frac{\log 8/10}{\log 2} = \frac{\log 8 - \log 10}{\log 2}$$

$$= \frac{0.9031 - 1}{0.3010} = \frac{-0.0969}{0.3010}$$

$$= -0.3219 = -0.322$$

Now, Calculation of average time (Y) when x = 3, be

$$Y = ax^b$$

$$Y = 100 \times (3)^{-0.322}$$

Taking log on both sides

$$\log Y = \log 100 + (-0.322) \log 3$$
$$\log Y = 2 + (-0.322) \times (0.4771)$$
$$\log Y = 2 - 1536$$

Therefore,

$$Y = \text{anti log } (1.8464) = (7015 + 6) = 70.21$$

Therefore $Y = 70.21$

80% Average Time Curve

Cummulative Units	*Average Time*	*Total Time*	*Marginal Time*
1	100	100	100(100 – 0)
	80	160	60(160 – 100)
	70.2	210.6(3 × 70.2)	50.6(210.6 – 160)
4	64	256(64 × 4)	45.4(256 – 210.6)

ILLUSTRATION 7

A customer has asked your company to prepare a bid on supplying 800 units of a new product. Production will be in batches of 100 units. You estimate that costs for the first batch of 100 units will average ₹ 100 a unit. You also expect that a 90% learning curve will apply to the cumulative labour cost on this contract.

Required:

(a) Prepare an estimate of the labour costs of fulfilling this contract.
(b) Estimate the incremental labour cost of extending the production run to produce an additional 800 units.
(c) Estimate the incremental labour cost of extending the production run from 800 units to 900 units.

Solution

(a) Statement Showing labour cost at 800 units

Cummulative units	*Average Cost per unit*	*Total Cost*	*Incremental Cost*
100	100	10,000	—
200	90	18,000	8,000
400	81	32,400	14,400
800	72.90	58,320	25,920

(b) Calculation of incremental labour cost to produce additional 800 units

Average cost for the first 1600 units = 72.90 × 90% = ₹ 65.61
Therefore, total cost = 65.61 × 1,600 = ₹ 1,04,976
Therefore, incremental cost = Total Cost of 1,600 units – Total Cost of 800 units
= (1,04,976 – 58,320) = ₹ 46,656

(c) Calculation of incremental Labour Cost of Production exceeding from 800 units to 900 units

We know

$$Y = ax^b$$

Where

$$a = 10,000$$
$$x = 9$$

$$b = \frac{\log 9/10}{\log 2} = \frac{\log 9 - \log 10}{\log 2}$$

$$= \frac{0.9542 - 1}{0.3010} = \frac{0.0458}{0.3010}$$

$$= -0.15216$$

Therefore $Y = 10000\ X(9)^{-0.15216}$

Taking log on both sides

$\log Y = \log 10{,}000(9)^{-0.15216}$

$\log Y = \log 10{,}000 + \log 9^{-0.15216}$

$\log Y = 4 + (-0.15216) \times (0.9542)$

$\log Y = 4 - 0.14519$

Therefore, $Y =$ Antilog 3.8548

= 7145 + 13 = 71.58

Hence, Average Cost per unit = ₹ 71.58

Therefore, Cost of 900 units = 900 × ₹ 71.58

= ₹ 64,422

Therefore, required incremental cost from 800 units to 900 units

= Total Cost of 900 units – Total Cost of 800 units

= ₹ 64,422 – ₹ 58,320 = ₹ 6,102

ILLUSTRATION 8

Comforts Ltd. makes household appliances. It is now examining a three-year old contract to make electrical bread toasters for sale through a departmental store. During the entire contract period, it will receive for its toaster a fixed price of ₹ 40 per piece for whatever quantity it can produce in the 3 years. Skilled labour is the constraint and this cannot be increased above that currently available in the Company for making the toaster.

Capital investment required ₹ 50,000 payable down cash with nil scrap value.

Additional Overheads	₹ 25,000 per annum
Material	₹ 30 per toaster
Labour (Skilled)	₹ 5 per hour.

The production manager envisages a learning curve effect for labour in the form of $y = at\ x^{-0.3}$ where y = average labour hours per unit, a = labour hours per first unit and x = cumulative production. He estimates that the first toaster will take 10 hours to produce and the fixed amount of skilled labour available will enable 5,000 toaster to be produced in the first year. Assume all cash infows to arise at year end and the cost of capital is 15%. What is your advice?

Solution

Statement of Net Present Value

Year	*1st year*	*2nd year*	*3rd year*
Revenue	5,000 × 40 = 2,00,000	8,460 × 40 = 3,38,400	10,550 × 40 = 4,22,000
***Less:* Cost**			
Material	1,50,000	2,53,800	3,16,500
Labour	19,425 = 3,885 × 5	19,425 = 3,885 × 5	19,425 = 3,885 × 5
Fixed overhead	25,000	25,000	25,000

Year	*1st year*	*2nd year*	*3rd year*
Cash Inflow	5,575	40,175	61,075
Present value factor	0.869	0.756	0.657
Present value of cash inflow	4,845	30,372	40,127

Present Value of Cash Inflow = 4845 + 30,372 + 40,127
= 75,344
Less: Present Value of Cash Outflow = 50,000
Net Present Value (N.P.V) = 25,344

Comment: Project should be accepted sinθ N.P.V is positive.

Working Notes

(i) Calculation of total labour hours available in first year

Statement of Learning Curve (just for under standing)

Quantity	*Average time per unit*	*Total hours*	*Incremental Hours*
1	10	10	—
	8	16	6
4	6.4	25.6	
5	—	—	
—	—	—	
—	—	—	
—	—	—	
5,000	—	3,885 (see below)	

Labour hour available in first year

$$Y = ax^b$$

Multiply both sides by X

$$xy = ax^b \times X$$
$$xy = ax^{b+1}$$

Taking log on both sides

$$Y = ax^b$$
$$\log xy = \log ax^{-0.3+1}$$
$$\log xy = \log 10(5000)^{0.7}$$
$$\log xy = \log 10 + 0.7 \log 5000$$
$$\log xy = 1 + 0.7 \times 3.699$$
$$\log xy = 3.5893$$
$$xy = \text{Antilog } 3.5893$$
$$= 3882 + 3 = 3885$$
$$xy = 3885$$

Therefore, the available labour hours in the first year are 3885 which are sufficient to produce 5000 toasters only in the first year.

(ii) The Number of Toaster to be produce in second year from 3885 labour hours

Labour hours available in first year = 3885 hours
Labour hours available in second year = 3885 hours
Total hours available up to 2nd year = 7770 hours

Which are to be utilized to produce the number of toaster up to second year with the application of equation method.

$$X \times Y = ax^b \times X$$
$$= ax^{b+1}$$
$$7770 = 10(x)^{0.7}$$

Taking log on both sides

$$\log 7770 = \log 10(x)^{0.7}$$
$$\log 7.77 \times 10^3 = \log 10 + \log x^{0.7}$$
$$3 + \log 7.77 = 1 + 0.7 \times \log x$$
$$3 + 0.8904 = 1 + 0.7 \times \log x$$
$$3.8904 - 1 = 0.7 \times \log x$$
$$\log x = \frac{2.8904}{0.7}$$
$$\log x = 4.1291$$
$$x = \text{Anti log } 4.1291$$
$$x = 1346 \times 10$$
$$x = 13460$$

Hence, total number of toasters produced upto

Second year	= 13,460
Less: first year	= 5,000
No. of toasters produced in 2nd year	= 8,460

(iii) Calculation of number of toasters to be produced up to third year.

Labour hours available in third year = 3885

Total labour hours available up to third year = 3 × 3885 hours = 11655 hours

Now,

$$XY = ax^{b+1}$$

i.e.,

$$11655 = 10(x)^{0.7}$$
$$\log 11655 = \log 10 + \log x^{0.7}$$

Therefore $X = 24010$

Hence, the total number of toasters produced

up to 3rd year = 24010

up to 2nd year = 13460

No. of toasters to be produced in 3rd year = 10550

ILLUSTRATION 9

An electronics firm has developed a new type of fire alarm system. A first unit assembled has a material cost of ₹ 18.000 and took 400 hours of direct labour to assemble. Labour rate is ₹ 25 per hour. This type of assembly is known to experience a learning curve effect of 80% (index of learning = 0.3219). Demonstration of this unit to potential customers resulted in an order for 20 units during the next quarter. The firm wishes to popularize this system and will therefore pass on the benefit of cost savings due to learning effect to the customers while setting the sale price.

(i) Determine the price to be set for the first lot of 20 units to be sold. The initial unit will not be sold as this is required for demonstration. The firm follows a practice of imputing a fixed overhead at 125% of direct labour cost and will set the selling price to earn a 20% gross margin on sale price.

(ii) Assume that a further order for a lot of 60 units was received on a contract basis from a single customer. The price was set on the basis of the contracted total. However, after delivery of 30 units against the contract, the contract was cancelled. Determine the deferred learning cost that may have to be written-off consequent to the cancellation of contract for balance not supplied.

Solution

Given data: X = 1, Y = 400 hours : Material cost ₹ 18,000;
Labour rate = ₹ 25 per hour. P = 80% (b = 0.3219)

First order lot 20 units. Since the first unit is not for sale to supply the first lot of 20, a total of 21 units would have been assembled. For the next contract of 60 units a total of 1 + 20 + 60 = 81 units would have to be assembled. For contract terminated halfway the total units assembled to date would 51 units.

Particulars	*X = 1*	*X = 21*	*X = 51*	*X = 81*
Y average labour hours	400	150.12	112.821	97.212
Total labour hours	400	3,153	5,754	7,874
Incremental total hours	400	2,753	2,601	4,721
			(over 21)	(over 21)
Average labour incremental	137.65	86.7	76.68	

Pricing for the first sale lot of 20 units: (₹ per unit)

Material cost		18,000.00
Direct labour	(137.65 × 25)	3,441.25
Overheads	(@ 125% labour)	4,301.56
Total cost		25,742.81
Add: Profit 20% on sales or 25% on cost		6,435.70
Selling price		32,178.51

Price quoted for the contract lot of 60 units and for a 30 units:

Particulars	*Full lot 60*	*Half lot 30*
Material	18,000	18,000
Direct labour	1,967	2,168
Overheads	2,459	2,710
Totai cost	22,426	22,878
Add: Profit margin	5,606	5,719
Selling price	28,032	28,597

On the expectation of a full contract of 60 units the price quoted would have been ₹ 28,032.50 per unit. If it is expected that only 30 units will be supplied, then the price to be quoted is ₹ 28,597.50 per unit.

		(₹)
Actual cost of 30 units	(30 × 22,878)	6, 86,340
Less: Cost recovered based on full contract	(30 × 22,426)	6,72,780
Under recovered cast to be written off		13,560

SOLVED PROBLEMS

PROBLEM 10.1

Engine Ltd. manufactures engine mounting for wide bodied airlines. They have been asked to bid on a prospective contract for 90 engine mounting for the Jet aircraft. They have just completed an initial run of 30 of these mounting at the following costs:

		₹
Direct materials		20,000
Direct Labour	(6,000 hours @ ₹ 4)	24,000
Tooling cost	(re-usable)	3,000
Variable Overheads	(₹ 0.50 per Labour hour)	3,000
Fixed	(₹ 0.50 per labour hour)	6,000
	Total	56,000

An 80% learning curve is thought to be pertinent in this case. The marketing director believes that the quotation is unlikely to be accepted if it exceeds ₹ 1,10,000 and as the company is short of work, he believe the contract to be vital.

Required: Comment whether is it worth accepting at 1,10,000 State your assumptions clearly.

Solution

Statement of Learning Curve (80%)

Cummulative produce	*Average time per unit*	*Total time*	*Incremental hours*
30	200(*i.e.*, 6,000/30)	6,000	—
60	160(*i.e.*, 80% of 200)	9,600(*i.e.*, 160 × 60)	3,600
120	128(*i.e.*, 80% of 160)	15,360(*i.e.*, 120 × 128)	5,760

Incremental time for next 90 units = total time for first 120 units total time for first 30 units
= 15,360 – 6,000 = 9,360 hours

Statement of Revenue Cost

Cost to be incurred:

Material (20,000/30 × 90) = 60,000
Labour (9,360 × 4) = 37,440
Variable overhead (9,360 × 0.5) = 4,680
Tooling cost = NIL
Fixed overhead = NIL
Revenue Cost = 1,02,120

As relevant cost is less than quoted price. Hence, its better to accept the offer i.e. as the relevant cost ₹ 1,02,120 is less than quoted price ₹ 1,10,000. Hence it better to accept the offer.

PROBLEM 10.2

Company has accepted an order for making 15 items of a specialized machine at a price of ₹ 4 lacs each. The delivery is to be completed within 4 months. The company works 23 days a monthly and the normal direct wages per day amounts to ₹ 10,000. However in case of need, the company can work overtime up to 8 days during the said period at double the normal rate of wages. Overheads amount to ₹ 12,000 per normal working day but no overheads are charged on overtime working days. The material cost is ₹ 2,40,000 per machine. The company has estimated that it will take 10 working days to manufacture the first machine. The company is expected to experience a learning effect of 90% (b = 0.152). The contract stipulates a penalty of ₹ 40,000 per machine delivered beyond the schedule of 4 months.

Required: Calculate the costs and advise the company whether it is preferable to work only during normal working days and pay penalty for any delayed delivery of the machines or to work overtime to avoid paying penalty.

Solution

Statement of Comparative Cost (14th and 15th)

Overtime Premium		*Penalty*	
Overtime premium (8 × 10,000)	80,000	Extra cost (40,000 × 2)	80,000
Overhead cost	Nil	Overhead (12,000 × 8)	96,000
Total	80,000	Total	1,76,000

Hence, its better to introduce overtime working days

Working Notes:

Normal wages rate = 10,000 per day
Working days = 4 × 23 days = 92 days
Basic wages = 10,000 per day
Overtime premium = 10,000 per day
Overtime payment = 20,000 per day

Statement of Learning Curve

Cummulative Produce	*Average time per unit*	*Total time*
1	10	10
2	9	18
4	8.1	32.40
8	7.29	58.32
13	6.772	88.03
14	6.694	93.716
15	6.625	99.375
16	6.561	104.976

For first 15 machines:

$$Y = a(x)^b$$
$$\text{Log } Y = \log 10(15)^{-0.152}$$
$$\text{Log } Y = 1 + \log(15)^{-0.152}$$
$$\text{Log } Y = 1 - 0.152 \log 15$$
$$\text{Log } Y = 1 - 0.152 \log 15$$

By solving above equation, we get $Y = 6.625$

For first 14 machines

$$Y = ax^b$$
$$\text{Log } Y = \log 10\ (14)^{-0.152}$$
$$\text{Log } Y = 1 + \log(14)^{-0.152}$$
$$\text{Log } Y = 1 - 0.152 \times \log 14$$

By solving above equation, we get $Y = 6.694$

For first 13 machines

$$Y = ax^b$$
$$Y = 10(13)^{-0.152}$$

$$\text{Log } Y = \log 10 + \log (13)^{-0.152}$$
$$\text{Log } Y = 1 - 0.152 \times \log 13$$

By solving above equation, we get $Y = 6.772$

Hence, from above it is cleared that 14th and 15th machine cannot be completed within scheduled time.

PROBLEM 10.3

A company has 10 direct workers, who work for 25 days a month of 8 hours per day .The estimated down time is 25% of the total available time. The company received an order for a new product. The first unit of the new product requires 40 direct labour hours to manufacture the product. The company expects 80% (index is – 0.322) learning curve for this type of work. The company uses standard adsorption costing the cost data are as under:

Direct materials	₹ 60 per unit
Direct labour	₹ 6 per direct labour hour
Variable Overheads	₹ 1 per direct labour hour
Fixed overheads	₹ 7,500 per month

Required:

1. Calculate the cost per unit of the first order of 30 units.
2. If the company receives a repeat order for 20 units, what prices will be quoted to yield a profit of 25% on selling price?

Solution

(i) Calculation of Cost per unit of first 30 units

	₹
Material	60
Labour (13.38 × 6)	80.28
Variable Overheads	13.38
Fixed Overheads (13.38 × 5)	66.90
Required Cost	220.56

(ii) Calculation of Quoted Price of next 20 units

	₹
Material (60 × 20)	1,200
Wages (166.1 × 6)	996.6
Variable OH (166.1 × 1)	166.1
Fixed overheads (166.1 × 5)	830.5
Cost	3,193.20
Profit (l/3 of cost)	1,064.40
Selling price	4,257.60

Working Notes:

(*i*) *Calculation of Recovery Rate*

= Fixed Overhead/Budgeted Hours

= ₹ 7,500/[(2000 – 500 (Down Time)] = ₹ 5 per hour

(*ii*) Statement of Learning Curve

Cummulative Produce	*Average Time per unit*	*Total Time*	*Incremental Time*
1	40	40	
4			
8			

Cummulative Produce	*Average Time per unit*	*Total Time*	*Incremental Time*
16			
30	13.38	401.40	
—			
—			
50	11.35	567.50	166.1

For first 30 units $Y = ax^b = 40(30)^{-0.322}$

Taking log on both sides

$\text{Log } Y = \log 40(30)^{-0.322}$

$\text{Log } Y = \log 40 + \log (30)^{-0.322}$

$\text{Log } Y = 1.6021 - 0.322 \times \log 30$

$\text{Log } Y = 1.1264$

$Y = \text{anti log } 1.1264$

$Y = 13.38$

For first 50 units $Y = ax^b = 40 \times (50)^{-0.322}$

Taking log on both sides

$\text{Log } Y = \log 40 - 0.322 \log 50$

$\text{Log } Y = \text{Anti log } 1.055$

$Y = 11.35$

PROBLEM 10.4

An electronic firm which has developed a new type of fire-alarm system has been asked to quote for a prospective contract.

Required: Prepare separate price quotations for each of the following.

Order	*Number of Fire-alarm systems*
First	100
Second	60
Third	40

The firm estimates the following cost per unit for the first order:

Direct materials ₹ 500

Direct Labour

Deptt. A (Highly automatic) 20 hours at ₹ 10 per hour.

Deptt. B (skilled labour) 40 hours at ₹ 15 per hour.

Variable Overheads 20% of direct labour

Fixed overheads absorbed:

Deptt.A ₹ 8 per hour

Deptt B ₹ 5 per hour

Determine a price per unit for each of the three orders, assuming the firm uses a mark-up of 25% on total costs and allows for an 80% learning curve. Extract from 80% Learning Curve table:-

X	1.0	1.3	1.4	1.5	1.6	1.7	1.8	1.9	2.0
Y(%)	100.0	91.7	89.5	87.6	86.1	84.4	83.0	81.5	80.0

X represents the cumulative total volume produced to date expressed as a multiple of the initial order. Y is the learning curve factor, for a given X value, expressed as a percentage of the cost of the initial order.

Solution

Statement showing Price per unit for each of three order

Particulars	*1st 100 units (₹)*	*2nd 60 units (₹)*	*3rd 40 units (₹)*
Direct material	50,000	30,000	20,000
Direct Labour			
Highly automatic Dept – A	20,000	12,000	8,000
Skilled Dept – B	60,000	22,656	13,344
Variable OH	16,000	6,931.20	4,268.80
Fixed OH			
Dept – A	16,000	9,600	6,400
Dept – B	20,000	7,552	4,448
Total Cost	1,82,000	88,739.20	56,460.8
Add: Profit Margin	45,500	22,184.80	14,115.20
Selling Price	2,27,500	1,10,924	70,576
Selling Price per unit	2,275	1,848.73	1,764.40

Working Note:

Statement of Learning Curve

Cummulative Unit	*Average Time per unit*	*Total Time*	*Incremental Time*
100 (=1)	40(100%)	4,000	—
130 (=1.3)	—	—	—
160 (=1.6)	34.44(86.1%)	5,510.40	1,510.4
200 (=2)	32(80%)	6,400	889.6

PROBLEM 10.5

(a) Your company has been approached by a customer to supply four units of a new product made to the customer's individual specification. The company experiences a 90% learning rate. The estimated labour time for the first unit of this product is 150 hours and the company's direct labour cost ₹ 5 per hour. (a) Estimate the labour cost for this order, (b) After receiving the first order, if the customer places a repeat order, what will be the labour cost for the second order, (c) If the customer had ordered all eight units at the same time, calculate the labour cost per unit for the combined order.

Solution:

(a) Calculation of Labour Cost

Units Produced (1)	*Cum. Production* (2)	*Avg. Time per unit (hrs.)* (3)	*Total Labour Time* (4) = (2) × (3)
1	1	150.0	150.0
1	2	135.0 (90% of 150)	270.0
2	4	121.5 (90% of 135)	486.0

Estimated Labour Cost for the order = 486 × ₹ 5 = ₹ 2,430

Labour Cost per unit = ₹ 607.50

(b) The first order relates to four units. The repeat order will be for another four units. Thus, average labour hours for 8 units will be:

Average time per unit = 90% of 121.5 = 109.35 hrs.

Average time for 8 units = 109.35 × 8 = 874.80

Less: time spent on this order 486.00

388.80

Total labour cost for second order = 388.8 × ₹ 5 = 1 ,944 or ₹ 486 per unit, i.e., 1,944 ÷ 4

(c) Labour Cost of Combined Order

Units Produced (1)	*Cum. Production (2)*	*Avg. Time per unit (hrs) (3)*	*Total Labour Time (4) = (2) × (3)*
1	1	150.0	150.0
1	2	135.0	270.0
2	4	121.5	486.0
4	8	109.35	874.8

Estimated labour cost for the order = 874.8 x ₹ 5 = ₹ 4,374

Estimated labour cost per unit (4,374 ÷ 8) = ₹ 546.75

PROBLEM 10.6

You have been asked about the application of the learning curve as a management accounting technique. You are required to: illustrate the use of learning curves for calculating the expected average unit cost of making: (i) 4 machines; and (ii) 8 machines.

Using the data given below.

Data:

Direct labour needed to make the first machine 1,000 hours	
Learning curve	80%
Direct labour cost	₹ 3 per hour
Direct materials cost	₹ 1,800 per machine
Fixed cost for either size order	₹ 8,000

Solution

(i) *Calculation of average time to be taken for different given levels.*

(a) Equation Approach, i.e., $y = (a)(x)^{-b}$

Learning coefficient for 80%

$$b = \frac{\log\text{(learning coefficient)}}{2} = \frac{\log(0.80)}{\log 2} = -0.3219$$

For 4 units $y = (1{,}000)$

$\log y = 3.0000 - 0.3219(0.6021)$

$= 3.0000 - 0.1938$

$= 2.8062$

y = Antilong 2.8062 = 640 hours per unit of cumulative production at this level.

For 8 units, $y = (1000)(8)^{-0.3219}$

= 512 hours per unit of cumulative production at this level.

(b) Doubling Approach: 80% learning curve, when the first unit required 1,000 hours.

Incremental qty. (units)	*Total number of units (units)*	*Average time to produce all units to date (Hrs.)*	*Computations*
1	1	1,000	(1,000 × 1)
1	2	800	(1,000 × 0.80)
2	4	640	(800 × 0.80)
4	8	512	(64 × 0.80))

(ii) Average unit cost for making:

(a) (*i*) 4 machines:

	₹
Direct material	1,800
Direct labour (640 hrs × ₹ 3)	1,920
Fixed cost (₹ 8,000 ÷ 4)	2,000
	5,720

(b) (*ii*) 8 machines:

Direct material	1,800
Direct labour (512 hrs. x ₹ 3)	1,536
Fixed cost (₹ 8,000 ÷ 8)	1,000
	4,336

PROBLEM 10.7

H Ltd. has produced its first 10 units of product B. The customer is enquiring about the cost of the further 30 units of Product B. The total cost of the original 10 units was:

	₹
Materials	3,000
Variable labour costs (500 hours at ₹ 10 per hour)	5,000
Variable overheads*	1,000
Other overheads**	1,000
Machine tool costs***	2,000
Total cost	12,000

*Directly affected by variable labour costs.

** Estimated at 20% of variable labour costs.

***All machine tools can still be used although all costs recovered on first order.

Use an 80% learning curve to estimate the total costs for a new batch of 30 units to Product B.

Solution

Machine cost is ignored, since it is already absorbed by the first batch.

Table showing the labour cost projection considering 80% learning effect

Incremental Qty. (Units)	*Cumulative Qty. (units)*	*Average Labour hours for the batch of 10 units (hours)*	*Cumulative Labour Cost (₹)*	*Calculation of Labour (₹)*
10	10	500	₹ 5,000	500 hrs. × 1 batch × ₹ 10
10	20	500 × 0.80	8,000	400 hrs. x 2 batches × ₹ 10
20	40	500 × 0.80 × 0.80	12,800	320 hrs. × 4 batches × ₹ 10

For 30 units:

Labour cost = ₹ 12,800 – ₹ 5,000 = ₹ 7,800

Variable overheads = 20% of ₹ 7,800 = ₹ 1,560

Other overheads = 20% of ₹ 7,800 = ₹ 1,560

Total estimated cost for additional 30 units:

Material	₹	9,000
Labour		7,800
Variable overheads		1,560
Other overheads		1,560
		19,920

PROBLEM 10.8

You have been asked to give a quote for the production of 50 units of a new product. Estimates for the assembly of the first unit are:

Direct materials	₹	100
Direct Labour	₹	50
Variable overhead	₹	30

Notes:

1. Labour costs are ₹ 5 an hour.
2. Variable overhead is based on labour hours (activity based) at a rate of ₹ 3 per labour hour.
3. The company quotes prices on a 20 per cent mark-up on the estimated costs to cover fixed overheads and profits.
4. The company operates an 80 per cent learning curve.
   (i) The company wishes to estimate the marginal cost of making the 50 units and hence calculate the quoted price per unit.
   (ii) What will be the impact, if the company decides to ignore the learning curve effect? Present the comparative data showing the price per unit.

Solution

(i) Calculation of average time to be taken for different given levels:

Equation approach, i.e. $y = ax^{-b}$

The company operates at 80% learning curve.

So, Learning coefficient for 80%

$$b = \frac{\log(0.80)}{\log 2}$$

For 50 units, $y = ax^{b}$

$$= (10)(50)^{-0.3219}$$

$$\log y = 1.000 - 0.3219(1.6990)$$

$$= 1.0000 - 0.5469$$

$$= 0.4531$$

$$y = \text{Antilog } 0.4531 = 2.839 \text{ or } 2.84 \text{ hrs.}$$

So, Total time for 50 units = 50 x 2.84 hrs = 142 hrs

Hence, the estimated marginal cost of 50 units.

Direct materials (50 × 100)	₹	5,000
Direct labour (142 hrs × ₹ 5)		710
Variable overhead (142 × ₹ 3)		426
Total		6,136

Hence marginal cost of 50 units = ₹ 6,136

Therefore, price to be quoted for 50 units = 6,136 x 1.20 = ₹ 7,363.20

So, Price quoted per item = ₹ 7,363.20 ÷ 50 = ₹ 147.26

Barsands should, therefore, quote a price of ₹ 147.26 per item for the batch of 50 items.

(ii) If the company did not appreciate that learning curve effect was present, then the estimated priced based on the first unit cost would be:

	Price based on 1st unit costs	*Priced based on learning curve*
Direct material	₹ 100.00	₹ 100.00
Direct labour 10 × 5; (2.84 × 5)	50.00	14.20
Variable overhead (10 × 3); (2.84 × 3)	30.00	8.52
Total	180.00	122.72
Add: 20% Mark-up	36.00	24.54
Price	216.00	147.26

Hence ignoring the learning curve effect would lead the substantial overpricing to the competitors advantage.

PROBLEM 10.9

A company with two production departments has set the following standards for the forthcoming year:

Particulars	*Department*	
	S	*W*
Direct labour hours available per period	6,000	4,000
Standard wage rate per hour	₹ 6	₹ 5
Expected learning curve	80%	70%
Standard variable overheads per hour	₹ 9	₹ 5
Standard fixed overhead per hour	₹.12	₹ 8
Direct labour hours required for first 100 units	18	9

The direct materials are introduced in Department S. The company is able to negotiate the following prices for purchase of direct materials during the year.

Level of output	*Price of direct materials per (unit of output)*
100	₹ 72.00
200	₹ 64.80
800	₹ 54.00

Overtime, if required, is paid at time and a half. The overhead rates as given above does not include overtime premium. It is the policy of the company to add profit margin as under in quoting the prices:

Department	*Percentage on total labour & overhead cost*
S.	25%
W.	15%
Sub-contracted work	5% on sub-contract price

The company has received a special order. Special tooling costs of the order amount to ₹ 1,200. If this order is for 200 units or less, it will be executed in the period which has a workload of 3840 direct labour hours in Department S and 2100 direct labour hours in Department W. For the work which is done in Department W, a subcontract price of ₹ 50 per unit is quoted by an associate company.

Required:

(i) If the company decides to get the work executed entirely within the company, what price, on cost plus basis, should be quoted for the order, if it consists of: (*i*) 100 units (*ii*) 200 units.

(ii) Assuming that the initial order placed by the customer is for 200 units, what lowest price should be quoted for a repeat order of 600 units? Assume that this order will be executed when there are no capacity constraints.

(iii) State the output level at which the company should close down Department W to get the work executed through sub-contractors.

Solution

Statement of Learning Curve

(Department – S) 80%			*(Department – W) 70%*		
Cummulative Produce	*Average Time per unit*	*Total Time*	*Cummulative produce*	*Average time per unit*	*Total Time*
100	18	1,800	100	9	900
200	14.40	2,880	200	6.3	1,260
400	11.52	4,608	400	4.41	1,764
800	9.216	7,372.8	800	3.087	2,469.6

Statement of Hours avalability

Particulars	*Department – S*	*Department – W*
Hours available	6,000	4,000
Less: regular working	(3,840)	(2,100)
Balance	2,160	1,900
(*i*) *less:* first 100 units	1,800	900
Balance	360	1,000
(*ii*) *less:* first 200 units	2,880	1,260
Balance surplus (Defcit)	(720)	640

Statement of Cost and Price per unit (Absorption)

First 100 units		*First 200 units*	
"S" Dept	₹ Per unit	"S" Dept	₹ per unit
Material	72	Material	64.80
Wages (18 × 6)	108	Wages (14.40 × 6)	86.40
Variable-OH (18 × 9)	162	Variable-OH (14.4 × 9)	129.6
Fixed-OH (18 × 12)	216	Fixed-OH (14.4 × 12)	172.80
		Overtime premium (2160/200)	10.80
"W" Dept		*"W" Dept*	
Labour cost (9 × 5)	45	Material	
Variable-OH (9 × 5)	45	Wage (6.3 × 5)	31.5
Fixed-OH (9 × 8)	72	Variable-OH (6.3 × 5)	31.5

		Fixed-OH (6.3 × 8)	50.4
		Overtime	NIL
Tooling Cost (1200/100)	12	Tooling Cost (1200/200)	6
Total	732	Total Cost	583.8
(+) Profit Margin "S" Dept – 486 × 25% = 121.5 "W" Dept – 162 × 15% = 24.3	145.8	(+) Profit "S" Dept – 399.6 × 25% = 99.90 "W" Dept – 113.4 × 15% = 17.01	116.91
Price	877.80	Price	700.71

PROBLEM 10.10

A company has designed a Prototype Electronic Starter for which the following information are available:

Direct Labour hours	260 hours
Direct material cost	₹ 30,000
Direct labour rate	₹ 20 per hour
Variable overhead	130% of direct labour
Fixed overhead	70% of direct labour

Based on the demonstration of the prototype, the company has received order for 50 units during first six months and another 75 units during the following six months thereafter.

A learning curve effect of 80% is applicable. It is expected that in view of large volume, a 5% discount on material cost will be available in first six months and a 10% discount thereafter. The rates of overhead will remain unchanged and the same percentages would apply.

The company sets the selling price with a 40% mark upon cost. Determine the selling price per unit for the first 50 units and the next 75 units.

(The index of learning rate of learning curve effect of 80% is 0.3219)

Solution

Incremental Labour Cost/unit

Hours *X*	*Y(x)*	*L(x)*	*M(x)*	*Incremental Cost/unit* (₹)
1	260	260	260	5200
51	73,334	3,740	69.9	1392
126	54,811	6,906	42.21	844

Selling Price Computation

Particulars	*1st lot of 50* (₹)	*2nd lot of 75* (₹)
Direct material	28,500 (30,000 – 1,500)	27,000 (30,000 – 3,000)
Direct Labour (as per statement)	1,392	844
Variable overhead	1,810	1,097
Fixed overhead	974	591
Total cost	32,676	29,532
Mark up 40%	13,070	11,813
	45,746	41,345

PROBLEM 10.11

A company has 10 direct worker, who work for 25 days a month of 8 hours per day. The estimated down time is 25% of the total available time. The company received an order for a new product. The first unit of the new product requires 40 direct labour hous to manufacture the product. The company expects 80% (index is - 0.322) learning curve for this type of work. The company uses standard absorption costing and the cost data are as under:

Direct labour hour	₹ 60 per unit
Direct material cost	₹ 6 per direct labour hour
Variable overhead	₹ 1 per direct labour hour
Fixed overhead	₹ 7,500 per month

Required:

(i) Calculte the cost per unit of the first order of 30 unils.

(ii) It the company receives a repeat order for 20 units, what price will be quoted to yield a profit of 25% on selling price?

Solution

(i) Computation of Cost per unit of the first order of 30 units

Particulars		₹
Direct Material Cost	(30 units × ₹ 60)	1,800.00
Direct Labour Cost	(401.4 hours × ₹ 6)	2,408.40
Variable Overheads	(401.4 hours × ₹ 1)	401.40
Fixed Overheads	(401.4 hours × ₹ 5)	2,007.00
Total Cost of 30 units		6,616.80
Cost per unit	(₹ 6,616.80/30 units)	220.56

(ii) Cost per unit, when a repeat order for 20 units is also placed.

Particulars		₹
Direct Material Cost	(20 units × ₹ 60)	1,200.00
Direct Labour	(567.5 hours – 401.40 hours) × ₹ 6	996.60
Variable Overheads	(166.1 hours × ₹ 1)	166.10
Fixed Overheads	(166.1 hours × ₹ 5)	830.50
Total Cost of 20 additional units		3,193.20
Cost per unit	(₹ 3, 193.20/20 units)	159.66

Price to be quoted to yield a profit of 25% on selling price.

It Selling Price is ₹ 100 then profit is ₹ 25 and cost of ₹ 75.

Hence Selling Price unit = $\frac{100}{75} \times 159.66$ = ₹ 212.88.

Working Notes:

(*i*) *By the theory of learning curve*

$$Y_x = KX^s$$

Hence X is the cumulative number of units or lots produced. Y is the cumulative average unit time of those X units. K is the average time of the first unit or lot, s is the improvement exponent or the learning coefficient or the index of learning.

Taking log on both sides of relation (i) we have

$$\log Y = \log K + s \log X$$

(*ii*) Time required for 30 units order (when the time required for first unit is 40 hours)

$$\log 40 + (-0.322) \log 30 = 1.6021 + (-0.322)(1.4771) = 1.6021 - 0.4756$$
$$= 1.1264$$

Antilog of 1.1264 =13.38

Hence hours required for 30 unit =13.38

Total time required for 30 units = 30 units × 13.38 hours = 401.4

(*iii*) Time required for 50 units order (when the time required for first unit is 40 hours)

$$\log 40 + (-0.0322) \log 50 = 1.6021 + (-0.0322)\ 1.6990 = 1.055$$

Antilog of 1.055 = 11.35

Hence hours required per unit 11.35 hours

Total time required for 50 units = 11.35 hours × 50 units = 567.5 hours

(iv) Fixed overhead recovery rate per labour hour

Total labour hours	(10 men × 25 days × 8 hrs)	2,000
Less: 25% downtime	(in hrs.)	500
Total effective hours		1,500
Total fixed overheads per month (₹)		7,500
Fixed overhead recovery rate per labour hour (₹)	(₹ 7,500/1500 hrs)	5

PROBLEM 10.12

SV Ltd. which has a fairly full order book is approached by a customer with the offer of a contract for a model that is a variant, in terms of dimensions and materials used, of one of its existing products.

Though the customer expects to pay a normal price for the model he wants SV Ltd. to take account of an 80% learning curve in its price calculation; this level has been shown to be reasonable in SV Ltd's industry for relevant work.

The Prospective contract is for a total 464 units made up of an initial order of 160 units, two subsequent orders of 80 unit each, and three subsequent orders of 48 units each. SV Ltd. estimates the following costs for the initial order.

Direct materials:

P- 8 mtr.	At ₹ 3.50 per mtr.
Q-12Kg.	At ₹ 1.00 per Kg.

Direct Wages:

Department	*Hours*	*₹ per hour*
1	100	
2	320	
3	160	1.00

Variable overhead: 20% of direct wages.

Department	*Fixed Overhead Recovery Rate per hour (₹)*
1	2.00
2	1.00
3	2.00

The nature of the work in the three production departments is as follows:- Department 1 uses highly automatic machines. Although the operators on these machines need to be fairly skilled, their efficiency only affects the quality of the work but can have little impact on the quantity of his departments output which is largely machine controlled. Department 2 and 3 the skill of operators is a major determinant of the volume of output.

Required: Calculate the cost per unit for:

(i) the initial order of 160 units
(ii) the second, third and fourth orders, if given successively but without guarantee of further orders and
(iii) the whole contract of six orders if given from the start but on the same basis of production and delivery.

Note: An 80% learning curve on ordinary graph paper would show the following relationship between the X-axis (volume) Y-axis (Cumulative average price of elements subjects to the learning curve):

X represents the cumulative total volume produced to date expressed as a multiple of the initial order. Y is the learning curve factor, for a given X value, expressed as a percentage of the cost of the initial order.

X	Y%	X	Y%
1.0	100.0	2.1	78.9
1.1	960	2.2	77.8
1.2	93.3	2.3	76.8
1.3	91.7	2.4	76.0
1.4	89.5	2.5	74.9
1.5	87.6	2.6	74.0
1.6	86.1	2.7	73.2
1.7	84.4	2.8	72.3
1.8	83.0	2.9	71.5
1.9	81.5	3.0	70.7
2.0	80.0	3.1	70.0

X represents the cumulative total volume produced to date expressed as a multiple of the initial order. Y is the learning curve factor, for a given X value, expressed as a percentage of the cost of the initial order.

Solution

Statement of Learning Curve of "Dept-2" (80%)

Cummulative Product	*Average Time per unit*	*Total Time*	*Incremental Time*
160(=1)	2 (=100)	320	—
176(1.1)	1.92(96%)	337.9_	17.92
240(1.5)	1.752(87.6%)	420.48	100.48
320(2)	1.6(80%)	512	91.52
368(2.3)	1.536(76.8%)	565.25	53.25
416(2.6)	1.48(74%)	615.68	50.43
464(2.9)	1.43(71.5%)	663.52	47.84

Statement of Learning Curve of "Dept-3" (80%)

Cummulative Product	*Average Time per unit*	*Total Time*	*Incremental Time*
160 (=1)	1(100%)	160	—
240 (=1.5)	0.876(87.6%)	210.24	50.24
320 (=2)	0.8(80%)	256	45.76
368 (=2.3)	0.768(76.8%)	282.624	26.62
416 (=2.6)	0.74(74%)	307.84	25.22
464 (=2.9)	0.715(71.5%)	331.76	23.92

(a) Calculation Cost of Initial Order of 160 units

		₹
Material:		
P – 8 × 3.50	= 28	
Q – 12 × 1.00	= 12	40
Wages:		
Dept-I – 100 × 1.25	= 125	
Dept-II – 320 × 1.50	= 480	
Dept-III – 160 × 1.00	= 160	765
Variable overheads		= 153
Fixed Overheads:		
Dept-I – 2 × 100	= 200	
Dept-I1 – 1 × 320	= 320	
Dept-III – 0.80 × 160	= 128	648
Total Cost	=	**1606**

(b) Statement showing Second, Third and Fourth Order Cost

Particulars	*2nd 80 units (₹)*	*3rd 80 units (₹)*	*4th 48 units (₹)*
Material	20	20	12
Direct Wages:			
Dept-I	62.5	62.50	37.50
Dept-II	150.72	137.28	79.875
Dept-III	50.24	45.67	26.62
Variable OH:	52.69	49.11	28.80
Fixed OH			
Dept-I	100	100	60
Dept-II	100.48	91.52	53.25
Dept-III	40.192	36.60	21.30
Total Cost	**576.82**	**542.68**	**319.35**

(c) Statement showing cost of whole contract (464 units)

	₹	₹
Direct material	=	116
Direct wages		
Dept-I – (290 × 1.25)	= 362.50	
Dept-II – (663.52 × 1.50)	= 995.28	
Dept-III – (331.76 × 1)	= 331.76	1,689.54

Variable Overheads	=	337.91
Fixed Overheads		
Dept-I – (2 × 290)	= 580	
Dept-II – (1 × 663.52)	= 663.52	
Dept-III – (0.80 × 331.76)	= 265.41	1,508.93
Total Cost	=	3,652.34

PROBLEM 10.13

SV Ltd., which has a fairy full order book is approached by a customer with the offer of a contract for a model that is a variant, in terms of dimensions and materials used, of one of its existing products. Through the customer expects to pay a normal price for the model, he wants SV Ltd. to take account of an 80% learning curve in its price calculation; this level has been shown to be reasonable in SV Ltd's industry for relevant work. The Prospective contract is for a total 464 units made up of an initial order of 160 units, two subsequent orders of 80 units each, and three subsequent orders of 48 units each. SV Ltd. estimates the following costs for the initial order:

Direct materials:

P-8 mtr. at ₹ 3.50 per mtr.
Q-12kg. at × ₹ 1.00 per kg.

Direct wages:

Department	*Hours*	*₹ per hour*
1	4	1.25
2	50	1.50
3	15	1.00

Variable overhead: 20% of direct wages

Fixed overhead Department	*Rate per hour (₹)*
1	2.00
2	1.00
3	0.80

The nature of the work in the three production departments is as follows:

Department 1 uses highly automatic machines. Although the operators on these machines need to be fairly skilled. Their efficiency only affects the quality of the work but can have little impact on the quantity of his department's output which is largely machine-controlled. Department 2 is partially mechanized, whilst Department 3 is an assembly department.

In both departments 2 and 3 the skill of operators is a major determinant of the volume of output.

The terms of the contract price allow for:

Direct materials cost *plus* 2.5% profit margin
Conversion cost *plus* 12.5% profit margin

You are required to calculate the price per unit for

(a) the initial order of 160 units;

(b) the second, third and fourth orders, if given successively but without guarantee of further orders, and

(c) the whole contract of six orders it given from the start but on the same basis of production and delivery.

Note: An 80% learning curve on ordinary graph paper would show the foiiowing relationship between the X-axis (volume) and Y-axis (cumulative average price of elements subjects to the learning curve):

x	*y%*	*x*	*y%*
1.0	100.0	2.1	78.9
1.1	96.0	2.2	77.8
1.2	93.3	2.3	76.8
1.3	91.7	2.4	76.0
1.4	89.5	2.5	74.9
1.5	87.6	2.6	74.0
1.6	86.1	2.7	73.2
1.7	84.4	2.8	72.3
1.8	83.0	2.9	71.5
1.9	81.5	3.0	70.7
2.0	80.0	3.1	70.0

Solution:

(a) Initial Order (₹)

Deptt. 2			
Labour Costs	(50 hrs @ 1.50)	75	
Variable Overhead	(20%)	15	
Fixed Overhead	(50 × ₹ 1)	50	140
Dept. 3			
Labour Costs	(15hrs@ ₹ 1)	15	
Variable Overhead	(20%)	3	
Fixed Overhead	(15 × 0.80)	12	30
Total cost affected by l.c. i.e., subject to reduction on(subsequent orders.)			170
Other Labour Costs			
Dept.1	(4 hrs. @ ₹ 1.25)	5	
Variable Overheads	20%	1	
Fixed Overheads	(4 × ₹ 2)	8	14
Total Conversion Cost			184
Materials	P(8 × 3.5)	28	
	Q(12 x ₹ 1)	12	40
Total Cost			224
Profit	(2.5% of ₹ 40)	1	
	(12.5%of ₹ 184)	23	24
			248

Selling price per unit for initial order = 248/160 = 1.55

Note: Department 1 is highly automatic as such not subject to LC effect.

(b) Second order of 80 units

Total output = 240 units (i.e., 160 + 80).

Thus the output due to second order increased by 50%.

160= 1.0= 100%

240 = 1.5* = 87.6% (overall average time)

*240/160 = 1.5 (1.5 = 87.6% as per given table)

Cumulative reducible cost*.			223.38
Less: Charged to first order			170.00
Reducible cost for this order			53.38
Wages/Overhead of Deptt. 1	(50% of ₹ 14)		7.00
Total Conversion Cost			60.38
Materials	(50% of ₹ 40)		20.00
Total Cost			80.38
Profit	(2.5% of ₹ 20)	0.50	
	(12.5% of ₹ 60.38)	7.55	8.05
			88.43

*(1.5 × ₹ 170) = ₹.255 (₹ 255 × 87.6%)

Selling price for second order of 80 units = ₹ 88.43 / 80 units = ₹ 1.11 per unit.

Third order of 80 units

Total cumulative output 320 units (i.e., 2 times of the first order of 160 unit.)

Therefore L.C. as per given table will be 80% (overall average time).

Cumulative reducible cost*			272.00
Less: Charged to 1st and 2nd orders			223.38
Reducible cost of this order			48.62
Wages/Overhead of Dept. I	(50% of ₹ 14)		7.00
Total Conversion Cost			55.62
Materials	(50% of ₹ 40)		20.00
Total Cost			75.62
Profit	(2.5% of ₹ 20)	0.50	
	(12.5% of ₹ 55.62)	6.95	7.45
Selling Price of this order			83.07

*(2.0 × ₹ 170) = ₹ 340

(80% of 340) = ₹.272

Selling Price per unit= ₹ 83.07/80 units = ₹ 1.04

Fourth order of 48 units

Total cumulative output = 360 units (i. e., 2.3 times of first order of 160 units) = 76.8% (overall average time)

(₹)

Cumulative reducible cost*			300.29
Less: Charged to previous three orders			272.00
Reducible cost of this order			28.29
Wages/overhead of Dept.	(18/160) × ₹ 14		4.20
Total conversion cost			32.49
Materials	(48/160) × ₹ 40		12.00
Total cost			44.49
Profit	(2.5% ₹ 12)	0.30	
	(12.5% of ₹ 32.)	4.06	4.36
Selling price for fourth order of 48 units			48.85

*(₹ 170 × 2.3) = ₹ 391
(76.8% of ₹ 391) = ₹ 300.29
Selling price per unit = ₹ 48.85/48 units = ₹ 1.02

(c) Total Contract

Orders	*Total units*
1 × 160	160
2 × 80	160
3 × 48	144
	464

464 units or 2.9 times of initial order of 160 units
Cumulative Average Time = 71.5% of initial order time.

			(₹)
Reducible costs*			352.50
Labour/Overhead Deptt.1	(2.9 x 14)		40.60
Total conversion cost			393.10
Materials	(2.9 × ₹ 40)		116.00
Total maximum cost			509.10
Profit	(2,5% of ₹ 116)	2.90	
	(12.5% of ₹ 393.10)	49.14	52.04
Total selling price of 464 units			561.14

*(2.9 × ₹ 170) = ₹ 493
(71.5% of ₹ 493) = ₹ 352.50